Marketing Essentials Online Learning Center

Log on to marketingessentials.glencoe.com

New Student Edition Features

- A Matter of Ethics
- Global Marketing
- Net Marketing
- Market Tech
- DECA Resources

Reading and Skills Assessment

- Read-and-Study Strategies
- Focus on the Main Ideas and Concepts
- Reading and Note-Taking Support With Study Organizers
- New Section and Chapter Assessments

Online Learning Center

- Curricula Correlations
- Answer Keys
- Teacher Forum
- Math Review and Practice
- Marketing Internship Project Outlines

New Technology Resources

- TeacherWorks™
- **Exam**_View_® Pro
- Interactive Chalkl
- Online Student E

D1504955

Teacher Wraparound Edition

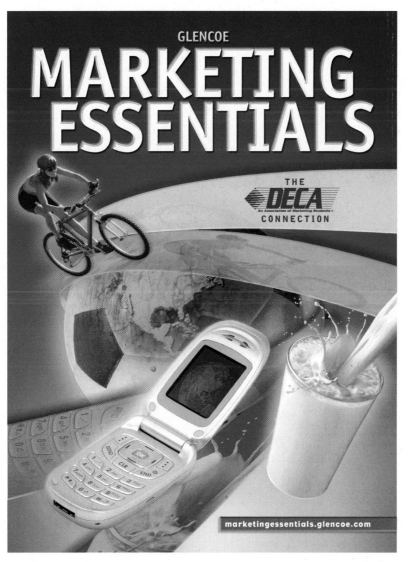

GLENCOE

MARKETING ESSENTIALS

THE **DECA** CONNECTION

marketingessentials.glencoe.com

Lois Schneider Farese

Grady Kimbrell

Carl A. Woloszyk, Ph.D.

Mc Graw Hill **Glencoe**

New York, New York   Columbus, Ohio   Chicago, Illinois   Peoria, Illinois   Woodland Hills, California

TEACHER MANUAL

Glencoe

The *McGraw·Hill* Companies

Send all inquiries to:
Glencoe/McGraw-Hill
21600 Oxnard Street, Suite 500
Woodland Hills, CA 91367

ISBN 0-07-861257-8 (Student Edition)
ISBN 0-07-868914-7 (Teacher Wraparound Edition)

1 2 3 4 5 6 7 8 9   079   09 08 07 06 05

About the Authors

Lois Schneider Farese is a nationally recognized secondary marketing educator and DECA advisor from Allendale, New Jersey. She has been involved in organizing and running New Jersey regional and state DECA conferences and has also participated as series director and event manager at state and national DECA conferences. The State Officer Action Team presented Farese with the Outstanding Service Award for her dedication, professionalism, and commitment to New Jersey DECA in 1993, 1996, and 1999, as well as with the Honorary Life Membership Award in 1990 for setting a new level of professionalism for local advisors. She was inducted into the DECA Hall of Fame in 1996.

Farese was named "Teacher of the Year" in 1981 by the Marketing Education Association of New Jersey. In 1993 and 1999, the University of Richmond recognized Farese for her contributions to the intellectual growth and achievement of students who graduated from her marketing program. In 2000, Farese was the nominee from Northern Highlands Regional High School for the Princeton Prize for Distinguished Secondary School Teaching.

Farese holds a bachelor's degree in business and distributive education and two master's degrees from Montclair State University in New Jersey.

Grady Kimbrell, a nationally recognized author and consultant on career education, began his career in education teaching high school business in Kansas. After relocating to Southern California, Kimbrell taught business courses and coordinated students' in-class activities with their on-the-job experience. He later directed the work experience program for the high schools of Santa Barbara, California.

A pioneer in the use of computers as a tool for educational research, Kimbrell has assisted school districts with a wide variety of research and evaluation activities. His research into on-the-job work activities led to the development of a new type of career interest inventory used in career guidance. In addition, Kimbrell has served on numerous state instructional program committees and writing teams, designed educational computer programs, and produced educational films.

Kimbrell holds degrees in business administration, educational psychology, and business education.

Carl A. Woloszyk is a professor emeritus from Western Michigan University with an extensive background in marketing education. He has served as a state department of education consultant for marketing and cooperative education, DECA and Delta Epsilon Chi state advisor, a career and technical administrator for a regional education service agency, and a secondary marketing teacher-coordinator. As a secondary marketing teacher-coordinator, he taught beginning and advanced marketing courses. His students have received numerous awards at district, state, and national DECA conferences. Woloszyk has served as a director for National DECA; member and president of the Marketing Education Foundation; President, Cooperative Work Experience Education Association of ACTE; and as a state representative to MarkED, a national marketing research and curriculum development center for marketing education. He is a charter and board member of the Michigan Marketing Educators' Association. He has received the Marketing Education Professional Award from the national Marketing Education Association for Exemplary Service to Marketing Education.

Woloszyk holds a master's degree from Eastern Michigan University and an educational specialist degree in occupational education from the University of Michigan. He received his doctorate in business and distributive education from Michigan State University.

Reviewers

Dennis Bristow
Professor of Marketing
St. Cloud State University
St. Cloud, Minnesota

Monica Caillouet
East Ascension High School
Gonzales, Louisiana

Deborah Deacon
Stoneham High School
Stoneham, Massachusetts

Jennifer Killlingsworth
West Hall High School
Oakwood, Georgia

Liberty A. Lacy
Woodland High School
Woodland, Washington

Atkins D. Trey Michael, III
Marketing Education Consultant
North Carolina Department of Public
   Instruction

Tom Scharine
Oregon High School
Oregon, Wisconsin

Michael T. Seltzer
Oxford Academy
Cypress, California

James W. Todd
Mac Arthur High School
San Antonio, Texas

Michelle Totra
Lindbergh High School
St. Louis, Missouri

Dana Young
Yuma High School
Yuma, Colorado

Contributing Writer

Priscilla McCalla
Professional and Program Development Director
DECA
Reston, Virginia

Contents

Inside the Student Edition

Inside the Teacher Edition

Program Resources

Effective Learning Tools
From Glencoe

Unit Opener

In this Unit You Will Find lists the chapters students will be covering in the unit and the chapter titles.

Spark Students' Interest Start With a Visual!

Every unit opens with a magazine advertisement that illustrates a key concept. **Analyze the Ad** ties the ad to the unit content and encourages students to explore its message.

The Marketing Plan tells students which aspects of the marketing plan the unit will address.

The Marketing Wheel is a visual representation of the National Marketing Education Standards. It illustrates the foundations and functions of marketing. The four marketing foundations are broad areas essential to understanding marketing concepts. These include: Business, Management, and Entrepreneurship; Communication and Interpersonal Skills; Economics; and Professional Development. The seven marketing functions are more specific and relate to how marketing is practically applied in the business world. These functions are: Distribution, Financing, Marketing-Information Management, Pricing, Product/Service Management, Promotion, and Selling.

In this Unit tells students the marketing foundations and functions that will be the focus of this unit.

Prepare Students for the World of Marketing With the *Marketing Internship*

Units close with the **Marketing Internship**, a simulated DECA event. Each internship gives a background scenario and a project assignment with a suggested strategy to use. You can find further guidelines at the Online Learning Center at **marketingessentials.glencoe.com**

Build Your Portfolio invites students to record their work and demonstrate what they mastered in the Marketing Internship project. They will build a portfolio containing samples of their best work, which they can present when they apply for real marketing internships.

Online Action tells students where to go to find DECA events-related information at the Online Learning Center.

Integrate *Standards* and *DECA Prep*

The Chapter Opener *Marketing Essentials* has a consistent chapter/section structure. Each chapter is divided into two or three sections. Each section has a self-contained lesson and self-assessment.

The DECA Connection points out which DECA events are related to the chapter's content. It also lists the performance indicators that are used in judging those events.

Chapter Objectives tells students what they are about to learn. These objectives preview the most important content of each chapter.

Guide to the Photo is divided into two parts. Market Talk introduces the chapter content. Quick Think follows up with a question that prompts students to start thinking about the chapter's content.

Promote *Reading* and *Writing* Skills

The Section Opener

Read and Study provides students with strategies to make their reading and studying more effective. The feature is divided into three sections:
- **Before You Read** prompts students to predict or connect to the content by thinking about what they already know.
- **The Main Idea** clearly and concisely states the primary concept in the section.
- **Study Organizer** gives students a note-taking method for organizing the material as they read.

Key Terms allows a preview of the marketing vocabulary words that will be introduced in the section. Key terms will be in boldface type and highlighted in the text.

While You Read focuses students' attention with a question or statement to connect with what they read.

The Section Opener image content

SECTION 1.1

OBJECTIVES
- Define marketing
- Explain the four foundations of marketing
- List the seven functions of marketing
- Understand the marketing concept

KEY TERMS
- marketing
- goods
- services
- marketing concept

Marketing and the Marketing Concept

READ and STUDY

BEFORE YOU READ
Connect Do you think you have ever been influenced by marketing? Explain why or why not and give examples if necessary.

THE MAIN IDEA
Marketing is an umbrella term that includes many activities and has many functions. To be a successful marketer, you need to understand the foundations, functions, and basic tools of marketing.

STUDY ORGANIZER
Draw an umbrella shape like the one below to organize the marketing concepts you will read about in this section.

WHILE YOU READ
Connect Relate the definition of marketing to the functions of marketing and to the marketing concept.

4 UNIT 1 · THE WORLD OF MARKETING

The Scope of Marketing
You already know a lot about marketing because it is all around you. You have been a consumer for many years and you have made decisions about products you liked and did not like. As you study marketing, you will analyze what businesses do to influence consumers' buying decisions. That practice will help you make the transition from thinking like a consumer to thinking like a marketer.

sponding through planned, personalized communication. The selling process influences purchasing decisions and enhances future business opportunities.

The Marketing Concept
The **marketing concept** is the idea that a business should strive to satisfy customers' needs and wants while generating a profit for the firm. The focus is on the customer. For an organization to be successful, all seven functions of marketing need to support this idea.

The personnel responsible for those functions must understand the marketing concept and reach for the same goal in order to send a consistent message to the customer. The message is that the customer satisfaction is

the best possible service to its customers. Businesses that stress the marketing concept with all employees are successful.

Customer Relationship Management (CRM)
In today's marketplace, customer relationship is most important. Customer relationship management (CRM) is an aspect of marketing that combines customer information (through database and computer technology) with customer service and marketing communications. Marketers who specialize in CRM try to create more meaningful one-on-one communications with the customer by applying customer data (demographic, industry, buying history, etc.) to every communication.

1.1 AFTER YOU READ

Reviewing Key Terms and Concepts
1. Name two ideas that can be marketed.
2. Where do exchanges take place?
3. What is the main difference between consumers and industrial users?

Integrating Academic Skills
Math
4. A customer purchases two tables at $149.99 each and would like them to be delivered. Your company charges customers $50 for delivery and the state imposes a 5 percent sales tax on furniture, but not on the delivery charge. What is the total amount due from the customer?

Economics
5. List at least three ways the Internet has changed marketing functions.

Online Action! Check your answers at marketingessentials.glencoe.com/1/read

marketingessentials.glencoe.com

Chapter 1 · Marketing Is All Around Us 7

The Section Close

The *Teacher Wraparound Edition* includes answers to After You Read questions, but students can also check their own answers by visiting **marketingessentials.glencoe.com**.

Review and Recall important material and terms.
Integrate Academic Skills with the world of marketing.

Review and *Reinforce*
Key Concepts

The Chapter Close

Each chapter closes with summaries, vocabulary and concept review activities.

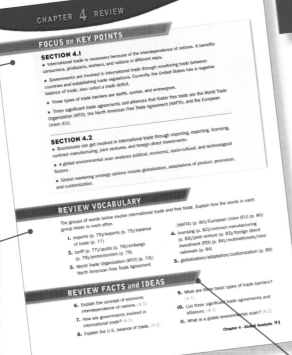

Focus on Key Points reviews the chapter highlights by section.

Review Vocabulary calls on students to define the key terms introduced throughout the chapter. They may be asked to write sentences, play games, or use some other method to demonstrate their understanding of the terms.

Careers in Marketing takes excerpts from interviews with people discussing their careers in marketing. The page highlights school-to-work transition with lists of skills, aptitudes, and career and education paths. It includes a Thinking Critically question to stimulate students and an Online Action project related to careers in marketing.

Review Facts and Ideas asks questions to test students' recall and understanding of material in the chapter.

Review, Apply, and Assess

Build Skills activities and questions strengthen **Workplace Skills, Technology Applications,** and **Math Practice.** Each is based on a marketing situation.

Apply Concepts activities ask students to take what they have learned and apply it to a realistic situation. The students will use word processing programs and other technology.

Help Students Practice and Prepare for DECA Events

The DECA Connection hones students role-playing skills because it is modeled after real DECA events.

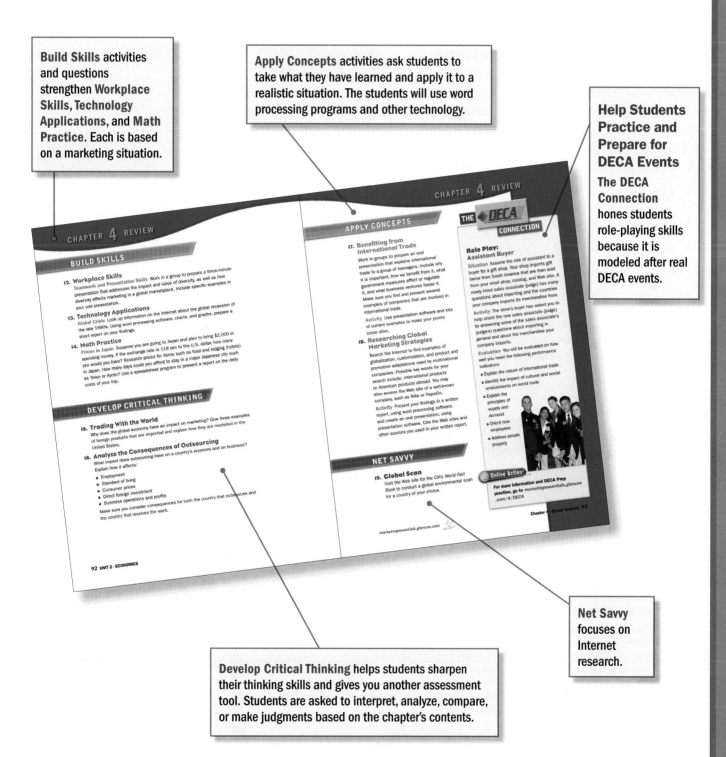

Develop Critical Thinking helps students sharpen their thinking skills and gives you another assessment tool. Students are asked to interpret, analyze, compare, or make judgments based on the chapter's contents.

Net Savvy focuses on Internet research.

Bring the *World of Marketing* to Your Classroom

***Marketing Essentials* Features** introduce students to real marketing situations. Questions strenghten creative and critical thinking skills. **Online Action** sends students to **marketingessentials.glencoe.com** for additional information, assistance, and project suggestions. Your students will:

- Explore Marketing Across all Industries
- Explain Globalization
- Analyze Marketing Strategies

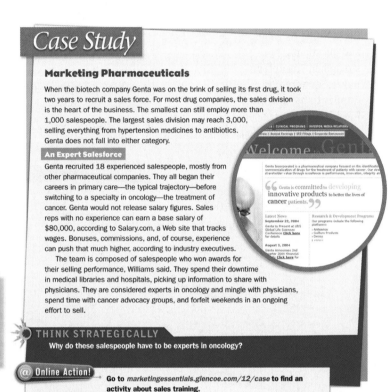

Case Study

Marketing Pharmaceuticals

When the biotech company Genta was on the brink of selling its first drug, it took two years to recruit a sales force. For most drug companies, the sales division is the heart of the business. The smallest can still employ more than 1,000 salespeople. The largest sales division may reach 3,000, selling everything from hypertension medicines to antibiotics. Genta does not fall into either category.

An Expert Salesforce

Genta recruited 18 experienced salespeople, mostly from other pharmaceutical companies. They all began their careers in primary care—the typical trajectory—before switching to a specialty in oncology—the treatment of cancer. Genta would not release salary figures. Sales reps with no experience can earn a base salary of $80,000, according to Salary.com, a Web site that tracks wages. Bonuses, commissions, and, of course, experience can push that much higher, according to industry executives.

The team is composed of salespeople who won awards for their selling performance, Williams said. They spend their downtime in medical libraries and hospitals, picking up information to share with physicians. They are considered experts in oncology and mingle with physicians, spend time with cancer advocacy groups, and forfeit weekends in an ongoing effort to sell.

Case Study offers a real-world story about a marketing decision or situation a business must face.

THINK STRATEGICALLY

Why do these salespeople have to be experts in oncology?

@ Online Action!

Go to *marketingessentials.glencoe.com/12/case* to find an activity about sales training.

GLOBAL MARKET

CHINA

Growing E-Clout of China

With 1.3 billion people, China has the largest population in the world, a huge potential e-commerce market. The Chinese economy is expanding, and computer sales are increasing. In 2003, 80 million Chinese were online, and that number is expected to almost double by 2006 as 800,000 Chinese become Internet users each week. International Data Corporation (IDC) estimated that there would be 84.2 million Web-enabled PCs in China by the end of 2004. Investment in Chinese Web portals is increasing dramatically. U.S. Web titans Yahoo and eBay have both entered the Chinese market, and Google opened a Chinese-language site in early 2004.

Governmental Help The Chinese government gives help to companies developing Web technologies. This provides a competitive advantage over businesses from free market economies like the United States. Web portals in the United States get most of their income from advertising. Chinese portals take advantage of the high rate of cellular phone use to sell services like messaging, games, even video greeting cards—all displayed on cell phones. Retailing and business-to-business sales lag far behind such services in the United States because of credit card and delivery obstacles.

Global Market focuses on a real-world, international business situation. Marketing horizons have expanded, and many businesses now operate globally and face new challenges.

CRITICAL THINKING

Do you think the U.S. government should make grants to technology companies to help them compete? Why or why not?

@ Online Action!

Go to *marketingessentials.glencoe.com/9/global* for an activity on international marketing and computer technology.

Integrate *Ethics* and *Technology*

A MATTER OF ETHICS

Sealing a Deal

A software firm in a medium-sized city has been growing, in part thanks to its popular sports-based video games. The company has decided to sell stock and become a publicly traded company. It can use the money it raises to fund new research and development, but it will also have to meet a lot of new accounting requirements. The people who own the company stock will want complete information about the company's financial performance.

Pitching and Wooing

Accounting firms in the city are desperately trying to get the contract with the software company. They treat executives and software designers to expensive dinners and tickets to NBA games. One company is so determined to win the contract that it makes a secret offer to one of the senior executives. It promises to hire the executive's daughter, who recently graduated from college, but has been having trouble getting a job.

THINKING ETHICALLY

How far can a company go to win over a potential customer?

@ Online Action!

Go to *marketingessentials.glencoe.com/ 12/ethics* to find an activity about ethics and sales.

A Matter of Ethics gives students an opportunity to ponder a situation where ethics will count.

MARKET TECH

FOSE—A High-Tech Trade Show

FOSE stands for Federal Office Systems Expo. This exposition has high-tech companies exhibiting their wares for government officials and procurement officers. In 2004 it was held at the Washington (D.C.) Convention Center. Some 500 vendors selling everything from printers, scanners, and software to GPS-equipped digital cameras and high-tech motion-detector systems showcase their products there. Close to 19,000 people attended FOSE in 2004.

Bringing Home Leads

According to Tom Temin, editor-in-chief of *Government Computer News* and *Washington Technology* and senior vice president for editorial at *PostNewsweek Tech Media*, "the show was more of a breeding ground for networking and mining sales leads than a place for vendors to close deals. There are deal shows, and this one is not one of those." Large and small companies used gimmicks to get prospects to stop at their booths. One company had a cartoonist, two others had slot machines promising gifts and awards for prizes, while another scanned badges for a raffle.

THINK LIKE A MARKETER

If you had a small company that specialized in software to track agricultural goods, would you pay to exhibit at this show? Why or why not?

@ Online Action!

Go to *marketingessentials.glencoe.com/ 12/tech* to find an activity about technology and sales.

Market Tech explains how the technology works, notes the strategy, and evaluates the success of the technology. This feature concludes with a Think Like a Marketer question.

NET MARKETING

Micropurchases for Microprices

Web purchases of more than a few dollars go through traditional credit-card-based billing systems. But what if you sell something that only costs 25 cents? Credit charges and fees cost more than that.

Micropayment carriers offer billing services to Web marketers including writers, artists, and musicians who want to offer very low-cost products online. Consumers open an account with an initial payment of $20 or more, and purchases are then deducted from the account. Obstacles to success include convincing Web surfers to open accounts to pay for such tiny purchases and keeping costs low to make a profit. But the market is potentially huge.

Micropayments for Words

RedPaper.com is a membership Web site that operates like an eBay for words; members buy articles, poems, and stories for less than $1. RedPaper developed its own micropayment system rather than contracting for the service. With 26,000 members, that makes sense.

THINK LIKE A MARKETER

Name one disadvantage of micropayments.

@ Online Action!

Go to *marketingessentials.glencoe.com/ 7/net* to find a project on Internet pricing.

Net Marketing highlights a new or innovative Internet marketing technique. Each Net Marketing feature concludes with a Think Like a Marketer question.

The National Marketing Education Standards

In this era of accountability for education, there has been a groundswell of interest in the development of standards. Due to the request of many of its members, the Marketing Education Resource Center (MarkED) updated its standards in 2000 through a national project involving hundreds of marketing educators and professionals throughout the nation.

Marketing Essentials Correlation to the Standards

If you are using, or plan to use, the National Marketing Education Standards to guide changes in your marketing curriculum, you can be assured that *Marketing Essentials* aligns with the standards. *Marketing Essentials* provides numerous opportunities for students, teachers, and school districts to meet the National Marketing Education Standards. Correlations on each unit interleaf show the close alignment between *Marketing Essentials* and the National Marketing Education Standards.

Mission of Marketing Education

The mission of Marketing Education is to enable students to understand and apply marketing, management, and entrepreneurial principles; to make rational economic decisions; and to exhibit social responsibility in a global economy.

The A*S*K* Institute

The *Institute for the Assessment of Skills and Knowledge for Business* (A*S*K Business Institute) is a joint initiative of DECA and MarkED. It operates as a quasi-independent agency providing objective, industry-based proof of learning for students of business. The Institute is administered by MarkED with guidance from a variety of public and private organizations nationwide.

Premises of the Curriculum

The Marketing Education curriculum should:

- Encourage students to think critically.
- Stress the integration of and articulation with academics.
- Be sequenced so that broad-based understandings and skills provide a foundation to support advanced study of marketing.
- Enable students to acquire broad understandings of and skills in marketing so that they can transfer their skills and knowledge between and among industries.
- Enable students to understand and use technology to perform marketing activities.
- Stress the importance of interpersonal skills in diverse societies.
- Foster a realistic understanding of work.
- Foster an understanding and appreciation of business ethics.
- Utilize a variety of types of interactions with the business community.

The Marketing Education Curriculum

The marketing education curriculum is divided into two primary parts: Foundations and Functions. The **Foundations** are fundamental to an understanding of marketing and can be viewed as co-requisites and as prerequisites for marketing. The content of the Marketing Foundations must be mastered in order for marketing-specific content to have relevance to student learning. There are four broad-based foundational areas: Business, Management, and Entrepreneurship; Communication and Interpersonal Skills; Economics; and Professional Development.

The **Functions** define the discipline of marketing as applied in business operations. They address marketing from the perspective of how it is practiced. Each function is viewed from its relationship to the marketing of a good, service, or idea. The seven functions are Distribution, Financing, Marketing-Information Management, Pricing, Product/Service Management, Promotion, and Selling.

Understanding the Standards

Since students can demonstrate their understanding in a variety of ways, the National Marketing Education Standards are supported by a series of performance indicators: learner expectations for each standard. They require students to demonstrate both their knowledge and skill.

The development approach to learning is exemplified through these performance expectations. For each standard, there are performance expectations for five curriculum planning levels: entry level, career-sustaining, marketing specialist, marketing supervisor, and manager/entrepreneur. The levels serve as building blocks for curriculum development and indicate the complexity of course/program content, ranging from development of employability skills to development of skills needed to manage/own a small business. At a minimum, a high school marketing curriculum would address performance indicators at the first two levels. Depending on time available and ability level of students, high school instructors could incorporate performance indicators from the specialist level. Post-secondary instructors would be responsible for the performance indicators at the specialist and higher levels.

The complete list of performance indicators for the Foundations can be found in the **National Curriculum Planning Guide**. To order the guide, contact MarkED at **www.mark-ed.com**.

FOUNDATIONS

Business, Management, and Entrepreneurship Understands fundamental business, management, and entrepreneurial concepts that affect business decision making

Communications and Interpersonal Skills Understands concepts, strategies, and systems needed to interact effectively with others

Economics Understands the economic principles and concepts fundamental to marketing

Professional Development Understand concepts and strategies needed for career exploration, development, and growth

FUNCTIONS

Distribution Understands the concepts and processes needed to move, store, locate, and/or transfer ownership of goods and services

Financing Understands the financial concepts used in making business decisions

Marketing-Information Management Understands the concepts, systems, and tools needed to gather, access, synthesize, evaluate, and disseminate information for use in making business decisions

Pricing Understands concepts and strategies utilized in determining and adjusting prices to maximize return and meet customers' perceptions of value

Product/Service Management Understands the concepts and processes needed to obtain, develop, maintain, and improve a product or service mix in response to market opportunities

Promotion Understands the concepts and strategies needed to communicate information about products, services, images, and/or ideas to achieve a desired outcome

Selling Understands the concepts and actions needed to determine client needs and wants and respond through planned, personalized communications that influences purchase decisions and enhances future business opportunities

National Marketing Education Standards Scope and Sequence

MARKETING FOUNDATION TOPICS	PERFORMANCE INDICATOR	LOCATION
Marketing Foundation: Economics		
Basic Concepts	Determine forms of economic utility created by marketing activities.	Sections 1.2, 1.3
	Explain the principles of supply and demand.	Sections 3.2, 25.1
	Explain the concept of economic resources.	Section 3.1
	Distinguish between economic goods and services.	Section 3.1
	Describe the nature of economics and economic activities.	Sections 3.1, 3.2
Economic Systems	Explain the types of economic systems.	Sections 3.1, 5.1
	Explain the concept of private enterprise.	Sections 3.1, 5.1
	Explain the concept of competition.	Sections 3.1, 5.1, 5.2
	Determine factors affecting business risk.	Section 5.1
	Identify factors affecting a business's profit.	Section 5.1
	Explain the relationship between government and business.	Sections 3.2, 6.1
	Explain the concept of private enterprise.	Section 33.1
Cost-Profit Relationships	Explain the concept of productivity.	Section 5.2
Economic Indicators/Trends	Explain the concept of Gross Domestic Product.	Section 5.1
	Explain measures used to analyze economic conditions.	Section 5.1
	Explain the nature of the Consumer Price Index.	Section 5.1
	Determine the impact of business cycles on business activities.	Section 5.2
International Concepts	Explain the nature of international trade.	Section 4.1
	Evaluate influences on a nation's ability to trade.	Section 4.1
	Identify the impact of cultural and social environments on world trade.	Section 4.2
Marketing Foundation: Communication, Interpersonal Skills		
Fundamentals of Communication	Explain the nature of effective communications.	Section 8.1
	Apply effective listening skills.	Section 8.1
	Make oral presentations.	Section 8.2
	Handle telephone calls in a businesslike manner.	Section 8.2
	Explain the nature of written communications.	Section 8.2
	Use communications technology/systems.	Section 8.2
Staff Communications	Explain the nature of staff communications.	Section 10.2
Group Working Relationships	Treat others fairly at work.	Sections 6.2, 11.1
	Foster positive working relationships.	Sections 10.1, 11.2
Customer Relationships	Handle customer inquiries.	Section 14.2
Participate as a Team Member	Participate as a team member.	Section 10.2
Marketing Foundation: Professional Development		
Self-Understanding	Demonstrate ethical work habits.	Section 6.2
	Identify personality traits important to business.	Section 10.1
	Adjust to change.	Section 10.1
	Demonstrate appropriate creativity.	Section 20.2
	Identify desirable personality traits important to business.	Sections 33.1, 37.2
Self-Development	Assess personal interests and skills needed for success in business.	Section 37.1
Career Planning	Explain employment opportunities in marketing.	Section 1.3
	Explain employment opportunities in business.	Sections 33.2, 37.3
	Identify tentative occupational interest.	Section 37.1
	Analyze employer expectations in the business environment.	Section 37.2
	Identify sources of career information.	Sections 37.2, 38.1

Job-Seeking Skills	Utilize job-search strategies.	Section 38.
	Complete a job application.	Section 38.2
	Write a letter of application.	Section 38.2
	Prepare a résumé.	Section 38.2
	Interview for a job.	Section 38.2
	Write a follow-up letter after job interviews.	Section 38.2
Continuing Development	Identify skills needed to enhance career progression.	Section 1.3, Section 37.2

Marketing Foundation: Business, Management and Entrepreneurship

Business Fundamentals	Describe marketing functions and related activities.	Section 1.1
	Explain marketing and its importance in a global economy.	Section 1.1, Section 1.3, Section 4.1, Section 22.2
	Explain the role of business in society.	Section 2.2, Section 3.1, Section 5.2
	Explain the concept of management.	Section 11.1
	Describe the role of management in the achievement of quality.	Section 11.2
	Explain the nature and scope of purchasing.	Section 23.1
	Explain the nature of the buying process.	Section 23.2
	Conduct vendor search.	Section 23.2
	Describe the nature of profit-and-loss statements.	Section 27.1
	Explain the types of business ownership.	Section 33.2
	Explain the concept of accounting.	Section 36.2
	Explain the nature of balance sheets.	Section 36.2
	Explain the nature of environmental regulations.	Section 6.1, 6.2
	Explain the nature of trade regulations.	Section 4.1, 4.2
	Describe legal issues affecting businesses.	Sections 32.2, 33.2, 5.1
Technological Tools	Identify ways that technology impacts business.	Section 9.1
	Demonstrate basic word-processing skills.	Section 9.2
	Demonstrate basic database skills.	Section 9.2
	Demonstrate basic spreadsheet skills.	Section 9.2
	Demonstrate basic presentation software skills.	Section 9.2
	Demonstrate basic search skills on the Web.	Section 9.2
Business Risks	Identify speculative business risks.	Section 33.1
	Explain the types of business risk.	Section 33.1, Section 34.1
	Explain the nature of risk management.	Section 34.1
	Explain routine security precautions.	Section 34.2
	Describe the concept of insurance.	Section 34.2
Organizing	Plan and organize the work efforts of others.	Section 35.2
Leading	Explain the nature of leadership in organizations.	Section 10.2, Section 11.2
	Explain the nature of management/supervisory training.	Section 11.1
	Encourage team building.	Section 11.2
	Explain the concept of staff motivation.	Section 11.2
Controlling	Interpret financial statements.	Section 36.
	Describe the nature of cash-flow statements.	Section 36.2
Planning	Explain the nature of a business plan.	Section 35.1, Section 36.1
	Explain external planning considerations.	Section 35.1
	Develop business plan.	Section 35.2

Marketing Function: Distribution

Nature and Scope	Explain the nature of channels of distribution.	Section 21.1
	Explain the nature of channel members relationships.	Section 21.1
	Explain the nature and scope of distribution.	Section 21.2, Section 22.1

Order Fulfillment	Use information system for order fulfillment.	Section 16.3
Warehousing/Stock Handling	Explain the shipping process.	Section 22.1
	Explain storing considerations.	Section 22.2
	Explain the nature of warehousing.	Section 22.2
	Explain the receiving process.	Section 24.1
	Explain stock handling techniques used in receiving deliveries.	Section 24.1
Management of Distribution	Explain the nature of channel strategies.	Section 21.2
	Select channels of distribution.	Section 21.2
Inventory Control	Explain the nature of inventory control systems.	Section 24.2
	Explain the types of inventory control systems.	Section 24.2

Marketing Function: Financing

Nature and Scope	Explain the nature and scope of financing.	Section 35.3, Section 36.1
Extending Credit	Explain the purpose and importance of credit.	Section 16.2, Section 32.2
Obtaining Business Credit	Explain the purposes and importance of obtaining credit (business).	Section 32.2
	Determine financing needed to start a business.	Section 35.3
	Describe sources of financing for businesses.	Section 35.3

Marketing Function: Marketing Information Management

Nature and Scope	Describe the need for marketing information.	Section 28.1
	Explain the nature of marketing research in a marketing-information function.	Section 28.1, Section 29.1
	Describe the use of technology in the marketing-information management function.	Section 29.2
Information Gathering	Identify information monitored for marketing decision making.	Section 28.2
	Describe sources of secondary data.	Section 29.1
	Collect marketing information from others.	Section 29.2
Information Processing	Use data for information analysis.	Section 29.1
Marketing Planning	Explain the nature of sales forecasts.	Section 28.2
	Explain the nature of marketing plans.	Section 35.2

Marketing Function: Pricing

Nature and Scope	Explain legal considerations for pricing.	Section 25.2
	Explain the nature and scope of the pricing function.	Section 25.1, Section 26.1, Section 27.1
Determining Prices	Determine discounts and allowances that can be used to adjust base prices.	Section 16.3, Section 27.2
	Select approach for setting a base price.	Section 25.1, Section 26.2
	Determine cost of product (break-even, ROI, markup, price).	Section 25.1, Section 26.2
	Explain factors affecting pricing decisions.	Section 25.2, Section 26.2
	Calculate break-even point.	Section 25.2
	Identify strategies for pricing new products.	Section 26.1
	Set prices.	Section 26.2, Section 27.1

Marketing Function: Product Service Management

Nature and Scope	Explain the nature and scope of the product/service management function.	Section 30.1
	Identify the impact of product life cycles on marketing decisions.	Section 30.2
Quality Assurances	Explain warranties and guarantees.	Section 32.1
	Identify consumer protection provisions of appropriate agencies.	Section 32.1
Product Mix	Explain the concept of product mix.	Section 30.1
	Plan product mix.	Section 30.1
Positioning	Describe factors used by marketers to position products/businesses.	Section 30.2
	Explain the nature of branding.	Section 31.1

Retail Product Considerations	Plan purchases.	Section 23.1

Marketing Function: Promotion

Nature and Scope	Explain the role of promotion as a marketing function.	Section 17.1
	Identify the elements of the promotional mix.	Section 17.1
	Describe the use of technology in the promotion function.	Section 20.2
Advertising	Explain the types of advertising media.	Section 19.1
	Evaluate the effectiveness of advertising.	Section 19.1
	Calculate media costs.	Section 19.2
	Select advertising media.	Section 19.2
	Explain the components of advertisements.	Section 20.1
Publicity/Public Relations	Develop public relations plan.	Section 17.1
	Analyze costs/benefits of participation in community activities.	Section 17.1
	Obtain publicity.	Section 17.1
Sales Promotion	Develop sales promotion plans.	Section 17.2
	Analyze the use of specialty promotion.	Section 17.2
	Explain the use of visual merchandising to create an image.	Section 18.1
	Explain the types of display arrangements.	Section 18.1
	Explain the relationship of merchandising and visual merchandising (display).	Section 18.2
	Prepare merchandise for display.	Section 18.2
	Maintain displays.	Section 18.2
Management of Promotion	Explain the use of advertising agencies.	Section 20.1

Marketing Function: Selling

Nature and Scope	Explain the nature and scope of the selling function.	Section 12.1
	Explain key factors in building a clientele.	Section 12.2
Product Knowledge	Analyze product information to identify product features and benefits.	Section 2.2
	Analyze product information for use in selling.	Section 12.1
Process and Techniques	Address the needs of individual personalities.	Section 2.1
	Identify customer's buying motives for use in selling.	Section 12.1
	Facilitate customer buying decision.	Section 12.1
	Determine customer/client needs.	Section 12.2, Section 13.2
	Differentiate between consumer and organizational buying behavior.	Section 12.2
	Explain the selling process.	Section 13.1
	Prepare for the sales presentation.	Section 13.1
	Establish relationship with client/customer.	Section 13.1
	Assess customer/client needs.	Section 13.2
	Demonstrate product.	Section 14.1
	Recommend specific product.	Section 14.1
	Convert customer/client objections into selling points.	Section 14.2
	Close the sale.	Section 15.1
	Sell good/service/idea to individuals.	Section 15.1
	Facilitate customer buying decisions.	Section 15.1
	Demonstrate suggestion selling.	Section 15.2
	Plan follow-up strategies for use in selling.	Section 15.2
	Address the needs of individual personalities.	Section 16.2
Support Activities	Process sales documentation.	Section 15.2, Section 16.1
	Calculate miscellaneous charges.	Section 16.2
Management of Selling Activities	Analyze technology for use in the sales function.	Section 16.1

Planning *Your* Marketing Course

The information in the Unit Planning Guide gives you a comprehensive overview of the unit content. You can easily identify unit objectives and unit enrichment resources. You will find program resources available to you for each chapter in the unit. Refer to these pages to make the most of the numerous instructional materials included with *Marketing Essentials.*

Enrichment Resources This is a list of resources related to the unit content.

Unit Objectives A bulleted list presents the performance-based objectives each student should be able to achieve once the unit is completed.

Teacher Classroom Resources A comprehensive list of chapter resources provides a quick reference for planning your instruction.

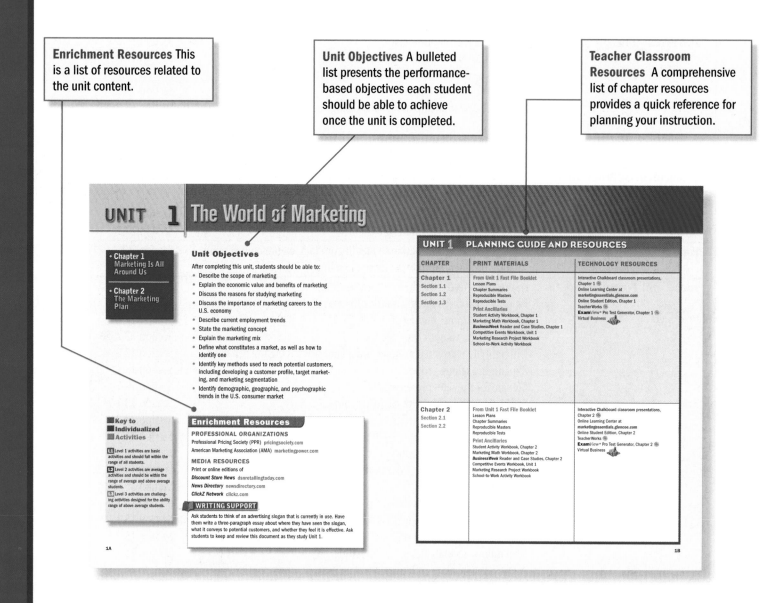

Helping You Meet
National Marketing Education Standards

On the second two pages of each unit planning guide, you will find a table presenting correlations between *Marketing Essentials* content and the National Marketing Education Standards. Relevant performance indicators and associated assessment activities are listed by chapter and section.

Performance Indicators
Performance indicators from the National Marketing Education Standards are detailed for each section of every chapter in the unit.

Assessment Correlations In-text assessment activities related to each performance indicator are detailed by section and chapter assessment.

National Marketing Education   Standards Assessment Correlation

CHAPTER	SECTION	PERFORMANCE INDICATOR	SECTION ASSESSMENT		CHAPTER ASSESSMENT						UNIT LAB
			Reviewing Key Terms and Concepts	Integrating Academic Skills	Review Facts and Ideas	Build Skills	Develop Critical Thinking	Apply Concepts	Workplace Skills	Net Savvy	Marketing Internship
Chapter 1 Marketing Is All Around Us	1.1	Describe marketing functions and related activities (BME)	1, 2, 3	✓	11–14	20, 21	23	26, 25	✓	✓	✓
		Explain marketing and its importance in a global economy (BME)	2, 3	✓	11–19			25		✓	
	1.2	Determine forms of economic utility created by marketing activities (ECO)	1, 2, 3	✓	10	20, 21	23	25	✓	✓	
	1.3	Explain employment opportunities in marketing (PD)	3			21	24				
		Identify skills needed to enhance career progression (PD)			20	24	26	✓			
Chapter 2 The Marketing Plan	2.1	Explain marketing and its importance in a global economy (BME)	1, 2, 3		8, 10						
		Explain the concept of competition (ECO)									✓
		Identify factors affecting a business's profit (ECO)									✓
		Address the needs of individual personalities (SEL)	1, 2	✓	8, 9, 13, 14	16, 17	19	21, 22	✓	✓	
	2.2	Explain the role of business in society (BME)	1		13, 14	16	20		✓	✓	
		Identify factors affecting a business's profit (ECO)									✓
		Analyze product information to identify product features and benefits (SEL)	2, 3	✓	12, 15		19	21, 22			✓

BME Business, Management, Entrepreneurship **ECO** Economics **PD** Professional Development **SEL** Selling

Online Action! Check the latest updates for national standards and for your state's standards at marketingessentials.glencoe.com

1C

Legend The legend explains the acronyms that follow each performance indicator. The acronyms represent the four foundations and seven functions of marketing.

Check for Updates Go to marketingessentials.glencoe.com's Teacher Center and click on Standards Correlations and Updates to find out the latest on national and states standards.

Convenient Teaching Plan

Introduction

Marketing students bring a variety of learning styles and needs to the classroom. The *Teacher Wraparound Edition* of *Marketing Essentials* provides you with a broad range of activities to fit your classroom's learning styles and needs. The *Teacher Wraparound Edition* is designed to assist both new and experienced teachers. It provides a wide range of suggestions, resources, and useful professional notes in a convenient format.

The Four Step Plan

Each section of each chapter in the *Teacher Wraparound Edition* provides a lesson plan divided into four steps: **Focus, Teach, Assess,** and **Close**. This proven master approach is designed to help you develop the chapter concepts in a manner that is both organized and consistent, with a framework that makes it easy for you to teach the material.

Build Background suggests a chapter opening discussion intended to draw the students in by referring to something familiar to them.

Prepare to Read offers a directed class activity to help students approach the chapter, preparing them in an organized manner for the reading.

The DECA Connection gives teachers the information they need to present each DECA feature to their classes and points out online resources for additional teaching tips.

Exploring the Sections

FOCUS

The first step in the four-step teaching plan is **Focus**.

● **Introducing the Section** prepares students and addresses the central objective of the section.

● **Read and Study** suggests ways to lead students and ideas on how to model effective reading strategies.

TEACH

The second and core step in the four-step teaching plan is **Teach**.

● **Concept Development** illustrates real-world applications which can help to maintain students' connections to the material.

● **Individualized Math Skills** reinforces the link between academics and career.

ASSESS

Assess provides a variety of review and evaluation activities and tools specifically designed to accommodate a wide range of learning abilities.

● **Review Guide** offers guided reviews of concepts and key terms; It also recommends additional activities that range from basic to advanced.

These activities are found in supplemental teaching materials, including the *Student Activity Workbook*, the *Competitive Event Workbook*, and the *BusinessWeek Reader and Case Studies*.

CLOSE

This step in the teaching plan summarizes content and suggests exercises to review the main points of each section.

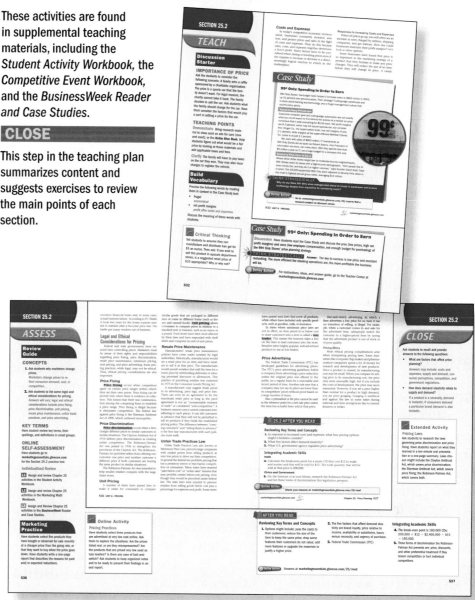

Additional Elements of the Teacher Wraparound Edition

Formative Assessment provides alternative or supplemental assessments, ranging from basic to advanced, to use for students with different learning styles or learning paces. It suggests remedial strategies for you if the results indicate the students have not learned the information.

Apply Concepts poses questions that use the chapter material in realistic situations.

Mini-Quiz provides you with a short set of questions to review each chapter's key content.

Individualized Practice helps students absorb concepts in the text through application.

Enrichment takes the lesson beyond the textbook. Each exercise asks students to apply a concept to a real-world situation.

Careers in Marketing includes additional Lifelong Learning and Primary Source activities. This edition directs you to the right Web sites for instructions and ideas.

Features sections help you teach the points made in the Case Study, Global Market, Market Tech, A Matter of Ethics, and Net Marketing features. The *Teacher Wraparound Edition* includes answers to the feature questions.

Photo Guide provides the answers for each question and recommends a follow-up discussion or activity.

Build Vocabulary appears throughout the *Teacher Wraparound Edition*. It selects some of the most difficult words in the section and lets you preview them with students.

Varied Assessments Reach All Students

Understanding Assessment

As a marketing educator, you need a variety of ways to assess what your students have learned. Student progress has traditionally been measured by written tests that evaluate recall of subject content. When you wish to use traditional testing methods, turn to the **Exam**View testbank on the *Marketing Essentials* CD-ROM, which allows you to build customized tests to assess student understanding. Additionally, you have available **Reproducible Tests** as traditional assessment modes. However, it is necessary to assess more than students' rote learning skills.

Using Alternative Assessment

Today's curriculum focuses on the acquisition of knowledge and skills that will help students function in the workplace. These skills include critical thinking, problem solving, communication, and human relations. The acquisition of those skills is not so easily evaluated using the traditional paper-and-pencil test. The focus of assessment, therefore, has shifted more and more toward alternative assessment.

Alternative assessment, sometimes known as performance-based assessment, is a continuum of testing strategies that allow you to observe students' behavior. Most performance-based assessments ask students to demonstrate their mastery of material by performing a specific task. Alternative assessment aims to reveal what each student can do with his/her knowledge in context. It is an excellent tool to meet the needs of students with diverse learning styles, cultural backgrounds, English proficiency levels, and ability levels. *Marketing Essentials* provides a multitude of activities, projects, and situations that will help you to create opportunities for alternative assessment:

- **Marketing Internship**, a *DECA* simulation in each unit, offers an assignment or project using technology and research.

- **Build Your Portfolio**, found in each unit, offers two options for creating work that will build students' portfolios, providing a tangible record of marketing work completed.

- Features offer questions that can be used to assess students. **Case Study** offers **Think Strategically**, while **Critical Thinking** questions are included in **Global Market** and **Careers in Marketing**. Such questions can give you insight into students' reasoning and problem-solving abilities.

- **Integrating Academic Skills** asks students to analyze situations and use information to solve problems.

- Each Chapter Review offers a variety of materials that can be used as alternative assessments: **Build Skills** focuses on workplace and technological skills as well as academic skills; **Develop Critical Thinking** provides two questions which can be used independently; **Apply Concepts** offers two alternative activities in which students apply information they learned in the text to real-world problems.

ASSESSMENT STRATEGIES	ADVANTAGES	DISADVANTAGES

Objective measures
Multiple choice
Matching
Item sets
True/False
	Reliable, easy to validate
	Objective, if designed
	  effectively
	Low cost, efficient
	Automated administration
	Lends to equating
		Measures cognitive
		  knowledge effectively
		Limited on other measures
		Not a good measure of
		  overall performance

Written measures
Essays
Restricted response
Written simulations
Case analysis
Problem-solving exercises
	Face validity (real life)
	In-depth assessment
	Measures writing skills and
	  higher level skills
	Reasonable developmental costs
	  and time
		Subjective scoring
		Time consuming and
		  expensive to score
		Limited breadth
		Difficult to equate
		Moderate reliability

Oral measures
Oral examinations
Interviews
	Measures communications
	  and interpersonal skills
	In-depth assessment with
	  varied stimulus materials
	Learner involvement
		Costly and time consuming
		Limited reliability
		Narrow sample of content
		Scoring difficult, need
		  multiple raters

Simulated activities In-basket Computer simulations	Moderate reliability Performance-based measure	Costly and time consuming Difficult to score, administer, and develop

Portfolio and product analysis
Work samples
Projects
Work diaries and logs
Achievement records
	Provides information not
	  normally available
	Learner involvement
	Face validity (real life)
	Easy to collect information
		Costly to administer
		Labor and paper intensive
		Difficult to validate or
		  equate
		Biased toward best samples
		  or outstanding qualities

Performance measures
Demonstrations
Presentations
Performances
Production work
Observation
	Job-related
	Relatively easy to
	  administer
	In-depth assessment
	Face validity
		Rater training required
		Hard to equate
		Subjective scoring
		Time consuming if breadth
		  is needed

Performance records References Performance rating forms Parental rating	Efficient Low cost Easy to administer	Low reliability Subjective Hard to equate Rater judgment

Self-evaluation	Learner involvement and
	  empowerment
	Learner responsibility
	Measures dimensions not
	  available otherwise
		May be biased or
		  unrealistic

Reading: The First Skill

"Today a reader, tomorrow a leader."
—Margaret Fuller, American writer and philosopher, 1810–1850

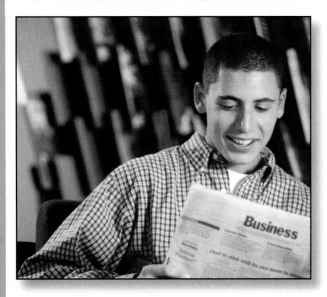

Students who are proficient readers usually go on to master a wide variety of transferable skills. Good readers become lifelong learners as they acquire a set of skills that will prepare them for the challenges of the 21st century.

Research-Based Instruction

The Standards for the English Language Arts state that "all students must have the opportunities and resources to develop the language skills they need to pursue life's goals and to participate fully as informed, productive members of society." The federal government also recognizes the importance of reading for success in life. The No Child Left Behind act (NCLB) emphasizes reading instruction based on scientifically proven methods. NCLB legislation also holds schools and school districts accountable for student progress in this area. Each year, students are given assessments to ensure that they have met the standards of academic proficiency developed by the state.

Accountability

The current emphasis on accountability for student achievement affects you as a teacher of Marketing because reinforcement of basic literacy skills is a responsibility shared by all educators. As the leading publisher of educational materials, Glencoe is committed to providing teachers and students with a variety of effective reading and related literacy strategies.

Integrating Language Arts

To help you incorporate literacy skills (reading, writing, listening, speaking, and viewing) into your Marketing classroom, we have provided a correlation to the language arts standards covered in *Marketing Essentials*. As you teach Marketing with and through the *Standards for the English Language Arts** you will help strengthen your students' literacy performance.

Correlation of *Marketing Essentials* and Standards for the English Language Arts

DESCRIPTION	CORRELATION
Students read a wide variety of print and non-print texts to build an understanding of texts, of themselves, and of the cultures of the United States and the world; to acquire new information; to respond to the needs and demands of society and the workplace; and for personal fulfillment.	Global Market Chapters 4, 8, 10, 37, 38
Students adjust their use of spoken, written, and visual language (e.g., conventions, style, vocabulary) to communicate effectively with a variety of audiences and for different purposes.	Think and Write Chapters 8, 10, 11, 37, 38
Students employ a wide range of strategies as they write and use different writing process elements appropriately to communicate with different audiences for a variety of purposes.	Chapter Review Chapters 8, 10, 11, 37, and 38
Students apply knowledge of language structure, language conventions (e.g., spelling and punctuation), media techniques, figurative language, and genre to create, critique, and discuss print and non-print texts.	Chapter Review Think and Write Think Ethically Think Strategically
Students conduct research on issues and interests by generating ideas and questions, and by posing problems. They gather, evaluate, and synthesize data from a variety of sources (e.g., print and non-print texts, artifacts, people) to communicate their discoveries in ways that suit their purpose and audience.	Chapter Review Net Savvy Think Like a Marketer Think Strategically
Students use a variety of technological and information resources (e.g., libraries, databases, computer networks, video) to gather and synthesize information and to create and communicate knowledge.	Chapter Review Market Tech Net Marketing
Students develop an understanding of and respect for diversity in language use, patterns, and dialects across cultures, ethnic groups, geographic regions, and social roles.	Global Market Chapters 4, 8, and 10

* THE INFORMATION ABOVE IS PUBLISHED WITH PERMISSION OF THE STANDARDS FOR THE ENGLISH LANGUAGE ARTS, COPUBLISHED BY THE NATIONAL COUNCIL OF TEACHERS OF ENGLISH AND THE INTERNATIONAL READING ASSOCIATION.

Strategies for Reading

The chart below lists the many reading strategies and activities that you will find throughout Glencoe's *Marketing Essentials*. Reading specialists have recognized that understanding is increased when students follow pre-reading, during reading, and post-reading strategies. (Some strategies may be effective in all three stages.)

BEFORE READING STRATEGIES			
STRATEGY	**PURPOSE**	**ACTIVITIES**	**LOCATION**
Set the Purpose	Provide students with purpose for reading	Objectives	Chapter Opener Section Opener
Activate Prior Knowledge	Prompt students to recall known or related information in a new context	Before You Read	Section Opener
Predict	Ask students to anticipate the content based on visual clues	Quick Think	Chapter Opener
Identify the Main Idea	Focus attention on key concepts	The Main Idea Study Organizer	Section Opener Section Opener
Pre-Teach Vocabulary	Explain enriched or above-grade vocabulary	Key Terms	Section Opener
DURING READING STRATEGIES			
Build Comprehension	Reinforce and extend understanding of text material	The Main Idea While You Read	Section Opener Section Opener
Identify Key Terms	Help students review and reinforce important concepts	Key Terms	Section Opener
Learn With Visuals	Support alternative learning styles Help students practice interpreting content using graphics	Analyze the Ad Guide to the Photo Photo or Ad Caption and Question	Unit Opener Chapter Opener Text Feature
Organize to Learn	Outline main ideas and key subpoints	Study Organizer	Section Opener

AFTER READING STRATEGIES			
STRATEGY	**PURPOSE**	**ACTIVITIES**	**LOCATION**
Summarize	Understand and explain key ideas in original words	After You Read Review Vocabulary Review Facts and Ideas	End-of-Section Feature Chapter Review Chapter Review
Question	Develop critical thinking and reasoning skills	Develop Critical Thinking Quick Think	Chapter Review Chapter Opener
Discuss	Grasp details and nuances of concepts; share alternative and interpretive views with other students	Think Like a Marketer Think Strategically Develop Critical Thinking Apply Concepts	In-text Feature In-text Feature Chapter Review Chapter Review
Make Connections	Recognize and build relationships between text and real world	Analyze the Ad Guide to the Photo Marketing Internship	Unit Opener Chapter Opener Unit Closer
Write	Assess comprehension; extend understanding of concepts; offer new interpretations	Think and Write Apply Concepts Marketing Internship Build Your Portfolio	Unit Opener Chapter Review Unit Closer Unit closer

Reading for All Students

Today's classroom is composed of students with various backgrounds, skill levels,and characteristics that affect their ability to read and process information at grade level. These students include:

- Struggling and striving readers
- English Language Learners (ELLs)
- Students with physical disabilities
- Students with learning difficulties
- Gifted and talented students

Universal Design for Learning

Every student needs to develop reading skills in order to succeed in school and in the workplace. To help meet this goal, Glencoe has developed Inclusion in the Marketing Classroom. This booklet contains reading and learning strategies designed to reach students of all performance levels and abilities. The booklet follows the Universal Design for Learning, a classroom approach that emphasizes how making a classroom inclusive helps every student-challenged or not-to learn and grow.

To help make your classroom more inclusive, you may wish to adapt some of the strategies summarized in the chart on page TM27.

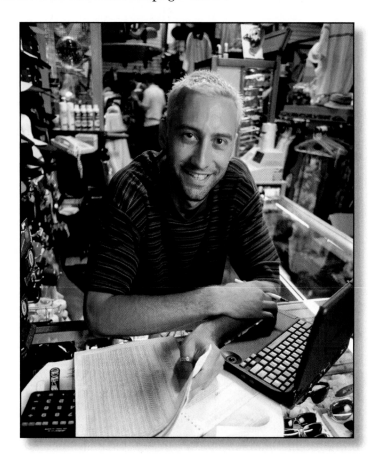

CLASSROOM INCLUSION STRATEGIES

STRATEGIES	MARKETING ACTIVITIES	LOCATION
Identify essential course content • Provide a course outline. • Have students use lesson organizers. • Use guided notes and handouts in class.	Objectives Study Organizer Focus on Key Points	Chapter and Section Openers Section Opener Section Opener
Use a variety of instructional methods and groupings • Have peers teach peers. • Use cooperative learning. • Allow small group discussions.	Apply Concepts Marketing Internship	Chapter Review Unit Closer
Provide information in multiple formats • Demonstrate ideas verbally, physically, and in writing. • Use pictures, posters, and other visuals to convey main ideas. • Use color to help students identify important ideas and organize information. • Use graphic organizers to help students visualize relationships among information.	Study Organizer Analyze the Ad Guide to the Photo	Unit Opener Chapter Opener Section Opener
Use multiple methods of assessment • Oral reports • Written reports • Multimedia presentations • Student portfolios	Apply Concepts Build Your Portfolio	Chapter Review Unit Closer
Use technology • Put content online so students can use screen readers to access information. • Use text to speech software. • Use CDs and multimedia to provide multiple ways to access information	Apply Concepts Technology Applications	Chapter Review Chapter Review

Build Academic Skills

Academic skills are crucial for success both inside and outside the classroom. The workplace is a diverse, interdependent environment, requiring a variety of skills. When you integrate academic skills into the marketing curriculum, you will help your students develop connections between school and the real world.

The No Child Left Behind Act

The No Child Left Behind Act of 2001 emphasizes student achievement in basic academic subjects and introduces strict accountability measures for schools in the form of standardized testing. Traditionally, the core academic subjects have been language arts, science, and mathematics. No Child Left Behind expands the list to the following:

- English
- Reading/language arts
- Mathematics
- Science
- Foreign languages
- Civics and government
- Economics
- Arts
- History
- Geography

25.2 AFTER YOU READ

Reviewing Key Terms and Concepts

1. In response to increased costs and expenses, what four pricing options might a business consider?
2. What five factors affect demand elasticity?
3. What U.S. government agency regulates price advertising?

Integrating Academic Skills

Math
4. Calculate the break-even point for a music CD that cost $12 to make and market and that will be sold for $15. The total quantity that will be sold at that price is 200,000.

Civics and Government
5. On the Internet or at your library, research the Robinson-Patman Act and list three forms of discrimination this legislation prevents.

@ Online Action! Check your answers at *marketingessentials.glencoe.com/25/read*

Chapter 25 - Price Planning **537**

marketingessentials.glencoe.com

The Importance of Integrating Academics into the Curriculum

In a recent survey of high school graduates–many of whom had gone directly to work rather than into postsecondary education–more than half the respondents said their high schools should have more strongly emphasized language arts, reading, mathematics, and science.

Unfortunately, some of these students–like so many others–did not see the relevance and value of much of their coursework while they were in high school. By explicitly integrating academic skills into the marketing curriculum, you can demonstrate the real-world necessity of learning these skills and the relationship between these skills and a successful business career.

Integrated learning offers the following additional benefits to students:

- It provides examples of real-world learning and thus establishes patterns of lifelong learning.

- It improves the academic achievement of all students—those who will begin their careers directly after high school, those who will go on to some postsecondary education or training, and those who will obtain four-year college degrees.

- It helps students make realistic plans for their own careers and educations.

How to Integrate Academic skills into the Marketing Curriculum

Integrate academic skills into the marketing curriculum by making them a regular part of your classroom activities. Include academic components in all class assignments: have students read class assignments and texts, write letters and reports, give presentations, and perform mathematics exercises. Make your expectations clear, telling students that grammar, spelling, and quality of presentation will be part of the evaluation criteria right along with subject content. Stress that clear writing, accuracy, and attention to detail are skills students will need for success not only in school, but also in the workplace.

Additionally, use assessments that require using academic skills. Ask students to write coherently to answer questions; expect them to solve math problems correctly; and include economic principles and geographic identification in assessments on the global marketplace. In other words, in both assignments and evaluations, underscore the connections between academics and marketing.

CHAPTER 26 REVIEW

BUILD SKILLS

13. Workplace Skills

Human Relations You work for a department store in the women's dress department. A customer approaches you with two dresses that are identical, except that the one from the petite department is not marked down, while the other one is. None of the petite dresses have been marked down because the buyer for that department did not elect to do so. How will you handle this customer who wants to buy that dress style in the petite size?

14. Technology Applications

Computer Skills Set up a spreadsheet to demonstrate bundle pricing of a computer and needed software. Show the savings to a customer when buying the advertised bundle price as compared with buying each item separately.

15. Math Practice

Incentives Promotional discounts are given to stores by manufacturers to place products in preferred locations or to pay for ads, displays, or in-store demonstrations. Calculate the store's net cost to stock the following items and the percentage of the discount given.

Item	Purchase Amount	Discount Amount	Net Cost to Store	Percent Discount
Snowboards	$5,650	$847.50		
CD Players	$535	$42.80		

Build Critical Thinking Skills

One of the factors that determines workplace success is an person's ability to deal with the varied demands of the fast-paced business world. This requires insightful decision making, creative problem solving, and interactions with diverse groups: employees, management, investors, customers, or clients. Thus, teaching critical thinking equips your students with the skills necessary to achieve success.

The Value of Critical Thinking

Critical thinking is the process of reasonably or logically deciding what to do or believe. It involves the ability to:

- Compare and contrast
- Solve problems
- Make decisions
- Analyze and evaluate
- Synthesize and transfer knowledge
- Engage in metacognition

Critical thinking skills are important for the following reasons:

- They help students investigate their own problem-solving mechanisms.
- They help students find creative resolutions.
- They lead students to compare and contrast what they know with unknowns.
- They allow students to make decisions about their own learning while making them aware of their processes.

Teaching Critical Thinking

All learning requires thinking. Benjamin Bloom's *Taxonomy of the Cognitive Domain* is probably the most widely recognized schema of levels of thinking. Each of Bloom's six cognitive categories lists various thinking skills and indicates the types of behavior students are expected to perform to fulfill specific learning goals.

CATEGORY	GOAL	EXPECTED STUDENT RESPONSE	APPROPRIATE QUESTIONS/ PROMPTS
Knowledge	Identify and recall of information	Define, recognize, recall, identify, label, show, collect, understand, examine	Who...? What...? When...? Where...? How...? Describe....
Comprehension	Organize and select facts and ideas	Translate, interpret, explain, describe, summarize, extrapolate	Retell in your own words.... What is the main idea of...?
Application	Use facts, rules, and principles	Apply, solve, show, experiment, predict	How is...an example of...? How is...related to...?
Analysis	Separate a whole into component parts	Connect, relate, differentiate, classify, arrange, check, group, distinguish, organize, categorize, detect, compare, infer	Classify...according to.... How does... compare/ contrast with...?
Synthesis	Combine ideas to form a new whole	Produce, propose, design, construct, combine, formulate, compose, plan, hypothesize	What would you predict/ infer from...? What might happen if you combined...with...?
Evaluation	Develop opinions, judgments, or decisions	Appraise, judge, criticize, decide	What do you think about...? Prioritize....

Integrating Critical Thinking

The text of *Marketing Essentials* and this *Teacher Wraparound Edition* provide many opportunities for you to integrate critical thinking skills into your daily lessons. Each **Careers in Marketing** feature, for example, includes a critical thinking question, and each chapter review include critical thinking questions. Here are some additional guidelines for incorporating critical thinking:

- **Focus on open-ended problems** with no right answers to open up the possibilities, foster intellectual growth, and provide a safe environment for creative problem solving.

- **Promote metacognition** through helping students become aware of their own thought processes and pointing out when they are thinking critically. Take every opportunity to show them the complexity of their thinking while they read and respond to content. For example, if students are to research a topic and answer questions about it, tell them they are analyzing and evaluating, something they do frequently in their personal lives: analyzing and evaluating music, television programs, goals, and relationships.

- **Encourage student growth** by giving feedback, supporting experimentation with ideas, offering new approaches to problem solving

- **Organize cooperative learning groups** so students can get and give feedback, try out new ideas in a safe environment, and see how others solve problems.

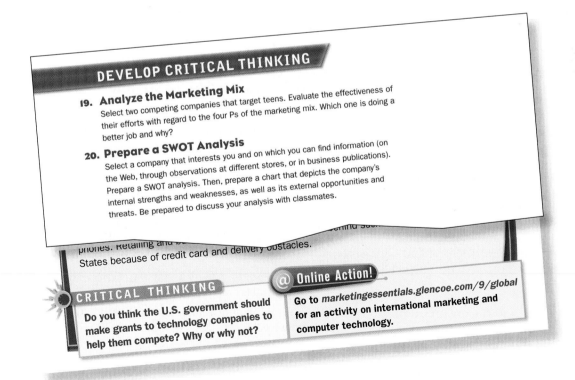

DEVELOP CRITICAL THINKING

19. Analyze the Marketing Mix
Select two competing companies that target teens. Evaluate the effectiveness of their efforts with regard to the four Ps of the marketing mix. Which one is doing a better job and why?

20. Prepare a SWOT Analysis
Select a company that interests you and on which you can find information (on the Web, through observations at different stores, or in business publications). Prepare a SWOT analysis. Then, prepare a chart that depicts the company's internal strengths and weaknesses, as well as its external opportunities and threats. Be prepared to discuss your analysis with classmates.

phones. Retailing and ____ ____ behind sac____
States because of credit card and delivery obstacles.

CRITICAL THINKING
Do you think the U.S. government should make grants to technology companies to help them compete? Why or why not?

@ Online Action!
Go to *marketingessentials.glencoe.com/9/global* for an activity on international marketing and computer technology.

Build Workplace Skills

Today's marketing environment is highly competitive and demands skilled employees. Professionals need decision-making and creative problem-solving skills, as well as the ability to interact with diverse groups. *Marketing Essentials* responds to these demands and helps students develop skills in the following areas:

- **Communication**
- **Information Technology**
- **Interpersonal and Collaborative Skills**
- **Self-Awareness**
- **Responsibility and Flexibility**

CHAPTER 2 REVIEW

BUILD SKILLS

16. Workplace Skills
Customer Service Skills Try to recall a businessperson or a salesperson who was able to establish a bond with you or one of your friends or family members during a business transaction at a store or a business office. List three things the person did to accomplish this.

17. Technology Applications
Age Groups Use spreadsheet software to create a chart that depicts the age groups reported by the U.S. Census Bureau's estimates as of July 2003:
Total population 290,808,777
Under 5 years 19,769,279
5 to 13 years 36,752,056
14 to 17 years 16,522,171
18 to 24 years 28,899,571
Include the 25 and older age group in your chart.

18. Math Practice
The 80/20 Rule Here are the sales figures for ten customers (1) $75,000; (2) $700,000; (3) $815,000; (4) $70,000; (5) $60,000; (6) $30,000; (7) $25,000; (8) $53,750; (9) $40,000; and (10) $25,000. Explain the 80/20 rule using the above ten sales figures.

THE FOUNDATION	MARKETING ESSENTIALS
Basic Skills—reading, writing, mathematics, speaking and listening.	The following chapters deal specifically with mathematics. **Chapters 7, 16, 27, and 29** The following chapter deals specifically with reading, writing, speaking, and listening. **Chapter 8**
Thinking Skills—creative thinking, decision making, problem solving, knowing how to learn, and reasoning.	The following chapters deal specifically with thinking skills. **Chapters 1–38**
Personal Qualities—individual responsibility, self-esteem, self-management, sociability, and integrity.	The following chapters deal specifically with personal qualities. **Chapters 10, 11, 37, and 38**
Resources—allocated time, money materials, space and staff.	The following chapters deal specifically with resources. **Chapters 11, 16, 19, 22, 25, 33, 35, and 36**
Interpersonal skills—work in teams, teach others, serve customers, lead, negotiate, and work with people from culturally diverse backgrounds.	The following chapters deal specifically with interpersonal skills. **Chapters 10, 11, 12, 13, 14, 15, 33**
Information—acquire and evaluate data, organize and maintain files, interpret and communicate information, use computers to process information.	The following chapters deal specifically with information. **Chapters 2, 4, 7, 9, 16, 25, 28, 29**
Systems—understand social, organizational, and technological systems; monitor and correct performance; design and improve systems.	The following chapters deal specifically with systems. **Chapters 11, 21, 22, 24, 28, and 29**
Technology—select equipment and tools, apply technology to specific tasks, and maintain and troubleshoot technologies.	The following chapters deal specifically with technology. **Chapters 9, 16, 23, 24, and 29**

Use Cooperative Learning

Introduction

Studies show that students learn faster and retain more information when they are actively involved in the learning process. Cooperative learning is one method that gets students actively involved in learning and at the same time allows for peer teaching.

Using Cooperative Learning

Your marketing course provides many opportunities for students to learn and apply the skills necessary for positive interpersonal relationships. Through the use of cooperative learning, the teacher can offer a structured method of teaching team-building, collaborative social skills, and team decision making while teaching basic concepts—essential skills for the workplace.

Cooperative Learning in this Text

In *Marketing Essentials*, students and teachers have a variety of materials to assist with cooperative learning activities. Many of the features and section and chapter assessment activities can be completed in a cooperative learning environment. These activities include the **Case Study**, **Building Academic Skills, Building Workplace Skills, Integrating Academic Skills, The DECA Connection, Internet Connection**, and the **Marketing Internship.**

The Benefits of Cooperative Learning

• Cooperative learning emphasizes working toward group goals as opposed to the traditional emphasis on individual competition and achievement.

• Students discover that not only must they learn the material themselves, but also they are responsible for helping everyone in the group learn the material.

• Cooperative learning increases academic achievement and develops essential social skills.

• Students discover how to work with people of all types.

• Students learn valuable problem-solving, team-building, and creativity skills that transfer to real-world occupations and work environments.

• People who help each other and work together toward a common goal generally begin to feel more positive about each other and interact constructively when performing collective tasks.

• Students do not feel as isolated, and they gain self-esteem.

• Students have the opportunity to perceive other students as colleagues rather than competitors. As a result, they recognize the value of helping others rather than working competitively.

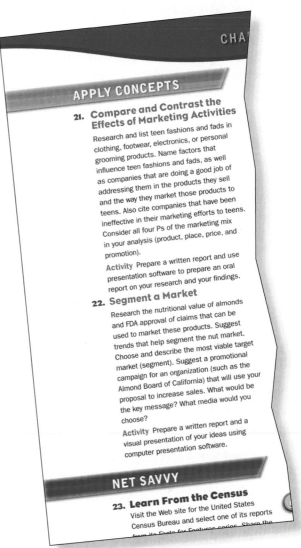

CHA...

APPLY CONCEPTS

21. Compare and Contrast the Effects of Marketing Activities

Research and list teen fashions and fads in clothing, footwear, electronics, or personal grooming products. Name factors that influence teen fashions and fads, as well as companies that are doing a good job of addressing them in the products they sell and the way they market those products to teens. Also cite companies that have been ineffective in their marketing efforts to teens. Consider all four Ps of the marketing mix in your analysis (product, place, price, and promotion).

Activity Prepare a written report and use presentation software to prepare an oral report on your research and your findings.

22. Segment a Market

Research the nutritional value of almonds and FDA approval of claims that can be used to market these products. Suggest trends that help segment the nut market. Choose and describe the most viable target market (segment). Suggest a promotional campaign for an organization (such as the Almond Board of California) that will use your proposal to increase sales. What would be the key message? What media would you choose?

Activity Prepare a written report and a visual presentation of your ideas using computer presentation software.

NET SAVVY

23. Learn From the Census

Visit the Web site for the United States Census Bureau and select one of its reports

Integrate Technology

Technology affects how all people work, interact, and live. It will affect your students if they become marketing professionals. For example, they may keep records with a computer, advertise on the Internet, or telecommute. It will also affect them as consumers. An increasing number of people are buying products on the Web. It is critical that your students become familiar and comfortable with technology now in order to prepare for successful careers.

Activities

Marketing Essentials helps you integrate technology into your teaching with computer-based activities:

- All features and figures provide a link to **marketingessentials.glencoe.com** to assist students in answering the associated questions and to further research the topic or find a project.

- The **Market Tech** feature in each chapter discusses an innovative way marketers use technology today. It includes a Think Like a Marketer question.

- The **Net Marketing** feature discusses a variety of topics related to Internet marketing and closes with a Think Like a Marketer question.

- The Chapter Review includes a **Technology Applications** exercise to teach how to use technology in real-world situations.

- **Net Savvy** in each Chapter Review provides an exercise to be completed using the Internet.

- The *Student Activity Workbook* supplement to *Marketing Essentials* includes a computer activity for each chapter in the textbook.

- PowerPoint presentations are encouraged throughout the text.

Using the Internet Effectively

There are steps you can take to use the Internet effectively in the classroom:

- Look for sites that are created by the government or universities (their URLs typically end in .gov or .edu). These are reliable sites with factual integrity and stability.

- Find out who created the site and why they did it. If the purpose and creator of the Web site are unclear, its content may be unreliable.

- Use multiple search engines when you are looking for information on a topic. This will help you find as many of the pertinent sites as possible.

- Combine your Internet research with traditional research methods. Ask librarians and experts for information and sources. Use books and magazines.

Meet Individual Needs and Learning Styles

One of your greatest challenges as a teacher is to provide a positive learning environment for all students in your classroom. Because each student has his or her own unique set of abilities, perceptions, and needs, the learning styles and physical abilities of your students may vary widely.

Assisting Students with Individual Needs

To help you provide all your students with a positive learning experience, this text provides a variety of activities. This diversity will stimulate student interest, motivate learning, and facilitate understanding. The *Teacher Wraparound Edition* provides independent practice activities which reinforce chapter learning by allowing students to progress at their own pace.

Teaching Students With Special Needs

The term *special needs* is most often used to describe students who face specific physical or behavioral challenges. However, it can also be used in a wider sense to describe students who have greater difficulty learning than do the majority of their fellow students.

Students in your classroom may have orthopedic impairments, hearing or vision impairments, learning disabilities, or behavior disorders—all of which may interfere with their ability to learn. The learning styles of your students may also vary. Some students may be visual learners; others may learn more effectively through hands-on activities. Some students may work well independently, while others need the interaction of others. Students may come from a variety of cultural backgrounds, and some may be second language learners.

Once you determine the special needs of your students, you can identify the areas in the curriculum that may present barriers to them. In order to remove those barriers,

you may need to modify your teaching methods. On the following pages are two charts. The first, **Meeting Special Needs**, describes some of the special needs you may encounter with your students and identifies sources of information. It also includes teaching tips for accommodating students' needs.

The second chart, **Eight Ways of Learning**, will help you identify your students' learning styles. The chart gives a description of each type of learner, describes the likes of each type, what each type is good at, and how each learns best, and names some famous learners who fit each type. Once you have identified each student's learning style, you can modify your teaching strategies to best suit his or her needs.

Meet Special Needs

SUBJECT	DESCRIPTION	SOURCES OF INFORMATION
Second Language Learners	Certain students often speak English as a second language, or not at all. Customs and behavior of people in the majority culture may be confusing for some of these students. Cultural values may inhibit some of these students from full participation in the classroom.	• *Teaching English as a Second Language Electronic Journal* • *Mainstreaming and the Minority Child* • *Internet TESL Journal*
Behavior Disorders	Children with behavior disorders deviate from standards or expectations of behavior and impair the functioning of others and themselves. These children may also be gifted or have learning disabilities.	• *Exceptional Children* • *The Journal of Special Education*
Visual Impairments	Children with visual impairments have partial or total loss of sight. Individuals with visual impairments are not significantly different from their sighted peers in ability range or personality. However, blindness may affect cognitive, motor, and social development.	• *Journal of Visual Impairment & Blindness* • *RE:view* • American Foundation for the Blind
Hearing Impairments	Children with hearing impairments have partial or total loss of hearing. Individuals with hearing impairments are not significantly different from their peers in ability range or personality. However, the chronic condition of deafness may affect cognitive, motor, social, and speech development.	• *American Annals of the Deaf* • *Journal of Speech, Language, and Hearing Research* • *Sign Language Studies*
Physical Impairments	Children with physical impairments fall into two categories—those with orthopedic impairments (use of one or more limbs severely restricted) and those with other health impairments.	• *Teaching Exceptional Children* • *Research and Practice for Persons with Severe Disabilities* • *Physical Disabilities: Education and Related Services*
Gifted	Although no formal definition exists, these students can be described as having above average ability, task commitment, and creativity. They rank in the top 5 percent of their classes. They usually finish work more quickly than other students and are capable of divergent thinking.	• *Journal for the Education of the Gifted* • *Gifted Child Quarterly*
Learning Disabilities	All students with learning disabilities have a problem in one or more areas, such as academic learning, language, perception, social-emotional adjustment, memory, or ability to pay attention.	• *Journal of Learning Disabilities* • *Learning Disability Quarterly*

TEACHING STRATEGIES

TIPS FOR INSTRUCTION

- Remember that students' ability to speak English does not reflect their academic ability.
- Try to incorporate students' cultural experiences into your instruction. The help of a bilingual aide may be effective.
- Include information about different cultures in your curriculum to help build students' self-image.
- Avoid cultural stereotypes.
- Encourage students to share their cultures in the classroom.

- Work for long-term improvement; do not expect immediate success.
- Talk with students about their strengths and weaknesses, and clearly outline objectives.
- Structure schedules, rules, room arrangement, and safety for a conducive learning environment.
- Model appropriate behavior for students and reinforce proper behavior.

- Modify assignments as needed to help students become independent.
- Teach classmates how to serve as guides for the visually impaired.
- Tape lectures and reading assignments for the visually impaired.
- Encourage students to use their sense of touch; provide tactile models whenever possible.
- Verbally describe people and events as they occur in the classroom for students with visual impairments.

- Limit unnecessary noise in the classroom.
- Provide favorable seating arrangements so students with hearing impairments can see speakers and read their lips (or interpreters can assist); avoid visual distractions.
- Write out all instructions on paper or on the board; overhead projectors enable you to maintain eye contact while writing.
- Avoid standing with your back to the window or light source.

- With the student, determine when you should offer aid.
- Help other students and adults understand students with physical impairments
- Learn about special devices or procedures and if any special safety precautions are needed.
- Allow students to participate in all activities including field trips, special events, and projects.

- Emphasize concepts, theories, relationships, ideas, and generalizations.
- Let students express themselves in a variety of ways including drawing, creative writing, or acting.
- Make arrangements for students to work on independent projects.
- Make arrangements for students to take selected subjects early.

- Provide assistance and direction; clearly define rules, assignments, and duties.
- Allow for pair interaction during class time; utilize peer helpers.
- Practice skills frequently. Distribute outlines of material presented to class.
- Allow extra time to complete tests and assignments.

Eight Ways of Learning

TYPE	DESCRIPTION	LIKES TO...
Verbal/Linguistic Learner	Intelligence is related to words and language, written and spoken.	read, write, tell stories, play word games, and tell jokes and riddles.
Logical/Mathematical Learner	Intelligence deals with inductive and deductive thinking and reasoning, numbers, and abstractions.	perform experiments, solve puzzles, work with numbers, ask questions, and explore patterns and relationships.
Visual/Spatial Learner	Intelligence relies on the sense of sight and being able to visualize an object, including the ability to create mental images.	draw, build, design, and create things, daydream, do jigsaw puzzles and mazes, watch videos, look at photos, and draw maps and charts.
Naturalistic Learner	Intelligence has to do with observing, understanding, and organizing patterns in the natural environment.	spend time outdoors and work with plants, animals, and other parts of the natural environment; good at identifying plants and animals and at hearing and seeing connections to nature.
Musical/Rhythmic Learner	Intelligence is based on recognition of tonal patterns, including various environmental sounds, and on sensitivity to rhythm and beats.	sing and hum, listen to music, play an instrument, move body when music is playing, and make up songs.
Bodily/Kinesthetic Learner	Intelligence is related to physical movement and the brain's motor cortex, which controls bodily motion.	learn by hands-on methods, demonstrate skill in crafts, tinker, perform, display physical endurance, and challenge self-physically.
Interpersonal Learner	Intelligence operates primarily through person-to-person relationships and communication.	have lots of friends, talk to people, join groups, play cooperative games, solve problems as part of a group, and volunteer help when others need it.
Intrapersonal Learner	Intelligence is related to inner states of being, self-reflection, metacognition, and awareness of spiritual realities.	work alone, pursue own interests, daydream, keep a personal diary or journal, and think about starting own business.

TEACHING STRATEGIES

IS GOOD AT...	LEARNS BEST BY...	FAMOUS LEARNERS
memorizing names, dates, places, and trivia; spelling; using descriptive language; and creating imaginary worlds.	saying, hearing, and seeing words.	Maya Angelou—poet Abraham Lincoln—U.S. President and statesman Jerry Seinfeld—comedian Mary Hatwood Futrell—international teacher, leader, orator
math, reasoning, logic, problem solving, computing numbers, moving from concrete to abstract, thinking conceptually.	categorizing, classifying, and working with abstract patterns and relationships.	Stephen Hawking—physicist Albert Einstein—theoretical physicist Marilyn Burns—math educator Alexa Canady—neurosurgeon
understanding the use of space and how to get around in it, thinking in three-dimensional terms, and imagining things in clear visual images.	visualizing, dreaming, using the mind's eye, and working with colors and pictures.	Pablo Picasso—artist Maria Martinez—Pueblo Indian famous for black pottery Faith Ringgold—painter, quilter, and writer I.M. Pei—architect
measuring, charting, mapping, observing plants and animals, keeping journals, collecting, classifying, participating in outdoor activities.	visualizing, hands-on activities, bringing outdoors into the classroom, relating home/classroom to the natural world.	George Washington Carver—agricultural chemist Rachel Carson—scientific writer Charles Darwin—evolutionist John James Audubon—conservationist
remembering melodies; keeping time; mimicking beat and rhythm; noticing pitches, rhythms, and background and environmental sounds.	rhythm, melody, and music.	Henry Mancini—composer Marian Anderson—contralto Midori—violinist Paul McCartney—singer, songwriter, musician
physical activities such as sports, dancing, acting, and crafts.	touching, moving, interacting with space, and processing knowledge through bodily sensations.	Marcel Marceau—mime Jackie Joyner-Kersey—Olympic gold medalist in track and field Katherine Dunham—modern dancer Dr. Christian Bernard—cardiac surgeon
understanding people and their feelings, leading others, organizing, communicating, manipulating, mediating conflicts.	sharing, comparing, relating, cooperating, and interviewing.	Jimmy Carter—U.S. President and statesman Eleanor Roosevelt—former first lady Lee Iococca—president of Chrysler Corporation Mother Teresa—winner of Nobel Peace Prize
understanding self, focusing inward on feelings/dreams, following instincts, pursuing interests, and being original.	working alone, doing individualized projects, engaging in self-paced instruction.	Marva Collins—educator Mara Montessori—educator and physician Sigmund Freud—psychotherapist Anne Sexton—poet

Integrate Ethics

Helping students learn about ethical behavior and how to consider the effects of a decision before it is made are important topics for your marketing course. *Marketing Essentials* includes an entire chapter devoted to legal and ethical issues.

The Benefits of Integrating Ethics

The goal of teaching ethical decision-making skills is not to teach values. It is to help students clarify their ethical beliefs and learn how to evaluate ethical situations in light of those beliefs. Establish your classroom so it is a relatively risk-free environment in which students can discuss and make ethical decisions. Students need to learn how to evaluate their actions and to ask questions such as, "Will I think well of myself if I take this action?" and "Would I want others to know about my actions?"

The Ethical Decision Model

Your students will learn to analyze ethical situations better if they have a model to use in deliberating the issues and the people affected by a decision. Several decision models exist, but the basic steps for an ethical decision model are as follows:

❶ Determine the ethical issue

❷ Identify the actions for handling the situation

❸ Identify the people affected by the situation

❹ Analyze how the situation affects the people involved

❺ Decide which of the actions to take.

Classroom Strategies

A Matter of Ethics features recount real-world situations posing ethical conundrums. This feature can be a catalyst for a lively classroom discussion. You may choose the **Case Study** feature as a springboard or have students bring in newspaper or magazine articles which suggest ethical dilemmas. Have students analyze the situations in class and, perhaps, write short reports on their analyses and conclusions. Some formats, such as learning groups, role plays, and debates, are particularly well suited to teaching the concept of ethics.

COOPERATIVE LEARNING GROUPS Small groups of students are especially well suited to discuss cases and share their ideas about ethical issues. Divide students into groups of four or five. Observe groups to be sure that all students are participating. Allow each group to reach its own conclusions, and then ask a member of each group to share that group's ideas with the class.

ROLE PLAYS AND DEBATES Have your students role-play ethical situations, using their own ideas about how to respond to a given situation. Discuss class responses to the role play, guiding students in using the ethical decision model. Set up debate teams to present different sides of an ethical issue.

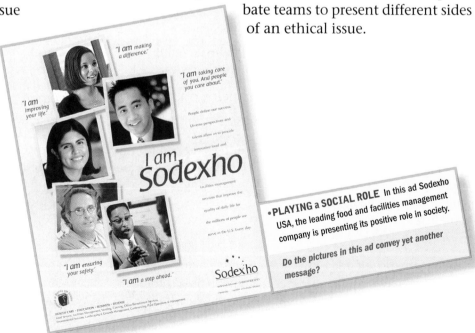

"I am making a difference."

"I am taking care of you. And people you care about."

"I am improving your life."

I am Sodexho

"I am ensuring your safety."

"I am a step ahead."

Sodexho

• **PLAYING a SOCIAL ROLE** In this ad Sodexho USA, the leading food and facilities management company is presenting its positive role in society. Do the pictures in this ad convey yet another message?

Integrate Cultural Diversity

Textbook Resources

The content of *Marketing Essentials* is designed to help students recognize and discuss issues of cultural diversity. During class activities, you may also find it appropriate to integrate questions related to cultural diversity. For example, you might expand a class discussion by asking:

- Would your response change if the customer or vendor were not a native speaker of English? If so, how?
- Would you direct your employee differently if his or her ethnic background were different from yours?
- Would your decision change if your co-worker were a male or female? From your own ethnic background? From a different background? Why?

Integrating Cultural Diversity

As future marketers, your students will be faced with a diverse marketplace in which people of many different cultures are both workers and consumers. Cultural knowledge may be the difference between success and failure in marketing products in the global economy. For students to become productive workers and responsible citizens, they must be open to cultural differences.

As students learn about skills needed to be successful in a marketing career, they should keep in mind the wide diversity of the people they are likely to encounter in every aspect of their working and personal lives. In the classroom and in one-on-one conferences, you can help your students consider the diversity of the U.S. population, not only in terms of ethnicity, but also in terms of customs, attitudes, religious beliefs, language backgrounds, and physical capabilities. High school students need to understand that ability and success are not related to skin color or gender.

Multicultural Education

Multicultural education incorporates the idea that all students—regardless of their gender and social class, and their ethnic, racial, or cultural characteristics—should have an equal opportunity to learn in school. Learning about other cultures concurrently with their own culture helps children recognize similarities and appreciate differences, without perceiving inferiority or superiority of one or the other. To foster cultural awareness:

- Recognize that all students are unique, having special talents and abilities
- Promote uniqueness and diversity as positive
- Know, appreciate, and respect the cultural backgrounds of your students
- Use authentic situations to provide for cultural learning and understanding
- Make sure people of all cultures are represented fairly and accurately
- Make sure that historical information is accurate and nondiscriminatory
- Make sure that materials do not include stereotypical roles
- Make sure there is gender equity
- Welcome parent and community involvement
- Use current news stories or advertisements to call students' attention to cultural differences that influence the marketing of products

Integrate Global Marketing

American businesses are operating in an increasingly international environment. The rapid expansion of the Internet into all corners of the globe has made it imperative that we integrate a global perspective into all our marketing courses. In a global economy, business rivals and great sales opportunities may be several time zones away.

Marketing Essentials is designed to provide your students with the international perspective that is so important to success in marketing. One unit in the text is devoted to international marketing. Also, the feature **Global Market** addresses some aspect of globalization and poses a critical thinking question. More and more, throughout *Marketing Essentials*, online activities involve working with or researching worldwide Internet sites.

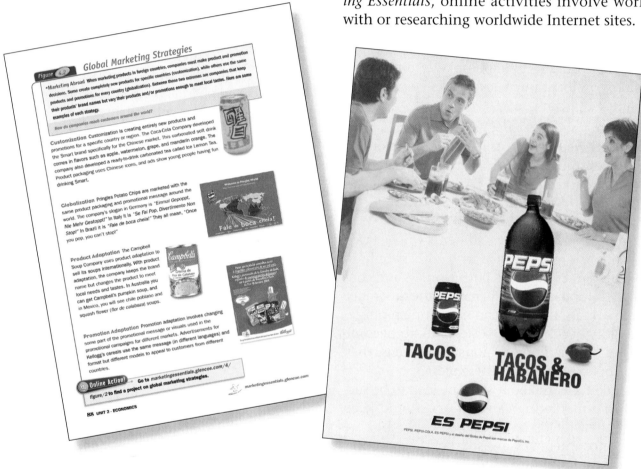

Integrate E-Commerce

The expansion of the international marketplace is largely related to the increasing scope of e-commerce. Today's marketers are facing an international marketplace that is rapidly becoming more competitive, specialized, and reliant on the Internet.

Coverage of technology is integrated throughout *Marketing Essentials*. **Net Marketing** features present an Internet marketing example or issue. In addition, the Chapter Review section in each chapter has a **Net Savvy** question which requires students browse the Internet in order to respond. Many of the **Case Study** features deal with firms that are technologically based or have made e-commerce a key component of their operations.

The Best DECA Prep Available

DECA is an association of marketing students. It is a co-curricular club with chapters in more than 6,000 high schools. DECA's membership includes representation from all 50 states, four U.S. territories, the District of Columbia, two Canadian provinces, Mexico, and Europe. All DECA activities further student development in one or more of the following areas: leadership development, social intelligence, vocational understanding, and civic consciousness. Through the integration of individual and group DECA activities with the marketing education instructional program, students' skills are cultivated to ensure they have great potential to become future leaders in the areas of marketing and management.

Leadership Skills

The structure of a DECA chapter encourages leadership development. Each chapter elects officers who, with the membership, identify an annual program of work. The identified program of work often includes committee chairpeople to organize and execute the activities. Chapter activities encourage all members to act responsibly as a leader or member of a group and typically focus on the advantages of participation in a free enterprise system, marketing research, an individual's civic responsibility within the community.

National DECA provides opportunities for local chapter officers and members to receive additional leadership and chapter development training. Annual Regional Conferences are held in the fall. In the spring, students may attend the Leadership Development Academy at the Career Development Conference (CDC). During the summer, a State Officer Leadership Institute is available.

Competitive Events

One part of the DECA program of student activities is the competitive events program. The events are both competency and curriculum based and assist students in the refinement of workplace skills required for entry and/or advancement in the field of marketing. All events are centered around those skills expected by employers in all marketing fields—effective communication skills, ability to solve problems, ability to make decisions, and ability to function responsibly as either a leader or member or a team. Some events are for individuals and others require students to function as members of a group. The competitive events program provides recognition for student excellence at the local, state, and national level of competition. The recognition received by both individuals and teams within a DECA chapter serve as a showcase of the marketing education program to the local school and community.

DECA Team Events	*Marketing Essentials*
DECA Written Events	
Business and Financial Services Marketing	All chapters
Entrepreneurship	Chapters 33–36
Food Marketing Research	Chapters 25–32
General Marketing Research	Chapters 28–29
Hospitality and Recreation Marketing Research	Chapters 25–29
Retail Marketing Research	Chapters 25–29
DECA Participating Events	
Entrepreneurship	Chapters 33–36
Fashion Merchandising Promotion Plan	Chapters 17–20
DECA Project Events	
Civic Consciousness	All chapters
Creative Marketing Research	Chapters 28–29
Learn and Earn	Chapters 37–38
Public Relations	Chapters 17–18
DECA Quiz Bowl	All chapters
Free Enterprise	Chapters 1–6
International Marketing	All chapters

DECA Preparation *Marketing Essentials* is designed to be one of your primary DECA preparation resources. The table above lists DECA's team events and the corresponding chapters in *Marketing Essentials* that will help students prepare for the events.

Team Events

Team projects and events may be completed by teams composed of one to three DECA members. All team events require completion of a written manual. Each year, DECA identifies a specific topic for each team event category. All events must include research related to the topic and follow the identified format. Excellence in the written events is evaluated on both the quality of the written report and performance during an interview conducted by a judge from the business community.

When completed, the written manuals could be included in a students' portfolios and would be of significant interest to both educators and business-people reviewing the portfolio.

Through their research and writing, team event participants are expected to
- function as leaders or members of a group.
- prepare complex reports.
- demonstrate initiative and creativity.
- communicate recommendations based on their research to business executives.

DECA COMPETITIVE EVENT OCCUPATIONAL AREAS

- Advertising and Visual Merchandising Services
- Apparel and Accessories Marketing
- Finance and Credit Services
- Food Marketing
- General Marketing
- Hospitality and Tourism Marketing
- Retail Merchandising
- Quick Serve Restaurant Management
- Full Service Restaurant Management
- Vehicles and Petroleum Marketing

Occupational Areas These are DECA's competitive event occupational areas. Students participate in the event categories in their areas of occupational interest within the field of marketing.

Individual Series Events

As participants in the individual series event program, students are evaluated on their proficiency in handling simulated business situations. Each event is directly related to competencies mastered through classroom instruction and/or related job experience. The following are the instructional areas included in DECA's competitive events program:

- **Economic Concepts and Principles**—economics, marketing, and business
- **Basic and Social Skills**—mathematics, communications, human relations, and career development
- **Marketing Functions**—financing, pricing, promotion, product/service management, distribution, selling, marketing-information management)

A typical individual series event includes a comprehensive written exam and two role-play events. In each series students are presented with a business situation. Students must then use the skills acquired through participation in their marketing class to make decisions and spontaneously react to the situation. A business executive judges students' performance while playing the role of the second party in the role play.

THE DECA CONNECTION

Using *Marketing Essentials* to prepare for DECA

Marketing Essentials is designed to be one of your primary DECA preparation resources. The text and end-of-chapter activities are devoted to preparing students for DECA. For example, Unit 11, Entrepreneurship and Finance, gives students step-by-step instructions on how to prepare for DECA's entrepreneurship written event, which requires students to write a business proposal for a new business.

In addition, each Chapter Assessment includes a DECA Connection Role Play in which students practice for DECA's participating events. Students are given a marketing situation to contemplate. For example, students may have to create a promotion plan for a product or make a distribution decision. They are asked to come up with a plan or solution and present it to the teacher who, in the role-play situation, represents a manager, a staff member, or other marketing personnel. Role-play activities provide the teacher with a list of performance indicators to use as criteria in evaluating students' performances. The Student Activity Workbook includes an additional DECA Role Play activity for every chapter.

If your students are competing in one of DECA's marketing research events, you will find the *Marketing Essentials* Marketing Research Project Workbook and invaluable preparation resource.

In addition to *Marketing Essentials*, there are several resources available that provide added training for students preparing for competition. Two of these resources are the Career Competency in Marketing Series published by Glencoe/McGraw-Hill and the event-specific Student Training Guides available through DECA Images (**www.deca.org**).

TEACHING STRATEGIES

THE DECA CONNECTION

COMPETITIVE EVENT CORRELATION

ROLE PLAYS

Course Plannning Guide

ONE SEMESTER COURSE		
Week	**Chapter**	
1	Chapter 1	Marketing Is All Around Us
2	Chapter 2	The Marketing Plan
3	Chapter 3	Political and Economic Analysis
	Chapter 4	Global Analysis
4	Chapter 5	The Free Enterprise System
	Chapter 6	Legal and Ethical Issues
5	Chapter 7	Basic Math Skills
	Chapter 9	Technology Applications for Marketing
6	Chapter 12	Preparing for the Sale
	Chapter 13	Initiating the Sale
7	Chapter 14	Presenting the Product
	Chapter 15	Closing the Sale
8	Chapter 16	Using Math in Sales
	Chapter 17	Promotional Concepts and Strategies
9	Chapter 18	Visual Merchandising and Display
	Chapter 19	Advertising
10	Chapter 21	Channels of Distribution
	Chapter 22	Physical Distribution
11	Chapter 23	Purchasing
	Chapter 24	Stock Handling and Inventory Control
12	Chapter 25	Price Planning
	Chapter 26	Pricing Strategies
13	Chapter 28	Marketing Research
	Chapter 30	Product Planning
14	Chapter 31	Branding, Packaging, and Labeling
	Chapter 33	Entrepreneurial Concepts
15	Chapter 35	Developing a Business Plan
	Chapter 36	Financing the Business
16	Chapter 37	Identifying Career Opportunities
	Chapter 38	Finding and Applying for a Job

Course Plannning Guide

FULL-YEAR COURSE—SIX-WEEK GRADING SYSTEM		
Grading Period	**Chapter**	
First	Chapter 1	Marketing Is All Around Us
	Chapter 2	The Marketing Plan
	Chapter 3	Political and Economic Analysis
	Chapter 4	Global Analysis
	Chapter 5	The Free Enterprise System
	Chapter 6	Legal and Ethical Issues
Second	Chapter 7	Basic Math Skills
	Chapter 8	Communication Skills
	Chapter 9	Technology Applications for Marketing
	Chapter 10	Interpersonal Skills
	Chapter 11	Management Skills
	Chapter 12	Preparing for the Sale
Third	Chapter 13	Initiating the Sale
	Chapter 14	Presenting the Product
	Chapter 15	Closing the Sale
	Chapter 16	Using Math in Sales
	Chapter 17	Promotional Concepts and Strategies
	Chapter 18	Visual Merchandising and Display
Fourth	Chapter 19	Advertising
	Chapter 20	Print Advertisements
	Chapter 21	Channels of Distribution
	Chapter 22	Physical Distribution
	Chapter 23	Purchasing
	Chapter 24	Stock Handling and Inventory Control
	Chapter 25	Price Planning
Fifth	Chapter 26	Pricing Strategies
	Chapter 27	Pricing Math
	Chapter 28	Marketing Research
	Chapter 29	Conducting Marketing Research
	Chapter 30	Product Planning
	Chapter 31	Branding, Packaging, and Labeling
	Chapter 32	Extended Product Features
Sixth	Chapter 33	Entrepreneurial Concepts
	Chapter 34	Risk Management
	Chapter 35	Developing a Business Plan
	Chapter 36	Financing the Business
	Chapter 37	Identifying Career Opportunities
	Chapter 38	Finding and Applying for a Job

Course Plannning Guide

FULL-YEAR COURSE—NINE-WEEK GRADING SYSTEM		
Grading Period	**Chapter**	
First	Chapter 1	Marketing Is All Around Us
	Chapter 2	The Marketing Plan
	Chapter 3	Political and Economic Analysis
	Chapter 4	Global Analysis
	Chapter 5	The Free Enterprise System
	Chapter 6	Legal and Ethical Issues
	Chapter 7	Basic Math Skills
	Chapter 8	Communication Skills
	Chapter 9	Technology Applications for Marketing
	Chapter 10	Interpersonal Skills
Second	Chapter 11	Management Skills
	Chapter 12	Preparing for the Sale
	Chapter 13	Initiating the Sale
	Chapter 14	Presenting the Product
	Chapter 15	Closing the Sale
	Chapter 16	Using Math in Sales
	Chapter 17	Promotional Concepts and Strategies
	Chapter 18	Visual Merchandising and Display
	Chapter 19	Advertising
	Chapter 20	Print Advertisements
Third	Chapter 21	Channels of Distribution
	Chapter 22	Physical Distribution
	Chapter 23	Purchasing
	Chapter 24	Stock Handling and Inventory Control
	Chapter 25	Price Planning
	Chapter 26	Pricing Strategies
	Chapter 27	Pricing Math
	Chapter 28	Marketing Research
	Chapter 29	Conducting Marketing Research
Fourth	Chapter 30	Product Planning
	Chapter 31	Branding, Packaging, and Labeling
	Chapter 32	Extended Product Features
	Chapter 33	Entrepreneurial Concepts
	Chapter 34	Risk Management
	Chapter 35	Developing a Business Plan
	Chapter 36	Financing the Business
	Chapter 37	Identifying Career Opportunities
	Chapter 38	Finding and Applying for a Job

GLENCOE
MARKETING ESSENTIALS

Everything a Marketing Program Should Be!

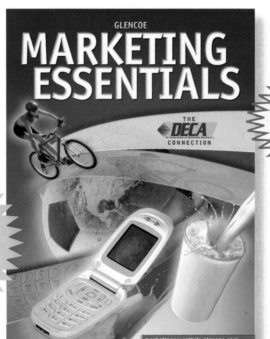

Student Edition Available Online!

Correlated to the National Marketing Education Standards!

DECA Preparation in Every Chapter!

THE DECA CONNECTION
An Association of Marketing Students

Role Play: Marketing Intern

Situation You are to assume the role of intern for a marketing consulting firm. A customer (judge) is considering turning his/her hobby of making special occasion chocolate candies into a full time career. The customer (judge) is fairly inexperienced in business matters and has come to your company for help and advice in developing a marketing plan for the proposed business.

Activity You must explain to the customer (judge) the importance and function of a good marketing plan.

Evaluation You will be evaluated on how well you meet the following performance indicators:

- Explain the nature of marketing plans

THE DECA CONNECTION
An Association of Marketing Students

Performance indicators represent key skills and knowledge. Relating them to the concepts explained in this chapter is your key to success in DECA events. These acronyms represent DECA events that involve knowledge of concepts in this chapter.

AAAL	FMAL	MMS	TMDM
AAML	FMDM*	QSRM	TSE*
ADC*	FMML	RMAL	VPM
BSM	FSRM	RMML	
EMDM	HMDM*	SMDM*	

In all these DECA events, you should be able to follow the following performance indicators:

- Distinguish between economic goods and services
- Determine the forms of economic utility that marketing creates
- Explain the concept of marketing strategies
- Explain the concept of market and market identification

DECA PREP

Check your understanding of DECA performance indicators with the DECA activity in this chapter's review. For more information and DECA Prep practice, go to *marketingessentials.glencoe.com/1/DECA*

PROGRAM RESOURCES

No other program brings so many rich resources to every class you teach

One look will prove it! Glencoe *Marketing Essentials* offers you more than any other marketing program. You can see the difference throughout the text with

- Twelve new **Marketing Internship Labs**

- Two new **DECA preparation activities** in every chapter

- Integrated coverage of E-commerce and of the globalization of business.

Program resources include

- *Competitive Events Workbook* that helps you prepare your students for state and national marketing education competitions.

- *BusinessWeek Reader and Case Studies* that employ active reading models to reinforce contemporary marketing topics

- *Marketing Research Project Workbook* with a Teacher Manual to help your students prepare for DECA research events

A Truly Readable Marketing Text!

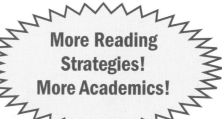

More Reading Strategies! More Academics!

Teacher Classroom Resources

The Student Activity Workbook with its **Teacher Annotated Edition** provides Vocabulary Review, Fact and Idea Review, Marketing Applications, Role Plays for DECA preparation, and Computer Activities for spreadsheet, database, and word processing programs.

The Marketing Research Project Workbook with its **Teacher Manual** offers a detailed, step-by-step procedure for students to follow in conducting a marketing research project.

The Marketing Math Workbook with its **Teacher Annotated Edition** provides supplementary math activities for every unit in the student text. The workbook offers marketing math pretests; table, graph, and spreadsheet activities; sales transaction practice; promotional budgeting activities; buying, distribution, and pricing activities; marketing research computations; financial statement calculations; and numeric keypad drills.

The Marketing Career Portfolio features 12 sample portfolio projects and a resource booklet with suggestions for managing the portfolio development process.

BusinessWeek **Reader with Case Studies** with its **Teacher Annotated Edition** contains *BusinessWeek* articles related to each chapter's content. These activities model for students the kind of thinking and questioning processes that skillful readers use. Each *BusinessWeek* Case Study includes activities for vocabulary, prereading, critical thinking, discussion, and performance assessment.

The School-to-Work Activity Workbook helps students relate their class work to on-the-job experience. It provides activities for every chapter and involves your students in work-site analysis and working with mentors.

TECHNOLOGY FOR YOUR CLASSROOM

The Marketing Essentials Interactive Chalkboard and PowerPoint Presentation provides over 1,000 high-interest, visually motivating slides. Each chapter presentation includes text highlights, charts, graphs, and figures, as well as study organizers that help students read and study each section.

TeacherWorks gives you instant access to all these print resources in one easy-to-use CD-ROM. This software allows instructors to plan lessons in a calendar format. It includes customizable built-in lesson plans and and links to printable program resources.

The ExamView® CD-ROM is one of the most comprehensive test packages on the market. It provides an accurate and exhaustive source of text items for a wide variety of examination styles. It contains thousands of questions, organized around learning objectives and categorized by chapter and unit.

The *Marketing Essentials* Online Learning Center at marketingessentials.glencoe.com provides resources to enrich and enhance learning:

- Practice tests
- Math review and practice
- Annotated marketing plan
- Internet resources
- Research activities
- DECA practice and tips

On the teacher site, you will find answer keys, standards updates, and curricula correlations.

Virtual Business–Retailing

Virtual Business – Retailing 2.0 is a software-based simulation of a convenience store that offers students hands-on control over the management and marketing of a business. Students have control over pricing, promotion, location, merchandising, market research, and more.

Three Great Ways to Use Virtual Business– Retailing 2.0 In Your Classroom

Pick your favorite or combine all three! Have your students work individually or in groups.

LESSON-BASED INSTRUCTION

A series of great lessons let your students break down the task of running a business into easy-to-understand pieces. Each lesson focuses on one decision, such as pricing, purchasing, or advertising. All other decisions are handled by the computer so the student can learn one thing at a time. Printable assignments and worksheets guide the students through each lesson and let you document each student's success.

PROJECT-BASED INSTRUCTION

Students start their own business from scratch and manage it from a single store to a chain of stores. Students work toward milestones, and their progress is recorded in a "project portfolio" that can be used to track and assess performance. Students gain ownership over the growth of their business through creative activities such as designing the signage and layout of their storefront. They print views of their store and include them in their growing portfolio. The project culminates in presentations by the students.

MULTIPLAYER CLASSROOM COMPETITIONS

Let your students compete directly against each other via your network and learn how to run their business in an ultra-real, ultra-fun competitive environment. Students compete with each other for the highest profit within a simulated economy. A price cut by a team on one side of your classroom may steal customers from the store run by students on the other side of your classroom. You automatically get a journal comparing the performance of each team complete with a log of the actions taken. Report templates are provided for students to assess how they did, what they learned, and what they would do differently next time.

Virtual Business–Management

Virtual Business–Management is a software-based simulation that focuses on human resource management. Students have control over the hiring and firing for all employees in this highly interactive simulation. In certain lessons students run an international business and explore exchange rates, tariffs and more.

HOW IT WORKS

■ Students manage a distribution business in a highly visual simulation.

■ Lessons let students learn one concept at a time.
■ Modular design lets you complement, not replace, your current curriculum.
■ Students work individually or in teams.

STUDENTS WILL LEARN TO

■ Review résumés and make hiring decisions.
■ Adjust wages to ensure an adequate pool of job applicants.
■ Decide whether to hire experienced workers or train new workers on the job.
■ Balance staffing of different positions to optimize work flow.
■ Assess employees performance versus other employees.
■ Deal with surprises such as competitors raising wages to steal employees.
■ Evaluate the cost effectiveness of using telecommuters.
■ Control wage costs to ensure overall profitability of the business.
■ Evaluate locating a business in a foreign country given wage differences and tariffs.

Glencoe Marketing Education

Glencoe Marketing Series

- *Retailing*
- *Sports and Entertainment Marketing*
- *Hospitality and Tourism*
- *Fashion Marketing*
- *E-Commerce*

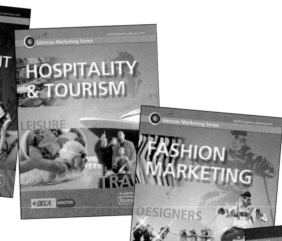

Glencoe Marketing Education Texts

- *Entrepreneurship and Small Business Management*
- *Marketing Essentials*
- *Business Plan Project Workbook*

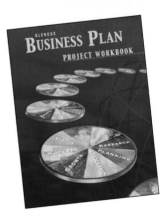

Innovative and Comprehensive

Proven, consistant features in all texts:

- **Competitive Events Preparation** Special feature activities prepare students for competitive events

- **Standards** Correlations to key curriculum and/or industry standards

- **Current Trends** Integrated coverage of current trends and contemporary issues in marketing

- **Real-world features** Thought-provoking stories focusing on creative and innovative approaches to marketing

- **Focus on Technology** An emphasis on the role of technology as a means of enhancing and enabling marketing practices

- **Focus on Ethics** Features to stress the importance of incorporating ethics into marketing decision making

- **Customizable Assessments** Easy-to-use and customizable assessment tools

- **Basic Skills** Activities reinforce basic skills and help students apply skills to real workplace situations

- **Focus on Reading** Strategies to improve student reading skills

- **Additional Activities** Activities to enrich and extend classroom learning by reteaching and reinforcing key concepts

- **Presentation Resources** Classroom presentations that provide visual reinforcement with important text and graphics

- **International Perspective** Integrated activities/features with focus on a global marketing perspective

---

Optional Package Resources

PARTNERSHIPS	TECHNOLOGY	STANDARDS
• DECA	• Online Learning Centers	• Alignments and Correlations for state and national standards
• *BusinessWeek*	• Marketing education Web site	
• FBLA	• **Exam***View*® Pro	• Latest updates available at **marketingessentials.glencoe.com**
• BPA	• Interactive Chalkboard with PowerPoint® Presentations	
• FGI	• *Virtual Business*	
• Standard & Poor's	• TeacherWorks	

Customize Your Marketing Program

GLENCOE TEXTS	Entrepreneurship	Economics	Selling and The Sales Process	International Trade	Business Plans	Feasibility Analysis	Market Research	Types of Businesses	Legal Issues	Government Regulation	Site Selection	Layout Planning	Visual Merchandising	Marketing Strategies	Marketing Plan	Marketing Mix	Pricing	Promotional Mix	Promotional Plans
Marketing Essentials	●	●	■	■	■	●	■	●	■	■	●	●	■	■	■	■	■	■	■
Entrepreneurship and Small Business Management	■	●	●	■	■	■	●	■	■	■	■	■	●	■	■	●	●	●	●
Retailing	●	●	■	●	●	●	●	■	●	●	■	■	■	■	■	■	■	■	■
Sports and Entertainment Marketing	●	●	■	●	■	●	■	■	●	●	●	■	■	■	■	■	■	■	■
Fashion Marketing	●	■	■	■	■	●	■	■	●	■	■	●	■	■	●	■	■	■	■
Hospitality and Tourism	■	■	■	●	■	■	■	■	■	●	●	■	■	■	■	■	■	■	■
E-Commerce	■	■	●	■	■	■	■	■	■	●	■	■	●	●	■	■	●	●	●

■ = advanced level   ● = introductory level

With Glencoe's Marketing Texts

	MARKETING CONCEPT																												
Advertising	Branding, Packaging, Labeling	Management Planning	Purchase Planning	Inventory Management	Production Management	Distribution	Managing Operations	Staffing and Company Policies	Motivating Employees	Obtaining Financing	Math Skills	Accounting	Record Keeping	Risk Management	Social/Ethical Responsibility	Marketing Careers	Budget Planning	Globalization	E-Tailing	Technology	Retailin	Licensing	Sponsorships	Target markets	Store Image	Web Site Developmen	Customer Service	Elements of Design
■	■	●	■	■	■	■	●	●	●	●	●	●	●	■	●	■	■	■	■	■	●	●	●	■	●	●	■	●
●	●	■	●	●	●	●	■	■	■	■	■	■	■	■	●	●	●	●	●	●	●	●	●	■	●	●	■	●
■	●	■	■	■	■	■	■	●	●	●	●	●	■	●	■	●	●	■	■	●	■	●	●	●	●	■	■	●
■	■	●	●	●	●	●	●	■	●	●	●	●	■	●	■	●	■	■	■	■	●	●	●	■	●	●	●	●
■	■	●	■	■	■	●	●	●	●	●	●	●	●	■	●	●	●	■	■	●	●	●	●	■	●	●	●	■
■	●	■	●	●	●	■	■	■	■	■	■	●	■	●	■	■	■	■	■	●	■	●	●	■	●	●	■	■
■	●	●	●	●	■	●	●	●	■	●	●	●	■	●	●	■	■	●	■	●	■	●	●	■	■	■	■	■

BRIEF CONTENTS

CONTENTS

Table of Contents

CONTENTS

CONTENTS

CONTENTS

CONTENTS

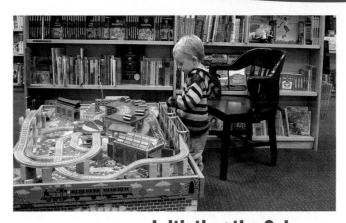

Table of Contents

CONTENTS

CONTENTS

SPIDER-MAN © 2004 Marvel Characters Inc.

CONTENTS

Table of Contents

CONTENTS

Table of Contents

CONTENTS

Table of Contents

xiv

CONTENTS

CONTENTS

Table of Contents

CONTENTS

Table of Contents

xvii

Understanding the Unit

Unit Opener

Marketing Essentials has 12 units that group the 38 chapters by theme. Each unit opens with an advertisement that shows marketing in action.

The Unit Opening Advertisement shows an advertisement that relates to the unit content.

Analyze the Ad guides you through an analysis of how the ad works. The activity in **Think and Write** will get you ready for the chapters ahead.

The Marketing Plan guides you through all the steps of the marketing strategy process.

The Marketing Wheel illustrates basic marketing concepts. The four marketing foundations are important building blocks: Business, Management, and Entrepreneurship; Communication and Interpersonal Skills; Economics; and Professional Development. The marketing functions are what marketers do: Distribution, Financing, Marketing-Information Management, Pricing, Product/Service Management, Promotion, and Selling.

The Marketing Internship

Each unit closes with a simulated DECA event called **Marketing Internship.** Each internship gives you a background scenario, an assignment, and a suggested strategy. After that, you make all the decisions—you're the marketer!

Build Your Portfolio helps you collect your reports, charts, and plans from each Marketing Internship to create a portfolio of your best work. You can use the portfolio when you apply for real internships and jobs.

Online Action sends you to marketingessentials.glencoe.com, to find more information about DECA events.

TO THE STUDENT

Understanding the Chapter

Each *Marketing Essentials* chapter opens with a list of chapter objectives, a photo related to the chapter content, and information about DECA events.

Chapter Objectives preview the most important things to remember about each chapter.

The DECA Connection lists the DECA competitive events that relate to the chapter and explains how you will be evaluated in these competitions.

Guide to the Photo has two parts: **Market Talk** tells you how the photograph relates to the chapter, then **Quick Think** asks a question you can answer based on your own experience.

DECA Prep directs you to the DECA activity that closes every chapter.

Understanding the Section

Each chapter is divided into two or three sections that group the chapter material by topic.

Objectives lists the concepts you will cover in the section.

Key Terms lists the vocabulary words you will learn in the section. Look for them in the text—they will be highlighted and in boldface type.

Read and Study makes your reading and studying more productive. It has three sections:
* **Before You Read** encourages you to think about what you might already know about the subject.
* **The Main Idea** tells you the primary concept you will be learning.
* **Study Organizer** gives you ideas for taking notes as you read.

While You Read connects the material you are reading with something you already know.

After You Read is a self-check of what you have read. You can check your answers on the Internet, at marketingessentials.glencoe.com.

Chapter Review

Each chapter closes with a variety of exercises and activities to assess how well you have absorbed the material. It will help you remember, apply, and use what you have learned.

Focus on Key Points reviews the chapter highlights. Read them to make sure you have not missed an important concept.

Review Vocabulary helps you memorize the definitions of the vocabulary words in the chapter.

Review Facts and Ideas asks questions to test your recall and understanding of chapter material.

Build Skills gives you a chance to practice workplace skills, technology applications, and math. Each activity is based on the world of marketing.

Apply Concepts asks you to take what you have learned and apply it to a realistic situation.

The DECA Connection asks you to role-play a marketing scenario, just like you would in a real DECA competition.

Develop Critical Thinking are questions to help you interpret, analyze, compare, or make judgments based on what you learned in the chapter.

Net Savvy focuses on sharpening your Internet research skills.

TO THE STUDENT

Understanding the Features

Each chapter has features that demonstrate how the marketing concepts work in the real world. A question and an activity follow each feature.

Case Study

Case Study offers a real-world story about a marketing decision or a situation facing a company.

GLOBAL MARKET

Global Market tells a story of a real-world, international business scenario. Largely because of the Internet and increased global access, marketing horizons have expanded, and many businesses now operate in multiple countries.

MARKET TECH

Market Tech goes beyond the Internet and tells you about other creative uses of technology. Each Market Tech feature briefly explains how the technology works, notes the strategy, and evaluates the success of the technology.

NET MARKETING

Net Marketing highlights a new or innovative Internet marketing technique that uses original ideas.

A MATTER OF ETHICS

A Matter of Ethics lets you ponder a situation that challenges you to pick the right thing to do.

CAREERS IN MARKETING

Careers in Marketing is an interview with someone who works in one of the many jobs in marketing. You will learn how people chose their careers, what education they have, what skills are most important in their jobs, and what they do to succeed.

Reading Strategies

Use this menu for reading strategies to get the most from your reading.

Before You Read . . .

SET A PURPOSE
- Why are you reading the textbook?
- How does the subject relate to your life?
- How might you be able to use what you learn in your own life?

PREVIEW
- Read the chapter title to preview the topic.
- Read the subtitles to see what you will learn about the topic.
- Skim the photos, charts, graphs, or maps. How do they support the topic?
- Look for key terms that are boldfaced. How are they defined?

DRAW FROM YOUR BACKGROUND
- What have you read or heard concerning new information on the topic?
- How is the new information different from what you already know?
- How will the information that you already know help you understand the new information?

While You Read . . .

PREDICT
- Predict events or outcomes by using clues and information that you already know.
- Change your predictions as you read and gather new information.

CONNECT
- Think about people, places, and events in your own life. Are there any similarities with those in your textbook?
- Can you relate the textbook information to other areas of your life?

QUESTION
- What is the main idea?
- How do the photos, charts, graphs, and maps support the main idea?

VISUALIZE
- Pay careful attention to details and descriptions.
- Create graphic organizers to show relationships that you find in the information.

NOTICE COMPARE AND CONTRAST SENTENCES
- Look for clue words and phrases that signal comparison, such as *similarly*, *just as*, *both*, *in common*, *also*, and *too*.
- Look for clue words and phrases that signal contrast, such as *on the other hand*, *in contrast to*, *however*, *different*, *instead of*, *rather than*, *but*, and *unlike*.

NOTICE CAUSE-AND-EFFECT SENTENCES
- Look for clue words and phrases, such as *because*, *as a result*, *therefore*, *that is why*, *since*, *so*, *for this reason*, and *consequently*.

NOTICE CHRONOLOGICAL SENTENCES
- Look for clue words and phrases, such as *after*, *before*, *first*, *next*, *last*, *during*, *finally*, *earlier*, *later*, *since*, and *then*.

After You Read . . .

SUMMARIZE
- Describe the main idea and how the details support it.
- Use your own words to explain what you have read.

ASSESS
- What was the main idea?
- Did the text clearly support the main idea?
- Did you learn anything new from the material?
- Can you use this new information in other school subjects or at home?
- What other sources could you use to find more information about the topic?

THE DECA CONNECTION

What is DECA?

DECA is a national association for students of marketing. It was formed in 1946 to improve the education of students in business subject areas, in particular marketing, entrepreneurship, and management.

DECA, which stands for the Distributive Education Clubs of America, offers students the opportunity to develop their leadership and professional skills. This is done through on-the-job experience, activities and projects sponsored by individual schools or chapters, and a series of competitive events in specific occupational areas. All activities apply the concepts of marketing to real-life situations. It is likely that DECA will be an integral part of your learning experience as you explore the world of marketing.

What is DECA's mission statement?

The mission of DECA is to enhance the co-curricular education of students with interests in marketing, management, and entrepreneurship. DECA helps students develop skills and competence for marketing careers, build self-esteem, experience leadership, and practice community service. DECA is committed to the advocacy of marketing education and the growth of business and education partnerships.

How can DECA help me?

Even though some activities may take time outside of school, DECA should be considered a co-curricular activity instead of an after-school activity. The basis for the projects and events will come from your classroom learning. Information from events that you take back to the classroom will enhance not only your learning experience, but that of your classmates as well.

DECA also offers scholarships and other recognition awards to exceptional students. In general, success in DECA events is a positive addition to your résumé or portfolio.

To the Student

DECA can help you:

- Develop strong leadership abilities
- Understand the importance of making ethical decisions in your personal life and future career
- Focus on enhancing effective public speaking and presentation skills
- Understand the need for diversity in the global marketplace
- Enhance those skills that are necessary for a career in marketing or as an entrepreneur
- Increase your self-confidence, especially when presenting or speaking in public
- Investigate different career opportunities available in the marketing field
- Develop good social and business etiquette

How are DECA activities related to my marketing class?

Marketing Essentials is designed to prepare you for a career or further study of marketing. It is also helpful in preparing for DECA activities. You will notice that the DECA logo and DECA approved activities are prominently featured throughout your book. The DECA Connection feature is modeled after DECA individual or team projects. It will let you practice applying the knowledge that you have gained from your marketing class. DECA activities can also enhance your classroom learning, because they help you develop stronger communication and analytical skills.

DECA sponsors competitive events in approximately 30 occupational areas. These areas include:

- Advertising and Visual Merchandising Services Series
- Apparel and Accessories Marketing Series
- Finance and Credit Services Series
- Food Marketing Series
- General Marketing Series
- Hospitality and Tourism Marketing Series
- Retail Merchandising Series
- Quick Serve Restaurant Management Series
- Full Service Restaurant Management Series
- Vehicles and Petroleum Marketing Series
- Sports and Entertainment
  Marketing Management Team
  Decision Making Pilot Event
- Travel and Tourism Marketing
  Management Team
  Decision Making Pilot Event

The World of Marketing

Unit Objectives

After completing this unit, students should be able to:

- Describe the scope of marketing
- Explain the economic value and benefits of marketing
- Discuss the reasons for studying marketing
- Discuss the importance of marketing careers to the U.S. economy
- Describe current employment trends
- State the marketing concept
- Explain the marketing mix
- Define what constitutes a market, as well as how to identify one
- Identify key methods used to reach potential customers, including developing a customer profile, target marketing, and marketing segmentation
- Identify demographic, geographic, and psychographic trends in the U.S. consumer market

Key to Individualized Activities

L1 Level 1 activities are basic activities and should fall within the range of all students.

L2 Level 2 activities are average activities and should be within the range of average and above average students.

L3 Level 3 activities are challenging activities designed for the ability range of above average students.

Enrichment Resources

PROFESSIONAL ORGANIZATIONS

Professional Pricing Society (PPR) pricingsociety.com

American Marketing Association (AMA) marketingpower.com

MEDIA RESOURCES

Print or online editions of

Discount Store News dsnretailingtoday.com

News Directory newsdirectory.com

ClickZ Network clickz.com

WRITING SUPPORT

Ask students to think of an advertising slogan that is currently in use. Have them write a three-paragraph essay about where they have seen the slogan, what it conveys to potential customers, and whether they feel it is effective. Ask students to keep and review this document as they study Unit 1.

UNIT 1 PLANNING GUIDE AND RESOURCES

CHAPTER	PRINT MATERIALS	TECHNOLOGY RESOURCES
Chapter 1 Section 1.1 Section 1.2 Section 1.3	**From Unit 1 Fast File Booklet** Lesson Plans Chapter Summaries Reproducible Masters Reproducible Tests **Print Ancillaries** Student Activity Workbook, Chapter 1 Marketing Math Workbook, Chapter 1 *BusinessWeek* Reader and Case Studies, Chapter 1 Competitive Events Workbook, Unit 1 Marketing Research Project Workbook School-to-Work Activity Workbook	Interactive Chalkboard classroom presentations, Chapter 1 Online Learning Center at **marketingessentials.glencoe.com** Online Student Edition, Chapter 1 TeacherWorks **Exam***View*® Pro Test Generator, Chapter 1 Virtual Business
Chapter 2 Section 2.1 Section 2.2	**From Unit 1 Fast File Booklet** Lesson Plans Chapter Summaries Reproducible Masters Reproducible Tests **Print Ancillaries** Student Activity Workbook, Chapter 2 Marketing Math Workbook, Chapter 2 *BusinessWeek* Reader and Case Studies, Chapter 2 Competitive Events Workbook, Unit 1 Marketing Research Project Workbook School-to-Work Activity Workbook	Interactive Chalkboard classroom presentations, Chapter 2 Online Learning Center at **marketingessentials.glencoe.com** Online Student Edition, Chapter 2 TeacherWorks **Exam***View*® Pro Test Generator, Chapter 2 Virtual Business

National Marketing Education

CHAPTER	SECTION	PERFORMANCE INDICATOR
Chapter 1 **Marketing Is All Around Us**	1.1	Describe marketing functions and related activities (BME)
		Explain marketing and its importance in a global economy (BME)
	1.2	Determine forms of economic utility created by marketing activities (ECO)
	1.3	Explain employment opportunities in marketing (PD)
		Identify skills needed to enhance career progression (PD)
Chapter 2 **The Marketing Plan**	2.1	Explain marketing and its importance in a global economy (BME)
		Explain the concept of competition (ECO)
		Identify factors affecting a business's profit (ECO)
		Address the needs of individual personalities (SEL)
	2.2	Explain the role of business in society (BME)
		Identify factors affecting a business's profit (ECO)
		Analyze product information to identify product features and benefits (SEL)

BME Business, Management, Entrepreneurship   **ECO** Economics   **PD** Professional Development   **SEL** Selling

Standards Assessment Correlation

SECTION ASSESSMENT		CHAPTER ASSESSMENT						UNIT LAB
Reviewing Key Terms and Concepts	Integrating Academic Skills	Review Facts and Ideas	Build Skills	Develop Critical Thinking	Apply Concepts	Workplace Skills	Net Savvy	Marketing Internship
1, 2, 3	✓	11–14	20, 21	23	26, 25	✓	✓	✓
2, 3	✓	11–19			25		✓	
1, 2, 3	✓	10	20, 21	23	25	✓	✓	
3			21	24				
			20	24	26	✓		
1, 2, 3		8, 10						
								✓
								✓
1, 2	✓	8, 9, 13, 14	16, 17	19	21, 22	✓	✓	
1		13, 14	16	20		✓	✓	
								✓
2, 3	✓	12, 15		19	21, 22			✓

@ **Online Action!** Check the latest updates for national standards and for your state's standards at marketingessentials.glencoe.com

Unit Overview

Use Unit 1 as a base of knowledge throughout the text. Chapter 1 defines marketing, explains the benefits of marketing, and provides an overview of careers in marketing. Chapter 2 lays the foundation for marketing principles and practices. It focuses on the marketing concept, four Ps of the marketing mix, target marketing, and market segmentation.

MAKING IT RELEVANT

Have students share examples of marketing—billboards, radio and TV commercials, print advertisements, decals on vehicles, and banners. Ask them why marketing is so prevalent in society. Let them know that, in the free market, every business has to fight for its customers and success.

Unit Launch Activity

Have students share their first impressions of the ad on this page. Ask students to list reasons West Virginia would market itself as a seasonal destination for recreational tourists.

Reasons will vary but may include location, costs of winter sports and lodging compared to other areas, beauty, and so on.

In this unit you will find

- **Chapter 1**
  Marketing Is All Around Us

- **Chapter 2**
  The Marketing Plan

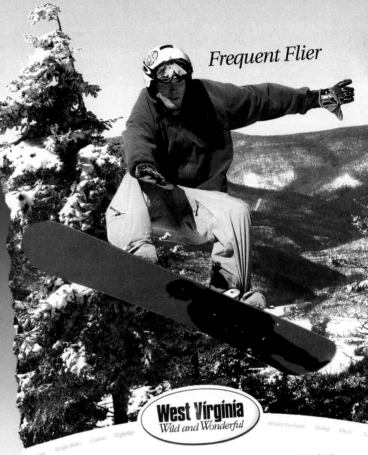

Frequent Flier

West Virginia
Wild and Wonderful

Camping Sleigh Rides Cabins Nightlife Winter Festivals Skiing Music Tubing

Picture yourself cruising and then –BAM – you're right in the middle of an awesome jump.
Let our mountain air clear your mind and send your spirits soaring.

www.callwva.com   FREE TRAVEL GUIDE   1 - 800 - CALL WVA

xxvi

OUT OF TIME?

If class time is too short to cover all the chapters in this unit, go to Unit 1 in your Fast File Teacher Resources booklet and find the Chapter Summaries for Chapters 1 and 2.

DECA UNIT PROJECT

Entering the World of Marketing

After completing this unit, have students select the DECA competitive events in which they want to compete. Have them interview a person employed in that area. Students should draft questions relating to the information in Chapters 1 and 2. After they have conducted the interviews, ask students to share their research.

Assessment Guidelines Prepare a rubric for evaluation that includes managing time, working independently, presenting work in neat and orderly manner, and submitting work on time.

Enrichment Assign and review Unit 1 activities in the Competitive Events Workbook.

Marketing

ANALYZE THE AD

This ad invites readers to visit the state of West Virginia for a vacation. What is the main theme? How does the picture work with the words?

Market Talk Marketing promotes and sells products such as food and clothing, or services such as a haircut or a vacation in West Virginia. Do you think marketing promotes ideas, as well?

Think and Write Print ads use powerful visual components and interesting, catchy writing to draw in the reader. Read the slogans in this ad. Do you think they work? Why or why not? Look through magazines or newspapers and write down three slogans you think are effective. Next, select a state or a country that interests you and write a slogan for it that would encourage tourism.

@ Online Action! Go to *marketingessentials.glencoe.com/ u1/ad* for an extended activity.

Functions of Marketing

In this unit

Foundations of Marketing
- Economics

Functions of Marketing
- Pricing
- Promotion
- Selling

marketingessentials.glencoe.com

1

Marketing Plan

ANALYSIS
1
- SWOT
- Economic
- Socio-Cultural
- Technological
- Competitive

STRATEGY
2
- Promotion
- Place
- Price
- Product

IMPLEMENTATION
3
- Organization
- Management
- Staffing

BUDGET
4
- Cost of sales
- Cost of Promotion
- Income and expenses

CONTROL
5
- Evaluation
- Performance Measures
- Performance Analysis

Marketing Plan

RELATE THE UNIT TO THE MARKETING PLAN
The four Ps of the marketing mix include product, place, pricing, and promotion. Inform students that Chapters 1 and 2 provide an overview of marketing practices and principles.

MARKETING PLAN OVERVIEW
Ask students to choose the marketing plan of a product or place and describe the message it conveys to consumers. Many students will find that marketing messages describe not only the item being sold but also a lifestyle or attitude.

Functions of Marketing
Point out to students that Chapters 1 and 2 will touch on one of the foundations of marketing (economics) and three of the functions (pricing, promotion, and selling).

- **Economics** Financing, pricing, distributing, and selling are all interwoven to keep a business successfully afloat.

- **Pricing** Price is a determining factor in both customer satisfaction and business profit.

- **Promotion** Showcasing the potential of a good or service to fulfill a need or a want grabs would-be consumers' attention. Clear communication offers the greatest chance for potential customers to hear about and buy a marketed product or service.

- **Selling** Offering customers the right product or service requires intense business development in terms of employing concepts and strategies that work. Selling occurs in any market, even in the business-to-business environment.

ANALYZE THE AD

Ask students to share their opinions of the visual components of the West Virginia tourism ad.

Market Talk Students should agree that the idea of West Virginia being a great tourism destination is as marketable as a pair of shoes. Ask students to think of a few examples of how advertising a product (shoes) is different from advertising a service or an idea.

Think and Write To help the creation of slogans, ask students to consider the aspects of a state or country that personally interests them—for example, beaches in Hawaii or mountains in Washington.

@ Online Action! For instructions, ideas, and answer guide, go to the Teacher Center at **marketingessentials.glencoe.com**

CHAPTER 1

Chapter Overview

Chapter 1 provides the foundation for all subsequent study in this textbook. It defines the term *marketing* and outlines the foundations and functions of this field. This chapter introduces these key concepts: marketing mix (the four Ps), utility, market share, and target market.

BUILD BACKGROUND

Point out that most students have been marketed to since they were very young, so they already know a lot about marketing from the viewpoint of the potential customer. Ask them to suggest things they bought or things bought for them throughout their lives. Ask: Why did they want these particular things?

Why It's Important

This chapter provides a foundation for learning about the world of marketing. Illustrate this by reading through the chapter objectives with the class. Then, ask whether students think they will study marketing from the viewpoint of a potential buyer or in some other way. If necessary, lead them to see that chapter content looks at all aspects of marketing.

Prepare to Read

On the board, work with students to make a simple outline of the section, assigning the red headings roman numerals and the blue headings capital letters. Students can make their own copies of this outline, leaving space on their papers between headings. They can then use the outline for their notes as they read the chapter. Encourage continuing use of this study skill.

CHAPTER 1
Marketing Is All Around Us

Chapter Objectives

After reading this chapter, you should be able to:

- Define marketing
- Explain the four foundations of marketing
- List the seven functions of marketing
- Understand the marketing concept
- Analyze the benefits of marketing
- Apply the concept of utility
- Describe the concept of market
- Differentiate consumer and industrial markets
- Describe market share
- Define target market
- List the components of the marketing mix

GUIDE TO THE PHOTO

Market Talk In the United States, it is rare to be far from an ad of some sort. A passing hiker in a national park might be wearing a T-shirt with a corporate logo. A sign on the side of a country road could announce fresh eggs for sale. In a mall or a major city, the marketing is much more intense. Everywhere you look, you see signs, brands, and ads.

Quick Think Promotion is only one aspect of marketing. How would you define marketing and all the activities that fall under its umbrella?

GUIDE TO THE PHOTO

Market Talk As students offer examples of products, record these examples in a cluster diagram on the board. Ask students if they can draw any conclusions about marketing from the diagram. For example, do they think that ads on the sails of sailboats are effective? What kinds of ads do they think might be featured on the sails?

Quick Think Student definitions of marketing and marketing activities will vary. Accept all reasonable answers.

 Follow Up Ask the class to write down their definitions of marketing and then save these for review—and revision—after study of this chapter.

Performance indicators represent key skills and knowledge. Relating them to the concepts explained in this chapter is your key to success in DECA events. These acronyms represent DECA events that involve knowledge of concepts in this chapter.

AAAL	FMAL	MMS	TMDM
AAML	FMDM*	QSRM	TSE*
ADC*	FMML	RMAL	VPM
BSM	FSRM	RMML	
EMDM	HMDM*	SMDM*	

In all these DECA events, you should be able to follow the following performance indicators:

- Distinguish between economic goods and services
- Determine the forms of economic utility that marketing creates
- Explain the concept of marketing strategies
- Explain the concept of market and market identification
- Select target market

All the events with an asterisk (*) also include this performance indicator:

- Describe the nature of target marketing in a specific industry

Some events include additional performance indicators. These are:

FMDM	Target financial products for specific markets
SMDM	Identify target markets for a sports/entertainment event
ADC	Develop a customer/client profile
HMDM	Determine potential lodging markets
EMDM	Identify online target market
TSE	Design a customer/client profile

DECA PREP

Check your understanding of DECA performance indicators with the DECA activity in this chapter's review. For more information and DECA Prep practice, go to *marketingessentials.glencoe.com/1/DECA*

CHAPTER 1 Classroom Resources

For the Teacher

- TeacherWorks
- marketingessentials.glencoe.com
- Interactive Chalkboard
- **Exam*View*®** Pro Test Generator
- Fast File Unit 1

For the Student

- ***Marketing Essentials*** Online Edition
- Student Activity Workbook
- Marketing Math Workbook
- Marketing Research Project Workbook
- School-to-Work Activity Workbook
- Competitive Events Workbook
- ***BusinessWeek*** Reader and Case Studies
- marketingessentials.glencoe.com

DECA events that require knowledge of marketing are described here. Discuss the performance indicators to make sure students understand how to demonstrate their understanding.

The event acronyms stand for:

AAAL:	Apparel and Accessories Marketing Series, AL
AAML:	Apparel and Accessories Marketing Series, ML
ADC:	Advertising Campaign Event
BSM:	Business Services Marketing Series
EMDM:	E-Commerce Management Team Decision Making Event
FMAL:	Food Marketing Series, AL
FMDM:	Financial Analysis Management Team Decision Making Event
FMML:	Food Marketing Series, ML
FSRM:	Full Service Restaurant Management Series
HMDM:	Hospitality Services Management Team Decision Making Event
MMS:	Marketing Management Series
QSRM:	Quick Serve Restaurant Management Series
RMAL:	Retail Merchandising Series, AL
RMML:	Retail Merchandising Series, ML
SMDM:	Sports and Entertainment Marketing Management Team Decision Making Event
TMDM:	Travel and Tourism Marketing Management Team Decision Making Event
TSE:	Technical Sales Event
VPM:	Vehicles and Petroleum Marketing Series

DECA PREP

Find timed DECA Prep activities correlated to the Competitive Events Workbook for students and DECA tips for teachers at **marketingessentials.glencoe.com/1/DECA**

FOCUS

Introducing the Section

COLLABORATIVE ACTIVITY

To illustrate that marketing is all around us, bring to class mail order catalogs or ask students to bring in a sampling of catalogs. Examine these with the class, discussing the variety of products offered. Point out that these are all examples of marketing. If you have Internet access in class, pull up several Web sites and point out the advertising that goes with them. Explain that this too is marketing.

Preteaching Key Terms

Have students skim the section and find each term and its definition in the text. As terms and definitions are offered, write these on the board and have students record the information in their notebooks.

- marketing
- goods
- services
- marketing concept

Critical Thinking

Ask students to explain how they are part of the marketing process.

OBJECTIVES

- Define marketing
- Explain the four foundations of marketing
- List the seven functions of marketing
- Understand the marketing concept

KEY TERMS

- marketing
- goods
- services
- marketing concept

Marketing and the Marketing Concept

READ and STUDY

BEFORE YOU READ

Connect Do you think you have ever been influenced by marketing? Explain why or why not and give examples if necessary.

THE MAIN IDEA

Marketing is an umbrella term that includes many activities and has many functions. To be a successful marketer, you need to understand the foundations, functions, and basic tools of marketing.

STUDY ORGANIZER

Draw an umbrella shape like the one below to organize the marketing concepts you will read about in this section.

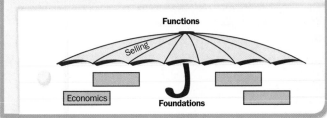

WHILE YOU READ

Connect Relate the definition of marketing to the functions of marketing and to the marketing concept.

The Scope of Marketing

You already know a lot about marketing because it is all around you. You have been a consumer for many years and you have made decisions about products you liked and did not like. As you study marketing, you will analyze what businesses do to influence consumers' buying decisions. That practice will help you make the transition from thinking like a consumer to thinking like a marketer.

4 UNIT 1 - THE WORLD OF MARKETING

READ and STUDY

BEFORE YOU READ

List examples that students offer, classifying these according to whether they were or were not influenced. Point out that even if they did not buy the product(s), they were still exposed to these marketing efforts.

THE MAIN IDEA

Encourage students to define *umbrella term* from context, the other words that surround it.

STUDY ORGANIZER

Model the study organizer for students. A full-size, downloadable study organizer can be found at marketingessentials.glencoe.com

 WHILE YOU READ Have students think of a product they like or use. As they read, students should keep this product in mind, noting how this specific example relates to the general definition of marketing.

● **MARKETING IDEAS** The definition of marketing includes marketing ideas, such as eating healthful foods.

What other ideas have you seen marketed?

Marketing is a broad term that includes many activities and requires many skills. **Marketing** is the process of planning, pricing, promoting, selling, and distributing ideas, goods, or services to create exchanges that satisfy customers. Note that marketing is a process. This means it is ongoing and it changes. As a marketer, you need to keep up with trends and consumer attitudes. The products, ideas, or services you develop and the way you price, promote, and distribute them should reflect these trends and attitudes. All functions of marketing support this effort. Current marketing practices focus on customers and maintaining a close relationship with them.

Ideas, Goods, and Services

Marketing promotes ideas, goods, and services. Politicians, for example, use marketing techniques to promote their platform, or ideas. **Goods** are tangible items that have monetary value and satisfy your needs and wants such as cars, toys, furniture, televisions, clothing, and candy. Intangible items that have monetary value and satisfy your needs and wants are **services**. Intangible means you cannot physically touch them. In most cases, services involve a task, such as cooking a hamburger or cutting hair. Banks, dry cleaners, amusement parks, movie theaters, and accounting offices all provide economic services.

Every time someone sells or buys something, an exchange takes place in the marketplace. The marketplace is the commercial environment where such trades happen. It is the world of shops, Internet stores, financial institutions, catalogs, and much more.

Foundations of Marketing

The practice of marketing depends on four key areas of knowledge. These are the four foundations of marketing. The marketing wheel on page 1 includes these four foundations.

The topics you will study in *Marketing Essentials* are based on these four foundations of marketing:

Chapter 1 - Marketing Is All Around Us **5**

Review Guide

CONCEPTS

Ask students to name the four foundations of marketing. Then have volunteers help classmates review this material by reading aloud the information under the appropriate headings in the text.
business, management, entrepreneurship; communication and interpersonal skills; economics; professional development

KEY TERMS

Have students work in small groups to review key terms, their spellings, and their definitions.

ONLINE SELF-ASSESSMENT

Have students go to marketingessentials.glencoe.com for the Section 1.1 practice test.

Individualized Review

L1 Assign and review Chapter 1 activities in the Student Activity Workbook.

L2 Assign and review Chapter 1 activities in the Marketing Math Workbook.

L3 Assign and review Chapter 1 activities in the *BusinessWeek* Reader and Case Studies.

Marketing Practice

Ask students to select two products they use in their everyday lives. Have students specify to whom they believe the product is marketed and how they think pricing decisions are made for this product. Have students summarize their findings in a one-page report.

1. **Business, management, entrepreneurship** Understanding the basics of business, management, and entrepreneurial concepts that affect business decision making
2. **Communication and interpersonal skills** Understanding concepts, strategies, and systems needed to interact effectively with others
3. **Economics** Understanding the economic principles and concepts that are basic to marketing
4. **Professional development** Understanding concepts and strategies needed for career exploration, development, and growth

Seven Functions of Marketing

The seven functions include distribution, financing, marketing information management, pricing, product/service management, promotion, and selling. The marketing wheel on page 1 also includes these functions. These functions define all the aspects that are part of the practice of marketing.

Distribution

Distribution is the process of deciding how to get goods in customers' hands. Physically moving and storing goods is part of distribution planning. The main methods of transportation are by truck, rail, ship, or air. Some large retail chains store products in central warehouses for later distribution. Distribution also involves the systems that track products so that they can be located at any time.

Financing

Financing is getting the money that is necessary to pay for setting up and running a business. Business owners often obtain bank loans to start a new business. Some also form corporations and may sell shares (or stock) of the business. Financing also involves decisions such as whether to offer credit to customers. Most retailers offer customers payment options such as MasterCard or Visa, while other stores offer their own credit services.

Marketing Information Management

Good business and marketing decisions rely on good information about customers, trends, and competing products. Gathering this information, storing it, and analyzing it are all part of marketing information management. Collecting information is done on a continual basis and through special marketing research studies. This is what marketers do to find out about customers, their habits and attitudes, where they live, and trends in the marketplace. Have you ever been asked to complete a questionnaire about the service at a restaurant or other type of business? If so, you have participated in marketing research. Companies conduct research so they can be successful at marketing and selling their products.

Pricing

Pricing decisions dictate how much to charge for goods and services in order to make a profit. Pricing decisions are based on costs and on what competitors charge for the same product or service. To determine a price, marketers must also determine how much customers are willing to pay.

Product/Service Management

Product/service management is obtaining, developing, maintaining, and improving a product or a product mix in response to market opportunities. Marketing research guides product/service management toward what the consumer needs and wants.

Promotion

Promotion is the effort to inform, persuade, or remind potential customers about a business's products or services. Television and radio commercials are forms of promotion. This type of promotion is called advertising. Promotion is also used to improve a company's public image. A company can show that it is socially responsible by recycling materials or cleaning up the environment. Promotion concepts and strategies are used to achieve success in the marketplace.

 Extended Activity

Functions of Marketing

Ask interested students to work in groups of two to five. Have each group choose a product or service and research each of the functions of marketing for that product or service: distribution, financing, marketing information management, pricing, product/service management, and promotion. Have groups present one of the functions of marketing of the product to the class in a three- to five-minute oral report.

Selling

Selling provides customers with the goods and services they want. This includes selling in the retail market to you, the customer, and selling in the business-to-business market to wholesalers, retailers, or manufacturers.

Selling techniques and activities include determining client needs and wants and responding through planned, personalized communication. The selling process influences purchasing decisions and enhances future business opportunities.

The Marketing Concept

The **marketing concept** is the idea that a business should strive to satisfy customers' needs and wants while generating a profit for the firm. The focus is on the customer. For an organization to be successful, all seven functions of marketing need to support this idea.

The personnel responsible for those functions must understand the marketing concept and reach for the same goal in order to send a consistent message to the customer. The message is that the customer satisfaction is most important. Everyone in an organization needs to recognize that repeat customers keep a company in business. For example, the switchboard operator in a large corporation or the pizza delivery person must understand the marketing concept and be mindful of the company's goals. Everyone in an organization is an extension of that firm and must provide the best possible service to its customers. Businesses that stress the marketing concept with all employees are successful.

Customer Relationship Management (CRM)

In today's marketplace, customer relationship is most important. Customer relationship management (CRM) is an aspect of marketing that combines customer information (through database and computer technology) with customer service and marketing communications. Marketers who specialize in CRM try to create more meaningful one-on-one communications with the customer by applying customer data (demographic, industry, buying history, etc.) to every communication.

1.1 AFTER YOU READ

Reviewing Key Terms and Concepts
1. Name two ideas that can be marketed.
2. Where do exchanges take place?
3. What is the main difference between consumers and industrial users?

Integrating Academic Skills
Math
4. A customer purchases two tables at $149.99 each and would like them to be delivered. Your company charges customers $50 for delivery and the state imposes a 5 percent sales tax on furniture, but not on the delivery charge. What is the total amount due from the customer?

Economics
5. List at least three ways the Internet has changed marketing functions.

 Online Action!

Check your answers at *marketingessentials.glencoe.com/1/read*

marketingessentials.glencoe.com

Chapter 1 - Marketing Is All Around Us **7**

AFTER YOU READ

Reviewing Key Terms and Concepts
1. Answers will vary. Possibilities include conserving natural resources, adopting of energy-saving measures in the home, or voting for a particular political party.
2. Exchanges take place in the marketplace.
3. Consumers as a rule purchase smaller quantities for their own use than industrial users purchase.

Integrating Academic Skills
4. $364.98; [($149.99 × 2) × 0.05] + $50 = $364.98
5. Answers will vary. Possible answers include the fact that the Internet easily reaches a global audience, it provides advanced means of inventory control, it can serve as marketing tool, it can serve in customer relationship management, and it can analyze market trends and desires.

Online Action! Answers at **marketingessentials.glencoe.com/1/read**

Extended Activity

Customer Relationship Management

Encourage students to give specific examples of how companies have tried to develop and keep them as customers. Possibilities include the practice of addressing customers by name in print advertising pieces and on the covers of catalogues, offering savings such as free shipping, and assigning code numbers to aid claiming frequent customer perks by phone or online.

FOCUS

Introducing the Section

COLLABORATIVE ACTIVITY

Have students work in small groups to brainstorm and list examples of new and improved products that they have looked at or purchased recently. In what ways is each product said to be different from the original? Can they spot any trends? For example, are food products said to be better for those who eat them? In what way(s)? Ask groups to report their findings to the class in a brief oral presentation.

Preteaching Key Terms

Write the key term *utility* on the board. Point out that it comes from the Latin verb *to use.* Explain that when used in marketing, the term has a specialized meaning. Have one student skim the section to find the word and read the definition aloud to the class.

Build Vocabulary

Ask volunteers to suggest other words that have the same root as the word *utility.* Then have volunteers check dictionaries and add any words found there. Possibilities include *use, useful, useless, user, utilize, utilitarian.*

 Critical Thinking

Ask students to brainstorm reasons why prices drop when products become more popular.

OBJECTIVES

- Analyze the benefits of marketing
- Apply the concept of utility

KEY TERM

- utility

The Importance of Marketing

READ and STUDY

BEFORE YOU READ

Use Prior Knowledge When did you last shop at a mall? Did you witness any promotion effort? Did you compare prices? What role did this play in your decision to buy?

THE MAIN IDEA

Marketing is a key part of our economy because it supports competition and offers benefits to consumers.

STUDY ORGANIZER

Reproduce the figure below. As you read this section, note the benefits of marketing and list the five utilities on lines jutting out from one of the ovals.

```
     Utility
  Added Value              Benefits of
                           Marketing
       Form
          Place
```

Economic Benefits of Marketing

Through the study of marketing you will realize just how important marketing is and how much it affects your life and the lives of other consumers. Its impact is even more dramatic when you consider how it affects our economy and standard of living.

Marketing plays an important role in an economy because it provides the means for competition to take place. In a competitive marketplace, businesses try to create new or improved products at lower prices than their competitors. Those efforts force

WHILE YOU READ

Connect List your own experiences and observations about how marketing benefits you personally.

8 UNIT 1 - THE WORLD OF MARKETING

READ and STUDY

BEFORE YOU READ

Point out that at this time, many students have begun to take increasing responsibility for earning money and determining how to spend it. Have them share their responses to the questions with the class.

THE MAIN IDEA

Ask a volunteer to read the main idea aloud and then ask aloud any questions it brings to mind.

STUDY ORGANIZER

As you begin to teach this section, keep students on task by filling out the ovals in the organizer. Make your own study organizer on the board, or download the one provided at **marketingessentials.glencoe.com**

WHILE YOU READ Encourage students to share their observations in class.

THE ONE AND ONLY EASY-TO-HOLD,
EASY-TO-OPEN, EASY-TO-POUR PAINT CONTAINER

The biggest idea in paint could only come from one brand, Dutch Boy.® The Twist & Pour™ paint container makes every painting job easier, with its revolutionary easy-to-hold, easy-to-open, and easy-to-pour design. It's another neat idea from Dutch Boy. For a Twist & Pour retailer near you, call 1.800.828.5669 or visit www.dutchboy.com.

Easy to hold   Easy to open   Easy to pour

Dutch Boy

• **NEW PRODUCTS** One of the major economic benefits of marketing is the proliferation of new and improved products.

List three new and improved products you have seen marketed lately.

them to be efficient and responsive to consumers. In addition, businesses look for ways to add value to a consumer's shopping experience. Let's look at the economic benefits of marketing to the economy and to consumers.

New and Improved Products

Marketing generates competition, which in turn fosters new and improved products. Businesses always look for ways to satisfy customers' wants and needs and to keep customers interested. This creates a larger variety of goods and services. For example, personal computers have gotten smaller, lighter, more powerful, and less expensive. As more people use computers, this market continues to grow.

Lower Prices

Marketing activities increase demand, and this helps to lower prices. When demand is high, manufacturers can produce products in larger quantities. This reduces the unit cost of each product. This is because the fixed costs (such as the rent on a building) remain the same whether the company produces 10 units or 10,000 units. When a company produces a larger quantity of a product, it spends less per unit on fixed costs. The company can charge a lower price per unit, sell more units, and make more money. Here is an example using a fixed cost of $20,000.

Quantity Produced	Fixed Cost Per Unit
10,000	$2.00
($20,000 ÷ 10,000)	
200,000	.10
($20,000 ÷ 200,000)	

As you can see, the increased quantity significantly reduces the fixed cost per unit.

In addition, when products become popular, more competitors enter the marketplace. To remain competitive, marketers find ways to lower their prices. Look at the DVD market for some examples of this phenomenon. DVD players were introduced in 1997. Since then, there has been an explosion in the sales and rentals of DVDs and DVD players. Combination DVD/CD/MP3 players were very costly products when they were introduced on the market, but now they can be purchased for less than $100.

Added Value and Utility

The functions of marketing add value to a product. This added value in economic terms is called **utility**. Utilities are the attributes of a product or service that make it capable of satisfying consumers' wants and needs.

There are five economic utilities involved with all products: form, place, time, possession, and information. Although form utility is not directly related to marketing, much of what goes into creating new products, such as marketing research and product design, makes it an integral part of the marketing process.

Chapter 1 - Marketing Is All Around Us **9**

TEACH CONTINUED

Discussion Starter

NEW AND IMPROVED PRODUCTS
Ask students to give examples of how consumer demand can influence what changes are made to existing products.

Concept Development

ADDED VALUE AND UTILITY
Ask students to generate a short list of products that your classroom might use. Choose one product and, as a class, determine the following: 1.) Form utility (what raw materials were used to make this product), 2.) Place utility (where this product would be distributed), 3.) Time utility (when this product would be sold), 4.) Possession utility (how the product would be paid for), 5.) Information utility (how to get information to potential customers).

Individualized Math Skills

L1 Ask students to explain how *fixed costs* and *unit costs* are related.
Fixed costs remain the same no matter how many units are produced. The greater the number of units produced, the cheaper it becomes to manufacture them.

L2 Ask students to imagine that the fixed costs at a store selling scarves are $7,500. If the company makes 300 scarves, what is the unit cost?
$25; $7,500 ÷ 300 = $25

L3 Ask students to imagine a store selling scarves that has fixed costs of $7,500. The unit cost is $25. How many scarves will have been sold if the unit price drops to $12.50?
600 scarves; $7,500 ÷ $12.50 = 600

ASSESS

Review Guide

CONCEPTS

Ask students to name each of the five economic utilities.

form utility, place utility, time utility, possession utility, and information utility

KEY TERMS

Have students work in small groups to review key terms, their spellings, and their definitions.

ONLINE SELF-ASSESSMENT

Have students go to marketingessentials.glencoe.com for the Section 1.2 practice test.

Individualized Review

L1 Assign and review Chapter 1 activities in the Student Activity Workbook.

L2 Assign and review Chapter 1 activities in the Marketing Math Workbook.

L3 Assign and review Chapter 1 activities in the *BusinessWeek* Reader and Case Studies.

Marketing Practice

Divide the class into five groups. Give the class an example of a particular product, service, or idea. Assign each group one type of utility. Have each group research the utility for each product and create a poster or other visual summary of the results of their research. Have groups present their findings in class and post their visual summaries in one place in the classroom.

MARKET TECH

Supermarket Personal Shopper

Albertsons introduced its Shop 'n' Scan technology by testing it—first in a handful of stores in Chicago, then expanding the test to more than 100 stores in the Dallas area. The tests started in October 2002. By October 2004 the company was planning to roll out the system in other cities.

The system enables customers to use hand-held scanners to scan and bag their purchases as they shop at several Jewel-Osco stores.

Focus on the Shopper

The technology has some other customer-friendly features. A portable computer keeps a running total of the prices of the items in the cart. Customers can also use an express pay station to ring up their purchases.

Company Goals

These customer-focused developments are in keeping with the overall policies and objectives of the company:

- Focusing on customers
- Building efficiency
- Capitalizing on technology

The company has had success with Shop 'n' Scan. According to the *Wall Street Journal*, shoppers using the technology bought, on average, twice as many groceries as shoppers using regular carts.

THINK LIKE A MARKETER

How does this technology add value (utility) to a customer's shopping experience?

@ Online Action!

Go to *marketingessentials.glencoe.com/1/tech* to find a project on technology as added value.

Form Utility

Form utility involves changing raw materials or putting parts together to make them more useful. In other words, it deals with making or producing things. The manufacturing of products involves taking things of little value by themselves and putting them together to create more value. If you consider the value of a zipper, a spool of thread, and several yards of cloth, each would have some value, but not as much as when you put all three together by making a jacket.

Form utility involves making products that consumers need and want. Special features or ingredients in a product add value and increase its form utility. For example, electronic controls on the steering wheel of an automobile add value to the final product.

Place Utility

Place utility involves having a product where customers can buy it. Businesses study consumer shopping habits to determine the most convenient and efficient locations to sell products.

Some businesses use a direct approach by selling their products through catalogs, and other businesses rely on retailers to sell their products. The Internet offers even more options to businesses that want to sell their products directly to their customers without the use of any intermediaries.

Time Utility

Time utility is having a product available at a certain time of year or a convenient time of day. For example, supermarkets and other food stores offer convenient shopping hours or they are open 24-hours a day. Retailers often have extended shopping hours during the busiest shopping season of the year, from Thanksgiving till Christmas. Marketers increase the value of products by having them available when consumers want them.

Possession Utility

How do you come into possession of the items you want? You generally buy them for

marketingessentials.glencoe.com

MARKET TECH

Supermarket Personal Shopper

Discussion Lead a discussion on potential problems with this technology and approach.

THINK LIKE A MARKETER **Answer:** The new approach adds both time and place utility. Ideally, the scanner allows shoppers to avoid the regular checkout lines, thus saving time, while the prompts from the scanner remind the shopper of earlier purchases of related items that might be purchased again.

@ Online Action! For instructions, ideas, and answer guide, go to the Teacher Center at marketingessentials.glencoe.com

Follow Up Widen the discussion by asking the class to consider how a person employed as a supermarket checker might be influenced by this system.

a price. The exchange of a product for money is possession utility. Retailers may accept alternatives to cash, such as personal checks, debit or credit cards, in exchange for their merchandise. They may even offer installment or layaway plans (delayed possession in return for gradual payment). Every one of these options adds value to the product being purchased. In fact, without these options, some customers would not be able to buy the items they want. In business-to-business situations, companies also grant their customers credit. They may give them a certain period (for example, 30 days) to pay a bill. This adds value to the products they sell.

Possession utility is involved every time legal ownership of a product changes hands. Possession utility increases as purchase options increase. The Internet also provides consumers with options to pay by providing secure sites where credit cards are accepted.

Information Utility

Information utility involves communication with the consumer. Salespeople provide information to customers by explaining the features and benefits of products. Displays communicate information, too. Packaging and labeling inform consumers about qualities and uses of a product. The label on a frozen food entrée will tell you the ingredients, nutritional information, directions for preparation, and any safety precautions needed.

Advertising informs consumers about products, tells where to buy products, and sometimes tells how much products cost.

Many manufacturers provide owners' manuals that explain how to use their products. Businesses have Web sites on the Internet where they provide detailed information about their companies and their products.

1.2 AFTER YOU READ

Reviewing Key Terms and Concepts
1. How does marketing help to lower prices?
2. In what way is marketing related to form utility?
3. Which utility is added by drive-through windows at fast-food restaurants?

Integrating Academic Skills
Math
4. In a business-to-business transaction, the seller offers the buyer a 2 percent discount for paying a bill early. Assuming the buyer took advantage of this offer, how much would be discounted on a $10,000 invoice?

Writing
5. Write a brief story (two to three paragraphs) about a young person shopping at the local mall that incorporates all the benefits of marketing.

 Online Action! Check your answers at *marketingessentials.glencoe.com/1/read*

marketingessentials.glencoe.com

CLOSE

Have students complete the following statement:

The added value to a product that marketing provides is called _____ .
utility

Extended Activity
Information Utility
Provide students with the following examples of companies that take information utility into the realm of social responsibility. For example, many cosmetics companies follow the lead of The Body Shop, making it part of their marketing strategy to state that they do not test their products on animals. The Adopt-a-Highway program cleans up the environment while providing some advertising by giving the name of the company or organization pledged to maintain a particular stretch of road. Ask students to think of other examples where marketing and social responsibility could combine.

 AFTER YOU READ

Reviewing Key Terms and Concepts
1. Marketing helps lower prices by encouraging competition.
2. Form utility creates the products that are marketed.
3. time utility

Integrating Academic Skills
4. $200; $10,000 × .02 = $200
5. Compositions should indicate familiarity with these benefits: new and improved products, lower prices, and added value and utility.

Online Action! Answers at **marketingessentials.glencoe.com/1/read**

11

SECTION 1.3

Introducing the Section

COLLABORATIVE ACTIVITY

Lead a discussion asking students for examples of recent marketing trends they may have noted through the media or by observing others.

Answers will vary; possible responses might include reduced-carb foods, organic foods, legal music downloading services, the miniaturization of portable electronics such as cell phones and MP3 players.

Preteaching Key Terms

Read each term aloud and then work with students to skim the section to find each term in context. Have a volunteer read the definition while everyone in the class records it.

- market
- consumer market
- industrial market
- market share
- target market
- customer profile
- marketing mix

Build Vocabulary

Ask students to think about the words *segmentation* and *target* as they are used in relation to the word *market*. Ask students why marketers might use visual references to discuss abstract concepts.

OBJECTIVES

- Describe the concept of market
- Differentiate consumer and industrial markets
- Describe market share
- Define target market
- List the components of the marketing mix

KEY TERMS

- market
- consumer market
- industrial market
- market share
- target market
- customer profile
- marketing mix

Fundamentals of Marketing

READ and STUDY

BEFORE YOU READ

Predict How do you think marketers decide where to advertise their products?

THE MAIN IDEA

The term *market* refers to all the people who might buy a product or service. The marketing mix is a set of four tools or strategies the marketer uses to influence buying decisions.

STUDY ORGANIZER

Draw two diagrams like the ones below. In the first diagram, record four terms about the concept of market. In the second diagram, record the four Ps of the marketing mix.

WHILE YOU READ

Connect Jot down examples of ads you have seen or heard and how they relate to your reading.

Market and Market Identification

The terminology found in this section is the foundation for future work and study in marketing. You need to commit these terms to memory so you can use them correctly when discussing marketing principles and practices. You will find that these terms are used throughout this textbook. So let's begin your journey into becoming a marketer.

12 UNIT 1 - THE WORLD OF MARKETING

READ and STUDY

BEFORE YOU READ

As volunteers offer ideas, record these on the board. Adjust this listing as study continues.

THE MAIN IDEA

Ask what question is raised by this statement of the main idea, if necessary leading students to see that as they read, they should look for information about the four tools or strategies that make up the marketing mix.

STUDY ORGANIZER

Make your own study organizer on the board, or download the one provided at marketingessentials.glencoe.com. Encourage students to fill out the ovals as they read.

 WHILE YOU READ Point out that in thinking about these examples, students will begin to think as marketers rather than as consumers.

Marketers know that their product or service cannot appeal to everyone. To do their job, they look for people who might have an interest in or a need for their product. They also look at people who have the ability to pay for their product. These people often share other similar needs and wants. All people who share similar needs and wants and who have the ability to purchase your products are called a **market**.

You could be part of the market for video games, but not be part of the market for an expensive car. Even though you may want an expensive car, you may not have the means to buy one. If you liked video games and had the resources to buy or rent them, you would be part of the video game market.

Consumer Versus Industrial Markets

There are different types of markets. A market can be described as a consumer market or an industrial market.

The **consumer market** consists of consumers who purchase goods and services for personal use. Consumers' needs and wants generally fall into a few categories that address their lifestyles. For the most part, consumers are interested in products that will save them money, make their life easier, improve their appearance, create status in the community, or provide satisfaction related to some other personal motivation.

The **industrial market** or business-to-business (B-to-B) market includes all businesses that buy products for use in their operations. The goals and objectives of business firms are somewhat different from those in the consumer market. Most relate to improving profits. Companies want to improve productivity, increase sales, decrease expenses, or in some other way make their work more efficient.

Companies that produce products for sale in the consumer market consider the reseller of their products to be part of the industrial

Our new packaging is designed to help your business grow.

Freshen up your meat case with fresh PERDUE® Breaded Chicken Breast items. Growing your business has never been easier. Call today to find out more about the brand that always brings you more. 1-800-992-7043. Email us at tradeinfo@perdue.com.

There's always more in store with PERDUE

Perdue Farms Incorporated · Salisbury, MD 21802 USA · www.perdue.com®

• ADVERTISING in the INDUSTRIAL MARKET
This ad, published in *Supermarket News*, highlights advantages to businesses who sell chicken to customers.

How do the objectives for purchases in the industrial market differ from those in the consumer market?

TEACH

Discussion Starter

MARKET SHARE
Ask students to consider a scenario, where two companies carry the bulk of market share for a product. Even though there may be other products on the market, marketing for these products is often framed in terms of direct competition. Have students consider the advantages and disadvantages of having only one major competitor.

TEACHING POINTS
Demonstrate Bring to class ads or slogans that show direct competition.

Explain Ask students to name their favorite brand of a common product, such as jeans or soap. Explain that these kinds of preferences are the basis of determining market share.

Critical Thinking
Ask students how the needs of the consumer market might differ from the needs of other markets such as business-to-business markets.

AD GUIDE ## ADVERTISING in the INDUSTRIAL MARKET

Discussion Lead a discussion asking students to suggest three words to describe this ad, stressing that students consider the audience for the ad. Ask students to brainstorm ways in which this ad might change if directed to consumers.

Caption Answer Objectives for purchases in the consumer market are personal and include things such as saving money, making life easier, improving one's appearance, or creating status in the community. Objectives in the industrial market relate to improving the bottom line—profit, which may include: grow business, improve productivity, increase sales, decrease expenses, or in some other way help to improve the company's operations.

TEACH CONTINUED

Individualized Math Skills

L1 Have students calculate the total percentages in **Figure 1.1**.
Total: 100

L2 Have students use **Figure 1.1** to determine the difference between the largest and smallest market share.
19.1 percent; 26.3 percent for Others − 7.2 percent for Fuji Film = 19.1 percent

L3 Have students use **Figure 1.1** to estimate how much money Sony earned from 21.1 percent of the market share.
$44 billion; if 10 percent of $212 billion is about $22 billion, then 20 percent is around $44 billion.

Concept Development

TARGET MARKET AND MARKET SEGMENTATION

To reinforce the concept of target market, have students look at their class as a whole. Divide the class into small groups and have them imagine that a company that sells class rings has targeted their class. What are some facts the company can use in their marketing effort? Allow time for groups to share ideas.
Possibilities include age, gender, interests, and region.

TEACHING POINTS

Demonstrate Bring to class ads or slogans that directly address their target market by name (such as ads directed toward children).

Critical Thinking

Ask students why different marketing plans might reuse the same elements for different audiences.

Figure 1.1 Market Share

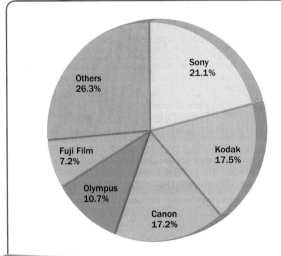

• **Who Leads in the Camera Market?** A company's percentage of total sales in a given market is its market share.

How do you think businesses use the concept of market share in their marketing programs?

Sony 21.1%
Others 26.3%
Fuji Film 7.2%
Olympus 10.7%
Kodak 17.5%
Canon 17.2%

@ Online Action! Go to *marketingessentials.glencoe.com/1/figure/1* to find a project on market share.

---

market. Therefore, they require two distinct marketing plans to reach each market.

Market Share

A market is further described by the total sales in a product category. Examples of categories are video games, fax machines, cameras, ice cream, or soft drinks. For example, everyone who bought digital still cameras in February 2004 from photo specialty, electronic/appliance stores, computer/office superstores, mass merchandisers, the Internet, and through mail order were part of the $211,464,600 digital still camera market.

A company's **market share** is its percentage of the total sales volume generated by all companies that compete in a given market. Knowing one's market share helps marketers analyze their competition and their status in a given market. (See Figure 1.1.) Market shares change all the time as new competitors enter

the market and as the size of the market increases or decreases in volume.

Target Market and Market Segmentation

Businesses know they cannot convince everybody to buy their product or service They look for ways to offer their product or service to the people who are most likely to be interested. This involves segmenting, or breaking down the market into smaller groups that have similar needs. Market segmentation is the process of classifying customers by needs and wants.

You already know that a market can be segmented into a consumer and an industrial market. Within those markets, further segmentation is possible. You will learn about market segmentation in Chapter 2. The goal of market segmentation is to identify the group of people most likely to become customers. The group that is identified for a specific

14 UNIT 1 - THE WORLD OF MARKETING

marketingessentials.glencoe.com

Figure 1.1 Market Share

Discussion On this particular graph, the divisions mark out the percentage of the market held by various companies. Lead a discussion asking students why consumers might be interested in market share.

Caption Answer Answers will vary; students may suggest that successful businesses make it a goal to try to maintain or grow their market share.

@ Online Action! For instructions, ideas, and answer guide, go to the Teacher Center at **marketingessentials.glencoe.com**

• **MARKET SEGMENTATION** A professional photographer shops for a top-performance camera to use as a work tool while an amateur would look for a basic, easy-to-use model.

How would marketing efforts differ for these two types of cameras and customers?

marketing program is the **target market**. Target markets are very important because all marketing strategies are directed to them. When a business does not identify a target market, its marketing plan has no focus. Identifying the target market correctly is a key to success.

Consumers Versus Customers

A product may have more than one target market. For example, manufacturers of children's cereal know that they need to target children and parents differently. They have two target markets: one is the children (consumers) who will be asking for the cereal and eating it. The other is the parents (customers) who need to approve of it and will be buying it. To reach the children, marketers might advertise on Saturday morning television programs specifically designed for children. The advertising message might be how much fun it is to eat this cereal. To reach parents, print advertising in magazines such as *Family Circle* or *Parenting* might be used, and the ad message might stress health benefits.

To develop a clear picture of their target market, businesses create a **customer profile**. A customer profile lists information about the target market, such as age, income level, ethnic background, occupation, attitudes, lifestyle, and geographic residence. Chapter 2 focuses on this aspect of marketing. Marketers spend a lot of money and time on research to collect data so that they understand the characteristics of their target market's customer profile. This information helps them make intelligent marketing decisions.

An easy and fun way to understand customer profiles is to look at magazines. If you thumb through a magazine's articles and advertisements, you will know who reads the publication. According to *Seventeen* magazine's

Chapter 1 - Marketing Is All Around Us **15**

Enrichment

CREATING CUSTOMER PROFILES

Ask students to work in groups to give an example of or create a product that is marketed to a distinct group of people. Have students use visual displays to create a short description of their product and their customer profile(s).

 Critical Thinking

Ask students: What is your customer profile for a grocery retailer? Have students create their own customer profiles and share them in class.

 Virtual Business

Introduce students to the concept of marketing segmentation using Knowledge Matters' Virtual Business Retailing visual simulation, *Targeted Marketing*. In this simulation, students learn the concept of targeted marketing and how particular media lend themselves to it. Students discover how well-targeted marketing campaigns produce the same results as broader campaigns for less cost.

PHOTO GUIDE | **MARKET SEGMENTATION**

Discussion Lead a discussion about products that are marketed to different groups of consumers. Encourage students to give examples.

Caption Answer Answers will vary; marketing efforts will probably include more technical and specialized ads for the professional photographer and promote ease-of-use and accessibility in ads for the amateur photographer.

Follow Up Encourage students to research and find ads that are geared to professionals in a particular field. Have students share their findings in class.

TEACH CONTINUED

Concept Development

MARKETING MIX
Read the text covering the four Ps, stopping as needed to stress key points. As each P is defined in the text, record the term and definition on the chalkboard. Students should write terms and definitions in their notebooks.

TEACHING POINTS
Clarify To reteach the concept of the marketing mix, select a product and review its characteristics, such as name, packaging, and ingredients. Each time you cover an element of the marketing mix, write it on the board.

Build Vocabulary

Give students time to commit all the marketing-related terms from this chapter to memory. Consider playing a simple matching game, with students matching term with definition. Remind students that they will be using these terms again and again for the remainder of this course.

A MATTER OF ETHICS

Targeting Children

You may have observed young children mesmerized by television commercials or seen children crying when a parent refuses to buy a product that a child had seen advertised on television.

Messages to Children
Businesses that target young children generally create images that their products are fun and enjoyable.

Messages to Parents
Some of these same companies target parents and send a different message about their products—stressing qualities that parents deem important, such as education, safety, or health.

THINKING ETHICALLY
Do you think targeting children with food products and toys is ethical? Should advertising to children should be restricted? Why or why not?

@ Online Action!
Go to *marketingessentials.glencoe .com/1/ethics* to find a project on ethical marketing techniques.

Web site, the magazine targets teen girls and young women who are interested in beauty, fashion, and entertainment. It is larger than any competitor in the 12- to 17-year-old market and 97.9 percent of its readers have accessed the Internet regularly.

Marketing Mix
The **marketing mix** includes four basic marketing strategies called the four Ps: **p**roduct, **p**lace, **p**rice, and **p**romotion. These are

---

tools marketing professionals or businesses use and control in order to influence potential customers. Marketers control decisions about each of the four Ps and base their decisions on the people they want to win over and make into customers. Because of the importance of customers, some would add a fifth P to the list: people. Marketers must first clearly define each target market before they can develop marketing strategies.

The four elements of the marketing mix are interconnected. Actions in one area affect decisions in another. Each strategy involves making decisions about the best way to reach, satisfy, and keep customers and the best way to achieve the company's goals.

Let's look at what each marketing mix component involves. Follow Figure 1.2 to see each of the four Ps illustrated and explained for Tropicana's Light 'n Healthy® brand orange juice.

Product
Product decisions begin with choosing what products to make and sell. Much research goes into product design. A product's features, brand name, packaging, service, and warranty are all part of the development. Companies also need to decide what to do with products they currently sell. In some cases, those products require updating or improvements to be competitive. By developing new uses and identifying new target markets, a company can extend the life of a product. In the orange juice example illustrated in Figure 1.2, Tropicana chose health conscious men and women as the target market for a new juice. It produced a lower-calorie, lower-carbohydrate orange juice and it selected a name—Light 'n Healthy—that would appeal to its target market.

Place
The means of getting the product into the consumer's hands is the place factor of the marketing mix. Knowing where one's customers shop helps marketers make the

 marketingessentials.glencoe.com

A MATTER OF ETHICS Targeting Children

Discussion Ask students to share their responses to this feature. Lead a discussion on the issues and implications of marketing to children.

THINKING ETHICALLY **Answer:** Answers will vary; encourage students to back up their responses with examples of advertising that they believe to be ethical and fair, and or examples of what they believe to be unethical, exploitive, or unfair.

@ Online Action! For instruction, ideas, and answer guide, go to the Teacher Center at **marketingessentials.glencoe.com**

Follow Up Have students work in pairs to research and bring to class examples of advertising aimed at children and then evaluate their findings for the class.

Figure 1.2 — Marketing Mix for a New Juice

• **Light 'n Healthy's Four Ps** Tropicana's marketing department develops strategies for each brand of orange juice in its product line. The four Ps of the marketing mix focus on the customer profile for a specific target market. The Light 'n Healthy brand targets men and women who are health conscious and want to stay physically fit.

Would you have made different choices about the four Ps to introduce this product? If so, what would you have done differently?

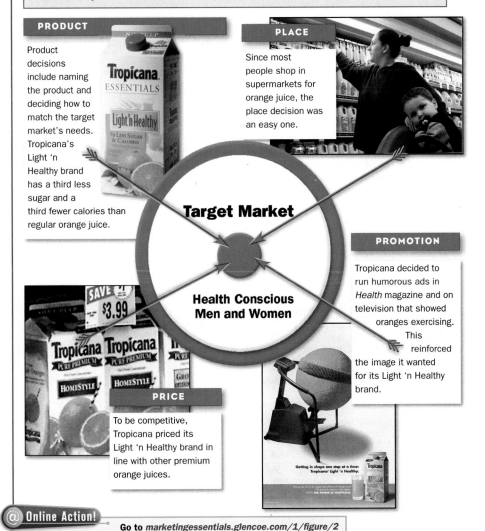

PRODUCT

Product decisions include naming the product and deciding how to match the target market's needs. Tropicana's Light 'n Healthy brand has a third less sugar and a third fewer calories than regular orange juice.

PLACE

Since most people shop in supermarkets for orange juice, the place decision was an easy one.

Target Market

Health Conscious Men and Women

PROMOTION

Tropicana decided to run humorous ads in *Health* magazine and on television that showed oranges exercising. This reinforced the image it wanted for its Light 'n Healthy brand.

PRICE

To be competitive, Tropicana priced its Light 'n Healthy brand in line with other premium orange juices.

 Online Action! Go to *marketingessentials.glencoe.com/1/figure/2* to find a project on the marketing mix.

 marketingessentials.glencoe.com

Chapter 1 - Marketing Is All Around Us 17

TEACH CONTINUED

Concept Development

PRODUCT DECISIONS

To help students internalize this important information, read each of the explanations for product, place, promotion, and price at random, leaving out any direct references to the products of the marketing mix and have students tell which of the four Ps is being discussed.

TEACHING POINTS

Clarify Tell students that product image and packaging are two product decisions that promote product sales. Bring in ads that show examples of these two product decisions to share with the class.

Figure 1.2 — Marketing Mix for a New Juice

Discussion Use information on the graphic featuring Tropicana brands to lead a discussion of the four Ps. Have students give examples of other possible product decisions.

Caption Answer Answers will vary; student responses should demonstrate an understanding of each of the four Ps of the marketing mix: product, place, promotion, and price.

Online Action! For instructions, ideas, and answer guide, go to the Teacher Center at **marketingessentials.glencoe.com**

ASSESS

Review Guide

CONCEPTS

Ask students to complete the following statement:

In order for a product to succeed, the four Ps must be directed to _____ .

the target market

KEY TERMS

Have students work in small groups to review key terms, their spellings, and their definitions.

ONLINE SELF-ASSESSMENT

Have students go to marketingessentials.glencoe.com for the Section 1.3 practice test.

Individualized Review

L1 Assign and review Chapter 1 activities in the Student Activity Workbook.

L2 Assign and review Chapter 1 activities in the Marketing Math Workbook.

L3 Assign and review Chapter 1 activities in the *BusinessWeek* Reader and Case Studies.

Marketing Practice

Invite interested students to research and learn about several wireless companies and what products and services they have to offer. Ask: Do any offer good deals but contain hidden costs (for example, a charge for the musical selections that signal an incoming call)? Encourage researchers to share their findings with the class.

Case Study

Pay as You Go Wireless Phones

The Roxy i90c phone from Boost is created for active young women. The Roxy brand represents freedom, fun, and individual expression, all of which are reflected in the design and custom features of the Roxy phone.

The Right Ring Tones

The Roxy wireless phone features ring tones such as *Funky Town, Girls Just Wanna Have Fun,* and *California Dreamin'.* The phone is preloaded with Java™ games, including Tetris® and Snood® from THQ and Blazing Boards™ by Cybiko. As with all Boost Mobile's models, the Roxy wireless phone comes with Boost 2WAY™, the long-range walkie-talkie feature.

Price and Place

Advertisements for the Roxy phone focus on girls involved in sports. The suggested retail price is $199, which includes $25 in wireless service credits that are loaded on activation. The limited edition Roxy phone is available at select Quiksilver Boardrider Club stores, select Surf & Specialty stores that carry the Quiksilver and Roxy brands, as well as Best Buy, Good Guys, Wherehouse Music, and Nextel Retail Stores. Boost Mobile customers pay for the minutes only as they need them through the purchase of Re-Boost™ cards, which are available in $20, $30, and $50 denominations and may be purchased as needed at all authorized Boost Mobile retailers (such as Nextel and Target) and 7-Eleven stores.

THINK STRATEGICALLY

Identify the target market and provide a customer profile for the Roxy brand wireless phone. Explain Boost Mobile's marketing mix decision (four Ps) for the Roxy phone and its Mobile service.

@ Online Action! Go to *marketingessentials.glencoe.com/1/case* to find a project on customer profiles.

---

place decision. Place strategies determine how and where a product will be distributed. For global companies, it may mean making decisions about which products will be sold in which countries and which retail outlets or other means of selling the product will best reach the customer. Can the product be sold directly to the consumer, or are intermediaries necessary? Other place decisions include deciding which transportation methods and what stock levels are most effective.

In the Tropicana orange juice example, the place decision was to sell 64-fluid-ounce containers of the Light 'n Healthy brand in food stores that have refrigerated cases. You see these products primarily in supermarkets, convenience stores, and mass merchandise retailers with food departments, such as Smart & Final, Wal-Mart, or Costco.

 marketingessentials.glencoe.com

Case Study   Pay as You Go Wireless Phones

Discussion Make four columns on a board and head each one with one of the four Ps. Then have students offer details from the Case Study. Lead students in discussing and deciding in which column each detail belongs.

THINK STRATEGICALLY

Answer: The target market is young, active, independent women who are comfortable with technology. Boost Mobile loaded the product with features that appeal to its target market and made it available in places its target market frequents. It has priced the phone competitively and advertised to its target market using sports.

@ Online Action! For instructions, ideas, and answer guide, go to the Teacher Center at marketingessentials.glencoe.com

Price

Price is what is exchanged for the product. Price strategies should reflect what customers are willing and able to pay. To that end, marketers must consider the price they will charge their industrial customers, including resellers. Pricing decisions also take into account prices the competition charges for comparable products.

Pricing Strategies

Price strategies therefore include arriving at the list price or manufacturer's suggested retail price, as well as discounts, allowances, credit terms, and payment period for industrial customers.

On occasion, a company may use special promotional pricing that would adjust the suggested retail price. A manufacturer may decide to use a promotional price for a fixed period of time, for example. This technique is frequently used to launch new products.

Promotion

Promotion refers to decisions about advertising, personal selling, sales promotion, and publicity.

Promotional Strategies

Promotional strategies deal with how potential customers will be told about a company's products, including the message, the media selected, special offers, and the timing of the promotional campaigns. Figure 1.2 highlights the Tropicana Light 'n Healthy ad campaign. In that campaign, images were carefully created to match a key feature of the product. Ads for orange juice with added calcium or vitamins might have different graphics and might run in different magazines.

1.3 AFTER YOU READ

Reviewing Key Terms and Concepts

1. What is the difference between consumer and industrial markets?
2. What is the relationship among market segmentation, target markets, and customer profiles?
3. Name the four Ps of the marketing mix and explain the importance of a target market for each of them.

Integrating Academic Skills

Math

4. If total sales in the ice cream category were $4.4 billion and Breyers's sales were $650,417,792, what would be its market share? Round your answer to the tenth decimal place.

Language Arts

5. Write a customer profile for a magazine of your choice. Support your description by describing sample articles and advertisements from the magazine.

 Online Action!

Check your answers at *marketingessentials.glencoe.com/1/read*

CLOSE

Have students go back to the definitions of marketing and marketing activities they wrote for the Quick Think at the beginning of this chapter. Ask them to change or add to their definition according to what they have learned. Have volunteers share their before-and-after responses with the class.

 Online Activity

The Marketing Mix on the Web

Ask students to find an example of a product or service that is marketed online. Ask students to write a one-page report explaining how each component of the marketing mix (product, price, place, and promotion) contributes to the marketing mix, and to explain who the target market is for the product.

AFTER YOU READ

Reviewing Key Terms and Concepts

1. Consumer markets purchase goods and services for personal use, while the industrial markets purchase products or services for use in their business operations.

2. Market segmentation refers to the breaking down of a market into smaller groups that have similar needs, and then pitching marketing efforts to this group. The group chosen is called the target market.

Online Action! Answers at **marketingessentials.glencoe.com/1/read**

Customer profile refers to specific information, such as age, income, etc., about the target market.

3. The four Ps (product, place, price, and promotion) are the means through which sellers reach their target market. The product, price, and promotion have to appeal to the target market, and the place has to be where the target market will buy.

Integrating Academic Skills

4. 14.78 percent

5. Customer profiles will vary; accept responses that show an understanding of how to determine a customer profile, which is specific information about the target market.

19

Lifelong Learning

CAREER INFORMATION

Have students go to marketingessentials.glencoe.com and find the Chapter 1 Careers page and click on the link for the American Marketing Association's Career Strategies and Tips. Ask students to select one article, read it, and write a three-paragraph summary.

MARKETING AND PEOPLE SKILLS

People skills are required for very technical jobs, but especially in marketing, where communication skills enable you to determine and reach your target market in order to successfully market and sell your product, service or idea. These skills can be learned and improved through work experience, public speaking, and communication classes.

Primary Source

Ask students to go to marketingessentials.glencoe.com and find Chapter 1 resources. Ask them to click on the link for the American Marketing Association's marketing dictionary and read definitions of any marketing career-related terms they find.

THINKING CRITICALLY

MBA-level marketing courses might be helpful for many careers because most careers involve some of the core skills essential to marketing, such as communication skills.

@ Online Action!

For instructions, ideas, and answer guide, go to the Teacher Center at marketingessentials.glencoe.com

CAREERS IN MARKETING

CHARLES SPIVEY
ARTIST DEVELOPMENT

? What do you do at work?
Artist development is all about helping my client take the next step, depending on where he or she is in his or her career. Some already have a couple albums under their belt, while others are looking to record a first demo. Fundamentally, I am a people broker. If a client needs a new Web site, I connect her to the best Web people I know. If a singer needs a new headshot, I hand him over to my best photographer. If a band needs 200 people at a show, I talk to every newspaper and radio person I know and get them to push the band.

? What skills are most important to you?
People skills, without a doubt, are the most important aspects of my job. I know that PR means public relations but I think it means people relations. Know your clients, know your friends, and know your business partners. They're all people and want to be treated like people, not profit centers. My undergraduate education had nothing to do with music, PR, or management, but my MBA course load of marketing classes has certainly paid big dividends. The best lessons I've learned have come from other people in the business—people I admire and look up to.

? What is your key to success?
It's important to set high goals and be tenacious, but also have the ability to accept failure and see it as an opportunity to grow. Sure I want to succeed every time I pick up the phone to market my clients, but I have to be willing to accept the rejection that often comes in the music business; I just dust myself off and come back for more.

Aptitudes, Abilities, and Skills

Strong interpersonal skills, resourcefulness, creativity, contact management, and organization

Education and Training

MBA degrees provide core-level skills that are valuable in a variety of careers.

Career Path

Entry-level opportunities abound for MBA graduates in virtually every field you can imagine.

THINKING CRITICALLY

Why might MBA-level marketing courses be helpful, even in a career that was not specifically the focus of those courses?

 @ Online Action!

Go to *marketingessentials.glencoe.com/1/careers* to find a career-related activity.

Test-Taking Strategies

Give the students opportunity to ask for clarification of any concepts they missed in their online self-assessments for each section. List their questions on the board, and have volunteers define and lead the class in discussing and determining answers to each one.

FOCUS on KEY POINTS

SECTION 1.1

● Marketing is defined as the process of planning and executing the conception, pricing, promotion, and distribution of ideas, goods, and services to create exchanges that satisfy individual and organizational objectives.

● There are four foundations and seven functions of marketing. The marketing concept is a focus on customers' needs and wants while generating a profit.

SECTION 1.2

● Three benefits of marketing are new and improved products, lower prices, and added value (utility). Five economic utilities are form, place, time, possession, and information.

SECTION 1.3

● A market is defined as all people who share similar needs and wants and who have the ability to purchase given products.

● Market share is a firm's percentage of total sales of all competitors in a given market.

● The four Ps of the marketing mix are product, place, price, and promotion. Marketing decisions and strategies for the four Ps are based on the target market.

REVIEW VOCABULARY

Define each of the following terms in writing.

1. marketing (p. 5)
2. goods and services (p. 5)
3. marketing concept (p. 7)
4. utility (p. 9)
5. market (p. 13)

6. consumer and industrial markets (p. 13)
7. market share (p. 14)
8. target market (p. 15)
9. customer profile (p. 15)
10. marketing mix (p. 16)

REVIEW FACTS and IDEAS

11. Define marketing. (1.1)
12. Identify and explain the four foundations of marketing. (1.1)
13. List the seven functions of marketing. (1.1)
14. Explain the marketing concept. (1.1)
15. What is meant by *utility* and what are the five economic utilities? (1.2)

16. What is a market and in what ways can a market be identified? (1.3)
17. What is market share? (1.3)
18. Define a target market. (1.3)
19. What are the four components of the marketing mix? (1.3)

Chapter 1 - Marketing Is All Around Us 21

REVIEW FACTS and IDEAS

11. the process of planning, pricing, promoting, selling, and distributing ideas, goods, or services to create exchanges that satisfy customers

12. 1.) business, management, entrepreneurship: understanding the basics of starting and running a business, basics that affect business decisions 2.) communication and interpersonal skills: understanding the concepts, strategies, and systems needed for effective business interactions 3.) economics: understanding the basic principles and concepts of marketing 4.) professional development: understanding concepts and strategies for career exploration, development, and growth

13. distribution, financing, marketing information management, pricing, product/service management, promotion, selling

14. the idea that a business should strive to satisfy customers' needs and wants while making a profit

15. Added value of a product or service that makes it capable of satisfying a customer's wants and needs. Economic utilities include form, place, time, possession, and information.

16. All the people who share similar needs and wants and have the ability to purchase products to satisfy these. Markets are either consumer markets, made up of those who purchase goods and services for personal use, or industrial, which includes all business-to-business purchasing.

17. a company's percentage of the total sales volume generated by all companies that compete in a given market

18. Target markets are the group of people most likely to buy a particular product. All marketing efforts are directed toward identifying and then marketing to this group.

19. product, place, price, and promotion

FOCUS on KEY POINTS

Call students' attention to each of the three sections in turn. Have a volunteer read the key points of a section aloud. Explore any additional questions students have about each point. For example, in Section 1.1 you might, have a student find those parts of the text that name and explain the four foundations of marketing and the seven functions of marketing. Read these aloud to the class.

REVIEW VOCABULARY

See glossary for definitions of **1–10**. A sample answer might read:

1. *Marketing* is the process of planning, pricing, promoting selling, and distributing ideas, goods, or series to create exchanges that satisfy customers.

BUILD SKILLS

20. Workplace Skills

Answers should indicate that the customer is correct. The best strategy is probably to acknowledge that the customer is right, and then discuss the immediate needs the customer might have for the technology. The salesperson should find out as much as possible about the customer's needs and should the customer decide not to buy, invite the customer to visit again.

21. Technology Applications

Slide presentations should indicate students' understanding of the broad definition of marketing as well as familiarity and comfort with using all the marketing vocabulary introduced in this chapter.

22. Math Practice

56.9 percent. Encourage students to use a calculator to perform calculations with multiple-digit numbers.

DEVELOP CRITICAL THINKING

23. The Cost of Marketing

Examples will vary. Accept answers that show student research and understanding of the different types of marketing within the marketing concept.

24. Explain the Marketing Concept

Essays will vary; student responses should show an understanding of the marketing concept, or the idea that a business should strive to satisfy customers' needs and wants while making a profit.

BUILD SKILLS

20. Workplace Skills

The Right Choice Assume you are a salesperson in a computer store. A customer is hesitant about buying a mid-priced laptop computer you are showing. The customer's objection is that it will sell for much less in a year. Do you think the customer is correct? What would you say?

21. Technology Applications

Understanding Market Functions With two or three classmates, use a word processing program to write a short report about a new fruit beverage that you believe will be popular with teenagers. Assume your team develops this new product and wants to start selling it. Consider all seven marketing functions (distribution, financing, information management, pricing, product/service management, promotion, and selling) in your report and explain for each function how it applies to the marketing of your new product.

22. Math Practice

Figure the Market Share Calculate Nikon's market share if total sales in the digital camera market are $211,464,600 and Nikon's sales are $120,305,671? Round your answer to the tenth decimal place.

DEVELOP CRITICAL THINKING

23. The Cost of Marketing

It is often said that marketing costs represent about 50 percent of the selling price of an item. Select a product that you have recently purchased or a product that interests you and research (on the Internet, in magazines and newspapers, etc.) what type of marketing has been done for this product. List all the examples you can find. Do you think all the items on the list were good marketing ideas? Why or why not?

24. Explain the Marketing Concept

Write a 200-word essay to convince a friend that maketing is more than just merchandising—displaying products in stores. Include how important consumers are to marketers by explaining the marketing concept.

Formative Assessment

Formative assessment is an essential component of classroom work. This type of assessment provides information that is then used as feedback to modify teaching and meet student needs.

L1 Have the students define marketing.

L2 Have students recall the components of the marketing mix.

L3 Have students create a fictional product, target market, and customer profile.

Reteach If the results of this formative assessment seem low, consider the following activity:

Choose an example of a good or service of interest to learners and walk students through the marketing of that item, using the definitions of marketing terms throughout the three sections as a roadmap.

APPLY CONCEPTS

25. Understand Target Markets and the Marketing Mix

Select an existing product that interests you. Look at how it is advertised in print or on television and the Internet. Research your product's price and where it is sold. Identify its target market and the four Ps of its marketing mix. Then change the target market for the product.

Activity Show how the four Ps of the marketing mix must be revised to focus on your newly defined target market. Prepare a written report and an oral presentation using presentation software.

26. Research Customer Relationship Management

Use magazine articles, Internet sources, and your own observations to research efforts made by companies to develop close relationships with customers. Analyze the effectiveness of customer relationship management (CRM). What pitfalls have been experienced by companies and what successes have been reported?

Activity Prepare a three-page written report, complete with citations from appropriate sources, to document the research you have done on the topic of CRM.

NET SAVVY

27. Check an Online Dictionary

Visit the American Marketing Association's (AMA) Web site and use its online dictionary to review its definition of marketing, as well as other key marketing terms covered in this chapter.

marketingessentials.glencoe.com

Role Play: Benefits of Marketing

Situation You are to assume the role of a marketing student at your local high school. Your marketing teacher (judge) has asked you to put together a presentation about the importance of marketing in our society. This presentation will be made to a group of incoming freshmen that have little knowledge of marketing or of its importance.

Activity You are to prepare an outline of your presentation on the importance of marketing and present it to your marketing teacher (judge) for approval.

Evaluation You will be evaluated on how well you meet the following performance indicators:

- Explain marketing and its importance in a global economy
- Describe marketing functions and related activities
- Determine forms of economic utility created by marketing activities
- Explain types of business activities
- Prepare simple written reports

 Online Action!

For more information and DECA Prep practice, go to *marketingessentials.glencoe.com/1/DECA*

APPLY CONCEPTS

25. Understand Target Markets and the Marketing Mix

Reports and presentations should demonstrate an understanding of the four Ps (product, place, price, and promotion) and how one or more of the Ps must be adjusted to reach a different target market.

26. Research Customer Relationship Management

Reports should demonstrate an understanding of customer relationship management (CRM), which is using technology, customer service, and communication to improve relationships with customers. Successes might include brand loyalty, while a pitfall might be cost.

NET SAVVY

27. Check an Online Dictionary

Work with the class to access and explore this valuable resource.

MINI-QUIZ

Read these sentences aloud and ask students whether they are true or false. Students can respond to quiz items in writing or orally.

1. The words *marketing* and *advertising* have very similar definitions. (false)

2. Place utility refers to having a product in a place where it is easy for customers to buy it. (true)

3. A market share refers to what a company's stock is worth. (false)

4. In a market economy such as ours, prices must be competitive but not so low that the company loses money. (true)

For an expanded chapter quiz, go to Chapter 1 in the TeacherWorks CD-ROM and to Chapter 1 in the **Exam***View*® Pro Test Generator CD-ROM.

The students should be evaluated on the performance indicators noted in the role play. For another DECA role play, go to the Competitive Events Workbook or the Student Activity Workbook, or go to **marketingessentials.glencoe.com/1/DECA**

 Online Action! For instructions, ideas, and answer guide, go to the Teacher Center at **marketingessentials.glencoe.com**

DECA Advisors Corner

DECA's Competitive Events Program is directly tied to and enhances your classroom curriculum. There are a number of individual and team competitive events covering all areas of marketing. Participation in DECA's Competitive Events Program offers students opportunities for achievement, confidence building, success, recognition, scholarships, and other awards.

Chapter Overview

Chapter 2 focuses on SWOT analysis and its place in the marketing plan. The text then discusses the overall marketing plan and then market segmentation, the key to any successful marketing effort.

BUILD BACKGROUND

Ask students to obtain driving directions between their school and some other place, such as a local attraction or another school. Ask them to mark the route on a roadmap. Ask the class the advantages of this kind of advance planning, such as that it reduces the chances of getting lost or being late. Draw a comparison between the driving directions or roadmap and the big idea of this chapter, the importance of a marketing plan.

Why It's Important

All successful marketing is based on a good marketing plan. The segmentation and targeting that result from researching the market and creating a marketing plan are integral to success in marketing any idea, service, or product.

Prepare to Read

Model for students how to skim the chapter, reading aloud headings and calling attention to any visuals and captions. Talk about any questions raised by this preview as these occur.

The Marketing Plan

Chapter Objectives

After reading this chapter, you should be able to:

- Conduct a SWOT analysis
- List the three key areas of an internal company analysis
- Identify the factors in an environmental scan
- Explain the basic elements of a marketing plan
- Explain the concept of market segmentation
- Analyze a target market
- Differentiate between mass marketing and market segmentation

GUIDE TO THE PHOTO

Market Talk Marketers understand that for a product or service to be successful, they first have to find out who needs it or has an interest in it. Marketers must determine their potential customers among diverse groups of people.

Quick Think There are 24.3 million teenagers in the U.S. They spend $120 billion each year. Many have regular jobs and weekly income. List three ways you would research this market.

24 UNIT 1 - THE WORLD OF MARKETING

GUIDE TO THE PHOTO

Market Talk Point out that the group pictured in the photograph could be considered a target market for a certain product or idea. Ask students how this market might be further broken down into even smaller components.

Quick Think Answers will vary; students may suggest that they can research this market by looking at media directed to or about the target market, administering and analyzing surveys, and observing and interviewing individuals in the target market.

Follow Up Have students brainstorm and suggest ideas, goods, and services that might appeal to the target market displayed in the photograph.

Performance indicators represent key skills and knowledge. Relating them to the concepts explained in this chapter is your key to success in DECA events. Keep this in mind as you read this chapter and write some notes each time you encounter material that helps you master a key concept.

These acronyms represent DECA events that involve knowledge of concepts in this chapter.

AAAL	FSRM*	TSE	FMAL
FMML	VPM	TMDM	RMAL
RMML	SMDM	BSM	FMDM
HMDM*	ADC	QSRM*	
AAML	MMS	EMDM	

In all these DECA events you should be able to follow these performance indicators:

- Explain the nature of marketing plans
- Explain the role of situational analysis in the marketing-planning process
- Conduct a SWOT analysis for use in the marketing-planning process
- Conduct an environmental scan to obtain marketing information
- Forecast sales
- Develop a marketing plan
- Describe measures used to control marketing planning
- Evaluate a marketing plan
- Conduct marketing audits

All the events with an asterisk (*) also include this performance indicator:

- Forecast servings of each food item

DECA PREP

Check your understanding of DECA performance indicators with the DECA activity in this chapter's review. For more information and DECA Prep practice, go to *marketingessentials .glencoe.com/2/DECA*

DECA events that require marketing plan knowledge and skills are described here. Discuss the performance indicators to make sure students understand how to demonstrate their understanding.

The event acronyms stand for:

AAAL: Apparel and Accessories Marketing Series, AL

AAML: Apparel and Accessories Marketing Series, ML

ADC: Advertising Campaign Event

BSM: Business Services Marketing Series

EMDM: E-Commerce Management Team Decision Making Event

FMAL: Food Marketing Series, AL

FMDM: Financial Analysis Management Team Decision Making Event

FMML: Food Marketing Series, ML

FSRM: Full Service Restaurant Management Series

HMDM: Hospitality Services Management Team Decision Making Event

MMS: Marketing Management Series

QSRM: Quick Serve Restaurant Management Series

RMAL: Retail Merchandising Series, AL

RMML: Retail Merchandising Series, ML

SMDM: Sports and Entertainment Marketing Management Team Decision Making Event

TMDM: Travel and Tourism Marketing Management Team Decision Making Event

TSE: Technical Sales Event

VPM: Vehicles and Petroleum Marketing Series

DECA PREP

Find timed DECA Prep activities correlated to the Competitive Events Workbook for students and DECA tips for teachers at **marketingessentials.glencoe.com /2/DECA**

CHAPTER 2 Classroom Resources

For the Teacher

- TeacherWorks
- marketingessentials.glencoe.com
- Interactive Chalkboard
- **Exam***View*® Pro Test Generator
- Fast File Unit 1

For the Student

- *Marketing Essentials* Online Edition
- Student Activity Workbook
- Marketing Math Workbook
- Marketing Research Project Workbook
- School-to-Work Activity Workbook
- Competitive Events Workbook
- *BusinessWeek* Reader and Case Studies
- marketingessentials.glencoe.com

FOCUS

Introducing the Section

COLLABORATIVE ACTIVITY

Have students work in small groups to brainstorm and list companies that they consider successful. Have groups share lists with the rest of the class. Ask: Have any companies been listed more than once? Do any dominate? Why did students make the choices they did? Point out that now the students are learning to think like marketers. Explain that there are formal means by which businesses can evaluate themselves and use the information as part of a marketing plan, a roadmap for all their business efforts.

Preteaching Key Terms

Assign two of the key terms to each of four students. Have each student find the two words in context and read definitions to classmates.

- SWOT analysis
- environmental scan
- marketing plan
- executive summary
- situation analysis
- marketing strategy
- sales forecasts
- performance standard

Critical Thinking

Ask students to come up with reasons why a threat could also be considered an opportunity. Encourage students to share their responses in class.

OBJECTIVES

- **Conduct a SWOT analysis**
- **List the three key areas of an internal company analysis**
- **Identify the factors in an environmental scan**
- **Explain the basic elements of a marketing plan**

KEY TERMS

- SWOT analysis
- environmental scan
- marketing plan
- executive summary
- situation analysis
- marketing strategy
- sales forecasts
- performance standard

WHILE YOU READ

Connect Conduct a SWOT analysis on yourself. What are your strengths and weaknesses? What outside opportunities and threats may impact your personal goals?

Marketing Planning

READ and STUDY

BEFORE YOU READ

Connect Suppose you are organizing a magazine sale for a school fund-raiser. Your goal is to raise $500 in one month. How would you organize the task and plan to meet your goal?

THE MAIN IDEA

A company starts its marketing planning with a look at itself and at the world around it. Marketers use this information to create a marketing plan to reach their goals.

STUDY ORGANIZER

Follow the outline below to identify the steps of a marketing plan.

Elements of a Marketing Plan
I. Executive summary
II. Situation analysis
III.
IV.
V.

SWOT Analysis

Good marketing relies on good plans. A company's planning efforts begin with a critical look at itself and its business environment, or the market in which it operates. This assessment lists and analyzes the company's strengths and its weaknesses. It also includes the opportunities and the threats that surround it. In other words, this analysis lists everything that can foster the business's success and what could make it fail. The acronym

READ and STUDY

BEFORE YOU READ

Work as a class to create a plan. Consider who will buy the subscriptions, the price of them, the percentage the school will receive from each sale, the number of orders necessary to reach the goal, and record-keeping.

THE MAIN IDEA

Point out that a company uses information about the world around it to make a marketing plan.

STUDY ORGANIZER

Make your own study organizer on the board, or download the one at marketingessentials.glencoe.com. As study continues, you and the class should work together to complete the outline.

 WHILE YOU READ Help students perform their SWOT analyses by modeling a sample analysis.

for strengths, weaknesses, opportunities, threats is also the name of this process: **SWOT analysis**.

This internal and external awareness will help a business deal with weaknesses and prepare it to handle threats such as competition or a changing marketplace. An accurate analysis also will help a company be more competitive because it provides guidance and direction. The company will develop strategies around the SWOT analysis.

Internal Strengths and Weaknesses

Strengths and weaknesses are internal factors that affect a business operation. The internal analysis centers around three Cs: company, customers, and competition. It is important to review these factors objectively and fairly. For this reason, some firms bring in outside consultants to conduct this phase of the analysis.

Company Analysis

Questions that are part of a company's internal analysis are about what a company does well and what areas are weak. This includes a review of the staff (both management and other personnel), the company's financial situation, its production capabilities, and each aspect of the marketing mix (product, promotion, place, and pricing). Here are a few sample questions that could be used as part of a company analysis:

Staff-Related Questions

- What is the company's mission statement? Does everyone know it? Is everyone on staff following it?
- How experienced are the company executives? What have they accomplished?
- Does the company have too much or not enough staff in each area to provide the quality of service it should? Should staff be re-assigned?
- What is the quality of the staff? Are there formal training and assessment programs?
- How effective is its sales force?

Financial Questions

- Has the company been profitable? In which areas and why?
- Are there enough financial resources to achieve the company's goals?
- What is the company's sales history? Are sales increasing or decreasing?

Production Capability Questions

- How are adjustments made in production due to an increase or decrease in sales orders?
- Has the research and development (R & D) department created successful new products?
- What percentage of sales come from products that are five years or older?
- What changes in technology are required to remain competitive?

Marketing Mix (Four Ps) Questions

Product
- What new products have been successful and why?
- Does the company own a patent on any of those products?
- Are any patents expiring in the future?

Price
- What are the present pricing strategies?
- Are the pricing strategies working?

Promotion
- How is the company positioned in the marketplace?
- What are the promotional strategies and have they been successful?
- What is the company's reputation and image among consumers?

Place
- Do products easily reach customers?
- Who helps the company with distribution?

The answers to these questions might reveal such strengths (or core competencies) as talented and well-trained employees, quality workmanship, and an excellent service record.

TEACH

Discussion Starter

INTERNAL STRENGTHS AND WEAKNESSES

Ask a class, ask students to discuss why an organization might hire an outside company to perform analysis to best determine strengths and weaknesses. Answers might include because a third party can be more objective.

TEACHING POINTS

Extend Point out that awareness of the strengths and weaknesses of competitors can help a company shape its marketing plan.

Build Vocabulary

Give students the following list of words: *external, weaknesses, opportunities, strengths, internal, threats*. Point out that the words on the list can be divided into pairs, each pair a word and its opposite in meaning. Have the students study the list, form these pairs, and be prepared to explain their choices.

strengths, weaknesses; internal, external; opportunities, threats

Extended Activity

SWOT Analysis

Ask students to begin to perform a basic company analysis for the company or organization of their choice. Encourage students to use the Internet, school or public libraries, periodicals, and other resources to identify a business and to try to answer some of the questions about staff, production, and the marketing mix that are posed in the text.

TEACH CONTINUED

Enrichment

CUSTOMER PROFILES

Ask students to select an ad. You can ask students to research ads on their own or provide some in class. Students can also use the ads provided in their textbook. Have students construct a customer profile for the ad they selected.

Build Vocabulary

Preview the following term by reading it in context. Ask students to provide a short definition or synonym.

- **segment** part or portion

Online Activity

Online Inventory

Internet companies sell millions of items per year and offer an amazing array of goods. Tell students that recent purchases from these companies by one individual include a used textbook on English grammar, a cashmere shawl, an omelet pan, and a small square of fabric advertised as a piece of a religious burial shroud. Few of these companies maintain huge warehouses full of inventory. Interested students might work in small groups to research how the company determines the needs of its customers, orders are placed, how they are filled, and how products get to the customer. Allow time for groups to share findings.

Case Study

Amazon.com

Amazon.com was one of the first online discount book retailers, and it enjoys a positive reputation and excellent name recognition. After being in business for seven years, it finally made a profit in 2001. Some of its strengths at that time included an increase in sales outside North America. In mid-2004, sales at sites outside the United States rose 50 percent to $595 million. They climbed 13 percent to $792 million in the United States. In 2004, Amazon agreed to buy Joyo.com, China's largest online retailer of books, music, and videos, to gain access to the world's second-biggest Internet market in terms of users. Amazon expects sales from foreign sites in China, Canada, France, Germany, and Great Britain to surpass U.S. sales in the future.

Amazon's Other Strengths

Other strengths were: expanded product selections (electronics, apparel, toys, and more) and successful pricing strategies, which included discounted prices and free shipping for orders over $25. However, this very same pricing strategy was also considered a weakness because it produced low gross profit margins. (Gross profit margin is the percentage of sales revenue left after paying for the cost of the goods or services sold.)

THINK STRATEGICALLY

What strategies do you think Amazon.com should adopt to capitalize on its new strengths?

@ Online Action! → Go to *marketingessentials.glencoe.com/2/case* to find a research project on companies' strengths and weaknesses.

Customer Analysis

Customers are a great source of information. Studying their buying habits may reveal patterns that offer insights into product offerings and pricing strategies. Here are a few questions that help in the analysis of customers.

- Who are the customers?
- How do groups of customers differ from one another?
- What, when, where, and how much do they buy?

- How do customers rate the company on quality, service, and value?
- How satisfied is each customer segment?
- What customer segments are not having their needs met?
- Is your customer base increasing or decreasing? Why?

Catalog companies use database technology to see buying patterns, which allow them to produce interest-specific catalogs. Companies with this technology and know-how

 marketingessentials.glencoe.com

Case Study   Amazon.com

Discussion Point out that many marketers make profits by selling relatively few higher-priced items at a large profit, but a profit also can be made by selling a greater quantity of items that are cheaper to produce and sell at a lower price. Ask the class to come up with other examples of products that decrease in price the less costly they become to produce.

THINK STRATEGICALLY   **Answer:** Students may suggest that Amazon should continue its efforts to keep prices low, to offer perks like free shipping, and to make their range of merchandise broader still while serving the larger world market that resulted from acquiring the huge Joyo.com and other foreign companies.

 Online Action!   For instructions, ideas, and answer guide, go to the Teacher Center at **marketingessentials.glencoe.com**

have a major advantage over their competitors because they can structure their product selection, pricing, and promotional messages to very specific targeted audiences.

To monitor customer satisfaction, many firms ask customers to complete a questionnaire or some form of survey after making a purchase. Data from this research helps companies pinpoint areas that need improvement.

Monitoring customer satisfaction reveals both strengths and weaknesses. Take, for example, the case of an eye doctor. Suppose that a strength is the amount of personal attention the doctor gives each patient. Patients report that the doctor spends a lot of time answering their questions. This strength also creates a weakness: complaints about the time patients spend in the eye doctor's waiting room. The solution seems simple: schedule fewer patients in a given time period so there is less overlap. This poses another problem that may generate complaints from patients wishing to make appointments. Under that new policy, patients might have to wait two weeks or more before they can get an appointment. So, what appeared to be a quick and easy solution is not so simple.

Competitive Position

A company may find that it has certain strengths and weaknesses when compared to its competitors. A company's market share may be greater than its competitors', which would be a major strength. If a company loses market share to its competitors, it would be a weakness. Questions that help a company analyze its internal competitive position are:

• **COMPARE and CONTRAST** FedEx, the United States Postal Service, and DHL all compete in the same market and provide similar services.

What do they do to keep or increase their market share?

TEACH CONTINUED

Concept Development

COMPETITION

After students have read the section on competition, ask them to consider how studying competitors is an important part of creating a marketing plan.

Studying competitors allows companies to generate comparisons and goals in relation to their market and their competitors. Analyzing how a competitor approaches the market can help companies determine what approaches to take in their own marketing plan.

TEACHING POINTS

Clarify Point out that market share is a tool that can be used to identify competitors and set quantifiable goals in a marketing plan.

Online Activity

Measuring Customer Satisfaction

Ask interested students to find online sites or surveys that rate products or services. Have students predict how companies can use the information and feedback generated on these sites in formulating their own marketing plan. Encourage students to find and print out an online consumer survey directed to their age group or demographic and share it with the class. Be sure to caution students against submitting their personal e-mail information over the internet.

AD GUIDE   **COMPARE and CONTRAST**

Discussion Lead a discussion on which of these ads students find to be most effective, and why.

Caption Answer DHL stresses how, being newer, it must work harder and offer more services than any other company; FedEx emphasizes the value of its long experience, suggesting that using its services has, with many customers, become a tradition; and USPS promises ease of use and familiarity.

Follow Up Walk the students through analysis of the USPS ad, asking what is implied by the statement at the top of the ad (possible answer: that USPS has taken all the hassle out of shipping).

TEACH CONTINUED

Concept Development

ENVIRONMENTAL SCAN

After students have read this section, ask them to consider the word *environment*. Have them brainstorm what the word makes them think of. Many students will mention physical or concrete surroundings. Tell students that in the same way that they are sensitive to their physical surroundings, marketers need to be sensitive to their business environment. Ask students to list the components of an environmental scan.

An environmental scan includes political, economic, socio-cultural, and technological surroundings.

Extended Activity

Understanding Economic Influences

Ask students to research and report on their local or state economies. Encourage students to use the library, newspapers, magazines, and online resources in their research. Have students summarize what they learned about their economy in a one-page report and moderate a discussion in class to determine if students have a basic understanding of how economic criteria such as employment rate and economic growth or slowing are considered when making marketing plans.

Online Activity

Researching Spam

Ask students who are interested in Internet marketing to research changes in legislation regarding e-mail spam. Have students share the results of their research in class, or use a word processing program to summarize their findings in a one-page report.

- What market share does the company have?
- What advantages does the company have over its competitors?
- What core competencies does the company possess? Does it have a better reputation, own a patent, have special resources, or better distribution capabilities?
- Are competitors taking business away from the company? How? New products? Better promotion?

External Opportunities and Threats

Companies must always look for opportunities to create competitive advantage due to external factors.

Competition

To stay competitive, companies need to know what their competitors are doing at all times. Changes in a competitor's financial situation and problems in the marketplace can provide opportunities. For example, Smart & Final, a discount supermarket chain based in the western United States, enjoyed increased customer traffic and increased sales when a labor strike crippled three competitors (Vons, Ralphs, and Albertsons) in 2004. The obvious weakness of Vons, Ralphs, and Albertsons (their inability to end the strike quickly) opened the door for competitors to take business away from them.

Companies that conduct a SWOT analysis on an ongoing basis are in a better position to react and make adjustments to their marketing mix. To assist in this process, companies must continually scan the external environment.

Environmental Scan

An **environmental scan** is an analysis of outside influences that may have an impact on an organization. This is a methodical look at the world that typically includes four areas: political, economic, socio-cultural, and technological (sometimes referred to with the acronym PEST). Understanding how each of

these areas is changing or is likely to change in the future can lead to a better appreciation of potential opportunities or threats for the firm. An alert business owner may use a change in one of these four aspects as an opportunity to be first to market products customers want.

Political

Political issues center around government involvement in business operations. Companies must be alert to changes in laws and regulations that affect their industries. Global companies need to understand the political structure and regulations of each foreign country in which they conduct business. To assess potential political risks and new opportunities, it is important to see what changes are likely in the laws governing your business operation, as they will have an impact on marketing plans. Here are a few examples of issues and current regulations that may affect certain industries in a positive way (opportunity) or in a negative way (threat):

- **Do Not Call Registry** The U.S. government passed this legislation in 2003. It gives people the ability to demand that telemarketers not call their phone numbers. This regulation forced many businesses to rethink part of their marketing strategies. Telemarketing companies had to adjust their data files to comply with the law.
- **Downloading Music from the Internet** The problem of illegal downloading of music created a whole industry with online companies that now provide legal downloading of music for a fee. This new industry may hurt music stores but has become an opportunity for companies like Apple's iTunes, RealNetworks' RealRhapsody, and Roxio's Napster.

Economic

The current state of the economy is of interest to all businesses: If the economy is robust, businesses are more likely to invest in new products and markets. An economy that is in a recession or slowing down sends a completely different message to the company's

•KNOWING YOUR MARKET
General Motors, one of the largest auto manufacturers in the United States, has added a navigation and emergency assistance system to some of its cars.

How may this technology affect auto companies?

"Out of nowhere, there was a voice and she said help was on the way."

In the moments after the crash, Michelle Creager heard two scared little voices. And one reassuring one.
On their way to the babysitter's, the Creagers' minivan hit a slick spot on a two-lane highway, plunged down an embankment and slammed into a tree, deploying the air bags and landing in a steep ditch filled with water.

Critically injured, Michelle drifted in and out of consciousness. Four-year-old Evan was still inside the vehicle, while two-year-old Jacob got out of his child safety seat and was crawling through the ditch.

decision makers. Upcoming marketing programs may be altered or scrapped altogether in a weak economy. Factors, such as the unemployment rate, inflation, retail sales figures, productivity, and consumer confidence, are tools to estimate the current status of the economy. The value of the dollar in relation to foreign currencies affects imports and exports. Here are some economic factors marketers would consider opportunities or threats:

- An economy in recession poses a threat to nearly all companies. Most companies slow or stop plans for new facilities and often reduce research and development (R&D) efforts.
- If unemployment figures decrease and consumer confidence increases, companies may see an opportunity to grow their business.
- Changes in foreign currency rates could be seen as a threat or an opportunity

depending on whether this makes the company's products or services cheaper or more expensive in their foreign target market.
- Illegal dumping (selling imported products at a very low price) in a given market is a threat to all businesses in that industry.
- Changes in trade restrictions, such as lowering or raising tariffs (taxes) on imported goods, could be considered a threat or an opportunity, depending on where a company does business.

Socio-Cultural

A socio-cultural analysis is based on customers and potential customers. Changes in their attitudes, lifestyles, and opinions provide a multitude of opportunities and threats. Socio-cultural analysis covers changes in all demographic factors, such as age, income, occupation, education level, and marital status. Here are two examples.

Chapter 2 - The Marketing Plan 31

SECTION 2.1

TEACH CONTINUED

Enrichment

POLITICAL ISSUES AND THE MARKET
Have students who are interested in how politics affects marketing to do further research on this topic. For example, students might research how local or national laws have affected commerce. Have researchers orally report their findings to the rest of the class. Encourage students to provide examples of this kind of technological change.

Extended Activity
Exploring Socio-Cultural Change
Have interested students research or create an example of a marketing survey that seeks to determine the attitudes of consumers toward a product, service, or idea. Give the example of a political survey as a type of survey that is used to determine the attitude of citizens or consumers toward an idea, such as a school bond measure that would be funded by a tax on a certain product. Encourage students to share the results of their research in class.

Virtual Business
Introduce staffing to students using Knowledge Matters' Virtual Business Retailing visual simulation, *Staffing*. In this simulation, students learn how staffing levels affect customer satisfaction and profitability.

AD GUIDE **KNOWING YOUR MARKET**

Discussion Ask students to consider what emotions are being appealed to in this ad. Students may mention the fears connected with a serious auto accident, the responsibility of caring for the young, the fear of being helpless.

Caption Answer This technology encourages companies to integrate it into existing products to fulfill customer needs. Auto companies that offer the OnStar option can consider it a strength. They can pose a threat to competitors. The competitors might decide to develop their own, similar technology, or pay OnStar to use the service.

 Follow Up Ask for opinions about the ad and the approach it takes. Responses will differ, but many students may feel manipulated or refer to the approach as a scare tactic. Ask students to suggest other ads that appeal to human fears or weaknesses.

Concept Development

TECHNOLOGICAL CHANGE

After students have read the section on changes in an environmental scan, ask them to consider how the speed at which technology changes might affect the other aspects of a marketing plan. Encourage students to give examples of this kind of technological change.

The speed at which technology changes affects the speed by which those products must be promoted, advertised, and sold. Examples will vary but might include new software programs and applications.

TEACHING POINTS

Explain Point out to students that evaluating technological change means that companies must determine whether new technologies can be used against them or for them, as well as innovating technology for their business itself.

- The United States is becoming a more ethnically and racially diverse country. Marketing plans need to meet this change. For example, in the area of home buying, minority consumers are expected to account for nearly two-thirds of all new home purchases by 2010.
- Obesity is an issue in the United States, as it causes many health problems. Consumer advocates for healthier eating habits have criticized fast-food chains.

Technological

Changing technology may be a threat for one industry or company, but an opportunity for others. A perfect example is digital photography. To be competitive, traditional photo companies like Kodak are looking for ways to adapt to this new technology. Camera companies are making more digital cameras. Other companies are seizing the opportunity to capitalize on this new technology by developing products to support it. Printer companies like Epson and Hewlett-Packard have developed products to make it easy for consumers to print their own digital photographs. Companies that keep abreast of the newest technological breakthroughs can use that knowledge to be more competitive. Here are a few examples:

- **Computer Automation** The home of the future may be completely automated. You may be able to call from your cell phone to change your thermostat so your home is warm when you arrive.
- **Satellite Technology** Cars now offer satellite radio and navigation systems that direct you to your destinations, as well as SOS systems such as OnStar that help you in an emergency.

Writing a Marketing Plan

Marketing is a complicated activity that relies on many different tasks. For this reason, marketers create a marketing plan. A **marketing plan** is a formal, written document that directs a company's activities for a specific period of time. It details analysis

---

NET MARKETING

Take Me Out to the Webcast

Major League Baseball (MLB) is betting that fans will pay to see games on their PCs. Distribution deals worth a combined $49 million were announced in March 2004 with Internet service providers AOL and MSN to stream live games and highlights over the Web. The league also signed marketing deals with three cable operators (Charter, Cablevision, and Comcast) to attract cable customers to the MLB Webcasts of more than 240 games a month. Fans can also access archived games for later replay. There's a big potential market. Broadband subscribers in the United States will grow from 27 million in 2004 to 46 million in 2008, says Jupiter Research. Plus, the recent success of streamed college basketball games on AOL suggests that people might finally be ready to log on rather than tune in to sports.

THINK LIKE A MARKETER

Which age group is most likely to be interested in this new way of viewing games? Why?

@ Online Action!

Go to *marketingessentials.glencoe.com/ 2/net* to find a research project on technology and growth opportunities.

  marketingessentials.glencoe.com

NET MARKETING

Take Me Out to the Webcast

Discussion Lead a discussion by asking students to consider which markets are most and least likely to respond to Webcasts.

THINK LIKE A MARKETER Answer: Students may suggest that teenagers to those in their early twenties would be most interested in this way of viewing games. Reasons might include the fact that this group is comfortable with and has access to technology.

@ Online Action! For instructions, ideas, and answer guide, go to the Teacher Center at **marketingessentials.glencoe.com**

GLOBAL MARKET

The Tesco Strategy

The British supermarket chain Tesco is aiming for long-term growth. It is best known as a grocery store, but it sees its future as something much bigger than the four food groups.

Expand and Diversify According the company's Web site, Tesco is expanding even more into international markets, such as Japan, Turkey, Poland, Hungary, and the Czech Republic. At the end of the 2003/2004 fiscal year, about half of its stores were outside the United Kingdom. The company says it is now the world's biggest online grocery store.

Tesco has also started stocking non-food products, including consumer electronics, and housewares. It sells financial services, such as mortgages, insurance, and even do-it-yourself wills. Its online services include music downloads, DVD rentals, and a flower delivery service.

The Company's Mission Tesco claims its core purpose is "creating value for customers, to earn their lifetime loyalty." The company says it has two values that drive the way it does business: "No one tries harder for customers;" and "Treat people how we like to be treated."

CRITICAL THINKING

In what way are Tesco's core purpose and values related to its marketing objectives and strategies?

@ Online Action!

Go to *marketingessentials.glencoe.com/2/global* to find a research project on global marketing.

---

and research efforts and provides a roadmap for how a product will enter the market, be advertised, and sold. A marketing plan also communicates the goals, objectives, and strategies of a company to members of the management team. The specifics in the plan let managers know their responsibilities, budget, and timelines for completion. A marketing plan helps a company monitor a company's performance. A small retail business may develop a simple marketing plan for a year, but a large manufacturer with global sales would prepare a marketing plan that covers five years.

Elements of a Marketing Plan

Marketing plans may differ from company to company. However, there are some basic elements that will be found in all marketing plans. Those elements include an executive summary, a situation analysis, marketing goals/objectives, marketing strategies, and implementation, as well as a system for evaluation and control. See Figure 2.1 for a complete outline of a marketing plan. Follow the annotations on the figure to see how a plan can be built.

Executive Summary

An **executive summary** is a brief overview of the entire marketing plan. It briefly addresses each topic in the plan and gives an explanation of the costs involved in implementing the plan. The executive summary may also be used to provide information to people outside the organization, especially those who may be investing in the company or organization.

marketingessentials.glencoe.com

Chapter 2 - The Marketing Plan **33**

SECTION 2.1

TEACH CONTINUED

Individualized Practice

ELEMENTS OF A MARKETING PLAN

Have students use the Net Marketing feature on page 32 to help them complete these practice activities.

L1 Ask students to create and write objectives for a marketing plan for a Webcast of a sports event.

L2 Ask students to perform a situation analysis for a Webcast of a Major League Baseball sports event. Have students summarize their findings in a one-page report.

L3 Ask students to come up with marketing strategies for a Webcast of a Major League Baseball sports event. Have students present their strategies in a five-minute oral presentation.

Critical Thinking

Ask students: Why is an executive summary useful to investors in particular?

GLOBAL MARKET

The Tesco Strategy

Discussion Ask the class to brainstorm all the ways that a company like Tesco might become first in market position.

CRITICAL THINKING **Answer:** Its marketing objectives are to create customer satisfaction and lifetime loyalty. Their values involve keeping the customer satisfied. They do this by selling nonfood products at the lowest prices and keeping up with changes in customer buying habits.

@ Online Action! For instructions, ideas, and answer guide, go to the Teacher Center at marketingessentials.glencoe.com

TEACH CONTINUED

Concept Development

ELEMENTS OF A MARKETING PLAN

A marketing plan outlines goals, objectives, and strategies of a business or organization. Ask students to identify the main audience for a marketing plan. Answers may include that the main audience for marketing plans is employees. Remind students that all employees should direct their efforts toward fulfilling the company's goals. The plan lets employees know what their roles and responsibilities are regarding those goals.

TEACHING POINTS

Explain Explain to students that the type of business or organization will determine the complexity of the plan and the period of time covered by the plan. A small manufacturer might develop a marketing plan for a year, whereas a large, multinational corporation might prepare one for five years. The longer time period allows for longer or more complex product development.

Extend Tell students that another audience for marketing plans might be potential or current investment advisors.

 Critical Thinking

Ask students: Does writing down a long-term plan help you accomplish your own goals?

Figure 2.1 **Elements of a Marketing Plan**

• **How to Build a Marketing Plan** A marketing plan is an essential planning tool for a company. This document defines the company's overall goals, determines strategies for achieving those goals, and, at the end of a predetermined period of time, assesses how well those goals were achieved. Below are the basic elements found in a marketing plan.

How can a small company benefit from writing a marketing plan?

This is the introduction to the marketing plan. Its clarity and brevity sell the plan to readers.

This part provides a snapshot of the company's present position. It often reports the results of a SWOT analysis and an environmental scan.

I. Executive summary

II. Situation analysis
   A. SWOT analysis
   B. Environmental scan

III. Objectives
   A. Company's mission
   B. Marketing objectives
   C. Financial objectives

This section defines specific goals to be met. To be effective, objectives must be single-minded, specific, realistic, and measurable, and must contain a time frame.

IV. Marketing strategies
   A. Positioning and points of difference
   B. Marketing mix (four Ps)
      1. Product
      2. Promotion
      3. Price
      4. Place (distribution)

This is where the company defines how it is going to meet its objectives with a marketing mix: the four Ps.

V. Implementation
   A. Organization
   B. Activities and responsibilities
   C. Timetables

This part outlines how the company will put its plans into effect.

VI. Evaluation and control
   A. Performance standards and measurements
      1. Marketing objectives
      2. Financial objectives
      3. Marketing mix strategies
   B. Corrective action

This part tells how the marketing plan will be evaluated and what measures might be necessary if objectives are not met.

VII. Appendix   *Supplemental materials are included in the appendix.*

 Online Action!   Go to *marketingessentials.glencoe.com/2/figure/1* to find a project on marketing plans.

marketingessentials.glencoe.com

Figure 2.1 *Elements of a Marketing Plan*

Discussion Have students follow as the content of **Figure 2.1** is read aloud. Lead a discussion about how company logos can be used to demonstrate goals.

Caption Answer Marketing plans are necessary for all companies, large or small, because all have the common goals of providing the best product at the lowest price while still making a profit.

 Online Action!   For instructions, ideas, and answer guide, go to the Teacher Center at **marketingessentials.glencoe.com**

Situation Analysis

Situation analysis is the study of the internal and external factors that affect marketing strategies. The information from a company's SWOT analysis and from the environmental scan becomes the basis for this portion of the marketing plan.

Goals and Objectives

Objectives let everyone know what the marketing plan will accomplish. To be useful, an objective must be single-minded (have only one topic for each objective), specific, realistic, measurable, and have a time frame. For example, you cannot include increasing sales and increasing profits in the same objective. Each topic needs to be a separate objective.

Specific means that the objective provides enough detail that there can be no misunderstanding. You cannot use, "to be better than a competitor" as an objective because what is "better" to one person may not be to another.

Measurable means that the objective includes a way to evaluate it. For example, you cannot simply say you want to increase sales. You need to identify the percentage increase in dollar or unit sales to make that objective measurable. Thus, you could use, "to increase dollar sales by 15 percent as compared to the same time last year."

Finally, you must include a time frame, such as in six months, or as compared to last year's sales. Without a time frame, you would not know if an objective was actually reached.

Marketing objectives must be in line with the organization's goals and mission. If an organization's goal is to double its business in five years, marketing objectives must coincide with that goal and provide the means to reach it.

A company's mission statement provides the focus for a firm's goals with its explanation of the company's core competencies, values, expectations, and vision for the future.

Marketing Strategies

A **marketing strategy** identifies target markets and sets marketing mix choices that focus on those markets. All strategies need to take the customer's needs and wants into account, as well as the objectives of the marketing plan.

A company's or product's position in the marketplace determines the appropriate marketing strategy. The positioning of the product or service will drive decisions for each of the four Ps.

An effective marketing strategy should be focused on the key points of difference. The key point of difference is the advantage a company, a product, or service has over its competition. The point of difference could be the quality of the product, a superior distribution system, a more creative ad campaign, or a more competitive pricing structure.

This competitive advantage is what will make the company successful. The marketing mix elements can help create points of difference with respect to competition.

The results of the SWOT analysis should provide enough information to identify the specific target market and suggest ideas to create the necessary point(s) of difference to be competitive.

Implementation: Make the Plan, Work the Plan

Implementation is putting the marketing plan into action and managing it. This means obtaining the financial resources, management, and staffing necessary to put the plan into action. A timetable shows when each part goes into play.

This part of the marketing plan outlines a schedule of activities, job assignments, **sales forecasts** (the projection of probable, future sales in units or dollars), budgets, details of each activity, and who will be responsible for each activity.

This phase of the plan requires excellent communication among members of the management team so that tasks are completed on a timely basis.

Evaluation and Control

In the evaluation section of the marketing plan, measures that will be used to evaluate the plan are discussed. It is important to

---

 Extended Activity

Phases of the Marketing Process

Ask students to discuss which phase of the marketing plan is the most important. Tell students that in order to keep the economic system vital, new products must be continuously developed. Also, factors that influence the marketing process are changing all the time. For example, internal changes in a company as well as changes in its customers and competition are ongoing, as are the external changes in the areas of politics, culture, society, economy, and technology. Have students share their opinions in class.

ASSESS

Review Guide

CONCEPTS

Ask students to explain the relationship between a SWOT analysis and a marketing plan.

A SWOT analysis is an essential part of a marketing plan.

KEY TERMS

Have students work in small groups to review the spellings and definitions of key terms.

ONLINE SELF-ASSESSMENT

Have students go to **marketingessentials.glencoe.com** for the Section 2.1 practice test.

Individualized Review

L1 Assign and review Chapter 2 activities in the Student Activity Workbook.

L2 Assign and review Chapter 2 activities in the Marketing Math Workbook.

L3 Assign and review Chapter 2 activities in the *BusinessWeek* Reader and Case Studies.

Marketing Practice

Have students work in small groups to choose one component of SWOT analysis and create a brief role play in which the person conducting the study meets with the company's employees to conduct that part of the analysis. As they work out their scene, students should review the questions provided under this heading in the text.

CLOSE

Write the following analogy on the board and have students choose the correct response to complete it:

A SWOT analysis is to a marketing plan as
(a) a glass is to water
(b) a limb is to a tree
(c) a puppy is to a dog
(b); because the SWOT analysis is an integral part of the whole marketing plan.

Extended Activity

Marketing Audit

Have interested students research the components of a marketing audit. Encourage students to perform an informal marketing audit on a company of their choice.

---

explain exactly how a specific objective will be measured and who will be responsible for providing that evaluation.

Performance Standards and Evaluation

Performance standards are the measuring stick. A **performance standard** is an expectation for performance that reflects the plan's objectives. As part of the planning process, the control section suggests actions that should be considered if objectives are not met. In the control phase, the company's goal is to reduce the gap between planned performance standards and actual performance.

Let's say sales did not reach the sales forecast numbers. One reason for this discrepancy could be recent changes in economic conditions. In such a situation, a company may revise its sales forecast to make it more realistic.

Appendix

The appendix is the section of the marketing plan that includes supplemental materials such as detailed financial statements, samples ads, and other materials that support the plan.

Conclusion

The marketing process is ongoing. Think of it as a circular pattern that keeps going through the three phases of the marketing process of planning, implementation, and control. The key question at the end of the process is "Did we accomplish the objectives listed in the marketing plan within the boundaries of the plan.

A marketing audit evaluates a company's marketing objectives, strategies, budgets, organization, and performance. It identifies problem areas in marketing operations. A marketing audit happens on a formal basis once a year and informally on a continuous basis.

2.1 AFTER YOU READ

Reviewing Key Terms and Concepts

1. What is a SWOT analysis and why is it helpful?
2. How can a business use a SWOT analysis and an environmental scan to create a marketing plan?
3. Why are evaluation and control important elements of a marketing plan?

Integrating Academic Skills

Math

4. If a company's current sales revenue is $1,386,000 and its marketing objective is to increase sales by 10 percent in the next year, what is the dollar sales goal for the following year?

Economics

5. How can a country's current economic situation impact a business's marketing plan?

 Online Action!
Check your answers at *marketingessentials.glencoe.com/2/read*

AFTER YOU READ

Reviewing Key Terms and Concepts

1. A SWOT analysis is a critical examination by a business of itself and its business environment. It is helpful because it enables a business to prepare for and deal with threats and weaknesses, as well as provide guidance and direction.

2. When a company conducts a SWOT analysis and an environmental scan, it can develop strategies to deal with its weaknesses and challenges and best use its strengths and opportunities.

3. The evaluation and control phase of a marketing plan assesses how well the company has met its objectives. This phase also sets the stage for the next marketing plan.

Integrating Academic Skills

4. $1,524,600; $1,386,000 × .10 = $138,600; $138,600 + $1,386,000 = $1,524,600

5. In times of a healthy and robust economy, businesses are more likely to invest in new products and markets; in an economy that is either in or heading toward a recession, marketing plans may be placed on hold, changed, or dismissed altogether until the economy improves.

Online Action! Answers at **marketingessentials.glencoe.com/2/read**

Market Segmentation

OBJECTIVES

- Explain the concept of market segmentation
- Analyze a target market
- Differentiate between mass marketing and market segmentation

KEY TERMS

- market segmentation
- demographics
- disposable income
- discretionary income
- geographics
- psychographics
- mass marketing

READ and STUDY

BEFORE YOU READ

Predict How do marketers find out who their customers are?

THE MAIN IDEA

The key to marketing and selling goods, services, or ideas is to know who your customer or audience is. This is called a target market and the process to find that specific market is called market segmentation. The factors that define a particular market are demographic, geographic, psychographic, and behavioral.

STUDY ORGANIZER

Use a chart like the one below to list differences between mass marketing and market segmentation.

Mass Market Versus Market Segmentation

Mass Market	Market Segmentation
Definition	Ways to segment 1. Demographics 2. 3. 4.

Identifying and Analyzing Markets

Businesses look for ways to connect with current and potential customers. The surest way to make that connection is to know them well. This means knowing where they live, their income level, age, ethnic background, activities, values, and what interests them. When a company looks at its customers this way, it can identify groups of people who have many things in common.

WHILE YOU READ

Connect Think of yourself as a consumer. What are your key characteristics?

FOCUS

Introducing the Section

COLLABORATIVE ACTIVITY

Ask whether anyone can define the term used as the title of this section, *market segmentation*, reminding students that they heard it first in Chapter 1. Then ask students to brainstorm different ways a market can be segmented.

Market segmentation is the breaking of a market into smaller groups based on common characteristics and then marketing to one particular group.

Preteaching Key Terms

Read each key term aloud and have students skim this section to find that word and its definition. A volunteer can then read the definition aloud for the class.

- market segmentation
- demographics
- disposable income
- discretionary income
- geographics
- psychographics
- mass marketing

READ and STUDY

BEFORE YOU READ

Point out to the class that they themselves are a market. Encourage students to keep this idea in mind as they read.

THE MAIN IDEA

Talk about each key term that is part of the main idea, rechecking definitions in context as needed.

STUDY ORGANIZER

Model the study organizer for students. Make your own organizer on the board, or download the one at **marketingessentials.glencoe.com**. Fill out the differences as study continues.

WHILE YOU READ

Encourage students to start their notes on their characteristics now and add to them as they work through this section.

Discussion Starter

IDENTIFYING AND ANALYZING MARKETS

Have students list at least some of these characteristics: age, gender, income, marital status, ethnic background, education, and occupation. Inform students that these and other characteristics make up their demographic characteristics.

TEACHING POINTS

Clarify Tell students that as their demographic characteristics change, they are reclassified in different kinds of terms to marketers.

Concept Development

DEMOGRAPHICS

Read the paragraph introducing the section on demographics aloud. Ask students to brainstorm specific ways that marketers might be able to differentiate and identify potential customers.

Critical Thinking

Ask students to think of reasons why today's marketers are so interested in Generation Y. Encourage interested students to do more research on this segment of the population and provide examples of marketing targeted toward members of Generation Y.

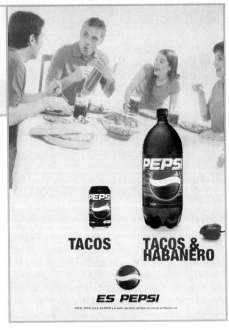

• **PEPSI for EVERYBODY** PepsiCo, Inc. does extensive market research as do many other large corporations. This research reveals how the market for a given product is segmented. This information plays an important role in determining where and how a product is advertised.

Which market is PepsiCo trying to reach with this ad? How?

Marketers analyze groups of customers to see if any of them can be further broken down into smaller, more precise clusters. The process of classifying people who form a given market into even smaller groups is called **market segmentation**. Let's look at the market for jeans. A marketer might ask, "Who buys jeans? At what price? What special features do they want?" Depending on the answers to these questions, the market for jeans could be segmented:

- **By age** jeans for kids, teens, and adults.
- **By price** marketers need to reach different income levels (often referred to as socio-economic groups).
- **By desired features** tight fit, comfortable fit, newest fashion, or a unique design.

To meet the needs of these different market segments, jeans manufacturers develop a unique marketing mix, including different products, promotions, stores for distribution, and price points. For example, Levi's jeans are available in relaxed fit, regular fit, 501 original, loose straight, loose boot cut, low rise straight, and low rise boot cut.

The next question marketers ask is, "Which of these segments should we target?" It is usually too costly to target all the potential target markets. So, it is very important to identify those markets in which the company has an advantage that enables it to survive against its competition over a long period of time. This is what marketers call a sustainable competitive advantage.

Companies study data generated by governments, private research firms, trade associations, and their own research to determine if a given target market is large enough to justify the expense. For example, United States census data might reveal that there are enough teenagers to justify making jeans for that segment of the market. To get a handle on the jeans market, additional research would reveal more about this market segment: their buying behavior, interests, activities, opinions about

---

AD GUIDE PEPSI for EVERYBODY

Discussion Lead a discussion of market segmentation by asking students to give their first impressions of this ad. Ask them to brainstorm to whom the ads might be directed.

Caption Answer Pepsi is attempting to reach a Spanish-speaking family demographic with this ad by featuring their product in a family-specific setting with appropriate ethnic cuisine as well as using the Spanish language.

Follow Up Encourage students to find and bring in to class other ads that are directed to a particular market segment. Have students identify the market segment to whom the ad is directed.

fashion, values, status, household income levels, ethnic background, and any other factor that might help marketers create a customer profile. The more specific the information is, the easier it is to design the jeans, price them, create the appropriate promotions, and sell them in the right outlets. The same factors that help segment a market are used to describe a target market. They are: demographics, geographics, psychographics, and behavioral factors.

Demographics

Demographics refer to statistics that describe a population in terms of personal characteristics such as age, gender, income, marital status, ethnic background, education, and occupation.

Age

Marketers can easily use age to segment the market by creating age ranges. The United States census provides information that might help in deciding on the age categories. Here are common labels used to segment the population by generation:

Baby Boom Generation
The 76 million babies born in the United States between 1946 and 1964 are known as the baby boomers. As baby boomers get older, their income and spending power increase. Therefore, they are prime targets for all types of products.

Generation X (or the Baby Bust Generation)
They followed the Baby Boom Generation. Most members of Generation X are children of dual-career households or divorced parents. They have been bombarded with media from an early age, and they are savvy purchasers and skeptical consumers. To reach this group, marketers must use sharp images, music, a sense of humor, and meet them on their own terms.

Generation Y
They are the sons and daughters of the later baby boomers. Generation Y is also known as the Echo Boomers or Millennium Generation. According to the United States census, this group is more racially and ethnically diverse with a lot of spending power. Fashions and

information about products get passed along via the Internet, as almost all of the members of this generation have e-mail and surf the Web.

Gender

Gender helps to create market segments as well. Jockey, at one time a men's underwear company, doubled its sales when it entered the women's market with Jockey underwear for women.

Income

Marketers want to know how much money they have to spend on different products. For this reason, they look at two types of income measurement: disposable income and discretionary income. **Disposable income** is the money left after taking out taxes. Marketers who produce and distribute products that are necessities are interested in changes in consumers' disposable income. **Discretionary income** is the money left after paying for basic living necessities such as food, shelter, and clothing. Marketers who sell luxury and premium products are interested in changes in consumers' discretionary income.

Marital Status

The U.S. Census indicates that married couples have slipped to 50.7 percent of total households, compared with 80 percent in the 1950s. Reasons for this reduction in married couples can be attributed to several factors. People are older when they get married for the first time, divorcing more, living longer, and remarrying less. Married couples with kids represent 25 percent of the population.

Ethnic Background

The U.S. population is becoming more multicultural and ethnically diverse, mainly as a result of increased immigration. The Caucasian population is declining, relative to other ethnic populations. African American, Hispanic, and Asian American populations make up 28 percent of the U.S. population. By 2025 these ethnic groups will represent 37.2 percent of all Americans.

Extended Activity

Determining Lifestyle

Have students research and select a print or online periodical that is targeted to a particular interest group. Examples might include magazines that are geared to a particular sport or to a music consumer. Ask students to predict and summarize the prospective audience for the periodical in a one-page response. Encourage students to support their conclusions with examples from the periodical.

Individualized Practice

MARKET SEGMENTATION

L1 Introduce students to the concept of psychographics by asking them how they spend their leisure time or what their values are.

L2 Ask students whether they believe that senior citizen or child discounts are fair. Have students support their positions in a one-page essay.

L3 Ask students to name some products that are promoted to both genders or one or more ethnic groups with the same approach or slightly different approach. Answers may include toys, food, or clothing. Ask students to discuss in a one-page report what they feel ads can do to perpetuate or counter gender or ethnic stereotypes.

Enrichment

ADVERTISING TO CHILDREN

Ask interested students to research laws and regulations about advertising to children. Moderate a class discussion about whether it is ethical to market to children. Some students will argue that children should learn early that advertising is meant to influence them and begin to make judgments about what they see. Those against advertising aimed at children may point out that children can not easily distinguish between fact and fiction, determine what is good for them and what is not, or make the distinction between program and advertising. They might further argue that when a child is exposed to advertising, a responsible adult should be with them to talk about what they are seeing.

Review Guide

CONCEPTS

Ask students to recall three factors marketers can use to segment a market. demographics, geographics, or psychographics

KEY TERMS

Have students work in small groups to review the spellings and definitions of key terms.

ONLINE SELF-ASSESSMENT

Have students go to marketingessentials.glencoe.com for the Section 2.2 practice test.

Individualized Review

L1 Assign and review Chapter 2 activities in the Student Activity Workbook.

L2 Assign and review Chapter 2 activities in the Marketing Math Workbook.

L3 Assign and review Chapter 2 activities in the *BusinessWeek* Reader and Case Studies.

Marketing Practice

Provide examples of advertisements to teams of two to four students or ask students to find advertisements on their own. Have each team identify the ways they think the marketer has segmented the market to reach the group or individuals being targeted by their selected advertisement. Encourage students to share their ads in class.

Geographics

The term **geographics** refers to segmentation of the market based on where people live. Geographics relate closely to demographics because of the similarity among people who live in a certain area. To segment a market geographically, you can refer to local, regional, national, or even global markets. For example, a small, independent restaurant generally caters to people who live in its vicinity. Some products, such as Coca-Cola and Pepsi, are marketed nationally and internationally.

- If you were interested in marketing to Latinos, it would be good to know the top Hispanic markets, which are Los Angeles, New York, Miami, Chicago, and Houston. If you were to introduce a new line of Hispanic products, the best place to market test them would be in these geographic areas.
- Fifty-five percent of the African American population live in the South. However, the city with the largest number of people identified as African American is New York City with 2.3 million. Chicago is second with 1.1 million, followed by Detroit, Philadelphia, Houston, Los Angeles, Baltimore, Memphis, Washington, D.C., and New Orleans. Any company that wants to reach African Americans would want to make sure it has distribution outlets in those key cities.
- If you were interested in marketing to children, it would be good to know where a large number of them live. According to the U.S. Census, Utah and Alaska had the highest proportion of their populations in the 5-to-13 age group (15 percent each). States with 14 percent were Texas, Arizona, California, and Idaho.
- In 2003, the population 65 years of age and older could be found in the greatest numbers in California (3.8 million), Florida (2.9 million), New York (2.5 million), Texas (2.2 million), and Pennsylvania (1.9 million).

- The states with a median household income of at least $50,000 in 2002 were Maryland ($55,912), Alaska ($55,412), Minnesota ($54,931), New Hampshire ($53,549), Connecticut ($53,325), New Jersey ($53,266), Delaware ($50,878), and Massachusetts ($50,587). Banks and other financial institutions would be interested in these geographic areas, as many of these states' residents would be prime candidates for investments and insurance. Makers of luxury items would also target these geographical areas.

Psychographics

Psychographics involves grouping people with similar lifestyles, as well as shared attitudes, values, and opinions. Consumer lifestyles include how people spend their time and money. Attitudes, values, and opinions require special research to learn more about a group's personality traits and motivation.

Activities

If you made a list of all of your present activities, you would come to realize just how many market segments can be identified by psychographics. A good way to get a feel for market segmentation by activities is to visit the magazine section of a bookstore. For each interest group and activity, you will find at least one related magazine, which represents a market segment.

Attitudes

Consumers' attitudes, such as taking responsibility for one's health, eating healthier, and becoming physically fit, are trend-setting issues for marketers in the twenty-first century.

Personality & Values

More advanced study of psychographics includes the study of personality characteristics and values.

Behavioral

Segmenting the market based on product-related behavior involves looking at the benefits desired by consumers, shopping patterns, and usage rate. For example, many people, regardless of their socio-economic status,

---

Online Activity

Diversity in Demographics

Refer students to the U.S. Census report, which can be found online or in public libraries. Have students list some of the kinds of information that can be found in the report. Students especially interested in the ethnic component of demographics might do research on breakdowns within each ethnic population and prepare an informal report for the class.

desire luxury and premium merchandise. The luxury market is a growing consumer trend as individuals define themselves more and more through the products and brands they buy.

For example, MasterCard research revealed five groups of online consumers: confident core users, cautious shoppers, mainstream users, curious but not convinced, and technology skeptics. The overriding finding was that enhanced security measures influenced a shopper's online purchase decision. Each group had different levels of concern about security.

How Marketers Use Consumers' Behavioral Patterns

Astute marketers study shopping patterns to determine usage rates. Jupiter Research, a market research company, has determined that most teenagers spend less than $50 a month on entertainment and that teenage girls spend 15 percent more on music than teenage boys.

Companies classify their customers according to the percentage of sales each group generates. Many businesses find that the 80/20 rule applies. The 80/20 rule means that 80 percent of a company's sales are generated by 20 percent of its loyal customers.

Mass Marketing Versus Segmentation

When products have universal appeal and few features to differentiate them from competitors, mass marketing is used. **Mass marketing** involves using a single marketing strategy to reach all customers.

A New Marketing Trend

Since most products can be segmented by demographics, psychographics, geographics, or buying behavior, mass marketing is not as popular as it once was. The current trend is niche marketing, which means that markets are narrowed down and defined with extreme precision. Even products that use one slogan in their advertising, such as *Got Milk?* ads, will use different models or themes to reach different segments of the market.

Ask volunteers to share their notes about themselves as consumers that they took as they read through this chapter. Ask: Do any descriptions show up in almost everybody's notes? What are some unique features that students would like to share? Have students describe which categories these features fall under.

Critical Thinking

Ask students to identify the five types of online consumers.

2.2 AFTER YOU READ

Reviewing Key Terms and Concepts

1. Which type of income, disposable or discretionary, is more important to businesses that sell expensive watches, second homes, and financial services?

2. Of what significance are the combined African American, Hispanic, and Asian-American populations to marketers?

3. A recent study shows that teens are drinking more bottled water and reducing the amount of carbonated beverages they drink. Which psychographic or lifestyle trend does this study support?

Integrating Academic Skills

Math

4. If 93 percent of the U.S. population of 290,890,777 (2003 estimate) snacks at least once a day, how large is the market for snack food?

Civics and Government

5. Why does the United States conduct a census of its residents every ten years?

 Online Action!

Check your answers at *marketingessentials.glencoe.com/2/read*

marketingessentials.glencoe.com

AFTER YOU READ

Reviewing Key Terms and Concepts

1. These businesses depend on the customer's discretionary income, the money left over after the necessities (such as food, clothing, shelter) have been purchased.

2. Each represents a potential market segment. By 2025, these groups will represent 37.2 percent of the U.S population.

3. attitudes, taking responsibility for one's health

Integrating Academic Skills

4. 270,528,422; 290,890,777 × .93 = 270,528,432.61

5. The census, mandated by the Constitution, gives the government fairly up-to-date information regarding who citizens are,

where they live, their ages, and so on. This information is vital in serving the nation's population, by providing statistics on things such as how many people will draw Social Security benefits in a given year, how many children will enter school at a given time, and so on.

 Online Action! Answers at **marketingessentials.glencoe.com/2/read**

Lifelong Learning

CAREER INFORMATION

Have students go to marketingessentials.glencoe.com, find the Chapter 2 Careers page, and then click on the link for the American Marketing Association's Career Strategies and Tips. Ask students to select one article to read and write a one-page summary.

MARKETING AND SETTING GOALS

Explain that in the context of the feature, a *measurable goal* is whether the product sells, and the creative pursuits are all the ways used to sell it. Point out that this definition suggests working with marketing plans offers the opportunity to use a wide range of skills related to setting and achieving goals.

Primary Source

Ask students to go to marketingessentials.glencoe.com and find Chapter 2 resources. Ask them to click on the link for the American Marketing Association's marketing dictionary and read definitions of any terms related to the marketing plan they find.

THINKING CRITICALLY

Study of psychology includes examination of all types of human behavior. The more understanding a person has about other people, the more likely that person will be able to reach and persuade them.

@ Online Action!

For instructions, ideas, and answer guide, go to the Teacher Center at marketingessentials.glencoe.com

---

ROBERT MARCUM
MARKETING COORDINATOR
ARGOS, KLEIN AND HAMMERSMITH

? What do you do at work?
I'm an employee of a consulting firm that focuses on using all types of marketing disciplines to help organizations achieve their goals. These include media relations, grassroots marketing, Internet communications, lobbying, investor relations, and advertising. My job mostly entails three things: leading and executing the communications programs for various clients, handling operations issues such as managing local staff, and pursuing new business.

? What skills are most important to you?
A lot of what marketing people do is apply a measurable goal to creative pursuits: writing, oration, design, etc. Therefore, if you want to succeed in marketing, you'd better have an eye for design, write well, or be a persuasive conversationalist.

? What kind of training do you recommend?
Read, read, read. Observe, observe, observe. Read everything. Read books on marketing. Read magazines to figure out how journalists craft stories. The best marketers are generally very observant people. Study psychology and learn to empathize with others. Marketing and communications are about evaluating an audience, and then communicating to that audience according to what you know about them in order to inspire the audience to do or think something so that you can further an organization's goals.

Aptitudes, Abilities, and Skills

Strong and outgoing personality, creativity, writing and communication skills

Education and Training

Degrees in marketing, communication, and psychology

Career Path

Marketing and communications positions range from entry-level assistant to upper-level executives. Entry-level positions provide real-world experience and a first step on the ladder upward.

THINKING CRITICALLY

Why is it valuable for marketing professionals to study psychology?

@ Online Action!

Go to *marketingessentials.glencoe.com/2/careers* to find a career-related activity.

Test-Taking Strategies

Let students know that they can use the graphic organizers found in each section to provide quick, visual reminders of the contents of the chapter. Tell students that they can create graphic organizers on their own to organize the information that they learn.

FOCUS on KEY POINTS

SECTION 2.1

● A SWOT analysis identifies a company's internal strengths and weaknesses, as well as external opportunities and threats. Internal strengths and weaknesses involve analysis of the company, its customers, and its competitive position. External opportunities and threats include political, economic, socio-cultural, and technological factors.

● A marketing plan is a written document that directs the marketing activities of a company for a specific period of time. The elements of a marketing plan are an executive summary, a situation analysis, marketing goals/objectives, marketing strategies, implementation, as well as evaluation and control, and appendix.

SECTION 2.2

● Market segmentation classifies people in a given market into smaller groups. Four methods of segmenting a market are demographics, geographics, psychographics, and buying behavior.

● Demographics can be broken down into age, gender, income, marital status, and ethnic background. Geographics relates to similarities among people who live in a certain area. Psychographics groups people with similar lifestyles, attitudes, values, and opinions.

REVIEW VOCABULARY

Review the definition of each key term and explain where each term belongs in the marketing plan.

1. SWOT analysis (p. 27)
   market segmentation (p. 38)

2. environmental scan (p. 30)
   demographics (p. 39)

3. executive summary (p. 33)
   disposable income (p. 39)

4. situation analysis (p. 35)
   discretionary income (p. 39)

5. marketing strategy (p. 35)
   geographics (p. 40)

6. sales forecast (p. 35)
   psychographics (p. 40)

7. performance standard (p. 36)
   mass marketing (p. 41)

REVIEW FACTS and IDEAS

8. Explain the purpose of a SWOT analysis. (2.1)

9. List the three key areas involved in an internal company analysis. (2.1)

10. Identify the factors in an external environmental scan. (2.1)

11. What are the basic elements found in all marketing plans? (2.1)

12. Explain market segmentation. (2.2)

13. How can a market be analyzed using demographics? Using geographics? (2.2)

14. What factors are involved in analyzing a market according to psychographics? (2.2)

15. Differentiate between mass marketing and market segmentation. (2.2)

Chapter 2 - The Marketing Plan 43

REVIEW FACTS and IDEAS

8. The purpose of a SWOT analysis is to help the company analyze its own strengths and weakness and the opportunities and threats in its environment.

9. The three key areas involved in an internal company analysis are company, customers, and competition (three Cs).

10. The factors in an external environmental scan are political, economic, socio-cultural, and technological (PEST).

11. The basic elements of a marketing plan include: summary, situation analysis, objectives, marketing strategies, implementation, evaluation, and control.

12. Market segmentation is classifying people in a given market into smaller groups based on common characteristics.

13. Using demographics to analyze a population involves segmenting it in terms of personal characteristics such as age, gender, income, marital status, ethnic background, education, and occupation. Analyzing according to geographics involves segmenting it based on where people live.

14. The market is examined according to similar lifestyles and shared attitudes, values, and opinions. Evaluating according to buying patterns involves studying benefits desired by the buyer and how often they make particular purchases.

15. Mass marketing refers to the using of a single marketing plan in efforts to reach all customers while market segmentation involves breaking the mass market into smaller parts based on shared characteristics and then aiming specific marketing efforts at a smaller group.

FOCUS on KEY POINTS

For both Section 2.1 and Section 2.2, have a different student read each key point aloud. Allow time after each reading for questions or comments, encouraging peer tutoring as classmates respond to each other's remarks.

REVIEW VOCABULARY

See glossary to find definitions for the key terms in **1–7.** A sample answer might read:

1. A *SWOT analysis* is an analysis of internal strengths and weaknesses, as well as external opportunities and threats. It belongs in the situation analysis portion of the marketing plan.

CHAPTER 2 REVIEW

BUILD SKILLS

16. Workplace Skills

Answers will vary but should list three things the salesperson did to establish rapport, such as looking the customer in the eye, asking questions about product use, or sharing personal experiences.

17. Technology Applications

Answers should indicate the ability to make use of the program used to create spreadsheets. Spreadsheets should demonstrate an understanding of how to collate and chart demographic information.

18. Math Practice

The two largest figures on this list represent the top 20 percent of customers; 80 percent of the company's sales ($700,000 + $815,000) are generated by the top 20 percent of customers.

DEVELOP CRITICAL THINKING

19. Analyze the Marketing Mix

Responses should indicate knowledge of the four Ps (product, place, price, and promotion) and how they apply to this situation. Judgment of which one is doing a better job should be supported with facts such as profit comparisons as well as the student's personal reasons.

20. Prepare a SWOT Analysis

Student charts and their responses during discussion should display an understanding of the components of SWOT analysis. Analyses should include appropriate strengths, weaknesses, threats, and opportunities.

BUILD SKILLS

16. Workplace Skills

Customer Service Skills Try to recall a businessperson or a salesperson who was able to establish a bond with you or one of your friends or family members during a business transaction at a store or a business office. List three things the person did to accomplish this.

17. Technology Applications

Age Groups Use spreadsheet software to create a chart that depicts the age groups reported by the U.S. Census Bureau's estimates as of July 2003:

Total population 290,808,777

Under 5 years 19,769,279

5 to 13 years 36,752,056

14 to 17 years 16,522,171

18 to 24 years 28,899,571

Include the 25 and older age group in your chart.

18. Math Practice

The 80/20 Rule Here are the sales figures for ten customers (1) $75,000; (2) $700,000; (3) $815,000; (4) $70,000; (5) $60,000; (6) $30,000; (7) $25,000; (8) $53,750; (9) $40,000; and (10) $25,000. Explain the 80/20 rule using the above ten sales figures.

DEVELOP CRITICAL THINKING

19. Analyze the Marketing Mix

Select two competing companies that target teens. Evaluate the effectiveness of their efforts with regard to the four Ps of the marketing mix. Which one is doing a better job and why?

20. Prepare a SWOT Analysis

Select a company that interests you and on which you can find information (on the Web, through observations at different stores, or in business publications). Prepare a SWOT analysis. Then, prepare a chart that depicts the company's internal strengths and weaknesses, as well as its external opportunities and threats. Be prepared to discuss your analysis with classmates.

Formative Assessment

Formative assessment is an essential component of classroom work. This type of assessment provides information that is then used as feedback to modify teaching and meet student needs.

L1 Ask students to work in pairs to explain the key terms in this chapter to one another.

L2 Ask students to name and describe the four components of SWOT analysis.

L3 Have students work in small groups to choose a product and create a marketing plan for it.

Reteach If the results of this formative assessment seem low, consider the following activity: Ask students to read the section subheads aloud and construct an outline which includes at least one key point under each heading.

APPLY CONCEPTS

21. Compare and Contrast the Effects of Marketing Activities

Research and list teen fashions and fads in clothing, footwear, electronics, or personal grooming products. Name factors that influence teen fashions and fads, as well as companies that are doing a good job of addressing them in the products they sell and the way they market those products to teens. Also cite companies that have been ineffective in their marketing efforts to teens. Consider all four Ps of the marketing mix in your analysis (product, place, price, and promotion).

Activity Prepare a written report and use presentation software to prepare an oral report on your research and your findings.

22. Segment a Market

Research the nutritional value of almonds and FDA approval of claims that can be used to market these products. Suggest trends that help segment the nut market. Choose and describe the most viable target market (segment). Suggest a promotional campaign for an organization (such as the Almond Board of California) that will use your proposal to increase sales. What would be the key message? What media would you choose?

Activity Prepare a written report and a visual presentation of your ideas using computer presentation software.

NET SAVVY

23. Learn From the Census

Visit the Web site for the United States Census Bureau and select one of its reports from its Facts for Features series. Share the report you selected with your class.

marketingessentials.glencoe.com

CONNECTION

Role Play:
Marketing Intern

Situation You are to assume the role of intern for a marketing consulting firm. A customer (judge) is considering turning his/her hobby of making special occasion chocolate candies into a full time career. The customer (judge) is fairly inexperienced in business matters and has come to your company for help and advice in developing a marketing plan for the proposed business.

Activity You must explain to the customer (judge) the importance and function of a good marketing plan.

Evaluation You will be evaluated on how well you meet the following performance indicators:

- Explain the nature of marketing plans
- Conduct SWOT analysis for use in a marketing planning process
- Explain the concept of a market and market identification
- Explain the nature of sales forecasts
- Select a target market

 Online Action!

For more information and DECA Prep practice, go to *marketingessentials.glencoe* *.com/2/DECA*

APPLY CONCEPTS

21. Compare and Contrast the Effects of Marketing Activities

Student reports and presentations should demonstrate an understanding of the teen demographic as well as an understanding of how to apply the four Ps of the marketing mix to their analysis. Presentations can be evaluated according to how well goals were met, quality of research, and mastery of the presentation software.

22. Segment a Market

Student presentations should express an understanding of a market segment as well as the components of the marketing plan. Presentations can be evaluated according to how well goals were met, quality of research, and mastery of the presentation software.

NET SAVVY

23. Learn From the Census

Student reports will vary but should demonstrate an understanding of how to use the U.S. Census Bureau Web site.

MINI-QUIZ

Have students write or volunteer answers as you read each item aloud.

1. A SWOT analysis is a marketing plan. (false)

2. A target market is as big as a market can get. (false)

3. External factors, political, economic, social, and technological, all affect a company's marketing efforts. (true)

4. Customer profiles help determine marketing strategies. (true)

5. Small companies have no need for marketing plans. (false)

For an expanded chapter quiz, go to Chapter 2 in the TeacherWorks CD-ROM and to Chapter 2 in the **ExamView®** Pro Test Generator CD-ROM.

 CONNECTION

Students should be evaluated according to the performance standards noted in the role play. For another DECA role play, go to the Competitive Events Workbook or the Student Activity Workbook, or go to marketingessentials.glencoe.com/2/DECA

 Online Action! For instructions, ideas, and answer guide, go to the Teacher Center at marketingessentials.glencoe.com

DECA Advisors Corner

Present an activity in marketing terms, where a new DECA chapter is the product. Work with your own DECA chapter to create a SWOT analysis and then a marketing plan. Secure the name of a school where you hope to create a DECA chapter and assign marketing tasks to chapter officers.

MARKETING INTERNSHIP

A SIMULATED ◆DECA PRODUCT AND SERVICE MANAGEMENT EVENT

SET-UP

Discuss this internship's basic background to make sure students understand the simulation. Introduce students to the NASCAR Web site, and let them know that this fastest-growing sport attracts the largest audiences of all sports. You may want to ask students who are NASCAR fans to discuss their attachment to the sport and explain how it is different from other sports.

PROCEDURES

You may want to list procedures on the board and talk about any questions the students might have. Remind the students that a suggested outline for their project is available at **marketingessentials.glencoe.com/u1/ internship.**

TIME MANAGEMENT

Set goals, block schedules, and milestones. Assign interim deadlines for each step of the project.

ASSESSMENT

The rubrics for evaluation of the written, oral, and computer presentations are available at **marketingessentials.glencoe.com/u1/ internship.**

Conduct a SWOT Analysis for NASCAR

 BASIC BACKGROUND

NASCAR wants to begin holding races in the New York City area and attract teenagers as new fans. It would also like to sign sponsorship deals with high-tech and financial services companies. A few of your clients fit that description.

You work with a large bank, an Internet company, a mobile phone service provider, and a teen apparel retailer.

Which Company Is the Right Sponsor? Before suggesting a sponsorship to any of these clients, you need to conduct a complete analysis of NASCAR. Official sponsors have exclusive rights, which means a competing company could not be a sponsor in that category. For example, if McDonald's is the sponsor for fast food at an event, no other fast food company would be permitted to sponsor that event.

 YOUR OBJECTIVE

Once you know more about NASCAR, you will be in a better position to suggest a client for a sponsorship deal. The bank has branches in four states. The Internet company is a small auction site specializing in sports memorabilia. The cell phone company sells phones and plans with walkie-talkie and messaging features. The apparel retailer is a chain found in major shopping malls around the country.

ASSIGNMENT AND STRATEGY

- **Conduct research** Research NASCAR and its marketing activities. How successful is NASCAR as a business entity? How well does it follow the marketing concept? Who are NASCAR's official sponsors? Do any of them compete with your clients? What is the customer profile of NASCAR's target market?

  Do the demographic, psychographic, geographic, and behavior factors that describe a fan match the target markets of any of your clients? You will need to conduct research at a library and on the Internet. You could review news coverage of NASCAR to learn more about its operations.

- **Develop a SWOT analysis** Use the format for conducting a SWOT analysis to analyze NASCAR's current situation. How effective are its marketing

READ to WRITE

Marketing Activities

Ask students to research and write about an athlete and his or her marketing activities. Ask them to consider what qualities make this athlete an effective spokesperson for the products he or she represents. Students can then organize their findings in a one- to two-page essay. For example, you may want to discuss the Lance Armstrong Foundation and the Nike-sponsored LIVESTRONG™ yellow wristband that stirred a cultural phenomenon around the world. It started out as a reference to Armstrong's cancer story and quickly grabbed hold of the hearts of many people, from professionals to kids to other athletes. Tell students to be sure to discuss in their essays why they think that particular athlete was chosen to market the products and how the athlete's representation may help to improve the products' image or sales.

mix strategies (product, place, price, promotion)? Are there any external threats or opportunities that might impact NASCAR now or in the future?

- **What your project should include** Select a client for NASCAR sponsorship and a specific type of sponsorship. Note the benefits of sponsorship for the client.

  Develop other creative marketing strategies the client could use to make the investment worthwhile.

  Conclude with a strong argument as to why your ideas are feasible and how your company can make it happen for the client you selected.

 YOUR REPORT

Use a word processing program and presentation software to prepare a double-spaced report and an oral presentation for the client you selected. See a suggested outline and key evaluation points at *marketingessentials.glencoe.com/internship*

marketingessentials.glencoe.com

BUILD YOUR PORTFOLIO

Option 1 Internship Report
Once you have completed your Marketing Internship project and presentation, put your written report and a few printouts of key slides from your oral presentation in your Marketing Portfolio.

Option 2 Analyzing a Company
Analyze a company of your choice. Research how the company follows the marketing concept. What does a SWOT analysis reveal? What is the company's market share and who are its competitors? Who are its target markets? What would you suggest to improve its marketing mix strategies? Prepare a written report and an oral presentation using word processing and presentation software. See a suggested outline and key evaluation points at *marketingessentials.glencoe .com/portfolio*

@ Online Action!
Go to *marketingessentials.glencoe .com/Unit/1/DECA* to review the SWOT analysis concepts that relate to DECA events.

Marketing Internship **47**

Unit Review

Have each student select a consumer item that is demonstrable in class, such as a folder, a pen, or a shoe. Have students determine the item's intended consumer market by using the library and Internet to research their answer. Ask: Has the market changed over the years? Items will vary, as will their markets. For example, the athletic shoe is no longer just for competitive athletes, but marketed and purchased by consumers with fashion and comfort in mind. Yet, the ballpoint pen has remained virtually unchanged for decades.

STEP AHEAD
Ask students how marketing and marketing plans influence the free enterprise system and the global economy. Answers will vary but may suggest that marketing helps a business compete nationally and internationally.

Internship Wrap-Up

Ask students what considerations a business should make before sponsoring a NASCAR race team. Have students give their responses in a ten-minute oral report. Encourage the use of presentation software and other visual aids. Answers will vary; responses may include that both parties align on demographics, psychographics, and geographics data.

BUILD YOUR PORTFOLIO

Explain to students that portfolios provide evidence of their knowledge and skills in working with data, people, and concepts. A portfolio is a valuable career tool. Point out to students to present a portfolio in a professional and organized manner. Encourage students to check the portfolio information available at **marketingessentials.glencoe.com/u1/internship**.

Peer Review
Fellow students who share common interests can serve as reviewers of the final portfolios. This review can be completed through the use of a checklist. Go to **marketingessentials.glencoe.com/u1/internship** to find a suggested checklist.

Chapter 3
Political and Economic Analysis

Chapter 4
Global Analysis

Unit Objectives

After completing this unit, students should be able to:

- Summarize the key principles on which a modified free enterprise system is based
- Explain how supply and demand interact to set prices
- Identify various types of economics
- Identify various economic measurements
- Discuss the role of the government and the consumer in a market economy
- Identify the factors of production and relate them to the three basic questions that all economies must answer
- List the goals of a healthy economy, and explain how they are measured
- Describe the four phases of the business cycle

Key to Individualized Activities

L1 Level 1 activities are basic activities and should fall within the range of all students.

L2 Level 2 activities are average activities and should be within the range of average and above average students.

L3 Level 3 activities are challenging activities designed for the ability range of above average students.

Enrichment Resources

PROFESSIONAL ORGANIZATIONS

American Economic Association acaweb.org

National Association for Business Economics nabc.org

MEDIA RESOURCES

Print or online editions of

BusinessWeek businessweek.com

The Economist economist.com

WRITING SUPPORT

Ask students to write a report about the free enterprise system. They should first explain their understanding of it, and then describe its advantages and disadvantages. The final paragraph should give an overall opinion about it. Ask students to keep and review this document as they study Unit 2.

UNIT 2 PLANNING GUIDE AND RESOURCES

CHAPTER	PRINT MATERIALS	TECHNOLOGY RESOURCES
Chapter 3 Section 3.1 Section 3.2	**From Unit 2 Fast File Booklet** Lesson Plans Chapter Summaries Reproducible Masters Reproducible Tests **Print Ancillaries** Student Activity Workbook, Chapter 3 Marketing Math Workbook, Chapter 3 *BusinessWeek* Reader and Case Studies, Chapter 3 Competitive Events Workbook, Unit 2 Marketing Research Project Workbook School-to-Work Activity Workbook	Interactive Chalkboard classroom presentations, Chapter 3 Online Learning Center at marketingessentials.glencoe.com Online Student Edition, Chapter 3 TeacherWorks **Exam**View® Pro Test Generator, Chapter 3 Virtual Business
Chapter 4 Section 4.1 Section 4.2	**From Unit 2 Fast File Booklet** Lesson Plans Chapter Summaries Reproducible Masters Reproducible Tests **Print Ancillaries** Student Activity Workbook, Chapter 4 Marketing Math Workbook, Chapter 4 *BusinessWeek* Reader and Case Studies, Chapter 4 Competitive Events Workbook, Unit 3 Marketing Research Project Workbook School-to-Work Activity Workbook	Interactive Chalkboard classroom presentations, Chapter 4 Online Learning Center at marketingessentials.glencoe.com Online Student Edition, Chapter 4 TeacherWorks **Exam**View® Pro Test Generator, Chapter 4 Virtual Business

National Marketing Education

CHAPTER	SECTION	PERFORMANCE INDICATOR
Chapter 3 **Political and Economic Analysis**	3.1	Explain the types of economic systems (ECO)
		Explain the concept of economic resources (ECO)
		Distinguish between economic goods and services (ECO)
		Describe the nature of economics and economic activities (ECO)
	3.2	Explain the concept of productivity (ECO)
		Explain the concept of Gross Domestic Product (ECO)
		Explain the measures used to analyze economic conditions (ECO)
		Explain the nature of the Consumer Price Index (ECO)
		Determine the impact of business cycles on business activities (ECO)
Chapter 4 **Global Analysis**	4.1	Explain the nature of international trade (ECO)
		Evaluate influences on a nation's ability to trade (ECO)
		Determine the relationship between government and business (ECO)
	4.2	Identify the impact of cultural and social environments on world trade (ECO)
		Explain the nature of trade regulations (BME)

BME Business, Management, Entrepreneurship   **ECO** Economics

Standards Assessment Correlation

SECTION ASSESSMENT		CHAPTER ASSESSMENT						UNIT LAB
Reviewing Key Terms and Concepts	Integrating Academic Skills	Review Facts and Ideas	Build Skills	Develop Critical Thinking	Apply Concepts	Workplace Skills	Net Savvy	Marketing Internship
2	✓	21	27	29, 30	31		✓	✓
1, 3	✓	22, 23	27	29	31		✓	✓
1, 2, 3		22, 23		29, 30				
2, 3	✓	23, 24	26	29	31, 32	✓	✓	✓
1		22	27	29, 30	31, 32		✓	✓
2	✓		27		31		✓	
1, 2, 3	✓	24	26, 27	29	31, 32	✓	✓	✓
	✓			29	32		✓	
3		22, 23, 25	26	29, 30	32	✓		✓
1, 2, 3	✓	6, 7	12	15	17, 18	✓		✓
2, 3	✓	7, 9	13	15	17, 18			✓
2, 3		7, 9, 10	13	16	17			✓
1, 2, 3	✓	6, 11	12, 13	15, 16	17	✓	✓	✓
3		8, 10		16	17			

Online Action! Check the latest updates for national standards and for your state's standards at **marketingessentials.glencoe.com**

Unit Overview

Unit 2 discusses some of the most basic principles of economic and political systems. Chapter 3 deals with the free enterprise system, characterized by private ownership, competition, profit, and risk. Chapter 4 compares the free enterprise system with other economic systems and the various political systems that go with them.

MAKING IT RELEVANT

Inform students that business is becoming increasingly international. Ask them to brainstorm reasons this is so.

Answers may include modern transportation, communication, immigration, and Internet sales resulting in increased international business.

Unit Launch Activity

Have students share their first impressions of the ad on this page. Ask students to discuss the rise in popularity and coverage of organic food and nutrition news in society. They might broaden the discussion of the ad about how peoples' lifestyle choices and health care costs have intersected to influence a portion of the economy.

OUT OF TIME?

If class time is too short to cover all the chapters in this unit, go to Unit 2 in your Fast File Teacher Resources booklet and find the Chapter Summaries for Chapters 3 and 4.

In this unit you will find

- **Chapter 3**
  Political and
  Economic
  Analysis

- **Chapter 4**
  Global Analysis

What keeps beautiful things beautiful?

All those water words borrowed from the beauty world.
Dewy, moisture, shiny, hydrated.
Those things that promise to keep you young and beautiful.
What's in them? Water, mostly. Water is the original beauty product.
It makes you, and everything on earth, look and feel alive.
So which is the fairest water of them all?
Every drop of Evian comes from a spring, deep in the heart of the Alps.
It's naturally filtered for over fifteen years through pristine
glacial rock formations. So it has a neutral pH balance
and a unique blend of minerals, including calcium, magnesium and silica.
No water is better than Evian to help you feel young,
fresh and beautiful.
So when you choose a bottled water to believe in, consider the source.

evian your natural source of youth:

48

 UNIT PROJECT

Marketing Competitive Events

Have students conduct a business survey of local business owners. The survey should focus on why they opened their businesses and how the current economy and government are helping or hindering their success at the present time.

Assessment Guidelines Prepare a rubric for evaluation that includes completeness of original survey, organized information and survey results, analyzed and reported survey findings in comprehensive paper or presentation, and connected workplace and classroom relationships.

Enrichment Assign and review Unit 2 activities in the Competitive Events Workbook.

Marketing Plan

ANALYZE THE AD

Evian is drinking water bottled from a spring in the French Alps. The French food producer Danone sells Evian as a high-quality, healthful drink, and beauty aid. How does this relate to this ad's visual component?

Market Talk The market for bottled water is expanding. Many consumers are willing to pay more for bottled water. Not all bottled water originates from natural springs. Would you choose bottled spring water? Why or why not?

Think and Write Grocery shelves stock bottled water from the United States and from springs around the world. Visit the Web sites of four major bottled water brands. Note their slogans or other marketing messages, then write a paragraph comparing and contrasting how the brands try to appeal to consumers.

@ Online Action! Go to *marketingessentials.glencoe.com/ u2/ad* for an extended activity.

Functions of Marketing
- Marketing-Information Management
- Financing
- Selling
- Distribution
- Product/Service Management
- Promotion
- Pricing

Foundations
- Professional Development
- Economics
- Business, Management, Entrepreneurship
- Communication, Interpersonal Skills

marketingessentials.glencoe.com

ANALYSIS
1
- SWOT
- Economic
- Socio-Cultural
- Political
- Technological

STRATEGY
2
- Promotion
- Place
- Price
- Product

IMPLEMENTATION
3
- Organization
- Management
- Staffing

BUDGET
4
- Cost of sales
- Cost of Promotion
- Incomes and Expenses

CONTROL
5
- Evaluation
- Performance Measures
- Performance Analysis

In this unit

Foundations of Marketing
- Economics

49

Marketing Plan

RELATE THE UNIT TO THE MARKETING PLAN

The four Ps of the marketing mix include product, place, pricing, and promotion. Inform students that the principles explored in Chapters 3 and 4 will help students understand and appreciate why marketing is necessary in a free market economy.

MARKETING PLAN OVERVIEW

Ask students to discuss how a marketing plan would vary in different economies. Answers will vary; students might state that a marketing plan is more aggressive in a free market economy than in a command economy.

Functions of Marketing

Point out to students that Chapters 3 and 4 will help students understand the role of economics as a foundation of marketing.

- **Economics** Financing, pricing, distributing, and selling are all interwoven to keep a business successfully afloat. Economic health, political stability, and socio-cultural differences are some of the factors that affect marketing nationally and internationally.

ANALYZE THE AD

Answers will vary; one possible answer is that the ad's visual component suggests that water is essential to the beauty of the flower—and to human beauty. Ask students to share their opinions.

Market Talk Students might say they would pay more to be sure their water is free from contaminants or that it tastes better. Others might say they would not pay more because their tap water tastes fine. Students might also discuss how origin plays into consumer buying decisions.

Think and Write Students might mention marketing water as a health, beauty, convenience, or athletic product. To facilitate the students' assignment, ask them to think about how demographics, health education, and socio-economic status play into grocery stores' decision to stock goods.

@ Online Action! For instructions, ideas, and answer guide, go to the Teacher Center at **marketingessentials.glencoe.com**

Chapter Overview

In this chapter students will examine different types of economies, including the free enterprise system, and develop key economic concepts such as resources and the ways in which economies are evaluated.

◈ BUILD BACKGROUND ◈

Ask students to name some of the things they or someone they know has purchased. Ask whether students have ever bought something made in another country. How did they know this? Answers may include that product tags and labels or print materials that accompany products give origins. Ask the class to recall the wording of some of these notices, or to share any labels they may have with them.

Why It's Important

Understanding a country's economy helps you understand how that country uses its resources and how it functions in the marketplace. Government and consumers both have a role in the economy.

Prepare to Read

Have students quickly skim the chapter and jot down three to five questions or comments raised by the headings, photos, graphs, and so forth. Share any of these offered by volunteers, and then ask the class to save their work for reference both as they study the chapter and after they have finished it.

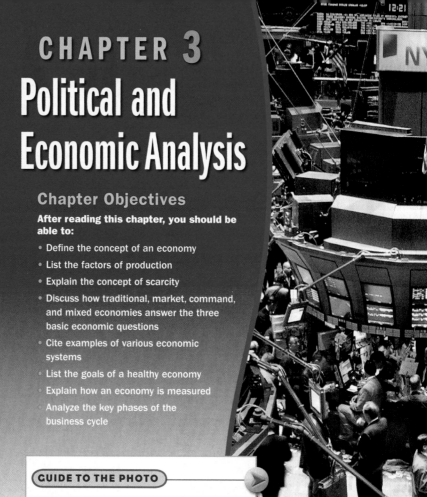

CHAPTER 3
Political and Economic Analysis

Chapter Objectives

After reading this chapter, you should be able to:

- Define the concept of an economy
- List the factors of production
- Explain the concept of scarcity
- Discuss how traditional, market, command, and mixed economies answer the three basic economic questions
- Cite examples of various economic systems
- List the goals of a healthy economy
- Explain how an economy is measured
- Analyze the key phases of the business cycle

◢ GUIDE TO THE PHOTO ◣

Market Talk The stock exchange is one place to take an economy's pulse. When investors are optimistic about the economy, they may buy more stocks. This is a way to own a small part of a company and share in its profits. Investors and consumers usually react to economic and political news and adjust their spending or investing accordingly.

Quick Think Why would a weak economy in some countries affect other countries' economies?

50 UNIT 2 - ECONOMICS

GUIDE TO THE PHOTO

Market Talk Read aloud the explanation of how an exchange functions. Ask students to describe what is happening in the photo. Then survey what they know about stock exchanges. Many students will be familiar with the New York Stock Exchange from seeing news clips of various people given the honor of ringing the opening and closing bells.

Quick Think Buying and selling take place not only within a country but between and among countries. Economic problems in one place can affect all countries that buy or sell to it. These ripple effects can touch many other countries, affecting the world economy.

Follow Up Have students observe or read reports on the stock market for several days. Encourage students to share reactions in class.

Performance indicators represent key skills and knowledge. Relating them to the concepts explained in this chapter is your key to success in DECA events. Keep this in mind as you read this chapter and write some notes each time you encounter material that helps you master a key concept.

These acronyms represent DECA events that involve knowledge of concepts in this chapter.

AAAL	FMAL	MMS	TMDM
AAML	FMDM	QSRM	TSE
ADC	FMML	RMAL	VPM
BSM	FSRM	RMML	
EMDM	HMDM	SMDM	

In all these DECA events you should be able to follow these performance indicators:

- Explain the concept of economic resources
- Describe the nature of economics and economic activities
- Explain the types of economic systems
- Determine the relationship between government and business
- Explain the concept of productivity
- Analyze the impact of specialization/division of labor on productivity
- Explain measures used to analyze economic conditions
- Explain the consumer price index
- Explain the concept of gross domestic product
- Determine the impact of business cycles on business activities
- Describe the nature of current economic problems

DECA PREP

Check your understanding of DECA performance indicators with the DECA activity in this chapter's review. For more information and DECA Prep practice, go to *marketingessentials .glencoe.com/3/DECA*

Chapter 3 - Political and Economic Analysis **51**

CHAPTER 3 Classroom Resources

For the Teacher

- TeacherWorks
- marketingessentials.glencoe.com
- Interactive Chalkboard
- **Exam*View*** ® Pro Test Generator
- Fast File Unit 1

For the Student

- *Marketing Essentials* Online Edition
- Student Activity Workbook
- Marketing Math Workbook
- Marketing Research Project Workbook
- School-to-Work Activity Workbook
- Competitive Events Workbook
- *BusinessWeek* Reader and Case Studies
- marketingessentials.glencoe.com

THE

CONNECTION

DECA events that require knowledge of economic systems are described here. Discuss the performance indicators to make sure students understand how to demonstrate their understanding.

The events acronyms stand for:

AAAL: Apparel and Accessories Marketing Series, AL

AAML: Apparel and Accessories Marketing Series, ML

ADC: Advertising Campaign Event

BSM: Business Services Marketing Series

EMDM: E-Commerce Management Team Decision Making Event

FMAL: Food Marketing Series, AL

FMDM: Financial Analysis Management Team Decision Making Event

FMML: Food Marketing Series, ML

FSRM: Full Service Restaurant Management Series

HMDM: Hospitality Services Management Team Decision Making Event

MMS: Marketing Management Series

QSRM: Quick Serve Restaurant Management Series

RMAL: Retail Merchandising Series, AL

RMML: Retail Merchandising Series, ML

SMDM: Sports and Entertainment Marketing Management Team Decision Making Event

TMDM: Travel and Tourism Marketing Management Team Decision Making Event

TSE: Technical Sales Event

VPM: Vehicles and Petroleum Marketing Series

DECA PREP

Find timed DECA Prep activities correlated to the Competitive Events Workbook for students and DECA tips for teachers at **marketingessentials.glencoe.com /3/DECA**

SECTION 3.1

FOCUS

Introducing the Section

COLLABORATIVE ACTIVITY

Write the word *economy* in the center of the board and circle it. Ask the class to offer other words and ideas that come to mind when they see this word. Create a cluster diagram of responses on the board. Encourage students to copy and save this diagram.

Preteaching Key Terms

Work with students to skim the section to find the key terms and their meanings. Have a volunteer read each term and definition aloud as fellow students take notes.

- economy
- resources
- factors of production
- infrastructure
- entrepreneurship
- scarcity
- traditional economy
- market economy
- command economy

OBJECTIVES

- Define the concept of an economy
- List the factors of production
- Explain the concept of scarcity
- Discuss how traditional, market, command, and mixed economies answer the three basic economic questions
- Cite examples of various economic systems

KEY TERMS

- economy
- resources
- factors of production
- infrastructure
- entrepreneurship
- scarcity
- traditional economy
- market economy
- command economy

What Is an Economy?

READ and STUDY

BEFORE YOU READ
Connect Do you think economic decisions affect your daily life? How?

THE MAIN IDEA
An economy is how a nation makes economic choices that involve how the nation will use its resources to produce and distribute goods and services to meet the needs of its population.

STUDY ORGANIZER
Create a diagram like the one below to record information about market economies and command economies.

Market Economy

Both Market and Command Economies

Command Economy

WHILE YOU READ
Connect Choose a country that interests you and note how its economy works as you study this chapter.

Economic Systems

An **economy**, or economic system, is the organized way a nation provides for the needs and wants of its people. A nation chooses how to use its resources to produce and distribute goods and services. Countries with different economic systems have different approaches when making these choices. A country's resources determine economic activities such as manufacturing, buying, selling, transporting, and

READ and STUDY

BEFORE YOU READ
Remind students that the U.S. economy is a market economy. Tell students that all of them benefit as consumers because many goods and services are produced by and available from our economic system.

THE MAIN IDEA
Stress that the term *economics* refers to how a country or area provides for the needs and wants of its people.

STUDY ORGANIZER
Make your own organizer or download the one provided at **marketingessentials.glencoe.com**. Work with students to make sure that the overlapping portion contains characteristics of both types of economies.

WHILE YOU READ Tell students to also look for connections between the economy of a country and that country's government.

investing. These broad categories of resources are common to all nations and affect how business is done across the world.

Resources

Resources are all the things used in producing goods and services. Economists use the term **factors of production** when they talk about resources. Factors of production comprise four categories: land, labor, capital, and entrepreneurship.

Land

Land includes everything contained in the earth or found in the seas. Coal and crude oil are natural resources, and so is a lake and all of the living things in the lake. Trees and plants, as well as the soil in which they grow, are natural resources. These natural resources are used as the raw material for making goods and creating services that are marketed to customers. Some countries' climate and geography are perfect for attracting tourists. Switzerland is a choice destination for skiing and enjoying mountain landscapes. For this country, the tourist trade is a viable industry that helps to support the economy.

Labor

Labor refers to all the people who work. Labor includes full- and part-time workers, managers, and professional people in both the private and public sectors. Companies may spend a lot of money training employees because a well-trained labor force is an asset to a company. Economies with well-educated and well-trained labor have an advantage over other nations in attracting business.

Capital

Capital includes money to start and operate a business. It also includes the goods used in the production process. Factories, office buildings, computers, and tools are all considered capital resources. Raw materials that have been processed into a more useful form (such as lumber or steel) are also considered capital. Without the capital to run a business, marketers would not have the funds or the resources

needed to develop, to advertise, and to transport goods. Capital includes **infrastructure**, which is the physical development of a country. This includes its roads, ports, sanitation facilities, and utilities, especially telecommunications. These things are necessary for the production and distribution of goods and services in an economy. Think of the challenges of trying to run an international business without dependable phone service.

Entrepreneurship

Entrepreneurship refers to the skills of people who are willing to invest their time and money to run a business. Entrepreneurs organize factors of production to create the goods and services that are part of an economy. They are the employers of a population.

•ECONOMICS and the SHOPPING MALL
Your local shopping mall is a good place to observe economic principles. Labor is represented by salespeople employed in stores and also by all the people who manufactured the products for sale. Capital is at work here, too, as money was invested in manufacturing products and selling them.

Do you think there are examples of the other two factors of production (land and entrepreneurship) in a shopping mall? Explain your answer.

Chapter 3 - Political and Economic Analysis **53**

TEACH

Discussion Starter

RESOURCES

As a group, work with the class to discuss natural resources and why they are important to economics. Explain that they provide the raw materials to manufacture goods or perform sevices.

Concept Development

FACTORS OF PRODUCTION

Have students practice identifying factors of production. First, have students review the factors by rereading the relevant parts in their texts. Then read the following scenario aloud as they listen. Finally, reread each sentence in the scenario, having students identify which of the four factors is described in it.

1. You and a friend want to start a small business for the summer.
entrepreneurship

2. You plan to make and sell custom skateboards.
entrepreneurship

3. Both you and your friend have taken woodworking and metalworking classes in school.
labor

4. Your skateboards will be unique because you will finish them with a heavy clear varnish.
labor

5. You will decorate the boards by suspending dried herbs and leaves in the varnish.
land

6. You have been able to buy materials for making fifteen boards.
capital

7. You will work out of your friend's garage.
capital

Concept Development

SCARCITY

To introduce the students to the concept of scarcity, ask students to research and name differences in infrastructure between heavily industrialized nations and lightly industrialized nations.

TEACHING POINTS

Clarify Explain to students that strong infrastructure enables the flow of commerce from one place to another within a geographic area.

Critical Thinking

Ask students to consider why increasing literacy is an important issue in developing and industrialized countries. Have students share their responses in class.

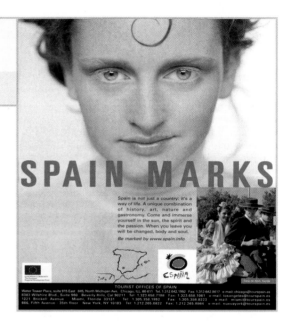

• **SPAIN** Tourism contributes greatly to Spain's economy. Spain wants to attract tourists.

What resources or factors of production make Spain a good vacation spot?

SPAIN MARKS

Spain is not just a country; it's a way of life. A unique combination of history, art, nature and gastronomy. Come and immerse yourself in the sun, the spirit and the passion. When you leave you will be changed, body and soul.

Be marked by www.spain.info

TOURIST OFFICES OF SPAIN

Water Tower Place, suite 915 East 845, North Michigan Ave. Chicago, ILL. 60 611 Tel. 1.312.642.1992 Fax 1.312.642.9817 e-mail chicago@tourspain.es
8383 Wilshire Blvd., Suite 960 Beverly Hills, Cal 90211 Tel 1.323.658.7188 Fax 1.323.658.1061 e-mail losangeles@tourspain.es
1221 Brickell Avenue. Miami, Florida 33131 Tel. 1.305.358.1992 Fax. 1.305.358.8223 e-mail: miami@tourspain.es
666, Fifth Avenue - 35th floor. New York, NY 10103 Tel 1.212.265.8822 Fax 1.212.265.8864 e-mail: nuevayork@tourspain.es

Scarcity

Different economies have different amounts of resources. The United States has an educated labor force, a great deal of capital, an abundance of entrepreneurs, and many natural resources. Most underdeveloped nations are not that fortunate. They might have natural resources to spare but not the capital or the skilled labor to develop them.

Even the United States, with its wealth of resources, cannot meet the needs and wants of all its citizens. Many citizens live below poverty level. Businesses go bankrupt on a regular basis. It is apparent that nations have unlimited wants and needs for growth and development but limited resources to meet them. The difference between wants and needs and available resources is called **scarcity**. Scarcity forces nations to make economic choices.

How Does an Economy Work?

Nations must answer three basic questions when deciding how to use their limited resources. The way nations answer these questions defines their economic system.

1. Which goods and services should be produced?
2. How should the goods and services be produced?
3. For whom should the goods and services be produced?

Economists have studied the way nations answer the three basic economic questions and have classified economic systems into three broad categories: traditional, market, and command economies.

However, no economy is purely traditional, purely market, or purely command. Elements of all three systems are found in all economies.

Traditional Economies

In a **traditional economy**, traditions and rituals answer the basic questions of what, how, and for whom. The answers are often based on cultural or religious practices and ideals

54 UNIT 2 - ECONOMICS

• **A TRADITIONAL ECONOMY** Bhutan, one of the world's smallest and least developed countries, has a traditional economic system based on agriculture and forestry. However, lately it has expanded its tourism industry which brings in elements of a market economy.

What benefits would this change provide for Bhutanese people?

that have been passed from one generation to the next. Typically, these activities are assigned through tradition rather than by choice.

1. **What?** In a traditional economy there is little choice as to what to produce. If people belong to a community of farmers, they farm for generations.
2. **How?** Again, this is bound by traditions. The potter whose family has made clay pots for generations will continue to follow the practices of his or her ancestors.
3. **For whom?** Tradition regulates who buys and sells and where and how the exchange takes place.

Market Economies

In a pure **market economy**, there is no government involvement in economic decisions. Individuals and companies own the means of production and businesses compete for consumers. The government lets the market answer the three basic economic questions.

1. **What?** Consumers decide what should be produced in a market economy through the purchases that they make in the marketplace. Products that do not satisfy consumers' needs are not purchased and therefore will not achieve success.
2. **How?** Businesses in a market economy decide how to produce goods and services. Businesses must be competitive and produce quality products at lower prices than their competitors. It is necessary for them to find the most efficient way to produce their goods and services and the best way to encourage customers to buy these products.
3. **For whom?** In a market economy, the people who have more money are able to buy more goods and services. To obtain money, people are motivated to work and invest the money they make.

Command Economies

A **command economy** is a system in which a country's government makes economic decisions and decides what, when, and how much will be produced and distributed. Under this system, the government controls the factors of production and makes all decisions about their use. In a command economy, the

Individualized Practice

ECONOMIC SYSTEMS

L1 Return to the cluster diagram around *economics* that you and the class made at the beginning of this section. Ask for additions, making sure that students add *factors of production* and indicate knowledge of the four elements (land, capital, labor, entrepreneurship) that fall under it.

L2 Have students write a two-paragraph account discussing two jobs in which they would be considered skilled labor and two others in which they would be considered unskilled.

L3 Using a tree as an example, students should write a one-paragraph explanation of the difference between land and capital as they relate to factors of production.

Enrichment

DEVELOPMENT AND CONSERVATION

Ask students to consider the following two issues:

1. As it moves from a traditional economy, the island country of Sri Lanka, off the coast of India, has lost 90 percent of its forests to logging.
2. During the war between the Soviet Union and Afghanistan in the 1980s, Russian forces destroyed the herds belonging to nomadic people in the northern part of the country. To survive, these people turned to logging, destroying almost all of that region's ancient forests.

Students interested in these issues might research other examples as well as examples of current conservation efforts.

PHOTO GUIDE **A TRADITIONAL ECONOMY**

Discussion Ask students to describe the characteristics of the kind of economy Bhutan now has (traditional) and what type of economy it is moving toward (market).

Caption Answer The tourism industry may provide work outside the traditional economy for a number of Bhutanese, and this budding market economy may create jobs in marketing and sales.

Follow Up Ask students to consider what might be lost in the transition from traditional economies to market economies. (Possible responses: knowing where you belong in society, traditions, folk arts and crafts, natural resources)

Enrichment

ECONOMIC PHILOSOPHIES

Share with students the following information: The modern idea of a communist state grew out of economic conditions in which great wealth and privilege was concentrated in the hands of a very few people while the bulk of the population lived in poverty. Early efforts to change these conditions led to the rise of several different schools of thought regarding communism.

Encourage interested students to research the history of communism in one particular country—such as China, Russia, or Cuba—and how that political or economic system differs or differed from the ideal.

Concept Development

DEVELOPING ECONOMIES

Divide students into three groups. Assign each group one of the three economic systems: capitalism, socialism, and communism. Tell each group to imagine that they are the leaders of a small developing nation. The nation has natural resources of fresh water and natural gas and its major agricultural products are corn, soybeans, and citrus fruits. About one-third of the population lives well, while the remaining two thirds live in poverty. Direct groups to use their economic systems to make decisions regarding what to produce, how to produce, and how to distribute what is produced. Have groups share their ideas with the class.

NET MARKETING

E-Commerce Readiness

International e-commerce is flourishing because even small businesses find that having a Web site can generate sales from around the country and abroad. Amazon.com has gone international and has Web sites in Canada, the United Kingdom, Germany, Japan, and France. If a business is interested in reaching out to the global marketplace, it needs to review the Internet readiness of the countries where it wishes to expand. Most European countries have access to the Internet, but in developing countries the number of Internet hosts is significantly lower. Canada, the United States, and the United Kingdom top the charts with regard to Internet providers. You can check a country's Internet readiness by visiting the CIA *World Fact Book* Web site and selecting Communications from the menu. It lists the number of Internet providers and Internet users for each country. For example, in 2002, Angola had one Internet service provider and an estimated 60,000 users. By comparison, the United States had 7,000 Internet service providers and 165.75 million users in 2002.

THINK LIKE A MARKETER

How could a developing country, such as Angola, use the Internet to improve its economy?

@ Online Action!

Go to *marketingessentials.glencoe.com/3/net* to find a project on e-commerce.

---

government is responsible for answering the three basic economic questions.

1. **What?** One person (often a dictator) or a group of government officials (a central planning committee) decides what products are needed based on what they believe is important.
2. **How?** Since the government owns all means of production, it runs all businesses. It decides how goods and services will be produced. It controls all employment opportunities and workers' benefits. In the most extreme command economy, the government tells people where they will work and how much they will get paid.
3. **For whom?** The government decides who will receive what is produced. In principle, wealth is shared equally among all people to ensure that everyone's basic needs are met. The idea is that all people are equal and are offered the same opportunities. The government provides subsidies

for housing and food for everyone, as well as medical care, education, and jobs for everyone who wants to work.

Mixed Economies

No economy is purely a traditional, market, or command economy. Every economy has influences that make it at least somewhat mixed. The United States is considered a mixed economy with leanings toward a market economy. In a pure market economy, there is no government interference at all. However, there is some government involvement in the U.S. economy through the laws and regulations that businesses must follow. There are also regulations to protect our food, air, and water supplies, and to protect consumers from unsafe products. There are labor laws that determine at what age people can start working, and the minimum wage they earn. The U.S. government provides social programs for those who need help, such as welfare and Medicaid

 marketingessentials.glencoe.com

NET MARKETING

E-Commerce Readiness

Discussion Ask students to discuss why they think the vast majority of current Internet users are from the United States, Canada, and Western Europe.

THINK LIKE A MARKETER **Answer:** Students might suggest that a country such as Angola could use the Internet to identify and purchase products not yet available in its own market and to market products it may produce. A developing country might also profit in general from this access to other nations.

@ Online Action!

For instructions, ideas, and answer guide, go to the Teacher Center at **marketingessentials.glencoe.com**

for the poor and Medicare for the elderly. Because of these characteristics, the U.S. economy is technically a mixed economy.

Since all economies in the world today are mixed, a meaningful economic classification depends on how much a government interferes with the free market. The three political philosophies that have shaped world economies are capitalism, socialism, and communism.

Capitalism

Capitalism is a political and economic philosophy characterized by marketplace competition and private ownership of businesses. It is the same as free enterprise. Government in a capitalist society is also concerned about its people and cares for those who cannot care for themselves. The number of social services, however, does not match that of a socialist country.

Political Foundations of Capitalism

The political system most frequently associated with capitalism is democracy. Nations that practice democracy believe that political power should be in the hands of the people. There is usually more than one political party from which to choose representatives to run the government in a democratic country. People in a democracy are free to elect those candidates who agree with their philosophy on how the government and the economy should be run. The United States and Japan are two examples of countries that are classified as capitalist and have a democratic form of government.

Communism

Communism is a social, political, and economic philosophy in which the government, usually authoritarian, controls the factors of production. There is no private ownership of property or capital. The theory behind these practices is that goods owned in common (by the government representing the community as a whole) are available to all as needed and society is classless.

Characteristics of a Communist Country

In a communist country all people who are able to work are assigned jobs. Theoretically, there is no unemployment.

Employees who do not go to work continue to get paid under this system. The government decides the type of schooling people will receive and also tells them where to live. Housing accommodations are assigned according to need. Food and housing subsidies keep prices low, so everyone has a place to live and food to eat. Medical care is free. However, there is a little or no economic freedom associated with communism. In this system there is no financial incentive for people to increase their productivity.

There are very few communist countries left in the world today. The economies of such countries have collapsed in recent years. The few countries that can still be classified as communist include Cuba and North Korea. China, which is still politically dominated by a communist party, is allowing more and more free enterprise practices. Vietnam and Laos are also following that path.

Socialism

Socialism is a term that originally referred to a system on its way to the communist ideal of a classless society. Today, most countries that are defined as socialist have democratic political institutions. They differ from capitalist nations in the increased amount of government involvement in the economy. The main goal is to meet basic needs for all and to provide employment for many.

Characteristics of Socialist Countries

Socialist countries tend to have more social services to ensure a certain standard of living for everyone. Medical care is free or low cost, as is education. These countries have systems for pensions and elderly care. Businesses and individuals pay much higher taxes than those in capitalist countries, so all contribute to financing government services.

The Role of Government in Socialist Countries

The government runs key industries and makes economic decisions. State-controlled, noncompetitive companies are often found in industries such as telecommunications, natural resources (such as gas, water, and power),

TEACH CONTINUED

Discussion Starter

CAPITALISM

Ask students the different ways they have made money before getting a payroll job. Responses may include babysitting, cutting lawns, making holiday gifts, or bake sales. Inform students that all of these activities mean that they were taking advantage of a free enterprise system.

Concept Development

ECONOMIES IN TRANSITION

Ask students to brainstorm some of the difficulties that can take place in moving from one economic system to another. Ask students to think of ways in which governments and neighboring governments can facilitate this transition.

 Extended Activity

Economic Freedom

Ask students if they believe it is possible to have economic freedom without a democratic form of government. Have students research facts and situations to support their opinions. Then moderate a class discussion.

 Critical Thinking

Ask students to consider in what kind of community communism might be a workable system of government. Let students know that smaller nations or communities often do well with certain aspects of a socialist economy.

Review Guide

CONCEPTS

Have students work in small groups to improvise a brief scenario in which they go shopping in a traditional, command, or market economy. Ask students to share their role plays with the class.

KEY TERMS

Have students work in small groups to review the spellings and definitions of key terms.

ONLINE SELF-ASSESSMENT

Have students go to marketingessentials.glencoe.com for the Section 3.1 practice test.

Individualized Review

L1 Assign and review Chapter 3 activities in the Student Activity Workbook.

L2 Assign and review Chapter 3 activities in the Marketing Math Workbook.

L3 Assign and Review Chapter 3 activities in the *BusinessWeek* Reader and Case Studies.

Marketing Practice

Ask students to work with a partner to explain the relationship between the government of a country and that country's economy. Have both students present their fiindings to the class in a ten-minute oral presentation. Encourage students to use visual aids.

Case Study

Transforming an Economic System: The Reunification of Germany

East Germany was a country of 18 million people whose standard of living, technology, and productivity had fallen far behind that of its western counterpart during more than four decades of Soviet Union-imposed command economics. After the reunification, wages in eastern Germany quickly rose to near the western levels. Western Germany's welfare and pension systems and its business regulations were extended to the east, despite warnings that they were too demanding for the east's lower level of economic development.

A Tough Road to the West

Nearly 20 percent of eastern Germans are still officially unemployed, compared with about nine percent in western Germany. Rethinking eastern Germany's economy became urgent when the European Union (EU) included ten former Soviet satellite countries that had also converted to a market economy. Many Germans fear that vigorous, cheap competition from Poles, Czechs, and other new EU citizens will further harm eastern Germany's economy, increase its reliance on government handouts, and weigh down the overall German economy. About four percent of western Germany's gross domestic product is transferred to the east every year, a massive drain on the nation's finances.

THINK STRATEGICALLY
What can the German government do to fight competition from other new members of the EU?

 Online Action! Go to *marketingessentials.glencoe.com/3/case* to find a project on German reunification.

transportation, and banking. Canada, Germany, and Sweden are generally characterized as having socialist elements in their economies.

Economies in Transition

The breakup of the former Soviet Union probably provides the best example of societies making the difficult change from command to market economies. Most Eastern European countries that were once communist satellites have moved toward global market economies and more democratic forms of government. This means that the state-owned industries have been privatized in many of these nations. Privatization refers to the process of selling government-owned businesses to private individuals.

This process generates much-needed revenue for the governments involved. It also

marketingessentials.glencoe.com

Case Study   Transforming an Economic System: The Reunification of Germany

Discussion Have a student read the Case Study aloud. Lead a discussion about the main points of the article, such as that the former East Germany, a command economy, after reunification has proved to be a financial drain on the socialistic/market economy of the former West Germany.

THINK STRATEGICALLY **Answer:** They might try to move the former East Germany's economy closer to a market economy as quickly as possible.

Online Action! For instructions, ideas, and answer guide, go to the Teacher Center at marketingessentials.glencoe.com

demonstrates a high level of commitment to making the transition to a market system.

A Move Toward Privatization

Today, many socialist countries are selling some of their state-run businesses to help balance their budgets as the costs of national health care, unemployment, and retirement programs soar.

Great Britain has sold its national phone company, national steel company, national sugar company, and several others. Another example of such a transfer, also called privatization, is British Airways. Since its privatization in 1987, the company has been increasing exponentially and has become Europe's number-one airline. These sales generated approximately $63 billion for Great Britain.

Developing Economies

Developing economies are mostly poor countries with little industrialization that are trying to become more prosperous and develop their infrastructure. Much of their success depends on improving the education levels of their labor force and on directing and using foreign investment efficiently.

Chad, a country in central Africa, is a good example of this situation. It is a traditional economy based on agriculture and farming. Cotton, cattle, and gum arabic are its primary exports. However, with an oil field and pipeline project paid for by foreign investors, Chad has begun to develop its oil reserves for export. This investment will help generate much-needed funds for this poor nation to use to improve its infrastructure and its labor resources.

SECTION 3.1

CLOSE

Have students complete at least one of the following activities:

1. Ask students to return to the cluster diagram about economy that each one made at the beginning of this section. Encourage students to add to or modify their definitions of economy according to what they have learned.

2. Ask students to express in their own words the relationship between marketing and the free enterprise system.

3.1 AFTER YOU READ

Reviewing Key Terms and Concepts

1. Explain how the infrastructure of a country is related to the factors of production.
2. What three broad categories do economists use to classify all economic systems?
3. In which economic system does the government let the market answer the three basic economic questions?

Integrating Academic Skills

Math

4. In a country with a population of 290,342,554, how many people would be considered below the poverty line if the percentage in that category was 12.7 percent?

Civics and Government

5. Write a letter to a pen pal in a socialist country to learn more about that country's economic and political system. Be sure to include pertinent questions about taxes, as well as social services for its residents.

 Online Action!

Check your answers at *marketingessentials.glencoe.com/3/read*

AFTER YOU READ

Reviewing Key Terms and Concepts

1. A solid infrastructure, which includes good roads and bridges, reliable utilities such as electricity, telecommunications, and so on, is necessary if a country is to produce necessary goods and services for its people.

2. The three categories are traditional, command, and market.

3. The free enterprise system (market economy).

Integrating Academic Skills

4. 36,873,504; 290,342,554 × .127 = 36,873,504

5. Answers will vary; students should demonstrate an understanding of socialism. Encourage students to review the Case Study on reunification of Germany in this section before they compose their questions.

 Online Action!   Answers at **marketingessentials.glencoe.com/3/read**

FOCUS

Introducing the Section

COLLABORATIVE ACTIVITY

Ask students to discuss what they know about today's economy. Can they give examples of characteristics of recessions or economic booms? Point out that a depression points to a slow economy, while characteristics of a good economy may include high employment, productivity, and stable prices.

Preteaching Key Terms

Read each term aloud and have the class skim the section to find its definition, which a volunteer can then read aloud.

- productivity
- gross domestic product (GDP)
- gross national product (GNP)
- inflation
- consumer price index (CPI)
- producer price index (PPI)
- business cycle
- expansion
- recession
- depression
- recovery

Build Vocabulary

Two often misused terms by students are *net* and *gross*. Call attention to the term *gross*, and have a volunteer look it up in a dictionary. Ask: Which definition most closely applies to the word as it is used in this section? (Answer: with nothing taken out or deducted.) Explain that *gross* refers to the amount of money taken in before costs such as salaries, raw materials, rent, etc., are deducted. Ask whether anybody knows the term that refers to amount of money left after expenses have been paid (net). Have students work with a partner to write a sentence using both words.

60

OBJECTIVES

- List the goals of a healthy economy
- Explain how an economy is measured
- Analyze the key phases of the business cycle

Understanding the Economy

KEY TERMS

- productivity
- gross domestic product (GDP)
- gross national product (GNP)
- inflation
- consumer price index (CPI)
- producer price index (PPI)
- business cycle
- expansion
- recession
- depression
- recovery

Cause and Effect
Note how economic measurements affect each other and how all of them influence business cycles.

READ and STUDY

BEFORE YOU READ
Predict What do you think constitutes a healthy economy?

THE MAIN IDEA
Aspects of an economy such as consumers, businesses, and governments affect each other and the economy in general. Companies need current economic information to make good marketing decisions.

STUDY ORGANIZER
Draw a chart like the one below and use it to take notes about economic measurements.

The Economy and Marketing

If you are a marketer and you want to perform a useful SWOT analysis (see Chapter 2), you need to consider the economic factors that will influence your marketing planning. An understanding of how to measure an economy and what factors contribute to economic strength or weakness is essential. It is only then that you can appreciate how the economy, consumers, businesses, and government influence each other.

READ and STUDY

BEFORE YOU READ
Record students' predictions on the board for review after study of this section.

THE MAIN IDEA
Help set purpose for study by asking students to be alert for examples of this interdependence of consumers, businesses, governments, and the economy.

STUDY ORGANIZER
Make your own organizer or download the one provided at **marketingessentials.glencoe.com**. Work with students to fill in the ovals as they study this material.

WHILE YOU READ
Review the term *business cycle* as you go over this statement with students.

When Is an Economy Successful?

A healthy economy has three goals: increase productivity, decrease unemployment, and maintain stable prices. All nations analyze their economies to keep track of how well they are doing. This analysis allows businesses, consumers, and governments to make appropriate economic decisions.

Economic Measurements

Accurate information about an economy is essential to the whole process. The key economic measurements that nations routinely use to determine their economic strength are labor productivity, gross domestic product, gross national product, standard of living, inflation rate, and unemployment rate.

Labor Productivity

Productivity is output per worker hour that is measured over a defined period of time, such as a week, month, or year. Businesses can increase their productivity in a number of ways.

They can invest in new equipment or facilities that allow their employees to work more efficiently. Providing additional training or financial incentives can also boost staff productivity. Businesses can also reduce their work force and increase the responsibilities of the workers who remain. This makes an organization more financially efficient and more effective. Higher productivity improves a company's profit.

Specialization and division of labor are key concepts related to increasing productivity. An assembly line is an example of specialization and division of labor whereby each part of a finished product is completed by a person who specializes in one aspect of its manufacturing. The theory behind this method of production is that the work can be completed faster and more efficiently when people specialize in their respective areas.

Gross Domestic Product

Most governments study productivity by keeping track of an entire nation's production

It's an engine for economic growth. This V8 engine is part of a very powerful system. Built by the team at Toyota Motor Manufacturing, Alabama, it will provide the power for one of over 100,000 Tundra trucks being manufactured at our plant in Indiana.* It's all part of our commitment to investing in the places where we do business. A commitment that has grown to include eight U.S. manufacturing facilities, research and design centers, sales and marketing operations, and a network of local suppliers and dealers. As a result, Toyota is responsible for creating more than 190,000 jobs across America, and with two new plants under construction in Texas and Tennessee, we'll continue to create opportunities for economic growth.** Local manufacturing, local investment, local jobs – it's a pretty powerful combination.

toyota.com/usa

TOYOTA

• **WHAT IS PRODUCED WHERE** Toyota, a Japanese car manufacturer, produces cars in Japan that are exported and sold in the United States. Toyota has also built factories in North America.

If you buy a car manufactured by Toyota in Alabama, is this car part of the U.S. GDP? Is the same car also part of the U.S. GNP?

Chapter 3 - Political and Economic Analysis **61**

TEACH

Discussion Starter

ECONOMIC MEASUREMENTS

Explain that economic measurements, called indicators, can indicate whether an economy is weak or strong. After students read this section, ask them to come up with examples of positive and negative economic indicators.

employment, worker productivity, prices, GDP

TEACHING POINTS

Illustrate   To illustrate the concept of productivity, ask students how they would measure their own performance if their job were to wash cars for three hours. Students should understand that their productivity is measured in output per worker hour—in this case, the number of cars washed per hour.

Individualized Practice

COMMUNICATION SKILLS

Tell students that they have been asked to suggest ways to increase productivity in a company mailroom. Each day the mailroom handles approximately 500 pieces of mail. These are sorted and delivered to 100 employees.

L1   Have students work in groups of two to three people to discuss improvements. Possible suggestions include implementing sorting methods by floor or last name.

L2   Ask students to suggest ways to improve the process. Have students write a two-paragraph memo communicating suggestions to managers.

L3   Ask students to form small groups and make a formal presentation of their ideas to the class in a role-play of the company executives. The speakers must be prepared to speak persuasively, answer questions, and defend their ideas.

TEACH CONTINUED

Individualized Practice

GROSS DOMESTIC PRODUCT

Have students find The U.S. Bureau of Economic Analysis Web site home page and use it to complete their levelled activity:

L1 Have students make a list of categories found on the home page.
National, International, Regional, Industry

Have them come to class prepared to tell where they found the category Gross National Product.
National

L2 Have students bring in a list of articles found under each of the main categories: National, International, Regional, and Industry.
You may have to print out the list of most recent articles.

L3 Tell students to read the article featured under Latest News Release. Then have them summarize it in their own words and share its contents with the class.
Student summaries should demonstrate an understanding of the article.

Concept Development

STANDARD OF LIVING

Ask students to consider why objective, measurable, economic factors such as GNP and GDP, as well as more subjective factors, such as health care availability, both enter into a nation's standard of living.
Both standards contribute to the quality of life.

TEACHING POINTS

Extend Ask students to brainstorm and share other factors that are included in quality of life.

---

output. Today the principal way of measuring that output in the United States is gross domestic product. **Gross domestic product (GDP)** is the output of goods and services produced by labor and property located within a country. The U.S. Bureau of Economic Analysis publishes a report on the United States' GDP. According to its 2003 report, the GDP grew 3.1 percent that year, which was its best showing since 2000. Total output was $11 trillion, which was $1 trillion more than in 2001.

The GDP is made up of private investment, government spending, personal spending, net exports of goods and services, and change in business inventories (see Figure 3.1). Private investment includes spending by businesses for things like equipment and software, as well as home construction. Government spending includes money spent by local, state, and federal governments. Personal spending includes all consumer expenditures for goods and services. Expanding inventories show that businesses are producing goods that are being stored in their warehouses—that adds to the GDP. Inventories that are shrinking indicate that people are buying more than what was actually produced, so you subtract that figure from the GDP.

As a review, here is the calculation for GDP: Add private investment, government spending, and personal spending, then you either add a trade surplus or subtract a trade deficit and you either add expanding inventories or subtract shrinking inventories.

Since 1991, the United States has been using GDP as its primary measurement of productivity. Before 1991, it used a measurement called gross national product. **Gross national product (GNP)** is the total dollar value of goods and services produced by a nation, including goods and services produced abroad by U.S. citizens and companies. Note the difference between GNP and GDP: With the GNP, it is not where the production takes place but who is responsible for it. For example, Ford is a U.S. corporation that has a plant in England. The portion of Ford's production that occurs in England is included in the U.S. GNP, but not in its GDP.

Standard of Living

A country's standard of living is a measurement of the amount and quality of goods and services that a nation's people have. It is a figure that reflects their quality of life. To calculate the standard of living, you divide the GDP or GNP of a country by its population to get the per capita GDP or GNP. Most industrialized nations enjoy a high standard of living because they have a high level of production.

Some marketers also look at additional factors to get a broader picture of a nation's standard of living. Since some countries provide more in terms of social services for their citizens, social benefits, such as free education and health care provided by the government may be reviewed. Number of households per 1,000 inhabitants with durable goods, such as washing machines, refrigerators, dishwashers, and autos, can be included in the analysis.

Inflation Rate

Inflation refers to rising prices. A low inflation rate (one to five percent each year) is good because it shows that an economy is stable. Double-digit inflation (10 percent or higher), on the other hand, devastates an economy. When inflation gets that high, money does not have the same value it did with lower inflation. The period from the mid-1960s to the early 1980s was a highly inflationary period. Prices tripled in the United States during that time. People who live on a fixed income such as a monthly Social Security check are especially hurt by high inflation.

Controlling inflation is one of a government's major goals. When inflation starts to go up, many governments raise interest rates to discourage borrowing money. The result is a slowdown in economic growth, which helps to bring inflation down.

Two measures of inflation used in the United States are the consumer price index and the producer price index. The **consumer price index (CPI)** measures the change in price over a period of time of some 400 specific retail goods and services used by the average urban household. It is also called the cost of living index. Food, housing, utilities,

---

Online Activity

Bureau of Economic Analysis

Go to the Web site of the U.S. Bureau of Economic Analysis. Print out the page called Frequently Asked Questions. Assign students, pairs, or groups a particular question from the page. Tell them to read the answer to the questions, then bring the answer to class for an informal question-and-answer session.

Figure 3.1 The Gross Domestic Product

• **The United States GDP** GDP, or gross domestic product, is the output of goods and services produced by labor and property located within a country. Here is a look at what made up the U.S. economy in 2003.

Why is consumer confidence so important to the United States' GDP?

15.7% Private Investment is the smallest of the three segments. Investment by businesses is critical to the overall health of the economy.

18.6% Government Spending includes everything the government spends money on: entitlements (Social Security, Medicare, veterans' benefits), defense (weapons, military operations), discretionary spending (NASA, Park Service), and interest payments on the national debt (the deficit).

The deficit: The federal government usually has to borrow money to pay its bills. For example, during the 2003 calendar year, it borrowed $395 billion, which amounts to 2.8 percent of the GDP.

70.4% Personal Spending is the foundation of the economy. Consumer spending includes almost everything people purchase (from a cup of coffee to medical insurance). This is why consumer confidence is so important. Confident consumers spend more money.

Note
If you are saying, "But this adds up to more than 100 percent," you are correct. Two items can shrink the economy's total production: imports and diminishing inventories. When we import more than we export, the resulting trade deficit is subtracted from the GDP. Expanding inventories add to the GDP. Shrinking inventories subtract from the GDP.

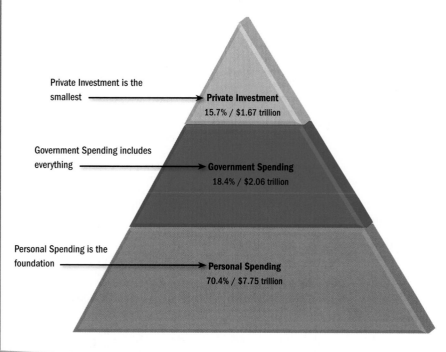

Private Investment is the smallest ——→ **Private Investment**
15.7% / $1.67 trillion

Government Spending includes everything ——→ **Government Spending**
18.4% / $2.06 trillion

Personal Spending is the foundation ——→ **Personal Spending**
70.4% / $7.75 trillion

 Online Action!
Go to *marketingessentials.glencoe.com/3/figure/1*
to find a project on the GDP.

 marketingessentials.glencoe.com

Chapter 3 - Political and Economic Analysis 63

Enrichment

GROSS DOMESTIC PRODUCT
Ask students to research the GDP for one country over the course of ten years. Have students prepare a five-minute oral report comparing and contrasting the changes in GDP across that period. Have students use presentation software or other visual aids in their presentations.

SOCIAL SECURITY
Social Security is a part of government expenditures that serves the retired, elderly, and the disabled. Ask students to research the issue of Social Security such as its origins or current problems, and present their research to the class in a ten-minute report.

Concept Development

INFLATION
Ask students to research and chart the U.S. consumer price index (CPI) and producer price index (PPI) over a six-month period and create a visual aid for the class.

TEACHING POINTS
Extend Inform students that from 1976–1980, the Carter Administration intervened to create jobs for the unemployed. However, oil price hikes in the Middle East caused a large increase in cost of living, and inflation ballooned. Ask interested students to research other inflation trends and how different parts of the government attempt to control it. Have students report their findings informally in class.

Figure 3.1 The Gross Domestic Product

Discussion Ask students to discuss the meaning of this figure. Ask: Are they surprised by anything they read or see? Have students explain their responses.

Caption Answer Consumer confidence means that consumers are spending more money, which results in heightened demand and productivity.

Online Action! For instructions, ideas, and answer guide, go to the Teacher Center at **marketingessentials.glencoe.com**

Follow Up Have interested students research the GDP of the country of their choice and create a similar figure.

TEACH CONTINUED

Individualized Practice

DECISION-MAKING SKILLS

Tell students to use the following scenario to complete their levelled activity:
They work for a small company that makes a component needed in the manufacture of automobile side airbags. The company is thinking of borrowing $1 million to expand its business. However, the federal government just increased interest rates by .75 to control inflation. The rate will be fixed.

L1 Ask students what effect increasing interest rates might have on the economy. It may slow it down.

L2 Tell students that the economy appears to be in recovery, but the increase in interest rates may slow down economic activity. Ask them to recommend whether to continue the expansion in a formal one-page memo.
Recommendations will vary, but some students may indicate that they should borrow money now before interest rates rise again; others may suggest waiting until the interest rate falls.

L3 Tell students that the company recently received a contract for one million parts. The contract will need to be fulfilled in two years. If the company produces the parts earlier, it will receive a $250,000 bonus. Have students orally present recommendations for expanding the business at this point.

---

transportation, and medical care are a few of its components. The core CPI excludes food and energy prices, which tend to be unpredictable. The **producer price index (PPI)** measures wholesale price levels in the economy. It is often a trendsetter, as producer prices generally get passed along to the consumer. When there is a drop in the PPI, it is generally followed by a drop in the CPI.

Unemployment Rate

All nations chart unemployment, or jobless rates. The higher the unemployment rate, the greater the chances of an economic slowdown. The lower the unemployment rate, the greater the chances of an economic expansion. This is true because when more people work, there are more people spending money and paying taxes. Businesses and government both take in more money, and the government does not have to provide as many social services.

Other Economic Indicators and Trends

The Conference Board provides additional indicators to help economists evaluate the performance of the U.S. economy. The Conference Board is a private business research organization that is made up of businesses and individuals who work together to assess the state of the economy. Three Conference Board indicators are the consumer confidence index, the consumer expectations index, and the jobs index, which measures consumers' perceptions regarding the number of jobs available. Consumers are polled to see how they feel about personal finance, economic conditions, and buying conditions. Retail sales are studied to see if consumer confidence polls match consumer actions in the marketplace. Along those same lines, the rate of housing starts is reviewed, as are sales of trucks and autos. These are big expenditures that tend to be affected by the economy and interest rates.

Wages and new payroll jobs provide additional information about the strength of the economy at any given point in time. When everyone is employed, supply and demand theory predicts that wages should increase

---

due to the shortage of workers. Economists study these factors, because they may affect inflation and other economic indicators.

The Business Cycle

History shows that sometimes an economy grows, which is called expansion, and at other times it slows down (contraction). These recurring changes in economic activity are called the **business cycle** (see Figure 3.2).

The business cycle includes the following key phases: expansion, recession, trough, and recovery, at which time expansion begins again. **Expansion** is a time when the economy is flourishing, sometimes referred to as a period of prosperity. Nationwide there is low unemployment, an increase in the output of goods and services, and high consumer spending. This is a good time for new businesses to start up or expand their operations. Expansion continues until it reaches a peak. A peak signifies the end of expansion and the beginning of a recession.

A **recession** is a period of economic slowdown that lasts for at least two quarters, or six months, according to financial experts. The National Bureau of Economic Research (NBER) defines a recession as a significant decline in activity spread across the economy, lasting more than a few months. During a recession, companies reduce their workforces and consumers have less money to spend. Since consumers are spending less, producers make fewer goods and services. Research and development (R&D) is cut back, and future plans for expanding business operations are generally put on hold. Recessions can end relatively quickly or last for a long time. According to the NBER, a recession begins immediately after the economy reaches a peak of activity and ends as the economy reaches its trough. A trough is when the economy reaches its lowest point in a recession, after which economic activity begins to rise.

A **depression** is a period of prolonged recession. During a depression, it becomes nearly impossible to find a job, and many businesses are forced to shut down. During a depression, consumer spending is very low,

---

Critical Thinking

Ask students to identify some ways that the government can improve a depressed economy. Answers might include reducing interest rates, cutting taxes, or instituting federally funded programs.

Figure 3.2 · The Business Cycle

•The Four Key Phases of the Cycle Throughout history, economies have followed a pattern of expansion and contraction called the business cycle. There are four phases in the business cycle: expansion (ended by a peak), recession, trough, and recovery. The length and intensity of each of the phases depends on many factors such as wars, natural disasters, and industrial innovation.

Which phase do you think the United States is in now?

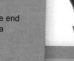

Expansion
During an expansion (prosperity), unemployment is low and consumer confidence and spending are high. Businesses prosper and invest in new product development and research and development. A peak marks the end of this phase and the beginning of a recession.

Recovery
During a recovery, the economy begins to grow again. Jobs are created and consumers begin to spend. With greater demand, the production of goods and services increases. This phase may last a long time.

Recession
During a recession, the economy slows. Businesses lay off workers. Consumer confidence and spending are low. With little demand, the production of goods and services decreases and businesses have little money to invest. A depression is a period of prolonged and deep recession.

Trough
A trough is the low point in the business cycle, marking the transition from recession to recovery. During a trough, the economy stops slowing and may show signs that a recovery is near.

 Online Action! Go to *marketingessentials.glencoe.com/3/figure/2* for a project on the business cycle.

TEACH CONTINUED

Concept Development

THE BUSINESS CYCLE
After students have read this section, ask them to name three factors that affect the business cycle and give an example of each.
business—by expanding and contracting operations; consumers—by spending more or less; government—by setting interest rates

TEACHING POINTS
Extend Explain that layoffs cannot only affect local and national economies, but can damage individual and community self-esteem. Have interested students investigate the human side of mass company layoffs in communities where that company is the major industry (such as auto plants or factories).

 Extended Activity

Unemployment
Have students work in groups to research state laws and services for unemployment. Ask students to research how the state standards differ from or supplement the national services available and present anything they learned to the class in a three- to five-minute oral report.

Figure 3.2 · The Business Cycle

Discussion The Great Depression of the 1930s seems to hold a place in the United States' collective memory. Ask students what they know about this period. Then encourage those interested in doing further research to write a report and present it to the class.

Caption Answer Answers will vary depending on current economic factors.

Online Action! For instructions, ideas, and answer guide, go to the Teacher Center at **marketingessentials.glencoe.com**

Follow Up Have interested students report on lesser-known depressions and recessions and present their findings to the class.

ASSESS

Review Guide

CONCEPTS

Ask students to identify and explain the four steps in the business cycle.
Prosperity (expansion), recession, depression, and recovery are the phases of the business cycle. Prosperity, or expansion, refers to the time when the economy is growing; recession is a period of economic slowdown; depression is a period of prolonged recession; recovery is the period of renewed economic growth that follows.

KEY TERMS

Have students review key terms, their spellings, and their definitions in small groups.

ONLINE SELF-ASSESSMENT

Have students go to marketingessentials.glencoe.com for the Section 3.2 practice test.

Individualized Review

L1 Assign and review Chapter 3 activities in the Student Activity Workbook.

L2 Assign and review Chapter 3 activities in the Marketing Math Workbook.

L3 Assign and review Chapter 3 activities in the *BusinessWeek* Reader and Case Studies.

Marketing Practice

Ask students to create a two-page report on the current economic climate of the United States or another country. Reports should refer to economic indicators such as GDP, unemployment, inflation, and productivity.

GLOBAL MARKET

CHINA

China Anxiously Seeks a Soft Economic Landing

After a decade with the economic throttle wide open, China is overheating, and the country's leaders are grappling with ways to slow the breakneck growth without choking it off. This is difficult for China's leaders, who are fairly new to the market economy game and who lack many of the finely tuned policy tools available to central bankers in the West and in Japan. Prime Minister Wen Jiabao has sought to assure foreign investors that China is taking significant steps to achieve a soft landing. The global recovery now depends on China as one of its twin engines, along with the United States. A hard landing—a steep decline in economic growth leading to higher urban unemployment and a sharp drop in imports—would rattle economies across Asia and the world.

Many Asian nations now depend heavily on selling to China, especially after China's overall imports jumped 40 percent in 2003. The Chinese accounted for a third of all the growth in Japan's exports, and a similar share of South Korea's, and they took two-thirds of the growth in Taiwan's exports. A sharp slowing of growth in China would hit those economies hard.

CRITICAL THINKING

How do you classify China politically and economically? What is its new role in the global economy?

@ Online Action!

Go to *marketingessentials.glencoe.com/3/global* to find a project on China's economy.

---

unemployment is very high, and production of goods and services is down significantly. Poverty results because so many people are out of work and cannot afford to buy food, clothing, or shelter. The Great Depression of the early 1930s best illustrates this phase of the business cycle.

Recovery is the term used to signify a period of renewed economic growth following a recession or depression. This is where the cycle begins again with economic expansion. The GDP begins to increase. During this stage, business picks up, people find jobs, and the demand for goods increases. Thus, recovery is characterized by reduced unemployment, increased consumer spending, and moderate expansion by businesses. Periods of recovery differ in length and strength.

Factors That Affect Business Cycles

Business cycles are affected by the actions of businesses, consumers, and the government. In turn, businesses, consumers, and the government are affected by business cycles.

Businesses tend to react to business cycles by expanding their operations during periods of recovery or expansion and curtailing their operations during periods of recession. During an expansion they may invest in new properties, equipment, and inventories, as well as hire more employees. When the economy moves into a recession, one of the first things a business does is lay off workers. Businesses also cut back on inventories to match lowered demand for goods and services in a recession or depression. This has a ripple effect in the economy

 marketingessentials.glencoe.com

GLOBAL MARKET

China Anxiously Seeks a Soft Economic Landing

Discussion Ask students what they already know about China and its economy and list their responses on the board. Then read the article in class, and discuss what students learned or what misperceptions were corrected. Point out that along with the United States, China is a "twin engine" of world trade, active in both importing and exporting.

CRITICAL THINKING
Answer: Answers will vary; students might describe China as a communist or totalitarian society but still recognize the country as a major player in the global economy.

@ Online Action!
For instructions, ideas, and answer guide, go to the Teacher Center at marketingessentials.glencoe.com

as business suppliers feel the effects of lost revenues.

During a period of recession, consumers' biggest fear is losing their jobs; the other big fear is a decrease in wages. These fears result in a loss of consumer confidence in the economy, which reduces consumer spending. Reduced consumer spending causes businesses to reduce their operations in response to lower demand. The opposite is true during periods of prosperity and recovery. During those periods, consumers are more optimistic. They spend more money on material goods and luxury items. Businesses will also respond by producing more goods. This cycle shows how important consumers are to an economy—consumer spending accounts for more than two-thirds of the U.S. GDP.

Government's Influence Over Business Cycles

A government influences business cycles through its policies and programs. Taxation has a strong bearing on what happens in an economy. As the government requires more money to run programs, higher taxes are needed. When taxes are raised, businesses and consumers have less money with which to fuel the economy. When the economy needs a boost, the government may reduce interest rates, cut taxes, or institute federally funded programs to spark a depressed economy. When an economy worsens, the Federal Reserve generally responds by lowering interest rates to encourage businesses and consumers to spend. Mortgage rates are low because the commercial banks' prime lending rate reflects the Fed's funding rate. For example, when the Federal Fund rate was at one percent, the prime lending rate was around four percent and mortgage rates were between five and six percent. If inflation becomes a problem, interest rates might be increased to discourage buying on credit.

Another action a government can take to spur economic growth is illustrated by Japan's decision to hand out free shopping coupons to its citizens. In 1999, Japan slashed income tax rates and distributed nearly $6 billion in shopping coupons to encourage people to spend. The government took these dramatic actions to spur consumption and revive an economy that was in its worst recession in 50 years.

3.2 AFTER YOU READ

Reviewing Key Terms and Concepts

1. How can businesses increase productivity?
2. Explain the difference between GNP and GDP.
3. What three factors affect business cycles?

Integrating Academic Skills

Math

4. If a country's GDP is $10 billion and its population is 250,000, what is its per capita GDP?

Civics and Government

5. Write a short newspaper article for the school newspaper regarding the current economy of the United States and why it is important for teenagers to understand economic indicators.

 Online Action!

Check your answers at *marketingessentials.glencoe.com/3/read*

CLOSE

Ask students to explain why it is so important to be able to measure an economy and chart its movement at any given time.

Once an economy is evaluated and placed in the context of the business cycle, economists, political leaders, and others can make decisions leading to economic improvements.

Critical Thinking

Ask students to imagine that they have each been given $1,000. Would they spend it or save it? Why? Does their choice indicate anything about the economy of the present day? Have students share their answers in class.

AFTER YOU READ

Reviewing Key Terms and Concepts

1. Businesses can increase productivity by investing in new equipment or facilities, educating staff for greater productivity, providing financial incentives to workers, or reducing the workforce and increasing responsibilities of those workers who remain.

2. GDP is the output of goods and services produced by labor and property located in a country. GNP is the total dollar value of goods and services produced by a nation, including goods and services produced abroad by U.S. citizens and companies.

3. The three factors are consumers, businesses, and the government.

Integrating Academic Skills

4. The per capita GDP is $40,000; $10 billion ÷ 250,000 = $40,000.

5. Articles should make the point that knowledge of economics is essential to becoming an informed voter, to electing officials whose economic plans are in accordance with one's own beliefs.

Online Action!   Answers at **marketingessentials.glencoe.com/3/read**

CAREERS IN MARKETING

Lifelong Learning

CAREER INFORMATION

Have students go to marketingessentials.glencoe.com and find the Chapter 3 Careers page and then click on the link for the American Marketing Association's Career Strategies and Tips. Ask students to select one article to read and write a three-paragraph summary.

FREE ENTERPRISE

Sales is an important part of the free enterprise system. Studying and analyzing your customer, consumer issues, and developments in your market will help marketers and consumers decide what to sell and what to buy. Sales experience provides an excellent practical introduction to a country's basic economic system.

Primary Source

Ask students to go to marketingessentials.glencoe.com and find Chapter 3 resources. Ask them to click on the link for the American Marketing Association's marketing dictionary and read definitions of any terms they find that are related to economies and the free enterprise system.

THINKING CRITICALLY

Experience as a sales representative enhances understanding of the customer, the market, marketing strategies and techniques, and the business cycle.

@ Online Action!

For instructions, ideas, and answer guide, go to the Teacher Center at marketingessentials.glencoe.com

---

CAREERS IN MARKETING

OLIVIER TRAVERS
INTERNET MARKETING CONSULTANT
PUBLISHER,
THEENDOFFREE.COM

What do you do at work?
I typically act as the hub of communication between team members and contractors who handle marketing, development, and design. Most clients already have an Internet presence they want to grow or improve. I help clients determine what types of technical services they require, and in many cases, which vendors will be able to provide the best and most efficient services. I have a background in sales and channel marketing so I'm always interested in helping companies set up partnerships and affiliate programs, as well as launch and grow outbound sales efforts.

What skills are most important to you?
Salesmanship, listening skills, empathy, self-motivation and autonomy, and the ability to keep learning on the fly. Nothing beats working as a sales rep before getting into marketing and consulting. It gives you a firm grasp of how customers think, what a sales cycle is, how to close a sale, and it forces you to be pragmatic and realistic.

What is your key to success?
Personal networking, providing value to people who will partner with me or will send me leads in the future. Also, the ability to connect the dots between various disciplines: marketing, sales, business operations, and online technology.

Aptitudes, Abilities, and Skills

Creativity, sales ability, tenacity, personal organization, and time and project management skills

Education and Training

Advanced degrees in marketing and general business are helpful.

Career Path

Marketing careers often begin with entry-level sales positions in companies of all types and sizes.

THINKING CRITICALLY

How does working as a sales representative prepare you for a career in marketing?

@ Online Action!

Go to marketingessentials.glencoe.com/3/careers to find a career-related activity.

 marketingessentials.glencoe.com

Test-Taking Strategies

Have students review the After You Read section review questions they completed at the end of each section in this chapter. Ask students to work in groups to clarify their answers to each question in the section reviews. Encourage groups to share answers.

FOCUS on KEY POINTS

SECTION 3.1

● An economy is how a nation chooses to use its resources to produce and distribute goods and services to provide for the needs and wants of its people.

● The four factors of production are land, labor, capital, and entrepreneurship. Due to the possibility of scarcity, all nations must answer three fundamental economic questions: what will be produced, how will it be produced, and who should get what is produced. These questions are answered differently in traditional, market, command, and mixed economies.

● Economic/political philosophies of capitalism, socialism, and communism tend to encourage different types of economic systems.

SECTION 3.2

● The characteristics of a healthy economy are high productivity, stable prices, and low unemployment. Economic indicators such as productivity, gross domestic product (GDP), standard of living, CPI, consumer confidence, and unemployment rates can measure an economy.

● The key phases of the business cycle are expansion, peak, recession, trough, and recovery. Economic business cycles affect businesses, consumers, and governments and they in turn affect business cycles, both domestically and globally.

REVIEW VOCABULARY

List a synonym or a brief definition for each key term.

1. economy (p. 52)
2. resources (p. 53)
3. factors of production (p. 53)
4. infrastructure (p. 53)
5. entrepreneurship (p. 53)
6. scarcity (p. 54)
7. traditional economy (p. 54)
8. market economy (p. 55)
9. command economy (p. 55)
10. productivity (p. 61)
11. gross domestic product (GDP) (p. 62)
12. gross national product (GNP) (p. 62)
13. inflation (p. 62)
14. consumer price index (CPI) (p. 62)
15. producer price index (PPI) (p. 64)
16. business cycle (p. 64)
17. expansion (p. 64)
18. recession (p. 64)
19. depression (p. 64)
20. recovery (p. 66)

REVIEW FACTS and IDEAS

21. What is an economy? (3.1)
22. Name the factors of production necessary to create goods and services in an economy. (3.1)
23. Explain the concept of scarcity. (3.1)
24. What are the three goals of a healthy economy? (3.2)
25. Describe the key phases of a business cycle. (3.2)

Chapter 3 - Political and Economic Analysis 69

REVIEW FACTS and IDEAS

21. An economy is the organized way a country provides for the wants and needs of its people.
22. The four factors of production include land, labor, capital, and entrepreneurship.
23. Scarcity occurs when the people's wants and needs are greater than the resources available.
24. The three goals of a healthy economy are to increase productivity, decrease unemployment, and maintain stable prices.
25. Prosperity, or expansion, refers to the time when the economy is growing; recession is a period of economic slowdown; depression is a period of prolonged recession; recovery is the period of renewed economic growth that follows.

FOCUS on KEY POINTS

Call attention to each point in turn. Have a volunteer read the point and then encourage students to ask questions or request clarification. Close by reading the point one last time to help students synthesize the information.

REVIEW VOCABULARY

See glossary for definitions of **1–20.** A sample answer might read:

1. An *economy* is the organized way a nation provides for the needs and wants of its people.

BUILD SKILLS

26. Workplace Skills

Answers should include that interest rates are usually low during periods of recession, when it is hoped that the low rates will stimulate the economy by encouraging investing. As the economy improves, rates go up.

27. Technology Applications

Reports should demonstrate an understanding of the country's economic indicators. Students should cite and give credit to any sources they use. Students should also demonstrate facility with using the software to organize and present their findings.

28. Math Practice

$510, $465; $1,200 − ($450 + $150 + $50 + $40) = $510; $450 + ($450 × 0.10) = $495; $1,200 − ($495 + $150 + $50 + $40) = $465.

DEVELOP CRITICAL THINKING

29. What Is Your Role in the Economy?

Student answers will vary but should show an understanding of the concepts of economy, goods and services, labor, and their role as a consumer and a citizen.

30. Evaluate the Impact of Economics on Marketing

Student reports will vary but should demonstrate that marketers must be aware of the general economic situation in order to reach consumers. For example, in a slow economy, marketers might appeal to the concept of value in order to make more sales or increase market share and profit without increasing price.

BUILD SKILLS

26. Workplace Skills

Human Relations Assume you work in a bank and an elderly couple on a fixed income asks you why the interest rate is so low on their savings account. How would you explain the basis for fluctuations in interest rates?

27. Technology Applications

Compare Two Economic Systems Select a foreign country and compare its economic system with that of the United States. Use the Internet to research all economic aspects of this country. If you lived in that country, how different would your life be? Why? Be prepared to share your insights with classmates. Use a word processing program and presentation software to prepare an oral report for your class.

28. Math Practice

Fixed Income Madeline, a retiree, lives on a fixed income of $1,200 a month. Each month she spends $450 for rent, and she budgets $150 for food, $50 for clothing, and $40 for various needs. She deposits the money that is left over into her savings account. How much money does she put into her savings each month? If her rent is increased by ten percent, how much money does she have left to put into her savings?

DEVELOP CRITICAL THINKING

29. What Is Your Role in the Economy?

Consider the part you play in the U.S. economy. Consider the following questions:
- What goods and services do you consume?
- What labor do you provide?
- What are some of your rights as citizens and consumers?
- What are some of your responsibilities?

30. Evaluate the Impact of Economics on Marketing

How is the current economy affecting the way businesses market their goods and services? Select two specific examples that interest you and examine these businesses in relation to the economy. Are they part of an industry that is expanding? Are there any new laws that affect them? Do they face global competition? How do these factors influence the marketing strategies of these companies?

Formative Assessment

Formative assessment is an essential component of classroom work. This type of assessment provides information that is then used as feedback to modify teaching and meet student needs.

L1 Ask students to work in pairs to explain the key terms in this chapter to one another.

L2 Ask students to define and give examples of the different types of economies.

L3 Have students compare and contrast the economic system of two different countries, or of one country which has changed its economic system.

Reteach If the results of this formative assessment seem low, consider the following activity:

Ask students to read section subheads aloud and name two important ideas listed under each subhead.

CHAPTER **3** REVIEW

APPLY CONCEPTS

31. Researching Different Economic Systems

Select a foreign country that either has gone through a major transformation from a command economy to a market-oriented economy or is an emerging country that is trying to become more industrialized. What obstacles did the nation have to overcome? What is its current economic situation? What is the future of this nation's economy?

Activity Write a three-page report using a word processing program. Cite your sources in a written bibliography. Be prepared to share your findings with classmates in an oral presentation.

32. Analyzing the Current U.S. Economy

Using government Internet sites and other sources, research the current U.S. productivity, GDP, standard of living, inflation, CPI, interest rates, and unemployment rates. Use the figures you gather to determine the business cycle phase of the U.S. economy at the present time.

Activity Using presentation software, create an oral report based on your findings. For all facts presented, cite the source of that data directly on the presentation slide and in a written bibliography.

NET SAVVY

33. What Is the Current State of the Economy?

Visit the Web site for the United States Department of Commerce to find current information on economic indicators. Prepare a list of the economic indicators that are provided at this Web site.

marketingessentials.glencoe.com

THE CONNECTION

Role Play: Assistant Manager

Situation Assume the role of assistant manager of an online business that specializes in antique prints, matting, and custom framing. Your customers can call your toll-free phone line or communicate by e-mail. You do business through the business's Web site. The business's owner (judge) has just received an e-mail from one of your best customers requesting that you look for a special print.

Activity You are to compose an e-mail to assure the customer that you will make every effort to obtain the print and that regular communication will be maintained about the progress of the search.

Evaluation You will be evaluated on how well you meet the following performance indicators:

● Write business letters

● Use communications technologies/systems (e.g., e-mail, faxes, voice mail, cell phones, etc.)

● Explain the nature of written communications

● Handle customer inquiries

● Demonstrate a customer-service mindset

 Online Action!

For more information and DECA Prep practice, go to *marketingessentials.glencoe .com/3/DECA*

APPLY CONCEPTS

31. Researching Different Economic Systems

As students make their choices, move among them offering suggestions as needed, guiding them to choices about which they will be able to gather sufficient information. Make sure they understand that the completed report will be judged both on content and on use of the word processing program to create a professional-appearing document.

32. Analyzing the Current U.S. Economy

Make sure students understand that assessment of presentations will be based on both the report's content and on the quality of the oral presentation. Encourage a practice run-through to make sure equipment required is in good working order.

NET SAVVY

33. What Is the Current State of the Economy?

Help students make inferences about the economy based on these indicators.

MINI-QUIZ

Have students write or volunteer answers as you read each item aloud.

1. Name the four factors of production.
(land, labor, capital, and entrepreneurship)

2. What are the three goals of any economy?
(stable prices; low unemployment; high productivity)

3. Name the four stages of the business cycle.
(prosperity, or expansion, recession, depression, recovery)

For an expanded chapter quiz, go to Chapter 3 in the TeacherWorks CD-ROM and to Chapter 3 in the **ExamView**® Pro Test Generator CD-ROM.

THE CONNECTION

Students should be evaluated according to the performance standards noted in the role play. For another DECA role play, go to the Competitive Events Workbook or the Student Activity Workbook, or go to **marketingessentials.glencoe.com/3/DECA**

 Online Action! For instructions, ideas, and answer guide, go to the Teacher Center at **marketingessentials.glencoe.com**

DECA Advisors Corner

DECA's Free Enterprise Event encourages class participation and allows students to expand on the subjects presented in this chapter. Students will formulate and give presentations about the free enterprise system to organized groups or the general public and record their experiences in a written manual. Students can use different media to document their experiences.

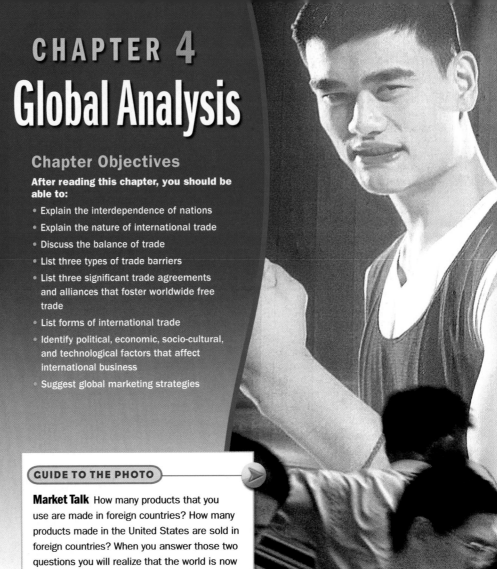

CHAPTER 4

Chapter Overview

This chapter explores international trade in the context of the interdependence of nations—what is called the global marketplace. It examines the effects of international trade on the United States and the countries with whom the U.S. trades. Students also examine government involvement in international trade, how politics affects the global market, and the practical side of doing business abroad.

BUILD BACKGROUND

Tell the class that in the 1960s, social commentator Marshall McLuhan coined the term *global village* to refer to the contemporary world, where electronic communications made all the people on earth neighbors. Ask students whether they think that this description is more or less true today. Have them provide examples to support their opinions.

Why It's Important

For today's marketing student, the whole world is the marketplace. Learning how to move through that world, made up as it is of many different countries, each with its own laws and rules and culture, is essential to successful marketing.

Prepare to Read

Call students' attention to the title of this chapter, Global Analysis, and the titles of the two sections, *International Trade* and *The Global Marketplace*. Then give the class a couple of minutes to jot down any comments, questions, or other ideas called to mind by these titles. Have students save these notes to return to after study of the chapter.

CHAPTER 4
Global Analysis

Chapter Objectives

After reading this chapter, you should be able to:

- Explain the interdependence of nations
- Explain the nature of international trade
- Discuss the balance of trade
- List three types of trade barriers
- List three significant trade agreements and alliances that foster worldwide free trade
- List forms of international trade
- Identify political, economic, socio-cultural, and technological factors that affect international business
- Suggest global marketing strategies

GUIDE TO THE PHOTO

Market Talk How many products that you use are made in foreign countries? How many products made in the United States are sold in foreign countries? When you answer those two questions you will realize that the world is now a global marketplace.

Quick Think What factors should a company consider when deciding if it should get involved in international trade?

GUIDE TO THE PHOTO

Market Talk Lead a discussion asking students to name familiar imported products or to give examples of products that the United States imports or exports.

Quick Think Write suggestions on the board as they are offered. Answers may include laws of the host country regarding marketing, or the socio-cultural customs and accepted behaviors of a particular country.

 Follow Up Ask students: If they could market one product of their choosing in any foreign country, what product and country would they choose? Why?

Performance indicators represent key skills and knowledge. Relating them to the concepts explained in this chapter is your key to success in DECA events. Keep this in mind as you read this chapter.

These acronyms represent DECA events that involve knowledge of concepts in this chapter.

AAAL	FMAL	MMS*	TMDM*
AAML*	FMDM*	QSRM*	TSE*
ADC*	FMML*	RMAL	VPM
BSM	FSRM*	RMML*	
EMDM*	HMDM*	SMDM*	

In all these DECA events you should be able to follow these performance indicators:

- Explain the nature of international trade
- Identify the impact of cultural and social environments on world trade
- Explain marketing and its importance in a global economy

Events with an asterisk (*) include:

- Evaluate influences on a nation's ability to trade

Some events include other indicators:

EMDM	Describe the impact of e-commerce on international trade
SMDM	Describe the impact of international policies on sports and entertainment marketing
FMDM	Identify global exchange services
RMAL	Explain the effect of international trade on retailing
AAAL	Explain the effect of international trade on retailing
VPM	Explain the effect of international trade on retailing
FMAL	Explain the effect of international trade on food marketing

DECA PREP

Check your understanding of DECA performance indicators with the DECA activity in this chapter's review. For more information and DECA Prep practice, go to *marketingessentials.glencoe.com/4/DECA*

marketingessentials.glencoe.com

Chapter 4 - Global Analysis **73**

DECA events that require knowledge of global analysis are described here. Discuss the performance indicators to make sure students understand how to demonstrate their understanding.

The events acronyms stand for:

AAAL:	Apparel and Accessories Marketing Series, AL
AAML:	Apparel and Accessories Marketing Series, ML
ADC:	Advertising Campaign Event
BSM:	Business Services Marketing Series
EMDM:	E-Commerce Management Team Decision Making Event
FMAL:	Food Marketing Series, AL
FMDM:	Financial Analysis Management Team Decision Making Event
FMML:	Food Marketing Series, ML
FSRM:	Full Service Restaurant Management Series
HMDM:	Hospitality Services Management Team Decision Making Event
MMS:	Marketing Management Series
QSRM:	Quick Serve Restaurant Management Series
RMAL:	Retail Merchandising Series, AL
RMML:	Retail Merchandising Series, ML
SMDM:	Sports and Entertainment Marketing Management Team Decision Making Event
TMDM:	Travel and Tourism Marketing Management Team Decision Making Event
TSE:	Technical Sales Event
VPM:	Vehicles and Petroleum Marketing Series

DECA PREP

Find timed DECA Prep activities correlated to the Competitive Events Workbook for students and DECA tips for teachers at **marketingessentials.glencoe.com/4/DECA**

CHAPTER 4   Classroom Resources

For the Teacher

- TeacherWorks
- **marketingessentials.glencoe.com**
- Interactive Chalkboard
- **Exam*View*®** Pro Test Generator
- Fast File Unit 2

For the Student

- ***Marketing Essentials*** Online Edition
- Student Activity Workbook
- Marketing Math Workbook
- Marketing Research Project Workbook
- School-to-Work Activity Workbook
- Competitive Events Workbook
- ***BusinessWeek*** Reader and Case Studies
- **marketingessentials.glencoe.com**

FOCUS

Introducing the Section

COLLABORATIVE ACTIVITY

Ask students to work in groups to name items that they have seen that were made or manufactured in some other country. List these as they are suggested. When you have a number of items listed, ask students how consumers might react if the products were no longer available for import.

Preteaching Key Terms

Pronounce each term for students, and then have students skim the selection to find the term and its definition in context. Select a student to read that word and its definition aloud to the class.

- international trade
- imports
- exports
- balance of trade
- free trade
- tariff
- quota
- embargo
- protectionism
- World Trade Organization (WTO)
- North American Free Trade Agreement (NAFTA)
- European Union (EU)

OBJECTIVES

- Explain the interdependence of nations
- Explain the nature of international trade
- Discuss the balance of trade
- List three types of trade barriers
- List three significant trade agreements and alliances that foster worldwide free trade

KEY TERMS

- international trade
- imports
- exports
- balance of trade
- free trade
- tariff
- quota
- embargo
- protectionism
- World Trade Organization (WTO)
- North American Free Trade Agreement (NAFTA)
- European Union (EU)

WHILE YOU READ

Connect Observe signs of global trade as you shop for groceries, clothes, and other items.

International Trade

READ and STUDY

BEFORE YOU READ

Connect Consider all the reasons why international trade is flourishing around the world.

THE MAIN IDEA

Since no country has all the resources it needs, nations rely on each other to provide goods and services that they do not have. This interdependence, along with trade agreements among countries, creates a global marketplace.

STUDY ORGANIZER

On a chart like the one below, organize the key concepts related to international trade.

International Trade

Balance of Trade	Trade Barriers	Trade Agreements
_____	_____	_____
_____	_____	_____
_____	_____	_____
_____		

Nature of International Trade

The global marketplace exists because countries need to trade with one another. It continues to expand because of the reduction of trade restrictions throughout the world. This new global marketplace makes all people and businesses in the world both potential customers and potential employees or employers.

READ and STUDY

BEFORE YOU READ

Ask students to share their responses. For example, they might consider the effects of the Internet on the needs and wants of people all over the world.

THE MAIN IDEA

Go over the points made here: 1) No country has all of the resources it needs. 2) This creates interdependence. 3) In some cases, written trade agreements have been drawn up between countries. 3) Countries benefit from these exchanges of goods and services.

STUDY ORGANIZER

Make your own organizer or download the one provided at marketingessentials.glencoe.com. Show students how to begin filling out the blanks.

WHILE YOU READ Tell students that they can take notes while they are shopping.

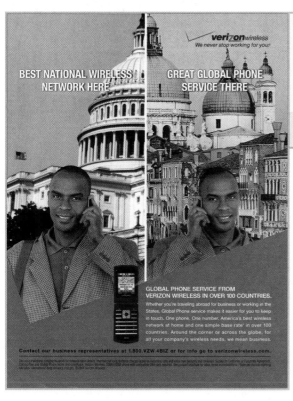

• **VERIZON GLOBAL** Companies do not necessarily have to establish a business abroad to cash in on the global market. Verizon, a U.S. leading wireless communication company, tries to fulfill business travelers' needs.

Why do you think Verizon decided to market global phone service?

International trade is the exchange of goods and services among nations. **Imports** are goods and services purchased from other countries. Conversely, **exports** are goods and services sold to other countries. These exchanges occur among businesses, but they are controlled by the governments of the countries involved.

Interdependence of Nations

Most countries do not produce or manufacture all the goods and services they need. They get some of their goods and services from other nations. This economic interdependence

happens because each country possesses unique resources and capabilities. The principle of economic independence is fundamental to marketing in a global environment.

Absolute Advantage and Comparative Advantage

Any nation that takes part in international trade may have an economic advantage over its trading partners. There are two types of advantages in international trade—absolute and comparative.

Absolute advantage occurs when a country has natural resources or talents that allow it to

Chapter 4 - Global Analysis **75**

75

TEACH CONTINUED

Concept Development

BENEFITS OF INTERNATIONAL TRADE

Ask students to list some of the benefits of international trade. Have students volunteer examples of each type of benefit.

Answers may include increased competition, which leads to better quality goods and lower prices, higher employment rates, improvement in standards of living, and increased purchasing options.

Build Vocabulary

Point out to students that the word *interdependence* is composed of the root *dependence* and the prefix *inter-,* which means "between or among." Ask students to compare this prefix with *intra-,* which means "within, or on the inside." Then put these sentences on the board:

1. We will study *interstate* commerce.

2. We will study *intrastate* commerce.

Ask which word means within a state (intrastate) and which means between or among states (interstate).

Critical Thinking

Ask students to explain why a skilled labor force is considered an exportable resource.

MARKET TECH

Wi-Fi in Europe: Not So Hot

The Starbucks coffee shop in London has a high-speed Wi-Fi (wireless fidelity) network that its customers can use to surf the Web at a price of 5.50 pounds (about $10.31 or €8.25) an hour. The Starbucks shop is one of thousands of coffee shops, airport lounges, hotels, and other public places worldwide where consumers can use laptops or personal organizers with Wi-Fi connections to surf the Internet.

Prices Influence Interest

Analysts say high prices in Europe are putting off many potential users. By comparison, Wi-Fi spots in the United States are a lot less expensive and are aimed at a wide audience. For example, McDonald's offers Wi-Fi access for less than $5 (€4) an hour in the United States. One of the reasons given for the high price in Europe is that Wi-Fi services are aimed at business travelers who are not concerned about price.

Europe is adding more Wi-Fi hot spots in airports and hotels, where business travelers spend much of their time. The average price in European hotels for business travelers was about $20 per day in 2004.

THINK LIKE A MARKETER

Assume you work for a U.S. company, such as Verizon or T-Mobile, both of which offer Wi-Fi service. How would you recommend they price their service in foreign countries?

@ Online Action!

Go to *marketingessentials.glencoe.com/4/tech* for an activity on technology and international business.

---

produce an item at the lowest cost possible. China produces 80 percent of all the silk in the world, which gives it absolute advantage in the silk market.

Comparative advantage is the value that a nation gains by selling what it produces most efficiently. When countries specialize in products or services well suited to their capabilities, they may gain a comparative advantage in international trade. Businesses in those countries produce these goods and services to satisfy economic needs in an international economy.

The United States has a comparative advantage in producing high-tech goods and services because of this country's infrastructure, raw materials, and educated labor force. These products include airplanes, computers, high-tech machinery, entertainment, and telecommunications.

Some emerging nations have large, unskilled labor forces available at a low cost. Labor-intensive industries—ones that rely on labor as opposed to machinery—do well in such an environment. Emerging nations can produce labor-intensive products such as toys, clothing, and shoes at a lower cost than most industrialized nations. They have a comparative advantage when manufacturing these goods. It is more cost effective for high-wage countries like the United States to buy those items from emerging nations rather than making them themselves.

Benefits of International Trade

Consumers, producers, workers, and nations benefit from international trade in different ways. Consumers benefit from the competition that the foreign companies offer. This competition encourages the production of high-quality goods with lower prices. The variety of goods increases as more producers market their goods in other countries.

Many producers expand their business by conducting operations in other countries. Almost one-third of the profits of U.S. businesses come from international trade and foreign investment.

 marketingessentials.glencoe.com

MARKET TECH

Wi-Fi in Europe: Not So Hot

Discussion Lead a discussion asking students to speculate about why Wi-Fi sites in Europe have not caught on to the extent expected.

THINK LIKE A MARKETER **Answer:** Students might suggest that a company create more competitively priced sites at gathering spots for the general public while keeping the higher-priced sites at places like hotels and airports.

@ Online Action! For instructions, ideas, and answer guide, go to the Teacher Center at **marketingessentials.glencoe.com**

Follow Up Ask students to describe the target market for these Wi-Fi sites. Answers might include business travelers, who will use the facility for work and are willing to pay its cost.

Workers also benefit from international trade. Increased trade can lead to higher employment rates both at home and abroad. For example, according to the U.S. Chamber of Commerce, Toyota, a Japanese company, has generated 500,000 jobs in the United States.

Nations as a whole benefit from international trade. Increased foreign investment in a country often improves the standard of living for that country's people. Individuals have more options to choose from when making purchasing decisions.

Government Involvement in International Trade

All nations control and monitor their trade with foreign businesses. The U.S. government monitors imports through the customs division of the U.S. Treasury Department. All goods that enter the United States from a foreign country are subject to search and review by U.S. customs officials. Other countries also check incoming goods. All U.S. citizens and firms must meet the customs requirements of foreign countries when visiting or when exporting goods.

Balance of Trade

Nations must keep track of their international trade to be aware of their economic status. The difference in value between exports and imports of a nation is called its **balance of trade**. A positive balance of trade, or trade surplus, occurs when a nation exports more than it imports. A negative balance of trade, or trade deficit, occurs when a nation imports more than it exports.

Trade Deficit

The large U.S. trade deficit may seem surprising because the United States is the world's biggest exporter. Some analysts believe this situation exists because Americans purchase more goods and services than people of other nations. Others believe that the United States is now focusing more on providing services than on manufacturing and farming, making it more economical to import goods that were once domestically manufactured.

Negative Consequences of a Trade Deficit

An unfavorable balance of trade reduces a nation's revenue. When more money leaves a country than comes in, that country is in debt, or is a debtor nation. To survive as a debtor nation, the United States relies on foreign investors who buy U.S. securities. Another effect of a negative balance of trade can be increased unemployment. People may lose their jobs as foreign competitors take business away from domestic firms. If domestic businesses do not become competitive, they will fail.

Trade Barriers

Many countries around the world favor and practice **free trade**, or commercial exchange between nations that is conducted on free market principles, without restrictive regulations. However, nations sometimes impose trade barriers or restrictions when they want to limit trade. These controls restrict the flow of goods and services among nations. The three main types of trade barriers are tariffs, quotas, and embargoes.

Tariffs

A **tariff** (sometimes called a duty) is a tax on imports. Tariffs may be used to produce revenue for a country. Revenue-producing tariffs were used in the United States as a primary source of income for the government before income taxes were established in 1913. These tariffs exist today, but they are as low as 25 cents or less per item or pound.

Another type of tariff is protective. A protective tariff is generally high. Its purpose is to increase the price of imported goods so that domestic products can compete with them. Protective tariffs can prevent foreign businesses from trading with the United States. This would protect domestic jobs and new domestic industries from foreign competition.

Chapter 4 - Global Analysis 77

Concept Development

BALANCE OF TRADE

Ask students to explain which of these options is better and why:

1. When a country imports more than it exports
2. When a country exports more than it imports

It is better when a country exports more than it imports because it means that the country's businesses are selling more abroad than its consumers are buying from foreign producers.

Enrichment

ETHICS AND INTERNATIONAL TRADE

Inform students that when engaging in trade, many U.S. companies take ethical considerations into account, such as whether the efficiency of production is dependent on an oppressive government, low wages, or poor working conditions for a labor force. Ask students to research human rights and international trade and give a five-minute oral presentation about what they learned.

 Critical Thinking

Ask students to explain why a country might choose to restrict imports of products that can also be produced domestically. Have students share their responses in class and propose examples of restricted products.

Enrichment

EMBARGOES

Tell students that when the U.S. ended its trade embargo on Vietnam in 1995, allowing American products to be sold there, the Coca-Cola company flew a 30-foot-tall inflatable Coke bottle to a Vietnamese celebration, and PepsiCo released a photo of a giant Pepsi can placed in the main part of Ho Chi Minh City. Ask students to guess what the purpose of these public relations ads might have been.

Possible answer: to attract consumers in a new market.

Build Vocabulary

Ask students to preview the following words by reading them in context and provide a synonym.

• **impose** set, decree
• **subsidized** financed

Concept Development

TRADE AGREEMENTS AND ALLIANCES

Trade increase due to expanding globalization has led to the need for controlling bodies. After students have read this section, ask them to list the advantages and disadvantages of trade organizations and trade agreements.

TEACHING POINTS

Clarify Ask students to name the number one trading partner of the United States (Canada). Tell students that NAFTA reduced trade barriers such as tariffs and quotas between Mexico, Canada, and the United States to make it less expensive and easier to perform trade. The EU performs a similar function for its members.

Case Study

The New Calcutta

Rapid changes are taking place in Calcutta (Kolkata), which shows how the outsourcing of jobs from the United States is helping to transform India. Long neglected by investors, Calcutta is attracting technology companies ranging from International Business Machines Corp. (IBM) to India's Wipro Ltd., thanks to its educated workforce and low costs. Software engineers who had gone abroad for opportunity are returning. Even though Calcutta is still poverty stricken, changes around the city are encouraging. The changes include brand new offices springing up on vacant land outside the city, huge housing developments, and new malls complete with cinemas and cafés.

Stressing the Positives

In the past, Calcutta suffered from a reputation for labor unrest. So, the city stressed the positive. Unlike many parts of India, Calcutta's power supply is fairly reliable. Costs are even lower than in Bangalore or Bombay (Mumbai). There is a huge supply of talent from nearby engineering schools such as the prestigious Indian Institute of Technology. To ease apprehensions about possible labor stoppages, the government made software and office services legally equivalent to a public utility so that in the event of a general strike, the government will ensure their work goes on as usual.

 THINK STRATEGICALLY

Evaluate Calcutta as a site for a U.S. tech company by conducting an environmental scan.

 Online Action! Go to *marketingessentials.glencoe.com/4/case* for an activity on international business and economic development.

Quotas

An import **quota** limits either the quantity or the monetary value of a product that may be imported. For example, the U.S. government could place a quota on foreign automobiles, limiting the number that may be imported. This would control the number of cars that could enter the U.S. market from other countries. In theory, such a measure would give U.S. auto manufacturers a better chance to sell their own cars.

Sometimes one trading partner voluntarily puts quotas on exports to improve its relations with another country. In the 1980s, Japan placed quotas on its auto exports to the United States to improve trade relations between the two nations.

Embargoes

An **embargo** is a total ban on specific goods coming into and leaving a country. A government can impose an embargo for

78 UNIT 2 - ECONOMICS

 marketingessentials.glencoe.com

Case Study   The New Calcutta

Discussion Ask students to state what has been the biggest drawback about outsourcing jobs to Calcutta (labor unrest). Then ask how the governments can address outsourcing issues.

THINK STRATEGICALLY   **Answer:** Environmental scans will vary; students should consider political, economic, socio-cultural, and technological aspects of Calcutta. Have students review the material on marketing plans and environmental scans in Chapter 2 before they begin their analysis.

 Online Action!   For instructions, ideas, and answer guide, go to the Teacher Center at **marketingessentials.glencoe.com**

health reasons. The U.S. government embargoed Chilean grapes in 1989 as a precaution after inspectors found poisoned fruit in a shipment. That embargo was lifted within a week.

Embargoes are also used for political reasons. Such embargoes based on political differences can last for a very long time. The United States lifted its 30-year embargo on Vietnam in 1994 so that trade relations could start again between the two nations. The U.S. embargo against Cuba—imposed in 1960 when Fidel Castro created a communist state—still remains in effect. In 2000, President Clinton signed a law that relaxed restrictions on food sales to Cuba. As a result, U.S. exports to Cuba were $1 million a day in January 2004.

Protectionism

Trade regulations can have many political and economic consequences. **Protectionism** is a government's establishment of economic policies that systematically restrict imports in order to protect domestic industries. Protectionism is the opposite of free trade. Imposing tariffs and quotas is one method of practicing protectionism.

Protectionism and Subsidies

A government can accomplish the same goal by subsidizing domestic industries, thus allowing them to be more competitive against foreign competition.

For example, the United States and Europe subsidize their farmers. Those subsidies allow farmers to overproduce products that they can sell or donate overseas. All excess output can then be sold internationally at very low prices. Naturally this displeases the foreign competitors who cannot compete with those low prices in the global marketplace.

Sometimes, when one country imposes a tariff or quota, the other country retaliates. For example, in November 2003, the United States imposed new import quotas on Chinese dressing gowns, knitwear, and bras in order to protect domestic textile firms that produce

those products. After those quotas were announced, China cancelled a trade mission to the United States to buy farm products such as cotton, wheat, and soybeans.

Trade Agreements and Alliances

Governments make agreements with each other to establish guidelines for international trade and to set up trade alliances. Some milestones in the movement toward worldwide free trade are the formation of the World Trade Organization, the North American Free Trade Agreement, and the creation of the European Union.

The World Trade Organization

The **World Trade Organization (WTO)** is a coalition of nations that makes rules governing international trade. The WTO had 148 members as of October 2004.

The WTO was formed in 1995 as the successor to the General Agreement on Tariffs and Trade (GATT). GATT was an international trade agreement designed to open markets and promote global free trade. It reduced tariffs and created a common set of trading rules. GATT had no enforcement power, so it created the WTO to police the agreement and resolve disputes among nations. For example, in 2004, the WTO ruled in favor of Brazil, which had alleged that U.S. cotton subsidies violated international trade rules and hurt Brazilian farmers by depressing global prices.

The WTO also manages world trade by studying important trade issues and evaluating the health of the world economy. It deals with activities that GATT was unable to address, including intellectual property rights, investment, and services.

The WTO, For or Against?

Supporters of the WTO and free trade stress that globalization and the expansion of trade have created enormous wealth in both rich and previously poor countries.

Free trade supporters believe global prosperity can be maintained and expanded only through a borderless economy. This requires a

 Extended Activity

The European Union

Inform students about the history of the EU. The European Union consists of a number of democratic European countries committed to working together for peace and prosperity. EU countries still make many of their own economic decisions, but they leave other decisions to Europe-wide institutions such as the European Parliament and the European Central Bank. The idea for the EU was proposed in 1950, but the European Union did not become a reality until 1992. As of 2004, there were 25 member states in the EU. Tell students that individual countries vote on whether to become part of the EU. Lead a discussion about why countries might or might not want to become part of the European Union.

ASSESS

Review Guide

CONCEPTS

Ask students to give the acronyms and names of the trade agreements and alliances covered in Section 4.1. Then have volunteers help classmates review this material by reading aloud the information under the appropriate headings in the text. WTO: World Trade Organization; NAFTA: North American Free Trade Agreement; EU: European Union

KEY TERMS

Have students work in small groups to review key terms, their spellings, and their definitions.

ONLINE SELF-ASSESSMENT

Have students go to marketingessentials.glencoe.com for the Section 4.1 practice test.

Individualized Review

L1 Assign and review Chapter 4 activities in the Student Activity Workbook.

L2 Assign and review Chapter 4 activities in the Marketing Math Workbook.

L3 Assign and review Chapter 4 activities in the *BusinessWeek* Reader and Case Studies.

Marketing Practice

Ask students to work in groups of three to five. Have students choose one nation and research its major industries, resources, imports, and exports. Have students give a five- to 15-minute presentation on the country's economy and its prospects for international trade.

CLOSE

Ask students to describe the global marketplace discussed at the beginning of this section.

The global marketplace is the term used to describe international trade.

Online Activity

Border Safety

Studies indicate that our ports and the amount of goods that moves through them are a weak spot in U.S. border defense. Ask students to use the Internet to research current domestic security concerns regarding international trade and present their findings to the class.

---

set of rules that is universally accepted. Advocates argue that such a system is the only way to ensure fairness and avoid damaging trade wars.

Critics of the WTO raise concerns about democracy, labor rights, and the environment. They charge that the WTO makes decisions affecting all of society on a commercial basis. They do not like giving a nonelected body the power to overrule governments on issues of environmental protection and labor rights. Some of the more radical critics want the organization disbanded. Others want to transform it into a body that addresses social and environmental concerns as well as economic ones.

North American Free Trade Agreement

The **North American Free Trade Agreement (NAFTA)** is an international trade agreement among the United States, Canada, and Mexico. It went into effect on January 1, 1994.

The main goal of NAFTA is to get rid of all trade barriers and investment restrictions among the three countries by 2009. Tariffs were eliminated immediately on thousands of goods traded between Mexico and the United States, including food, clothing, and automobiles.

European Union

The **European Union (EU)** is Europe's trading bloc. In 1992, the Maastricht Treaty created the EU to establish free trade among the member nations, as well as a single European currency (the euro) and a central bank. Other treaty provisions relate to fair competitive practices, environmental and safety standards, and security matters.

In 2004, the EU added ten new members, including Poland, Hungary, the Czech Republic, and the Slovak Republic. To be considered part of the EU, these countries had to conform to the EU's political, economic, and legal standards.

4.1 AFTER YOU READ

Reviewing Key Terms and Concepts

1. Explain the nature of international trade.
2. What are two key reasons why embargoes are imposed?
3. What is the common goal or purpose of the WTO, NAFTA, and the EU trade agreements?

Integrating Academic Skills

Math

4. If a Japanese company reported an 8.8 percent increase in net profit from last year's 426 billion yen, what would be this year's net profit in yen?

History

5. Why does the United States have an embargo against Cuba?

 Online Action!

Check your answers at *marketingessentials.glencoe.com/4/read*

marketingessentials.glencoe.com

AFTER YOU READ

Reviewing Key Terms and Concepts

1. International trade is the exchange of goods and services between nations.

2. Two reasons are health reasons, as in contaminated products, and political or diplomatic reasons.

3. The common goal of all three agreements is to establish trade guidelines and set up trading alliances.

Integrating Academic Skills

4. 38 billion yen
5. The embargo is political in nature; Cuba is a communist country and U.S. policy does not support communist countries.

Online Action! Answers at **marketingessentials.glencoe.com/4/read**

The Global Marketplace

READ and STUDY

BEFORE YOU READ

Connect Suppose you have manufactured a new product and you want to sell it in a foreign country. List three things you would need to know to accomplish your goal.

THE MAIN IDEA

Doing business in a foreign country can be very different from doing business in the United States. Besides language barriers, there are many other factors that must be considered in international business. Without this understanding, costly problems may arise.

STUDY ORGANIZER

Create a chart like the one below to list factors that affect international business.

(International Business) (Global Environment) (Market Strategies)

OBJECTIVES

- List forms of international trade
- Identify political, economic, socio-cultural, and technological factors that affect international business
- Suggest global marketing strategies

KEY TERMS

- licensing
- contract manufacturing
- joint venture
- foreign direct investment (FDI)
- multinationals
- mini-nationals
- globalization
- adaptation
- customization

Doing Business Internationally

The global marketplace has been growing with the increasing acceptance of capitalism around the world, advances in technology such as Internet connections, and the reduction of trade barriers. Global news coverage is instantaneous, connecting people throughout the world. These factors have encouraged businesses to venture into foreign countries. In this section, you will see what it takes for a business to become a global player.

Connect Think of one example for each type of international business transaction this section describes.

Chapter 4 - Global Analysis **81**

FOCUS

Introducing the Section

COLLABORATIVE ACTIVITY

Divide students into groups of three to five. Ask groups to choose the one foreign country to which they would most like to market a product or service and then explain their choice in an informal class discussion.

Preteaching Key Terms

Assign three key terms each to groups of three students. Have students study the words in context and then write a sentence for each term. They can then present sentences and word definitions to the rest of the class.

- licensing
- contract manufacturing
- joint venture
- foreign direct investment (FDI)
- multinationals
- mini-nationals
- globalization
- adaptation
- customization

READ and STUDY

BEFORE YOU READ

Ask students to write down their lists without discussion. Encourage them to return to the lists at the end of this section, changing and adding as needed based on what they have learned.

THE MAIN IDEA

Set purpose by asking students to read Section 4.2 to see what some of those costly problems might be.

STUDY ORGANIZER

Make your own organizer or download the one provided at **marketingessentials.glencoe.com.** Model for students how to fill in the organizer by filling in the first factor.

WHILE YOU READ

Ask students to share their examples of the types of transactions in class.

TEACH

DOING BUSINESS INTERNATIONALLY

After students have read this section, read the material under this heading aloud to the class and ask volunteers to explain two ways of getting involved in international trade.

Answers may include importing, exporting, licensing, contract manufacturing, and foreign direct investment.

TEACHING POINTS

Clarify Point out that each of these ways of closing business involves a different amount of risk and control. Help students see that in this context, *risk* refers to the possibility of losing one's investment, while *control* refers to how much say a business owner has, even over that owner's own business, when operating in a foreign country.

Enrichment

MOVING OPERATIONS

Explain to students that the U.S. has laws designed to create a safe workplace and to provide a certain amount of pay. Some companies have moved operations to other countries where wages are lower and there are fewer restrictions. Ask students to share any information they have heard or read about U.S. companies moving their operations out of the country.

Trade agreements by governments set the guidelines for businesses to operate in the global marketplace. Getting involved in international trade can mean importing, exporting, licensing, contract manufacturing, joint ventures, or foreign direct investment. Each option offers a different level of risk and control. Figure 4.1 shows how the profit potential increases as the levels of financial commitment, risk, and marketing control increase with the different market entry options.

Importing

Importing involves purchasing goods from a foreign country. Products imported for the U.S. market must meet the same standards as domestic products, including those imposed by the Food and Drug Administration. If these standards are met, most products can be imported without prior government approval.

A quota can limit entry of certain goods into the country. Quotas exist on cotton, peanuts, and sugar. Once a quota is reached for a certain item, no more of that item may enter the country. Any shipment in excess of the quota is quarantined by U.S. Customs. Knowing the details of importing is difficult and U.S. businesses usually hire customs brokers—specialists licensed by the U.S. Treasury Department. Customs brokers know the laws, procedures, and tariffs governing imports. They handle over 90 percent of imports because of the complex procedures involved.

Exporting

A domestic company that wishes to enter into the global marketplace with minimal risk and control might consider exporting. Domestic companies that want to export their goods and services can get help from the United States government, through its Internet export portal and at its BuyUSA site.

Licensing

Licensing involves letting another company (licensee) use a trademark, patent, special formula, company name, or some other intellectual property for a fee or royalty. This type of market entry has its pros and cons. With licensing, a foreign company makes the

Figure 4.1 **Doing Business Internationally**

•**Level of Risk and Control** International trade includes importing, exporting, licensing, contract manufacturing, joint ventures, and foreign direct investment. Each of these options involves a different level of risk and control. As you can see, the greatest level of risk and marketing control occurs when a company makes a direct investment in a foreign country.

What advice would you give to a small or medium-sized company interested in international trade?

@ Online Action! Go to *marketingessentials.glencoe.com/4/ figure/1* to find a project on international trade.

marketingessentials.glencoe.com

Figure 4.1 **Doing Business Internationally**

Discussion Ask students to discuss why they feel that marketing in a foreign country might increase the risk for a certain product or company.

Caption Answer Answers will vary. Students may feel that keeping risk low, for example focusing on exporting, is the way for a smaller company to enter this market.

@ Online Action! For instructions, ideas, and answer guide, go to the Teacher Center at **marketingessentials.glencoe.com**

•OPENING a GLOBAL BUSINESS Starting an import-export business is one way to capitalize on the global marketplace.

What might you need to know before starting such a business with Japan?

product using the information or guidelines provided by the licensor. If the product is a success in the foreign country, the licensor has gained entry with minimal risk. If the product fails, the licensor's name is tarnished.

A special type of licensing is franchising. In a franchise agreement, a franchisor grants the franchisee the rights to operate under the company name. The agreement involves following specific guidelines for operation to foster a unified image of the franchisor. Many fast-food chains, like McDonald's, Wendy's and Burger King, have franchised operations in foreign countries.

Contract Manufacturing

Contract manufacturing has become popular as emerging countries offer facilities, know-how, and inexpensive labor. **Contract manufacturing** involves hiring a foreign manufacturer to make your products, according to your specifications. The finished goods are either sold in that country or exported. Many U.S. companies that sell clothing, toys,

golf clubs, and computers use contract manufacturers in emerging countries to manufacture their products.

The major benefit is lower wages, which allow companies to be more competitive in their pricing. One of the pitfalls of contract manufacturing is that proprietary information must be given to these companies. Golf clubs are an example. In China, molds of new golf club heads have been stolen by workers and sold to counterfeiters. The counterfeit clubs are then sold as copies or knockoffs in the United States and abroad for much less than the brand-name clubs.

Joint Ventures

A **joint venture** is a business enterprise that companies set up together. In some countries, foreign investors are not permitted to own 100 percent of a business. If you want to conduct business in those countries, you must find a local business partner, thus creating a joint venture. This is often a good idea even when it is not mandated by law. Domestic

Chapter 4 - Global Analysis 83

Concept Development

CONTRACT MANUFACTURING

After students have read the section on contract manufacturing, ask them to list one advantage and disadvantage of this manufacturing method.

advantage: lower wages, competitive prices; disadvantage: possibility of knockoffs, or counterfeit products

TEACHING POINTS

Clarify Explain the relationship between contract manufacturing and knockoffs. In contract manufacturing, one company engages a foreign manufacturer to produce product to the company's specification. A knockoff is an illegally manufactured item that is made to look like a brand-name product.

Enrichment

JOINT VENTURES

After students have read this section, ask them if they were surprised to find that foreign businesses have part ownership of U.S. companies. Explain that many corporations have global branches and interests. Ask students to use the Internet and other sources to research a business enterprise that involves businesses from one or more countries and to present a summary of that company to the class in a five-minute presentation.

Discussion Lead a discussion about this photo by asking students what kind of research an entrepreneur might do before beginning a business venture in Japan.

Caption Answer Answers may include political, economic, socio-cultural, and technological issues and trends.

 Follow Up Ask students to research and give a brief oral report on retail business etiquette in Japan or another country of their choice.

Critical Thinking

Ask students: Should intellectual property—ideas, written work, and so on—be protected and licensed in the same way that products are? Why?

Individualized Practice

GLOBAL ENVIRONMENTAL SCAN

L1 Ask students to imagine that they have just become employed in a marketing job. The company they work for is considering marketing its product, a new brand of healthful cat food, in foreign markets. Have students return to and reread the material on the environmental scan in Chapter 2. Ask students to give an example of the political and economic factors, socio-cultural differences, and technological levels they might consider.

L2 Ask students to imagine that they have just become employed in a marketing job. The company they work for is considering marketing its product, a new brand of healthful dog food, in foreign markets. Have each student choose a country and conduct an environmental scan, and report his or her findings in a two- to three-page written memo.

L3 Ask students to imagine that they work a company based in Ireland, where they manufacture and sell gift items with Irish themes, such as china mugs decorated with shamrocks and other items of this type. The company is considering marketing its products in the United States. Have students perform an environmental scan and report their findings in a five-minute oral presentation.

business partners know the market and procedures for conducting business in their own country.

For example, Viacom Inc., which owns CBS, Nickelodeon, and MTV, has a minority share in a joint venture with Shanghai Media Group.

Foreign Direct Investment

All the joint ventures described above are considered foreign direct investments. A **foreign direct investment (FDI)** is the establishment of a business in a foreign country.

Sometimes that may involve no more than setting up an office with a staff to maintain a presence in that country. Higher levels of direct investment involve acquisitions of existing foreign companies and construction of facilities such as manufacturing plants and retail stores. Sony, a Japanese company, has invested in several countries. It has direct foreign investment of approximately $8 billion in China. In the United States, Sony has 11 manufacturing facilities. Honda, another Japanese company, has a manufacturing plant in Alabama.

Multinationals and Mini-Nationals

Multinationals are large corporations that have operations in several countries. About one-third of the world's private-sector assets are controlled by some 37,000 transnational corporations with over 170,000 foreign affiliates. Gillette, Procter & Gamble, Unilever, Nike, PepsiCo, and Coca-Cola are multinational firms. Gillette has manufacturing operations in 14 countries. The products from these operations are distributed in more than 200 countries.

Mini-nationals are midsize or smaller companies that have operations in foreign countries. The key characteristic that sets multinationals and mini-nationals apart from domestic businesses is foreign investments in factories, offices, and other facilities abroad that are used for operations. All these investments are referred to as FDIs.

Global Environmental Scan

Recall the factors involved in an environmental scan (see Chapter 2). How would you use those factors to evaluate a country's marketing opportunities and threats?

A global environmental scan is in order. This includes analysis of political and economic factors, sociocultural differences, and technological levels.

Political Factors

Political factors include a government's stability, its trade regulations and agreements, and any other laws that impact a company's operation.

Government Stability

A government's stability is an important factor when considering international business operations. If there are changes in the government, investors become wary. For example, when Luiz Inácio Lula da Silva, a left-wing politician, won Brazil's presidential election in 2002, stock prices in Brazil plunged. Stocks regained strength when businesses saw that President da Silva supported continued economic reform.

Trade Regulations and Laws

A business must keep abreast of new trade regulations, which can force companies to reconsider doing business in a country. Changes in trade regulations include reduced tariffs, laws to protect intellectual property, and an increase in the percentage of business ownership allowed by foreign investors. For example, on January 1, 2004, the United States-Chile Free Trade Agreement went into force. Under this agreement, Chile must have stronger standards for the protection of intellectual property rights. This means that Chile will need to adopt rules similar to those in the United States for copyrights, trademarks, patents, and trade secrets.

Domestic laws must be followed by foreign marketers. For example, toys cannot be advertised in Greece. These regulations are important for retailers like Toys "R" Us.

Extended Activity

Business and Politics

Remind students that political change might result in changes in economic and political policy, both of which can affect business. Ask interested students to research how recent major political changes have affected stock markets in the United States and other countries and report their findings in a five-minute oral presentation.

Economic Factors

Key economic factors relevant to doing business in another country include infrastructure, the quality and cost of labor, employee benefits, taxes, the standard of living, and foreign exchange rates.

Infrastructure

Things like undependable telephone service or inadequate roads would rule out a location for some businesses. Yet these same infrastructure factors would be an opportunity for companies involved in building roads, energy plants, and telecommunications systems. For example, Poland and the Czech Republic had to carry out environmental cleanup to meet the entry requirements for membership in the European Union. U.S. companies that have expertise in that area could partner with companies in Poland and the Czech Republic to help them with these projects.

Labor Force

If you are establishing a business in another country, you must consider the quality and cost of the labor force available there. You need to know the educational and skill levels of the workers, as well as the customary wages and employment laws. For example, India has been supporting technology education and now has a pool of highly qualified workers whose wages are lower than those for similar workers in the United States. U.S. companies like AOL, Yahoo, and Google have recognized this opportunity and now look to India for computer programming and other computer-related expertise.

Employee Benefits

In most countries, employers are responsible for paying for mandated employee benefits above and beyond wages. Many companies shy away from investing in France because of labor policies. France restricts the work week to 35 hours and requires companies to consult with employees before downsizing or restructuring. Payroll taxes and employee benefits are high, so that the cost of the total employee

package is higher in France than in other European countries.

Taxes

Other costs include taxes on property and profits. Countries that want to attract foreign investment may offer reduced taxes for a period of time as an incentive. Switzerland offered corporate tax breaks in 1997 and since

marketingessentials.glencoe.com

A MATTER OF ETHICS

Is the Price Right?

Suppose an international company is a direct purchaser of many products it sells. Because of its size, it is also able to negotiate great prices from suppliers. For example, it has been able to get low prices on raw materials for its suppliers.

Economies of Scale

In the case of clothing, this large international company visits mills around the world to get the best deal it can on fabric. Its supplier of jeans, for example, benefits because it is able to get a great price on the fabric.

Lower Than Low Prices

As a result, jeans that used to sell for $30 are now selling for under $10. The company's competitors cannot keep up with such low prices for jeans because their manufacturers pay regular prices for the fabric.

THINKING ETHICALLY

Is it ethical for a large business to use its clout to secure low prices on raw materials for its suppliers too?

@ Online Action!

Go to *marketingessentials.glencoe.com/4/ethics* for an activity on ethics and international business.

TEACH CONTINUED

Concept Development

TRADE REGULATIONS AND LAWS

Since each country possesses a different set of economic laws. trade organizations can facilitate economic interaction between nations by setting up common standards. Ask students to use the internet and other sources to research trade regulations in a country of their choice. Have students share what they learned with a partner.

Individualized Practice

COMMUNICATION SKILLS

Have students consider the challenges firms face when doing business in a foreign country.

L1 Have students list two to five problems that might arise from the cultural differences, such as communication difficulties, prejudice, different economic laws, and company policy regarding hours, holidays, and time off.

L2 Have students identify the source or cause of two challenges and write a short summary of each. For example, communication problems might be caused by a language barrier.

L3 Have students choose one potential challenge and develop strategies to deal with the problem in a one-page memo. For example, the language barrier could be breached by providing instruction and training in more than one language, and/or by having managers who are proficient in both languages.

A MATTER OF ETHICS   Is the Price Right?

Discussion Lead a discussion on this question, encouraging students to view it from the standpoint of a customer, of an executive or stockholder in the large company, and of a small competing business that manufactures and sells only jeans.

THINKING ETHICALLY **Answer:** Answers will vary; students not troubled by the practice may cite free enterprise. Others may see this as a monopolistic practice that should be regulated by government control.

@ Online Action! For instruction, ideas, and answer guide, go to the Teacher Center at marketingessentials.glencoe.com

Follow Up Ask: Do any existing U.S. laws or trade regulations address issues such as these? Ask interested students to do research and report their findings.

TEACH CONTINUED

Concept Development

SOCIO-CULTURAL FACTORS

After students have read this section, form the class into groups of three to four. Have groups research business etiquette in the country of their choice and use presentation software to give a 10-minute presentation on their findings.

TEACHING POINTS

Model Bring in ads or articles from the Internet or other sources that appeal to cultural biases or stereotypes.

Enrichment

TECHNOLOGICAL FACTORS

Explain to students that in countries that do not have well-developed telecommunications infrastructure, the cost of telephone service is very high. Ask students to determine what kind of market the lack of infrastructure might benefit.

wireless or cell phone technology

Critical Thinking

Ask students to consider how technology influences socio-cultural factors such as language usage. Have students discuss their thoughts and opinions in class.

---

then has experienced a growth in foreign direct investment. Some large companies, like Procter & Gamble, Starbucks, and Google, have their European headquarters in Switzerland.

Standard of Living

Standard of living can be a consideration if a business is eyeing a country as a market rather than a manufacturing site. When Honda entered China's consumer market, it recognized that most Chinese people could not afford cars. The company targeted the motorcycle market instead and was very successful.

The number of middle-income workers is increasing in poorer nations. This increases the demand for all types of ordinary consumer goods. U.S. products like soaps, detergents, breakfast cereals, snack foods, and soft drinks are gaining popularity among consumers in emerging nations.

Foreign Exchange Rate

The foreign exchange rate is the price of one country's currency if you were to buy it with another country's currency. Exchange rates vary every business day. The exchange rate for a nation's currency based on the U.S. dollar is an important factor to consider. Changes in an exchange rate affect businesses that sell abroad. If the dollar strengthens in value against other currencies, that means it costs more yen, euros, or pesos to buy one dollar. It also means it costs more yen, euros, or pesos to buy one dollar's worth of U.S.-made products. International sales of U.S.-made products are likely to fall. If the reverse happens—if the U.S. dollar is devalued—U.S. products are more attractive in the global marketplace. The devaluation of the dollar in 2004 affected the profits of many international companies that do business in the United States. For example, Honda Motor Co. reported a drop in net income in April 2004, which it attributed to lower sales, rising costs, and the effects of a stronger yen against the U.S. dollar.

Socio-cultural Factors

Marketers must be savvy with cultural diversity and a foreign society's value system.

Before conducting business in a foreign country, a cross-cultural analysis should be performed. This analysis should include sociocultural factors such as language and symbols, holidays and religious observances, and social and business etiquette.

Language and Symbols

Differences in language and customs make international trade more challenging than doing business at home. Cultural symbols are often different. In the United States, the number 13 is considered unlucky. Many hotels do not include a 13th floor. In China and Japan, the number four is unpopular because it relates to death. Marketers in these countries who sell multiple units of a product should consider groups of six or eight, never four.

Holidays and Religious Observances

Holidays and religious observances are part of a country's culture too. In India, the cow is sacred, so little beef is sold there. Fast-food companies like McDonald's adapt to India's culture by selling chicken, fish, and vegetarian burgers. Marketers must heed these cultural differences when creating, naming, and packaging products, as well as when designing ad campaigns for them.

Social and Business Etiquette

Social and business etiquette is important when doing business abroad. A common practice in one country may take on a different meaning elsewhere. Gift giving is one area of concern. A gift may be considered part of business etiquette in the Far East; however, it might be considered an illegal bribe in the United States or Canada.

Technological Factors

Technology is changing the ways that businesses can get involved in international trade. Studying a country's technology means taking into consideration even the most basic factors such as measurement systems and electric voltage standards. A thorough look at the use of computers, faxes, voice mail, cellular phones, and the Internet is important. A

Extended Activity

Global Marketing Strategies

Show students products, packaging, or Web sites that offer content in more than one language. Explain to students that the Internet allows marketers an easy way to reach the entire world. Form students into teams of three to four and assign them a country to research. Students should identify or create a product that they believe would sell well in that particular country. Ask students to create a presentation to package, promote, and sell that product to the country they chose.

• A NEW FORM of CUSTOMIZATION: TRANSCREATION Marvel Enterprises, Inc. and Gotham Entertainment Group, an Indian publishing licensee of Marvel Comics, launched *Spider-Man India*, the first-ever comics transcreation: They re-invented the origin of Spider-Man so that he is an Indian boy in Bombay (Mumbai), dealing with local challenges and problems.

Why do you think the Spider-Man story was re-invented instead of translated?

Concept Development

ADAPTATION

After students read this section, ask them to brainstorm ideas why food and food products lend themselves well to product adaptation.

Food preferences vary by culture, but all cultures need food.

TEACHING POINTS

Demonstrate If possible, bring in an example of packaging or an ad for a foreign food product.

Extend Tell students that one marketing strategy involves giving products foreign names to lend them an air of exoticism. For example, some or food products may be referred to by a French or French-sounding name because of the association some may have between French culture and food.

Enrichment

CULTURAL MARKETING

Ask students to use the Internet and other resources to locate products that are marketed to different ethnic groups within the United States. Have students create a five-minute presentation or summarize what they learned in a one-page report.

---

visit to the CIA's *World Fact Book* Web site provides information about the number of telephones (main lines and mobile), radio and television broadcast stations, Internet service providers, and Internet users in a given country. These facts can help you decide if setting up a Web site in a specific country would be worthwhile.

Global Marketing Strategies

In planning and making decisions about the four Ps (see Chapter 1) of the marketing mix, global marketers need to consider all the factors analyzed for the environmental scan. The possibilities for marketing strategies that involve product and promotion decisions range from complete standardization, called globalization, to new product development, which is complete customization. Figure 4.2 shows examples of the global marketing strategies for product and promotion decisions.

Globalization

Globalization is selling the same product and using the same promotion methods in all countries. Only a small portion of products that are common to all global customers can use this marketing strategy. Coca-Cola and other soft drink companies can use a globalization

marketing strategy by offering the same version of its products with the same advertising message in countries around the world.

How Globalization Works

The reason these companies are able to use the same product and same promotion is that they have uncovered a common need that transcends different cultures. They are able to identify a global consumer. One of the benefits of globalization is global brand recognition. An example of a company that answers common needs across the globe is Microsoft. While users do need computer programs to function in different languages, the basic applications remain the same; likewise Internet search engines such as Yahoo and Google. The success of e-commerce has increased the power of globalization in some instances, particularly where technology is involved.

Adaptation

Companies study the characteristics of a country and find ways to target consumers with similar needs and wants. That often requires adapting their products or promotions to each country where they do business. Sometimes, only the product is changed, while in other cases, only the promotion is changed.

Chapter 4 - Global Analysis 87

ASSESS

Review Guide

CONCEPTS

Ask students to explain the difference between globalization, adaptation, and customization.

In globalization, the product is sold as is, without modification for particular countries. In adaptation, the product or the promotion of it are changed to suit the country. Customization is the creating of an entirely new product for a specific foreign market.

KEY TERMS

Have each student work with a partner to review the spellings and definitions of key terms.

ONLINE SELF-ASSESSMENT

Have students go to marketingessentials.glencoe.com for the Section 4.2 practice test.

Individualized Review

L1 Assign and review Chapter 4 activities in the Student Activity Workbook.

L2 Assign and review Chapter 4 activities in the Marketing Math Workbook.

L3 Assign and review Chapter 4 activities in the *BusinessWeek* Reader and Case Studies.

Marketing Practice

Have students choose a product they know well or use a lot. Ask them to assume they have the opportunity to market it worldwide. Which marketing strategies would they use: globalization, adaptation (either product or promotion or both), or customization? Ask students to summarize their opinions in a one-page response.

Figure 4.2 *Global Marketing Strategies*

• **Marketing Abroad** When marketing products in foreign countries, companies must make product and promotion decisions. Some create completely new products for specific countries (customization), while others use the same products and promotions for every country (globalization). Between these two extremes are companies that keep their products' brand names but vary their products and/or promotions enough to meet local tastes. Here are some examples of each strategy.

How do companies reach customers around the world?

Customization Customization is creating entirely new products and promotions for a specific country or region. The Coca-Cola Company developed the Smart brand specifically for the Chinese market. This carbonated soft drink comes in flavors such as apple, watermelon, grape, and mandarin orange. The company also developed a ready-to-drink carbonated tea called Ice Lemon Tea. Product packaging uses Chinese icons, and ads show young people having fun drinking Smart.

Globalization Pringles Potato Chips are marketed with the same product packaging and promotional message around the world. The company's slogan in Germany is *"Einmal Gepoppt, Nie Mehr Gestoppt!"* In Italy it is *"Se Fai Pop, Divertimento Non Stop!"* In Brazil it is *"Fale de boca cheia!"* They all mean, "Once you pop, you can't stop!"

Product Adaptation The Campbell Soup Company uses product adaptation to sell its soups internationally. With product adaptation, the company keeps the brand name but changes the product to meet local needs and tastes. In Australia you can get Campbell's pumpkin soup, and in Mexico, you will see chile poblano and squash flower (*flor de calabaza*) soups.

Promotion Adaptation Promotion adaptation involves changing some part of the promotional message or visuals used in the promotional campaigns for different markets. Advertisements for Kellogg's cereals use the same message (in different languages) and format but different models to appeal to customers from different countries.

@ Online Action! Go to *marketingessentials.glencoe.com/4/figure/2* to find a project on global marketing strategies.

Figure 4.2 *Global Marketing Strategies*

Discussion Ask students to give their opinions on the effectiveness of each of the ads in the figure, giving both real-life examples and their first impression. Have students defend and discuss their opinions in small groups.

Caption Answer Answers may include by customizing products, marketing existing products globally, or adapting the product or the promotion of the product.

@ Online Action! For instructions, ideas, and answer guide, go to the Teacher Center at marketingessentials.glencoe.com

Adaptation is a company's use of an existing product and/or promotion to which changes are made to better suit the characteristics of a country or region.

Product Adaptation

Changing a product to meet different consumer needs and/or to reflect the cultural differences in a foreign market is product adaptation. In some cases, a product's brand name is changed. For example, Unilever's Sunsilk hair products are called *Seda* (which means silk) in Latin America. In addition, Sunsilk's ingredients are formulated to match consumers' needs (prevalent hair types) in different countries.

Promotion Adaptation

A promotion adaptation strategy involves changing the advertising message to reflect the values, familiar images, and cultural differences in a foreign market. In some cases, the advertising is changed to adhere to government regulations. For example, McDonald's is careful to use only adults in its advertising in Sweden, where advertising to children is prohibited.

Another facet of adaptation is the use of adaptation pricing policy. This pricing technique requires a careful competitive analysis so that a product's price can be accurately set to match and compete with the prices of comparable local products.

Customization

Customization involves creating specially designed products or promotions for certain countries or regions. Each geographical area where a product is sold or a service is offered becomes a unique market segment.

4.2 AFTER YOU READ

Reviewing Key Terms and Concepts

1. Give an example of a political factor that could discourage a business from engaging in international trade with a given country.
2. Give an example of how a country's poor infrastructure can create opportunities for foreign companies.
3. Which socio-cultural factors make doing business abroad difficult?

Integrating Academic Skills
Math

4. Assume the currency exchange rate between the United States and Canada is 1.25, which means US$1 dollar is equal to CN$1.25 in Canadian currency. If a T-shirt costs $20 at a Gap store in Montréal, how much should it cost at a Gap in Detroit?

Foreign Language

5. Translate a magazine ad or advertising slogan into a foreign language you are studying. Then, translate back into English. Note any problems and suggest any changes as necessary.

 Online Action!

Check your answers at *marketingessentials.glencoe.com/4/read*

marketingessentials.glencoe.com

Chapter 4 - Global Analysis **89**

AFTER YOU READ

Reviewing Key Terms and Concepts

1. Possible answers include an unstable economy, change in political party, or a more drastic political change such as a coup or a civil war.

2. If roads are bad, bridges in disrepair, electricity and phones unreliable, a foreign company that can replace, repair, or create new infrastructure could prosper.

3. learning about and then acting according to a different language and symbol system, holidays and religious observances, and social and business etiquette

Integrating Academic Skills

4. It should cost $16 in Detroit; $20 ÷ 1.25 = $16

5. Answers will vary. Students might explain to the class whether their translations are word-for-word or if rewording was necessary, and why.

 Online Action! Answers at **marketingessentials.glencoe.com/4/read**

Lifelong Learning

CAREER INFORMATION

Have students go to marketingessentials.glencoe.com and find the Chapter 4 Careers page. They can then click on the link for the American Marketing Association's Career Strategies and Tips. Ask students to select one article, read it, and summarize it in three short paragraphs.

SKILLS FOR THE GLOBAL MARKETPLACE

Qualities that might help a person succeed at a marketing job in the global marketplace include a sound marketing background, the ability to speak one or more foreign languages, flexibility, interest in other people and how they live, an outgoing personality, and sensitivity to the feelings of others.

Primary Source

Ask students to go to marketingessentials.glencoe.com and find Chapter 4 Resources. Ask them to click on the link for the American Marketing Association's marketing dictionary and read the definitions of terms relating to international trade and the global marketplace.

● THINKING CRITICALLY

Studying abroad or participating in multicultural awareness and sensitivity training will help individuals build skills for the global marketplace.

@ Online Action!

For instructions, ideas, and answer guide, go to the Teacher Center at marketingessentials.glencoe.com

---

CAREERS IN MARKETING

LEE DULANEY
SENIOR ACCOUNT EXECUTIVE
CREATIVE ALLIANCE

(?) What do you do at work?
My job is to coordinate all of Creative Alliance's advertising account services for Yum! Brands' KFC franchisees in the Caribbean and Central and South America. Creative Alliance handles all the TV, radio and in-store POP (point of purchase) advertising for this diverse region. I also act as agency producer for TV and radio, because of my background in broadcast/video production.

(?) What skills are most important to you?
A willingness to learn and the ability to think on your feet are just two of the skills that I believe are the basis for everything. In a marketing capacity, be it national or international, you need to be able to listen and learn about your client, and the consumer your client is trying to reach. In an international marketing capacity, it's crucial that you try your best to understand the culture of your target audience. What motivates them? How do they spend their disposable income? Organizational skills and the ability to prioritize are also critical, because you can often have three or four campaigns in production at any given time.

(?) What is your key to success?
Being able to communicate, listen and follow-through are three very important keys. You also have to make the effort to understand cultural nuances and customs. A marketing idea that works in the United States may not work in, say, the Caribbean or Latin America.

Aptitudes, Abilities, and Skills

International marketers must be able to step inside the mindset of other cultures. Research skills are a must.

Education and Training

Degrees in marketing, advertising, foreign languages, and general business are helpful.

Career Path

Entry-level marketing positions can lead to global careers like this one, particularly if the person has foreign language skills.

● THINKING CRITICALLY

Why is spending time abroad prior to launching a career in international marketing helpful?

@ Online Action!

Go to *marketingessentials.glencoe.com/4/careers* to find a career-related activity.

 marketingessentials.glencoe.com

▨ Test-Taking Strategies

Suggest to students that when they take a test, they should take care not to get stuck on one question if they are not sure of the answer. Instead, they should first go all the way through the test, completing those items for which they know the answers. They can then go back through and address each item that requires more thought.

FOCUS on KEY POINTS

SECTION 4.1

● International trade is necessary because of the interdependence of nations. It benefits consumers, producers, workers, and nations in different ways.

● Governments are involved in international trade through monitoring trade between countries and establishing trade regulations. Currently, the United States has a negative balance of trade, also called a trade deficit.

● Three types of trade barriers are tariffs, quotas, and embargoes.

● Three significant trade agreements and alliances that foster free trade are the World Trade Organization (WTO), the North American Free Trade Agreement (NAFTA), and the European Union (EU).

SECTION 4.2

● Businesses can get involved in international trade through importing, exporting, licensing, contract manufacturing, joint ventures, and foreign direct investments.

● A global environmental scan analyzes political, economic, socio-cultural, and technological factors.

● Global marketing strategy options include globalization, adaptations of product, promotion, and customization.

REVIEW VOCABULARY

The groups of words below involve international trade and free trade. Explain how the words in each group relate to each other.

I. imports (p. 75)/exports (p. 75)/balance of trade (p. 77)

2. tariff (p. 77)/quota (p. 78)/embargo (p. 78)/protectionism (p. 79)

3. World Trade Organization (WTO) (p. 79)/ North American Free Trade Agreement (NAFTA) (p. 80)/European Union (EU) (p. 80)

4. licensing (p. 82)/contract manufacturing (p. 83)/joint venture (p. 83)/foreign direct investment (FDI) (p. 84)/multinationals/mini-nationals (p. 84)

5. globalization/adaptation/customization (p. 89)

REVIEW FACTS and IDEAS

6. Explain the concept of economic interdependence of nations. (4.1)

7. How are governments involved in international trade? (4.1)

8. Explain the U.S. balance of trade. (4.1)

9. What are three basic types of trade barriers? (4.1)

10. List three significant trade agreements and alliances. (4.1)

II. What is a global environmental scan? (4.2)

Chapter 4 - Global Analysis 91

REVIEW FACTS and IDEAS

6. The concept of economic interdependence of nations is that no one nation has all the resources it needs and wants and so must get some of its resources from other nations.

7. Governments make the laws and trade agreements that are essential for smooth functioning of international trade.

8. The term *balance of trade* refers to the difference between a country's imports and exports. The U.S. currently has a trade deficit because it imports more than it exports.

9. Three basic types of trade barriers are quotas, tariffs, and embargoes.

10. Three significant trade agreement and alliances are the World Trade Organization, the North American Free Trade Agreement (NAFTA), and the European Union (EU).

II. A global environmental scan analyzes political, economic, socio-cultural, and technological factors.

FOCUS on KEY POINTS

Divide students into pairs. Have each student take turns reading aloud a key point from Section 4.1 and have them explain it in their own words. Have everyone switch partners and do the same for Section 4.2.

REVIEW VOCABULARY

See glossary for definitions of the terms used in **I–5.** A sample answer might read:

5. *Globalization, adaptation,* and *customization* are all global marketing strategies.

BUILD SKILLS

12. Workplace Skills
Presentations will vary; students should demonstrate an understanding of the value of diversity.

13. Technology Applications
Reports will vary; students should demonstrate an understanding of a recession and the ability to use word processing software.

14. Math Practice
You would have 236,000 yen; $2,000 \times 118 = 236,000$. Spreadsheets should include prices for items such as food and lodging and demonstrate an understanding of how to determine the amount of money needed for the stay.

DEVELOP CRITICAL THINKING

15. Trading With the World
Examples will vary but should express an understanding of importing and how the marketing of products is often modified or changed to better appeal to other cultures or countries.

16. Analyze the Consequences of Outsourcing
Responses will vary but should include how outsourcing can affect the employment, standard of living, consumer prices, direct foreign investment, and the business operations and profits of both countries involved in the outsourcing.

BUILD SKILLS

12. Workplace Skills
Teamwork and Presentation Skills Work in a group to prepare a three-minute presentation that addresses the impact and value of diversity, as well as how diversity affects marketing in a global marketplace. Include specific examples in your oral presentation.

13. Technology Applications
Global Crisis Look up information on the Internet about the global recession of the late 1990s. Using word processing software, charts, and graphs, prepare a short report on your findings.

14. Math Practice
Prices in Japan Suppose you are going to Japan and plan to bring $2,000 in spending money. If the exchange rate is 118 yen to the U.S. dollar, how many yen would you have? Research prices for items such as food and lodging (hotels) in Japan. How many days could you afford to stay in a major Japanese city such as Tokyo or Kyoto? Use a spreadsheet program to present a report on the daily costs of your trip.

DEVELOP CRITICAL THINKING

15. Trading With the World
Why does the global economy have an impact on marketing? Give three examples of foreign products that are imported and explain how they are marketed in the United States.

16. Analyze the Consequences of Outsourcing
What impact does outsourcing have on a country's economy and on business? Explain how it affects:

- Employment
- Standard of living
- Consumer prices
- Direct foreign investment
- Business operations and profits

Make sure you consider consequences for both the country that outsources and the country that receives the work.

Formative Assessment
Formative assessment is an essential component of classroom work. This type of assessment provides information that is then used as feedback to modify teaching and meet student needs.

L1 Have students use each key term in a sentence.

L2 Collaborate to write a narrative about an importing business started by two teenagers. Give the first sentence and then let the class take it from there.

L3 Have students choose one of the ads from this chapter and write a one-page narrative about its creation, using at least three key terms in their story.

 Reteach **If the results of this formative assessment seem low, consider the following activity:**

Students can share with a partner the questions they wrote for the Prepare to Read for each section, adding newly acquired facts and insights.

APPLY CONCEPTS

17. Benefiting from International Trade

Work in groups to prepare an oral presentation that explains international trade to a group of teenagers. Include why it is important, how we benefit from it, what government measures affect or regulate it, and what business ventures foster it. Make sure you find and present several examples of companies that are involved in international trade.

Activity Use presentation software and lots of current examples to make your points come alive.

18. Researching Global Marketing Strategies

Search the Internet to find examples of globalization, customization, and product and promotion adaptations used by multinational companies. Possible key words for your search include: *international products* or *American products abroad.* You may also access the Web site of a well-known company, such as Nike or PepsiCo.

Activity Present your findings in a written report, using word processing software, and create an oral presentation, using presentation software. Cite the Web sites and other sources you used in your written report.

NET SAVVY

19. Global Scan

Visit the Web site for the CIA's *World Fact Book* to conduct a global environmental scan for a country of your choice.

marketingessentials.glencoe.com

THE CONNECTION

Role Play: Assistant Buyer

Situation Assume the role of assistant to a buyer for a gift shop. Your shop imports gift items from South America that are then sold from your retail shop, catalog, and Web site. A newly hired sales associate (judge) has many questions about importing and the countries your company imports its merchandise from.

Activity The store's buyer has asked you to help orient the new sales associate (judge) by answering some of the sales associate's (judge's) questions about importing in general and about the merchandise your company imports.

Evaluation You will be evaluated on how well you meet the following performance indicators:

- Explain the nature of international trade
- Identify the impact of cultural and social environments on world trade
- Explain the principles of supply and demand
- Orient new employees
- Address people properly

 Online Action!

For more information and DECA Prep practice, go to *marketingessentials.glencoe .com/4/DECA*

APPLY CONCEPTS

17. Benefiting From International Trade

Student presentations should demonstrate an understanding of international trade. Presentations can be evaluated on content, especially quality of research in finding interesting examples, as well as competence with the software.

18. Researching Global Market Strategies

Student findings should demonstrate the ability to make use of Internet resources as well as the word processing software. Remind students to credit any sources taken from the Internet.

NET SAVVY

19. Global Scan

Encourage students to share the results of their country in class.

MINI-QUIZ

Read these sentences aloud and have students volunteer the missing words.

1. _____ refers to the fact that all countries depend on each other for resources that they themselves lack. (Interdependence)

2. Two types of advantages in international trade are comparative and _____. (absolute)

3. A trade deficit occurs when a country's _____ are greater than its _____. (imports, exports)

4. The business activity in the global market that carries the lowest risk is _____. (exporting)

5. Offering a product for sale worldwide without making any changes or modifications to the product is called _____. (globalization)

For an expanded chapter quiz, go to Chapter 4 in the TeacherWorks CD-ROM and to Chapter 4 in the **Exam***View*® Pro Test Generator CD-ROM.

THE CONNECTION

Students should be evaluated according to the performance standards noted in the role play. For another DECA role play, go to the Competitive Events Workbook or the Student Activity Workbook, or go to marketingessentials.glencoe.com/4/DECA

Online Action! For instructions, ideas, and answer guide, go to the Teacher Center at marketingessentials.glencoe.com

DECA Advisors Corner

Consider either an actual or an electronic exchange with DECA chapters abroad. Such partnerships can help chapter members learn more about and feel comfortable in the global marketplace.

MARKETING INTERNSHIP

A SIMULATED DECA PRODUCT AND SERVICE MANAGEMENT EVENT

SET-UP

Discuss the basic background to make sure students understand the simulation. Direct students to financial or industry Web sites and publications about global food retailers in order to assess the marketing strategies of successful food retailers in their countries of interest. Let students know opportunities in other countries remain untapped while the United States continues as a hotly contested battleground for market share.

PROCEDURES

You may want to list procedures on the board and talk about any questions the students might have. Remind the students that a suggested outline for their project is available at marketingessentials.glencoe.com/u2/internship.

TIME MANAGEMENT

Set goals, block schedules, and milestones. Assign interim deadlines for each step of the project.

ASSESSMENT

The rubrics for evaluation of the written, oral, and computer presentations are available at marketingessentials.glencoe.com/u2/internship.

Conduct a Global Environmental Scan

BASIC BACKGROUND

Friendly Supermarkets is looking to expand its operations globally. An article in *Supermarket News* (May 31, 2004) identified four countries that have potential for growth in this area: Russia, China, India, and Japan. Multinational competitors include Wal-Mart (United States), Carrefour (France), Tesco (United Kingdom), and Metro (Germany).

The Ideal Destination

The marketing director has indicated that Friendly is not interested in countries where the market is saturated, such as Brazil, Poland, Hungary, and South Africa. It is also not interested in areas where there are aggressive price promotions, such as western Europe, or where there is political unrest, such as the Persian Gulf region. For its first venture, it wants the location to be one that has the greatest potential with the least risk.

YOUR OBJECTIVE

You will be working in a team. Your objective is to give Friendly Supermarkets well-researched advice on how to proceed. The company needs to know which country to pick, how to set up its business there, and how to give the local customers what they want. There is a good chance Friendly's marketing plan for the United States will not apply overseas.

ASSIGNMENT AND STRATEGY

- **Get the background** Research the four countries and the competition. Consider the stability of the governments and their attitudes toward foreign investors. Look at the countries' economic philosophies (traditional, market, command), economic health, factors of production, infrastructure, and technology. Consider Friendly's potential customers. What sociocultural factors, such as languages, customs, and religion, would affect the four Ps of the marketing mix? Consider the competition. Local and multinational competitors may already be growing in these countries. What are the successful competitors doing differently?

- **Conduct an analysis** Use your research to conduct an environmental scan for each country. Look for opportunities and threats.

READ to WRITE

The Chinese Market

Have students research how large companies such as PepsiCo, Volkswagen, or Wal-Mart gained a stronghold in China. Have them write a two-page response about special dealings with the government and considerations made especially for the Chinese market. During their research, ask students to consider how the United States views China. They might have to research economic trends in China from World War II to the present in order to grasp how consumerism has gained ground in the Chinese economy. Students might also consider the future of the Chinese market for American consumer goods. For example, what issues exist for companies wishing to market products to the Chinese? What factors must they take into consideration? Have students answer these questions in their written responses.

Come to a consensus as a team about which country Friendly Supermarkets should invest in first. Rank the second, third, and fourth choices. Support your recommendations with facts.

- **What your project should include** Choose a country for Friendly Supermarkets' international expansion and explain why it is the best choice. Which city or region should Friendly try first? Should the company go it alone or work with a local partner? Should Friendly use its existing products and promotions, adapt them somewhat, or customize them for the local population? How should it answer the other P questions: place, price, and promotion?

 YOUR REPORT

Use a word processing program and presentation software to prepare a double-spaced report and an oral presentation for Friendly Supermarkets. See a suggested outline and key evaluation points at *marketingessentials.glencoe.com/internship*

BUILD YOUR PORTFOLIO

Option 1 Internship Report
Once you have completed your Marketing Internship project and presentation, include your written report and a few printouts of key slides from your oral presentation in your Marketing Portfolio.

Option 2 Searching the Globe Select a special product, such as a locally made soft drink or handcrafted jewelry, to market in a foreign country. Conduct environmental scans (PEST) of several countries before choosing the best one for the product. Investigate competitors and target markets. Conduct a SWOT analysis. Prepare a written report and an oral presentation using word processing and presentation software. See a suggested outline and key evaluation points at *marketingessentials.glencoe.com/portfolio*

Online Action!

Go to *marketingessentials.glencoe.com/Unit/2/DECA* to review global environmental scan concepts that relate to DECA events.

marketingessentials.glencoe.com

Marketing Internship **95**

Unit Review

Have students prepare a display of products, ads, and articles related to doing business in domestic and in global marketplaces. Ask students to supply materials and captions that present a complete picture of the following key concepts: types of businesses, current business practices (including ethical and social issues), and conducting business in the global marketplace.

STEP AHEAD
Now that students have learned about different types of economies, ask whether they think it is a good idea for businesses from different economies to work together. Students should agree that international business offers profitability but that companies must conduct research and forecasting.

Internship Wrap-Up

Have students conduct a global environmental scan on a domestic company of their choice. Encourage students to follow the steps used in their Friendly Supermarkets internship to complete their analysis.

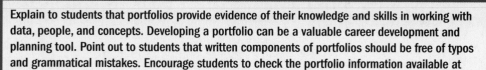

BUILD YOUR PORTFOLIO

Explain to students that portfolios provide evidence of their knowledge and skills in working with data, people, and concepts. Developing a portfolio can be a valuable career development and planning tool. Point out to students that written components of portfolios should be free of typos and grammatical mistakes. Encourage students to check the portfolio information available at **marketingessentials.glencoe.com/u2/internship.**

Peer Review
Fellow students who share common interests can serve as reviewers of the final portfolios. This review can be completed through the use of a checklist. Go to **marketingessentials.glencoe.com/u2/internship** to find a suggested checklist.

- **Chapter 5**
  The Free Enterprise System

- **Chapter 6**
  Legal and Ethical Issues

Unit Objectives

After completing this unit, students should be able to:

- Discuss the importance of international trade and government methods to encourage or discourage it
- Explain how businesses can get involved in international trade, and what factors they should consider before doing so
- Tell what a business is, and explain its basic functions
- Identify and classify different types of business
- Discuss business ethics and areas in which businesses are thought to have social responsibility

■ Key to
■ Individualized
▨ Activities

L1 Level 1 activities are basic activities and should fall within the range of all students.

L2 Level 2 activities are average activities and should be within the range of average and above average students.

L3 Level 3 activities are challenging activities designed for the ability range of above average students.

Enrichment Resources

PROFESSIONAL ORGANIZATIONS

Business Marketing Association (BMA) marketing.org

Organization of Women in International Trade owit.org

MEDIA RESOURCES

Print or online editions of

CultureGrams onlineedition.culturegrams.com

International Business Ethics Institute (IBEI) business-ethics.org

▶ WRITING SUPPORT

Ask students to write about international business from the point of view of both a consumer and a business. Have them describe the benefits and drawbacks for both the consumer and the business. Ask students to keep and review this document as they study Unit 3.

UNIT 3   PLANNING GUIDE AND RESOURCES

CHAPTER	PRINT MATERIALS	TECHNOLOGY RESOURCES
Chapter 5 Section 5.1 Section 5.2	**From Unit 3 Fast File Booklet** Lesson Plans Chapter Summaries Reproducible Masters Reproducible Tests **Print Ancillaries** Student Activity Workbook, Chapter 5 Marketing Math Workbook, Chapter 5 *BusinessWeek* Reader and Case Studies, Chapter 5 Competitive Events Workbook, Unit 3 Marketing Research Project Workbook School-to-Work Activity Workbook	Interactive Chalkboard classroom presentations, Chapter 5 Online Learning Center at **marketingessentials.glencoe.com** Online Student Edition, Chapter 5 TeacherWorks **Exam***View*® Pro Test Generator, Chapter 5 Virtual Business
Chapter 6 Section 6.1 Section 6.2	**From Unit 3 Fast File Booklet** Lesson Plans Chapter Summaries Reproducible Masters Reproducible Tests **Print Ancillaries** Student Activity Workbook, Chapter 6 Marketing Math Workbook, Chapter 6 *BusinessWeek* Reader and Case Studies, Chapter 6 Competitive Events Workbook, Unit 3 Marketing Research Project Workbook School-to-Work Activity Workbook	Interactive Chalkboard classroom presentations, Chapter 6 Online Learning Center at **marketingessentials.glencoe.com** Online Student Edition, Chapter 6 TeacherWorks **Exam***View*® Pro Test Generator, Chapter 6 Virtual Business

National Marketing Education

CHAPTER	SECTION	PERFORMANCE INDICATOR
Chapter 5 **The Free Enterprise System**	5.1	Explain the types of economic systems (ECO)
		Explain the concept of private enterprise (ECO)
		Explain the concept of competition (ECO)
		Determine factors affecting business risk (ECO)
		Identify factors affecting a business's profit (ECO)
	5.2	Explain the relationship between government and business (ECO)
		Explain the principles of supply and demand (ECO)
Chapter 6 **Legal and Ethical Issues**	6.1	Explain the role of business in society (BME)
		Explain marketing and its importance in a global economy (BME)
	6.2	Explain the role of business in society (BME)
		Treat others fairly at work (CIS)
		Demonstrate ethical work habits (PD)
		Explain the nature of environmental regulations (BME)

BME Business, Management, Entrepreneurship   **CIS** Communication, Interpersonal Skills   **ECO** Economics   **PD** Professional Development

Standards Assessment Correlation

SECTION ASSESSMENT		CHAPTER ASSESSMENT						UNIT LAB
Reviewing Key Terms and Concepts	Integrating Academic Skills	Review Facts and Ideas	Build Skills	Develop Critical Thinking	Apply Concepts	Workplace Skills	Net Savvy	Marketing Internship
1		11	18	20	22		✓	
1, 2		11, 14, 15	17		22	✓		
	✓	12	17	21	22	✓	✓	
	✓		18, 19	21	22			
3		13, 16	18	21	22		✓	
1, 3	✓	11, 16	17		22	✓	✓	
		13	18	20	22		✓	
	✓	19	21, 22	24, 25	26, 27	✓	✓	✓
	✓	18, 19			26			
2, 3	✓	19	21	24, 25	26, 27	✓	✓	✓
		19, 20	21	24	26	✓		
1, 2, 3	✓	19, 20	21	24	26, 27	✓	✓	✓
2, 3		18	22	25				

@ **Online Action!** Check the latest updates for national standards and for your state's standards at **marketingessentials.glencoe.com**

Unit Overview

Unit 3 explores international business and the basic functions of business. Chapter 5 takes the student into the global marketplace with a discussion of international trade principles and practices. Chapter 6 spells out the three major functions of business: production, marketing, and management. Then it presents the types of businesses and the social responsibilities of business to society, with regard to the environment, consumers, and ethics.

MAKING IT RELEVANT

Inform students that a business is not self-sufficient. Rather environment, consumers, and even other countries influence the way a business operates.

Unit Launch Activity

Have students share their first impressions of the ad on this page. Ask students to discuss the relationship between organized sporting events such as football games and insurance.

OUT OF TIME?

If class time is too short to cover all the chapters in this unit, go to Unit 3 in your Fast File Teacher Resources booklet and find the Chapter Summaries for Chapters 5 and 6.

In this unit you will find

- **Chapter 5**
  The Free Enterprise System

- **Chapter 6**
  Legal and Ethical Issues

THE BAYOU IS NO ORDINARY FOOTBALL GAME.

STATE FARM® IS PROUD TO BE THE TITLE SPONSOR OF THE BAYOU CLASSIC. Honor. Pride. Tradition. Things that matter long after the season ends. The State Farm Bayou Classic® is a time-honored battle on the gridiron. It's a symbol of pride that we're excited to bring to the community. From kick-off to the thrilling finish, everyone knows this is more than just a football game. WE LIVE WHERE YOU LIVE®

LIKE A GOOD NEIGHBOR   STATE FARM IS THERE®

Providing Insurance and Financial Services

statefarm.com®

State Farm Insurance Companies • Home Offices: Bloomington, IL

DECA UNIT PROJECT

Marketing Competitive Events

Have students in your DECA chapter study a U.S. firm that does business abroad or a foreign-owned company that does business in the United States. To begin their research, tell students to acquire a copy of the firm's annual report. Have them review the annual report to discover how the topics covered in this unit relate to their selected company.

Assessment Guidelines Prepare a rubric for evaluation for the research report that includes clearly defined objective, demonstrated knowledge of the topic, clearly identified concepts, and end product produced.

Enrichment Assign and review Unit 3 activities in the Competitive Events Workbook.

Marketing Plan

RELATE THE UNIT TO THE MARKETING PLAN
The four Ps of the marketing mix include product, place, pricing, and promotion. Unit 3 places them in the context of ethics and international business.

MARKETING PLAN OVERVIEW
Ask students if it is necessary for a business to have an ethical marketing plan. Opinions about the relationship between profit and ethics will vary; students should note that unethical business methods do not usually work in the long term.

Functions of Marketing
Point out to students that Chapters 5 and 6 will help them understand two foundations of marketing: economics, as well as business, management, and entrepreneurship.

- ⬤ **Economics** Infrastructure, cost of labor, taxes, and currency exchange rate are all economic factors a business must consider.

- ⬤ **Business, Management, Entrepreneurship** Production, marketing, and management create the unified triangle in business. A business categorizes itself by its size, its profit orientation, its market served, and its product or service.

(ANALYZE THE AD)

Is this ad promoting a football game or an insurance company? Both! Why would State Farm sponsor this annual matchup between two Louisiana football teams?

Market Talk All insurance companies sell similar products and services, so each one has to find a way to differentiate itself from the others. What statement is State Farm making about itself in this ad?

Think and Write Insurance companies have to compete in a free enterprise system. Some try to appeal to customers with their prices, others emphasize their services. Research three large insurance companies and note their slogans and messages to consumers. List two ways the companies you selected try to set themselves apart.

@ Online Action! Go to *marketingessentials.glencoe.com/u3/ad* for an extended activity.

Marketing Plan

1 ANALYSIS
- SWOT
- Economic
- SocioCultural
- Technological
- Competitive

2 STRATEGY
- Promotion
- Place
- Price
- Product

3 IMPLEMENTATION
- Organization
- Management
- Staffing

4 BUDGET
- Cost of sales
- Cost of Promotion
- Incomes and Expenses

5 CONTROL
- Evaluation
- Performance Measures
- Performance Analysis

In this unit

Foundations of Marketing
- Economics
- Business, Management, Entrepreneurship

(ANALYZE THE AD)

Interpretations of the State Farm ad will vary; ask students to brainstorm about other slogans or concepts that might be used to market insurance policies.

Market Talk With such slogans as "We live where you live" and "Like a good neighbor, State Farm is there," the company claims it knows its customers as people, rather than just customers. It takes the personal approach to marketing an intangible service.

Think and Write To facilitate this assignment, you may want to discuss the challenges of marketing a tangible versus an intangible service. For example, you could bring to class magazine ads for each type of service. Ask students to identify the challenges in marketing the intangible. Advertisements for intangible services often focus on the value offered to the customer.

@ Online Action! For instructions, ideas, and answer guide, go to the Teacher Center at
marketingessentials.glencoe.com

Chapter Overview

In this chapter, students will learn about the characteristics and basic principles of the free enterprise system and place it within the context of marketing, the U.S. economy, and the global marketplace.

BUILD BACKGROUND

Ask students to share ways that they have earned money. (Possibilities include baby sitting, doing yard work, selling hand-made crafts.) List responses as they are offered. Point out that all are examples of free enterprise.

Why It's Important

The free enterprise system is the economic system of the United States and many other countries. It underlies many businesses and business ventures. Knowledge of the free enterprise system is essential to any study of marketing.

Prepare to Read

Have students preview the photos in this chapter. Then ask them to provide words that describe what they learn from the photos, and begin a word list on the board. Students may suggest words such as choice, variety, manage, competition, and environment.

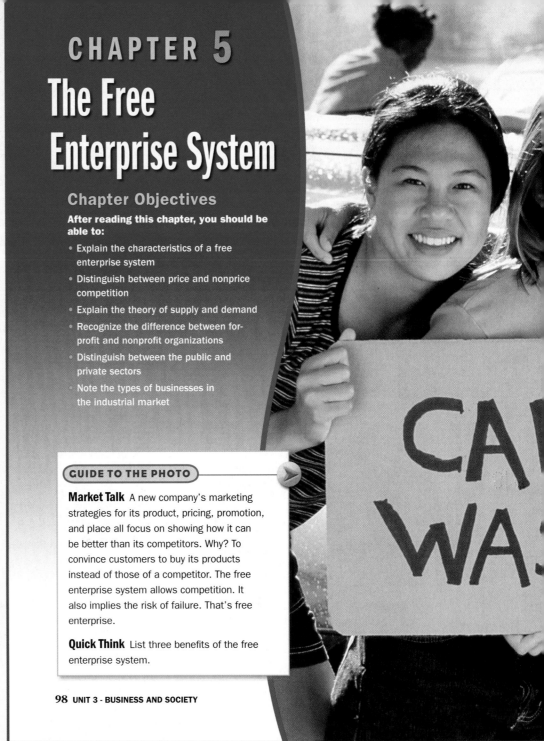

CHAPTER 5
The Free Enterprise System

Chapter Objectives

After reading this chapter, you should be able to:

- Explain the characteristics of a free enterprise system
- Distinguish between price and nonprice competition
- Explain the theory of supply and demand
- Recognize the difference between for-profit and nonprofit organizations
- Distinguish between the public and private sectors
- Note the types of businesses in the industrial market

GUIDE TO THE PHOTO

Market Talk A new company's marketing strategies for its product, pricing, promotion, and place all focus on showing how it can be better than its competitors. Why? To convince customers to buy its products instead of those of a competitor. The free enterprise system allows competition. It also implies the risk of failure. That's free enterprise.

Quick Think List three benefits of the free enterprise system.

GUIDE TO THE PHOTO

Market Talk Use a challenge or contest analogy to spark a discussion about competition: In a challenge sports event or political contest, there is often a winner and a loser. There are also often degrees of winning or losing, such as first place, second place, and so on.

Quick Think Ask students to save their lists of benefits to add to or modify as they read.

 Follow Up Ask students to think of times when they chose between two competing products. How did they make their choices?

Performance indicators represent key skills and knowledge. Relating them to the concepts explained in this chapter is your key to success in DECA events. Keep this in mind as you read this chapter and write some notes each time you encounter material that helps you master a key concept.

These acronyms represent DECA events that involve knowledge of concepts in this chapter.

AAAL	FMAL	MMS	TMDM
AAML	FMDM	QSRM	TSE
ADC	FMML	RMAL	VPM
BSM	FSRM	RMML	
EMDM	HMDM	SMDM	

In all these DECA events you should be able to follow these performance indicators:

- Explain the concept of private enterprise
- Identify factors affecting a business's profit
- Determine factors affecting business risk
- Explain the concept of competition
- Explain the principles of supply and demand
- Describe the concept of price
- Determine the relationship between government and business
- Explain the concept of organized labor and business
- Describe types of business activities

Some events include additional performance indicators. These are:

BSM Describe factors that influence the demand for services

SMDM Describe factors that influence the demand for services

DECA PREP

Check your understanding of DECA performance indicators with the DECA activity in this chapter's review. For more information and DECA Prep practice, go to *marketingessentials .glencoe.com/5/DECA*

marketingessentials.glencoe.com

Chapter 5 - The Free Enterprise System **99**

DECA events that require knowledge of the free enterprise system are described here. Discuss the performance indicators to make sure students understand how to demonstrate their understanding.

The events acronyms stand for:

AAAL: Apparel and Accessories Marketing Series, AL

AAML: Apparel and Accessories Marketing Series, ML

ADC: Advertising Campaign Event

BSM: Business Services Marketing Series

EMDM: E-Commerce Management Team Decision Making Event

FMAL: Food Marketing Series, AL

FMDM: Financial Analysis Management Team Decision Making Event

FMML: Food Marketing Series, ML

FSRM: Full Service Restaurant Management Series

HMDM: Hospitality Services Management Team Decision Making Event

MMS: Marketing Management Series

QSRM: Quick Serve Restaurant Management Series

RMAL: Retail Merchandising Series, AL

RMML: Retail Merchandising Series, ML

SMDM: Sports and Entertainment Marketing Management Team Decision Making Event

TMDM: Travel and Tourism Marketing Management Team Decision Making Event

TSE: Technical Sales Event

VPM: Vehicles and Petroleum Marketing Series

DECA PREP

Find timed DECA Prep activities correlated to the Competitive Events Workbook for students and DECA tips for teachers at **marketingessentials.glencoe.com /5/DECA**

CHAPTER 5 **Classroom Resources**

For the Teacher

- TeacherWorks
- marketingessentials.glencoe.com
- Interactive Chalkboard
- **Exam*View*®** Pro Test Generator
- Fast File Unit 3

For the Student

- *Marketing Essentials* Online Edition
- Student Activity Workbook
- Marketing Math Workbook
- Marketing Research Project Workbook
- School-to-Work Activity Workbook
- Competitive Events Workbook
- *BusinessWeek* Reader and Case Studies
- marketingessentials.glencoe.com

FOCUS

Introducing the Section

COLLABORATIVE ACTIVITY

Ask students to name products they frequently buy or would like to buy, and write the product names on the board. When the list reaches 10–12 items, ask students to name a competitive product for each.

Preteaching Key Terms

Assign key terms to student pairs. Have the pairs find the words in context, define them, and then present their words and definitions to the class.

- free enterprise system
- patent
- trademarks
- copyright
- competition
- price competition
- nonprice competition
- monopoly
- nonprofit
- business risk
- profit
- supply
- demand

Build Vocabulary

Write the word *free* on the board and ask volunteers to write definitions under it. You will probably have several definitions. Then call on a volunteer to look up the word in a dictionary. Ask: How did the class list of definitions compare to the dictionary?

OBJECTIVES

- Explain the characteristics of a free enterprise system
- Distinguish between price and nonprice competition
- Explain the theory of supply and demand

KEY TERMS

- free enterprise system
- patent
- trademark
- copyright
- competition
- price competition
- nonprice competition
- monopoly
- nonprofit
- business risk
- profit
- supply
- demand

Market-Oriented Economic Systems

READ and STUDY

BEFORE YOU READ
Connect Why do you think the free enterprise system is called "free"?

THE MAIN IDEA
Countries that are active in the global marketplace have market-oriented economic systems and follow the principles of the free enterprise system: competition, property ownership, risk, and the profit motive. Pricing in a free enterprise system is determined primarily by supply and demand theory.

STUDY ORGANIZER
Use a chart like the one below to take notes about the characteristics of a free enterprise system.

	Ownership	Business Ownership
		Intellectual Property
Freedoms		

WHILE YOU READ

Connect List two everyday examples of business life in a free enterprise system.

Basic Principles

Our nation's founders believed that individuals should have freedom of choice. They defined rights that are central to our society. For example, in the United States, we have the freedom to elect the people who represent us in our government. We have the freedom to make decisions about where we work and how we spend our money. Workers have the freedom to organize and negotiate with business, as part of a labor union. Consumers

100 UNIT 3 - BUSINESS AND SOCIETY

READ and STUDY

BEFORE YOU READ
Students can connect their definitions of *free* to make their predictions about the free enterprise system.

THE MAIN IDEA
Have students read the main idea in small groups. As questions arise, record these on the board.

STUDY ORGANIZER
Make an organizer or download the one at **marketingessentials.glencoe.com**. Show students how to begin filling out this graphic aid.

Have students write down possible examples of business life as they read.

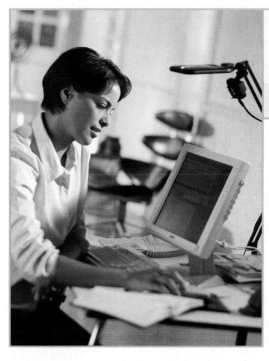

•CHOOSING WHERE YOU WORK In a free enterprise system, some people choose not to work in an office environment. They create their own businesses and sometimes work out of their homes.

Why is this flexibility an important part of our system?

TEACH

Discussion Starter

FREEDOM OF OWNERSHIP
Ask students to think for a few minutes about the things they would like to own as adults. Have students share their responses.

TEACHING POINTS
Predict Work with the group to list businesses that students think they might like to own one day. Ask them to describe the advantages and disadvantages of owning each business. Save this list of businesses for more discussion about competition.

Clarify Tell students that different economic systems have different ways of dividing up and managing work. Point out to students that ours is an economic system that allows them to choose where and how they work.

have the freedom to purchase goods and services and to invest their money in banks or businesses.

The basis of the free enterprise system is the freedom to own personal property, to compete, to take risks, and to make a profit. A **free enterprise system** encourages individuals to start and operate their own businesses in a competitive system, without government involvement. The marketplace determines prices through the interaction of supply and demand. The free enterprise system we have today in the United States is modified because the government does intervene in business on a limited basis. It does this to protect citizens, while supporting the basic principles of free enterprise.

Freedom of Ownership
Individuals in our free enterprise system are free to own personal property, such as cars, computers, and homes, as well as natural resources such as oil and land. You can buy anything you want as long as it is not prohibited by law. You can also do what you want with your property in a free enterprise system. You can give it away, lease it, sell it, or use it yourself.

Business Ownership
The free enterprise system encourages individuals to own businesses. There are all types of business, as you will see in Section 5.2. You may have heard of people who have started and run their own businesses. These individuals are called entrepreneurs. Others may not want to be involved in running a business, but they support business by investing their money in parts or shares of business. These shares of a business are called stocks, and the investors are called stockholders. Company stocks are bought and sold daily.

PHOTO GUIDE   CHOOSING WHERE YOU WORK

Discussion Ask students to brainstorm advantages and disadvantages of working at home.

Caption Answer Work flexibility allows people to set their own hours or to fulfill other obligations such as childcare or doctor's appointments.

Follow Up Ask students to describe the work environment of someone they know (or have observed) who works at home.

TEACH CONTINUED

Concept Development

INTELLECTUAL PROPERTY RIGHTS

Ask students to give examples of intellectual property rights.

Intellectual property rights include creative works such as writing (copyright), inventions (patents), processes (trade secrets), and identifiers (trademarks).

TEACHING POINTS

Demonstrate Bring to class an example—photograph or illustration—of each kind of intellectual property discussed here: patents, trademarks, copyright, and trade secret (if possible).

Individualized Practice

INTELLECTUAL PROPERTY SYMBOLS

L1 Have students work together to make a poster using the symbols ©, ®, and TM, and show an example (cut out or copied) from a book or a package.

L2 Have students make a poster defining the symbols ©, ®, and TM, and show an example of each.

L3 Have students make a three-column chart with the headers patent, trademark, and copyright. For each column, have them include the symbol, its definition, and show at least two examples.

•CREATING YOUR OWN BUSINESS
Another way to be your own boss is to open a store.

What are the pros and cons of opening a business?

When a company is doing well, stock prices generally increase because more people want to buy that stock.

There are, however, some restrictions on how and where businesses may operate. Businesses may be restricted in where they can locate. Most kinds of businesses are zoned out of areas intended for private housing. Manufacturers may be forced to comply with certain environmental and safety measures.

Intellectual Property Rights

Intellectual property rights are protected in a free enterprise system. Patents, trademarks, copyrights, and trade secrets are intellectual property rights. If you get a **patent** on an invention, you alone own the rights to that item or idea. To ensure that protection, you would apply for a patent in the U.S. Patent and Trademark Office. If granted, you would have the exclusive rights to make, use, or sell that invention for up to 20 years. During this time, anyone who wanted to manufacture your product would have to pay you for its use through a licensing agreement. A **trademark** is a word, name, symbol, sound, or color that identifies a good or service and that cannot be used by anyone but the owner. Unlike a patent, a trademark can be renewed forever, if it is being used by a business. A **copyright** involves anything that is authored by an individual, such as writings (books, magazine articles, etc.), music, and artwork. It gives the author the exclusive right to reproduce or sell the work. A copyright is usually valid for the life of the author plus 70 years. A trade secret is information that a company

PHOTO GUIDE   CREATING YOUR OWN BUSINESS

Discussion Ask students to describe what they can infer about the people in this photo by their expressions and body language.

Caption Answer Answers will vary; pros may include autonomy, creativity, and degree of control; and cons may include long working hours, too many tasks and responsibilities, and the risk of failure.

Follow Up Name a local small business with which students may be familiar, and discuss the potential pros and cons of ownership.

keeps and protects for its use only, but it is not patented. Coca-Cola's formula for Coke is a trade secret.

When a company wants to use another's name, symbol, creative work, or product, it must get permission to do so and pay a fee for the use. A licensing agreement protects the originator's name and products. A T-shirt manufacturer might be granted a licensing agreement with the National Football League (NFL) so that it can produce T-shirts with NFL logos on them. The company will have to pay NFL Properties a fee for this privilege. It will also have to agree to certain standards to protect the NFL's reputation. In addition, the NFL has control over all team logos and how the teams can use them.

Competition

Businesses that operate in a free enterprise system try to attract new customers and keep old ones. Other businesses try to take those same customers away. This struggle for customers is called **competition**.

Competition is an essential part of a free enterprise system. It is one of the means by which the free enterprise system functions to benefit consumers. Competition forces businesses to produce better-quality goods and services at reasonable prices.

Businesses constantly look for ways to develop new products and improve old ones to attract new customers. Competition results in a wider selection of products from which to choose. The results of these efforts is an

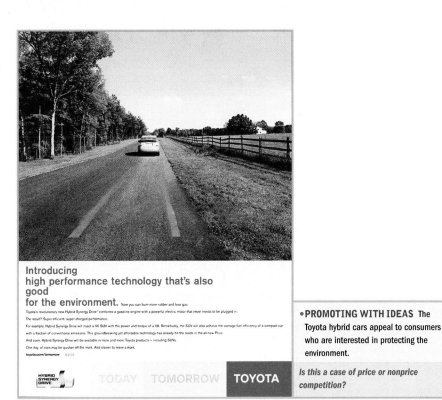

Introducing high performance technology that's also good for the environment. Now you can burn more rubber and less gas.

Toyota's revolutionary new Hybrid Synergy Drive™ combines a gasoline engine with a powerful electric motor that never needs to be plugged in.

The result? Super-efficient, super-charged performance.

For example, Hybrid Synergy Drive will inject a V6 SUV with the power and torque of a V8. Remarkably, the SUV will also achieve the average fuel efficiency of a compact car with a fraction of conventional emissions. This groundbreaking yet affordable technology has already hit the roads in the all-new Prius.

And soon, Hybrid Synergy Drive will be available in more and more Toyota products – including SUVs.

One day, all cars may be quicker off the mark. And slower to leave a mark.

toyota.com/tomorrow

HYBRID SYNERGY DRIVE TODAY TOMORROW **TOYOTA**

• **PROMOTING WITH IDEAS** The Toyota hybrid cars appeal to consumers who are interested in protecting the environment.

Is this a case of price or nonprice competition?

Chapter 5 - The Free Enterprise System **103**

TEACH CONTINUED

Concept Development

COMPETITION

Tell students that there are many ways businesses can compete. To illustrate, name a popular local restaurant. Ask why individuals like the restaurant. They may name the food, the prices, and the service. Point out that these are all ways that a particular place succeeds over its competition.

TEACHING POINTS

Extend Refer to the list of businesses students began on page 101. Ask if they want to add any businesses to the list. Then have them name competitors for each business.

Model Help students see competition in another type of business with an opening sentence such as: "I like to buy clothes at XYZ Store. They are easy to find, the service is good, and the prices are just right." Ask students to make a similar statement about a competitor. Continue as students demonstrate the different ways businesses can compete.

AD GUIDE **PROMOTING WITH IDEAS**

Discussion Make sure all students are aware of what a hybrid vehicle is (a vehicle containing both an electric battery and a gasoline engine). Such a vehicle also possesses the capacity to automatically switch between these two as driving conditions dictate. Discuss the advantages of this kind of a vehicle.

Caption Answer This is an example of nonprice competition, appealing as it does to those who are willing to spend more in order to do their part in cleaning up the environment.

Follow Up Have students compare the prices of hybrids, electric, and conventional vehicles.

TEACH CONTINUED

Concept Development

MONOPOLIES

Read the definition of *monopoly* aloud. Have students brainstorm examples of either past or possible present monopolies. Ask students to explain why a monopoly is not compatible with the free enterprise system.

The free enterprise system does not allow monopolies because they prevent competition.

TEACHING POINTS

Clarify Remind students that healthy competition can lead to the development of better products and make them more accessible to consumers.

Concept Development

RISK

Ask students to name some incidents in which they take a risk: In a sport? Beginning a new class? Learning to drive? Making a new friend? Talk about risk taking and how it feels to succeed and to fail. Lead students to see the connection between daily risks and business risks.

TEACHING POINTS

Model Set an example for students by telling about a time you took a risk and about the outcome. This example might initially be about failure, but in the end taught you a valuable lesson.

•**THE MARKET DETERMINES SUCCESS** In the 1980s, Coca-Cola changed the formula of its leading soda and launched New Coke in a highly publicized effort. The resulting flop of New Coke remains a classic example of product failure.

What do you think is a common cause of product failure?

increase in the nation's output of goods and services, as well as in its standard of living.

There are two basic ways businesses compete: price competition and nonprice competition.

Price and Nonprice Competition

Price competition focuses on the sale price of a product. The assumption is that, all other things being equal, consumers will buy the products that are lowest in price.

The marketing strategies used by Wal-Mart and Southwest Airlines are examples of price competition. Wal-Mart's "Always Low Prices. Always." slogan stresses price as the primary focus of its competitive advantage, as does Southwest's focus on low fares. Companies that run sales and offer rebates also use price competition. A $5,000 rebate offer by an auto manufacturer and a retailer's one-day sale offering a 15 percent discount storewide are examples of price competition.

In **nonprice competition**, businesses choose to compete on the basis of factors that are not related to price. These factors include the quality of the products, service, financing, business location, and reputation. Some nonprice competitors also stress the qualifications or expertise of their personnel. Businesses that use nonprice competition may charge more for products than their competitors do.

Examples of nonprice competition in advertising stress a company's reliability, tradition, superior know-how, and special services. An example of nonprice competition among dot-com companies are offers of free shipping and same-day delivery.

These examples of price and nonprice competition suggest that businesses adopt one strategy or the other. In our value-oriented society, however, it is not uncommon for businesses to try to do both. As competition increases, you may see more price-oriented

104 UNIT 3 - BUSINESS AND SOCIETY

PHOTO GUIDE THE MARKET DETERMINES SUCCESS

Discussion Have students brainstorm products or services that they liked that were not successful. Ask: How do they account for this?

Caption Answer Answers will vary. Some students may say that many people approach anything new with distrust. Others may say that if the product is good enough, it will not fail. Students may consider that success of a new product also depends on marketing and sales efforts, the strength, quality, and sales ability of any competition, and the mood of the public.

Follow Up When it became clear that the new product was not a success, Coca-Cola began to market the old product in new ways. Ask students to research the change in marketing techniques.

competitors offering services they never offered in the past.

Monopolies

When there is no competition and one firm controls the market for a given product, a monopoly exists. A **monopoly** is exclusive control over a product or the means of producing it.

Monopolies are not permitted in a free enterprise system because they prevent competition. A company can charge whatever it wants without competition. It can also control the quality of a product and who gets it. Without competition, there is nothing to stop a company from acting without regard to customer wants and needs.

One of the most publicized monopoly cases in recent history involved Microsoft, the computer software company. A federal judge declared Microsoft's Windows operating system was a monopoly. Its technology dominance was said to have stifled innovation and hurt consumers.

The U.S. government has allowed a few monopolies to exist, mainly in industries where it would be wasteful to have more than one firm. These regulated monopolies, however, are on the decline.

Currently, utility companies are being deregulated. This will allow customers to choose their own electric and natural gas suppliers. In order for this deregulation to work, the government will still control natural gas and electric companies by imposing price restrictions, preventing the formerly regulated monopolies from charging excessive prices.

Risk

Along with the benefits that come from competition and private ownership of property, businesses also face risk. **Business risk** is the potential for loss or failure. As the potential for earnings gets greater, so does the risk. For example, putting money in the bank with guaranteed interest rates is less risky than investing in the stock market where the value of shares and stocks fluctuates. Simply starting a company is a risk. If you wanted to open your own business, you would probably put your savings into the enterprise. You make money if the business is successful; but if the business fails, you lose all your savings. One out of every three businesses in the United States fails after one year of operation.

Businesses also run the risk of being sued or having their name tarnished by bad publicity (warranted or not). Natural disasters could also ruin a business. You will learn more about business risks and how to manage them in Chapter 34.

When an industry develops and profits are great, more people enter that industry. This increases competition and the risk of failure for individual firms. You may have read of businesses closing operations in effort to reduce losses and become more competitive. For example, Levi Strauss & Co. closed its manufacturing plants in North America and now contracts with foreign manufacturers to make its garments.

Risk is also involved in the development of new products. Product introductions are costly and risky; up to 85 percent of new products fail in the first year.

Profit

Profit is the money earned from conducting business after all costs and expenses have been paid. Profit is often misunderstood. Some people think the money a business earns from sales is its profit. That is not true. The range of profit for most businesses is one percent to five percent of sales; the remaining 95 to 99 percent goes to pay costs, expenses, and business taxes.

Profit is the motivation for taking the risk of starting a business. It is the potential reward for taking that risk. It is also the reward for satisfying the needs and wants of customers and consumers. Businesses may use their profits to pay owners or stockholders, or they may elect to reinvest those profits in their businesses.

Profits are good for our economy in many ways. The concept of profit is the driving force in our free enterprise system. It encourages

TEACH CONTINUED

Concept Development

PROFIT

To emphasize the concepts of risk and profit, tell students to imagine they will start a new business: making and selling T-shirts to other students in the school. Each student has $100 of imaginary money to invest or keep. Ask them how much of their $100 they are willing to invest in this venture, stressing that if the business is a success, those who invested the most will receive the greatest profit. Start off by asking for $100 investments. If there are few or none of these, begin to lower the price until you reach $5 and, if necessary, $1. You many find that many students are unwilling to invest any money while others pledge to invest higher amounts.

TEACHING POINTS

Demonstrate Ask the class what they observed during this activity, leading them to see that the whole concept of risk and profit takes on a different meaning when it is one's own money on the line.

Virtual Business

Introduce the concept of supply and demand to students using Knowledge Matters' Virtual Business Retailing visual simulation *Supply and Demand*. In this simulation, students will compute the capacity of a town to support retail stores.

Online Activity

Technology Monopoly

The government's legal action against Microsoft lasted for years and cost the taxpayers millions. To give some sense of the enormity of the action, ask students to use the Internet to find words and phrases connected with the case and bring in the results of these searches.

TEACH CONTINUED

Individualized Practice

SUPPLY AND DEMAND

L1 Have students suggest some possible prices for T-shirts that a school marketing club might sell to other students. Then, they can determine the demand for the T-shirts at each price.

L2 Ask students to suggest the number of students that would buy the shirts at each of the suggested prices. Ask students to prepare a supply and demand curve.

L3 Ask students to prepare a supply and demand curve for the T-shirts. Tell them to identify the equilibrium price, and provide a rationale for their curve.

Individualized Math Skills

L1 Ask students to explain what is wrong with this statement: A small company's first quarter sales totaled $2,468; these profits were divided among the four owners, so each person earned around $600.

The total sales figure would be reduced by operating costs, expenses, and business taxes. Only between one and five percent of the profits would be left for the owners.

L2 If a company's profits for a quarter were $600,300, and the company has one owner, which figure comes closest to the profit that owner would make for the quarter? a) $600,000; b) $60,000; c) $6,000 d) $600

d) $600

L3 A company is owned by five people. Total sales for one quarter were $250,000. If each of the owners made $250, what percent of total sales was profit?

5 percent

---

people to develop new products and services in the hope of making a profit. Without profit, few new products would be introduced.

Profit remains high when sales are high and costs are kept low. This encourages companies to work in an efficient way that helps to conserve precious human and natural resources. Profits provide money for a company to keep its facilities and machinery up-to-date. Then the business can produce goods more efficiently.

Economic Cost of Unprofitable Firms

An unprofitable business faces many problems. One of the first things businesses do when their profits decline is lay off employees. Investors in publicly traded companies can lose money if the stock value falls below what they paid for it.

Government also suffers when business profits decline. Poorly performing businesses pay less money to the government in taxes. When businesses lay off workers, there is a rise in unemployment. This causes an increase in the cost of social services and puts more stress on such agencies.

Economic Benefits of Successful Firms

Profitable businesses hire more people. Employees may have higher incomes, better benefits and higher morale. Investors earn money from their investments, which they spend or reinvest. Vendors and suppliers make more money, too. As employment and profits climb, the government makes more money from taxation of individuals and businesses. Companies and individuals are also more likely to donate to charities when they are doing well.

Remember that profitable companies attract competition, which is beneficial to the consumer. To satisfy consumer wants and needs, they try to offer new products, the lowest prices, the highest quality, and the best service.

When people earn higher incomes, they have more money to spend. There is increased demand not only for expensive products such as cars and homes, but also for services provided by a variety of businesses, from hair salons to travel agencies.

Supply and Demand

In a market-oriented economy, supply and demand determine the prices and quantities of goods and services produced. To understand how prices are determined, you have to look at supply and at demand and at how they interact. See Figure 5.1.

Supply is the amount of goods producers are willing to make and sell. The law of supply is the economic rule that price and quantity supplied move in the same direction. This means that as prices rise for a good, the quantity supplied generally rises, and as the price falls, the quantity supplied by sellers also falls. Thus, suppliers want to supply a larger quantity of goods at higher prices so their businesses can be more profitable.

Demand refers to consumer willingness and ability to buy products. The law of demand is the economic principle that price and demand move in opposite directions. As the price of a good increases, the quantity of the good demanded falls. And as the price falls, demand for the good increases.

When supply and demand interact in the marketplace, conditions of surplus, shortage, or equilibrium are created. These conditions often determine whether prices will go down, go up, or stay the same.

Surpluses

Surpluses of goods occur when supply exceeds demand. If the price of a product is too high or seems unreasonable to customers, they may decide not to buy it. Their decisions will affect the market. When this happens, businesses respond by lowering their prices in order to encourage people to buy more of the product. To do so, they may run sales or special promotions.

One of the best examples of surpluses can be found in the produce section of a supermarket. Peaches, apples, broccoli, or other produce may be priced very low one week due to supply. When a given crop is in season, there is often an excess supply, and farmers lower their prices to sell large quantities. Supermarkets that buy large quantities of the crop at the low price do the same. The surplus affects the price all the

---

Extended Activity

Adapting to Shortages

Ask students to work in groups of three to five to research shortages of items in a particular region or country over a specific period of time. You might give the example of food, nylon, or fuel shortages for domestic uses during World War II. Another example you might put forth might be the unexpected shortage of flu vaccine in the United States in the winter of 2004. Have interested students research the effects of the shortages and how individuals, governments, or organizations responded to such shortages and share their findings in an informal 10-minute oral presentation.

Figure 5.1 — Supply and Demand Theory

• **Supply and Demand** Supply and demand interact to determine the price customers are willing to pay for the goods producers are willing to make.

How do supply and demand work?

DEMAND

Demand refers to consumer willingness and ability to buy products. According to the law of demand, if the price drops, demand for a product usually increases. This is reflected in the demand schedule. It provides the points to plot a demand curve.

SUPPLY

Supply is the amount of goods producers are willing to make and sell. The law of supply states that at a higher price, producers will offer a larger quantity of products for sale. At a lower price, they will offer fewer products. This is reflected in the supply schedule. It provides the points to plot a supply curve.

Demand Schedule for Athletic Shoes Sold at Retail	
Price per Shoe	Number Demanded
$155	600
140	800
125	1,100
110	1,500
95	2,000
80	3,000
65	3,400
50	4,600
35	6,200

Supply Schedule for Athletic Shoes Sold at Retail	
Price per Shoe	Number Supplied
$155	6,000
140	5,800
125	5,600
110	5,400
95	5,000
80	4,400
65	3,400
50	2,000
35	1,000

EQUILIBRIUM

Equilibrium exists when the amount of product supplied is equal to the amount of product demanded. On the graph, this is the point where the supply and demand curves meet. It is also the point where both producer and consumer are satisfied with the price. The equilibrium price, therefore, is the price at which customers are willing to buy and producers are willing to sell.

Demand and Supply Curves for Athletic Shoes at Retail

 Online Action!

Go to *marketingessentials.glencoe.com/5/ figure/1* to find a project on supply and demand theory.

marketingessentials.glencoe.com

Chapter 5 - The Free Enterprise System **107**

Figure 5.1 — Supply and Demand Theory

Discussion Ask volunteers to read the introductory text in this figure's subheads aloud. Clarify any questions students might have.

Caption Answer As prices rise, demand drops; as supply increases, prices drop. The equilibrium point is where consumers are willing to buy and suppliers are willing to sell.

Online Action! For instructions, ideas, and answer guide, go to the Teacher Center at marketingessentials.glencoe.com

CLOSE

Ask students to respond to the following question in a one-page essay: Knowing what you know now about the free enterprise system, would you entertain the idea of starting your own business? Encourage students to provide details to support their opinions.

Essays will vary; students should provide reasons for their decision. For example, students who might wish to start their own business might cite the opportunity for profit and innovation inherent in the system; those who do not wish to start their own business might cite statistics regarding new business failure (two out of every three businesses fail in the first year) or that the average profit that can be expected is 2 to 5 percent.

way down the line. You can see how a produce shortage affects produce prices. When there is a poor season for oranges, you will find that the price of oranges is higher. For produce, extreme weather conditions such as drought or flood can affect supply. However, if the product in question is a necessity, customers will pay the price determined by the market.

Shortages

When demand exceeds supply, shortages of products occur. When shortages occur, businesses can raise prices and still sell their merchandise. An oil shortage increases the price of gasoline, so consumers who want to drive their vehicles pay the higher price. Price increases also raise the cost of doing business, which in turn affects profits. For example, in 2004, rubber prices increased significantly due to strong demand from China. The increased prices affected all types of companies, such as surgical-glove makers, producers of hoses and conveyor belts, and tire manufacturers.

Equilibrium

When the amount of a product being supplied is equal to the amount being demanded, equilibrium exists. When supply and demand are balanced, everyone wins. Customers are able to purchase goods and services at a fair price, and retailers experience a steady flow of business. Customers buy the entire stock of the product that is available. Retailers clear their shelves of merchandise. Everyone's needs and wants are satisfied in the most efficient manner possible.

There are exceptions to the rules of supply and demand, which you will learn about in Chapter 25 on price planning. There, you will see how demand elasticity and the law of diminishing returns affect supply and demand theory.

5.1 AFTER YOU READ

Reviewing Key Terms and Concepts

1. Provide an example of how freedom of ownership may be limited by government.
2. What are intellectual property rights and how does the law protect these rights?
3. In supply and demand theory, when is equilibrium achieved?

Integrating Academic Skills

Math

4. A discount retailer reported a profit of $93 million on sales of $4.6 billion. What percentage of sales was its profit?

Economics

5. If the local hair salon increased its price for a hair cut from $25 to $50, what might happen to demand for that service? What should happen if the opposite occurred—if the price was reduced from $50 to $25? What other factors could influence consumer demand in these situations?

 @ Online Action!

Check your answers at *marketingessentials.glencoe.com/5/read*

AFTER YOU READ

Reviewing Key Terms and Concepts

1. Students may suggest environmental protection and zoning laws as examples.
2. These rights include patents, copyrights, trademarks, and trade secrets. Once the first three are registered with the government, they are protected. Trade secrets cannot be registered.

3. Equilibrium is achieved when the amount of a product being supplied is equal to the amount being demanded.

Integrating Academic Skills

4. 2 percent; $93 million profit ÷ sales of $4.6 billion is 0.0202, or 2 percent

5. If the salon increases its price, demand should go down. If the opposite occurs, demand should go up. Other factors include quality of the haircut, location of the shop, customer loyalty, and ability to grant appointments in a reasonable amount of time.

 Online Action! Answers at **marketingessentials.glencoe.com/5/read**

Business Opportunities

READ and STUDY

BEFORE YOU READ
Connect Can you think of some businesses that are not interested in making a profit?

THE MAIN IDEA
The major functions of a business are production or procurement, marketing, management, and finance. The analysis of these key functions is an excellent basis for determining the strengths and weaknesses of a company as part of a SWOT analysis.

STUDY ORGANIZER
In charts like the one below, record the various ways to classify businesses and the major functions of business.

- Types of Business
  - Size and Scope — Large Versus Small
  - Purpose

OBJECTIVES
- Recognize the difference between for-profit and nonprofit organizations
- Distinguish between the public and private sectors
- List the major types of businesses in the industrial market

KEY TERMS
- domestic business
- global business
- for-profit business
- nonprofit organization
- public sector
- private sector
- industry
- derived demand
- wholesalers
- retailers
- production
- management
- finance
- accounting

Types of Business

In a free enterprise system, there are many opportunities to invest or work in many different types of businesses. In order to view those opportunities, it is a good idea to start by classifying businesses. To understand their differences, you will need to know the terminology associated with business classification. Keep in mind that a business may be classified in more than one

WHILE YOU READ

Connect List four businesses in your community. How would you classify each one?

FOCUS

Introducing the Section

COLLABORATIVE ACTIVITY
Have students work as a group to review the definition of a SWOT analysis. A SWOT analysis is a critical examination by a business of itself and its business environment. Also known as Strengths, Weaknesses, Opportunities, Threats.

Preteaching Key Terms

Have students find the terms in the text and read them in context. Then have them write the definitions.

- domestic business
- global business
- for-profit business
- nonprofit organization
- public sector
- private sector
- industry
- derived demand
- wholesalers
- retailers
- production
- management
- finance
- accounting

Building Vocabulary

Have student groups read the section's objectives. Ask them to share with the class two pairs of terms they will learn to analyze in this section (e.g., for-profit and nonprofit organizations; public and private sectors.) Discuss some of the nonprofit organizations in your area (i.e., how they make money, and what they do with the money they make).

READ and STUDY

BEFORE YOU READ
Students may have heard of the Red Cross, Doctors Without Borders, or other such organizations.

THE MAIN IDEA
Read this statement with students, discussing each point in turn. If applicable, have students preview text for the definition of *procurement*.

STUDY ORGANIZER
Model the study organizer by filling out the first blank, or download the one provided at
marketingessentials.glencoe.com

WHILE YOU READ Suggest that students make notes about each business as they proceed through this section.

TEACH

Discussion Starter

SIZE AND SCOPE

Have students choose one business from among the four they listed as they prepared to read this section. Ask volunteers to describe the business they chose. Then point out that in marketing there are some standard ways to describe a business. Knowing marketing terms aids in the fluency of business language.

TEACHING POINTS

Demonstrate Give students help with outlining by putting the following on the board. Have the class copy it, leaving spaces for notes between each item. As students read, encourage them to take notes to fill in the outline.

I. Ways to Classify Businesses

  A. Size and Scope
    1. Large Versus Small Business
    2. Domestic Versus Global

  B. Purpose
    1. For Profit Versus Nonprofit
    2. Public Versus Private

  C. Industry & Markets
    1. NAICS
    2. Consumer, Industrial, and Service Markets

•CLASSIFYING BUSINESSES Qantas Airlines flies many routes around the globe as well as in Australia.

What type of company is Qantas, domestic or global?

Only Qantas can entertain you all the way to Australia.

Sit back, relax and enjoy your own personal entertainment system. With 12 video channels, 16 audio channels, the very latest movies and quality kids programming, the journey will be over before you know it. That's the spirit. **The Spirit of Australia.** QantasUSA.com

QANTAS

category. A business can be classified by its size and scope, by its purpose, and by its place within the industry.

Size and Scope

One of the easiest ways to describe a business is by its size. It is large or small? The scope of a business refers to the extent of its business operation. Some businesses serve a small neighborhood, while others do business globally. Now we will look at these two ways to categorize businesses.

Large Versus Small Businesses

A small business is one that is operated by only one or a few individuals. It generally has fewer than 100 employees. A large business is usually one that employs more than 1,000 people. Nationwide, there are millions of small businesses, or "mom-and-pop" operations. They include neighborhood grocery stores, florists, gift shops, photocopy and print shops, and secretarial services. This category also contains many Internet start-up companies and dot-com businesses that often start off with small budgets and staffs. About 95 percent of all U.S. businesses are classified as small businesses. These types of businesses employ more than half of the private-sector (non-government) workforce.

AD GUIDE   **CLASSIFYING BUSINESSES**

Discussion Have students study both the words and image in this ad. Ask students to brainstorm what Qantas is offering? Answers may include all sorts of electronic extras to make the long flight between the United States and Australia comfortable and pleasant.

Caption Answer Qantas is a global company.

Follow Up Encourage students to research other Qantas or airline ads. Can they find a common thread among them? Encourage students to share their research results in class.

NET MARKETING

Web Sites Created by Kids

A 14-year old entrepreneur designs Web sites for other small businesses and has four clients. Other teenagers who are building Web sites are doing so to promote a cause or provide help for others. Peter Grunwald of the Internet research firm Grunwald Associates estimates there are about two million sites created by kids aged 6 to 17.

Getting Started

Terra Lycos is a company that promotes site building. People start with its free service and then can upgrade for a charge. The company offers two sites—Angelfire.com and Tripod.com—that host personal sites.

Kids do not have to know computer code—software programs make site building easy.

THINK LIKE A MARKETER

List three reasons why teenagers would use Terra Lycos's service.

@ Online Action!

Go to *marketingessentials.glencoe.com/ 5/net* to find an activity on Internet marketing and the free enterprise system.

Concept Development

PURPOSE

Ask students to identify the different kinds of business organizations explained in this section and to give an example of each type of organization.

The different kinds of organizations are for-profit businesses, nonprofit organizations, public enterprise, and private enterprise. Examples will vary. A for-profit business such as Microsoft seeks to make a profit. A nonprofit organization such as the Sierra Club uses the revenue it earns to fund the cause identified in its charter. A public school is an example of a government-funded enterprise. A business not associated with government agencies, such as a private bank or corporation, is part of the private sector.

TEACHING POINTS

Give some examples of nonprofit businesses that are not mentioned in the text such as UNICEF, SPCA, homeless shelters, student vocational organizations (such as DECA), professional organizations (such as the Small Business Association), and the Special Olympics. Then ask students to volunteer reasons why someone might want to work for a business that does not have profit as a main motive for operation.

Answers might include idealism, ethics, personal satisfaction, a desire to improve a particular industry, and so on.

Domestic Versus Global

A business that sells its products only in its own country is considered a **domestic business**. Because a domestic business limits its scope of operation to one country, its opportunities for growth are limited to customers within that country. A **global business** sells its products in more than one country. The advent of the Internet, along with faster transportation and financial transfers, makes it easier to do business globally. Products produced in one country are now finding greater acceptance around the world. The trend among large and small businesses is toward a more global market.

Purpose

A business firm serves the needs of its customers in order to make a profit. However, there are other organizations that function like a business but have a different purpose. To understand this difference, we need to distinguish between for-profit and nonprofit organizations, and between public and private enterprise.

For-Profit Versus Nonprofit Organizations

A **for-profit business** seeks to make a profit from its operations. A **nonprofit organization** functions like a business but uses the money it makes to fund the cause identified in its charter. Nonprofit organizations generate revenue through gifts and donations. Some even sell goods or services, which generate income. They usually do not have to pay taxes on their income. They also have expenses. They pay employees and rent for their office space. Other expenses may include supplies, printing, and postage for letters sent requesting donations. The Red Cross, the Boy Scouts of America, DECA, and other nonprofit organizations strive to generate more income than expenses, just like a for-profit business. However, unlike profit-oriented businesses, nonprofit organizations use that extra money to fund their respective causes. Thus, their organizational

marketingessentials.glencoe.com

Chapter 5 - The Free Enterprise System 111

NET MARKETING

Web Sites Created by Kids

Discussion Have a volunteer read this article for the rest of the class. Lead a discussion about what might motivate young people to build Web sites.

THINK LIKE A MARKETER Answer: Possible reasons include for technology help, for advice to beginners, and to research other Web sites.

@ Online Action! For instructions, ideas, and answer guide, go to the Teacher Center at **marketingessentials.glencoe.com**

Follow Up Encourage students to look at the Web sites mentioned in this article and report their findings to the class.

TEACH CONTINUED

Individualized Practice

HOW TO CLASSIFY

To demonstrate how to classify, have students complete one of these activities.

L1 Have student groups take a poll of how they commute to school. Have them classify the results and show them in a table.

L2 Have student groups take a classroom poll of an item students bought for themselves. Have them classify the results and show in a chart or pie graph.

L3 Have students poll classmates for a business in which they might have an interest. Tell students to classify the types of businesses named and show them in a chart or graph.

Build Vocabulary

Preview the following word by reading it in context:

* **endowment** donated income

Then have students explain what the word means. Check a dictionary as needed.

Critical Thinking

Have students work in pairs to name a business, local or national, and classify it according to the NAICS system.

---

goal is not to make a profit but rather to use that money for their cause. Many people who feel strongly about helping others seek to start or work for a nonprofit organization. Although there are many unpaid volunteers, a staff of paid workers is often also needed to manage the operation of a nonprofit organization.

Public Versus Private

In addition to charitable institutions, other organizations operate like businesses but are not intended to earn a profit. Most local, state, and federal government agencies and services, such as public schools and public libraries, fall into this category. Their main purpose is to provide service to the people in the country or community in which they operate. At the federal level, there are military agencies, like the Army and the Air Force; social agencies, like Social Security and Medicare; and regulatory agencies, like the Food and Drug Administration and the Environmental Protection Agency. Government-financed agencies like

Case Study

Entrepreneurship and Science

The Wisconsin Alumni Research Foundation (WARF) is a little-known nonprofit organization that was founded in 1925 by Harry Steenbock and eight other alumni of the University of Wisconsin-Madison. Each of the nine founders contributed $100 to hold patents developed by the university. Today, patent royalties and investment income have piled up a $1.3 billion endowment, which returns $40 million a year to the university for scientific research.

A 1923 Discovery

This all came about after Steenbock discovered, in 1923, that irradiating food increased its vitamin D content, which would eliminate rickets, a crippling bone disease. The Quaker Oats Company offered $1 million ($10.8 million in today's dollars) to purchase the rights to this process. But Steenbock reckoned the university could reap far more if the foundation held on to the patent and licensed the technology to Quaker Oats. Vitamin D still accounted for 70 percent of the $38.7 million in patent royalties earned in 2003. Today, inventors get 20 percent of the royalties generated by their invention. WARF collects the remaining 80 percent but agrees to defend the patent against challenges (which can cost $1 million or more).

THINK STRATEGICALLY

How can WARF be helpful to a scientist who has an idea for curing cancer or another life-threatening disease?

@ Online Action!

Go to *marketingessentials.glencoe.com/5/case* to find an activity about scientific research and the free enterprise system.

Case Study   Entrepreneurship and Science

Discussion Ask students to brainstorm reasons why universities and other educational and nonprofit research organizations might seek to hold patents.

THINK STRATEGICALLY   **Answer:** The foundation might fund the research.

@ Online Action!   For instructions, ideas, and answer guide, go to the Teacher Center at **marketingessentials.glencoe.com**

Follow Up   Have interested students research WARF online to learn about other technologies and report their findings to the class.

Hi. Lo. Pick a color.

Free Shipping

Free Return Shipping

365-Day Return Policy

110% Price Protection

★CONVERSE at Zappos.com
the web's most popular shoe store!

www.zappos.com

•ZAPPOS'S ADVANTAGE
This ad advertises Converse sport shoes. But it also advertises Zappos.com, a shoe e-tailer.

Would you shop at Zappos.com? Why or why not?

Concept Development

CONSUMER, INDUSTRIAL, AND SERVICE MARKETS

Ask students to explain the difference between wholesalers and retailers and to give an example of each.

Examples will vary. Wholesalers, or distributors, obtain goods from manufacturers and sell them to industrial users, retailers, or other wholesalers. Retailers buy goods from wholesalers or manufacturers and resell them to the consumer.

Individualized Math Skills

L1 Have students select a product, such as a pair of sneakers. Then look in various advertisements to find a price, and share it with the class.

L2 Have students select a product, and find a price for the same item at three different e-tailing sources. Have students report their findings to the class.

L3 Have students compare three e-tailing sites for best prices and make a chart demonstrating price variances.

---

these are part of the **public sector**. Businesses not associated with government agencies are part of the **private sector**.

Public-sector organizations purchase one-third of all goods and services sold in the United States each year. Just think about all the products and supplies purchased in the operation of your public school system and you will see why businesses seek out customers in the public sector.

Industry and Markets

Businesses are often classified according to the industry they represent, the products they sell, and the markets they target. The government provides a system for classifying types of business by industry and sector. Products and markets are classified according to intended use. All of these classifications are interrelated based on the customers served.

NAICS

According to the U.S. Department of Labor, an **industry** consists of a group of establishments primarily engaged in producing or handling the same product or group of products or in rendering the same services. For 60 years, the U.S. government used the Standard Industrial Classification (SIC) system to collect data on businesses and analyze the U.S. economy. However, rapid changes in

services and technology made a new system necessary. The United States, Canada, and Mexico jointly developed the North American Industry Classification System (NAICS). In a nutshell, it states that "establishments that do similar things in similar ways are classified together." NAICS uses a six-digit hierarchical coding system to classify all economic activity into 20 industry sectors. For example, the information sector includes the industries involved in communications, publishing, and motion pictures, as well as Internet companies. Some of the subcategories of the Internet industry are Web search portals, Internet publishing and broadcasting, electronic shopping, and electronic auctions. The information in the NAICS can be helpful to businesses looking for new marketing opportunities and to individuals who may want to find employment or invest in those sectors.

Consumer, Industrial, and Service Markets

As you read in Chapter 2, the consumer market consists of customers who buy goods for personal use. The industrial market consists of business customers who buy goods for use in their operations. The two are interrelated because of the economic concept of derived demand. For example, when consumers decide to buy more automobiles, dealers

Chapter 5 - The Free Enterprise System 113

Concept Development

INDUSTRY AND MARKETS

Tell students that a good example of derived demand is electric cars, such as Honda Civic Hybrid, and Toyota Prius Hybrid. Have them research to find out the length of the waiting list to purchase one of these cars at a local dealer.

TEACHING POINTS

Paraphrase In their own words, have students provide definitions of consumer market, industrial market, and service market.

Extend Have students name another product that is currently trendy—an item of clothing, footwear, or music. Lead a discussion about derived demand if that item suddenly sold way beyond its production expectations.

Concept Development

THE FUNCTIONS OF BUSINESS

Ask students to name the four functions involved in the management of an organization.

Production and procurement, marketing, management, and finance

---

need more cars, so auto manufacturers will need an increased supply of auto components, such as tires, radios, batteries, and electronic parts. Companies that make such parts experience an increased demand as a result of consumer decisions to buy more cars. This is called derived demand. **Derived demand** in the industrial market is based on, or derived from, the demand for consumer goods and services. Because of this relationship between consumer and industrial demand, industrial companies look for opportunities to increase their business by studying consumer trends. Service-related businesses function in both consumer and industrial markets.

Businesses that are involved in the industrial market include extractors, construction and manufacturing businesses, wholesalers, retailers, and service-related firms.

Extractors are businesses that take something from the earth or sea. They include agriculture, forestry, fishing, and mining. The products are sold primarily to other businesses.

Construction companies build structures such as houses, office buildings, and manufacturing plants. Manufacturing involves producing goods to sell to other manufacturers or to wholesalers and retailers. **Wholesalers** obtain goods from manufacturers and resell them to industrial users, other wholesalers, and retailers. Wholesalers are also called distributors. **Retailers** buy goods from wholesalers or directly from manufacturers and resell them to the consumer. For the most part, retailers cater to the consumer market.

Service-related businesses are companies that provide intangible products to satisfy needs and wants of consumers and/or businesses. Consumer services include such things as dry cleaning, hair styling, entertainment, transportation, insurance, and personal needs, such as lawn-cutting, child care, and housekeeping. Business services follow the same concept. That is why you have firms that specialize in accounting, marketing, management, insurance, shipping, and finance. There are also professional services—those provided by

professionals such as doctors, dentists, and lawyers.

Internet-related services, such as Web portals, Web casting, Web site design, and Web advertising have created opportunities that did not exist many years ago. For example, e-commerce (short for "electronic commerce") is the buying and selling of products through the use of electronic networks, usually the Internet. Even traditional retailers are adapting their marketing to e-commerce, creating e-tailing.

The Functions of Business

Regardless of the type of business, there are four main functions involved in an organization's operation. They are production or procurement, marketing, management, and finance. The ways each business performs these activities may differ. However, all four are essential for running a business or organization. The success of a business is dependent on how well these activities are coordinated, managed, and performed.

A company that has a great product but is poorly managed will not succeed. A company will also fail if it lacks the resources to pay for experienced personnel or to maintain inventory levels so products are available for sale. Poor financial record keeping can lead to poor management decisions, which may result in poor performance. If inaccurate accounting causes investors to believe that a company is more profitable than it really is, a corporation's reputation may be damaged. That in turn can lead to bad publicity and lower stock prices. Thus, the four business functions must be viewed in relation to one another. As you evaluate strengths and weaknesses during a SWOT analysis, review all four activities. For now, we will look at the role each plays in a firm's operation. Keep in mind that all these functions must be performed well for a company to be successful.

Production and Procurement

The process of creating, expanding, manufacturing, or improving on goods and services

---

 Extended Activity

Production of Goods and Services

Ask students to research all the stages of production for a product or service of their choice. You might suggest a CD or a food product such as sliced bread for a product, and a car wash for a service.

GLOBAL MARKET

FRANCE

A Hidden Champion

Hidden champions is a term that was coined by a German business consultant, Hermann Simon. A hidden champion is a small to medium-sized company that is narrowly focused on a small, highly specialized market. Such companies are usually not well known, yet are very profitable. One example of a hidden champion is the French company Essilor.

Staying the Course Essilor manufactures ophthalmic lenses, which is the formal name for contact lenses and lenses for eyeglasses. Over the years, Essilor has reinforced its single focus and avoided branching out into eyeglass retailing. Instead, the company concentrated its efforts on going global. Today, Essilor is the industry's leader. Besides staying specialized and having a clear strategy, Essilor kept innovations coming. For example, Essilor invented progressive lenses. These alternatives to bifocal lenses have a gradual change in correction power from top to bottom. Like most other hidden champions, Essilor invests a notable four to five percent of its annual sales on research and development. Other characteristics of hidden champions include tight financial management, superior customer service, and foresight.

CRITICAL THINKING

How would you evaluate this hidden champion based on the functions of business?

@ Online Action!

Go to *marketingessentials.glencoe.com/5/global* to find an activity on global marketing and free enterprise.

---

is called **production**. A songwriter creates a song. A farmer grows wheat. Ford Motor Company manufactures cars. Van conversion companies improve new vans to make them more suitable for a disabled driver, or for camping and travel. Thus, production, as a function of business, is found in industries such as farming, mining, forestry, manufacturing, and service-related operations.

When evaluating this function of business in a SWOT analysis, look for innovation, speed to market, efficiency, and level of success with products. Companies that want to be leaders in an industry produce the most innovative products and do so before their competitors do. Efficiency helps to keep prices down and sales up, which makes for a profitable company.

Hewlett-Packard is a good example of an industry leader in printers. The computer equipment maker has 9,000 patents, and anything that is not patented is protected by trade secrets. As a result, it is the industry leader in printers. In 2004, the printer division accounted for 80 percent of Hewlett-Packard's earnings.

Procurement

Procurement involves buying and reselling goods that have already been produced. Retail and wholesale businesses function in this capacity. A supermarket (retailer) buys cans of soup, fresh produce, frozen foods, dairy products, and the other nonfood items for resale. Most of these products were purchased from manufacturers, while a few may have been

---

GLOBAL MARKET

A Hidden Champion

Discussion Ask students to brainstorm which function or functions of business are described by the phrases "research and development" and "superior customer service."

CRITICAL THINKING **Answer:** Students may suggest that Essilor exhibits an effective balance between production, marketing, management, and financing.

@ Online Action! For instructions, ideas, and answer guide, go to the Teacher Center at **marketingessentials.glencoe.com**

Follow Up Read the article with students stopping as needed to stress and clarify key points. Have a student use a dictionary to define *ophthalmic*.

TEACH CONTINUED

Concept Development

PRODUCTION AND PROCUREMENT

After reading the first paragraph, ask students to list the activities involved in production.

creating, expanding, manufacturing, improving goods

TEACHING POINTS

Extend Help students distinguish the difference between production (the making of product) and procurement (buying product already produced).

Demonstrate Have students look around the room and point out things that are produced. As they name items, ask if they can describe (or take their best guess at) how the item was produced.

Individualized Math Skills

L1 For this activity, have students consider a company that has assets of $100,000 and liabilities of $75,000. Ask students to calculate how much equity the company should have in order for the owners to own more of the company than the creditors.

$50,000 or more

L2 Have student pairs create a financial table with columns labeled Assets, Liabilities, and Equity. Have students create appropriate figures that would show the owners' profit.

L3 Divide students into pairs. Have students create a financial table with columns labeled Assets, Liabilities, and Equity. Have partners describe a business, with its assets, liabilities, and equity, while the other partner enters the numbers in the table and evaluates the business for success.

ASSESS

Review Guide

CONCEPTS

1. Ask students to recall the three large categories that are used to classify businesses.

size and scope, purpose, and industry and markets

2. Ask students to name the four functions of business.

production or procurement, marketing, management, and finance

KEY TERMS

Students can work in small groups to review definitions of terms, if necessary finding them again in context and talking about meanings.

ONLINE SELF-ASSESSMENT

Have students go to marketingessentials.glencoe.com for the Section 5.2 practice test.

Individualized Review

L1 Assign and review Chapter 5 activities in the Student Activity Workbook.

L2 Assign and review Chapter 5 activities in the Marketing Math Workbook.

L3 Assign and review Chapter 5 activities in the *BusinessWeek* Reader and Case Studies.

Marketing Practice

Have students choose a company of interest or one that produces a product they use. Ask students to research the product and then define it for the class using what they have learned in this section.

---

purchased from wholesalers. Wholesalers buy goods from manufacturers for resale to other wholesalers and retailers. Even businesses that appear to manufacture their own products may actually be buying those products from other companies and putting their names on the labels. You may buy a Dell printer thinking that Dell manufactured that printer. However, another company like Lexmark may have made that product with minor changes and re-branded it a Dell.

SWOT Analysis, Wholesalers, and Retailers

In a SWOT analysis, you would evaluate wholesalers and retailers on their merchandising ability.

The five "rights" of merchandising are having:

- the right goods
- at the right time
- in the right place
- at the right price
- in the right amount.

Predicting customer demand and product preferences is a difficult task, as is determining the price at which those products will sell.

Marketing

All activities from the time a product leaves the producer or manufacturer until it reaches the final consumer are considered marketing activities.

All types of business, regardless of size, scope, intended purpose, and products sold use marketing activities in their operations. Manufacturers, service operations, wholesalers, and retailers buy goods for use in their operations and sell their finished products to customers.

The Role of Marketing Activities

All related marketing activities support the buying and selling functions. For example, research helps to determine what products to make and/or purchase, as well as how to price and promote them. Promotion helps to educate potential customers about a company's products and is used to stimulate sales.

Aeropostale, a New York-based chain of retail apparel stores, spends heavily for consumer research. Since it is a teen-oriented company, it must keep up with teens' changing tastes in clothing. To do so, it runs high school focus groups, in-store product tests, and an online research program. The Internet-based research is conducted with 100,000 online shoppers who are asked for their input in crating new styles. It runs this program 20 times a year and averages 3,500 participants.

In a SWOT analysis, you would evaluate the four Ps of the marketing mix and how well they focus on the intended market(s). They should also be reviewed in relation to the company's objectives and sale performance.

Management

Management is the process of achieving company goals by effective use of resources through planning, organizing, and controlling.

Planning involves establishing company objectives and forming strategies to meet those objectives. Management will determine the corporate culture and mission or vision for a firm.

Organizing involves specific operations, such as scheduling employees, delegating responsibilities, and maintaining records.

Controlling has to do with overseeing and analyzing operating budgets to suggest the most cost-effective measures for a company to follow. Analysis of financial reports, such as cash flow and profit and loss statements, is part of its controlling function.

A SWOT analysis would evaluate the personnel who run a company. The CEO or owner in a smaller operation, as well as the key managers and their expertise, are important indicators.

Finance and Accounting

Finance is the function of business that involves money management. **Accounting** is the discipline that keeps track of a company's financial situation. If you want to analyze a company's finances, you would study its balance sheet, profit and loss statement, and possibly its cash flow statement.

 Online Activity

Consumer Research

Ask students to research consumer research firms and find consumer research opportunities online. Ask any students who have participated in online consumer research to describe their experiences. Have them explain how they became involved in the market research, what kinds of questions they answered, and whether they were compensated in anyway. Remind students that they should never give their Social Security number, credit information, bank account information or any PIN numbers while participating in online consumer surveys or focus groups.

Balance Sheet

A balance sheet reports a company's assets, liabilities, and owner's equity. Assets are things a company owns. Liabilities represent money owed by a business to its creditors.

If most of a company's liabilities have not been paid for yet, a company's financial situation would not be positive. For example, if a company had assets of $100,000 and liabilities of $75,000, its owner's equity would be only $25,000. In this case, creditors own more of the company than the owners.

Profit and Loss Statements

Profit and loss statements reflect the ongoing operations of a firm. They include income from sales revenue and investments,

as well as costs and expenses of doing business. A profitable company generates more income than it pays out for costs of goods and expenses to run the business. When a business suffers a loss, its costs and expenses exceed its revenue.

Financial Statements and the SWOT Analysis

In a SWOT analysis, both financial statements provide important information regarding how well a business is doing financially.

A profitable business with high owner's equity allows a company to grow. It can invest in more research and devel-opment. It can expand its operations by building new facilities or acquiring other business. Why? Because it has the money to do so.

CLOSE

Ask students if they have formed any new or additional ideas of where their own marketing job interests might lie. Encourage students to use the terms they have learned in this section in formulating their responses.

Extended Activity

Company Earnings

Tell students that balance sheets and profit and loss statements are both components of company earnings statements, which are often released both quarterly and year-end. These earnings statements are used by investors and the financial community to determine the company's performance. Have interested students research past quarterly or year-end earnings for a public or private company online or in print media and summarize the results in a brief (one-paragraph) response.

5.2 AFTER YOU READ

Reviewing Key Terms and Concepts

1. Of what significance are small businesses to the U.S. economy?

2. Why would DECA, an international association of marketing students, be classified as a nonprofit organization?

3. What information is reported in a company's balance sheet? In its profit and loss statement?

Integrating Academic Skills

Math

4. Determine the net worth (owner's equity) of a company that has assets of $500,000 and liabilities of $200,000.

History

5. Research how the Red Cross, a nonprofit organization, began internationally and in the United States, and identify its fundamental principles and any interesting historical facts about its operations. Prepare a written report on your findings.

 Online Action!

Check your answers at *marketingessentials.glencoe.com/5/read*

marketingessentials.glencoe.com

Chapter 5 - The Free Enterprise System **117**

 AFTER YOU READ

Reviewing Key Terms and Concepts

1. About 95 percent of all U.S. businesses are classified as small. These businesses employ about 95 percent of all the private sector (non-government) workforce.

2. DECA is a nonprofit because the money it makes is not distributed as profit but rather used to further the education of marketing students.

3. A balance sheet reports a company's assets, liabilities, and owner's equity. A profit and loss statement reports the ongoing operations of a firm, including its income from sales revenue and investments and the costs of doing business.

Integrating Academic Skills

4. The net worth (owner's equity) of a company that has assets of $500,000 and liabilities of $200,000 is $300,000. ($500,000 − $200,000)

5. Reports will vary. Students might first access the Red Cross Web site and click under Frequently Asked Questions to get basic information to begin their research.

Online Action! Answers at **marketingessentials.glencoe.com/5/read**

Lifelong Learning

CAREER INFORMATION

Have students go to marketingessentials.glencoe.com and find the Chapter 5 Careers page. They can then click on the link for the American Marketing Association's Career Strategies and Tips. Ask students to select one article, read it, and summarize it in three short paragraphs.

MULTIPLE LANGUAGES

Second-language learning is a good way to prepare for a marketing career in a global economy. Any second language must be practiced regularly outside the classroom for the speaker to gain and maintain fluency. Reading, viewing, or listening to media in the second language is also an excellent way to gain exposure to that language.

Primary Source

Ask students to go to marketingessentials.glencoe.com and find Chapter 5 Resources. Ask them to click on the link for the American Marketing Association's marketing dictionary and read the definitions of terms relating to the free enterprise system.

● THINKING CRITICALLY

Specialized knowledge gives one the ability to understand the culture and trends of the target market.

@ Online Action!

For instructions, ideas, and answer guide, go to the Teacher Center at marketingessentials.glencoe.com

---

CAREERS
IN MARKETING

MICHAEL SARAY
DIRECTOR, HISPANIC COUNCIL, DIRECT MARKETING ASSOCIATION

? What do you do at work?
Many direct marketers realize the importance of the Hispanic market and MSHM helps them get started. Typically, we do not do primary research, but instead we look for the relevant information regarding market size and consumer attitudes. With the relevant information in hand, we develop a strategic plan that considers strengths and weaknesses, consumer awareness, and media options. Once the communication platform is developed, we create the actual message. This involves integrating the words and the images so that the consumer is motivated to act. We do this with mail pieces, the Internet, and television and print advertising.

? What skills are most important to you?
I have a good education with a bachelor of commerce degree and an MBA. This has taught me to be analytic and consider the whole picture. Make sure that you take every opportunity you can to improve your technical and computer skills. The most important training is informal and on the job. There is always something to be learned from those around you.

? What is your key to success?
Be passionate about your work. Listen and understand what people are telling you. Be an expert in your area. Never stop learning.

Aptitudes, Abilities, and Skills

Strong research, communication, and writing skills, creativity, organization, and time management skills

Education and Training

Degrees in marketing, communication, or general business; MBAs are also helpful.

Career Path

Entry-level marketing positions often deal with the basics of the field and might be thought of as apprenticeships of sorts. Higher-level marketing positions are often filled from this pool of talent.

● THINKING CRITICALLY

How can specialized knowledge of a particular market—in this case, the Hispanic consumer—be an asset?

@ Online Action!

Go to *marketingessentials.glencoe.com/ 5/careers* to find a career-related activity.

◢ Test-Taking Strategies

Staying up all night cramming for a test may seem effective, but it can lead to exhaustion before the testing even begins. Encourage students to schedule study time numerous days in advance of the test to ensure a good night's sleep the night before the test.

FOCUS on KEY POINTS

SECTION 5.1

- The characteristics of a free enterprise system are freedom of ownership, freedom to compete, freedom to make a profit, and freedom to take risks. Price competition involves competing with a lower price, while nonprice competition involves factors other than price, such as special services and an excellent reputation.

- The economic cost of unprofitable businesses includes loss of jobs, loss of revenue to investors and to the government, and increased government costs for social services. The possible benefits of successful firms include increased employment, better returns for investors, more sales revenue for supporting companies, more tax revenue for the government, higher charitable donations, and more competition.

- Supply and demand interact to create price. Theory suggests that as prices rise, demand drops. As prices increase, supply increases. The equilibrium point is where the supply and demand curves meet. At that point, consumers are willing to buy and suppliers are willing to sell.

SECTION 5.2

- Businesses can be classified on the basis of size and scope, purpose, and place within industry.

- Unlike profit-oriented businesses, which keep their profits, nonprofit organizations use the money they make (profit) to fund the causes identified in their charters. The public sector consists of all organizations and agencies funded by the government. The private sector consists of all nongovernmental organizations and businesses. The major types of businesses that comprise the industrial market are extractors, construction companies, manufacturers, wholesalers, retailers, and service-related companies.

REVIEW VOCABULARY

Explain how the terms in the groups below relate to each other.

1. free enterprise system (p. 101) business risk and profit (p. 105)
2. patents, trademarks, and copyrights (p. 102)
3. competition (p. 103), monopoly (p. 105), price, and nonprice competition (p. 104)
4. supply and demand (p. 106)
5. domestic and global business (p. 111)
6. for-profit and nonprofit organizations (p. 111)
7. public sector and private sector (p. 113)
8. industry (p. 113) and derived demand (p. 114)
9. retailers and wholesalers (p. 114)
10. production (p. 115), management, finance, and accounting (p. 116)

REVIEW FACTS and IDEAS

11. What are the key characteristics of a free enterprise system? (5.1)
12. Provide examples of price and nonprice competition. (5.1)
13. Explain the basic theory of supply and demand. (5.1)
14. What are three major categories for classifying businesses? (5.2)
15. How do for-profit businesses and nonprofit organizations differ? (5.2)
16. What are the differences between the public and private sectors? (5.2)

Chapter 5 - The Free Enterprise System 119

CHAPTER **5** REVIEW

REVIEW FACTS and IDEAS

11. The key characteristics are ownership of property (both business and intellectual), competition, risk, and profit.

12. Examples will vary. Wal-Mart is one example of price competition with its slogan, "Always Low Prices. Always." Neiman Marcus, with high quality merchandise and excellent service, exemplifies nonprice competition.

13. As demand increases, so do prices. As demand declines, so do prices. As supply increases, prices go down; but as supply decreases, prices go up. The equilibrium point is where suppliers are willing to sell and consumers are willing to buy.

14. The three major categories are size and scope, purpose, and industry and markets.

15. For-profit businesses strive to make money; nonprofits use the money made to fund the causes listed in their charters.

16. The public sector includes all government agencies; the private sector includes all nongovernmental organizations and businesses.

FOCUS on KEY POINTS

Ask volunteers to read aloud each summary. After each one is read, give students a few minutes for questions or clarification.

REVIEW VOCABULARY

Answers will vary. See glossary for definitions of **1–10.** A sample answer might read:

1. All businesses are not guaranteed success in a *free enterprise system* because there is *business risk* involved.

CHAPTER 5 REVIEW

BUILD SKILLS

17. Workplace Skills

Reports will vary. Make sure students call ahead to determine the proper person and arrange a suitable time for the interview. Encourage students to take notes during the interview, review them immediately after, and use them to write the report.

18. Technology Applications

The demand curve should go down as prices go up from $50 to $250. The supply curve should go up as prices increases. The range for the amount demanded/supplied is from 0 to 5,000 jackets.

19. Math Skills

4%; $2,456,700 − (1,246,100 + 1,112,332) = $98,268

DEVELOP CRITICAL THINKING

20. Supply and Demand

Answers will vary but should demonstrate an understanding of supply and demand.

21. SWOT Analysis and Free Enterprise

Students might imagine that they were considering buying stock in a company or making a major purchase from a company. The SWOT analysis gives evidence regarding the health of the company in question.

BUILD SKILLS

17. Workplace Skills

Communication Conduct a telephone interview with a representative of your local chamber of commerce. Ask what new businesses have joined the organization in the past year. Also, ask about the economic, political, and other conditions facing businesses in your community. Write about your findings in a one-page report.

18. Technology Applications

Creating Charts Using a spreadsheet program like Excel, create a chart to depict supply and demand curves for a jeans jacket. When graphing your chart, select an equilibrium point and note it in ink on the completed chart. The price range is from $50 to $250. The range for the amount demanded/supplied is from 0 to 5,000 jackets.

19. Math Skills

How Much Profit? Determine the profit a company makes with sales of $2,456,700, costs of $1,246,100, and expenses of $1,112,332. What percentage of sales does the profit represent?

DEVELOP CRITICAL THINKING

20. Supply and Demand

Provide examples of supply and demand theory at work. Think of products or services that interest you. For example, you may select music-related products such as MP3 players, or music-related services such as music download sites. Other possibilities include sports or fashion apparel, cars, or tutoring services. Then, try to think of one example each to illustrate surplus, shortage, and equilibrium.

21. SWOT Analysis and Free Enterprise

Select a business of your choice and review its four major functions: production or procurement, marketing, management, and finance. Identify the company's strengths and weakness for each of those functions as part of a SWOT analysis. Why is this an important process to follow in a free enterprise system?

Formative Assessment

Formative assessment is an essential component of classroom work. This type of assessment provides information that is then used as feedback to modify teaching and meet student needs.

L1 Have students write a paragraph using five key terms.

L2 Have students perform a SWOT analysis of a new auto company. Potential customers want to be sure that the company will be in business for a long time so there will be no problems regarding service, parts, and resale value.

L3 Have students perform a SWOT analysis on a company of their choice and then write a report to a consumer rights group outlining the results of their SWOT study.

Reteach If the results of this formative assessment seem low, consider the following activity: Read aloud the subheads of each section and have students name facts from each one.

APPLY CONCEPTS

22. Designing a Plan

A small, family-owned paint and wallpaper store that has been in existence for three generations is facing stiff competition from some retail giants. Within 15 miles of the store are five Home Depots, five Sherwin-Williams paint stores, three Sears, and a newly opened Lowe's store. The owners know they cannot compete on price, so they need a cost-effective plan to compete on some other basis.

Activity Your job is to develop that plan and present it to the owners in a written document and an oral presentation, complete with examples and visuals to support your ideas.

23. Researching Intellectual Property Rights

Conduct research on the nature of patents, copyrights, and trademarks in the United States. Since 1790, how many patents have been issued? Which industries and companies hold the most patents? How long does it take to get a patent approved? What are some of the current issues with patents, copyrights, and trademarks? What can a business do if its patent, copyrighted material, or trademark has been copied by a competitor? Provide examples.

Activity Prepare a written report using a word processing program. Cite all your sources.

NET SAVVY

24. Industry Classification

Visit the Bureau of Labor Statistics Web site, which provides background information on NAICS. Select an industry of your choice to review. Report your findings.

Role Play:
The Free Enterprise System

Situation You are to assume the role of sales associate for a locally owned sporting goods store located in a small, but rapidly growing community. Your store sells a limited line of sporting goods that concentrates on items of interest and use to local athletes. Your store has enjoyed the unique position of having no competing stores within your immediate trading area. You have learned that another local merchant plans to add a limited line of sporting goods to its merchandise offerings.

Activity You are to respond to another sales associate (judge) who questions why the other merchant would want to compete with your store.

Evaluation You will be evaluated on how well you meet the following performance indicators:

- Explain the concept of private enterprise
- Explain the concept of competition
- Explain the types of economic systems
- Describe current business trends
- Demonstrate a customer-service mindset

 Online Action!

For more information and DECA Prep practice, go to *marketingessentials.glencoe .com/5/DECA*

APPLY CONCEPTS

22. Designing a Plan

Plans will vary. All plans, regardless of specific details, should stress ways to compete based on nonprice factors, such as quality and uniqueness of goods sold, personalized services offered, and hours of operation.

23. Researching Intellectual Property Rights

Reports will vary. Written reports should contain the information requested here, which can be found on the U.S. Patent and Trademark Office Web site, additional topic searches on the Internet, and review of indices of news publications.

NET SAVVY

24. Industry Classification

Findings will vary. Encourage peer tutoring by forming pairs made up of different learners. As pairs plan their reports, make sure the preparation and the presentation are shared equally.

 DECA CONNECTION

Students should be evaluated on the performance indicators noted in the role play. For another DECA role play, go to the Competitive Events Workbook, the Student Activity Workbook, or go to **marketingessentials.glencoe.com/5/DECA**

Online Action! For instructions, ideas, and answer guide, go to the Teacher Center at **marketingessentials.glencoe.com**

 DECA Advisors Corner

To prepare students for DECA competitions, create a game show with competency-based questions. Offer a DECA novelty item, such as a T-shirt to the winner. To prepare students for occupation-specific questions, use the resources available at **marketingessentials.glencoe.com**

MINI-QUIZ

Read these sentences aloud and have students volunteer the missing word.

1. One characteristic of the _____ is the private citizens' right to own businesses. (free enterprise system)

2. The major ways to classify businesses are _____, purpose, and _____. (size and scope; industry and markets)

3. The four functions of business are production or procurement, marketing _____, and _____. (management; finance)

For an expanded chapter quiz, go to Chapter 5 in the TeacherWorks CD-ROM and to Chapter 5 in the **Exam***View*® Pro Test Generator CD-ROM.

Chapter Overview

Chapter 6 discusses the government roles in regulating business and protecting consumers. Students learn about business and individual responsibilities in creating an ethical workplace, product, and marketplace against the backdrop of the governmental protective structure.

BUILD BACKGROUND

Ask students to do a quick-write. Explain that you will give them a phrase and they will have a couple of minutes to write words and phrases that come to mind. Read students the phrase *corporate responsibility*. Then have students volunteer to share a point from their quick-writes and note whether responses are positive or negative.

Why It's Important

Knowledge of how the combined actions of government, corporations, and labor work together to create an ethical business environment is essential to any successful marketing effort.

Prepare to Read

Read each chapter objective aloud to students. Ask students to make additional generalizations about what they will learn based on these objectives.

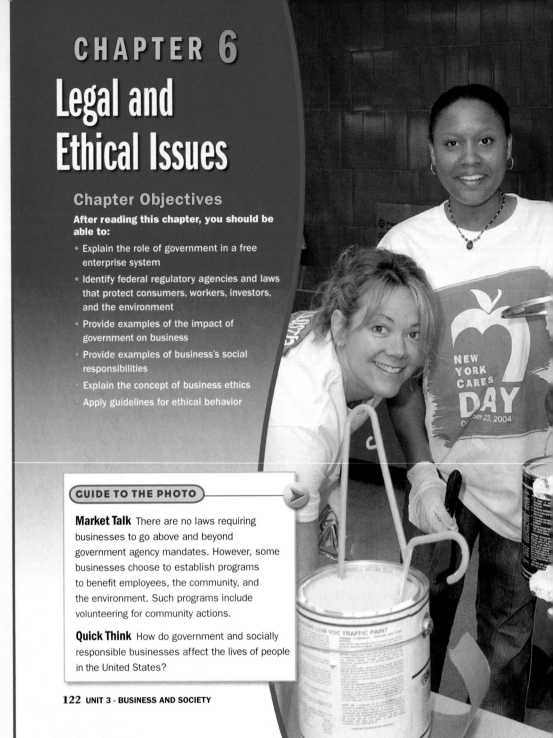

CHAPTER 6
Legal and Ethical Issues

Chapter Objectives

After reading this chapter, you should be able to:

- Explain the role of government in a free enterprise system
- Identify federal regulatory agencies and laws that protect consumers, workers, investors, and the environment
- Provide examples of the impact of government on business
- Provide examples of business's social responsibilities
- Explain the concept of business ethics
- Apply guidelines for ethical behavior

GUIDE TO THE PHOTO

Market Talk There are no laws requiring businesses to go above and beyond government agency mandates. However, some businesses choose to establish programs to benefit employees, the community, and the environment. Such programs include volunteering for community actions.

Quick Think How do government and socially responsible businesses affect the lives of people in the United States?

GUIDE TO THE PHOTO

Market Talk Ask students to use their own words to define socially responsible and ethical business behavior. Responses might contain the idea of going beyond imposed standards.

Quick Think Answers will vary. The government and socially responsible businesses can play a role in creating and enforcing ethical business standards and developing community goodwill.

 Follow Up Encourage students to think about whether their opinions about ethical behavior change as they read. Have students discuss their responses in class.

marketingessentials.glencoe.com

Performance indicators represent key skills and knowledge. Relating them to the concepts explained in this chapter is your key to success in DECA events.

These acronyms represent DECA events that involve knowledge of concepts in this chapter.

AAAL	FMAL	MMS*	TMDM*
AAML*	FMDM*	QSRM*	TSE*
ADC*	FMML*	RMAL	VPM
BSM	FSRM*	RMML*	
EMDM*	HMDM*	SMDM*	

In all these DECA events you should be able to follow these performance indicators.

- Determine the relationship between government and business
- Explain the role of business in society
- Describe current business trends
- Describe legal issues affecting businesses

All the events with an asterisk (*) also include these performance indicators:

- Explain the nature of personnel regulations
- Explain the nature of workplace regulations (including OSHA, ADA)
- Explain the nature of trade regulations
- Explain the nature of environmental regulations
- Explain the nature of businesses' reporting requirements

Some events include additional performance indicators. These are:

FMML Explain the nature of health and sanitation laws affecting food marketing

FSRM Explain the nature of health and sanitation laws

QSRM Explain the nature of health and sanitation laws

DECA PREP

Check your understanding of DECA performance indicators with the DECA activity in this chapter's review. For more information and DECA Prep practice, go to *marketingessentials.glencoe.com/6/DECA*

Chapter 6 - Legal and Ethical Issues **123**

DECA events that require knowledge of legal and ethical issues are described here. Discuss the performance indicators to make sure students understand how to demonstrate their understanding.

The events acronyms stand for:

AAAL: Apparel and Accessories Marketing Series, AL

AAML: Apparel and Accessories Marketing Series, ML

ADC: Advertising Campaign Event

BSM: Business Services Marketing Series

EMDM: E-Commerce Management Team Decision Event

FMAL: Food Marketing Series, AL

FMDM: Financial Analysis Management Team Decision Making Event

FMML: Food Marketing Series, ML

FSRM: Full Service Restaurant Management Series

HMDM: Hospitality Services Management Team Decision Making Event

MMS: Marketing Management Series

QSRM: Quick Serve Restaurant Management Series

RMAL: Retail Merchandising Series, AL

RMML: Retail Merchandising Series, ML

SMDM: Sports and Entertainment Marketing Management Team Decision Making Event

TMDM: Travel and Tourism Marketing Management Team Decision Making Event

TSE: Technical Sales Event

VPM: Vehicles and Petroleum Marketing Series

DECA PREP

Find timed DECA Prep activities correlated to the Competitive Events Workbook for students and DECA tips for teachers at **marketingessentials.glencoe.com/6/DECA**

CHAPTER 6   Classroom Resources

For the Teacher

- TeacherWorks
- marketingessentials.glencoe.com
- Interactive Chalkboard
- **Exam***View*® Pro Test Generator
- Fast File Unit 3

For the Student

- *Marketing Essentials* Online Edition
- Student Activity Workbook
- Marketing Math Workbook
- Marketing Research Project Workbook
- School-to-Work Activity Workbook
- Competitive Events Workbook
- *BusinessWeek* Reader and Case Studies
- marketingessentials.glencoe.com

FOCUS

Introducing the Section

COLLABORATIVE ACTIVITY

Ask students to work in small groups to write a preliminary statement of what they consider the role of government in business in a free enterprise system. Groups should save their statements for reference when they have completed this chapter.

Preteaching Key Terms

Have the class skim the section to find each key term in context. Ask the student who finds a key term to point it out on its page, then choose another student to read that term and its definition aloud to the class.

- Food and Drug Administration (FDA)
- Consumer Product Safety Commission (CPSC)
- Equal Employment Opportunity Commission (EEOC)
- Occupational Safety and Health Administration (OSHA)
- Securities and Exchange Commission (SEC)
- Environmental Protection Agency (EPA)
- Federal Trade Commission (FTC)

 Critical Thinking

Ask students to consider why many industries set their own standards for product compliance.

OBJECTIVES

- Explain the role of government in a free enterprise system
- Identify federal regulatory agencies and laws that protect consumers, workers, investors, and the environment
- Provide examples of the impact of government on business

KEY TERMS

- Food and Drug Administration (FDA)
- Consumer Product Safety Commission (CPSC)
- Equal Employment Opportunity Commission (EEOC)
- Occupational Safety and Health Administration (OSHA)
- Securities and Exchange Commission (SEC)
- Environmental Protection Agency (EPA)
- Federal Trade Commission (FTC)

 WHILE YOU READ

Connect List three ways local, state, and national governments serve and protect businesses.

Government and Laws

 READ and STUDY

BEFORE YOU READ

Predict What are two ways government can affect business?

THE MAIN IDEA

In a free enterprise system, the government plays a role in safeguarding its own principles and providing for the health, general welfare, and safety of its citizens.

STUDY ORGANIZER

Use a chart like the one below to take notes about the U.S. government and its role in the free enterprise system.

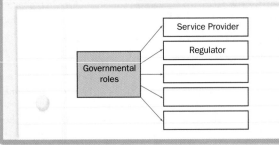

The Roles of Government

The stability of a government and its policies shape the political climate of a country. Government actions have a great impact on business and its operations. Thus, it is important to understand how government functions and how it affects businesses.

The stability of a government, of its structure, and of its legal system is always part of the analysis of a business (the environmental scan). The government plays the roles of a provider of services, a customer, a regulator, an enforcer of free

---

 READ and STUDY

BEFORE YOU READ

If necessary, encourage responses with a statement such as: A strong government can have a favorable impact on business; a weakened or divisive government can have a negative effect on business.

THE MAIN IDEA

Read this statement aloud. Remind students of earlier SWOT analyses. Have them consider ways U.S. government efforts to regulate business might provide business opportunities.

STUDY ORGANIZER

Make your own organizer or download the one at marketingessentials.glencoe.com. Help students begin by reading the examples together.

WHILE YOU READ Lead students to the words *service provider* and *regulator* to help them make associations between governments and business.

enterprise, and a monitor of the economy. All these roles involve laws and regulations that have consequences for business.

Structure of the United States Government

In the United States, each of the three branches of government—executive, legislative, and judicial—limits the power of the other two. This provides a system of checks and balances that prevents any one branch of government from becoming too powerful. Comparable branches of government exist at the state and local levels. Business owners and trade groups must follow the actions of all branches and levels of government, because they all affect business operations.

Executive Branch

The executive branch of the federal government includes the Office of the President; Executive Departments (for example, Interior, Commerce, Defense), as well as independent agencies and corporations, boards, commissions, and committees; and quasi-official agencies. Each administration tends to have different initiatives and issues that impact business due to economic times and political agendas.

The U.S. Department of Agriculture (USDA) is an agency that is part of the executive branch. It provides the inspection, grading, and certification of beef, lamb, pork, and veal, for example. The meat grades are used as a marketing tool by retailers and restaurants to distinguish the better cuts from less expensive ones. The USDA also provides a grading service for dairy products. States may contract with the USDA to have grading and inspection carried out by inspectors who are trained and licensed by the USDA.

Legislative Branch

The legislative branch of the U.S. government is the U.S. Congress. It is made up of the Senate and the House of Representatives. Members of Congress debate and vote on laws and regulations. Lobbyists try to influence the way legislators vote on bills that affect their interests.

•**USDA INSPECTORS at WORK** The USDA, a government agency founded in 1862 by President Abraham Lincoln, controls the safety and quality of meat, poultry, and egg products.

Why do you think a USDA grade could be used in marketing?

For example, even before the appearance of mad cow disease in the United States, some politicians, farm groups, and the Consumer Federation of America lobbied for mandatory country of origin labeling (COOL) on meat products. Lobbyists for the food industry asked Congress to at least postpone COOL for a few years. In 2004, Congress granted the meat, produce, and peanut industries a two-year reprieve in the implementation of the mandatory labels.

Judicial Branch

The judicial branch of government is responsible for interpreting, applying, and administering the laws of the United States. The judicial system consists of a network of courts at all levels of government.

When the legislative or executive branches of government enact laws or regulations

Chapter 6 - Legal and Ethical Issues **125**

Individualized Practice

THE ROLE OF SERVICE PROVIDER AND CUSTOMER

L1 Ask students to explain the relationship between government services like Medicare or Department of Homeland Security measures and the citizens of the United States.
The government pays for these services with taxpayers', or citizens', money.

L2 Ask students to do some research and then explain what it means to bid on a government contract and why this procedure is required on most contracts.
Companies seeking the contract bid for, or tell the price for which they will do, the job. This puts them in competition. The government seeks to insure the most prudent use of taxpayer money.

L3 Ask students to review the definitions of capitalist and socialist systems of government and write a 200-word report to describe their in relation to government services.

Concept Development

THE ROLE OF REGULATOR

After students have read this section, ask volunteers to give examples of different types of regulation.
Answers might include laws, licensing, zoning, and locally or federally mandated standards for product or service quality.

---

that negatively affect businesses, those businesses may appeal to the judicial branch of government. Any court decision may create opportunities for some and threats to others. In 2004, four regional telephone companies (Verizon, BellSouth, Qwest Communications, and SBC Communications) appealed the part of the Telecommunications Act of 1996 that required them to make their phone networks available to competitors at heavy discounts. This provision was originally established to combat the near-monopoly the regional companies had in local telephone service.

The Role of Service Provider and Customer

The government must spend a lot of money to carry out its responsibility to ensure the safety and general welfare of people in the United States. As a matter of fact, approximately one-third of the country's gross domestic product is generated by government expenditures.

To keep the country safe, the Department of Homeland Security spends money on border protection, disaster recovery, and on other measures such as airport security. For example, to improve the country's infrastructure, federal, state, and local governments fund the construction of roads and bridges.

Businesses that provide products and services for any government installation, project, or institution must adhere to certain guidelines. Why? Because it is taxpayers' money that the government is spending.

The Role of Regulator

In the United States, most laws are designed to protect the safety, health, and welfare of individuals. At the federal, state, and local levels, these laws are carried out by government agencies. The government acts as a regulator to protect consumers, employees, investors, and the environment and this affects businesses. (See Figure 6.1.) Note that businesses must comply or suffer the legal consequences.

Protecting Consumers

At the state and local levels, government agencies are involved with consumer protection. People who perform certain services, such as hairstylists, manicurists, and electricians, must be licensed. Local zoning laws about where homes, businesses, and farms can be located protect real estate investments and quality of life for residents. Health departments inspect restaurants and other food-handling businesses to protect consumers. If a business fails these inspections, it is cited and required to correct the problems identified. Failure to do so can result in closure of the business.

The Food and Drug Administration and the Consumer Product Safety Commission are two federal agencies that protect consumers.

The **Food and Drug Administration (FDA)** regulates the labeling and safety of food, drugs, and cosmetics sold in the United States.

The FDA approves new products and reviews products already on the market. For example, in 2004 the FDA banned a dietary supplement, ephedra, because of health risks associated with products that contain that ingredient. The government first issued a warning telling consumers to stop taking ephedra products immediately and asking companies to voluntarily stop selling products that contained ephedra and ephedrine alkaloids. The actual ban became effective 60 days after issuance. Obviously, this ruling had a negative impact on manufacturers of products that contained ephedra.

The FDA also responds to petitions for action. For example, the Grocery Manufacturers of America asked the FDA to provide definitions for low-carb food items.

The **Consumer Product Safety Commission (CPSC)** is responsible for overseeing the safety of products such as toys, electronics, and household furniture. The CPSC is not responsible for oversight of food, drugs, cosmetics, medical devices, tobacco products, firearms and ammunition, motor vehicles, pesticides, aircraft, boats, and fixed site amusement rides. The CPSC was established under the Consumer Product Safety Act of 1972. That act gives the commission the authority to set standards for products that are

---

 Online Activity

Product Recalls

Review the meaning of the word *recall* in this context. Make sure students understand that a recall means a product is taken off the market after it has been on the market and sold to customers. Customers can return a recalled item for exchange or a return of their investment. Ask interested students to go to the Consumer Product Safety Commission Web site for up-to-date recall and product notices. Have students report on a recent product recall or product notice in a five-minute oral presentation.

Figure 6.1 The Government's Regulatory Role

- **The Music Industry Versus Copyright Violators** The music industry's struggle to protect copyrighted music—and the right of musicians to make a living—illustrates the regulatory roles of the different branches of the federal government.

If it's legal is it ethical?

The law U.S. copyright law gives ownership and the right to reproduce, distribute, or license an original work to the creator of that work. Originally written to protect authors, the law now covers software, sound recordings, and motion pictures.

◀ **The infringement** The development of the Internet and file-sharing software made it possible for music lovers to download their favorite recordings for free.

The cases: Mitch Bainwol, Chairman, CEO, RIAA, testifies before the Senate The recording industry fought back, filing suit in federal court. The Recording Industry Association of America (RIAA), a trade group, has sued more than 4,000 individuals for illegally downloading music from popular music Web sites. In 2001, it won a case against Napster for its role in the music downloads and succeeded in shutting down the popular site.

◀ **File-sharing software** Since the ruling against Napster, the computer industry has developed peer-to-peer file sharing software, which enables files to be shared without the use of a central computer. It was Napster's use of a central computer that led to the guilty verdict. Now, free music Web sites, such as Kazaa, advertise that because the sites do not actually host the file sharing, they are legal. Congress is attempting to pass legislation that will provide additional protection for musicians and for the music industry.

@ Online Action!

Go to *marketingessentials.glencoe.com/6/figure/1* to find a research project on the government's regulatory process.

Figure 6.1 The Government's Regulatory Role

Discussion Ask students to share what they know about file sharing. Have students list the advantages and disadvantages of file-sharing software for consumers.

Caption Answer Lead students to conclude that what is "legal" and what is "ethical" do not always coincide.

@ Online Action! For instructions, ideas, and answer guide, go to the Teacher Center at **marketingessentials.glencoe.com**

Follow Up Ask students what they know about downloading copyrighted music and to share their opinions. Lead a discussion about musicians who are against it, and those who do not have a problem with consumers downloading their music for free. Ask interested students to research some of the issues involved in file sharing and report back to the class.

TEACH CONTINUED

Individualized Practice

THE FDA

Write these sentences on the board. Students will use these statements to complete the levelled activities.

1. The FDA may issue food warnings to consumers.

2. The FDA regulates the labeling and safety of food, drugs, and cosmetics sold in the U.S.

3. The FDA reviews products on the market.

4. The FDA can ban foods or drugs from sale.

L1 Have students classify these sentences according to whether they are main ideas or details.

Sentences 1, 3, and 4 are details. Sentence 2 is the main idea.

L2 Have students draw a main idea/detail graphic organizer and identify the main idea and at least three details.

L3 Have students write the main idea on a piece of paper. Then have them do research outside the class to provide at least three more details to add to the description of the FDA.

Concept Development

THE ROLE OF REGULATOR

After reading about the Consumer Product Safety Commission, lead discussion about the value of setting and monitoring safety standards in products. Talk with students about reasons why such a commission would be necessary.

Possible reasons are that even though products are tested, problems don't show up until they are used for periods of time, or by large numbers of people, or in untested conditions.

127

Concept Development

PROTECTING WORKERS

This section includes a discussion of several acts of legislation under the EEOC. Ask students to list the laws discussed in this section.

Lists should include: Civil Rights Act, Equal Pay Act, Age Discrimination in Employment Act, Rehabilitation Act, Americans With Disabilities Act, and Civil Rights Act.

TEACHING POINTS

Research Have students work in small groups. Assign each student group one of the acts on the list. Have them work together to research the act and report their findings to the class.

Enrichment

FAMILY AND MEDICAL LEAVE ACT

Different states and countries have different laws and regulations regarding family and medical leave. Encourage interested students to choose a state or foreign country and research what options and rights working individuals have in relationship to family and medical leave. Have students share their results in an informal oral presentation.

Critical Thinking

Ask students to brainstorm and list reasons why an individual might need the FMLA. Have students share their opinions on how this legislation might be viewed as ethical legislation.

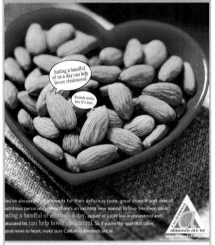

•ALMONDS: GOOD for YOUR HEALTH This ad uses a health claim to promote a food product.

Which government agency had to approve this health claim before it could be used in this advertisement?

considered hazardous and to recall dangerous products. Product recalls are published at the CPSC Web site.

The Consumer Product Safety Commission covers many areas. It also enforces the Federal Hazardous Substances Act, the Flammable Fabrics Act, the Poison Prevention Packaging Act, and the Refrigerator Safety Act. Of prime concern with all these acts is the safety of children. It is a good idea for businesses to test their products before marketing them to the public. Businesses should also keep up with new guidelines in the labeling of their products, especially with regard to directions for their safe use.

Protecting Workers

The Equal Employment Opportunity Commission and the Occupational Safety and

Health Administration are among the groups responsible for protecting employees at the federal level. Companies also must comply with minimum wage standards and other laws and regulations established by state and federal governments, such as the Family and Medical Leave Act. There are also laws to protect employees who report illegal practices by their employers. These laws protecting whistleblowers are covered later in this section.

The **Equal Employment Opportunity Commission (EEOC)** is responsible for the fair and equitable treatment of employees with regard to hiring, firing, and promotions. Some of the laws it enforces are Title VII of the Civil Rights Act, the Equal Pay Act of 1963, the Age Discrimination in Employment Act of 1967 (ADEA), Sections 501 and 505 of the Rehabilitation Act of 1973, Titles I and V of the Americans with Disabilities Act of 1990 (ADA), and the Civil Rights Act of 1991.

Businesses must adhere to the policies established by the United States Department of Labor. The **Occupational Safety and Health Administration (OSHA)** provides guidelines for workplace safety and enforces those regulations. For example, construction workers must wear hard hats for protection.

The Family and Medical Leave Act (FMLA) of 1993 requires employers that qualify to grant eligible employees up to a total of 12 workweeks of unpaid leave during any 12-month period for one or more of the following reasons: the birth and care of the newborn child of the employee; placement with the employee of a son or daughter for adoption or foster care; to care for an immediate family member (spouse, child, or parent) with a serious health condition; or to take medical leave when the employee is unable to work because of a serious health condition.

Protecting Investors

The **Securities and Exchange Commission (SEC)** regulates the sale of securities (stocks and bonds). It is responsible for licensing brokerage firms and financial advisers. It also investigates any dealings among corporations, such as mergers, that affect the value of stocks.

AD GUIDE   **ALMONDS: GOOD for YOUR HEALTH**

Discussion Ask the class to speculate about why a business association (of California almond growers) might have issued this ad. One possible answer is to dispel the belief that all nuts are high in fat and cholesterol and therefore unhealthy.

Caption Answer Students should note that because the ad is for a food and makes health-related claims, the FDA had to approve it.

Follow Up Have students find ads for other products that discuss cholesterol and share them with the class.

This type of regulation helps protect investors from deceptive practices. The SEC requires that all information about the corporation that is given to investors be truthful. This requirement protects both the investor and the corporation. Companies whose shares are traded on the stock exchange must publish a company's prospectus and an annual report. A prospectus is a document offered to potential investors for their review when they are making a decision about whether to invest in a company. Corporations must prepare an annual report at least once a year to show its investors how the company has performed. On a more frequent basis, such corporations report their profits and stock dividends for publication in the media.

Protecting the Environment

The **Environmental Protection Agency (EPA)** was established in 1970 to protect human health and our environment. Its responsibilities include monitoring and reducing air and water pollution, as well as overseeing hazardous waste disposal and recycling.

For example, the 1970 Clean Air Act was amended in 1990, making it more effective. In 2004, new rules to improve air quality were added. One of those rules involves stringent pollution controls on diesel engines used in industries such as construction, agriculture, and mining. Two other industries that will have similar emission standards are diesel locomotives and marine diesel engines.

Environmental laws cover problem areas such as acid rain, asbestos, lead poisoning, mercury, mold, ozone depletion, pesticides, and radon. They also address littering. For example, new laws regarding distribution of advertising materials went into effect on April 1, 2001. A company can be fined if it distributes advertising materials inappropriately. For example, businesses are no longer allowed to place advertising leaflets on vehicles.

Enforcer of the Free Enterprise System

The **Federal Trade Commission (FTC)** has the responsibility of enforcing the principles of a free enterprise system and protecting consumers from unfair or deceptive business practices. As an independent agency, it reports to Congress on its actions. Its commissioners are nominated by the President and confirmed by the Senate. The FTC runs three bureaus: the Bureau of Consumer Protection; the Bureau of Competition; and the Bureau of Economics.

Bureau of Consumer Protection

The Bureau of Consumer Protection is responsible for enforcing consumer protection laws and trade regulation rules. It investigates individual companies and industry-wide operations and initiates lawsuits against companies that violate these laws and regulations.

There are six divisions with special responsibilities: advertising, enforcement, financial, marketing, international, and planning and information.

• FMLA The Family and Medical Leave Act is making it possible to have flexible work arrangements and encourages work/home life balance.

What consequence does FMLA have on employees? On business?

Chapter 6 - Legal and Ethical Issues **129**

TEACH CONTINUED

Concept Development

PROTECTING INVESTORS

Ask students to explain how the Securities and Exchange Commission protects both corporations and investors. If a business or corporation is found in violation of SEC regulations, the consequences can range from fines to imprisonment.

The SEC protects corporations and their investors from internal and external fraud by requiring that all information about the corporation given to the investors be truthful.

 Extended Activity

Protecting the Environment
Have students choose either an industry or a region of the country affected by EPA regulations and do a before-and-after study. Make sure researchers consider factors other than EPA regulations that also affected their topic. For example, many industries relocated abroad. What part did an abundance of cheap, nonunion labor in other countries play in this decision? Ask students to write a short report and share it with the class.

As an alternate activity, have students research local laws regarding littering, recycling, and disposing of trash. Encourage students from different towns or who have lived elsewhere to share the local laws in another location.

PHOTO GUIDE   FMLA

Discussion Remind students that, in addition to covering maternity/paternity leave, the act also covers caring for aged relatives. Ask students to share their thoughts on this legislation.

Caption Answer Students may suggest that flexibility allows employees to better balance their work and personal lives. Happier and more productive employees lead to better business results.

Follow Up Students might research articles reporting on companies and individuals that make use of the FMLA. Have students share their findings with the class.

TEACH CONTINUED

Enrichment

ENFORCER OF THE FREE ENTERPRISE SYSTEM

Assign each of the three subdivisions of the Federal Trade Commission to a different student and have those students investigate the subdivisions and review their findings review their findings with the rest of the class.

TEACHING POINTS

Model Set an example of self-review by asking questions such as:

- What are clothing label requirements?
- What is predatory pricing?

Have students find the answers in the text and read them aloud.

Concept Development

BUREAU OF CONSUMER PROTECTION

The Bureau of Consumer Protection is the division of the Federal Trade Commission which deals with the enforcement of consumer protection and trade laws and regulations. The Bureau is divided into six different divisions. After students have read this section, ask them to name the six divisions of the Bureau.
Advertising Division, Enforcement Division, Financial Practices Division, Marketing Practices Division, International Division of Consumer Protection, and the Division of Planning and Information

- The Advertising Division enforces truth-in-advertising laws.
- The Enforcement Division ensures compliance with the laws involving the Internet; the U.S. Postal Service; textile, wool, fur, and care labeling; and energy use. For example, clothing labels must identify the fabric content, country of origin, and care instructions.
- The Financial Practices Division covers the Truth-In-Lending Act, as well as leasing and privacy issues.
- The Marketing Practices Division is responsible for responding to fraudulent activities and scams. The Telemarketing Sales Rule, the 900-Number Rule, the Funeral Rule, and the Magnuson-Moss Act are a few of the laws enforced by the Marketing Practices Divisions.
- The International Division of Consumer Protection promotes consumer confidence in the international marketplace through cross-border cooperation and information sharing.

Case Study

Car Emissions

California's plan for sharp cuts in automotive emissions of global warming gases could eventually lead much of the coastal United States to turn to vehicles that are substantially cleaner, and also probably more fuel efficient, than those in the rest of the nation.

New Jersey, Rhode Island, and Connecticut have said they intend to start following California's rules instead of the federal government's. New York, Massachusetts, Vermont, and Maine already do so. Other states are also considering doing so in order to comply with federal ozone emission regulations.

Regulation's Cost

"It would be a logistical and engineering challenge, and a costly problem to make different vehicles for different states," said Dave Barthmuss, a spokesman for General Motors. "It is more cost effective for us to have one set of emissions everywhere."

The California plan would require auto manufacturers to reduce global warming emissions from their new vehicles by 29.2 percent over the next decade, phasing in from the 2009 to the 2015 model years. The California Air Resources Board has estimated that the cost for these changes would run around $1,047 per vehicle.

The California regulators are adamant that the plan is not a fuel economy measure because the federal government has authority over that issue.

THINK STRATEGICALLY

Use this proposed legislation to explain how government functions and its impact on business. How does this affect marketing?

@ Online Action! Go to *marketingessentials.glencoe.com/6/case* to find an activity on ethics, consumption, and consumerism.

Case Study   Car Emissions

Discussion Led by California, several states are creating legislation that would require that cars in future have even lower harmful emissions than emission levels set by the federal government. Ask students to discuss their responses to and opinions about this kind of legislation.

THINK STRATEGICALLY   **Answer:** Students may cite the increasing popularity of hybrid cars, especially in California; the marketing campaigns to advertise them, and the long waiting lists to purchase them.

@ Online Action!   For instructions, ideas, and answer guide, go to the Teacher Center at **marketingessentials.glencoe.com**

• The Division of Planning and Information helps consumers get information. There are help lines where consumers can report identity theft and other fraud-related complaints.

Bureau of Competition

The FTC's antitrust responsibilities involve prevention of anti-competitive mergers and business practices. Some of the acts that the bureau enforces include the following:

- The Federal Trade Commission Act, which prohibits unfair methods of competition.
- The Sherman Antitrust Act (1890), which outlawed all contracts and agreements that would limit trade or competition in interstate commerce. It also prevents one company from undercharging for an item or service in order to put the competition out of business. This practice is known as predatory pricing.
- The Clayton Antitrust Act (1914), which reduced loopholes in the Sherman Antitrust Act and covered mergers and acquisitions.
- The Hart-Scott-Rodino Amendment to the Clayton Act (1976), which requires companies to notify antitrust agencies before planning a merger.
- The Robinson-Patman Act (1936), which prohibits price discrimination.

Distribution laws also fall under the FTC's jurisdiction. Several states have similar laws, which may be challenged in the future, especially with the growth of the Internet and e-commerce.

Another example of distribution law is the sale of tobacco products to minors. It is illegal to sell tobacco products or distribute samples to underage customers. On July 1, 2004, a new state law went into effect that requires California retailers to obtain a state license to sell tobacco products. Retailers that do not comply are subject to fines and may even be arrested.

MARKET TECH

Item Pricing

New technology now makes it possible for digital bar code scanners to apply an adhesive price sticker to a product at the point-of-purchase station. This technology makes it possible for retailers to give consumers the proper price label by unit for each product they buy, no matter how small.

Legal Roots for Technology

Several large chains, such as Wal-Mart and Home Depot, have gotten into legal tangles in the past few years over the lack of consistent unit price labeling for all items on their shelves.

In Wal-Mart's case, Massachusetts resident Colman Herman won a multimillion-dollar legal settlement in a class-action suit with Wal-Mart Corp. over the chain's alleged failure to comply with the state's item-pricing regulation. The settlement agreement says Wal-Mart will spend $5.6 million over the next three years to bring its Massachusetts stores into compliance with the regulation.

The legal victory in the Wal-Mart case and the ensuing outcry from retailers about the high costs associated with item pricing prompted revisions to the original regulation that forced retailers to label items on the shelves. Retailers are now allowed to stop marking prices on individual items if they install the new bar code scanners. Then, the choice is the consumers'.

THINK LIKE A MARKETER

In what way did technology help to change the item-pricing regulation?

@ Online Action!

Go to *marketingessentials.glencoe.com/6/tech* to find an activity on ethics and technology.

ASSESS

Review Guide

CONCEPTS

Have students work in small groups. Assign each group an area for review according to the headings in this section. Each group can review the assigned section, and then present its concepts to the rest of the class.

KEY TERMS

Have students review key terms, their spellings, and definitions with a partner.

ONLINE SELF-ASSESSMENT

Have students go to **marketingessentials.glencoe.com** for the Section 6.1 practice test.

Individualized Review

L1 Assign and review Chapter 6 activities in the Student Activity Workbook.

L2 Assign and Review Chapter 6 activities in the Marketing Math Workbook.

L3 Assign and Review Chapter 6 activities in the *BusinessWeek* Reader and Case Studies.

Marketing Practice

Ask students to imagine that a friend from another country has plans to move to the U.S. and start a small business. What advice would they offer this friend? Have students summarize their advice in a one-page response.

MARKET TECH

Item Pricing

Discussion Ask students to brainstorm other issues that bar code technology might help solve.

THINK LIKE A MARKETER **Answer:** Students should note that technology in effect solved the issue by providing the bar coding as well as the scanner that retailers used.

@ Online Action! For instructions, ideas, and answer guide, go to the Teacher Center at marketingessentials.glencoe.com

CLOSE

Ask students to write a two-paragraph response on how the U.S. government reulates legal and ethical business practices. Encourage students to support their responses with examples from the section or from their own research.

Extended Activity

Monitor of Our Economy
Make sure students understand the meaning and importance of economic stability in the United States and the rest of the world. Have students work in pairs to write a summary of each of the two sections. Then have student pairs share their summaries.

Bureau of Economics

The Bureau of Economics studies the impact of its actions on consumers and reports its findings to Congress, to the executive branch, and to the public. Its reports cover antitrust, consumer protection, and regulation. In certain instances, it may also provide information on pending bills to help policy makers in the legislative branch.

Monitor of Our Economy

To ensure economic stability of the United States, the government monitors our economy and controls our monetary supply through the Federal Reserve System. This is our nation's central bank. When the Federal Reserve Board of Governors thinks that the economy is moving too fast or too slowly, it reacts to correct the problem. When prices are going up too fast, the board may increase interest rates to slow economic activity. Higher interest rates generally make it more difficult to borrow money and therefore discourage expansion by businesses.

Business Supporter

The role of the Small Business Administration (SBA) is to support business and encourage our free enterprise system. The SBA provides counseling and educational materials to prospective business owners. Additional support comes in the form of loan guarantees for some business owners who cannot get conventional loans.

International Issues

Foreign governments may not provide the legal protection or the framework necessary to ensure that business operations are conducted in a safe and secure manner. Thus, it is important to analyze U.S. government's role in promoting free enterprise and its ability to enforce those principles in the context of international business. For example, limited intellectual property protection in China and a challenging legal system make it a tough place for U.S. companies to do business.

6.1 AFTER YOU READ

Reviewing Key Terms and Concepts

1. How does the role of government influence marketing?
2. Name some of the responsibilities and functions of the Food and Drug Administration.
3. What are the three bureaus of the Federal Trade Commission?

Integrating Academic Skills

Math

4. The Truth in Lending legislation requires banks and other lending institutions to clearly disclose their annual interest rates. If the monthly interest rate on an outstanding credit card is 1.5 percent, what is the annual interest rate?

Government and Civics

5. Research the current status of the country-of-origin labeling (COOL) legislation and write a one-page report on it.

@ Online Action! Check your answers at *marketingessentials.glencoe.com/6/read*

AFTER YOU READ

Reviewing Key Terms and Concepts

1. Answers may include: It requires that unsolicited e-mails include a way for recipients to indicate that they do not want to be part of any future mass mailings. It also states that senders of spam can no longer conceal their identities.

2. It regulates the labeling and safety of food, drugs, and cosmetics sold in the U.S; approves new products and reviews existing products in these areas; and responds to petitions for action by marketing and consumer groups.

3. The three bureaus include Bureau of Consumer Protection, Bureau of Competition, and Bureau of Economics.

Integrating Academic Skills

4. Assuming there is no compound interest, the annual interest rate is 8%; 1.5% per month × 12 months

5. Answers will depend on the current status of this legislation. Students might visit the USDA Web site to check this answer.

 Answers at **marketingessentials.glencoe.com/6/read**

Social Responsibility and Ethics

OBJECTIVES

- Provide examples of business's social responsibilities
- Explain the concept of business ethics
- Apply guidelines for ethical behavior

FOCUS

Introducing the Section

COLLABORATIVE ACTIVITY

Prior to beginning reading, have students work in groups to define *ethics* and *social responsibility* in their own words. As a class, evaluate the similarities of definitions offered, and prepare students to learn more about both concepts.

READ and STUDY

BEFORE YOU READ
Predict Why do you think it is a good idea for companies to be civic-minded and ethical?

THE MAIN IDEA
Socially responsible businesses see their role extending into community issues. Civic-minded companies are concerned with their workers, customers, communities, and the environment. Business ethics are part of social responsibility and play a role in decisions made by businesses that affect the same stakeholders.

STUDY ORGANIZER
As you read, jot down an outline of the concept of social responsibility, ethics in business, and the guidelines for ethical behavior.

In the workplace

Business and Social Responsibility

KEY TERMS

- flextime
- telecommuting
- Ad Council
- green marketing
- ethics
- Better Business Bureau
- price gouging
- whistle-blowing

Preteaching Key Terms

Have students review the list of key terms and guess what they might mean. You can get them started by modeling the first one: "*Flex* might be from 'flexible.' *Time* might refer to putting in time on the job, as in punching a time clock. So, *flextime* could mean that an employee has some choice about when to work, like starting and ending the day early."

- flextime
- telecommuting
- Ad Council
- green marketing
- ethics
- Better Business Bureau
- price gouging
- whistle-blowing

Business and Social Responsibility

Social responsibility and ethics have become important business topics as trust has deteriorated due to corporate scandals. Corporate scandals and unethical behavior have a very negative effect on consumer confidence and the image of a company. It is essential to see the role of business in society not only as a provider of goods and services but also as an integral part of the society at large.

WHILE YOU READ
Connect List two business practices that demonstrate social responsibility and ethics.

Chapter 6 - Legal and Ethical Issues **133**

Critical Thinking
Ask students what benefits a company might receive through socially responsible behavior.

READ and STUDY

BEFORE YOU READ
Students may express that civil and ethical behavior keeps a company on the right side of the law.

THE MAIN IDEA
Have a different student read aloud each of the three sentences, stopping for any necessary clarification.

STUDY ORGANIZER
Make your own organizer or download the one at **marketingessentials.glencoe.com.** Show students how to begin filling out this graphic aid.

WHILE YOU READ Have students save their responses and evaluate whether they still have the same opinion after reading this section.

TEACH

IN THE WORKPLACE

Flextime, telecommuting, family leave, child care, health care benefits, and time off with pay are all potential benefits and trends in today's workplace. Ask students to choose one of these trends, identify it, and give an example of it in class.

Answers will vary. A sample answer might be: Flextime is a work schedule arrangement that allows workers to choose work hours that fit their personal needs. For example, a worker might want to begin work early in the morning in order to leave in the mid-afternoon in order to take classes or to fulfill family obligations.

TEACHING POINTS

Extend Explain to students that technology can help make telecommuting and job sharing available to more industries as more and more individuals choose to work from home.

Anyone can choose to go into business in a free enterprise system, but everyone must abide by local, state, and federal laws that apply to businesses. Some of those laws encourage fair business practices, while others protect consumers, workers, investors, and the environment.

Apart from following the law, should businesses have any further social responsibility? Some businesses feel they should. They believe their role in society includes actions affecting employees, consumers, the communities in which they operate, and the environment. These civic-minded businesses set themselves apart from others on the basis of management's vision of their role in the workplace, marketplace, community, and environment.

In the Workplace

Many businesses recognize their employees' needs outside the workplace and try to accommodate them. In so doing, they create a user-friendly workplace environment. Some employee benefits offered by socially responsible companies include flextime, telecommuting, extended family leave, on-site child care, health care benefits, and time off with pay.

Flextime

Flextime allows workers to choose their work hours. Possible arrangements include early start/early finish (e.g. 7 A.M.–3 P.M.), late start/late finish (e.g. 10 A.M.–6 P.M.), and even four-day workweeks (often four 9- or 10-hour days followed by a three-day weekend).

Telecommuting

Telecommuting involves working at home, usually on a computer. Completed jobs are transmitted by e-mail or mail-in disk. For working parents this benefit provides some flexibility in their child care arrangements. For the company, it helps reduce office space requirements. Because telecommuting employees do not have to travel to work, this arrangement is also good for the environment.

Extended Family Leave

Some companies offer employees family leave without pay beyond the time required by the Family and Medical Leave Act. In some professions and under some employee contracts, the time off could be for as long as one year. Such a policy allows companies to retain valued employees who are encouraged to stay with a company that allows such flexibility.

On-Site Child Care

On-site child care is a benefit that has grown in popularity with the increase in two-income families. Some employers have expanded it to include on-site schools and on-site clinics for children who are ill. Any form of the benefit tends to reduce employee absenteeism and employee turnover.

Health Care Benefits

With rising health costs, health care insurance paid for by employers is a major employee benefit. Some health care benefits cover employees and their dependents and even extend into retirement. Employee health care is often a major issue during contract negotiations with employee unions.

Time Off With Pay

Time off with pay includes vacations, sick days, and personal days. Paid vacations are generally part of an employee's contract. The time allotted for the paid vacation is generally based on the length of time an employee has been with the company.

In the Marketplace

Consumers are the focal point of a company that follows the marketing concept. Such businesses are concerned about consumers' perceptions of a company, as well as issues that impact consumers.

Providing Information

Socially responsible companies cooperate with the government and consumer groups to provide important information to consumers. For example, the National Consumers League and the Food and Drug Administration created a public education campaign about the safe and proper use of over-the-counter pain relievers.

Online Activity

Ad Council

Have students research the Ad Council online. They will find a list of campaigns on their Web Site. Have students select a campaign, and write a paragraph telling its purpose and its target. Encourage students to share their findings with the class. Discuss the similarities in their findings.

The **Ad Council** is a nonprofit organization that helps produce public service advertising campaigns for government agencies and other qualifying groups.

Employing Self-Censorship

In the broadcast industry, standards are established by the Federal Communications Commission (FCC). Beyond those regulations, network executives establish their own policies for self-regulation. For example, many broadcast networks (CBS, ABC, NBC, Fox) and cable channels (like CNN and MTV) have no-advocacy policies. Each station reviews commercials that might be considered controversial. If the commercial is not socially acceptable, is inaccurate, or poses a legal liability, it is rejected.

Anything that is broadcast comes under FCC scrutiny. This includes radio as well.

Responding to Consumer Concerns

Socially responsible companies look for ways to respond to consumers' concerns. As an example, a United States government report identified obesity as a major consumer problem. That prompted many companies to seek solutions.

In the Community

Businesses in the United States have many means of providing community support. Multinational companies view their role in the global community as well.

Local Businesses

Socially responsible local businesses support community efforts. You may know of a local business that funds a Little League team or that sponsors a holiday food drive for the needy. Local companies will act as drop-off

• **McDONALD'S and FITNESS** McDonald's is making a very publicized effort to offer healthier menus at its fast-food restaurants.

Why do you think the company logo is so small in this ad?

Chapter 6 - Legal and Ethical Issues **135**

Concept Development

IN THE MARKETPLACE

Help students to distinguish the difference between advertising for profit and advertising for public service.

TEACHING POINTS

Demonstrate Bring in some public service advertisements from magazines or newspapers. Help students identify their message and their market.

Extend Ask students: Would you buy a product with an advertising campaign that offended you? Why or why not? In discussing their opinions, encourage students to cite examples of advertising that they feel is offensive.

Individualized Math Skills

L1 Have students select a product, such as a pair of sneakers, and look in magazine, newspaper, or Internet advertising to find a price for the product and share it with the class.

L2 Have students select a product, and find a price for the same item at three different e-tailing sources, then report their findings to the class.

L3 Have students compare three e-tailing sites for best prices and make a chart demonstrating price variances.

AD GUIDE	McDONALD'S and FITNESS

Discussion Ask students what the words "Go Active" might mean in the context of this ad. Ask: How does the image help them determine this?

Caption Answer Answers will vary; students might propose that the ad wants to target health-conscious consumers and to minimize the public perception that fast food is bad for your health.

Follow Up Encourage students to visit the McDonald's Web site. Ask them to identify the target market in the Internet advertising they see.

TEACH CONTINUED

Concept Development

IN THE COMMUNITY

Ask students to name organizations or groups in the community that involve people their age that are funded by local or other businesses or organizations. Ask: How do these groups benefit the community? How does the community benefit from the involvement of the businesses? Encourage students to share their answers in class.

Individualized Math Skills

L1 Ask students to calculate the answer to the following scenario: BW Publications Worldwide is a nonprofit that donates one-fourth of their yearly revenue to women's shelters. This year, they donated $3,950 to the shelters. How much is BW's yearly revenue?
$15,800; $3,950 × 4 = $15,800

L2 Ask students to calculate the answer to the following: Paul Newman's "Newman's Own" brand has raised $150 million for charities since 1982. If 10 percent of this amount came from sales of Paul Newman's Popcorn, how much money did the sale of popcorn contribute?
$15 million; $150 million × 0.10 = $15 million

L3 Ask students to calculate the answer to the following scenario: Ben & Jerry's donates 7.5% of its income to charity. If Ben & Jerry's earned $3 million in revenue last year and the same the year before, how much of that amount was given to charity?
$600,000; ($3,000,000 × 0.075) × 2 = $600,000

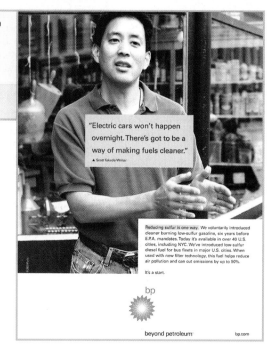

• PETROLEUM DEFENDS ITSELF British Petroleum is one of the largest oil companies in the world. As such, it produces and sells a product that is necessary but harmful to the environment.

How does BP handle this issue and the competition from alternative energy?

"Electric cars won't happen overnight. There's got to be a way of making fuels cleaner."
▲ Scott Takeda/Writer

Reducing sulfur is one way. We voluntarily introduced cleaner burning low-sulfur gasoline, six years before E.P.A. mandates. Today it's available in over 40 U.S. cities, including NYC. We've introduced low-sulfur diesel fuel for bus fleets in major U.S. cities. When used with new filter technology, this fuel helps reduce air pollution and can cut emissions by up to 90%.

It's a start.

bp

beyond petroleum   bp.com

---

centers for a Community Food Bank or for the Marine Corps Toys for Tots Program.

Large Companies

Many large companies have guidelines and initiatives that clearly define how they see their role in supporting community causes. Ben & Jerry's, the ice cream manufacturer, donates 7.5 percent of its pretax earnings to the disadvantaged and the needy. The company also contributes to groups that strive for social change and environmental protection.

Paul Newman started his own company, Newman's Own. Newman's Own donates its profits and royalties after taxes to educational and charitable causes.

International Businesses

The United Nations has a Division of Economic and Social Affairs. An outgrowth of that division is the World Business Council for Sustainable Development (WBCSD), which is a coalition of international companies with a mission "to provide business leadership as a catalyst for change toward sustainable development, and to promote the role of eco-efficiency, innovation, and corporate social responsibility." Some international companies that are members of the WBCSD include Time Warner, AT&T, Bayer, BP, Coca-Cola, Unilever, Dow Chemical, and Shell.

In the Environment

Socially responsible companies are concerned about our environment and have programs to work toward saving the earth for future generations. Two major issues involve cleaner fuel and green marketing.

Cleaner Fuel

Alternatives to the traditional transportation fuels of gasoline and diesel fuel are currently being developed. Some vehicle fuels, because

136 UNIT 3 - BUSINESS AND SOCIETY

AD GUIDE **PETROLEUM DEFENDS ITSELF**

Discussion Ask students to tell what they know about cleaner fuels and green marketing. Ask students to brainstorm different kinds of energy sources.

Caption Answer Point out to students that the ad seems to take a two-pronged approach, by 1) stating that they are all for electricity as the fuel of the (perhaps distant) future and 2) pointing out their work in attempting to make fossil fuels cleaner.

Follow Up Ask students to research alternative fuel sources and to share their findings with the class.

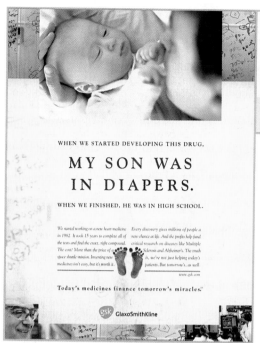

TEACH CONTINUED

Enrichment

GREEN MARKETING AND SUSTAINABILITY

After making sure students are clear on the meaning of *sustainability,* have them research material on the Web site of the World Business Council for Sustainable Development and follow any interesting links. Have students share their findings with classmates.

Concept Development

BUSINESS ETHICS

Before beginning to read, ask students to tell what they think ethics in consumerism and ethics in marketing might mean. Ask if they think they are related.

TEACHING POINTS

Organize Have students work in small groups to illustrate how consumers, consumer groups, government, and business leaders share the responsibility for protecting consumer rights.

Extend Have students discuss the meaning of the statement "Ethical companies are proactive."

---

of physical or chemical properties, create less pollution than do today's gasolines. These are called clean fuels. They include certain types of alcohol, electricity, natural gas, and propane.

Green Marketing

Consumer concern over the environment is increasing, and marketers are paying attention. The growing importance of ecological issues has brought about green marketing. In **green marketing**, companies make an effort to produce and promote environmentally safe products. Such products are often labeled as ozone-safe, recyclable, environmentally friendly, or biodegradable. Green marketing strategies have become an increasingly important way for companies to build consumer loyalty. A significant number of consumers are willing to pay more for products that are environmentally friendly.

Business Ethics

A major aspect of social responsibility is business ethics. **Ethics** are guidelines for good behavior. Ethical behavior is based on knowing the difference between right and wrong—and doing what is right. Ethical behavior is truthful and fair and takes into account the well-being of everyone. There is often a fine line between legal issues and ethical issues, especially when cultural differences are involved. Ethical businesses follow the laws established for their operations.

Ethics and Consumerism

Consumerism involves the relationship of marketing to those who buy a company's goods or services. Consumerism is the societal effort to protect consumer rights by putting legal, moral, and economic pressure on business. Individual consumers, consumer groups,

Critical Thinking

Tell students that some consumer advocates have become well known for their work. Ask students whether consumers should accept the reports of either consumer or industry product advocates without question.

AD GUIDE   **PRICE GOUGING**

Discussion Ask a student to read the ad copy aloud, and then have a volunteer state the message in his or her own words. Explain that *price gouging* means pricing products unreasonably high when consumers do not have other choices.

Caption Answer Allow students to offer their opinions. Some students may feel the need to do additional research on the topic to form a balanced opinion.

Follow Up Encourage students to research recent or past instances of price gouging in the pharmaceutical industry or in other industries.

TEACH CONTINUED

Enrichment

ETHICS IN MARKETING

Ask students who are interested in a particular field to research ethical guidelines or concerns for that business. Encourage students to research trade associations, trade publications, and other online sources. Have students use the Internet and other sources to do their research and summarize their findings in a one-page report. Encourage students to discuss their findings in class.

Concept Development

SELF-REGULATION

Ask students if they believe it was necessary for General Mills to act ethically and recall all of their canned beans when one batch was discovered to perhaps contain bacteria. What does this marketing exchange do for their public image?

Point out that their responsible actions were probably better for business than the sale of all of those canned beans, and better than the possibility of causing illness or death.

Have interested students research other instances of food contamination and report their findings to the class in a five-minute oral report.

Online Activity

Better Business Bureau

Encourage students to go online to find up-to-date news from the Better Business Bureau. Have students choose one news item and summarize it in one to two paragraphs.

---

government, and socially responsible business leaders share this effort.

The greatest growth in consumerism took place from the early 1960s until about 1980. It involved all areas of marketing. President John F. Kennedy's Consumer Bill of Rights dominated the beginning of this consumer period. It stated that consumers have four basic rights:

- To be informed and protected against fraud, deceit, and misleading statements, and to be educated in the wise use of financial resources
- To be protected from unsafe products
- To have a choice of goods and services
- To have a voice in product and marketing decisions made by government and business

Ethics in Marketing

Consumerism and corporate scandals have prompted businesses to address the many ethical issues and topics that involve marketing in general, as well as specific functions and activities. It is important to study ethics because you may be faced with ethical dilemmas as an employee or business owner. Whether you choose the right course of action may affect your career and company. Ethical principles are important in business because they reflect the management of the company and the trust between a company and its stakeholders.

Self-Regulation

Ethical companies are proactive. They join organizations that help to create an ethical business environment. The **Better Business Bureau** (BBB), established in 1912, is one of the oldest nonprofit organizations to set up self-regulation among businesses. To be a member of the BBB, a business must "agree to follow the highest principles of business ethics and voluntary self-regulation, and have a proven record of marketplace honesty and integrity." The BBB has a strict Code of Advertising as well as one for online businesses that defines what is acceptable and not acceptable with regard to truth in advertising.

Another comprehensive guide for marketing ethics is the Code of Ethics adopted by

---

the American Marketing Association (AMA). Ethical companies subscribe to the AMA's Code of Ethics which is a guideline for ethical professional conduct. Its basic rule is "not knowingly to do harm," and it includes "all relevant publics: customers, organizations, and society." The Code addresses honesty and fairness, rights and duties in all areas of marketing, and organizational relationships. Let's look at two examples of how ethical businesses comply with the AMA's Code of Ethics in the areas of marketing exchange and product development.

- **Marketing exchange** "products and services offered are safe and fit for their intended uses." In 2002, General Mills recalled 4,080 cans of Old El Paso Traditional Variety Refried Beans in five states. They did so because they discovered that one batch of those products may have been underprocessed and could have contained bacteria that would make people sick. Even though there were no reports of illness, General Mills acted ethically and removed those products from retailers' shelves.

- **Product Development and Management** "disclosure of all substantial risks associated with product or service usage." Some people are highly allergic to certain products, especially nuts. As a result, food companies have been diligent in product labeling that provides allergy warnings. For example, the Morning Start brand Apple Crisp breakfast bar includes the following warning on its packages: "Allergy Information: This product is manufactured in a facility that uses peanuts and other nuts and seeds."

Ethical Issues Related to Marketing Functions

Ethical issues can always arise when doing business. Let us look at a few ethical issues that involve specific marketing functions, such as pricing, distribution, promotion, management of marketing information, and selling.

Extended Activity

Protecting Informants

Have interested students perform research online, or using other sources, about legislation designed to protect individuals who inform the government about illegal or unethical actions. Ask students to consider why governments have enacted laws to protect these individuals.

Price gouging is not covered in the AMA's Code of Ethics; however, it is a major concern in the pharmaceutical industry, as well as when a natural disaster creates a need for products such as bottled water or flashlights. **Price gouging** is pricing products unreasonably high when the need is great or when consumers do not have other choices.

In the pharmaceutical industry, patented prescription drugs are granted monopoly status for a period of time. How companies price their patented product during that time is an area of dispute. Pharmaceutical companies argue that high prices are due to the time and money spent on research and development to come up with the medicine. Many consumer groups think price gouging exists when consumers must pay extraordinarily high prices for drugs they need to stay alive.

Some states have laws that govern price gouging during disasters, like hurricanes or tornadoes. Products in high demand, such as hotel rooms, bottled water, flashlights, food, and fuel, are often priced higher due to the unusual demand created by the catastrophe.

Management of marketing information involves issues of privacy. Industries that maintain customer data bases containing your personal information have a responsibility to keep that information private. Banking, finance companies, medical practices, marketing research companies, and any other industry that collects personal data must not share that information with anyone unless you give them permission to do so. For years, it was unethical; now, it is also against the law.

Product research and marketing research must report their findings honestly by disclosing all the facts involved in the research design and results.

Selling practices that come under scrutiny because of ethical issues often involve bribes,

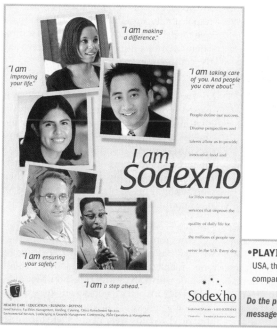

"I am making a difference."

"I am improving your life."

"I am taking care of you. And people you care about."

I am Sodexho

"I am ensuring your safety."

"I am a step ahead."

HEALTH CARE · EDUCATION · BUSINESS · DEFENSE

Sodexho

●**PLAYING a SOCIAL ROLE** In this ad Sodexho USA, the leading food and facilities management company, is presenting its positive role in society.

Do the pictures in this ad convey yet another message?

TEACH CONTINUED

Concept Development

ETHICS IN MARKETING
List these words and phrases on the board:

- bribes
- kickbacks
- favors
- high-pressure tactics

Ask students: Do these sound like ethical tactics for making a sale? Initiate in-class discussion of each tactic, including why it is unethical, if not illegal.

Enrichment

REAL-LIFE BUSINESS ETHICS
Bring in to the class news stories about a business that is having ethical, financial, or legal problems. Encourage students to discuss the situation from many points of view, using concepts they have read in the text. Lead the discussion to illustrate all the different people or things who would be affected by the situation.

 Online Activity

E-Commerce Ethics
Ask interested students to investigate some of the ethical issues involved in e-commerce. Have students summarize their findings in note form and report their discoveries to the class.

AD GUIDE   PLAYING a SOCIAL ROLE

Discussion Ask students whether they think actual employees of the company talk and feel the way the people are portrayed in the ad.

Caption Answer Answers will vary; students might note that the pictures convey the diversity of the company's workforce.

Follow Up Have students look through newspaper and online ads for other examples showing employee diversity.

Review Guide

CONCEPTS

Ask students to explain the difference between the social responsibility of business and business ethics, giving an example of each.

Answer suggestion: Social responsibility refers to a business's effort to recognize and accommodate employees' needs outside the workplace, such as a need for reliable childcare. Business ethics refers to the guidelines for good behavior adopted by a business, such as not allowing employees to bribe or mislead customers.

KEY TERMS

Students can work in small groups to review definitions of terms in context and then compose a sentence for each one.

ONLINE SELF-ASSESSMENT

Have students go to marketingessentials.glencoe.com for the Section 6.2 practice test.

Individualized Review

L1 Assign and review Chapter 6 activities in the Student Activity Workbook.

L2 Assign and review Chapter 6 activities in the Marketing Math Workbook.

L3 Assign and review Chapter 6 activities in the *BusinessWeek* Reader and Case Studies.

Marketing Practice

Ask students to imagine they have been offered a well-paying job in a company that has a reputation for less-than-ethical marketing tactics. Have them work in pairs to role-play a scene when they tell a parent or other concerned adult why they are or are not taking the job.

A MATTER OF ETHICS

Gouging? Or Marketing Tactics?

In June 2004, an investigation revealed price gouging affecting a federally funded program called the Special Supplemental Nutrition Program for Women, Infants, and Children (WIC). This program provides government vouchers to needy families to buy specific foods that meet the program's nutritional guidelines.

Higher Prices

Specialty WIC stores have been pricing their products 10 to 20 percent higher than regular supermarkets have priced them. Some WIC stores sent sales representatives to hospitals to sign up new mothers as customers. At that time, gifts could be offered such as baby strollers, diapers, and baby clothes, as well as free transportation.

THINKING ETHICALLY

Should the government step in to regulate WIC stores, or would that go against the principles of the free enterprise system?

@ Online Action!

Go to *marketingessentials.glencoe.com/6/ ethics* to find a research activity on ethics and marketing.

---

kickbacks, favors, and high-pressure tactics used to close a sale. Cultural differences complicate those issues.

For example, in some Asian countries, businesspeople expect to receive a gift as part of customary practice. The same gift given in the United States might be considered a bribe and thus be illegal.

Another issue involving bribes and kickbacks is defining what they are. Is taking a client out to dinner a bribe? Is giving a customer a free gift for buying a product considered a kickback? Some companies avoid these ethical issues by imposing strict rules against offering any type of gift to customers. Their buyers are also not permitted to accept any gifts, no matter how inexpensive they are.

High-pressure selling tactics and failure to follow through on promises made to close a sale are examples of unethical selling practices. One of the reasons for this unethical behavior can be undue pressure to meet sales quotas established by high-level management. Sales representatives feel pressured to produce, so they hound customers and make promises they cannot keep, just to make a sale.

Managerial and Personnel Issues

Management ultimately makes the decisions about major ethical issues that confront a business. From the top level right on down to the supervisory level, managers must take responsibility for establishing and creating a role model for ethical practices within a firm. Their decisions impact how customers view the company, as well.

Proper Accounting and Reporting

The Sarbanes-Oxley Act of 2002 was passed in response to the corporate scandals that involved misuse of company funds and unethical corporate governance. Accounting and proper reporting of corporation's financial situation are addressed by this new legislation. Company executives and their consulting firms can be held accountable for misinformation.

Whistle-Blowing

Provisions in the Sarbanes-Oxley Act of 2002, as well as many other laws involving management and personnel issues, include whistle-blowing protection. **Whistle-blowing** involves reporting an illegal action of one's employer. If you discovered that financial records were being altered in order

 marketingessentials.glencoe.com

A MATTER OF ETHICS   Gouging? Or Marketing Tactics?

Discussion Ask students what practice in WIC's approach to customers seems questionable. Answers may include the offering of free gifts and perks such as rides to their stores.

THINKING ETHICALLY **Answer:** If necessary, help students see that the free enterprise system is not the issue here but rather the inflated prices at taxpayer expense.

@ Online Action! For instructions, ideas, and answer guide, go to the Teacher Center at marketingessentials.glencoe.com

Follow Up Have students periodically look for continuing developments in this instance of price gouging.

to cover up extravagant personal purchases made by the top executives, would you report it? If you did, you would be a whistle-blower. If you got fired for your whistle-blowing, you would have recourse under several federal laws governing whistle-blowing.

Making a decision to be a whistle-blower involves personal ethics. Employees and managers who face such decisions find it easier to report offenses when a company has specific guidelines for making ethical decisions and a way to report offenses.

Guidelines for Ethical Behavior

Companies with an interest in ethical business behavior have or are developing guidelines to help employees make ethical decisions. It is important to remember that people make the decisions and that business ethics are closely related to personal ethics for that reason.

To make the right ethical choices, employees at all levels should follow a decision-making process that includes the following:

1. Get the facts.
2. Identify all parties concerned.
3. Think of all your alternatives.
4. Evaluate your alternatives by asking yourself the following questions:

- Is it in compliance with the law?
- Does it go against company policy?
- How does it affect everyone involved?
- Is it right, fair, and honest?
- Will it build good will for the company?
- Am I comfortable with it? Can I live with my decision?
- How will it hold up to public scrutiny?

CLOSE

Ask students to work in groups to present this scenario: They work for a clothing company. On a business trip abroad, they visit one of this company's suppliers, a manufacturer of men's sweaters. There they have seen sweatshop conditions and learned of worker exploitation by paying less than a living wage to people who do not complain for fear of losing their jobs. In the role play, they should talk about the situation among themselves, discuss how they might approach their employer, and review their options as they attempt to right the wrongs they have seen. Suggested response: Students should explore issues of personal and company ethics and allude to the aid of organizations such as the Fair Labor Association.

Critical Thinking

Ask students to consider what recourse they would have if a supervisor or coworker were to request that they do something morally or legally wrong.

6.2 AFTER YOU READ

Reviewing Key Terms and Concepts

1. Name six employee benefits that demonstrate social responsibility in the workplace.
2. What can businesses do in the marketplace to demonstrate social responsibility?
3. What things can a local business do to support the community?

Integrating Academic Skills

Math

4. If an employee took a $1.79 candy bar from her employer every day and worked five days a week for 50 weeks of the year, how much would that pilfering cost the company? If 20 employees did the same thing, how would that affect the company's profits?

Civics and Government

5. Research the legal and ethical issues about what can and cannot be said when advertising and promoting products. Prepare a one-page written report on your findings.

 Online Action!

Check your answers at *marketingessentials.glencoe.com/6/read*

marketingessentials.glencoe.com

Chapter 6 - Legal and Ethical Issues **141**

AFTER YOU READ

Reviewing Key Terms and Concepts

1. flextime, telecommuting, extended family leave, on-site child care, health insurance, paid vacation and sick time

2. They provide information to consumers, employ self-censorship by establishing ethical practices, and respond to consumer concerns with new products and company initiatives.

3. support a local sports team, hold food and blood drives, promote and support after school programs, donate supplies to local schools

Integrating Academic Skills

4. The single employee pilfering would cost the company $447.50 per year. The company would lose $8,950 a year if 20 employees did the same thing.

($1.79 × 5 days a week = $8.95; $447.50 × 50 weeks a year = $447.50; $447.50 × 20 employees = $8,950.)

5. Reports should demonstrate an understanding of legal and ethical product advertising issues. Encourage students to choose a product that interests them and focus on it. Stress that they should credit the sources they consult.

 Online Action! Answers at **marketingessentials.glencoe.com/6/read**

CAREERS
IN MARKETING

Lifelong Learning

CAREER INFORMATION

Have students go to marketingessentials.glencoe.com and find the Chapter 6 Careers page. They can then click on the link for the American Marketing Association's Career Strategies and Tips. Ask students to select one article, read it, and summarize it in three short paragraphs.

WRITING AND LISTENING

Writing and listening are especially important skills in careers that have to do with ethics or litigation. These activities help in the development of critical thinking skills which can be employed to solve problems in any aspect of business. Encourage students to develop their writing and listening skills in any class environment and in the workplace.

Primary Source

Ask students to go to marketingessentials.glencoe.com and find Chapter 6 Resources. Ask them to click on the link for the American Marketing Association's marketing dictionary and read the definitions of terms relating to legal and ethical issues.

⬤ THINKING CRITICALLY

Cultivating a mentor can lead to increased skills, job recommendations, and positive references from a person who probably has some standing in the field.

Online Action!

For instructions, ideas, and answer guide, go to the Teacher Center at marketingessentials.glencoe.com

---

CAREERS
IN MARKETING

KARL HAMPE
DIRECTOR, LITIGATION & INVESTIGATIVE SERVICES BDO SEIDMAN, LLP

❓ What do you do at work?
I identify new opportunities to provide accounting and economic consulting services to assist attorneys involved in complex business litigation. I also manage large-scale engagements and provide testimony on specialized topics relating to the accounting and economic aspects of litigation.

❓ What skills are most important to you?
Listening and writing skills are the foundation of the ability to identify new opportunities, secure new business, and deliver high quality work. Both listening and writing skills require ongoing sharpening and, frankly, humility—because everyone needs to recognize that he or she can always improve in these areas. Listening and writing skills are also catalysts for creative and critical thinking, which enables us to provide innovative responses to complex problems in litigation matters.

❓ What is your key to success?
Exceed the client's expectations while adhering to strict integrity. To do that, you must understand the client's expectations, develop a response that is creative, accurate, well presented, and delivered on time, and then make sure to take credit for a job well done.

Aptitudes, Abilities, and Skills

Writing, communication, and listening skills are essential in this career

Education and Training

Degrees in business, communication, and psychology, with at least some focus on the liberal arts.

Career Path

Most litigation and investigative specialists have a background in law and in business.

⬤ THINKING CRITICALLY

What are some of the benefits of identifying a mentor in your chosen field and working to emulate that person's skills?

Online Action!

Go to *marketingessentials.glencoe.com/6/careers* to find a career-related activity.

marketingessentials.glencoe.com

Test-Taking Strategies

Students may already have developed strategies for studying subjects which require that they commit facts to memory. These strategies might include creating anagrams or visualizing amusing scenes to aid recall. Encourage students to share any strategies of these that work for them with classmates.

FOCUS on KEY POINTS

SECTION 6.1

● The government plays a critical role in enforcing the free enterprise system and providing for the health, safety, and welfare of its citizens. The three branches of the U.S. government are the executive, legislative, and judicial branches. The Food and Drug Administration (FDA) and the Consumer Product Safety Commission (CPSC) are two federal agencies that protect consumers. Employment protection at the federal level includes the Equal Employment Opportunity Commission (EEOC) and the Occupational Safety and Health Administration (OSHA). The Securities and Exchange Commission (SEC) protects investors and the Environmental Protection Agency (EPA) protects the environment. The Federal Trade Commission (FTC) has the responsibility of enforcing the principles of a free enterprise system and protecting consumers from unfair or deceptive business practices.

SECTION 6.2

● Socially responsible businesses have policies and programs that address issues in the workplace, marketplace, community, and environment. Business ethics are guidelines for good behavior. Ethical businesses are community-conscious.

REVIEW VOCABULARY

For each of the following terms, define its meaning or explain its function in one sentence.

1. Food and Drug Administration (FDA) (p. 126)

2. Consumer Product Safety Commission (CPSC) (p. 126)

3. Equal Employment Opportunity Commission (EEOC) (p. 128)

4. Occupational Safety and Health Administration (OSHA) (p. 128)

5. Securities and Exchange Commission (SEC) (p. 128)

6. Environmental Protection Agency (EPA) (p. 129)

7. Federal Trade Commission (FTC) (p. 129)

8. flextime (p. 134)

9. telecommuting (p. 134)

10. Ad Council (p. 135)

11. green marketing (p. 137)

12. ethics (p. 137)

13. Better Business Bureau (BBB) (p. 138)

14. price gouging (p. 139)

15. whistle-blowing (p. 140)

REVIEW FACTS and IDEAS

16. Explain the role of government in a free enterprise system. (6.1)

17. How is the U.S. government structured? (6.1)

18. Name the federal regulatory agencies that have been established to protect consumers, workers, investors, and the environment, as well as the one that enforces the free enterprise system. (6.1)

19. What are business ethics, and how are they related to the law? (6.2)

20. Provide examples of ethical issues in marketing, management, and personnel. (6.2)

Chapter 6 - Legal and Ethical Issues 143

CHAPTER **6** REVIEW

REVIEW FACTS and IDEAS

16. The government provides services for, regulates, and enforces free enterprise in a free enterprise system.

17. The government is structured into three branches: executive, legislative, and judicial.

18. consumers: FDA and Consumer Product Safety Commission; workers: EEOC and OSHA; investors: SEC; environment: EPA; free enterprise: FTC

19. Ethics are guidelines for good behavior, so business ethics include fair business practices as well as social responsibility. Ethical businesses also follow laws that relate to their operations, and they sometimes try to exceed standards set in those laws.

20. Examples of ethical issues in marketing might include: marketing: truth-in-advertising; management: recalling a product with potential to harm; personnel: asking an employee to do an unethical task.

FOCUS on KEY POINTS

Ask volunteers to define the terms *legal* (Section 6.1) and *ethical* (Section 6.2) in their own words. Then read each point aloud, stopping after each one for discussion or clarification.

REVIEW VOCABULARY

See glossary for definitions of **1–15.** A sample answer might read:

1. The *Food and Drug Administration (FDA)* regulates the labeling and safety of food, drugs, and cosmetics sold in the United States; approves new products; and reviews products already on the market.

CHAPTER 6 REVIEW

BUILD SKILLS

21. Workplace Skills

Letters should clearly state the issue and offer adequate supporting evidence. The tone of the letter should be professional, serious, and respectful.

22. Technology Applications

Plans will vary but should demonstrate proficiency with the software and an understanding of how recycling benefits the environment.

23. Math Practice

It would take 166.$\overline{6}$ pounds; $10 \div \$.06 = 166.\overline{6}$

DEVELOP CRITICAL THINKING

24. Considering the Use of a Law Degree

Answers should demonstrate an understanding of the idea that lawyers can help organizations and businesses comply with the law.

25. Examining the Benefits of Recycling

Answers should show evidence of research and present information about the environmental benefits of recycling.

BUILD SKILLS

21. Workplace Skills

Writing Write a letter to the appropriate federal regulatory agency to complain about an unfair business practice, an ethical issue, or another topic of concern to you, such as identity theft.

22. Technology Applications

Examining the Benefits of Recycling Visit the Web site for the Environmental Protection Agency and conduct additional research to examine the benefits of recycling on the environment. Work in groups to create a promotional plan to educate the public about those benefits. Use presentation software to share your promotional plan and the sources you used with classmates.

23. Math Practice

The Price of Recycling If the local recycling plant pays $.06 per pound for aluminum cans, how many pounds of cans would it take to get $10?

DEVELOP CRITICAL THINKING

24. Considering the Use of a Law Degree

Review this chapter's main points. Research the type of courses a law student would take to study for a law degree or J.D. (juris doctor). An efficient way to perform this research is to key the words *juris doctor courses* on an Internet search engine. Be sure to compare several programs and course listings before forming an opinion about which courses are typically required. From your research and your review, make a list of all the ways a law degree could be useful for business and marketing employment. Compare your list with your classmates'.

25. Examining the Benefits of Recycling

Visit the Web site for the Environmental Protection Agency and conduct additional research to examine the benefits of recycling for the environment. Work in groups to create a promotional plan to educate the public about those benefits. Share your promotional plan and the sources you used with classmates in an oral presentation.

 Formative Assessment

Formative assessment is an essential component of classroom work. This type of assessment provides information that is then used as feedback to modify teaching and meet student needs.

L1 Review Key Terms for this chapter. Students can work in groups to write a short play about a topic or topics in this chapter. They should use ten of the key terms in their dialogue.

L2 Have students write a one-page story featuring a legal or ethical issue raised in the chapter.

L3 Students should write either an essay or a poem giving their opinion of the relationship between our federal government and the free enterprise system.

 If the results of this formative assessment seem low, consider the following activity: Assign the material under each of the headings in the text to a different student who is then responsible for reviewing that material for the class.

APPLY CONCEPTS

26. Investigating the Price for Medicine

Many U.S. citizens are visiting Canada to buy their prescription drugs at greatly reduced prices. Investigate the issues surrounding the prices of prescription drugs in the United States. Present all sides of the issue—the consumer's side, the pharmaceutical firm's side, and the role of government.

Activity Use word processing to prepare a three-page written report on this issue.

27. Developing a Socially Responsible Company

Work in groups to research the code of ethics established by organizations such as the BBB and AMA, as well as by socially responsible businesses. Use those examples to develop a code of ethics for your school store, a local business, or a hypothetical business. Begin with a paragraph on the importance of ethics in business. Include ethical issues and scenarios to help guide employees into taking the ethical course of action.

Activity Prepare your code of ethics in writing for publication. Share your work with classmates in an oral presentation.

NET SAVVY

28. Product Recalls

Visit the Consumer Product Safety Commission Web site. List and explain five current product recalls from that Web site.

CONNECTION

Role Play: Legal and Ethical Issues

Situation You are to assume the role of an experienced sales associate for a men's clothing store. You have been assigned the duty of orienting a new sales associate (judge) about the types of clothing the store carries and the importance of reading the labels attached to them. The new sales associate (judge) wonders why clothing labels are so important.

Activity You are to explain to the new sales associate (judge) the importance of the care labels and fiber content labels in the garments that your store sells.

Evaluation You will be evaluated on how well you meet the following performance indicators:

● Describe the nature of selling regulations

● Explain business ethics in selling

● Determine the relationship between government and business

● Explain the role of business in society

● Orient new employees

 Online Action!

For more information and DECA Prep practice, go to *marketingessentials.glencoe .com/6/DECA*

Chapter 6 - Legal and Ethical Issues **145**

APPLY CONCEPTS

26. Investigating the Price for Medicine

All sides should be presented in a fairly even-handed manner. Supporting details should be interesting and to the point. The tone should be serious. The appearance of the report should illustrate comfort with the use of the word processing program.

27. Developing a Socially Responsible Company

Presentations will vary but should demonstrate an understanding of the concept of ethics. The tone of students' documents and their presentations should reflect that of the official materials they studied as they prepared this assignment.

NET SAVVY

28. Product Recalls

Answers will vary but should demonstrate an understanding of product recalls. Consider making this an ongoing project, with interested students updating classmates as new information is posted.

MINI-QUIZ

Read these sentences to students and have them tell whether each is true or false.

1. *Legal* and *ethical* mean almost the same thing. (false)

2. Consumerism refers to efforts to protect the public from misleading advertising and inferior or harmful products. (true)

3. Ours is not a totally free enterprise system but rather one that is modified by laws. (true)

For an expanded chapter quiz, go to Chapter 6 in the TeacherWorks CD-ROM and to Chapter 6 in the **Exam***View*® Pro Test Generator CD-ROM.

 CONNECTION

The students should be evaluated according to the performance standards noted in the role play. For another DECA role play, go to the Competitive Events Workbook or the Student Activity Workbook, or go to **marketingessentials.glencoe.com/6/DECA**

 Online Action! For instructions, ideas, and answer guide, go to the Teacher Center at **marketingessentials.glencoe.com**

DECA Advisors Corner

Ask members to brainstorm local volunteer organizations that they might work with individually or as a chapter. Then schedule time with a different organization each month for the rest of the school year. Personal satisfaction, chapter recognition, and organizations' appreciation are all likely results.

SET-UP

Discuss the basic background to make sure students understand the simulation. Direct students to the Ad Council Web site to see examples of ads. You may want to bring up examples such as the local radio or television public service announcements for public transportation or other community services.

PROCEDURES

You may want to list procedures on the board and talk about any questions the students might have. Remind the students that a suggested outline for their project is available at **marketingessentials.glencoe.com/u3/ internship.**

TIME MANAGEMENT

Set goals, block schedules, and milestones. Assign interim deadlines for each step of the project.

ASSESSMENT

The rubrics for evaluation of the written, oral, and computer presentations are available at **marketingessentials.glencoe.com/u3/ internship.**

MARKETING INTERNSHIP

A SIMULATED **DECA** PRODUCT AND SERVICE MANAGEMENT EVENT

Write a Proposal for a Civic-Minded Project

➡ BASIC BACKGROUND

Your firm is a member of the American Association of Advertising Agencies. One of your firm's responsibilities as a member is to donate its time and resources to create public service ads when assigned them by the Ad Council. Now your firm would like to submit its own idea to the Ad Council for a public service ad on behalf of a government agency or a nonprofit organization.

Marketing for Social Change As part of the initiative, your firm is asking every employee to submit proposals for consideration by management. According to the Ad Council, "The objectives of these ads are education and awareness of significant social issues in an effort to change the public's attitudes and behaviors and stimulate positive social change."

➡ YOUR OBJECTIVE

Your objective is to complete a proposal for a project that would meet the Ad Council's criteria and the criteria of the firm's civic-minded initiative. The firm wants its public service ads to be just as well planned and interesting as its work for a paying customer. Your idea will need a design element as well as an effective message.

➡ ASSIGNMENT AND STRATEGY

- **Conduct research** Research the Ad Council. Learn more about its purpose, mission, and past campaigns. Review the acceptable topics, which include educational issues and community health and safety. Review possible clients. They may be government agencies or nonprofit organizations.

- **Develop your concept** Develop a plan to help the client. Include the purpose and objectives, as well as the rationale for selecting that particular topic and beneficiary. Explain the main purpose of the proposed project and specific objectives you expect to accomplish.

  Be sure your objectives are simple, specific, and measurable. Include a time line for the project, as well as all the

READ to WRITE

Public Service Announcements

Direct students to the Ad Council Web site. Ask the students to view the featured public service announcement (PSA) and then view other PSAs. Ask students to select a PSA and research and define the issue it discusses in a one-page response. Students should discuss in their responses reasons a corporation or company might have sponsored or placed such ads. Have students analyze the PSA from the viewpoints of both society and the company that sponsors the ad. Students might discuss what benefits the company receives from sponsoring an ad or taking a position on a particular issue.

organizational details required for its completion. Explain how the project will be evaluated.

- **What your project should include** Describe the project that you are proposing in detail and its potential benefits. Include samples of proposed marketing materials. For example, include a sample advertisement, complete with headline, illustration(s), and a slogan, or a Web page design and site map of what would be included on a Web site. Conclude with a persuasive argument why the firm should select your proposal as its submission to the Ad Council.

YOUR REPORT

Use a word processing program and presentation software to prepare a double-spaced report and an oral presentation for your supervisors. See a suggested outline and key evaluation points at *marketingessentials.glencoe.com/internship*

marketingessentials.glencoe.com

BUILD YOUR PORTFOLIO

Option 1 Internship Report Once you have completed your Marketing Internship project and presentation, include your written report and a few printouts of key slides from your oral presentation in your Marketing Portfolio.

Option 2 Promoting Free Enterprise Evaluate advertisements by states or local areas that attempt to attract businesses and/or tourists. Research other ways local communities try to promote economic growth, such as hosting golf tournaments or a state fair. Select a state or community that needs economic help. Then design a marketing strategy around specific objectives, including ways to evaluate the effectiveness of the plan. See a suggested outline and key evaluation points at *marketingessentials.glencoe .com/portfolio*

@ Online Action!

Go to *marketingessentials.glencoe .com/Unit/3/DECA* to review public service concepts that relate to DECA events.

Marketing Internship **147**

Unit Review

Now that students have completed the chapters in Unit 3, ask them to review their answers to the Analyze the Ad on page 97. Would they answer them differently now? Why or why not?

Have students make a list of companies that are known for their socially responsible, ethical conduct. Examples may include Target, Ben & Jerry's, and Working Assets. Ask students to debate whether such behavior affects a company's profits. Have students write a three-paragraph report about the marketing benefits for a company of ethical conduct.

STEP AHEAD

Now that the students have learned how and where a business operates and about ethical business behavior, ask students what skills are required to operate a business successfully.

Answers will vary but may include strong communication skills, interpersonal skills, and management skills.

Internship Wrap-Up

Ask the class to discuss advertisements or public service announcements of social concerns that opened their eyes to issues they were oblivious to before. Have students prepare a print or broadcast ad for a community or nonprofit organization of their choice using graphic design software, audiovisual equipment, or other technology.

BUILD YOUR PORTFOLIO

Explain to students that portfolios provide evidence of their knowledge and skills in working with data, people, and concepts. Developing a portfolio is a valuable career tool. Point out to students to regularly update their portfolio to reflect their latest and best work. Encourage students to check the portfolio information available at **marketingessentials.glencoe.com/u3/internship**.

Peer Review

Fellow students who share common interests can serve as reviewers of the final portfolios. This review can be completed through the use of a checklist. Go to **marketingessentials.glencoe.com/u3/internship** to find a suggested checklist.

Unit Objectives

After completing this unit, students should be able to:

- Perform essential math functions with whole numbers, fractions, and decimal numbers
- Effectively communicate by speaking, listening, writing, and reading
- Discuss the uses of computers in business and in marketing
- Facilitate understanding of others through personal attitude and interpersonal skills
- Explain the basic functions of management and discuss effective management techniques

Key to Individualized Activities

L1 Level 1 activities are basic activities and should fall within the range of all students.

L2 Level 2 activities are average activities and should be within the range of average and above average students.

L3 Level 3 activities are challenging activities designed for the ability range of above average students.

Enrichment Resources

PROFESSIONAL ORGANIZATIONS

Marketing Research Association mra-net.org

National DECA deca.org

MEDIA RESOURCES

Print or online editions of

BusinessWeek businessweek.com

Fast Company fastcompany.com

PC Magazine pcmag.com

WRITING SUPPORT

Ask students to write an essay about how the classes they are taking in school can help them in a professional marketing job. Students should list at least three courses and their benefits. Ask students to keep and review this document as they study Unit 4.

UNIT 4 PLANNING GUIDE AND RESOURCES

CHAPTER	PRINT MATERIALS	TECHNOLOGY RESOURCES
Chapter 7 Section 7.1 Section 7.2	**From Unit 4 Fast File Booklet** Lesson Plans; Chapter Summaries; Reproducible Masters; Reproducible Tests **Print Ancillaries** Student Activity Workbook; Marketing Math Workbook; *BusinessWeek* Reader and Case Studies, Chapter 7; Competitive Events Workbook, Unit 4; Marketing Research Project Workbook; School-to-Work Activity Workbook	Interactive Chalkboard classroom presentations **marketingessentials.glencoe.com** Online Student Edition, Chapter 7 TeacherWorks **Exam***View*® Pro Test Generator, Chapter 7 Virtual Business
Chapter 8 Section 8.1 Section 8.2	**From Unit 4 Fast File Booklet** Lesson Plans; Chapter Summaries; Reproducible Masters; Reproducible Tests **Print Ancillaries** Student Activity Workbook; Marketing Math Workbook; *BusinessWeek* Reader and Case Studies, Chapter 8; Competitive Events Workbook, Unit 4; Marketing Research Project Workbook; School-to-Work Activity Workbook	Interactive Chalkboard classroom presentations **marketingessentials.glencoe.com** Online Student Edition, Chapter 8 TeacherWorks **Exam***View*® Pro Test Generator, Chapter 8 Virtual Business
Chapter 9 Section 9.1 Section 9.2	**From Unit 4 Fast File Booklet** Lesson Plans; Chapter Summaries; Reproducible Masters; Reproducible Tests **Print Ancillaries** Student Activity Workbook; Marketing Math Workbook; *BusinessWeek* Reader and Case Studies, Chapter 9; Competitive Events Workbook, Unit 4; Marketing Research Project Workbook; School-to-Work Activity Workbook	Interactive Chalkboard classroom presentations **marketingessentials.glencoe.com** Online Student Edition, Chapter 9 TeacherWorks **Exam***View*® Pro Test Generator, Chapter 9 Virtual Business
Chapter 10 Section 10.1 Section 10.2	**From Unit 4 Fast File Booklet** Lesson Plans; Chapter Summaries; Reproducible Masters; Reproducible Tests **Print Ancillaries** Student Activity Workbook; Marketing Math Workbook; *BusinessWeek* Reader and Case Studies, Chapter 10; Competitive Events Workbook, Unit 4; Marketing Research Project Workbook; School-to-Work Activity Workbook	Interactive Chalkboard classroom presentations **marketingessentials.glencoe.com** Online Student Edition, Chapter 10 TeacherWorks **Exam***View*® Pro Test Generator, Chapter 10 Virtual Business
Chapter 11 Section 11.1 Section 11.2	**From Unit 4 Fast File Booklet** Lesson Plans; Chapter Summaries; Reproducible Masters; Reproducible Tests **Print Ancillaries** Student Activity Workbook; Marketing Math Workbook; *BusinessWeek* Reader and Case Studies, Chapter 11; Competitive Events Workbook, Unit 4; Marketing Research Project Workbook; School-to-Work Activity Workbook	Interactive Chalkboard classroom presentations **marketingessentials.glencoe.com** Online Student Edition, Chapter 11 TeacherWorks **Exam***View*® Pro Test Generator, Chapter 11 Virtual Business

National Marketing Education

CHAPTER	SECTION	PERFORMANCE INDICATOR
Chapter 7 **Basic Math Skills**	7.1	Solve basic math problems (PRI, SEL)
		Solve math problems involving fractions (PRI, SEL)
	7.2	Operate a calculator (PRI, SEL)
		Solve mathematical problems involving percentages (PRI, SEL)
		Read charts and graphs (PRI, SEL)
Chapter 8 **Communication Skills**	8.1	Explain the nature of effective communications (CIS)
		Apply effective listening skills (CIS)
	8.2	Make oral presentations (CIS)
		Handle telephone calls in a businesslike manner (CIS)
		Explain the nature of written communications (CIS)
		Use communications technology/systems (CIS)
Chapter 9 **Technology Applications for Marketing**	9.1	Identify ways that technology impacts business (BME)
	9.2	Demonstrate basic word processing skills (BME)
		Demonstrate basic database skills (BME)
		Demonstrate basic spreadsheet skills (BME)
		Demonstrate basic presentation software skills (BME)
		Demonstrate basic search skills on the Web (BME)
Chapter 10 **Interpersonal Skills**	10.1	Foster positive working relationships (CIS)
		Identify personality traits important to business (PD)
		Adjust to change (PD)
	10.2	Participate as a team member (CIS)
		Explain the nature of leadership in organizations (BME)
		Explain the nature of staff communications (CIS)
Chapter 11 **Management Skills**	11.1	Explain the concept of management (BME)
		Explain the nature of management/supervisory training (BME)
	11.2	Foster positive working relationships (CIS)
		Describe the role of management in the achievement of quality (BME)
		Encourage team building (BME)
		Explain the concept of staff motivation (BME)
		Explain the nature of leadership in organizations (BME)

BME Business, Management, Entrepreneurship   **CIS** Communication, Interpersonal Skills   **PD** Professional Development   **PRI** Pricing   **SEL** Selling

Standards Assessment Correlation

SECTION ASSESSMENT		CHAPTER ASSESSMENT						UNIT LAB
Reviewing Key Terms and Concepts	Integrating Academic Skills	Review Facts and Ideas	Build Skills	Develop Critical Thinking	Apply Concepts	Workplace Skills	Net Savvy	Marketing Internship
1, 2, 3			14		19, 20	✓		
3		10			19			
1			16				✓	
2	✓	12	14			✓	✓	
3	✓	13		17	19		✓	
1, 2, 3				28		✓		✓
1, 2	✓	17		27				
			24			✓		✓
		20						✓
2		19, 21, 22						✓
			25			✓	✓	✓
1	✓	24, 29		33		✓		✓
	✓		32	33	35		✓	
					36			
					36			
					35			✓
	✓		30, 32			✓	✓	
1		7, 8, 10	13			✓		
		7	14		19			✓
3	✓	7, 9	14	16				✓
1, 3	✓							
2		11	13			✓		✓
		9, 10, 12	13			✓	✓	✓
2	✓	16, 17, 18						✓
1, 3								
			21			✓		✓
3		19			27		✓	✓
3		20	21			✓		✓
3	✓	20	21	25		✓	✓	✓
1, 2		19		24				✓

148D

Unit Overview

Unit 4 introduces students to the concepts of business, marketing, and technology as well as the basic skills necessary for success in the real world of work.

Chapter 7 provides a review of basic mathematical skills and Chapter 8 includes information on important communication skills. Chapter 9 discusses current computer technology used in marketing, while Chapter 10 familiarizes students with teamwork and interpersonal skills. Lastly, Chapter 11 introduces management functions and techniques.

MAKING IT RELEVANT

Inform students that, while understanding the concepts of marketing are key, one cannot succeed in the profession of marketing without certain skills.

Unit Launch Activity

Review the ad on this page. Survey students about "one stop shopping" as this concept relates to MNI. Ask them how such a business is effective and efficient for a company seeking exposure in all the "right" places.

OUT OF TIME?

If class time is too short to cover all the chapters in this unit, go to Unit 4 in your Fast File Teacher Resources booklet and find the Chapter Summaries for Chapters 7, 8, 9, 10, and 11.

148

In this unit you will find

- **Chapter 7**
  Basic Math
  Skills

- **Chapter 8**
  Communication
  Skills

- **Chapter 9**
  Technology
  Applications
  for Marketing

- **Chapter 10**
  Interpersonal
  Skills

- **Chapter 11**
  Management
  Skills

OCCUPY THE EXECUTIVE SUITE.

Advertise locally in the nation's best business magazines in your priority markets with one simple media buy exclusively through MNI. In 48 top local markets, the MNI Executive Network delivers an exclusive group of business leaders who invest for success. If you want your message to reach business decision-makers, call your MNI representative or Robert Reif, National Ad Director at 877.ASK.4MNI.

LOCAL ADS. NATIONAL MAGS.

MEDIA NETWORKS, INC.

www.mni.com

148

 UNIT PROJECT

Human Resources Manual

Put chapter members into teams to develop a training and policy manual used for running a business. This could be for a local business or the school store. The manual should be set up like those issued by Human Resources Departments. After studying this unit, have students decide which concepts apply to the manual.

Assessment Guidelines Prepare a rubric for evaluation that includes various forms of written communication (e.g., organization, purpose, details, grammar and mechanics, and voice/tone), demonstrates knowledge of the topic, and clearly outlines the concepts.

Enrichment Assign and review Unit 4 activities in the Competitive Events Workbook.

Marketing

ANALYZE THE AD

One of the goals of marketing is getting a message to a specific audience. Media Networks, Inc. sells ad space in business magazines. What does it promise?

Market Talk Ad placement firms specialize in newspaper, magazine, broadcast, or Internet advertising. They can advise clients on the best places to feature their messages and the most efficient way to spend their advertising budgets.

Think and Write Just like communication between people, advertising is more effective if it says exactly what it means. List three ways Media Networks, Inc. gets its message across to potential customers.

@ Online Action! Go to *marketingessentials.glencoe.com/u4/ad* for an extended activity.

Functions of Marketing

Marketing Plan

1 ANALYSIS
SWOT
Economic
Socio-Cultural
Technological
Competitive

2 STRATEGY
Promotion
Place
Price
Product

3 IMPLEMENTATION
Organization
Management
Staffing

4 BUDGET
Cost of sales
Cost of Promotion
Incomes and Expenses

5 CONTROL
Evaluation
Performance Measures
Performance Analysis

In this unit
Foundations of Marketing
- Communication, Interpersonal Skills
- Professional Development
- Business, Management, Entrepreneurship

149

RELATE THE UNIT TO THE MARKETING PLAN

The four Ps of the marketing mix include product, place, pricing, and promotion. Unit 4 identifies the skills necessary to execute the mix, including math, communication, computer applications, interpersonal, and management skills.

MARKETING PLAN OVERVIEW

Ask students to identify how the skills taught in each chapter are required to execute a marketing plan.

Examples may include math for pricing and communication for promotion. Management and interpersonal skills would be necessary to work with a team and computers would be required to do business in the modern world.

Functions of Marketing

Point out to students that Unit 4 will help them understand these foundations of marketing: business, management, and entrepreneurship; professional development; and communication and interpersonal skills.

- **Business, Management, Entrepreneurship** A modern-day manager must provide the workplace with adequate communication channels and working technology. Without these, output and efficiency suffer.

- **Professional Development** Solid, modern workplace skills require the employees to interact, communicate with clarity, and manage their workload with efficiency.

- **Communication, Interpersonal Skills** At its essence, marketing conveys a clear and concise message about a company, concern, or cause.

ANALYZE THE AD

Answers may include that Media Networks, Inc., promises it will get an advertiser's message into the offices of top decision-makers.

Market Talk Ask students to discuss the complexity of this advertising message. In their opinion, is the message in the ad adequately communicated by the visual, or does the viewer have to read the copy in order to understand the message?

Think and Write To facilitate this assignment, students might want to look ahead at Chapter 8, Communication Skills, and skim it for ideas if they have difficulties writing their paragraph. They might want to brainstorm how advertising is an effective mode of communication and decide where advertising techniques overlap interpersonal communication techniques.

@ Online Action! For instructions, ideas, and answer guide, go to the Teacher Center at **marketingessentials.glencoe.com**

Chapter Overview

Chapter 7 explains the basic math skills used in marketing, including writing numbers in words and working with fractions, decimals, and percentages. Students will learn how to use a calculator to solve math problems and how to read different types of graphs.

BUILD BACKGROUND

Initiate a discussion about math skills. Ask students what math skills they use in their everyday lives. Ask students to name math skills they think might be used in marketing. Tell students they will learn the basic math skills used in purchasing, advertising and promotion, distribution, pricing, selling, entrepreneurship, and finance.

Why It's Important

Virtually every job in marketing and business requires a knowledge of basic math skills. In addition, today's jobs require the use of various tools, such as calculators and computers, to analyze information. Understanding these tools and fundamental math skills will be essential to success in a marketing career.

Prepare to Read

Ask students to write down all the major headings of the chapter in outline form. Tell students to write down what they already know about each topic. They will then fill in new information as they read the chapter, leaving them with a thorough chapter outline.

CHAPTER 7
Basic Math Skills

Chapter Objectives

After reading this chapter, you should be able to:

- Write numbers in words, using commas and hyphens correctly
- Understand fractions
- Perform basic math operations with decimal numbers and round answers
- Convert fractions to decimal equivalents
- Use a calculator to solve math problems
- Convert percentages to decimals and decimals to percentages
- Read graphs used to present mathematical data

GUIDE TO THE PHOTO

Market Talk Everyday tasks, even figuring out the odds of winning a prize at a fair, relate to math concepts. Marketers use basic math skills in every phase of marketing, including purchasing, advertising and promotion, distribution, pricing, selling, entrepreneurship, and finance.

Quick Think If you are working with a calculator, what is the point of estimating the answer to a math problem?

150 UNIT 4 - SKILLS FOR MARKETING

GUIDE TO THE PHOTO

Market Talk Lead a discussion about the basic math skills a vendor at an amusement park would need to make a sale (making change, using a calculator, etc.). Ask students to share their experiences using math in a sales capacity. Ask: What would the challenges be in conducting a sales transaction at a vendor booth as opposed to at a retail store? What math skills would be needed in any sales job?

Quick Think Estimating can save time or effort and is helpful in confirming the accuracy of your answer.

Follow Up Ask students to go to a craft fair, farmer's market, or similar sales environment and interview vendors about the math skills they use to conduct business. Have students write two to three paragraphs summarizing their interview.

Performance indicators represent key skills and knowledge. Relating them to the concepts explained in this chapter is your key to success in DECA events. Keep this in mind as you read this chapter and write some notes each time you encounter material that helps you master a key concept.

These acronyms represent DECA events that involve knowledge of concepts in this chapter.

AAAL	FMAL	MMS*	TMDM*
AAML*	FMDM*	QSRM*	TSE*
ADC*	FMML*	RMAL	VPM
BSM	FSRM*	RMML*	
EMDM*	HMDM*	SMDM*	

In all these DECA events you should be able to follow these performance indicators:

- Calculate net sales
- Interpret descriptive statistics for marketing decision making
- Calculate media costs
- Calculate miscellaneous charges

All the events with an asterisk (*) also include these performance indicators:

- Calculate financial ratios
- Forecast sales
- Determine discounts and allowances that can be used to adjust base prices
- Analyze cost/benefits of company participation in community activities
- Prepare a promotional budget
- Analyze sales reports
- Analyze operating results in relation to budget/industry

DECA PREP

Check your understanding of DECA performance indicators with the DECA activity in this chapter's review. For more information and DECA Prep practice, go to *marketingessentials.glencoe.com/7/DECA*

marketingessentials.glencoe.com

CHAPTER 7 Classroom Resources

For the Teacher

- TeacherWorks
- **marketingessentials.glencoe.com**
- Interactive Chalkboard
- **Exam*View*®** Pro Test Generator
- Fast File Unit 4

For the Student

- *Marketing Essentials* Online Edition
- Student Activity Workbook
- Marketing Math Workbook
- Marketing Research Project Workbook
- School-to-Work Activity Workbook
- Competitive Events Workbook
- *BusinessWeek* Reader and Case Studies
- **marketingessentials.glencoe.com**

DECA events that require knowledge of basic math skills are described here. Discuss the performance indicators to make sure students understand how to demonstrate their understanding.

The events acronyms stand for:

AAAL: Apparel and Accessories Marketing Series, AL

AAML: Apparel and Accessories Marketing Series, ML

ADC: Advertising Campaign Event

BSM: Business Services Marketing Series

EMDM: E-Commerce Management Team Decision Making Event

FMAL: Food Marketing Series, AL

FMDM: Financial Analysis Management Team Decision Making Event

FMML: Food Marketing Series, ML

FSRM: Full Service Restaurant Management Series

HMDM: Hospitality Services Management Team Decision Making Event

MMS: Marketing Management Series

QSRM: Quick Serve Restaurant Management Series

RMAL: Retail Merchandising Series, AL

RMML: Retail Merchandising Series, ML

SMDM: Sports and Entertainment Marketing Management Team Decision Making Event

TMDM: Travel and Tourism Marketing Management Team Decision Making Event

TSE: Technical Sales Event

VPM: Vehicles and Petroleum Marketing Series

DECA PREP

Find timed DECA prep activities correlated to the Competitive Events Workbook for students and DECA tips for teachers at **marketingessentials.glencoe.com/7/DECA**

FOCUS

Introducing the Section

COLLABORATIVE ACTIVITY

To prepare for reading this section, have students work as a group to brainstorm math skills that might be needed in marketing.

Answers should include writing numbers in words, using fractions and decimals, rounding numbers, and converting fractions to decimals.

Next, write math skills on the board and have students write down a scenario in which each skill might be used. Ask volunteers to share their scenarios with the class.

Preteaching Key Terms

Ask a volunteer to read the key terms aloud. Have students write down a number that they think is an example of each term. Tell students they can check their guesses as they read the section.

- digit
- fractions
- numerator
- denominator
- mixed number
- decimal number

Build Vocabulary

Preview the following words by reading them in context under the heading Writing Whole Numbers. Discuss the meaning of these words with the students.

- **inventory**
  stock of goods

- **symbol**
  something that represents something else

- **whole number**
  number without fractions or decimals

152

OBJECTIVES

- Write numbers in words, using commas and hyphens correctly
- Understand fractions
- Perform basic math operations with decimal numbers and round answers
- Convert fractions to decimal equivalents

KEY TERMS

- digit
- fractions
- numerator
- denominator
- mixed number
- decimal number

WHILE YOU READ

Connect Think of three situations when you would use fractions.

Math Fundamentals

READ and STUDY

BEFORE YOU READ

Predict Why do you think math skills relate to the study of marketing?

THE MAIN IDEA

Virtually every job in marketing and business requires a good understanding of math fundamentals; the sharper your math skills, the more successful you will be.

STUDY ORGANIZER

Use a chart like the one below to write down examples of rounding from three decimal places to the nearest tenth, converting a fraction to a decimal, and calculating the area of a rectangular room.

Rounding From Three Decimal Places to the Nearest Tenth	Converting a Fraction to a Decimal	Calculating the Area of a Rectangular Room
4.888 = 4.9		

Writing Whole Numbers

A company needs to know exactly how many of each product remains in its warehouse, so it takes inventory. When taking inventory, count using whole numbers.

The numbering system we use is composed of ten basic symbols called digits: 0, 1, 2, 3, 4, 5, 6, 7, 8, and 9. Each **digit** represents a number and can be combined to represent larger numbers, such as 14; 215; 7,901; and 36,852.

READ and STUDY

BEFORE YOU READ

Ask students to think about what they have learned about marketing in the previous chapters. Lead a discussion about how math skills might relate to the marketing concepts they have learned so far.

THE MAIN IDEA

Ask students to brainstorm problems that might occur if they get a job in marketing but have poor math skills.

STUDY ORGANIZER

Model for students how to fill in an example number. A full-size, downloadable study organizer can be found at marketingessentials.glencoe.com

 WHILE YOU READ Model for students how they can write down sample marketing situations as they read the section on fractions.

These numbers are all whole numbers because they can be written without fractions or decimals. Each digit in a whole number represents *how many* of something. The digit on the far right represents the number of ones. The next digit to the left represents the number of tens. So, in the number 25, there are five ones and two tens.

Knowing the place name for each digit and for groups of digits is necessary for reading numbers and writing them in words. You use this skill, for example, when you write a check. The check format requires that amounts be written in both figures and words. Follow these five steps when you read whole numbers or write them in words:

1. Separate the number into groups of three digits: units, thousands, and millions. Very large numbers may include groups of digits for billions, trillions, and so on.

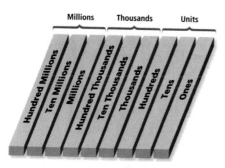

Millions   Thousands   Units

Hundred Millions / Ten Millions / Millions / Hundred Thousands / Ten Thousands / Thousands / Hundreds / Tens / Ones

2. Separate the groups with commas.

Name of the three-digit group

36,750 ⟶ thirty-six thousand, seven hundred fifty

Comma

The name of this group is understood to be units, but it is not written.

3. When writing the names of whole numbers, never use the word *and*.

360 ⟶ three hundred sixty

No *and*

4. Use hyphens in numbers less than 100 that are written as two words.

29 ⟶ twenty-nine

Use a hyphen.

5. When a three-digit group is made up of only zeros, do not write the name of the group.

3,000,375 ⟶ three million, three hundred seventy-five

Since there are no thousands, no words are written.

Fractions

The marketing research department of a soap company did a survey and found that two-thirds of the people who bought its new dish detergent thought it did a better job than the competition. This means that, for every three people surveyed, two were pleased with the new product, and one was not. Many jobs in business, especially in marketing, require a good understanding of fractions.

Fractions are numbers used to describe or compare parts of a whole. The top number, the **numerator**, represents the number of parts being considered. The bottom number, the **denominator**, represents how many parts in a whole. For example, the shaded area in the rectangle below is ³⁄₅ (three-fifths) of the total rectangle.

Numerator, the number of parts being considered

$$\frac{3 \text{ shaded parts}}{5 \text{ total parts}} = \frac{3}{5}$$

Denominator, the number of parts in a whole

TEACH

Discussion Starter

WRITING WHOLE NUMBERS

Ask students to imagine they are managers of a retail store. They must compile a math test as part of the employee application. What questions would they use to test potential employees' knowledge of whole numbers? Lead a discussion about why it is important to have basic knowledge of whole numbers when working in retail.

TEACHING POINTS

Demonstrate Bring to class examples of job ads that require math skills. Be sure to include ads for a variety of jobs.

Role Play Divide students in pairs and have one student pretend to be a store manager conducting an interview and have the other student be a potential employee. Have the interviewer ask the interviewee about his or her math skills.

Enrichment

VISUAL AIDS

Have students work in groups to create flash cards, computer programs, or other visual aids that might help them with the concepts taught in this section. Encourage students to share their projects as study aids.

Online Activity

Math in Marketing

Ask students to use the Internet to find a job description of a marketing position. Have students research what math skills are involved in this position and what skills a person is required to have to be considered for the job.

Critical Thinking

Ask students if they like or dislike math. Why do they like or dislike it? How would they feel if math were an everyday part of their job? Have students share their responses in class.

SECTION 7.1

TEACH CONTINUED

Individualized Math Skills

FRACTIONS

L1 Write a fraction on the board and point to the numerator and the denominator, asking students to identify each part. Then write a mixed number on the board and ask students to identify the components.

L2 Draw a circle on the board with three out of four sections shaded and ask students to identify the shaded region (3/4). Repeat with a circle entirely shaded in (1/1 or 1), and with two circles: one circle entirely shaded and one half shaded (1 1/2).

L3 Write five to 10 fractions on the board and have students draw shaded figures representing each fraction on a piece of paper.

TEACHING POINTS

Demonstrate Ask students to name a fraction, and then demonstrate on the board or with a computerized diagram its corresponding shaded figure.

Concept Development

DECIMAL NUMBERS

Ask students to cut or rip a piece of paper into four pieces, then write a different decimal number on each piece to make four flashcards. Students should then choose partners and take turns showing their partner a flashcard and having the partner read the decimal number aloud. After students have read all four of their partner's cards, have them choose new partners and repeat. Then, lead a discussion about any problems students had in reading the decimal numbers.

Micropurchases for Microprices

Web purchases of more than a few dollars go through traditional credit-card-based billing systems. But what if you sell something that only costs 25 cents? Credit charges and fees cost more than that.

Micropayment carriers offer billing services to Web marketers including writers, artists, and musicians who want to offer very low-cost products online. Consumers open an account with an initial payment of $20 or more, and purchases are then deducted from the account. Obstacles to success include convincing Web surfers to open accounts to pay for such tiny purchases and keeping costs low to make a profit. But the market is potentially huge.

Micropayments for Words

RedPaper.com is a membership Web site that operates like an eBay for words; members buy articles, poems, and stories for less than $1. RedPaper developed its own micropayment system rather than contracting for the service. With 26,000 members, that makes sense.

> **THINK LIKE A MARKETER**
> Name one disadvantage of micropayments.
>
> **@ Online Action!**
>
> Go to *marketingessentials.glencoe.com/ 7/net* to find a project on Internet pricing.

In the example below, the number of circles is 2/7 (two-sevenths) of the total number of shapes.

 $$\frac{2 \text{ circles}}{7 \text{ shapes}} = \frac{2}{7}$$

Here are more examples illustrating the same principle.

 $$\frac{\text{Number of shaded parts}}{\text{Total number of parts}} = \frac{3}{8}$$

 $$\frac{3 \text{ shaded parts}}{\text{Total number of parts}} = \frac{3}{3} = 1$$

One whole circle is shaded.

 $$\frac{5 \text{ shaded triangles}}{4 \text{ triangles in a square}} = \frac{5}{4} \text{ of a square}$$

A fraction can describe a number greater than 1.

When the numerator is greater than the denominator, the fraction describes a number greater than 1. It can be written as a **mixed number**, which is a whole number and fraction together.

$$\frac{6}{5} = 1\frac{1}{5}$$ ← Mixed number

Numerator is greater than denominator.

Decimal Numbers

A **decimal number** is another way to write a fraction or mixed number whose denominator is a power of 10 (10, 100,

marketingessentials.glencoe.com

Micropurchases for Microprices

Discussion Lead a discussion about the use of micropayment services. Ask students to name the advantages and disadvantages of using micropayment versus traditional credit-card-based billing systems.

THINK LIKE A MARKETER **Answer:** Answers will vary, but may include the difficulty of getting people to sign up and keeping costs low.

@ Online Action! For instructions, ideas, and answer guide, go to the Teacher Center at **marketingessentials.glencoe.com**

PRACTICE 1

What fraction of each shape is shaded?

1. 2. 3.

4. 5.

Answer each question with a fraction:

6. If you spend seven hours a day sleeping, what fraction of the day are you asleep?
7. You have saved $69 of the $159 you need to buy a new printer. What fraction of the money do you still need to save?
8. Your class has 14 male and 17 female students. What fraction of your class is female?
9. If one-third of your family's income is spent on housing, what fraction is left for other expenses?
10. Seventy-five cents represents what fraction of one dollar?

Note: Answers to all practice sets at *marketingessentials.glencoe.com*

1000, etc). The decimal number 5.3 means $5 + 0.3$ or $5 + \frac{3}{10}$ or $5\frac{3}{10}$. The decimal number 935.47 can be broken down as $900 + 30 + 5 + \frac{4}{10} + \frac{7}{100}$.

Knowing place names is necessary for reading decimals and writing them in words. Decimal place names apply to digits to the right of the decimal point.

Decimal point   Decimal placement names

 marketingessentials.glencoe.com

To read a decimal number or write it in words, follow the steps below. Use 15.083 as an example.

1. Begin with the whole number to the left of the decimal point (*fifteen*).
2. Read or write *and* for the decimal point.
3. Read or write the number to the right of the decimal point as a whole number (*eighty-three*).
4. Use the name of the decimal place of the final digit (*thousandths*).

The result is *fifteen and eighty-three thousandths*.

There is another way to read numbers with decimal points. You may hear decimal numbers read using the whole number and only the names of the digits in the decimal places, with *point* for the decimal point. For example, 9.7 could also be read as *nine point seven*; 15.083 might be read as *fifteen point zero eight three*.

Why You Should Know How to Write Numbers

Why is it important for you to know how to write decimals and fractions, and to understand the relationship between the two?

Understanding the relationship between decimal numbers and fractions is important when you are writing a check. After writing the amount in decimal form, you must write it again, using words for the dollars and a fraction for the cents. (See example on page 156.)

PRACTICE 2

Write the decimals as words. Write the money amounts as words and fractions. Write the words as decimals.

1. 9.8   5. $67.40
2. 0.3   6. $457.89
3. 23.67   7. $112.07
4. 0.056

8. Two thousand, one hundred sixty-four and eight tenths
9. Three hundred four and seven hundredths
10. Four hundred twenty-one dollars and thirty-seven cents

Chapter 7 - Basic Math Skills **155**

Enrichment

USING MATH SKILLS

Ask students to interview the manager of a store or other business and ask what math skills he or she requires of employees. Have students write a two- to three-paragraph summary of their interview. Alternatively, students can research careers that require math skills and write a summary of that career.

PRACTICE 1 ANSWERS

1. $\frac{5}{10}$ or $\frac{1}{2}$
2. $\frac{1}{3}$
3. $\frac{2}{4}$ or $\frac{1}{2}$
4. $\frac{11}{16}$
5. $\frac{16}{16}$ or 1
6. $\frac{7}{24}$
7. $\frac{90}{159}$
8. $\frac{17}{31}$
9. $\frac{2}{3}$
10. $\frac{75}{100}$ or $\frac{3}{4}$

PRACTICE 2 ANSWERS

1. Nine and eight-tenths
2. Three-tenths
3. Twenty-three and sixty-seven hundredths
4. Fifty-six thousandths
5. Sixty-seven and $\frac{40}{100}$ dollars
6. Four hundred fifty-seven and $\frac{89}{100}$ dollars
7. One hundred twelve and $\frac{07}{100}$ dollars
8. 2,164.8
9. 304.07
10. $421.37

Critical Thinking

Ask students to think of instances in which they use fractions in their everyday lives. You might suggest cooking or keeping time as common uses for fractions. Have students share their answers with the class.

TEACH CONTINUED

Concept Development

ADDING AND SUBTRACTING DECIMAL NUMBERS

Write a variety of decimal numbers on slips of paper, being sure to vary the amount of numerals before and after the decimal point in each number. On each slip of paper, write an addition or subtraction sign before each number. Then write a decimal number on the board and choose a student to write the number from his or her slip of paper on the board under your number and then add or subtract it and write the new total. Then, have the next student come up and add or subtract their number from the total. Continue until all students have added or subtracted their number.

TEACHING POINTS

Model Write two decimal numbers on the board to start, and then add or subtract the numbers as a model to the students. Remind students to line up the decimal points and add zeros as needed to fill places where there are no numbers.

Critical Thinking

Ask students why it is important to understand how to add and subtract decimal numbers when dealing with money. Ask: What might happen if they added or subtracted money incorrectly while shopping or at work? Have students share their responses in class.

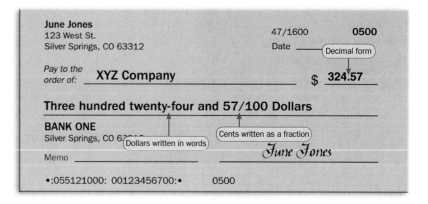

June Jones
123 West St.
Silver Springs, CO 63312

47/1600   **0500**

Date _____ (Decimal form)

Pay to the order of: **XYZ Company** _____ $ __324.57__

Three hundred twenty-four and 57/100 Dollars

BANK ONE
Silver Springs, CO 6____

(Dollars written in words)   (Cents written as a fraction)

Memo _____   *June Jones*

•:055121000: 00123456700:•   0500

Adding and Subtracting Decimal Numbers

To add or subtract decimal numbers, first list the numbers vertically, keeping the decimal points in line with each other. Then add or subtract as you would with whole numbers. Sometimes you may need to write zeros to fill a column.

1.45 + 3.4 = ?

(Align decimal points vertically.)

$$\begin{array}{r} 1.45 \\ + \ 3.40 \\ \hline 4.85 \end{array}$$

← (Write 0s as needed.)
← (Add as with whole numbers.)

13.4 − 7.56 = ?

(Align decimal points vertically.)

$$\begin{array}{r} 13.40 \\ - \ 7.56 \\ \hline 5.84 \end{array}$$

← (Write 0s as needed.)
← (Subtract as with whole numbers.)

Multiplying Decimal Numbers

The Carpet Store was having a sale on carpeting priced by the square yard. What is the area of carpeting for a room that is 9.6 yards long and 4.25 yards wide?

To multiply decimal numbers, use the following two-step process.

156 UNIT 4 - SKILLS FOR MARKETING

• **REPRESENTING NUMBERS** More and more people pay bills online or use electronic funds transfer, but writing checks is still an essential skill. On a check, the amount must be written in words and as a decimal number.

What other math skills are required to manage a checking account?

PHOTO GUIDE | REPRESENTING NUMBERS

Discussion Lead a discussion about the skills required to write a check. Ask volunteers to share their experiences writing checks. Ask: What types of math skills are required when paying bills online or electronically?

Caption Answer Answers may include addition, subtraction, and estimating skills.

(Follow Up) Ask students to research their bank's or any bank's online bill-paying services and share their findings with the class.

PRACTICE 3

Complete the following addition and subtraction problems with decimal numbers.

1. 7.3 + 8.2 =
2. 6.7 + 9 =
3. 9.8 + 7.05 =
4. 20.04 + 7.7 =
5. 0.08 + 4.075 =
6. 0.04 + 0.25 =
7. 3.71 + 0.6 + 1.89 + 11 =
8. 7.6 − 3.6 =
9. 54.9 − 27 =
10. $10 − $3.99 =
11. 7.5 − 2.11 + 26.045 =
12. 33.4 − 9.428 =

13. Maps To Go paid the following shipping charges in the first week of April: FedEx—$14.75, $28.00, $14.75; UPS—$23.69, $84.27, $47.88, $119.57, $63.74. What was their total shipping charge for that week?

14. Luis was given a roll of paper 35 yards long. He was asked to make four banners for the upcoming student elections. Two banners need to be 13.75 yards in length, one banner is to be 7.5 yards, and the final banner is to be 2 yards in length. How much more paper will he need?

---

1. Multiply the two numbers as if they were whole numbers. Pay no attention to the decimal points yet.

2. Add the number of decimal places in the two numbers being multiplied. Then, working from the right, count off the same number of decimal places in the product and insert the decimal point. Note: When counting off places from the right, you may have to add a zero in order to place the decimal point.

$9.6 \times 4.25 = ?$

$$
\begin{array}{r}
4.25 \\
\times\ 9.6 \\
\hline
2550 \\
3825 \\
\hline
40.800
\end{array}
$$

4.25 has two decimal places.
9.6 has one decimal place.

Place the decimal three places to the left.

Since 40.800 = 40.8, the answer is 40.8 square yards.

$$
\begin{array}{r}
0.25 \\
\times\ 0.3 \\
\hline
0.075
\end{array}
$$

0.25 has two decimal places.
0.3 has one decimal place.

Add a 0 in the product in order to have three decimal places.

Multiply amounts of money as you would other decimal numbers. Remember to include the dollar sign in your answer.

$$
\begin{array}{r}
\$4.98 \\
\times\ \ \ \ 2 \\
\hline
\$9.96
\end{array}
$$

Write the dollar sign.

Rounding Decimal Numbers

Sometimes you may have to round a decimal number. This is especially common when multiplying with amounts of money, as when figuring tax amounts, discounts, and so on.

Use the following steps to round decimal amounts.

Round 16.842, 16.852, and 16.892 to the nearest tenth.

1. Find the decimal place you are rounding to.

16.842   16.852   16.892

Tenths place

2. Look at the digit to the right of that place.

16.842   16.852   16.892

Digit to the right

Chapter 7 - Basic Math Skills **157**

PRACTICE 3 ANSWERS

1. 15.5	**11.** 31.435
2. 15.7	**12.** 23.972
3. 16.85	**13.** $396.65
4. 27.74	**14.** 2 yards
5. 4.155	
6. 0.29	
7. 17.2	
8. 4	
9. 27.9	
10. $6.01	

Individualized Math Skills

MULTIPLYING DECIMAL NUMBERS

Duplicate for your students a newspaper ad that lists the prices for many products, such as a grocery store or electronics store ad.

L1 Ask students to choose a product and calculate the price if they bought two. Have them choose another product and calculate the price to buy 10. Repeat with various numbers.

L2 Tell students they have $100 to spend on the products in the ad. Have them prepare a budget listing which products they will buy and the quantity of each, with the subtotals for each type of product and the grand total.

L3 Tell students they will purchase a certain quantity of a product in the ad (for example, six cans of tomato sauce). There is 7.5 percent sales tax on the purchase. Have students calculate the price for the items plus sales tax. Repeat with various products and quantities. Students should multiply the total by 0.075 and add the result to the total.

TEACHING POINTS

Explain Explain to students that multiplying prices is the same as multiplying regular decimal numbers. Remind them to include the dollar sign in their final answer.

Model Choose a product from the ad and multiply it by a quantity as a model for the students. Also model how to multiply and add sales tax.

Critical Thinking

Ask students how rounding numbers may affect business applications such as sales data, purchase orders, or pricing. Have students share their responses in class.

TEACH CONTINUED

Concept Development

ROUNDING DECIMAL NUMBERS

Write a decimal number on the board that has four numerals to the right of the decimal point (numerals should vary). Using calculators or working on paper, have students multiply the number by two and record the answer. Then have them round the original number to the thousandths place and multiply by two, again. Repeat, having students round to the hundredths, tenths, and finally to a whole number, and multiply by two. Ask students to observe the difference between each answer. Ask: Which answer is the most accurate, based on the original number? Lead a discussion about how accuracy decreases as a number is rounded.

TEACHING POINTS

Model Do the exercise as a group on the board, and then repeat the exercise with a new number, having students perform the calculations themselves.

PRACTICE 4 ANSWERS
1. 43.2
2. 55.692
3. 1.57
4. 14.3374
5. 0.00082
6. 27.6
7. 68.7
8. 12,345
9. $0.96
10. $22.00
11. $49.17

3. If the digit to the right is less than 5, leave the first digit as is. If the digit is 5 or greater, round up.

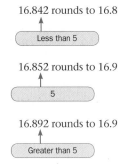

16.842 rounds to 16.8

Less than 5

16.852 rounds to 16.9

5

16.892 rounds to 16.9

Greater than 5

When you are working with amounts of money, use the same steps to round your answer to the nearest cent (the nearest hundredth).

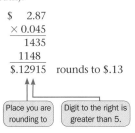

$$\begin{array}{r} \$\ \ 2.87 \\ \times\ 0.045 \\ \hline 1435 \\ 1148\ \ \\ \hline \$.12915 \end{array}\ \ \text{rounds to }\$.13$$

Place you are rounding to

Digit to the right is greater than 5.

Dividing Decimal Numbers

Division of decimal numbers is similar to division of whole numbers. Follow the steps below to divide decimal numbers.

1. Set up the division problem as you would with whole numbers.

69.7 divided by 1.724 = $1.724\overline{)69.7}$

2. Shift the decimal point in the divisor so that the divisor becomes a whole number. The divisor is the number you are dividing by. Then shift the decimal point in the dividend the same number of decimal places. The dividend is the number to be divided. Write zeros in the dividend, if necessary, in order to place the decimal point.

Write 0s.

$1.724\overline{)69.700} \longrightarrow 1724\overline{)69700.}$

Shift the decimal point three places to the right.

PRACTICE 4

Complete the following multiplication problems with decimal numbers. Round any money amounts to the nearest cent.

| 1. | 4.8 | 2. | 27.3 | 3. | 3.14 | 4. | 29.26 | 5. | 8.2 |
| | × 9 | | × 2.04 | | × .5 | | × 0.49 | | × .0001 |

6. 2.76 × 10 = **7.** 0.687 × 100 = **8.** 12.345 × 1,000 =

9. Gasoline costs $2.02 per gallon when you pay with a credit card, but $1.94 when you pay with cash. How much do you save on a 12-gallon purchase if you pay with cash?

10. Every month you deposit $75 into a savings account for insurance costs. Your insurance expenses for this year were four equal payments of $219.50. How much remained in your savings account after the last payment?

11. Your phone company charges a $3.95 monthly long distance service fee plus $0.07 per minute for long distance phone calls. How much will you pay if you have 646 minutes of long distance calls for the month?

 Critical Thinking

Ask students to think of reasons why it is easier to add, subtract, multiply, and divide decimals than fractions. Ask: Are there any cases where it would be easier to work with fractions? Have students discuss their responses in class.

3. Place a decimal point in the answer space directly above its new position in the dividend. Then divide as with whole numbers.

Place the decimal point in the answer.

$$1724. \overline{)\ 69700.}$$

Sometimes you may need to write extra zeros after the decimal point in order to complete the division.

40.429 rounds to 40.43 (rounded to nearest hundredth)

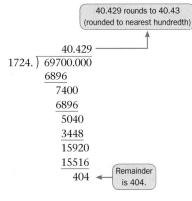

$$
\begin{array}{r}
40.429 \\
1724. \overline{)\ 69700.000} \\
6896 \\
\hline
7400 \\
6896 \\
\hline
5040 \\
3448 \\
\hline
15920 \\
15516 \\
\hline
404
\end{array}
$$

Remainder is 404.

Some decimal answers will continue infinitely as you write zeros to the right of the decimal point. *Repeating decimals* will repeat a number or pattern of numbers.

These digits repeat.

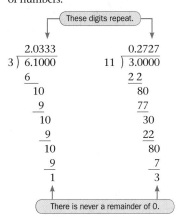

$$
\begin{array}{r}
2.0333 \\
3\, \overline{)\ 6.1000} \\
6 \\
\hline
10 \\
9 \\
\hline
10 \\
9 \\
\hline
10 \\
9 \\
\hline
1
\end{array}
\qquad
\begin{array}{r}
0.2727 \\
11\, \overline{)\ 3.0000} \\
2\,2 \\
\hline
80 \\
77 \\
\hline
30 \\
22 \\
\hline
80 \\
77 \\
\hline
3
\end{array}
$$

There is never a remainder of 0.

PRACTICE 5

Complete the following division problems. Round answers to the nearest thousandth.

1. 438 ÷ 15 =
2. 40.7 ÷ 3.7 =
3. 2.685 ÷ 8.25 =
4. 7.8 ÷ 0.035 =
5. 0.01 ÷ 2 =
6. 4.002 ÷ 0.75 =
7. If you are paid $11.02 per hour, how many hours must you work to pay for a computer that is priced at $495.90?
8. Compare the cost of Brand X and Brand Y laundry detergent. Which is the better buy? Brand X is $6.59 for 64 ounces. Brand Y is $10.79 for 96 ounces.

Converting Fractions to Decimals

Decimals are easier than fractions to add, subtract, multiply, and divide. To convert any fraction to a decimal, simply divide the numerator by the denominator.

Numerator
Denominator

$$\frac{1}{4} = 1 \div 4 = 4\, \overline{)\ 1.00}$$

$$
\begin{array}{r}
0.25 \\
4\, \overline{)\ 1.00} \\
8 \\
\hline
20 \\
20 \\
\hline
0
\end{array}
$$

$$\frac{2}{3} = 2 \div 3 = 3\, \overline{)\ 2.000}$$

$$
\begin{array}{r}
0.666 \\
3\, \overline{)\ 2.000} \\
1\,8 \\
\hline
20 \\
18 \\
\hline
20 \\
18 \\
\hline
2
\end{array}
$$

There is never a remainder of 0.

In its decimal form, $\frac{2}{3}$ is a repeating decimal. When working with repeating decimals, you may round to the nearest hundredth in most cases. Thus, $\frac{2}{3} = 0.67$.

Chapter 7 - Basic Math Skills **159**

TEACH CONTINUED

Concept Development

CONVERTING FRACTIONS TO DECIMALS

Write various fractions on squares of paper. The fractions should vary in value from 0 to 1. Draw a line across the length of the board and label one end "0" and the other end "1." Give students one square and have them go up to the board and tape their fraction to where it falls on the number line. (Expect students to have trouble with this task.) Then, have students take their squares back to their desks and convert their fraction to a decimal number. Now have students try again to place their fraction on the number line. When all fractions are posted on the board, lead a discussion about how converting fractions to decimals makes it easier to compare values. For example, it may be easier to see that 0.33 is larger than 0.25 than it is to see that 1/3 is larger than 1/4.

PRACTICE 5 ANSWERS
1. 29.2
2. 11
3. 0.325
4. 222.857
5. 0.005
6. 5.336
7. 45 hours
8. Brand X

Critical Thinking

Ask students to imagine what would happen to a business that had mismanaged the math in its accounts with clients. Ask students what impact that would have on the way clients viewed the business.

ASSESS

CONCEPTS

Ask students to give examples of digits, fractions, mixed numbers, and decimal numbers, labeling the parts of each. Then ask students to write the numbers in words.

KEY TERMS

Have students review key terms, their spellings, and definitions in small groups.

ONLINE SELF-ASSESSMENT

Have students go to marketingessentials.glencoe.com for the Section 7.1 practice test.

Individualized Review

L1 Assign and review Chapter 7 activities in the Student Activity Workbook.

L2 Assign and review Chapter 7 activities in the Marketing Math Workbook.

L3 Assign and review Chapter 7 activities in the *BusinessWeek* Reader and Case Studies.

Marketing Practice

Have students look through magazine or newspaper ads and make a list of items they would like to buy. Then have them write out mock checks for each item, entering their purchases in a check register, starting with a preset balance and having them subtract each purchase. Ask students to write two to three paragraphs about why it is important to keep track of purchases in business.

Case Study

Selling Music and Style

When Apple Computer introduced the first iPod in late 2001, music lovers rejoiced. About the size of a deck of cards and weighing only 6.5 ounces, it could store a thousand songs in the form of digital sound files, and the sound reproduction quality was excellent. The iPod was perfectly placed to ride the wave of popularity of downloading music from the Internet. The company sold almost 3 million iPods by 2004, contributing to a turnaround in profits for the company. That same year, Apple released a model with 40 GB of memory. It could store up to 10,000 songs.

iPod and iTunes: Two Peas in a Pod

Apple also developed iTunes, a Web service for low-cost downloading of music that pays a royalty to musicians and music producers. Fifty million songs had been sold on the service by March of 2004. iTunes gained the support of popular musicians, who were happy to encourage use of a service that provides legal paid downloads. In return, close association with hip rock musicians gave a big boost to iPod's and iTunes' market appeal.

In early 2004, Apple brought out the iPod mini, weighing only 3.6 ounces, which came on the market with prerelease orders of over 100,000. With 4GB of memory, the mini still stores a thousand songs. Sleekly designed and available in five colors, it quickly became a fashion accessory. Again, the hipness angle paid off for Apple.

THINK STRATEGICALLY

Apple has benefited from the free publicity generated by having famous people praise and use its product and service. Can you think of a situation in which having a celebrity endorse your product might harm your sales?

@ Online Action! Go to *marketingessentials.glencoe.com/7/case* to find a project on the use of celebrities in advertising.

Calculating Surface Measurements

When planning the installation of new carpeting or the use of space in an office, warehouse, or retail store, you will need to calculate the area of floor surface.

The area of a surface is the number of squares of a certain measure that the surface covers. If you measure the length and width in feet, the area will be expressed in square feet. If you measure in inches, the area will be expressed in square inches.

To compute the area of a rectangle or square, multiply the length of one side by the length of the side next to it. The shorter length is commonly called the width. The formula for the area of a rectangle is

$$A = l \times w$$

 marketingessentials.glencoe.com

Case Study Selling Music and Style

Discussion Ask volunteers to share their experiences with iPods and/or iTunes. Did the popular musicians who supported Apple influence their desire to own an iPod? Why might a product such as iPod benefit from endorsement by hip rock musicians?

THINK STRATEGICALLY
Answer: Answers will vary; students might note that negative publicity for a celebrity might negatively affect public perception of the endorsed product.

@ Online Action! For instructions, ideas, and answer guide, go to the Teacher Center at marketingessentials.glencoe.com

Follow Up Have students ask what images, celebrities, etc., they think of when they think of iPod.

where A stands for area, l for length, and w for width.

The formula for the area of a square is really the same, but because there is no difference in the length and width, it may be written

$$A = s^2$$

where A stands for area and s for side.

Business Applications of Surface Measurements

Calculating surface is a business skill that is useful for retailers to figure out the floor space they need or how this space can be rearranged. It is also necessary for fabric retailers and wholesalers, contractors, and anybody who sells, distributes, or manufactures products that need to have an exact area measurement. For example, how would you go about deciding how much fabric you would need to re-upholster a sofa? You would care-fully measure each area that needs to be covered. You would then have several geometric shapes with perimeter measurements. With that information you would be able to calculate the area measurement of each shape, add them up to know what amount of fabric you would need.

> **PRACTICE 6**
>
> The owner of a retail store wishes to replace the carpeting. The store measures 86 feet long and 50 feet wide. The store also includes two fitting rooms measuring each two feet wide by three feet long. The new carpet is priced at $35 per square yard and sales tax is 7 percent. Calculate the total surface area of the floor, and estimate the cost of material to replace the carpet, including sales tax. (Remember that 9 square feet are equivalent to 1 square yard.)

7.1 AFTER YOU READ

Reviewing Key Terms and Concepts

1. Write the whole number 3,010,049 in words, using commas and hyphens correctly.
2. Round $6.875 to the nearest cent and to the nearest dollar.
3. Convert the fraction ⅛ to its decimal equivalent.

Integrating Academic Skills

Math

4. Create a place value chart ranging from the thousands place to the thousandths place. Why is there no "ones" place to the right of the decimal point?
5. Prepare a lesson explaining why the decimal number 2.25 correctly represents $2.25 when talking about money, but does not correctly represent 2 hours and 25 minutes when talking about time. What other examples can you give where this occurs?

 Online Action!

Check your answers at *marketingessentials.glencoe.com/7/read*

marketingessentials.glencoe.com

CLOSE

Have students complete the following statements:

1. In a fraction, the _____ expresses the number of parts considered, and the _____ expresses the number of parts in a whole.
   numerator, denominator
2. A fraction or mixed number whose denominator is a multiple of 10 is known as a _____ .
   decimal number

PRACTICE 6 ANSWER

$17,892.78

 Online Activity

Numbers in the News
Have students look through an online newspaper or business publication to find examples of digits, fractions, mixed numbers, and decimals.

AFTER YOU READ

Reviewing Key Terms and Concepts

1. Three million, ten thousand, forty-nine.
2. $6.88, $7.00
3. 0.125

Integrating Academic Skills

4. Left to right, place value chart should read: thousands, hundreds, tens, ones, decimal, tenths, hundredths, thousandths. Ones are not present because they represent a whole number.

5. Lessons will vary; lessons should include the understanding that a decimal number is a fraction whose denominator is a multiple of ten. $1.00 is a multiple of ten, 60 minutes is not. Other examples will vary.

Online Action! Answers at *marketingessentials.glencoe.com/7/read*

FOCUS

Introducing the Section

COLLABORATIVE ACTIVITY

To prepare for reading this section, write the following sales figures on the board:

Gross Monthly Sales for 2005

Month	Sales
January	$8,670
February	7,955
March	8,995
April	11,690
May	13,200
June	13,567
July	14,688
August	16,780
September	16,555
October	14,500
November	15,600
December	17,800

Ask students to think of ways they could present a comparison of these sales figures. List students' answers on the board. Answers may include percentages, bar graphs, line graphs, circle graphs, and pie charts.

Preteaching Key Terms

Ask a volunteer to write the key terms on the board. Ask students to predict the meaning of each term and write it down or draw an example of the term on a piece of paper.

- percentage
- bar graph
- line graph
- circle graph
- pie chart

Tell students they can check their predictions as they read the section.

OBJECTIVES

- Use a calculator to solve math problems
- Convert percentages to decimals and decimals to percentages
- Read graphs used to present mathematical data

KEY TERMS

- percentage
- bar graph
- line graph
- circle graph
- pie chart

Interpreting Numbers

READ and STUDY

BEFORE YOU READ

Predict What marketing situations might require the use of charts and graphs?

THE MAIN IDEA

Today's marketing jobs require the use of various tools to analyze information and make decisions. Calculators, computers to create graphic displays, algebraic thinking, and statistics are all important tools of the marketing professional.

STUDY ORGANIZER

In a chart like the one below, write in your own example of calculating tax on a sale, estimating for a gratuity, and a simple chart or graph to illustrate and compare data.

Calculating Tax on a Sale	Estimating for a Gratuity	A Simple Chart or Graph to Illustrate and Compare Data

WHILE YOU READ

Analyze List five situations in which you would use a calculator to solve a problem.

Using a Calculator

Calculators simplify the computation that is common in both the business world and in people's personal lives. Many people find calculators vital when paying bills, creating budgets, and balancing their checkbooks. There are two basic types of calculators. The most widely used type employs the algebraic entry system. This is the type of calculator used in the problems that follow. The other type uses the reverse-entry system.

162 UNIT 4 - SKILLS FOR MARKETING

READ and STUDY

BEFORE YOU READ

Lead students in finding examples of marketing situations requiring the use of charts and graphs. Ask a volunteer to write situations on the board.

THE MAIN IDEA

Ask a volunteer to list important math-related tools for the marketing professional.

STUDY ORGANIZER

Model the study organizer for students by doing a sample calculation together as a class. A full-size, downloadable study organizer can be found at **marketingessentials.glencoe.com**

WHILE YOU READ Model for students how to create a list of five situations as they read the section and get ideas.

The basic difference is that with the reverse-entry system, you enter the first amount and press the enter key, then the second amount, and then the operation (added to, subtracted from, multiplied by, or divided into the first amount). If you have a calculator that uses the reverse-entry system, read the instruction book that accompanies your calculator very carefully. You will get a very different answer if you enter numbers as if using algebraic entry.

If you expect to be hired in sales or any other marketing job, you will almost certainly use a calculator. Besides simply knowing which buttons to press, you will be expected to work with accuracy, know how to work with fractions and amounts of money, and have an understanding of how the calculator computes with multiple operations.

Estimate, Then Operate

When using a calculator, many people follow the guess-and-check method. They estimate first, then enter the problem in the calculator. Finally, they check the displayed answer against the estimate.

$$388 + 995 = ?$$

Estimate: $400 + 1,000 = 1,400$
Enter the problem:
 1,383

(Displayed answer)

Check: 1,388 is reasonably close to the estimate of 1,400.

$$480 \times 112 = ?$$

Estimate: $500 \times 100 = 50,000$
Enter the problem:
 53,760

(Displayed answer)

Check: 53,760 is reasonably close to the estimate of 50,000.

It is important to estimate your answers when you use a calculator because you may make errors when entering numbers or even press the wrong operation key. It is a good idea to have an estimate of the answer in mind. For example, if you are expecting an answer of about 300, you will know something is wrong if the displayed answer on your calculator is 3,300.

Another way to ensure accuracy when using a calculator is to check the display after you enter each number and before you press the operation key. If you have made an error, press the Clear Entry key Ⓒ to remove the last entry. Suppose you want to multiply 5.8 × 7.2, but you enter ⑤ . ⑧ ✕ ⑦ ②. Press Ⓒ to delete the last two keystrokes. Then you can reenter the second number correctly. The first number will remain in the calculator. Press the Equals key ═, and the answer will be displayed: 41.76.

How to Make Entries

Keep in mind as you enter digits that you can disregard leading zeros to the left of the decimal point (as in 0.6 or 0.375) and final zeros after the decimal point (as in 9.250 or 41.500). You do not need to enter these zeros. The calculator will display all the digits needed.

Number	Keystrokes Entered	Display
0.785	. ⑦ ⑧ ⑤	0.785
5.10	⑤ . ①	5.1

When dealing with mixed numbers or fractions, you must first convert the fractions to decimal form. Do this by dividing the numerator by the denominator. For example, to enter $5\frac{1}{4}$, first enter ① ÷ ④. Then add the whole number by entering ✛ ⑤.

When solving problems dealing with money, remember to write the dollar sign in the answer. You may also have to round the displayed answer to the nearest cent.

Display	Answer Written as Money Amount
5.25	$5.25
25.368216	$25.37 (Round to nearest cent)
46.0194	$46.02 (Round to nearest cent)
76514.1	$76,514.10

TEACH

Discussion Starter

ESTIMATE, THEN OPERATE

Ask students to imagine they are working for a company and part of their job involves making a series of calculations using a calculator. Because they must work quickly, they don't have time to double-check their work. How might estimating, then operating be useful in their job? Lead a discussion about how estimating can help prevent errors when using a calculator.

TEACHING POINTS

Demonstrate Read students a series of math problems in quick succession and have them use calculators to get answers. When students have finished with all the problems, read the correct answers aloud. Ask students how many errors they had.

Role Play Have students team up in pairs. Give each pair a list of dollar amounts and have one student pretend to be working at a cash register and adding up amounts using a calculator. Have the other student pretend to be the consumer and estimate the answer. Have students check answers against each other. Then have students switch roles and repeat the activity using different dollar amounts.

Critical Thinking

Ask students which concepts in this chapter are familiar to them. Have students consider which concepts they use frequently in their lives, and why. Have them then consider which concepts they use infrequently, and why. Ask students to share their responses in groups of three to four.

Concept Development

PERCENTAGES

Divide students into groups of two or three and have them make a list of different school, home, work, or other situations in which percentages are used. Have students write out on paper a scenario involving calculating percentages. Have groups exchange problems and practice solving percentage problems. Lead a discussion about any problems groups may have encountered when calculating percentages.

Answers may include sales tax, tipping a server, calculating interest on a loan, etc.

TEACHING POINTS

Demonstrate Bring in examples of real-life percentages, such as sales tax on a receipt, ads for interest rates on loans, a card showing tipping amounts, etc.

Individualized Math Skills

PERCENTAGES

L1 Ask students to explain what a percentage is (parts per hundred) and how to convert a number to a percentage (multiply the number by 100).

L2 Ask students to convert the following decimal numbers to percentages using a calculator:

a.) .89 (89%)
b.) 3.6 (360%)
c.) .005 (0.5%)
d.) 8.15 (815%)

L3 Ask students to convert the following fractions to decimals and then to percentages:

a.) 1/4 (0.25, 25%)
b.) 2/5 (0.4, 40%)
c.) 1 1/8 (1.125, 112.5%)
d.) 1/18 (0.28, 28%)

A calculator can operate on only two numbers at a time. However, you can perform a string of involved calculations on more than two numbers if you are very careful. When only addition and subtraction are involved, the calculator will perform these operations as they are entered.

⑧．⑥＋．②⑤＋①①．⑨
⊖③．⑥②⊜　17.13

When only multiplication and division are involved, the calculator will also perform these operations as they are entered.

⑦⑦⑤✕．⑨⑥÷⑤✕
①．⑨⑥⊜　291.648

However, when a calculation involves a combination of addition or subtraction with multiplication or division, not all calculators work the same way. You will need to check how your calculator performs the operations in this type of problem. Most calculators will do the operations as they are entered.

$6 + 4 \times 6$ will be calculated as
$6 + 4 \times 6 =$

$10 \times 6 = 60.$

$6 \times 4 + 6$ will be calculated as
$6 \times 4 + 6 =$

$24 + 6 = 30.$

$9 - 5 \times 2 + 6 \div 7$ will be calculated as
$9 - 5 \times 2 + 6 \div 7 =$

4×2

$8 + 6$

$14 \div 7 = 2.$

Ten-Key by Sight or Touch

Ten-key calculators have been popular for many years. They use algebraic entry. Most computer keyboards have a 10-key keypad along the right side of the board. (There are actually more than 10 keys; the 10-key designation refers to the digits 0 through 9.) With practice, you can learn to operate a 10-key keypad by touch, just as you learned to type the alpha characters on a keyboard by touch. This allows very fast operation and is a valuable skill for online point-of-sale entries, accounting, using spreadsheet programs, and other computer-related applications.

While learning to use a 10-key keypad, keep your fingers close to the home row of keys—the 4, 5, and 6 keys. Try to keep your arm, wrist, and hand in a straight line; do not rest your wrist on your desk. Relax your fingers, and press the keys lightly. Frequent,

• **CHECKING the CHECKER** To be sure that the amount they are charged for a multi-purchase sale is accurate, some people take a calculator when they go shopping.

What math skills are required to check the checker?

PHOTO GUIDE　　**CHECKING the CHECKER**

Discussion Lead a discussion about checking the checker when you go shopping. Ask students if they have ever used a calculator or witnessed someone else using a calculator when shopping. Ask: What are the reasons for bringing a calculator when shopping? Have students discuss their responses in class.

Caption Answer Answers might include addition, subtraction, multiplication, and the ability to calculate percentages.

Follow Up Ask students to visit a store and interview a checker about his or her experiences with a shopper who used a calculator during checkout.

short periods of practice are most effective in developing speed with accuracy. Courses for developing skill on a 10-key keypad are available at many community colleges and on the Internet.

Percentages

Two percent of a company's revenue goes to pay for insurance. This means that $2 of every $100 that comes in goes to pay for insurance. **Percentage** means parts per 100. Thus, a number expressed as a percentage represents the number of parts per 100.

To write a whole number or a decimal number as a percentage, multiply it by 100. A simple way to do this is to move the decimal point two places to the right.

> Move the decimal point two places to the right.

$0.705 = 0.7 \times 100 = 70\%$ or $0.70 = 70\%$
$0.05 = 0.05 \times 100 = 5\%$ or $0.05 = 5\%$
$2.5 = 2.5 \times 100 = 250\%$ or $2.50 = 250\%$

> Write 0s as needed.

You can use a calculator to do this operation.

. 7 × 1 0 0 = $70 = 70\%$
2 . 5 × 1 0 0 = $250 = 250\%$

Converting Fractions to Percentages

To write a fraction or mixed number as a percentage, first convert the fraction to decimal form. Do this by dividing the numerator by the denominator. If there is a whole number, add it to the converted fraction. Then multiply by 100. You can use a calculator to do this operation.

$\frac{1}{2}$ = 1 ÷ 2 × 1 0 0 = $50 = 50\%$
$\frac{3}{8}$ = 3 ÷ 8 × 1 0 0 =
  $37.5 = 37.5\%$
$4\frac{2}{5}$ = 2 ÷ 5 + 4 × 1 0 0 =
  $440 = 440\%$

Converting Percentages to Decimals

Sometimes it may be easier to complete a math problem by changing a percentage to a decimal. You can change a percentage to a decimal number by dividing by 100. A simple way to do this is to move the decimal point two places to the left.

> Move the decimal point two places to the left.

$24.8\% = 24.8 \div 100 = .248$
  or $24.8\% = 0.248$
$0.5\% = 0.5 \div 100 = 0.005$
  or $0.5\% = 0.005$

> Write 0s as needed.

You can use a calculator to do this operation.

12.6% = 1 2 . 6 ÷ 1 0 0 =   0.126
1.4% = 1 . 4 ÷ 1 0 0 =   0.014

You can also convert a percentage with a fraction or mixed number to a decimal by using a calculator.

$7\frac{1}{4}\%$ = 1 ÷ 4 + 7 ÷ 1 0 0 =
  0.0725

Percentage Problems

Percentage problems are often encountered on a marketing job. For example, you may be asked to figure a tip, a discount amount, or the amount of sales tax. You may have to figure the total selling price, including the tax. Maybe you will be asked to figure the percentage of commission on your total sales.

Most percentage problems will involve finding a percentage of a number. To do that, multiply the decimal equivalent of the percentage by the number.

> Decimal equivalent of $5\frac{1}{2}\%$

$5\frac{1}{2}\%$ of $35 = 0.055 \times \$35$

> *of* tells you to multiply.

Chapter 7 - Basic Math Skills 165

SECTION 7.2

TEACH CONTINUED

Concept Development

CONVERTING PERCENTAGES TO DECIMALS

Ask students to perform the following calculation: 25×60 percent. Lead a discussion about any problems students had in attempting this calculation. Were they able to simply multiply by 60 percent? What step must be taken before multiplying by a percentage?

They must first convert 60 percent to a decimal in order to multiply.

Did any students try to multiply 25×60? If so, ask: How is this answer $(1,500)$ different from the correct answer (15)? Why is it important to know how to correctly perform math problems involving percentages?

TEACHING POINTS

Explain Explain that some calculators have a percentage key, and it may not be necessary to convert percentages to decimals on such calculators. It is important that students understand how their calculators perform percentage operations. However, students should still learn to convert percentages to decimals for manual calculations or when using a calculator without a percentage key.

Demonstrate Write various percentages on the board and ask volunteers to convert each percentage to a decimal.

Extended Activity

Sales Tax in Your State

Ask students to go online to research sales tax in their state and, if applicable, the additional local sales tax. Ask students to write a one-page summary of the sales tax and what kinds of products are excluded from the tax. Have students calculate the sales tax in your city for $10; $100; $1,000; and $10,000 to get an idea of how sales taxes can add up with more expensive purchases.

Online Activity

Ten-Key Tutorial

Have students find an online ten-key tutor, and use the tutor to help them learn and practice ten-key keypad operation by touch.

Concept Development

READING CHARTS AND GRAPHS

Give students newspapers or magazines containing charts and graphs. Then separate them into small groups of two or three and have each group identify and write down the data presented in each chart or graph. Lead a discussion about what type of information is commonly presented in charts and graphs, and what type of charts and graphs are most common (bar graphs, line graphs, circle graphs, etc.).

TEACHING POINTS

Demonstrate Cut out a few examples of various types of charts and graphs and hang them on the board for students to use as a reference.

Model Choose one chart or graph and model for students how to identify the information presented in it.

Build Vocabulary

Preview the following words by reading them in context under the heading Reading Charts and Graphs. Discuss the meaning of these words with the students.

- **parallel**
  always the same distance apart and never meet

- **proportional**
  in the correct relationship of size, quantity, or degree

- **variable**
  able to change

- **geometric**
  using simple shapes

Follow these steps to solve percentage problems.

1. Estimate the answer.
2. Translate the problem into a math statement.
3. Do the calculations.
4. If necessary, round money amounts to the nearest cent.
5. Check your answer.

Read the instructions for your calculator to find out how to use its percent key.

Three types of percentage problems are explained below. Solve the first problem by estimating the answers. The other problems can be solved with a calculator without the use of a percent key.

1. Suppose you and three friends have enjoyed a delicious dinner at a restaurant. When the waiter brings the check, you decide to treat your friends and pay for dinner. To figure the gratuity (tip), you will not need to dig out a calculator because you know how to estimate. The total on the check is $93.58, including tax. You know that a 15 percent gratuity is usual, so you round the total to $100. You know that 10 percent of $100 is $10, and 15 percent is 1½ times 10 percent. Your estimate for the gratuity is $15, and a good estimate is all that is needed. You leave $115.

2. Suppose you have sold a set of golf clubs listed at $395.99 to someone eligible for a 15% discount. How much in dollars and cents will you allow as a discount on the golf clubs?
   - *First: Estimate the answer.* Round the list price to $400. Figure that 10% of $400 is $40. Since 15% is 1½ times 10%, estimate the discount at about $60 (1½ times $40).
   - *Second: Translate the problem into a math statement.*
     15% of $395.99 = 0.15 × $395.99
   - *Third: Do the calculations.*
     0.15 × $395.99 = $59.3985

- *Fourth: Round the answer to the nearest cent, if necessary.*
  $59.3985 rounds to $59.40
- *Finally: Check the answer against your estimate.* The amount $59.40 is reasonably close to the estimate of $60. The discount is $59.40.

3. If sales tax is 6½%, how much tax should you collect on the sale of the golf clubs? Before you can figure the tax, you have to find out the net selling price.

   List price − discount = net price
   $395.99 − $59.40 = $336.59
   Now you can proceed, following the guidelines given above.
   - *Estimate:* Round 6½% to 7% and $336.59 to $300. A 7% sales tax means that $7 tax is collected on every $100 in sales. So you can estimate the tax to be $21 (3 × $7).
   - *Translate:* 6½% of $336.59 = 0.065 × $336.59
   - *Calculate:* 0.065 × $336.59 = $21.8784
   - *Round:* $21.8784 rounds to $21.88
   - *Check:* $21.88 is reasonably close to the estimate of $21. The sales tax to be collected is $21.88.

Reading Charts and Graphs

Often in marketing, people need to use numbers to describe market trends, growth of sales, and other data. Graphs are a way of presenting such information that is easier to understand. It is easier to tell that one bar is longer than another, or that a line is going up or down, than it is to try to understand data by reading lists of numbers. Usually a graph shows the relationship between two kinds of data, or statistical information.

Bar Graphs

A **bar graph** is a drawing made up of parallel bars whose lengths are proportional to the qualities being measured. The bar graph in Figure 7.1 shows cell phone ownership by

---

Extended Activity

Price Comparison
Ask students to research and compare prices on a product at two different Web sites or retail stores. Have students calculate the effect of any promotions, coupons, tax, shipping, etc., on the product's cost. Have students present their findings to the class.

GLOBAL MARKET

Foreign Exchange

Selling products abroad is a long-range goal for many marketers in the United States. One factor that makes doing business in another country complicated is the currency exchange rate, or the amount in dollars that another country's money is worth.

The world's major currencies change in value in relation to each other every day. When the euro (the European currency) was introduced in 1999, it was worth 89¢ U.S. But the euro's value has crept up since its introduction. In late 2003, the euro was worth $1.23, an increase of 38 percent.

When the value of the U.S. dollar is low against the euro, as it was in late 2004, American goods are cheaper for buyers using the euro. This helps increase American exports.

Sometimes, governments keep the value of their currencies low so their products are cheaper for others to buy. The Chinese government often does this. The practice makes Chinese goods very cheap for Americans, but makes American goods expensive in China.

Manufacturers selling abroad must be good predictors of trends in the exchange rate. If a sports shoe maker believes the dollar's value is declining, he or she may want to ship more shoes to Europe. But if the dollar's value rises instead, the company may earn a lower profit than expected.

CRITICAL THINKING
You manufacture snowboards and you want to sell in foreign countries. How will you choose in which country to start?

@ Online Action!
Go to *marketingessentials.glencoe.com/7/global* to find a project on foreign exchange.

---

different age groups. The bottom of the graph lists the age groups. Each group is represented by a bar of a certain height. There is a vertical line along the left side of the graph indicating the percentage of individuals in each age group who own cell phones.

To discover what percentage of 18- to 24-year-olds own cell phones, simply draw an imaginary line across the top of the bar that represents that age group. Then note where that line intersects the left side of the graph. As you can see, 66 percent of 18- to 24-year-olds own cell phones.

Look at the bar representing cell phone ownership for 30- to 39-year-olds. Compare it to the bar for 40- to 49-year-olds. They are the same, at 76 percent, representing the highest percentage on the chart. The relative heights of the bars gives an instant picture of the cell phone ownership of various age groups.

Line Graphs

Another kind of graph you have probably seen often in magazines and newspapers is a line graph. A **line graph** uses a line that joins points representing changes in a variable quantity, usually over a specific period of time. It is very useful for charting sales, prices, profits, output, and things that people expect to change over time. The information is useful in predicting future trends so that businesses can make plans to prepare for them.

The line graph shown in Figure 7.1 charts the changes in cell phone ownership for

---

Individualized Practice

GRAPHS

L1 Ask students to write a paragraph explaining why it is better to use a graph to present data instead of just listing numbers.
Answers will vary but should explain that a bar graph gives an instant visual picture and makes it easier to compare data.

L2 Make copies of a bar graph or circle graph to give to students. Ask students to read the graph and write down the number each bar or piece of the circle represents.

L3 Give students the following data and have them create a circle graph representing the data using software or other programs.

Consumers' Favorite Ice Cream Flavors		
	Men	Women
Vanilla	41%	37%
Chocolate	36%	45%
Strawberry	20%	14%
Other	3%	4%

TEACHING POINTS

Demonstrate Bring in examples of various graphs and pass them around the class or model them to students.

Critical Thinking

Ask students when is a better time to sell American goods abroad—when the dollar is low or high against other countries' currencies? Answers should reflect it is better to sell when the dollar is low against other currencies.

GLOBAL MARKET

Foreign Exchange

Discussion After students have read Global Market, ask them to discuss how currency exchange impacts global trade.

CRITICAL THINKING **Answer:** Answers will vary but should include doing market research to determine the best market for your product.

@ Online Action! For instructions, ideas, and answer guide, go to the Teacher Center at **marketingessentials.glencoe.com**

Follow Up Ask students to research the current value of the U.S. dollar compared to the currency of five other countries. Have students present their findings to the class.

TEACH CONTINUED

Enrichment

CHARTS AND GRAPHS

Ask each student to choose a company to research. Have them research their company, including the organization of the company and its performance in the previous year. Have students write a two-page overview of their company, supporting their paper with charts and graphs that present data about the company, such as sales figures, product assortment, profits, expenses, etc. Students should include at least one example of a bar graph, line graph, and circle graph.

Concept Development

FREQUENCY TABLES

Make copies of a graph. Lead a discussion about the type of information found in the graph and have students work backwards from the graph to create a frequency table listing the data in the graph. Have students choose a partner to compare frequency tables with. Did students differ in the way they set up their tables? Discuss different ways of presenting the same information.

TEACHING POINTS

Model Show students how to work backwards to create a frequency table from the data in a graph.

Critical Thinking

Ask students to suggest reasons why it might be important to be able to present data in chart or graph format in their professions.

Figure 7.1 *Charts and Graphs*

U.S. Cell Phone Ownership by Age Group

(Age groups: 18–24: 66%, 25–29: 71%, 30–39: 76%, 40–49: 76%, 50–59: 73%, 60–69: 60%, 70–79: 50%, 80+: 32%)

• How to Use Charts and Graphs
Bar graphs, line graphs, and circle, or pie graphs are used to display different kinds of data. Here's how to choose the best type of graph to show your results.

How are graphs used?

Bar Graphs
Bar graphs are best for comparing groups. The groups or items being compared do not need to affect each other. They are also a fast way to show big differences. Notice how easy it is to see which age groups own the most cell phones.

Worldwide Cell Phone Sales, 2nd Quarter 2004

- Motorola 14.7%
- Nokia 27.7%
- Samsung 13.9%
- Siemens A.G. 6.4%
- Sony/Ericsson 6.4%
- LG Electronics 6.1%
- Others 24.8%

Total units sold: 164 million

Circle Graphs
A circle, or pie, graph is used to show how a part of something relates to the whole. This kind of graph shows percentages effectively. It's easy to see from this circle graph that Nokia has the largest market share of the cell phone market.

Change in Cell Phone Ownership, '95–'04

(Percentage owning cell phones; lines for 40–49 yr. olds, 18–24 yr. olds, 60–69 yr. olds)

Line Graphs
Line graphs are used to show how one thing is influenced by another. They are especially useful in showing how things change over time. Line graphs are helpful when predicting future trends because they clearly show patterns from the past. This line graph shows that sales of cell phones are increasing for all but one age group.

 Online Action! Go to *marketingessentials.glencoe.com/7/figure/1* for a project on graphs.

168 UNIT 4 - SKILLS FOR MARKETING

Figure 7.1 *Charts and Graphs*

Discussion After students read **Figure 7.1**, discuss the three different types of graphs. Ask students to explain why the data presented in each graph is suited to that type of graph.

Caption Answer Graphs are used to compare information, to show how things change over time, and to show how a part relates to a whole.

 Online Action! For instructions, ideas, and answer guide, go to the Teacher Center at **marketingessentials.glencoe.com**

Follow Up Have students use a spreadsheet, word processing, or graphics program to create different kinds of charts and graphs.

different age groups over a nine-year period. Along the bottom of the graph are the years. Along the left side are the percentages of cell phone ownership. As you can see by following the lines, cell phone ownership increased steadily during that time period for all but 18- to 24-year-olds. This kind of information can help marketers determine how to market their product and help stores decide how much merchandise to order for the following year.

Circle Graphs

A **circle graph** is a geometric representation of the relative sizes of the parts of a whole. Businesses often choose such a graph to compare things like the cost of different aspects of manufacturing, the expenditures of one specific department, or the way income from sales is used by a company.

Circle graphs offer a visual that is easy to understand when considering how a large figure is broken down into several parts. A circle graph is better known as a **pie chart**, because it looks like a pie cut into slices of different sizes. The proportions of the different slices are sometimes expressed as percentages of the whole circle and sometimes as dollar amounts.

The pie chart in Figure 7.1 shows a percentage breakdown of cell phone sales among the major cell phone manufacturers. Even without reading the numbers, you can easily see which company accounted for the largest share of the cell phone market. You can also see that the second- and third-largest market shares were very close to each other, but not very close to the market leader.

This kind of chart enables companies to see at a glance how successful they were compared to other companies. The companies can then determine whether the current market position meets their goals. If not, they can institute new marketing strategies to help them reach their goals.

Frequency Tables

A frequency table lists numbers, fractions, or percentages observed for different intervals. In practical terms, a frequency table can reveal

information for things like consumer buying behavior. For example, the frequency table shown in Figure 7.2 was constructed from survey information about the primary uses of the Web. Information in a frequency table can be presented in graphic form to make it easier to understand.

> **PRACTICE 7 (PROJECT)**
>
> The information in the following frequency table is data from a survey by age group on the uses of the Web. Based on this information, create a bar graph for the age ranges of 11–20 and 21–25.
>
> **PRIMARY USE OF THE INTERNET**
> Percentage of Responses
>
> | | Ages 11–20 | Ages 21–25 |
> |---|---|---|
> | Education | 17% | 16% |
> | Shopping | 8% | 12% |
> | Entertainment | 19% | 17% |
> | Work | 8% | 15% |
> | Communication | 12% | 10% |
> | Personal information | 16% | 17% |
> | Time-wasting | 16% | 11% |
> | Other | 4% | 2% |
> | Total responses: | 100% | 100% |

Algebraic Thinking

Charts and graphs are used to organize information so we can analyze it and make decisions. But how do we analyze numbers to make sense of them? Using algebraic thinking, we look for patterns and relationships, which are called functions in mathematics. We also use symbols to represent variables, numbers we are not sure of or those that will change. For example, Sheila, a marketing analyst, does a study and finds that 30 percent of those who buy a new car will purchase four new tires after two years. Sheila's company needs to plan ahead, so she wants to know how many tires this group will purchase three years from now. Sheila lets n stand for the number of new cars purchased next year, and t stand for the number of tires purchased in three years. Then, she writes an equation: $t = n \times 30\% \times 4$. So if she estimates that 1 million new cars are sold next

TEACH CONTINUED

Concept Development

DESCRIPTIVE STATISTICS

Give students a list of 30 test scores. Have students figure out the mean, median, and mode of the test scores. Then have them figure out the dispersion of the test scores. Ask students to consider how these statistics can help a teacher in evaluating the effectiveness of a test. Lead a discussion about the importance of statistics in evaluating data.

TEACHING POINTS

Extend Ask students to find a list of statistics in a newspaper or online. Have students write two to three paragraphs explaining how the statistics were compiled and how the statistics are meant to be used.

> **PRACTICE 7 ANSWER**
>
> Student graphs should reflect appropriate percentages and an understanding of the elements of a bar graph. See below for examples of how students' graphs should appear.

169

ASSESS

CONCEPTS

Ask students to recall how to convert percentages to decimals and decimals to percentages and ask volunteers to do examples on the board. Ask students to identify different types of graphs and explain how to read them.

KEY TERMS

Have students review key terms, their spellings, and definitions in small groups.

ONLINE SELF-ASSESSMENT

Have students go to marketingessentials.glencoe.com for the Section 7.2 practice test.

Individualized Review

L1 Assign and review Chapter 7 activities in the Student Activity Workbook.

L2 Assign and review Chapter 7 activities in the Marketing Math Workbook.

L3 Assign and review Chapter 7 activities in the *BusinessWeek* Reader and Case Studies.

Marketing Practice

Ask students to invent a product they would like to market. Ask students to research similar products on the market and compile data that would be useful in marketing their product, such as sales data for similar products, the existing market for the product, consumer demographic information, etc. Have students create a proposal for marketing their product, making use of graphs and statistics. Students should then present their proposals to the class.

170

---

year, she knows that this group will purchase $1{,}000{,}000 \times 0.30 \times 4 = 1.2$ million tires in three years.

Descriptive Statistics

Statistics are used to describe and summarize data, thus making the data more meaningful and easier to understand. If you ever read the sports page of your local newspaper, you know something about statistics. Professional baseball, basketball, and football standings indicate the ranking of teams by games won and lost. They also show the percentage of wins for each team. Box scores for a baseball game include statistics on each team member's times at bat, hits, runs batted in, and runs scored.

Business Applications of Descriptive Statistics

In business, statistics are used in analyzing data. For example, Sam is doing a study to track how many people use the Internet to make purchases. He collects data on thousands of people and uses statistics to find:

- The distribution
- The central tendency
- The dispersion

The distribution is a summary of the frequency of values for a variable such as age. This may be presented in a frequency distribution table listing the percentage of customers making Internet purchases by age group.

Customers by Age	Percentage
18–28	12%
29–38	23%
39–48	28%
49–58	16%
59–68	11%
69 and up	10%

The central tendency of a distribution is an estimate of the center of a distribution of

---

Figure 7.2 *Main Reasons for Using the Web*

Purpose for Use	Count, or Frequency, of Uses	Percent of Responses
Education	2,020	16%
Shopping	1,725	13%
Entertainment	1,977	15%
Work	2,168	17%
Communication	1,165	9%
Personal information	2,421	19%
Time-wasting	1,219	9%
Other	286	2%
Total responses:	**12,981**	**100%**

• Frequency Tables Display Counts Frequency tables are used to show counts for particular categories or intervals. This frequency table shows the number of Web site uses, or hits, by purpose of visit.

What was the most frequent purpose for using the Web? How might marketers use this information?

@ Online Action! Go to *marketingessentials.glencoe.com/7/ figure/2* for a project on frequency tables.

Figure 7.2 *Main Reasons for Using the Web*

Discussion After students read **Figure 7.2**, discuss the information in the frequency table. Have students brainstorm other ways to present the data and discuss which way would work better.

Caption Answer According to the table, the most frequent purpose for using the Web was work. Marketers might use this information to identify useful sites for particular jobs or professions and place ads for products that might interest individuals in those jobs and professions on those sites.

@ Online Action! For instructions, ideas, and answer guide, go to the Teacher Center at marketingessentials.glencoe.com

Follow Up Ask students to create and conduct a survey. Using the survey results, have students construct a frequency table and then a graph presenting their results.

values. Here are the three main types of estimates of central tendency:

- Mean
- Median
- Mode

The mean, sometimes called the arithmetic mean, is the most common way of describing central tendency. Most people know this as the average. The mean is computed by adding up all the values and dividing by the number of values. Thus, the average of the values 4, 8, 13, 28, 35, 44, and 56 is 188 divided by 7 = 26.86, rounded to 27.

The median is the exact middle of a set of values. The median in the set of values above is 28. Notice that it is very close to the mean of 27.

The mode is the most frequently occurring value. You would not look for a mode in a set of only seven values, but it can be useful when there is a large number of values. For example, suppose you take a final exam in your marketing class. When the exams are corrected and graded, the scores range from 65 to 95. No more than two students receive the same score, except that 5 students scored 81. Thus, 81 is the most frequently occurring value and is the mode.

Dispersion is the spread of values around the central tendency. The simplest way to measure the dispersion is with the range. The range is the highest values minus the lowest value. With final exam scores between 65 and 95, the range is 30. This is how far the scores are dispersed from the center of the scores.

Have students complete the following statement:

Charts and graphs make it possible to _____ .

see information and thus grasp it more readily

Critical Thinking

Ask students to list the advantages and disadvantages of using a calculator to determine results. Have students discuss their responses in class.

 7.2 AFTER YOU READ

Reviewing Key Terms and Concepts

1. Use a calculator to find the decimal equivalent of $1/3$. Round to the nearest thousandth.
2. What is the decimal equivalent of 40%? What is the percentage equivalent of 1?
3. Why are graphs used to represent numerical data? What are three common forms of graphic representation?

Integrating Academic Skills

Mathematics

4. Employees who work overtime are often paid time-and-a-half. How do you write time-and-a-half as a percentage? If your regular pay rate is $13.50 per hour, how much will you receive for overtime?

History

5. Use the Internet to learn about the prime rate. Define the prime rate. Using historical information about the prime rate for the last 10 years, create a line graph.

 Online Action!
Check your answers at *marketingessentials.glencoe.com/7/read*

AFTER YOU READ

Reviewing Key Terms and Concepts

1. The decimal equivalent of $1/3$ is 0.333.
2. The decimal equivalent of 40 % is .40; the percentage equivalent of 1 is 100 percent.
3. Graphs present information in a way that is easy to understand. Three common forms of graphic representation are bar graphs, line graphs, and circle graphs.

Integrating Academic Skills

4. Time-and-a-half is written as 150%, you will receive $20.25; $13.50 × 1.5 = $20.25
5. The prime rate is the interest rate charged by banks to their most creditworthy customers. Graphs will vary and should include data from the last 10 years.

Online Action! Answers at **marketingessentials.glencoe.com/7/read**

CAREERS IN MARKETING

Lifelong Learning

CAREER INFORMATION

Have students go to marketingessentials.glencoe.com and find the Chapter 7 Careers page and click on the link for the American Marketing Association's Careers Strategies and Tips. Ask students to select one article, read it, and summarize it in three to four short paragraphs.

BASIC MATH SKILLS

Taking courses in business math and accounting can give students skills they can use when completing tax returns, making a budget, buying groceries, calculating interest, and choosing benefits. Encourage students to master the math concepts in the text. Tell students that they will need to analyze such information as part of a marketing career.

Primary Source

Ask students to go to marketingessentials.glencoe.com and find Chapter 7 Resources. Ask them to click on the link for the American Marketing Association's marketing dictionary and read the definitions of the math-related terms they find.

THINKING CRITICALLY

Explain to students that tax laws and audit and financial planning requirements are constantly changing. It is important for a CPA to stay up to date on current laws and regulations.

@ Online Action!

For instructions, ideas, and answer guide, go to the Teacher Center at marketingessentials.glencoe.com

---

CAREERS IN MARKETING

RAY LINDLE
CPA
KOSSE AND LINDLE

 What do you do at work?
I have 34 years of accounting experience. My CPA practice focus is in the construction, wholesale, manufacturing, and service industries. I supervise and perform audit field work, reviews, and prepare financial reports and business income tax returns. I also provide succession planning, tax planning for business owners, and litigation support services. I hold NASD Series 6 & 63 securities licenses.

 What skills are most important to you?
Being able to analyze the numbers beyond the profit statement. It is important to be able to visualize options to achieve a goal. Of course an in-depth knowledge of tax laws is mandatory to planning. When I can help a client achieve profitability by exploring the past and coming up with options for the future then I can feel satisfied. It is also important to understand an owner's long-term objectives, so that I can help them plan for the future, such as retirement or succession.

Also, a CPA is now mandated 150 hours of college before he or she can sit for the licensing exam, but this is just the start. I continually take continuing professional education courses in excess of the annual requirement of 40 hours. Tax classes are a must, and audit and financial planning requirements are constantly changing.

 What is your key to success?
Providing your clients not only what they think they need, but also ideas and suggestions which they may not have thought of yet. My clients are my friends and I need to remember that my goal is to know their long-term business and personal goals and help them achieve both.

Aptitudes, Abilities, and Skills

Analytical and research skills, attention to detail, proficiency in mathematics

Education and Training

Bachelor's and Master's degrees in accounting and general business help pave the way for the CPA exam.

Career Path

Most accountants begin entry-level work with a CPA firm; occasionally, entrepreneurial students can set up shop quickly as a bookkeeper, doing basic work while studying for the CPA exam.

THINKING CRITICALLY

Why do you think this career requires such extensive on-going training?

@ Online Action!

Go to *marketingessentials.glencoe.com/7/careers* for a career-related activity.

Test-Taking Strategies

Read aloud an example of a math problem or question from each chapter heading and subheading. Have students write down their answer and then read the correct answer aloud. Instruct students to spend extra time working on any sections for which they were unable to answer the math problem correctly.

FOCUS on KEY POINTS

SECTION 7.1

● The placement name for each digit and for groups of digits is necessary for reading numbers, writing numbers, and for writing a check. A fraction is a number used to describe a part of a whole amount.

● A decimal number is a fraction or mixed number whose denominator is a power of 10. Rounding decimal numbers is common when multiplying with amounts of money, as when figuring tax, discounts, and gratuities. Decimal equivalents of fractions are used in many marketing jobs. To convert a fraction to a decimal, divide the numerator by the denominator.

SECTION 7.2

● Nearly everyone in marketing uses a calculator, and there are two basic types. The most commonly used calculator uses the algebraic entry system. The other type uses the reverse-entry system.

● Charts and graphs present data in a way that is easier to understand than a long series of numbers. They are used to describe market trends, growth of sales, and other data.

REVIEW VOCABULARY

1. What is the name for the ten basic symbols used in our numbering system? (p. 152)

2. Name the numbers at the top and bottom of a fraction. (p. 153)

3. What is another way to write a fraction with a denominator that is a power of 10? (p. 154)

4. Representing a number as parts per 100 is representing it as a what? (p. 165)

5. Name four ways to present numbers graphically. (pp. 166–169)

REVIEW FACTS and IDEAS

6. How are commas used to write numbers in words? When are hyphens used in writing numbers in words? (7.1)

7. What are fractions? What does the denominator tell you? The numerator? (7.1)

8. What rule must you follow when adding or subtracting decimal numbers? Multiplying decimal numbers? Dividing decimal numbers? (7.1)

9. List the steps for rounding decimal numbers. To what place do you usually round money? (7.1)

10. Explain how to convert $2/5$ to its decimal equivalent. (7.1)

11. The use of a calculator increases accuracy and efficiency. Why is it important to estimate your answer when using a calculator? (7.2)

12. How do you convert a percentage to a decimal? A decimal to a percentage? (7.2)

13. Graphs are used to illustrate data. Give an example of how each of the following types of graphs might be used in business: Bar graph, line graph, circle graph. (7.2)

Chapter 7 - Basic Math Skills 173

5. Four ways to present a number graphically are a bar graph, line graph, circle graph, and frequency table.

REVIEW FACTS and IDEAS

6. Commas are used to separate whole numbers into groups of three digits. Hyphens are used to write whole numbers less than 100 that are written as two words.

7. A fraction is a number that describes a part of some standard amount. The denominator describes how many parts are in the whole. The numerator describes how many parts are being considered.

8. Adding or subtracting: Align the decimals. Multiplying: Add the number of decimals in the two factors, then counting from right to left, insert the same number of decimals in the product. Dividing: Shift the decimal in the divisor to create a whole number and then shift the decimal in the dividend a corresponding number of places.

9. Locate the place you are rounding to; look at the digit to the right of that place; if that digit is less than five, leave the first digit as is and drop all digits that follow; if that digit is five or greater, round the first digit up and drop all digits that follow. Round money to the hundredths place.

10. You would divide 2 by 5, which yields 0.4.

11. An estimate will enable you to spot an error in data entry.

12. Percentage to decimal: Divide by 100 (move decimal point two places to the left). Decimal to percentage: Multiply by 100 (move the decimal point two places to the right).

13. A bar graph uses bars of different heights to represent differences in categories (variables) and thus allows for comparisons. A line graph uses points connected by a line to show growth or decline in one variable over time and helps to illustrate a trend. A circle graph is used to show the relationship of the parts to the whole, such as in a budget.

FOCUS on KEY POINTS

Ask volunteers to read the summaries aloud and give the classroom one example for each concept.

REVIEW VOCABULARY

1. The ten basic symbols used in our numbering systems are called digits.

2. The number at the top of a fraction is the numerator. The number at the bottom of a fraction is the denominator.

3. A decimal number is another way to write a fraction with a denominator that is a power of 10.

4. Representing a number in parts per 100 is representing it as a percentage.

BUILD SKILLS

14. Workplace Skills

Answers will vary. Some students are apt to see it as fair because everyone is taking the same percentage cut. Others may argue that those who are paid less cannot afford the cut and should have a lower rate of cut than those who are paid more.

15. Technology Applications

Reports will vary. Accept all reports that show an understanding of software programs and their various math applications.

16. Math Practice

The cost per pencil is $.33. You would charge $.34 for one pencil, otherwise it would be cheaper for a customer to buy the pencils singly.

DEVELOP CRITICAL THINKING

17. How Are the Different Graphs and Charts Used?

Summaries will vary. Accept all summaries showing understanding of the three types of graphs and their uses.

18. What Is the Difference Among Calculators?

Reports will vary. Accept all reports including research on both graphing and financial calculators.

BUILD SKILLS

14. Workplace Skills

Human Relations You work for a small company. Hourly wages at the company range from $11 per hour to $55 per hour. Lately, the company has experienced financial difficulty. A task force has been set up to provide possible solutions to avoid layoffs. One suggestion from management is that each employee take a voluntary cut in wages of 3 percent. Is this a fair solution? Why or why not?

15. Technology Applications

Math Software Prepare a short oral report on software programs for math applications in daily business life. Make sure you consider many different kinds of job situations. Include information about which type of job makes use of each type of software you list.

16. Math Practice

Working With a Calculator Use a calculator to solve the following problem: Your store is advertising pencils at three for $1.00. What is the cost per pencil if you round to the nearest cent? If a customer wanted to buy just one pencil, what would you charge? Why?

DEVELOP CRITICAL THINKING

17. How Are the Different Graphs and Charts Used?

Using business magazines and newspapers, locate and make copies of a bar graph, a line graph, and a circle graph. Briefly summarize the information that each graph communicates in a few written paragraphs.

Bring your examples to class and be ready to discuss and share them with your classmates.

18. What Is the Difference Among Calculators?

Research graphing calculators and financial calculators at a local retailer or on the Internet. You might also consider asking your math teacher about the various functions available for calculators. Use a word processing program to prepare a one-page report summarizing the features of each type of calculator.

 ## Formative Assessment

Formative assessment is an essential component of classroom work. This type of assessment provides information that is then used as feedback to modify teaching and meet student needs.

L1 Review key terms. Have students write down or draw an example of each term.

L2 Read aloud various scenarios involving key terms. Have students identify the key terms involved in each scenario.

L3 Have students create a list of math problems and questions testing understanding of each chapter concept. Have students exchange tests and fill in answers.

 Reteach **If the results of this formative assessment seem low, consider the following activity:**

Read the chapter heads and subheads aloud and have students write down two important facts they know about each concept.

APPLY CONCEPTS

19. Using Circle Graphs

Assume that you are accepting a full-time job in your locality that pays $2,600 after taxes per month. Using your local newspaper, determine what it will cost you to rent a one-bedroom apartment. Estimate your other living costs for one month such as food, clothing, transportation, utilities, insurance, miscellaneous.

Activity Use a computer program to create a circle graph representing this data.

20. Research Refrigerator Offers

Assume that you are looking for a new refrigerator for your apartment. Using newspaper and magazine ads or searching on the Internet, find the same refrigerator offered by two different stores in your area. Compare the offers on the two refrigerators, including rebates, discounts, and other sales promotions to determine which is the better offer.

Activity Write a short, one-page report comparing and contrasting the offers and defend your decision to buy one refrigerator over the other.

NET SAVVY

21. Inflation

Use a search engine to locate an inflation calculator that is based on the consumer price index (CPI). Begin with a basket of items costing $100 in 1950. Compute the inflated cost for 1960, 1970, 1980, 1990, and 2000. Enter your data into a spreadsheet program such as Excel. Create both a bar graph and a line graph based on your data. Which graph do you think is most effective in presenting your data? Why?

THE DECA CONNECTION

Role Play: Sales Associate

Situation You work at a large department store. You are preparing for the school year and want to purchase some new clothes. One of the employee benefits your store offers is a 20 percent discount on store purchases. You want to purchase a pair of jeans that cost $65.00, a pair of shoes that cost $95.00, 2 tops that cost $40.00 each, and a jacket that costs $125.00. You must also add the sales tax of 7.5 percent to your total purchase.

Activity You must determine the amount of money you will spend and save by taking advantage of your employee discount to make your back-to-school purchases.

Evaluation You will be evaluated on how well you meet the following performance indicators:

- Explain the nature of personnel regulations
- Explain the nature of wage and benefit programs
- Calculate miscellaneous charges
- Make decisions
- Prepare simple written reports

 Online Action!

For more information and DECA Prep practice, go to *marketingessentials.glencoe.com/7/DECA*

APPLY CONCEPTS

19. Using Circle Graphs

Graphs will vary; each graph should include all living costs.

20. Research Refrigerator Offers

Reports will vary. Accept all reports comparing two refrigerators and including sufficient information on the two offers.

NET SAVVY

21. Inflation

Answers and graphs will vary. Accept all answers showing an understanding of inflation as well as bar and line graphs.

THE DECA CONNECTION

The students should be evaluated on the performance indicators noted in the role play. For another DECA role play, go to the Competitive Events Workbook or the Student Activity Workbook, or go to **marketingessentials.glencoe.com/7/DECA**

 Online Action! For instructions, ideas, and answer guide, go to the Teacher Center at **marketingessentials.glencoe.com**

DECA Advisors Corner

Utilize school display space throughout the year to display awards, trophies, pictures from trips, and other memorabilia to showcase your DECA chapter activities. This is an excellent way to improve the image of your DECA chapter and recognize student achievement.

MINI-QUIZ

Read these sentences to the students and have them volunteer the missing words.

1. In the number 6,035,274, the digit 5 represents the _____ place. (thousands)

2. The number 376, 023 rounded to the nearest ten thousand is _____ . (380,000)

3. A _____ graph best shows changes over time. (line)

For an expanded chapter quiz, go to Chapter 7 in the TeacherWorks CD-ROM and to Chapter 7 in the **Exam*View*®** Pro Test Generator CD-ROM.

Chapter Overview

Chapter 8 covers the basic communication skills essential to clear expression of thought in the business world and in daily life, including face-to-face interaction as well as written and electronic forms of communication.

⊘ BUILD BACKGROUND ⊘

Ask students for examples of people working together for a common goal. They may bring up examples such as sports teams, musicians in a band, firefighters, or even social activists. Then ask the class about the importance of communication to these cases. Can a team of people work effectively without communication? Emphasize that in a business, co-workers must convey their ideas effectively to each other, as well as to their customers.

Why It's Important

Individuals are asked to communicate their ideas with others both on and off the job. Communicating clearly and appropriately will help students be more productive and effective in all areas of their lives.

Prepare to Read

Ask a volunteer to write all of the major headings on the board in outline format. Tell students to fill in the secondary (blue) headings as they preview or read the chapter. They will then have a thorough chapter outline to use as study notes.

CHAPTER **8**
Communication Skills

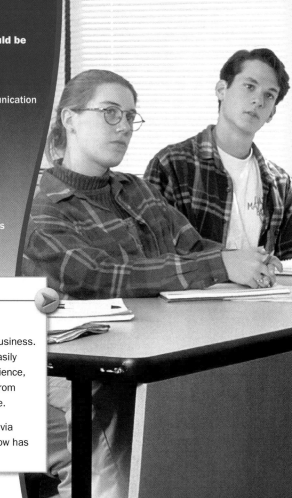

Chapter Objectives

After reading this chapter, you should be able to:

- Define effective verbal and nonverbal communication
- Explain the role of listening in communication
- Explain why awareness of cultural differences is important
- Define reading for meaning
- Explain how to organize and present your ideas
- Demonstrate professional telephone communication skills
- Explain how to write effective business letters and persuasive messages

▸ GUIDE TO THE PHOTO

Market Talk Communicating clearly is necessary for success in school or in business. The ability to send a message that is easily understood by the market, or by an audience, is critical to all aspects of marketing—from advertising to sales to customer service.

Quick Think Business communication via e-mail has increased in recent years. How has this affected formal letter writing?

GUIDE TO THE PHOTO

Market Talk Let students know that a marketing message can be communicated to the general public or to a specific target market. For example, ads for computer parts, or underground bands, may pique the interest of industry professionals or fans but mean nothing to the general public.

Quick Think Students may suggest that the advent of e-mail has made formal letter writing and phone calls less common. Using e-mail does not require postage, it can be transmitted at any hour, and it allows for easy tracking.

Follow Up Ask students for some drawbacks to using e-mail instead of a formal letter or telephone call. Drawbacks may include the likelihood of careless mistakes, the chance of e-mails being sent accidentally, and the possibility of them being forwarded without your knowledge.

Performance indicators represent key skills and knowledge. These acronyms represent DECA events that involve knowledge of concepts in this chapter.

AAAL	FMAL	MMS*	TMDM*
AAML*	FMDM*	QSRM*	TSE*
ADC*	FMML*	RMAL	VPM
BSM	FSRM*	RMML*	
EMDM*	HMDM*	SMDM*	

In all these DECA events you should be able to follow these performance indicators:

- Explain the nature of effective communication
- Apply effective listening skills
- Use proper grammar and vocabulary
- Explain the nature of effective verbal communications
- Address people properly
- Handle telephone calls in a businesslike manner
- Persuade others
- Make oral presentations
- Explain the nature of written communications
- Write business letters
- Prepare simple reports
- Follow directions
- Explain the nature of staff communication
- Explain the use of interdepartmental/company communications
- Describe ethical considerations in providing information

All the events with an asterisk (*) also include these performance indicators:

- Give directions for completing job tasks
- Conduct staff meetings

DECA PREP

Check your understanding of DECA performance indicators with the DECA activity in this chapter's review. For more information and DECA Prep practice, go to *marketingessentials.glencoe.com/8/DECA*

marketingessentials.glencoe.com

Chapter 8 - Communication Skills **177**

DECA events that require knowledge of communication skills are described here. Discuss the performance indicators to make sure students understand how to demonstrate their understanding.

The event acronyms stand for:

AAAL: Apparel and Accessories Marketing Series, AL

AAML: Apparel and Accessories Marketing Series, ML

ADC: Advertising Campaign Event

BSM: Business Services Marketing Series

EMDM: E-Commerce Management Team Decision Making Event

FMAL: Food Marketing Series, AL

FMDM: Financial Analysis Management Team Decision Making Event

FMML: Food Marketing Series, ML

FSRM: Full Service Restaurant Management Series

HMDM: Hospitality Services Management Team Decision Making Event

MMS: Marketing Management Series

QSRM: Quick Serve Restaurant Management Series

RMAL: Retail Merchandising Series, AL

RMML: Retail Merchandising Series, ML

SMDM: Sports and Entertainment Marketing Management Team Decision Making Event

TMDM: Travel and Tourism Marketing Management Team Decision Making Event

TSE: Technical Sales Event

VPM: Vehicles and Petroleum Marketing Series

DECA PREP

Find timed DECA Prep activities correlated to the Competitive Events Workbook for students and DECA tips for teachers at **marketingessentials.glencoe.com/8/DECA**

CHAPTER 8   Classroom Resources

For the Teacher

- TeacherWorks
- marketingessentials.glencoe.com
- Interactive Chalkboard
- **Exam***View*® Pro Test Generator
- Fast File Unit 4

For the Student

- *Marketing Essentials* Online Edition
- Student Activity Workbook
- Marketing Math Workbook
- Marketing Research Project Workbook
- School-to-Work Activity Workbook
- Competitive Events Workbook
- *BusinessWeek* Reader and Case Studies
- marketingessentials.glencoe.com

FOCUS

Introducing the Section

COLLABORATIVE ACTIVITY

To prepare for reading this section, have students create a poster illustrating the different ways they communicate every day. They may include talking in person, using phones, trading text messages, and using e-mail. Ask students to include in their poster when they would use each method, and why.

Preteaching Key Terms

Have students predict the meanings of the following terms:

- communications
- channels/media
- feedback
- barriers
- setting
- distractions
- emotional barriers
- jargon

Have the class review their predictions as they read the chapter.

Extended Activity

Barriers

Ask students to brainstorm and share examples of common barriers to communication among individuals from different cultures. Answers might include physical barriers such as clothing or ornaments that obscure eyes, faces, or hands, linguistic barriers such as the use of slang, and cultural barriers such as body language or the misinterpretation of body language or activities.

OBJECTIVES

- Define effective verbal and nonverbal communication
- Explain the role of listening in communication
- Explain why awareness of cultural differences is important
- Define reading for meaning

KEY TERMS

- communication
- channels/media
- feedback
- barriers
- setting
- distractions
- emotional barriers
- jargon

Defining Communication

READ and STUDY

BEFORE YOU READ

Predict Write two words that you associate with the word *communicate*. Add to or change the list as you read.

THE MAIN IDEA

Effective communication—sending and receiving messages that are understood in the same way by both sender and receiver—is a key component of marketing. Understanding the communication process and improving listening and reading skills will lead to greater success on the job and in the marketplace.

STUDY ORGANIZER

Copy the chart below and use it to take notes about the listening process.

The Listening Process

Listening → Things that Help the Process → Message
Listening → Things that Stop the Process

WHILE YOU READ

Connect Do you prefer writing, speaking, or some other method of communication?

The Communication Process

Communication is the process of exchanging messages between a sender and a receiver. These messages can be about information, ideas, or feelings. The skills used to send and receive these messages are called communication skills. They include listening, reading, speaking, and writing. Good communication skills are key to effective communication, in which the speaker or writer presents the message clearly and concisely so that

178 UNIT 4 - SKILLS FOR MARKETING

READ and STUDY

BEFORE YOU READ

Let students know that communication is not only speaking, but also listening, making gestures, reading, and writing, making and seeing art, and other forms of expression.

THE MAIN IDEA

Have students discuss the factors that they contribute to effective communication.

STUDY ORGANIZER

Model the study organizer by filling in the chart as you teach. A full-size, downloadable study organizer can be found at **marketingessentials.glencoe.com**

 WHILE YOU READ Ask students to think about the ways they communicate as they read the chapter.

the listener or reader can understand it easily. Effective communication is vital in every aspect of business, including developing job skills, training employees, working as a team, networking, and marketing products.

Businesses now compete around the globe, which means they must make their messages understood by people of different cultural backgrounds.

Channels or Media

Channels, or **media**, are the avenues through which messages are delivered. Examples include face-to-face conversations, telephone calls, written memos, letters, reports, and e-mail. Advertising channels include television, radio, print media, and the Internet. Channels differ in terms of message-carrying capacity (how much content they can carry), the speed with which the message is delivered, cost of the message, and its accuracy, or quality of content. The choice of medium depends on the relative importance of these factors in the delivery of the message.

Feedback

A receiver's response to a message is known as **feedback**. For example, if your boss asks you to post a report on the company Web site, you will probably ask some questions about what to include, when to post it, and so on. Your questions are feedback to your boss. Feedback in communication allows participants to clarify the message and make sure that all parties gave the message the same meaning.

Barriers

Barriers to communication are obstacles that interfere with the understanding of a message. They can be verbal barriers, such as using vague or unclear language or using a language or dialect that is unfamiliar to the receiver of the message. For example, what do you call a carbonated, sugary beverage that comes in cans and bottles? Depending on where you live, you might call this drink *soda, pop, soda pop,* or even something else. Marketing professionals need to make sure the language that they are using is appropriate for and

•CULTURAL NORMS Different cultures have different gestures to show respect or greeting.

What are some gestures that you use to demonstrate greeting or respect?

able to be understood by their audience. This applies to cross-cultural marketing as well. For example, the Spanish language has many dialects, and people from different Spanish-speaking countries, such as Cuba, Mexico, Spain, and the Dominican Republic often use different Spanish words to express the same concept. So when businesses are trying to target the Hispanic market, it is important for them to know something about the cultural backgrounds of potential customers.

Setting

The **setting** is the circumstance under which communication takes place. These circumstances include place, time, sights, and sounds. The setting can help or hinder the ability to exchange messages. For example, a salesperson at an electronics store may find it difficult to explain the features of a video camera to a customer if the music department across the aisle has a stereo playing at full volume.

Listening

Listening for understanding is one of the most valuable communication skills. Listening is the active mental process by which a

Chapter 8 - Communication Skills **179**

TEACH CONTINUED

Concept Development

TECHNIQUES FOR EFFECTIVE LISTENING

Have students watch a televised interview. It can be hard news, entertainment, or a talk show. Ask them to take notes about feedback given by the interviewer. Both verbal and nonverbal communication should be recorded. Then ask them to watch the feedback given by the person being interviewed. Is it different than the interviewer? Have students share their findings in class.

TEACHING POINTS

Role Play Carry on a "bad" conversation with a student. Do not pause, give nonverbal communication, or acknowledge understanding. Ask the student what you could have done differently to be a better communicator.

Demonstrate On a chalkboard, dry-erase board, or screen projection, make a chart listing examples of positive and negative feedback. Example: looking at a person's eyes and looking around him or her.

Critical Thinking

Ask students how they can be good listeners in difficult circumstances, such as noisy, dark, or uncomfortable settings.

---

person recognizes, assimilates, assesses, and evaluates what is heard. (See Figure 8.1 for a list of barriers to listening.) Situations in which listening plays an important role include handling customer complaints, understanding feedback, recognizing clients' needs, following directions, and resolving conflicts with coworkers.

Techniques for Effective Listening

Listening, like all skills, must be learned. The following techniques will improve your listening skills and help you to be an effective listener.

Identify the Purpose

Prepare to listen by learning and reviewing the purpose of the communication. Managers planning a group meeting, for example, send out an agenda in advance so everyone will know the meeting's purpose. When a customer sets up a meeting, it is especially important to understand the meeting's purpose so that you will be prepared to respond to the customer's questions.

Look for a Plan

When you listen to a structured speech, think about how the speaker has organized the presentation. Be alert at the beginning of the speech, because the speaker may give an outline of the main ideas of the talk. If you see a structure or pattern, it will be easier to see how the different parts of the message fit together.

Face-to-face conversations are often informal and unplanned, so just stay focused on the message instead of thinking about structure.

Give Feedback

When you are conversing about business, listen carefully and then give feedback to show whether you have understood the message. Without interrupting, you can nod your head, raise an eyebrow, smile, or frown. Look for an opportunity to ask questions when the speaker pauses or completes his or her point. Think through what has been said and summarize your understanding of the message. Acknowledge your understanding respectfully or ask the speaker for clarification if you are uncertain.

When a speaker is giving instructions, it may be better to interrupt with questions than to wait for a pause. In that way, a confusing point can be clarified, and you can follow the remainder of the directions. However, before interrupting, you should be sure that the speaker is comfortable with this approach.

Search for a Common Interest

Effective listening is easier when you are interested in the ideas being discussed. If you find the subject boring and are tempted to tune out, resist the temptation. Try to find something that interests you or that you can use. Tuning out can become a bad habit and can cause you to miss some important information.

Evaluate the Message

It is important to know how to respond appropriately to a message. To do so, you must evaluate it. For example, if a customer shares a personal point of view with you, even if you disagree, it would be inappropriate to make a sudden judgment. Doing so could be destructive to your relationship. Instead, try to view the message from the speaker's point of view. Listen carefully and try to understand the new information even if it conflicts with what you believe. Relax and do not become defensive. Recognize that your customer's experience may be unlike yours. Different experiences may cause differences in perception. Ask polite but probing questions to understand the message better. Try to identify any parts of the speaker's message with which you do agree.

Listen for More Than Verbal Content

Listen for more than just words in the speaker's message. What is communicated by the speaker's rate of speech, pitch, volume, and voice quality?

Awareness of cultural differences will help in the understanding of vocal cues. In the United States and other Western countries, including Canada, Australia, and Great Britain, speakers are expected to look at and speak directly to listeners. In many Asian countries, however, speakers show respect by averting their eyes, speaking in soft tones, and approaching their subject indirectly. A speaker

---

Online Activity

Reading Online

Ask students to visit the Web site of a local or national newspaper. Ask them to compare the news, entertainment, sports, business, ads, and other sections, and identify their different purposes. How is each section read differently? What is each section trying to communicate? Have students share their responses in class.

Figure 8.1 Barriers to Listening

• How Listening Can Fail Barriers to listening stop the communication process. They prevent the listener from receiving and understanding the messages sent to them.

How can you be a good listener?

Distractions Distractions interfere with the ability to listen well. You may be distracted by thoughts about another subject. Focus your attention on the speaker's words.

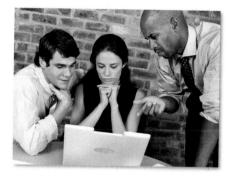

Emotional Barriers When you have a negative emotional reaction to something someone says, it prevents you from concentrating on what is being said. To overcome this barrier, try to keep an open mind.

Planning a Response This is a very common block to listening. If you are trying to figure out what to say when other people are still speaking, you will not take in all that they are saying. To overcome this barrier, listen carefully until the other person has finished, then respond.

Online Action! Go to *marketingessentials.glencoe.com/8/figure/1* to find a project on listening skills.

marketingessentials.glencoe.com

Chapter 8 - Communication Skills **181**

TEACH CONTINUED

Enrichment

UNDERSTANDING TONE
Tell students that in e-mail, memos, and other forms of written communication, there is no nonverbal communication. As a result, it can be hard to identify tone, which can help you tell when someone is sarcastic or joking. Ask students if they have ever misunderstood someone's tone or had their tone misunderstood. Ask: How did they solve the problem? Have students share their responses in class.

TEACHING POINTS
Extended Have students list verbal or nonverbal cues they would give a speaker to show him or her that they have understood his or her tone.

Build Vocabulary

Preview the following words that have to do with verbal communication by reading them in context. Have students research and suggest a brief definition for each word. Ask students to demonstrate them by adjusting their voices.

- **rate of speech**
  quickness of speaking
- **pitch**
  tone of voice
- **volume**
  loudness
- **voice quality**
  clarity and smoothness of voice

Figure 8.1 Barriers to Listening

Discussion After students have read **Figure 8.1,** discuss the three barriers to listening. Ask students to come up with everyday examples of each barrier illustrated in this figure and role-play situations reflecting them. For example: 1.) Distractions: blaring music or television program 2.) Emotional barriers: being hungry or tired 3.) Planning a response: a telemarketer who gives stock answers

Caption Answer You can be a good listener by identifying the purpose, looking for a plan, giving feedback, searching for a common interest, evaluating the message, listening for more than verbal content, listening for a conclusion, and taking notes.

Online Action! For instructions, ideas, and answer guide, go to the Teacher Center at **marketingessentials.glencoe.com**

Critical Thinking
Ask students: Have you ever spoken to someone who just wouldn't listen? Ask students to identify the barriers and think of what could be done to overcome them.

ASSESS

Review Guide

CONCEPTS

Ask students to list the primary elements of communication.

Answers include the following: senders and receivers, messages, channels, feedback, blocks, and setting.

KEY TERMS

Have students write a brief guide to effective listening and reading using each of the key terms.

ONLINE SELF-ASSESSMENT

Have students to go marketingessentials.glencoe.com for the Section 8.1 practice test.

Individualized Review

L1 Assign and review Chapter 8 activities in the Student Activity Workbook.

L2 Assign and review Chapter 8 activities in the Marketing Math Workbook.

L3 Assign and review Chapter 8 activities in the *BusinessWeek* Reader and Case Studies.

Marketing Practice

Have students pair up and conduct mock interviews as though they were on a televised talk show. The interviewer and interviewee should practice giving feedback, using both verbal and nonverbal techniques. Then have the students swap roles.

---

in Canada who wants to say "No" will simply say "No." In Korea, a person who wants to communicate the same message may say, "That might be very difficult." Both statements mean "No," but the messages reflect cultural differences.

Listen for a Conclusion

Listen carefully for the speaker's conclusion. You may want to take action based on it. Do not jump to your own conclusion before the speaker has finished presenting the facts that support his or her conclusion. Be prepared to check your understanding by asking well-thought-out questions. If the situation is a formal one, wait to ask questions at the right time. Intelligent questions indicate not only interest but also respect for the speaker's work.

Take Notes

Try to identify a plan in the presentation of formal meetings. Then structure your notes according to the plan. Take notes on the main points presented at business meetings. Important points are often preceded by signal words such as *first, second, next, then, another, therefore,* and *thus.* If there is a summary or a recap at the end of the meeting, listen carefully and check your notes to make sure you understood the main ideas.

Barriers to Listening for Understanding

A barrier to receiving a message can be environmental, such as a plane flying overhead, or it may involve attitudes and characteristics of the listener. Common barriers to listening include the following:

- **Distractions** Distractions are things that compete with the message for the listener's attention. These can include noises, conversations, and competing thoughts. One way to overcome this barrier is to move away from the distractions—to change the setting.
- **Emotional barriers** Emotional barriers are biases against the sender's opinions that prevent a listener from understanding. Poor listeners close their minds to

---

things with which they disagree. Good listeners always listen with an open mind, even when they do not agree with the speaker's ideas.

- **Planning a response** Planning a response occurs when the receiver of the message stops listening and instead begins to think about what to say next. A person cannot focus on the message and plan a response at the same time.

Listeners must be aware of and actively avoid or overcome any barriers in order to concentrate on the message.

Reading

Reading, like listening, is an active mental process of receiving and understanding a message. Reading skills are essential on any job; in fact, they are usually needed to get a job in the first place. Applicants must read help-wanted ads or search online for job postings. In the workplace, reading skills are needed to interpret information in schedules, graphs, training manuals, e-mails, and reports.

Know the Purpose of Your Reading

Many of the techniques for effective listening also apply to reading. For instance, it is helpful when reading to look for a plan, search for an interest, and evaluate the message. A technique that is especially valuable in building good reading skills is to keep in mind the purpose for your reading. Good readers know why they are reading. This awareness determines how they read.

Reading for Meaning

Reading for meaning requires that a person read carefully, figure out the meaning of new words, search for answers, and analyze and evaluate information—often in a short period of time. Most job-related reading assignments involve reading for meaning. For example, you may be required to search for sources online or read through a large report to find information about marketing trends. Another job-related reading task is checking facts. There are three

---

 Extended Activity

Reading for Meaning

Bring examples of reading material, such as newspapers novels, store catalogs, and news or entertainment magazines. Ask students to skim a page or article in one minute, then test their recall by asking them to summarize it. Have students compare their techniques for reading for meaning.

strategies that can improve the ability to read for meaning:

1. **Focus your mind** The mind does not focus on a subject automatically. It must be trained. Monitoring your thoughts when you read can keep you focused. Think about how each paragraph relates to your purpose for reading.

2. **Summarize as you read** As you finish each paragraph and section of the text, mentally review what you have just read and summarize it. If you do not understand the text, go over it again. If it is still unclear, jot down a question so that you can follow up on it later.

3. **Make connections** Think about how the material relates to ideas or information with which you are familiar.

4. **Form mental pictures** Try to form pictures of the people, places, things, and situations described. This can help you remember the material in a form that is meaningful to you.

5. **Build your vocabulary** You may come across words that are unfamiliar when reading.

Skipping over these words may cause you to miss key points in the message. Try to figure out the meaning by the way the word is used in the sentence. Always keep a dictionary nearby and learn how to use both the thesaurus and dictionary included in office computer software. Looking up words will improve your vocabulary and your understanding of what you are reading.

In job-related reading, you may come across **jargon**, specialized vocabulary used by members of a particular group. Because these words or meanings are not commonly used, they are often not listed in standard dictionaries. For example, the word *market* as used by marketing professionals is jargon because it has a specific meaning for marketers. A market, to marketers, is a group of people or organizations that share a need for a particular product and have the willingness and ability to pay for it. Learning the jargon used in your field will make it easier for you to do job-related reading.

8.1 AFTER YOU READ

Reviewing Key Terms and Concepts

1. What listening techniques can help you better understand messages you receive?
2. What are two barriers that could interfere with receiving a message?
3. List three ways to improve reading for meaning.

Integrating Academic Skills

Math

4. Assume that the average number of waking hours per day is 16. If we spend 70 percent of our waking hours communicating, how many hours do we spend communicating each day?

Language Arts

5. Listen to a news report. Apply two techniques for effective listening, such as listening for a conclusion and taking notes. Summarize the report in a short paragraph.

 Online Action!

Check your answers at *marketingessentials.glencoe.com/8/read*

marketingessentials.glencoe.com

Chapter 8 - Communication Skills **183**

AFTER YOU READ

Reviewing Key Terms and Concepts

1. Listening techniques include the following: identifying the purpose, looking for a plan, giving feedback, searching for a common interest, evaluating the message, listening for more than verbal content, listening for a conclusion, and taking notes.

2. Barriers to communication include distractions, emotional blocks, and planning a response.

3. Ways to improve reading for meaning include: focusing your mind, summarizing as you read, making connections, forming mental pictures, and building your vocabulary.

Integrating Academic Skills

4. 11.2 hours per day; $16 \times .70 = 11.2$

5. Reports will vary but should demonstrate an understanding of the techniques for effective listening.

Online Action! Answers at **marketingessentials.glencoe.com/8/read**

CLOSE

1. **Ask students to explain what reading and listening have in common.** Reading and listening both involve the process of trying to understand a message.

2. **As a class, create a set of instructions for an everyday task such as peeling an orange or driving a car. Challenge students to be as clear as possible in their directions, and to utilize visual aids or graphics if appropriate.**

 Critical Thinking

Ask students: Why might you recall reading for pleasure more easily and accurately than reading for meaning?

FOCUS

Introducing the Section

COLLABORATIVE ACTIVITY

To prepare for reading this section, ask students to list their favorite writers. They can be magazine columnists, newspaper reporters, bloggers (people who create and maintain online journals on a particular topic), or novelists. Have the class write down what they like about their favorite writers' work. Can students apply the same techniques in their own writing, both in business and everyday contexts?

Preteaching Key Terms

Read the key terms aloud, or ask a volunteer to read them. Ask students to predict the meanings of these terms:

- persuade
- enumeration
- generalization

Tell students they can check their predictions as they read this section.

 Critical Thinking

Ask students: Have you ever been in a conversation about a subject with which you were not familiar? What is the best strategy for handling such a situation? Have students share their responses in class.

OBJECTIVES

- **Explain how to organize and present your ideas**
- **Demonstrate professional telephone communication skills**
- **Explain how to write effective business letters and persuasive messages**

KEY TERMS

- persuade
- enumeration
- generalization

Elements of Speech and Writing

READ and STUDY

BEFORE YOU READ

Predict List three ways businesspeople communicate.

THE MAIN IDEA

Speaking and writing are ways to send messages—a key component of marketing. Building professional speaking and writing skills will help to ensure that your business messages are communicated successfully.

STUDY ORGANIZER

Use a chart like the one below to write tips for effective speaking in one circle, and tips for effective writing in the other circle. Write all the tips that apply to both in the space that overlaps.

Tips for Effective Communication

Effective Speaking | Speaking Writing | Effective Writing

WHILE YOU READ

Connect As you read, list ideas about how you could improve your speaking and writing skills.

Speaking

Speaking is an important part of most jobs. People use speech to ask questions at meetings, to answer the telephone, and to discuss plans at a meeting. In marketing, speaking has applications in customer relations, presenting marketing plans, and television advertising. Because speaking is an important part of most business and marketing, it is important to know how to speak effectively.

184 UNIT 4 - SKILLS FOR MARKETING

READ and STUDY

BEFORE YOU READ

Lead students in listing ways businesspeople communicate. Answers might include in-person meetings, telephone calls, conference calls, e-mails, instant messages, facsimiles, and presentations.

THE MAIN IDEA

Ask a volunteer to read the main idea aloud. Have students discuss how building speaking and writing skills can help an individual's personal relationships as well as business relationships.

STUDY ORGANIZER

Model the study organizer for students. A full-size, downloadable study organizer can be found at **marketingessentials.glencoe.com**

WHILE YOU READ Encourage students to maintain their lists of ideas in a journal.

Show Respect

In most business situations, the most important rule is to show courtesy and respect for others. Whether handling a customer complaint or addressing a coworker at a meeting, you should maintain a cordial tone.

Know the Purpose

As with listening and reading, it is helpful when speaking to know your purpose. In most business situations, speaking is done to inform, persuade, or entertain.

- **Inform** Conversations with customers and general business meetings are often held to inform others—to pass on information. When speaking to inform, be clear and concise—get to the point.
- **Persuade** Marketing involves sending messages that persuade others to change how they think or what they do. To **persuade** someone is to convince that person to change a perception in order to get him or her to do what you want. As you prepare an oral presentation, determine what your listeners' needs are. Then, talk about how you, your company, or your product can satisfy those needs. Persuasive speaking is also important in conflict resolution, when there is a need to present a point of view or suggest a solution.
- **Entertain** Sometimes the purpose of speaking is to entertain others. Salespeople frequently need to entertain clients or customers. It is not necessary to be a comedian to joke and tell stories. This kind of informal speaking helps create a comfortable atmosphere, build friendships, and improve customer relations.

Using Your Voice and Nonverbal Cues

Good communicators use their voices effectively, modulating tone and pace to improve delivery. Some people, such as news or sports commentators, have a natural talent for delivery. With practice, you too can improve communication by better controlling your voice.

•TELEPHONE SKILLS Many of today's marketing jobs require the ability to communicate clearly over the telephone.

What are some advantages and disadvantages of telephone communication?

Other nonverbal cues that can enhance presentation are body language and eye contact. When speaking, maintain eye contact with your listeners as much as possible.

Speaking Formally

The general rules for effective speaking apply to all professional speaking. Whether the speech is used to present a marketing plan to the department or to give a speech to an audience of 500 people, the guidelines are the same. A good speech has a formal structure, or organization. It begins with an opening statement, which summarizes the topics to be covered. It ends with a concluding statement that reviews the main points. In between, four basic patterns can be used to structure the message.

Enumeration

Enumeration is listing items in order. This strategy is often used when giving directions or explaining a process with steps. Use

TEACH

Discussion Starter

USING YOUR VOICE AND NONVERBAL CUES

Ask students to consider the following scenario and share their answers to the corresponding questions in class: You are in charge of helping a candidate for public office improve his or her public speaking skills. What specific suggestions would you make regarding the modulation of tone or speed? What nonverbal cues would you recommend?

TEACHING POINTS

Clarify Bring a videotape of a speech, and point out the speaker's vocal strengths and use of nonverbal cues to enhance presentation. Consider announcements from the press and government.

Concept Development

SPEAKING FORMALLY

Ask students to watch commercials on TV and pay attention to whether the ads use one of the four strategies of formal speaking: enumeration, generalization, cause and effect, compare and contrast. Have them share their findings in class, and discuss which techniques are most popular and most effective.

PHOTO GUIDE   TELEPHONE SKILLS

Discussion Ask students if they ever receive marketing phone calls. Have them give general critiques about the calls they receive, noting the aspects of a bad or good sales call. Ask: Is there such thing as a good sales call?

Caption Answer An advantage of telephone communication is that parties can communicate instantaneously no matter where they are on the globe. Disadvantages include that the parties must be free at the same moment and that they cannot communicate nonverbally.

Follow Up Ask students why telemarketing companies often have a high employee turnover rate.

Individualized Math Skills

L1 Give students the following problem: If an audience of 500 students pays $7.50 each to hear a speech, what is the gross income?
$3,750; 500 × $7.50 = $3,750

L2 Give students the following problem: A campus events group has $10,000 remaining in its annual budget. If it books three speakers at $750 and two bands at $1,500, how much money will remain?
$4,750; $10,000 − ($750 × 3) − ($1,500 × 2) = $4,750

L3 Tell students that a public speaker will be paid $2,000 to give a commencement speech. Ask: If travel costs are $109 for plane tickets each way, two nights in a $149 hotel room, and $30 for a rental car, how much profit will the speaker net?
$1,454; $2,000 − ($109 × 2) − ($149 × 2) − $30 = $1,454

Concept Development

SPEAKING ON THE TELEPHONE

Inform students that talking on a cell phone while driving a car is illegal in many cities. Have students research the technological options for hands-free conversation and compile a list of devices with their prices and features. Ask: which devices do they recommend, and why?

Critical Thinking

Inform students that results of surveys and statistics can be twisted to give distorted views. Ask students to give examples of misleading statistics or generalizations.

---

signal words, such as *first, second, third,* or *next,* to help the listener. These signal words show the relationship between what you have already said and what you will say next.

Generalization with Examples

Many speakers use generalizations to make a point. A **generalization** is a statement that is accepted as true by most people. Speakers support generalizations with evidence and examples; this creates confidence in the listener. For example, when you make a general statement such as, "People agree that high definition television (HDTV) has great picture quality that's worth the added cost," you could support the claim with evidence such as, "In a Sony survey conducted in 2002, 80 percent of the HDTV owners surveyed said picture clarity is worth the higher price." Using evidence to support your generalizations also helps your listeners remember the main points. Signal words, such as *for instance* and *for example,* will help get your point across.

Case Study

Talking About Price

Selling successfully requires persuasive, informative, and entertaining speech. You must keep the purpose of your communication in mind, and organize your presentation to serve that purpose. It is essential to read the customer's body language and listen carefully to his or her needs.

The Five Ws and H

Prices for many goods and services are negotiable. A salesperson's communication skills are tested when it comes to negotiating price. Michelle Nichols, a well-known consultant on selling, reminds salespeople to remember the five Ws and H: who, what, when, where, why, and how.

- **Who** mentions price? Conventional wisdom is that the first person to mention price loses, but there are times when you have to break the ice. Practice different ways of broaching the topic.
- **What** is the price? Read your customer to decide at what price to begin negotiations. Start too high and he or she may lose interest. Too low, and you cut off potential profit.
- **When** is price mentioned? Mention price before the customer is sufficiently interested and he or she may walk away. Too late, and you may find he or she cannot afford it. You will have wasted your time. If the customer asks, it's the right time to begin discussing it.
- **Where** to talk about it? Where a sale can be completed. If you're selling cars, for example, wait until you're back in the office.
- **Why** mention it? Clearly, if you don't, there can be no sale.
- **How** to talk about it? Lightly, even with humor. If the customer is spending a significant amount, it will not help you to make him or her feel heavy or unhappy about it.

THINK STRATEGICALLY
Which of the five Ws and H is the most difficult and why?

@ Online Action! Go to *marketingessentials.glencoe.com/8/case* to find a research project on sales communication skills.

Case Study   Talking About Price

Discussion Have students read the Case Study and discuss the five Ws and H. Ask: In the students' experiences, do salespeople seem to heed Nichols' advice when they sell clothes, DVDs, electronic devices, or other items?

THINK STRATEGICALLY **Answer:** Answers will vary; students should give reasons for their choice of which of the five Ws and H is the most difficult.

@ Online Action! For instructions, ideas, and answer guide, go to the Teacher Center at **marketingessentials.glencoe.com**

Cause and Effect

When you present an issue in terms of cause and effect, you attempt to demonstrate that one event or situation is the cause of another. For example, you can show how implementing your marketing plan will allow the client to meet a sales goal. This pattern can be used effectively to persuade the listener. Use signal words or phrases, such as *therefore, consequently,* and *as a result* to help the listener understand the sequence.

Compare and Contrast

Another pattern often used to persuade a listener is compare and contrast. In this pattern, new concepts are explained by showing how they are similar to or unlike those listeners already know. This approach is particularly useful when working in cross-cultural situations. Signal words or phrases such as *similarly, however, nevertheless,* and *on the other hand,* help to make the differences and similarities clear.

Speaking on the Telephone

In most telephone conversations, your listener cannot see you, so you cannot rely on facial expressions and body language to help get your message across. The message is communicated solely by voice, so a pleasant voice is very important.

Whether answering or initiating the call, greet the other person in a cheerful but formal way. For example, you might say, "Customer Relations, this is Maria. How may I help you?" This greeting signals to the caller that he or she has reached the right number. Use a pleasant tone, enunciate clearly, and speak directly into the mouthpiece. Speak loudly enough for the other person to hear, but do not shout. Be courteous and respectful, and never interrupt when the other person is speaking.

It is also necessary that you convey all the necessary information. It may be a good idea to write down key points before a phone call. Telephone customer service representatives and telemarketers use scripts.

Be prepared to take a message. Note the time of the call, the caller's name and message,

and the return phone number. Repeat the telephone number to the caller to make sure it is correct. Most companies make use of voice mail so that callers may leave a message when the person is unavailable.

Writing

Much business and marketing communication is in written form. A written message is necessary when there is a large volume of material and presenting it verbally would be impractical. Writing is also necessary when a permanent record of the communication is required. For instance, legal documents, manuals describing company policy, and letters confirming the terms of a deal are all written.

Writing takes more time and thought than a conversation. One advantage of writing a message rather than speaking it is that there is more time to organize the message. There are different forms of business writing—e-mail, letters, reports—each with specific uses and conventions. Marketing writing takes many forms, including print ads, scripts, and packaging.

Basic Considerations in Writing

As with listening, reading, and speaking, it is important when writing to know the precise reason for the message. The three basic considerations in writing are:

1. **Know your audience** Before you begin writing, think about who will receive your message. What do you know about them? Do they have the same experiences as you? Why will they read your message? What do they know about the subject? Answering these questions will help you to write a meaningful message.
2. **Know your purpose** Why are you writing? Most of your marketing writing is done to inform, confirm, inquire, answer, or persuade. Marketing messages are often written to persuade. Some messages, of course, combine two or more of these purposes.
3. **Know your subject** To write effective messages, you need in-depth knowledge and you must know how to relate what

TEACH CONTINUED

Concept Development

BASIC CONSIDERATIONS IN WRITING

Ask students to think of three potential audiences for written communication. (For example, letter of recommendation to a colleague's potential employer, an article for an academic journal, or an e-mail to a friend.) Have them explain how the tone, references, and style of writing would be adjusted for each audience.

TEACHING POINTS

Demonstrate Choose a well-known and well-documented public figure such as Martin Luther King, Jr. or Winston Churchill, and compare his or her published personal letters to his or her public speeches. You might also use contemporary public figures and compare comments made during informal interviews with written essays or speeches.

 Extended Activity

Understanding Audiences
Have students create a list of television shows. They should mix variety, news, comedies, sports, and other programming. Then ask students to list which of the purposes of speech each program has: to inform, to persuade, or to entertain. Does the class agree? Can there be a mixture? Instruct speakers to think about the purpose of speech on a daily basis.

 Extended Activity

Practice Communication
Assign the following roles to students: a businessperson talking to potential client and a businessperson talking to a customer who owes money; a musician talking between songs during a concert and a musician talking to her lawyer; an athlete talking to opponents during a game and an athlete talking to coach during practice. Have student pairs volunteer to act out these role plays in class. Have the class suggest which of the situations in these role plays might benefit from a written component.

TEACH CONTINUED

Concept Development

DEVELOPING A WRITING STYLE

Inform students that different businesses will have different writing styles. For example, a financial services business' press release will have a very different tone than a record company's announcement about a new CD. Ask students why they think the tones would be different.

Different tones appeal to different audiences.

TEACHING POINTS

Demonstrate Bring in a tabloid and a financial magazine to show the class. Compare headlines, lead sentences, and tone.

Clarify While some businesses will be more casual in their writing than others, it should be reinforced that proper grammar and spelling are important in all situations.

 Online Activity

Writing to Persuade

Ask students to investigate the Web sites of nonprofit organizations such as Greenpeace, The Red Cross, or Save the Manatees. Ask: How does the writing on these sites persuade those who view the site to become involved? What techniques are used? Have students share their findings in class.

MARKET TECH

Push-to-Talk Marketing

Following the popularity of push-to-talk buttons on cell phones, another push-to-talk technology is now in use in marketing.

Technology company eStara offers VoIP (Voice over Internet Protocol) service, allowing users to respond verbally to printed communication. A customer can click on a button on a Web page and initiate a live conversation using his or her Internet connection.

On-Demand Live Service

Another option is for the user to key in his or her phone number and click the same button to receive a call back from a customer service employee. The technology is gaining popularity with marketers who can no longer make unsolicited calls to consumers as a result of legislation restricting telemarketing.

Testing Banner Ads

The VoIP service also allows advertisers to test the effectiveness of Web banner ads, based on how many calls they generate. In one survey of customers using the technology to buy something online, 25 percent said they would have quit the transaction if they hadn't had the push-to-talk option.

THINK LIKE A MARKETER

Why is it a plus for marketers to be able to move from a written communication like Web advertising or e-mail to an actual conversation?

@ Online Action!

Go to *marketingessentials.glencoe.com/ 8/tech* to find a project on VoIP technology.

you know to what the customer wants to know. You may be well educated on certain subjects, but almost every new assignment will require further research.

Developing a Writing Style

Writing style differs from industry to industry. The executives of a company generally establish the company's writing style, which usually includes guidelines on when to use formal and informal communication. You can read company letters, official e-mail, memos, and reports to gain a feel for how the firm wishes to present itself to its clients.

In business writing, it is generally best to use a direct yet respectful conversational style. Whether writing to inquire, inform, or persuade, your writing should be crisp, clear, and easy to read. Be professional in tone, but do not use big words to impress others. Use a word processing program with spelling and grammar checkers to eliminate common errors. Always review your writing one final time to ensure that all errors are corrected. If you have a tendency to overlook minor mistakes, ask a colleague to proofread your work.

Personalize your message by using the name of the person who will receive it. The receiver will have a warmer feeling toward you if you do. When writing to someone outside your company, be formal until you have permission to be more informal and personal in your writing.

You may want to use jargon in your messages to people in your professional field. However, when writing to a mixed audience, it is best to avoid jargon. If jargon is necessary, clearly define any technical words.

Use Language Effectively

Pay attention to the words and phrases used by your clients, vendors, and associates. If they are different from the ones you generally use, translate your ideas and feelings into language that makes sense to them. Using the words and phrases familiar to your audience in your communications can be a powerful persuasive technique.

marketingessentials.glencoe.com

MARKET TECH

Push-to-Talk Marketing

Discussion After students read Market Tech, lead a discussion about why it might be better to have customers initiate conversations with marketers rather than have marketers initiate conversations with customers.

 THINK LIKE A MARKETER Answer: Verbal communication is more persuasive than written communication because it is generally easier to listen than read. Also, if the verbal communication is in person or over the telephone, a speaker can listen to feedback and adjust his or her presentation.

@ Online Action! For instructions, ideas, and answer guide, go to the Teacher Center at marketingessentials.glencoe.com

Organize Your Thoughts

Construct your persuasive message in three parts: an opening paragraph, a persuasive body, and a concluding paragraph. In the opening paragraph, grab your readers' attention. State clearly why you are writing and involve them in some way, perhaps addressing them as *you* if appropriate.

Begin each body paragraph with a topic sentence. Follow with three to five sentences in which you develop a single point. Use connectives, such as *therefore* and *so you see*. Ethical writing requires honesty, so be sure to acknowledge any significant point of view that may differ from your own. There is nothing wrong with presenting evidence showing that your view is more likely to result in the desired outcome. If you can, quote a recognized expert or survey to add support for your case. Try to create a vivid image to help your reader see your point of view.

Your concluding paragraph should be positive and interesting and should strongly support the message outlined in your introduction. Restate the points made in the body, citing the evidence in support of each point. Emphasize the overall reason your position, product, or service is worth considering. Finally, state exactly what action should be taken next to achieve the mutually acceptable outcome.

Forms of Written Communication

Most business writing takes the form of letters, e-mail, memos, and reports. Each of these formats follows its own very specific rules of style and format.

Letters

Communication with people outside the company is usually done with business letters or e-mail. Letters are the more formal of the two. They are used for purposes such as official announcements, thank yous, and confirmations of business transactions. In direct-mail marketing, targeted letters are often written addressing the needs or interests of specific groups.

E-Mail

E-mail has become the method of choice for fast, informal communication with those inside and outside the company. Marketers often use e-mail for informal contacts between the firm and the client. E-mail has the advantage of speed over other forms of written communication. With e-mail, documents can be attached to, or sent along with, the message.

A MATTER OF ETHICS

Ethics in Communication

In cases where others are affected, the writer or speaker has an ethical responsibility to make sure the message is clear and understood.

Suppose you supervise a large car manufacturing company with many different departments. You ask the engineering department to send you a memo evaluating recent complaints about a possible manufacturing defect in one model. You also ask for a recommendation for action.

Targeting Questions and Answers

The engineering department sends you a detailed report with a lot of objective data on the different components of the car but no recommendation for action. Three weeks later, you receive several reports of fatal injuries in accidents involving the same car model and the same car parts.

THINKING ETHICALLY

Does this engineering department bear any responsibility in this lack of communication? Why or why not?

@ Online Action!

Go to *marketingessentials.glencoe.com/8/ethics* to find a project on communication and ethics.

---

 marketingessentials.glencoe.com

Individualized Practice

FORMS OF WRITTEN COMMUNICATION

L1 Ask students to explain why e-mail has become the method of choice for fast, informal communication in the business world.

Answers will vary, but may include that e-mail is received almost instantaneously, saves postage costs, can be sent at any hour, and is easily kept on record.

L2 Have students explain why letters are still the favored format for official announcements, "thank yous", and confirmations of business transactions.

Answers will vary, but may include the more formal feel of paper communication and the feeling of permanency that e-mails do not have. Letters are also more secure.

L3 Ask students to discuss potential drawbacks of e-mail.

Answers may include accidental erasure, easy forwarding, easy inclusion of errors, occasional corruption, accidental deletion, and security issues.

Enrichment

E-MAIL POLICIES

Ask students to research why many companies have strict e-mail policies. Encourage students to identify the reasons for these common rules:

- Save only essential e-mail.
  E-mail can quickly build up and take up hard drive space.

- Do not forward e-mail without the sender's expressed permission.
  Personal messages may not be meant for others.

- Seek permission and use extreme care when forwarding confidential e-mails.
  Company messages are often not meant for outside release.

A MATTER OF ETHICS — Ethics in Communication

Discussion Lead a discussion on the topic by asking whether people consider the effect of their work on others. Ask students how this consideration relates to ethics.

THINKING ETHICALLY **Answer:** Answers will vary; students may suggest that the supervisor should have followed up on the engineering department's report and asked whether the car should be recalled or not.

@ Online Action! For instructions, ideas, and answer guide, go to the Teacher Center at marketingessentials.glencoe.com

Follow Up Divide students into two groups and have them debate whether the engineering department should be held responsible for the fatal injuries.

ASSESS

Review Guide

CONCEPTS

Ask students to describe the four basic patterns for formal speeches and give examples of each.

Answers should include definitions and examples of enumeration, generalization with examples, cause and effect, and compare and contrast.

KEY TERMS

Have students review key terms and write a sentence for each using them in context.

ONLINE SELF-ASSESSMENT

Have students go to marketingessentials.glencoe.com for the Section 8.2 practice test.

Individualized Review

L1 Assign and review Chapter 8 activities in the Student Activity Workbook.

L2 Assign and review Chapter 8 activities in the Marketing Math Workbook.

L3 Assign and Review Chapter 8 activities in the *BusinessWeek* Reader and Case Studies.

Marketing Practice

Form students into small groups. Assign each group simple statements such as "people should eat more fruit" or "pets are good" or approve any statements that students propose. Give the groups 10 to 15 minutes to create an oral presentation using one or more of the patterns of formal speech. Have groups give their presentations to the class, which should identify the patterns used and rate their effectiveness.

While e-mail norms differ from company to company, a typical interoffice e-mail contains the following:

- An informative subject title
- A traditional (not personal) greeting
- A concise, clearly stated body
- A statement regarding the type of response needed
- A formal closing and signature (for the signature, type your name, company, address, phone and fax number, and e-mail address)

Although e-mail has a reputation for speed and informality, it is important to remember that, like all written communication, it leaves a permanent record. Business e-mails are official documents. They are the property of the company or firm.

Many companies now have strict e-mail policies. The following rules are found in most e-mail policies:

- Save only essential e-mail.
- Do not forward e-mail without the sender's express permission.
- Seek permission and then use extreme care when forwarding confidential e-mails.
- Use only copyrighted materials that you have permission, or have paid, to use.

When writing business e-mail, follow the guidelines for business writing described above. Compose your messages carefully. Use conventional business language and style. Use the company computer only for business communication, not for private messages.

Memos

A memorandum, or memo, is a written message to someone in the company. It is usually brief and covers only one subject. Most memos are written in a simple format that has a standard set of headings. The standard headings include the sender's and receiver's names, the date, the subject, and a message in paragraph form. In many businesses, e-mail has taken the place of memos.

Business Reports

Business reports usually cover lengthy topics, such as yearly sales, survey results, or problems that need attention. Some, called in-house reports, are meant to be read only by company employees. Others, such as reports to stockholders, are written for a wider audience and are more formal. An in-house report can be written by a company department to let management know the results of a project, or a report might move from one department to another. For example, the sales department may produce a report to tell the design department how customers like a product. Several people may give input to produce the report, but one person is usually responsible for writing the final document.

Many of the techniques used in preparing a speech are also appropriate in preparing a report. Enumeration, generalization with example, cause and effect, and compare and contrast are patterns of organization that work well for reports. A simple report can be brief, perhaps as short as one page. Complex reports include more data and may use a variety of charts and graphs.

Company Publications

Many companies produce internal publications for their employees. These might be newsletters or employee handbooks that outline policies and procedures. Some companies produce external publications, such as promotional brochures about the company or individual products. A communications department usually writes internal publications, while a marketing department writes external publications.

Meetings and Parliamentary Procedure

Parliamentary procedure is a structure for holding group meetings (such as DECA's) and making decisions. Parliamentary procedure favors the opinion of the majority of a group, but the viewpoint of the minority is not overlooked. Parliamentary procedure has a specific structure.

Extended Activity

Meetings and Parliamentary Procedure

Ask students if they perceive parliamentary procedure to be an awkward structure that might actually get in the way of communication rather than streamlining or enabling communication. Have them develop variations on the rules or make new rules for running meetings. Ask students to make guidelines for their systems and share them with the class. Encourage them to try using their systems at campus organization meetings.

A Quorum

A quorum is a proportion of the membership needed to conduct official business. It may be a set number of members, like 20, or a percentage of members, like 51 percent.

Order of Business

The meeting follows a standard order of business, which is called an agenda. The standard format for a meeting is as follows

1. **Call to order** This statement alerts all members that the meeting is beginning and that they should be quiet.
2. **Minutes of the meeting** The secretary reads the minutes, which are a written record that outlines the decisions made at the last meeting.
3. **Treasurer's report** The treasurer reports the money that the organization received since the last meeting and the money it spent, as well as the current balance.
4. **Committee reports** Each committee presents a report to let the entire membership know what they have done and what they plan to do.
5. **Old business** Any issues that were discussed but were not decided on become old business.
6. **New business** New ideas are brought up at the end of the meeting.
7. **Adjournment** This is the official end of the meeting. The secretary records the time of adjournment in the minutes.

The Motion

After being allowed to speak by the chairperson, one member makes a motion, or a proposal. Another member must second the motion. A period of discussion follows.

8.2 AFTER YOU READ

Reviewing Key Terms and Concepts

1. Name the three most common purposes for speaking, and give an example of how each can be applied in a business situation.
2. What are three basic considerations in writing an effective message?
3. What is the difference between persuading and influencing?

Integrating Academic Skills

Mathematics

4. Communication on the Internet travels at the speed of light—186,000 miles per second. The Earth is approximately 8,000 miles in diameter. How long would it take an e-mail to circle the Earth one time? Round your answer to the nearest one-thousandth of a second.

Social Studies

5. Identify a political issue that is being debated at the local, state, or national level. Write a letter to persuade your government representative to vote for or against the issue. Construct your letter using the three parts outlined in your text.

@ Online Action!
Check your answers at *marketingessentials.glencoe.com/8/read*

marketingessentials.glencoe.com

CLOSE

Ask students to recall and list answers to the following questions:

- **What is the four-step plan for training?**

  1.) Explain the task that is to be performed. 2.) Demonstrate how to perform the task. 3.) Let the trainee try doing the task. 4.) Provide a critique that explains what he or she did correctly.

- **What are the common company policies regarding e-mail?**

  Save only essential e-mail, do not forward e-mail without the sender's permission, seek permission and then use extreme care when forwarding confidential e-mails, use only copyrighted materials that you have permission, or have paid, to use.

Online Activity

Research Businesses

Ask students to look online for business reports of large companies and share their results. Such reports may include profits, expansion, and number of employees. Ask: Why might a company post such information for the public to see online? Answers might include in order to communicate with potential investors.

AFTER YOU READ

Reviewing Key Terms and Concepts

1. Three common purposes are to inform, to persuade, to entertain. Examples will vary.

2. Three basic considerations in writing an effective message are know your reader, know your purpose, and know your subject.

3. Persuading is the process of getting others to do what you want them to do. Influencing is getting others to consider your message as they make a decision.

Integrating Academic Skills

4. $\pi \times 8{,}000 \div 186{,}000 = 0.135$ seconds

5. Letters will vary; all letters should include the salutation, body, and closing.

@ Online Action! Answers at **marketingessentials.glencoe.com/8/read**

CAREERS IN MARKETING

Lifelong Learning

CAREER INFORMATION

Have students go to marketingessentials.glencoe.com and find the Chapter 8 Careers page and click on the link for the American Marketing Association's Careers Strategies and Tips. Ask students to select one article, read it, and summarize it in three short paragraphs.

COMMUNICATION SKILLS

Speech, debate, and drama groups or classes can allow students and others to experience the range of emotions public speaking can elicit and can teach different speaking techniques, such as elocution. Many find that this practice leads to increased comfort when they are speaking in front of a group.

Primary Source

Ask students to go to marketingessentials.glencoe.com and find Chapter 8 Resources. Ask them to click on the link for the American Marketing Association's marketing dictionary and find and read the definitions of the communications-related terms they find.

THINKING CRITICALLY

Answers will vary; students might suggest that respect for others and the ability to communicate with and satisfy the needs of many different types of clients requires diplomacy.

@ Online Action!

For instructions, ideas, and answer guide, go to the Teacher Center at marketingessentials.glencoe.com

---

CAREERS IN MARKETING

MARIAN DOUGLAS PEARCE, APR, CCC
ACCOUNT EXECUTIVE
SEMAPHORE, INC.

? What do you do at work?
I spend a considerable amount of my time talking to clients on the phone, in meetings, or via e-mail. After determining their needs, I develop a marketing plan to achieve their goals and objectives. I collaborate with the creative team (an art director and copywriter) to develop the product (ad, billboard, etc.) that best suits their needs. I also am responsible for creating project and annual marketing budgets and account administration tasks such as billing, filing, and supplier coordination.

? What skills are most important to you?
Time management skills, organization, and diplomacy. If I were not organized, I could not keep up with all the projects we have in the agency at one time. An account executive must be diplomatic when it comes to giving the client what they want but giving them what they need to accomplish their goals. I recommend learning the basics of all integrated marketing communications. I received my undergraduate degree in advertising and public relations management and minored in marketing. Training in business administration basics such as accounting will help you understand the budgeting and billing processes that are a daily part of an account executive's routine. And training in presentation skills is a must.

? What is your key to success?
I treat my clients the way that I would like to be treated. I respect them and their ideas because they intrinsically know their business better than I can ever know.

Aptitudes, Abilities, and Skills

Organization, strong interpersonal skills, diplomacy, the ability to manage and wisely use resources

Education and Training

Degrees in marketing, communication, and general business courses.

Career Path

Account executives can be recruited from within. As an entry-level sales position, account executive jobs are usually paid on a commission-only basis. Established account executives are often in high demand.

THINKING CRITICALLY

Why is diplomacy such an important skill in this career?

Online Action!

Go to *marketingessentials.glencoe.com/8/ careers* to find a career-related activity.

Test-Taking Strategies

Encourage students to read test questions carefully before writing an answer to be sure that they understand the intent. Determining exactly what the test-giver wants to assess will increase students' chance of giving the right answer. Point out to students that strategies for being a good listener can also be helpful in test taking. For example, identifying the purpose of a question can help you understand what the test-giver is looking for.

FOCUS on KEY POINTS

SECTION 8.1

● The global economy has brought new pressures on companies to communicate with customers and vendors around the world. Overcoming cultural barriers to listening with understanding is now more important than ever.

● As the volume of information to be absorbed increases, reading for meaning—the ability to differentiate what is important from what is not—is becoming an important business skill.

SECTION 8.2

● Most business and marketing jobs require the ability to communicate a message clearly, concisely, and courteously by speaking and writing.

● Persuasion is used to convince others of the value or importance of an idea or thing—an essential skill in marketing. The simplest and often most effective way to persuade others is to learn their needs and propose a way to fulfill them.

REVIEW VOCABULARY

Define each of the following terms in a short sentence.

1. communication (p. 178)
2. channels/media (p. 179)
3. feedback (p. 179)
4. barriers (p. 179)
5. setting (p. 179)
6. distractions (p. 182)
7. emotional barriers (p. 182)
8. jargon (p. 183)
9. persuade (p. 185)
10. enumeration (p. 185)
11. generalization (p. 186)

REVIEW FACTS and IDEAS

12. List three examples of barriers to listening (8.1)
13. Explain three ways to improve listening skills. (8.1)
14. Why is it important for businesspeople to be aware of cultural differences? (8.1)
15. What three techniques will help you read for understanding? (8.1)
16. List three professional telephone skills. (8.2)
17. Explain the different uses of letters, e-mail, memos, and reports. (8.2)
18. What are the three basic considerations in business writing? (8.2)
19. Describe a method of organizing and presenting your ideas. (8.2)

Chapter 8 - Communication Skills 193

REVIEW FACTS and IDEAS

12. Barriers to communication include distractions, emotional blocks, and planning a response.

13. Ways to improve listening skills should include three of the following: Identify the purpose, look for a plan, give feedback, search for a common interest, evaluate the message, listen for more than verbal content, listen for a conclusion and take notes.

14. Businesspeople need to be aware of cultural differences to ensure good communication.

15. The three techniques to help you read for understanding are focusing your mind, forming pictures, and improving your vocabulary.

16. Answers may include three of the following skills: a cheerful but formal greeting indicating the caller has reached the right number, a pleasant tone, clear enunciation, careful listening, and accurate message taking.

17. Letters are used to communicate with people outside the company. E-mail is the method of choice for fast, informal communication to people inside or outside the company. Memos are usually brief, cover only one subject, and are sent within a company. Business reports cover lengthy topics such as yearly sales, survey reports, or problems that need attention.

18. The three basic considerations are know your reader, know your purpose, and know your subject.

19. Answers will vary; possible answers include: Formal speaking, in which the speaker uses enumeration, generalization, cause and effect, or compare and contrast to persuade the listener; an e-mail message, including a greeting, one or more paragraphs explaining the point, outlining the necessary response, and a formal closing; or a letter, containing an opening paragraph, a persuasive body, and a concluding paragraph.

FOCUS on KEY POINTS

Ask students to read the summaries aloud and have volunteers restate each point in their own words in class.

REVIEW VOCABULARY

See glossary for definitions of **1–11.**
A sample answer might read:

1. *Communication* is the process of exchanging messages between a sender and a receiver.

BUILD SKILLS

20. Workplace Skills
Presentations will vary, but should include specific examples of how body language, tone, and mannerisms affect communication.

21. Technology Applications
E-mails will vary, but should include saving only essential e-mail, not forwarding e-mail without the sender's permission, seeking permission and then using extreme care when forwarding confidential e-mails, and using only copyrighted materials that you have permission, or have paid, to use.

22. Math Practice
It will cost $1,040; $200 + $150 + ($15 × 46) = $1,040

DEVELOP CRITICAL THINKING

23. Following Directions
Situations will vary; students should realize that being a better listener can help one accomplish tasks more accurately.

24. Communicating in Person
Answers will vary; students may suggest that despite advances in computers and technology, people still need the personal touch.

BUILD SKILLS

20. Workplace Skills
Public Speaking Using presentation software or visual aids, prepare a five-to-ten-minute presentation on how body language, tone, and mannerisms affect communication.

21. Technology Applications
Writing Effective E-Mails Imagine that employees at your work have been using company e-mail to send personal or social messages.

Use an e-mail or word processing program to compose an e-mail memo that instructs employees on the appropriate use of interoffice e-mail.

22. Math Practice
Determine Costs You have been asked to make the arrangements for a conference meeting for your company. A local conference center charges $150 to rent a room for a half day and $200 to rent a room for a full day. They charge $15.00 per person for each lunch served and $30.00 per person for each dinner served.

How much will it cost to rent the facility for one and one-half days and to provide lunch for 46 conference attendees on the first day?

DEVELOP CRITICAL THINKING

23. Following Directions
Describe a situation where you have had to follow directions to complete a task. Explain how you listened to the instructions (or read them) and how you made sure to follow each step.

List three ways improving your listening skills could help you accomplish tasks at school or at work?

24. Communicating in Person
Even though high-tech communication channels are available, many businesspeople still prefer face-to-face meetings for important transactions. Explain why you think businesspeople in your culture and other cultures might sometimes prefer to communicate in person.

 Formative Assessment

Formative assessment is an essential component of classroom work. This type of assessment provides information that is then used as feedback to modify teaching and meet student needs.

L1 Have students write or demonstrate the patterns used to organize a formal speech.

L2 Ask students to state the difference between persuading and influencing someone, and then give an example.

L3 Have students write a memo about the proper use of phones on the job.

 Reteach **If the results of this formative assessment seem low, consider the following activity:**

Read each of the key terms aloud. Have students define the key terms and use them in a sentence. Clear up any confusion students may have.

APPLY CONCEPTS

25. Prepare a Business Letter

Your high school debate team is having a raffle. The money from the raffle will be used to send your team to district, state, and national debate tournaments.

Activity Use a word processing program to write a business letter from your high school debate club to local business owners soliciting donations for your annual raffle.

26. Research Public Speaking

Use the Internet to research Toastmasters International, an organization for public speakers. Describe how its logo communicates its goals. Lists the four skills this organization will help you develop or strengthen.

Activity Use a graphic-design or word-processing program to create a brochure to persuade your classmates that membership in this organization will benefit them.

NET SAVVY

27. The Internet and Government

Do an Internet search to discover what the U.S. government is doing to fight spam, or unwanted e-mail, on the Internet. Write a brief report on your findings. Then use the Web to find the e-mail addresses of the senators from your state. Send them an e-mail expressing your view on the issue.

THE DECA CONNECTION

Role Play: Customer Service

Situation You are to assume the role of assistant manager of an online business that specializes in antique prints, matting, and custom framing. Your customers have the choice of using your toll-free phone line or communicating by e-mail. You do business through the business's Web site. The business's owner (judge) has just received an e-mail from one of your best customers requesting that you look for a special print to add to an existing collection.

Activity Compose an e-mail response to the customer for the owner's (judge's) approval.

Evaluation You will be evaluated on how well you meet the following performance indicators:

- Write business letters
- Use communications technologies/systems (e.g., e-mail, faxes, voice mail, cell phones, etc.)
- Explain the nature of written communications
- Handle customer inquiries
- Demonstrate a customer-service mindset

 Online Action!

For more information and DECA Prep practice, go to *marketingessentials.glencoe .com/8/DECA*

CHAPTER **8** REVIEW

APPLY CONCEPTS

25. Prepare a Business Letter
Business letters will vary and should be polite, well-organized, and have proper spelling and grammar.

26. Research Public Speaking
Brochures will vary and should include four skills that Toastmasters will help members develop or strengthen.

NET SAVVY

27. The Internet and Government
Findings and e-mails regarding spam will vary but might include the following elements: an informative subject title; a traditional (not personal) greeting; a concise, clearly stated body; a statement regarding the type of response needed, and a formal closing and signature.

THE DECA CONNECTION

The students should be evaluated on the performance indicators noted in the role play. For another DECA role play, go to the Competitive Events Workbook or the Student Activity Workbook, or go to **marketingessentials.glencoe.com/8/DECA**

 Online Action! For instructions, ideas, and answer guide, go to the Teacher Center at **marketingessentials.glencoe.com**

DECA Advisors Corner

To make your fundraising projects more meaningful to your students, give them a personal incentive: Establish individual DECA accounts for each chapter member. Funds earned into that student's account should be used for chapter activities. Funds can cover part of the cost of a conference or field trip.

MINI-QUIZ

Read these sentences to the students and have them volunteer the missing word(s).

1. The substance of any communication is the _____ . (message)

2. In job-related reading, you may come across _____, specialized vocabulary used by members of a particular group. (jargon)

3. A _____ is a proportion of a business' membership needed to conduct official business. (quorum)

For an expanded chapter quiz, go to Chapter 8 in the TeacherWorks CD-ROM and to Chapter 8 in the **Exam***View*® Pro Test Generator CD-ROM.

Chapter Overview

Chapter 9 focuses computers and common software applications that are used in business and marketing. This chapter also discusses both current and anticipated uses of specialized computer technology in marketing.

BUILD BACKGROUND

Discuss with students the abundance of pop-up ads encountered when surfing the Web. Why do they think there are so many? Talk about the power of the Web as a marketing tool, and how it allows people to respond immediately to ads or information.

Why It's Important

Every person who works in marketing (or other forms of business) will probably use computers as a tool. Likewise, every person who uses technology is subject to marketing, from internet pop-up ads to spam or mailed ads to customer profiling from retailing outlets.

Prepare to Read

Ask a volunteer to write all of the major headings in this Chapter on the board in outline format. Tell students to fill in the secondary (blue) headings as they preview or read the chapter. They will then have a thorough chapter outline to use as study notes.

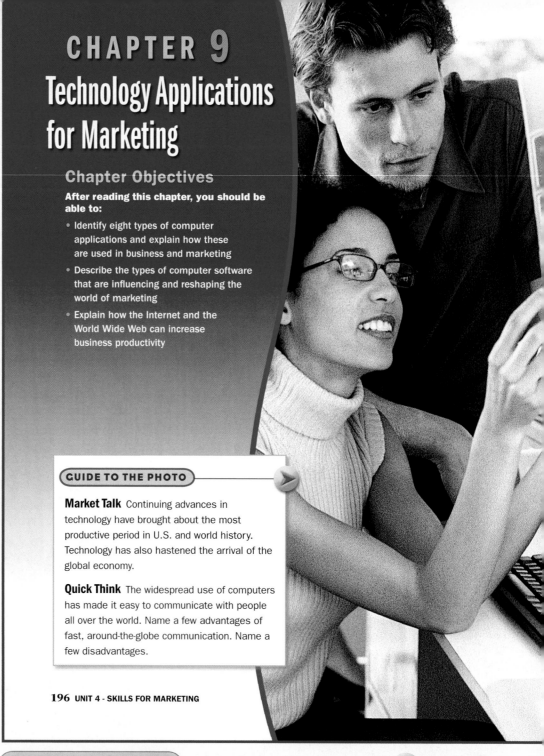

CHAPTER 9
Technology Applications for Marketing

Chapter Objectives

After reading this chapter, you should be able to:

- Identify eight types of computer applications and explain how these are used in business and marketing
- Describe the types of computer software that are influencing and reshaping the world of marketing
- Explain how the Internet and the World Wide Web can increase business productivity

GUIDE TO THE PHOTO

Market Talk Continuing advances in technology have brought about the most productive period in U.S. and world history. Technology has also hastened the arrival of the global economy.

Quick Think The widespread use of computers has made it easy to communicate with people all over the world. Name a few advantages of fast, around-the-globe communication. Name a few disadvantages.

196 UNIT 4 - SKILLS FOR MARKETING

GUIDE TO THE PHOTO

Market Talk Lead a discussion about how computers and technology have affected marketing and business during the students' lifetime. Examples may include ATMs, downloadable movie trailers, commercials in supermarket lines, and music videos being played at the end of television programs.

Quick Think Student responses may include increased competition, inaccuracy, and reduced face-to-face interaction.

Follow Up Ask students if they can think of places where people are not subject to marketing.

Performance indicators represent key skills and knowledge. Relating them to the concepts explained in this chapter is your key to success in DECA events.

These acronyms represent DECA events that involve knowledge of concepts in this chapter.

AAAL	FMAL	MMS	TMDM*
AAML	FMDM	QSRM	TSE
ADC	FMML	RMAL	VPM
BSM*	FSRM	RMML	
EMDM	HMDM*	SMDM*	

In all these DECA events you should be able to follow these performance indicators:

- Use communication technologies/systems
- Describe ethical considerations in providing information
- Identify ways that technology impacts business
- Demonstrate basic word processing skills
- Demonstrate basic presentation software skills
- Demonstrate basic database skills
- Demonstrate basic spreadsheet skills
- Demonstrate basic search skills on the Web
- Explain how technology impacts the industry

Events with an asterisk (*) also include:

- Use check authorization system

Some events include other indicators:

EMDM   Explain the nature of the Internet
Use e-mail functions
Demonstrate basic desktop publishing
Integrate software applications
Create and post a Web page
Describe tools used in Web site creation
Explain basic programming languages
Select a Web host

DECA PREP

Check your understanding of DECA performance indicators with the DECA activity in this chapter's review. For more information and DECA Prep practice, go to *marketingessentials.glencoe.com/9/DECA*

DECA events that require knowledge of technology applications for marketing are described here. Discuss the performance indicators to make sure students understand how to demonstrate their understanding.

The events acronyms stand for:

AAAL: Apparel and Accessories Marketing Series, AL

AAML: Apparel and Accessories Marketing Series, ML

ADC: Advertising Campaign Event

BSM: Business Services Marketing Series

EMDM: E-Commerce Management Team Decision Making Event

FMAL: Food Marketing Series, AL

FMDM: Financial Analysis Management Team Decision Making Event

FMML: Food Marketing Series, ML

FSRM: Full Service Restaurant Management Series

HMDM: Hospitality Services Management Team Decision Making Event

MMS: Marketing Management Series

QSRM: Quick Serve Restaurant Management Series

RMAL: Retail Merchandising Series, AL

RMML: Retail Merchandising Series, ML

SMDM: Sports and Entertainment Marketing Management Team Decision Making Event

TMDM: Travel and Tourism Marketing Management Team Decision Making Event

TSE: Technical Sales Event

VPM: Vehicles and Petroleum Marketing Series

DECA PREP

Find timed DECA prep activities correlated to the Competitive Events Workbook for students and DECA tips for teachers at **marketingessentials.glencoe.com/9/DECA**

CHAPTER 9   Classroom Resources

For the Teacher

- TeacherWorks
- marketingessentials.glencoe.com
- Interactive Chalkboard
- **Exam**View® Pro Test Generator
- Fast File Unit 4

For the Student

- *Marketing Essentials* Online Edition
- Student Activity Workbook
- Marketing Math Workbook
- Marketing Research Project Workbook
- School-to-Work Activity Workbook
- Competitive Events Workbook
- *BusinessWeek* Reader and Case Studies
- marketingessentials.glencoe.com

SECTION 9.1

FOCUS

Introducing the Section

COLLABORATIVE ACTIVITY

To prepare for reading this section, have students think of different types of marketing projects. Examples may include billboard campaigns, skywriting, television commercials, and other forms of marketing. Have them discuss ways computers are involved in each, such as design and correspondence.

Preteaching Key Terms

Read the key terms aloud, or ask a volunteer to read them. Ask students to use each term in a sentence.

- word processing programs
- database programs
- spreadsheet programs
- desktop publishing programs
- graphics and design programs
- presentation software
- home page
- hypertext markup language (HTML)
- communications programs

Tell students they can check their understanding of the concepts as they read the section.

OBJECTIVES

- Identify eight types of computer applications and explain how these are used in business and marketing

KEY TERMS

- word processing programs
- database programs
- spreadsheet programs
- desktop publishing programs
- graphics and design programs
- presentation software
- home page
- hypertext markup language (HTML)
- communications programs

Computer Applications

READ and STUDY

BEFORE YOU READ

Predict Are computers necessary for a marketing project to be successful?

THE MAIN IDEA

Your career success will probably require an understanding and skillful use of computers and of certain key software applications.

STUDY ORGANIZER

In a chart like the one below, note the eight types of software discussed in this section.

Computer Program	Uses
Word processing program	Letters and memos

WHILE YOU READ

Connect Name three computer applications you use often.

Types of Applications

There is a computer application for just about every purpose you can imagine. For personal use, daily planner and calendar applications manage time, and financial software manages money. Some applications serve as address books, while others help manage photos. Virtually all businesses use computer applications. Medical practices use programs to schedule patients and

READ and STUDY

BEFORE YOU READ

Lead students in discussing the importance of computers in marketing. Stress that even in the most non-technological marketing project, computers are probably used for planning via e-mail or doing research online.

THE MAIN IDEA

Ask a volunteer to read the main idea aloud and ask another student to retell it in his or her own words.

STUDY ORGANIZER

Model the study organizer for students by filling in one type of software and its uses. A full-size, downloadable study organizer can be found at marketingessentials.glencoe.com

 WHILE YOU READ Have students take note of the three computer applications they use most often and look for them as they read through the section.

track billing. Hotels use applications to manage room assignments and generate bills.

Software is constantly being written, tested, and marketed to meet every conceivable business need.

Word Processing Programs

Word processing programs are software applications designed to create documents that are primarily text but that may contain a few graphics. The benefits of a word processing program include being able to determine the format of a document and see on screen exactly how the document will look when printed out. This is called WYSIWYG, for "What You See Is What You Get." Word processing programs also help correct mistakes in spelling and grammar, give accurate word counts, and add design elements, among dozens of other features. The most common word processing program is Microsoft Word. Others include WordPerfect, Nisus Writer Express, and Mariner Write. Businesses use word processing programs to

- Write letters and memos
- Produce research papers and reports
- Develop business and marketing plans
- Write contracts
- Take notes and record meeting minutes
- Create announcements

Database Programs

Database programs are applications that store and organize information. They are like filing cabinets, but with much greater flexibility. Database programs allow users to sort, find, choose (or filter), and organize information. A single database can hold information about the products a company sells, the orders the company has received, shipments of those products, and its customers. The power of a database is its ability to link that information together. Database software ranks among the most popular business applications. Common database software includes Filemaker Pro, Microsoft Access, 4D, and Oracle. Marketers use database programs to

- Maintain customer lists for automated mass mailings
- Keep information about guests and vendors for parties and events
- Catalog furniture and assets for insurance records
- Manage time and track billable hours
- Catalog personnel records
- Scan the Internet to find suppliers and customers
- Track the searches and purchases of clients visiting Web sites

Suppose you are using a database of your company's mailing list. That mailing list contains the names and addresses of more than 3,000 customers. With one keystroke, the database can alphabetize the list by last name, group the addresses by zip code, or display only those customers who use post office boxes. Including purchase histories in the database would allow you to quickly pull up a list of all customers who made purchases during a certain month or who purchased a certain dollar amount of merchandise.

Spreadsheet Programs

Spreadsheet programs are used to organize, calculate, and analyze numerical data. With spreadsheets, you can perform financial and scientific calculations, organize numeric information, illustrate data with charts and graphs, and create professional-looking reports. Spreadsheets also graphically display the relationship of data in the form of charts and graphs that are often easier for people to understand than tables of raw data. Microsoft Excel is the one of the most popular spreadsheet programs. Others include Quattro Pro and XESS. Businesspeople use spreadsheets for many purposes:

- Develop a budget
- Analyze financial performance
- Track loans or mortgages
- Track stock and bond performance
- Schedule projects
- Manage business assets

TEACH

Discussion Starter

TYPES OF APPLICATIONS

Ask students to consider the following scenario: A new bookstore is about to open its doors. The fixtures have been installed, the stock has arrived, and workers have been hired. However, the computer system has not arrived. Discuss with students what this absence will mean to the business.

TEACHING POINTS

Explain In the above situation, the computer will most likely be for cash register transactions, inventory, communicating via e-mail, and conducting research.

 Online Activity

Operating Monopoly
Ask students to use the Internet to research why, in the late 1990s and early 2000s, the American government found it necessary to break up Microsoft's grip on computer users, held through its dominant Windows® operating system.

 Critical Thinking

Ask students to list the benefits of designing with a computer instead of on paper. Answers may include being able to alter work more easily and give it to printers in a ready format. As a follow up, have students research the different kinds of software that designers use, select one, and create a brief summary of its features and uses.

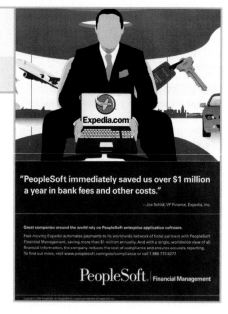
TEACH CONTINUED

Individualized Math Skills

For each problem below, tell students to consider an employee whose hourly wage is $8.

L1 Ask students to calculate how much an employee would be paid for 40 standard hours of work—a standard work week.
$320; $8 × 40 = $320

L2 If an employee who is paid $8 per hour works from 10 a.m. to 7 p.m. with a one-hour break for lunch, what is the gross amount she is paid per day?
$64; 8/hour × (9 hours − 1 hour) = $8/hour × 8 hours = $64)

L3 For overtime, employees are paid one-and-one-half times the hourly wage for time worked after eight hours in a single workday. If a coworker becomes sick and the employee above is asked to work two extra hours, how much gross pay will she receive in that day?
$88; 64 + ($8 × 1.5 × 2) = $64 + $24 = $88

 Online Activity

Online Timesheets
Have students research online systems for keeping track of employees' working hours. Ask students to think about and explain why the method they have chosen to research is popular. Answers may include being able to log in from remote locations and having records available from afar.

- Produce profit and loss statements
- Calculate and produce a payroll
- Track client/customer responses to marketing promotions
- Build relationship marketing based on customer value profiles
- Track sales and service
- Conduct marketing research

A spreadsheet consists of a grid of rows and columns. Users enter data and formulas into cells on the grid, and the program performs calculations with speed and accuracy not possible by hand or with a calculator. When you change one piece of information, the spreadsheet will automatically update all related numbers. This allows users to test different scenarios. For example, you can see how adjusting the price of a product would affect projected sales, taxes, and the overall budget.

Desktop Publishing Programs

The invention and rapid development of **desktop publishing programs** illustrates both the computer's creative potential and its usefulness for business. Part word processor and part graphics application, desktop publishing programs enable users to edit and manipulate both text and graphics in one document. This is how books, magazines, and flyers are designed and produced. Desktop publishing software can produce documents that are creative, eye-catching, attractive, professional, and easy to read. The two most popular commercial desktop publishing programs are Adobe InDesign and QuarkXPress. Marketing uses desktop publishing to

- Create layouts for newsletters, books, brochures, and advertisements
- Create professional-looking forms, such as invoices and project planning sheets

Businesses can save money by using desktop publishing programs in-house to produce printed materials.

Graphics and Design Programs

Graphics and design programs are software applications for creating and modifying

---

PHOTO GUIDE **FAST RESULTS**

Discussion Lead a discussion about the ad's selling point. Clarify that it suggests that Expedia.com immediately saved over $1 million by using PeopleSoft's services.

Caption Answer Expedia.com can use financial management software to handle its many online transactions and to analyze the use and profitability of its products.

Follow Up Ask students what other businesses could use the services of financial management software applications.

images, including drawings, designs, and photographs. Designers can create all graphic elements themselves with the drawing tools provided by the software, or they can use photos and ready-made artwork, often called clip art. These images are usually grouped together in categories like business, food, sports, people, places, animals, cartoons, and holidays.

There are thousands of graphics programs, with some of the most common being Adobe Photoshop, Adobe Illustrator, CorelDRAW, Flash, and Macromedia Freehand. Graphics programs can be used by marketers and businesses to

- Design marketing promotion materials
- Create logos and letterheads

- Illustrate floor plans and furniture arrangements
- Create professional-looking illustrations and photographic prints
- Create images for presentations or for Web pages and Internet ads

Presentation Software

Presentation software produces slide shows or multimedia presentations. This software helps users organize ideas and concepts to be presented in a meeting. Presentation software can be used by businesses and marketers to

- Prepare verbal and visual copy for meetings

• **SHOW and TELL** Presentation software has become an indispensable tool in many business meetings.

How could you use such software in your schoolwork?

Chapter 9 - Technology Applications for Marketing **201**

Concept Development

PRESENTATION SOFTWARE

Ask students if they have ever been in an audience for a presentation made with a computer. Ask students to name the benefits and drawbacks of using presentation software.

Answers will vary, but students may compliment use of interesting graphics and criticize the simple and boring projection of outline heads, for example. They may also note that no matter how excellent a computerized presentation is, it's up to the speaker to make it effective and present it well.

TEACHING POINTS

Demonstrate Show students how you use presentation software in class.

Extend Suggest to students that computer presentations can also be shown online to audiences far away.

Extended Activity

Graphics and Design Programs
Ask students to research research clip art and to discuss the advantages and disadvantages of using clip art. Answers will vary; benefits may include having a variety of graphics that are ready to use. One drawback is that another company or individual may use the art or that the art is not original.

PHOTO GUIDE   **SHOW and TELL**

Discussion Lead a discussion about how presentation software has become an indispensable tool in many business meetings. Point out that many meeting rooms have been specially equipped for such technology, with screens and input jacks that feed directly into laptop computers.

Caption Answer Answers will vary, but students may suggest that using computers can improve oral reports and other presentations.

Follow Up Ask students to compile a list of things that presenters should not do. For example, they should not write down the presentation word for word or feel compelled to use every font, color, and trick that the software includes.

TEACH CONTINUED

Concept Development

WEB PAGE EDITORS

After students have read the section on Web page editors, ask volunteers to talk about their favorite Web sites. Ask: What do they like most about them, in terms of both content and aesthetics?

Answers will depend on personal tastes, but most students should agree on the importance of organization and ease of navigation.

TEACHING POINTS

Demonstrate Show the Glencoe *Marketing Essentials* Online Learning Center, **marketingessentials.glencoe.com**. Ask students how the site benefits instructors, students, and the company itself.

Build Vocabulary

Preview the following phrases by reading them in context in the Global Market feature. Ask the students to predict or explain what they think these words mean.

- **free market economies**
  economies where buying and selling can be carried out without restrictions on price, etc.

- **business-to-business sales**
  selling conducted between two commercial entities

 Online Activity

Regulating the Internet
Inform students that in addition to helping Web technologies, the Chinese government heavily regulates Internet usage. Have students research reports on the Chinese government's attempts to control the Internet usage and habits of Chinese citizens.

 GLOBAL MARKET

Growing E-Clout of China

With 1.3 billion people, China has the largest population in the world, a huge potential e-commerce market. The Chinese economy is expanding, and computer sales are increasing. In 2003, 80 million Chinese were online, and that number is expected to almost double by 2006 as 800,000 Chinese become Internet users each week. International Data Corporation (IDC) estimated that there would be 84.2 million Web-enabled PCs in China by the end of 2004. Investment in Chinese Web portals is increasing dramatically. U.S. Web titans Yahoo and eBay have both entered the Chinese market, and Google opened a Chinese-language site in early 2004.

Governmental Help The Chinese government gives help to companies developing Web technologies. This provides a competitive advantage over businesses from free market economies like the United States. Web portals in the United States get most of their income from advertising. Chinese portals take advantage of the high rate of cellular phone use to sell services like messaging, games, even video greeting cards—all displayed on cell phones. Retailing and business-to-business sales lag far behind such services in the United States because of credit card and delivery obstacles.

CRITICAL THINKING

Do you think the U.S. government should make grants to technology companies to help them compete? Why or why not?

@ Online Action!

Go to *marketingessentials.glencoe.com/9/global* for an activity on international marketing and computer technology.

- Present and discuss ideas interactively via the Internet with clients in other cities or countries
- Create slide shows using pictures or Web pages
- Add voice narration to accompany visual material

Presentation software can incorporate a series of slides, film clips, and streaming video. Presentations can include text, bulleted lists, graphs, photos, screen shots from the company Web page, and even interactive problem and decision situations. Colorful graphics and concise text can be used in marketing promotions and sales presentations to persuade clients and close sales. Voice narration can create the feeling of attending a conference, even when participants are thousands of miles apart.

As global interaction in the business world increases, programs like this simplify communication and cut down on travel time. Some examples of presentation software programs are Microsoft PowerPoint and Apple Keynote.

Web Page Editors

The Web has become an integral part of our world. Many businesses use their Web sites to promote their companies and products and to stay connected to their customers. Web sites generally contain an initial **home page** which is the entry point for a Web site. It gives general information to introduce the company, person, or product. The home page has links to other pages containing additional information, such as product details and contact information.

 marketingessentials.glencoe.com

 GLOBAL MARKET

Growing E-Clout of China

Discussion Ask students to discuss why the Chinese government might encourage e-commerce. Students might state that it promotes business locally and internationally.

CRITICAL THINKING **Answer:** Opinions will vary. Some may believe that the government should not be involved with private businesses. Others will think that the benefits outweigh any negative effects of government involvement.

@ Online Action! For instructions, ideas, and answer guide, go to the Teacher Center at **marketingessentials.glencoe.com**

The home page can also link to an online store or other interactive resources such as online questionnaires.

At first, creating a Web page meant writing very specific, detailed, and complicated code, called **hypertext markup language (HTML)**. Today, Web editing programs enable people to create Web pages as if they were using a word processor or a desktop publishing program. Some of the most popular of these applications are Macromedia Dreamweaver, Adobe GoLive, and Microsoft FrontPage.

Communications Programs
Communications programs enable users to electronically communicate with

Case Study

Online Radio

Radioparadise is an online radio station run out of the home of Bill and Rebecca Goldsmith. A 30-year veteran of FM radio, Bill Goldsmith loves his new career. He uses a laptop computer to program the station to play an eclectic mix of musical styles. There is no advertising, but satisfied listeners contributed $120,000 in 2003, enough to cover all the station's costs and still give the Goldsmiths a comfortable lifestyle. As sound and Internet technology continue to become more powerful and less expensive, opportunities for online radio entrepreneurs are likely to expand.

A New trend

Internet radio is gaining in popularity. Not long ago, online sound quality was poor and it often dropped out due to connection problems. But digital audio file quality has improved, and broadband technology makes connections more stable. Most new computers have built-in sound capability, so no new equipment is required. You can sit at your computer, do your homework, and listen to your favorite band. Online listening is growing at an average rate of 43 percent a year. Yahoo's music site and radio network, Launchcast, gets one million listeners a week. Nineteen million people tune in to Internet radio each week.

Just like other broadcasters, Internet radio stations are legally required to pay music companies for the copyrighted music they play.

Global Reach

More than 6,500 stations are available online from more than 130 countries. They are an easy and inexpensive way for immigrants to stay in touch with their home countries. They can also help students learn the language and music of the cultures they are studying.

THINK STRATEGICALLY

If you were the owner of an online radio station, how would you plan to earn money from your site?

@ Online Action! Go to *marketingessentials.glencoe/9/case* to find an activity about online technology and marketing.

marketingessentials.glencoe.com

Chapter 9 - Technology Applications for Marketing **203**

Case Study Online Radio

Discussion Have students read the Case Study and discuss why people may choose to listen to online radio instead of commercial radio. Suggest that online radio can be more specifically targeted toward the listener, rather than directed toward a mass market.

THINK STRATEGICALLY **Answer:** Answers will vary. Suggest to students that an online radio station owner can earn money from asking for donations, selling advertisements, and offering products such as T-shirts or baseball caps that are related to the station.

@ Online Action! For instructions, ideas, and answer guide, go to the Teacher Center at marketingessentials.glencoe.com

Review Guide

CONCEPTS
Ask students how the Internet can be received via broadband technology.
It can be received through special phone or cable lines.

KEY TERMS
Have students review key terms, their spellings, and definitions in small groups.

ONLINE SELF-ASSESSMENT
Have students go to **marketingessentials.glencoe.com** for the Section 9.1 practice test.

Individualized Review

L1 Assign and review Chapter 9 activities in the Student Activity Workbook.

L2 Assign and review Chapter 9 activities in the Marketing Math Workbook.

L3 Assign and review Chapter 9 activities in the *BusinessWeek* Reader and Case Studies.

Marketing Practice

Have small groups of students pretend to be a business of their choice. Tell them to look at similar business sites and create a plan or an outline for a site for their imaginary business. Ask them to keep in mind its role in marketing—facilitating the movement of goods or services from the company to the consumer.

CLOSE

Ask students to recall and provide answers to the following questions:

- **What does WYSIWYG mean?**
  "What you see is what you get" allows a word processor user to know exactly what a document will look like when it is printed out.

- **What is a desktop publishing?**
  Desktop publishing is part word processor and part graphics application that enables users to edit and manipulate text and images in one document.

Critical Thinking

Ask students: Do you think that it is possible to be effective in business or marketing without being familiar with computer applications? Encourage students to share their responses in class.

---

others around the world through their computers. The key to any communication software is connecting to some kind of network.

Broadband Technology

Broadband technology is a high-speed connection that transmits information through special phone or TV cable lines. It dramatically reduces the time it takes for a computer to send and receive data over a network. This extra bandwidth can be used to send files attached to e-mails and can turn text-based instant messaging sessions into audio chats or even video conference calls where participants use small cameras and can see and hear each other in real time.

Videoconferencing

Videoconferencing has many practical advantages. Perhaps the greatest professional advantage to videoconferencing is that it can reduce the need for expensive business travel. Travel time and expenses can be dramatically reduced by holding videoconferences rather than meeting in person.

Communications Programs

Communications programs include e-mail software such as Microsoft Outlook and Qualcomm Eudora; instant messaging software such as AOL Instant Messenger; and video-conference software, including Apple iChat and Microsoft NetMeeting.

9.1 AFTER YOU READ

Reviewing Key Terms and Concepts

1. List eight types of software applications commonly used by businesses.
2. What is a database program? What advantage does such a program offer a business that gathers a large quantity of data?
3. When might a business use presentation software? Name two examples of this type of software.

Integrating Academic Skills

Mathematics

4. You are comparing the cost of two high-speed Internet services. The cable company charges a $59.95 one-time connection fee, plus $34.95 per month. It provides free connection hardware if you keep the service for one year. The phone company charges $89.95 for the connection fee and hardware, plus $29.95 per month. What is the difference in the cost of the two plans for a 12-month period?

Geography

5. Using the Internet or reference materials in a library, research the geography and culture of a country you know little about but would like to visit. Then use word processing software to write a tourism advertisement describing the points of interest that a visitor should not miss.

@ Online Action!
Check your answers at *marketingessentials.glencoe.com/9/read*

Reviewing Key Terms and Concepts

1. The eight types of software applications are word processing, database, spreadsheet, desktop publishing, graphics, design, presentation, and communications.

2. Database programs are applications that store and organize information. For businesses that work with large quantities of data, they can link theinformation together.

3. Answers will vary, but a business might use presentation software at employee meetings. Examples of software include Microsoft PowerPoint and Apple Keynote.

Integrating Academic Skills

4. $30; Cable: $59.95 + ($34.95/month × 12 months) = $479.35; Phone company: $89.95 + ($29.95/month × 12 months) = $449.35; $479.35 − $449.35 = $30

5. Tourism advertisements will vary; student creations should effectively describe the country of their choice.

@ Online Action! Answers at **marketingessentials.glencoe.com/9/read**

Computer Technology and Marketing

READ and STUDY

BEFORE YOU READ
Connect How do you think computer technology will change marketing and business in the future?

THE MAIN IDEA
Technological advances are changing the scope of marketing. With innovations that speed up the transfer of information and increase the use of the Internet, businesses are finding new marketing opportunities and can offer better service to customers.

STUDY ORGANIZER
In a chart like the one below, list the five types of specialized computer technology marketers use.

Point-of-Sale (POS) System

Computer Technology for Marketing

OBJECTIVES
- Describe the types of computer software that are influencing and reshaping the world of marketing
- Explain how the Internet and the World Wide Web can increase business productivity

KEY TERMS
- enterprise resource planning (ERP)
- Internet
- Internet service providers (ISPs)
- Wi-Fi
- World Wide Web
- hypertext transfer protocol (HTTP)
- uniform resource locator (URL)
- firewall
- site map

Interactive Technology for Marketing

Marketing applications for computer technology appear endless. In addition to the software applications discussed in Section 9.1, many other computer applications are shaping the way we conduct business. These include point-of-sale systems, interactive touch-screen computers, interactive TV, just-in-time schedulers, customer relationship management and enterprise resource planning systems, and the Internet.

WHILE YOU READ

Analyze Think of the ways you have used the Internet.

Chapter 9 - Technology Applications for Marketing **205**

FOCUS

Introducing the Section

COLLABORATIVE ACTIVITY
To prepare for reading this section, have students work as a group on a collaborative list of places where they have seen Web sites listed. Examples might include cereal box tops, top edges of NBA basketball backboards, and television commercials for just about anything. Ask students why marketers would encourage this type of Web site placement.

Preteaching Key Terms

Read the key terms aloud, or ask a volunteer to read them. Ask students to predict the meanings of these terms and phrases.

- enterprise resource planning (ERP)
- Internet
- Internet service providers (ISPs)
- Wi-Fi
- World Wide Web
- hypertext transfer protocol (HTTP)
- uniform resource locator (URL)
- firewall
- site map

Tell students they can check their predictions as they read this section.

 Online Activity

Internet Marketers
Ask interested students to research an Internet marketing company. Have students report on techniques, clientele, and other characteristics of the company in a five-minute oral presentation.

READ and STUDY

BEFORE YOU READ
Lead students in discussing how computer technology will change marketing and business in the future. Answers might include more individualized marketing via personalized records.

THE MAIN IDEA
Ask students to provide examples of computer technology changing marketing.

STUDY ORGANIZER
Model the study organizer for students by filling in a kind of technology as the lesson progresses. A full-size, downloadable study organizer can be found at **marketingessentials.glencoe.com**

WHILE YOU READ Ask students to recall personal experiences of Internet marketing as they read the section.

TEACH

Concept Development

INTEGRATED MARKETING SOFTWARE

Ask the class if any students have purchased items online. Ask them for their experiences with customer relationship marketing. Ask: Were they able to check the status of their orders or track the shipping? If students answer yes, ask if they needed a non-automated response. Ask students if it was easy to get a phone number or e-mail response, and have students share their positive or negative experiences.

TEACHING POINTS

Extend Inform the class that many point-of-sale systems are operated by customers rather than clerks. Ask students to consider why supermarkets, post offices, and other locations might be increasing their use of point-of-sale systems.

Enrichment

INTERACTIVE TV

Inform students that interactive television is often used in hotels. It allows guests to order movies, play video games, and check out from the hotel without leaving their rooms. Ask students why such technology might have started in the hospitality industry.

Answers will vary, but may include competition driving the evolution of customer service.

Point-of-Sale Systems

A common use of computers in retailing is the point-of-sale (POS) system. This system consists of cash registers and peripherals, such as scanners, touch screens, handheld checkout devices, printers, and electronic kiosks. Scanners feed information directly from merchandise tags or product labels into a computer to update inventory. See Chapter 16 for more information on POS systems.

Integrated Marketing Software

Capturing customer information, viewing customers' sales histories, and customizing promotions are the core of customer relationship management (CRM). New CRM applications are Internet-enabled, fully integrated Web service applications. A customer can place an order online and check the progress of the order on the Web or by telephone. In addition to tracking the business the customer is doing with the firm, CRM can also track the customer's satisfaction level at each step in the sales process.

Enterprise Resource Planning (ERP)

Enterprise resource planning (ERP) software is even more sophisticated. Using new ERP software, all parts of a company's business management are integrated, including planning, manufacturing, sales, marketing, invoicing, and payroll. Applications are now available to help management with such activities as inventory control, order tracking, customer service, finance, and human resources. ERP vendors are now integrating CRM software into their ERP suites. Both CRM and ERP applications can help generate marketing reports and solve marketing problems.

Interactive Touch-Screen Computers

A touch screen is a computer display screen that responds to human touch. This allows the user to interact with the computer by touching words or pictures on the screen. (See Figure 9.1.) In retail marketing, there is a strong move toward the greater use of this kind of interactive technology. Interactive computers are on shelves in retail stores and

in stand-alone kiosks at malls and airports. The customer reads and responds to questions on the touch-sensitive screen. In this way, the "computerized salesperson" directs the customer to the correct product.

Customers like touch screens, and the maintenance costs to business are very low. However, it would be a mistake to think all sales can be made via touch-screen technology. The computer-assisted transactions discussed here are used for products, goods, and services that are fairly standard and receptive to programmable decision making. Costly or complex products need a degree of personal contact that is not possible without a real person.

Interactive TV

Interactive TV marries television with Internet-style interactivity. Such systems combine satellite dishes, DVD players, and television set-top boxes equipped with modems, microprocessors, hard drives, operating systems, and software, including browsers to make the TV behave more like a computer.

Advertisers like the idea of interactive television because consumers can instantly get more information about products through their TVs. Viewers can actually interact with the programming. For example, when a viewer sees an ad for pizza and decides he is hungry he can click a link to have that company's pizza delivered right to the door.

The Click Stream

Interactive TV also benefits marketers because of the click stream. Every click of the remote control goes into a database for later analysis. From this data, a picture of individual viewers and what motivates them emerges. TV programmers can use this data to check viewers' reaction to content and use that information in deciding what to show in the future. Over time, psychological profiles of individual viewers can be developed, providing an enormous amount of information. Today, companies are developing and testing ways in which interactive television can be used for advertising and promotion.

 Critical Thinking

The Digital Divide

Ask students if they believe that the Internet increasingly favors individuals from wealthier classes who can afford the latest computers and broadband access. How might such a class disparity be reduced? Ask interested students to perform research on this topic and report their findings to the class.

Figure 9.1   Marketing with Interactive Technology

> •**Conversing With a Computer**   Interactive technology, in which a customer interacts with a computer to get a desired result, is dramatically changing the way products and services are marketed. Applications of this technology are making sales and ordering more streamlined and efficient. They allow market research to capture an enormous amount of data, and, by using these data, advertisers are able to more effectively reach their markets. Let's look at some of the ways interactive technology is being put to use in marketing.
>
> *What's the importance of interactive technology to marketers?*

Touch-Screen Computers, Computerized Salespeople
Touch-screen computers allow customers to locate product information without the help of salespeople. The computers can check inventory and prices, suggest other merchandise a customer might like, and even connect to a wedding gift registry created in another state.

Interactive TV
With interactive TV, viewers can vote for their favorite TV character, access information related to a program, download reality show contestant biographies, or link to an online store. Sports fans can use interactive TV to get up-to-the-minute results for their favorite teams or athletes.

E-Commerce
E-commerce allows customers to view products, compare prices, and order—all at the click of a mouse. This young man can compare prices and styles at hundreds of hip-hop "stores" in a matter of minutes without leaving his home. Information he supplies when placing his order is captured in a database and used by a marketer to generate future sales.

@ Online Action!
Go to *marketingessentials.glencoe.com/9/figure/1* to find a research project on marketing with technology.

 marketingessentials.glencoe.com

TEACH CONTINUED

Individualized Practice

MARKETING WITH INTERACTIVE TECHNOLOGY

L1 Ask students to write a 100-word paragraph on why customers may prefer interacting with touch-screen computers than talking to an actual salesperson.
Answers will vary, but may include that it is a low-pressure situation that allows a customer to go at his or her own speed in privacy.

L2 Have students compare and contrast marketing information-gathering techniques by writing a two- to three-paragraph response to the following question: Does a business gain more information from a customer using a touch-screen computer or through talking to a salesperson? Explain.
Students should note that every step taken by a customer on a computer can be saved and studied. Personal interaction cannot be analyzed as easily.

L3 Ask students to design a touch-screen computer interface for a business such as a shoe store. What questions would be asked? What information could be gained and used? Have students prepare a five-minute presentation on their interface.
Presentations will vary; all presentations should include an appropriate and effective interface.

Figure 9.1   Marketing With Interactive Technology

Discussion Lead a discussion of the forms of marketing with interactive technology. Ask students if there are advantages to using touch-screen computers, interactive TV, or e-commerce instead of talking to a salesperson. Then have them share experiences with each example from the discussion.

Caption Answer Interactive technology provides an unobtrusive and inexpensive way for marketers to encourage sales from and also collect information about their customers.

@ Online Action! For instructions, ideas, and answer guide, go to the Teacher Center at **marketingessentials.glencoe.com**

Concept Development

INTERNET CONNECTIVITY

Have students discuss their level of connectivity and compare that to Internet use in heavily connected countries such as South Korea. What do students think about the relationship between a country's Internet technology and its commerce? Ask students to explain their opinions.

TEACHING POINTS

Extend Present your experiences with the Internet, from your very first exposure to your current setup. Share initial reservations, difficulties with installation, personal benefits, and other details.

Enrichment

THE WORLD WIDE WEB

Discuss with students how the World Wide Web is not regulated. Users can add or take away from it as they wish. Encourage students to debate the benefits and drawbacks of this lack of regulation. Benefits may include freedom of speech and commercial opportunities. Drawbacks may include Web sites with ignorant or hateful content and business scams.

Internet Connectivity

The **Internet**, it appears to be the world's biggest computer network, but it is actually a network of networks, across which information flows freely.

The Internet began life as a research project for the U.S. Defense Department. Over time, it became popular among researchers at universities. Then it took on a life of its own, growing slowly at first and then exploding in popularity in the 1990s. Telephone companies provided connectivity to the first commercial Internet service providers. During this time, most people connected to the Internet using a dial-up modem connected to telephone lines. The first modems were quite slow, but improved technology brought faster modems and more reliable service.

Broadband Connection

In the 1990s, high-speed connectivity became affordable for home users. This service, called broadband, uses technology that moves much more data per second along a phone line. Two types of broadband technology were introduced: the digital subscriber line (DSL) and Internet access via cable TV. Both are provided by **Internet service providers (ISPs)**, which are companies that provide Internet access for businesses, organizations, and individuals. Estimates in 2004 showed that 48 million Americans have broadband connections in their homes.

Yet another technology is being developed for faster Internet access. New modems transmit data across the power grid. Introduced in 2004 by the publicly owned electric power utility in Manassas, Virginia, this new service is known as broadband-over-power-lines (BPL). All you have to do to connect is plug into any electric outlet. Because the power lines are already in place, the cost of BPL connection is expected to remain lower than DSL or cable connections. With 40 million people still using dial-up connections, there may be a sizable market for BPL.

Wireless Connectivity

Wireless routers provide Internet connectivity without a physical connection. This technology, called **Wi-Fi**, (short for wireless fidelity) establishes a wireless Internet connection using radio frequencies.

Hundreds of millions of people around the world are expected to join the online community over the next few years. As of 2004, 945 million people used the Internet, according to the *Computer Industry Almanac.* That figure is expected to hit 1.1 billion by 2005, 1.3 billion by 2006, and close to 1.5 billion by 2007.

The World Wide Web

Although the terms are often used synonymously, the **World Wide Web** and the Internet are actually two different things. The Web is a subset of the Internet and is a collection of interlinked electronic documents. These pages are viewed with a browser. A browser is any piece of software that tells the computer what Web content to display. Web pages contain links that prompt the browser to load a new page.

Researcher Tim Berners-Lee invented the technology behind the Web. He developed the **hypertext transfer protocol (HTTP)** that links documents together and the **uniform resource locator (URL)**, which is the protocol used to identify and locate Web pages on the Internet. It is also known as a Web address.

Today there are billions of pages on the Web. Hundreds of thousands of new Web pages are added every week. Because the World Wide Web does not have a system for locating or categorizing content, companies have developed an assortment of Web directories and search engines to help users find what they are looking for.

Search Engines

Two of the most popular search engines are Google and Yahoo. Each has a database of more than four billion Web pages. Many of the most useful and common Web pages are known to all search engines, but there are also

Critical Thinking

Ask students how Internet connectivity can affect a community's culture. Students may note that having access to arts and ideas from around the world can enrich a user's outlook.

Online Activity

Online Clickstream

Have students visit an online retail site. Ask students to consider what sort of information the site can save from each person who browses the site and how that information can be used by the business for the user's future visits or for other customers. Have students write a one-page report on their findings.

many sites and pages that are identified only by one or two search engines. That means it can be useful to check search sites like Teoma and Vivisimo to find sites eluding Google and Yahoo.

Search engines try to return results that relate well to your search terms. But they are also designed to make money for the company. To do that, search engines will place paid advertisers near or high up in the results listings.

Electronic Mail

E-mail represents another revolutionary change prompted by the development of the Internet. The popularity of e-mail is attributable to its instant delivery and to the fact that the sender and receiver do not have to be available at the same time.

For example, an appliance store employee can e-mail an order for new merchandise to a shipper in a different time zone. The shipper can acknowledge the order when she arrives at work, and the merchandise can be prepared for shipment almost immediately.

Intranets and Extranets

An intranet is a private, secure network, usually within a company or organization, that contains proprietary company data and can be accessed only by internal users. Some businesses have developed networks for their customers, employees, partners, and suppliers. These networks, called extranets, enable customers to access data stored on an internal server. A firewall protects the security of sensitive information. A **firewall** is a hardware and software checkpoint for all requests for or inputs of data, incoming and outgoing. The firewall reviews the message to make sure that the data content is safe and acceptable for others to view.

Protecting Digital Data

Anyone who has used a computer for a while knows that digital data is not always safe. Sometimes hard disks crash, and the data stored on them cannot be retrieved. Sometimes files are corrupted and cannot be read. Sometimes files are accidentally deleted. The longest-lasting media for backup files are CDs and

---

NET MARKETING

From Server to Web Portal?

AOL (America Online) was the first major commercial Internet service provider (ISP). In the late 1990s, AOL had more than half the market. As Internet users became more sophisticated, other providers offered more transparent access to the Internet with less advertising to sift through. They also offered faster broadband connections. At the end of 2003, AOL had 24 million subscribers, down from a high of 35 million.

One way AOL is fighting this trend is by focusing more attention on its Web site, AOL.com. The site has some public areas, but its main purpose is to provide subscribers with services such as e-mail access away from their dial-up location. Now AOL is offering low-cost membership for its site-based services to people using other ISPs. There are also plans for AOL to mimic Yahoo as a free Web portal that depends on advertising revenues rather than subscriber fees for income.

THINK LIKE A MARKETER

How could a free public Web portal be more profitable for AOL than a system with subscribers paying monthly fees?

@ Online Action!

Go to *marketingessentials.glencoe.com/9/net* to find an activity about Internet marketing.

marketingessentials.glencoe.com

Chapter 9 - Technology Applications for Marketing **209**

NET MARKETING

From Server to Web Portal?

Discussion Lead a discussion about the unique challenges faced by a business that succeeds during an industry's boom. Examples may include Sony's Betamax system during the early era of home video or Vision selling skateboards when the sport boomed during the 1980s.

THINK LIKE A MARKETER **Answer:** Answers will vary, but students may suggest that AOL can earn more money from advertisers and content consumers than subscribers.

@ Online Action! For instructions, ideas, and answer guide, go to the Teacher Center at **marketingessentials.glencoe.com**

Concept Development

ELECTRONIC MAIL

Inform students that while e-mail has many benefits, it also has many disadvantages, such as unwanted spam, attached viruses, and even e-mail scams. Ask students how they deal with such issues and what can be done about them.

Answers will vary, but students may suggest deleting e-mail from strangers and using anti-virus software.

TEACHING POINTS

Clarify Share with students typical subject lines of spam e-mails that can be deleted without even opening them. Examples may include "your e-mail" or "fantastic opportunity."

Demonstrate Share with students a virus-detection program and explain how it works.

Critical Thinking

Ask students to brainstorm and name reasons why a person or group might create and unleash a destructive or malicious virus program. Do they think it should be punishable by law? Lead a discussion on the ethics of viruses in class.

ASSESS

Review Guide

CONCEPTS

Ask students to discuss how the Internet and the World Wide Web can increase business productivity.
Answers will vary, but may include instant communication, expanded resources, and an international customer base.

KEY TERMS

Have students review key terms and use them in complete sentences that relate to marketing technology concepts.

ONLINE SELF-ASSESSMENT

Have students go to marketingessentials.glencoe.com for the Section 9.2 practice test.

Individualized Review

L1 Assign and review Chapter 9 activities in the Student Activity Workbook.

L2 Assign and review Chapter 9 activities in the Marketing Math Workbook.

L3 Assign and review Chapter 9 activities in the *BusinessWeek* Reader and Case Studies.

Marketing Practice

Divide students into groups of three or four. Have each group select a product and ask them to create an online marketing strategy for it. Make sure you approve all products. Ask students to consider e-mail, Web sites, and other options. Instruct them to share their ideas with the class in a 10- to 15-minute presentation.

DVDs. Many people use removable, external hard drives because they can be stored off-site, yet are quick and easy to retrieve and access. External drives back up your data with the push of a single button.

Computer files are also vulnerable to viruses, worms, and spyware. Viruses and worms can destroy your data, and spyware can track wherever you go on the Web. It can force you to visit certain sites, and it can collect personal information. Viruses, worms, and spyware can sneak into your system in an attachment to an innocent-looking e-mail message. The best way to protect your data is to use reputable anti-virus and anti-spyware software.

Spam

In 2003, Congress passed the CAN-SPAM law, which bans certain spamming techniques and requires senders to include a valid address. Although the law has made it easier to install filters to block spam, unwanted e-mail is still a problem. The law has merely driven major spammers offshore, beyond the reach of U.S. anti-spam laws.

Web Site Development

A business develops a Web site to inform consumers about the company and its products, enable the business to sell its products, provide related resources, and handle services and inquiries after the sale.

Any Web site's domain name comes from the Internet Corporation for Assigned Names and Numbers (ICANN). The domain name is the part of a URL that identifies a server or service provider. Top-level domains are three-letter extensions, which follow the dot in a Web address. Examples of top-level generic domains include .com and .biz for businesses and .org for nonprofit organizations.

Companies should plan to incur several costs to develop Web sites, including domain name registration, development and maintenance of the Web site, and subscription to a server (if one is not available in-house).

Most business Web sites have similar components that include a branding logo, content, a shopping cart for electronic purchases, a secured payment system for purchases, and general policies related to privacy, shipping, returns, and collection of sales taxes.

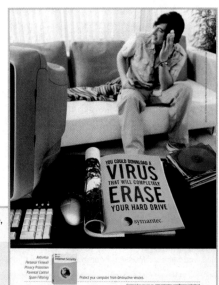

•SECURITY While computers have become indispensable, they are also vulnerable to virus attacks and data theft.

Name several reasons why the user of a home computer would want to purchase an Internet security software package.

AD GUIDE **SECURITY**

Discussion Lead a discussion about virus attacks and data theft. Describe to students cases of widespread viruses such as the "I love you" virus, which halted businesses for days in the year 2000.

Caption Answer Answers will vary; reasons for a home computer user to purchase Internet security software packages might include preventing a virus from crippling or corrupting personal files or actually damaging hardware. Another reason is to protect personal information that may be kept on one's computer.

Follow Up Ask students if they think they should back up their computer data. Why or why not?

When developing a Web site, the designer creates a site map. A **site map** outlines what can be found on each page within the Web site. This concept in Web site design is known as global navigation. The site map guides a viewer to the desired information and provides links to different parts of the Web site.

A Web site designer prepares a layout grid for every page within a Web site. Layout grids identify all the Web page elements, such as the title of the page, the branding logo, the placement of banner ads, the content, related links, and a navigation bar for movement within the site.

E-Commerce

E-commerce is the process of conducting business transactions on the Internet.

E-commerce sales figures have risen dramatically over the years. In 2000, $28 billion was spent in online shopping in the United States. That translates to less than one percent of the total retail sales figures for the year. In 2003, that had risen to nearly $56 billion, closing in on two percent of all retail sales.

As e-commerce grows, it is redefining the relationship between the seller and the buyer. E-commerce can exist B2B (business to business) or B2C (business to customer). Web markets differ from traditional markets in that they are open for business 24 hours a day, seven days a week. They are also unencumbered by costly middlemen and distribution channels. Additionally, suppliers all over the globe can compete if they can deliver the quality, price, quantity, and service demanded by the customer and are deemed trustworthy financially and ethically.

CLOSE

Ask students to recall and provide answers to the following questions:

- **What is a click stream?**
  In interactive TV, every click of the remote control goes into a database for later analysis.

- **What is "CAN-SPAM"?**
  A law passed by Congress in 2003 that bans certain spamming techniques and requires senders to include a valid address.

Online Activity
Domain Names
Inform students that they are about to form online stores. Have them think of potential names for their stores, then look them up online to see if the domains are being used. How does one make sure that his or her domain name is original? Is it acceptable for a business' name to be similar to that of an existing site?

9.2 AFTER YOU READ

Reviewing Key Terms and Concepts
1. Give four examples of specialized computer systems used for marketing.
2. What are five common uses of the Internet in the workplace?
3. What are three important procedures to follow to protect digital data?

Integrating Academic Skills
Mathematics
4. For four nations, the following ratios show the numbers of people in millions who have access to the Internet compared to the population in millions. Calculate the percent of the population that has access to the Internet for each country: United States, 185.9/290.34; Australia, 13.05/19.73; Japan, 77.95/127.21; China, 95.8/1,280

Language Arts
5. Do research using consumer magazines and the Internet to learn more about interactive TV. Go to a store to see the features demonstrated. Based on the information you gather, decide if you think the benefits of interactive TV outweigh its potential for invasion of privacy. Use a word processing program to write a paper persuading the reader of your point of view. Use the elements required when writing a paper to persuade.

 Online Action!

Check your answers at *marketingessentials.glencoe.com/9/read*

AFTER YOU READ

Reviewing Key Terms and Concepts
1. Four examples are point-of-sale systems, integrated marketing software, interactive touch-screen computers, and interactive TV.

2. Five common uses include the World Wide Web, electronic mail, information retrieval, intranets and extranets, and electronic commerce.

3. Three important procedures to follow are: back up files regularly, install anti-virus software, and install a firewall.

Integrating Academic Skills
4. United States: 185.9 ÷ 290.34 = 64%;
   Australia: 13.05 ÷ 19.73 = 66%;
   Japan: 77.95 ÷ 127.21 = 61%;
   China: 95.8 ÷ 1,280 = 7%

5. Papers will vary; students should show evidence of research as well as an understanding of the advantages and disadvantages of interactive TV.

 Online Action!   Answers at **marketingessentials.glencoe.com/9/read**

CAREERS
IN MARKETING

Lifelong Learning

CAREER INFORMATION

Have students go to marketingessentials.glencoe.com and find Chapter 9 Careers page and click on the link for the American Marketing Association's Careers Strategies and Tips. Ask students to select one article, read it, and make a poster presenting its main points.

TECHNOLOGY APPLICATIONS FOR MARKETING

Inform students that most businesses do not create and maintain their own Web sites; they hire specialists to do it for them. Let students know that many businesses do what they specialize in, and let specialists handle the online presence of the business. Other businesses choose to handle their online presence in-house.

Primary Source

Ask students to go to marketingessentials.glencoe.com and find Chapter 9 Resources. Ask them to click on the link for the American Marketing Association's marketing dictionary and read the Web- and computer-related definitions they find.

⊙ THINKING CRITICALLY

Answers will vary; students may say when the Web was young, degrees were not as important because education was not up to date with the rapidly evolving technology.

@ Online Action!

For instructions, ideas, and answer guide, go to the Teacher Center at marketingessentials.glencoe.com

---

ERIC MATHIASEN
SENIOR SOFTWARE
ANALYST
ORBITZ.COM

? **What do you do at work?**
My first role is that of change or configuration manager. It is my responsibility to make sure changes to the site software have been approved by our software testing team and then are prepared and made active on our Web site in as smooth and problem-free a process as possible. My second function is to work on the installation and deployment of existing site software to new servers or new software to existing servers. My third function is to help track down problems with the Web site when they occur.

? **What skills are most important to you?**
Investigation and tracking. Investigation is important for both finding problems and for finding solutions. Researching problems is a big part of what I do, and to be a good researcher you have to be curious, creative, and persistent. Tracking is important to most professional jobs to make sure you complete all tasks and also to make sure you don't repeat past mistakes.

? **What is your key to success?**
First, be persistent. Don't give up just because things are harder than you expected. Second, stay aware of unexpected opportunities—you never know where a great idea may come from. Third, don't be afraid of failure. Especially when you're starting out, you can learn as much and often more from trying and failing than you can from easy success.

Aptitudes, Abilities, and Skills

Computer and technical skills, organization, strong research and reading skills

Education and Training

A four-year degree in computer science is a good starting point; graduate degrees in related sciences can also be helpful.

Career Path

Entry-level positions might consist largely of routine Web site maintenance and management; these positions can lead to more robust, creative roles.

⊙ THINKING CRITICALLY

Why do you think it is harder now for someone to break into a Web-related career without a college degree?

@ Online Action!

Go to *marketingessentials.glencoe.com/ 9/careers* for an activity about careers in computer technology.

 marketingessentials.glencoe.com

 Test-Taking Strategies

Give students the opportunity to ask for clarification as needed while the lesson is being taught. List concepts on the board and have the class write sentences demonstrating their understanding of each. Call on a student to read a sentence for each concept, and discuss them as a class.

FOCUS on KEY POINTS

SECTION 9.1

● Computer software applications satisfy business needs for communications, accounting and record keeping, publishing, and graphic design.

SECTION 9.2

● Computer technologies developed especially for marketing fulfill needs in the areas of point-of-sale systems, integrated marketing programs, interactive touch-screen computers, interactive TV, and the Internet.

REVIEW VOCABULARY

Define each of the words below.

1. word processing programs (p. 199)
2. database programs (p. 199)
3. spreadsheet programs (p. 199)
4. desktop publishing programs (p. 200)
5. graphics and design programs (p. 200)
6. presentation software (p. 201)
7. home page (p. 202)
8. hypertext markup language (HTML) (p. 203)
9. communications programs (p. 203)
10. enterprise resource planning (ERP) (p. 206)
11. Internet (p. 208)
12. Internet service providers (ISPs) (p. 208)
13. Wi-Fi (p. 208)
14. World Wide Web (p. 208)
15. hypertext transfer protocol (HTTP) (p. 208)
16. uniform resource locator (URL) (p. 208)
17. firewall (p. 209)
18. site map (p. 211)

REVIEW FACTS and IDEAS

19. How are software applications used in business? (9.1)
20. Give three examples of uses for database programs. (9.1)
21. How can graphics programs be used in marketing? (9.1)
22. Name two examples of interactive technology that are relevant to marketing activities. (9.2)
23. Describe common uses of the Internet in marketing. (9.2)
24. What are the essential components of a Web site? (9.2)

Chapter 9 - Technology Applications for Marketing 213

REVIEW FACTS and IDEAS

19. Software applications are used to meet every conceivable business need.

20. Database programs can: maintain customer lists for automated mass mailings; keep information about guests and vendors for parties and events; catalog furniture and assets for insurance records; manage time and track billable hours; catalog personnel records; scan the Internet to find suppliers and customers; and track the searches and purchases of clients visiting Web sites.

21. Marketers can use graphics programs to: design marketing promotion materials; create logos and letterheads; illustrate floor plans and furniture arrangements; create professional-looking illustrations and photographic prints; and create images for presentations or for Web pages and Internet ads.

22. Some examples of interactive technology include: point-of-sale systems, interactive touch-screen computers, interactive TV, just-in-time schedulers, customer relationship management and enterprise resource planning systems, and the Internet.

23. The Internet is used for e-commerce by marketers that sell their products or services online. E-mail sent over the Internet also aids marketers by notifying customers of their purchases, shipping status, etc.

24. Most Web sites contain a branding logo, content, a shopping cart for electronic purchases, a secured payment system for purchases, and general policies related to privacy, shipping, returns, and collection of sales taxes.

FOCUS on KEY POINTS

Ask students to read the summaries aloud and give the classroom one real-life example for each concept.

REVIEW VOCABULARY

See glossary for definitions of 1–18. A sample answer might read:

1. *Word processing programs* are used to create text documents.

213

BUILD SKILLS

25. Workplace Skills
Presentations should demonstrate an understanding of what equipment the business requires and the associated costs.

26. Technology Applications
Responses should show an understanding of the four different kinds of connectors.

27. Math Practice
1,500,000; 25 operations per millisecond $\times$ 1,000 milliseconds per second $\times$ 60 seconds per minute = 1,500,000 operations per minute

DEVELOP CRITICAL THINKING

28. Technology and Success
Reports should show an understanding of how the technology named could help the chosen company.

29. Investing in Technology
Responses should show an understanding of the technology budget.

BUILD SKILLS

25. Workplace Skills
The Digital Workplace Work in a group. First, pick a type of business to open together. Then, talk to computer salespeople and use the Internet to find out what computer equipment and software applications are necessary to run that business and how much the technology costs. Make a three- to five-minute presentation of your results to the class.

26. Technology Applications
Wires Do some research on the Internet about the different kinds of connectors (such as wireless transmitters and USB, serial, and Ethernet cables) used to connect computers with monitors, printers, broadband connections, and other computer equipment. Using word processing software, describe four different types of connectors and the equipment they're most often used with.

27. Math Practice
Faster Than Fast A millisecond (ms) is a unit of time used to describe how long it takes a computer to complete an operation. 1 second = 1000 ms. If a computer can execute 25 operations per millisecond, how many operations can it complete in one minute? (Remember, there are 60 seconds in one minute.)

DEVELOP CRITICAL THINKING

28. Technology and Success
Look in the business section of a newspaper and find an article about a large corporation that is losing money and why it is failing. Think about how computers and software applications could help the company. Using a word processing program, write a one-page report outlining your recommendations for technology that can help make the corporation profitable again.

29. Investing in Technology
Imagine you run a business that makes skateboards. You have a budget of $200,000 to invest in increased productivity this year. Improved manufacturing software and the equipment to go with it costs $140,000. A desktop publishing package would cost $55,000. You're also considering design software for $40,000 and more powerful servers that could speed up your office computers and make them more secure for $30,000. You don't have enough employees in your information technology division to take care of any additional software. How do you decide how to spend the productivity budget?

 Formative Assessment
Formative assessment is an essential component of classroom work. This type of assessment provides information that is then used as feedback to modify teaching and meet student needs.

L1 Have students describe how the Internet and World Wide Web are influencing and reshaping the world of marketing in a one-paragraph response.

L2 Have students evaluate Web sites for rival businesses in a one-page report.

L3 Have students design a fictional home page for an online service company.

 Reteach If the results of this formative assessment seem low, consider the following activity:
Have students define the key terms and rephrase the definitions in their own words. Clear up any confusion students may have.

APPLY CONCEPTS

30. Analyzing Computer Use in Marketing Careers

Choose a possible marketing career and use the Internet to research how computers are used in it. Speculate on what new uses computers might have in the future in that career.

Activity Use a word processing program to write a one- to two-page report and present your report orally to the class. Use presentation software, if possible, for supplemental graphics.

31. Data Entry Procedures

Using a spreadsheet program, create a document to track monthly travel expenses for a salesperson. Include columns for miles, parking fees, meals, lodging, airfare, car rentals, and miscellaneous. Enter data in each column. Each entry should be dated. Provide a total for each expense as well as a total for the month.

Activity Save your electronic document on a disk, memory card, or e-mail it to your teacher, so it can be shared and discussed in class.

NET SAVVY

32. The Choice Is Yours

Your boss has asked you to research computer technology that is available for persons with special needs. This is called adaptive or assistive computer technology. Prepare a memo to outline your findings.

marketingessentials.glencoe.com

THE CONNECTION

Role Play:
Technology Applications

Situation You are to assume the role of cashier at a large supermarket. Your store has recently added a computerized grocery ordering system to the company Web site. This system allows customers to place their grocery orders online, specify a delivery date and time, and select from various payment options. A customer (judge) has complained about the amount of time that it takes to shop for groceries after work.

Activity You are to explain to the customer (judge) the new online shopping service your supermarket is offering.

Evaluation You will be evaluated on how well you meet the following performance indicators:

● Identify ways that technology impacts business

● Analyze technology for use in the sales function

● Describe current business trends

● Use an information system for order fulfillment

● Handle customer inquiries

 Online Action!

For more information and DECA Prep practice, go to *marketingessentials.glencoe.com/9/DECA*

Chapter 9 - Technology Applications for Marketing **215**

APPLY CONCEPTS

30. Analyzing Computer Use in Marketing Careers
Reports will vary and should show evidence of how technology is used in marketing careers.

31. Data Entry Procedures
Spreadsheets will vary; students should demonstrate understanding of how to use the software.

NET SAVVY

32. The Choice Is Yours
Memos and findings will vary but should show evidence of research into assistive or adaptive computer technology.

THE CONNECTION

The students should be evaluated on the performance indicators noted in the role play. For another DECA role play, go to the Competitive Events Workbook or the Student Activity Workbook, or go to **marketingessentials.glencoe.com/9/DECA**

Online Action! For instructions, ideas, and answer guide, go to the Teacher Center at **marketingessentials.glencoe.com**

DECA Advisors Corner

Have students list two ways that your chapter can use computers and/or technology for each of the following: (1) to create newsletters and flyers, (2) to increase membership, (3) to improve your school store (if applicable), (4) to build community and business support, and (5) to save time and money.

MINI-QUIZ

Read these sentences to the students and have them volunteer the missing word(s).

1. _____ programs are used to organize, calculate, and analyze numerical data. (Spreadsheet)

2. Part word processor and part graphics application, _____ programs enable users to edit and manipulate both text and graphics in one document. (desktop publishing)

3. The Internet began as a research project for _____. (the U.S. Defense Department)

For an expanded chapter quiz, go to Chapter 9 in the TeacherWorks CD-ROM and to Chapter 9 in the **ExamView**® Pro Test Generator CD-ROM.

Chapter Overview

Chapter 10 provides an overview of the key personal traits, interpersonal skills, and elements of teamwork that facilitate job success.

BUILD BACKGROUND

Discuss with students how people living longer, traveling more often, and communicating more easily affect the workforce. There has never been a more diverse workplace or marketplace. Inform students that it is important for workers to receive training to handle the changing environment.

Why It's Important

Being prepared to work well with others and knowing how to avoid and resolve conflict will help an individual be more effective, productive, and happy both on and away from the job.

Prepare to Read

Discuss the chapter objectives with students. Have students skim the chapter, looking at pictures, reading captions, and noting headings. Ask students for subjects they expect to be covered. Allow them to discuss topics that interest them regarding the subject matter.

CHAPTER 10
Interpersonal Skills

Chapter Objectives

After reading this chapter, you should be able to:

- Recognize the personal traits necessary for ethical action in the workplace
- Identify important interpersonal skills
- Perform effectively in diverse environments
- Manage conflict by using appropriate negotiation skills
- Discuss how to receive and handle customer complaints
- Identify skills needed to be a good team member and provide leadership
- Name six aspects of successful teamwork

GUIDE TO THE PHOTO

Market Talk Good interpersonal skills help employees establish relationships with coworkers and clients. In the diverse marketplace, good interpersonal skills are highly valued. They enable people to work effectively with people of different cultural, religious, and socioeconomic backgrounds.

Quick Think If you were assigned to travel to a foreign country on business, how would you prepare for your interactions with your counterparts there?

GUIDE TO THE PHOTO

Market Talk Lead a discussion about interpersonal skills. According to students, what are good interpersonal skills? Have them give examples from their experiences, touching on relationships with people of different ages, genders, cultures, and other backgrounds.

Quick Think Answers will vary; students might talk to others who conduct business in that country or contact someone in the embassy.

 Follow Up Ask students to describe the qualities of three people who they think demonstrate good interpersonal skills.

THE DECA CONNECTION

Performance indicators represent key skills and knowledge. Relating them to the concepts explained in this chapter is your key to success in DECA events.

These acronyms represent DECA events that involve knowledge of concepts in this chapter.

AAAL	FMAL	MMS	TMDM
AAML	FMDM	QSRM	TSE
ADC	FMML	RMAL	VPM
BSM	FSRM	RMML	
EMDM	HMDM	SMDM	

In all these DECA events you should be able to follow these performance indicators:

- Treat others fairly at work
- Develop cultural sensitivity
- Foster positive working relationships
- Participate as a team member
- Show empathy for others
- Use appropriate assertiveness
- Demonstrate problem-solving skills
- Maintain a positive attitude
- Demonstrate interest and enthusiasm
- Demonstrate responsible behavior and initiative
- Demonstrate honesty and integrity
- Demonstrate ethical work habits
- Demonstrate orderly and systematic behavior
- Demonstrate self-control
- Set personal goals
- Use time-management principles
- Use feedback for personal growth
- Explain the concept of self-esteem

DECA PREP

Check your understanding of DECA performance indicators with the DECA activity in this chapter's review. For more information and DECA Prep practice, go to *marketingessentials .glencoe.com/10/DECA*

THE DECA CONNECTION

DECA events that require knowledge of interpersonal skills are described here. Discuss the performance indicators to make sure students understand how to demonstrate their understanding.

The event acronyms stand for:

AAAL: Apparel and Accessories Marketing Series, AL

AAML: Apparel and Accessories Marketing Series, ML

ADC: Advertising Campaign Event

BSM: Business Services Marketing Series

EMDM: E-Commerce Management Team Decision Making Event

FMAL: Food Marketing Series, AL

FMDM: Financial Analysis Management Team Decision Making Event

FMML: Food Marketing Series, ML

FSRM: Full Service Restaurant Management Series

HMDM: Hospitality Services Management Team Decision Making Event

MMS: Marketing Management Series

QSRM: Quick Serve Restaurant Management Series

RMAL: Retail Merchandising Series, AL

RMML: Retail Merchandising Series, ML

SMDM: Sports and Entertainment Marketing Management Team Decision Making Event

TMDM: Travel and Tourism Marketing Management Team Decision Making Event

TSE: Technical Sales Event

VPM: Vehicles and Petroleum Marketing Series

DECA PREP

Find timed DECA Prep activities correlated to the Competitive Events Workbook for students and DECA tips for teachers at **marketingessentials.glencoe.com /10/DECA**

CHAPTER 10 Classroom Resources

For the Teacher

- TeacherWorks
- marketingessentials.glencoe.com
- Interactive Chalkboard
- **ExamView**® Pro Test Generator
- Fast File Unit 4

For the Student

- *Marketing Essentials* Online Edition
- Student Activity Workbook
- Marketing Math Workbook
- Marketing Research Project Workbook
- School-to-Work Activity Workbook
- Competitive Events Workbook
- *BusinessWeek* Reader and Case Studies
- marketingessentials.glencoe.com

SECTION 10.1

FOCUS

Introducing the Section

COLLABORATIVE ACTIVITY

To prepare for reading this section, have students talk about times they have worked as part of a team. As a class, make a list of skills needed to work in a group. The list should include, but not be limited to, the list of key terms. Ask students to provide an example of each skill being utilized.

Preteaching Key Terms

Read the key terms aloud, or ask a volunteer to read them. Ask students to predict the meanings of these terms.

- self-esteem
- initiative
- time management
- assertiveness
- flexibility
- ethics
- equity
- negotiation
- empathy

Tell students to check their predictions as they read this section.

 Critical Thinking

Ask students how a positive attitude can lead to success.

OBJECTIVES

- Recognize the personal traits necessary for ethical action in the workplace
- Identify important interpersonal skills
- Perform effectively in diverse environments
- Manage conflict by using appropriate negotiation skills

KEY TERMS

- self-esteem
- initiative
- time management
- assertiveness
- flexibility
- ethics
- equity
- negotiation
- empathy

WHILE YOU READ

Evaluate Yourself Make a list of personal traits that you feel you need to improve to be successful in building relationships with people of different backgrounds.

Personal Strengths and Interpersonal Skills

READ and STUDY

BEFORE YOU READ

Connect List five ways your interpersonal skills have helped you form relationships in the past.

THE MAIN IDEA

Self-development and good interpersonal skills are essential in handling a variety of work situations effectively and in working with people of diverse backgrounds.

STUDY ORGANIZER

In a chart like the one below, write down the personality traits and interpersonal skills that are important in good working relationships.

Personal Traits

Friendliness, courtesy, tact

Building Personal Strengths for Good Working Relationships

Successfully interacting with others depends on many factors. A positive self-image, understanding the rules of acceptable behavior, and awareness of the different cultural, religious, and socioeconomic backgrounds of those you are working with are some of these factors.

READ and STUDY

BEFORE YOU READ

Lead students in finding examples of ways interpersonal skills have helped them form friendships. Answers might include compassion, encouragement, and flexibility.

THE MAIN IDEA

Ask a volunteer to read the main idea aloud and ask another student to retell it in his or her own words.

STUDY ORGANIZER

Model the study organizer for students by filling in a personality trait or skill. A full-size, downloadable study organizer can be found at marketingessentials.glencoe.com

WHILE YOU READ Tell students to keep their lists of personal traits and take note of which ones appear in the section. Ask students what they can do to improve their traits.

Self-Esteem and Self-Awareness

Self-awareness is how you perceive yourself. **Self-esteem** is how you perceive your worth or value as a person. It is one of the basic building blocks of successfully interacting with others. Having self-esteem is important because it allows you to believe in yourself and improves your attitude at work.

How do you demonstrate self-esteem in the workplace? When you value yourself and know how you would like to be treated, it allows you to treat others the same way—with respect, friendliness, and patience. Another way you show self-esteem is in your work habits and grooming. Dressing appropriately and behaving in a confident yet courteous way shows that you respect yourself and your work. Arriving at work on time shows that you value yourself as a professional.

Setting goals for your career and personal development is another important aspect of self-awareness and self-esteem. You cannot get anywhere if you do not know where you are headed.

Positive Attitude

Your attitude is your mental outlook, which shapes the way you view people and situations. People with a positive attitude welcome a difficult assignment as a challenge. They look for something positive even when they experience setbacks. They also accept constructive criticism as a way to improve.

Initiative and Responsibility

Initiative means taking action and doing what needs to be done without being asked. If you come up with a new idea, initiative allows you to act on it. Initiative shows that you are enthusiastic about your work.

Accepting responsibility means being willing to be held accountable for your actions. After taking the initiative to begin a job, you must accept responsibility for completing it. Employers and customers value responsible employees because they fulfill their promises.

Self-Control

People who exercise self-control take careful, measured steps and do not act on impulse or emotion. Self-control in the workplace allows you to stop and analyze a situation before reacting to it. This is important when handling conflict. Self-control and orderly behavior inspire confidence in customers and in coworkers. People who cannot control themselves tend to be perceived as overly emotional, irresponsible, inattentive, and uninterested in the customer. They are not likely to be taken seriously.

Creativity

Creativity is the ability to use the imagination to invent. Creativity is used in marketing to think of new products and new ways to present products. It also allows you to find new ways of doing your job. Creativity helps you analyze problems from a new and fresh perspective.

Time Management

Time management means budgeting your time to accomplish tasks on a certain schedule. Time management principles involve establishing goals, setting deadlines, allocating enough time for each task, tackling the most difficult task first, and being realistic. In order to be effective in your work, you must be able to use time wisely. Managing time well is an example of responsible behavior. To manage your time, follow these guidelines:

1. Make a list of the tasks you need to complete.
2. Determine which task is most important considering the time frame you have.
3. Continue to rank the tasks.
4. Create a schedule based on your list.

When you are working on one task, do not let yourself worry about another one. You may, however, be able to work on more than one job at a time. Managing multiple tasks at once is called multitasking.

TEACH

Discussion Starter

BUILDING PERSONAL STRENGTHS FOR GOOD WORKING RELATIONSHIPS

Ask students to consider the following scenario: As a member of a start-up marketing company, make a list of skills you would want your boss to have. Then make a list of skills you would want your employees to have. Ask students to justify their responses and discuss the similarities and differences between their lists.

TEACHING POINTS

Clarify Let students know that *interpersonal* means between persons or involving relations between persons. In contrast, *intrapersonal* means existing within one's mind or self. Have students form small groups and discuss the difference.

Critical Thinking

Ask students: How can a person develop creativity? Answers might include trying new activities and surrounding oneself with creative people.

Online Activity

Time Management

Ask students to look up the keyboard *time management* in a search engine online. Have them find out what online services are available to help users manage their time and what strategies are used. Ask: Do you think such strategies would be helpful to you at home, at work, and at school? Have students share their responses in class.

Concept Development

STRESS MANAGEMENT

Inform students that many companies offer employees massage therapy, yoga, and other forms of stress relief. Such activities can cost considerable time and money. Ask students to give reasons why a company might be willing to accept the cost.

Healthy and happy workers are more productive, and these stress-relieving incentives may increase company loyalty.

TEACHING POINTS

Demonstrate Lead students through a relaxation technique such as deep breathing or visualizing.

Explain Point out to the class that pressure is not always bad. Tell students that pressure situations should be looked at as challenges, and that they can be occasions to succeed and learn. Ask them to share examples of how pressure contributed to success from their own lives.

Build Vocabulary

Preview the following words by reading them in context. Ask students to explain what each word means and use it in a sentence.

- **anxiety**
  the state of being uneasy, apprehensive, or worried about what may happen

- **mechanism**
  the working parts of a larger system

- **hormone**
  an organic or synthetic substance that triggers a specific effect in the body

•CREATIVE SOLUTIONS Creativity enables you to find new ways of doing things. It is a valuable trait to have in many different kinds of work.

What applications does creativity have in marketing?

Stress Management

Stress is a reaction to outside pressure. It can be mental or physical. An example of mental stress might be your reaction if your boss asked you to produce a ten-page research report on competing products by 9:00 A.M. the next day—when you had tickets to a game. Stress can energize, motivate, and excite us. The negative aspects of stress, though, are often harmful. Stress-related anxiety triggers the fight-or-flight mechanism in our bodies. Although this reaction may keep us alive in an emergency, it becomes dangerous when it occurs too often.

New research suggests that a hormone released by bodies under stress suppresses the immune system. Highly stressed people catch colds and flu more often than those who can handle or relieve their stress. Learning to manage stress is a valuable workplace skill.

Stress Relief

Researchers who have studied stress agree that three main elements help prevent stress: regular exercise, a balanced diet, and enough sleep. They also suggest engaging in recreation, making reasonable compromises, and accepting what you cannot change. When you are dealing with stress away from work, try getting a massage or watching a television program or movie. Getting involved in activities you enjoy, such as sports, reading, or listening to music, is a good way to relieve stress. Helping someone in need can help relieve stress by putting things in perspective.

Assertiveness

Assertiveness is standing up for what you believe. People will respect you if you can be assertive without being pushy or aggressive. Show confidence and speak with authority.

PHOTO GUIDE **CREATIVE SOLUTIONS**

Discussion Lead a discussion about creativity on the job. Ask students if they think creativity is something that employers can look for when they hire people or if it is a skill that can be acquired. Have students explain their answers.

Caption Answer Creativity can be used to develop approaches, ideas, and slogans that are new, clever, and catchy. It can also help in problem solving.

Follow Up Ask students why individuals might be afraid to be creative at work. Answers might include that they might be afraid to fail or be criticized. Ask students what they think about this type of working environment.

For example, suppose you are working with a client who ridicules your opinion. In a very professional and respectful way, you should reassert your contribution. Be sure to point out its strengths in a clear and precise manner. Offer credible support for any claim that you make; valid evidence will put you in a strong position to influence others. Assertiveness is a skill that takes time to learn. Confidence in being assertive comes with experience.

Flexibility

Flexibility allows you to adapt to changing circumstances. A flexible person can learn from others, accept criticism, and grow. To develop flexibility, listen with an open mind. Be willing to try new approaches.

As you will see in the next section, flexibility will help you be a productive team member. Businesses value employees with this trait because flexibility enables a business to move forward and adapt to changing markets.

Ethics in the 21st-Century Workplace

Ethics are the basic values and moral principles that guide the behavior of individuals and groups. In most cultures, ethical behavior includes honesty, integrity, and a sense of fair play. Ethical behavior also means treating all people with respect. People who practice ethical behavior gain the trust of coworkers and clients.

Honesty

Honesty in the workplace is an important part of ethical behavior. It includes telling the truth, maintaining confidentiality, and not spreading gossip. Respect for company property and making an effort to prevent theft are other aspects of workplace honesty. Honesty is the basis for trust, which is essential to a good business relationship.

Respect

The number-one rule when speaking to business clients or customers is to show respect. That applies to interactions with

---

A MATTER OF ETHICS

Doing the Right Thing

Charlene has been working as a cashier at Johnson Drugs for six months. She loves her job. She gets along well with her supervisor and coworkers, but she has not made friends with any of them yet.

A new employee, Simone, has been very friendly with Charlene. Charlene likes Simone and the fact that she now has a friend at work, but Charlene often hears Simone making fun of a coworker. It seems wrong to Charlene, but she is not sure what to do about it. Simone seems to be doing a good job otherwise.

What's Right?

Charlene does not want to confront Simone and risk losing her friendship. When Charlene considers telling her supervisor, she feels she would be tattling on Simone and perhaps getting her in trouble. Still, just keeping quiet does not feel good, either. Going to work is not very much fun anymore.

☀ THINKING ETHICALLY

What is the right thing for Charlene to do in this situation? How can she deal with the situation in a way that is fair to Simone and her other coworkers? How would you handle a similar situation?

@ Online Action!

Go to *marketingessentials.glencoe .com/10/ethics* to find a project on interpersonal skills in the workplace.

TEACH CONTINUED

Concept Development

ASSERTIVENESS

Ask the class to contrast assertiveness with aggression, having students share their personal experiences with each of them. Assertiveness is standing up for what you believe; aggression is being hostile. Experiences will vary.

TEACHING POINTS

Extend Let students know that being assertive does not mean being perfect. It is just as important for individuals to admit when they are wrong as it is for them to stand up for what they believe is right.

Enrichment

MODERN WORKPLACE ETHICS

Inform students that ethics are a hot topic in the workplace. Point out the 1989 Exxon oil spill, the 2001 financial scandal at Enron, and textile manufacturers' use of overseas sweatshops as examples of unethical or damaging situations affecting a company's profile. Have students research those cases or find their own examples of recent unethical situations and how companies have acted to regain the public's esteem. Have them compare those large-scale cases to more personal ones that an individual worker might face. Ask: What can one learn from such events?

Critical Thinking

Ask students what consumers can do to affect a company's unethical practices. Answers may include asking the company to change its practices, boycotting its goods or services, and publicizing unethical or illegal acts.

A MATTER OF ETHICS   Doing the Right Thing

Discussion Lead a discussion on this topic by asking students to give examples of ethical dilemmas faced at work or at school.

☀ **THINKING ETHICALLY**   **Answer:** Answers will vary. Students might suggest that Charlene confront Simone in a friendly way to try to resolve the matter and then talk to a supervisor if Simone refuses to change her behavior.

@ **Online Action!**   For instructions, ideas, and answer guide, go to the Teacher Center at *marketingessentials.glencoe.com*

Follow Up   Have the class compile a list of ways for Charlene to react to Simone's actions. Role-play with the students different options, and ask them to compare the strengths and weaknesses of each option.

Concept Development

MANAGING CONFLICT

Reinforce with students that negotiation requires listening and speaking skills. Have students recall and name some elements of listening for meaning and speaking well.

Answers will vary; possible answers include giving verbal feedback and enumerating the speaker's points.

TEACHING POINTS

Model Role-play with students the proper tone of negotiation. Give students negative statements such as "You really messed up the order" and have them come up with alternative positive phrasings of the statements.
Example: "Next time, let's double check the order before sending it."

Clarify Talk to students about negative and positive reinforcement. Ask: Which do they react better to and why? What cases can they make for using different reinforcement?

• NEGOTIATING CONFLICTS When negotiating conflict resolution, all parties must be willing to work together to find a fair solution.

What is the key to negotiation?

coworkers as well. You demonstrate respect by listening with an open mind to the other person's point of view, then addressing any differences of opinion with courtesy and tact. This is especially important if there is a disagreement or conflict, for instance, when handling a customer complaint. While it may not always be easy to be courteous and pleasant, you must practice showing respect to others.

Fairness and Equity

People expect to be treated the way others are treated. **Equity** means that everyone has equal rights and opportunities. Never give special privileges to an employee for reasons that are unrelated to his or her work performance.

Sometimes a business establishes standards to maintain fairness. Equality is also protected through both federal and state laws. Such standards and laws can prevent discrimination in procedures such as hiring and firing. For example, employment laws forbid discrimination due to gender, age, religion, or national origin. Federal laws include the Americans with Disabilities Act of 1990, which protects qualified individuals with disabilities from discrimination. If an employee believes that he or she has been the victim of discrimination, the employee can file a complaint with the United States Equal Employment Opportunity Commission (EEOC).

Avoiding Stereotypes

It is important to become aware of prejudices we may have and to eliminate them.

Learning about others' interests and experiences helps you understand them better. Interests often reflect values. Experiences shape how we think and view the world. With this understanding, you will find it easier to understand others, and they will be much more likely to understand you. Good workplace relationships and success in marketing are based on mutual understanding.

Managing Conflict

Like stress, conflict in the workplace can be productive or counterproductive. Counterproductive conflict can cause lost time and resources and a decrease in efficiency. Productive conflict can energize a person, group, or organization. Managing conflict requires understanding, skill, knowledge, and experience.

Conflict and Negotiation

Companies can help prevent conflict by creating an atmosphere in which all employees are accepted despite differences in beliefs, values, backgrounds, or experiences. However, no company can completely prevent conflict. When conflicts arise, they must be negotiated.

Negotiation is the process of working with the parties to a conflict to find a resolution. Negotiating requires a willingness to work together. The key to successful negotiation is clear communication. As you learned in

---

PHOTO GUIDE | **NEGOTIATING CONFLICTS**

Discussion Lead a discussion about negotiating conflict resolution. Ask: Can a conflict be resolved if all sides are not willing to work together?

Caption Answer The key to negotiation is a willingness to work together.

Follow Up Ask students to think of cases of conflict resolution from their history class. What can they learn from these conflicts and their resolutions? (Examples will vary, but may include treaties between warring countries. Students may state that forcing resolution upon parties does not settle conflicts.)

Chapter 8, there are four basic skills involved in the communication process: listening, reading, speaking, and writing. Negotiation involves two of these skills: listening and speaking.

Speaking

The first step in negotiation is defining as clearly as possible the problem as each person sees it. Facts and feelings must be presented from each individual's perspective. This usually goes more smoothly when "I statements" are used. For example, avoid the aggressive tone in "You make me mad when you. . . ." Instead, say "I become upset when you. . . ." Instead of saying "Your description of the problem is confusing," say "I am confused about what the problem is." Placing blame should

Case Study

Coming to an Agreement

Herb Cohen is a successful negotiator who has worked for U.S. government agencies, famous sports figures, and large corporations. He has written several best-selling books on negotiation. The most recent is titled *Negotiate This! By Caring, But Not T-H-A-T Much*. It highlights skills Cohen used to help settle an NFL strike and as a consultant during the 1980 Iran hostage crisis. These skills can be applied to issues that arise in everyday life and in the workplace.

Imagine that your mom wants you to wash the dishes. You ask if you can play basketball first, while it is still light outside. That is negotiating! You both win. You play ball and the dishes get washed, too. You probably both feel good about the outcome, an important result of successful negotiation. Negotiating is not about getting your own way, but about coming to agreement.

The Negotiating Process

Cohen emphasizes the importance of caring about your position, but not so much that it prevents you from compromising. Be clear about what you are willing to give up, and what you are not. It is important to make concessions—to give in a little—early in the process. Cohen cautions people not to assume they know what is important to the other person. If you assumed that your mom would be satisfied only if you did the dishes right away, you might not ask if you could play ball first. Thus, you would lose out as a result.

THINK STRATEGICALLY

Suppose you and a friend are planning to spend Saturday afternoon together. Each of you wants to see a movie, but no movies in your neighborhood appeal to both of you. How can you use negotiation skills to decide what to do?

@ Online Action! Go to *marketingessentials.glencoe.com/10/case* to find a project on negotiations.

Case Study — Coming to an Agreement

Discussion Have students read the Case Study and discuss the negotiating they have done recently. Examples can come from relationships with family, friends, or coworkers.

THINK STRATEGICALLY **Answer:** Answers will vary. Students may suggest that one person chooses one week, and the other will choose the following week. Another compromise might be for one person to choose the movie and the other to choose where to go for dinner.

@ Online Action! For instructions, ideas, and answer guide, go to the Teacher Center at **marketingessentials.glencoe.com**

ASSESS

Review Guide

CONCEPTS

Ask students to list the four guidelines for managing time well.
1.) Make a list of the tasks you need to complete. 2.) Determine which task is most important considering the timeframe you have. 3.) Continue to rank the tasks. 4.) Create a schedule based on your list.

KEY TERMS

Have students form small groups, review key terms, and write scenarios that illustrate them.

ONLINE SELF-ASSESSMENT

Have students go to **marketingessentials.glencoe.com** for the Section 10.1 practice test.

Individualized Review

L1 Assign and review Chapter 10 activities in the Student Activity Workbook.

L2 Assign and review Chapter 10 activities in the Marketing Math Workbook.

L3 Assign and review Chapter 10 activities in the *BusinessWeek* Reader and Case Studies.

Marketing Practice

Emphasize to students the importance of empathy in marketing. Let them know that unless they understand their market, they cannot communicate effectively with potential clients. Ask students to think of ways to better understand their markets and to choose one way, then create a short presentation explaining their choice. Answers will vary; student choices may include spending time with members the market, conducting focus groups, or hiring consultants.

223

CLOSE

Ask students to recall and provide answers to the following questions:

- **What are some positive effects of stress?**

  Stress can energize, motivate, and excite us.

- **What are the six simple techniques for negotiating conflict resolution?**
  1. Show respect.
  2. Recognize and define the problem.
  3. Seek a variety of solutions.
  4. Collaborate.
  5. Be reliable.
  6. Preserve the relationship.

Extended Activity

Conflict Resolution

Ask students to research select online or written guides that define and give tips for resolving conflicts in written communication. Have them compare and contrast those solutions to resolving conflicts in person.

---

be avoided because it puts people on the defensive. Participants should take some time to plan ahead what they will say. If possible, set a time and place to meet that is convenient for everyone involved. A quiet, neutral place with few distractions is ideal.

Listening

Listening is an active process in which all of your attention is focused on the speaker. Encourage the speaker to share his or her feelings and thoughts. Maintaining eye contact with the speaker shows that you are interested and want to understand what is being said. Planning a response before the speaker's point is made is a distraction that often causes misunderstandings.

Try to empathize, or show empathy, with the person who is speaking. **Empathy** is an understanding of a person's situation or frame of mind. Remember that people of different ages, genders, cultures, and abilities may have had experiences that are unfamiliar to you. Do not make the mistake of assuming that certain viewpoints and behaviors are universal. There are many people in the world with ideas that are very different from yours.

Six simple techniques for negotiating conflict resolution can be helpful:

1. Show respect
2. Recognize and define the problem
3. Seek a variety of solutions
4. Collaborate
5. Be reliable
6. Preserve the relationship

The problem is solved only when both sides reach a common understanding and agreement about what actions are to be taken. Never assume you understand the other person without asking some verification questions. For example, you might ask "Is this what you meant by. . . ?" or "Did I understand correctly when. . . ?"

10.1 AFTER YOU READ

Reviewing Key Terms and Concepts

1. Name five personality traits that help to develop good working relationships.
2. Define ethics and name four ways to apply ethical behavior in the workplace.
3. Explain the two key communication skills necessary to resolve conflict.

Integrating Academic Skills

Math

4. Your company's health insurance plan costs $585 per employee per month. There are 64 employees. Another health insurance company would charge 10 percent less. What would be the total savings per year?

English

5. You were asked to promote a golf tournament for charity. Write a paragraph to explain how you will schedule the steps needed to complete the project.

 @ Online Action! Check your answers at *marketingessentials.glencoe.com/10/read*

marketingessentials.glencoe.com

AFTER YOU READ

Reviewing Key Terms and Concepts

1. Five personality traits that help to develop good working relationships include the following: self-esteem and self-awareness, positive attitude, initiative and responsibility, self-control, and creativity.

2. Ethics are the basic values and moral principles that guide the behavior of individuals and groups. Four ways to apply them include honesty, respect, integrity, and a sense of fair play.

3. The two key communication skills necessary to resolve conflict are speaking and listening.

Integrating Academic Skills

4. $3,744; $585 × 64 × .10 = $3,744

5. Paragraphs should demonstrate an understanding of effective time management.

@ Online Action! Answers at **marketingessentials.glencoe.com/10/read**

Working Together: Leadership and Teamwork

FOCUS

OBJECTIVES

- Discuss how to receive and handle customer complaints
- Identify skills needed to be a good team member and provide leadership
- Name six aspects of successful teamwork

READ and STUDY

BEFORE YOU READ
Predict What do you think are some advantages to working on a team versus working individually?

THE MAIN IDEA
By developing the skills of a good team member, you will help your team achieve its goals.

STUDY ORGANIZER
Draw the chart below. As you read this section, write in six aspects of good teamwork.

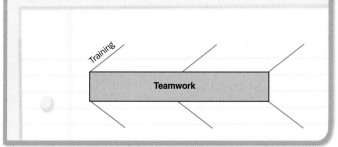

KEY TERMS

- teamwork
- cross-training
- consensus
- agreement

Introducing the Section

COLLABORATIVE ACTIVITY
To prepare for reading this section, have students discuss a time they have worked in a team. Ask: What were their experiences like? As students recount their stories, have them write down descriptors about the interpersonal skills of the employees or people they worked with. Afterwards, have students share their descriptions in small groups.

Preteaching Key Terms

Read the key terms aloud, or ask a volunteer to read them. Ask students to predict their meanings.

- teamwork
- cross-training
- consensus
- agreement

Tell students they can check their predictions as they read this section.

Interpersonal Skills in Marketing

Good working relationships between employees and customers or clients depends on the interpersonal skills of the employees. As an employee, you should be familiar with your company's basic procedures in responding to concerns raised by customers. It is also important to know when you need to refer the customer to someone else. This may happen when an issue needs to be resolved by a manager or when a question involves information that your department does not have.

WHILE YOU READ

Connect Focus on each aspect of teamwork and how you can improve your own ability to be a good team member.

Chapter 10 - Interpersonal Skills **225**

Critical Thinking

Ask students if the elements of teamwork change according to the size of the team. Why or why not? Answers will vary, but may include varying levels of responsibility.

READ and STUDY

BEFORE YOU READ
Lead students in discussing the advantages of working as a team. Have students form small groups to describe the benefits. Answers may include combining different skills and generating more ideas.

THE MAIN IDEA
Ask a volunteer to give an example of how he or she has helped a team achieve its goals.

STUDY ORGANIZER
Model the study organizer for students by writing in elements of teamwork, such as training. A full-size, downloadable study organizer can be found at marketingessentials.glencoe.com

WHILE YOU READ Model for students how they can take notes about being a good team member as they read through the section.

TEACH

WORKING TOGETHER: LEADERSHIP AND TEAMWORK

Ask students to consider the following situation: A group of marketing students is asked to raise money for its school club, so they decide to hold a bake sale. Ask students to consider the tasks needed to organize such an event and what skills will be required to accomplish each task.

Answers may include handling publicity, organizing materials, coordinating workers, providing manual labor, and handling money. The event can only be held successfully if each task is handled adequately.

TEACHING POINTS

Model Tell students that one model for teamwork is a racecar pit crew, which can prepare a car in a matter of seconds. Talk about the preparation and execution of such a pit stop.

Extend Have students discuss other models of teamwork from their own experiences or observations.

TRAINING

After students have read the section on training, tell them that there are companies that organize motivational speaking events geared toward professionals from all types of businesses. Often, the speakers are star athletes and coaches. What do students think successful people from the sports world can offer to people in the workforce?

Answers will vary, and may include lessons in leadership, teamwork, and attitude.

Addressing Customers' Concerns

To respond promptly and intelligently to customer concerns, you need to be familiar with company procedures. You should know how to handle the following situations:

- **Requests and questions** You will need to learn the proper procedures for handling customer requests and questions. You will also need to know what you should say to customers if you cannot answer their questions yourself.
- **Directions** You will need to be able to give clear and concise directions to your store or office.
- **Management's role** You will need to know under what circumstances a manager should be called to talk to a customer.
- **Business policies** You will need to be able to explain business policies to customers. These may include return or exchange procedures and the company policy on checks or credit cards.

Addressing Customers' Complaints

Most customers never let the company or store know they have a complaint. Only four to eight percent of customers who have a concern or complaint share their problem with the firm.

If a customer brings you a concern, you have an opportunity to learn something that may improve service. You may also prevent damage to the firm and stop the problem from recurring.

Complaints cover a range of issues. Some are genuine errors on the part of the firm, such as a faulty item or a bad service experience. Others stem from misunderstandings, such as poorly written directions on a product's package. The customer may suggest how the firm can improve its service. Your company should develop a procedure to follow when dealing with customer complaints. If not, follow these guidelines:

- **Listen** First, listen completely and openly to the customer's complaint so that you are sure you understand it.

- **Take the customer aside** If the customer is talking loudly, try to take him or her aside—if possible, into a separate room. A sales counter or desk can seem like a barrier. Standing side by side in a quiet place may ease the tension.
- **Repeat** When appropriate, repeat the facts of the complaint to show that you understand. If you can explain what caused the problem for the customer, state it clearly. Do not place blame on anyone.
- **Get help** If you feel you need assistance from a supervisor, let the customer know this and seek assistance promptly.
- **Establish a plan** Try to reach an agreement with the customer about the next course of action. Suggest only action that is consistent with the company's policy. Then be absolutely certain to follow through on the action agreed upon.

Teamwork

A team is a group of people who work together to achieve a goal. **Teamwork** is work done by a group of people to achieve a common goal.

Teamwork is becoming increasingly important in the business world. According to football coach Vince Lombardi, "Individual commitment to a group effort—that is what makes a team work, a company work, a society work, a civilization work." The following are six aspects of teamwork. (See Figure 10.1 for more detail.)

Training

To be an effective team member, you must have training for all the tasks you will perform. You have probably heard of cross-training in sports. **Cross-training** means preparing to do many different activities.

On the job, people are cross-trained for many tasks on a team. This gives the team flexibility and diverse strengths. Work becomes more enjoyable when you know you will not be doing the same activity every day.

Team Planning

Before you start working on a project, make a plan as a team. Team planning involves setting

Online Activity

Research Events

Have students look up Web sites for the planning of the following events: running a marathon, organizing a party, and going on an overseas trip. Have students make a list of what the different plans have in common.

goals, assigning roles, making agreements, sharing responsibility, and communicating regularly.

Team Goals

Team members must be involved in defining a goal in order to feel committed to it. This results in greater company loyalty and stronger team spirit.

Members should reach a consensus about goals. A **consensus** is a decision to which each member agrees. Therefore, all team members must be allowed to state their opinions. The final agreement may require team members to make a compromise. Being flexible as an individual helps you learn to compromise as a team member.

Assigning Roles

Team projects often work more smoothly if the team appoints a leader who coordinates tasks.

Each person on the team needs to know which part of the process he or she is responsible for each day. Members are usually assigned tasks based on their skills and experience.

Agreements

An **agreement** is a specific commitment that each member makes to the group. When team members make agreements, the team becomes more cohesive and stronger. A team's agreements must be consistent with its goals.

It is important that each team member feel connected to the company's goals as well as to the team's goals. Team loyalty and positive peer pressure help to encourage people to keep their agreements.

Shared Responsibility and Shared Leadership

Shared responsibility and shared leadership mean that each member must feel responsible for the whole team's efforts. Shared leadership also allows all team members to perform some management functions.

Feedback

When giving feedback, make sure you are respectful. If you are overly critical, the feedback

---

MARKET TECH

Customer Relationship Marketing (CRM)

The more companies know about their customers, the better they can serve them. A wise business develops a database with information about where customers live and what products they purchase. This is part of customer relationship marketing (CRM), which focuses on the customer as key to the success of a business.

Amazon.com Example

When a customer signs in to a personal Amazon.com account and begins browsing the virtual bookshelves, he or she leaves a digital trail. Amazon uses CRM software to collect information about which books the customer looks at and which he or she buys. The company can then direct advertising of similar items to the customer.

A Network of Customer Information

After asking permission, businesses can share information about customers' preferences and buying habits with other businesses. This expands the network of knowledge about the customer. Each piece of information helps to round out the picture, so that the business knows how to sell to each customer better.

THINK LIKE A MARKETER

Besides purchases made, what type of customer information is valuable to marketers?

 Online Action!

Go to *marketingessentials.glencoe.com/10/tech* to find a project on customer relationship marketing.

TEACH CONTINUED

Individualized Math Skills

L1 Ask students to describe the costs for an online boutique to send an e-mail newsletter.

Costs may include the purchasing of a mailing list and fees of a mass-mailing service.

L2 Ask students if a mailing list of 50,000 e-mail addresses costs $1,000 and a company charges $25 to send 1,000 e-mails, what is the total cost?

$2,250; $1,000 + (50,000 × $25 ÷ 1,000) = $1,250; $1,000 + $1,250 = $2,250

L3 If the business expects 2 percent of the e-mails to respond with an average order of $15, would buying and sending an e-mail newsletter be worth it?

50,000 × .02 × $15 = $15,000. Yes.

Online Activity

E-mail Marketing

Ask students to research the costs of buying and sending e-mail lists. Have them make a list of factors to study when considering such an activity.

MARKET TECH

Customer Relationship Marketing (CRM)

Discussion After students have read Market Tech, lead a discussion about customer relationship marketing. Ask: Are there any drawbacks to businesses sharing information about their customers?

THINK LIKE A MARKETER **Answer:** Valuable information for marketers might include their customers' location, favorite brands, ages, and household demographics.

Online Action! For instructions, ideas, and answer guide, go to the Teacher Center at **marketingessentials.glencoe.com**

227

Review Guide

CONCEPTS
Ask students to list the customer concerns a worker should be able to handle. Requests and questions, directions, management's role, and business policies.

KEY TERMS
In small groups, have students review key terms, their spellings, and definitions.

ONLINE SELF-ASSESSMENT
Have students go to marketingessentials.glencoe.com for the Section 10.2 practice test.

Individualized Review

L1 Assign and review Chapter 10 activities in the Student Activity Workbook.

L2 Assign and review Chapter 10 activities in the Marketing Math Workbook.

L3 Assign and review Chapter 10 activities in the *BusinessWeek* Reader and Case Studies.

Marketing Practice

Have students describe the teamwork they see at a local restaurant. Have students break down the process of serving a customer into tasks that are completed by different individuals. Ask students to infer and explain how the failure of any one team member can slow or damage the entire process. Have students share their responses in class.

For example, a dishwasher can ruin the customer's dining experience by leaving a stain on a cup.

Figure 10.1 **Teamwork**

• **Succeeding Together** As many businesses move away from a top-down management style toward a team approach, it is important for employees to understand how a team works and what's expected of individual members.

What are some of the interpersonal skills you need to be a valuable team member?

TRAINING
Individual members of a team need to keep up with the team. This means having the necessary skills to do your job and staying current with best practices in your field.

TEAM PLANNING
Teams are usually assigned projects. Planning how to carry out those projects is the team's responsibility. Teams often include individuals with different strengths; for instance, an advertising team may include an illustrator, a copywriter, a production coordinator, and a marketing specialist.

TEAM GOALS
The team sets goals. For an advertising team, that might mean completing a new ad or an entire advertising campaign by a certain date. Team goals must be aligned with the goals of the company.

DELEGATION/AGREEMENTS
Members of the team are assigned different tasks, depending on their skills. Each team member agrees to complete the assigned task. On an advertising team, the graphic artist lays out graphics on a computer, the copywriter develops slogans and copy, and the production coordinator works with outside vendors.

SHARED RESPONSIBILITY/LEADERSHIP
Everyone on the team shares responsibility for achieving the team's goal. Members of the team usually select a manager, or owner, to keep track of schedules and handle any difficulties that come up.

@ Online Action!
Go to *marketingessentials.glencoe.com/10/figure/1* to find a project on teamwork.

 marketingessentials.glencoe.com

Figure 10.1 **Teamwork**

Discussion After students have read Figure 10.1, have small groups of students choose real or imagined advertising campaign and come up with specific examples of each of the five aspects of teamwork that might be used in implementing the campaign.

Caption Answer Answers will vary, but may include tact, leadership, perspective, experience, and a sense of humor.

@ Online Action! For instructions, ideas, and answer guide, go to the Teacher Center at marketingessentials.glencoe.com

Follow Up Have students discuss their own experiences of working in a team, whether in class, on sports teams, at work or within their own family.

will not serve its purpose. Instead, it will alienate the team member being evaluated.

Leadership Skills

One definition of leadership is helping members of a group achieve their goals. Leaders need self-confidence and a willingness to take the initiative. They need creativity to solve new or unusual problems. Leaders need problem-solving, social judgment, and communication skills. Problem-solving skills include being able to define the problem, gather information, analyze the problem, and generate plans for a solution. Good leaders understand people and social systems and are able to motivate others to work together. Conflict resolution is also important in helping members of a group work together. Leaders need to communicate their vision to others and be sensitive to their motivations and needs.

Being a Valuable Team Member

What makes a person a good team member? The following list describes valuable attitudes and actions.

- Make the team's goals your top priority.
- In meetings, listen actively and offer suggestions.
- Build positive group dynamics with team members.
- Continue to communicate with team members outside meetings.
- Follow up on what you have been assigned to do.
- Work to resolve conflicts among team members.
- Respect the other members of your team.
- Try to inspire other employees to get involved.

 10.2 AFTER YOU READ

Reviewing Key Terms and Concepts

1. Define teamwork and explain how this concept applies to the business world.
2. What personal strengths and interpersonal skills are required of a good leader?
3. What personal traits and interpersonal skills make a person a good team member?

Integrating Academic Skills

Math

4. Your business has decided to start recycling paper products. In exchange, the recycling company will donate 20 boxes of new paper each year to your business. You currently order 150 boxes of paper per year, at $50 per box. If you start recycling with the company, how much money will you save each year?

Economics

5. Research the economic benefits of teamwork in business. Does teamwork increase productivity? How are employees and customers affected?

 Online Action!   Check your answers at *marketingessentials.glencoe.com/10/read*

marketingessentials.glencoe.com

Chapter 10 - Interpersonal Skills **229**

SECTION 10.2

CLOSE

Ask students to answer the following questions:

- **What is shared responsibility and shared leadership?**
  Shared responsibility means that each member must feel responsible for the team's efforts. In shared leadership, team members take action to bring the whole team's performance up to the standards the team has agreed on.

- **What is customer relationship marketing?**
  Customer relationship marketing focuses on the customer as the key to the success of any market-related business.

 Online Activity

Team Spirit
Have students look up the Web sites for two to three marketing companies online. Ask students to make a list of their references to teamwork on the sites.

AFTER YOU READ

Reviewing Key Terms and Concepts

1. Teamwork is work done by a group of people to achieve a common goal. It is becoming increasingly important in the business world.

2. Personal strengths and interpersonal skills needed by a good leader include problem solving, social judgment, and communication.

3. Personal traits and interpersonal skills required by a good team member include listening, building positive group dynamics, conflict resolution, respect, inspiring, and making the team's goals one's top priority.

Integrating Academic Skills

4. $1,000; 20 × $50 = $1,000

5. Answers will vary. Students might conclude that teamwork allows workers to be more efficient and productive. It can also improve workers' morale and customer satisfaction.

Online Action!   Answers at **marketingessentials.glencoe.com/10/read**

229

Lifelong Learning

CAREER INFORMATION

Have students go to **marketingessentials.glencoe.com** and find the Chapter 10 Careers page and click on the link for the American Marketing Association's Careers Strategies and Tips. Ask students to select one article, read it, and make a poster or presentation showing its main points.

INTERPERSONAL SKILLS

School and extracurricular activities such as team sports, clubs, work, and internships are some of the many places and situations in which you can practice and learn how to relate to and communicate with others. Being able to communicate with others is key to developing the teamwork and customer service skills that are essential to many jobs.

Primary Source

Ask students to go to **marketingessentials.glencoe.com** and find Chapter 10 Resources. Ask them to click on the link for the American Marketing Association's marketing dictionary and read the definitions of the terms related to interpersonal skills they find.

● THINKING CRITICALLY

Give a brief description of the training vendors might provide. Suggest that it may entail more role-playing and practicing than a typical classroom education.

@ Online Action!

For instructions, ideas, and answer guide, go to the Teacher Center at **marketingessentials.glencoe.com**

CAREERS
IN MARKETING

CARSON LEDFORD
OWNER
TECHNOLOGY PLUS
SALES AND SERVICE

❓ What do you do at work?
I started the company with myself as the only employee and tried to cover all aspects of the business from service provider to bookkeeping. Now with five full-time employees, I focus mainly on sales and customer service. I still maintain a hands-on role, spending about 20 percent of my time in the field providing service to the customer.

❓ What skills are most important to you?
In the beginning when I was the only employee, my technical skills in electronics were the most valuable. The ability to understand the products I serviced and be able to repair them was a must. As my role in the company has changed, I have found my people skills to be more valuable than any other. The most important part of that process is being able to communicate with the customer in a manner that does not confuse them. I believe that good, constant communication with the customer throughout a project is the key to quality solutions.

❓ What is your key to success?
Customer service! Customer service! Customer service! The willingness to provide a quality and affordable service to the customer has been what sets us apart from our competition. We utilize technology, not hide behind it, which allows us to respond quickly to customers' needs. We always return calls promptly to our customers.

● THINKING CRITICALLY

What kind of training might vendors provide to companies such as this, and how would it differ from traditional classroom education?

@ Online Action!

Go to *marketingessentials.glencoe.com/10/careers* to Pnd a research project on technology services.

Aptitudes, Abilities, and Skills

Technical knowledge, sales ability, strong communication skills

Education and Training

Bachelor's and Master's degrees in computer science and technology are helpful, along with general business degrees to aid in the non-technical side of the business.

Career Path

Many technology professionals begin as freelancers or start their own companies; for others, careers can begin with entry-level IT positions within established companies.

 marketingessentials.glencoe.com

▱ Test-Taking Strategies

Ask students to consider what the team goal of a class is. Ask: Is it to do well on tests or to learn information? Have students compare the two goals and determine what their benefits are. Tell students that knowing the goals of a class is key to succeeding on tests.

FOCUS on KEY POINTS

SECTION 10.1

● Good interpersonal skills are necessary for building effective working relationships with coworkers and clients.

● Personality traits such as assertiveness and creativity help people work effectively with others.

● Ethical behavior in today's workplace involves demonstrating respect for people of diverse backgrounds.

● Conflict negotiation requires good communication skills.

SECTION 10.2

● Teamwork means a group of people work together toward a goal.

● Understanding the team goals, the roles assigned to individual team members, and shared responsibilities will help make you a valuable team member.

REVIEW VOCABULARY

Use the following pairs of terms in sentences that show you understand their meanings. Explain how all these words relate to the concept of self-esteem.

1. initiative (p. 219)—time management (p. 219)
2. assertiveness (p. 220)—flexibility (p. 221)
3. consensus (p. 227)—agreement (p. 227)
4. ethics (p. 221)—equity (p. 222)
5. negotiation (p. 222)—empathy (p. 224)
6. teamwork (p. 226)—cross-training (p. 226)

REVIEW FACTS and IDEAS

7. Which personality traits discussed in the text do you feel you need to work on to become a better friend and coworker? (10.1)
8. Explain the importance of initiative to good working relationships. (10.1)
9. How will asking about others' interests and experiences help to prevent bias? (10.1)
10. What is the one thing that a team must do before it can begin its work? (10.2)
11. How can sharing responsibility and leadership be helpful in achieving team goals? (10.2)
12. What are five conventions that can help teams overcome obstacles? (10.2)

Chapter 10 - Interpersonal Skills **231**

REVIEW FACTS and IDEAS

7. Personality traits will vary; positive traits include self-esteem and self-awareness, positive attitude, initiative and responsibility, self-control, and creativity.

8. Initiative shows that you are enthusiastic about your work and can do what needs to be done without being asked.

9. Asking about others' interests and experiences helps you understand them better.

10. Before a team can act, it must have clearly defined goals.

11. Sharing responsibility and leadership helps employees feel more powerful because it actually gives them more power.

12. Students should list five of the following conventions that help a team overcome obstacles: making the team's goals top priority, listening and offering suggestions, building positive group dynamics, communicating with team members, following up on your work, resolving conflicts among team members, respecting other team members, and inspiring other employees to get involved.

FOCUS on KEY POINTS

Ask volunteers to read the summaries aloud and give the classroom one real-life example of each concept.

REVIEW VOCABULARY

Sentences should demonstrate that students understand the words' meanings. See glossary for definitions of **1-6.** A sample answer might read:

1. *Initiative* is taking action and doing what needs to be done without being asked, while *time management* is budgeting your time to accomplish tasks on a certain schedule.

BUILD SKILLS

13. Workplace Skills
Paragraphs will vary; student responses might suggest addressing all three employees generally, and giving positive reinforcement to the good worker while he or she is away from the other two.

14. Technology Applications
One-page reports will vary; students should demonstrate an understanding of stress management and relaxation techniques, negotiating conflict resolution, or gender equity. Internet sources should be listed.

15. Math Practice
$1,799 × .12 = $215.88;
$1,799 − $215.88 = $1,583.12

DEVELOP CRITICAL THINKING

16. Why Is Cross-Training Important to Teamwork?
One-page essays will vary; students may suggest that having a multi-faceted background allows one to be better prepared to handle new or unexpected tasks.

17. How Can Business Benefit From Stress Management?
One-page papers will vary; students may suggest that stress management will allow workers to be more productive and content in adverse conditions.

BUILD SKILLS

13. Workplace Skills
Interpersonal Communication You are the new manager of a photocopy shop that has three other employees. One of them is an excellent worker, but two who were recently hired often arrive late and tend to make a lot of mistakes. Write a paragraph describing how you will handle the situation and what you will say to your employees.

14. Technology Applications
Researching on the Web Use the Internet to research one of the following topics: (1) Stress management and relaxation techniques; (2) Negotiating conflict resolution; or (3) Gender equity in the workplace. Write a one-page report summarizing your findings.

15. Math Practice
Cross-Training With Math Math is a basic skill that can be helpful to you as a team member. Assume that your boss asks you to determine how much will be discounted from the price of a color printer that has a list price of $1,799 and a discount of 12 percent. What answer would you give her?

DEVELOP CRITICAL THINKING

16. Why Is Cross-Training Important to Teamwork?
Assume that you are employed by a public relations firm as an assistant publicist. Your company is organized into teams. Through regular team meetings and human relations workshops, all the members of your team have some understanding of the roles played by the other team members. The day before a press kit is due to an important client, the senior publicist assigned to produce the press kit calls in sick with the flu. What should you do? Write a one-page essay explaining your answer and why cross-training is valuable in this situation.

17. How Can Business Benefit From Stress Management?
Assume that you work for a shipping company that gets very busy during the holiday season. A month before the company expects its heaviest traffic, your boss calls a meeting and asks for suggestions on how best to handle the increased business. Prepare a short, one-page paper recommending that the human resources department offer a course in stress management. Explain your recommendation.

 Formative Assessment
Formative assessment is an essential component of classroom work. This type of assessment provides information that is then used as feedback to modify teaching and meet student needs.

L1 Review key terms for this chapter. Ask students to write one sentence for each key term.

L2 Provide various marketing scenarios to the students, for example, advertising campaigns or public relations damage control. For each situation, have students describe ways marketing teams would work together to approach these scenarios.

L3 Ask students to create situations that illustrate workplace interpersonal skills.

 Reteach If the results of this formative assessment seem low, consider the following activity:
Read the sections' subheads aloud and have students name two key facts or important details for each.

CHAPTER 10 REVIEW

APPLY CONCEPTS

18. Use Time Management Principles

Imagine that you are an event planner. You have been given the job of planning a marketing career fair to be held at a large convention center. The event is scheduled for the weekend of November 6 and 7, which is six weeks from today.

Activity Use time management principles to create a schedule for planning a marketing career fair to be held six weeks from today. Present the schedule to your class using presentation software.

19. Research Training Opportunities

You have just been hired as the new sales representative for a start-up athletic gear manufacturing company. There is currently no human resources department in the company. Your boss has given you a budget for training and asked you to find appropriate courses in assertiveness and self-esteem, which he considers useful to the job.

Activity Use the Internet to research training in assertiveness and self-esteem. Find out what kinds of classes are available and how they relate to success in business. Pick one and, using a word processing program, prepare the information to present for your boss's approval. Present this information to the class.

NET SAVVY

20. Etiquette

Locate Web sites explaining cultural customs and beliefs that differ from those in the United States. Select one country. Write a 200-word business etiquette guide.

marketingessentials.glencoe.com

THE DECA CONNECTION

Role Play:
Motel Front-Desk Clerk

Situation You are to assume the role of front-desk clerk for a family-owned motel in a popular resort area. The main attraction for the motel is that it offers fun family activities like miniature golf tournaments, cookout nights, etc. The staff is a small one, but shares a sense of friendly teamwork. Recently, the housekeeping staff have complained that they don't hear about upcoming activities planned for guests and feel generally uninformed about activities at the motel.

Activity The motel owner (judge) has asked you for some ideas about ways to make the housekeeping staff feel more a part of the motel's activities.

Evaluation You will be evaluated on how well you meet the following performance indicators:

● Encourage team building

● Explain the nature of staff communication

● Handle employee complaints and grievances

● Assess employee morale

● Address people properly

 Online Action!

For more information and DECA Prep practice, go to *marketingessentials.glencoe.com/10/DECA*

THE DECA CONNECTION

The students should be evaluated on the performance indicators noted in the role play. For another DECA role play, go to the Competitive Events Workbook or the Student Activity Workbook, or go to **marketingessentials.glencoe.com/10/DECA**

 Online Action! For instructions, ideas, and answer guide, go to the Teacher Center at **marketingessentials.glencoe.com**

DECA Advisors Corner

This chapter lends itself to any of DECA's competitive events. By selecting an Individual Series Event, you can have students demonstrate their interpersonal skills in handling problems from customer relations to employee conflict resolution. DECA's team events require students to develop team abilities and the ability to interact with business professionals.

APPLY CONCEPTS

18. Use Time Management Principles

Schedules and presentations will vary; students might estimate the length of each task and counting backwards from the deadline.

19. Research Training Opportunities

Reports and presentations will vary; students should explain the importance of assertiveness and self-esteem and list ways to cultivate these traits in employees.

NET SAVVY

20. Etiquette

Etiquette guides will vary; student guides should demonstrate an understanding of and a tolerance for cultural customs and beliefs that differ from those of the United States.

MINI-QUIZ

Read these sentences to the students and have them volunteer the missing word(s).

1. _____ means budgeting your time to accomplish tasks on a certain schedule. (Time management)

2. Stress is a reaction to _____. (outside pressure)

3. The Americans With Disabilities Act of 1990 protects qualified individuals with disabilities from _____. (discrimination)

For an expanded chapter quiz, go to Chapter 10 in the TeacherWorks CD-ROM and to Chapter 10 in the **Exam*View*®** Pro Test Generator CD-ROM.

Chapter Overview

Chapter 11 explores types of management structures, including horizontal and vertical organization, and self-managed work teams. The chapter also looks at the basic management functions of planning, organizing, and controlling with a discussion of effective management techniques.

BUILD BACKGROUND

Ask students to recall times they have worked in groups at work, school, sports, music, or other situations. Have them discuss ways decisions are made by the team, and ask them to consider how that model would work in a business setting.

Why It's Important

Every profession has particular management functions that evolve with the state of technology and the diverse workforce. A basic understanding of management structure and functions is essential for business success.

Prepare to Read

Have students skim the chapter, looking at pictures, reading captions, and noting headings. Ask questions to ensure that students have an understanding of the chapter structure.

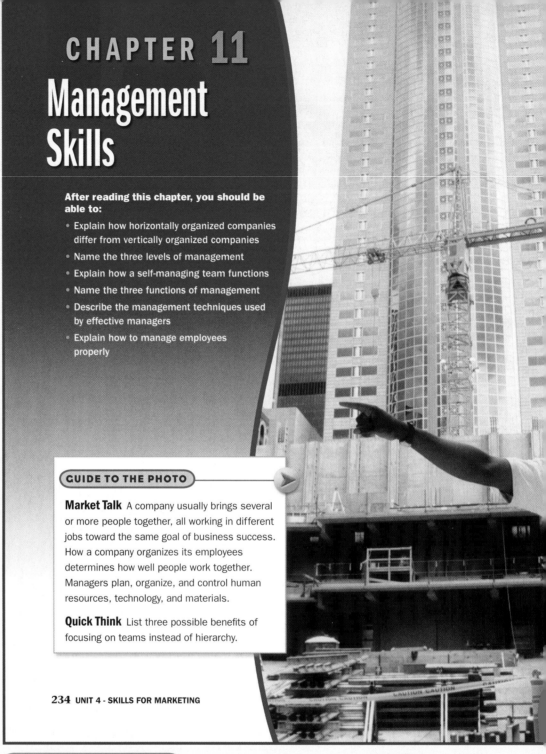

CHAPTER 11
Management Skills

After reading this chapter, you should be able to:

- Explain how horizontally organized companies differ from vertically organized companies
- Name the three levels of management
- Explain how a self-managing team functions
- Name the three functions of management
- Describe the management techniques used by effective managers
- Explain how to manage employees properly

GUIDE TO THE PHOTO

Market Talk A company usually brings several or more people together, all working in different jobs toward the same goal of business success. How a company organizes its employees determines how well people work together. Managers plan, organize, and control human resources, technology, and materials.

Quick Think List three possible benefits of focusing on teams instead of hierarchy.

234 UNIT 4 - SKILLS FOR MARKETING

GUIDE TO THE PHOTO

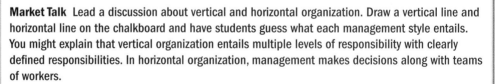

Market Talk Lead a discussion about vertical and horizontal organization. Draw a vertical line and horizontal line on the chalkboard and have students guess what each management style entails. You might explain that vertical organization entails multiple levels of responsibility with clearly defined responsibilities. In horizontal organization, management makes decisions along with teams of workers.

Quick Think Three possible benefits might include greater efficiency, increased employee satisfaction, and less supervision by management.

Follow Up Have students describe the vertical management style of your classroom. Ask: How would procedures change if it were managed horizontally?

THE DECA CONNECTION

Performance indicators represent key skills and knowledge. Relating them to the concepts explained in this chapter is your key to success in DECA events. These acronyms represent DECA events that involve knowledge of concepts in this chapter.

AAAL	FMAL	MMS*	TMDM*
AAML*	FMDM*	QSRM*	TSE*
ADC*	FMML*	RMAL	VPM
BSM	FSRM*	RMML*	
EMDM*	HMDM*	SMDM*	

In all these DECA events you should be able to follow these performance indicators:

- Explain the concept of management
- Describe the nature of business records
- Describe the nature of budgets
- Describe crucial elements of a quality culture
- Develop project plan
- Explain the nature of overhead/operating costs
- Describe the nature of managerial control (control process, types of control, what is controlled)
- Identify routine activities for maintaining business facilities and equipment
- Orient new employees

All the events with an asterisk (*) also include these performance indicators:

- Describe the role of management in the achievement of quality
- Explain the nature of managerial ethics
- Determine hiring needs
- Establish personnel policies
- Explain the nature of leadership in organizations
- Assess employee performance
- Explain ways to build employee morale

DECA PREP

Check your understanding of DECA performance indicators with the DECA activity in this chapter's review. For more information and DECA Prep practice, go to *marketingessentials.glencoe.com/11/DECA*

THE DECA CONNECTION

DECA events that require knowledge of management skills are described here. Discuss the performance indicators to make sure students understand how to demonstrate their understanding.

The events acronyms stand for:

AAAL: Apparel and Accessories Marketing Series, AL

AAML: Apparel and Accessories Marketing Series, ML

ADC: Advertising Campaign Event

BSM: Business Services Marketing Series

EMDM: E-Commerce Management Team Decision Making Event

FMAL: Food Marketing Series, AL

FMDM: Financial Analysis Management Team Decision Making Event

FMML: Food Marketing Series, ML

FSRM: Full Service Restaurant Management Series

HMDM: Hospitality Services Management Team Decision Making Events

MMS: Marketing Management Series

QSRM: Quick Serve Restaurant Management Series

RMAL: Retail Merchandising Series, AL

RMML: Retail Merchandising Series, ML

SMDM: Sports and Entertainment Marketing Management Team Decision Making Event

TMDM: Travel and Tourism Marketing Management Team Decision Making Event

TSE: Technical Sales Event

VPM: Vehicles and Petroleum Marketing Series

DECA PREP

Find timed DECA Prep activities correlated to the Competitive Events Workbook for students and DECA tips for teachers at **marketingessentials.glencoe.com/11/DECA**

CHAPTER 11 Classroom Resources

For the Teacher

- TeacherWorks
- **marketingessentials.glencoe.com**
- Interactive Chalkboard
- **Exam*View*®** Pro Test Generator
- Fast File Unit 4

For the Student

- ***Marketing Essentials*** Online Edition
- Student Activity Workbook
- Marketing Math Workbook
- Marketing Research Project Workbook
- School-to-Work Activity Workbook
- Competitive Events Workbook
- ***BusinessWeek*** Reader and Case Studies
- **marketingessentials.glencoe.com**

Management Structures

FOCUS

Introducing the Section

COLLABORATIVE ACTIVITY

To prepare students for reading this section, divide the class into three groups: one half of the class, and two quarters of the class. Tell them that they have five minutes to design a school flag. Afterwards, discuss their work. Ask: Were specific people assigned to certain tasks? Was there one overseer who talked to leaders of other groups? Explain that in business there are different types of management.

Preteaching Key Terms

Read the key terms aloud, or ask a volunteer to read them. Ask students to predict the meanings of these terms and phrases:

- management
- vertical organization
- top management
- middle management
- supervisory-level management
- horizontal organization
- empowerment

Tell students they can check their predictions as they read this section.

Critical Thinking

Ask students why sales and marketing positions are often the precursors of management positions.

OBJECTIVES

- Explain how horizontally organized companies differ from vertically organized companies
- Name the three levels of management
- Explain how a self-managing team functions

KEY TERMS

- management
- vertical organization
- top management
- middle management
- supervisory-level management
- horizontal organization
- empowerment

READ and STUDY

BEFORE YOU READ

Predict What are the benefits of having fewer managers in a business?

THE MAIN IDEA

There are two ways of organizing a business: the traditional or vertical organization with an emphasis on hierarchy, and the horizontal organization with a focus on teams.

STUDY ORGANIZER

In a chart like the one below, take notes on the types of business organization.

WHILE YOU READ

Compare Note differences between vertical and horizontal organization.

Leadership in the 21st Century

Business leaders in the United States and around the world expect many changes in the coming years as a result of globalization. New leaders come from diverse backgrounds. Global competition is creating companies and managers who are united by common goals and ideals.

READ and STUDY

BEFORE YOU READ

Lead students in discussing the benefits of having fewer managers in business. Answers might include faster decision making and closer relationships between managers and workers.

THE MAIN IDEA

Ask a volunteer to give examples of horizontally or vertically managed businesses.

STUDY ORGANIZER

Model the study organizer for students. A full-size, downloadable study organizer can be found at marketingessentials.glencoe.com

WHILE YOU READ Show students how they can take notes to differentiate between vertical and horizontal organization.

Types of Management Structure

Management can be defined simply as getting work done through the effort of others. More often, management is considered the process of reaching goals through the use of human resources, technology, and material resources. To facilitate effective management, businesses are generally organized either vertically or horizontally.

Vertical Organization

For a long time, the role of management was to keep an eye on workers. In large, traditional companies, managers reported to higher levels of management. Most managers were responsible for the proper operation of a particular department. The up-and-down structure of this kind of organization is called vertical organization. **Vertical organization** refers to a chain-of-command, hierarchical structure where the tasks and responsibilities of each level of the organization are clearly defined.

Management Levels

In the traditional, vertically organized company, there are three basic levels of management: top management, middle management, and supervisory-level management. Those who make decisions that affect the whole company are **top management**. CEO (chief executive officer), president, COO (chief operating officer), CFO (chief financial officer), and vice president are some top management titles. The functions of top (or senior) management include setting a direction for the company as a whole, identifying resources and methods for meeting goals, and controlling the systems and structures of the company.

GLOBAL MARKET

INDIA

Cultural Adjustments

In 1995, Ranjini Manian founded Global Adjustments, a company that capitalizes on international business both abroad and in India. Global Adjustments offers cross-cultural training for professionals who move to India and for Indian professionals preparing to travel or relocate abroad. The company is based in Chennai (formerly called Madras) in southern India and counts companies such as Ford India, Citibank, Verizon, Morgan Stanley, Siemens, and BMW among its clients.

Management and Etiquette Tutorials The services for foreign professionals arriving in India range from help with finding a place to live or an office to rent, to advice on respecting the Indian custom of blessing new living or working quarters with a religious ceremony. Also available are courses on history and culture, tours of temples and of an Indian home, and even a tutorial Indian lunch to teach foreigners how to eat with their fingers according to Indian custom. Global Adjustments publishes a monthly newsletter with articles about life and culture in India.

Indian professionals can also prepare to travel abroad through Global Adjustments' course on Western management style, dining etiquette, and interview and phone skills.

CRITICAL THINKING

What consequences would a lack of knowledge about local culture have on a company?

@ Online Action!

Go to *marketingessentials.glencoe.com/ 11/global* to find a research project about globalization and the Internet.

GLOBAL MARKET

Cultural Adjustments

Discussion Ask students if they have ever gone to a foreign Web site. Let them know that there are many foreign versions of American sites, such as Amazon.com in Japan or Nike's European home page. Ask: What might they expect to find at such sites?

CRITICAL THINKING **Answer:** Answers will vary; students may suggest that businesses may have a hard time being successful if they fail to tailor their marketing approach to the specific needs and customs of a local culture.

@ Online Action! For instructions, ideas, and answer guide, go to the Teacher Center at *marketingessentials.glencoe.com*

TEACH

Discussion Starter

IMPORTANCE OF MANAGEMENT STRUCTURES

Have students consider the following scenario: A shoe factory loses all communication with its managers. No e-mail, cell phones, or facsimiles can get through. Ask students how long the factory could remain functional under these circumstances.

Answers will vary, but students should agree that a business, like any team, cannot function without communication from its leadership because it would not know its purpose or role in the company's plans.

TEACHING POINTS

Clarify Compare business managers to a baseball team manager who gives teammates tasks, goals, and training to help the entire club. Ask students how the two roles are different and similar.

Concept Development

TYPES OF MANAGEMENT STRUCTURE

1. Have students research theories of motivation, such as Maslow's Hierarchy of Needs, McClelland's Achievement Motivations, and Herzberg's factors. Ask students to write brief reports on how these theories demonstrate vertical organization.

2. Ask students to identify the advantages and disadvantages of working on a self-managed work team in horizontal organization.
   Advantages include shared responsibility and greater adaptability. Disadvantages are difficulty getting along and keeping everyone on goal.

ASSESS

CONCEPTS

Ask students to explain why vertical organization became popular in the 1980s. Answers will vary but may suggest the need for a more efficient and responsive business model.

KEY TERMS

Have students review key terms and use them to create a business memo to employees.

ONLINE SELF-ASSESSMENT

Have students go to marketingessentials.glencoe.com for the Section 11.1 practice test.

Individualized Review

L1 Assign and review Chapter 11 activities in the Student Activity Workbook.

L2 Assign and review Chapter 11 activities in the Marketing Math Workbook.

L3 Assign and review Chapter 11 activities in the *BusinessWeek* Reader and Case Studies.

Marketing Practice

Inform the class that a friend is starting an online clothing boutique. The small company will cater to the latest fashions while also showcasing the work of up-and-coming artists. Ask students: What type of management organization would you suggest and why? Have students work in groups of three to five and then present their findings to the class.

• **BRAINSTORMING**
Brainstorming is an important activity for self-managing teams.

What else do self-managing teams do?

Middle management implements the decisions of top management. Middle management plans how the departments under them can work to reach top management's goals.

In **supervisory-level management**, managers supervise the activities of employees who carry out the tasks determined by the plans of middle and top management. Supervisors assign duties, monitor day-to-day activities in their department, and evaluate the work of production or service employees.

Horizontal Organization

Beginning in the 1980s, many companies downsized to increase their efficiency and productivity.

These companies needed more than staff cuts to become more efficient. The answer was a new type of management structure—horizontal organization.

In **horizontal organization**, top management shares decision making with self-managing teams of workers who set their own goals and make their own decisions.

Self-Managing Teams

At the heart of horizontal organization is a restructuring of the traditional management hierarchy. Levels of management are eliminated, and the number of supervisors is reduced. This is known as flattening the organization. Instead of reporting up a chain of command, employees are organized into teams that manage themselves.

Self-managing teams in a horizontal organization gather information, analyze it, and take collective action. They are responsible for making decisions, completing tasks, and coordinating their activity with other groups in the company.

Encouraging team members to contribute to and take responsibility for the management process is known as **empowerment**. Empowerment reinforces team spirit and contributes to company loyalty. It can also increase productivity and profits.

Organization by Process

A second characteristic of horizontal companies is organization by process. Self-managing teams are organized around particular processes, such as developing new products or providing customer support. Teams made up of people with different specializations replace functional divisions, like the finance department or engineering department.

PHOTO GUIDE | **BRAINSTORMING**

Discussion Lead a discussion about the role of brainstorming in business. Ask students to share ways to record and present new ideas.

Caption Answer Self-managing teams may also gather information, analyze it, take action, make decisions, complete tasks, and coordinate their activities with other groups in the company.

Follow Up Ask students to describe an atmosphere that is conducive to brainstorming. Answers may suggest that the environment have a relaxed and positive atmosphere where people feel free to share ideas.

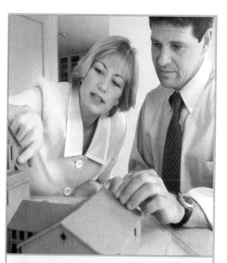

•TEAMWORK This team is working on the design of a new building.

In a horizontal organization, who would be the manager of this team?

Customer Orientation

The third characteristic of horizontal organization concerns the team's focus. In vertical organizations, workers tend to look to management for direction. In horizontal companies, workers are more likely to focus on the customer.

For example, you can buy Starbucks coffee beans in Starbucks coffee shops, or you can buy them in grocery stores and supermarkets. Different marketing teams within Starbucks focus on each different type of customer. One team is concerned with the wants and needs of the individual who buys beans in the Starbucks store. Another is concerned with the needs of the supermarket chain. By focusing on these different customers instead of on a product or process, managers have direct access to customer feedback. The ideal result is to have satisfied customers, high productivity, large profits, and contented investors.

11.1 AFTER YOU READ

Reviewing Key Terms and Concepts
1. What is the principal difference between the structure of a vertical company and the structure of a horizontal company?
2. What are the three levels of management in a vertical organization?
3. Explain two advantages of horizontal organization.

Integrating Academic Skills
Math
4. Your company produces and markets electronic equipment. Sales last year totaled $2,446,320. The company goal is to increase sales by 12 percent this year. Your division goal is to achieve 25 percent of total sales. What is the dollar value of your division goal?

Social Studies
5. An automobile company is considering locating a new assembly plant in your state. The plant would add about 10,000 jobs and require workers of all different education and training levels. What section of the state would you suggest and why?

 Online Action! Check your answers at *marketingessentials.glencoe.com/11/read*

marketingessentials.glencoe.com

Chapter 11 - Management Skills 239

CLOSE

Ask students to complete the following sentences:

* _____ is the process of reaching goals through the use of human resources, technology, and material resources.
  management

* Self-managing teams in a _____ organization gather information, analyze it, and take collective action.
  horizontal

PHOTO GUIDE

TEAMWORK

Discussion Have students list some of the teams that would contribute to the introduction of a new building. Teams may include architecture, interior design, engineering, safety, and marketing.

Caption Answer Neither person is manager. A horizontal organization is managed by a team.

Follow Up Inform students that many buildings are designed every year, but very few are actually constructed. Have students discuss possible reasons why this might be.

AFTER YOU READ

Reviewing Key Terms and Concepts
1. Vertical companies are organized in departments; orders come from management above. Horizontal companies are organized into self-managing teams that set their own goals and make their own decisions.
2. The three levels of management are top management, middle management, and supervisory-level management.

3. Advantages of horizontal organization include increased efficiency and productivity, less management, employee empowerment, and customer orientation.

Integrating Academic Skills
4. $684,969.60; $2,446,320 × 1.12 = $2,739,878.40; $2,739,878.40 × .25 = $684,969.60
5. Answers will vary; responses might include some analysis of cost, workforce, and transportation.

Online Action! Answers at **marketingessentials.glencoe.com/11/read**

FOCUS

Introducing the Section

COLLABORATIVE ACTIVITY

To prepare for reading this section, place students into teams of three to four and tell them they have been asked to organize a school campus clean-up campaign. Within teams, have them decide how to best change the school's cleanliness. After five minutes, have each group list the steps they took to make their decisions.

Preteaching Key Terms

Read the key terms aloud, or ask a volunteer to read them. Ask students to define the terms and phrases in their own words.

- planning
- organizing
- controlling
- mission statement
- remedial action
- exit interview

Tell students they can check their definitions as they read this section.

Build Vocabulary

Preview the following words by reading them in context. Ask students to explain what each word means and use it in a sentence.

- comprehensive
  dealing with all relevant details

- incorporate
  to combine or join with something already formed

 Critical Thinking

Ask students: Is it easier to teach new skills to a new employee or teach a skilled employee a new skill? Have students explain their reasoning.

OBJECTIVES

- **Name the three functions of management**
- **Describe the management techniques used by effective managers**
- **Explain how to manage employees properly**

KEY TERMS

- planning
- organizing
- controlling
- mission statement
- remedial action
- exit interview

WHILE YOU READ

Practice Consider how you would use each effective management technique that you read about.

Management Functions

READ and STUDY

BEFORE YOU READ
Predict What interpersonal skills should a manager have?

THE MAIN IDEA
As more employees fulfill management positions, understanding basic management functions is essential to your success in the field of marketing.

STUDY ORGANIZER
Draw the chart below. As you read this section, write in management functions and techniques.

What Managers Do

Managers make decisions in addition to supervising and directing the actions of others. Management decisions affect all employees. This means that communicating and motivating people are among the most important of management skills.

Basic Management Functions

All managers perform certain basic functions of planning, organizing, and controlling (see Figure 11.1). **Planning**

READ and STUDY

BEFORE YOU READ
Lead students in discussing the interpersonal skills that a manager should have. Skills mentioned may include communicating and motivating.

THE MAIN IDEA
Ask a volunteer to read the main idea aloud and ask another student to retell it in his or her own words.

STUDY ORGANIZER
Model the study organizer for students. A full-size, downloadable study organizer can be found at
marketingessentials.glencoe.com

 WHILE YOU READ Suggest that students think of one business scenario and apply the various management techniques to it as they read the section.

Figure 11.1 · Management Functions

• **Three Basic Functions** Whether a company is organized vertically or horizontally, the management functions remain the same. Managers plan, organize, and control. Below are the management functions required of the manager, or owner, of a marketing team developing an ad campaign for a new car. In this case, the company structure is horizontal.

What skills are necessary to be a manager?

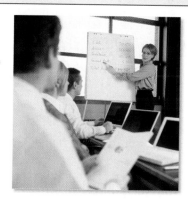

Planning At the planning stage, the team develops a plan covering the entire life of the ad campaign, from market research to tracking the campaign's effectiveness. The manager, or owner, of the team must be sure that the team's plans and goals are aligned with the company's overall plans.

Organizing Once the plan is set, the manager organizes its execution. With input from other members of the team, the owner delegates responsibilities, determines schedules, makes sure that the efforts of the individual team members are coordinated, and keeps everyone on track to meet team goals.

Controlling When the project is complete, the manager should determine its effectiveness. If it was not successful, the manager must find out what went wrong.

Online Action! Go to *marketingessentials.glencoe.com/11/ figure/1* to find a project on management functions.

marketingessentials.glencoe.com

Chapter 11 - Management Skills **241**

TEACH

Discussion Starter

BASIC MANAGEMENT FUNCTIONS

Ask students if they have ever had to make a difficult decision. Perhaps they made a promise to do one thing and then something better came along. How did they resolve the problem? Have the class come up with a step-by-step process for handling such situations. Then have them compare it to the process outlined on page 242.

TEACHING POINTS

Role Play Have students come up with a situation which involves making a decision and use the decision-making process shown on page 242 to make their decision.

Clarify Inform the class that managers often discuss their situations with other managers. Ask students who they confer with when they have difficult choices to make.

Online Activity

Mission Statements
Instruct students to look up the mission statements of various companies online. What style of writing do they use? What content do they share? From their research, have students write brief guidelines about writing a mission statement.

Figure 11.1 · Management Functions

Discussion After students read **Figure 11.1**, have them discuss the three functions of management. Ask them to come up with examples of the functions for other situations, such as a bakery introducing a new line of cookies or a video game company creating a new line of games.

Caption Answer Skills will vary, but may include communication, organization, ability to handle multiple tasks, and attention to detail.

Online Action! For instructions, ideas, and answer guide, go to the Teacher Center at **marketingessentials.glencoe.com**

Follow Up Divide students into groups of three or four and assign them various group-oriented tasks for completion. Have group members take turns acting as the group's manager. Ask students to share what they learned from the exercise.

TEACH CONTINUED

Concept Development

ORGANIZING

Ask students: If a large company employs hundreds of middle-level managers, thousands of supervisors, and tens of thousands of employees, how do they stay on the same page—that is, keep informed of goals and news?
Answers will vary, but may include regular meetings between managers, a detailed employee guide, a corporate intranet, or a corporate newsletter.

TEACHING POINTS

Demonstrate Bring to class a job orientation or a training manual. Go over its table of contents and ask students to share their experiences of being hired for a job.

Enrichment

EFFECTIVE MANAGEMENT TECHNIQUES

Have students discuss what is appropriate behavior in the workplace. Ask the class to compile a list of rules and make a guidebook. Examples of topics might include punctuality, respectfulness, and open-mindedness.

TEACHING POINTS

Explain Remind students that employees should be encouraged to ask questions while on the job. Give examples of ways supervisors could promote clarification, such as by asking, "Do you have any questions?" or "Is everything clear?"

---

involves setting goals and determining how to reach them. **Organizing** includes establishing a time frame in which to achieve the goal, assigning employees to the project, and determining a method for approaching the work. **Controlling** refers to setting standards and evaluating performance.

All three of these management functions involve making decisions. Following a formal decision-making process can be helpful when making complicated decisions. This process usually includes the following steps:

1. Define the problem.
2. Identify the options available.
3. Gather information and determine the consequences of each option.
4. Choose the best option.
5. Take action.
6. Evaluate the results.

Planning

Good management planning at any level is realistic, comprehensive, and flexible. It includes plans for the short- and long-range uses of people, technology, and material resources.

To be effective, a management plan should be a written statement that identifies resources that can be used to meet a given goal. The plan should be clear and direct. When completed, the plan should be distributed to and discussed with everyone who is involved.

Organizing

Organizing is a coordinated effort to reach a company's planning goals. It involves assigning responsibility, establishing working relationships, hiring staff to carry out the work, and directing the work of employees.

Controlling

Controlling is the process of comparing what you planned with actual performance. It involves three basic activities: setting standards, evaluating performance according to those standards, and solving any problems revealed by the evaluation.

Before setting standards, many companies compose a mission statement. A **mission statement** is a brief description of the ultimate goals of a company. A mission statement summarizes why a company exists. It identifies products or services offered and the target market.

After a company establishes goals in a mission statement, it adopts standards that are consistent with the goals. Here are some examples of standards:

- Financial standards—profit, cash flow, sales
- Employee standards—productivity, professional conduct, dress
- Customer satisfaction standards—sales returns, customer complaints, repeat business, referrals
- Quality control standards—production line checks for defects in materials or workmanship, repair requests, recalls

Managers use standards to evaluate both company and individual performance. When performance does not meet established standards, managers must identify and solve the problem.

Effective Management Techniques

Whether you become a supervisor in a traditionally organized vertical company or a member of a self-managing team, you will need to develop management skills. The most effective management techniques are usually a matter of common sense.

Give Clear Directions

Directing others requires good communication skills. Good communication is necessary at every level of management. Even the best employees will not be productive if they do not know what they are expected to do.

A supervisor should give all the direction required for each job and encourage employees to ask questions about instructions.

Be Consistent

If you have decided that a job must be completed in a certain way, make sure that all

---

 Online Activity

Business and the Law
Inform students that part of management's job is to make sure that business records conform to state and federal laws. Have students conduct research on the Internet to find out the guidelines that must be followed by businesses in their state.

Case Study

Always Making It Better

Dell Inc. founder Michael Dell learned about keeping costs low and marketing directly to consumers as a young boy selling stamps to collectors. He began the computer business as a 19-year-old college student, selling out of his Texas condo. In the 20 years before he stepped down as CEO, Dell's company reached $40 billion a year in sales.

Driven to Improve

Dell's management has always focused on continuous improvement. Many technology companies spend a significant fraction of revenues on research and development, looking for the "next big thing." At Dell, the goal has been to do better at what is already being done—sell more, cut costs more, improve quality control. When a project concludes successfully, the person responsible gets a little praise, followed by a long discussion of how it could have been done better. This has worked well for employees who have grown up within the company culture.

Even Management Can Improve

Michael Dell does not exempt himself from the drive to improve. In 2001, he and company president Kevin Rollins discovered that employee perceptions of them were quite negative. Dell and Rollins responded by promising that there would be change, and they invited more input from other managers before they made any decisions. Their honesty and responsiveness had an enormous effect on others in management.

THINK STRATEGICALLY

New employees often have difficulty adapting to Dell's management style, and they soon move on. Do you think a management model that depends on filling positions from within the company can be successful in the long run? Why or why not?

@ Online Action! Go to *marketingessentials.glencoe.com/11/case* to find a research project on management models.

---

employees follow this standard. Do not make exceptions unless there is a good reason to do so.

Treat Employees Fairly

Whenever possible, do what is best for your employees. Set reasonable standards of performance and apply those standards to everyone. You do not need to say yes to every employee request. However, you should always consider the employees' point of view when making decisions. Listen to suggestions from your employees, and consider acting on them. Take time to explain your reasoning if you believe an employee is wrong. Employees will be more productive when treated fairly.

Be Firm When Necessary

Each situation requiring disciplinary action is different. A friendly suggestion may be all

Concept Development

CONTROLLING

Give students a list of different businesses. They can range from a bookstore to an accounting firm to a landscaping service. Have students create a group of employee standards for each, paying attention to productivity, professional conduct, and dress. Ask: How do they differ? What do they have in common?

Extended Activity

Personal Standards

Ask students what types of personal standards they hold themselves to. Categories may include finance, work, spirituality, and relationships. How do they enforce these standards? Have students discuss their methods in a one-page expository response.

Critical Thinking

Remind the class that a manager should treat all team members equally. Ask students if this should apply to new employees as well.

Case Study Always Making It Better

Discussion Have students read the Case Study and discuss the controlling model of Dell Computer. Ask: What are its benefits and drawbacks? List student suggestions on the board. Benefits might include constant improvement. Drawbacks might include hurting the feelings of certain employees.

THINK STRATEGICALLY **Answer:** Answers will vary; students may suggest that a management model that hires only from within will not be successful in the long run. It prevents new ideas and energies from entering the business.

@ Online Action! For instructions, ideas, and answer guide, go to the Teacher Center at *marketingessentials.glencoe.com*

TEACH CONTINUED

Enrichment

DELEGATE RESPONSIBILITY

Reinforce to the class that it is often hard for supervisors to give up control by delegating. Have students come up with strategies for helping a manager be less controlling. Methods may include surrounding oneself with capable workers, starting training programs, and realizing that accepting help is not a sign of weakness.

Build Vocabulary

Preview the following words by reading them in context. Ask students to explain what each word means.

- **delegate**
  to entrust authority or power to a person acting as one's agent or representative

- **foster**
  to help to grow or develop

- **specialization**
  a concentrated or limited line of endeavor

Concept Development

HUMAN RESOURCES

Inform students that employees in human resources have access to information that other workers do not have. For example, human resources will keep on file an employee's personal information, performance evaluations, and disciplinary actions. Ask students what type of person should be working in human resources.

Answers may include someone who is tactful, keeps a secret, and knows boundaries.

---

that is necessary to get most employees on the right track. Others may not respond to the friendly approach, and you may have to be direct and firm. Give whatever directions are appropriate, and be certain the employee understands what you expect.

Sometimes employee problems are caused by the inappropriate behavior of one employee toward another. In this case, have a discussion with the employees to solve the problem. Listen to what both parties have to say and be reasonable but firm.

Set a Good Example

Set a good example in everything you do on the job. Doing this one simple thing will make your supervisory job much easier.

Delegate Responsibility

Some supervisors and middle managers do too much work themselves. If a manager is taking work home almost every night, it usually means resources are not being managed well. The manager is probably not delegating enough tasks to others, even though there are capable employees with lighter workloads who would be willing to do more.

As a supervisor, never try to do everything yourself. Organize your work responsibilities, and then decide which ones you can delegate to others. Decide which employee can best handle each task. Take time to teach employees how to do new tasks. Follow up by monitoring and evaluating the tasks that have been delegated. This will allow you more time to concentrate on the most important tasks.

Foster Teamwork

As mentioned earlier, teamwork is especially important in horizontally organized companies. As a manager or group owner, you can foster teamwork in a number of ways. Encourage team members to step outside their areas of specialization and learn about other aspects of the process for which they are responsible. Try to promote honest discussion before decisions are made. Listen respectfully to the comments and opinions of other team members, and encourage others in the group to do likewise. Respond to the comments and

concerns of team members to develop a feeling of trust. Treat all team members equally. A team will not succeed if some members are treated unfairly.

Be Ethical

Ethical behavior involves understanding how your actions affect others and striving to make honest and just decisions. Management is responsible for promoting ethical behavior by example.

Employee Motivation

Motivating employees is a key skill for any manager. The more people feel that they are appreciated, the harder they work. Managers should provide frequent feedback to employees and formally evaluate them each year. Identifying long-term goals and rewarding employees who help meet them are important ways to motivate those you manage.

Rewards

It is important to reward smart work, not busy work. A person who looks busy may not necessarily be getting the work done. To get results, reward results.

Identify those workers who value not only speed but quality. Ask them to suggest ways to improve job performance.

Enthusiastic long-term employees are the key to success in most companies. Reward loyalty by investing in continuing education for employees and promoting from within.

Encourage Creativity

A reasonable amount of conformity is necessary in every company in order to maintain standards, but do not let conformity stifle creativity. Encourage employees to be creative, and remind them that they will not be penalized for mistakes. Sometimes, it is necessary to take risks when avoiding conformity.

Human Resources

Without effective managers, team members, employees at all levels, the best technology, and material resources would be of little value.

Critical Thinking

Inform students that current employees may refer job applicants and are often rewarded if the applicant gets the job. Ask students why current employees are a good source of referrals.

NET MARKETING

Online B2B Marketing

Beginning in the 1990s, online business-to-business (B2B) exchanges allowed purchasing managers to buy supplies through Web sites that access hundreds of vendors rather than by visiting a showroom or meeting a salesperson. About 1,500 online exchanges opened, but by 2001, most were gone because they did not offer their customers service that was personal enough. Purchasing managers wanted familiar suppliers with whom they felt comfortable. The online exchanges that have survived are the ones that have adapted to industry needs.

Zero to Sixty in the Click of a Mouse

For example, Covisint is the auto industry B2B exchange, connecting 22,000 companies. Automakers have instant access to these suppliers. The speed and low cost of Web-based ordering and invoicing are especially useful in auto manufacturing, where parts are ordered many times a day.

An exchange serving trucking companies uses onboard global positioning software to match truckers with shippers in towns they pass through. This increases the efficiency of moving products around the country.

THINK LIKE A MARKETER

Why do you think exchanges are well adapted to the industrial market?

@ Online Action!

Go to *marketingessentials.glencoe.com/11/net* to find a research activity about purchasing through B2Bs.

Most companies have a human resources (HR) department that handles recruitment, hiring and firing, training, and other personnel matters. Employee personnel records are generally maintained in a file within the human resources office. These records include records related to an employee's hiring, participation in training programs, performance evaluations, disciplinary action, and commendations.

Recruiting

Recruiting is the process of locating a pool of applicants and selecting employees from this group. Prospective employees can be recruited from a number of different sources, depending on the type of job opening. Sources include current employees, walk-in applicants, media advertising, state employment services, public and private employment agencies, schools, and the Internet.

Current Employees

Most employees welcome the opportunity for a promotion, and many are happy with a lateral move, or transfer. Notices of job openings should be posted where all employees can see them. The notice should include the job title and duties, qualifications, contact name, and sometimes the salary. Current employees are also a good source for referrals.

Walk-Ins

Some applicants simply walk into the human resources office and ask to be considered for one or more types of jobs. They usually complete an application form and may be given information on any jobs that might soon become available. They may take the company's employment tests.

marketingessentials.glencoe.com

Chapter 11 - Management Skills 245

Concept Development

RECRUITING

Discuss with students why current employees are good candidates for job vacancies.

Answers may include that workers are already familiar with the business and its culture; it encourages them to work hard, and shows them that their work is recognized and rewarded.

Individualized Math Skills

L1 Ask students to explain the costs of hiring employees.

Answers may include wages, insurance, and training.

L2 If a manager makes $12 per hour and clerks make $7 per hour, how much would it cost a tea shop to have one manager and three clerks work 8-hour shifts during a day?

$264; ($12 $\times$ 8) + ($7 $\times$ 8 $\times$ 3) = $96 + $168 = $264

L3 If the cost of employees for a tea shop is $264 per day and the shop makes $2.50 profit off each drink, how many drinks must be sold to pay for the cost of employees in one day?

106 drinks; $264 $\div$ $2.50 = 105.6

 Virtual Business

Introduce the concept of business turnaround to students using Knowledge Matters' Virtual Business Retailing visual simulation, *Turnaround*. In this simulation, students take over the management of a business with specific problems and work as a team to restore the business to profitability.

NET MARKETING

Online B2B Marketing

Discussion After students have read Net Marketing, lead a discussion about business-to-business marketing. Let them know that many businesses known for retail have special services for other businesses. For example, Office Depot has stores for everyday customers, but also has special prices and services meant for business accounts.

THINK LIKE A MARKETER

Answer: Answers will vary but might include such factors as price, quality of equipment, and customer service.

@ Online Action!

For instructions, ideas, and answer guide, go to the Teacher Center at **marketingessentials.glencoe.com**

TEACH CONTINUED

Concept Development

RECRUITING

Have students act as human resources managers for a large auto dealer that is recruiting new mechanics. Ask: What are some ways they can use the Internet?

Answers may include posting a notice on the auto dealer site, sending e-mails to colleagues, or using an online job board or a newspaper's classifieds section to advertise the positions.

TEACHING POINTS

Extend Ask students why they think a state employment office would help jobseekers find openings.

Answers may suggest that employed individuals contribute to the state economy.

Critical Thinking

Inform students that commercial radio stations in America are increasingly becoming owned by a handful of large companies. Ask students to consider what role managers might have on the diversity and quality of music being played on the air.

Media Advertising

Most companies use media advertising, in newspapers and on the Internet, to recruit applicants. Blind advertisements that do not disclose the name of the company are usually not very effective. The nature of the job and required qualifications should be clearly indicated in an advertisement.

State Employment Services

State employment offices provide pre-screening and testing of prospective applicants. Both state offices and private employment agencies try to match listings of applicants with job openings. State or public agency services are free, but private agencies charge a fee when an applicant is hired.

Schools

High schools can be a good source for jobs that do not require specialized skills. Vocational and technical schools are sources for applicants who have learned a variety of specialized skills. Colleges are the recruiting field for applicants with higher-level skills.

Discrimination and the Law

Laws that prohibit discrimination govern both employers and recruitment agencies. These laws apply even before an employee is hired, so it is important to avoid discriminatory remarks and actions in all recruiting efforts. Federal law prohibits employers from discriminating on the basis of race, color, religion, gender, national origin, age, sexual orientation, or

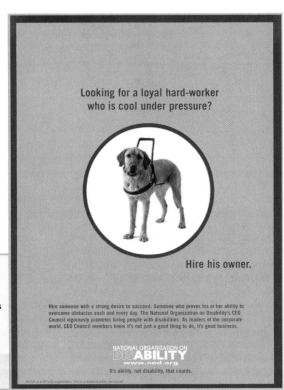

• ABILITY, NOT DISABILITY
Unemployment is one of the most profound issues facing the disability community. Only 32 percent of Americans with disabilities aged 18 to 64 are working, but two-thirds of those that are unemployed would rather be working.

Do you think it is legal to avoid hiring a disabled job applicant? Explain.

Looking for a loyal hard-worker who is cool under pressure?

Hire his owner.

Hire someone with a strong desire to succeed. Someone who proves his or her ability to overcome obstacles each and every day. The National Organization on Disability's CEO Council vigorously promotes hiring people with disabilities. As leaders of the corporate world, CEO Council members know it's not just a good thing to do, it's good business.

NATIONAL ORGANIZATION ON
DISABILITY
www.nod.org
It's ability, not disability, that counts.

246 UNIT 4 - SKILLS FOR MARKETING

AD GUIDE — ABILITY, NOT DISABILITY

Discussion Lead a discussion about why employers might not hire people with disabilities. Reasons may include that the workplace is not properly equipped for those workers or that some workers feel uncomfortable around people with disabilities.

Caption Answer No. The U.S. Equal Employment Opportunity Commission enforces and regulates laws that prohibit discriminating on the basis of race, religion, gender, national origin, age, sexual orientation, or disability.

Follow Up Ask students what the National Organization on Disability might do for job seekers with disabilities.

• **THE INTERVIEW** For the company, the purpose of a job interview is to determine whether an applicant can perform well on the job.

As a manager, how would you prepare to interview several applicants for the same job?

disability. The U.S. Equal Employment Opportunity Commission enforces and regulates these laws.

Hiring New Employees

For the employer, the purpose of the interview is to determine whether an individual has the skills and abilities to perform well on the job.

It is a good idea to conduct at least two interviews with applicants who seem well-qualified. It is also a good idea to have at least two people interview final applicants. Prepare interview questions in advance. Ask only questions that are job related. If you are interviewing more than one applicant for the same job, ask each of them exactly the same questions in exactly the same order. You will need to allow the applicant to ask questions, too.

It is the interviewer's responsibility to explain such things as wages and benefits.

When the time comes for managers to interview job applicants, they should check to make sure that they will be following all the laws that govern the hiring process. They should remember which kinds of questions are illegal or unacceptable.

Before hiring an applicant, most employers do some pre-employment testing. This may include some type of aptitude test to predict how well an applicant would be able to perform certain tasks. Some companies give personality tests, and many companies will ask prospective employees to be tested for illegal drug use.

Orientation and Training Programs

Orienting new employees includes more than simply training them for their positions. It is important to make new employees feel valued and welcome and to familiarize them with the working environment.

Orientation may take as little as a couple of hours or as long as a few days. It commonly includes the following:

- Tour of the company and introduction to coworkers
- Discussion of the company's history, mission, and values
- Description of what the company does
- Training on equipment, such as cash registers and computers
- Information on where facilities are located
- Information about payroll, benefits, and company policies

All new employees need on-the-job training. As a supervisor, you may train new employees yourself or delegate this task to an experienced employee. Make sure that all job duties are explained and that new employees understand how to complete them.

Scheduling Employees

Employee scheduling is the process of determining which employees should work at

Chapter 11 - Management Skills **247**

TEACH CONTINUED

Concept Development

HIRING NEW EMPLOYEES

Have students break into pairs and role-play the interviewing process for a job of their choice. Start by having students develop a list of questions and appropriate tests, then have them take turns interviewing each other.

 Online Activity

Preparing for the Interview
Have students look online for lists of common interview questions and other tips for preparing for the interview. Ask them to work in groups of three to four and make guidelines for effective job interviews to present to the class.

PHOTO GUIDE   **THE INTERVIEW**

Discussion Lead a discussion about the purpose of a job interview. Ask: Can the interviewer truly know whether an applicant can perform well on the job?

Caption Answer Answers might include that in order to ensure fairness, a manager should prepare to interview every applicant in the same way.

Follow Up   Ask students who have jobs about their experiences with job interviews. Ask: Did they make any mistakes during their interview?

ASSESS

Review Guide

CONCEPTS

Ask students to explain what managers do.

Managers make decisions in addition to supervising and directing the actions of others.

KEY TERMS

Have students review key terms, their spellings, and definitions in small groups. Ask them to write complete sentences using each.

ONLINE SELF-ASSESSMENT

Have students go to marketingessentials.glencoe.com for the Section 11.2 practice test.

Individualized Review

L1 Assign and review Chapter 11 activities in the Student Activity Workbook.

L2 Assign and review Chapter 11 activities in the Marketing Math Workbook.

L3 Assign and review Chapter 11 activities in the *BusinessWeek* Reader and Case Studies.

Marketing Practice

Have students role play managers of a newly formed sporting goods or sports clothing manufacturer. Have them write a mission statement for the company, making sure it mentions the products and services offered and identifying a target market.

---

what times. Very small companies can handle the scheduling of employees quite simply without any special computer program. Today, though, most companies use some type of computer scheduling.

Handling Complaints and Grievances

Employee complaints or grievances should be taken just as seriously as customer complaints. Most employee complaints fall into one of three categories: complaints about other employees, complaints about the quality of the company's product or service, or complaints about their own work situation. Complaints about other employees should be handled with care and discretion. Conflicts in the workplace can damage morale and productivity.

Some employees do, indeed, care enough about the quality of the company's products or services to bring problems to the attention of management. The complaining employee should be kept informed at every step. If the complaint proves justified, the employee should be rewarded.

Complaints involving the employee's work situation are usually fairly easy to resolve when the issue is salary. Every company should have a pay range for each job and a way to deviate from this range for truly outstanding work. For other work situation complaints, gather the facts, report the findings to the complaining employee, make your decision, and clearly explain to the employee the reasons and nature of your decision.

Assessing Employee Performance

Assessment enables a manager to develop better workers and a more efficient and profitable company.

In many companies, newly hired employees are placed on probation for a period of three to six months. Near the end of the probationary period, the employee is evaluated. If performance is satisfactory, the employee's status is changed to permanent. Usually, all

---

employees are evaluated yearly. In many companies, the employee completes a self-evaluation form, and the supervisor completes the same form on the employee. Then a meeting is scheduled so that the supervisor and the employee can compare and discuss any differences in their completed forms.

Remedial Action

Whenever a supervisor notices that an employee's performance or behavior is substandard, it is the supervisor's responsibility to discuss the matter with the employee. Sometimes, remedial action is necessary. **Remedial action** is a means of encouraging appropriate workplace behavior in order to improve employee performance. Two approaches to remedial action are preventive discipline and corrective discipline.

Preventive Discipline

Preventive discipline focuses on managing employees in a way that prevents behavior that might require directly disciplining an employee. Its intent is to encourage employees to follow the rules. Preventive techniques might include involving employees in setting standards, encouraging employees to meet standards, and communicating standards clearly. Providing training programs for self-discipline and having a method for controlling absences are also helpful.

Corrective Discipline

In some cases, corrective discipline is necessary. Corrective counseling is sometimes effective. This involves a discussion between the employee and a human resources counselor about the problem and what must be done to correct it. When this fails, more severe forms of remedial action are required. This usually begins with an oral warning and an explanation of what will be required. Next is a written warning to the employee with a copy for the employee's personnel file. If the problem is not resolved, the third action is suspension from work without pay. The suspension usually lasts from one to five days

---

 Critical Thinking

Ask students why customer satisfaction will be a top priority and management will become more diverse in the future. Students might say that customer satisfaction will be key as technology and transportation give consumers more options, and management will become more diverse to reflect the changing population and global market.

and comes with a warning that if the problem is not corrected, the employee may be fired.

Dismissing Employees

Sooner or later, all companies have to face the task of firing an employee for poor performance or bad behavior. Before this decision is made, certain procedures must be followed. In most cases, a supervisor or manager must give the employee verbal and written warnings that her performance or behavior is not acceptable. These warnings should be included on the employee's performance assessment form in the personnel file. The employee may be placed on probation and given time to change.

When a decision is made to dismiss a worker, a letter of dismissal should be written, along with separate checks for final salary and severance pay.

The Exit Interview

When an employee leaves the company, the human resources department will typically arrange an **exit interview**. An exit interview provides the opportunity for both the employee and manager to obtain valuable feedback. Exit interviews are often conducted with human resources personnel rather than the employee's supervisor. An employee always has the right not to participate in an exit interview.

An employee leaving voluntarily may have feedback on overall work conditions that will help the company retain workers in the future.

If the employee is being dismissed, the reason should be discussed in the exit interview. Usually, an employee will be entitled to advance notice of termination. As a manager, you must decide whether to have the employee continue working or leave immediately.

SECTION 11.2

CLOSE

Ask students to recall and provide answers to the following questions:

- **What is the difference between preventive discipline and corrective discipline?**
  Preventive discipline focuses on managing employees in a way that prevents behavior that might require disciplining an employee. Corrective discipline is action taken after an employee has broken rules.

- **What are some sources of prospective employees?**
  Sources include current employees, walk-ins, media advertising, state employment services, public and private employment agencies, schools, and the Internet.

Online Activity

21st Century Management

Ask interested students to research an Internet marketing company. Have students report on techniques, clientele, and other characteristics of the company in a five-minute oral presentation.

11.2 AFTER YOU READ

Reviewing Key Terms and Concepts

1. What are the basic functions of management?
2. What does it mean to delegate responsibility?
3. What is the purpose of assessing employee performance?

Integrating Academic Skills

Math

4. Retail store clerks are negotiating with their company management for a 7.5 percent increase in their hourly wage. Assume that the average hourly wage of a clerk is $13.75 and that the company has 45 clerks who each work a 40-hour week, for 50 weeks per year. The clerks receive an additional two-week paid vacation each year. What would such a pay raise cost the company per year?

Language Arts

5. Choose a clothing store whose products you purchase or like. Do research to learn what ethical policies the company follows in terms of working conditions for those who produce the clothing. Write a one-page report on what you learn.

 Online Action!

Check your answers at *marketingessentials.glencoe.com/11/read*

marketingessentials.glencoe.com

AFTER YOU READ

Reviewing Key Terms and Concepts

1. The basic functions of management are planning, organizing, and controlling.

2. Delegating means giving jobs or duties to other people to do, rather than trying to do it all yourself.

3. The purpose of assessing employee performance is to develop better workers and a more effective and profitable company.

Integrating Academic Skills

4. $96,525; $13.75/hour × .075 = $1.03125/hour; $1.03125 × 1,800 hours/week = $1,856.25/week; $1,856.25 × 52 weeks/year = $96,525

5. Reports will vary but should demonstrate an understanding of ethical policies regarding working conditions.

 Online Action! Answers at **marketingessentials.glencoe.com/11/read**

Lifelong Learning

CAREER INFORMATION

Have students go to **marketingessentials.glencoe.com** and find the Chapter 11 Careers page and click on the link for the American Marketing Association's Careers Strategies and Tips. Ask students to read one article, and summarize the article.

INTERPERSONAL SKILLS

The ability to communicate well is an essential skill for managers, who must ensure that their employees work together to achieve goals. Many companies offer communication skills workshops for workers; individuals can find resources on how to improve their skills online, in books, and from their human resources department.

Primary Source

Ask students to go to **marketingessentials.glencoe.com** and find Chapter 11 Resources. Ask them to click on the link for the American Marketing Association's marketing dictionary and read the definitions of the terms they find that are related to management skills.

THINKING CRITICALLY

A marketing career is based on relationships, and marketers should have good social skills in order to establish and maintain relationships.

@ Online Action!

For instructions, ideas, and answer guide, go to the Teacher Center at **marketingessentials.glencoe.com**

DAN REED
MUSIC DIRECTOR/
OPERATIONS MANAGER
WXPN-FM

? What do you do at work?
I am the music director and operations manager of WXPN in Philadelphia, a non-commercial radio station. I'm also the talent coordinator of the "World Café," a daily syndicated music show. I'm responsible for all of the contact with the music industry, including new music acquisition, relationships with management and labels, booking artists, and special events coordination. Everything I do is geared toward marketing because if there isn't an audience, there isn't a radio station or show. The biggest creative part of my job is understanding the audience and making sure that they know what we're doing—that's marketing in its purest form.

? What skills are most important to you?
I was fortunate enough to attend a high school that had a radio station, so my early, mistake-ridden, trial-and-error training came in 10th, 11th, and 12th grades. I also worked at my college radio station. Besides about 16 years in the radio business, I also worked for five years in the concert business, which has become invaluable experience. Contacts are important—the art of the schmooze should be considered. Get real world experience—a degree is fine, but hardcore work experience is paramount.

? What is your key to success?
I work hard, and I let my opinions be heard. Any media or marketing organization runs on ideas, so always be thinking. I've tried to make people believe in me and my work ethic, and I've never backed off tough decisions. Having a sense of humor is very important—I think that laughter has allowed me to disarm many a detractor.

Aptitudes, Abilities, and Skills

Strong interpersonal skills, an outgoing personality, tenacity, and a tough work ethic

Education and Training

A bachelor's degree can be helpful, but real-world experience is often more important.

Career Path

Positions such as this one can begin virtually anywhere within an organization; Reed suggests that individuals seek out new ways to make themselves valuable to the company.

THINKING CRITICALLY

Why do you think "the art of the schmooze" is important in a marketing career?

Online Action!

Go to **marketingessentials.glencoe.com/11/careers** for a career-related activity.

Test-Taking Strategies

Suggest that students create their own chapter tests as a way to review the chapter. They will revisit the content in the process, and they can take each other's tests for further review.

CHAPTER 11 REVIEW

FOCUS on KEY POINTS

SECTION 11.1

● The global marketplace will influence the kind of leadership companies will need in the future.

● Businesses are organized in one of two ways: vertically or horizontally.

● Traditional, vertically organized companies have three levels of management: top management, middle management, and supervisory-level management.

● Horizontal companies have top and middle management. Horizontally organized companies have self-managed teams that set their own goals and make their own decisions.

SECTION 11.2

● Basic management functions are planning, organizing, and controlling.

● Effective management techniques involve properly training employees, letting them know what is expected of them, and treating them fairly.

● In the case of poor performance or unacceptable behavior, the employee should receive warnings. These warnings should be included in the employee's personnel file. A letter of dismissal should be given to the employee at dismissal time, along with the final salary amount due.

REVIEW VOCABULARY

Define each of the following terms in a short sentence.

1. management (p. 237)
2. vertical organization (p. 237)
3. top management (p. 237)
4. middle management (p. 238)
5. supervisory-level management (p. 238)
6. horizontal organization (p. 238)
7. empowerment (p. 238)
8. planning (p. 240)
9. organizing (p. 242)
10. controlling (p. 242)
11. mission statement (p. 242)
12. remedial action (p. 248)
13. exit interview (p. 249)

REVIEW FACTS and IDEAS

14. How do horizontally organized companies differ from traditionally organized companies? (11.1)

15. What are the three levels of management? (11.1)

16. How does a self-managing team function? (11.1)

17. What are the three functions of management? (11.2)

18. What management techniques are used by effective managers? (11.2)

19. What methods can be used to motivate employees? (11.2)

Chapter 11 - Management Skills 251

REVIEW FACTS and IDEAS

14. In horizontal organizations, the traditional hierarchy of management is flattened and replaced by teams that manage themselves.

15. The three levels of management are top management, middle management, and supervisory-level management.

16. Self-managing teams set their own goals and make their own decisions. They are organized by process and are customer oriented.

17. The three functions of management are planning, organizing, and controlling.

18. Effective managing techniques include: giving clear directions, training new employees, being firm when necessary, setting a good example, delegating responsibility, fostering teamwork, and motivating employees.

19. Some methods to motivate employees include: provide frequent feedback to employees and formally evaluate them each year. Reward: (a) real solutions, not quick fixes; (b) smart work, not busy work; (c) simplification, not complication; (d) quiet effectiveness, not complaining; (e) quality work, not just fast work; (f) creativity, not mindless conformity; (g) loyalty.

FOCUS on KEY POINTS

Ask volunteers to read each of these summaries aloud and rephrase the concepts in their own words.

REVIEW VOCABULARY

See glossary for definitions of 1–13. A sample answer might read:

1. *Management* can be defined simply as getting work done through the effort of others.

BUILD SKILLS

20. Workplace Skills

Answers will vary; possible options for Angela may include speaking with Lou, speaking with other team members, or speaking with the personnel department.

21. Technology Applications

Summaries and Web addresses will vary but should demonstrate an understanding of what makes the job a management opportunity.

22. Math Practice

132 square feet; 16 feet × 6 cubicles = 96 square feet; 96 square feet + (3 × 12) square feet hallway space = 132 square feet

DEVELOP CRITICAL THINKING

23. Organizational Plans

Answers will vary but may mention that different management styles may suit different cultures.

24. Rewarding Job Performance

Rewards programs will vary; students should give reasons for their opinions on material and nonmaterial rewards.

BUILD SKILLS

20. Workplace Skills

Working in Teams Angela is a member of a six-person team. One of the team members, Lou, often arrives at work late. The other team members seem not to notice. Angela feels the quality of Lou's work is being affected by his late arrival. What should she do?

21. Technology Applications

Internet Job Ads Use the Internet to find recruiting sites. Locate an ad for a management opportunity in marketing. Use a word processing program to write a summary of your findings, including the qualifications necessary to apply for the job. Also include the Web address of the site.

22. Math Practice

Plan Office Space Calculate the square feet of space required to organize an office area to accommodate six employees. Each cubicle will be 16 square feet. Plan for three cubicles on each side (for a total of six cubicles) and a 3-foot wide hallway down the middle.

DEVELOP CRITICAL THINKING

23. Organizational Plans

Business organizational structures can mimic existing social structures. For example, a U.S. company doing business with a company in a hierarchical society might use a straightforward, vertically organized management structure to enhance communication with its target market and vendors.

Why might globalization encourage companies to use a mix of both vertical and horizontal organization?

24. Rewarding Job Performance

A material reward for a job well done might include a raise, bonus, or promotion. Do you think nonmaterial rewards such as praise and public recognition motivate and encourage employees as much as financial compensation? Explain your answer. What other types of reward might an employer use to motivate and encourage employees? List a few examples and explain why you think they would be applicable to work situations.

Formative Assessment

Formative assessment is an essential component of classroom work. This type of assessment provides information that is then used as feedback to modify teaching and meet student needs.

L1 Have students write down the functions of management.

L2 Have students compare horizontal management to vertical management.

L3 Have students explain why horizontal management is more effective than vertical management in the modern field of marketing.

 Reteach If the results of this formative assessment seem low, consider the following activity:

Read each of the key terms aloud. Have students define the key terms and use them in a sentence.

APPLY CONCEPTS

25. Plan an Event

Assume that your school is going to organize a talent show fund-raiser. You will need to form a committee to solicit prizes, advertise, sell tickets, hold a drawing, distribute prizes, and determine expenses and profit.

Activity Create a vertical or horizontal organization plan for your committee. Use visual aids and/or a word-processing program to explain your choice of organization and show how your organization will accomplish the goals of your committee.

26. Develop a Mission Statement

Assume that you are the manager of a new independent retail music store with seven employees.

Activity Use a word processing program to create a mission statement explaining the goals of your business.

NET SAVVY

27. Does the Company Benefit?

You and several coworkers would prefer to work at home and avoid the commute to the office. Browse the Web to research the advantages and disadvantages for the company of having employees work from their homes.

Use a word processing program to write a one-page report that could serve as a basis for a discussion with company management.

marketingessentials.glencoe.com

THE DECA CONNECTION

Role Play:
Management Trainee

Situation You are to assume the role of management trainee for a chain of CD and video stores. Your chain of stores is a dynamic and growing one. As a result of this growth, the company is constantly seeking individuals for management positions. The manager of the store where you are assigned (judge) will be making a presentation to some potential management trainees.

Activity You are to prepare information about your company and some of the traits upper management seeks in the individuals it hires for management positions. You are to review your ideas with your store manager (judge).

Evaluation You will be evaluated on how well you meet the following performance indicators:

● Explain the concept of management

● Identify desirable personality traits important to business

● Analyze employer expectations in the business environment

● Explain the nature of managerial ethics

● Make oral presentations

 Online Action!

For more information and DECA Prep practice, go to *marketingessentials.glencoe.com/11/DECA*

Chapter 11 - Management Skills **253**

APPLY CONCEPTS

25. Plan an Event
Organization plans will vary but should clearly relate to how goals will be accomplished.

26. Develop a Mission Statement
Mission statements will vary; all statements should describe the ultimate goals of the company.

NET SAVVY

27. Does the Company Benefit?
Reports will vary; all reports should show student understanding of the benefits and drawbacks of telecommuting.

THE DECA CONNECTION

The students should be evaluated on the performance indicators noted in the role play. For another DECA role play, go to the Competitive Events Workbook or the Student Activity Workbook, or go to marketingessentials.glencoe.com/11/DECA

 Online Action! For instructions, ideas, and answer guide, go to the Teacher Center at marketingessentials.glencoe.com

DECA Advisors Corner

Your DECA chapter can serve your community by conducting an Operation Holiday Help project in the fall. This project provides training and employment for all students in your school who want to work during the holiday season. Contact members of your local retail business community and/or your local Chamber of Commerce to get them involved in the project.

MINI-QUIZ

Read these sentences to the students and have them volunteer the missing word(s).

1. _____ managers supervise the activity of employees who carry out the tasks determined by the plans of middle and top management. (Supervisory-level)

2. In _____ management, top management shares decision making with self-managing teams of workers. (horizontal)

3. _____ is the process of comparing what you planned with actual performance. (Controlling)

For an expanded chapter quiz, go to Chapter 11 in the TeacherWorks CD-ROM and to Chapter 11 in the **Exam***View*® Pro Test Generator CD-ROM.

MARKETING INTERNSHIP

SET-UP
Discuss the basic background to make sure students understand the simulation. Have students discuss the challenges they have experienced traveling, whether it is packing the proper amount of clothing for a weekend trip or navigating in areas where they may not know the language.

PROCEDURES
You may want to list procedures on the board and talk about any questions the students might have. Remind the students that a suggested outline for their project is available at marketingessentials.glencoe.com/u4/internship.

TIME MANAGEMENT
Set goals, block schedules, and milestones. Assign interim deadlines for each step of the project.

ASSESSMENT
The rubrics for evaluation of the written, oral, and computer presentations are available at marketingessentials.glencoe.com/u4/internship.

MARKETING INTERNSHIP

A SIMULATED **DECA** *PRODUCT AND SERVICE MANAGEMENT EVENT*

Design a Program for Savvy Business Travelers

BASIC BACKGROUND
Cameo Creations recently began expanding its operations internationally and has found that its staff is ill-prepared for the rigors of travel and the expertise needed to conduct business abroad. Although there are many outside consultants and seminars available, the company prefers to keep its training in-house. It wants your firm to propose an interactive training program in a technology that can be used whenever a new employee is hired.

Working Abroad Some topics that were discussed during the initial interview with Cameo Creations executives include: cross-cultural differences in management, communication and interpersonal relations; safety when traveling abroad; foreign currency conversion; jet lag; and technology needed to conduct business in foreign countries, e.g., the right type of cell phone or a bringing a power adapter for laptop computers.

YOUR OBJECTIVE
Your objective is to design a reusable training program for Cameo Creations' employees that travel abroad and to convince company executives that your proposal meets their needs. You will need to include the most current information available on technology and the tools that can make international business easier.

ASSIGNMENT AND STRATEGY
- **Conduct research** Research the topics the client wants included in its training program. Research consulting companies that provide cross-cultural workshops to see what topics they generally cover. Interview global business travelers and review business magazines, such as *Business-Week, Sales and Marketing Management,* and *Forbes,* and the magazines' Web sites to learn about the practical issues a person needs to know.
- **Design a training program** Select one foreign country or region of the world to use as the basis of your proposal. Outline the topics covered in this program and explain why

READ to WRITE

Virtual Travel
Ask students to research the viability of technological alternatives to travel, such as teleconferences and online chat rooms. Have them list the benefits and drawbacks related to each technological or travel alternative and present them in a one- or two-page report. Remind students to consult recent copies of business and technology online periodicals, newspapers, or trade journals that discuss the virtual business world's advances. Ask students to include in their reports situations they believe require face-to-face meetings, and therefore travel, and situations when travel alternatives are an option. Have them explain their reasoning.

you would include them. Describe the interactive activities for participants. Decide on a length and schedule for the program, and how you could evaluate participants. Include a list of the computer equipment and software that the client will need for this training program.

- **What your project should include** To make your project complete, prepare a sample scenario that can be used for role playing exercises to train participants in interpersonal skills when doing business abroad. Include a sample test that can be used to evaluate a participant at the end of the training program. Prepare a flyer that would be distributed to participants to outline the program's major topics.

YOUR REPORT

Use a word processing program and presentation software to prepare a double-spaced report and an oral presentation for your supervisors. See a suggested outline and key evaluation points at *marketingessentials.glencoe.com/internship*

marketingessentials.glencoe.com

BUILD YOUR PORTFOLIO

Option 1 Internship Report
Once you have completed your Marketing Internship project and presentation, include your written outline and a few printouts of key slides from your oral presentation in your Marketing Portfolio.

Option 2 Design Business Seminars Typical business seminars include selling techniques, management skills, customer service, communications skills, and computer training. Create a new kind of seminar and explain why it could succeed. Decide where it will be offered and what the fee will be. Describe the presenters and draw up an outline. Come up with a plan to promote it. Prepare a written report and an oral presentation using word processing and presentation software. See a suggested outline and key evaluation points at *marketingessentials.glencoe.com/portfolio*

@ Online Action!

Go to *marketingessentials.glencoe.com/Unit/4/DECA* to review employee training concepts that relate to DECA events.

Marketing Internship 255

Unit Review

Now that students have completed the chapters in Unit 4, ask them to review their answers to the Analyze the Ad questions on page 149. Would they answer them differently? Why or why not?

Have students consider the skills covered by this unit and ask them to list which ones are their strengths or weaknesses. Ask them to consider how they can strengthen or develop the skills. Then have students write a three-paragraph essay about the skills that they can bring into a marketing-related profession.

STEP AHEAD

Have students consider the skills needed to succeed in marketing. Ask them: How do the same skills relate to selling?

Internship Wrap-Up

Ask students to write a two-page memo explaining why regular and continuous training is important for both employees and employers. Have them explain the benefits to the employer and the employee.

BUILD YOUR PORTFOLIO

Explain to students that portfolios provide evidence of their knowledge and skills in working with data, people, and concepts. Developing a portfolio can be a valuable career tool. Point out the importance of using high-quality paper and printouts for making a good impression. Encourage students to check the portfolio information available at **marketingessentials.glencoe.com/u2/internship**.

Peer Review
Fellow students who share common interests can serve as reviewers of the final portfolios. This review can be completed through the use of a checklist. Go to **marketingessentials.glencoe.com/u4/internship** to find a suggested checklist.

Unit Objectives

After completing this unit, students should be able to:

- Identify and execute the seven steps of the sales process
- Explain the process and techniques of both retail and business-to-business selling
- Identify ways to prepare for selling
- Demonstrate appropriate techniques to initiate a sale and determine customer needs
- Handle customer objections during the selling process
- Demonstrate effective suggestion selling and sale closing techniques
- Perform the cashiering and math procedures of retail and business-to-business sales transactions
- Evaluate sales as a profession for career-planning purposes

Key to Individualized Activities

L1 Level 1 activities are basic activities and should fall within the range of all students.

L2 Level 2 activities are average activities and should be within the range of average and above average students.

L3 Level 3 activities are challenging activities designed for the ability range of above average students.

Enrichment Resources

PROFESSIONAL ORGANIZATIONS

American Marketing Association marketingpower.com

National Association of Sales Professionals (NASP) nasp.com

MEDIA RESOURCES

Print or online editions of

Selling Power sellingpower.com

Sales & Marketing Management salesandmarketing.com

WRITING SUPPORT

Ask students to write a few paragraphs stating if they believe whether a salesperson is born or trained. Do they believe some people are better suited for sales, or is selling a taught skill? Students should list at least three reasons for this opinion. Ask students to keep and review this document as they study Unit 5.

UNIT 5 PLANNING GUIDE AND RESOURCES

CHAPTER	PRINT MATERIALS	TECHNOLOGY RESOURCES
Chapter 12 Section 12.1 Section 12.2	**From Unit 5 Fast File Booklet** Lesson Plans; Chapter Summaries; Reproducible Masters; Reproducible Tests **Print Ancillaries** Student Activity Workbook; Marketing Math Workbook; *BusinessWeek* Reader and Case Studies, Chapter 12; Competitive Events Workbook, Unit 5; Marketing Research Project Workbook; School-to-Work Activity Workbook	Interactive Chalkboard classroom presentations **marketingessentials.glencoe.com** Online Student Edition, Chapter 12 TeacherWorks **Exam***View*® Pro Test Generator, Chapter 12 Virtual Business
Chapter 13 Section 13.1 Section 13.2	**From Unit 5 Fast File Booklet** Lesson Plans; Chapter Summaries; Reproducible Masters; Reproducible Tests **Print Ancillaries** Student Activity Workbook; Marketing Math Workbook; *BusinessWeek* Reader and Case Studies, Chapter 13; Competitive Events Workbook, Unit 5; Marketing Research Project Workbook; School-to-Work Activity Workbook	Interactive Chalkboard classroom presentations **marketingessentials.glencoe.com** Online Student Edition, Chapter 13 TeacherWorks **Exam***View*® Pro Test Generator, Chapter 13 Virtual Business
Chapter 14 Section 14.1 Section 14.2	**From Unit 5 Fast File Booklet** Lesson Plans; Chapter Summaries; Reproducible Masters; Reproducible Tests **Print Ancillaries** Student Activity Workbook; Marketing Math Workbook; *BusinessWeek* Reader and Case Studies, Chapter 14; Competitive Events Workbook, Unit 5; Marketing Research Project Workbook; School-to-Work Activity Workbook	Interactive Chalkboard classroom presentations **marketingessentials.glencoe.com** Online Student Edition, Chapter 14 TeacherWorks **Exam***View*® Pro Test Generator, Chapter 14 Virtual Business
Chapter 15 Section 15.1 Section 15.2	**From Unit 5 Fast File Booklet** Lesson Plans; Chapter Summaries; Reproducible Masters; Reproducible Tests **Print Ancillaries** Student Activity Workbook; Marketing Math Workbook; *BusinessWeek* Reader and Case Studies, Chapter 15; Competitive Events Workbook, Unit 5; Marketing Research Project Workbook; School-to-Work Activity Workbook	Interactive Chalkboard classroom presentations **marketingessentials.glencoe.com** Online Student Edition, Chapter 15 TeacherWorks **Exam***View*® Pro Test Generator, Chapter 15 Virtual Business
Chapter 16 Section 16.1 Section 16.2 Section 16.3	**From Unit 5 Fast File Booklet** Lesson Plans; Chapter Summaries; Reproducible Masters; Reproducible Tests **Print Ancillaries** Student Activity Workbook; Marketing Math Workbook; *BusinessWeek* Reader and Case Studies, Chapter 16; Competitive Events Workbook, Unit 5; Marketing Research Project Workbook; School-to-Work Activity Workbook...	Interactive Chalkboard classroom presentations **marketingessentials.glencoe.com** Online Student Edition, Chapter 16 TeacherWorks **Exam***View*® Pro Test Generator, Chapter 16 Virtual Business

National Marketing Education

CHAPTER	SECTION	PERFORMANCE INDICATOR
Chapter 12 **Preparing for the Sale**	12.1	Explain the nature and scope of the selling function (SEL)
		Analyze product information for use in selling (SEL)
		Identify customer's buying motives for use in selling (SEL)
		Facilitate customer buying decisions (SEL)
	12.2	Determine customer/client needs (SEL)
		Explain key factors in building a clientele (SEL)
		Differentiate between consumer and organizational buying behavior (SEL)
Chapter 13 **Initiating the Sale**	13.1	Explain the selling process (SEL)
		Prepare for the sales presentation (SEL)
		Establish relationship with client/customer (SEL)
	13.2	Determine customer/client needs (SEL)
		Assess customer/client needs (SEL)
Chapter 14 **Presenting the Product**	14.1	Demonstrate product (SEL)
		Recommend specific product (SEL)
	14.2	Convert customer/client objections into selling points (SEL)
		Handle customer inquiries (CIS)
Chapter 15 **Closing the Sale**	15.1	Close the sale (SEL)
		Sell good/service/idea to individuals (SEL)
		Facilitate customer buying decisions (SEL)
	15.2	Demonstrate suggestion selling (SEL)
		Process sales documentation (SEL)
		Plan follow-up strategies for use in selling (SEL)
Chapter 16 **Using Math in Sales**	16.1	Analyze technology for use in the sales function (SEL)
		Process sales documentation (SEL)
	16.2	Calculate miscellaneous charges (SEL)
		Explain the purpose and importance of credit (FIN)
		Address the needs of individual personalities (SEL)
	16.3	Determine discounts and allowances that can be used to adjust base prices (PRI)
		Use information system for order fulfillment (DIS)

CIS Communication, Interpersonal Skills   **DIS** Distribution   **FIN** Financing   **PRI** Pricing   **SEL** Selling

Standards Assessment Correlation

SECTION ASSESSMENT		CHAPTER ASSESSMENT						UNIT LAB
Reviewing Key Terms and Concepts	Integrating Academic Skills	Review Facts and Ideas	Build Skills	Develop Critical Thinking	Apply Concepts	Workplace Skills	Net Savvy	Marketing Internship
1	✓	19, 20, 21	25		31	✓		✓
2		22, 23	25		30, 31	✓	✓	✓
3	✓		25		30	✓	✓	✓
3			25		30	✓	✓	✓
1, 2	✓		25, 26	28		✓		✓
3	✓		26		30			✓
		24	26	28				✓
1, 2, 3		6, 7		16	18			✓
		8	14	16	18, 19			
2	✓	8	13	17	18, 19	✓	✓	
1, 2, 3	✓	9, 10, 12	14, 15	17	18		✓	
1, 2		11, 12	14, 15		18		✓	
1, 2, 3		10, 11, 12	18	20	22, 23			
	✓			20	22			
3	✓	13, 15, 16	17	21		✓		
1, 2, 3		15, 16	17, 18			✓		
	1, 2, 3	✓	10, 11	15			✓	
3	✓		15, 16	18		✓		
3			15			✓		
1, 2	✓	12, 13	15			✓		
			15	19		✓		
3	✓	14	15, 16			✓		
	✓		14, 15	17, 18		✓	✓	
1	✓	8	14	18		✓		
2	✓	9, 11			19, 20		✓	
				18			✓	
			14			✓	✓	
1, 2, 3	✓		16		19			

UNIT 5

Unit Overview

Unit 5 introduces aspects of selling to the students. Chapter 12 helps students prepare for the sale by introducing the concept of feature-benefit selling and the importance of customer knowledge and prospecting. Chapter 13 introduces students to all the steps of the sale, concentrating on approaching customers and determining their needs. Chapter 14 teaches the principles and practices of presenting the product and handling customers' objections. Chapter 15 includes closing the sale, suggestion selling, and the concept of relationship marketing. Chapter 16 reviews the mathematics involved in retail and business-to-business selling.

MAKING IT RELEVANT

Inform students that the success of every business depends on selling. Regardless of the quality of a good or a service, a business that does not succeed in selling will fail.

Unit Launch Activity

Have students share their first impressions of the ad on this page. Ask students to discuss the tone of the V8 vegetable juice ad. Ask them to describe the atmosphere of the image and the text. In their opinion, what does the casual, fun tone suggest about V8?

OUT OF TIME?
If class time is too short to cover all the chapters in this unit, go to Unit 5 in your Fast File Teacher Resources booklet and find the Chapter Summaries for Chapters 12, 13, 14, 15, and 16.

256

In this unit you will find

HALF THE CARBS OF ORANGE JUICE.

(PUT THAT IN YOUR JUICER AND SQUEEZE IT.)

100% JUICE

V8
100% VEGETABLE JUICE

V8. DRINK IT. FEEL IT.™

256

 UNIT PROJECT

Sales Presentation
The culmination of this unit should be an actual sales presentation based on the sales training manuals that students write as an ongoing project while working on the unit. To make the presentations more instructive, record them, if possible, and play them back for class or DECA chapter evaluation.

Assessment Guidelines Prepare a rubric for evaluation that includes teamwork (e.g., clear team roles, balance of work allotted, good transitions among presenters), presentation style and delivery (e.g., good eye contact, quality verbal and nonverbal styles, persuasive speaking), information/content delivered, and visual aids/graphics used.

Enrichment Assign and review Unit 5 activities in the Competitive Events Workbook.

Marketing Plan

RELATE THE UNIT TO THE MARKETING PLAN

The four Ps of the marketing mix include product, place, pricing, and promotion. Unit 5 will help students apply these aspects to the process of selling.

MARKETING PLAN OVERVIEW

Ask students to relate the marketing plan to selling. Students should understand that the ultimate goal of a marketing plan is to facilitate sales.

Functions of Marketing

Point out that Unit 5 will help students understand the marketing foundation of communication and interpersonal skills as well as the function of selling.

- **Communication, Interpersonal Skills** Selling requires open channels of communicating between customer and seller. The variety of methods and strategies used to communicate, in the end, lead the prospect to give the seller a commitment.

- **Selling** All marketing is selling a concept, cause, good, or service. Selling requires initiating, determining, and closing a sale.

Marketing Plan

ANALYSIS
1. SWOT
   Economic
   Socio-Cultural
   Technological
   Competitive

STRATEGY
2. Promotion
   Place
   Price
   Product

IMPLEMENTATION
3. Organization
   Management
   Staffing

BUDGET
4. Cost of sales
   Cost of Promotion
   Incomes and Expenses

CONTROL
5. Evaluation
   Performance Measures
   Performance Analysis

ANALYZE THE AD

The makers of V8 vegetable juice saw an opportunity to gain customers when low-carbohydrate diets became popular. What tone does this ad have?

Market Talk V8 is a "shelf-stable bottled juice," while consumers head to the refrigerator or freezer cases to buy orange juice. Why do you think V8 feels it can compete directly with orange juice?

Think and Write Imagine you work at a health-food store and a customer asks you which is the best choice, V8 or a sports drink. What would you need to know about these two products and about your customer to give a helpful answer?

@ Online Action! Go to *marketingessentials.glencoe.com/ u5/ad* for an extended activity.

Functions of Marketing

- Marketing-Information Management
- Financing
- Selling
- Professional Development
- Economics
- Business, Management, Entrepreneurship
- Communication, Interpersonal Skills
- Pricing
- Distribution
- Foundations
- Product/Service Management
- Promotion

Concepts • Technology • Academic Concepts

In this unit

Foundations of Marketing
- Communication, Interpersonal Skills

Functions of Marketing
- Selling

marketingessentials.glencoe.com

257

ANALYZE THE AD

The ad has a playful message in its ad copy, with a confident, challenging tone. Overall, the ad offers the viewers a friendly message with a casual writing style.

Market Talk Answers will vary. Students could note that customers do not necessarily differentiate between shelf-stable juice and refrigerated or frozen juice. V8 simply sees an opportunity to convince people to try something different and to capitalize on the low-carb diet trend.

Think and Write Answer will vary. To lead students in this assignment, you might bring to class a few examples of ads that directly refer to competitors. Analyze their messages from a visual point of view and considering the slogan and other written content.

@ Online Action! For instructions, ideas, and answer guide, go to the Teacher Center at **marketingessentials.glencoe.com**

Chapter Overview

Chapter 12 covers how a salesperson prepares for the sale. Personal selling is defined, and three basic sales situations are reviewed: retail, business-to-business, and retailing sales situations. The twin goals of selling are also discussed.

BUILD BACKGROUND

Have students write summaries of positive and negative experiences they have had with salespeople. This can open discussion about the twin goals of selling and the types of salespeople.

Why It's Important

Researching products and customers is important when selling any type of product or idea. Finding customers and knowing key selling concepts are also essential to selling.

Prepare to Read

Ask a volunteer to write all of the major headings of each section on the board in outline format:

What Is Selling?
Getting Ready to Sell

Tell students to fill in the secondary (blue) headings as they preview or read the chapter. They will then have a thorough chapter outline to use as study notes.

Preparing for the Sale

Chapter Objectives

After reading this chapter, you should be able to:

- Define selling and different types of selling situations
- Explain the purpose and goals of selling
- Define consultative selling
- Differentiate between rational and emotional buying motives
- List three levels of customer decision making
- Name sources of product information
- Explain the main focus of preparation in business-to-business selling and in retail selling

GUIDE TO THE PHOTO

Market Talk Product knowledge is what sales skills rest on. In the food industry, salespeople need to know what the products are, their shelf life, and how they are prepared. An apparel salesperson needs to know how garments were manufactured, their style, and specific features such as warmth or ease of care.

Quick Think If you worked in the produce section of a grocery store, what questions would customers ask?

GUIDE TO THE PHOTO

Market Talk How much knowledge does the class think the average salesperson has or should have about his or her product or service? Have students give examples from their experiences.

Quick Think Student responses will vary; answers may include questions about nutrition information, flavor, and freshness.

 Follow Up Ask students to list, in order of importance, what qualities they look for in a salesperson.

An Association of Marketing Students

Performance indicators represent key skills and knowledge. Relating them to the concepts explained in this chapter is your key to success in DECA events. These acronyms represent DECA events that involve knowledge of concepts in this chapter.

AAAL*	FMAL*	MMS	TMDM
AAML*	FMDM	QSRM	TSE
ADC	FMML*	RMAL*	VPM*
BSM	FSRM	RMML*	
EMDM*	HMDM	SMDM	

In all these DECA events you should be able to follow these performance indicators:

- Explain the nature and scope of the selling function
- Explain company selling policies
- Prepare for the sales presentation
- Acquire product knowledge for use in selling
- Identify product features and benefits
- Identify a customer's buying motives for use in selling
- Differentiate between consumer and organizational buying behavior
- Prospect for customers
- Write sales letters

All the events with an asterisk (*) also include this performance indicator:

- Explain the use of brand names in selling

Some events include additional performance indicators. These are:

BSM Describe customer buying process for services

SMDM Describe customer buying process for services

DECA PREP

Check your understanding of DECA performance indicators with the DECA activity in this chapter's review. For more information and DECA Prep practice, go to *marketingessentials .glencoe.com/12/DECA*

Chapter 12 - Preparing for the Sale 259

An Association of Marketing Students

DECA events that require knowledge of preparing for the sale are described here. Discuss the performance indicators to make sure students understand how to demonstrate their understanding.

The events acronyms stand for:

AAAL: Apparel and Accessories Marketing Series, AL

AAML: Apparel and Accessories Marketing Series, ML

ADC: Advertising Campaign Event

BSM: Business Services Marketing Series

EMDM: E-Commerce Management Team Decision Making Event

FMAL: Food Marketing Series, AL

FMDM: Financial Analysis Management Team Decision Making Event

FMML: Food Marketing Series, ML

FSRM: Full Service Restaurant Management Series

HMDM: Hospitality Services Management Team Decision Making Event

MMS: Marketing Management Series

QSRM: Quick Serve Restaurant Management Series

RMAL: Retail Merchandising Series, AL

RMML: Retail Merchandising Series, ML

SMDM: Sports and Entertainment Marketing Management Team Decision Making Event

TMDM: Travel and Tourism Marketing Management Team Decision Making Event

TSE: Technical Sales Event

VPM: Vehicles and Petroleum Marketing Series

DECA PREP

Find timed DECA Prep activities correlated to the Competitive Events Workbook for students and DECA tips for teachers at **marketingessentials.glencoe.com /12/DECA**

CHAPTER 12 Classroom Resources

For the Teacher

- TeacherWorks
- marketingessentials.glencoe.com
- Interactive Chalkboard
- *ExamView*® Pro Test Generator
- Fast File Unit 6

For the Student

- *Marketing Essentials* Online Edition
- Student Activity Workbook
- Marketing Math Workbook
- Marketing Research Project Workbook
- School-to-Work Activity Workbook
- Competitive Events Workbook
- *BusinessWeek* Reader and Case Studies
- marketingessentials.glencoe.com

FOCUS

Introducing the Section

COLLABORATIVE ACTIVITY

To prepare for reading this section, have students work in groups of four to five to prepare role-play infomercials for school sweatshirts. Have each group stress product features, customer benefits, rational motives, and emotional motives in their script and perform their infomercials in front of the class. Have students limit their infomercial to 15 minutes.

Preteaching Key Terms

Read the key terms aloud, or ask a volunteer to read them. Ask students to predict the meanings of these phrases:

- personal selling
- business-to-business selling
- telemarketing
- consultative selling
- feature-benefit selling
- product features
- customer benefits
- rational motive
- emotional motive
- extensive decision making
- limited decision making
- routine decision making

Tell students they can check their predictions as they read this section.

 Extended Activity

Personal Selling

Ask students to describe their ideal salesperson. Have students share their descriptions in class.

OBJECTIVES

- Define selling and different types of selling situations
- Explain the purpose and goals of selling
- Define consultative selling
- Differentiate between rational and emotional buying motives
- List three levels of customer decision making

KEY TERMS

- personal selling
- business-to-business selling
- telemarketing
- consultative selling
- feature-benefit selling
- product features
- customer benefits
- rational motive
- emotional motive
- extensive decision making
- limited decision making
- routine decision making

WHILE YOU READ

Connect Think about the last time you shopped. What motives did you have for your purchase, and what product information was important to you?

What Is Selling?

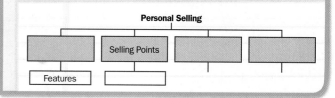 **READ and STUDY**

BEFORE YOU READ

Connect When was the last time you purchased something with the help of a salesperson? What was the item and how did the salesperson help you?

THE MAIN IDEA

Selling is a function of marketing that involves one-on-one contact with customers. To be effective in sales, a salesperson must possess product knowledge, as well as an understanding of customers' motives for buying and of the decision-making process.

STUDY ORGANIZER

Create a chart like the one below to record important information about selling situations and customers' decision making.

Personal Selling

| | Selling Points | | |

| Features | | |

Selling

Personal selling is any form of direct contact between a salesperson and a customer. The key factor that sets it apart from other forms of promotion is this two-way communication between the seller and the buyer. This communication can take place in a retail setting, in a business-to-business setting, and in telemarketing (over the phone). Salespeople need to research their products and their customers. The more a salesperson

READ and STUDY

BEFORE YOU READ

Help students provide detailed accounts of their purchasing experiences. Details might include the person describing product features or mentioning that it is the last one left.

THE MAIN IDEA

Ask a volunteer to read the main idea aloud and ask another student to explain it in his or her own words.

STUDY ORGANIZER

Model the study organizer for students by filling in the first rectangle. A full-size, downloadable study organizer can be found at **marketingessentials.glencoe.com**

 WHILE YOU READ Suggest that students recall their recent shopping experiences while reading through the section.

knows about both, the better prepared and the more effective she or he will be at offering customers solutions to their problems and meeting their needs. Certain aspects of a salesperson's job will vary depending on where the selling takes place.

Retail Selling

Retail selling is unique because customers come to the store. The salesperson should be available to answer any questions about the product or its features.

Business-to-Business Selling

Business-to-business selling may take place in a manufacturer's or wholesaler's showroom (inside sales) or a customer's place of business (outside sales). In the latter case, it is up to the salesperson to make contact with the customer. Sales representatives, in most cases, will call to make an appointment prior to their visit. In other cases, a sales representative may make a cold call, which means he or she will appear without an appointment.

Telemarketing

The last type of personal selling situation is **telemarketing**, which is the process of selling over the telephone.

In 2003, Congress passed legislation making it more difficult for telemarketers to operate. The new law prohibits telemarketers from calling any phone number that has been registered with the national Do Not Call Registry, established by the Federal Communications Commission. This new law has significantly reduced the number of people telemarketers may contact.

Goals of Selling

The purpose and goals of selling are the same regardless of the sales situations. They are to help customers make satisfying buying decisions, which create ongoing, profitable relationships between buyer and seller. This is important because repeat business is crucial to the success of any company. It is easier and less expensive to keep current customers happy than it is to generate new customers. If a business is successful at keeping customers

happy, the customers are likely to pass along positive recommendations to other business associates, friends, and family.

Consultative Selling

Salespeople accomplish these goals by engaging in a process called consultative selling. **Consultative selling** is providing solutions to customers' problems by finding products that meet their needs. A customer may say that she is having a problem with her feet because she stands all day in her new job. Possessing the relevant product knowledge allows an alert salesperson to suggest shoes designed for comfort and support.

Consultative selling goes even further in business-to-business selling. To comply with OSHA standards, an ice cream manufacturer must provide insulated clothing to protect employees who work in freezers that are 20 degrees below zero. In this situation, the sales representative for the insulated clothing company would recommend the garments that had the capacity to keep workers warm in such a cold work environment. Analysis of customer needs combined with product knowledge is the essence of consultative selling. To be effective in consultative selling, you need to be trained in feature-benefit selling.

Feature-Benefit Selling

Matching the characteristics of a product to a customer's needs and wants is a concept called **feature-benefit selling**. Many people believe that customers do not buy products; rather, they buy what the products will do for them. Leather shoes are purchased for their appearance, easy care, comfort, and longevity (see Figure 12.1).

Product Features

A salesperson needs to learn how a product's features will benefit the customer. **Product features** may be basic, physical, or extended attributes of the product or purchase. The most basic feature of a product is its intended use. A person buys an automobile for transportation and a watch to tell time.

Chapter 12 - Preparing for the Sale 261

Individualized Practice

CUSTOMER DECISION MAKING

Have all students list three or four different types of products. They will use this list to complete their leveled activity.

L1 Ask students to write as many rational and emotional motives for buying each of these items.

L2 Ask students to write as many rational and emotional motives for buying each of these items. Then have students write selling sentences that connect product features with those motives for buying the products.

L3 Have students select one of the products to use as the basis for a magazine ad, complete with headline (main buying motive) and ideas for illustrations (photos or artwork) that would help demonstrate the most important buying motives. Have students present their ads in a 10-minute oral presentation in class.

Concept Development

CUSTOMER BUYING MOTIVES

Have students create a bulletin board display of selected advertisements arranged according to buying motive. The ads on one side should depict rational motives, those on the other, emotional motives.

 Online Activity

Features and Benefits

Have students research various product and retail sites and find a feature-benefit chart. Ask students to share the chart with the class.

Figure 12.1 *Feature-Benefit Chart*

- **Warm and Dry** A feature-benefit chart combines product features with corresponding benefits, creating selling points. This chart shows the features and benefits for Columbia Sportswear's Canyon Meadows Jacket.

What other important product feature is needed to complete this chart?

Product Feature	Customer Benefit
100% nylon Hydro Rip	Durable, water/wind resistant, washable
100% nylon Hydro Plus shell	Durable, water/wind resistant, washable
65% polyester & 35% cotton jersey lining	Comfortable, washable
Designed to fold into zippered pouch that is part of the jacket	Packable, great for hiking and trail trips
Radial sleeve and articulated elbow	Free range of motion, comfortable
Colors: abalone, wink, Columbia navy, tilt blue	Unisex colors, offers variety
Sizes: 7/8, 10/12, 14/16, 18/20, 4/5, 6/6x, 2T, 3T, 4T	Children's sizes, covers full age range
Limited warranty	Covers defects in materials and workmanship in outerwear manufactured by Columbia Sportswear Company.

@ Online Action! Go to *marketingessentials.glencoe.com/12/ figure/1* to find a project on feature-benefit charts.

Consumers look for qualities of a product that differentiate competing brands and models. In buying a vehicle, a consumer might consider the car's engine, gas consumption, appearance, stereo system, and tires, and whether the car has an automatic transmission, air bag, power steering, and antilock brakes.

Additional features add more value to a product and provide the reasons for price differences among product models. An iron that turns itself off after sitting unused will cost more than a basic model without this feature. Extended product features for a vehicle might include the warranty, service policy, and available financing. Customers might consider the reputation of a company to be an extended feature because there is reduced risk in doing business with a secure and well-established company. Customers are faithful to a reputable company that stands behind its products.

Figure 12.1 *Feature-Benefit Chart*

Discussion After students read **Figure 12.1**, discuss the importance of the product features to the customer. Ask: In the end, might a person buy the jacket just because it looks cool or functional or put it back on the rack just because he or she thinks it is unattractive? Ask students to explain their responses.

Caption Answer Answers will vary, but might include price or country of origin.

@ Online Action! For instructions, ideas, and answer guide, go to the Teacher Center at marketingessentials.glencoe.com

Follow Up Have students create a feature-benefit chart of a clothing item of their choice. Encourage students to use spreadsheet or graphic design software to create their charts.

Customer Benefits

When the features of a product are developed into customer benefits, they become selling points. **Customer benefits** are the advantages or personal satisfaction a customer will get from a good or service. It is a salesperson's job to analyze the product features from the customer's point of view to determine the benefits. A salesperson will need to answer two questions about each product feature:

1. **How does the feature help the product's performance?** The answer to this question represents the first step in developing a customer benefit. For example, air pockets in the heel of a running shoe cushion the impact on pavement.
2. **How does the performance information give the customer a personal reason to buy the product?** What value is the product to the customer? In the case of the running shoe, the air pockets give the wearer more comfort when running or walking and help to protect the foot from injury.

After identifying the features of a product and their benefits, you should put together a feature-benefit chart. This is a chart in which each product feature is listed with its corresponding customer benefits. In preparing such a chart, remember that the more useful a feature, the more valuable the product is to the customer. Figure 12.1 on page 262 shows a feature-benefit chart for a jacket.

Customer Buying Motives

Salespeople must know what motivates customers to buy and what decisions customers make before the final purchase.

Customers may have rational or emotional motives for making purchases. A **rational motive** is a conscious, logical reason for a purchase. Rational motives include product dependability, time or monetary savings, health or safety considerations, service, and quality. An **emotional motive** is a feeling experienced by a customer through association with a product. Emotional motives are feelings such as social approval, recognition, power, love, or prestige. Many buying decisions involve a combination of both buying motives.

Successful salespeople determine customers' rational and emotional motives in a potential buying situation. Then they suggest the features and benefits of the product that best matches those motives.

Customer Decision Making

Some customers need no help from salespeople, and others require significant time and effort. This difference has its roots in three distinct types of decision making—extensive,

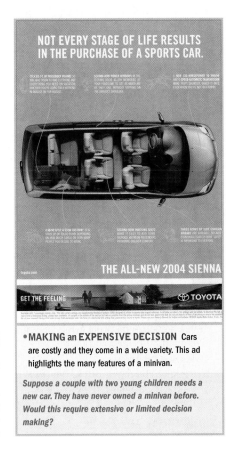

NOT EVERY STAGE OF LIFE RESULTS IN THE PURCHASE OF A SPORTS CAR.

THE ALL-NEW 2004 SIENNA

GET THE FEELING   TOYOTA

• **MAKING an EXPENSIVE DECISION** Cars are costly and they come in a wide variety. This ad highlights the many features of a minivan.

Suppose a couple with two young children needs a new car. They have never owned a minivan before. Would this require extensive or limited decision making?

Chapter 12 - Preparing for the Sale **263**

CLOSE

Ask students to recall and provide answers to the following questions:

- **What are the purpose and goals of selling?**
  To help customers make satisfying buying decisions and create ongoing, profitable relationships between buyer and seller.

- **What is consultative selling?**
  Providing solutions to customers' problems by finding products that meet their needs.

Online Activity

Fan Sites

Have students find Web sites made by customers who are loyal to specific brands and products. For example, there are fan sites dedicated to Subaru WRX cars, Apple computers, and Spam (the food product). Ask students to discuss why Subaru, Apple, and Hormel might support such sites with advertisements or logo placement in a one-paragraph response.

---

limited, and routine. How a person makes a decision is affected by the following factors:

- Previous experience with the product and company
- How often the product is purchased
- The amount of information necessary to make a wise buying decision
- The importance of the purchase to the customer
- The perceived risk involved in the purchase (for example, uncertainty about how the product will function)
- The time available to make the decision

Extensive Decision Making

Extensive decision making is used when there has been little or no previous experience with an item. This category includes those goods and services that have a high degree of perceived risk, are very expensive, or have high value to the customer. A consumer who is buying a first home will use extensive decision making.

Limited Decision Making

Limited decision making is used when a person buys goods and services that he or she has purchased before but not regularly. There is a moderate degree of perceived risk involved, and the person often needs some information before buying the product.

Consumer goods and services in this category might include a second car, certain types of clothing, furniture, a vacation, and household appliances.

Routine Decision Making

Routine decision making is used when a person needs little information about a product. The perceived risk may be low because the item is inexpensive, the product is bought frequently, or satisfaction with the product is high. Some consumer goods and services in this category are grocery items, newspapers, and dry cleaning services. Customers who have developed brand loyalty for a product will use routine decision making.

12.1 AFTER YOU READ

Reviewing Key Terms and Concepts

1. What sets personal selling apart from other forms of promotion?
2. Identify a basic, a physical, and an extended product feature for a camera.
3. What factors influence the level of customer decision making?

Integrating Academic Skills

Math

4. When buying advertising time on television or in magazines, advertisers calculate the cost per thousand (CPM) people reached by the ad. If the cost of advertising was $100,000 and the reach or circulation was 10,000,000 people, what would be the CPM? (Note: M is the Roman numeral for 1,000.)

Civics and Government

5. Research the provisions of the Do Not Call Registry and note its impact on sellers and telemarketers. Prepare a one-page written report on your findings.

 Online Action!

Check your answers at *marketingessentials.glencoe.com/12/read*

AFTER YOU READ

Reviewing Key Terms and Concepts

1. In personal selling, there is two-way communication between the buyer and the seller.

2. Answers will vary; a sample answer might read: Basic feature: it takes photos. Physical feature: red-eye reduction. Extended feature: warranty.

3. Factors that influence the level of customer decision making might include: experience with the product and company, how often the item is purchased, amount of information necessary to make a wise buying decision, importance of purchase to the customer, and perceived risk involved in the purchase.

Integrating Academic Skills

4. $10; $100,000 ÷ 10,000 = $10

5. Reports will vary; accept all reports that show understanding of the Do Not Call Registry.

 Online Action! Answers at **marketingessentials.glencoe.com/12/read**

Getting Ready to Sell

OBJECTIVES

- Name sources of product information
- Explain the main focus of preparation in business-to-business selling and in retail selling

KEY TERMS

- pre-approach
- prospect
- referrals
- endless chain method
- cold canvassing
- sales quotas

 READ and STUDY

BEFORE YOU READ

Predict Suppose you are starting tomorrow as a tire salesperson. Where would you find information about car tires?

THE MAIN IDEA

As a salesperson, you will need to prepare for the sale by learning about the industry and the products you will be selling. In specific sales situations, you may also need to find customers. The tools and techniques for accomplishing these tasks are covered in this section. You will also review company policies and ethical and legal issues in sales.

STUDY ORGANIZER

Use a chart similar to the one below to take notes about sources of product and industry information and methods of prospecting.

Pre-approach

Product Information — Company Policies

The Pre-Approach

The **pre-approach** is the preparation for the face-to-face encounter with potential customers. In preparing to assist customers, salespeople study their products, keep abreast of industry trends and competitors, research potential customers, and develop familiarity with their company's policies and procedures. They also review ethical and legal issues involved in their selling situation.

 WHILE YOU READ

Summarize List three things to remember in preparing for the sales process.

Chapter 12 - Preparing for the Sale **265**

FOCUS

Introducing the Section

COLLABORATIVE ACTIVITY

To prepare for reading the section, have students share what they know about an upcoming movie of their choice. Then have them classify sources of their information into one of four categories: direct experience, written materials, other people, and formal training. Let students know that businesses prepare to sell their product through these ways.

Preteaching Key Terms

Read the key terms aloud, or ask a volunteer to read them. Ask students to predict the meanings and compose sentences using these phrases:

- pre-approach
- prospect
- referrals
- endless chain method
- cold canvassing
- sales quotas

Tell students they can check their predictions as they read this section.

Critical Thinking

Ask students to explain why the pre-approach is an important part of the sales process.

READ and STUDY

BEFORE YOU READ

Lead students in discussing where they would find information on car tires. Sources might include trade magazines, manufacturer catalogs, and conversations with current salespeople.

THE MAIN IDEA

Ask a volunteer to read the main idea aloud and ask another student to rephrase it in his or her own words.

STUDY ORGANIZER

Model the study organizer for students by filling in sources as you progress through the lesson. A full-size, downloadable study organizer can be found at **marketingessentials.glencoe.com**

WHILE YOU READ Have students save their lists of ways to prepare for the sales process and compare them to what is recommended in this section.

TEACH

Discussion Starter

PRODUCT INFORMATION

Have students pretend they are about to start working at a clothing store. Ask them to brainstorm where they can find information about a particular garment, such as whether to wash or dry-clean it. Answers may include the care label or hangtag.

TEACHING POINTS

Clarify Reinforce the idea that many businesses encourage employees to buy and use the company's merchandise. Some retailers require their clerks to wear clothes they sell. Explain that this helps the employees become familiar with the products, shows off the products, and also makes the store or company look good.

◆ Extended Activity

Finding Product Information
Have students choose a product that interests them. Ask students to use consumer and trade magazines, newspapers, online forums, and other sources to develop their product knowledge. Have students then present their product knowledge in a five-minute oral presentation or a feature-benefit chart.

Product Information

Developing product knowledge is easy if you know where to look for the information. Salespeople can generally find all the product information they need through four main sources: direct experience, written publications, other people, and formal training.

Some businesses offer discounts to their salespeople to encourage employees to buy and use the company's merchandise. You can also get direct experience with a product by studying display models or visiting the manufacturing facility to see how the product is made.

Printed materials include user manuals, manufacturer warranties and guarantees, catalogs, and promotional materials. Labels provide important information for clothing items or prepackaged goods. Manufacturers, retailers, and wholesalers often have Web sites where products may be explained and purchased.

Formal training may be the best way to educate salespeople on certain products. Most industrial sales representatives receive much

---

Case Study

Marketing Pharmaceuticals

When the biotech company Genta was on the brink of selling its first drug, it took two years to recruit a sales force. For most drug companies, the sales division is the heart of the business. The smallest can still employ more than 1,000 salespeople. The largest sales division may reach 3,000, selling everything from hypertension medicines to antibiotics. Genta does not fall into either category.

An Expert Salesforce

Genta recruited 18 experienced salespeople, mostly from other pharmaceutical companies. They all began their careers in primary care—the typical trajectory—before switching to a specialty in oncology—the treatment of cancer. Genta would not release salary figures. Sales reps with no experience can earn a base salary of $80,000, according to Salary.com, a Web site that tracks wages. Bonuses, commissions, and, of course, experience can push that much higher, according to industry executives.

The team is composed of salespeople who won awards for their selling performance, Williams said. They spend their downtime in medical libraries and hospitals, picking up information to share with physicians. They are considered experts in oncology and mingle with physicians, spend time with cancer advocacy groups, and forfeit weekends in an ongoing effort to sell.

THINK STRATEGICALLY
Why do these salespeople have to be experts in oncology?

@ Online Action! Go to *marketingessentials.glencoe.com/12/case* to find an activity about sales training.

 marketingessentials.glencoe.com

Case Study Marketing Pharmaceuticals

Discussion Have students read the Case Study and discuss the pros and cons of having such a small and highly paid sales team. Pros may include prestige and publicity, while cons may include smaller outreach.

Caption Answer Genta's salespeople have to be experts because their clientele is made up of educated specialists and informed advocates.

@ Online Action! For instructions, ideas, and answer guide, go to the Teacher Center at marketingessentials.glencoe.com

Figure 12.2 How to Develop Employer Leads

• **Finding a Buyer** Many firms generate leads for their sales staff. Leads help salespeople locate potential customers.

How do companies find leads?

1 EMPLOYERS ATTEND TRADE SHOWS

Employers can get leads by attending trade shows. Retailers and other interested business-to-business buyers attend trade shows to learn about new products they may want to buy to resell or to use in their businesses. Attendees are usually good leads for the shows' vendors. Trade shows are often sponsored by trade associations. For instance, the Super Show is sponsored by the Sporting Goods Manufacturers Association (SGMA), the members of which are producers of athletic clothing, footwear, and sports equipment.

2 EMPLOYERS GIVE LEADS

Employers give leads to the sales representatives responsible for the territories in which the prospects are located. Special forms may be used to communicate this information and to track the follow-up action taken by the sales representatives.

3 SALESPEOPLE ACT ON LEADS

Salespeople call to learn more about the prospects. Salespeople make appointments with qualified leads. They then report back to their employer. That way the employer knows that the leads have been followed.

Online Action! Go to *marketingessentials.glencoe.com/12/ figure/2* to find a project on employer leads.

TEACH CONTINUED

Individualized Math Skills

L1 Inform students that they are sales reps for a paper company that specializes in selling to schools. If the company takes three months off for summer vacation, what percentage of the year is spent in downtime?
25%; $3 \div 12 = .25 = 25\%$

L2 Inform students that a customer wants five boxes of high-quality photo paper and 20 boxes of printer paper. If a box of printer paper costs $25 and the photo paper costs twice as much, how much is the total?
$750; $(5 \times 50) + (20 \times 25) = \$250 + \$500 = \$750$

L3 Inform students that there is a special deal in which customers who order $500 worth of products or more receive 10 percent credit toward their next purchase. If a customer ordered $750 worth of products, how much credit does the customer receive?
$75; $\$750 \times .10 = \$75$

Critical Thinking

Ask students: Is it ethical for a salesperson to take his or her customers when moving to a new job? Have students share their responses in class.

Figure 12.2 How to Develop Employer Leads

Discussion After students read **Figure 12.2**, have them discuss the ways employers help salespeople locate leads. Ask students why trade shows might be a good source of leads. Answers might include that people who attend trade shows are interested in the field.

Caption Answer Companies find leads through employers who attend trade shows and pass them to salespeople who follow up on them.

Online Action! For instructions, ideas, and answer guide, go to the Teacher Center at **marketingessentials.glencoe.com**

TEACH CONTINUED

Concept Development

INDUSTRY TRENDS

How do skate shops, surf shops, and street wear boutiques know what's cool? Inform students that the Action Sports Retailer trade shows attract store buyers from around the world. Store buyers can set up appointments or meet with sales reps from established and up-and-coming companies that arrange equipment demos, endorsed athlete signings, and fashion shows. Ask students why a retailer might send a group of employees to such a trade show.

To find out the latest trends and items.

TEACHING POINTS

Clarify Tell students that if you were a new shoe manufacturer, your booth would have catalogs and samples. Ask students what else might be involved.

Answers might include a video display, demos by sponsored athletes, or giveaways.

Enrichment

IDENTIFYING PROSPECTS

Ask students to select a business and prospect for new customers. Suggest the library and the Internet to find identify trade shows, journals, organizations, and other sources that may provide leads for new customers. Have students create an outline that lists the sources and their potential.

MARKET TECH

FOSE—A High-Tech Trade Show

FOSE stands for Federal Office Systems Expo. This exposition has high-tech companies exhibiting their wares for government officials and procurement officers. In 2004 it was held at the Washington (D.C.) Convention Center. Some 500 vendors selling everything from printers, scanners, and software to GPS-equipped digital cameras and high-tech motion-detector systems showcase their products there. Close to 19,000 people attended FOSE in 2004.

Bringing Home Leads

According to Tom Temin, editor-in-chief of *Government Computer News* and *Washington Technology* and senior vice president for editorial at *PostNewsweek Tech Media*, "the show was more of a breeding ground for networking and mining sales leads than a place for vendors to close deals. There are deal shows, and this one is not one of those." Large and small companies used gimmicks to get prospects to stop at their booths. One company had a cartoonist, two others had slot machines promising gifts and awards for prizes, while another scanned badges for a raffle.

THINK LIKE A MARKETER

If you had a small company that specialized in software to track agricultural goods, would you pay to exhibit at this show? Why or why not?

@ Online Action!

Go to *marketingessentials.glencoe.com/ 12/tech* to find an activity about technology and sales.

---

of their product knowledge through formal training sessions. Information might be funneled informally to the sales staff as new merchandise is received or selected for promotion. Some of this information and even training may be provided by the vendors/manufacturer of the product(s).

Industry Trends

Sales representatives read periodicals related to their trade to gain insight into the industry. As a sales representative for an apparel manufacturer, you might read *Women's Wear Daily*. At the retail level of selling, a sales representative may read consumer fashion magazines, such as *Vogue*, to stay current with up-to-date colors and trends.

Prospecting

Looking for new customers is called prospecting. A **prospect**, or a lead, is a potential customer. Many types of businesses require salespeople to find prospects, while others do not.

Prospecting is especially important in business-to-business selling situations. Salespeople are evaluated on how many new accounts they open through prospecting efforts.

Employer Leads

Some firms employ entire telemarketing teams to generate leads for their sales staffs. They also attend trade shows, where they display their products for review by buyers in the industry.

Interested buyers provide information for follow-up. Other firms rely entirely on their salespeople to find new customers. Many employers do what they can to help locate potential customers for their salespeople.

Directories

The Yellow Pages list businesses that may be potential customers for certain industrial goods and services. Business-to-business sales representatives can use trade and professional

 marketingessentials.glencoe.com

MARKET TECH

FOSE—A High-Tech Trade Show

Discussion After students read Market Tech, lead a discussion about why businesses use gimmicks to get prospects to stop at their booths. Answers might include to make their booths stand apart from the rest. Have students discuss what kind of gimmicks they may have seen or might use.

THINK LIKE A MARKETER

Answer: Answers will vary; students might agree that the show is worthwhile because it would give you an opportunity to show your wares to the Department of Agriculture and other government agencies.

@ Online Action! For instructions, ideas, and answer guide, go to the Teacher Center at marketingessentials.glencoe.com

directories to locate potential customers. One well-known directory frequently used by sales representatives is the *Thomas Register of American Manufacturers*.

Newspapers

Newspapers provide good leads for some salespeople. For example, engagement announcements provide bridal shops, caterers, florists, and printers with prospects.

Commercial Lists

Salespeople may buy lists of potential customers from companies that specialize in categorizing people by such criteria as education, age, income, credit card purchases, and location. Lists of businesses categorized according to net sales, profits, products, and geographic locations are also available.

Customer Referrals

Satisfied customers often give salespeople **referrals**—the names of other people who might buy the product. Referrals open the market to potential customers whom you might not have reached without a recommendation. When salespeople ask previous customers for names of potential customers, they are said to be using the **endless chain method**. Some companies offer discounts or gifts to customers who give referrals.

Cold Canvassing

In **cold canvassing**, potential customers are selected at random, such as by going door-to-door or selecting names from a telephone directory. This is also sometimes called blind prospecting.

Preparing for the Sale in Business-to-Business Selling

In business-to-business (B-to-B or B2B) sales, pre-approach activities vary depending on whether the sales call is with a previous customer or a new prospect. When dealing with previous customers, salespeople analyze past sales records and review their notes about the buyer's personality, family, interests, and hobbies.

marketingessentials.glencoe.com

A MATTER OF ETHICS

Sealing a Deal

A software firm in a medium-sized city has been growing, in part thanks to its popular sports-based video games. The company has decided to sell stock and become a publicly traded company. It can use the money it raises to fund new research and development, but it will also have to meet a lot of new accounting requirements. The people who own the company stock will want complete information about the company's financial performance.

Pitching and Wooing

Accounting firms in the city are desperately trying to get the contract with the software company. They treat executives and software designers to expensive dinners and tickets to NBA games. One company is so determined to win the contract that it makes a secret offer to one of the senior executives. It promises to hire the executive's daughter, who recently graduated from college, but has been having trouble getting a job.

THINKING ETHICALLY

How far can a company go to win over a potential customer?

@ Online Action!

Go to *marketingessentials.glencoe.com/12/ethics* to find an activity about ethics and sales.

When dealing with a new customer, the salesperson must do some homework before jumping into the selling process. Questions that the salesperson should research include the following:

Concept Development

PROSPECTING

Ask students which type of prospecting they would prefer using: cold canvassing or the endless chain method, and why. Most students would agree that the endless chain method is easier because it allows you to use the name of a mutual acquaintance to get your foot in the door.

TEACHING POINTS

Demonstrate Bring newspapers to class to illustrate their usefulness as a source of leads. Find the section with engagement announcements, which could be used by bridal shops, caterers, florists, and printers who are looking for new clients.

Extend Ask students whether it is ethical for commercial list providers to include the e-mail addresses of Web users who have not consented to be sent business-related spam. Have students discuss their responses in class.

Online Activity

Researching Companies

Have students look up Dun & Bradstreet on the Web to see what services the company offers. Ask: What businesses can use them? Have students share their findings in class.

A MATTER OF ETHICS Sealing a Deal

Discussion Lead a discussion on this topic by asking questions about gift-giving and nepotism, or favoritism. Let students know that gifts and favors to clients are accepted in other countries and cultures.

THINKING ETHICALLY **Answer:** Answers will vary; many students will agree that bribery is going too far and is not appropriate for business.

@ Online Action! For instructions, ideas, and answer guide, go to the Teacher Center at **marketingessentials.glencoe.com**

Follow Up Tell the class that Salt Lake City organizers were penalized for attempting to bribe the Olympic Planning Committee. Have students research the story and write a short paper about the situation or present their findings orally to the class.

269

ASSESS

Review Guide

CONCEPTS

Ask students to recall the four main sources of product information.

direct experience, written publications, other people, formal training

KEY TERMS

Have students review key terms, their spellings, and definitions in small groups.

ONLINE SELF-ASSESSMENT

Have students go to marketingessentials.glencoe.com for the Section 12.2 practice test.

Individualized Review

L1 Assign and review Chapter 12 activities in the Student Activity Workbook.

L2 Assign and review Chapter 12 activities in the Marketing Math Workbook.

L3 Assign and review Chapter 12 activities in the *BusinessWeek* Reader and Case Studies.

Marketing Practice

Have students work in groups of three to five to choose one product for the subject of a role play. The role play should demonstrate a training session for salespeople for the new product. It should exhibit knowledge of the product and product features as well as knowledge of the product's audience or consumer. Students can also practice sales techniques on one another in the training session role play.

- Does the prospect need this product or service?
- Does the prospect have the financial resources to pay?
- Does the prospect have the authority to buy?

To find answers to these questions, you can make inquiries by calling other sales representatives who sell noncompeting lines. You can read the company's annual reports or subscribe to the database listings of a company like Dun & Bradstreet, which monitors businesses' financial situations. All these things are part of qualifying a prospect. Qualified prospects are prospective customers that meet the necessary requirements established by your firm to conduct business.

Some of the concerns above can be addressed during your telephone conversation with the prospect. By asking tactful questions such as what competing products the prospect carries, you can determine satisfaction with the present supplier. You may find that your product could better satisfy your prospect's needs. Other questions might help to determine how your product could help improve the prospect's business. That will help you in your consultative selling because you will be in a position to offer solutions to current needs and problems.

• SALES TRAINING Formal training may be used to disseminate product information to new and seasoned sales staff. Role playing is often used.

What other information might be important to cover in the formal training of a new sales employee?

Preparing for the Sale in Retail Selling

Since the customer comes to you in retail selling situations, the preparation centers around the merchandise and work area. Retail sales associates are often responsible for merchandising, stock keeping, and housekeeping. Those activities include:

- Straightening, rearranging, and replenishing the stock
- Adjusting price tickets before and after special sales
- Learning where stock is located and how much is available
- Arranging displays
- Vacuuming the floor, dusting the shelves, and keeping the selling area neat and clean

Company Policies and Training

Sales management establishes the guidelines and policies under which salespeople function. Some of their specific duties involve scheduling sales staff, overseeing and evaluating their performance, and training them.

Training

A four-step process is often used by sales managers who are ultimately responsible for training new sales personnel. The four steps are explanation, demonstration, trial, and critique. A sales technique is first explained and then is demonstrated by the person conducting the training. In the next step, the new sales associate performs the newly learned task or demonstrates product knowledge in a role-playing format. The final step involves constructive criticism by the trainer. This plan for sales training works well at all levels of selling. It also helps to reinforce the concept of consultative selling with new and seasoned sales associates when new products are being introduced.

Compensation and Sales Quotas

Salespeople are compensated by straight commission, straight salary, or salary plus commission.

PHOTO GUIDE — SALES TRAINING

Discussion Lead a discussion about the formal training of sales staff. Ask students why role-playing is used to help sales staff learn how to react to different sales situations.

Caption Answer In addition to product information, other information might include sales tactics and techniques, company policies, and legal and ethical selling issues.

Follow Up Ask students why experienced sales staff may go through formal training with the new employees. Answers may include to update them with the latest policies and to build familiarity with the new sales staff.

Commission salespeople get paid only when they sell something. Salaried salespeople get paid a set amount regardless of how much they sell. Salary plus commission salespeople generally have a set salary, and their commission rate is lower than those who are paid only commission.

Regardless of the methods of compensation, sales managers often establish sales quotas. **Sales quotas** are dollar or unit sales goals set for the sales staff to achieve in a specified period of time. A plan for meeting a yearly sales quota may be to establish sales quotas for a week, month, or quarter.

Legal and Ethical Issues

Commission sales and sales quotas can create pressure on the sales staff to produce sales. If not schooled properly in selling ethics and legal issues, sales associates may engage in hard-sell tactics or may lie to a prospective customer. For example, if a salesperson knows that it will take four weeks for delivery of an order and promises two-week delivery just to make the sale, that is both illegal and ethically wrong.

It is important to remember that a sales order or purchase order is a legal agreement, a contract between the buyer and seller and signed by both parties. It contains all the elements of a legal contract: an offer, an acceptance, consideration (price and terms), competent parties (buyer and seller), legal form, and legal subject matter.

Another aspect of a sales contract is full disclosure of the facts. In a contract providing services, all services and materials that will be used should be clearly identified.

 12.2 AFTER YOU READ

Reviewing Key Terms and Concepts

1. In all selling situations, what can salespeople do to prepare for the sale?
2. What is prospecting?
3. Which of the three sales compensation methods would you prefer? Why?

Integrating Academic Skills

Math

4. Mark has a choice as to how he will be compensated in his new sales position. He may elect to be paid a straight commission of eight percent of sales or a salary of $55,000 plus a two percent commission on sales. Which is a better deal for Mark if sales are projected to be $1,000,000 in his territory? Which method of compensation would you recommend? Why?

Writing

5. To prepare for a sales demonstration with a product of your choice, write a letter to the product's manufacturer. Introduce yourself and tell the reason for writing the letter. Explain why you selected that company's product for your research. Identify the specific information you are requesting. Request the information in a way that makes it easy for the reader to comply.

 Online Action!
Check your answers at *marketingessentials.glencoe.com/12/read*

marketingessentials.glencoe.com

Chapter 12 - Preparing for the Sale **271**

 CLOSE

Ask students to recall and provide answers to the following questions:

- **What are sales quotas?**
  Dollar or unit sales goals set for the sales staff to achieve in a specified period of time.

- **What is the four-step process of training?**
  Explanation, demonstration, trial, and critique.

Extended Activity

Sales Quotas
Tell students that sales quotas are generally set high in an effort to motivate salespeople to achieve growth. Ask students if they believe this is fair and to write their responses in a two-paragraph essay.

AFTER YOU READ

Reviewing Key Terms and Concepts

1. In all selling situations, salespeople can prepare for the sale by studying their products, keeping abreast of industry trends and competitors, researching potential customers, and developing familiarity with their company's policies and procedures.

2. Prospecting is looking for potential customers.

Online Action! Answers at **marketingessentials.glencoe.com/12/read**

3. Answers will vary; students should explain why they prefer straight commission, straight salary, or salary plus commission.

Integrating Academic Skills

4. Answers will vary: Straight commission: $1,000,000 $\times$ .08 = $80,000; Salary plus commission: $55,000 + ($1,000,000 $\times$ .02) = $75,000. Mark would potentially make

more with straight commission, but since there is no guarantee that sales will always be $1,000,000, more cautious students may recommend the salary plus commission.

5. Letters will vary; all letters should include an introductory paragraph, a second paragraph that explains why the student chose his or her company, and a third paragraph that asks for specific information.

271

Lifelong Learning

CAREER INFORMATION

Have students go to marketingessentials.glencoe.com and find the Chapter 12 Careers page and click on the link for the American Marketing Association's Careers Strategies and Tips. Ask students to select one article, read it, and make a poster presenting its main points.

PREPARING FOR THE SALE

Inform students that sales jobs have highs and lows that often depend on whether or not sales are made. Keeping a sense of perspective is important to keep from being overwhelmed by the pressure to find customers and to make and close the sale. Being prepared will help ensure that the sales process goes smoothly.

Primary Source

Ask students to go to marketingessentials.glencoe.com and find Chapter 12 Resources. Ask them to click on the link for the American Marketing Association's marketing dictionary and read the definitions of the terms they find which are related to preparing for the sale.

● THINKING CRITICALLY

Answers will vary, but students may agree that the toughest part is always being under pressure to achieve set goals.

@ Online Action!

For instructions, ideas, and answer guide, go to the Teacher Center at marketingessentials.glencoe.com

NANCY NORTHERN
UNDERWRITING SALES
PUBLIC RADIO
PARTNERSHIP

(?) What do you do at work?
I find prospects that will benefit the most from on-air exposure on one of Public Radio Partnership's three radio stations. It is then my responsibility to "court" them. I will send an introduction letter, detailing who I am and a very brief description of how my product can help their business. After sending a few mailers, I follow up with a phone call and attempt to set up an in-person meeting. At this meeting we discuss the prospect's marketing challenges, strengths, weaknesses, and goals for the future.

(?) What skills are most important to you?
Communication is a skill that is necessary in a sales position. You must be able to communicate with your prospects, your clients, and your audience. Another essential skill is writing. Every proposal that I present to a client must be easy to understand while expressing the specific desires of my client. In addition, on-air time restrictions require me to express a large amount of information in a very short period of time.

(?) What is your key to success?
I read books on the market, advertising, marketing, and specific client categories that I am targeting as often as possible. I also attend sales seminars and networking events. Hard work and thick skin are key. Sales can be a very difficult job. There are a lot of highs and lows and a ton of nos. I do not take nos personally; a good sales person can't. I have perseverance and dedication and I am really bad at giving up.

Aptitudes, Abilities, and Skills

Outgoing personality, writing and communication skills, persistence, and self-motivation

Education and Training

Degrees in general business and marketing can be helpful.

Career Path

Sales positions are easy to find, and since many are commission-only, they can be easy to land. Excellent performance within a sales position leads to quick advancement, as a company's sales force is its life blood.

● THINKING CRITICALLY

What do you think would be the toughest aspect of a career in sales?

@ Online Action!

Go to *marketingessentials.glencoe.com/12/careers* to find a career-related activity.

 marketingessentials.glencoe.com

Test-Taking Strategies

Suggest to students that when taking tests, they first go through the test to determine the number and type of questions as well as the desired length of the answer. In this way, they can pace themselves and make sure they are not caught off guard by questions that require a longer response towards the end of the test-taking period.

FOCUS on KEY POINTS

SECTION 12.1
- Three types of selling situations are retail, business-to-business, and telemarketing.
- Matching the characteristics of a product to a customer's needs and wants is feature-benefit selling. Customers may have both rational and emotional motives for making a purchase. Three forms of customer decision making are extensive, limited, and routine.

SECTION 12.2
- To prepare for a sale, salespeople study their products, industry trends, competitors, and customers, as well as company policies and legal and ethical selling issues.
- A prospect or lead is a potential customer.
- To prepare for business-to-business selling, research the customer and meet with qualified prospects. For retail selling, learn about products, merchandising, stockkeeping, and housekeeping.

REVIEW VOCABULARY

Define each of the key terms below.

1. personal selling (p. 260)
2. business-to-business selling (p. 261)
3. telemarketing (p. 261)
4. consultative selling (p. 261)
5. feature-benefit selling (p. 261)
6. product features (p. 261)
7. customer benefits (p. 263)
8. rational motive (p. 263)
9. emotional motive (p. 263)
10. extensive decision making (p. 264)
11. limited decision making (p. 264)
12. routine decision making (p. 264)
13. pre-approach (p. 265)
14. prospect (p. 268)
15. referrals (p. 269)
16. endless chain method (p. 269)
17. cold canvassing (p. 269)
18. sales quotas (p. 271)

REVIEW FACTS and IDEAS

19. Define personal selling and name three settings where it may occur. (12.1)

20. What are the purpose and goals of selling? (12.1)

21. Explain the concept of feature-benefit selling and how it is related to consultative selling. (12.1)

22. Name five sources that can be used in prospecting. (12.2)

23. What is the difference between the endless chain and cold canvassing methods of prospecting? (12.2)

24. What is the focus of the pre-approach in business-to-business and in retail sales? (12.2)

Chapter 12 - Preparing for the Sale 273

REVIEW FACTS and IDEAS

19. Personal selling is any form of direct contact occurring between a salesperson and a customer. Three settings: retail stores, business-to-business, and telemarketing.

20. The purpose and goals of selling are to help customers make satisfying buying decisions that create ongoing, profitable relationships between the buyer and seller.

21. To perform consultative selling, one must know how to match characteristics of a product to a customer's needs and wants.

22. Employee leads, telephone directories, trade and professional directories, newspapers, and commercial lists.

23. Endless chain processing is based on customer referrals, while cold canvassing uses no leads.

24. The pre-approach in business-to-business sales includes analysis of the customer's needs, qualifying new customers, and making appointments to meet the new customers. The pre-approach in retail sales includes merchandising, stockkeeping, and housekeeping to learn the inventory.

FOCUS on KEY POINTS

Ask volunteers to read the summaries aloud and rephrase them in their own words. Have students give examples of the different types of selling situations, buying motives, customer decision making, and ways to prepare for a sale.

REVIEW VOCABULARY

See glossary for definitions of **1–18.**
A sample definition might read:

1. *Personal selling* is any form of direct contact between a salesperson and a customer.

BUILD SKILLS

25. Workplace Skills
Role plays will vary, but should include the four-step training process, define consultative selling, and touch on ethical behavior.

26. Technology Applications
Telephone scripts will vary; scripts should confirm that the restaurants, hotels, and country clubs sell the baked goods that the company sells.

27. Math Skills
The second shirt costs $20 and the third shirt costs $13.33. The total cost is $79.38; $40 + ($40 × .50) + ($40 × .33) = $40 + $20 + $13.33 = $73.33; $73.33 × 1.0825 = $79.38

DEVELOP CRITICAL THINKING

28. Job Skills
Lists of qualities will vary; general qualities might include positive and organized, and specific qualities might include a certain amount of experience in certain industries. Conclusions will vary, but might include that there are a lot of sales positions to be filled.

29. Buying Motives
Answers will vary. Gift givers might have emotional buying motives. Those who want to capture the holidays on film or digital media may have rational motives.

BUILD SKILLS

25. Workplace Skills
Human Relations As the senior salesperson for a mobile phone company, you are responsible for training a new sales associate in consultative selling and selling ethics. Conduct a role play to demonstrate how you would cover those two topics with a classmate who will play the role of a new sales associate.

26. Technology Applications
Prepare a Script Write the telephone script for a company that wants to qualify the leads it received before passing them along to the sales staff. Assume you work for a local commercial bakery that services independent restaurants, as well as those found in hotels and country clubs, in three adjacent states.

27. Math Skills
Calculating Discounts A store is having a sale: Buy one shirt (priced at $40), get the second one at half price and the third one at one-third of the price.

How much does the second shirt cost? The third shirt? Add an 8.25 percent sales tax. What is the total cost to a customer buying three shirts?

DEVELOP CRITICAL THINKING

28. Job Skills
Scan the newspaper's want ads and ads on monster.com and list the various qualities and skills required for sales positions. Organize your list into three categories:

- General and specific qualities for retail
- General and specific qualities for business-to-business
- General and specific qualities for telemarketing sales positions

What conclusions do you draw from your research?

29. Buying Motives
Suppose you are working as a salesperson in the camera department of a large retailer during the holiday season. What buying motives do you think you will observe among your customers?

Formative Assessment
Formative assessment is an essential component of classroom work. This type of assessment provides information that is then used as feedback to modify teaching and meet student needs.

L1 Have students explain the three levels of customer decision making.

L2 Have students provide various examples of each of the three levels of customer decision making from their experience.

L3 Have groups of students role play sales situations while the remainder of the class identifies the levels of customer decision making being shown.

 Reteach If the results of this formative assessment seem low, consider the following activity:

Read each of the key terms aloud. Have students define the key terms and use each of them in a sentence. Clear up any misunderstandings.

APPLY CONCEPTS

30. Writing a Sales Letter

One way to generate leads is to write sales letters to prospective customers. Your prospective customers are DECA chapter advisors and members. Your company is an art gallery that runs auctions for fund-raising projects.

Activity Use your knowledge of buying motives and consultative selling to write a convincing sales letter to generate an interest in this form of fund-raising. Include a means of contacting your company for follow-up by one of your sales representatives.

31. Learning Company Policies and Selling Ethics

Select a company that is of interest to you and to which you have access. Interview the person responsible for orienting new sales associates. Ask questions about company policies, as well as unethical selling practices and sales regulations with which a new employee should be familiar. Also ask about the type of training that is provided.

Activity Prepare a background report on this company. Describe what it sells and how it sells its products. Include the types of sales personnel it employs.

NET SAVVY

32. Finding the Unique Features

Select a product of interest to you that is also fairly new. Use the Internet to research and create a list of all the unique features of your product.

marketingessentials.glencoe.com

THE DECA **CONNECTION**

Role Play: Preparing for the Sale

Situation Assume the role of part-time employee of a camera store. You want to do a good job, so you spend all the time you can reading about the different cameras your store sells. Your manager (judge) has noticed you studying the camera information and customers asking for you by name. The manager (judge) has also noticed that your sales figures are growing steadily.

Activity The manager (judge) has asked you to explain your selling method so the manager (judge) can encourage the other employees to do the same.

Evaluation You will be evaluated on how well you meet the following performance indicators:

- Acquire product information for use in selling
- Analyze product information to identify product features and benefits
- Prepare for the sales presentation
- Explain key factors in building a clientele
- Explain the selling process

Online Action!

For more information and DECA Prep practice, go to *marketingessentials.glencoe .com/12/DECA*

APPLY CONCEPTS

30. Writing a Sales Letter
Letters will vary, but should include information about the purpose of the fund raiser and contact information.

31. Learning Company Policies and Selling Ethics
Background reports will vary, but should describe the company's goods or services, how it sells its products, and its sales force.

NET SAVVY

32. Finding the Unique Features
Products and their features will vary; students should list them in an organized manner.

MINI-QUIZ

Read these sentences to the students and have them volunteer the missing word(s).

1. Businesses that simply reorder goods and services without much thought are using _____ decision making. (routine)

2. Satisfied customers often give sales-people _____, or the names of other people who might buy the product. (referrals)

3. _____ salespeople get paid only when they sell something. (Commission)

For an expanded chapter quiz, go to Chapter 12 in the TeacherWorks CD-ROM and to Chapter 12 in the **ExamView**® Pro Test Generator CD-ROM.

THE DECA **CONNECTION**

The students should be evaluated on the performance indicators noted in the role play. For another DECA role play, go to the Competitive Events Workbook or the Student Activity Workbook, or go to marketingessentials.glencoe.com/12/DECA

Online Action! For instructions, ideas, and answer guide, go to the Teacher Center at **marketingessentials.glencoe.com**

DECA Advisors Corner

Group students in twos or threes and have them develop various presentations based on the core principles of DECA to present to local businesspeople. Have students invite them to become business members of your local DECA chapter.

Chapter Overview

Chapter 13 introduces students to the steps of the sales process. It then explores in detail the first two steps of the sales process: approaching the customer and determining needs.

BUILD BACKGROUND

Have students recall a sales situation in which the customer used limited decision making. Ask them what happened when the customer entered the store, showed interest in an item, made a purchase, and left the store. Have students compare their sales situations.

Why It's Important

Knowing the steps of a sale and understanding the customer's wants and needs will help you become a more effective salesperson and a wiser consumer.

Prepare to Read

List the section objectives for students. Have students skim the chapter, looking at pictures, reading captions, and noting headings. Ask questions to ensure that students have an understanding of the chapter structure.

CHAPTER 13
Initiating the Sale

Chapter Objectives

After reading this chapter, you should be able to:

- List the seven steps of a sale
- Explain the importance and purposes of the approach in the sales process
- Demonstrate how business-to-business sales representatives conduct the initial approach
- Name three methods for making the initial approach in retail sales
- Explain why determining needs is an essential step in the sales process
- List three methods for determining needs

GUIDE TO THE PHOTO

Market Talk The approach to the customer is the critical first step in the sales process. It gives the salesperson the opportunity to establish a relationship with the customer, to initiate a conversation, and to focus the customer's attention on the product. The approach can make or break a sale, so it is important to make a good first impression.

Quick Think What might you say to open a conversation with a customer?

GUIDE TO THE PHOTO

Market Talk Lead a discussion with students about first impressions. Have them talk about how important first impressions are in social settings and compare that to first impressions in selling situations. Have students describe their impressions of the salesperson in this ad.

Quick Think Answers will vary but may include, "May I help you?" or "Hello."

Follow Up Ask students if they prefer being greeted or left alone when they enter a retail store. Students' preferences will probably fall somewhere between being hounded and being ignored.

Performance indicators represent key skills and knowledge. Relating them to the concepts explained in this chapter is your key to success in DECA events. These acronyms represent DECA events that involve knowledge of concepts in this chapter.

AAAL*	FMAL	MMS	TMDM
AAML*	FMDM	QSRM	TSE
ADC	FMML	RMAL	VPM
BSM	FSRM	RMML	
EMDM	HMDM	SMDM	

In all these DECA events you should be able to follow these performance indicators:

- Explain the selling process
- Establish relationships with clients/customers
- Address the needs of individual personalities
- Determine customer/client needs
- Assess customer/client needs

All the events with an asterisk (*) also include these performance indicators:

- Determine the size and fit of children's apparel
- Determine the size and fit of women's apparel
- Determine the size and fit of men's apparel
- Determine the size and fit of shoes

Some events include additional performance indicators. These are:

VPM	Interpret test results to customers
FMDM	Explain the process of selling stocks
SMDM	Identify risks perceived by customers in purchasing services
TMDM	Determine client's travel preferences/needs

DECA PREP

Check your understanding of DECA performance indicators with the DECA activity in this chapter's review. For more information and DECA Prep practice, go to *marketingessentials.glencoe.com/13/DECA*

CHAPTER 13 Classroom Resources

For the Teacher

- TeacherWorks
- marketingessentials.glencoe.com
- Interactive Chalkboard
- **Exam*View*®** Pro Test Generator
- Fast File Unit 5

For the Student

- ***Marketing Essentials* Online Edition**
- Student Activity Workbook
- Marketing Math Workbook
- Marketing Research Workbook
- School-to-Work Activity Workbook
- Competitive Events Workbook
- ***BusinessWeek* Reader and Case Studies**
- marketingessentials.glencoe.com

DECA events that require knowledge of initiating the sale are described here. Discuss the performance indicators to make sure students understand how to demonstrate their understanding.

The events acronyms stand for:

AAAL:	**Apparel and Accessories Marketing Series, AL**
AAML:	**Apparel and Accessories Marketing Series, ML**
ADC:	**Advertising Campaign Event**
BSM:	**Business Services Marketing Series**
EMDM:	**E-Commerce Management Team Decision Making Event**
FMAL:	**Food Marketing Series, AL**
FMDM:	**Financial Analysis Management Team Decision Making Event**
FMML:	**Food Marketing Series, ML**
FSRM:	**Full Service Restaurant Management Series**
HMDM:	**Hospitality Services Management Team Decision Making Event**
MMS:	**Marketing Management Series**
QSRM:	**Quick Serve Restaurant Management, Series**
RMAL:	**Retail Merchandising Series, AL**
RMML:	**Retail Merchandising Series, ML**
SMDM:	**Sports and Entertainment Marketing Management Team Decision Making Event**
TMDM:	**Travel and Tourism Marketing Management Team Decision Making Event**
TSE:	**Technical Sales Event**
VPM:	**Vehicles and Petroleum Marketing Series**

DECA PREP

Find timed DECA Prep activities correlated to the Competitive Events Workbook for students and DECA tips for teachers at **marketingessentials.glencoe.com/13/DECA**

FOCUS

Introducing the Section

COLLABORATIVE ACTIVITY

Ask students to describe poor sales experiences they have had or witnessed. As they share their stories, write down the salespeople's qualities on the board: pushy, stuck-up, clueless, and so on. Ask students how the salespeople can improve on every category.

Preteaching Key Terms

Have teams of students draw vocabulary terms out of a hat or bowl and then write them on a sheet of paper. Have students guess the meaning of each word and write their guesses beside the word. Record the words and guesses on the board. Leave this list up so students can see how close their definitions were to the actual definitions as they work through the chapter.

- service approach
- greeting approach
- merchandise approach

 Critical Thinking

Ask students why different products might require different sales approaches.

OBJECTIVES

- List the seven steps of a sale
- Explain the importance and purposes of the approach in the sales process
- Demonstrate how business-to-business sales representatives conduct the initial approach
- Name three methods for making the initial approach in retail sales

KEY TERMS

- service approach
- greeting approach
- merchandise approach

WHILE YOU READ

Connect Think about selling situations where all seven steps of a sale were involved. Recall how the salesperson incorporated each step into the selling process.

The Sales Process

READ and STUDY

BEFORE YOU READ

Connect Reflect on ways salespeople have approached you. How effective were their methods?

THE MAIN IDEA

There are seven main steps to the sales process. There are also different styles and methods for approaching customers. What type of approach is appropriate depends on the sales situation. These elements are the foundation of sales skills.

STUDY ORGANIZER

Prepare a chart similar to the one below to identify the steps of a sale.

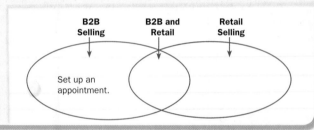

The Selling Process

Selling is the process of matching customer needs and wants to the features and benefits of a product or service. The salesperson plays a vital role in this process by gathering information about the customer, then advising the customer about which products would best suit his or her needs and lead to a decision to buy.

READ and STUDY

BEFORE YOU READ

Have students recall ways salespeople have approached them. Ask: Which methods are the most effective?

THE MAIN IDEA

Ask a volunteer to read the main idea aloud. Have students discuss which sales styles might be appropriate for different situations, such as a fancy jewelry store or a neighborhood comic book store.

STUDY ORGANIZER

Make your own organizer or download the one at marketingessentials.glencoe.com. As study continues, work with the class to identify the steps.

WHILE YOU READ

Encourage students to be attentive to the characteristics of sales situations they experience.

1. **Approaching the customer** greeting the customer face-to-face
2. **Determining needs** learning what the customer is looking for in order to decide what products to show and which product features to present first in the next step of the sale
3. **Presenting the product** educating the customer about the product's features and benefits
4. **Overcoming objections** learning why the customer is reluctant to buy, providing information to remove that uncertainty, and helping the customer to make a satisfying buying decision
5. **Closing the sale** getting the customer's positive agreement to buy
6. **Suggestion selling** suggesting additional merchandise or services that will save your customer money or help your customer enjoy the original purchase
7. **Relationship building** creating a means of maintaining contact with the customer after the sale is completed

In this chapter, we will concentrate on the first two steps in the sales process: (1) the approach and (2) determining the customer's needs. The other five steps will be examined in later chapters.

Approaching the Customer

Salespeople can make or break a sale during their first few minutes with a customer; therefore, the initial approach is critical. Customers who are turned off by the approach will be difficult to win over later on.

The approach sets the mood or atmosphere for the other steps of the sale. It has three purposes: to begin conversation, to establish a relationship with the customer, and to focus on the product.

To begin conversation, you need to be alert to customers' interests. This may be easier in business-to-business selling because you can conduct research prior to the initial meeting. In retail selling, you must observe the customer from the moment he or she enters the store.

To establish a relationship, treat the customer as an individual. You should not stereotype a person because of age, sex, race, religion, appearance, or any other characteristic.

You must be perceptive about the customer's buying style. Some customers like to do business quickly. Others prefer a more methodical, slower pace. In any case, a customer likes to feel important.

To put a customer at ease and establish a positive atmosphere you should be enthusiastic, courteous, and respectful. Show sincere interest by maintaining good eye contact and showing genuine friendliness. Always ask business-to-business customers if it is a good time to see them. This courtesy is appreciated by busy businesspeople.

The Approach in Business-to-Business Selling

In business-to-business selling, the salesperson sets up an appointment in the pre-approach stage of the sale. Arriving early for the appointment will show your customer that you are interested and give you time to organize your thoughts. Introduce yourself and your company with a firm handshake and a smile. Use the customer's name. Some salespeople may give a business card to the customer.

The initial approach depends on your prior dealings with the customer or the work you did in the pre-approach. When meeting with customers you visit frequently, you can be more personal. Comments on recent happenings in the customer's industry or personal recollections about the customer's family, interests, or hobbies can create a smooth initial meeting. Learning what is appropriate to say regarding personal matters is critical. When personal conversation is not appropriate, you can still engage in small talk to establish a relationship with the customer.

Prior research on the prospect conducted in the pre-approach may suggest other possible opening comments. You can also discuss current topics in the industry.

Chapter 13 - Initiating the Sale 279

Critical Thinking

Ask students to describe why it might not be a good idea for a salesperson to be too familiar or joke around when first approaching a customer. Answers may include that the salesperson is not familiar with the customer's mood or sense of humor.

TEACH

Discussion Starter

THE SELLING PROCESS

Ask students: If every sales situation is different, how can there be the same steps each time? Let them know that the steps provide an effective starting point and sales strategy.

TEACHING POINTS

Extend Compare the seven steps of selling to the structure of a jazz song or plans to plant a garden. Remind students that there is room to improvise in all situations.

Clarify Let students know that time spent on each step can vary, and that it may loop back to various sections more than once if the customer buys more than one item.

Concept Development

APPROACHING THE CUSTOMER

Have students consider the three purposes of the sales approach: to begin conversation, to establish a relationship with the customer, and to focus on the product. Ask students which purpose is the most important and why.
Answers will vary. Some students may argue that there can be no sale without a conversation. Others may suggest that the sale is what matters most. Long-sighted students may believe that long-term relationships are the true goal.

TEACHING POINTS

Explain Tell students that not every customer is expected to make a purchase. Some may simply be browsing. However, sales associates and stores may still generate future sales by making a good impression.

Enrichment

THE APPROACH IN RETAIL SELLING

Let students know that there are professional journals meant to help salespeople excel. Ask students to look up issues of *Personal Selling Power, Sales & Marketing Management,* and other publications for articles about the approach in retail selling. Have them present their findings to the class.

TEACHING POINTS

Extend Ask students: Can salespeople who are in totally different industries use the same journals about selling?

Answers will vary, but most will say that the selling process is similar, even if the products—such as homemade candy and industrial chemicals—are not.

PHOTO GUIDE

THE MERCHANDISE APPROACH

Discussion Discuss with students how to tell if a customer is interested in an item. Indicators may include him or her studying it, picking it up, returning to it several times, or asking about it.

Caption Answer The salesperson might point out features such as insoles or wheels or ask if the customer has ever used rollerblades.

Follow Up Pick an item in the classroom and ask students to sell it with a merchandise approach. For example, they might point out the throwback borders on the globe or the decorations on someone's backpack. Have students enact their approaches in class.

Case Study

Beware of Bias

Wanting to take a pro-active approach with his team, Harry Bradford, a regional sales VP with GlaxoSmithKline turned to Orlando-Ward Associates, a San Diego-based workplace training organization that specializes in live-action drama to address diversity and other interpersonal workplace issues.

Here is an example of a vignette used in such training: You are making your first sales call to Dr. Lee's office in the Chinatown section of San Francisco. Approaching a young Asian woman behind the desk, you say who you are and ask to speak with Dr. Lee for a moment. After a brief pause the woman looks up from her paperwork and deadpans: "You're speaking with Dr. Lee right now." Whoops! After you apologize profusely, Dr. Lee responds that she would be happy to meet with you—about a year from now.

Role Play as Training

After each vignette was presented during the half-day program, the producing director led a discussion with the reps to identify the mistakes made and to brainstorm about more thoughtful approaches. Next, reps were invited to participate in replays, in which the scene is re-enacted but this time with a program participant playing the role of the sales rep. The rep's task is to handle the situation more effectively, without making errors based on cultural or gender stereotypes.

THINK STRATEGICALLY
Why are live-action drama and role playing good sales training methods?

@ Online Action! Go to *marketingessentials.glencoe.com/13/case* to find a research project on avoiding stereotyping.

The Approach in Retail Selling

When customers are in an obvious hurry, you should approach them quickly. When customers seem undecided, encourage them to look around and ask questions.

The Three Methods of Approach in Retail Selling

There are three methods you can use in the initial approach to retail customers: the service approach, the greeting approach, and the merchandise approach. You must evaluate the selling situation and the type of customer to determine which method is best.

Service Approach

With the **service approach**, the salesperson asks the customer if he or she needs assistance. One way to use this method is to ask, "How may I help you?" An open-ended question such as this one offers the customer a greater opportunity to respond with more

 marketingessentials.glencoe.com

Case Study   Beware of Bias

Discussion Have students read the Case Study and then discuss the importance of sales training. Let them know that such training can be costly, but that it can save money by eliminating problems in the long run.

THINK STRATEGICALLY **Answer:** Live-action drama and role playing are effective sales training methods because they force participants to think on their feet. Also, many people learn more through participatory action and experience than they do from books, lectures, and other forms of education.

@ Online Action! For instructions, ideas, and answer guide, go to the Teacher Center at **marketingessentials.glencoe.com**

than "yes" or "no." It is acceptable when the customer is obviously in a hurry or if you are an order-taker for routine purchases. In most other sales situations, this type of question is ineffective because it usually elicits a negative response, such as "No, I'm just looking." In this case, you lose control of the sales situation. If such a situation occurs, take a moment to remind the customer to ask any questions that he or she may have later on.

Greeting Approach

With the **greeting approach**, the salesperson simply welcomes the customer to the store. This lets the customer know that the salesperson is available for any questions or assistance. The greeting can be a simple one, such as "Good morning."

When you greet the customer, it is important to use a rising tone in your voice. A falling tone sounds unfriendly and would start the sales process off on the wrong note. It is extremely important that the salesperson smile and be friendly.

• **THE MERCHANDISE APPROACH** The merchandise approach can be used only when a customer demonstrates interest in a product.

What might you say to this customer to demonstrate the merchandise approach?

NET MARKETING

Business E-Mail

Once considered merely a nuisance, spam and other unwanted e-mail have become a costly burden for enterprises. E-mail can spread destructive computer viruses to millions of users in a matter of hours.

An Expensive Problem

Ferris Research estimates that in 2003, the total cost of spam to U.S. businesses in lost productivity was $10 billion. The MX Logic Threat Center reported that 74.4 percent of all e-mail traffic filtered by the company was spam. By 2006, industry analysts expect the economic impact of computer viruses to approach $60 billion worldwide.

THINK LIKE A MARKETER

Assume you work for a company that sells software and services to block spam and provide antivirus protection. Write an attention-getting statement that you could use in conjunction with your greeting and initial approach in a business-to-business selling situation.

@ **Online Action!**

Go to *marketingessentials.glencoe.com/ 13/net* to find a project on e-mail security.

marketingessentials.glencoe.com

Chapter 13 - Initiating the Sale **281**

NET MARKETING

Business E-Mail

Discussion After students have read Net Marketing, lead a discussion about the effects of spam. Discuss not only the memory taken up and viruses that are transmitted through spam but also the work time spent sorting through an e-mail inbox.

THINK LIKE A MARKETER **Answer:** Statements will vary; responses should demonstrate an understanding of spam and antivirus software and employ a business-to-business selling approach.

@ **Online Action!** For instructions, ideas, and answer guide, go to the Teacher Center at **marketingessentials.glencoe.com**

ASSESS

Review Guide

CONCEPTS

Ask students to recall the salesperson's role in the selling process.

To gather information about the customer, advise the customer about which products best suit his or her needs, and lead to a decision to buy.

KEY TERMS

Have students review key terms and role play examples of each approach.

ONLINE SELF-ASSESSMENT

Have students go to **marketingessentials.glencoe.com** for the Section 13.1 practice test.

Individualized Review

L1 Assign and review Chapter 13 activities in the Student Activity Workbook.

L2 Assign and review Chapter 13 activities in the Marketing Math Workbook.

L3 Assign and review Chapter 13 activities in the *BusinessWeek* Reader and Case Studies.

Marketing Practice

Have pairs of students take turns being a salesperson for a stationery store. Have one approach the other in a business-to-business situation. Then have them switch roles and approach each other in a retail situation.

Role plays will vary; the business-to-business approach might focus on how the goods can save the customer's business money, and the retail approach should be service-, greeting-, or merchandise-centered.

CLOSE

Ask students to answer the following questions:

- **What are the first two steps of the sales process?**
  The approach and determining the customer's needs.

- **What are the three methods of approaching retail customers?**
  The service, greeting, and merchandise approaches.

- **What are some characteristics of the sales approach in business-to-business situations?**
  Answers may include having an appointment, meeting at the customer's place of work, and knowing that the sale is being made for business purposes.

Critical Thinking

Ask students: What does the merchandise approach require of a salesperson? Answers may include that he or she must be familiar with both the merchandise and the layout of the store.

If the customers need help, they will tell you how you can assist them. If they are just looking, they will let you know. The greeting approach establishes a positive atmosphere and opens the lines of communication.

Merchandise Approach Method

With the **merchandise approach**, the salesperson makes a comment or asks questions about a product in which the customer shows interest. This method can be used only if a customer stops to look at a specific item. You may open with a statement about the product's features and benefits.

Using Conversation Skills

In the merchandise approach, the salesperson walks up to the customer and starts talking about the merchandise without asking whether the customer wants assistance. The opening comment used in the merchandise approach should be appropriate to the situation. Ideally, it should give the customer some information that is not immediately apparent to the eye.

Notice what interests the customer and make that the focus of your conversation. If a customer is looking at a label, you might say, "That shirt is made of a cotton and polyester blend, so it's machine washable." If a customer is simply looking at an item and you have no indication of the exact interest, you can talk about the item's popularity, its unusual features, or its special values. You can also ask a question about the item, such as "Is that the size you need?" or "Were you looking for a comfortable children's jacket?"

The merchandise approach is usually the most effective initial approach in retail sales because it immediately focuses attention on the product. It also gives you an opportunity to tell the customer something about the features and benefits of the merchandise.

Customers may not see the desired style, size, or color on the selling floor. The merchandise approach can easily clear up any confusion, let the customer know what is available, and open a dialogue with the customer.

13.1 AFTER YOU READ

Reviewing Key Terms and Concepts

1. Do you think all seven steps of a sale are followed in every sale? Why or why not?
2. Why is the initial approach in business-to-business selling different from a retail approach?
3. What are the advantages of the merchandise approach?

Integrating Academic Skills

Math

4. Assuming there is no sales tax on clothing, how much would you charge a customer who needs only two pairs of socks when the sign indicates six pairs are $15.99?

Language Arts

5. Write two merchandise approaches for the product you researched in Chapter 12. Save this work as part of your sales project for this unit.

 Online Action! Check your answers at *marketingessentials.glencoe.com/13/read*

marketingessentials.glencoe.com

 AFTER YOU READ

Reviewing Key Terms and Concepts

1. All seven steps do not have to be followed in every sale. Some customers are pre-sold and know exactly what they want. Also, the salesperson may do such a good job matching products with a customer's needs that there are no objections.

2. In retail selling, the customers arrive in the store location. In business-to-business selling, salespeople go to the customer's place of business to make a presentation. Also, a business-to-business meeting is usually made by appointment.

3. The merchandise approach immediately focuses attention on the product and gives the salesperson an opportunity to tell the customer about its features and benefits.

Integrating Academic Skills

4. $5.33; $15.99 \div 6 = $2.665 \times 2 = $5.33

5. Answers will vary; merchandise approaches should point out the features of the product being sold.

Online Action! Answers at *marketingessentials.glencoe.com/13/read*

Determining Needs in Sales

FOCUS

OBJECTIVES

- Explain why determining needs is an essential step in the sales process
- List three methods for determining needs

READ and STUDY

BEFORE YOU READ

Predict Name three ways you might determine a customer's needs.

THE MAIN IDEA

Determining needs is an early step in the sales process because it frames the rest of the sales presentation. It is also the one step that continues throughout the sales process as you try to match a customer's needs with solutions found in your product line.

STUDY ORGANIZER

Prepare a chart like the one below to review when and how to determine needs in the sales process.

```
           ┌─────────────────────┐
           │  Determining Needs  │
           └─────────────────────┘
       ┌──────────┐         ┌──────────┐
       │   When   │         │   How    │
       └──────────┘         └──────────┘
   _____   _____
   _____   _____
```

KEY TERMS

- nonverbal communication
- open-ended questions

Determining Needs

In this step of the sale, your job is to uncover the customer's problems or reasons for wanting to buy. In some instances, their motives or needs may be quite obvious, but that is not always the case. It is your job to determine those needs so you can offer one or more solutions. Discovering your customer's motivation for buying will help you in the next step of the sale when you are helping the customer select the right product.

WHILE YOU READ

Connect Has a salesperson ever helped you make a choice? What was the sales approach?

Chapter 13 - Initiating the Sale **283**

Introducing the Section

COLLABORATIVE ACTIVITY

To prepare for reading this section, have students work in groups to describe different types of customers. They may include the person who is in a hurry, someone who has to buy a gift but has no idea what to buy, or someone who has time to waste. Ask: How can they identify the types of customers?

Answers may include observing nonverbal communication, listening to their conversations or comments, and asking questions.

Ask students to role-play customers and salespeople in different situations.

Preteaching Key Terms

Read the key terms aloud or ask a volunteer to read them and predict their meanings.

- nonverbal communication
- open-ended questions

Have students give examples of each phrase.
Standing with arms crossed while tapping one's toes is an example of nonverbal communication. An open-ended question example might be, "What do you think about velour tops?"

Online Activity

Determining Needs Online

Have students research what methods online stores use to ascertain the needs of its customers. Students might suggest that asking for key words and offering options is similar to questioning.

READ and STUDY

BEFORE YOU READ

Lead students in listing ways to determine a customer's needs: observing, listening, questioning.

THE MAIN IDEA

Ask a volunteer to read the main idea aloud and ask another student to rephrase it in his or her own words.

STUDY ORGANIZER

Model the study organizer for students. Have them fill out the chart as they read the section. A full-size, downloadable study organizer can be found at marketingessentials.glencoe.com

WHILE YOU READ Answers will vary; but students' experiences should reflect observing, listening, or questioning.

TEACH

Discussion Starter

IMPORTANCE OF DETERMINING NEEDS

Ask students to consider the following scenario: A couple enters a gift store just before closing time and begins to leisurely look through books and T-shirts. If they buy something, the salesperson doesn't mind staying open late. If they are merely browsing, she would like to close the store. Ask students how the salesperson should approach and handle this situation.

Tell students that they can observe the customers' actions, listen to their comments, or ask them if they might like to buy something.

Concept Development

HOW TO DETERMINE NEEDS

Review with students the five listening skills to use when talking to customers: maintaining good eye contact, providing verbal and nonverbal feedback, giving undivided attention, listening with empathy and an open mind, and not interrupting. Ask students to visit local stores and write two- to three-paragraph reports on how well the clerks demonstrated good listening skills.

TEACHING POINTS

Role Play Have conversations with students as if you were a shopper and they were salespeople. As you explain your needs, have them practice the five listening skills.

Critical Thinking

Ask students if new employees should allow more experienced ones to ask questions. Why or why not?

🌐 GLOBAL MARKET

Skateboarding in Brazil

BRAZIL

Skateboarding might seem like an all-American sport, but it is also very popular and competitive around the world. Brazil has a thriving skateboarding market. Brazilian skaters started out by making their own skateboards with roller skate trucks and wheels, inspired by American products they often could not afford. However, what started as tinkering has now become a national industry.

Homegrown Success Brazil's government is protective of small firms and trademarks and offers incentives to promote internal commerce. Skateboard products are sold mostly through specialty stores. With imports heavily taxed, domestic brands sell far better than U.S. competitors. Government policies and taxation were determining factors in the creation of domestic skateboard brands and in the growth of the Brazilian skateboard market. Skateboarding shoes, accessories, and clothing are now also manufactured in Brazil for Brazilian brands. The largest board brands are Son, Formigao, Perfect Line, and Stage. Truck brands are Crail, Tracker, and Crazy. The largest wheel manufacturer is Moska. Some of these companies have now expanded into exporting their goods throughout South America and to the United States.

CRITICAL THINKING

How does knowledge regarding a customer's motivation and value system help in determining their needs?

@ Online Action!

Go to *marketingessentials.glencoe.com/13/global* to find a research project on customer motivation.

When to Determine Needs

The salesperson's focus should be to determine the customer's needs as early in the sales process as possible. Here is an example of what can happen when a salesperson does not determine needs early on.

Salesperson: "This is one of our most popular tennis rackets. It's perfect for you—the grip is the correct size and the large sweet spot can improve your game."

Customer: "That's very interesting; but, I'm not buying the racket for myself. It's actually a gift for my nine-year-old daughter."

After the initial approach, the salesperson could have asked, "Are you interested in a racket for yourself?"

The answer to that simple question could have guided the salesperson into additional questions about the person for whom the

racket was being purchased. It also could have helped the salesperson decide which racket to show the customer and which features to emphasize.

In retail selling, the salesperson should begin to determine needs immediately after the approach. In business-to-business selling, needs can be determined in the pre-approach. In both situations, the salesperson should continue determining needs throughout the sales process.

How to Determine Needs

There are three methods used to determine customer needs: observing, listening, and questioning. (See Figure 13.1.)

Observing

When you observe a customer, you look for buying motives that are communicated nonverbally. **Nonverbal communication** is

 marketingessentials.glencoe.com

🌐 GLOBAL MARKET

Skateboarding in Brazil

Discussion Let students know that the success of Bob Burnquist, Lincoln Ueda, and other Brazilian pro skateboarders in America help fuel the sport's popularity in their home country. Lead a discussion on how this can impact marketing.

CRITICAL THINKING **Answer:** Such knowledge can help a salesperson in determining customer needs because the salesperson can then form a basis upon which to ask appropriate questions.

@ Online Action! For instructions, ideas, and answer guide, go to the Teacher Center at **marketingessentials.glencoe.com**

expressing yourself without the use of words. Facial expressions, hand motions, eye movement, and other forms of nonverbal communication can give you clues about a customer's mood and interest in a product.

Observing how long a customer in a retail store looks at a product can give you an initial idea about the level of interest.

In a business-to-business selling situation, you can generally get ideas about a buyer's interests by looking around his or her office.

Listening

Listening helps you pick up clues to the customer's needs. You can use this information for the product presentation. Here's an example.

Customer: "I want a copier for my home business that is simple to use and reliable. My last copier broke down often, which was a problem. I usually make one or two copies at a time. However, occasionally I may make up to 50 copies at once."

From these statements, you have learned that the customer is not looking for a top-of-the-line copier. Since the copier is for a home business, size is a factor.

Questioning and Engaging the Customer

When you begin determining needs, first ask general questions about the intended use of the product and any previous experience with it. Build your questions around words like *who, what, when, where, why,* and *how.* You might ask the following questions of someone who wants to purchase a copier:

- Who will be using the copier?
- What type of copier is the person presently using?

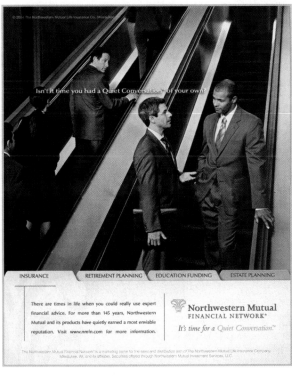

Isn't it time you had a Quiet Conversation™ of your own?

INSURANCE · RETIREMENT PLANNING · EDUCATION FUNDING · ESTATE PLANNING

There are times in life when you could really use expert financial advice. For more than 145 years, Northwestern Mutual and its products have quietly earned a most enviable reputation. Visit www.nmfn.com for more information.

Northwestern Mutual
FINANCIAL NETWORK®
It's time for a Quiet Conversation.™

• **DETERMINING CUSTOMER NEEDS** The sales step of determining customer needs helps a salesperson match those needs with products or services.

What does this ad say about the company's policy of listening to customers' needs?

TEACH CONTINUED

Individualized Math Skills

Give students the following scenario: they are salespeople at a tennis store during a one-day sale offering special discounts and no sales tax. During the sale, 30 percent will be taken off the price of all rackets except for children's rackets, which are half off.

L1 Ask students: If a customer has a coupon for an extra 10 percent off all adult purchases, how much will he or she save on a purchase of $255?
$102; $255 × .60 = $153; $255 − $153 = $102

L2 Have students calculate the cost of one adult racquet priced at $180 and one child's racquet priced at $75.
$163.50; ($180 × .70) + ($75 × .50) = $126 + $37.50 = $163.50

L3 Tell students that a customer returns a child's racquet bought on sale for $37.50 for a higher performance one priced at $120, even though there will be no discount on it. How much will he owe the store if sales tax is 6.25 percent?
$87.66; $120 − $37.50 = $82.50; $82.50 × 1.0625 = $87.66

Concept Development

QUESTIONING

To practice questioning, have students write 10 questions that might be used to find out what type of athletic shoe a customer wants to buy. Suggest they begin by discussing experience with shoe models, intended use, and the functions the customer is looking for.

TEACHING POINTS

Role Play Role play as if you were shopping for a product either for home or for school, such as paper or vegetables. Have students use their questions to determine your needs and suggest models.

ASSESS

Review Guide

CONCEPTS

Ask students to describe open-ended questions and how they are used in sales. Open-ended questions require more than a yes or no answer and provide information about a customer's needs.

KEY TERMS

Have students review key terms and rephrase their definitions in their own words.

ONLINE SELF-ASSESSMENT

Have students go to marketingessentials.glencoe.com for the Section 13.2 practice test.

Individualized Review

L1 Assign and review Chapter 13 activities in the Student Activity Workbook.

L2 Assign and review Chapter 13 activities in the Marketing Math Workbook.

L3 Assign and review Chapter 13 activities in the *BusinessWeek* Reader and Case Studies.

Marketing Practice

Tell students they are working as salespeople at a nursery that specializes in orchids, a type of flower that is very difficult to grow. It is often unclear whether a customer has experience raising such delicate plants. Ask students to create tactful questions that can be asked to find out whether a customer knows what he or she is buying. Break students into groups of three or more and have them write scripts for a role play between a salesperson and a customer. Ask teams to act out the role plays in class.

286

Figure 13.1 — **Ways to Determine Customer Needs**

• **Observe, Listen, Question** Selling is based on matching a customer's needs or wants with the features and benefits of a product. In the step of the sales process known as determining needs, the salesperson gathers information in order to match the customer's needs and wants with a product. There are three ways to do that.

Is there one best way to determine customer needs?

Observing Customers provide many nonverbal cues about their product interests. By carefully observing a customer, a salesperson can learn a lot about the customer's interests. The salesperson can then use that information to guide the customer to products that might result in a decision to buy.

Listening When a customer is ready to talk, the salesperson should give the customer his or her undivided attention and maintain eye contact. Other guidelines that help to make the salesperson a good listener are not interrupting until the customer has finished, providing feedback, and listening with an open mind.

Questioning Questions can encourage a customer to talk. When asking questions, salespeople should begin with general questions, such as those beginning with *who, what, when, where, why,* and *how.* For instance, this salesperson might ask what color of shoe the woman is shopping for. Salespeople must be careful not to ask a question that is too personal or unintentionally offends the customer. That might quickly put an end to the sale.

@ **Online Action!** Go to *marketingessentials.glencoe.com/13/ figure/1* to find a project on determining customer needs.

marketingessentials.glencoe.com

Figure 13.1 — **Ways to Determine Customer Needs**

Discussion After students read **Figure 13.1**, discuss the ways to determine a customer's needs, such as observing, listening, or questioning. Let them know that they are not mutually exclusive; a combination of ways can be used.

Caption Answer Answers will vary; most students should agree that a combination of the three methods (observing, listening, and questioning) would usually work best.

@ **Online Action!** For instructions, ideas, and answer guide, go to the Teacher Center at **marketingessentials.glencoe.com**

- How much experience has the person had with copiers?
- How many copies will the person be making every week or month?

How to Refine Your Questioning

Once you have an idea of the customer's general needs, then you can ask more specific questions relating to the product. In the case of the copier, questions could be asked about the need to enlarge or reduce the size of the copy, as well as the need to collate and staple copies.

Open-ended questions are those that require more than a yes or no answer, such as "What do you dislike about the copier you're presently using?" The answer to such a question will provide valuable information about a customer's needs. Always bear in mind that some customers will be protective of their privacy; they may resent even general, non-personal questions.

Here are some other dos and don'ts guidelines for questioning:

1. Do ask open-ended questions that encourage customers to do the talking.
2. Do ask clarifying questions to make sure you understand customers' needs. To do this, use opening lines such as "Let me see if I understand you" or "Am I correct in assuming you're looking for a product that can . . .?"
3. Don't ask too many questions in a row. This will make customers feel as if they are being cross-examined.
4. Don't ask questions that might embarrass customers or put them on the defensive. Never ask, "How much do you want to spend?" Instead, ask about the intended use of the product and any past experience. That should give you enough information to determine the correct price range on your own.

CLOSE

Ask students to provide answers to the following questions:

- **What are some examples of nonverbal communication?**
  Answers will vary and may include tone, facial expressions, and eye movement.

- **When determining a customer's needs, around what three words should you base your questions?**
  The three words are what, when, and where.

Extended Activity

Determining Needs and the Sales Process
Tell students that a salesperson should begin determining a customer's needs as soon as possible. Ask students to think about how this helps the sales process. Have students write a one-paragraph response.

13.2 AFTER YOU READ

Reviewing Key Terms and Concepts

1. Why is determining needs an essential step in the sales process?
2. How can you use open-ended questions to encourage customers to do the talking?
3. You are a salesperson in a rug store that carries inexpensive area rugs, medium-priced area rugs, and very expensive handmade area rugs. How would you determine your customer's price range?

Integrating Academic Skills
Math

4. Based on your analysis of the customer's needs, a premium of $1,500 per year is required for long-term health care insurance for your client. Since your client cannot handle this yearly payment, you want to offer a quarterly payment schedule. There is a surcharge of $25 per quarter for this service. What are the quarterly payments for this client?

Language Arts

5. Use the product you researched in Chapter 12 to write five to ten questions that could be used to determine a customer's needs in the sale of that product. Save this work as part of your sales unit project.

 Online Action!

Check your answers at *marketingessentials.glencoe.com/13/read*

marketingessentials.glencoe.com

AFTER YOU READ

Reviewing Key Terms and Concepts

1. Determining needs is used to build the entire sales presentation and is the basis for consultative selling.
2. Asking open-ended questions allows the customer to talk about his or her needs.

3. Do not directly ask about his or her price range. Instead, ask about the rug's intended use to gain clues of how much he or she expects to pay.

Integrating Academic Skills

4. $400; $1,500 ÷ 4 = $375; $375 + $25 = $400
5. Answers will vary depending on the product used and should be in appropriate question format.

Online Action! Answers at **marketingessentials.glencoe.com/13/read**

CAREERS IN MARKETING

Lifelong Learning

CAREER INFORMATION

Have students go to marketingessentials.glencoe.com and find the Chapter 13 Careers page and click on the link for the American Marketing Association's Careers Strategies and Tips. Ask students to select one article, read it, and summarize it in three short paragraphs.

INITIATING THE SALE

Entrepreneurs have to sell. Their livelihood is based on their ability to determine the needs of clients and offer their skills and services as a solution. Customer research and feedback, as well as market trends, may help entrepreneurs in determining needs. The ability to determine needs quickly and accurately is a necessary skill for any entrepreneur.

Primary Source

Ask students to go to marketingessentials.glencoe.com and find Chapter 13 Resources. Ask them to click on the link for the American Marketing Association's marketing dictionary and read the definitions of the terms they find that are related to initiating the sale.

THINKING CRITICALLY

Training and classes other than college include trade schools, workshops, and internships.

@ Online Action!

For instructions, ideas, and answer guide, go to the Teacher Center at marketingessentials.glencoe.com

---

CAREERS IN MARKETING

MELISSA MCINTOSH, MJE
FOUNDER
1214 ENTERPRISES, INC.

? What do you do at work?
For my corporate clients in law, real estate, medicine, engineering, architecture, and construction, I can provide a full spectrum of design and print-brokering services so that they have one contact for all their marketing collateral needs. A big part of my job is focused on service: handholding a brochure all the way through the print process with an outside commercial printer, making 900 tweaks to a corporate logo to get it "just right," and making sure I pay attention to the small details.

? What skills are most important to you?
The ability to be flexible. Being able to keep from getting frustrated and to move between being a marketing consultant, tech support guru, and graphic artist. Having a background where I've worked with computers since the mid-80s and have learned a lot in the trial and error department has really helped.

? What is your key to success?
Very simple: hard, hard work. In any of the jobs I've had, either in education or business, and in owning my own company now, I have never bragged that I'm the smartest, most creative, most cutting edge, or whatever. But how I have always had an edge over the competition is that I'm willing to out-work them. If the "what does it take" requires evenings and weekends to get the job done just a bit better than the other guy, fine.

Aptitudes, Abilities, and Skills

Computer skills, sales and communication skills, versatility, an eagerness to learn and gain new experiences

Education and Training

Degrees in marketing, communication, language, and computer science are helpful.

Career Path

Before starting their own companies, many entrepreneurs work for companies that do the work they want to do. That is their training. To eventually run a marketing consulting firm, the best career track is to work in marketing, sales, and communications departments.

THINKING CRITICALLY

Other than college, what kind of training and classes might be worth pursuing?

@ Online Action!

Go to *marketingessentials.glencoe.com/ 13/careers* to find a career-related activity.

 marketingessentials.glencoe.com

Test-Taking Strategies

Break the class into four teams. List key terms on the board and have volunteers define and discuss them. Give a point to each team that gives the correct answer. This quiz format allows students an interactive forum for review.

FOCUS on KEY POINTS

SECTION 13.1

● Seven steps in the sales process are approach, determining needs, product presentation, overcoming objections, closing the sale, suggestion selling, and relationship building.

● Relationship building is important to create loyal customers.

● The approach step of the sale can make or break the sale.

● The three purposes of the approach are to begin a conversation, build a relationship, and focus on the product.

● The approach in business-to-business selling is different from that in retail selling.

● The three retail sales approaches are service, greeting, and merchandise.

SECTION 13.2

● Determining needs is a step in the sales process that should begin as soon as possible and continue throughout the process.

● Three methods that help in determining needs are observing, listening, and asking questions.

REVIEW VOCABULARY

Work in groups to develop a story about two salespeople using the following terms:

1. service approach (p. 280)
2. greeting approach (p. 281)
3. merchandise approach (p. 282)
4. nonverbal communication (p. 284)
5. open-ended questions (p. 287)

REVIEW FACTS and IDEAS

6. What are the seven steps of a sale? (13.1)
7. What are the main purposes of the approach step in the sales process? (13.1)
8. Write the dialogue and describe the actions that might be taken during an initial business-to-business sales approach by a sales representative from the XYZ Copier Company meeting a new prospect for the first time. (13.1)
9. Why is determining needs an essential step in the sales process? (13.2)
10. List three methods used for determining needs. (13.2)
11. What types of questions should be asked first when determining customer needs? (13.2)
12. What is the next step after a sales approach? (13.2)

CHAPTER **13** REVIEW

REVIEW FACTS and IDEAS

6. The seven steps are approach, needs determined, product presentation, overcoming objections, closing the sale, suggestion selling, and relationship building.

7. The main purposes of the approach are to begin a conversation, establish a relationship with the customer, and focus on the product.

8. Answers will vary but may include an introduction, a firm handshake, and a smile. The greeting may resemble, "Hi, I am _____ from the XYZ Copier Company. I am here to show you a way to reduce your expenses and improve your employees' productivity."

9. It is used for consultative selling that matches customers' needs with product features that solve their problems.

10. Three methods for determining customer needs are observing, listening, and questioning.

11. The types of questions that should be asked first are questions about intended use and experience.

12. The needs should be determined immediately after the approach.

FOCUS on KEY POINTS

Ask volunteers to read the summaries aloud and rephrase them in their own words. Have interested students enact the three retail sales approaches.

REVIEW VOCABULARY

Stories will vary; all stories should use all of the key terms. See glossary for definitions of **1-5.**

BUILD SKILLS

13. Workplace Skills

When role-playing salespersons, students should introduce themselves as sales representatives from the XYZ Corporation while using the appropriate greeting for each country: Japan: handshake and slight bow; Germany: firm, short handshake; Brazil: light handshake that lasts a long time; Singapore: slide palms together and bow.

14. Technology Applications

Reports will vary but might indicate whether the car dealer's vehicles use metric or English tools as well as tools that might be used for typical problems.

15. Math Practice

5 miles ÷ 10 miles/hour = ½ hour = 30 minutes; 8:00 A.M. + 30 minutes = 8:30 A.M. Students might suggest calling the customer to let him or her know that you are going to be late and allowing for a longer commute time to prevent the situation from happening again.

DEVELOP CRITICAL THINKING

16. Why Does the Approach Used in Business-to-Business Selling Differ From the Retail Approach?

A retail sales approach involves carefully determining the customer's needs and matching them. During an appointment with a gardening supply store, the business relationship is already present, an appointment has probably been made, and business can be attended to with less greeting and more listening and questioning.

17. Good Observations Lead to Sales

Answers will vary; possible responses may include observing his style as reflected in his haircut and clothing.

BUILD SKILLS

13. Workplace Skills

Human Relations Use the Internet to research different ways of greeting people. Conduct a role play with classmates to demonstrate the proper way to greet customers who are from Japan, Germany, Brazil, and Singapore in a business-to-business setting. Assume you are employed by the XYZ Corporation.

14. Technology Applications

Research During Pre-approach Imagine that you are a sales representative for a tool distributor such as Grainger and you have a meeting with a car dealer who repairs cars on the lot. Using the Internet, research the car dealerships and repair shops to determine the needs that might be met by items in your product line. Prepare a short, one-page report on your findings.

15. Math Practice

Budgeting Your Time You are stuck in traffic, and you are going to be late for your first meeting with a potential customer. You are traveling at ten miles an hour and have five miles to go. If it is 8:00 A.M., at what time can you expect to arrive if you keep traveling at that speed? What should you do? How could you prevent this situation from happening again?

DEVELOP CRITICAL THINKING

16. Why Does the Approach Used in Business-to-Business Selling Differ From the Retail Approach?

Imagine that you are a salesperson selling seeds to garden supply stores. Think of how you would approach the sale using a *retail sales approach*. Do you think that would be an effective approach? Why or why not?

17. Good Observations Lead to Sales

Salespeople must be good communicators in order to initiate conversations with potential customers and gather information about customers' wants and needs. But customers are not always willing to talk. Assume you are a men's clothing salesperson in a large department store and you have a customer who seems reluctant to talk. How might you determine his interests? What skills, besides communication, would you need to do this?

Formative Assessment

Formative assessment is an essential component of classroom work. This type of assessment provides information that is then used as feedback to modify teaching and meet student needs.

L1 Have students list the three methods of determining customer needs.

L2 Have students describe the methods of determining needs in the form of a story.

L3 Have students write plays in which they act out the methods of determining customer needs in both business-to-business and retail settings.

Reteach If the results of this formative assessment seem low, consider the following activity:

Read each of the key terms aloud. Have students define the key terms and use them in a sentence. Clear up any confusion students may have.

APPLY CONCEPTS

18. Approaching and Determining Needs

Role play the approach and determining needs steps of a sale with a classmate by using a personal product, such as a jacket, calculator, or purse. Assume you work for a retailer.

Activity Make a list of guidelines for listening, observing, and asking questions. At the conclusion of the role play, provide the salesperson with constructive criticism. Change the product and switch roles with your partner to repeat the assignment.

19. Research Selling Etiquette in Foreign Countries

Accepted business etiquette differs from country to country, including manner of greeting, preferred time of day to conduct business, and follow-up. Select one foreign country and conduct research on the Internet and with other sources regarding business etiquette and cultural difference when selling in foreign countries.

Activity What are some of the dos and don'ts? Using a word processing program, write a two-page report of your findings. Cite your sources.

NET SAVVY

20. Selling on the Internet

Select a company that sells its products on the Internet, such as Dell or Gateway computers. Assume the role of a customer and research the questions you should ask in order to decide on the best buy for your needs.

marketingessentials.glencoe.com

Role Play: Initiating the Sale

Situation You are to assume the role of an experienced employee for a toy store. The holiday season is a few months away, and many new employees have been hired who have had little or no sales training. The store manager (judge) knows that you are studying marketing and has asked you to offer some ideas for basic sales training on the steps of a sale.

Activity You are to present your ideas about training in the steps of a sale to the store manager (judge).

Evaluation You will be evaluated on how well you meet the following performance indicators:

● Explain the selling process
● Prepare for the sales presentation
● Determine customer/client needs
● Demonstrate suggestion selling
● Close the sale

 Online Action!

For more information and DECA Prep practice, go to *marketingessentials.glencoe.com/13/DECA*

Chapter 13 - Initiating the Sale **291**

APPLY CONCEPTS

18. Approaching and Determining Needs

Role plays and lists will vary; all students should demonstrate communication skills such as observing, listening, and questioning.

19. Research Selling Etiquette in Foreign Countries

Reports will differ according to country; all reports should include manner of greeting, preferred time of day to conduct business, and follow-up.

NET SAVVY

20. Selling on the Internet

Customers' questions will depend on the online company selected; all questions should reflect intended use and experience.

MINI-QUIZ

Read these sentences to the students and have them volunteer the missing word(s):

1. Always ask _____ customers if it is a good time to see them. (business-to-business)

2. With _____ approach, the salesperson asks the customer if he or she needs assistance. (service)

3. _____ approach is usually the most effective initial approach in retail sales. (merchandise)

For an expanded chapter quiz, go to Chapter 13 in the TeacherWorks CD-ROM and to Chapter 13 in the **Exam***View*® Pro Test Generator CD-ROM.

Students should be evaluated according to the performance standards noted in the role play. For another DECA role play, go to the Competitive Events Workbook or the Student Activity Workbook, or go to **marketingessentials.glencoe.com/13/DECA**

 Online Action! For instructions, ideas, and answer guide, go to the Teacher Center at **marketingessentials.glencoe.com**

DECA Advisors Corner

Select any of DECA's series events to reinforce the lessons in this chapter. The role-play situations dealing with sales and the sales process will give your students opportunities to master initiating the sales process and view it from both sides.

291

Chapter Overview

Chapter 14 covers two essential steps in the sales process: presenting the product and overcoming objections. It provides examples of what to do and say during the presentation process and suggests how to plan for and cope with objections.

BUILD BACKGROUND

Ask students to recall a time someone they know was approached by a salesperson. Have students share what the salesperson did to impress that person with the product's features.

Why It's Important

Presenting your product in the context of your customers' needs and anticipating and being able to manage customer objections will help ensure and promote successfulness in sales.

Prepare to Read

List and discuss the chapter objectives with students. Have students skim the chapter, looking at pictures, reading captions, and noting their heads. Ask questions to ensure that students have a basic understanding of the chapter structure.

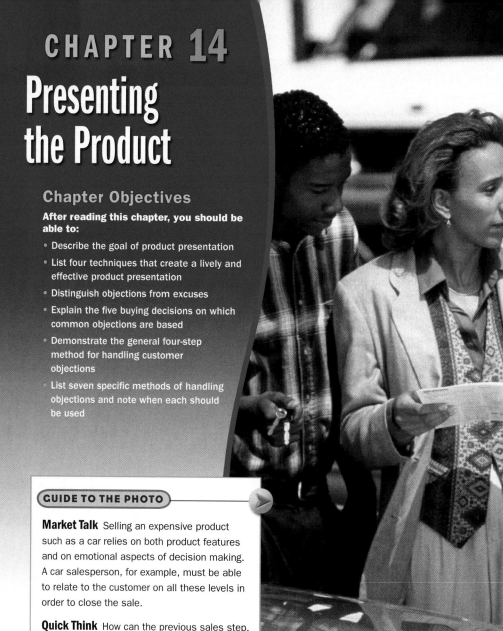

CHAPTER 14
Presenting the Product

Chapter Objectives

After reading this chapter, you should be able to:

- Describe the goal of product presentation
- List four techniques that create a lively and effective product presentation
- Distinguish objections from excuses
- Explain the five buying decisions on which common objections are based
- Demonstrate the general four-step method for handling customer objections
- List seven specific methods of handling objections and note when each should be used

GUIDE TO THE PHOTO

Market Talk Selling an expensive product such as a car relies on both product features and on emotional aspects of decision making. A car salesperson, for example, must be able to relate to the customer on all these levels in order to close the sale.

Quick Think How can the previous sales step, determining needs, help a salesperson do a better job at selling a car?

292 UNIT 5 - SELLING

GUIDE TO THE PHOTO

Market Talk Lead discussion about how making a major purchase requires more consideration and thought from a customer than a minor purchase does. For example, buying a car or house might take more careful research and comparison shopping than purchasing a CD or a food item.

Quick Think After determining a customer's needs, a car salesperson can present models that will most likely appeal to that customer.

 Follow Up Ask the class to research how the Internet has affected car selling. Answers may include that customers are better informed about features and costs.

THE DECA CONNECTION

Performance indicators represent key skills and knowledge. Relating them to the concepts explained in this chapter is your key to success in DECA events. These acronyms represent DECA events that involve knowledge of concepts in this chapter.

AAAL	FMAL	MMS	TMDM
AAML	FMDM	QSRM*	TSE
ADC	FMML*	RMAL	VPM
BSM	FSRM	RMML	
EMDM	HMDM*	SMDM	

In all these DECA events you should be able to follow these performance indicators:

- Recommend a specific product
- Demonstrate a product
- Create a presentation software package to support a sales presentation
- Analyze technology for use in the sales function
- Prescribe a solution to customer needs
- Convert customer/client objections into selling points

All the events with an asterisk (*) also include this performance indicator:

- Take a customer's food order

Some events include additional performance indicators. These are:

AAAL	Use style characteristics to sell men's and women's apparel
AAML	Use style characteristics to sell men's and women's apparel
VPM	Suggest needed parts/service as determined by testing
FMAL	Recommend quantities and cuts of meat to customers

DECA PREP

Check your understanding of DECA performance indicators with the DECA activity in this chapter's review. For more information and DECA Prep practice, go to *marketingessentials* .glencoe.com/14/DECA

Chapter 14 - Presenting the Product **293**

THE DECA CONNECTION

DECA events that require knowledge of presenting the product are described here. Discuss the performance indicators to make sure students understand how to demonstrate their understanding.

The events acronyms stand for:

AAAL:	**Apparel and Accessories Marketing Series, AL**
AAML:	**Apparel and Accessories Marketing Series, ML**
ADC:	**Advertising Campaign Event**
BSM:	**Business Services Marketing Series**
EMDM:	**E-Commerce Management Team Decision Making Event**
FMAL:	**Food Marketing Series, AL**
FMDM:	**Financial Analysis Management Team Decision Making Event**
FMML:	**Food Marketing Series, AL**
FSRM:	**Full Service Restaurant Management Series**
HMDM:	**Hospitality Services Management Team Decision Making Event**
MMS:	**Marketing Management Series**
QSRM:	**Quick Serve Restaurant Management Series**
RMAL:	**Retail Merchandising Series, AL**
RMML:	**Retail Merchandising Series, ML**
SMDM:	**Sports and Entertainment Marketing Management Team Decision Making Event**
TMDM:	**Travel and Tourism Marketing Management Team Decision Making Event**
TSE:	**Technical Sales Event**
VPM:	**Vehicles and Petroleum Marketing Series**

DECA PREP

Find timed DECA Prep activities correlated to the Competitive Events Workbook for students and DECA tips for teachers at **marketingessentials.glencoe.com /14/DECA**

CHAPTER 14 Classroom Resources

For the Teacher

- TeacherWorks
- **marketingessentials.glencoe.com**
- Interactive Chalkboard
- **Exam*View*®** Pro Test Generator
- Fast File Unit 5

For the Student

- *Marketing Essentials* Online Edition
- Student Activity Workbook
- Marketing Math Workbook
- Marketing Research Project Workbook
- School-to-Work Activity Workbook
- Competitive Events Workbook
- *BusinessWeek* Reader and Case Studies
- **marketingessentials.glencoe.com**

FOCUS

Introducing the Section

COLLABORATIVE ACTIVITY

To prepare for reading this section, divide students into groups of three to five to review the first two steps in the selling process: approaching the customer and determining needs. Ask: If students worked at a greeting card store, how would those steps affect product presentation? Have groups brainstorm and share answers in class.

Answers may include determining the customer's needs and then pointing out the appropriate section of the store, such as birthday, wedding, sympathy, etc.

Preteaching Key Terms

Read the key term aloud and ask students to provide a definition and examples as they read the text.

*   layman's terms

Extended Activity

Show the Product

Divide students into groups of three to six. Have the groups work together to brainstorm creative ideas for presenting and demonstrating product features for a product of your choice. Have students present their ideas to the class. One example: non-stick cookware. Presentation ideas might include setting up a table with a portable burner and having a person prepare foods with the cookware.

OBJECTIVES

*   Describe the goal of product presentation
*   List four techniques that create a lively and effective product presentation

KEY TERMS

*   layman's terms

Product Presentation

BEFORE YOU READ

Predict Do you think selling has a system or method? What might it be?

THE MAIN IDEA

The product presentation step of the sales process is where you get to share your product knowledge with customers. To be effective, you need to first determine customers' needs in order to match those needs with product features and benefits. There are a few techniques that will create an exciting and interesting presentation for your customers.

STUDY ORGANIZER

Copy the chart below. Use the chart to take notes about how to create an effective product presentation.

```
                    ┌──────────────────────────┐
                    │   Product Presentation   │
                    └──────────────────────────┘

    ┌──────────┐        ┌──────────────┐        ┌──────────┐
    │          │ ◄────► │ Show and Tell│ ◄────► │          │
    └──────────┘        └──────────────┘        └──────────┘

    ┌──────────┐        ┌──────────────────┐    ┌──────────┐
    │          │ ◄────► │ Make It Come Alive│ ◄──► │          │
    └──────────┘        └──────────────────┘    └──────────┘
```

WHILE YOU READ

Connect How can you use what you already know about product knowledge and communication skills to create an effective sales presentation?

Organizing the Product Presentation

Selling is, in many ways, like putting together a jigsaw puzzle. When you do a puzzle, you analyze the various parts by shape and size. You select the straight-edged pieces to use for the frame. When you sell, you analyze your customer's needs and buying motives. Then you use that information to begin framing your product presentation.

READ and STUDY

BEFORE YOU READ

Discuss with students the seven steps of selling. Let them know that the outline allows for changes to be made for each individual salesperson's strengths and personality.

THE MAIN IDEA

Ask a volunteer to talk about product presentation's placement in the seven steps of selling.

STUDY ORGANIZER

Have students fill in the chart as they read the chapter. A full-size, downloadable study organizer can be found at marketingessentials.glencoe.com

WHILE YOU READ

Have students recall what they already know about product knowledge and communication skills.

Show and Tell

Your first decision in the product presentation step of the sale is what product or products to show your customer. Then you must think about what you are going to say and how you are going to say it. This is the step of the sale where you have the opportunity to share your expertise with the customer. The preparation that you have put into learning about the product or products you sell and how to communicate their selling points will assist you now. In this step, you have the opportunity to match the product features to the customer's needs in consultative selling.

Which Products Do You Show?

After you have learned the customer's intended use of a product, you should be able to select a few samples that match those needs. (See Figure 14.1.) For example, you may select a technically advanced camera for a customer who wants a camera for professional use. Novice customers might want a fully automatic camera.

What Price Range Should You Offer?

When you do not know the customer's price range and your knowledge of the intended use is insufficient to determine a price range, begin by showing a medium-priced product. You can move up or down in price once you begin to get the customer's feedback.

It is not a good idea to introduce price early on in the product presentation unless it is a major selling point because you need time to show your clients/customers how valuable your product is to them. You know yourself that if it is something you really need and want, price becomes less of a factor in a purchase decision.

How Many Products Should You Show?

To avoid overwhelming your customer, show no more than three products at a time. It is difficult for most people to remember all the features of more than three items during a presentation. When a customer wants to see more than three, put away the displayed products in which the customer shows no interest.

marketingessentials.glencoe.com

MARKET TECH

Worth the Higher Price?

It wasn't long after the invention of the movie camera that people started making home movies, chronicling everything from birthdays to weddings, vacations to baseball games. Over time, the cameras have gotten much smaller and much less expensive. And now, like so many other products, camcorders are digital. Panasonic, Hitachi, and Sony all make DVD camcorders that let you record directly onto a mini DVD-R disc compatible with DVD players. All three companies' models offer useful features, such as a screen of thumbnail images that lets you easily find the video you want to play and a mechanism that prevents you from accidentally recording over your saved videos.

More Features

Sony charges $790 for its camcorder, approximately $130 more than its competitors. Why? Sony's model lets you know exactly how much time is left on your battery. It focuses faster and lets you record in near to total darkness. It also has a sharper, brighter screen and an AC adapter that powers the camera even while the battery is still in place. The company is betting that consumers will be willing to shell out extra money for these extra features.

THINK LIKE A MARKETER

What statements might a customer make that would give you reason to show the new DVD camcorder in the product presentation step of the sale? How would you handle the price objection for the Sony model?

@ Online Action!

Go to *marketingessentials.glencoe.com/14/tech* to find a project on selling technology.

MARKET TECH

Worth the Higher Price?

Discussion Lead a discussion about why certain people are willing to pay more for the latest technology even though it will often soon become better and cheaper.

THINK LIKE A MARKETER Answer: Answers will vary. A statement that might indicate an interest in the new DVD camcorder might be "Why don't they make a camcorder that lets you record directly onto a DVD?" or "I am so tired of the hassle involved in getting the video from my camcorder to play on my TV." To handle the price objection, you could use the superior point method and list the features that the Sony brand has over the competition.

@ Online Action! For instructions, ideas, and answer guide, go to the Teacher Center at *marketingessentials.glencoe.com*

TEACH

Discussion Starter

IMPORTANCE OF PRODUCT PRESENTATION

Ask the students to consider the following scenario: They are working at a record store that sells various genres of music. How would they know which new releases to suggest to customers?

Answers might include that from observing, listening to, or questioning students could determine what music the customers like and present suitable popular releases.

TEACHING POINTS

Role Play Ask students in your class a few questions related to their musical taste, and then recommend specific musical artists if possible. This should illustrate the inexact nature of the selling process.

Concept Development

WHICH PRODUCTS DO YOU SHOW?

After students have read this section, ask them if they would show the same product features or show the features in the same order to all customers during the product presentation. Have them explain their answers.

Answers will vary; some sales procedures may specify the same points be covered in a particular order, but most of the time the feature most important to that particular customer would be shown first.

Critical Thinking

Ask students to brainstorm ways that a sales associate can determine a customer's needs. Have students share their responses in class.

TEACH CONTINUED

Enrichment

TIPS FOR EFFECTIVE PRODUCT PRESENTATION

Ask small groups of students to choose a product and develop an effective way to present it. They should consider the display, possible demonstration, and ways to involve the customer. Ask the groups to create posters depicting their ideas, with the elements labeled and explained.

Concept Development

WHAT DO YOU SAY?

Have students practice using descriptive adjectives and active verbs. Pick an item in the classroom, such as a student's new shoes or backpack, and ask the class to list product features.

Descriptions will vary but should be clear and objective ("ergonomic," "made of brushed aluminum") rather than subjective ("cool," "pretty").

TEACHING POINTS

Extend Ask students: Why is it unwise to use slang or double meanings when selling to a customer? Answers might include that customers may not share the same appreciation of slang or misunderstand what you are trying to say.

 Online Activity

Retail Strategies
Have students look up online stores that sell retail display units. Ask them to take note of the retail strategies that are integrated into the units' design and write a report about the logic behind retail displays.

296

Figure 14.1 *Tips for Effective Product Presentation*

- **Matchmaking** The goal of a sales presentation is to match customer needs to the features and benefits of a product. Once you've learned something about your customer's interests and have selected products you believe will interest that customer, you're ready for the presentation. While no advice can guarantee success, the following tips will help to ensure that the process goes smoothly.

What are some other suggestions for product presentation?

DISPLAY AND HANDLE THE PRODUCT

Thinking of how the product will appear to a customer is important. For instance, if you are selling jewelry, an attractive display case will add to the product's appeal. Pick up the jewelry, perhaps showing how it appears in different lighting. Show the customer any special features of the product. When you handle a product, always demonstrate respect for what you are selling.

DEMONSTRATE

Show the customer how the product works. If it is a necklace, demonstrate how the clasp works. If you are selling a product with complicated parts or instructions, using sales aids, such as audiovisual presentations or brochures, helps.

INVOLVE THE CUSTOMER

If possible, let the customer try the product. In makeup sales, salespeople often give away free samples. In car sales, salespeople let the potential buyer drive the car. This allows the customer to experience the product and base the purchasing decision on that experience.

@ Online Action!
Go to *marketingessentials.glencoe.com/14/figure/1* to find a project on product presentation.

Figure 14.1 *Tips for Effective Product Presentation*

Discussion After students read **Figure 14.1**, discuss ways to present products effectively. Ask students to share examples from stores that they patronize.

Caption Answer Suggestions will vary, but may include testimonials, endorsements, and art.

@ Online Action! For instructions, ideas, and answer guide, go to the Teacher Center at **marketingessentials.glencoe.com**

Follow Up Ask students to volunteer to research and share examples of poor product presentation. Interested students can create an example of poor or effective product presentation to share with the class.

• **PRODUCT FEATURES and BENEFITS** A detailed knowledge of product features can help you find the right product for a customer's need.

Which features of this jacket might make it appropriate for snow sports?

What Do You Say?

In this step of the sales process, talk about the product's features and benefits. Tell your customer the product features that match his or her buying motives and needs. Use highly descriptive adjectives and active verbs when describing product features. Avoid unclear words, such as *nice, pretty,* and *fine.*

Avoid slang and double meanings. For example, when selling an expensive suit to a corporate executive, you might not say, "You look cool in that suit."

When selling industrial products, you might use the appropriate jargon to communicate with industrial buyers at their level

of expertise. When selling products to retail customers, you should use layman's terms. **Layman's terms** are words the average customer can understand.

Make the Presentation Come Alive

Planning is necessary for an effective product presentation. Consider how you will display and handle the merchandise. What will you do to demonstrate the product's selling points? What sales aids will add to your presentation? Finally, how will you involve the customer?

Chapter 14 - Presenting the Product **297**

Concept Development

USING SALES AIDS

Review with students how computer presentation software can be used as a sales aid. Talk about how presentation software is easily learned and how images, pictures, and music can be imported. Ask students what they would include in their programs.

Students may present entire lines of products, including features, testimonials, and sales strategies.

TEACHING POINTS

Extend Have students talk about possible reasons that computer presentation software is playing an increasingly important role in product presentations.

Answers may include the portability of laptops for in-store presentation, the fact that most businesses have computers and can play presentations on a CD-ROM or over the Internet, and that PowerPoint and other programs can be used on PCs and Macs.

Enrichment

INVOLVE THE CUSTOMER

Have students research retail stores where customers are allowed to try products. Ask students to take note of special accommodations that must be made for their usage. Have students share their findings informally in class.

Answers will vary but may include a fitting room for clothing, listening stations for CDs, or an artificial putting green for golf clubs.

TEACHING POINTS

Explain Tell student that certain kitchenware stores offer cooking classes that allow customers to use specialized items that they may never try otherwise. Encourage students to think of similar classes offered by other types of businesses.

Displaying and Handling the Product

Creatively displaying the product is the first step in an eye-catching presentation. Some products, of course, lend themselves more naturally to visual display. Others will challenge your creativity. Diamond rings, for example, look great on a black velvet display pad. An attractive display of vacuum cleaners, on the other hand, takes more creative planning.

The way you physically handle a product presents an image of its quality. Handle it with respect and use hand gestures to show the significance of certain features.

Demonstrating the Product

Demonstrating the product in use helps to build customer confidence. This is especially true if you are showing an item that requires manipulation or operation, such as a television, camera, or a computer. To demonstrate the features of a copier, you may show how it can enlarge or reduce a document, as well as organize and staple multiple copies.

To prove selling points or claims made by the manufacturer, you may need to demonstrate a product in a more dramatic way. To prove that a paper towel absorbs water, you can use it to clean up spills. At Saturn car dealerships, salespeople jump up and down on a car door that has been removed to show high durability and dent-proof construction.

Using Sales Aids

When it is impractical to demonstrate the actual product or when you want to emphasize certain selling points, you can use

• **PRODUCT DEMONSTRATION** Whenever possible, salespeople demonstrate a product's features and benefits. This helps to eliminate any doubts about a product's claims and makes for an effective presentation.

What difficulties or challenges might demonstrating a product present to a salesperson?

PHOTO GUIDE   PRODUCT DEMONSTRATION

Discussion Lead a discussion about the demonstration of products to customers. Ask students how the extra interaction allows a salesperson to learn more about the customers' needs and wants. Answers might include more conversation and more time spent together.

Caption Answer Answers will vary but may mention the difficulty of demonstrating a product out of the context in which it is meant to be used. Students might offer that demonstration of a product requires the salesperson to be more knowledgeable about his or her wares. If the product is of below-average quality, it might also present more harm than good to the selling process.

• **USING TECHNOLOGY** The SanDisk Cruzer Mini is just one of many forms of technology that can be used to enhance a product presentation.

Name another technological sales aid.

sales aids in your presentations. Sales aids include samples, reprints of magazine and newspaper articles, audiovisual aids, models, photographs, drawings, graphs, charts, specification sheets, customer testimonials, and warranty information. Computers play an increasingly important role in product presentations as many business-to-business sales representatives make use of computer presentation software.

With a riding lawnmower, you could show the customer complimentary letters or testimonials from satisfied customers as a sales aid, or whatever warranty the manufacturer offers. These tactics help consumers build confidence in the company because it shows that the company stands behind its products. If you were selling this product to retailers for resale purposes, you may even want to use samples of the lawnmower's blade to demonstrate

its effectiveness and durability or a video to demonstrate its important features and high-quality construction.

Be creative when determining which sales aids will help you in your particular product presentation. A manufacturer of industrial ovens might show a videotape of how quickly and efficiently the oven performs. An insurance salesperson might use graphs and charts to show how dividends will accumulate or to compare the benefits of one policy with another. He or she might even use a computer to personalize the presentation of that information for each customer and show different policy plans for that person.

Involving the Customer

It is best to get the customer physically involved with the product as soon as possible in the sales presentation. You could have

Chapter 14 - Presenting the Product 299

CLOSE

Ask students to recall and provide answers to the following questions:

- **What are layman's terms and why should a salesperson use them?**
  They are words an average customer can understand.

- **Why should a salesperson show no more than three products at a time?**
  It is difficult for most people to remember all the features of more than three items during a presentation.

Critical Thinking

Ask students to brainstorm ways a salesperson could demonstrate a rain jacket's water resistance and strength. Answers may include splashing water on the raincoat and letting potential customers try to tear a swatch of its fabric.

---

your customers hold and swing golf clubs, try on and walk around in a pair of shoes, use a computer keyboard or mouse, test-drive an automobile, or taste and smell food products. Some cosmetic companies offer free makeovers so customers can see how the products look on their faces.

For a jacket, have the customer try it on and move her arms around to feel the free range of motion the jacket permits. You can also involve your customer verbally during the sales presentation by confirming selling points. You might say, "This jacket is wind and water resistant. Don't you think that feature will come in handy on an outdoor trip?" Pause for the customer's answer. You should only ask a question that is guaranteed to produce a positive response. Getting the customer's agreement on several selling points helps to ensure that you are on the right track with the selected product.

Holding the Customer's Attention

When you involve a customer in the sale, you help the person make intelligent buying decisions. You also help yourself because a customer is generally more attentive when doing more than just listening to what you say.

If you are losing your customer's attention, ask a simple question. You might say, "Now that you've seen the features of this product, what do you think about it?" Regaining your customer's attention is essential if you are to continue with the sales presentation. The key is keeping the customer involved.

14.1 AFTER YOU READ

Reviewing Key Terms and Concepts

1. When you cannot determine a customer's intended price range, what price level of product should you show? Why?
2. For security purposes and to make your sales presentation effective, what would you do if a customer asks to see six pairs of expensive earrings?
3. How could you involve a customer in the product presentation when selling a copying machine for a business? Replacement windows for a home?

Integrating Academic Skills

Math

4. Your customer wants to buy 7 feet of fabric, and the price per yard is $12.50. How much would you charge?

Language Arts

5. Write a detailed plan that covers the product presentation for a product you have researched. For at least two product features, include what you will say, how you will demonstrate that feature, what sales aids you will use, how you will use them, and how you will involve your customer with each feature. When appropriate, incorporate sample dialogue. Prepare this plan using a word processing program.

 Online Action! Check your answers at *marketingessentials.glencoe.com/14/read*

 marketingessentials.glencoe.com

AFTER YOU READ

Reviewing Key Terms and Concepts

1. Show the middle price range so you can move up or down as required by the customer's needs.

2. Answers will vary. Most will remember that three is the limit for effective product presentation, so they can tell the customer that their store policy states or manager prefers that no more than three are shown at a time.

3. For a copying machine, you could have the customer use features such as double-sided copies, enlargement, reduction, collating, etc. For replacement windows, you could have the customer see how easy it is to open, close, or remove them for cleaning.

Integrating Academic Skills

4. $87.50; 7 × $12.50 = $87.50

5. Answers will vary depending on product selected; plans might include a list of features and ways to present them, as well as a sales script and a description of sales aids.

 Online Action! Answers at **marketingessentials.glencoe.com/14/read**

Objections

OBJECTIVES

- Distinguish objections from excuses
- Explain the five buying decisions on which common objections are based
- Demonstrate the general four-step method for handling customer objections
- List seven specific methods of handling objections and note when each should be used

KEY TERMS

- objections
- excuses
- objection analysis sheet
- paraphrase
- substitution method
- boomerang method
- superior-point method
- third-party method

Introducing the Section

COLLABORATIVE ACTIVITY

Ask students if they have ever gone shopping without the intention of buying anything. Have them list responses to salespeople who asked them if they wanted help. In small groups, have students come up with answers to each response. Allow groups to share their answers and discuss the effectiveness of the sales approaches they experienced.

Preteaching Key Terms

Read the key terms aloud, or ask a volunteer to read them. Ask students to predict the meanings of each term and to use each term in a sentence:

- objections
- excuses
- objection analysis sheet
- paraphrase
- substitution method
- boomerang method
- superior-point method
- third-party method

Tell students they can check their predictions as they read this section.

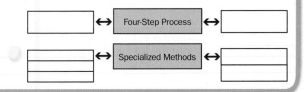

READ and STUDY

BEFORE YOU READ
Predict Why might objections be a useful sales tool?

THE MAIN IDEA
Learning how to handle objections during the sales process will make you a more effective salesperson. You will quickly see that objections are helpful in the sales process by providing an opportunity to further determine customers' needs and problems. Objections are easily managed once you know the basis for them, as well as the general and specific methods that work in various selling situations.

STUDY ORGANIZER
Copy the chart below. Use the chart to take notes about ways to handle objections.

| ↔ | Four-Step Process | ↔ | |
| ↔ | Specialized Methods | ↔ | |

Understanding Objections

Objections are concerns, hesitations, doubts, or other honest reasons a customer has for not making a purchase. Objections should be viewed as positive because they give you an opportunity to present more information to the customer.

Anticipating and planning potential answers to objections will help you feel more confident in your responses to customers. Selecting the most appropriate method for handling those objections will make you a superior salesperson.

WHILE YOU READ

Question What are some techniques you have used to handle objections?

READ and STUDY

BEFORE YOU READ
Lead a discussion explaining why objections can be a useful sales tool. Suggest that handling objections allows a salesperson to erase customers' doubts about a product or service.

THE MAIN IDEA
Ask a volunteer to read the main idea aloud and ask another student to retell it in his or her own words.

STUDY ORGANIZER
Model the study organizer for the class by filling in ways to handle objections. A full-size, downloadable study organizer can be found at **marketingessentials.glencoe.com**

WHILE YOU READ
Answers will vary; encourage students to compare their own responses to objections to the ones listed in the section.

TEACH

UNDERSTANDING OBJECTIONS

Ask the students if they have ever watched or participated in a debate (for example, a political debate). Have them recall aspects of the debate and list responses on the board. Ask students how debates can build skills in handling objections.

Explain that, after a person gives his or her statement, he or she faces a rebuttal and is given a chance to respond to it. Let students know that, in the same manner, salespeople anticipate and plan answers to customers' objections. Doing so increases their chances of finalizing a sale.

TEACHING POINTS

Explain Inform students that a salesperson's training often includes responses to objections. Let them know that these are taught through scripts and role-playing exercises. Ask students to think of other ways they can learn how to react to objections.

Answers may include films or talking with other salespeople.

Extend Ask students to differentiate objections from excuses.

Objections are concerns, hesitations, doubts, or other honest reasons a customer has for not making a purchase. Excuses are reasons for not buying or not seeing the salesperson.

Objections can be presented as either questions/inquiries or statements. An example of a question or inquiry would be, "Do you carry any other brands?" and a statement would be, "These shoes don't fit me properly." For direct inquiries, you simply answer the question posed. Objections which are statements may require more selling expertise.

Excuses are reasons for not buying or not seeing the salesperson. Customers often use excuses when they are not in the mood to buy or when concealing other objections.

It is often difficult to distinguish between objections and excuses. A statement or question that seems to be an objection may really just be an excuse. When you are faced with this in a retail selling situation, be polite and courteous. Encourage the customer to look around and ask you any questions he or she may have.

In a business-to-business selling situation, the procedure is different. Leave a business card if a potential customer refuses to see you when you make a call and ask if it is possible to see the person at a more convenient time.

There are cases when excuses are actually attempts to hide real objections. "I didn't plan to buy today" may really mean, "I don't like the styles you have available." When you suspect that may be the case, ask additional questions to get to the real reason for the disinterest in your product or products.

Plan for Objections

Objections can occur at any time during the sales process and should be answered promptly. A customer who must wait to hear responses to questions or concerns tends to become preoccupied with the objection. When that happens, you may lose the customer's attention and confidence.

Objections can guide you in the sales process by helping you redefine the customer's needs and determine when the customer wants more information. A customer may say, "This item is very expensive." What the person may really mean is, "Tell me why this

•**OVERCOMING OBJECTIONS** If a customer objects to the price of an eye shadow, you could apply the product to the customer's skin to show its effectiveness and explain that the price per use is low.

How can you find out what a customer objects to about a product?

product costs so much." This objection not only lets you know why the customer is reluctant to buy but also gives you an opportunity to bring out additional selling points.

You should therefore welcome objections; they are not necessarily the sign of a lost sale. Research shows a positive relationship between customer objections and a successful sales outcome.

You can prepare yourself for most objections that might occur in a sales situation by completing an **objection analysis sheet**, a document that lists common objections and possible responses to them. Although the actual objections may be slightly different from those you anticipated, thinking of responses ahead of time gives you an idea of how to handle other objections.

PHOTO GUIDE	OVERCOMING OBJECTIONS

Discussion Lead a discussion about what observations might help you determine how to respond to a customer's objections.

Caption Answer Answers will vary but may include that careful observation and asking questions can help you determine what a customer's objections are.

Follow Up Ask students to brainstorm what might happen if a sales associate misrepresented a product or its attributes while overcoming objections.

You can incorporate anticipated objections into your product presentation so they do not become objections. You must be cautious about this, however. You do not want to include so many objections in your product presentation that you introduce doubt, especially if none existed before. Saying, "I guess you're worried about the safety of this snowmobile," may introduce a fear that was not a previous concern.

A better way to handle the same situation would be to emphasize the safety features of the vehicle. You might say, "The suspension on this snowmobile is especially designed to keep it stable. It's very safe to operate."

Common Objections

When you list general customer objections you will see that they fall into certain categories. Most objections are based on key decisions the customer must make before buying—decisions about need, product, source, price, and time. This is true for both retail and business-to-business sales situations. The actual objections will vary because of the difference in purchase motivation.

The following are examples of customer objections in a retail situation. They provide a starting point for the creation of an objection analysis sheet.

Need

Objections related to need usually occur when the customer does not have an immediate need for the item or wants the item but does not truly need it. A comment such as, "I really want to get these sandals, but I really don't need another pair," is an objection based on a conflict between a need and a want.

Product

Objections based on the product itself are more common. They include concerns about things such as construction, ease of use, quality, color, size, or style. "I don't buy 100 percent cotton shirts because you have to iron them" is such an objection.

Source

Objections based on source often occur because of negative past experiences with the firm or brand. A business-to-business customer might say, "The last time I placed an order with your company, I received it two weeks after the promised date."

Price

Objections based on price are more common with expensive merchandise. You might

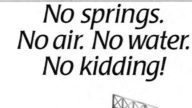

No springs.
No air. No water.
No kidding!

Weightless Sleep

No better bed than Tempur-Pedic.

Our Weightless Sleep bed embodies an entirely new sleep technology. It's recognized by NASA. And widely acclaimed by the media. It's recommended worldwide by more than 25,000 medical professionals. Moreover, our high-tech bed is preferred by countless stars and celebrities, people who demand the best.

Our scientists invented an amazing viscoelastic sleep surface: TEMPUR pressure-relieving material. It reacts to bodyshape, bodyweight, bodyheat. Nothing mechanical or electrical. Yet it molds precisely to your every curve.

Tempur-Pedic brings you a relaxing, energizing quality of sleep you've never experienced before. That's why 91% of our enthusiastic owners recommend us to their friends and relatives.

Please call us toll-free, without the slightest obligation, for a FREE DEMONSTRATION KIT!

 SPACE

Free Sample/Free Video/Free Info
FREE IN-HOME TRYOUT CERTIFICATE

YOURS FOR THE ASKING!

888-244-8332
Call toll-free or fax 866-795-9367

TEMPUR·PEDIC
PRESSURE RELIEVING
SWEDISH MATTRESSES AND PILLOWS

• **PROVIDING PROOF** In telemarketing, overcoming objections becomes even more challenging than in face-to-face sales situations.

If a customer calls the toll-free number in this ad and questions you about the mattress's construction, what would you say to eliminate any doubt about it?

Chapter 14 - Presenting the Product **303**

Concept Development

PLAN FOR OBJECTIONS

Divide the class into groups of two to five students. Ask each group to choose a type of retail business to simulate. Tell them to pick a product and then create an objection analysis sheet for it listing at least five objections and ways to handle them. Have groups object to other groups' products to see how well the sheets work.

TEACHING POINTS

Role Play Play the customer in a role play with students using the objection analysis sheets they created in the exercise above. Adjust their responses or create new ones as needed.

Extend Ask students: who writes the objection analysis sheet? Explain that the answers will vary but may include managers, salespeople, or a combination of the two.

Extended Activity

Handling Customer Objections Ask students about experiences (either real or fictional) they have had with or observed about persistent salespeople. Have students share their stories in class and discuss responses to the experiences. Then have students brainstorm objections and responses to objections to the products shown in the ads in this chapter.

TEACH CONTINUED

Enrichment

FOUR-STEP PROCESS FOR HANDLING OBJECTIONS

Have students go shopping with pre-planned objections to present to a salesperson. Ask them to record and evaluate the salesperson's methods for handling those objections. Have them prepare an oral and written report on their findings.

TEACHING POINTS

Role Play Inform students that the four-step process for handling objections can be used outside of business situations. In role plays with students, use the process in such situations as asking for help or asking someone to the movies.

Concept Development

RESTATE THE OBJECTIONS

Split the class into pairs and have students practice restating the objection, taking turns being the customer and salesperson. Emphasize to them the importance of paraphrasing and measuring one's tone so you don't sound incredulous, mocking, or condescending.

TEACHING POINTS

Demonstrate Read passages from the newspaper and paraphrase them. Take sentences from the front page, sports section, and other sections.

Role Play Have students provide objections to a sales situation. Restate the objections in two or three different ways.

304

A MATTER OF ETHICS

Getting Attention

Richard has recently started a small public relations business out of his home in a suburb of Chicago. He has just three employees. They are competing with some of the biggest names in the business, and Richard is having trouble getting the attention of the most desirable clients in town.

It occurs to Richard that if he signs up himself and his employees to volunteer at big charity events, such as a fund-raiser for cancer research or making repairs at homeless shelters, his firm would get some favorable mention as a sponsor. Richard figures he would not even have to tell his employees he had signed them up, because he could call just before the event and say everyone had suddenly "come down with a bad cold." Richard figures no one would be hurt if they did not show up to help... plus, his firm would get some great exposure.

THINKING ETHICALLY

Is it ethical for Richard to volunteer his firm for the charity events, then pull out? Why or why not? What would be a more ethical way for Richard to get attention for his public relations firm?

 Online Action!

Go to *marketingessentials.glencoe.com/14/ethics* to find a project on the ethics of getting publicity.

---

hear statements like, "That's more than I wanted to spend."

Time

Objections based on time reveal a hesitation to buy immediately. These objections are

---

sometimes excuses. Customers usually have a real reason for not wanting to make a purchase on the spot. A customer might say, "I think I'll wait until July when you have your summer sale to buy those sandals."

You will probably hear many different kinds of objections once you begin selling. You should note them for future reference.

Four-Step Process for Handling Objections

Successful salespeople have learned to use a very basic strategy when answering all objections. It consists of four basic steps for handling objections: listen, acknowledge, restate, and answer.

Listen Carefully

Remember to be attentive, maintain eye contact, and let the customer talk.

Acknowledge the Objections

Acknowledging objections demonstrates that you understand and care about the customer's concerns. Some common statements used to acknowledge objections are, "I can see your point," or, "Other customers have asked us the same question."

These acknowledgments make a customer feel that his or her objections are understandable, valid, and worthy of further discussion. It does not mean that you agree with the customer, but it acknowledges the objection. Disagreeing with the customer, or saying, "You're wrong," will put the customer on the defensive, and you might lose the sale.

Restate the Objections

To be sure you understand the customer, you can restate his or her objections in a number of ways:

"I can understand your concerns. You feel that.... Am I correct?"

"In other words, you feel that...."

"Let me see if I understand. You want to know more about...."

Do not repeat the customer's concerns word for word. Instead, paraphrase the

marketingessentials.glencoe.com

A MATTER OF ETHICS — Getting Attention

Discussion Ask students if they note who sponsors a charity event. How does this affect their perception of a business? Students may state that it shows the business's commitment to the community and suggests it is doing well enough to look after others.

THINKING ETHICALLY **Answer:** Most students will agree that it is unethical to make a commitment that you know you won't fulfill—especially to a charity. They may suggest that Richard get attention by attending the events. They may also suggest that he take part in events in Chicago, since they probably get more press than ones in the suburbs.

 Online Action! For instructions, ideas, and answer guide, go to the Teacher Center at **marketingessentials.glencoe.com**

Follow Up Ask students if a charity event is a good way to make contacts.

objections. To **paraphrase** is to restate something in a different way. A customer might say, "The style is nice, but I don't like the color." You could paraphrase the objection by asking, "Would you be interested in the jacket if we could find your size in another color?"

Answer the Objections

Answer each objection tactfully. Never answer with an air of superiority or suggest that the person's concern is unimportant.

Think of yourself as a consultant, using the objections to further define or redefine the customer's needs. When price is the objection, go back to determining the customer's needs. Offer a higher-priced item to a customer if it is warranted. Explain the features and benefits of the more expensive model and why that item is better suited to the customer.

Specialized Methods of Handling Objections

There are seven specialized methods for handling objections: substitution, boomerang, question, superior point, denial, demonstration, and third party.

Substitution

Sometimes a customer is looking for a specific brand or model of a product that you do not carry. Or maybe the product you show the customer is not to his or her liking. In any of those cases, you may want to use something called the **substitution method**, which involves recommending a different product that would satisfy the customer's needs. Assume a customer says, "I don't like the way this dress looks on me." In this case you may want to suggest a totally different design that is more becoming on your customer. "Here, why don't you try this dress. It has a completely different look. I think it will fit your style better than the one you just had on."

Boomerang

An objection can be returned to the customer in the same way that a boomerang

returns to the thrower. The **boomerang method** brings the objection back to the customer as a selling point. Here is an example:

Customer: "These ski gloves are so lightweight. They can't possibly keep me warm."
Salesperson: "The gloves are so light because of an insulation material called Thinsulate. The manufacturer guarantees that Thinsulate will keep you warmer than fiberfill insulation, without the bulk and extra weight."

When using the boomerang method, you must be careful not to sound as if you are trying to outwit the customer. Use a friendly, helpful tone to explain how the objection is really a selling point.

Question

The question method is a technique in which you question the customer to learn more about the objections. While answering your inquiries, the shopper may even come to realize that an objection may not be valid. Here is an example:

Customer: "I don't see the point of having two sinks in the bathroom, as featured in your suggested layout."
Salesperson: "Do you and another member of your family ever need to get ready to go out at the same time?"
Customer: "Yes."
Salesperson: "Does either one of you have to wait for the other to finish using the sink on those occasions?"
Customer: "Yes. I see your point."

Never ask questions in an abrupt manner; this may seem rude and create a defensive atmosphere.

Superior Point

The **superior-point method** is a technique that permits the salesperson to acknowledge objections as valid yet still offset them with other features and benefits. The superior-point method allows you to admit disadvantages in certain products but then present superior points to offset or compensate for them. This technique puts the

Chapter 14 - Presenting the Product **305**

SECTION 14.2

TEACH CONTINUED

Concept Development

SPECIALIZED METHODS OF HANDLING OBJECTIONS

Have students compare and contrast the boomerang method with the superior-point method.

Both the boomerang and superior-point methods take a negative comment and return with a positive one. In the boomerang method, the salesperson turns a negative comment into a positive one. In the superior-point method, the salesperson responds with a completely different positive comment.

Individualized Math Skills

L1 Let students know that 8 boxes of ski jackets have arrived at the store. If the postage for each box is $15.80, how much did it cost for them to be sent?
$126.40; $15.80 × 8 = $126.40

L2 Tell students that the new shipment of ski jackets has come from Canada. If the US$1 is worth CDN$1.4, how much would a CDN$180 jacket cost in American dollars?
US$128.57; CDN$180 × US$1 ÷ CDN$1.4 = US$128.57

L3 If the wholesale price of a ski jacket is $90 and there is a 10 percent discount on every jacket ordered over 30, how much would 45 jackets cost?
$3,915; $90 × 30 + ($90 × .90 × 15) = $2,700; $2,700 + $1,215 = $3,915

ASSESS

Review Guide

CONCEPTS

Ask students to define objections to a sale.

Objections are concerns, hesitations, doubts, or other honest reasons a customer has for not making a purchase.

KEY TERMS

Have students work in small groups to review key terms, their spellings, and their definitions.

ONLINE SELF-ASSESSMENT

Have students go to marketingessentials.glencoe.com for the Section 14.2 practice test.

Individualized Review

L1 Assign and review Chapter 14 activities in the Student Activity Workbook.

L2 Assign and review Chapter 14 activities in the Marketing Math Workbook.

L3 Assign and review Chapter 14 activities in the *BusinessWeek* Reader and Case Studies.

Marketing Practice

Have students role play that they are customers at a department store, and ask them to come up with six reasons not to buy certain items. Afterwards, have the students pretend to be salespeople. Ask the class to (1) distinguish objections from excuses and (2) come up with four-step responses to the objections. Have volunteers act out the objections and excuses in class.

Case Study

Overcoming the Price Objection

When handling the price objection in a business-to-business situation, sell value, not price. You can also conduct a comparison between your product and your competitors' lower-priced products. Take Kellogg Company, which works to educate its customers and potential customers about the benefits of doing business with them.

To maximize perceived value and respond to price objections, Kellogg uses facts about the company. It asks customers to consider the research and development that goes into products, the ongoing support the company will provide, the certainty of on-time delivery, the company's history and reputation, and its market knowledge. Taken together, those factors are worth a lot.

Selling Value as More Than Price

If you want to take this concept a step further, you may use a competitive comparison. This method of handling objections begins with a comparison of product features and return on investment. Then it adds all the value-added aspects of doing business with your company to show how price is not the only factor that should be considered. This competitive comparison method of handling objections can be difficult. It requires a cool head and thorough preparation. Showing customers this comparison of the total package helps a customer see that doing business with a company that has higher-priced products may suit its needs and address its overall situation better than the one with lower-priced products.

THINK STRATEGICALLY

Which of the two methods (perceived value and competitive comparison) would you use to handle a price objection if you were a Kellogg sales representative? Why?

@ Online Action! Go to *marketingessentials.glencoe.com/14/case* to find a research project on price objection.

---

customer in a position to decide between the different features and thus see additional reasons for buying. Here is an example:

Customer: "Your prices are higher than the prices of your competitors."
Salesperson: "That's true. Our prices are slightly higher, but with good reason. We use better quality wool in our garments that will last five to ten years longer than our competitors' garments. Plus, we guarantee the quality for

life. You can return the product if you ever have a problem with it and we'll repair it free of charge."

Denial

The denial method is when the customer's objection is based on misinformation. It is best to provide proof and accurate information in answer to objections. This method is also used when the objection is in the form of a question or inquiry. When using the denial method, you

 marketingessentials.glencoe.com

Case Study Overcoming the Price Objection

Discussion Have students read the Case Study and discuss ways to overcome the price objection. Let the class know that sales associates have to help customers see the product in a certain context.

THINK STRATEGICALLY **Answer:** Either option will work, but selling value is easier to use than competitive comparison, which requires more planning and practicing.

@ Online Action! For instructions, ideas, and answer guide, go to the Teacher Center at **marketingessentials.glencoe.com**

must back up the negative reply with proof and accurate facts. Consider an example:

Customer: "Will this shirt shrink?"

Salesperson: "No, it won't shrink because the fabric is made of 50 percent cotton and 50 percent polyester. The polyester will prevent shrinkage."

Demonstration

The demonstration exemplifies the adage "Seeing is believing." Here is an example:

Customer: "I can't believe that jacket can fold up into itself to become a zippered pouch."

Salesperson: "I'm glad you brought that up. Let me demonstrate how easy it is to stuff this jacket into the pocket pouch here and then zipper it up."

The demonstration method can be quite convincing and should be used when appropriate. Conduct only demonstrations you have tested, and make sure they work before using them on a customer in a sales situation.

Third Party

The **third-party method** involves using a previous customer or another neutral person who can give a testimonial about the product.

Customer: "I can't see how this machine can save me $1,000 in operating costs the first year."

Salesperson: "Frank Smith, one of my customers, questioned the same point when he bought his machine a year ago. He now praises its efficiency and says that his costs have gone down by $1,200. Here's a letter I recently received from him."

In any given sales situation, it is unlikely that you will use all seven methods of handling objections. You will create effective combinations over time that will work best for you.

14.2 AFTER YOU READ

Reviewing Key Terms and Concepts

1. Why should objections be answered promptly?

2. How can you prepare for objections?

3. Which specialized method of handling objections allows you to offset an objection with other features and benefits?

Integrating Academic Skills

Math

4. To overcome a price objection, demonstrate the savings a business-to-business customer will enjoy from purchasing 50 $150 jackets that will last for five years when compared to 50 $80 jackets that will be functional for only a maximum of two years.

Writing

5. Prepare an objection analysis sheet for a silk-and-wool designer blazer. List at least five objections, then write responses to depict methods for handling the objections. Use a word processing program to prepare your written document.

 Online Action!

Check your answers at *marketingessentials.glencoe.com/14/read*

marketingessentials.glencoe.com

Chapter 14 - Presenting the Product **307**

 AFTER YOU READ

Reviewing Key Terms and Concepts

1. So that the customer does not become preoccupied with the objection. When that happens, you may lose the customer's attention and confidence.

2. By anticipating them and preparing an objection analysis sheet, which lists common objections and possible responses to them.

3. The superior-point method is a technique that permits the salesperson to acknowledge an objection such as its high price as valid, yet still offset it with other features and benefits.

Integrating Academic Skills

4. The $150 jackets offer a savings of $500/year; ($150 × 50) ÷ 5 = $1,500/year;

($80 × 50) ÷ 2 = $2,000/year; $2,000 − $1,500 = $500/year

5. Answers will vary but should include at least five different objections and the responses to them. One response should depict the four-step method for handling objections.

Online Action! Answers at **marketingessentials.glencoe.com/14/read**

Ask students to recall and provide answers to the following questions:

- **What is the third-party method of handling objections?**

  Using a previous customer or another neutral person who can give a testimonial about the product.

- **What are the four steps in handling objections?**

  Listen, acknowledge, restate, and answer.

 Online Activity

Anticipating Objections

Ask students to research and give an example of ways that online ads anticipate customer objections. Have students share their findings with the class.

CAREERS
IN MARKETING

Lifelong Learning

CAREER INFORMATION

Have students go to marketingessentials.glencoe.com and find Chapter 14 Careers page and click on the link for the American Marketing Association's Careers Strategies and Tips. Divide students into small groups. Ask the groups to read one article and summarize it in a three-paragraph response.

PRESENTING THE PRODUCT

The ability to handle objections is not only part of the sales process but also an important life skill. Some of these techniques are effective when handling objections at school, at home, at work, or in the community. Encourage students to practice the four-step process in a variety of situations of promotion.

Primary Source

Ask students go to marketingessentials.glencoe.com and find Chapter 14 Resources. Ask them to click on the link for the American Marketing Association's marketing dictionary and find the terms related to product presentation and objections and compare their definitions to the ones in the chapter.

● THINKING CRITICALLY

Answers may include product shots, architectural design planning, lifestyle images, and portraits of the employees for press or other purposes.

 Online Action!

For instructions, ideas, and answer guide, go to the Teacher Center at marketingessentials.glencoe.com

DAVID MODICA
COMMERCIAL
PHOTOGRAPHER

? **What do you do at work?**
I specialize in making photographic images for business usage in advertising, documentation, historical preservation, and for competition. Clients come directly and through design and advertising agencies. I'm classified as a commercial photographer rather than a portrait/wedding photographer.

? **What skills are most important to you?**
Photographic skills are obvious necessities, and today those skills are centered around the digital imaging business. Commercial photographers have to know digital cameras and scanning and their applications to paper and Web production. This process starts with capture and runs through color correction and preproduction.

? **What is your key to success?**
Defining my business in great detail and finding a way to survive long enough to develop that business. That means taking jobs you don't necessarily want in the long run to pay bills and doing what is necessary to meet the people you want to work for. Network key industries, spend advertising money wisely, and get involved in your key geographic area.

Aptitudes, Abilities, and Skills

Camera skills, a visually oriented mind-set, knowledge of both the Web and print industries

Education and Training

Specialized courses in photography can be helpful, but hands-on experience, working with established photographers, is essential.

Career Path

Virtually all companies utilize the services of a photographer at some point—whether for a brochure, a newspaper ad, or a Web site. Ad agencies and design houses establish relationships with photographers for their projects.

● THINKING CRITICALLY

What are some of the ways businesses use photography to market their products and services?

@ Online Action!

Go to *marketingessentials.glencoe.com/14/careers* to find a research project on photography and marketing.

Test-Taking Strategies

Divide the class into two roughly equal teams. Have one team review the aspects of product presentation and the other, objections and ways to handle them. Ask each team to make a presentation to review the chapter. Encourage students to take notes during the presentations.

FOCUS on KEY POINTS

SECTION 14.1

● The goal of the product presentation is to match a customer's needs and wants to a product's features and benefits.
● When selecting products to show your customer during the product presentation, consider needs and price range, and limit your selection to three items at a time.
● To make your product presentation lively and effective, handle the product with respect, demonstrate product features, involve the customer, and use sales aids.

SECTION 14.2

● Objections are reasons or doubts that occur during a sales presentation.
● You should welcome objections in the sales process because they help clarify a customer's needs and provide an opportunity to introduce additional selling points.
● Common objections are based on five buying decisions: need, product, source, price, and time.
● The four-step method for handling customer objections is: listen, acknowledge, restate, and answer.
● There are seven specific methods of handling objections, each of which can be used in different selling situations: substitution, boomerang, question, superior-point, denial, demonstration, and third-party.

REVIEW VOCABULARY

Define each of the following words in a short sentence.

1. layman's terms (p. 297)
2. objections (p. 301)
3. excuses (p. 302)
4. objection analysis sheet (p. 302)
5. paraphrase (p. 305)
6. substitution method (p. 305)
7. boomerang method (p. 305)
8. superior-point method (p. 305)
9. third-party method (p. 307)

REVIEW FACTS and IDEAS

10. What is the goal of the product presentation? (14.1)
11. Describe some guidelines for what to say during the product presentation. (14.1)
12. What are four techniques that will make the product presentation lively and effective? (14.1)
13. Why are objections important to the sales process? (14.2)
14. List the five buying decisions on which common objections are based. (14.2)
15. Explain the process for handling customer objections. (14.2)
16. Name seven specific methods of handling objections. (14.2)

Chapter 14 - Presenting the Product 309

FOCUS on KEY POINTS

Ask volunteers to read the summaries aloud and give an example of each concept. Have interested students share their examples with the class.

REVIEW VOCABULARY

See glossary for definitions of **1–9.**
A sample answer might read:

1. *Layman's terms* are words the average customer can understand.

REVIEW FACTS and IDEAS

10. The goal of product presentation is to match a product's features and benefits to the customer's needs and wants.
11. Guidelines include the following: Tell your customer how the product features match his or her needs. Use highly descriptive adjectives and active verbs. Avoid unclear words such as pretty, nice, and fine. Choose words carefully. Avoid slang and double meanings. Use layman's terms.
12. Four techniques are displaying the product effectively and handling it with care, demonstrating product features, using sales aids, and involving the customer in the sale.
13. Objections help you refine the customer's needs and determine when the customer wants information, thus allowing you to bring out additional selling points.
14. The five buying decisions are need, product, source, price, and time.
15. The process for handling customer objections is to listen carefully, acknowledge the objections, restate the objections, and answer the objections.
16. The seven methods for handling objections include substitution (when the customer does not find what he or she is looking for), boomerang (when the objection can be turned into a selling point), question (to learn more about the objection), superior point (when the objection is valid but can be offset by other features and benefits), denial (when the objection is based on misinformation), demonstration (when seeing is believing), third party (when there is a neutral party or testimonial to remove doubt).

BUILD SKILLS

17. Workplace Skills

Possible answers include:

a. Demonstration method: "Let me show you."

b. Direct denial: "No, it is machine washable because of the fabrics used in its construction."

c. Question method: "Do you usually dry-clean? This machine-washable shirt will save you money."

d. Substitution method: "We have those very same pants in several colors. Would you like to see them?"

e. Third party: "That is exactly what Ms. Lee said when she was looking at this model. Shortly after buying it, she wrote us this letter stating that she never thought she would use all the special features, but now she doesn't know what she'd do without them."

18. Technology Applications

Charts comparing products will vary but should include features and prices. Students should pick one product to favor and be ready to defend it from objectors.

19. Math Practice

$1,209.36; 10¾ sq. yd. × 9 sq. ft./sq. yd. = 96.75 sq. ft; 96.75 sq. ft. × $12.50/sq. ft = $1,209.375

DEVELOP CRITICAL THINKING

20. Selling Points

a. The language is nonspecific and uses slang. You might instead say: "This suit is very flattering and is appropriate for work and evenings."

b. The language uses jargon and should be restated in layman's terms. You might instead say: "This jacket is made of very finely spun nylon, a high-quality fabric."

21. Communication Skills

Examples will vary; student answers should show an understanding of the four-step method for handling objections and the specific methods of handling objections.

---

17. Workplace Skills

Handling Objections Write a response for each of the following objections and note the specialized method you used.

a. "This is the smallest TV I've ever seen. How will I be able to see the picture?"

b. "Does this blouse need to be dry-cleaned?"

c. "These no-iron cotton dress shirts are awfully expensive."

d. "I like these pants, but I already have two pairs of black pants."

e. "This cell phone is too sophisticated for me; it has too many fancy features I don't need."

18. Technology Applications

Make a Chart Assume you work as a sales associate for an electronics retailer. Select two competing products to compare, focusing on their features and prices. Use spreadsheet, presentation, or word processing software to make a chart that shows this comparison for use in the product presentation step of the sales process. Share your chart with classmates and be prepared to answer their questions and handle objections from them.

19. Math Practice

Determine the Price Your customer wants to buy 6¾ square yards of wood flooring for one room of a house and 4 square yards for another room. The price per square foot is $12.50. How much would you charge the customer?

DEVELOP CRITICAL THINKING

20. Selling Points

Tell what is wrong with the following two selling statements and what you would say instead during a product presentation:

a. "This suit is great."

b. "This fabric is made of 420 denier nylon."

21. Communication Skills

Can you use the methods for handling objections in sales to handle objections in other aspects of life? Give three examples of situations when the methods could be useful. Explain which method or methods you would use in each situation, and what the results might be.

Formative Assessment

Formative assessment is an essential component of classroom work. This type of assessment provides information that is then used as feedback to modify teaching and meet student needs.

L1 Have students write or demonstrate all of the steps of handling a customer's objections.

L2 Have students write a narrative description of a customer objecting to a sale and a salesperson responding to the objections.

L3 Assign the different types of objects to pairs of students and have them write and role-play a sales situation including an objection and the salesperson's response.

 Reteach **If the results of this formative assessment seem low, consider the following activity:**

Read each of the key terms aloud. Have students define each of the key terms and use them in a sentence.

Timing the Close

Some customers are ready to buy sooner than others; therefore, you must be flexible. You may show a customer a product and almost immediately detect an opportunity to close the sale. Other times, you may spend an hour with a customer and still find that he or she is having difficulty making a decision.

Buying Signals

When attempting to close a sale, look for **buying signals**, the things customers do or say to indicate a readiness to buy. Buying signals include facial expressions, body language, and comments.

Trial Close

You may attempt a trial close to test the readiness of a customer and your interpretation of a positive buying signal. A **trial close** is an initial effort to close a sale.

Even if the close does not work, you will learn from the attempt. The customer will most likely tell you why he or she is not ready to buy. If the trial close does work, you will reach your goal of closing the sale. In both cases, you are in an excellent position to continue with the sales process.

General Rules for Closing the Sale

Professional salespeople recognize closing opportunities, help customers make a decision, and create an ownership mentality for the customer. You also want to avoid saying or doing a few things when closing a sale.

Recognize Closing Opportunities

Having a major obstacle removed usually makes a customer receptive to buying the product or service. You can also use effective product presentations to close the sale. Dramatic product presentations often prove important selling points and get a customer excited about owning the product. Take advantage of high customer interest at these times and attempt to close.

Help Customers Make a Decision

When a customer is having difficulty making a buying decision, stop showing additional merchandise. You should also narrow the selection of items by removing those things that are no longer of interest to the customer. You can do this by asking, "Which of these items do you like the least?" Once you get the selection

• **IS the CUSTOMER READY to BUY?**
A customer might like a product but be hesitant to buy it.

How would you assess if this customer is ready to make a purchase?

Chapter 15 - Closing the Sale **315**

PHOTO GUIDE — IS the CUSTOMER READY to BUY?

Discussion Lead a discussion on what signals indicate that a customer is ready to buy a product and how a sales associate could work off those signals to close the sale.

Caption Answer Answers may include comments that suggest ownership, the way she holds the merchandise, and facial expressions.

 Follow Up Ask students how long it should take for a customer to be ready to buy. One answer might be that there is no set schedule for a customer's readiness to buy. It can be immediate when he or she spots an item or hours later.

TEACH

Discussion Starter

IMPORTANCE OF CLOSING THE SALE

Because the customer is ready to purchase at different times in each selling situation, it is crucial for salespeople to recognize when it is time to close a sale. Ask students if it would be different to identify a customer's readiness to buy in a drill bit section of a hardware store or in a high-end clothing boutique.

TEACHING POINTS

Clarify Tell students that they have to use their observation and listening skills to determine whether a customer is ready to buy.

Concept Development

GENERAL RULES FOR CLOSING THE SALE

Review with students the general rules for closing a sale: recognize closing opportunities, help customers make a decision, create an ownership mentality, do not talk too much, and do not rush. Have students share examples from their own experiences.

TEACHING POINTS

Role Play With students acting as customers, act out ways to botch the four general rules for closing the sale.

Critical Thinking

Ask students to explain the purpose of a trial close. One answer might be that a salesperson delivers a trial close to determine whether a customer is ready to buy.

TEACH CONTINUED

Individualized Math Skills

Tell students to imagine they are working at a gift shop. The gift-wrap manager has invited a local scout troop to provide gift-wrapping services on weekends during holidays.

L1 During the holidays, the gift shop typically makes $4,500 over a weekend. If gift-wrapping increases holiday sales by 25 percent on weekends, how much more will the shop make?
$1,125; $4,500 × .25 = $1,125

L2 The gift shop is open from 11:00 A.M. to 7:00 P.M. on Saturday and 12:00 P.M. to 6:00 P.M. on Sunday. If each shift can be up to six hours and two scouts and a scout leader are needed to work the gift wrap table, how many scouts and leaders are required to work each day?
Four scouts and two leaders on Saturday; two scouts and one leader on Sunday.

L3 The gift shop averages 20 transactions an hour on weekends. If 35 percent of customers choose to get gifts wrapped, about how much money will the scout troop make on Saturday if the gift shop is open from 11:00 A.M. to 7:00 P.M. and the typical customer gets two gifts wrapped for $2 per gift?
$224; 20 transactions/hour × .35 = 7 transactions/hour; 7 transactions/hour × 2 gifts/transaction = 14 gifts/hour; 14 gifts/hour × $2/gift = $28/hour × 8 hours = $224

Extended Activity

Cultural Differences in Closing the Sale
Have interested students research close techniques that are common in other cultures, such as bartering. Have students share their research in a five-minute oral presentation.

---

down to two, you can help a customer decide by summarizing the major features and benefits of each product. You can also explain any advantages or disadvantages of the item being considered. Both methods help you to focus the decision making on important considerations.

Create an Ownership Mentality

Use words that indicate ownership, such as *you* and *your*. When presenting selling points, say things such as, "When your children are hiking with you and the weather changes,

you'll be happy that they have waterproof shoes like these." Look for minor agreements from the customer on selling points that lead up to the close.

Do Not Talk Too Much and Do Not Rush

If you think the customer is ready to make a buying decision, stop talking about the product.

On the other hand, don't rush a customer into making a buying decision. Be patient, courteous, polite, and helpful. Always

Case Study

The Electronic Close

Somewhere in the list of things mobile phones were one day supposed to become was the idea that they would replace credit cards.

Sour Chhor wants to make it happen, and he is closer than you might expect. He is the general manager of a group at Philips Electronics that is focused on developing a technology called near field communications (NFC). This technology is based on radio frequency identification (RFID) and could start turning common mobile phones into the spendthrift's best friend.

New Phone Functions

Consider using the phone to buy concert tickets. Not only will the phone handle payment but it will also become the ticket. Wave it in front of the turnstile at the concert venue, and the phone gets you in the door, where it can also be used to buy a T-shirt.

A Glimpse at the Future

NFC is potentially the next force that will push forward the concept of contactless payments. Credit card companies such as Visa, MasterCard, and American Express, as well as issuing banks like Citicorp's Citibank, J.P. Morgan Chase, and MBNA are testing this technology. ExxonMobil issues its SpeedPass RFID keychain to customers who use them to pay for gas and snacks at gas stations.

THINK STRATEGICALLY
How do you see the future of NFC and RFID technology in relation to the entire sales process? Will it be a positive or negative force?

@ **Online Action!** Go to *marketingessentials.glencoe.com/15/case* to find a research project on sales closes that do not involve human beings.

 marketingessentials.glencoe.com

Case Study   The Electronic Close

Discussion Ask students what it will take for sales through mobile phones to succeed. Responses might include people buying phones with the RFID technology and major stores promoting the process.

THINK STRATEGICALLY **Answer:** Answers will vary; many students will agree that it is a positive force toward making purchases easier for both customers and salespeople.

 @ **Online Action!** For instructions, ideas, and answer guide, go to the Teacher Center at **marketingessentials.glencoe.com**

GLOBAL MARKET

Hong Kong Octopus Is a Hit

The Octopus card, an electronic money card, has become a widely accepted electronic currency in Hong Kong. The card can be used to buy a newspaper at 7-Eleven, a meal at a fast-food restaurant, and even coffee at Starbucks. In all, more than 12,000 locations across Hong Kong accept the card.

A Hard-Working Card Octopus is a stored-value card and works like a debit card. Money is automatically subtracted from the card's monetary value when the card is held over a reading device. This device is a low-range radio transmitter that can be incorporated into doors, turnstiles, and countertops. Because reading devices can detect a card through leather and plastic, many people never remove their card but rather wave their purse or wallet over the reader. There is even a $35 Octopus wristwatch with the card technology built in.

Funds can be added to the cards at machines in subway stations, convenience stores, and via an automatic draw from a bank account.

CRITICAL THINKING

In which specialized closing method would the Hong Kong Octopus card be helpful?

@ Online Action!

Go to *marketingessentials.glencoe.com/15/global* to find a research project about proprietary debit cards.

---

remember that your primary interest is customer satisfaction.

Specialized Methods for Closing the Sale

Attempt to close the sale as soon as you recognize a buying signal. How you go about this depends on the selling situation. Certain selling situations warrant the use of specialized methods, including the which, standing-room-only, direct, and service closes.

Which Close

The **which close** encourages a customer to make a decision between two items. Follow the general rules for closing a sale and remove unwanted items to bring the selection down to two. Review the benefits of each item and then ask the customer, "Which one do you prefer?"

Standing-Room-Only Close

The **standing-room-only close** is used when a product is in short supply or when the price will be going up in the near future. This close should be used only when the situation honestly calls for it because it may be perceived as a high-pressure tactic. In many situations, a sales person can honestly say, "I'm sorry, but I can't promise that I'll be able to make you this same offer later." This approach is often used in selling high-demand real estate. Customers must often be prompted to act on a hot property that will be off the market quickly.

Direct Close

The **direct close** is a method in which you ask for the sale. You would use the direct close method when the buying signal is very strong. Here are a few direct close approaches: "Can I assume that we're ready to talk about the details of your order?" "It appears you like

---

GLOBAL MARKET

Hong Kong Octopus Is a Hit

Discussion Ask students to brainstorm other ideas for Octopus devices. Ideas may include key chains, necklaces, or other items that may be worn or carried easily.

CRITICAL THINKING **Answer:** The Octopus card would be most helpful with the service close. If a customer did not have enough cash on hand to make a purchase, a salesperson could suggest the Octopus.

@ Online Action! For instructions, ideas, and answer guide, go to the Teacher Center at **marketingessentials.glencoe.com**

Follow Up Let students know that certain colleges and other groups use such cards. Some offer extra money per deposit to encourage the card's usage over debit cards.

TEACH CONTINUED

Individualized Practice

SPECIALIZED METHODS FOR CLOSING THE SALE

Set this scene for students: You are a sales associate for an electronics boutique. It is the last day of the week, and you are $300 short of your weekly sales quota. You have just spent 30 minutes with a couple who are looking at portable TVs. They are having difficulty choosing between a model that is on sale for $349 and another model priced at $399. At this point, your supervisor asks you to take a lunch break because she expects the store to be busy in half an hour.

L1 Ask students to identify close options in the above situation.

Answers will vary; options may include taking a break, making a trial close, handing the customers off to another salesperson, or continuing to help the customers and asking for a break after the busy period.

L2 Have students identify at least three close options in the above situation and select the best one, explaining their decision in a one-page response.

Answers will vary and may include taking a break, making a trial close, handing the customers off to another salesperson, or continuing to help the customers and asking for a break after the busy period. Most will agree that the latter option is the best.

L3 Have small groups of students identify at least three options and role-play them in front of the class. Have the class decide which option is the best.

Most students should agree that continuing to help the customers and asking for a break after the busy period is the best option.

ASSESS

Review Guide

CONCEPTS

Ask students to recall the general rules for closing the sale.

Recognize closing opportunities, help customers make a decision, create an ownership mentality, do not talk too much, and do not rush.

KEY TERMS

Divide the key terms in two lists, and have half of the class study one of them. Have the halves quiz each other on the terms' spellings and meanings.

ONLINE SELF-ASSESSMENT

Have students go to **marketing.essentials.glencoe.com** for the Section 15.1 practice test.

Individualized Review

L1 Assign and review Chapter 15 activities in the Student Activity Workbook.

L2 Assign and review Chapter 15 activities in the Marketing Math Workbook.

L3 Assign and review Chapter 15 activities in the *BusinessWeek* Reader and Case Studies.

Marketing Practice

Divide the class into four groups. Assign a specialized method of closing the sale to each group. Have groups write scripts and present role plays that demonstrate their method in a retail situation. Have each group perform their role plays in class.

---

everything I have shown you. Now we just need to discuss the quantity you will need."

In a retail situation, you might ask about payment: For example, "How would you like to pay for this purchase—cash, check, or credit card?"

Service Close

Sometimes you may run into obstacles or instances that require special services to close the sale. The **service close** is a closing method in which you explain services that overcome obstacles or problems. Such services include gift wrapping, a return policy, special sales arrangements, warranties and guarantees, and bonuses or premiums. You might want to explain the store's return policy when a customer hesitates but seems to be willing to make the purchase anyway. This is an especially good idea when a customer is purchasing the item as a gift for someone else.

Special sales arrangements are used to close the sale when the customer needs help in paying for the item or order.

The Service Close in Business-to-Business Situations

In an industrial selling situation, the sales representative would talk about the terms of the sale, discussing points such as when payment is expected. For example, payment could be due 30 or 60 days after the date of the invoice.

A customer may also need information about credit terms to help him or her decide to buy. In other cases, the customer may need a sample to try out before purchasing large quantities. Sometimes, offering a sampling program is beneficial if it is a new purchase or the buyer is changing vendors and needs proof that your product is a better substitute for the one currently being used.

The Service Close in Retail

In a retail selling situation, the use of credit and checks, as well as special buying plans such as layaway, can be suggested. When a customer questions the quality of the

---

merchandise, perhaps you can explain that a warranty or guarantee is offered on the product. When your business offers the same quality merchandise at the same price as your competitors, your service may be the only factor that affects the buying decision.

Failure to Close the Sale

Do not assume that every sales presentation should result in a sale. Even the best salespeople can sell to only a fraction of the prospects they call on. Research suggests that perseverance is the way to succeed.

In a retail setting, invite the customer to shop in your store again. In a business-to-business selling situation, ask if you may call again. In business-to-business selling, the sale is rarely closed on the first call. Business-to-business salespeople may negotiate with large accounts for over a year before closing the sale. Also remember that every sales contract has the potential to become a successful sale in the future.

Get Feedback

Experienced salespeople capitalize on defeat and come away from an unsuccessful selling experience with something to show for it. It is important to keep in mind that even a customer who does not make a purchase is still a prospect for future business. Be alert to what purchases today's non-buyer might make in the future.

If you have established an excellent rapport with the buyer, you may be able to ask him or her what factors led to the decision to buy from another source. A request for constructive criticism may work for you if you have earned the buyer's respect.

Maintain a Positive Attitude

The attitude of the salesperson who has not made the sale should be no different than that of the successful salesperson. It is very important for the salesperson to smile and be friendly after failing to make a sale. In business-to-business selling situations, it is not uncommon for a buyer to be convinced

---

Online Activity

Web Returns

The service close entails explaining special services such as return policies on items that are to be given as gifts. Have students look up Web sites of local stores to see how they handle gift returns and summarize their findings in a five-minute oral report or one-paragraph analysis.

by a sales presentation but not yet ready to buy.

In such a situation, it is extremely important that the salesperson leave an opening for a return sales call. Return calls can increase sales costs, so consider the situation carefully before bowing out.

Preparing for Future Sales Calls

If you clearly sense an impending turndown, it is better to make a graceful exit, leaving the door open for a future sales call.

Some businesses send questionnaires or call customers to check on how well they were treated by the sales and service staff. The results of these surveys are passed on to salespeople so they can improve their sales techniques.

Success in Sales

One popular misconception about selling is that salespeople are born, not made. It is true that effective salespeople possess certain behavioral characteristics, including confidence, problem-solving ability, honesty, and a sincere desire to be helpful.

However, success in selling is the result of training, apprenticeship, and experience. Learning one's products and how to handle various situations comes with experience and hard work.

Ask students to recall and provide answers to the following questions:

- **What are buying signals?**
  The things customers do or say to indicate a readiness to buy, including facial expressions, body language, and comments.

- **When are special sales arrangements used to close the sale?**
  When the customer needs help in paying for the item or order.

Critical Thinking

Ask students to brainstorm some ways a salesperson can maintain a positive attitude. Answers will vary and may include a sense of perspective and stress management techniques.

15.1 AFTER YOU READ

Reviewing Key Terms and Concepts

1. Why are trial closes beneficial?
2. Why should a salesperson stop talking about a product once a customer gives strong buying signals?
3. A customer seems to be frustrated because she likes three of the items you have shown her. What specialized closing method would you use to make her buying decision easier?

Integrating Academic Skills

Math

4. To close the sale, you offer layaway as an option, which requires a 20 percent deposit. What would the required deposit be on a $350 coat?

Language Arts

5. Write two paragraphs explaining how and when to close a sale. Also write examples of three different specialized methods of closing using a product of interest to you.

 Online Action!

Check your answers at *marketingessentials.glencoe.com/15/read*

marketingessentials.glencoe.com

Chapter 15 - Closing the Sale **319**

AFTER YOU READ

Reviewing Key Terms and Concepts

1. Trial closes are beneficial because if they do not work, customers will most likely tell you why they are not ready to buy, and if they do work, you will close the sale.

2. After a customer has decided to buy, a salesperson should stop talking about the product because it may have a negative effect on the sale.

3. You would use the *which close* specialized closing method, where you would make her buying decision easier by narrowing the selection of items to two and review the benefits of each.

Integrating Academic Skills

4. $70; $350 × .20 = $70

5. Paragraphs will vary based on the product selected. Students should provide examples of the *which close*, the *direct close*, and the *standing-room-only close*.

 Online Action! Answers at **marketingessentials.glencoe.com/15/read**

FOCUS

Introducing the Section

COLLABORATIVE ACTIVITY

Have students imagine that they work at a men's dress suit store. Ask: After a customer buys a suit, what items can be sold to that customer through suggestion selling? Have students share their responses in class.

Answers will vary and may include ties, shirts, tie pins, cuff links, and belts.

Preteaching Key Terms

Read the key terms aloud or have a student volunteer to read them aloud. Ask students to look up their meanings and share examples from their experience.

- suggestion selling
- customer relationship management

Critical Thinking

Ask students: How does suggestion selling enhance customer satisfaction? Answers will vary; students may offer that suggestion selling allows a salesperson to give customers the best product or service available and also shows that the salesperson is looking out for the customers' needs.

OBJECTIVES

- Explain the importance of suggestion selling
- List the rules for effective suggestion selling
- Demonstrate appropriate specialized suggestion selling methods
- Discuss strategies for maintaining and building a clientele
- Explain the importance of customer service and follow-up
- Explain the concept of customer relationship management

KEY TERMS

- suggestion selling
- customer relationship management

Connect Have you ever experienced suggestion selling? Give examples.

Customer Satisfaction and Retention

READ and STUDY

BEFORE YOU READ
Predict What are some ways to maintain customer loyalty?

THE MAIN IDEA
The goal of selling is to help customers make satisfying buying decisions so that they buy from you again. In this section, you will learn how to create a relationship with your customers so that they will continue to do business with you in the future.

STUDY ORGANIZER
Prepare charts similar to the two below to summarize the key points to remember for suggestion selling and maintaining and building a clientele.

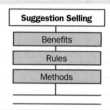

Effective Selling

Maintaining and building a clientele is crucial for future sales. The actual sale is just the beginning of a relationship with a customer. To keep customers, it is important to make a good impression, get to know your customers, and provide excellent customer service.

READ and STUDY

BEFORE YOU READ
Have students list stores or brands to which they are loyal and provide reasons why.

THE MAIN IDEA
Ask a volunteer to read the main idea aloud and ask another student to retell it in his or her own words.

STUDY ORGANIZER
Show students how they can outline the section according to the chart. A full-size, downloadable study organizer can be found at marketingessentials.glencoe.com

Experiences will vary, but may include clerks at a fast-food restaurant. Have students recall other examples as they read the section.

320

Suggestion Selling

Suggestion selling is selling additional goods or services to the customer. It involves selling customers other items that will ultimately save time and money or make the original purchase more enjoyable.

Consider the customer who buys an electronic toy for a child, takes it home, and only then realizes that he or she has no batteries for it. The salesperson would have had a sure sale with a suggestion to buy batteries.

Benefits of Suggestion Selling

Suggestion selling benefits the salesperson, the customer, and the company. You benefit because customers will want to do business with you again, and as a result of your efforts, your sales will increase. Since salespeople are often evaluated on their sales figures, you will be viewed as an effective salesperson. Your customer benefits because he or she is more pleased with the original purchase. The firm benefits because the time and cost involved in suggestion selling is less than the cost of making the original sale.

Consider the two purchases in the following chart. The second includes an extra item, a suggestion from the salesperson. Note that the extra time spent on suggestion selling significantly increased the firm's net profits. Expenses rose, but not in proportion to the sales volume. There are two reasons for this. First, less time and effort are needed for suggestion selling compared with the initial sale. Second, certain business expenses (such as utilities and rent) remain the same despite the extra sales activity.

Purchase 1		Purchase 2	
Pants	$75	Pants	$ 75
		Shirt	$ 35
Total	$75	Total	$110
Cost of goods	−$37	Cost of goods	−$55
Gross Profit	$38	Gross Profit	$55
Expenses	−$12	Expenses	−$15
Net profit	$26	Net profit	$40

Rules for Suggestion Selling

Here are five basic rules for suggestion selling:

1. **Use suggestion selling after the customer has made a commitment to buy but before payment is made or the order written.** Introducing additional merchandise before the sale has been closed can create pressure for the customer. The only exception to this rule involves products whose accessories are a major benefit. Let's say you are showing a retailer a new type of video game system. To clinch the sale, you may need to tell the retailer about the exciting new video games that will be sold in conjunction with that new system.

2. **Make your recommendation from the customer's point of view and give at least one reason for your suggestion.** You might say, "For your child to enjoy this toy immediately, you'll need two AAA batteries."

3. **Make the suggestion definite.** Don't ask, "Will that be all?" Instead say, "This oil is recommended by the manufacturer for this engine." In most cases, general questions invite a negative response.

4. **Show the item you are suggesting.** Merely talking about it is not enough. In many cases, the item will sell itself if you let the customer see and handle it. You may put a matching purse next to the shoes a customer has just decided to buy, particularly with some commentary. You might say, "This purse matches your shoes perfectly, doesn't it?"

5. **Make the suggestion positive.** You could say, "Let me show you the matching top to that skirt. It will complete the outfit beautifully."

Suggestion Selling Methods

Three methods are used in suggestion selling: offering related merchandise, recommending larger quantities, and calling attention to special sales opportunities. Figure 15.1 shows an example of using suggestion selling.

Chapter 15 - Closing the Sale 321

Online Activity

Online Suggestion Selling

Show students pages taken from online retail stores that state something like "customers who order the item that you ordered also buy this item." Ask students if they would consider more items as a result of this type of suggestion selling. Answers will vary; many will say yes because the suggestion selling is personalized.

TEACH

Discussion Starter

SUGGESTION SELLING

To prepare for reading this section, ask students what a clerk at a restaurant often says to you after you order a sandwich.

An answer might be "Would you like fries/ a beverage/soft drink with that?"

TEACHING POINTS

Clarify Let students know that suggestion selling requires little work from the clerk and very often increases an order.

Role Play Role-play suggestion selling examples from different types of stores: For example, a shoe store might have, "Would you like socks to go with those shoes?"; an electronic store might have, "Would you like batteries with that MP3 player?"; and a skateboard shop might have, "Would you like ball bearings to go with those wheels?"

Concept Development

SUGGESTION SELLING

Have students share or brainstorm examples of experiences in which a salesperson's suggestion selling might not be appreciated. Ask them to explain the circumstances.

Answers will vary and may include an electronics store salesperson pushing a warranty that costs almost as much as the product.

TEACH CONTINUED

Individualized Practice

SUGGESTION SELLING METHODS

Ask students to consider a situation in which an auto salesperson uses follow-up techniques.

L1 Have students identify follow-up techniques that could be used by auto dealers.

Answers may include sending customers letters thanking them for their business, including the customer in a satisfaction survey, and offering reduced pricing on the first routine maintenance service.

L2 Have students select a follow-up technique and describe it in a one-page memo to management. Ask them to cite the benefits of the suggested technique.

L3 Have students create a one-page letter that would be sent to customers as part of a follow-up technique used by an auto dealer.

Enrichment

SUGGESTION SELLING OPPORTUNITIES

Have students research cultural, religious or national holidays, such as Rosh Hashanah, Cinco de Mayo, Ramadan, Christmas, Kwanzaa, Hanukkah, Valentine's Day, Father's Day, and Mother's Day. Ask them to create a calendar listing those holidays and others in which special foods are eaten and/or gifts are given or exchanged. Have students then write a one- to two-page report about how a business of their choice can use the events to increase sales. Interested students can write their reports on a particular demographic or another country.

Figure 15.1 *Suggestion Selling*

- **Suggestion Selling in Business-to-Business Sales** Once customers decide to buy, it is a good practice to suggest something specific to help them enjoy their purchase. This practice is known as suggestion selling. Three methods are commonly used in suggestion selling. Let's examine how they might be used by a sales representative for a clothing manufacturer in a business-to-business sale.

What are some examples of suggestion selling?

UP-SELLING

A sales representative may suggest buying larger quantities of goods so a customer qualifies for special discounts, payment terms, or delivery charges. Retailers may also receive free merchandise.

CROSS-SELLING

The sales representative may suggest related merchandise to the retail store buyer. The rationale is that customers may need accessories and related items.

SPECIAL SALES OPPORTUNITIES

When a manufacturer runs a special promotion on products or wants to introduce a new product, it is up to the sales representative to share that information with the retailer.

 Online Action! Go to *marketingessentials.glencoe.com/15/figure/1* for a project on suggestion selling.

Figure 15.1 *Suggestion Selling*

Discussion After students read **Figure 15.1**, have them brainstorm ways that suggestion selling benefits the customer and business. Responses might include that suggestion selling helps a customer better enjoy his or her purchase and possibly prevents a second trip to the store.

Caption Answer Examples will vary; answers might include buying a second item for half-price, an accessory to go with an article of clothing, or extra memory for a digital camera.

Online Action! For instructions, ideas, and answer guide, go to the Teacher Center at **marketingessentials.glencoe.com**

Offering Related Merchandise

In some businesses, this method is called cross-selling. You use the opportunity at the end of a sale to introduce another product of possible interest to the customer. Introducing related merchandise is probably the easiest and most effective suggestion selling method.

Recommending Larger Quantities

Suggesting a larger quantity is often referred to as up-selling. This method works in retail settings when selling inexpensive items or when savings in money or time and convenience are involved.

In business-to-business sales situations, the salesperson may suggest a larger quantity so that the customer can take advantage of lower prices or special considerations.

Calling Attention to Special Sales Opportunities

Salespeople are obligated to communicate special sales opportunities to their customers.

In retail sales, routinely inform your customer of the arrival of new merchandise. Regular customers appreciate this special service because they like having the opportunity to see new merchandise before others do.

In business-to-business sales situations, sales representatives often show new items to their customers after they have completed the sale of merchandise requested. Thus, the salesperson establishes a rapport with the customer before introducing new merchandise.

Maintaining and Building a Clientele

Making a sale is the first step in maintaining and building a clientele. After-sale activities by the sales and customer service staff, as well as customer relationship management strategies employed by the company, are two key factors in building a clientele.

After-Sales Activities

After-sale activities include order processing, departure, order fulfillment, follow-up, and customer service. All these activities need to be handled in such a way that it generates repeat business.

Order Processing

In retail selling, bag the merchandise with care. Products such as glassware may require individual wrapping before bagging. Work quickly to bag your customer's merchandise and complete the payment process. In business-to-business sales, complete the paperwork quickly and leave a business card.

Departure

Before the customer departs or before you leave your client's office, reassure the person of his or her wise buying choices. If an item needs special care or specific instructions, take the time to educate your customer about it. You may want to remind the customer, for example, that to get the best results from a Teflon-coated frying pan, it should be preheated. Helpful comments like this will make your customer feel you are interested and concerned.

Always thank your customers. Even when a customer does not buy, express your gratitude for the time and attention given to you. Invite him or her back to the store, or ask for permission to call again in the near future.

Order Fulfillment

In a retail store, fulfillment is a simple process of the customer paying for merchandise and carrying it away. In e-commerce, mail order, or telemarketing sales, order fulfillment gets more complicated. It includes taking the order, financial processing (such as credit card information), picking the right product, packing it well, and shipping it according to the customer's preference. In some companies, fulfillment also includes customer service, technical support, managing inventory, and handling returns and refunds. The goal, of course, is to make the customer happy.

In the new e-commerce economy, success often depends as much on appropriate fulfillment strategies as it does on having the right product at the right price. Some of the most successful online retailers have established

Online Activity

Packaging

Have students research Web sites that provide information about bagging and packaging options. Ask them write a paragraph explaining how the packaging and protecting of products help a business' customer relations, giving specific examples of how items can be packaged and sent.

Concept Development

AFTER-SALES ACTIVITIES

Ask students to present their experiences of after-sales activities. Have them state if such actions by the salespeople make it more likely for them to give return business.

Examples will vary, most students should agree that departure, follow-up, and other after-sales activities are appreciated by most customers.

TEACHING POINTS

Model Share examples of after-sales activities you have experienced, such as follow-up calls, e-mails from e-tailers, or letters from educational publishers.

Build Vocabulary

Preview the following words by reading them in context in the section Maintaining and Building a Clientele. Have students explain what they think the words mean:

- fulfillment
  to carry out something promised, desired, or expected

- clientele
  all one's clients and customers, collectively

- empathetic
  of or characterized by the ability to share in a person's emotions, thoughts, or feelings

Critical Thinking

Ask students if there are cases where it is not ethical to suggest buying more quantities of a product. Answers will vary, but students may say that items that spoil or deteriorate quickly should not be sold in high quantities.

TEACH CONTINUED

Concept Development

KEEPING A CLIENT FILE

Let students know that client files are more important for business-to-business sales than retail sales. Ask students to brainstorm reasons why this might be. In business-to-business situations, sales-people and customers see each other more often, and build relationships that may last for years. Retail sales are often more casual, but can also develop into personal relationships.

TEACHING POINTS

Demonstrate On the chalkboard, create the outline of a customer file. Information might include name, marital status, children, and hobbies, which can be used to plan small talk for future customer visits. Have interested students create their own customer file for a store or store type of their choice.

Critical Thinking

Ask students why department stores hold sales on President's Day, Memorial Day, and other holidays in which gifts are not given. Answers will vary, but students may suggest that days off work or school are often spent shopping. Also, a holiday like Memorial Day coincides with the commencement of a new school year.

NET MARKETING

Partnership Selling

Digitizing traditional media such as music, photography, or art enables it to be marketed and purchased entirely over the Web. In 2002, IBM announced that the National Geographic Society (NGS) was digitizing and making commercially available 10,000 of its renowned images. NGS planned to add at least 3,000 images a year out of its database of more than 10 million images. IBM provided the computer technology and expertise, and National Geographic provided the images to make this partnership happen.

Better Customer Service

Customers such as advertising agencies, publishers, and others could view, analyze, sort, and purchase NGS images of culture and nature on demand. "IBM's solution is helping NGS serve our customers worldwide more effectively by making our images available in the digital marketplace," said Maura Mulvihill, the National Geographic's image collection vice president.

THINK LIKE A MARKETER

How does IBM demonstrate the concept of partnership selling in the digital marketplace?

@ Online Action!

Go to *marketingessentials.glencoe.com/15/net* to find a research activity about digitizing media.

---

their own fulfillment centers to ensure prompt delivery. Amazon.com, BarnesandNoble.com, and Dell Computer all have their own fulfillment centers. Another approach is to outsource fulfillment to a third party. This allows a company to concentrate their resources on marketing the products.

Follow-Up

The follow-up includes making arrangements to follow through on all promises made during the sales process. It also includes checking on your customer's satisfaction with his or her purchase. Here are a few follow-up ideas:

- Call the shipping department to confirm a special delivery date.
- Check to make sure that delivery occurs as promised.

- Call the customer and explain any delay.
- Phone the customer a week or two after the purchase to see if he or she is happy with the selection.
- Send a thank-you note with your business card attached.

Customer Service

Some firms have customer service departments to handle customer inquires and complaints. For example, in some auto dealerships, specific customer service representatives are assigned to each customer to handle appointments and questions with auto problems and regular servicing. In business-to-business sales, customer complaints should be provided to the sales representatives responsible for those customers.

324 UNIT 5 - SELLING

NET MARKETING

Partnership Selling

Discussion After students read Net Marketing, lead a discussion about partnerships. What are some other kinds of businesses that the National Geographic Society could have partnered with? Have students explain their responses. Answers may include other computer-related companies such as Apple or a photo agency such as Getty Images.

THINK LIKE A MARKETER Answer: IBM demonstrates the concepts of partnership selling by acting as a consultant and partner in helping companies solve their technology problems.

@ Online Action! For instructions, ideas, and answer guide, go to the Teacher Center at **marketingessentials.glencoe.com**

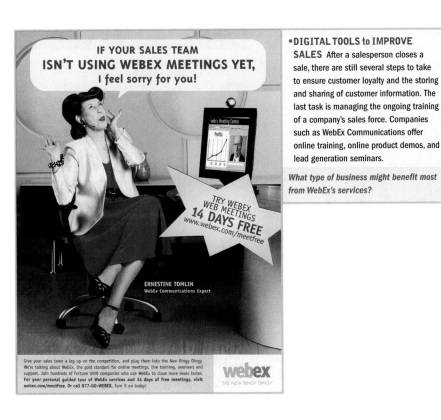

IF YOUR SALES TEAM
ISN'T USING WEBEX MEETINGS YET,
I feel sorry for you!

TRY WEBEX
WEB MEETINGS
14 DAYS FREE
www.webex.com/meetfree

ERNESTINE TOMLIN
WebEx Communications Expert

Give your sales team a leg up on the competition, and plug them into the *New Ringy Dingy*. We're talking about WebEx, the gold standard for online meetings, live training, seminars and support. Join hundreds of Fortune 1000 companies who use WebEx to close more deals faster. For your personal guided tour of WebEx services and 14 days of free meetings, visit webex.com/meetfree. Or call 877-GO-WEBEX. Turn it on today!

webex
THE NEW RINGY DINGY

• **DIGITAL TOOLS to IMPROVE SALES** After a salesperson closes a sale, there are still several steps to take to ensure customer loyalty and the storing and sharing of customer information. The last task is managing the ongoing training of a company's sales force. Companies such as WebEx Communications offer online training, online product demos, and lead generation seminars.

What type of business might benefit most from WebEx's services?

How these complaints are handled is crucial to maintaining clientele. Customers expect immediate action when they file a complaint. Positive customer-client relations require compassionate and understanding personnel and sales associates who are problem solvers. The main goal is customer satisfaction.

Keeping a Client File

You can use the time immediately after the sale to plan for your next encounter with the customer. Take notes on your conversation with the customer. Keep this in a file for future reference. In retail sales, note a customer's preference in color, style, and size, as well as the person's address and telephone number. In business-to-business selling, record personal information on the buyer's marital status, children, and hobbies to assist with future sales visits. Record changes in buying patterns that may lead to future sales. You also want to note any future service dates for appliances or cars so that you can send a reminder when the time comes. Also be sure to inform your company of any changes you uncover, such as changes in personnel responsible for buying, as well as address or telephone changes so that company files can be kept up to date.

Evaluate Your Sales Efforts

Even if your company has a formal method of reviewing your efforts, you should conduct

Chapter 15 - Closing the Sale **325**

AD GUIDE   DIGITAL TOOLS to IMPROVE SALES

Discussion Have students brainstorm advantages and disadvantages of having online training. Ask students to name some of the limitations an online-only training session might have.

Caption Answer A large business with up-to-date technology and many branches in one country or in multiple countries might benefit from using WebEx's services.

 Follow Up Have students research the specifics of WebEx's services and present a summary of them to the class.

Concept Development

CUSTOMER RELATIONSHIP MANAGEMENT (CRM)

Inform students that many online stores have a built-in program that, when you are logged in, recalls the types of products you are interested in and makes customized suggestions for you. Ask them for examples from sites such as Amazon.com or adidas.com, which recall your previous orders and make recommendations based on them.

TEACHING POINTS

Demonstrate If you or your school has an online account with such a retailer, show how the site recalls your previously purchased and recently viewed products.

Clarify Inform students that CRM can be practiced in brick-and-mortar stores as well as online ones. For example, a video store person may make recommendations based on your previous rentals or a shoe store may let you know if a shipment has come in from a shoe manufacturer that you have bought before. Ask students to think of other examples and share them with the class.

Critical Thinking

Ask students: What characteristics are needed by a person who works in customer service? Answers will vary, but may include empathy, a positive attitude, and the ability to handle multiple tasks at once.

ASSESS

Review Guide

CONCEPTS

Ask students to list the rules for effective suggestion selling.

1) Use suggestion selling after the customer has made a commitment to buy but before payment is made or the order is written. 2) Make your recommendation from the customer's point of view and give at least one reason for the suggestion. 3) Make the suggestion definite. 4) Show the item you are suggesting. 5) Make the suggestion positive.

KEY TERMS

Have students review the key terms and their definitions.

ONLINE SELF-ASSESSMENT

Have students go to marketingessentials.glencoe.com for the Section 15.2 practice test.

Individualized Review

L1 Assign and review Chapter 15 activities in the Student Activity Workbook.

L2 Assign and review Chapter 15 activities in the Marketing Math Workbook.

L3 Assign and review Chapter 15 activities in the *BusinessWeek* Reader and Case Studies.

Marketing Practice

Have students assume they work at a shop that offers cell phones, accessories, and plans. Ask them to develop examples of each type of suggestion selling: up-selling, cross-selling, and special sales opportunities.

Examples include selling multi-phone packages selling chargers with phones, or offering free phones with plans.

---

your own evaluation. In your evaluation, consider the following:

- What were the strong points of your sales presentation?
- What did you do wrong?
- How could you have improved your performance?
- What would you do differently next time?
- What can you do now to solidify your relationship with your customer if you made the sale?

Objective self-evaluation is a helpful tool in any career. Asking yourself these questions can help you improve your selling skills as well as your business skills in general. They will enable you to look forward to your next sales opportunity. That kind of attitude will help you become more effective with each sales contact. It will also help you become more successful in building a strong relationship with your customers.

Customer Relationship Management (CRM)

A popular trend among companies today is **customer relationship management** (CRM), which involves finding customers and keeping them satisfied. CRM provides companies with the means to develop and nurture customer relationships, including lead generation, sales support, customer service, and other after-sale activities.

Technology and CRM

Technology can play a role in this endeavor. Some companies purchase software that can be customized for their business. Others may subscribe to the services of Web-based companies for similar CRM services. For example, Siebel CRM OnDemand and salesforce.com host customer relationship management services. According to a case study at Siebel's Web site, General Orthodontic selected Siebel CRM OnDemand when General Orthodontic realized it needed to manage an overwhelming

---

number of new sales leads. Since it was a start-up company, it also had to keep costs down and still provide a high level of customer service if it wanted to be successful.

The value of a good relationship is not a new idea. Marketers have long recognized that identifying the needs of customers and satisfying them can be profitable. However, only recently have firms made a dedicated effort to use customer relationship management.

By examining successful partnerships in business and elsewhere, marketers have discovered that enduring relationships are built on trust and commitment and require a lot of time and effort to maintain.

Maintaining Contact

To maintain sales accounts, it is important to offer solutions to problems and to stay in contact, acting as a partner or consultant for your customers. For example, a manufacturer of artificial knees or hips may actually be present in the operating room during such a procedure in case there is a question or problem.

You may have seen commercials for IBM and American Express, where they stress their commitment to their customers in providing solutions to their problems, thus demonstrating consultative selling. That commitment signifies their role in relationship building. For example, IBM helped the National Geographic Society with its own photography e-commerce site.

Maintain Relationships

Relationship marketing is alive and well in both traditional and e-commerce marketing. Consider the example set by Harley-Davidson, the motorcycle manufacturer. The company established a club for its members, and it markets services such as motorcycle insurance and travel assistance to those members.

An e-commerce example of relationship marketing is Amazon.com's practice of collecting information about customers' book purchases and then e-mailing personalized

---

Extended Activity

Benefit Comparison

Have students look at Web sites or advertisements for at least three airline companies and research the types of frequent flyer plans available. Ask students to make a chart comparing the benefits of each airline frequent flyer plan.

---

information about promotions and merchandise within the customer's established range of interest.

Develop Customers Loyalty

Customer loyalty cannot be taken for granted, especially with the high level of competition in today's market. A company can stay close to its customers and keep them happy by having the sale be the first step in developing a relationship, not the final one.

Think of after-sale activities as part of an ongoing dialog with customers in preparation for future sales. This is simplified with the use of e-mail, which can be used to keep customers informed about sales, new products, and important company news.

Customer Loyalty and Reward Programs

Some companies also reward their regular customers through loyalty programs such as frequent flier programs. E-mailed questionnaires with prize entries or advance notice of special sales are other practices marketers have developed to create and reinforce loyalty. You can also send that information in the mail or have a customer service representative communicate with your customers by phone.

 15.2 AFTER YOU READ

Reviewing Key Terms and Concepts

1. Explain how suggestion selling can increase a firm's net profit.
2. List three related items that could be used for suggestion selling after a customer's decision to buy a bicycle.
3. How can a salesperson use the time immediately after the sale to plan for his or her next encounter with that customer?

Integrating Academic Skills

Math

4. You sold a $715 item via the Internet to a European customer, a Japanese customer, and a New Zealand customer. Use the chart below to calculate the total amount due for the product and applicable duties and customs for each of the three customers.

	Europe	Japan	New Zealand
Duties & Customs	20%	9%	50%

Language Arts

5. Write about suggestion selling and measures that can be taken to build and maintain clientele in the sale of a product of your choice. Provide examples of related merchandise that can be suggested in the sale of that product, and specific measures that can be taken in after-sale activities and customer relationship management.

 Online Action! Check your answers at *marketingessentials.glencoe.com/15/read*

marketingessentials.glencoe.com

Chapter 15 - Closing the Sale **327**

 CLOSE

Ask students to recall and provide answers to the following questions:

- **What is customer relationship management (CRM)?**
  The finding of customers and keeping them satisfied.

- **What is suggestion selling?**
  Selling additional goods or services to the customer.

Critical Thinking

Ask students why keeping and maintaining customer loyalty is a common challenge in the many industries. Answers may include increased competition and rapidly improving customer service due to technology and training.

AFTER YOU READ

Reviewing Key Terms and Concepts

1. Less time and effort are required for suggestion selling compared to the initial sale. Also, despite the extra sales, certain business expenses, such as utilities and rent, remain the same.

2. Answers will vary; bicycle-related items might include a helmet, basket, special seat, or apparel.

3. A salesperson can plan for his or her next encounter with the customer by taking notes on their conversation. The salesperson can then keep these notes on file for future reference.

Integrating Academic Skills

4. Europe: $715 × 1.2 = $858
   Japan: $715 × 1.09 = $770.35
   New Zealand: $715 × 1.5 = $1,072.50

5. Reports will vary depending on the products students have selected for the project. Answers should include specific after-sales measures and customer relationship management strategies.

Online Action! Answers at **marketingessentials.glencoe.com/15/read**

327

CAREERS
IN MARKETING

Lifelong Learning

CAREER INFORMATION

Have students go to marketingessentials.glencoe.com and find the Chapter 15 Careers page and click on the link for the American Marketing Association's Careers Strategies and Tips. Ask students to select one article, read it, and use visual art materials or graphic design software to create a poster that illustrates its main points.

CLOSING THE SALE

Students can apply their customer service and sales skills to other areas of their lives. Activities such as buying a car, choosing your educational path, renting a place to live, or joining a health club all involve dealing with sales or service representatives. Knowing how salespeople think can help you to get what you want and need.

Primary Source

Ask students to go to marketingessentials.glencoe.com and find the Chapter 15 Resources. Ask them to click on the link for the American Marketing Association's marketing dictionary and read the definitions of the terms they find which are related to closing the sale.

THINKING CRITICALLY

Working on smaller prospects may reap more immediate results and build loyalty, as well as lead to bigger prospects.

@ Online Action!

For instructions, ideas, and answer guide, go to the Teacher Center at marketingessentials.glencoe.com

---

EMILY EBERS-GERMER
SALES REPRESENTATIVE
EBERS & ASSOCIATES
BUSINESS PRINTING

(?) What do you do at work?
My job consists mainly of talking to my customers, setting goals, making cold calls, developing leads, and talking to people and letting them know what I do. Customer service involves keeping the customers I already have. Every one of them is important! I am pretty much available to all my customers by phone, fax, e-mail, cell phone, and through my Web site.

(?) What skills are most important to you?
If I were to hire someone, they would have to have sales experience. You can teach them about printing, but if someone does not have "it," it won't happen. "It" is personality, attitude, the ability to talk to anyone and put a smile on your face whether you mean it or not. You have to open your mouth and ask questions, and find out what people need and what you can do for them.

(?) What is your key to success?
I think my success has been mainly due to my customer service. No customer is too small for me to give them my undivided attention. My base of customers are small businesses. They usually stay with you; they are loyal.

Aptitudes, Abilities, and Skills

Organization and time management, strong people skills, an outgoing personality

Education and Training

Degrees in marketing and general business are helpful, as are industry-specific sales courses.

Career Path

Since most sales representative positions are commission-only, they can be relatively easy to land. Proving yourself in an entry-level sales position can quickly lead to virtually unlimited opportunities.

THINKING CRITICALLY

Why can sales reps find success by focusing on smaller prospects, rather than working to land larger accounts?

@ Online Action!

Go to *marketingessentials.glencoe.com/15/careers* to find a research project on customer service.

 marketingessentials.glencoe.com

Test-Taking Strategies

Ask students to write the chapter objectives on flash cards and quiz themselves to review the chapter concepts. When they are satisfied that they have learned a new concept, they can remove the card and concentrate on the concepts that remain. Students can also make cards to review vocabulary terms or mathematical formulas.

CHAPTER **15** REVIEW

FOCUS on KEY POINTS

SECTION 15.1

- Customer buying signals help a salesperson determine a customer's readiness to buy, which is important in trial closes.

- Close the sale as soon as the customer is ready to buy.

- Use success in answering objections or presenting a product as an opportunity to close.

- Help customers make a decision and create an ownership mentality.

- Three specialized methods for closing a sale include the which close, the standing-room-only close, and the service close.

SECTION 15.2

- Suggestion selling is important because it helps generate more sales revenue for a company and helps to create more satisfied customers.

- Three specialized suggestion selling methods are (a) offering related merchandise, also referred to as cross-selling; (b) selling larger quantities, also referred to as up-selling; and (c) calling attention to special sales opportunities.

- After-sales activities and customer relationship management (CRM) are important for maintaining and building a clientele. They include order processing, departure, order fulfillment, follow-up, customer service, and keeping a client file, as well as evaluating your sales efforts.

REVIEW VOCABULARY

Define each of the terms below in a short sentence.

1. closing the sale (p. 314)
2. buying signals (p. 315)
3. trial close (p. 315)
4. which close (p. 317)
5. standing-room-only close (p. 317)
6. direct close (p. 317)
7. service close (p. 318)
8. suggestion selling (p. 321)
9. customer relationship management (CRM) (p. 326)

REVIEW FACTS and IDEAS

10. What are customer buying signals? (15.1)
11. List two rules for closing a sale. (15.1)
12. Why is suggestion selling an important step in the sales process? (15.2)
13. What are two rules for suggestion selling? (15.2)
14. Explain the concept of customer relationship management. (15.2)

Chapter 15 - Closing the Sale **329**

REVIEW FACTS and IDEAS

10. Customer buying signals are the things customers do or say to indicate a readiness to buy. Examples include facial expressions, body language, and comments.

11. Answers should include two of the following: recognize closing opportunities, help the customer make a decision, create an ownership mentality, and do not rush the customer, and do not talk too much.

12. Suggestion selling will save the customer time and money or make the original purchase more enjoyable. It may also encourage customer loyalty by satisfying more of his or her needs.

13. Rules may include two of the following: Do suggestion selling after the customer commits to buy but before payment is made or the order is written; make your recommendation from the customer's point of view and give at least one reason for it; make the suggestion definite; show the item you are suggesting; and make the suggestion positive.

14. Customer relationship management (CRM) involves the finding of customers and keeping them happy. CRM helps businesses develop and nurture customer relationships by generating leads, supporting sales, serving customers, and handling after-sales activities.

FOCUS on KEY POINTS

Ask volunteers to read the summaries aloud and give the classroom a real-world example of each of the concepts.

REVIEW VOCABULARY

See glossary for definitions of **1–9**.
A sample definition might read:

1. *Closing the sale* is obtaining positive agreement from the customer to buy.

BUILD SKILLS

15. Workplace Skills

Role plays will vary; all role plays should demonstrate selling and completing the sale. The student who plays the salesperson should use cash, count back change, and properly fold, wrap, and bag merchandise. At the transaction's end, the student should thank the customer and invite him or her to return again.

16. Technology Applications

Presentations will vary, but should include ideas on how to help customer service representatives cross-sell after answering, inquiring, and problem solving.

17. Math Practice

37 meetings ; 30 meetings/month $\times$ 1.25 = 37.5 = approximately 37 meetings

DEVELOP CRITICAL THINKING

18. The Service Close

A service close is utilized to overcome obstacle or problems. For example, gift wrapping and return policies may be explained to a customer who is buying a gift.

19. Explaining and Evaluating Selling Policies

Reports on retailers will vary, but should evaluate their effectiveness, citing sales approaches, merchandise return policies, and payment options.

BUILD SKILLS

15. Workplace Skills

Making a Sale With another student playing the role of a customer, perform a role-play in which you demonstrate how you would sell an item of clothing to an individual customer. Be sure to complete the sales transaction, too.

If possible, use cash as the method of payment to demonstrate your ability to count back change and use a garment to demonstrate the proper way to fold, wrap, and bag merchandise after the sale.

In order to complete this sales role play, remember to end the sales transaction by thanking the customer and inviting him or her to return again.

16. Technology Applications

Prepare a Sales Presentation Suppose you have some ideas on how to help your company's customer service representatives to cross-sell when they finish answering customer inquiries or solving problems customers have with their phone service. Management likes your ideas and wants you to sell your ideas to the entire group of customer service representatives at the next meeting. Use presentation software to present your ideas.

17. Math Practice

Managing Time Mia is a sales associate for a public relations service firm. She attends an average of 30 client meetings a month. Her manager has recently asked sales associates to increase the number of client meetings they have each month by 25 percent. How many meetings will Mia then have?

DEVELOP CRITICAL THINKING

18. The Service Close

What are some situations that require a service close? List at least three examples and explain why a service close would be needed each time.

19. Explaining and Evaluating Selling Policies

Explain the selling policies of three comparable retailers and evaluate their effectiveness. You may want to consider studying the initial approaches used by sales associates, merchandise return policies, and payment options, as well as any other related selling policy that differentiates one store from the other. Use a word processing program to report your findings.

Formative Assessment

Formative assessment is an essential component of classroom work. This type of assessment provides information that is then used as feedback to modify teaching and meet student needs.

L1 Have students write or demonstrate at least three methods of closing a sale.

L2 Have students write a narrative description of two different methods of closing a sale.

L3 Have students write a script and act out three methods of closing a sale. Have the class identify each method and rate its execution by the salesperson.

Reteach If the results of this formative assessment seem low, consider the following activity:

Read each of the section headings aloud. Have students identify the major points of each section and explain them in their own words. Clear up any confusion students may have.

APPLY CONCEPTS

20. Closing the Sale

Different sales situations call for different closing techniques. If one technique does not work, you may want to try another one.

Activity Respond to the following comments in a role play with a classmate by selecting the most appropriate closing method. After the role play, ask your partner to evaluate your response in terms of the method selected and how effective it was.

a. "I like your product, but I don't have enough money in my store's budget at the current time to buy it right now."

b. "I have tried so many different brands of golf clubs that I can't make up my mind."

c. "My sister is very particular about perfume. What if she doesn't like this fragrance?"

d. "I like these shoes, but I am going to wait until they go on sale before buying them."

21. Maintaining Clientele

Select a business of your choice and note the purpose of the business and its clientele.

Activity Prepare an oral and visual presentation of the skills and strategies that sales personnel should use to build and maintain the firm's clientele. Use presentation software to help organize and deliver your ideas in an effective manner.

NET SAVVY

22. Employing Suggestion Selling

Visit a clothing retailer Web site to find products that can be used for suggestion selling in conjunction with the sale of an outdoor sports jacket. List three ways you would use suggestion selling for a product of your choice.

 marketingessentials.glencoe.com

THE DECA CONNECTION

Role Play: Closing the Sale

Situation You are to assume the role of assistant manager of a women's clothing store. The store has good traffic, and the number of sales per day is good. However, the dollar amount of each sale is decreasing. Your store manager (judge) has decided this is because the sales associates are not making effective use of suggestion selling.

Activity The store manager (judge) has asked you to make a presentation about the use of suggestion selling during the next staff meeting.

Evaluation You will be evaluated on how well you meet the following performance indicators:

- Demonstrate suggestion selling
- Assess customer/client needs
- Sell good/service/idea to individuals
- Close the sale
- Conduct staff meetings

@ **Online Action!**

For more information and DECA Prep practice, go to *marketingessentials.glencoe .com/15/DECA*

APPLY CONCEPTS

20. Closing the Sale

Role plays will vary and may include the following:

a. Students may offer extended credit terms, such as 30 or 50 days for payment.

b. Students could narrow the selection down to two sets and then compare the benefits of each.

c. Students should explain the store's refund policy.

d. Students could explain the fact that the customer's shoe size may not be available when the model goes on sale.

21. Maintaining Clientele

Presentations will vary; all presentations should note the purpose of the business and define its clientele.

NET SAVVY

22. Employing Suggestion Selling

Answers will vary; suggestion selling may include cross-selling a waterproofing spray, mentioning a new promotion on matching gloves, or up-selling a second jacket in a different color.

THE DECA CONNECTION

The students should be evaluated on the performance indicators noted in the role play. For another DECA role play, go to the Competitive Events Workbook or the Student Activity Workbook, or go to marketingessentials.glencoe.com/15/DECA

 Online Action! For instructions, ideas, and answer guide, go to the Teacher Center at marketingessentials.glencoe.com

DECA Advisors Corner

Teach students about the Technical Sales Event in the Marketing Representative Events, in which students organize and deliver a sales presentation. The logical presentation of a sale reinforces the competencies of this event.

MINI-QUIZ

Read these sentences to the students and have them volunteer the missing word(s).

1. The _____ is a closing method that encourages a customer to make a decision between two items. (which close)

2. _____ Include order processing, departure, order fulfillment, follow-up, and customer service. (After-sale activities)

For an expanded chapter quiz, go to Chapter 15 in the TeacherWorks CD-ROM and to Chapter 15 in the **Exam View**® Pro Test Generator CD-ROM.

Chapter Overview

Chapter 16 focuses on the concluding steps of the sales process—recording the transaction, presenting the customer with a sales receipt in retail sales, and the forms for a sale in business-to-business sales. It also covers the functions of cash registers, types of sales transactions, and the steps of filling out sales checks, purchase orders, and invoices.

BUILD BACKGROUND

Ask students to think about what happens when they buy something. Do they pay cash? Do they use credit cards? Do they get a receipt? What do they do with their receipts? Then, ask them to imagine being the sales person in these types of transactions. Ask: What would be the most challenging thing about each type of transaction—making change, processing credit cards, or creating receipts? Tell students that in this chapter they will get a chance to learn more about sales transactions and improve their ability to complete a sales transaction.

Why It's Important

Completing and recording the sale is the conclusion to most business transactions. Wrapping up a sale efficiently and documenting it correctly is key to success in marketing.

Prepare to Read

List the section objectives to discuss with students. Have students skim the chapter, looking at pictures, reading captions, and noting their heads. Ask questions to ensure that students have a basic understanding of the chapter structure.

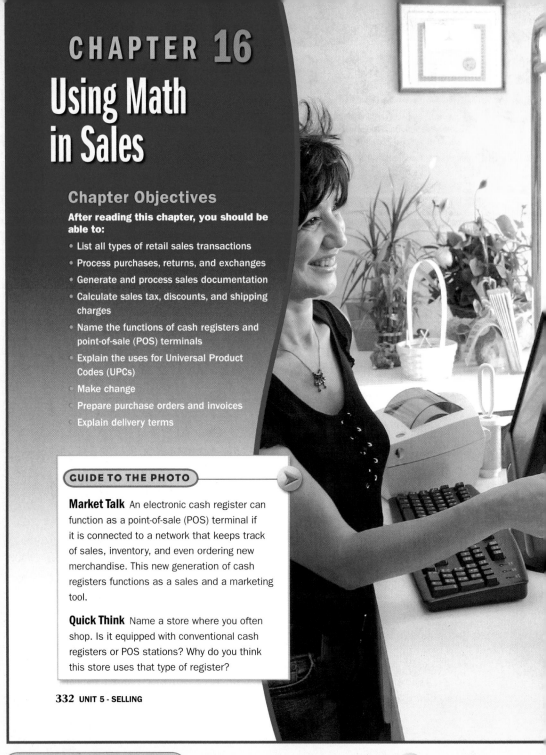

Using Math in Sales

Chapter Objectives

After reading this chapter, you should be able to:

- List all types of retail sales transactions
- Process purchases, returns, and exchanges
- Generate and process sales documentation
- Calculate sales tax, discounts, and shipping charges
- Name the functions of cash registers and point-of-sale (POS) terminals
- Explain the uses for Universal Product Codes (UPCs)
- Make change
- Prepare purchase orders and invoices
- Explain delivery terms

GUIDE TO THE PHOTO

Market Talk An electronic cash register can function as a point-of-sale (POS) terminal if it is connected to a network that keeps track of sales, inventory, and even ordering new merchandise. This new generation of cash registers functions as a sales and a marketing tool.

Quick Think Name a store where you often shop. Is it equipped with conventional cash registers or POS stations? Why do you think this store uses that type of register?

332 UNIT 5 - SELLING

GUIDE TO THE PHOTO

Market Talk Remind students of the non-computerized cash registers they may have seen in small stores or in the movies. Have students discuss different types of cash registers they see today. They may mention cash registers that look and function like computers.

Quick Think Student responses may include: Large stores selling CDs and books which use POS terminals to update store inventory as soon as a purchase is made, restaurants with preset buttons for food items, or even online stores which use POS terminals not only to update inventory but also to record customer preference information.

Follow Up Ask students to list the potential benefits of POS terminals. Answers might include: more accurate inventory, time saved by not having to physically count inventory, gathering information about customer preferences so that marketing can be targeted to those customers.

Performance indicators represent key skills and knowledge. Relating them to the concepts explained in this chapter is your key to success in DECA events. These acronyms represent DECA events that involve knowledge of concepts in this chapter.

AAAL*	FMAL*	MMS	TMDM*
AAML*	FMDM*	QSRM*	TSE*
ADC	FMML*	RMAL*	VPM*
BSM	FSRM*	RMML*	
EMDM	HMDM*	SMDM*	

In all these DECA events you should be able to follow these performance indicators:

- Calculate miscellaneous charges
- Process sales documentation
- Analyze technology for use in the sales function
- Prepare invoices
- Use information systems for order fulfillment

The events with an asterisk (*) also include:

- Process cash sales
- Process charge (credit) sales
- Accept checks from customers
- Operate register/terminal
- Prepare cash drawers/banks
- Open/close register/terminal
- Process special orders

Some events include additional indicators:

BSM	Make change
FMDM	Assist with currency exchange
TMDM	Maintain petty-cash fund
HMDM	Perform bucket (room rack) check and resolve discrepancies
RMAL/RMML	Process returns and exchanges
AAAL/AAML	Process returns and exchanges

DECA PREP

Check your understanding of DECA performance indicators with the DECA activity in this chapter's review. For more information and DECA Prep practice, go to *marketingessentials .glencoe.com/16/DECA*

DECA events that require knowledge of completing and recording the sale are described here. Discuss the performance indicators to make sure students understand how to demonstrate their understanding.

The events acronyms stand for:

AAAL: Apparel and Accessories Marketing Series, AL

AAML: Apparel and Accessories Marketing Series, ML

ADC: Advertising Campaign Event

BSM: Business Services Marketing Series

EMDM: E-Commerce Management Team Decision Making Event

FMAL: Food Marketing Series, AL

FMDM: Financial Analysis Management Team Decision Making Event

FMML: Food Marketing Series, ML

FSRM: Full Service Restaurant Management Series

HMDM: Hospitality Services Management Team Decision Making Event

MMS: Marketing Management Series

QSRM: Quick Serve Restaurant Management Series

RMAL: Retail Merchandising Series, AL

RMML: Retail Merchandising Series, ML

SMDM: Sports and Entertainment Marketing Management Team Decision Making Event

TMDM: Travel and Tourism Marketing Management Team Decision Making Event

TSE: Technical Sales Event

VPM: Vehicles and Petroleum Marketing Series

DECA PREP

Find timed DECA Prep activities correlated with the Competitive Events Workbook for students and DECA tips for teachers at **marketingessentials.glencoe.com /16/DECA**

CHAPTER 16 Classroom Resources

For the Teacher

- TeacherWorks
- marketingessentials.glencoe.com
- Interactive Chalkboard
- **Exam*View*®** Pro Test Generator
- Fast File Unit 5

For the Student

- **Marketing Essentials** Online Edition
- Student Activity Workbook
- Marketing Math Workbook
- Marketing Research Project Workbook
- School-to-Work Activity Workbook
- Competitive Events Workbook
- **BusinessWeek** Reader and Case Studies
- marketingessentials.glencoe.com

FOCUS

Introducing the Section

COLLABORATIVE ACTIVITY

Divide the class into small groups of two or three. Have each group of students discuss their employers' procedures and policies (or ones they have observed as customers) about paying for purchases with any of the following:

- cash
- checks
- debit cards
- credit cards

Have each group report their findings to the class.

Preteaching Key Terms

Assign six teams of students one vocabulary term each. Have teams predict the meaning of each term and write their predictions on the board. Leave this list on the board so students can see how close their definitions were to the actual definitions as they work through the chapter.

- sales check
- layaway
- on-approval sale
- cash-on-delivery (COD) sale
- sales tax
- allowance

Critical Thinking

Ask students: Is it better to pay for purchases using cash or credit? Have students give reasons for their answers. For example, dealing with cash may be simplest for the store, but shoppers may not want to carry large amounts of cash.

OBJECTIVES

- List all types of retail sales transactions
- Process purchases, returns, and exchanges
- Generate and process sales documentation
- Calculate sales tax, discounts, and shipping charges

KEY TERMS

- sales check
- layaway
- on-approval sale
- cash-on-delivery (COD) sale
- sales tax
- allowance

Sales Transactions

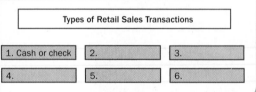
READ and STUDY

BEFORE YOU READ

Connect Imagine you have just finished shopping at your favorite store and are at the checkout counter. List and describe all the steps that take place before you leave the store.

THE MAIN IDEA

Today, there are many different ways of completing a purchase transaction, but one thing remains true: You still need basic math skills.

STUDY ORGANIZER

Draw the chart below. As you read this section, list six types of retail sales transactions.

Types of Retail Sales Transactions		
1. Cash or check	2.	3.
4.	5.	6.

WHILE YOU READ

Summarize List the differences in handling various methods of payment.

Types of Retail Sales Transactions

As a salesperson or cashier, you will handle several types of sales transactions. Most will be cash and debit or credit card sales, but you might also deal with layaway (or will-call) sales, on-approval sales, and cash-on-delivery (COD) sales. You will also handle returns, exchanges, allowances, sales tax, and shipping charges.

READ and STUDY

BEFORE YOU READ

Ask students to think about the last purchase they made. Ask: How did they pay? Make a chart on the board tallying the most common payment methods.

THE MAIN IDEA

Have students list two or three math skills needed to complete transactions.

STUDY ORGANIZER

Make an organizer or download the one at marketingessentials.glencoe.com. As study continues, you and the class should work together to complete the organizer.

WHILE YOU READ Model for the students a way to list differences by creating a chart.

Cash or Check Sales

A cash sale is a transaction in which the customer pays for the purchase with cash or a check. The simplest sale occurs when the customer pays in cash. The cashier records the transaction on the register, gives the customer change and a receipt, and wraps the purchase.

When a customer writes a check, you may need to verify his or her identity by requesting a driver's license and another form of identification. Every business has rules about accepting checks. You will have to learn the policy of your company or store.

Sales Checks

A **sales check** is a written record of a sales transaction that includes such information as the date of the transaction, the items purchased, the purchase prices, sales tax, and the total amount due. It is valuable to a customer as an itemized receipt.

In its most complete form, a sales check can contain customer information (name, address, and phone number) and details such as the time of the sale and the identity of the salesperson. While handwritten sales checks are becoming less common than printed ones, some small firms still use them. The salesperson records the transaction by hand in a sales check book that contains at least two copies of each form. One copy is given to the customer and one is retained by the business as a record of the sale.

Math Skills for Handwritten Sales Checks

Some math is necessary when preparing handwritten sales checks. The five steps of this process are shown in Figure 16.1. Occasionally, you will not be given a unit price, and you will need to calculate it on your own. This occurs when items are sold in multiple quantities, such as three reams of paper for $15. To find the selling price of one item in an instance like this, you divide the total price by the number of items: One ream of paper in this example would be $5 ($15 ÷ 3).

When the result of the division is uneven, any fraction of a cent is rounded up and charged to the customer. The price of one ream of paper when three reams are $13.99 is calculated as follows: $13.99 ÷ 3 = $4.6633 or $4.67.

Debit Card Sales

Businesses that have an encrypted, or coded, personal identification number (PIN) pad can ask customers whether they would like to pay with debit or credit. Customers who choose "debit" key in their private PIN. The terminal then dials out and checks to see whether there are enough funds in the customer's account to pay for the sale. If so, the funds are transferred to the merchant's account. The customer does not need to sign a sales draft.

Advantages of Debit Card Payments

The bank that issues the debit card charges the merchant only a flat rate, for example $.59 per sale, regardless of the amount of the sale. They are a convenience to many customers who cannot get approval for a credit card, who prefer not to use a credit card, or who do not carry either a checkbook or large amounts of cash. Most merchants prefer payment by debit card to payment by check because they have access to the money much sooner, there is no risk of insufficient funds, and the cost to the merchant is less than when the customer pays with a credit card.

Credit Card Sales

Statistics show that by accepting credit cards, businesses can increase sales by as much as 40 percent. Primarily because of this potential for increased sales, most businesses today accept one or more of the major credit cards, such as Visa, MasterCard, and American Express.

Credit Card Payment on the Internet

Credit cards are also the most frequently used method of payment for Internet purchases. Many Internet sites also allow the consumer to make purchases with a gift certificate that has a security code the customer must key in. For safety reasons, the payment data (card number, expiration date, security code,

TEACH

Discussion Starter

TYPES OF RETAIL SALES TRANSACTIONS

Ask students to brainstorm and describe different types of sales transactions. Have volunteers find each type of transaction in the text and read it to the class.

Enrichment

SECURITY IN SALES TRANSACTIONS

Ask students to imagine they are all section managers in a large department store. The department store has been losing money to fraud. People have passed counterfeit money, bad checks, and paid with stolen credit cards. The cashiers need to be trained to guard against fraud. Ask: How would the section managers design the training? What types of skills would be included?

TEACHING POINTS

Model Show students some of the methods people might use to pass bad checks or pay with stolen credit cards, such as saying they lost their identification cards.

Clarify Remind students that no method of fraud prevention in stores may be perfect all the time. Law enforcement and security officers are also needed to protect stores from fraud.

 Extended Activity

Demonstrate Sales Transactions

Have students read this section in class and divide the students into four groups. Ask the groups to fashion artificial currency, making sure the bills are of a standard size by giving them a blank template. Make sure each group makes the same number of each denomination of bills: $1, $5, $10, $20, $50, and $100. Also have on hand ten or more play "checks" and simple credit card/debit card receipts and distribute them evenly for each group. Once you have a set of artificial currency, checks, and receipts at your disposal, ask each group to organize the documents by category: currency, checks, and receipts. You can use these documents to demonstrate sales transactions through this section.

TEACH CONTINUED

Concept Development

SALES CHECKS

Bring to class or create an example of a sales check. Divide students into groups and have them label the parts of the sales checks, including information as the date of the transaction, the items purchased, the purchase prices, sales tax, and the total amount due.

TEACHING POINTS

Demonstrate Show students how to analyze a sales check yourself. Use a real sales check or create one to display on a board. Then ask students to point out the different parts.

Explain Ask students to think about what they might learn if they kept all their sales checks. Explain that keeping sales checks can help individuals budget because they can predict how much they typically spend on items in a given period of time.

Critical Thinking

Have students imagine that they are a business owner and must decide on preferred methods of payment for their store. Ask: What types of information do they need to gather to make a good decision?

Figure 16.1 *Sales Check—Multiple Purchases*

- **Adding Complexity** The basic sales check becomes more complicated when the customer buys several items, or several units of one item.

How can you be sure that the final sales check is accurate?

Step 1—Multiply unit price times quantity for each item and extend the amounts to the last column. Remember that the last two digits on the right are cents. Place a decimal point to their left, or enter them to the right of the vertical line dividing the last column into two unequal parts.

Step 2—Add item amounts to arrive at a merchandise subtotal. Enter this figure on the appropriate line.

Step 3—Calculate sales tax or look it up in a tax table. Sales tax must be paid by the buyer on all retail sales. It is calculated as a percentage of the merchandise subtotal. In most states, food and prescription medicine are exempt from sales tax, as are shipping charges.

Step 4—Calculate shipping charges. You need to decide if you will use U.S. mail or a specific express mail carrier.

Step 5—Add subtotal, tax, and shipping to get the purchase total. This is the amount the customer will pay.

ODEL'S CAMERA, INC.
1329 Walnut Street • Santa Barbara, CA 93101

NEW CUSTOMER ☐ YES ☐ NO	DATE 6/17/--
NAME	Joe Bundy
COMPANY	The Daily Times
ADDRESS	
CITY & STATE	
PHONE (RESIDENCE)	PHONE (OTHER)

SOLD BY	TYPE OF SALE
	CASH	CHECK ✓	C.O.D.	CARD TYPE	ACCOUNT	PURCHASE ORDER NO.

CODE	QTY	DESCRIPTION	PRICE	AMOUNT
6T	1	Olympus digital camera	399.00	399 00
4B	10	Fuji 100 color film	2.80	28 00
	8	Fuji 100 b/w film	3.00	24 00

SPECIAL INSTRUCTIONS	HANDLING	— —
	SUB TOTAL	451 00
	TAX	31 57
	SHIPPING	— —
	TOTAL AMOUNT	482 57
SHIP VIA:	PAID	500 00
PAID ON #	TC #	BALANCE	17 43
CC #		7932

 Online Action! Go to *marketingessentials.glencoe.com/16/figure/1* to find a project on sales checks.

marketingessentials.glencoe.com

Figure 16.1 *Sales Check—Multiple Purchases*

Discussion Ask students to look at **Figure 16.1**. Then, ask them to explain what each of the bold columns means: CODE, QTY, PRICE, DESCRIPTION, and AMOUNT. Also, make sure they understand the last six rows of the sales check: SUB TOTAL, TAX, SHIPPING, TOTAL AMOUNT, PAID, and BALANCE.

Caption Answer You can check your work when you are finished and use a calculator or computer when necessary.

Online Action! For instructions, ideas, and answer guide, go to The Teacher Center at **marketingessentials.glencoe.com**

Follow Up Ask students how conducting sales transactions could help to reinforce and improve basic math skills.

cardholder's identity) sent via the Internet are encrypted. This makes it more difficult for unauthorized individuals to gain access to a customer's card numbers.

Credit Card Payment Costs to the Merchant

If your company accepts credit cards, it pays a fee to the bank or agency that handles the billing and record keeping for each card transaction processed. This fee is a percentage of credit sales based on a sliding scale, which means that it varies according to the size of the store account and how the charges are processed.

Suppose your store had Visa sales of $100,000 in one month and that another store had Visa sales of only $2,000 in that same month. Your company would pay a smaller percentage for handling.

Overall, the cost of accepting credit cards typically varies from a low of 1.79 percent for MasterCard and Visa to 3.25 percent for American Express.

How Are Credit Card Payments Processed?

For many businesses, the amount of each credit card sale is electronically deposited in the business's bank account as the sale is made. A credit card sales check, or receipt, is issued by the cash register. With this procedure, the credit card company deducts its service charges from the store's bank account immediately, and the store normally has access to the customers' payment funds the next day. This process is much faster than physically delivering credit card sales checks to a bank.

If manually prepared credit card sales checks are used for these charges, they may be deposited when you deposit checks in your company account. A special deposit slip must be prepared for the bank so that your account is credited quickly.

Getting Credit Authorization

While credit cards are a convenient alternative to more traditional forms of payment, some fraud is always possible. Many retail businesses set a floor limit, a maximum amount a customer is allowed to charge to a credit card, to protect themselves against losses due to the use of stolen or fake credit cards. Illicit charges are disputed by the true cardholder and the credit card company, and the store is liable for only the amount of the floor limit.

Most modern cash registers include an integrated credit authorizer. An electronic credit authorizer can also be a device that reads data encoded on credit cards. The sales clerk inputs the amount of the sale into the device. The data are then transmitted to a computer,

---

PRACTICE 1: CREDIT CARD FEES

Calculate the impact credit card fees would have on the business described below.

1. At Carol's Pearls and Stones, Visa sales are usually between $13,000 and $15,000 per month. The Visa handling charge is a sliding scale. For $10,000–$14,999, it charges 3 percent of sales; for $15,000–$19,999, 2.5 percent; and for $20,000–$29,999, 2 percent.

   That means that for a purchase of $22,000, Visa collects a 3 percent fee on the first $14,999, a 2.5 percent fee on the next $5,000, and a 2 percent fee on the remaining $2,001. The total Visa collects is $614.99.
   a. Carol had $15,500 in Visa sales one month. How much more did she net than if sales had been $14,300?
   b. How much would Carol have netted in that month if her shop had done $21,000 in Visa sales?

2. Carol has decided to accept the Diners Club card in her shop. The handling charges are 1 percent higher than those for Visa at each sales level. If Carol had $19,000 in Diners Club sales, how much more would she pay in handling fees than she would have for the same amount in Visa sales?

3. Carol had $13,600 in cash sales, $14,800 in Diners Club sales, and $15,200 in Visa sales one month. What were her net sales after handling charges?

Note: Answers to all practice sets at *marketingessentials.glencoe.com*

TEACH CONTINUED

Individualized Math Skills

L1 Have students explain how to calculate unit price in their own words.
total price divided by number of items

L2 Have students find the total cost of a pair of boots whose sales price is $19.95 if the sales tax is 8.9%.
$21.72; $19.95 × .089 = $1.78; $19.95 + $1.78 = $21.72

L3 Ask students to calculate the monthly cost of accepting a credit card payment if the amount per month in sales is $100,000 and the interest rate is 2.1 percent.
$2,100; $100,000 × (100,000 × 0.021) = $2,100

TEACHING POINTS

Model Tell students that sometimes stores offer special deals to customers who buy more of an item, such as buying 3 shirts for $60, when just one shirt would cost $25. Ask students to think of other examples of these types of deals.

Demonstrate Some deals are better than others. Ask students which is the better deal: 3 shirts for $60 or 4 shirts for $75. Walk students through the process of dividing the price by the number of shirts to find the unit price and determine the better deal.
4 shirts for $75 is a better deal

PRACTICE 1 ANSWERS

1. a. $1,166.50; b. $20,405.01
2. $190.00
3. $42,553

 Online Activity

Cyber Shipping

Have each student select an online store and find out how that store calculates shipping costs. Ask students to report their findings to the class and to also note the different methods and costs of shipping.

TEACH CONTINUED

Concept Developement

RECORDING CREDIT OR DEBIT CARD SALES

To explain the importance of recording credit and debit card sales, ask students to imagine the things that could go wrong with electronic retail transaction recording systems. Answers might include power outages or computer viruses. Ask students what stores should do if their computers are down and a customer wants to make a purchase using a credit or debit card. Reminds students that there are usually three copies of each manually prepared sales check—one for the customer, one for the seller, and one for the bank or credit card agency. The salesperson might use a mechanical imprinter to transfer the customer's name and account number to the sales slip, or the salesperson might write the information on the sales check by hand.

TEACHING POINTS

Demonstrate Bring to class or create a sample sales slip. Have students work in pairs to record credit or debit card sales by hand. Students can take turns making up their purchases. If carbon paper is available, students can use it to make copies and label each copy: merchant copy, customer copy, and bank or credit card agency copy.

Clarify Remind students that as sales people they can help protect their businesses from credit card fraud by checking the customer's signature on the back of the card.

Critical Thinking

Ask students what advantages they see to using a computerized sales check versus a handwritten sales check. Answers might include that computers are more accurate or faster.

Case Study

Safety in Internet Sales

How can a small business sell products over the Internet and be certain it will be paid? How can a buyer be certain a Web merchant will not misuse credit card information? In the early days of Web marketing, credit card fraud frightened away many buyers and sellers.

eBay and PayPal

PayPal is a system developed in 1998 to provide safe transactions over the Internet. Originally, most of PayPal's customers were individuals involved in auctions on eBay— the huge Internet auction site. More recently, small online businesses, especially those run by individuals, have been signing up with PayPal. To buy a product from a PayPal client, a purchaser fills out a PayPal registration form, entering credit card and sometimes bank account information. PayPal verifies the information and opens an account for the purchaser.

When someone makes a purchase using PayPal, his or her credit card information is not shared with the merchant. In fact, it is not transmitted over the Web at all, where others might see it. The buyer feels safer making the purchase, and the seller is assured of being paid. PayPal has fraud protection that protects both seller and buyer, making it a more and more popular way to transact business.

THINK STRATEGICALLY

If PayPal charges one percent more to process each transaction than do credit card companies, why would it make sense for a small Web marketer to use them?

 Online Action! Go to *marketingessentials.glencoe.com/16/case* to find a research project on Internet sales.

---

which returns an approval or a disapproval in less than a minute.

Recording Credit or Debit Card Sales

As a salesperson in retail business, you will probably process many credit card sales. Electronic recording of credit card sales is now common and has replaced manually prepared credit card sales checks. There are usually three copies of each manually prepared sales check—one for the customer, one for the seller, and one for the bank or credit card agency. You might use a mechanical imprinter to transfer the customer's name and account number to the sales slip, or you might write the information on the sales check by hand.

Layaway Sales

Removing merchandise from stock and keeping it in a separate storage area until the customer pays for it is called **layaway**, or will-call. Layaway appeals to many shoppers and increases sales. The customer makes a

marketingessentials.glencoe.com

Case Study Safety in Internet Sales

Discussion After students have read the Case Study, lead a discussion about why new systems had to be invented to deal with Internet transactions. Expand the discussion by asking students to compare and contrast the pros and cons of purchasing something online with a credit card versus in a store with a credit card.

THINK STRATEGICALLY **Answer:** Answers will vary; possible answers may include that the fraud protection is a value-added service worth paying for and/or that the one percent may be less than the amount lost to fraud, when the small business uses other credit card companies.

Online Action! For instructions, ideas, and answer guide, go to the Teacher Center at marketingessentials.glencoe.com

deposit on the merchandise and agrees to pay for the purchase within a certain time period. The customer receives the merchandise when it is fully paid. If it is not paid for within the agreed-upon time, the goods are returned to stock. The deposit and any money paid need not be returned to the customer.

On-Approval Sales

An **on-approval sale** is an agreement permitting a customer to take merchandise (usually clothing) home for further consideration. Some department and specialty stores extend this special privilege to their regular customers. If the goods are not returned within an agreed-upon time, the sale is final. The customer must then send a check or return to the store to pay for the merchandise. Credit card information may be taken from the customer so that the sale can be processed if the customer keeps the item. This practice is a safe way for retailers to handle on-approval sales because there is much less risk involved.

Cash-on-Delivery Sales

A **cash-on-delivery (COD) sale** is a transaction that occurs when a customer pays for merchandise at the time of delivery. Because the customer must be on hand when the merchandise is delivered, however, COD sales are not as efficient as other types of sales transactions.

Sales Tax

A **sales tax** is a percentage fee placed by the government on the sale of goods and services. Rates differ from state to state. State taxes are sometimes combined with local charges.

Who Pays a Sales Tax?

Sales tax is paid only by the final user, or the individual customer who, in most cases, is also the consumer. It does not apply to goods bought for resale. Consumers pay the cost of sales taxes. A sales tax is a regressive tax. It is assessed at a flat rate that applies to persons of all income levels. Thus, although a low-income person and a person with a higher income pay

the same sales tax on the same item, the lower-income person is paying a higher percentage of his or her income in making the purchase. For this reason, some states exempt certain items, such as food, clothing, or medication from sales tax.

Sales Tax on the Internet

In the past several years, Internet sales have soared, and some states feel that they should have an easier time collecting tax on

---

Concept Development

RETURNS, EXCHANGES, AND ALLOWANCES

Ask students to generate a list of all the reasons they have ever returned an item to a store. Have a student record these reasons on the board. Ask students to discuss how returns, exchanges, and allowances each impact the store. Note that some items can be resold, while others cannot. Note that customer satisfaction may increase if customers are allowed to return items. Ask students what they think is a fair return policy. Answers will vary; students should demonstrate an understanding of returns.

Enrichment

SALES AND CUSTOMER SERVICE

Ask students to research the business pros and cons of layaway, on-approval sales, cash-on delivery sales, refunds, exchanges, and allowances. Suggest that they talk with customer service people at supermarkets, office supply stores, or home supply stores about some of the problems they face when dealing with customers. Then, have students set up different scenarios and role-play customers interacting with customer service representatives.

A MATTER OF ETHICS — Should You Tell Your Boss?

Discussion Lead students in a discussion of the best ways to communicate with bosses about errors. Ask those students who have had jobs to think of times they have talked with their bosses. Review ways to keep conversations friendly and professional.

THINKING ETHICALLY Answer: Mark did the right thing. If he had been too afraid to talk to his boss, more customers would have been overcharged. In addition, one of these customers might have noticed the error and complained. This could have hurt the business. Because Richard pointed out the error to his boss, his boss was able to come up with a solution that would be good for the business.

@ Online Action! For instructions, ideas, and answer guide, go to the Teacher Center at **marketingessentials.glencoe.com**

 Extended Activity

Sales Tax

Bring in or create a receipt and point out the sales tax if possible. Ask students to generate a list of items, determine their base price, then find the sales tax and total cost based on their own state's sales tax and the sales tax in another state.

CONCEPTS

Have students recall the different ways customers may complete a sales transaction and the special requirements of sales people in these transactions.

Students should discuss the steps a salesperson goes through to accept cash, checks, credit cards, and debit cards.

KEY TERMS

Have students review key terms, their spellings, and definitions in small groups.

ONLINE SELF-ASSESSMENT

Have students go to marketingessentials.glencoe.com for the Section 16.1 practice test.

Individualized Review

L1 Assign and review Chapter 16 activities in the Student Activity Workbook.

L2 Assign and Review Chapter 16 activities in the Marketing Math Workbook.

L3 Assign and Review Chapter 16 activities in the *BusinessWeek* Reader and Case Studies.

Marketing Practice

Bring in sample receipts. Make sure that names, addresses, or credit or debit card numbers are blacked out. Have students work in groups and distribute receipts to each group. Ask students to work together to classify the type of transaction each receipt represents and label each part of the receipt.

340

---

all state-to-state sales, including online sales. Legislation is being considered that would set up an Internet sales tax collection system.

The government does not want to put unreasonable burdens on small businesses selling through the Internet. Most of these mom-and-pop businesses do not have sophisticated computer software that could apply every state's unique tax policies to every transaction. But states complain that they cannot expect residents to keep perfect records of all their Internet transactions and to send the states the taxes that are due voluntarily.

Returns, Exchanges, and Allowances

A return is merchandise brought back for a cash refund or credit. Most businesses are happy to make exchanges because they want their customers to be satisfied. (See Figure 16.2.)

An **allowance** is a partial return of the sale price for merchandise that the customer has kept. These are usually given when there is a defect in the merchandise, such as a missing button.

Each of these situations requires a different type of sales transaction. Some businesses adopt a policy of no returns; however, most feel that accepting returns is an important part of good customer relations. Some businesses accept returns but only offer store credit that can be used to pay for other merchandise from the same business instead of a cash refund.

A transaction that involves returning an item for a replacement with the same price is an even exchange.

How to Handle Sales Tax in Return or Exchange Transactions

Suppose Duane decides he needs a laptop computer to help him keep up with his studies, but he wants a less expensive one than the one he was given for his birthday. The original computer was priced at $1,149 (excluding sales tax), and Duane wants to exchange it for

Figure 16.2 — *Refund Slip*

• **Refund Policy** Most businesses give customers refunds or exchanges under certain circumstances.

Why do stores often insist that the customer have a sales receipt before giving a refund?

Nicky's Dress Shop   **REFUND SLIP**

STORE NO.	DATE	ITEM RETURNED	AMOUNT	
	8/17/--	SKIRT	45	00

NAME Stacy McClintock
ADDRESS 777 Seaview Lane
CITY & STATE Marblehead, MA 01945

| | | TAX | 3 | 15 |
| TELEPHONE NO. 781-882-0252 | | | | |

CUSTOMER'S SIGNATURE *Stacy McClintock*

| | | TOTAL AMOUNT | 48 | 15 |

EMPLOYEE NO. 6P   AUTHORIZED BY *G. Smith*   REASON FOR RETURN Wrong color

No refunds after 30 days; No refunds without receipt.

@ Online Action! Go to *marketingessentials.glencoe.com/16/figure/2* to find a project on refunds.

Figure 16.2 — *Refund Slip*

Discussion Have students discuss why it is important for businesses to keep track of the reasons items are returned. Answers might include: so that business track which items their customers like and dislike and make orders based on this information, or so that they can check to see if the item is defective in some way, or so that they can help individual customers make better purchases in the future.

Caption Answer Store owners want to make sure the customer bought the item at their store and not another similar store. They also want to make sure of the price the customer originally paid for the item and to track inventory.

@ Online Action! For instructions, ideas, and answer guide, go to the Teacher Center at marketingessentials.glencoe.com

one priced at $895. To handle this transaction, you refund the difference, $254, plus the sales tax on $254. This procedure is reversed for a customer who wants to exchange an item for one that is more expensive. The customer pays the extra cost of the exchanged item and the extra sales tax on that amount.

Consider how a sales check is prepared. Each item is not taxed individually in multiple purchases; instead, the subtotal is used to calculate the sales tax. When looking at the sales check, simply find the item being returned, calculate the difference between that item and the item the customer is taking in exchange for the item returned, and determine the difference in tax on the two amounts. The customer has already paid tax on the original item, so tax is due only on the difference between the two items.

Shipping Charges

Not all purchases can be bought and carried home: Some items may be too bulky, and others are purchased via the phone or the Internet. Shipping is necessary and adds separate charges. Because delivery charges are generally exempt from sales tax, they are added after the sales tax has been calculated. The cost of shipping merchandise depends on the service used, the weight of the shipment, and the distance it is being sent.

PRACTICE 2

How much will be returned to or paid by the customer in each of the following cases? Assume a sales tax rate of 7 percent.

1. Mr. Williams returned a $330 lamp that did not put out enough light. He chose another style priced at $225. How much will you return to him?

2. Mrs. Crawford returned a $159 printer because it was apparently defective. She chose another model priced at $229. How much more will you charge her?

16.1 AFTER YOU READ

Reviewing Key Terms and Concepts

1. What is a sales check? What important information should it include?
2. How do the fees a merchant must pay for accepting credit card purchases compare with the fees for debit card purchases? What is the main reason merchants are willing to accept credit cards?
3. How are a return, an exchange, and an allowance different from each other?

Integrating Academic Skills

Math

4. A local department store had a 20 percent off everything sale. If you purchased items at $24.95, $5.95, and $34.99, what would be your total bill, assuming the sales tax rate is 5 percent?

Language Arts

5. Write an e-mail message to your boss explaining why your company should (or should not) accept credit card purchases over the Internet.

 Online Action!

Check your answers at *marketingessentials.glencoe.com/16/read*

marketingessentials.glencoe.com

Chapter 16 - Using Math in Sales **341**

CLOSE

Ask students to recall and provide answers to the following questions:

- **What are the primary elements of a sales check?**
  product code, quantity, product, unit price, price, subtotal, tax, shipping, total amount, amount paid, balance

- **List all types of sales transactions.**
  Cash sales, debit card sales, credit card sales, layaway (or will-call) sales, on-approval sales, and cash-on-delivery (COD) sales, returns, exchanges, and allowances.

Critical Thinking

Ask students: What are the benefits to merchants of accepting both credit and debit cards?

PRACTICE 2 ANSWERS

1. $112.35
2. $74.90

AFTER YOU READ

Reviewing Key Terms and Concepts

1. A sales check is a written record of a sales transaction that includes such information as the date of the transaction, the items purchased, the purchase prices, sales tax, and the total amount due. A sales check can also contain customer information and details such as the time of the sale and the identity of the salesperson.

Online Action! Answers at **marketingessentials.glencoe.com/16/read**

2. The bank that issues the card charges the merchant a flat rate of $.59 per sale, regardless of the amount of sale. Charges for credit card use are considerably higher, 1.79% to 3.25% or more. Merchants accept credit cards because accepting them increases sales up to 40%.

3. A return is merchandise brought back that generates a refund or credit to the buyer.

An exchange is merchandise brought back and replaced by other merchandise. An allowance is a partial return of the sale price for defective merchandise that the buyer chooses to keep.

Integrating Academic Skills

4. $55.35; ($24.95 + $5.95 + $34.99) ÷ 0.20 = $52.71; $52.71 + ($52.71 × 0.05) = $55.35

5. E-mails should include discussion of increased sales as well as increased costs.

Cash Registers

FOCUS

Introducing the Section

COLLABORATIVE ACTIVITY

To begin the lesson, bring several empty boxes to class to serve as "cash drawers." Create or have on hand "play" coins and currency, enough to constitute an opening cash fund and enough additional money for students to use for simulated purchases.

- Have students count out the opening cash funds for each drawer. Suggest appropriate amount, e.g., $75 or $100 in coins and currency.

- Model how students should place coins and currency in the drawer in appropriate order. Identify where such things as checks, food stamps, and coupons would go.

- Have students work in groups to set up their drawers and practice cash payments.

Preteaching Key Terms

Ask for a volunteer to read each of the key terms aloud as each student writes them on a sheet of paper. When they finish, write the terms on the board. Then have students guess at the meaning of each. Write their guesses next to each term. Leave this list on the board so that students can see how close their guesses were to the actual definitions as they work through the chapter.

- Universal Product Code (UPC)
- point-of-sale system
- till
- opening cash fund

OBJECTIVES

- Name the functions of cash registers and point-of-sale (POS) terminals
- Explain the uses for Universal Product Codes (UPCs)
- Make change

KEY TERMS

- Universal Product Code (UPC)
- point-of-sale system
- till
- opening cash fund

READ and STUDY

BEFORE YOU READ

Predict What do you think are some of the functions performed by cash registers and point-of-sale terminals?

THE MAIN IDEA

The cash register or the point-of-service station (POS) is the cashier's most important tool in completing a sales transaction. In some instances, it even assumes the cashier's role.

STUDY ORGANIZER

Draw the chart below. As you read this section, write in three methods of entering information in an electronic cash register and three safeguards against theft.

Electronic Cash Registers
Methods of Entering Information 1.　　　2.　　　3.
Safeguards Against Theft/Counterfeiting 1.　　　2.　　　3.

WHILE YOU READ

Compare Create a list of key differences among the methods of recording sales.

Cash Registers and Their Main Functions

After the sale of a product or service is finalized, we say the sale is closed. For accounting and tax purposes, a closed sale must be recorded. In most businesses, cash registers perform this function.

All cash registers, from the simplest to the most complex, perform three basic sales transaction functions:

READ and STUDY

BEFORE YOU READ

Ask students to recall and describe as many different kinds of cash registers as they can.

THE MAIN IDEA

Cash registers and point-of sales-terminals are essential to closing and recording the sale. Both record the sale and create a receipt.

STUDY ORGANIZER

Model the study organizer for students by filling in the first method. A full-size, downloadable study organizer can be found at marketingessentials.glencoe.com

WHILE YOU READ　While students read, ask them to note that the headings and subheadings can help them organize the different ways of recording sales.

1. **Recording sales** Cash registers provide a convenient way to enter information about a sale. This usually includes the department, the type of transaction, the salesperson, the amount of the sale, and the form of payment (cash, credit card, gift certificate, etc.). The salesperson also enters the amount of money given by the customer, and the cash register computes the amount of change the customer receives.

2. **Storing cash and sales documents** Cash registers provide a convenient, organized way to keep cash, personal checks, credit sales checks, and refund slips. Coupons and other sales-related documents may also be kept in the cash register drawer.

3. **Providing receipts** Cash registers automatically provide a receipt for the customer. This is the customer's record of the sale and proof of payment.

The Electronic Cash Register

Many businesses today utilize sophisticated electronic cash registers that perform multiple functions in addition to the three basic functions. These may include (1) figuring sales tax, (2) calculating discounts, (3) subtracting and crediting returns, (4) determining the amount due back to the customer, (5) tracking inventory, and, in some instances, even (6) automatically reordering stock.

Entering Data Into an Electronic Cash Register

Sales transaction data are entered into an electronic cash register in several ways:

- **Optical scanning** Supermarkets and other retailers, such as home improvement centers and discount chains, have improved their efficiency in recording sales transactions by installing optical scanners at checkout counters. Salesclerks drag items across the scanner so it can read the bar codes on the product packaging. If the scanner cannot read the code, the salesclerk must key the information manually.

- **Electronic wand entry** Many retailers (especially department and clothing stores) use electronic wands to enter sales transactions. The salesperson moves the point of the wand across the data printed on a tag attached to the article sold.
- **Manual key entry** Even with electronic cash registers, some businesses have their salespeople enter sales transactions manually, often by keying in a Universal Product Code (UPC) using the register keys. All registers provide a numeric keyboard for entry in case other input devices do not function properly.

Universal Product Codes

A **Universal Product Code (UPC)** is a combination bar code and number used to identify a product and manufacturer.

Every item a manufacturer sells must have a different item number. For example, different sizes of the same garment and different size containers of the same product must have distinct UPC codes.

UPCs have two parts: the machine-readable bar code and the human-readable UPC number. Bar codes, consisting of a series of vertical bars, are symbols printed on tags or on product packaging. The UPC number is the series of digits above or below the bar code.

The last number of the code is a check digit based on all the other digits: Every time a scanner reads an item, it uses a formula to calculate the check digit. If the check digit it calculates does not match the check digit it reads, the scanner signals that the item needs to be rescanned. After the coded information is scanned and entered into a register, it can be transferred to a computer for further processing.

Many electronic cash registers are linked to computers as part of a POS (point-of-sale) system. Using the data, the computer can update inventory records with each sale and automatically reorder items in short supply. It can store customer information and make it available for marketing or credit-check purposes. It can

Chapter 16 - Using Math in Sales 343

TEACH CONTINUED

Concept Development

THE CASH DRAWER

1. Have students generate a list of five purchase amounts and corresponding amounts tendered. Then have students calculate the amount of change given. For example, if the purchase is $14.49, the customer might tender $20.50.

2. Tell students that at the end of the working day, you must balance the cash drawer. Ask students to list what you need to do to make sure you have the right amount in your cash drawer.

This procedure involves totaling all the cash, checks, and credit slips in the drawer and then subtracting the opening cash fund and any refunds given to customers. The result is the day's receipts. If this figure matches the total on the register tape, the drawer is balanced.

TEACHING POINTS

Role Play Have students perform role play where one student is a sales associate and one student is a customer. The sales associate should convince the customer to open a store credit account.

Expand Explain that a store's receipt for the day is not equal to the amount of profit for the day. Explain that the money taken in is off set by the money expended on the products, the employees, and the cost of keep the store open—rent, electricity, water, etc.

---

also print out financial statements, sales trends, and sales personnel productivity reports.

POS systems have screens that show the names of items scanned and their prices. These displays are usually elevated and angled so customers can easily see the information. After all of the items have been scanned and totaled and tax has been added, the display will show the total amount of the sale. When the customer tenders payment, the amount tendered and the change due the customer are displayed.

Current Trends

Several new trends have emerged and are changing the way business sales transactions are conducted and recorded. Several retailing chains have begun to offer their customers the option of using a self-service checkout. In a self-service lane at a typical grocery store, customers scan their own merchandise and weigh their own produce. They then enter payment in a self-service cash register, which allows them to pay with cash or via credit or debit card.

Integration of Point-of-Sale Information

A **point-of-sale system** combines a cash register with a computer, making it possible to capture information about the transaction at the time of the sale, then apply it to different functions. POS information is now used to trigger replenishment of stock and manufacturing of replacement merchandise.

For example, suppose that on a Saturday afternoon at a store in Atlanta, Georgia, a teenage shopper purchases a plaid skirt, size 8. The clerk processes the transaction at a POS terminal. On the following Monday afternoon, in Hong Kong, a computer technician downloads the information about the sale. On Wednesday, a factory worker in Hong Kong, pulls the same size skirt off the assembly line and boxes it to be shipped to Atlanta. All this happens automatically without anyone at the Atlanta store having to order a replacement.

344 UNIT 5 - SELLING

Radio Frequency Identification

A new technology for sales transactions is radio frequency identification (RFID). With RFID, radio frequencies are used to read labels on products. An RFID tag is placed on cases and pallets by the manufacturer, who then labels each item with an Electronic Product Code (EPC). The tags are read by a radio signal reading machine as a customer passes his or her cart through checkout. This brand new technology makes it possible to read all the items in a cart simultaneously while they are still in the cart.

The Cash Drawer

Currency and checks collected in sales transactions are deposited in the till. The **till** is the cash drawer of a cash register.

Cash Drawer Arrangement

Usually, the till has ten compartments—five in the back and five in the front. Although some companies vary the arrangement, bills are usually kept in the back of the drawer and coins in the front.

In the section for bills, the first compartment on the left often remains empty. It is reserved for checks or other special items. The second compartment contains $20 bills, the third $10 bills, and the fourth $5 bills. The last compartment on the right is used for $1 bills. If a customer uses a larger bill, such as a $50 or a $100, many companies require that it be checked with a head cashier or a manager prior to being placed under the tray, where it is more secure.

In the section for coins, the first compartment on the left is used for silver dollars and half-dollars. The next compartment is for quarters, the following one for dimes, and the one after that for nickels. The last compartment on the right is for pennies.

This arrangement facilitates making change because the bill and coin compartments are related and in descending order of value. Each pair has at least one digit in common. The $20 bills are behind the quarters ($.25). The $10 bills are behind the dimes ($.10). The $5 bills

---

Extended Activity

Keeping Cash Safe

Have students research safety measures for transporting money from a store safe to the store cash register. For example, some stores only transport large amounts of cash when the store is closed and locked. Some use a pneumatic tube or a one-way drop box. Other students might research techniques con artists use at the cash register. For example, a common strategy is to ask unsuspecting cashiers, "Can I have change for a $5 bill?" Once change is given, another request is made and then another. By the time the requests are finished, the con artist is richer, and the clerk may not even realize there is a problem until the drawer is balanced. Have students share the results of their research in class.

are behind the nickels ($.05), and the $1 bills are behind the pennies ($.01).

Opening Cash Fund

At the beginning of each business day, the manager or other designated person provides a limited amount of money for the cash register, which is called the **opening cash fund**. This fund consists of the coins and currency, or bills, designated for the register for a given day's business. To verify the fund, the assigned person first counts the coins and places them, one denomination at a time, in the correct compartment; then he or she does the same with the currency.

As the coins and currency are counted, the amount is written down and then checked against the amount planned for the register. The change fund is even when the two amounts match exactly. When there is more than planned, the fund is over. If there is less than planned, the fund is short. An opening cash fund that is short or over should be reported immediately to the person who supplied the money so that it can be corrected or accounted for prior to the start of business transactions for that day.

Making Change

A salesperson who handles a large number of cash transactions may run short of certain denominations during the business day. Check your cash drawer during any downtime you have to see if you need any bills or coins, and request the change then. This procedure can prevent delays when customers are waiting for service.

Method 1: Making Change With a POS System

A POS system with a customer display makes it easy to count the correct change due the customer. You simply need to count out the change shown on the display. Begin with the largest denomination when using this type of machine. When the register displays $3.35 due the customer for a $16.65 purchase, select the change from the cash

---

MARKET TECH

Beyond Bar Codes

Radio frequency identification (RFID) may someday replace the bar codes used on products today. RFID uses miniature circuitry in a durable wireless transmitter called a tag. Some tags are so small that they can be embedded into almost anything—shipping pallets, clothing, credit cards, a tube of lipstick.

How Does It Work?

A tag can contain information about a product, the place of manufacture, its shipping history, and the date and time it was sold to the customer. Electronic readers take the information and feed it into a computer database. A computer can then perform a variety of operations. It can tell the retailer the last time a person purchased toothpaste or how often, and what type of books a customer bought.

RFID on the Road

RFID is already used by ten million motorists in the U.S. in the form of a tiny E-Zpass tag attached to their windshield. The E-Zpass tag allows them to drive through tollbooths and pay electronically.

THINK LIKE A MARKETER

How would RFID affect efficiency in delivering materials from suppliers to manufacturers? How might RFID affect marketing research, advertising, and selling?

@ Online Action!

Go to *marketingessentials.glencoe.com/ 16/tech* to find a project on radio frequency identification.

TEACH CONTINUED

Concept Development

MAKING CHANGE

Have students discuss how cashiering relates to customer service. Students should note that giving quick and accurate change will increase customer satisfaction with both the purchase and the store. On the other hand, if customers are kept waiting or are given incorrect change, they may think twice about shopping at that venue again.

TEACHING POINTS

Demonstrate Using real or created money, walk the class through making change without a customer display screen.

Role Play Have students create a role play where a customer is making a purchase with a cashier at a POS system. Make sure students understand the importance of good customer service when giving change.

Online Activity

Web Ads

Have students explore an online store. Have them print out examples of what they consider good advertising. This might include interesting descriptions of the product, detailed information about the product, graphic design of the ad, and flattering photos of the product. Have students share their findings with the class and make a class list of online advertising techniques.

MARKET TECH

Beyond Bar Codes

Discussion Tell students that as radio frequency identification becomes more common, rules and policies governing the use of the information gathered. Ask students what restrictions might be helpful in protecting privacy.

THINK LIKE A MARKETER **Answer:** RFIDs could increase distribution efficiency, making for more accurate inventory control. They could also help market researchers link the purchase of a product to specific customers and develop a profile of a typical buyer. Information about our personal tastes and decisions can guide advertising decisions and increase sales.

@ Online Action! For instructions, ideas, and answer guide, go to the Teacher Center at **marketingessentials.glencoe.com**

CONCEPTS

Review with students the three general functions of cash registers, the arrangement of cash in the cash drawer, the two methods of making change, and the uses for the UPC. Provide students with play money and have them work in small groups to review making change and arranging a cash drawer.

KEY TERMS

Have students review key terms, their spellings, and definitions in small groups.

ONLINE SELF-ASSESSMENT

Have students go to **marketingessentials.glencoe.com** for the Section 16.2 practice test.

Individualized Review

L1 Assign and review Chapter 16 activities in the Student Activity Workbook.

L2 Assign and review Chapter 16 activities in the Marketing Math Workbook.

L3 Assign and review Chapter 16 activities in the *BusinessWeek* Reader and Case Studies.

Marketing Practice

Have students research the different types of cash registers and their functions. Ask students to give five- to ten-minute oral presentations on how cash registers have been modified to accommodate the changing marketplace.

PRACTICE 3: MAKE CHANGE

How would you make or arrange for change in the following situations using the smallest number of bills and coins possible?

1. A customer gives you a $50 bill and a coupon worth $1 off one item to pay for a $23.19 purchase. What change would you give her?
2. A customer is buying two CDs that total $25.09, including tax. The smallest bills he has are two $20 bills, and he does not want too much change back. What is your response?
3. A customer gives you $30.25 for a $21.25 purchase. How would you count back the change?
4. You are a cashier at Caldwell Drugstore, and a customer gives you $10.75 to pay for a purchase of $3.55. Count the customer's change back to him. Why did he give you the change along with the $10 bill?

---

drawer by taking out three $1 bills, a quarter, and a dime. The customer knows from the display what change is due; so all you need to do is say aloud "$3.35" as you hand it to the customer.

Method 2: Making Change Without a Customer Display Screen

If your cash register does not have a customer display showing the change due, begin by announcing the total amount of the sale and then count up to the amount tendered. In doing this, be thorough and accurate, and follow these five steps:

1. Once the transaction has been entered in the cash register, announce to the customer the total amount of the sale. You might say, "That will be $16.65."
2. Announce the amount tendered when the customer offers payment in cash, saying, for example, "Out of a $20 bill."
3. Place the $20 on the cash drawer ledge and leave it there until you have given change to the customer. This eliminates most disputes over amount tendered.
4. Count silently while removing change from the cash drawer. The most common method is to count up from the purchase price, taking out smaller denominations of coins and currency first. Use as few coins as possible in making change.

5. Count aloud when handing the change to the customer. Say, "That's $16.65 out of $20. $16.75 (giving the customer a dime), $17 (giving a quarter), $18, $19, and $20 (giving three $1 bills, one at a time)."

Many customers avoid accumulating small change by tendering an odd amount of change to pay for their purchases. A customer might give you $20.39 for a sales total of $18.39. You would use the $.39 to cancel the "odd cents" of the sale and give change for the $20 bill. The same customer might also tender $20.50, in which case you would count the odd cents first, starting at $18.39.

Sales Tally

Salespeople and cashiers who use a cash register must account for the day's sales and money at closing. This process goes by a number of names, including *balancing the cash* and *balancing the till*.

Most cash registers automatically keep a sales tally, or summary of the day's sales. This makes the job of balancing the cash much simpler. The person responsible for each register counts the money and fills out a brief closing balance report. Then he or she removes the tape from the cash register and sends the money, report, and tape to management.

Safeguards Against Theft and Counterfeiting

Every employee who uses a cash register should be familiar with some safeguards

---

PRACTICE 3 ANSWERS

1. One penny, a nickel, three quarters, two $1 bills (or a $2 bill), a $5 bill, and a $20 bill.
2. Ask if the customer has $.09 in change or at least a dime.
3. By disregarding the exact change provided, the cashier is less likely to get confused. Disregard the $.25 and simply say, "That's $21 out of $30; twenty-two, twenty-three, twenty-four, twenty-five [counting back four $1 bills, one at a time], and $30 [giving back $5]."
4. "That's $3.55 out of $10.75; $.65, $.75 [handing back two dimes]," then say, "That leaves $3 out of $10; $4, $5 [handing back two $1 bills], and $10 [handing back a $5 bill]." By tendering the $.75, the customer reduces the amount of small change to be returned to him.

against the theft of money. The first rule is to always close the cash drawer between transactions. While you are counting change to a customer, always partially close the drawer. Remove the money tendered by the customer from the register ledge after giving change. You should always lock the register if you leave it.

A customer may interrupt you while you are counting change. It is best to ignore the interruption. Don't allow yourself to get distracted, because this may cause you to make incorrect change. You can respond politely once the transaction has been completed.

Counterfeit bills show up in almost every city at some time, and it is important that cashiers routinely check all currency, particularly larger denominations, such as $20, $50, and $100 bills.

The best way to guard against counterfeit money is to become very familiar with U.S. currency. Every company should have printed information on how to identify counterfeit money. Genuine currency has tiny red and blue fibers embedded throughout. The

portrait on a genuine bill appears lifelike and stands out distinctly from the background. Counterfeit portraits are usually lifeless and flat, with details merged into the background. Also, the fine-line printing on the border of a genuine bill is clear and unbroken. On a counterfeit, the lines on the border scrollwork may be blurred and indistinct.

New Currency Design

From time to time, changes are made to the design of U.S. currency to prevent counterfeiting. To make the currency more difficult to reproduce, in the late 1990s the U.S. Department of the Treasury redesigned most denominations with new security features. The redesigned bills include a polymer thread embedded vertically in the bill, concentric fine-line printing, a watermark, color-shifting ink, and an enlarged, off-center portrait. Beginning in 2003, subtle green, peach, and blue colors were featured in the background of $20 bills. The $5, $10, $50, and $100 bills were similarly redesigned. All the older bills will retain their value as long as they are in circulation.

CLOSE

Have students complete this statement:

Cash registers fill these three important functions of sales transaction: _____ . recording sales, storing cash, and providing receipts

Extended Activity

Counterfeiting and Fraud
Have interested students research what steps the U.S. government has taken through the years to identify and prevent the manufacturing of counterfeit currency, traveler's checks, checks, and other documents. Have students share their findings in an informal oral presentation in groups or in class.

16.2 AFTER YOU READ

Reviewing Key Terms and Concepts

1. What are three functions that all cash registers and POS terminals perform?

2. A customer gives you a $50 bill for a purchase of $34.29. Describe two ways you could count change back to her.

3. What is the Universal Product Code and how is it used?

Integrating Academic Skills

Math

4. The Big 12 Sports Mart sold 20 baseballs and 10 bats to a Little League team. The price for baseballs is $4.25 each and for bats is $17 each. Tax on sales is 7 percent. What is the total cost for the team?

History

5. Research the development of digital scanning technology and write a brief report.

 Online Action!

Check your answers at *marketingessentials.glencoe.com/16/read*

AFTER YOU READ

Reviewing Key Terms and Concepts

1. Recording sales, storing cash and sales documents, and providing receipts. Computers linked to cash registers also update inventory records with each sale.

2. With a POS system, you could simply say "$15.71" as you hand her the change. Without a POS system, you would say

"That's $34.29 out of $50. $34.30 (handing her a penny), $34.40, $34.50 (handing her two dimes, one at a time), $34.75, $35.00 (handing her two quarters, one at a time). $40 (handing her a $5 bill) and $50 (handing her a $10 bill).

3. A Universal Product Code (UPC) is a combination bar code and number used to identify a product and manufacturer.

Integrating Academic Skills

4. $272.85; ($4.25 × 20) + ($17 × 10) + [($4.25 × 20) + ($17 × 10)] × 0.07 = $272.85

5. Accept all reports that demonstrate student effort. Reports might include the invention of the UPC codes and the development of RFID tags.

Online Action! Answers at **marketingessentials.glencoe.com/16/read**

Purchase Orders, Invoices, and Shipping

FOCUS

Introducing the Section

COLLABORATIVE ACTIVITY

Give groups of students a blank purchase order and an office supply catalogue site. Tell students to imagine they work in a marketing office of five employees. They are out of copy paper, file folders, pens, and notebooks. Ask students to fill out a purchase order to replace supplies for a month. Emphasize that while there are reasonable and unreasonable purchase amounts, there are no right or wrong answers. The main point is to discover how to fill out a purchase order.

Preteaching Key Terms

Ask students predict at the meaning of these key terms:

- purchase order (PO)
- invoice
- terms for delivery
- free-on-board (FOB)

Tell students that they can check their predictions as they read the section.

Building Vocabulary

Preview the following words by reading them in context in the Purchase Order section:

- **vendor** seller, provider of a service
- **extension** increase in length or time

Discuss the meaning of these words with the students.

OBJECTIVES

- Prepare purchase orders and invoices
- Explain delivery terms

KEY TERMS

- purchase order (PO)
- invoice
- terms for delivery
- free-on-board (FOB)

WHILE YOU READ

Compare Make a list of similarities and differences between purchase orders and invoices.

READ and STUDY

BEFORE YOU READ

Predict What do you already know about purchase orders and invoices?

THE MAIN IDEA

Writing a purchase order, creating an invoice, and figuring shipping may be part of the sales process, particularly when dealing with business-to-business sales.

STUDY ORGANIZER

Draw the chart below. As you read this section, write in the six types of information needed to complete a purchase order or an invoice.

Information Needed	
Purchase Order	Invoice
1. Item number	

Purchase Orders

When a buyer for a business purchases supplies or merchandise from another business (business-to-business sale), the first step in the process is to prepare a purchase order. For vendors—those who sell to other businesses—the equivalent form is the invoice. The calculations for both forms are very similar to those performed by retail salespeople on sales checks.

A **purchase order (PO)** is a legal contract between the buyer and the supplier. This document lists the quantity, price,

READ and STUDY

BEFORE YOU READ

Ask students to discuss some of the reasons business-to-business transactions might be different from the transactions of everyday shoppers.

THE MAIN IDEA

Learning to calculate and verify purchase orders and invoices is an important part of completing and recording a business-to-business sale.

STUDY ORGANIZER

Model the study organizer for students. A full-size, downloadable study organizer can be found at marketingessentials.glencoe.com

WHILE YOU READ

Have students summarize characteristics of purchase orders and invoices as they read.

and description of the products ordered, along with the terms of payment and delivery. In Figure 16.3, notice the information routinely included in a purchase order:

- **Item number** The vendor's catalog designation for the merchandise ordered
- **Quantity** The number of units ordered
- **Description** What is being ordered

- **Unit** How the item is packaged and priced (individually, by the dozen, by the ream, etc.)
- **Unit cost** The price per unit
- **Total** The extension, or the result of multiplying the number of units by the cost per unit

Note that if you order several items on the same PO, the total of all extensions is entered at

Figure 16.3 *Purchase Order*

> • **A Legal Document** A purchase order is a legal contract between a buyer and a seller.
>
> *How would you determine the extension cost of an item from the unit cost?*

Invoice and ship to:	Mountain-Air Bicycle Shop			**PURCHASE ORDER NUMBER: 1004**	
	123 State Street				
	Van Nuys, CA 91423			**DATE:** Oct. 15, 20 - -	
Vendor:	Sure-Tread Tire Company				
	782 Via Camino				
	Mission Viejo, CA 91626				

ITEM NO.	QUANTITY	DESCRIPTION	UNIT	UNIT COST	TOTAL
T781	8	10-inch. wheels	ea.	$ 19.99	$ 159.92
K04	2	14-inch wheels	ea.	21.99	43.98
T77	4	20-inch wheels	ea.	24.99	99.96
				TOTAL AMOUNT:	$ 303.86
				TAX	0.00
				TOTAL DUE:	$ 303.86

Go to *marketingessentials.glencoe.com/16/figure/3* to find a project on purchase orders.

marketingessentials.glencoe.com

Figure 16.3 *Purchase Order*

Discussion After students have read **Figure 16.3**, ask volunteers to name and give the purpose of each element of the purchase order as you list them on the board.

Caption Answer You can multiply the number of units by the unit cost to determine the extension cost.

Online Action! For instructions, ideas, and answer guide, go to the Teacher Center at **marketing essentials.glencoe.com**

Follow Up Arrange to have a member of the school staff who deals with ordering supplies, books, or food products for the school talk to the class about the steps involved in creating a purchase order.

TEACH

Discussion Starter

IMPORTANCE OF PURCHASE ORDERS

Ask students to review the purchase order in **Figure 16.3**. Are there any elements of the purchase order that they feel are not necessary? Discuss the need for each part of the PO separately. For example, the addresses are needed to know where the items are going to and from. The unit cost is needed to avoid confusion in the cost of the item. Make sure students can state the purpose of each part of the PO.

TEACHING POINTS

Reinforce Bring a school purchase order to class. Without telling students any details about the transaction, have them describe what each part of the purchase order tells them.

Concept Development

INVOICES

Ask students how one business gets another business to pay for services. Explain that an invoice is an official request for payment. Many businesses will not pay another business unless they receive a formal invoice, even if they know that services have been rendered. Even a personal phone call is not enough. Have students provide reasons why invoices are so important.

They should mention that an invoice is the only official written record of the request for payment, the payment amount, and the date due.

Critical Thinking

Ask students: Why should a customer always check an invoice?

349

ASSESS

Review Guide

CONCEPTS

1. Ask students to recall the parts of a purchase order.

Item number, quantity, description, unit, unit cost, and total including extensions.

2. Have students also restate the primary difference between a purchase order and an invoice.

A purchase order is used by the buyer to requests an item or service. An invoice is used by the seller to request payment for an item or service.

KEY TERMS

Have students review key terms, their spellings, and definitions in small groups.

ONLINE SELF-ASSESSMENT

Have students go to marketingessentials.glencoe.com for the Section 16.3 practice test.

Individualized Review

L1 Assign and review Chapter 16 activities in the Student Activity Workbook.

L2 Assign and review Chapter 16 activities in the Marketing Math Workbook.

L3 Assign and Review Chapter 16 activities in the *BusinessWeek* Reader and Case Studies.

Marketing Practice

Accurate recording is an important part of tracking purchases for both vendors and customers. Ask students to research a company of their choice and write a one-page summary on how that company issues invoices and purchase orders.

---

the bottom of the total column. This amount is used to compute sales tax, if any.

Invoices

When filling an order based on a PO, a vendor will include an invoice with the delivered merchandise. An **invoice** is an itemized list of goods that includes prices, terms of sales, total, taxes and fees, and amount due. The invoice item numbers, quantities, unit costs, and extensions are correct when they match the PO.

Dating Terms

Dating terms state when a bill must be paid and the discount granted for paying early. Ordinary dating occurs when the dating terms are based on the invoice date. Consider, for example, ordinary dating of 2/10, net 30. This means that there will be a two percent discount if the buyer pays within ten days and that the invoice total must be paid within 30 days.

Shipping

As in retail sales transactions, shipping charges are not subject to tax. Therefore, you should add them after the tax is calculated. Shipping services vary greatly, from international companies that specialize in importing or exporting large quantities of goods to the U.S. Postal Service's regular mail service. Private package delivery companies and the post office's Express Mail service compete vigorously with each other in the extremely competitive overnight delivery market. They include Federal Express, UPS (United Parcel Service), and DHL Express.

Parcel Post

Parcel post is one type of standard surface package delivery that is offered by the U.S. Postal Service. Parcel post is a good option if there is time to take packages to the post office and if the customer is willing to wait for delivery.

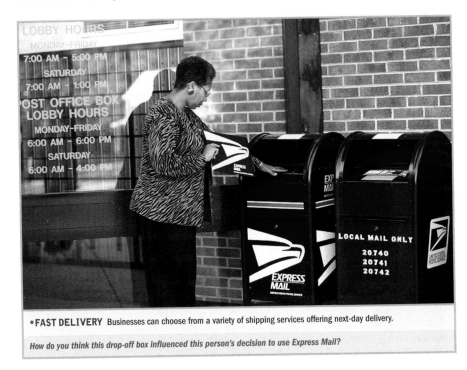

● **FAST DELIVERY** Businesses can choose from a variety of shipping services offering next-day delivery.

How do you think this drop-off box influenced this person's decision to use Express Mail?

PHOTO GUIDE — FAST DELIVERY

Discussion Lead a discussion about the pros and cons of using overnight delivery services. Point out that, while overnight delivery can be expensive, this service pays off in efficiency and speed. Challenge students to think of ways the Internet might be used in place of overnight delivery. Students may suggest E-mail, file transfer programs and .ftp sites, applications that allow you to operate a computer from a remote location.

Caption Answer The drop-off box provided convenience and ease of transaction.

Follow Up Have students research and compare at least two companies' rates for overnight delivery for a typical letter or document.

Cash on Delivery (COD)

With COD (cash on delivery) shipping, the postal carrier will collect the amount due from the customer and forward it to the company. The company must prepay the shipping charges. The amount due from the customer may include the total for both the merchandise and the shipping costs. The customer must pay a fee for the COD service, which varies depending on the amount collected.

Up to $500 may be collected on delivery by a postal carrier. Many businesses prefer using UPS for COD shipments. This is because UPS does not limit the amount that can be collected at delivery to $500 and the shipping charges do not have to be prepaid.

Delivery

Part of the selling arrangement negotiated between a buyer and seller involves delivery. This is an important negotiation point in business-to-business transactions. The issues are who will pay for delivery and when change of title (ownership) will take place. The final delivery arrangement between the buyer and seller, called **terms for delivery**, is part of every agreement in business-to-business sales.

Free on Board (FOB)

There are several possibilities for terms for delivery. All are variations of **FOB (free on board)**. FOB destination leaves title and ownership of the goods with the seller until the goods reach their destination. The seller pays for transportation. FOB shipping point makes the buyer responsible for shipping and for any damages during transit. With FOB factory freight prepaid, the seller pays for shipping but the buyer owns the goods in transit. With FOB destination charges reversed, the merchandise becomes the buyer's when goods are received. The buyer pays for shipping, but any damages are covered by the seller.

16.3 AFTER YOU READ

Reviewing Key Terms and Concepts

1. In business-to-business sales, who issues a purchase order (PO)? An invoice?

2. Define extension and explain how an extension is calculated on a purchase order or invoice.

3. You receive an invoice with the dating terms 2/10, net 30. What does that mean?

Integrating Academic Skills

Math

4. Calculate the extensions for these purchases: 50 reams of printer paper at $5.95 each, 36 pens at $2.20 each, and 24 printer cartridges at $32 each.

Arts

5. You are the buyer for a company that sells computer games. Your boss has asked you to prepare a rough drawing of a new logo to appear on company purchase orders. Prepare a sketch in keeping with the products your company sells.

 Online Action!

Check your answers at *marketingessentials.glencoe.com/16/read*

CLOSE

Have students complete the following statements:

- Much of the math that a buyer does is for _____ .
  purchasing

- Much of the math that a vendor does is for _____ .
  invoices

Extended Activity

Purchasing Orders and Invoices

Bring in a copy of a purchase order a department of the school has recently sent. Show students how the vendor would be likely to fill out the invoice. If possible, also show copies of actual invoices the school has received. Then, have students work in groups to create invoices for the purchase orders they created previously. When finished, have students discuss anything that was difficult about writing out the invoices.

Critical Thinking

Ask students to think about why cashiers count aloud when returning change. Ask: what purpose does this serve?

AFTER YOU READ

Reviewing Key Terms and Concepts

1. In business-to-business sales, buyer issues a purchase order (PO), and a vendor issues an invoice.

2. An extension is the cost of buying multiple items. It is calculated by multiplying the number of units by the cost per unit.

3. This means that you will receive a 2 percent discount if the invoice is paid within 10 days. The entire amount is due in 30 days.

Integrating Academic Skills

4. Paper, $297.50; pens, $79.20; cartridges, $768

5. Designs will vary. Accept all designs that show reasonable effort and understanding of logos.

Online Action! Answers at **marketingessentials.glencoe.com/16/read**

Lifelong Learning

CAREER INFORMATION

Have students go to **marketingessentials.glencoe.com** and find Chapter 16 Careers page and click on the link for the American Marketing Association's Careers Strategies and Tips. Ask students to select one article, read it, and summarize it in three short paragraphs.

USING MATH IN SALES

The information in this chapter informs students about the seller's side of the retail process. Learning the math involved in sales transactions can help students audit the work of salesclerks or computer purchasing programs during transactions. They can also develop the useful habit of double-checking receipts after purchase, which can help them manage expenses.

Primary Source

Ask students to go to **marketingessentials.glencoe.com** and find Chapter 16 Resources. Ask them to click on the link for the American Marketing Association's marketing dictionary and read the definitions of the terms they find which are related to completing and recording the sale.

 THINKING CRITICALLY

When you are using e-mail, people cannot see your facial expressions or hear the tone of your voice. Therefore, it is very important to make sure that the words you write are friendly and extra polite.

@ Online Action!

For instructions, ideas, and answer guide, go to the Teacher Center at **marketingessentials.glencoe.com**

CAREERS IN MARKETING

KEVIN SHARPLES
CUSTOMER SERVICE
MANAGER
STAGEPASS.COM INC.

(?) What do you do at work?
We communicate with customers, mostly by e-mail, which has its own unique challenges. The most important is how we address the customer's concerns while being extremely conscious of the tone of our e-mails. Customers generally want to hear that they are, first, understood and second, that there is someone there to help. Taking time to fully understand the problem from the customer's point of view is critical.

(?) What skills are most important to you?
Advertising may bring in business but customer service is what keeps them coming back and affects how they will speak to others regarding your company. The satisfaction comes in finding the resolution to their problem or answer to their question. It is then that you get the reward of a grateful customer, which usually builds loyalty. People remember how they are treated by a company, so the value of this department can never be overrated.

(?) What is your key to success?
It takes a person who doesn't take things personally and welcomes a chance to make a wrong a right. The reward is a very grateful, happy customer. If you've done your job, they usually are appreciative and leave you with a smile and personal satisfaction. The key is you have to care.

Aptitudes, Abilities, and Skills

Writing and communication skills, patience, and problem-solving strengths are all valuable.

Education and Training

General business degrees can be helpful, although many companies prefer to train their customer service and POS staff in-house.

Career Path

Many customer service and POS jobs are entry level and can lead to a variety of different positions within the company.

THINKING CRITICALLY

Why is careful communication so important in a field where most contact takes place via e-mail?

 @ Online Action!

Go to *marketingessentials.glencoe.com/16/careers* to find a research project on customer service.

marketingessentials.glencoe.com

Test-Taking Strategies

Encourage students to review test material in pairs or small groups. Students can share information, discuss chapter concepts, and quiz one another on chapter concepts and vocabulary words. This peer reinforcement can contribute to concept retention.

FOCUS on KEY POINTS

SECTION 16.1
● You may be called upon to handle several types of sales transactions. They may include cash sales, debit card or credit card sales, layaway sales, on-approval sales, and COD sales. You may also handle returns, exchanges, and allowances. Sales tax and shipping charges are normally added to the total price of products sold.

SECTION 16.2
● Most retail businesses today use electronic cash registers to record sales transactions. Many of these registers are linked to computers as part of a point-of-sale (POS) system. Electronic cash registers display the amount of change to be returned to the customer. Some businesses continue to use cash registers that do not display the amount of change to be returned to the customer. Therefore, knowing the two ways to count change as it is given to the customer is important. Some small businesses use handwritten sales checks to record sales.

SECTION 16.3
● To place an order, most companies prepare a purchase order. A purchase order includes the item number, quantity, description, unit, unit cost, and total (or extension) for each item ordered. When filling an order, a vendor prepares an invoice with the delivered merchandise. The invoice includes all of the information on a purchase order plus tax and shipping charges.

REVIEW VOCABULARY

Study each pair of terms and then, in your own words, tell how they are related to each other.

1. sales check (p. 335)—sales tax (p. 339)
2. layaway (p. 338)—on-approval sale (p. 339)
3. Universal Product Code (UPC) (p. 343)—point-of-sale system (p. 344)
4. till (p. 344)—opening cash fund (p. 345)
5. purchase order (PO) (p. 348)—invoice (p. 350)
6. terms for delivery (p. 351)—FOB (free on board) (p. 351)
7. cash-on-delivery sale (COD) (p. 339)—allowance (p. 340)

REVIEW FACTS and IDEAS

8. What are the various types of retail sales transactions? (16.1)
9. Name and explain the general content of sales checks and the basic ways of generating them. (16.1)
10. What is the arrangement of currency and coins in a cash register drawer? (16.2)
11. What are two methods of making change? (16.2)
12. What are two rules for safeguarding money at the cash register? (16.2)
13. Define Universal Product Code (UPC) and explain its uses. (16.2)
14. What are terms for delivery? Give three examples. (16.3)

Chapter 16 - Using Math in Sales 353

FOCUS on KEY POINTS

Ask volunteers to read the summaries aloud and give the classroom one real-life example for each key point.

REVIEW VOCABULARY

See glossary for definitions of **1-7.** Sentences should display an understanding of the relationships between the key terms.

REVIEW FACTS and IDEAS

8. Types of retail transactions include cash, credit or debit card, layaway or will-call, on-approval, COD, returns, exchanges, allowances, sales tax, and shipping charges

9. A sales check is a written record of a sales transaction that includes such information as the date of the transaction, the items purchased, the purchase prices, sales tax, and the total amount due. It is valuable to a customer as an itemized receipt. In its most complete form, a sales check can contain customer information (name, address, and phone number) and details such as the time of the sale and the identity of the salesperson.

10. Bills are kept in the back compartments, coins in the front. Denominations are arranged from larger to smaller, moving from left to right.

11. Counting up from the purchase price to the amount tendered, starting with the smallest denomination. When using the cash register display of change due, counting down from the largest denomination to the amount displayed.

12. Two rules for safeguarding money at the cash register include 1) Close the cash drawer between transactions. 2) Lock the register if you leave it.

13. A Universal Product Code (UPC) is a combination bar code and number used to identify a product and manufacturer.

14. Terms for delivery refers to the final delivery agreement between the buyer and the seller. Examples may include FOB destination, FOB shipping point, FOB factory freight prepaid, or FOB destination charges reversed.

BUILD SKILLS

15. Workplace Skills
Answers will vary depending on store's policy. Sample answers might include getting the customer's name and phone number for contact after the cash drawer is balanced.

16. Technology Applications
Accept reports that show student effort and understanding of POS systems.

17. Math Skills
The total cost of the merchandise is $6,104.88; (144 × $17.85) + (72 × $16.99) + (72 × $20.80) + (36 × $22.60) = $6,104.88

DEVELOP CRITICAL THINKING

18. Evaluate the Benefits of Technology
Answers will vary; but might include decreased labor costs and better inventory control, which contributes to profit.

19. Protect Your Business
Answers will vary; sample answers might include providing information about identifying counterfeit bills, and policies on obtaining proper ID for credit cards and checks.

BUILD SKILLS

15. Workplace Skills
Interpersonal Communication You work as a cashier, and today has been exceptionally busy. You give change to a woman for a $10 bill. She claims she gave you a $20 bill. Unfortunately, you neglected to leave the bill out while making change.

How would you handle this situation?

16. Technology Applications
Internet Search You work as a cashier in a children's clothing store where an older cash register requires entering the amount of each sale by hand. The owner of the store has asked you to research what POS systems would be appropriate for the store and how much these systems cost.

Use the Internet to do this research. Then use a word processing program to prepare a report.

17. Math Practice
Calculate a Sales Total You prepare a purchase order for the following: 144 shirts at $17.85 each, 72 shirts at $16.99 each, 72 shirts at $20.80 each, and 36 shirts at $22.60 each.

What is the total cost of the merchandise ordered?

DEVELOP CRITICAL THINKING

18. Evaluate the Benefits of Technology
The Universal Product Code (UPC) system was first used by grocery stores to speed checkout and help them keep track of their inventory.

Why do you think other retailers were so willing to adopt the system? What benefits does it provide them?

19. Protect Your Business
The loss to businesses from accepting counterfeit money is a serious problem, as counterfeiters use the latest technology to create ever-better reproductions.

If you were the head of a retail operation how would you protect yourself from this loss?

Formative Assessment

Formative assessment is an essential component of classroom work. This type of assessment provides information that is then used as feedback to modify teaching and meet student needs.

L1 Have students write or demonstrate all of the steps of the two methods of making change.

L2 Have students write a narrative description of two different types of sales transactions. One should be a sale to an individual customer, and one should be a business-to-business sale.

L3 Have students create a fictional sales check, purchase order, and invoice.

 Reteach **If the results of the formative assessment seem low, consider the following activity:**

Read each of the key terms aloud. Have students define the key terms and use them in a sentence. Clear up any confusion students may have.

APPLY CONCEPTS

20. Comparing Purchase Order and Invoice Forms

Ask several local businesses for copies of their purchase orders and invoice forms. Explain to the business owners that you are requesting this information in order to complete a class project. You might also ask about any available information regarding the use of these forms.

Activity Use a spreadsheet program to compare the formats based on ease of use.

21. Comparing Sales Tax Rates

Choose five different states and research the sales tax rates that are applied there.

Activity Create a chart using a spreadsheet program comparing these rates.

NET SAVVY

22. Evaluating Effective Internet Selling

Research how easy it is to purchase items on the Internet. Also research the privacy protection for Internet purchases. Choose three e-tailers that interest you and focus your research on their sites.

Write a brief report detailing your findings, focusing on the strategies you thought were most successful.

THE DECA CONNECTION

Role Play: Sales Associate

Situation You are to assume the role of an experienced sales associate for a gift shop located at the historic home of a well-known nineteenth-century author. The gift shop sells copies of the author's books, postcards, and other souvenir items. You are to help orient a new employee (judge) to the overall duties of a sales associate. The new employee (judge) has asked why math is necessary in selling since all the merchandise has price tickets and the register indicates the amount of change to give for cash transactions.

Activity You are to explain to the employee (judge) the importance of math for selling and how those skills will be useful.

Evaluation You will be evaluated on how well you meet the following performance indicators:

- Process cash and charge sales
- Process returns/exchanges
- Prepare cash drawers/banks
- Open/close register/terminal

 Online Action!

For more information and DECA Prep practice, go to *marketingessentials.glencoe.com/16/DECA*

APPLY CONCEPTS

20. Comparing Purchase Order and Invoice Forms

Spreadsheets will vary depending on forms collected. Accept all spreadsheets that show reasonable effort as well as an understanding of the components of both purchase orders and invoices.

21. Comparing Sales Tax Rates

Charts will vary. Accept all charts that show reasonable effort as well as an understanding of sales tax.

NET SAVVY

22. Evaluating Effective Internet Selling

Answers will vary based on the e-tailers chosen. Accept all reports that show reasonable research effort as well as an understanding of privacy protection strategies.

THE DECA CONNECTION

The students should be evaluated on the performance indicators noted in the role play. For another DECA role play, go to the Competitive Events Workbook or the Student Activity Workbook, or go to **marketingessentials.glencoe.com/16/DECA**

 Online Action! For instructions, ideas, and answer guide, go to the Teacher Center at **marketingessentials.glencoe.com**

DECA Advisors Corner

DECA's Learn and Earn Project can enhance students understanding of sales math. This project provides students with the opportunity to apply entrepreneurial skills to a sales or service project to be run as a real business venture in your community. Students will use their math skills while preparing their proposed budget and as they document the project earnings.

MINI-QUIZ

Read these sentences aloud and have students volunteer the missing words.

1. Coins and currency designated for the register for a given day's business are collectively called the _____. (opening cash fund)

2. The _____ is the maximum amount a salesperson may allow a customer to charge without getting special authorization. (floor limit)

3. A(n) _____ is a legal contract between the buyer and the supplier. (purchase order)

For an expanded chapter quiz, go to Chapter 16 in the TeacherWorks CD-ROM and to Chapter 16 in the **ExamView®** Pro test generator.

SET-UP

Discuss the basic background to make sure students understand the simulation. Ask students: What could be on the promotional CDs and DVDs? Answers may include movie-related products, previews for upcoming films, and promotional pieces (such as music videos).

PROCEDURES

You may want to list procedures on the board and talk about any questions the students might have. Remind the students that a suggested outline for their project is available at **marketingessentials.glencoe.com/u5/ internship.**

TIME MANAGEMENT

Set goals, block schedules, and milestones. Assign interim deadlines for each step of the project.

ASSESSMENT

The rubrics for evaluation of the written, oral, and computer presentations are available at **marketingessentials.glencoe.com/u5/ internship.**

MARKETING INTERNSHIP

A SIMULATED **DECA** *PRODUCT AND SERVICE MANAGEMENT EVENT*

Selling: LidRock Sales

 BASIC BACKGROUND

LidRock sells soft-drink lids that hold mini CDs and DVDs. The current target markets include movie theaters, fast-food chains, and convenience stores—anywhere fountain soft drinks are sold. The content may include songs by popular artists, movie clips, video games, and computer screen savers, as well as special offers by advertisers, such as Internet service providers and other companies that target the demographic that purchases the soft drinks.

Extra Costs LidRock charges about 70 cents for each lid. The pizza and pasta chain Sbarro has been selling soft drinks with CD lids since 2003. It charges up to $1.50 extra, depending on the drink size and what's on the CD. Regal Cinemas haven't raised the price for drinks with CDs and DVDs.

YOUR OBJECTIVE

Your job is to design a Web-based presentation to sell these lid-tops with CDs and DVDs to businesses you believe would be interested in this new promotional medium. Since travel is expensive, the Web-based presentation must include all the steps of the sale, as well as tips for selling them at the retail level and recommendations for CD and DVD content based on the individual prospects you identified.

ASSIGNMENT AND STRATEGY

- **Get the background** Conduct research on LidRock and other companies that sell CDs and DVDs as promotional products. Investigate prospective customers—what businesses could use lid-top CDs and DVDs as part of their promotional mix? What are the major selling points and anticipated objections for this new medium? Review companies that offer Web conferencing software to see how you can set up an interactive sales presentation.
- **Develop the presentation** Identify three prospective customers and the CDs or DVDs that you would suggest for each one. Begin the written script for LidRock's Web-based sales presentation with an appropriate and attention-getting approach. Explain how the product should be depicted. Anticipate objections and prepare suggested responses. In your

---

READ to WRITE

Explain New Marketing Media

Explain to students that CDs and DVDs are exceptional marketing tools because of their inexpensiveness and compactness. Ask students to research new media formats that companies might use for marketing purposes and to summarize their findings in a one-page report. To facilitate their assignment, you might ask students how independent musicians use new marketing tools to spread the word about their music even though they do not have big entertainment conglomerates backing them. You might suggest they resort to utilizing Web blogs, fan-based Web pages, online shared music playlists, and so on.

script, provide a few examples of methods for closing the sale. Offer ideas that might convince customers, such as establishing an on-going partnership or creating a related promotion. Be sure to include ideas for training the retail counterpersons who will be selling the fountain drinks. Explain what will be done as a follow-up to ensure success for the customers.

- **What your project should include** Design the Web-based presentation using computer presentation software. It should be interactive and visually interesting, and use the sales techniques you've learned.

YOUR REPORT

Use a word processing program to prepare a written script to accompany the Web-based computer presentation that could be shown to LidRock. Use presentation software for the Web-based presentation and your oral presentation to our client. See a suggested outline and key evaluation points at *marketingessentials.glencoe.com/internship*

marketingessentials.glencoe.com

Marketing Internship **357**

Unit Review

Now that students have completed the chapters in Unit 5, ask them to review their answers to the Analyze the Ad questions on page 257. Would they answer them differently? Why or why not?

Have students brainstorm ways of evaluating salespeople based on the key principles learned for each step of the selling process. Ask them to organize and compile their standards into a small one- to four-page guidebook.

STEP AHEAD
Ask students to compare and contrast marketing, selling, and promoting. Ask them to consider the concepts, methods, and goals of each.

Internship Wrap-Up

Ask the class to ponder how content on CD-ROMs or DVDs sold to coffee drinkers might differ from those sold to soda drinkers. They should consider if the coffee-drinking market is different from the soda-drinking market. They may suggest that coffee drinkers are an older, business-related audience; the popularity of coffee drinks makes the idea worth pursuing. Have students develop a sample ad for both markets. Encourage students to use graphic design software or art materials to create their ads.

BUILD YOUR PORTFOLIO

Explain to students that portfolios provide evidence of their knowledge and skills in working with data, people, and concepts. Developing a portfolio is a valuable career tool. Point out to students who complete technology-related work to present their portfolio online or on disc. Encourage students to check the portfolio information available at **marketingessentials.glencoe.com/u5/internship**.

Peer Review
Fellow students who share common interests can serve as reviewers of the final portfolios. This review can be completed through the use of a checklist. Go to **marketingessentials.glencoe.com/u5/internship** to find a suggested checklist.

Unit Objectives

After completing this unit, students should be able to:

- Explain the promotional mix concept and its role in marketing
- Discuss trade and consumer sales promotions
- Explain the nature and scope of public relations
- Write a news release
- Discuss the elements of visual merchandising and the artistic aspects of creating a display
- Explain the purpose and importance of advertising
- Identify the different types of advertising media
- Calculate media costs
- Prepare print advertising

Key to Individualized Activities

L1 Level 1 activities are basic activities and should fall within the range of all students.

L2 Level 2 activities are average activities and should be within the range of average and above average students.

L3 Level 3 activities are challenging activities designed for the ability range of above average students.

Enrichment Resources

PROFESSIONAL ORGANIZATIONS

Advertising Research Foundation (ARF) arfsite.org

Direct Marketing Association the-dma.org

MEDIA RESOURCES

Print or online editions of

Advertising Age adage.com

AdWeek adweek.com

Promo Magazine promomagazine.com

WRITING SUPPORT

Ask students to write an essay about whether it is an effective promotional strategy for a product to have a celebrity spokesperson. Why or why not? Have students supply at least three specific examples to present their case. Ask them to keep and review this document as they study Unit 6.

UNIT 6   PLANNING GUIDE AND RESOURCES

CHAPTER	PRINT MATERIALS	TECHNOLOGY RESOURCES
Chapter 17 Section 17.1 Section 17.2	**From Unit 6 Fast File Booklet** Lesson Plans; Chapter Summaries; Reproducible Masters; Reproducible Tests **Print Ancillaries** Student Activity Workbook Marketing Math Workbook *BusinessWeek* Reader and Case Studies, Chapter 17 Competitive Events Workbook, Unit 6 Marketing Research Project Workbook School-to-Work Activity Workbook	Interactive Chalkboard classroom presentations **marketingessentials.glencoe.com** Online Student Edition, Chapter 17 TeacherWorks **Exam***View*® Pro Test Generator, Chapter 17 Virtual Business
Chapter 18 Section 18.1 Section 18.2	**From Unit 6 Fast File Booklet** Lesson Plans; Chapter Summaries; Reproducible Masters; Reproducible Tests **Print Ancillaries** Student Activity Workbook Marketing Math Workbook *BusinessWeek* Reader and Case Studies, Chapter 18 Competitive Events Workbook, Unit 6 Marketing Research Project Workbook School-to-Work Activity Workbook	Interactive Chalkboard classroom presentations **marketingessentials.glencoe.com** Online Student Edition, Chapter 18 TeacherWorks **Exam***View*® Pro Test Generator, Chapter 18 Virtual Business
Chapter 19 Section 19.1 Section 19.2	**From Unit 6 Fast File Booklet** Lesson Plans; Chapter Summaries; Reproducible Masters; Reproducible Tests **Print Ancillaries** Student Activity Workbook Marketing Math Workbook *BusinessWeek* Reader and Case Studies, Chapter 19 Competitive Events Workbook, Unit 6 Marketing Research Project Workbook School-to-Work Activity Workbook	Interactive Chalkboard classroom presentations **marketingessentials.glencoe.com** Online Student Edition, Chapter 19 TeacherWorks **Exam***View*® Pro Test Generator, Chapter 19 Virtual Business
Chapter 20 Section 20.1 Section 20.2	**From Unit 6 Fast File Booklet** Lesson Plans; Chapter Summaries; Reproducible Masters; Reproducible Tests **Print Ancillaries** Student Activity Workbook Marketing Math Workbook *BusinessWeek* Reader and Case Studies, Chapter 20 Competitive Events Workbook, Unit 6 Marketing Research Project Workbook School-to-Work Activity Workbook	Interactive Chalkboard classroom presentations **marketingessentials.glencoe.com** Online Student Edition, Chapter 20 TeacherWorks **Exam***View*® Pro Test Generator, Chapter 20 Virtual Business

National Marketing Education

CHAPTER	SECTION	PERFORMANCE INDICATOR
Chapter 17 **Promotional Concepts and Strategies**	17.1	Explain the role of promotion as a marketing function (PRO)
		Identify the elements of the promotional mix (PRO)
	17.2	Develop sales promotion plans (PRO)
		Analyze the use of specialty promotion (PRO)
		Develop public relations plan (PRO)
		Analyze costs/benefits of company participation in community activities (PRO)
		Obtain publicity (PRO)
Chapter 18 **Visual Merchandising and Display**	18.1	Explain the use of visual merchandising (PRO)
		Explain the use of visual merchandising to create an image (PRO)
		Explain the types of display arrangements (PRO)
	18.2	Explain the relationship of merchandising and visual merchandising (display) (PRO)
		Prepare merchandise for display (PRO)
		Maintain displays (PRO)
Chapter 19 **Advertising**	19.1	Explain the types of advertising media (PRO)
		Evaluate the effectiveness of advertising (PRO)
	19.2	Calculate media costs (PRO)
		Select advertising media (PRO)
Chapter 20 **Print Advertisements**	20.1	Explain the use of advertising agencies (PRO)
		Explain the components of advertisements (PRO)
	20.2	Describe the use of technology in the promotion function (PRO)
		Demonstrate appropriate creativity (PD)

PD Professional Development   **PRO** Promotion

Standards Assessment Correlation

SECTION ASSESSMENT		CHAPTER ASSESSMENT						UNIT LAB
Reviewing Key Terms and Concepts	Integrating Academic Skills	Review Facts and Ideas	Build Skills	Develop Critical Thinking	Apply Concepts	Workplace Skills	Net Savvy	Marketing Internship
1, 2, 3	✓	25	30, 31	32	34, 35		✓	✓
3		26, 27	30, 31	32	34, 35		✓	✓
1, 2			30, 31		34, 35			✓
			30, 31	33	34, 35		✓	✓
1, 3		28		33				✓
	✓		29	33		✓		
3	✓				34			✓
1, 2, 3	✓	9, 10	18	21, 22		✓		
1, 2, 3	✓	9, 10	18	21, 22		✓		
2, 3	✓	11, 12	18, 19	22	23, 24	✓	✓	
1, 2, 3	✓	11, 12, 13	18, 19	21, 22		✓	✓	
1, 2, 3		14–17	18		23, 24	✓	✓	
1, 2, 3		17	18		23, 24	✓	✓	
1, 2		11, 12	18	21	23	✓		✓
1, 2, 3	✓	17	18, 19	21, 22		✓	✓	✓
1, 2	✓	16	18, 20	22	24	✓		✓
		13		22	23, 24			✓
	12		21					✓
1, 2, 3	✓	11, 13, 14			23			✓
			19				✓	✓
1, 2	✓	13, 14, 16, 17	18, 19		23, 24	✓		✓

@ **Online Action!** Check the latest updates for national standards and for your state's standards at marketingessentials.glencoe.com

Unit Overview

Unit 6 conveys the importance of promotional strategies when selling goods and services or developing a business image. First, Chapter 17 describes the concept of promotion and how promotional strategies are coordinated for the appropriate promotional mix. Chapter 18 provides an overview of visual merchandising and display concepts. Chapter 19 explains the different types of advertising media and teaches students how to calculate media costs. Lastly, Chapter 20 explains how advertising campaigns are developed and discusses the role of advertising agencies as well as the elements of print advertisements and techniques for developing effective layouts.

MAKING IT RELEVANT

Inform students that businesses spend a phenomenal amount of money annually on promotional activities that inform, persuade, or remind people about their products or services and improve their public image.

Unit Launch Activity

Have students share their first impressions of the ad on this page. Ask students if they find this ad visually clever. Ask them why or why not, and have them explain their opinions.

OUT OF TIME?
If class time is too short to cover all the chapters in this unit, go to Unit 6 in your Fast File Teacher Resources booklet and find the Chapter Summaries for Chapters 17, 18, 19, and 20.

UNIT 6

Promotion

In this unit you will find

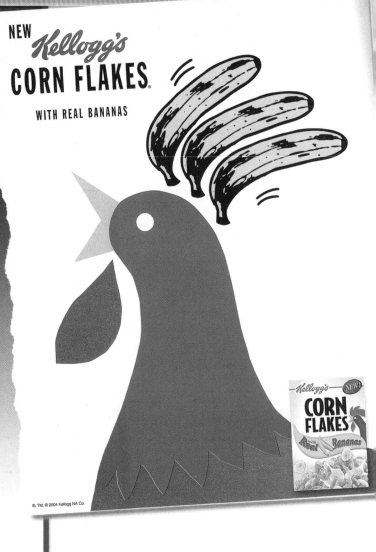

NEW *Kellogg's* CORN FLAKES.
WITH REAL BANANAS

®, TM. © 2004 Kellogg NA Co.

DECA UNIT PROJECT

Marketing Careers in Promotion
Have each chapter member interview three people involved in different aspects of promotion (e.g., an advertising copywriter, an artist, and a marketing manager), and write a report comparing and contrasting the duties, career paths, and job satisfaction levels of each position. The report should conclude with a statement as to whether the student would consider those professions as potential careers.

Assessment Guidelines Prepare a rubric for evaluation that includes completeness of notes taken during an interview, thoroughness of reporting and writing, depth of coverage, and personal experience integrated for appropriateness and relevance.

Enrichment Assign and review Unit 6 activities in the Competitive Events Workbook.

ANALYZE THE AD

Kellogg's did not stray far from its traditional Corn Flakes logo when it introduced a new variation of its cereal. What impression does this ad make?

Market Talk Ready-to-eat (RTE) cereals came onto the market in the late 1800s. Early on, there were only a few varieties, including Shredded Wheat and Corn Flakes. By 1989, cereal makers were introducing more than 100 new kinds of cereal each year.

Think and Write Visit the cereal aisle of your local grocery store. What brands get prime position, in front of your eyes? Which ones are on the top shelves or down by your feet? Choose a cereal you think could have a better display. List three things you would do to change the product's design and display and to promote it.

@ Online Action! Go to *marketingessentials.glencoe.com/u6/ad* for an extended activity.

Functions of Marketing

- Marketing-Information Management
- Financing
- Selling
- Pricing
- Distribution
- Promotion
- Product/Service Management

Foundations
- Professional Development
- Economics
- Business, Management, Entrepreneurship
- Communication, Interpersonal Skills

Academic Concepts • Technology

ANALYSIS
1
SWOT
Economic
Socio-Cultural
Technological
Competitive

STRATEGY
2
Promotion
Place
Price
Product

IMPLEMENTATION
3
Organization
Management
Staffing

BUDGET
4
Cost of sales
Cost of Promotion
Incomes and Expenses

CONTROL
5
Evaluation
Performance Measures
Performance Analysis

In this unit

Foundations of Marketing
- Communication, Interpersonal Skills

Functions of Marketing
- Promotion

marketingessentials.glencoe.com

359

RELATE THE UNIT TO THE MARKETING PLAN

The four Ps of the marketing mix include product, place, pricing, and promotion. Unit 6 explains promotion and its relationship to the other Ps.

MARKETING PLAN OVERVIEW

Let students know that promotion is a key component of any product's marketing plan. The cost of promotion is accounted for the final price of a product.

Functions of Marketing

Point out to students that Chapters 17, 18, 19, and 20 will deal with the marketing function of promotion and the marketing foundation of communication and interpersonal skills.

▸ **Promotion** Promotion is one of the key elements to the marketing mix. It plays an integral part in marketing, along with product, placement, and price.

○ **Communication, Interpersonal Skills** Promotion, one of the four Ps in the marketing mix, is used to communicate a marketing message. Various media are used in promotion, such as print, television, and e-mail. The effectiveness of the promotion depends to a great extent on the communication skills of those developing the promotion. Applying known strategies for effective writing and visual presentation is key to the successful promotion of a product.

ANALYZE THE AD

Students would have to be familiar with the original box of Corn Flakes in order to understand the new box's slight variation. This ad is both humorous (because of the bananas on top of the rooster's head) and traditional.

Market Talk Ask students to discuss how RTE cereals differentiate themselves visually, through ads, and by their placement together in stores. Discuss how placement and promotion work together to sell a product.

Think and Write Answers will vary depending on the cereals students find and the one they choose to promote. Students' suggestions should follow the guidelines for effective promotions, visual display, and design given in the unit.

@ Online Action! For instructions, ideas, and answer guide, go to the Teacher Center at **marketingessentials.glencoe.com**

Chapter Overview

This chapter explores the concept of the promotional mix as well as the five basic types of promotion: advertising, personal selling, direct marketing, sales promotion, and public relations.

BUILD BACKGROUND

Ask students to recall the most outrageous stories they have either heard or witnessed from a company promoting a new product. In their opinion, did the promotional technique work? If so, in what way did it work? Tell students they are going to learn in this chapter how promotional opportunities and techniques aid a company and how sales and public relations all dovetail with promotional strategies.

Why It's Important

You can have the best product in the world, but if it is not promoted well, all the work goes unnoticed in the marketplace. In order to stay competitive and profitable, businesses must have promotional strategies to showcase their investment.

Prepare to Read

List the section objectives to discuss with students. Have students skim the chapter, looking at the photographs, reading the captions, and noting the headings. Ask questions to ensure that the students have a minimal understanding of the chapter structure.

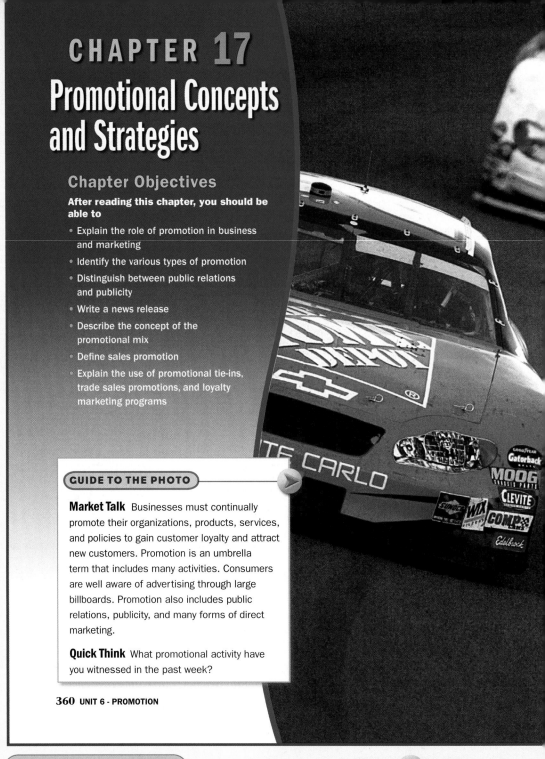

CHAPTER 17
Promotional Concepts and Strategies

Chapter Objectives

After reading this chapter, you should be able to

- Explain the role of promotion in business and marketing
- Identify the various types of promotion
- Distinguish between public relations and publicity
- Write a news release
- Describe the concept of the promotional mix
- Define sales promotion
- Explain the use of promotional tie-ins, trade sales promotions, and loyalty marketing programs

GUIDE TO THE PHOTO

Market Talk Businesses must continually promote their organizations, products, services, and policies to gain customer loyalty and attract new customers. Promotion is an umbrella term that includes many activities. Consumers are well aware of advertising through large billboards. Promotion also includes public relations, publicity, and many forms of direct marketing.

Quick Think What promotional activity have you witnessed in the past week?

360 UNIT 6 - PROMOTION

GUIDE TO THE PHOTO

Discussion Lead a discussion about how we as consumers learn about new products that have recently come to the market. Ask: What role does advertising play? What role does word-of-mouth play? What other ways do we come to learn about new products or services?

Quick Think Student answers will vary but may include examples of advertising or free samples.

Follow Up Ask students to name a new product or service they have recently become aware of and share how they learned about it.

Performance indicators represent key skills and knowledge. Relating them to the concepts explained in this chapter is your key to success in DECA events. These acronyms represent DECA events that involve knowledge of concepts in this chapter.

AAAL	FMAL	MMS*	TMDM*
AAML*	FMDM*	QSRM*	TSE*
ADC*	FMML*	RMAL	VPM
BSM	FSRM*	RMML*	
EMDM*	HMDM*	SMDM*	

In all these DECA events you should be able to follow these performance indicators:

- Explain the communication process used in promotion
- Explain the role of promotion as a marketing function
- Explain the types of promotion
- Identify the elements of the promotional mix
- Explain the nature of a promotional plan
- Coordinate activities in the promotional mix
- Write a news release

All the events with an asterisk (*) also include these performance indicators:

- Obtain publicity
- Develop a public relations plan
- Analyze use of specialty promotions
- Design a frequency marketing program

Some events include additional performance indicators. These are:

FMDM Promote sales through community service activities

SMDM Select strategies for maintaining fan support

DECA PREP

Check your understanding of DECA performance indicators with the DECA activity in this chapter's review. For more information and DECA Prep practice, go to *marketingessentials.glencoe.com/17/DECA*

DECA events that require knowledge of promotional concepts and strategies are described here. Discuss the performance indicators to make sure students understand how to demonstrate their understanding.

The events acronyms stand for:

AAAL: Apparel and Accessories Marketing Series, AL

AAML: Apparel and Accessories Marketing Series, ML

ADC: Advertising Campaign Event

BSM: Business Services Marketing Series

EMDM: E-Commerce Management Team Decision Making Event

FMAL: Food Marketing Series, AL

FMDM: Financial Analysis Management Team Decision Making Event

FMML: Food Marketing Series, ML

FSRM: Full Service Restaurant Management Series

HMDM: Hospitality Services Management Team Decision Making Event

MMS: Marketing Management Series

QSRM: Quick Serve Restaurant Management Series

RMAL: Retail Merchandising Series, AL

RMML: Retail Merchandising Series, ML

SMDM: Sports and Entertainment Management Team Decision Making Event

TMDM: Travel and Tourism Marketing Management Team Decision Making Event

TSE: Technical Sales Event

VPM: Vehicles and Petroleum Marketing Series

DECA PREP

Find timed DECA Prep activities correlated to the Competitive Events Workbook for students and DECA tips for teachers at **marketingessentials.glencoe.com /17/DECA**

CHAPTER 17 Classroom Resources

For the Teacher

- TeacherWorks
- **marketingessentials.glencoe.com**
- Interactive Chalkboard
- **ExamView**® Pro Test Generator
- Fast File Unit 6

For the Student

- *Marketing Essentials* Online Edition
- Student Activity Workbook
- Marketing Math Workbook
- Marketing Research Project Workbook
- School-to-Work Activity Workbook
- Competitive Events Workbook
- *BusinessWeek* Reader and Case Studies
- **marketingessentials.glencoe.com**

FOCUS

Introducing the Section

COLLABORATIVE ACTIVITY

Form students into groups of three to four. Ask each group to imagine that it has been asked for help by the local pet rescue and adoption center. The nonprofit organization needs to promote its upcoming Saturday festival, Pet Adoption in the Park. How can the organization promote this function without spending a lot of money? Ask groups to formulate a promotional plan to convince local citizens to attend this local function.

Preteaching Key Terms

List and review the vocabulary terms with the students. Acknowledge students' correct answers by writing a brief definition next to the terms they know. Place an asterisk by terms they do not know and return to the vocabulary list later when they come across these unfamiliar terms.

- promotion
- product promotion
- institutional promotion
- advertising
- direct marketing
- sales promotion
- public relations
- publicity
- news release
- promotional mix
- push policy
- pull policy

 Critical Thinking

Ask students how they think businesses can evaluate the effectiveness of their promotional strategies.

362

OBJECTIVES

- Explain the role of promotion in business and marketing
- Identify the various types of promotion
- Distinguish between public relations and publicity
- Write a news release
- Describe the concept of the promotional mix

KEY TERMS

- **promotion**
- **product promotion**
- **institutional promotion**
- **advertising**
- **direct marketing**
- **sales promotion**
- **public relations**
- **news release**
- **publicity**
- **promotional mix**
- **push policy**
- **pull policy**

WHILE YOU READ

Describe How would you describe the various types of promotion?

Promotion and Promotional Mix

READ and STUDY

BEFORE YOU READ

Predict What would happen if businesses could not promote their products or services?

THE MAIN IDEA

The combination of advertising, selling, sales promotion, direct marketing, and public relations makes up the promotional mix.

STUDY ORGANIZER

In a chart like the one below, take notes about the five elements of the promotional mix and give examples for each.

```
                    [ Promotional Mix ]

        (  Elements  )              (  Examples  )
```

The Concept of Promotion

Promotion is persuasive communication. Companies rely on promotion to inform people about their products and services. Companies also use promotional techniques to enhance their public image and reputation and persuade people that their products are valuable. Organizations such as nonprofits rely on promotional activities to educate the public about an issue or

362 UNIT 6 - PROMOTION

READ and STUDY

BEFORE YOU READ

Ask students to think of examples when a company may not have promoted an item enough or promoted it too much.

THE MAIN IDEA

To illustrate this idea, pick a product and analyze its promotional mix.

STUDY ORGANIZER

Fill in the elements of the chart as study progresses. A full-size, downloadable study organizer can be found at **marketingessentials.glencoe.com**

WHILE YOU READ Explain that the types of promotion are multifaceted, created to reach as many people as possible in as many venues possible.

trend or to advocate for change in a law or policy. The goals of promotional activities are summarized by the phrase *AIDA*—first attract Attention, then build Interest and Desire, and finally ask for Action.

A business uses **product promotion** to convince prospects to select its products or services instead of a competitor's brands. Promotional activities explain the major features and benefits of the product or service, identify where it is sold, advertise sales, answer customer questions, and introduce new offerings. Product promotion also helps companies foster good relations with existing customers, thereby enhancing their loyalty.

Institutional promotion is used to create a favorable image for a business, help it advocate for change, or take a stand on trade or community issues. As part of its institutional promotional efforts, for example, businesses maintain Web sites to provide news, product and general information, and to answer questions. Although institutional promotions do not directly sell a product or service, these activities do foster a favorable image for the company, which in turn may help sales efforts.

Types of Promotion in the Promotional Mix

The combination of advertising, selling, sales promotion, direct marketing, and public relations makes up the promotional mix. There are five basic categories in the promotion mix and each plays a vital role in promoting businesses and their products. (See Figure 17.1.)

1. Personal selling
2. Advertising
3. Direct marketing
4. Sales promotion
5. Public relations

Through advertising, direct marketing, public relations, and sales promotion, companies communicate with customers in ways other than direct contact. Personal selling, on the other hand, requires direct personal contact with the customer.

Personal Selling

Personal selling requires that a company employ sales representatives who generate and maintain direct contact with prospects and customers. It is one of the costliest forms of promotion. Direct contact can take the form of personal meetings, telemarketing, e-mail contact, and correspondence. Typically, personal selling takes place after—or as a result of—other promotional activities.

Advertising

Advertising is a form of nonpersonal promotion. Companies pay to promote ideas, goods, or services in a variety of media outlets. Advertising can be found everywhere, from magazines, newspapers, television, and Web sites to gymnasiums and city buses. With advertising, a company engages in a one-way communication to the prospect or customer.

Direct Marketing

Direct marketing is a type of advertising directed to a targeted group of prospects and customers rather than to a mass audience. The two forms of direct marketing are printed direct mail, which is sent via regular mail to a home or business, and electronic direct mail.

The goals of direct marketing are to generate sales or leads for sales representatives to pursue. Generally, direct marketing generates a response from the targeted customer by making a special offer, such as a coupon, discount, or special merchandise and delivery terms. Direct marketing gives recipients an incentive to respond by visiting a store or Web site, calling a toll-free number, returning a form, or sending an e-mail.

Both print and electronic direct marketing allows a business to engage in one-way communication with its customers about product announcements, special promotions, bulletins, customer inquiries, and order confirmations. However, as a result of consumer complaints about unwanted electronic direct mailings, Congress passed the CAN-SPAM Act of 2003. This act requires senders of unsolicited

TEACH

Discussion Starter

TYPES OF PROMOTION IN THE PROMOTIONAL MIX

Ask students to discuss why a business might use a promotional mix instead of relying on one form of promotion only. Different types of promotion appeal to and reach different members of a target audience. By using several types of promotion, a business can appeal to and reach a wider audience.

TEACHING POINTS

Explain Tell students that some forms of the promotional mix require fairly savvy interpersonal communication skills while others enlist creative types to create the persuasive campaign. For example, a public relations employee usually has good people skills and frequently works in the field; meanwhile, a copywriter may work best alone.

Clarify Inform students that not all promotional mix categories are created equally. For example, many consumers find the personal selling technique the most invasive and annoying form, due in part to telemarketers calling homes at inconvenient hours and unwanted advertisements filling up e-mail inboxes.

 Virtual Business

Introduce promotion to students using Knowledge Matters' Virtual Business Retailing visual simulation, *Promotion*. In this simulation, students explore the importance of promotion to their business.

 Extended Activity

Understanding Direct Marketing

Bring to class examples of flyers that have been sent or placed to residential addresses. Have students share their responses to the ads and determine both the product or service advertised as well as identify to whom the ads are addressed. Divide students into groups of three to five and have each student create a direct mail advertisement for one of the following services: car sales or service, grooming products, pet care products, nutritional supplements, dentistry, or take-out food. Have students display their creations in class.

Concept Development

BASIC TYPES OF PROMOTION

Organize the class into teams of five or six members. Ask teams to create a business that sells products to high school students. Assign each member to one of the five types of promotion (personal selling, advertising, direct marketing, sales promotion, and public relations) to develop ideas for a promotional mix. Assign a reporter to record the ideas. Have each group orally report on their promotional strategies for their business.

Enrichment

PERSONAL SELLING

Ask students if they or someone they know signed up for the National Do Not Call Registry. (The Federal Trade Commission, the nation's consumer protection agency, runs this program.) Ask: How might this registry affect a business that operates on conducting phone surveys for marketing agencies?

Answers might include limit the diverse pool of phone participants, influence the effectiveness of a product due to lack of market research, decrease telemarketing firms' bottom line, and so on.

Figure 17.1 **Elements of a Promotional Mix**

• **Several Strategies, Same Goal** The promotional activities chosen to promote a particular product are known as its promotional mix.

How do the elements in a promotional mix work together?

Advertising Advertising is a one-way communication about a product with a potential customer. Advertising can be done through radio, television, billboards, newspapers, and the Internet.

Direct marketing Direct marketing sends a promotional message to a specific group of customers. It takes the form of printed mail or e-mail.

Sales promotions Sales promotions are activities directed at business or retail customers to boost sales. Sales promotions include coupons, product samples, and point-of-purchase displays.

Public relations Public relations designed to influence opinion and to create a favorable public image of a person or a product. A campaign to encourage businesses to donate computers to schools is an example.

Personal selling Personal selling requires sales representatives to generate and maintain contact with customers through meetings, by phone, or by e-mail.

@ Online Action! Go to *marketingessentials.glencoe.com/17/figure/1* to find a project on the promotional mix.

marketingessentials.glencoe.com

Figure 17.1 **Elements of a Promotional Mix**

Discussion Give some examples of local businesses. Lead a discussion of the promotional mix by asking students the following questions about each identified business:

• What kind of advertising is done by this business?

• Does the business use personal selling to sell its products?

• Does the business use any sales promotions?

• How could the business use public relations to build and promote itself or its products?

Caption Answer The elements work together to communicate information and attract attention to particular audiences about images, products, services, and issues.

@ Online Action! For instructions, ideas, and answer guide, go to the Teacher Center at **marketingessentials.glencoe.com**

commercial e-mail to give recipients a way to opt out of e-mails, prohibits the use of deceptive subject lines and headers, and requires businesses to provide valid return addresses on their e-mails.

Sales Promotion

According to the American Marketing Association (AMA), **sales promotion** represents all marketing activities—other than personal selling, advertising, and public relations—that are used to stimulate purchasing and sales. The objectives of sales promotions are to increase sales, inform potential customers about new products, and create a positive business or corporate image.

Public Relations and Publicity

Public relations (PR) activities enable an organization to influence a target audience. Often, public relations campaigns try to create a favorable image for a company, its products, or its policies. However, companies can rely upon public relations strategies and techniques for many reasons. One of the goals of a public relations program is to cultivate media relations with reporters who cover a specific industry.

Writing News Releases

Although there are many media tools, one of the most important ones is the **news release**. A news release is an announcement that is sent to the appropriate media outlets.

GLOBAL MARKET

Puma's Advertising Approach

Puma AG is a German company that has an international reputation as an athletic footwear supplier for soccer, track, and baseball.

In 2003, the company had worldwide sales of $1.65 billion, but only 0.25 percent of the U.S. market share for athletic footwear. Puma trailed Nike, which had 45 percent, and Reebok International Ltd., with 9 percent of the U.S. market.

Using the Olympics as a Promotion Theme To increase its market share in the United States, Puma launched an advertising campaign timed to coincide with the 2004 Summer Olympics in Athens, Greece. The company bet that a fun, lighthearted advertising approach would bolster U.S. sales. The company ran 15- and 30-second television ads titled *Stick, Stick, Stick* and featuring Olympic athletes from Jamaica. As the athletes pass in front of different venues, such as markets or parks, viewers hear a loud "boing!" as the baton is passed off. Puma athletic shoes magically appear on the runner's feet.

CRITICAL THINKING

Compare Puma's ad to most other athletic shoes ads. How is it different?

 Online Action!

Go to *marketingessentials.glencoe.com/17/global* to find an activity about international marketing.

TEACH CONTINUED

Individualized Practice

SALES PROMOTION

L1 Ask students to recall a scenario when an advertisement convinced them to buy the product or when an advertisement turned them off to purchasing an item. Have students write a 150-word paragraph on why they believe this ad affected them in this way.

L2 Ask students to analyze an advertisement citing why marketers thought the ad would be appealing to consumers.

L3 Tell students that an advertising firm has asked them to come up with a creative, fun tagline to promote a client's new line of macadamia nut chocolate chip cookies. Come up with three options to propose to the firm. Ask the class to pick their favorite tagline.

Concept Development

PUBLIC RELATIONS AND PUBLICITY

After students have read the section on Public Relations and Publicity, ask them to imagine news stories that did not shed favorable light on someone famous or a well-known product. Can publicity cause more harm than good?

Answers may include stories about negative publicity, such as product recalls or legal troubles.

GLOBAL MARKET

Puma's Advertising Approach

Discussion Lead a discussion on advertising approaches by asking students the following question: When it comes to advertising a product, is the product's spokesperson or the general theme of the advertisement more important to them than the product itself?

CRITICAL THINKING **Answer:** Answers will vary. Most athletic footwear ads focus on individual endorsement, fashion, or competition. Puma's market share is relatively small in the United States, and the company is banking on ads that will attract viewers using a different, creative approach.

Online Action! For instructions, ideas, and answer guide, go to the Teacher Center at **marketingessentials.glencoe.com**

TEACH CONTINUED

Individualized Practice

PUBLIC RELATIONS

L1 Have students take a company with which they are familiar and create a list of five possible public relations efforts it might take to promote its reputation. Allow them to be creative with their scenarios.

L2 Have students select a peer. Have the students share their ideas to create a better institutional image for the school. Process all the ideas together and agree upon the top five. Then, ask students to give their list to the student council for possible implementation.

L3 Within the last several years, there have been highly publicized cases in which public relations efforts helped to counter bad publicity. Have each student research one case of damage control. Have students write a 150- to 400-word paper describing the situation, the company, the bad publicity, and all major public relations efforts taken to overcome it.

Critical Thinking

Ask students to consider examples of good publicity. Ask: What are some ways in which competitors can react to their competitors' successful promotional activities?

Figure 17.2 **News Releases**

- **Step-by-Step Directions** News releases sent via regular mail to media outlets should be double-spaced and printed on letterhead stationery. Margins should be about one-and-a-half inches to allow the editor to make notes. Always type copy so that it is clean, legible, and free of spelling errors. News releases distributed electronically or posted on the company's Web site are limited by the capability of the e-mail program or the Web site design.

What kind of news goes in a news release?

1 The first paragraph should answer the Who, What, When, Where, and Why questions.

2 The story with important facts should be developed within the next few paragraphs.

3 While identifying people in a news release include the full name and title or position of the person, but avoid using Mr., Ms., Mrs., Dr., etc. After you have used the complete name refer only to the last name in the remaining part of the news release.

4 More information that is slightly less important can follow.

5 The entire news release should be brief—usually one or two pages is enough. If the news release runs more than one page, write "more" at the bottom of each page except the final one. Identify and number each succeeding page at the top. On the last page, put "---30---" or "###" at the bottom to signify the end of the news release.

6 The news release should always include the name, address, and phone number of the contact person sending out the release. All pages should be numbered except for the first page.

MOTORCYCLE RIDING ACCESSORIES HIT THE WEB AT FULL SPEED

Dateline: July 15, 2004 ... Miami Beach, FL
Contact Name: Felix Mosqueda
Contact Phone: 1-888-309-5819
Web Address: http://www.moto-xtreme.com/

MIAMI BEACH, FL - July 15, 2004 - Motorcycle accessories are now just a click away at Moto-Xtreme.com. No more driving to the nearest city to find all of the name brand apparel, riding gear, helmets, boots, exhaust systems, tires and other sought-after accessories.

Enthusiasts of motorcycles, snowmobiles, scooters, personal watercraft and ATV's can search hundreds of products throughout the breathtaking selection at Moto-Xtreme.com, and have accessories delivered directly to their home.

With eighteen years' experience in the motorcycle business, and three years as an online Web source for accessories, the owners of Moto-Xtreme.com are very concerned about safety as well as style and quality. Bringing motorcycle riders the best possible products for safety and luxury is the number one goal at Moto-Xtreme.com.

"I'm X-tremely pleased with your pricing, selection and your speed of service!" states customer Andrew W. Bertsch.

Motorcycle riders will enjoy browsing the best buys, closeouts, discounts and new products sections at the site.

Also, the customer service group is knowledgeable, helpful, and available from 10 A.M. until 9 P.M., providing the best possible service to each individual. Shipping is available at only "a penny" on many major brands.

To learn more about Moto-Xtreme.com, please visit the Web site at: http://www.moto-xtreme.com/

For an interview or further information, please contact Steve Sharts at 1-888-309-5819.

@ Online Action! Go to *marketingessentials.glencoe.com/17/figure/2* to find a project on news releases.

 marketingessentials.glencoe.com

Figure 17.2 **News Releases**

Discussion Ask students to imagine they are local reporters for the newspaper. The release in **Figure 17.2** comes across their desk and they are to write a brief news story about its announcement. Have students brainstorm angles from which to approach the story in the release.

Caption Answer A news release announces newsworthy developments about a company or its products or services.

@ Online Action! For instructions, ideas, and answer guide, go to the Teacher Center at **marketingessentials.glencoe.com**

Follow Up Ask students to find a press release or news release about a company, product, or service that interests them. Have students share their releases in small groups.

The release announces newsworthy developments about the company's products or services, distribution channels, facilities and operations, partners, revenues and earnings, employees, and events. (See Figure 17.2.)

Publicity is one tactic that public relations professionals use. Publicity involves bringing news or newsworthy information about an organization to the public's attention. This process is known as placement.

Although a publicity campaign can be launched to achieve various goals, the main function of publicity is to develop a positive perception or awareness of the organization in the marketplace. The right kind of publicity can create and maintain a company's positive image; negative publicity can devastate it. People like to do business with respectable companies, so companies engage in such image-building activities as sponsoring cultural events, awarding scholarships, and donating land or equipment for public use.

Unlike advertising, the placement of publicity is free. For example, a one-minute story on the evening news about a company costs nothing; fifteen seconds of advertising time on the same broadcast, however, can cost thousands of dollars.

Cost is not the only advantage of publicity. Newspapers, television and radio news programs, and reporters are usually viewed as more objective than advertisers. People are more likely to pay attention to and believe news stories than advertisements. Publicity often appears as a media story or is incorporated into a larger story or report, which makes the information appear more credible to many people.

The disadvantage of publicity is that its content, unlike paid advertising, is not easily controlled by the business that issues it. The media select the context and story angle and decide when and how to present the content. Negative stories, such as one reporting on an accident or an unsafe product, are as likely to get publicized as positive ones about company successes or community contributions.

Whenever possible, businesses work to generate positive publicity and avoid negative publicity.

The Concept of Promotional Mix

To teach its promotional goals, an organization develops an effective **promotional mix**—a combination of strategies and a cost-effective allocation of resources. Most businesses use more than one type of promotion to achieve their promotional goals. How do companies decide which mix will be most effective? A business establishes a promotional mix by following a series of steps that range from identifying the target market to measuring the results.

The strategies in the mix are designed to complement one another. Advertising and direct marketing create awareness of a business's product, while public relations helps cultivate a favorable image and brand recognition. Sales promotional activities stimulate sales, reinforce advertising, and support selling efforts. Finally, personal selling builds on all of these previous efforts by completing the sale.

Elements of the promotional mix must be coordinated. For example, national advertising should be reinforced by local promotional efforts. Many consumer product manufacturers give or sell retailers decorations or in-store displays to reinforce a national campaign. At the local retail level, the national and local efforts need to be communicated to the store personnel. Sales personnel should be made aware of coupons, rebates, contests, and any other featured promotional items so that they can encourage customer participation. When promoted products are not available as advertised or when the sales staff is uninformed about a promotion, sales are lost and customers are dissatisfied.

Promotional Budget

In large companies, the marketing department has many roles. It determines the promotional mix, establishes the budget, allocates resources, coordinates the campaign,

Online Activity

Online Media Relations
Have students visit one or more Web sites of the company or organization of their choice. Ask students to find the section of the site that houses media relations content such as press releases or news releases. Ask students to summarize the information presented to the public in this portion of the site, and have them rate the news releases section of the site on usability, readability, and relevance.

ASSESS

Review Guide

CONCEPTS
Ask students to differentiate the elements of the promotional mix, including their advantages and disadvantages.
Answer suggestion: **Figure 17.1** on page 364 is a good example to use in order to answer the question. Allow students to broaden their definitions of "advantages" and "disadvantages" outside of the answers given in the running text.

KEY TERMS
Have students, in small groups, review key terms, their spellings, and definitions.

ONLINE SELF-ASSESSMENT
Have students go to **marketingessentials.glencoe.com** for the Section 17.1 practice test.

Individualized Review

L1 Assign and review Chapter 17 activities in the Student Activity Workbook.

L2 Assign and review Chapter 17 activities in the Marketing Math Workbook.

L3 Assign and review Chapter 17 activities in the *BusinessWeek* Reader and Case Studies.

Marketing Practice

Ask students to take a company's product that interests them and analyze the various promotional strategies used to gain a wider audience. They may have to research the media outlets to see which areas were possibly most successful. Since real data will not be available, students will have to base their opinions on empirical evidence.

Ask students to recall and give answers to the following questions:

- **Compare the communication process in advertising to the communication process in personal selling.**
  Advertising is considered a nonpersonal form of communication that is also known as one-way communication. Personal selling relies on attracting prospects through its advertising, sales promotion, or public relations activities; then, representatives will step in to sell to prospective customers.

- **Is a consumer more likely to encounter the push or pull policy?**
  The pull policy directs promotion towards consumers.

- **Explain the difference between advertising and direct marketing.**
  Advertising is any paid form of nonpersonal presentation and promotion of ideas, goods, or services by an identified sponsor to a mass audience. Direct marketing (print and electronic) is focused directly on individuals rather than a mass audience.

supervises any outside resources, and measures the results.

It is important to consider all aspects of the promotional mix when developing the promotional budget. Determining the ideal amount for the promotional budget can be difficult. There is no precise way to measure the exact results of spending promotional dollars. Often, a promotional budget is a percentage of sales. Sometimes, the budget is dictated by revenue and includes operational costs.

The Push-Pull Concept

Manufacturers often develop a promotional mix for each segment of the distribution channel. To promote a product to large retailers that sell its products, a manufacturer might want to use a mix of personal selling, advertising, and buying discounts. This type of promotion, known as the **push policy**, is used only with the next partner in the distribution channel. The manufacturer pushes the product to the retailer. The main purpose of the promotion is to convince a retailer to stock the products being promoted. A push strategy relies heavily on personal selling and sales promotion, especially at trade shows. It is a helpful strategy for manufacturers whose products do not have strong brand identity.

The same manufacturer might use a different promotional mix of local and national advertising, in-store displays, sales promotion, and public relations to reach consumers. The **pull policy** directs promotion towards consumers. This pull policy of promotion is designed to create consumer interest and demand. Consumer demand can pull or encourage retailers to carry the product being promoted. This strategy relies heavily on advertising geared to consumers, in addition to premiums, samples, and demonstrations.

17.1 AFTER YOU READ

Reviewing Key Terms and Concepts

1. What is promotion?
2. What is the difference between product and institutional promotion?
3. Describe the concept of promotional mix.

Integrating Academic Skills

Math

4. Your school store management team has established a promotional budget of $750 to be spent in the following manner: $300 for a print advertisement in the school yearbook; $125 for "two-for-one specials" on selected advertised items; $75 for premiums (pencils imprinted with the store name); $250 for a DECA scholarship to build public relations. What percentage of the budget is spent on each promotional category?

Social Studies

5. Watch the evening news on television. Write a 200-word report about a segment you think might be the result of corporate publicity.

 Online Action!   Check your answers at *marketingessentials.glencoe.com/17/read*

AFTER YOU READ

Reviewing Key Terms and Concepts

1. Promotion is persuasive communication. It is used to inform, persuade, or remind people about a company's products and its image.

2. Product promotion is used to convince people to buy or use a certain product. Institutional promotion does not directly sell a product, but is used to create a favorable image, which can result in sales.

3. The promotional mix is the combination of advertising, selling, sales promotion, direct marketing, and public relations used by an organization to meet its professional goals.

Integrating Academic Skills

4. Print Advertisement: 40%; two-for-one deal: 16.67%; Premiums: 10%; Public relations: 33.33%

5. Answers will vary; an uncritical representation of the company is a clue that a story is the result of corporate publicity.

Online Action!   Answers at **marketingessentials.glencoe.com/17/read**

Types of Promotion

OBJECTIVES

• Define sales promotion
• Explain the use of promotional tie-ins, trade sales promotions, and loyalty marketing programs

READ and STUDY

BEFORE YOU READ

Predict How do you think a sales force can benefit from promotions?

THE MAIN IDEA

A business must continually promote its products. Sales promotion includes different techniques to increase sales and inform customers about a company's products or services.

STUDY ORGANIZER

Draw a two-column chart like the one below to list examples for each type of sales promotion.

Sales Promotions

Trade Promotions   Consumer Promotions

KEY TERMS

• sales promotions
• trade promotions
• consumer promotions
• coupons
• premiums
• incentives
• promotional tie-ins

Sales Promotion

Sales promotions are incentives that encourage customers to buy products or services. Sales promotions can be used to encourage customers to try a new product, build awareness, increase purchases by current customers, or reward loyalty. Sales promotions are usually supported by advertising

Connect List three examples of how you have responded to sales promotions in the past.

Chapter 17 - Promotional Concepts and Strategies **369**

Discussion Starter

IMPORTANCE OF TRADE PROMOTIONS

Bring to class or ask students to gather samples of store or manufacturer promotional sales fliers often found in the newspaper or even in stores. Encourage students to read the fine print of the promotions to see how each varies and how this might impact a purchasing decision. Have students share their findings in class.

Concept Development

TRADE PROMOTIONS

If possible, schedule a field trip to a local trade show so that students have a better understanding of the purpose of trade shows. (Those students who go to the state and national DECA competitions will have the opportunity to visit the trade show at the convention in which textbooks and other educational materials, DECA merchandise, and school store merchandise will be displayed.)

Build Vocabulary

Ask students to preview the phrase *cooperative advertising* in context. Ask students if they believe they have witnessed this type of advertising before, and, if so, what manufacturers they speculate aided in paying for the local advertising pieces. Have students explain their answers.

activities. They may be either business-to-business (B2B) or business-to-consumer (B2C) oriented.

Trade Promotions

Trade promotions are sales promotion activities designed to get support for a product from manufacturers, wholesalers, and retailers. More money is actually spent on promoting to businesses than to consumers. Major trade promotions include promotional allowances, cooperative advertising, slotting allowances, sales force promotions, and trade shows and conventions. Good business ethics require that trade promotional payments and awards be offered in a uniform manner, that terms be clearly spelled out, and that no one be penalized for not achieving the goals, among other requirements.

Promotional Allowances

Promotional allowances represent cash payments or discounts given by manufacturers to wholesalers or retailers for performing activities to encourage sales. For example, promotional allowances are sometimes used to encourage wholesalers or retailers to stock a large quantity of a product. The cash payment or price discount gives wholesalers and retailers an incentive to sell, so they are more likely to promote the product to customers.

Cooperative Advertising

A manufacturer supports the retailer by helping to pay for the cost of advertising its product locally. This practice is known as cooperative advertising.

Slotting Allowances

A slotting allowance is a cash premium paid by a manufacturer to a retailer to help the retailer cover the costs of placing the manufacturer's product on the shelves. Slotting allowances can range from a few thousand dollars to several million dollars per product. In addition to buying space in the store, slotting allowances also pay for a retailer's discount specials on a product, charges for store shelves, penalties for poor sales, store advertising, and display costs.

Sales Force Promotions

Sales force promotions are awards given to dealers and employees who successfully meet or exceed a sales quota. Such quotas can apply to a specific period of time, such as a month, one day, or a year, or for a particular product or line of products.

Sales force promotions vary from business to business, but they may include cash bonuses or prizes such as merchandise or travel awards.

Trade Shows and Conventions

Trade shows and conventions showcase a particular line of products. One of the largest trade shows is the annual Consumer Electronics Show in Las Vegas, which attracts more than 190,000 manufacturers, retailers, product engineers, and developers. Many participating companies invest millions of dollars in their display booths. Trade shows provide businesses with opportunities to introduce new products, encourage increased sales of existing products, meet customers and partners in the distribution chain, and gain continued company and product support.

Consumer Promotions

Consumer promotions are sales strategies that encourage customers and prospects to buy a product or service. Consumer promotions support advertising, personal selling, and public relations efforts. Major consumer sales promotion devices include coupons, premium deals, incentives, product samples, sponsorships, promotional tie-ins, product placement, loyalty marketing programs, and point-of-purchase displays.

Coupons

Coupons are certificates that entitle customers to cash discounts on goods or services. Manufacturers use coupons to introduce new products, to enhance the sales of existing products, and to encourage retailers to stock and display both.

Coupons are placed on or inside product packages, or printed in newspapers and magazines. Increasingly, companies are

Extended Activity

Promotional Excitement

Ask students to brainstorm and share examples of different promotions or promotional contests they have witnessed or in which they have participated. Let students know that many consumer promotions create customer excitement and increase sales. Contests, sweepstakes, and rebates offer customers a promise of a material reward for purchasing the product. Ask students to keep an eye out for sweepstakes, contests, and other promotions and to bring examples to class. Have students label the kind of promotion offered and place the promotions on a bulletin board.

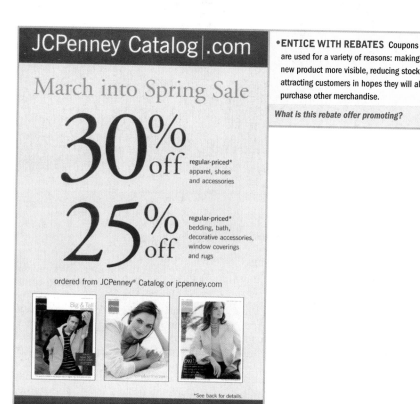

ENTICE WITH REBATES Coupons are used for a variety of reasons: making a new product more visible, reducing stock, or attracting customers in hopes they will also purchase other merchandise.

What is this rebate offer promoting?

using strategies to drive consumers online to download and print electronic coupons or to redeem printed coupons by purchasing merchandise sold online.

Stores that accept coupons send them to the manufacturers' headquarters or to a clearinghouse to be sorted and passed along to redemption centers. The centers, in turn, reimburse the stores for the face value of each coupon plus a handling charge of about eight cents per coupon. They then bill the manufacturers.

Premiums

Premiums are low-cost items given to consumers at a discount or for free. They are designed to increase sales by building product loyalty, and attracting new customers. They also can persuade nonusers to switch brands.

The fundamental concept behind premium marketing is that people will be more motivated to buy a product when they are offered an added-value gift in exchange. Three types of popular consumer premiums are factory packs, traffic builders, and coupon plans.

Factory packs, or in-packs, are free gifts placed in product packages, or as a container premium. This form of premium is especially popular with cereal manufacturers.

Traffic builders are low-cost premiums, such as pens, key chains, pocket calendars, and coffee mugs, that are given away to consumers for visiting a new store or for attending a special event.

Chapter 17 - Promotional Concepts and Strategies **371**

Individualized Practice

DEALS

L1 Ask students how a business uses different sales promotions instead of relying on one form of promotion.
Answers might include sales promotions increase demand and stimulate sales.

L2 Have students select one local company and list five characteristics of its image. This will require researching the company. Then have students write a 50-word summary of the company's image.

L3 Using such publications as *Advertising Age, Stores, Chain Store Age, BusinessWeek,* and *Inc.,* have students research the latest trends in sales promotion. They need to focus on one area only, such as clothing or jewelry. Have students develop an outline of their findings and then write a 250-word report based on their findings.

Enrichment

PUTTING ALL THE PROMOTIONS TOGETHER

Have students work together to prepare a promotional calendar for their school store for the school year. They should incorporate all the types of promotion into the calendar. Encourage students to use at least six illustrations in their calendar.

 Online Activity

Creating a Promotion

Ask students to create a chart with the various forms of consumer promotion. Then, have students use the Internet to scout company Web sites for promotional opportunities in each category.

- **PREMIUMS** Giveaways such as this one encourage customers to visit the store or service provider.

Which two goals does this premium offer seek to accomplish?

Totally Free Checking* and a Free Gift!

Open an Independent Bank checking account and get a Rolling Duffel Bag FREE! Get the whole set when you tell your friends!

Independent Bank
www.independentbank.com

Coupon plans are ongoing programs offering a variety of premiums in exchange for labels or coupons obtained from a product or label. A customer might send a manufacturer three soup-can labels in exchange for a recipe book.

Deals

Deals or price packs offer short-term price reductions that are marked directly on the label or package. The deal might feature two similar products bound together for the price of one or two related products, such as Bausch & Lomb's Renu contact lens cleaner and its multipurpose wetting solution.

Incentives

Businesses use **incentives** to promote many products because they create customer excitement and increase sales. Incentives generally are higher-priced products earned and given away through contests, sweepstakes, and rebates.

Contests are games or activities that require the participant to demonstrate a skill. Contest winners win such prizes as scholarships, vacations, and money.

Sweepstakes are games of chance. (By law in most states, no purchase is necessary in order to enter a contest or sweepstakes.)

Rebates are discounts offered by manufacturers to customers who purchase an item during a given time period. Auto and household appliance manufacturers frequently use rebates to encourage customers to buy their products.

Product Samples

Another form of consumer sales promotion is the product sample. A product sample is a free trial size of a product sent through the mail, distributed door-to-door, or given away at retail stores and trade shows. Detergents, toothpastes, shampoos, deodorants, and colognes are frequently promoted this way. Samples are especially important in promoting new products. Drug manufacturers frequently give samples to doctors and dentists so they can let their patients try new products.

Sponsorship

Sponsorship has become an integral part of promotion. The sponsoring company pays a fee for the right to promote itself and its products or services at or on a set location. The location can be a physical site (such as a stadium), an event (such as a concert), a group (such as a car racing team), or a person (such as a golfer or tennis player).

Sponsors often negotiate the right to use logos and names on retail products. A title sponsor is an organization that pays to have its name incorporated into the name of the sponsored location, such as the Mattel Children's Hospital at the University of California in Los Angeles.

Sponsorship is a high-profile promotional medium. Therefore, deals must be able to

AD GUIDE   PREMIUMS

Discussion Banks often offer a popular consumer premium for opening a checking account. Ask students which type of plan they think this ad promotes: factory packs, traffic builders, or coupon plan. Give some examples of items offered for their pursuit of services.

Caption Answer This premium wants both to sign up new customers and to have them recruit other potential customers.

Follow Up Ask students to make a list of three to five items they have purchased due to popular consumer premium offers. How satisfied were they with the "prize" in relation to the actual product? Would they buy the product again based upon the free item?

withstand public and media scrutiny. The effectiveness of the sponsorship is measured among those who actually view the title or logo.

Promotional Tie-Ins, Cross-Promotion, Cross-Selling

Promotional tie-ins are also known as cross-promotion and cross-selling campaigns. These activities involve sales promotional arrangements between one or more retailers or manufacturers. They produce mutually beneficially results.

Partners combine their resources (advertising and sales promotional activities) to conduct a promotion that will create additional sales for each partner. Promotional tie-ins as well as cross-promotional and cross-selling campaigns can be complex and involve several companies. This practice is becoming increasingly popular on the Internet; for example, a traditional marketer will offer an incentive for consumers to go online to make a purchase or receive a discount from an online marketer.

Product Placement

Product placement is a consumer promotion that involves using a brand-name product in a movie, television show, sporting event, or even in a commercial for another product. For example, in the *Survivor* television series, winning teams were given Doritos and Mountain Dew as treats. Strategic product placement helps an organization develop recognition for its products and gain increased exposure. One of the best-known examples for product placement took place in the Warner Brothers movie *You've Got Mail,* which featured America Online (AOL). The onscreen exposure in this movie is said to have cost AOL between $3 and $6 million. As a result, Warner Brothers was able to offset

---

NET MARKETING

Supermarket Shopping Online

Although online groceries represent only 5 percent of a $400 billion supermarket business, online sales are projected to grow in the future. Many customers prefer the ease of shopping online and filling their virtual shopping carts at home. Items ordered online are delivered the next day for about $10 per order. For some shoppers, the convenience is worth the cost.

Expansion Strategy

While several online grocers have failed in the past because of costly high-tech warehouses and rapid expansions, stores like Albertson's, Publix Super Markets, Inc., and Safeway are limiting their expenses by using individual stores rather than costly warehouses to fill orders. Their e-business segments are also expanding slowly, often one city or neighborhood at a time.

● THINK LIKE A MARKETER

Suggest how online grocers can promote online shopping and avoid high promotional costs.

@ Online Action!

Go to *marketingessentials.glencoe.com/17/net* to find an activity about Internet promotion and shopping.

NET MARKETING

Supermarket Shopping Online

Discussion After students have read Net Marketing, lead a discussion about online grocery shopping. Ask students if they think this version of shopping will increase in the future and to brainstorm why stores are slow to respond thus far.

● THINK LIKE A MARKETER Answer: Answers will vary but may include cross-promotions and a loyalty marketing program. Repeat buyers can receive electronic mailings announcing specials, coupons, and loyalty reward points. Ceiling banners, shopping bags, local TV ads, and weekly flyers can also be displayed in each retail location.

@ Online Action! For instructions, ideas, and answer guide, go to the Teacher Center at **marketingessentials.glencoe.com**

TEACH CONTINUED

Concept Development

CROSS-SELLING AND SPONSORSHIP

After students have read this section, ask volunteers to explain the difference between cross-selling and sponsorship. Cross-selling is a consumer sales promotion that involves promotional arrangements between one or more retailers or manufacturers. They combine their resources (advertising and other promotional activities) to do a promotion that creates additional sales for each partner. Sponsorship involves the promotion of a company in association with a property.

▢ Extended Activity

Consumer Promotions

This activity will help students reflect on the decision-making process by which companies decide which form of consumer promotion is most likely to benefit specific merchandise or specific services. Divide students into groups of three to six. Ask each group to choose a product or service and come up with a promotion strategy and plan for that product or service. Groups should use one of the following types of promotions mentioned in Section 17.1: coupons, premiums, incentives, product samples, sponsorships, promotional tie-ins, product placement, loyalty marketing programs, or point-of-purchase displays. Have each group present their findings to the class in an oral presentation. Encourage groups to use multimedia in their presentations.

Review Guide

CONCEPTS

Ask students to write the short answers to Section 17.2 objectives in their journals. Allow them to write the answers from memory first and then go back to use the book to fill in the holes.

KEY TERMS

Have students review key terms, their spellings, and definitions in small groups.

ONLINE SELF-ASSESSMENT

Have students go to **marketingessentials.glencoe.com** for the Section 17.2 practice test.

Individualized Review

L1 Assign and review Chapter 17 activities in the Student Activity Workbook.

L2 Assign and review Chapter 17 activities in the Marketing Math Workbook.

L3 Assign and review Chapter 17 activities in the *BusinessWeek* Reader and Case Studies.

Marketing Practice

Have students collect a week's worth of coupons and other premiums delivered in the newspaper, magazines, and mail. Have them create a log of these promotional items. The log should be descriptive; it might include type of consumer promotion, duration of offering, notes on its visual appeal, action likely to be taken on this item, and so on. Have students share their logs in class.

Case Study

Plastic That Pays Back

Credit card companies know that consumers are more loyal to brands than they are to their cards. They understand that consumers will respond to the card with the best (lowest) rate. Consumers will easily switch credit cards. It is not surprising, therefore, that credit card issuers align themselves with consumer brands.

Co-Branding

Many financial institutions offer credit cards branded with the names of consumer companies. This type of arrangement is known as co-branding.

The specifics of co-branded cards vary quite a bit, but generally, for each dollar you charge, you receive a point. Points can be redeemed at affiliated companies— for lattes with your Starbucks-branded card, for chinos with your Gap-branded card, or for flights with your Delta-branded card. The number of accounts offering rewards jumped from 35 million to 56 million in 2003 according to the industry-tracking Nielson Report. According to Synovate, a market-research firm, U.S. households received 263 million pitches for co-branded credit cards in the last quarter of 2003, up 35 percent from the same period the year before.

THINK STRATEGICALLY

Why are loyalty programs involving co-branded credit cards growing in popularity?

@ Online Action! Go to *marketingessentials.glencoe.com/17/case* to find an activity about financial marketing.

---

its production costs and create a realistic film, while AOL received international film exposure for its product and services. Another popular example is the movie character James Bond, who is known as much for his Rolex watch and Aston-Martin as he is for his prowess.

Loyalty Marketing Programs
Loyalty marketing programs, also called frequent buyer programs, reward customers for patronizing a company.

The airline industry instituted one of the first such promotions, the frequent flier program. These programs reward customers with free air travel once they have accumulated a designated amount of travel miles.

The hotel industry has adopted similar programs in which consumers can earn free lodging by spending a designated number of nights or dollar amount on lodging.

Customer loyalty means that customers are so satisfied with a brand or retailer that

374 UNIT 6 - PROMOTION

marketingessentials.glencoe.com

Case Study Plastic That Pays Back

Discussion Have students read the Case Study and discuss what makes them loyal to a brand. Would they change from one brand to another if the other one had co-branded with a company they particularly liked? Encourage students to use real-world examples to help illustrate this marketing alliance.

THINK STRATEGICALLY
Answer: Answers will vary. Co-branded credit cards provide frequent buyers with rewards on future purchases of co-branded products and services. Co-branded partners can combine resources and promote customer loyalty.

@ Online Action! For instructions, ideas, and answer guide, go to the Teacher Center at **marketingessentials.glencoe.com**

they continue to buy that brand or patronize that retailer even when they have others from which to choose. Loyalty marketing offers consumers incentives to continue to buy.

Both small and large businesses in many industries have adopted loyalty marketing programs. T.G.I Friday's, a restaurant chain, has a Gold Points card program; customers can earn points and trade them for dining certificates and catalog merchandise.

Online Loyalty Marketing

Online versions of loyalty marketing programs have also become popular. The Internet search engine Yahoo! awards points to Web surfers who buy from certain retailers or visit certain Web sites. Yahoo! has negotiated with the airline industry to allow consumers to convert their points into frequent flier miles.

Point-of-Purchase Displays

Point-of-purchase displays are displays designed primarily by manufacturers to hold and display their products. They are usually placed in high-traffic areas and promote impulse purchases.

By exposing potential customers firsthand to a company's products, point-of-purchase displays stimulate sales and serve as in-store advertising. A complete discussion of visual merchandising and display can be found in Chapter 18.

CLOSE

Ask students to recall and provide answers to the following:

- **Give examples of the locations where a sponsor might be found.**
  Physical site—stadium, hospital, museum, or performing arts center; event—concert, film festival, or yacht race; group—car racing team; and person—professional athlete

- **Give examples of trade promotions and consumer promotions.**
  Examples of trade promotions include promotional allowances, cooperative advertising, slotting allowances, sales force promotions, buying allowances, trade shows and conventions. Examples of consumer sales promotions include cross-selling, coupons, premiums, incentives, samples, sponsorship, product placement, loyalty marketing programs, and point-of-purchase displays.

17.2 AFTER YOU READ

Reviewing Key Terms and Concepts

1. Why do businesses use sales promotions?
2. Explain the difference between trade and consumer promotions.
3. What are the purposes of promotional tie-ins?

Integrating Academic Skills

Math

4. Promotional discounts are given to stores by manufacturers to place products in preferred locations or to pay for ads, displays, or in-store demonstrations. Calculate the store's cost to stock the following items and the percentage of the discount given.

Item	Purchase Amount	Discount Amount	Net Cost to Store	Percent Discount
Snowboards	$5,650	$847.50	_____	_____
CD Players	$535	$42.80	_____	_____

Language Arts

5. Perform an Internet search or visit a library to identify some of the advantages and disadvantages that manufacturers face when they issue product coupons. Identify and label them in a two-column table.

 Online Action! Check your answers at *marketingessentials.glencoe.com/17/read*

AFTER YOU READ

Reviewing Key Terms and Concepts

1. Sales promotions are used to encourage product trials, build product awareness, encourage more purchases, or reward loyalty.

2. Trade promotions are sales promotion activities designed to gain manufacturers', wholesalers', and retailers' support for a product. Consumer sales promotion activities are designed to encourage individual customers to buy a product.

3. Promotional tie-ins involve sales promotional arrangements between one or more retailers or manufacturers. This is designed to stimulate customer response to a product offered and combine the resources of each partner in the arrangement and enables companies to reach customers and prospects within market segments that they have in common, to share costs, and to capitalize on the brand awareness of popular consumer or business-to-business brands.

Integrating Academic Skills

4. Snowboards: Net Cost = $4,802.50, 15% discount; CD players: Net Cost = $492.20, 8% discount

5. Answers will vary. Tables should be organized and contain evidence of research.

Online Action! Answers at **marketingessentials.glencoe.com/17/read**

375

Lifelong Learning

CAREER INFORMATION

Have students go to marketingessentials.glencoe.com and find Chapter 17 Careers and click on the link for the American Marketing Association's Careers Strategies and Tips. Ask students to select one article, read it, and summarize it in three short paragraphs.

INVESTIGATING CAREER CHOICES

Newspapers, magazines, and Web sites often list entry-level positions in sales promotions and public relations. Many Web sites offer career advice and resources as well as the opportunity to browse available positions. Students can also use the print or online *Occupational Outlook Handbook* for detailed information about careers in sales, public relations, or marketing.

Primary Source

Ask students to go to marketingessentials.glencoe.com and find Chapter 17 Resources. Ask them to click on the link for the American Marketing Association's marketing dictionary and read the definitions of the promotions-related terms they find.

THINKING CRITICALLY

Answers will vary. A mentor provides career and professional advice and guidance. Teachers, school counselors, and business associations can help you find and choose mentors.

@ Online Action!

For instructions, ideas, and answer guide, go to the Teacher Center at marketingessentials.glencoe.com

376

CAREERS IN MARKETING

OLGA GARCIA
MANAGER,
CORPORATE RELATIONS
COORS BREWING
COMPANY

(?) What do you do at work?
My position is Manager, Corporate Relations, Coors Brewing Company. My emphasis is on the Latino community, developing relevant corporate initiatives and sales opportunities that enhance the company's image and build brand awareness.

(?) What skills are most important to you?
The ability to communicate effectively both written and verbally, in both Spanish and English, to a variety of audiences: the Latino public, the general market and Latino press, community leaders, internal departments, our distributors, agencies and senior management. A formal education (bachelor and masters degrees) in communications, journalism, government affairs and business administration is very important, as well as formal education in the Spanish language. Continuing education as a professional is critical to success, especially in leadership development.

(?) What is your key to success?
Ongoing evaluation of your career goals with a mentor. A good mentor can help you identify areas of improvement to realize your maximum potential and a game plan to help you achieve your career goals. The work-family life plan should be included in goals to set realistic expectations that can be achieved throughout your life cycle. And don't be afraid to move out of your comfort zone!

Aptitudes, Abilities, and Skills

Communication and interpersonal skills are crucial in this career.

Education and Training

Degrees in communication, business administration, and marketing are all helpful; Masters-level degrees can be especially beneficial.

Career Path

Careers such as this one often begin with entry-level positions within a company's marketing or public relations department, and evolve over time as the employee becomes familiar with the company's products and services, and how best to present them to the public.

THINKING CRITICALLY

How can a mentor help with your career development? How should you go about choosing a mentor?

@ Online Action!

Go to *marketingessentials.glencoe.com/ 17/careers* to find a career-related activity.

Test-Taking Strategies

Encourage students to "guess smart" if they do not know the answer to a multiple-choice question. Try to eliminate one or two choices that seem wrong, and then select one answer through this process of elimination.

FOCUS on KEY POINTS

SECTION 17.1

● Promotion is any form of communication a business uses to inform, persuade, or remind people about its products and its image. Promotion includes personal selling, advertising, direct marketing, sales promotion, and public relations.

● Public relations fosters a favorable image about a business, its products, or its policies. Publicity tries to place positive information in the media.

SECTION 17.2

● Sales promotion is a short-term incentive given to encourage consumers to buy a product or service. Sales promotions can be classified as either trade promotions or consumer sales promotions.

REVIEW VOCABULARY

Write a sentence for each of the following terms.

1. promotion (p. 362)
2. product promotion (p. 363)
3. institutional promotion (p. 363)
4. advertising (p. 363)
5. direct marketing (p. 363)
6. sales promotion (p. 365)
7. public relations (p. 365)
8. news release (p. 365)
9. publicity (p. 367)
10. promotional mix (p. 367)
11. push policy (p. 368)
12. pull policy (p. 368)
13. sales promotions (p. 369)
14. trade promotions (p. 370)
15. consumer promotions (p. 370)
16. coupons (p. 370)
17. premiums (p. 371)
18. incentives (p. 372)
19. promotional tie-ins (p. 373)

REVIEW FACTS and IDEAS

20. List the five basic types of promotion. (17.1)
21. What is the purpose of public relations? (17.1)
22. Explain the differences between trade promotions and consumer sales promotions. (17.2)
23. Explain the difference between contests, sweepstakes, and rebates. (17.2)
24. Explain the concept of product placement. (17.2)

Chapter 17 - Promotional Concepts and Strategies 377

REVIEW FACTS and IDEAS

20. The five basic types of promotion are personal selling, advertising, direct marketing, sales promotion, and public relations.

21. Public relations is designed to influence opinion and to create a favorable image of a person or product.

22. Trade promotions are incentives provided in business-to-business transactions; consumer sales promotions are aimed at individual purchases of a particular product or service.

23. Contests and sweepstakes are different kinds of games. Contests require participants to demonstrate a skill; sweepstakes are games of chance. Rebates are discounts offered by manufacturers to customers who purchase a product or service during a given time period.

24. Product placement is a consumer promotion that involves using a brand-name product in a movie, television show, sporting event, or commercial for another product. Its purpose is to develop consumer recognition of the product.

FOCUS on KEY POINTS

Ask volunteers to read the summaries aloud and encourage students to offer one real-life example for each concept.

REVIEW VOCABULARY

See glossary for definitions of **1–19.**
A sample answer might read:

1. *Promotion* is persuasive communication.

CHAPTER 17 REVIEW

BUILD SKILLS

25. Workplace Skills

Answers will vary, but should tactfully handle the situation presented. Students should be able to explain their positions in a way that is respectful of the boss and the company practice while asserting the importance of the charitable giving he or she already does.

26. Technology Applications

Answers will vary. Answers should demonstrate an understanding of the marketing use of e-coupons. An e-coupon is a keyword or a combination of numbers good for a discount when making a purchase over the Internet. A business usually e-mails the coupon to a potential or existing customer. The term is used less often for online or e-mailed coupons that are intended to be printed out and used in a store.

27. Math Practice

Advertising: $1,200,000 × .53 = $636,000;
Sales Promotion: $1,200,000 × .27 = $324,000;
Trade Promotion: $1,200,000 × .20 = $240,000.

DEVELOP CRITICAL THINKING

28. Understanding Promotional Devices

Answers will vary; possible answers might include: pro: redeemable at convenient locations, pique consumers' interest in a product; con: easily disposable, time restrictive.

29. Researching Publicity

Answers will vary; encourage students to utilize a variety of media outlets as research guides. Summaries and explanations should display an understanding of the concept of negative publicity.

BUILD SKILLS

25. Workplace Skills

Human Relations Each month at your company, a certain amount is automatically deducted from managers' paychecks and donated to established charities. Your boss has asked you to participate. You are reluctant because you already donate to your own charities, and you prefer to decide where your money goes. How would you explain your position?

26. Technology Applications

E-Coupons Perform an Internet search to find examples of electronic coupons and use a word processing program to prepare a brief report on the advantages of electronic coupons as promotional devices. Explain how e-coupons are used.

27. Math Practice

Figure Out Promotional Expenditures A large amount of money is spent annually on promotional activities in the United States. The average budget spent on any one campaign breaks down as follows: 53 percent for advertising, 27 percent for sales promotion, and 20 percent for trade promotion.

Use these percentages to calculate the amount a company will spend on each type of promotional expenditure to promote a product in the United States if its overall budget is $1.2 million.

DEVELOP CRITICAL THINKING

28. Understanding Promotional Devices

Research the advantages and disadvantages of coupons as promotional devices. Gather coupons from a local newspaper, magazines, or the Internet. Use these coupons to give specific examples of pros and cons.

29. Researching Publicity

Identify an event that resulted in negative publicity for a business or person. You can find examples by reading through national newspapers (in the business pages) and magazines, or by performing an Internet search. Even simple key words such as *negative publicity* will yield some examples. Summarize the situation for your chosen examples. Explore how the outcome could have been avoided or how negative publicity could have been minimized.

Formative Assessment

Formative assessment is an essential component of classroom work. This form of assessment provides information that is then used as feedback to modify teaching and meet student needs.

L1 Review key terms for this chapter. Ask students to write one sentence for each key term.

L2 Provide various examples of factors that affect public relations in story form. After each story, have the students identify which factors affect public relations.

L3 Ask students to create stories that illustrate effective sales promotional ideas of a product of their choice.

 Reteach If the results of this formative assessment seem low, consider the following activity:

Read the sections' objectives and subheads. Then, ask students to start drawing conclusions based on the concepts voiced.

APPLY CONCEPTS

30. Planning Promotions

Plan a promotion for a product of your choice. Describe your target market, as well as the public image you would like for your product. Choose a product name and explain why it will appeal to your audience. Describe where you will sell your product (catalog, retail store, discount store, or industry). Discuss any premiums you might offer to promote your product.

Activity Use a word processing program to write a report about your plan.

31. Analyzing Promotions

Choose a product that is heavily promoted in the marketplace. Answer the following questions in your analysis: What market is being targeted? What type of image is the company trying to project? What types of promotion are used? Are the promotions effective? Why or why not?

Activity Prepare an oral analysis of the product using presentation software.

NET SAVVY

32. Internet Promotions

Perform an Internet search to identify three different retail apparel companies that are of interest to you. Summarize at least one Web-based promotional effort used by each company this year. Include in your summaries what you think the goals of the promotions were.

marketingessentials.glencoe.com

THE **DECA** CONNECTION

Role Play:
Promotional Concepts and Strategies

Situation You are to assume the role of employee of a service station that also has an attached convenience store. The station owner (judge) is an enthusiastic fan of the local professional football team. The station owner (judge) has decided to celebrate the team's victories by offering free coffee on Monday's following a victory by the football team.

Activity The station owner (judge) has asked you to prepare a report with an outline for a promotional plan for the free coffee promotion.

Evaluation You will be evaluated on how well you meet the following performance indicators:

- Develop a sales promotion plan
- Analyze the use of specialty promotions
- Explain the types of promotion
- Identify the elements of the promotional mix
- Prepare simple written reports

 Online Action!

For more information and DECA Prep practice, go to *marketingessentials.glencoe.com/17/DECA*

Chapter 17 - Promotional Concepts and Strategies **379**

CHAPTER **17** REVIEW

APPLY CONCEPTS

30. Planning Promotions
Answers will vary; student plans should display an understanding of promotion, premiums, and related concepts.

31. Analyzing Promotions
Answers will vary; student analyses should reflect an understanding of the promotion used and its effectiveness.

NET SAVVY

32. Internet Promotions
Summaries will vary; student responses should reflect an understanding of Web-based promotion techniques.

MINI-QUIZ

Read these sentences aloud and have students volunteer whether they are true or false.

1. A promotional mix is a combination of different types of promotion used to sell a product. (true)

2. An activity designed to create goodwill toward a business is called public relations. (true)

3. A pre-written story about a company that is sent to the various media is called a press kit. (false, this is a news release)

For an expanded chapter quiz, go to Chapter 17 in the TeacherWorks CD-ROM and to Chapter 17 in the **ExamView®** Pro Test Generator.

THE **DECA** CONNECTION

Students should be evaluated according to the performance standards noted in the role play. For another DECA role play, go to the Competitive Events Workbook or the Student Activity Workbook, or go to marketingessentials.glencoe.com/17/DECA

 Online Action! For instructions, ideas, and answer guide, go to the Teacher Center at marketingessentials.glencoe.com

DECA Advisors Corner

To increase your DECA chapter's visibility, keep a camera handy in the classroom and in your student store (if applicable). Assign students public relations activities for the semester, such as taking pictures, videotaping activities, creating displays, or writing press releases for your local or school newspaper.

Chapter Overview

Chapter 18 introduces the importance of visual merchandising as a promotional strategy to attract potential customers and to create a desired business image. The chapter explains the concepts of visual merchandising and display, and identifies the ways in which cultural and ethnic differences impact visual merchandising. It presents the different types of displays, the key steps in display preparation, the artistic elements necessary for successful displays, and basic display maintenance principles.

⊘ BUILD BACKGROUND ⊘

Ask students to think about what first catches their attention when they walk into a store. Do students notice the merchandise or the display elements first? Tell students that they are going to learn more about visual merchandising and displays and their role in promotion.

Why It's Important

Promotion strategies such as visual merchandising and displays help sell products and services, attract potential customers, and create a desired image for an organization or business.

Prepare to Read

List the section objectives to discuss with students. Have students skim the chapter, looking at pictures, reading captions, and noting headings. Ask questions to ensure that students have a basic understanding of the chapter structure.

CHAPTER 18
Visual Merchandising and Display

Chapter Objectives

After reading this chapter, you should be able to:

- Explain the concept and purpose of visual merchandising
- Identify the elements of visual merchandising
- Describe types of display arrangements
- Understand the role of visual merchandisers on the marketing team
- List the five steps in creating a display
- Explain how artistic elements function in display design
- Describe the importance of display maintenance

▸ GUIDE TO THE PHOTO

Market Talk Window display is often the first contact the customer has with merchandise. This type of display is used especially in fashion retail. Displays can set the tone for the store (high-end, professional, or young and trendy). Window displays can even become a tradition, such as Chicago's Marshall Field's displays.

Quick Think Besides fashion retail, which other business categories rely heavily on displays?

GUIDE TO THE PHOTO

Discussion Lead a discussion about how fashion retail storefront or store window displays often celebrate a particular season. Ask: Which elements in the storefront or store window display help us identify the season? Students might name colors, fabric accents, lighting, graphics, props, and more.

Quick Think Student responses may include: computer equipment stores, audio and video equipment stores, bookstores, movie rental stores, etc.

 Follow Up Ask students to consider how a large store chain might vary its visual merchandising and display to appeal to different cultures or to reflect different seasons.

Performance indicators represent key skills and knowledge. Relating them to the concepts explained in this chapter is your key to success in DECA events. These acronyms represent DECA events that involve knowledge of concepts in this chapter.

AAAL*	FMDM	HMDM	RMML*
AAML*	FMML*	QSRM*	TMDM
FMAL*	FSRM*	RMAL*	VPM*

In all these DECA events you should be able to follow these performance indicators:

- Prepare store/department for special event
- Dismantle/Store displays/display fixtures/forms
- Create promotional signs

All the events with an asterisk (*) also include these performance indicators:

- Explain the use of visual merchandising in retailing
- Describe types of display arrangements
- Maintain displays
- Select and use display fixtures/forms
- Create displays

Some events include additional performance indicators. These are:

AAAL/AAML	Arrange trunk showing (apparel)
FMAL/FMML	Build food marketing displays
FSRM/QSRM	Explain display considerations in food service
RMAL	Plan/Schedule displays/themes with management
RMML	Inspect/Approve displays
VPM	Set up point-of-sale displays and handouts

DECA PREP

Check your understanding of DECA performance indicators with the DECA activity in this chapter's review. For more information and DECA Prep practice, go to *marketingessentials.glencoe.com/18/DECA*

marketingessentials.glencoe.com

Chapter 18 - Visual Merchandising and Display **381**

THE DECA CONNECTION

DECA events that require knowledge of visual merchandising and display are described here. Discuss the performance indicators to make sure students understand how to demonstrate their understanding.

The events acronyms stand for:

AAAL: Apparel and Accessories Marketing Series, AL

AAML: Apparel and Accessories Marketing Series, ML

FMAL: Food Marketing Series, AL

FMDM: Financial Analysis Management Team Decision Making Event

FMML: Food Marketing Series, ML

FSRM: Full Service Restaurant Management Series

HMDM: Hospitality Services Management Team Decision Making Event

QSRM: Quick Serve Restaurant Management Series

RMAL: Retail Merchandising Series, AL

RMML: Retail Merchandising Series, ML

TMDM: Travel and Tourism Marketing Management Team Decision Making Event

VPM: Vehicles and Petroleum Marketing Series

DECA PREP

Find timed DECA Prep activities correlated to the Competitive Events Workbook for students and DECA tips for teachers at **marketingessentials.glencoe.com/18/DECA**

CHAPTER 18 Classroom Resources

For the Teacher

- TeacherWorks
- marketingessentials.glencoe.com
- Interactive Chalkboard
- **ExamView®** Pro Test Generator
- Fast File Unit 6

For the Student

- *Marketing Essentials* Online Edition
- Student Activity Workbook
- Marketing Math Workbook
- Marketing Research Project Workbook
- School-to-Work Activity Workbook
- Competitive Events Workbook
- *BusinessWeek* Reader and Case Studies
- marketingessentials.glencoe.com

FOCUS

Introducing the Section

COLLABORATIVE ACTIVITY

Have students identify the elements of visual merchandising in promotion. Examples might include brand promotion; merchandise displays, including signs; colors; themes, especially seasonal; design and layout of store; lighting; fixtures; etc. Ask students to consider who determines the visual merchandising approach.

Preteaching Key Terms

Read each of the key terms aloud and ask students to write them on a sheet of paper. When they finish, write the terms on the board. Have students check their terms for any spelling errors. Then have students guess the meaning of each word. Write students' responses next to the terms. Leave this list on the board so students can review how close their guesses were to the actual definitions as they work through the section.

- visual merchandising
- display
- storefront
- marquee
- store layout
- fixtures
- point-of-purchase displays (POPs)
- kiosk

Critical Thinking

Have students think about the types of color and lighting used in the stores they frequent. Ask: What type of store were they in? What purpose did the color and lighting serve?

Display Features

OBJECTIVES

- Explain the concept and purpose of visual merchandising
- Identify the elements of visual merchandising
- Describe types of display arrangements
- Understand the role of visual merchandisers on the marketing team

KEY TERMS

- visual merchandising
- display
- storefront
- marquee
- store layout
- fixtures
- point-of-purchase displays (POPs)
- kiosk

WHILE YOU READ

Connect Think about one of your favorite stores. As you read this section, visualize and list examples of visual merchandising in that store.

READ and STUDY

BEFORE YOU READ
Predict Why are displays an important part of promotion?

THE MAIN IDEA
Visual merchandising and displays are important promotional strategies to sell products and services, attract potential customers, and create a desired business image.

STUDY ORGANIZER
Use a chart like the one below to take notes on the basics of merchandising and display.

Visual Merchandising and Display

Visual merchandising encompasses all of the physical elements that merchandisers use to project an image to customers. Visual merchandising promotes interest in merchandise or services, encourages purchasing, and reinforces customer satisfaction.

The term *visual merchandising* is sometimes used interchangeably with the term *display,* but they are not the same. Display is a much narrower concept and makes up only one element

---

READ and STUDY

BEFORE YOU READ
Ask students to give examples of different displays they have encountered.

THE MAIN IDEA
Ask students to consider what the word "display" means to them, then have them share their responses.

STUDY ORGANIZER
Model the study organizer for students by filling in the first blank. A full-size, downloadable study organizer can be found at marketingessentials.glencoe.com

WHILE YOU READ
Model for students how they can predict future content by analyzing the main headings on each spread.

of visual merchandising. **Display** refers to the visual and artistic aspects of presenting a product to a target group of customers. Visual merchandising, by contrast, encompasses the visual and artistic aspects of the entire business environment.

The Role of the Visual Merchandiser

Visual merchandisers are responsible for the total merchandise or service presentation, the overall business/brand image, and even the building and placement of design elements. They are active members of the marketing team that promotes a business and its products or services.

Elements of Visual Merchandising

One goal of visual merchandising is to create a positive shopping experience that will compel customers to return. Merchandisers consider four elements key to achieving this goal: storefront, store layout, store interior, and interior displays.

Storefront

The exterior of a business is known as the storefront. The **storefront** encompasses a store's sign or logo, marquee, banners, awnings, windows, and the exterior design, ambiance, and landscaping. Consider Target stores, which are typically large buildings with bold graphics, a logo, bright red colors, a convenient location near a main highway, and a large, well-lit parking lot to attract customers, provide safety, and assist with security. Storefronts project brand identity and help the company distinguish itself from its competitors and surrounding stores.

Signs

Signs are designed primarily to attract attention, advertise a business, and project brand identity. The design of the sign should be original and easily recognizable. The name, letters, logo, materials, and colors that are used help create the desired store's image. An upscale department store might use an elegant script,

 marketingessentials.glencoe.com

A MATTER OF ETHICS

Advertising Food to Children

According to government statistics, about 20 to 30 percent of children in the United States are either overweight or at risk of becoming overweight. The Kaiser Family Foundation reviewed more than 40 studies on the role of the media in childhood obesity.

Television and Fast Food

It found that kids today see an estimated 40,000 television ads a year, compared with about 20,000 a year in the 1970s. Many of today's ads are for candy, cereal, and fast food.

Although the report did not endorse one specific solution to the problem, it recommended that parents limit television viewing time for their children. In addition, the report recommended that food advertisements to children be reduced or regulated.

THINKING ETHICALLY

Do you think that it is ethical to target food ads to children? Why or why not? Should the government develop regulations? Why or why not?

@ Online Action!

Go to *marketingessentials.glencoe.com/18/ethics* to find an activity on ethics and promotion.

---

while a toy merchandiser would use bright primary colors to reinforce a youthful and playful image.

Marquee

A **marquee** is an architectural canopy that extends over a store's entrance. Marquees can be found over most theater entrances, where names of the latest plays or movies are

Chapter 18 - Visual Merchandising and Display **383**

A MATTER OF ETHICS — Advertising Food to Children

Discussion Lead students in a discussion about the importance of nutrition in children and the suitable number of hours or access children should have to television.

THINKING ETHICALLY **Answer:** Answers will vary. Some students might argue that it is the parents' responsibility, rather than the government's, to control the amount of time they watch television. In a free marketplace, pressure from the media, threats of legal action, as well as information from nutritionists and doctors about the need for exercise to reduce health problems might be as effective in changing eating habits as governmental regulation of advertising.

@ Online Action! For instructions, ideas, and answer guide, go to the Teacher Center at marketingessentials.glencoe.com

---

TEACH

Discussion Starter

ELEMENTS OF VISUAL MERCHANDISING

Ask students to imagine they are in a megastore and need to find three distinct items: batteries, cereal, and socks. Have students discuss the visual merchandising elements they would use to find each of these items without staff assistance.

TEACHING POINTS

Model Show students the ways people use signage to find the general section they are looking for by bringing in an example of a sign that directs customers toward a particular product.

Individualized Practice

STOREFRONT

L1 Ask students to recall an instance when a storefront enticed them to enter a store. Then have them recall an instance when a storefront turned them off from entering the store. Have students identify which elements worked and didn't work for them and why.

L2 Provide students with a number of photographs of storefronts. On a three-column chart, have students compare the storefronts of three stores using these categories: sign/logo, lighting, and exterior design.

L3 Provide students with a number of photographs of storefronts or ask students to choose their own. Ask each student to select a storefront with high personal appeal. Have the student write a one-page persuasive essay encouraging others to visit the store.

TEACH CONTINUED

Concept Development

STORE LAYOUT

To explain the concept of store layout, ask students to list distinct spaces found on a retail store floor space. Have a student record these types of spaces on the board. Ask students to discuss the purpose for each space and to consider the percentage that each space takes up.

TEACHING POINTS

Model Provide students with a floor plan of an average-sized retail store. As a class, divide the floor space into the four distinct spaces: selling space, storage space, personnel space, and customer space.

Enrichment

STORE INTERIOR

Present students with a number of images of specific style of retail store, such as a prestige retailer. Have students identify the elements of the store interior, such as color, lighting, paint, and fixtures.

 Virtual Business

Introduce promotion to students using Knowledge Matters' Virtual Business Retailing visual simulation, *Promotion*. In this simulation, students explore the importance of promotion to their business.

•**STORE DISPLAYS** Pet stores organize their displays for each type of pet. Cat food is usually close to accessories displays with cat litter, toys, and water bowls.

How does a display of related items help customers find exactly what they want?

highlighted. Marquees also can display the store's name and its key products as well as hours of operation and a phone number or URL address. A marquee is highly visible, and a company can exploit the space for advertising.

Entrances

Entrances are usually designed with customer convenience and store security in mind. Smaller stores normally have only one entrance, while larger ones have several. The average midsize business needs at least two entrances—one leading in from the street for pedestrians and another adjacent to the parking lot for patrons who drive.

Window Displays

Display windows are especially useful for visual merchandising. Window displays initiate the selling process, create excitement, and attract prospects.

Store Layout

Store layout refers to ways that stores use floor space to facilitate and promote sales and serve customers. A typical store layout divides a store into four distinct spaces:

- **Selling space** is used for interior displays, wall and floor merchandise, product demonstrations, sales transactions, and aisles for customer traffic flow.
- **Storage space** is for items that are kept in inventory or stockrooms.
- **Personnel space** is allocated to store employees for office space, lockers, lunch breaks, and restrooms.
- **Customer space** is designed for the comfort and convenience of the customer and may include sandwich, soda, and coffee shops, in-store restaurants, seating, lounges, and recreation areas for children.

Decisions are made about how much selling space to allocate and the type of interior and window displays to use for various products and related items. Store layout planners and visual merchandisers design traffic patterns to encourage browsing and impulse shopping.

Store Interior

Once the general placement of merchandise has been determined, store personnel can develop the visual merchandising approaches for the building's interior. Mannequins, decorations, comfortable seating, and innovative props are all valuable tools for creating a memorable shopping experience. The selection of floor and wall coverings, lighting, colors, store fixtures, interior signage, and graphics powerfully impact the customers' shopping experience and their image of the store.

Color, Lighting, Graphics, and Paint

Bright colors and light pastels (or plain white) appeal to different types of customers. Stores catering to teens might favor bright colors and lighting. Stores catering to adults often choose pastels and soft, subtle lighting effects. Superstores choose fluorescent or high-intensity

---

PHOTO GUIDE **STORE DISPLAYS**

Discussion Have students brainstorm reasons why the grouping of pet items is an example of effective promotion.

Caption Answer It is convenient for customers when related items are grouped together because they do not have to guess where items are located.

Follow Up Ask students if they have ever been in a store where items were disorganized. Have students discuss their reactions to that store in class.

discharge lighting, while prestige retailers might install expensive chandeliers.

Interior graphics and signage can be used to promote a particular product brand or a specific line of products, provide directions to various departments, or assist with a special promotional campaign, such as a demonstration, special sale, or a holiday promotion.

Walls are interior features that can be covered to reinforce store image. Walls are also used to display merchandise. Clothing can be hung high up on the walls. This technique has the advantage of both saving space and attracting customers with higher-than-eye-level displays.

Fixtures

The principal installations in a store are the **fixtures**. Fixtures are permanent or movable store furnishings that hold and display merchandise. Basic types of fixtures include display cases, tables, counters, floor and wall shelving units, racks, bins, and stands.

A business cultivating an upscale image might enhance its fixtures by painting them or covering them with textured materials (carpeting, fabric, cork, or reed, for example). A business catering to discount buyers would most likely use basic, unadorned shelf fixtures.

The width of a store's aisles is related to its fixtures. The width of aisles and positioning of the fixtures and displays influence traffic patterns and buying behavior.

Interior Displays

If interior displays are done exceptionally well, they enable customers to make a selection without the assistance of a sales clerk. So it is not surprising that these displays have an important place in the selling environment of today's self-service stores.

Five types of interior displays are closed displays, open displays, architectural displays, point-of-purchase displays, and store decorations. Figure 18.1 illustrates the five types of interior displays.

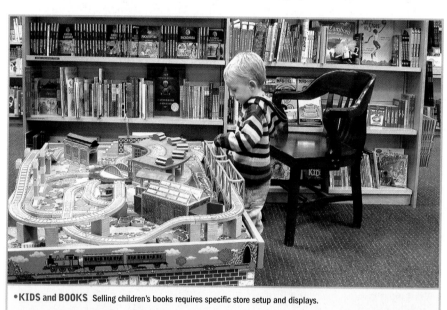

•**KIDS and BOOKS** Selling children's books requires specific store setup and displays.

List three components of a good book display and store setup for children's books.

Enrichment

INTERIOR DISPLAYS

Have students visit a department store and find an example of each of the five types of interior displays. Have students evaluate how well each display promotes the merchandise, assists the customers, and promotes the store image or brand. Ask students to take notes so that they can later discuss the reasons behind using each type of display.

Individualized Practice

DISPLAYS

L1 On a two-column chart, have students compare two promotional window displays using these categories: sign/logo, lighting, and featured products.

L2 Recall an instance when an institutional display prompted students to learn more about the group behind it. In a short exposition, have students identify the focus of the institutional display and its target audience.

L3 Ask students to list three events or occasions throughout the year that are featured in window displays.

 Critical Thinking

Tell students that reasons for using a certain type of display vary depending upon the merchandise featured. For example, personal cosmetics are often placed in closed displays for sanitary reasons. Have students suggest other items that are stored in closed displays and the reasons behind this decision.

PHOTO GUIDE KIDS and BOOKS

Discussion Discuss with students how store setups can be very market specific. Spark discussion by pointing out the physical size of the intended market and the size of the displayed books.

Caption Answer Three elements of a good book display and store setup for a children's book store might include: low-height bookshelves, shelves that accommodate a wide variety of book heights, and a soft sitting area with small chairs or beanbags as a readers' corner.

Follow Up Ask students to suggest the interior elements for a children's bookstore renovation. Have students choose three options to propose for interior elements.

Review Guide

CONCEPTS

- Have students recall the different elements of visual merchandising.
  brand promotion; merchandise displays, including signs; colors; themes, especially seasonal; design and layout of store; lighting; fixtures; etc.

- Have students recall the types of interior displays.
  store decorations, architectural display, open display, closed display, and point-of-purchase display/kiosk.

KEY TERMS

Have students review key terms, their spellings, and definitions in small groups.

ONLINE SELF-ASSESSMENT

Have students go to marketingessentials.glencoe.com for the Section 18.1 practice test.

Individualized Review

L1 Assign and review Chapter 18 activities in the Student Activity Workbook.

L2 Assign and review Chapter 18 activities in the Marketing Math Workbook.

L3 Assign and review Chapter 18 activities in the *BusinessWeek* Reader and Case Studies.

Marketing Practice

Bring in photographs of various store setups. Have students work in groups of three to four. Distribute an equal number of photographs to each group. Ask students to work together to classify the type of store each store setup represents and label each part of the photograph.

Figure 18.1 *Types of Interior Displays*

• **The Functions of Displays** Retailers use interior displays to show merchandise, provide customers with product information, get customers to shop at the store, reinforce advertising messages, and promote the store's image.

Why are interior displays so effective?

ARCHITECTURAL DISPLAYS

Architectural displays consist of model rooms that allow customers to see how merchandise might look in their homes.

STORE DECORATIONS

Store decorations are displays that often coincide with seasons or holidays. Banners, signs, props, and similar items are used to create the appropriate atmosphere.

OPEN DISPLAYS

Open displays allow customers to handle and examine merchandise without the help of a salesperson. Tables and shelves for groceries or countertop and shelf displays for cosmetics are examples.

CLOSED DISPLAYS

Closed displays allow customers to see but not handle merchandise. They are typical displays in places like jewelry stores, where security or breakage is a concern.

POINT-OF-PURCHASE DISPLAYS

Point-of-purchase displays are designed to promote impulse purchases. They are usually more effective at supporting new products than established ones.

Online Action! Go to *marketingessentials.glencoe.com/18/figure/1* to find a project on interior displays.

Figure 18.1 *Types of Interior Displays*

Discussion After students read **Figure 18.1**, discuss how the type of merchandise affects the type of display used. Have students name a type of store that primarily uses one type of display:

1. Store decorations (florist)
2. Architectural display (furniture)
3. Open display (bookstore)
4. Closed display (jewelry store)
5. Point-of-purchase display (drugstore)

Caption Answer Answers might include because they are immediate and appealing, and because customers tend to respond more to organized spaces.

Online Action! For instructions, ideas, and answer guide, go to the Teacher Center at marketingessentials.glencoe.com

As you can see in Figure 18.1, different sales situations call for different types of displays. Items such as clothing are difficult to showcase in a closed display. The cosmetic department is an example of a typical store area that combines many different displays. Items such as brushes and accessories may be part of an open display; other items could be contained in a closed display to prevent customers from sampling them inappropriately. Finally, a point-of-purchase display may feature a computerized touch screen terminal that can evaluate the best cosmetics for each customer's preferences, coloring, and skin type. These displays complement one another and create a positive, interactive buying experience.

Point-of-Purchase Displays

As explained in Chapter 17, **point-of-purchase displays (POPs)** are a consumer sales promotion device. Most POPs are manufactured units with bold graphics and signage that hold, display, or dispense products. Vending machines and automatic teller machines (ATMs) are examples of point-of-purchase units.

Interactive Kiosks

In recent years, interactive point-of-purchase or retail **kiosks** are playing a growing role in point-of-sale merchandising. Kiosks are typically four feet high, have pedestal-mounted, high-tech screens, and take up less than two square feet of store space. Immediate product availability, more reliable technology, and information services have led to their increased popularity. Photo-finishing stands for processing prints from digital cameras are among the most popular kiosks.

Props

Props, also called properties, are special display elements. Props are generally classified as decorative or functional. Decorative props include background scenery such as rakes, dried leaves, and a wheelbarrow used to project an autumn theme. Functional props include items that hold merchandise, such as mannequins and shirt forms.

 18.1 AFTER YOU READ

Reviewing Key Terms and Concepts

1. Why is display considered part of visual merchandising?
2. How does visual merchandising differ from display?
3. What are the four elements of visual merchandising?

Integrating Academic Skills

Math

4. Space productivity is measured by sales per square foot of selling space. What are the sales per square foot for a merchandise category that generated $259,645 in sales for a selling space of 1,602 square feet?

Art

5. Research the Internet and look at storefronts and advertising in magazines to find information and ideas about various display styles. Next, select a product category that interests you. Use a posterboard to draw a display for these products. You may use paint, collage, or any other medium you wish. Be creative.

 Online Action!

Check your answers at *marketingessentials.glencoe.com/18/read*

marketingessentials.glencoe.com

Chapter 18 - Visual Merchandising and Display **387**

CLOSE

Ask students to recall and provide answers to the following questions:

- **What are the four key elements of visual merchandising?**
  storefront, store layout, store interior, and interior displays

- **List all four of the distinct spaces in a store layout.**
  selling space, storage space, personnel space, and customer space

 Critical Thinking

Ask students why point-of-purchase displays (also called point-of-sale displays) often contain small items.

 Online Activity

Bricks and Clicks

Ask students to compare a brick-and-mortar storefront to its online equivalent, a home page. Ask them to evaluate the visual merchandising and displays of each. Which appeals to them more—the virtual store or the real store? Have students share their evaluations in class.

AFTER YOU READ

Reviewing Key Terms and Concepts

1. Displays are considered a form of visual merchandising responsible for attracting customers' attention, because they are creating a desire for a product, and helping to enhance sales.

2. Visual merchandising encompasses all the visual artistic elements of the selling environment. Display relates only to those visual and artistic elements that present the product to a target group of customers.

3. The four elements of visual merchandising include: 1) storefront; 2) store layout; 3) store interior; 4) interior displays.

Integrating Academic Skills

4. $259,645 ÷ 1,602 = $162.08 per square foot

5. Answers will vary for each type of display.

Online Action! Answers at **marketingessentials.glencoe.com/18/read**

Artistic Design

FOCUS

Introducing the Section

COLLABORATIVE ACTIVITY

As a class, discuss the four types of displays. Divide students into four groups. Using things they find in the classroom, have each group design and create one of the four different types of display:

- one-item display
- similar-products display
- related-merchandise display
- cross-mix merchandise display

Preteaching Key Terms

Write each of the key terms on a slip of paper. Place the slips in a hat or container. Have volunteers choose a key terms slip and state its meaning in their own words.

- color wheel
- complementary colors
- adjacent colors
- triadic colors
- focal point
- proportion
- formal balance
- informal balance

Online Activity

E-Tailer Displays

Have students explore the home pages of large department stores such as Macy's, Marshall Field's, Nordstrom, etc. Have students analyze the type of display used. For example, Marshall Field's uses a similar-products display of men's and women's sweaters on its home page.

OBJECTIVES

- List the five steps in creating a display
- Explain how artistic elements function in display design
- Describe the importance of display maintenance

KEY TERMS

- color wheel
- complementary colors
- adjacent colors
- triadic colors
- focal point
- proportion
- formal balance
- informal balance

READ and STUDY

BEFORE YOU READ

Predict What skills and talents would you need to design a store display?

THE MAIN IDEA

Visual merchandisers must know the rules of artistic design in order to create displays that help enhance sales, attract customers, and sustain customer loyalty.

STUDY ORGANIZER

As you read this section, identify the key steps in display in a flow chart like the one below.

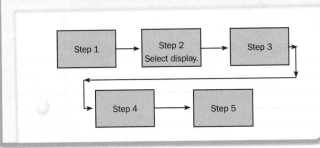

WHILE YOU READ

Connect Think about a display that attracted your attention in the past. List three things that attracted you to it.

Display Design and Preparation

In the retail environment, a display has about four to six seconds to attract a customer's attention, create a desire, and sell a product. This limited time frame means that a business must target its displays carefully to appeal to its customers.

When planning and preparing displays, retailers and merchandisers must carefully consider differences in cultural

388 UNIT 6 - PROMOTION

READ and STUDY

BEFORE YOU READ

Ask students to list ways to attract attention in visual display.

THE MAIN IDEA

Visual merchandisers must design displays that appeal to their target market, reflect a desired image, and enhance sales.

STUDY ORGANIZER

Model the study organizer for students by filling in the first key step. A full-size, downloadable study organizer can be found at marketingessentials.glencoe.com

 Ask students to expand on why they were attracted by the qualities in the displays.

and ethnic perceptions among their target markets.

Many will employ specialists in cross-cultural and ethnic design and marketing to adapt displays to the target market. All display design and selection involves the following five steps.

Step 1: Selecting Merchandise for Display

The merchandise selected will determine the theme and all other supporting elements of the display. Display merchandise must also be visually appealing and contemporary to attract customers. It must be appropriate for the season and for the store's geographic location.

Step 2: Selecting the Display

The merchandise selected largely determines the type of display that is used. There are four basic kinds of displays: those that feature just one item; similar products; related products, such as camping equipment; and a cross-mix of items, such as a display of a picnic scene, with tables, grills, grilling tools, and aprons.

Step 3: Choosing a Setting

Displays can be presented in a number of different settings. The setting a business selects will depend largely on the image it wants to project.

A realistic setting depicts a room, area, or recognizable locale. The scene could be a restaurant, a park, or a party. Props, such as tables, chairs, plants, risers, books, dishes, and mannequins provide the details.

A semirealistic setting suggests a room or locale but leaves the details to the viewer's imagination. A cardboard sun, a beach towel, a surfing poster, and a sprinkling of sand would be enough to invoke the rest of the beach scene in the viewer's mind.

An abstract setting does not imitate, or even try to imitate, reality. It focuses on form and color rather than reproducing actual objects. Wide bands of torn colored paper used as an accent behind or around merchandise can create an attractive visual image that has little or nothing to do with reality.

Step 4: Manipulating Artistic Elements

The artistic elements of a display include line, color, shape, direction, texture, proportion, motion, and lighting. These elements subtly influence your perception of a display.

Line

Lines within displays are created to direct the viewer's attention. Various types of lines create different impressions. Straight lines suggest stiffness and control, while curving lines suggest freedom and movement. Diagonal lines give the impression of action; vertical lines offer height and dignity; and horizontal lines convey confidence.

Color

Color selection is a critical step in developing displays. The colors selected for a display should contrast with those used on the walls, floors, and fixtures around them. For example, a store decorated in pastels should feature displays that use darker, stronger colors.

The standard **color wheel** shown in Figure 18.2 illustrates the relationships among colors. **Complementary colors** are found opposite each other on the color wheel and are used to create high contrast. Red and green, blue and orange, and yellow and purple are examples of complementary colors.

Adjacent colors, also called analogous colors, are located next to each other in the color wheel and share the same undertones. Successive adjacent colors (such as yellow-orange, yellow, and yellow-green) form families, or groups of colors, that blend well with each other. **Triadic colors** involve three colors equally spaced on the color wheel, such as red, yellow, and blue. Triadic color harmony, as shown by the triangle on the color wheel, creates vivid and contrasting colors. Triadic color schemes can be achieved by rotating the triangle within the color wheel.

Chapter 18 - Visual Merchandising and Display 389

Extended Activity

Model Settings

Model how to design a specific type of setting using objects found in the classroom. As a class, decide on the object/product to be promoted. Then decide which type of setting will be used to display it. Design the setting on the board.

TEACH

Discussion Starter

STEP 1: SELECTING MERCHANDISE FOR DISPLAY

Show students photos of various pieces of merchandise (athletic shoes, CDs, electric mixer, computer, bedding, etc.). As a class, have students discuss which type of display would best suit each piece of merchandise.

Answers might include the following: athletic shoes could be part of a similar product display or a related-merchandise display. An electric mixer could be part of a related-merchandise display or a cross-mix merchandise display.

TEACHING POINTS

Reinforce Remind students that merchandise selection also depends on the store's location, the demographic groups within the area, and the season.

Concept Development

STEP 2: SELECTING THE DISPLAY

1. Have students discuss how to display a select piece of merchandise, such as a flat-screen TV, using a realistic setting, a semirealistic setting, or an abstract setting.

2. Have students identify related merchandise that could be displayed with the following items:

- shampoos
  brushes and combs, hair styling products, other bath products

- computers
  printers, software, speakers

- hiking shoes
  socks, walking sticks, backpacks, energy snacks

Concept Development

STEP 4: MANIPULATING ARTISTIC ELEMENTS

Ask students to imagine they are designing a display for sweaters that are made of wool from the British Isles. Ask students to list the colors or patterns they will use as part of their display. Also, have students identify the type of display they will use to promote their product.

Students might choose a theme that would reflect the British Isles. They would probably choose a themed display to make their new product stand out.

TEACHING POINTS

Clarify Remind students that certain patterns, shapes, and color combinations have traditional or cultural identities becauseof flags or other associations. For example, the fleur-de-lis is associated with France, a shamrock is associated with Ireland, and a paisley pattern is associated with India.

Enrichment

MULTICULTURAL DISPLAY

As a class, develop a list of cultural and ethnic groups living in your area. From there, analyze which colors would most appeal to each group. Are there any colors that are traditionally used for certain events? Explain that visual merchandisers would use this information to "dress" their stores.

Answers will include a list of cultural and ethnic groups living in the area. Students should also identify some colors traditionally used for certain events.

 Figure 18.2 *The Color Wheel*

- **Color Matters** The color wheel is structured to show both similarities and differences in colors. Effective displays use colors that draw customers' attention but don't compete with the product.

How would you use this wheel to create triadic color harmony?

 Online Action! Go to *marketingessentials.glencoe.com/18/figure/2* to find a project on the use of color in merchandising.

Effective displays use color groupings to create visual calm or excitement. Colors from the warm side of the color wheel, such as red and yellow, convey a festive mood that works well with lower-priced merchandise. Colors from the cool side of the color wheel, such as blue and green, represent calm and refinement. They are often associated with higher-priced merchandise.

Shape

Shape refers to the physical appearance, or outline, of a display. Shape is determined by the props, fixtures, and merchandise used in the display. Squares, cubes, circles, and triangles are some of the shapes that display units may resemble. Displays that have little or no distinct shape—called mass displays—are also possible. Mass displays are often used by dollar stores, discounters, and supermarkets to display large quantities and indicate a low price.

Direction

A good display directs the viewer's eye to the merchandise, moving a viewer's attention

390 UNIT 6 - PROMOTION

marketingessentials.glencoe.com

Figure 18.2 *The Color Wheel*

Discussion After students have read **Figure 18.2**, discuss the concepts of complementary, adjacent, and triadic colors. Challenge students to discuss how this information is very important to visual merchandising and display. Answers might include that color choice is very important because the display colors must both complement the merchandise and contrast with the colors on the store interior.

Caption Answer You could use the color wheel to create triadic color harmony by choosing three primary, secondary, or intermediate colors and using them in a display.

Online Action! For instructions, ideas, and answer guide, go to the Teacher Center at **marketingessentials.glencoe.com**

Case Study

The Shopping Buddy

There is a revolution afoot in the world of food shopping: a technology-powered Shopping Buddy. The Shopping Buddy is a cart-based, wireless shopping aid. Several Stop & Shop stores in Massachusetts have started using this new technology. The Shopping Buddy talks the customer through the shopping experience.

Faster, Easier Shopping

The buddy reads the shopper's loyalty card, linking the card and the shopper's history to an 8-inch by 11-inch electronic tablet that is positioned on the cart handle. The wireless browser, combined with sensors embedded in the ceiling, enables the tablet to send and receive data to speed and simplify the shopping experience.

A Virtual Grocery List

The system alerts the shopper to items based on the shopper's preferences and history. It can even place the shopper's deli order and alert her or him when it is ready. It uses sophisticated technology to combine visual merchandising and loyalty marketing.

THINK STRATEGICALLY

How will the Shopping Buddy help increase sales at Stop & Shop stores?

@ Online Action!

Go to *marketingessentials.glencoe.com/18/case* to find an activity on technology and promotion.

---

seamlessly from one part of the display to another. This smooth visual flow is called direction. Effective displays create direction by using techniques such as color, repetition, and lighting patterns.

Effective displays should also have a **focal point**, an area in the display that attracts attention first, above all else. A good method of creating an effective focal point is to build the display elements in a triangular shape. The focal point is created by placing the strongest shape at the top, or apex, of the imaginary triangle in the display. A viewer's eyes will naturally travel to the strongest shape within a display. This arrangement helps keep the eyes moving up and over the merchandise. Displays that lack a focal point are said to be unfocused. Typically, an unfocused display contains too many items, too many shapes, or too many props outside the imaginary triangle.

marketingessentials.glencoe.com

Chapter 18 - Visual Merchandising and Display 391

Case Study   The Shopping Buddy

Discussion Have students read the Case Study and discuss the advantages (such as shopping convenience and time-saving options) and the disadvantages (such as lack of privacy) of the Shopping Buddy system.

THINK STRATEGICALLY **Answer:** The Shopping Buddy helps increase sales because it makes suggestions to shoppers based on their purchasing history. It also suggests other brands or merchandise to fulfill similar needs, or calls the shopper's attention to new merchandise.

@ Online Action! For instructions, ideas, and answer guide, go to the Teacher Center at marketingessentials.glencoe.com

TEACH CONTINUED

Individualized Practice

DESIGN ELEMENTS

L1 In short responses, have students describe the mood each of the following types of lines evoke:

- a group of vertically straight lines
- a group of wavy lines
- a group of circles
- a group of diagonal lines

L2 Have students draw a color sketch of the following displays: a one-item display, a similar-products display, a related-merchandise display, and a cross-mix display.

L3 Have students choose a display sketch from a magazine and adapt it for another international market, such as a Japanese market or British market. Have students address which elements they might change and which elements might stay the same.

Enrichment

EFFECTIVE DISPLAYS

Ask students to imagine they are designing a display for an organic oatmeal that includes Hawaiian macadamia nuts and dried pineapple. Ask students to list the props and colors they will use as part of their display. Also have students identify the type of display they will use to promote their product.

Students might choose a Polynesian theme. They would probably choose a one-item display to make their product stand out from the other oatmeal brands.

ASSESS

Review Guide

CONCEPTS

Have students recall the four different types of display and the three types of setting used in visual merchandising. displays: one-item, similar-products, related-merchandise, and cross-mix merchandise, settings: realistic, semi-realistic, and abstract

KEY TERMS

Have students review key terms, their spellings, and definitions in small groups.

ONLINE SELF-ASSESSMENT

Have students go to marketingessentials.glencoe.com for the Section 18.2 practice test.

Individualized Review

L1 Assign and review Chapter 18 activities in the Student Activity Workbook.

L2 Assign and review Chapter 18 activities in the Marketing Math Workbook.

L3 Assign and review Chapter 18 activities in the *BusinessWeek* Reader and Case Studies.

Marketing Practice

Give students examples of a fashion retail store that reflects a particular demographic. Ask them to note the merchandise, type of displays, setting, and artistic elements used. Have students adapt the visual merchandising to appeal to another demographic (such as another culture, age group, or gender). Have students prepare displays and present them to the class.

MARKET TECH

Payments by Fingerprint

The Piggly Wiggly grocery store chain has introduced a finger-scanning payment system at more than 100 stores in South Carolina and Georgia. The chain will begin offering a high-tech payment feature allowing customers to pay using their fingerprints. With a touch of the finger to a light-sensitive pad, patrons will be able to pay for their groceries, provided that they have an account in the store's system that can be debited.

Who Is Watching You?

According to Pay By Touch, the San Francisco-based firm whose technology is being used, the system takes 10 seconds to approve a payment by fingerprint. Pay By Touch claims customers' personal information is stored in a secure database and cannot be accessed by unauthorized parties. The company says other stores that have utilized the technology find that three-fourths of their customers sign up to use the fingerprint system. Many privacy advocates, however, oppose fingerprint payment technology. Some consumers are opposed to any technology that can be used to track shoppers.

THINK LIKE A MARKETER

What are the benefits for stores that use fingerprint technology? Can you think of some of the reasons why some consumer organizations do not like this new technology?

@ Online Action!

Go to *marketingessentials.glencoe.com/ 18/tech* to find an activity on technology and promotion.

marketingessentials.glencoe.com

Texture

A texture (smooth or rough) is the look of the surfaces in a display. The contrast between the textures used in a display creates visual interest. Products that are smooth, such as flatware, should be placed against backgrounds or props that are rough.

Proportion

Proportion refers to the relationship between and among objects in a display. The merchandise should always be the primary focus of a display. Props, graphics, and signs should be in proportion to the merchandise; they should not dominate the display.

Balance

Display designers also pay attention to balance when creating displays. They place large items with large items and small items with small items to create **formal balance** in a display. When a large item is placed on one side of a display, an equally large item should be placed on the other side for balance. To create **informal balance**, they will place several small items with one large one. An example of an informal display would be one in which an adult mannequin is placed next to several shallow baskets of flowers that are elevated on a prop to the mannequin's height.

Motion

Motion is playing an increasingly important role in display design. Animation can be achieved through the use of motorized fixtures, mannequins, and props. Motion should be used sparingly to accentuate merchandise, not overpower it.

Lighting

Proper lighting is critical to attractive displays. Lighting can help make merchandise appear more attractive. It is recommended that display lighting be two to five times stronger than a store's general lighting. Colored lighting can be used in displays to create

---

MARKET TECH

Payments by Fingerprint

Discussion Convenience and quick checkouts are something customers want from a grocery store. Identify the ways in which the Pay By Touch technology could be used in other service applications.

THINK LIKE A MARKETER **Answer:** Answers will vary. Pay By Touch creators believe it will make shopping easier by eliminating the need for cash, checks, or credit cards. They also believe it will build customer loyalty by offering targeted discounts and tracking customer purchases. Opponents might argue that tracking purchases or recording fingerprints are both an invasion of privacy.

 Online Action! For instructions, ideas, and answer guide, go to the Teacher Center at marketingessentials.glencoe.com

dramatic effects. Lighting used with reflective items such as crystal needs careful attention. Although the lighting in the dressing rooms is technically not part of a display, it should be considered as well. Dressing room lighting that is glaring and unflattering will negatively affect a consumer's buying decisions, no matter how well the merchandise is lit in a display.

Step 5: Evaluating Completed Displays

Do displays enhance the store's image, appeal to customers, and promote the product in the best possible way? Were a theme creatively applied? Were the color and signage appropriate? Was the result pleasing? These are just some of the factors that visual merchandisers consider when evaluating the effectiveness of displays.

Display Maintenance

Once a display has been constructed, it needs to be maintained and eventually dismantled. Individual businesses have different policies regarding the duration of displays. Most businesses check displays daily for damage, displacements, or missing items caused by customers handling the merchandise. Clothing items that are folded and stacked in a display should be organized and restocked frequently. Proper display maintenance can keep the merchandise fresh and attractive to customers.

Poor maintenance can create a negative image not only of the merchandise, but of the store as well. Display fixtures and props should be cleaned and merchandise dusted on a regular basis. Customers are not likely to be enthusiastic about purchasing items that are displayed on dusty or dirty fixtures.

18.2 AFTER YOU READ

Reviewing Key Terms and Concepts
1. Why is the first step in display preparation so important?
2. Name the four basic types of displays.
3. Why is a focal point so necessary in display preparation?

Integrating Academic Skills
Math
4. The *2002 Buyers Report* by Point of Purchase Advertising International estimated POP spending at over $17 billion. If $240 billion is spent on advertising in the United States annually, what percentage of the overall expenditures is the estimated spending on POP advertising?

Art
5. Visit a local supermarket or discount store to observe point-of-purchase (POP) displays. Ask permission to sketch the display on a poster board. Ask the store owner why and how product display choices were made. Annotate your sketch with these comments and answers.

 Online Action!

Check your answers at *marketingessentials.glencoe.com/18/read*

marketingessentials.glencoe.com   Chapter 18 - Visual Merchandising and Display **393**

CLOSE

Have students complete the following statements:

- Displays should enhance the store's image, appeal to customers, and _____ .
  promote the product

- Proper display maintenance keeps the merchandise fresh and _____ .
  attractive to customers

Critical Thinking

Tell students that certain colors are sometimes given gender identity through marketing. For example, pastels are traditionally seen as "softer" and hence "feminine." However, pale blue is seen as a masculine color. Ask students if they perceive certain colors as gender-specific and ask them to explain their answers.

Extended Activity

Design Associations

Ask students to reflect on their own experiences with design and color. Ask them what they think of when they think of the color purple or when they see a four-leaf clover. Have students share their associations in class.

AFTER YOU READ

Reviewing Key Terms and Concepts

1. Selecting the merchandise is important because that will determine the theme and all other elements of the display.

2. The four types of displays are: 1) one-item display, 2) similar-products display, 3) related-merchandise display, and 4) cross-mix merchandise display.

3. The focal point is important because it is the area that directs your eyes to focus on the merchandise presented in the display.

Integrating Academic Skills

4. 7 percent; $17,000,000,000 ÷ $240,000,000,000 = 0.07 = 7 percent

5. Sketches will vary; student annotations should demonstrate an understanding of point-of-purchase displays.

Online Action!   Answers at **marketingessentials.glencoe.com/18/read**

Lifelong Learning

CAREER INFORMATION

Have students go to marketingessentials.glencoe.com and find Chapter 18 Careers page and click on the link for the American Marketing Association's Careers Strategies and Tips. Ask students to select one article, read it, and summarize it in three short paragraphs.

VISUAL MERCHANDISING AND DISPLAY

People who work in non-retail service businesses, such as medical offices or employment agencies, need to be aware of the implications of display and the use of interior space. It can be helpful to know the terms that specialists use. Students can also apply the same concepts of color, lighting, texture, and space in their homes.

Primary Source

Ask students to go to marketingessentials.glencoe.com and find Chapter 18 Resources. Ask them to click on the link for the American Marketing Association's marketing dictionary and read the definitions of the terms related to visual merchandising and display.

THINKING CRITICALLY

Fine arts or visual design courses could educate the professional about the many artistic elements that work together as part of visual merchandising and display.

@ Online Action!

For instructions, ideas, and answer guide, go to the Teacher Center at marketingessentials.glencoe.com

394

CAREERS
IN MARKETING

NINA J. MONASTERO, AIA
MONASTERO & ASSOCIATES, INC. ARCHITECTURE AND INTERIOR DESIGN

? **What do you do at work?**
I am an architect and an interior designer who specializes in retail design. We strive to design all aspects of a customer's experience: the way the store environment is shaped, the colors and finishes used in the space, the retail fixtures used, the ways in which merchandise is displayed, the sounds, and the smells, so that all of a customer's senses are affected, and to some extent, controlled, to reinforce the store's message and entice purchases.

? **What skills are most important to you?**
It is imperative to have good listening skills. By that, I mean that I engage in active listening, whereby I make and maintain direct eye contact, don't interrupt, take notes where needed and reflect back on what I think I heard. When meeting with clients, I tend to listen much, much more than speak. Next, an innate design sense, or sense of style is important and should be supplemented by proper training in design, be it through architecture, interior design, graphic design, or industrial design coursework at the college level.

? **What is your key to success?**
Over the course of my career, I have always put my clients, their companies and their needs first, my ego second. My firm and I are not known for having a "style." Rather, we are known for designing the best solutions for our clients. I always try to put myself in their shoes and understand where their issues and ideas may be coming from.

Aptitudes, Abilities, and Skills

Strong interpersonal skills, an eye for design, and a strong sense of creativity

Education and Training

Courses in architecture and interior design can lay the groundwork, fine arts will add depth to the understanding of how space works.

Career Path

Designers usually begin their careers working for an established agency with a reputation. Once individuals have built portfolios of projects, they can think about moving to better opportunities within their companies, with another firm, or on their own as freelancers.

THINKING CRITICALLY

Why would fine arts courses be helpful to someone working in retail space design?

@ Online Action!

Go to *marketingessentials.glencoe.com/ 18/careers* to find a career-related activity.

Test-Taking Strategies

Suggest to students that they preview tests before they answer any test questions. This will get them thinking about the material. Have them note the point value of each question and use this information to figure out how to budget their time, spending more time on questions of greater value.

FOCUS on KEY POINTS

SECTION 18.1

● Visual merchandising is an important part of a business's total promotional mix. Visual merchandising and display must be coordinated with advertising, direct marketing, personal selling, and sales promotion efforts.

SECTION 18.2

● Visual merchandising and in-store displays help to sell products and build store and brand image. Businesses create effective displays by using prescribed steps and rules for artistic design to attract customers and to keep them coming back.

REVIEW VOCABULARY

Study each pair of terms and, in your own words, tell how they are related to each other.

1. visual merchandising (p. 382)—display (p. 383)

2. storefront (p. 383)—marquee (p. 383)

3. store layout (p. 384)—fixtures (p. 385)

4. point-of-purchase displays (p. 387)—kiosks (p. 387)

5. color wheel (p. 389)—complementary colors (p. 389)

6. adjacent colors (p. 389)—triadic colors (p. 389)

7. focal point (p. 391)—proportion (p. 392)

8. formal balance (p. 392)—informal balance (p. 392)

REVIEW FACTS and IDEAS

9. What is the purpose of visual merchandising? (18.1)

10. What are the key elements of visual merchandising? (18.1)

11. Why are interior displays important? (18.1)

12. Which type of interior display is most effective for new product introductions? (18.1)

13. What role do visual merchandisers play on the marketing team? (18.1)

14. What are the five steps involved in creating a display? (18.2)

15. What artistic elements function in display design? (18.2)

16. Locate complementary and adjacent colors on the color wheel. How do the colors contrast with each other? (18.2)

17. How is formal and informal balance achieved in a display? (18.2)

Chapter 18 - Visual Merchandising and Display **395**

REVIEW FACTS and IDEAS

9. It promotes interest in merchandise or services, encourages purchasing, and reinforces customer satisfaction.

10. The key elements include storefront, store layout, store interior, and interior displays.

11. Interior displays generate one out of every four sales.

12. Point-of-purchase displays are most effective for new product introductions.

13. Visual merchandisers are active members of the marketing team responsible for promoting a business and its products and services.

14. The five steps include selecting merchandise for display, selecting a type of display, choosing a display setting, manipulating artistic elements, and evaluating the display.

15. The artistic elements include line, color, shape, direction, texture, proportion, motion, and lighting.

16. Complementary colors lie opposite each other on the color wheel and create the greatest contrast. Adjacent colors can be found next to each other on the color wheel and contrast only slightly.

17. Formal balance is achieved by placing large items with large items and small items with small items. Informal balance is achieved by balancing a large item with several smaller ones in a display.

FOCUS on KEY POINTS

Ask volunteers to read the summaries aloud and give the classroom one real-life example for each concept.

REVIEW VOCABULARY

See glossary for definitions of **1–8.**
A sample sentence might read:

3. The arrangement of *fixtures* is part of the *store layout*.

CHAPTER 18 REVIEW

BUILD SKILLS

18. Workplace Skills

Answers will vary; preparation might involve research on the most recent skills for display specialist. Required skills may include: a person who has related education and/or experience in design layout, lighting, or animation, a good work history, demonstrates initiative, creativity, and flexibility.

19. Technology Applications

Answers will vary based on type of displays selected; students should demonstrate an understanding of the components effective in visual merchandising.

20. Math Practice

Cheryl spent $654.89 last year. She is considering a 52.7 percent increase this year.

DEVELOP CRITICAL THINKING

21. Technology and Displays

Answers will vary based on the stores selected; students should express benefits and features of the technology.

22. Evaluating Displays

Answers will vary based on the type of businesses selected; students should rate the artistic elements of each display.

BUILD SKILLS

18. Workplace Skills

Human Relations Assume that you are the visual merchandising coordinator for a large department store. You have been asked to update the required skills for display specialists. You must provide a rationale and explain your decisions at a meeting with upper management. How would you prepare for the meeting?

19. Technology Applications

Comparing Display Techniques Visit a department store to observe and evaluate its visual merchandising effectiveness. Review its storefront, store layout, and store interior.

Use a spreadsheet program to create a chart, evaluating the quality of each component.

20. Math Practice

Display Budget Cheryl owns a small fashion retail store in a suburban mall in Georgia. Last year she spent one percent of her profits ($65,489) on props for windows and store displays. This year, she forecasts her display costs at $1,000. How much did she spend last year? What percent increase is she considering this year?

DEVELOP CRITICAL THINKING

21. Technology and Displays

Visit a local supermarket, then a megastore. Briefly describe the technology, if any, that is used in displays, noting its purpose and benefits to both the store and the consumer. Then, make a list and compare and contrast how the technology you observed is used in both types of stores. Does one store use technology more effectively? Explain your evaluation.

22. Evaluating Displays

Visit a shopping mall to observe and evaluate three different window or interior displays. Using a scoring rubric for each display, evaluate and rate each display in terms of the artistic elements from this chapter.

Formative Assessment

Formative assessment is an essential component of classroom work. This type of assessment provides information that is then used as feedback to modify teaching and meet student needs.

L1 Have students write or demonstrate all of the steps of a display creation process.

L2 Have students write a narrative description of two different types of displays. One should be a cross-mix merchandise display.

L3 Have students create an abstract setting using classroom materials.

 Reteach   If the results of this formative assessment seem low, consider the following activity:

Read each of this key terms aloud. Have students define the key terms and use them in a sentence. Clear up any confusion students may have.

APPLY CONCEPTS

23. Explaining Display Objectives

Conduct an Internet search on the award-winning point-of-purchase (POP) displays recognized by Point of Purchase Advertising International (POPAI). Select one temporary, semipermanent, or permanent POP display to download, then review its objectives.

Activity Use a word processing program to prepare a brief report on your findings.

24. Preparing a Display

Interview a local business owner or manager regarding visual merchandising needs. Ask the business owner whether he or she would participate in a classroom project. Explain that this project involves preparing a display that fits the needs of the business.

Activity As a member of a display team, prepare a display at the local business with selected merchandise and specifications as determined by the business owner.

NET SAVVY

25. Research Display Fixtures

Perform an Internet search to find five suppliers of store fixtures. Write a summary of the products and services provided by each supplier, where the company is located, and its Web site address. Make sure to provide details such as prices and styles of fixtures.

CONNECTION

Role Play: Virtual Merchandising and Display

Situation You are to assume the role of assistant manager of an upscale women's designer boutique. The store is currently undergoing a complete renovation and image update. The store's designer (judge) has asked you for some ideas for the new bags and packaging, including shopping bags, hanging garment bags, and mailing packaging. You may include any other sizes of bags you think are necessary.

Activity You are to present your ideas for the new bags and packaging to the store's designer (judge).

Evaluation You will be evaluated on how well you meet the following performance indicators:

● Demonstrate appropriate creativity

● Demonstrate interest and enthusiasm

● Develop a project plan

● Recommend specific products

● Follow directions

 Online Action!

For more information and DECA Prep practice, go to *marketingessentials.glencoe .com/18/DECA*

APPLY CONCEPTS

23. Explaining Display Objectives

Answers will vary; all elements of the display must be discussed. Reports should show an understanding of POP displays.

24. Preparing a Display

Student displays should demonstrate an understanding of the principles of display. Encourage creativity in the displays.

NET SAVVY

25. Research Display Fixtures

Summaries will vary based on the five suppliers chosen; each summary should detail the types of store fixtures provided.

MINI-QUIZ

Read these sentences to the students and have them volunteer the missing words.

1. The store sign is important because it _____ . (makes the first impression)

2. The way a store's floor space is allocated to facilitate sales and best serve customers is called its _____ . (store layout)

3. _____ colors are found opposite each other on the color wheel and create the_____ . (Complementary; greatest contrast)

For an expanded chapter quiz, go to Chapter 18 in the TeacherWorks CD-ROM and to Chapter 18 in the **Exam*View*®** Pro Test Generator CD-ROM.

THE DECA CONNECTION

Students should be evaluated according to the performance standards noted in the role play. For another DECA role play, go to the Competitive Events Workbook or the Student Activity Workbook, or go to **marketingessentials.glencoe.com/18/DECA**

 Online Action! For instructions, ideas, and answer guide, go to the Teacher Center at **marketingessentials.glencoe.com**

DECA Advisors Corner

One approach to DECA Week is to highlight a different aspect of DECA each day during that week. Brainstorm with chapter members to plan specific activities for each day during the national DECA Week, and use the conceptual foundation of the organization, the DECA diamond.

Chapter Overview

This chapter introduces advertising and its purposes, and explains the different types of media. The chapter also gives an overview of how advertising rates are determined for newspaper, magazine, and online advertising. Key reasons for selecting a promotional media are also explored.

BUILD BACKGROUND

Post several print ads around the classroom. Include a mix of promotional and institutional ads with different target markets. Have students look at the ads, then close their eyes and say which ads they remember best. Tell students they have identified the purpose of advertising: to attract attention so that people will buy a product or accept an idea.

Why It's Important

Advertising spreads the word about a company and its products or services. Businesses use different types of advertising media to promote their image, products, or services.

Prepare to Read

List the section objectives to discuss with students. Have students skim the chapter, looking at pictures, reading captions, and noting headings. Ask questions to ensure that students have a basic understanding of the chapter structure.

CHAPTER 19
Advertising

Chapter Objectives

After reading this chapter, you should be able to:

- Explain the concept and purpose of advertising in the promotional mix
- Identify the different types of advertising media
- Discuss the planning and selection of media
- Identify media measurement techniques
- Explain techniques used to evaluate media
- Summarize how media costs are determined
- Explain promotional budget methods

GUIDE TO THE PHOTO

Market Talk There are many forms of advertising to fit all kinds of budgets. A large company such as Procter & Gamble typically spends 25 to 30 percent of its revenues on advertising, while a small firm might consider spending two percent. Types of ads vary greatly, from carefully crafted television national ad campaigns, to print ads in newspapers and magazines, to a much simpler and cheaper approach, such as leaflet distribution.

Quick Think When planning an advertising budget and strategy, do you think it is important to study how and where the competition is advertising?

GUIDE TO THE PHOTO

Market Talk Lead a discussion about the type of advertising visible in this photograph. Ask: is it promotional or institutional? Then have students identify the type of media used in this photograph. Students should identify the type of advertising as promotional and the type of media as print media, or more specifically, printed T-shirts.

Quick Think Answers will vary. Students should recognize they need to compare their advertising campaign against the campaign of their competition.

 Follow Up Ask students to name two businesses that have similar products but different advertising campaigns.

THE **DECA** CONNECTION
An Association of Marketing Students

Performance indicators represent key skills and knowledge. Relating them to the concepts explained in this chapter is your key to success in DECA events. These acronyms represent DECA events that involve knowledge of concepts in this chapter.

AAAL	FMAL	MMS*	TMDM*
AAML*	FMDM*	QSRM*	TSE*
ADC*	FMML*	RMAL	VPM
BSM	FSRM*	RMML*	
EMDM*	HMDM*	SMDM*	

In all these DECA events you should be able to follow these performance indicators:

- Explain the types of advertising media
- Explain the nature of direct advertising strategies
- Describe considerations in using databases in advertising
- Calculate media costs

All the events with an asterisk (*) also include these performance indicators:

- Select advertising media
- Buy advertisements
- Develop an advertising campaign
- Use past advertisements to aid in promotional planning
- Prepare promotional budget
- Manage promotional allowances

Some events include additional performance indicators. These are:

ADC   Select placement of advertisements
TMDM   Select placement of advertisements
FMDM   Select placement of advertisements

DECA PREP

Check your understanding of DECA performance indicators with the DECA activity in this chapter's review. For more information and DECA Prep practice, go to *marketingessentials .glencoe.com/19/DECA*

CHAPTER 19 Classroom Resources

For the Teacher

- TeacherWorks
- marketingessentials.glencoe.com
- Interactive Chalkboard
- **Exam***View*® Pro Test Generator
- Fast File Unit 6

For the Student

- ***Marketing Essentials*** Online Edition
- Student Activity Workbook
- Marketing Math Workbook
- Marketing Research Project Workbook
- School-to-Work Activity Workbook
- Competitive Events Workbook
- ***BusinessWeek*** Reader and Case Studies
- marketingessentials.glencoe.com

THE **DECA**
An Association of Marketing Students

CONNECTION

DECA events that require knowledge of advertising are described here. Discuss the performance indicators to make sure students understand how to demonstrate their understanding.

The events acronyms stand for:

AAAL: Apparel and Accessories Marketing Series, AL

AAML: Apparel and Accessories Marketing Series, ML

ADC: Advertising Campaign Event

BSM: Business Services Marketing Series

EMDM: E-Commerce Management Team Decision Making Event

FMAL: Food Marketing Series, AL

FMDM: Financial Analysis Management Team Decision Making Event

FMML: Food Marketing Series, ML

FSRM: Full Service Restaurant Management Series

HMDM: Hospitality Services Management Team Decision Making Event

MMS: Marketing Management Series

QSRM: Quick Serve Restaurant Management Series

RMAL: Retail Merchandising Series, AL

RMML: Retail Merchandising Series, ML

SMDM: Sports and Entertainment Marketing Management Team Decision Making Event

TMDM: Travel and Tourism Marketing Management Team Decision Making Event

TSE: Technical Sales Event

VPM: Vehicles and Petroleum Marketing Series

DECA PREP

Find timed DECA Prep activities correlated to the Competitive Events Workbook for students and DECA tips for teachers at **marketingessentials.glencoe.com /19/DECA**

FOCUS

Introducing the Section

COLLABORATIVE ACTIVITY

Ask students how many of them watch infomercials on television. Have them discuss the types of products that might be featured in infomercials.

Types of products might be exercise equipment, computers, skin care and kitchen appliances.

Next, have students identify the characteristics of infomercials.

Characteristics might include talk-show type setting, celebrity featured, a specific product or range of related products for sale, or call a number/visit a Web site to order.

Preteaching Key Terms

Divide the class into three groups. Give each group three key terms. Ask group members to discuss the meaning for each key term and present a definition. Have a volunteer write the group definitions on the board.

- promotional advertising
- institutional advertising
- media
- print media
- transit advertising
- broadcast media
- online advertising
- specialty media
- media planning

Extended Activity

Cross-Promotion

Give examples of cross-promotion by bringing in or showing a current advertising campaign that involves two products—for example, a current movie and associated merchandise that might be sold in the form of toys or food.

400

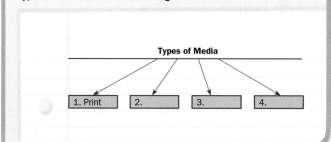
Advertising Media

OBJECTIVES

- Explain the concept and purpose of advertising in the promotional mix
- Identify the different types of advertising media
- Discuss the planning and selection of media

KEY TERMS

- promotional advertising
- institutional advertising
- media
- print media
- transit advertising
- broadcast media
- online advertising
- specialty media
- media planning

READ and STUDY

BEFORE YOU READ

Predict If a business did not advertise, how would potential customers learn about its products?

THE MAIN IDEA

Advertising is an important element of promotion. Businesses use different types of advertising media to promote their images, products, and services.

STUDY ORGANIZER

In a chart like the one below, organize your notes about the types of media used in advertising.

Types of Media

| 1. Print | 2. | 3. | 4. |

WHILE YOU READ

Connect Think about the many types of advertisements you have seen. How would you classify the different types?

Advertising and Its Purpose

Advertising is everywhere—television, radio, magazines, newspapers, stores, the World Wide Web, billboards, theaters, sports arenas, and even on highway road signs. The average person is exposed to more than 2,000 advertisements every week.

In advertising, advertisers control the message, where it will be seen or heard, and how often it will be repeated.

READ and STUDY

BEFORE YOU READ

Ask students to identify how customers could learn about a business's products without traditional advertising. Answers might include word of mouth, seeing a product they like, door-to-door salespeople, etc.

THE MAIN IDEA

Ask a student to consider what the word *promotion* means to him or her, then state it in his or her own words.

STUDY ORGANIZER

Model the study organizer for students by filling in the other types of media as you progress through the chapter. A full-size, downloadable study organizer can be found at **marketingessentials.glencoe.com**

WHILE YOU READ
Model for students how they can use their own experience as consumers when learning about the different types of advertisements.

Promotional and Institutional Advertising

There are two main types of advertising: promotional and institutional. **Promotional advertising** is when the goal is to increase sales. The targets of promotional advertising are consumers or business-to-business customers. Promotional advertising can introduce a new business, change a company image, promote a new product, advertise an existing one, or encourage the use of a particular service. Sometimes, the goal of promotional advertising is to encourage potential customers to ask for information, call for an appointment, go online, or enter a store. This is called generating leads or developing prospects.

Promotional advertising is an effective way to support direct selling efforts, sales promotion activities, visual merchandising, and display efforts.

Institutional advertising tries to create a favorable image for a company and foster goodwill in the marketplace. There are many institutional advertising techniques in use today. Connecting its name to a worthy cause helps a company make a favorable impression on its customers.

Mass Advertising Versus Targeted Advertising

Mass advertising enables companies to reach large numbers of people with their messages. Certain media, such as television and radio, lend themselves to mass advertising. Thanks to today's sophisticated technology, advertisers can also carefully target their messages to select audiences. This is known as targeted advertising. Advertising demonstrates the features and benefits of a product or service. As a result, business customers and general consumers are encouraged to buy the product or service.

Types of Media

Media are the agencies, means, or instruments used to convey advertising messages

• **A SPECIAL PLACE** State or city tourism offices have placed this ad to advertise Arizona as a good place to vacation.

List three characteristics of this ad.

Chapter 19 - Advertising **401**

AD GUIDE   **A SPECIAL PLACE**

Discussion Lead a discussion with students about how this ad advertises a vacation spot. Have students discuss how likely they would be to visit Arizona after seeing this ad.

Caption Answer Lists will vary; students might point out the unusual image of a shirt as a backdrop, the photography, and the slogan.

Follow Up Ask students to list three other products or services that can be advertised in a similar way.

TEACH

Discussion Starter

PROMOTIONAL AND INSTITUTIONAL ADVERTISING

Lead a discussion about effective advertising by asking students the following questions: Have you ever been asked to make a purchase or donate money to a cause based largely on an advertising campaign? What was the product or who was the group, and what factors might have induced you to buy the product or donate to the group?

TEACHING POINTS

Clarify Define the terms *promotional* and *institutional* for students. A good understanding of these terms will help focus the discussion. Ask each student to think of an example of promotional advertising and institutional advertising. Write the examples in a two-column chart. Answers might include: promotional—a Nike ad; institutional—a Nike clean-up day.

Concept Development

TYPES OF MEDIA

Bring in examples of a daily national newspaper and a local newspaper. Point out an insert, a full-page advertisement, and also a smaller advertisement. Have students identify what each type of advertisement has, and its effectiveness in promoting a product or service.

TEACHING POINTS

Clarify Remind students of the limitations of advertising in print media. Newspaper copy is often decided upon days in advance.

Concept Development

PRINT MEDIA

Ask students to recall an instance when a print advertisement enticed them to buy a product, such as a department store sale advertisement. Then have them recall an instance when a newspaper advertisement made them less interested in a product. Have students explain which elements of the advertisement appeal or do not appeal to them and why in a one-page expository essay.

Individualized Practice

MAGAZINE ADVERTISING

L1 Have students form pairs. Give each pair a magazine advertisement. Have the pair guess the type of magazine it came from and its target market, and have them also describe the format, the colors, and the paper stock the ad is printed on.

L2 Give each student an advertisement promoting a specific product, such as a bicycle. Have students guess the target market and magazine. Then have students adapt the advertisement for another target market. In a sketch and a paragraph, have them outline the revised advertisement.

L3 Have students read a business-to-business magazine, such as *CPC Packaging*—a cosmetics and personal care packaging trade magazine. In a short exposition, have students identify the focus of the advertisements in the magazine and how these advertisements might differ from ones in consumer magazines.

---

to the public. The four general categories of advertising media are print, broadcast, online, and specialty. Figure 19.1 illustrates examples of the different types of advertising media.

Print Media

Print media includes advertising in newspapers, magazines, direct mail, signs, and billboards. This is one of the oldest and most effective types of advertising.

Newspaper Advertising

Newspapers continue to be an important advertising outlet for many consumer-oriented products and services. In 2004, there were 1,456 daily newspapers in the United States. These local papers provide a timely way for companies to reach their target audiences. Many retailers and local companies rely on daily newspapers to advertise their products and services. These papers also offer a variety of options for the size, location, and frequency of insertion of ads. This flexibility enables companies to select the options that best suit their budgets and advertising goals.

Another type of local paper is called a shopper. Shoppers contain little editorial content, but they are delivered free to residents who live in specific areas.

National newspapers, such as *USA Today* and the *Wall Street Journal*, are distributed throughout the country. Advertisers can purchase ad space in the newspaper to reach the entire circulation or buy less expensive space targeted only to specific regions or cities.

Local and national papers often have online editions and sell advertising space for both formats. What are the advantages of newspaper advertising? It is estimated that 55 percent of adults in the United States read a newspaper every day. Advertisers want their ads to be seen, and this high number of readers is very important. Since a newspaper's reach is known, advertisers can target their advertising to people living in certain areas or with certain interests. A newspaper may even offer different neighborhood sections within the same city.

Responses to newspaper ads and coupon sales can be dated and easily tracked. The cost of newspaper advertising is another advantage. It remains relatively low because the paper and print quality is lower and the expense of printing is less than for magazines and direct mail.

Newspaper advertising does have limitations, however. Some newspapers are distributed to subscribers outside the business's target market. Also, newspapers have a limited shelf life because they are read and then thrown away each day. Many newspapers are still printed with black ink or with just a limited number of color pages. Ads are less visually appealing than those found in colorful magazines and direct mail.

Magazine Advertising

Magazines are distributed locally, regionally, or nationally. They can be published as weeklies, monthlies, and quarterlies. *U.S. News & World Report, Time,* and *Newsweek* are examples of national weekly magazines. Regional magazines are often developed to serve the needs of a metropolitan area or region. *Southern Living* is an example of a regional magazine. Some national magazines have regional, state, and city editions.

Magazines can also be classified as consumer or business-to-business. More than 3,000 consumer magazines such as *Reader's Digest, TV Guide, Seventeen, Forbes,* and *Sports Illustrated* are read for personal pleasure or interest. Advertisers can target their audiences through the characteristics of a magazine's subscribers.

Business-to-business magazines, also known as trade publications, interest professionals in specific fields. Examples include *Mass Market Retailers, Advertising Age,* and *Women's Wear Daily.* These publications are cost effective for advertisers who want to reach a target audience with little wasted circulation.

Both consumer and business-to-business magazines have a longer life span than newspapers. People tend to keep magazines for a more extended period of time. This increases the chance that they, and the ads in

---

Online Activity

Mass Advertising

As a class, discuss the differences between mass advertising and targeted advertising. Have students develop a list of mass advertisements and targeted advertisements and write them on the board. Answers might include an ad promoting winter wear for the whole family as a mass advertisement, but an ad promoting trendy winter wear for teens is more of a targeted advertisement.

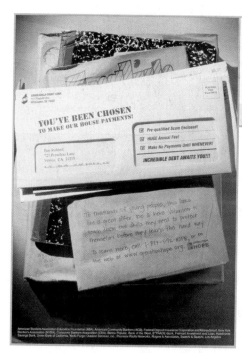

• **DIRECT MAIL and ETHICS** The Direct Marketing Association (DMA) encourages its members to follow ethical guidelines for the practice of direct mail advertising. In this ad, several banks and banking associations are promoting awareness of direct-mail scams.

Why does this group advertise Operation Hope?

TEACH CONTINUED

Concept Development

DIRECT MAIL

To explain the concept of direct mail, ask students to list types of direct mail they have received, either in printed or electronic form.

Answers will include catalogs, spam (unsolicited e-mail), newsletters, invitations to special events, etc.

Have a student record these types of direct mail on the board. Ask students to discuss the purpose of each type of advertisement.

TEACHING POINTS

Explain Customer response is when customers see or hear an advertisement and they are prompted to seek out the product or service.

Demonstrate Pile a large stack of direct mail on a desk in the room. Have students discuss their perceptions of this stack of direct mail. Is the term *junk mail* appropriate? Have students explain their answers.

 Critical Thinking

Ask students to consider which type of direct mail they find most useful—printed or electronic? Ask: Which type of direct mail is easiest to dispose of? Which type of direct mail do they prefer?

---

them, will be reread or passed along to others. People also read magazines more slowly and thoroughly than newspapers. Magazines are generally printed in color and have better print quality than newspapers. Magazines also offer a variety of presentation formats, including full-page ads, two-page spreads, gatefolds (a page folded into itself), return cards, and heavy stock inserts.

There are drawbacks to magazine advertising. The cost of advertising in magazines is higher than newspaper advertising. In addition, magazines are often printed a month or two in advance of publication. The deadline for submitting ads is several weeks or months before actual publication, and this requires careful planning.

Direct Mail

Direct marketing is a highly focused form of advertising. The two types of direct marketing are printed direct mail sent to a home or business and electronic direct mail delivered to an e-mail address. Such direct marketing is a good way to keep current customers aware of new products, services, and upcoming sales. It is also a cost effective way to generate leads and qualify prospective customers.

Printed direct-mail advertising takes many forms, including newsletters, catalogs, coupons, samplers, price lists, circulars, invitations to special sales or events, letters, and more. Large retailers and manufacturers send direct-mail catalogs and price lists to current and prospective customers.

The success of direct-mail advertising depends on carefully selecting its target. Direct mail is most effective with existing customers. However, in order to grow, a company must find new customers. Direct-mail advertisers seek new customers first by analyzing their existing customers to build a customer profile. Then, they acquire the names of people or organizations that fit the same profile. Direct

Chapter 19 - Advertising 403

AD GUIDE   DIRECT MAIL and ETHICS

Discussion Lead a discussion asking students how they feel about receiving direct mail advertising. Ask: What ethical considerations might apply to direct mail?

Caption Answer Operation Hope promotes individual financial literacy.

Follow Up Ask students if a direct-mail campaign has ever convinced them to buy a product or use a service.

TEACH CONTINUED

Individualized Practice

ANALYZING ADVERTISEMENTS

L1 Provide students with photocopies of two directory advertisements for similar services, such as dentists. On a two-column chart, have students compare the advertisements using these four categories: size, content, format, illustration/art.

L2 Tell students the following scenario: An advertising firm has asked students to suggest a design for a spectacular promoting a wildlife theme park. Have them come up with three options to propose to the firm, in both sketch form and accompanying paragraph outline. Ask the class to pick their favorite spectacular.

L3 Present students with a specific type of business, such as plumbing. In a one-page essay, have students analyze which type of print advertising would best suit the business's needs and why.

Extended Activity

Choosing Print Media

Have students share their responses to the following question in class. Ask students: In which print media would you advertise the following products?

- Fashion dolls for children aged 7–12 (children's magazines)
- New line of rain jackets magazines related to outdoor sports (sports section of a newspaper)
- Legal services (directory advertising, billboard and transit advertising)

Figure 19.1 *Advertising Media*

• **Promoting Images and Products** Media are the agencies, means, or instruments used to convey advertising messages to the public. Below are some examples of advertising media. The advertising media should be determined much in the same way as the advertising message: by the appeal and the target audience.

What are some other advertising media?

MAGAZINES AND NEWSPAPERS

Magazines offer a high level of reader involvement and messages that can be seen repeatedly. Online magazines represent a new advertising opportunity for marketers. Newspapers are a convenient way for a local advertiser to present a message in selected geographic areas.

DIRECT MAIL

Direct-mail advertising sends a message directly to your home or computer. It encourages customers to try new products and usually offers them an incentive for doing so.

TRANSIT ADVERTISING

Transit advertising uses public transportation facilities and vehicles to bring messages to people.

 Online Action!

Go to *marketingessentials.glencoe.com/19/figure/1* to find a project on advertising media.

 Figure 19.1 *Advertising Media*

Discussion Lead students in a discussion about the different types of advertising media. Spark the discussion by pointing out how some products are promoted across many types of media, while others tend to be promoted in one type of media.

Caption Answer Answers will vary but might include advertising on the Web, radio, and on specialty media.

 Online Action! For instructions, ideas, and answer guide, go to the Teacher Center at **marketingessentials.glencoe.com**

Follow Up Have students suggest three products or services that could be promoted with transit advertising.

marketing specialty firms sell lists of people's mailing addresses, phone numbers, and e-mail addresses. Names can be sorted according to many different demographic criteria to match the profile of existing customers.

Direct-mail advertising enables advertisers to be highly selective about who will receive the mailing and when the person receives it.

Direct-mail advertisers have a wide choice of printed advertisement formats, such as letters, catalogs, and postcards—limited only by postal regulations. Direct mail also includes electronic advertising campaigns. This flexibility enables direct mailers to test various creative approaches providing valuable input for perfecting future campaigns.

There are disadvantages to direct mail. It can yield a low level of response in relation to the number of items sent. A return of 10 percent for printed direct mail is usually considered excellent. Poorly planned and executed direct mail campaigns usually yield less than a one-half percent response.

Direct mail also has an image problem. Many people think of printed or electronic direct-mail advertising as junk mail.

The cost of printed direct mailing can be high because it includes producing and printing each piece of the mailing, collating it, buying mailing lists, and paying for postage to send it.

Directory Advertising

The best example of a directory that accepts advertising is the telephone directory. In the White Pages, businesses and residents receive a free alphabetical listing of their phone numbers and addresses. In the Yellow Pages, businesses pay for an alphabetical listing and, if desired, a display ad. The listings and ads appear under general category headings.

Directory advertising has some unique advantages. It is relatively inexpensive and can be used to target all demographic groups. For example, telephone directories are found in 98 percent of American households. Directories are usually kept for at least a year or until another is provided. This advantage, however, can also be a disadvantage. Advertisers cannot adjust their information, offers, or message until a new directory is distributed.

Outdoor Advertising

Both local, regional, and national businesses use outdoor signs for advertising. There are two types of outdoor signs: nonstandardized and standardized. Nonstandardized outdoor signs are used by companies at their places of business or in other locations throughout the community. An example is a sign displaying the company's logo at the entrance to its office building.

Standardized outdoor signs are purchased from advertising companies and are provided only in standard sizes. Examples are advertisements to be placed on billboards.

Other types of standardized outdoor signs are posters, painted bulletins, and spectaculars. Posters are pre-printed sheets put up like wallpaper on a wall or billboard. They are changed three to four times each year. Painted bulletins are painted signs that are changed every six months to a year. Spectaculars are outdoor signs purchased or rented from an advertising company. They use lights or moving parts to attract attention. They are common in densely populated metropolitan areas.

Outdoor advertising is highly visible and relatively inexpensive. It provides a 24-hours-a-day, 7-days-a-week message, and can be located to reach specific target markets. Drawbacks of outdoor advertising include limited viewing time, inability to target a specific audience, and increasing government regulations. Outdoor advertising is often restricted to roadways and areas zoned for commercial and industrial uses.

Transit Advertising

Transit advertising can be found on public transportation. It includes printed posters inside trains, taxis, and buses; ads on public benches, bus stop shelters, kiosks, newsstands, and trash cans; and station advertising located near or in subways and in railroad, bus, and airline terminals.

Chapter 19 - Advertising 405

TEACH CONTINUED

Individualized Practice

COMPARING ADVERTISEMENTS

L1 Videotape two TV advertisements for a specific type of product, such as laundry detergent. Have students watch the ads and compare them using these four categories: sound, action, color, and characters. Ask students to write a short exposition comparing the two advertisements.

L2 Have students think of ways they can get their products and services promoted on TV, and yet avoid customers zipping past them using VCRs or personal video recorders such as TiVo. Have students write a 150- to 200-word essay describing how they might accomplish this change.

L3 Present students with a specific type of professional—such as an attorney, dentist, or salesperson—to endorse a product. Have students create a 30-second advertisement for TV or radio. Ask student pairs to videotape or tape-record the advertisement. Review the advertisements as a class and discuss.

Critical Thinking

Ask students: What qualities do magazines possess that make consumers keep them longer and read them more thoroughly than newspapers? Have students share their answers in class. Encourage students to bring in examples from magazines to illustrate their answers.

TEACH CONTINUED

Concept Development

BROADCAST MEDIA

As a class, have students develop a chart of TV and radio viewing by answering the following questions:

- How much TV do you watch per week (hours)?
- How much radio do you listen to per week (hours)?
- Which shows do you regularly watch on TV?
- Which stations do you regularly listen to on the radio?
- Name a TV or radio jingle you know.

Have students write the answers to the questions on a sheet of paper. Then, as a class, compile the results into a TV and radio viewing chart. Discuss the reasons behind the results as a class.

Concept Development

RADIO ADVERTISEMENTS

Record a small number of radio ads during a specific time period, such as during a commuter drive time. Create a chart on the board with these categories: length, content, jingle/music, and personality. Have students complete the chart, using the radio advertisement elements.

TEACHING POINTS

Demonstrate To help get the activity started, demonstrate how to analyze one of the radio advertisements. Then add your information to the chart on the board.

Explain Some radio listeners tune in to particular stations so that they can listen to high-profile presenters or programs. Have students consider the effect these personalities or programs might have on the types of advertisements aired.

Transit advertising reaches a wide, and sometimes captive, audience. It is economical and has a defined market, usually in urban areas.

Broadcast Media

Broadcast media encompass radio and television. Over a lifetime of 70 years, the average person will spend nearly ten years watching television and almost six years listening to the radio. You can see why advertising through broadcast media is popular. Most of the 1,200 commercial television stations are affiliated with one of the major networks—ABC, CBS, NBC, or Fox. There are about 11,600 local cable systems. More than 66 percent of the estimated 98 million households with a television set are cable television subscribers.

Television Advertising

Television is the ultimate advertising medium for many businesses because it can combine all the creative elements necessary—sight, sound, action, and color—to produce a compelling advertising message. As a result, television is a very effective medium for demonstrating a product's features and benefits.

Television advertising allows companies to direct their advertising messages to audiences with a specific interest such as news, movies, or sports.

Most television advertisements are 30- or 60-second spots. An exception is the infomercial, which is a 30- or 60-minute advertisement. Infomercials promote products such as cookware, exercise equipment, and appliances, using a talk-show type setting. Viewers can order the advertised merchandise by calling a phone number, visiting a Web site, or writing to an address.

There are disadvantages to television advertising. Television has the highest production costs of any type of media and a high dollar cost for the TV time purchased. Prime-time and special event costs can be prohibitive. For example, a 30-second network TV ad for Super Bowl XXXVIII cost $2.25 million, while ABC charged $1.5 million for a 30-second ad during the 2004 Academy Awards.

Smaller companies cannot usually afford the production and placement costs of network television advertising, or they may be forced to buy time in less desirable time slots or rely on smaller and less expensive local or cable TV markets.

Radio Advertising

More than 10,000 AM and FM radio stations reach 96 percent of all people age 12 and over in a given week. This ability to reach a wide audience makes radio an extremely efficient and cost-effective advertising medium.

Radio is a mobile medium that can be heard just about anywhere. It is also a timely medium—radio advertisers can update their messages, ads, and offers daily, even hourly. Radio has the immediacy of newspapers without the high production costs of television.

Radio advertisers can carefully target their audience when they select the station on which to broadcast their ads. Most radio station programming targets a specific segment of the radio listening market.

Radio advertisements are presented in 10-, 20-, 30-, or 60-second time periods. These messages are effective in encouraging people to buy because the announcer or actors—along with background music, jingles, slogans, and sound effects—add excitement, drama, or humor.

However, products and services can only be described, not seen. Advertisers cannot rely on visual involvement to hold a listener's attention. That is why a catchy jingle is important. Radio advertisements also have a short life span.

Online Advertising

Online advertising is a form of advertising that uses either e-mail or the World Wide Web. It is still a small part of overall advertising spending, but it is growing steadily. Online advertising sales totaled $6.5 billion in 2003, generating 1.09 trillion impressions. An impression is a single appearance of an ad on a computer user's screen.

Electronic direct-mail advertising is sent via e-mail. Today, much advertising of this

---

 Critical Thinking

Reasons for using a certain type of advertisement vary, depending on the merchandise featured and the target audience. For example, children's shows are advertised on TV because promoters want to make use of the visual nature of TV. A newsprint or magazine ad for a children's show would be much less effective. Have students suggest other items that are primarily advertised on TV and the reasons behind this.

NET MARKETING

Rich Media Comes to PC Ads

Rich media ads—ones that combine animation, video, and sound with interactive features—are growing in popularity. Jupiter Research predicts that by 2008, advertisers will spend about 39 percent of their online advertising budgets on rich media. Rich media captured only 11 percent of online ad spending in 2003.

What Rich Media Can Do

Rich media ads provide instant, detailed feedback about how long PC users spend viewing an ad and what ad the user viewed next. The ads entice users to make an online purchase or submit demographic data in real time. DoubleClick, a company that distributes online ads, found that rich media ads generate better brand recognition and higher sales activity than static online ads.

AOL and Yahoo work with the Interactive Advertising Bureau to set standards for file size and load time to protect Web surfers with slower Internet connections.

THINK LIKE A MARKETER

How do rich media ads differ from print and broadcast ads in addressing a target market?

@ Online Action!

Go to *marketingessentials.glencoe.com/19/net* to find an activity on Internet advertising.

---

type is sent to pre-qualified groups of people. This is known as opt-in e-mail because recipients requested it or authorized it. Many of these e-mails enable the recipient to click through to a company's Web site. This enables companies to track exactly how many people visited their site by clicking on a link in the e-mail. It is also cost-effective, and it is easy to update and personalize the message for each recipient.

Banner and Pop-Up Ads

Most online advertising appears as banner ads. A banner ad comes in various shapes and sizes, but it is usually a rectangle seen at the top, bottom, or side of a Web page.

Similar to banner ads but smaller in size, button ads are placed in a strategic position on a Web page. Some advertisers use pop-up interstitial ads, which are TV-like spots that pop up between Web pages and are inserted in audio or video streams, either live or on-demand. A viewer must click on the ad to get

to the advertiser's Web site or close the ad window to resume surfing.

Online advertisers have found that bold colors, top-of-page placement, animation, calls to action, and limited frequency of exposures help increase that number of click-throughs. Even using these techniques, online advertisers report response rates as low as one percent. In other words, for every 100 banner ads, only one in 100 users clicks on the ad to visit the Web site.

Specialty Media

Specialty media, which are sometimes called giveaways or advertising specialties, are relatively inexpensive, useful items featuring an advertiser's name or logo.

To be successful as advertising tools, specialty items must be practical, used frequently, and placed in locations with high visibility. Common items that fit this description include hats, calendars, pens and pencils. Specialty items carry the identity of the

marketingessentials.glencoe.com

Chapter 19 - Advertising 407

NET MARKETING

Rich Media Comes to PC Ads

Discussion After students have read Net Marketing, ask volunteers to describe their own experience of viewing rich media advertising and share them with the class. Discuss whether this form of advertising seems to be increasing.

THINK LIKE A MARKETER Answer: Traditional print and TV ads target broad demographic groups, but do not allow any interactivity. Rich media could reinforce print and TV ads by repurposing photos, video, and music from those campaigns for online ads. Web ads can target specific groups known to visit certain Web sites.

@ Online Action! For instructions, ideas, and answer guide, go to the Teacher Center at *marketingessentials.glencoe.com*

ASSESS

Review Guide

CONCEPTS

Have students identify the four types of media.

print, broadcast, online, and specialty

Have students also list the subtypes of media in each category.

print: newspaper, magazine, direct mail, signs, directories, billboards, and transit; broadcast: radio and television; online: e-mail or Web; specialty: clothing, calendars, magnets, pens and pencils, etc.

KEY TERMS

Have students review key terms, their spellings, and definitions in small groups.

ONLINE SELF-ASSESSMENT

Have students go to **marketingessentials.glencoe.com** for the Section 19.1 practice test.

Individualized Review

L1 Assign and review Chapter 19 activities in the Student Activity Workbook.

L2 Assign and review Chapter 19 activities in the Marketing Math Workbook.

L3 Assign and review Chapter 19 activities in the *BusinessWeek* Reader and Case Studies.

Marketing Practice

Ask students to select a product that is mostly advertised in one medium, such as TV. Have students work independently or in groups of two to four to develop a marketing plan to promote the product in another medium, such as radio or the Internet. Presentations should be no longer than 15 minutes.

CLOSE

1. Have students complete these statements:

   • The choice of advertising media depends upon _____ .
     the type of product being advertised

   • In radio advertisements, there is no visual involvement to _____ .
     hold a listener's attention

2. Have students identify products and services that could be promoted in these broadcast media:

   • FM radio—rock 'n' roll
     TV shows, radio shows, concerts, movies, etc.

   • cable TV
     TV shows, consumer products, department store sales, etc.

   • online
     all of the above and more

Critical Thinking

Tell students that Internet "pop-up" ads are a type of ad that have generated a lot of consumer irritation. Have students describe an ad like these that they have seen either in class or outside of class, which they did not like. Ask them to explain the elements of the ad and why they did not like it in a two-paragraph response.

---

business sponsoring them and an advertising message.

The distribution of the items is usually limited. In addition, the items might be given to people who would never consider buying the product or patronizing the business.

Other Advertising Media

Businesses are constantly creating innovative means of transmitting their messages to potential customers. Examples include sports arena billboards, ads in movie theaters and home video rentals. Some advertisers, such as pharmaceutical manufacturers, use DVDs and CD-ROMs.

In-Store Advertising

Increasingly, in-store advertising techniques, such as electronic shelf ads, supermarket cart displays, instant coupon machines, floor mats, and sound systems are being used to advertise products within stores.

Media Planning and Selection

Media planning is the process of selecting the advertising media and deciding the time or space in which the ads should appear to accomplish a marketing objective. To select and compare different types of media, companies rely upon media planning software as well as media cost data and audience information.

To establish the media plan and select the right medium to use, advertisers address three basic questions:

1. Can the medium present the product and the appropriate business image?
2. Can the desired customers be targeted with the medium?
3. Will the medium get the desired response rate?

The media plan provides the opportunity to present a compelling message and project the desired business image to the target market.

19.1 AFTER YOU READ

Reviewing Key Terms and Concepts

1. Describe the two main types of advertising.
2. List the six different kinds of print media.
3. What is media planning?

Integrating Academic Skills

Math

4. In 2003, total advertising expenditures for TV (network, local, and cable) were $48.9 billion. What percentage was spent in each category if network TV totaled $20.4 billion, local TV $16.2 billion, and cable TV 12.3 billion?

History

5. Use the Internet or your local school or community library to research the history of print advertising over time. Prepare a two-page written report.

 Online Action!

Check your answers at *marketingessentials.glencoe.com/19/read*

marketingessentials.glencoe.com

AFTER YOU READ

Reviewing Key Terms and Concepts

1. The two main types of advertising are promotional and institutional advertising.

2. The six different kinds of print media are newspaper advertising, magazine advertising, direct mail, directory advertising, outdoor advertising, and transit advertising.

3. Media planning is the process of selecting the time and space in various media for advertising to accomplish an objective.

Integrating Academic Skills

4. Network TV = 41.7% (20.4/48.9 billion)

   Local TV = 33.1% (16.2/48.9 billion)

   Cable TV = 25.2% (12.3/48.9 billion)
   (Due to rounding, total percentage does not equal 100 percent.)

5. Answers will vary; reports should exhibit a chronological history of print advertisement.

Online Action! Answers at **marketingessentials.glencoe.com/19/read**

Media Measurement and Rates

OBJECTIVES

- Identify media measurement techniques
- Explain techniques used to evaluate media
- Summarize how media costs are determined
- Explain promotional budget methods

READ and STUDY

BEFORE YOU READ
Predict Suppose your company ran a four-color ad in *Newsweek* three months ago. How would you measure the response to that ad?

MAIN IDEA
Businesses need to reach as many targeted customers as possible within limited budgets. It is important to calculate costs and measure media effectiveness to best reach a potential audience.

STUDY ORGANIZER
Use a chart like the one below to take notes about media rates.

Media	How Rates Are Determined
Newspaper	

KEY TERMS

- audience
- impression
- frequency
- cost per thousand (CPM)

Media Measurement

Media planners must concern themselves with the correct medium to use and its costs as well as how to measure overall advertising effectiveness.

To understand media measurement, you need to become familiar with several key terms. First, the number of homes or people exposed to an ad is called the **audience**. A single exposure to an advertising message is called an **impression**. **Frequency** is the number of times an audience sees or hears an

WHILE YOU READ
Predict If you were charged with selecting advertising media, what kinds of information would you need?

Chapter 19 - Advertising **409**

FOCUS

Introducing the Section

COLLABORATIVE LEARNING
Have students work in groups to list how they think print and broadcast media pay for their publication costs and programming. Then write two headings on the board: *Print* and *Broadcast*. Ask students to help you list the factors that would influence advertising rates for each.

Preteaching Key Terms

Read the key terms aloud. After reading each term, suggest a synonym. Ask students to use the synonyms as hints at word meanings.

- **audience**
  clients

- **impression**
  exposure

- **frequency**
  ratio

- **cost per thousand (CPM)**
  rate

 Critical Thinking

Explain to students that advertising rates vary greatly. Therefore, it is difficult to quote exact rates for each type of media advertising. How might students find this type of information? Answers might include that they could gather a number of rates and develop an average rate from them.

READ and STUDY

BEFORE YOU READ
Lead students in measuring a response to an ad of your selection. Have them work in small groups to measure this response using audience, impression, frequency, and CPM.

THE MAIN IDEA
Ask a volunteer to read the main idea aloud and ask another student to retell it in his or her own words.

STUDY ORGANIZER
Model the study organizer for students by filling in the first part of the organizer. A full-size, downloadable study organizer can be found at marketingessentials.glencoe.com

WHILE YOU READ
Students may mention that costs, objectives, and measurement criteria would be important.

TEACH

MEDIA MEASUREMENT

Ask students which media measurement tool discussed in this section they understand the best. Ask: Which measurement tool do they feel they need to understand better? What course of action would best help them become familiar with the computations they need to understand better?

TEACHING POINTS

Clarify Explain that cost per thousand is referred to as CPM instead of CPT because the M stands for *mille*, the Latin word for thousand.

NEWSPAPER RATES

After students have read the section on media rates in general and newspaper rates specifically, ask them to decide which type of advertising would best promote the following products or services:

- puppies for sale
- gardening help wanted
- '78 Chevy for sale
- 1990s townhouse for rent
- scout leader wanted

Answers might include: Classified ads: gardening help wanted, scout leader wanted; Display ads: 1990s townhouse for rent, '78 Chevy for sale, puppies for sale.

TEACHING POINTS

Explain Explain to students how many products benefit from the visual advertising provided in display ads. However, wanted services often appear as classified ads.

---

advertisement. **Cost per thousand (CPM)** is the media cost of exposing 1,000 readers or viewers to an advertising impression. Cost per thousand is the comparison tool used to determine the effectiveness of different types of media.

The audience for print media is the total number of readers per issue. Readership in print media is measured by surveys or estimated by circulation. The audience figure is normally higher than its circulation because more than one person can read a single issue of a printed newspaper or magazine. From an advertiser's viewpoint, the audience figure better reflects the actual number of people exposed to an ad.

Television audience measurement is based upon diaries and meter data collected by Nielsen Media Research for a sample of TV viewers in more than 200 TV markets. The measurement of viewing behavior occurs during what are known as sweeps months—February, May, July, and November. The Arbitron Company measures radio audiences in more than 260 markets by collecting diaries of listening behavior. Online audiences are measured through surveys and computer software tracking systems to calculate the number of people who viewed a particular ad.

Knowing the potential audience, how frequently your advertisement will be seen, and its CPM can tell you whether the rates charged by various media are right for your advertising budget.

Media Rates

To reach customers, advertising uses a set format that is defined in terms of time (a 30-second television commercial) or space (a half-page newspaper ad). Media costs vary greatly, not just with type of media but also with geographical location and audience. For example, a quarter-page newspaper ad in a large city daily newspaper could cost four to eight times more than the same-sized ad in a small-town weekly. It is virtually impossible to quote exact rates for each type of media advertising.

Businesses can look up rates in the publications of Standard Rate and Data Service. This

---

company publishes rate cards for most major media according to general categories, such as print media or broadcast media.

Another service important to both advertisers and print media is the Audit Bureau of Circulations (ABC). Print media publishers subscribe to the ABC to verify their circulation figures. A circulation audit is critical to publishers because it enables them to verify circulation numbers to advertisers. Circulation figures are important selling points when publications try to attract and maintain their advertisers.

Newspaper Rates

Newspaper advertising rates are divided into two categories depending on whether the ad is a classified ad or a display ad.

Classified ads are grouped, or classified, into specific categories, such as help wanted, real estate, personals, or auto sales. They are effective for selling everything from services to houses to job openings. People or businesses that buy classified ads usually pay by the word or line of type.

Display ads enable the advertiser to depict the product or service being advertised. Advertisers use a mix of art or photographs, headlines, copy, and a signature or logo of the product or business. Display ads are generally larger than classified ads. Their cost is based upon the amount of space used and the ad's position in the newspaper.

Newspapers quote display advertising rates by the column inch. A column inch is an area that is one column wide by one inch deep. If a newspaper quotes a column inch rate, you simply multiply the number of inches by the number of columns to determine the total number of column inches. Then, multiply the total column inches by the rate. For example, if the rate for a column inch is $17, then a single ad (called an insertion) that measures four inches long by three columns will cost $204.

$$\$17 \times 4 \text{ inches} \times 3 \text{ columns} = \$204$$

Factors That Affect Rates

Advertising rates can vary depending on when an advertisement will appear in a paper.

Online Activity

Online Advertising

Have students find print ads for a particular product and find a similar product advertised online. Have students list any similarities and differences between the types of promotion and their effect on the audience.

A newspaper may charge a Monday through Thursday rate of $29 per column inch, a Friday rate of $30, a Saturday rate of $32, and a Sunday rate of $35 per column inch.

Where an ad appears is another factor. Display ads are usually sold at run-of-paper rates. Run-of-paper allows the newspaper to choose where to run an ad in the paper or magazine. However, for a higher rate, advertisers can run ads in guaranteed or preferred locations, such as the back cover. The use of color also affects the advertising rate. Color ads are sold at a higher price than black-and-white ads. The frequency of advertising affects the amount charged. The open rate, often referred to as the noncontract rate, is used for infrequent advertisers. It is the highest rate charged for a display ad.

Businesses that advertise in the newspaper frequently may contract with a newspaper to guarantee that they will use a certain amount of space for a specified time period. They are granted contract rates, which are discounted from the open rate. Contracts can be written in a number of ways. A yearly frequency contract guarantees that an advertiser will use a minimum number of column inches each week for 52 weeks. A bulk space contract guarantees that a minimum number of inches will be used when the advertiser chooses, within a 12-month period.

Comparing Rates

The cost per thousand (CPM) measurement is useful in comparing the cost of advertising to reach 1,000 readers in one newspaper with

Individualized Math Skills

Ask students to calculate the results for the following scenarios:

L1 Suppose the cost of an ad in *The Springfield Record* is $100, and the paper has a circulation of 50,000 people. What is its CPM rate?
$2

L2 Suppose the cost of an ad in *The Middletowner* is $200, and the paper has a circulation of 100,000 people. A second ad in *Review Weekly* costs $175, but the paper's circulation is 150,000 people. Which ad is the better deal?
CPM rate in *The Middletowner* is $2. The CPM rate in *Review Weekly* is $1.17. Therefore, the *Review Weekly* ad is the better deal.

L3 Suppose the cost of an ad in *Daily Journal* is $180, and the paper has a circulation of 300,000 people. A second ad in *Georgetown Times* costs $275, but the paper's circulation is 250,000 people. A third ad in *Metropolitan* costs $150, but the paper's circulation is 275,000 people. Which ad is the better deal?
CPM rate in *Daily Journal* is 60 cents. The CPM rate in *Georgetown Times* is $1.10. The CPM rate in *Metropolitan* is 55 cents. Therefore, the *Metropolitan* ad is the better deal.

GLOBAL MARKET

SAUDI ARABIA

Green Pastures

Almarai is the largest dairy foods company in the Middle East. The company was founded in 1976. Its headquarters are in Riyadh, Saudi Arabia. Almarai, whose name means *green pastures* in Arabic, has developed from a simple dairy farm into a large international business under the guidance of the governing royal family. Today, Almarai exports its dairy products all across the Middle East.

A Focus on Local Tastes Similar companies in developing countries often achieve notable success only to lose the competition for markets once multinational competitors decide to enter the race for customers. A multinational company with well-funded and experienced marketing and advertising departments is hard to beat. But Almarai won such a challenge against giant Nestle by tailoring its marketing and advertising to Middle Eastern preferences. The company's success rests on its focus on local taste for fresh, full-fat milk (sold in plastic bottles that look like old-fashioned glass milk bottles), regional products such as *labneh* (a soft cheese made from yogurt), and yogurt with no artificial color or flavor.

CRITICAL THINKING
Why might multinational companies find it difficult to market their products in a foreign market?

@ Online Action!
Go to *marketingessentials.glencoe.com/19/global* to find an activity on international advertising.

GLOBAL MARKET

Green Pastures

Discussion After students read Global Market, discuss the concept of cultural appeal. Discuss the idea that different cultures have different preferences and therefore require different advertising at times.

CRITICAL THINKING **Answer:** Local preferences and tastes can sometimes clash with multinational products, making it difficult for companies to expand in a particular market.

@ Online Action! For instructions, ideas, and answer guide, go to the Teacher Center at **marketingessentials.glencoe.com**

Follow Up Have students suggest three high-priced consumer items that were marketed in other countries before entering the American market.

Concept Development

MAGAZINE RATES

After students have read the section on magazine rates, ask them to imagine they are planning to run an ad in a popular teen magazine. Have students answer these questions about their ad:

- What size is the ad?
- How many colors will be used?
- What is the ad's preferred position?

Answers will vary, but should state the size, number of colors, and position in the magazine.

Build Vocabulary

Preview the following words by reading them in context with the magazine rates section.

- bleed
- black-and-white rates
- color rates
- premium position
- discounts

Discuss the meaning of these words with students.

---

the cost of advertising to reach 1,000 readers in another newspaper. The comparison is made by using the following formula:

Cost of the ad × 1,000/Circulation = CPM

Suppose the cost of an ad in the *Times* is $500, and the paper has a circulation of 500,000. Its CPM would be calculated as follows:

$500 × 1,000/500,000 = $500,000/500,000
= $1 per 1,000 readers

Suppose the cost of an ad in the *Tribune,* a competing paper, is $600, and the paper has a circulation of 300,000. Its CPM would be calculated as follows:

$600 × 1,000/300,000 = $600,000/300,000
= $2 per 1,000 readers

All other things being equal, an advertiser would probably choose the *Times* over the *Tribune* because it would cost less per 1,000 readers. Of course, all other things might not be equal. The *Tribune's* circulation could include more of the advertiser's target market, or the paper could offer a special ad placement. CPM is a convenient measure that enables advertisers to compare costs.

Magazine Rates

Magazine rates are based on circulation, the type of readership, and production techniques. To calculate the actual cost of magazine advertising, you need to become familiar with terms found on magazine advertising rate cards, including bleed, black-and-white rates, color rates, premium position, and discounts.

Bleed means that half- or full-page ads are printed to the very edge of the page, leaving no white border. Magazines generally charge between 15 to 20 percent extra for bleeds.

The lowest rates that magazines offer for display ads are black-and-white rates for black-and-white advertisements. Color rates are offered for color ads. Each time the magazine adds color to the ad, the rates increase.

412 UNIT 6 - PROMOTION

Magazine Rate Card

General Rates

RATE BASE: Rates based on a yearly average of 1,100,000 net paid A B C
A member of the Audit Bureau of Circulation

SPACE UNITS	BLACK & WHITE	BLACK & ONE COLOR	FOUR COLOR
1 page	$16,000	$19,630	$23,300
2 columns	11,620	14,560	18,170
½ page	10,130	13,550	17,200
1 column	5,920	9,530	12,180
½ column	3,020		
Covers			
Second Cover			$25,520
Third Cover			23,300
Fourth Cover			27,020

BLEED CHARGE: 15%
AGENCY COMMISSION: 15%
CASH DISCOUNT: 2% 10 days, net 30 days

Bleed accepted in color, black & white, and on covers, at an additional charge of 15%. No charge for gutter bleed in double-page spread.

Premium Positions: A 10% premium applies to advertising units positioned on pages 1, 2, and 3. A surcharge of 5% applies to bleed units in premium positions.

Rate Change Announcements will be made at least two months in advance of the black & white closing date for the issue affected. Orders for issues thereafter at rates then prevailing.

ISSUANCE AND CLOSING DATES

A. On sale date approximately the 15th of month preceding date of issue.

B. Black & white, black & one color, and four-color closing date, 20th of the 3rd month preceding date of issue. Example: Forms for August issue close May 20th.

C. Orders for cover pages noncancellable. Orders for all inside advertising units are noncancellable 15 days prior to their respective closing dates. Supplied inserts are noncancellable the 1st of the 4th month preceding month of issue. Options on cover positions must be exercised at least 30 days prior to four-color closing date. If order is not received by such date, cover option automatically lapses.

• **AD RATES** Ad rates are based on color.

Based on this magazine rate card, what is the cost of a half-page, four-color ad paid in ten days from the issuance of the invoice?

PHOTO GUIDE **AD RATES**

Discussion Lead a discussion about account executives in the publishing world and how they must solicit business to purchase ads. Ask students to brainstorm how account executives achieve this goal.

Caption Answer The ad would cost $16,856. ($17,200 × .02 = $344; $17,200 − $344 = $16,856)

Follow Up Ask students to speculate about what kind of information is used to determine ad rates.

Premium position refers to ad placement. Ads placed in premium positions, such as on the back cover or the inside of the first page, are more expensive to buy.

Rate Discounts

Frequency discounts are offered to advertisers who run the same ad several times during the year. The magazine may publish an entire schedule of rates for the number of times during the year an advertiser contracts to advertise. The rate per issue decreases as the frequency increases.

Another discount is a commission—a percentage of sales given by the magazine to the advertising agency for placing the ad for the advertiser. A typical commission is 15 percent.

Take a look at the rate card. You would calculate the cost of a full-page, four-color advertisement with bleed as follows:

$23,300	1 page, four-color rate
× .15	bleed
$ 3,495	extra for bleed

Case Study

Generating New Revenue

Magazines are trying to boost advertising revenues with new crossover and promotional tie-in deals. Some of the ideas include partnering with successful television channels and making distribution arrangements with mass merchandisers.

For example, the music video cable channel MTV crossed over from television to print by launching an MTV magazine. Major advertisers in the first edition included Nike, Pepsi, the NBA, and Procter & Gamble. The model for this crossover was ESPN. The sports station began *ESPN The Magazine* in 1998, and it has a circulation of 1.7 million.

Trying Something New

Time Inc., a large magazine publisher, is considering a new kind of distribution tie-in deal, including a new women's magazine. This new magazine would be sold only through mass retailers. To attract scarce ad dollars, magazine publishers are also partnering with the makers and sellers of consumer products. However, experience shows that only four out of ten new magazines survive.

Talk Show Crossovers

The publisher of the magazine *Rosie* hoped to profit from the popularity of talk show host Rosie O'Donnell. It shut down after a year and a half. In contrast, talk show host Oprah Winfrey's magazine *O* has been a success.

THINK STRATEGICALLY

Considering the survival rate for new magazines, why do media companies view crossovers to be a smart way to create new revenues?

 Online Action!

Go to *marketingessentials.glencoe.com/19/case* to find an activity on media advertising.

TEACH CONTINUED

Concept Development

MEDIA RATES

After students have read the section on rates, ask them to imagine they plan to advertise their new skateboard line both in print and online. Have students answer these questions about their ad:

- What is the ad's size?
- What is the ad's format?

Answers will vary but should state the size and format of the ad for each medium.

TEACHING POINTS

Clarify Unlike circulation, a Web site's appeal is measured by its monthly volume of visitors.

Enrichment

RADIO RATES

Have students listen to recordings of advertisements on a specific radio station. The recordings should illustrate each of the five radio times. Have students evaluate the types of advertising that appear during each radio time. Ask students to take notes so that they can later discuss the reasons behind advertising certain products or services during each time.

Case Study   Generating New Revenue

Discussion Have students read the Case Study and discuss the pros (increased exposure of their merchandise) and the cons (six out of 10 magazines fail to survive) of crossover advertising.

THINK STRATEGICALLY **Answer:** Because these "brand extensions" theoretically come with a built-in audience and consumer awareness, media companies view crossovers as a smart way to create revenue streams. The media companies don't have to spend hundreds of millions of dollars to create a new brand.

Online Action! For instructions, ideas, and answer guide, go to the Teacher Center at marketingessentials.glencoe.com

Critical Thinking

Whenever businesses begin to plan an ad, they need to consider how best to promote their merchandise. Have students choose a specific product, such as a car, and decide on the size, color, and placement that their ad needs to best promote the product.

ASSESS

Review Guide

CONCEPTS

Ask students to recall the different types of advertising media and the techniques used to evaluate their effectiveness. Have them summarize how media costs are determined.

KEY TERMS

Have students review key terms, their spellings, and definitions in small groups.

ONLINE SELF-ASSESSMENT

Have students go to **marketingessentials.glencoe.com** for the Section 19.2 practice test.

Individualized Review

L1 Assign and review Chapter 19 activities in the Student Activity Workbook.

L2 Assign and review Chapter 19 activities in the Marketing Math Workbook.

L3 Assign and review Chapter 19 activities in the *BusinessWeek* Reader and Case Studies.

Marketing Practice

Have students select three products or services they bought recently and their advertisements. Have students write a two-page report that explores the reasons behind how the advertising prompted them to purchase the product or service. Ask the students to relate these ideas to concepts presented in this chapter in their reports.

$23,300	1 page, four-color rate
+ 3,495	bleed
$26,795	for 1 page, four-color, with bleed

An ad agency placed the ad and it took the commission and the cash discount. The total cost of the above ad to the agency would be:

$ 26,795	1 page, four-color, with bleed
× .15	ad agency's commission
$ 4,019.25	

$ 26,795.00	1 page, four-color, with bleed
− 4,019.25	agency's commission
$ 22,775.75	net cost of ad to agency after commission
× .02	cash discount percentage if paid within 10 days of invoice
$ 455.52	cash discount
$ 22,775.75	net cost of ad to agency after commission
− 455.52	cash discount
$ 22,320.23	net cost to advertising agency for one full-page, four-color ad with bleed after cash discount and agency commission

As with newspapers, the CPM can be used to compare the cost of advertising in several magazines. If a magazine has a circulation of two million and charges $35,000 for a full-page, black-and-white ad, the CPM for such an ad would be $17.50.

$$\$35,000 \times 1,000/2,000,000 = \$17.50$$

Online Rates

Online advertising rates are based upon the type of format the customer desires. Banner ads, rich-media enhanced banner ads, button ads, and interstitial ads are some of the options. Online advertising rates are set on a CPM rate of page views. Rates vary based on the volume of monthly page views.

Radio Rates

When purchasing radio time, a business needs to decide what kind of radio advertising to use. There are three options: network radio advertising, national spot radio advertising, and local radio advertising. It is important to know the difference between spot radio and spot commercials. Spot radio refers to the geographical area an advertiser wants to reach with its advertising. Spot commercials are advertising messages of one minute or less that can be carried on network or spot radio.

Businesses with a national customer base usually choose network radio advertising or national spot radio advertising. Network radio advertising is a broadcast from a network studio to all affiliated radio stations throughout the country.

The following radio times are listed from most expensive to least expensive:

Class AA:	Morning drive time: 6 A.M. to 10 A.M.
Class A:	Evening drive time: 4 P.M. to 7 P.M.
Class B:	Home worker time: 10 A.M. to 4 P.M.
Class C:	Evening time: 7 P.M. to midnight
Class D:	Nighttime: midnight to 6 A.M.

Weekend rates may differ from weekday rates.

Rates are higher during early morning and late afternoon listening times, also called drive times. Radio stations also offer less costly, run-of-schedule (ROS) airtimes. ROS airtime allows a radio station to decide when to run the ad.

Television Rates

Advertising rates for television also vary with time of day. It is more expensive, for example, to advertise during the prime time hours of 7 P.M. to 10 P.M. than during other hours. The rates charged for other time slots, such as day (9 A.M. to 4 P.M.), late fringe (10:35 P.M. to 1:00 A.M.), or overnight (1 A.M. to 5 A.M.) are lower due to smaller numbers of viewers. Advertisers try to play their messages during the time slots that enable them to reach the most customers.

 Critical Thinking

Ask students why using several different forms of media is the best way to advertise a product or business. Ask them to consider when it would be most effective and appropriate to use just one medium for all advertising. Have students share their responses in class.

Promotional Budget

The promotional budget considers not only the cost for developing and placing or airing advertising but also the cost of staffing the department or campaign. The advertiser must consider short- and long-term benefits of the effort or campaign. Four common promotional budgeting methods are percentage of sales, all you can afford, following the competition, and objective and task.

1. In the percentage of sales method, the budget is decided based on a percentage of past or anticipated sales. For example, the current budget for advertising might be five percent of last year's sales or five percent of projected sales for the coming season. In either case, the advertising budget is tied to figures that could be too high or too low for current market condition.

2. If a company follows the all you can afford method, it first pays all expenses, then applies the remainder of funds available to promotional activities. This method is often used for only a short period of time. It is popular in small businesses, especially Internet and other start-up companies. The objective is to build sales and reputation quickly in the beginning.

3. When employing a following the competition method, an advertiser matches its competitor's promotional expenditures or prepares a budget based on the competitor's market share. This method is generally considered to be weak because it is based on the competitor's objectives.

4. With the objective and task method, the company determines goals, considers the necessary steps to meet goals, and determines the cost for promotional activities to meet the goals. This method considers a company's current situation and where it wants to be. This is the most effective of the four methods because it focuses on the company's goals and how it will reach them.

19.2 AFTER YOU READ

Reviewing Key Terms and Concepts

1. What is the cost per thousand (CPM) measurement?
2. What determines the rates television and radio stations charge for advertising?
3. Name the four methods used to create a promotional budget.

Integrating Academic Skills

Math

4. Calculate the CPM for an ad in a magazine that has a circulation of 1.7 million and charges $35,000 for a full-page, black-and-white advertisement.

Civics/Government

5. Perform an Internet or library search on how the government tries to prevent deceptive advertising. Find at least three laws, rules, or regulations established to assist the consumer with advertised products or services.

@ **Online Action!** Check your answers at *marketingessentials.glencoe.com/19/read*

CLOSE

Ask students to recall and to list answers to the following questions:

- What are the two types of newspaper ads?
  classified and display

- What are magazine rates based upon?
  circulation, quality of readership, and production technique

 Online Activity

Researching Web Sites
Ask students to select a Web site. Ask them to research how many hits that site has per day and report on what kind of advertising would do well on that site. Have students present their findings in a one-page report.

AFTER YOU READ

Reviewing Key Terms and Concepts

1. Cost per thousand (CPM) is the media cost of exposing 1,000 readers or viewers to an advertising impression.

2. Radio and TV rates are based on the time of day the advertisement is aired.

3. Four common promotional budgeting methods are percentage of anticipated sales, all you can afford, following the competition, and objective and task.

Integrating Academic Skills

4. $20.587; ($35,000 × 1,000) ÷ 1,700,000 = $20.587.

5. Answers will vary. However, students could cite laws related to labeling, online advertising, billboard advertising, prohibitions on some forms or types of advertising (such as tobacco, nearness to schools, etc.).

@ **Online Action!** Answers at **marketingessentials.glencoe.com/19/read**

Lifelong Learning

CAREER INFORMATION

Have students go to marketingessentials.glencoe.com and find the Chapter 19 Careers page and click on the link for the American Marketing Association's Careers Strategies and Tips. Ask students to summarize one article in three short paragraphs.

ADVERTISING

Since advertising affects so many decisions that students will make as consumers during their lifetimes, they can benefit from understanding its uses and applications. After taking this class, they can keep up with trends in advertising by reading a variety of publications, including *Adweek, Advertising Age, Marketing News,* and other industry-specific or general interest publications.

Primary Source

Ask students to go to marketingessentials.glencoe.com and find Chapter 19 Resources. Ask them to click on the link for the American Marketing Association's marketing dictionary and read the definitions of terms they find that are related to advertising.

THINKING CRITICALLY

Marketing professionals should be well-rounded people familiar with cultural trends. This familiarity will help them do a better job at connecting with their target audience.

@ Online Action!

For instructions, ideas, and answer guide, go to the Teacher Center at marketingessentials.glencoe.com

JUAN GUILLERMO TORNOÉ
PARTNER
HISPANIC DIVISION
WIZARD OF ADS, INC.

? What do you do at work?
I work in a marketing and advertising consulting firm, Wizard of Ads, Inc. I handle all the media research and negotiation for our mainstream clients, currently 40+ of them located in 38 cities across the United States and Canada. I personally research and negotiate each one of the individual markets where our clients are located, maximizing their advertising budgets' performance. From a couple thousand dollars to several million dollars per market, depending on the client's size, we get the most efficient and effective media buys for the dollar in each of those markets.

? What skills are most important to you?
Not diminishing formal education, which most certainly created an extremely strong foundation as well as an invaluable skills tool box, it has been through real-world work experiences that I have obtained the best training to do my job. I was blessed with the opportunity to work on and learn about message development, strategy, media negotiation, human persuasion, and "why people do the things they do" with the president of my company.

? What is your key to success?
I have realized that success is a journey, not a destination. I have had to learn to rejoice on each individual milestone accomplished, and then keep on moving toward the next one. The keys to reaching those milestones have been awareness of opportunities, the willingness to take risks, hard work, and perseverance.

Aptitudes, Abilities, and Skills

Creativity, writing and communication skills, and an analytical mind

Education and Training

Degrees in marketing, psychology, communication, and general business are helpful.

Career Path

Many careers at marketing and advertising agencies are launched through unpaid internships or entry-level assistant positions. Successful employees usually become responsible for large client accounts and entire ad campaigns.

THINKING CRITICALLY

Why would a marketing professional benefit from a study of art, sociology, and religion?

@ Online Action!

Go to *marketingessentials.glencoe.com/ 19/careers* to find a career-related activity.

 marketingessentials.glencoe.com

Test-Taking Strategies

Encourage students to review daily the section graphic organizers which they have filled out and/or used to take notes. This daily review will help many students to better retain the information they have read in the text.

FOCUS on KEY POINTS

SECTION 19.1
● The main purpose of advertising is to present a message that encourages the customer to buy the product or service or to accept an idea. Businesses must choose the most appropriate advertising media for their target market; for example, Web sites, newspapers, radio, or television. A business then prepares a media plan.

SECTION 19.2
● Choosing the correct medium to use from all the available types of media is a very complex effort. Media planners must concern themselves not only with the correct medium to use and its costs, but also with how to measure overall advertising effectiveness. Once a company decides on its promotional methods and goals, it must create a promotional budget.

REVIEW VOCABULARY

Organize the class into two teams for a game of "Marketing Tic-Tac-Toe." Team members will give the definition for the terms and will place an "X" or "O" on the board for each correct definition.

1. promotional advertising (p. 401)
2. institutional advertising (p. 401)
3. media (p. 401)
4. print media (p. 402)
5. transit advertising (p. 405)
6. broadcast media (p. 406)
7. online advertising (p. 406)
8. specialty media (p. 407)
9. media planning (p. 408)
10. audience (p. 409)
11. impression (p. 409)
12. frequency (p. 409)
13. cost per thousand (CPM) (p. 410)

REVIEW FACTS and IDEAS

14. What is advertising? (19.1)
15. List the four main categories of advertising media. (19.1)
16. What three basic questions are used to develop a media plan? (19.1)
17. What are the two forms of broadcast advertising? (19.1)
18. What is online advertising? (19.1)
19. What factors affect newspaper ad rates? (19.2)
20. What is the most effective way to create a promotional budget? (19.2)

REVIEW FACTS and IDEAS

14. Advertising is any paid form of non-personal promotion of ideas, goods, or services by an identified sponsor.
15. The four main categories of advertising media include: print, broadcast, online, and specialty media.
16. Can the medium present the product and the appropriate business image? Can the desired customers be targeted with the medium? Will the medium get the desired response rate?
17. The two main forms of broadcast advertising are radio advertising and television advertising.
18. Online advertising is advertising placed on the Internet.
19. Some factors are: when an ad will appear; in which part of the newspaper it will appear; use of color; and frequency of advertising.
20. Use the objective and task method.

FOCUS on KEY POINTS

Ask volunteers to read the summaries aloud and give the class one real-life example for each of the concepts.

REVIEW VOCABULARY

See glossary for definitions of **1–13.**
A sample answer might read:

1. *Promotional advertising* is advertising with the goal of increasing sales.

BUILD SKILLS

21. Workplace Skills

Answers will vary; students should be able to cite the benefits of effective advertising.

22. Technology Applications

Answers will vary. Students should cite advantages (i.e., extra revenue); disadvantages (i.e., inappropriate for learning environment); and suggest limitations on school use.

23. Math Practice

Reader's Digest = $3.16; ($35,000 × 1,000) ÷ 11,090,349 = $3.16

People = $9.64; ($35,000 × 1,000) ÷ 3,628,982 = $9.64

Cosmopolitan = $12.23; ($35,000 × 1,000) ÷ 2,860,024 = $12.23

Ebony = $19.45; ($35,000 × 1,000) ÷ 1,798,844 = $19.45

DEVELOP CRITICAL THINKING

24. Analyzing Printed Direct Mail

Answers will vary; students should demonstrate an understanding of how the ad relates to the target market.

25. Advertising a Start-Up

Answers will vary; students should be able to give reasons for their promotion strategy selection which demonstrate an understanding of the strategy.

CHAPTER 19 REVIEW

BUILD SKILLS

21. Workplace Skills

Communication A coworker believes that advertising is a waste of money and suggests that products would be cheaper without it. Develop a ten-minute oral presentation on the benefits of advertising.

22. Technology Applications

Ads in Schools and Gyms Research the Internet to find information about the advantages and disadvantages of advertising in school buildings and athletic facilities. What restrictions, if any, would you recommend for such advertising? Use a word processing program to develop a one-page paper on the topic.

23. Math Practice

CPM Calculations Calculate the CPM for a $35,000 ad in the following magazines based upon circulation figures from the first six months of 2003.

Magazine	Total Paid	CPM
Readers Digest	11,090,349	
People	3,628,982	
Cosmopolitan	2,860,024	
Ebony	1,798,844	

DEVELOP CRITICAL THINKING

24. Analyzing Printed Direct Mail

Analyze the printed direct mail that either you or your family receives in a two-week period, such as reply cards, incentive discounts, product samples, credit card offers, inserts with utility bills, or letters. Attach your analysis and the direct mail samples to a poster board for display.

25. Advertising a Start-Up

Suppose you and your best friend have created a new formula for a shampoo. You decide you want to manufacture several hundred bottles of this shampoo. Part of your business plan involves developing a promotion strategy. What type of advertising would you choose? Why?

Formative Assessment

Formative assessment is an essential component of classroom work. This type of assessment provides information that is then used as feedback to modify teaching and meet student needs.

L1 Have students identify the media measurement techniques.

L2 Have students write an evaluation of the effectiveness of two types of advertising.

L3 Have students create a billboard advertisement promoting a product or service of their choice.

Reteach If the results of this formative assessment seem low, consider the following activity:

Read each of the key terms aloud. Have students define the key terms and use them in a sentence. Clear up any confusion students may have.

APPLY CONCEPTS

26. Analyzing Radio Listening

Listen to your favorite radio station for one hour. List the products advertised, characterize the advertising approach taken, and identify the sponsor as either national or local.

Activity Use a spreadsheet computer program to prepare an advertising log for one hour of your radio listening.

27. Creating a Media Plan

Develop a media plan for a product of your choice using billboards, radio ads, magazines, television commercials, and/or newspapers for a one-month period. Assume that you have $125,000 to reach a target audience of 10,000 people. The CPM for an ad in each medium is as follows:

Billboard	$2.05
Radio ad, drive time	$8.61
Magazine, one-page color ad	$9.35
TV commercial, 30 seconds in prime time	$17.78
Newspaper, one-third page, black-and-white	$22.95

Activity Use a word processing program to develop a plan that identifies how you will use the above media.

NET SAVVY

28. Finding Resources

Perform an Internet search for *B to B: The Magazine for Marketing Strategists*. Select one of the business Web sites named on B2B's Top 100 list. Browse the Web site and prepare a summary about the resources that are available on the site.

THE **DECA** CONNECTION

Role Play:
Develop an Advertising Plan

Situation You are to assume the role of manager of the cosmetics department of a small, locally owned department store. You are to develop an advertising plan and coordinate an in-store promotional plan to announce the new lipstick colors for the upcoming spring season. The new colors are inspired by flowers and include shades of lilac, rose, hyacinth, violet, and hibiscus red.

Activity You are to select appropriate advertising media and make suggestions for an in-store promotion that will coordinate with one another. You are to present your ideas to the department store manager (judge).

Evaluation You will be evaluated on how well you meet the following performance indicators:

● Explain the types of advertising media

● Select advertising media

● Analyze use of specialty promotions

● Develop a sales promotion plan

● Demonstrate appropriate creativity

 Online Action!

For more information and DECA Prep practice, go to *marketingessentials.glencoe .com/19/DECA*

THE **DECA** CONNECTION

Students should be evaluated according to the performance standards noted in the role play. For another DECA role play, go to the Competitive Events Workbook or the Student Activity Workbook, or go to **marketingessentials.glencoe.com/19/DECA**

Online Action! For instructions, ideas, and answer guide, go to the Teacher Center at **marketingessentials.glencoe.com**

DECA Advisors Corner

Reinforce students' computer and advertising skills by getting them involved in one of DECA's online advertising competitions. Guidelines for the competitions are on the DECA Web site. These competitions encourage DECA members to seek knowledge beyond traditional advertising media.

APPLY CONCEPTS

26. Analyzing Radio Listening

Spreadsheets will vary; all should be listed by time and contain all elements: product advertised, advertising approach, and whether the sponsor is national or local.

27. Creating a Media Plan

Answers will vary; students should demonstrate an understanding of how different media will be used to promote the product.

NET SAVVY

28. Finding Resources

Answers will vary depending upon which business is selected.

MINI-QUIZ

Read these sentences to the students and have them volunteer the missing words.

1. Advertising designed to increase sales is known as _____ . (promotional advertising)

2. The main purpose of advertising is to present a message so well that a customer _____ . (buys the product or accepts the idea presented)

3. The _____ , or CPM rate, is the cost of exposing 1,000 readers to an advertisement. (cost per thousand)

For an expanded chapter quiz, go to Chapter 19 in the TeacherWorks CD-ROM and to Chapter 19 in the **ExamView®** Pro Test Generator CD-ROM.

Chapter Overview

Chapter 20 explains how advertising campaigns are developed and the changing role advertising agencies play in assisting businesses with the marketing of products. The essential elements of print advertisements, including headlines, copy, illustrations, signature, and slogans, are explained. Principles of ad layout and design are also discussed.

⊗ BUILD BACKGROUND ⊗

List common consumer products or the names of national chain retailers on the board and ask students to recall the advertising they have seen promoting these products or stores. Ask them to add to the list with brands they associate with memorable advertising campaigns. Have students discuss what they think makes certain ad campaigns memorable.

Why It's Important

Understanding advertising's role in marketing and how ad campaigns communicate with potential customers is key to successful marketing. Knowing what makes an effective print advertisement is an essential skill for any marketer.

Prepare to Read

Ask a volunteer to list the major headings from the two sections on the board in outline format:

The Advertising Campaign
Developing Print Advertisements
Developing Print Advertising Layouts

Suggest that students take notes as they read the chapter, listing subheads and key ideas and facts under the three major headings.

Print Advertisements

Chapter Objectives

After reading this chapter, you should be able to:

- Discuss how advertising campaigns are developed
- Explain the role of an advertising agency
- Identify the main components of print advertisements
- Explain the principles of preparing an ad layout
- List advantages and disadvantages of using color in advertising
- Describe how typefaces and sizes add variety and emphasis to print advertisements

▸ GUIDE TO THE PHOTO

Market Talk There are many different types of print ads. Magazines, newspapers, and direct mail are the most common venues for these ads. Preparing a print ad requires a high degree of expertise, since the writing style and graphics can vary greatly depending on the product and where the ad will run.

Quick Think Take a quick look at a daily newspaper and at a monthly magazine. Compare the types of ads you see.

420 UNIT 6 - PROMOTION

GUIDE TO THE PHOTO

Market Talk Point out to students that as members of a marketing team, they may be asked their opinion about various aspects of an advertising campaign under development. Have students discuss what elements they think contribute to effective print advertisements.

Quick Think Student responses may include: Magazine ads are more likely to be larger and printed in full color. Newspaper advertisements are usually designed to reach a local audience, so they more often deal with specific products or services available in a local area.

 Follow Up Ask students to find ads in newspapers and magazines that serve different purposes, such as promoting a locally available product or service, or building general brand awareness for a national brand.

Performance indicators represent key skills and knowledge. Relating them to the concepts explained in this chapter is your key to success in DECA events. These acronyms represent DECA events that involve knowledge of concepts in this chapter.

AAAL	FMAL	MMS*	TMDM*
AAML*	FMDM*	QSRM*	TSE*
ADC*	FMML*	RMAL	VPM
BSM	FSRM*	RMML*	
EMDM*	HMDM*	SMDM*	

In all these DECA events you should be able to follow these performance indicators:

- Explain components of advertisements
- Write promotional messages that appeal to targeted markets
- Create a Web site

All the events with an asterisk (*) also include this performance indicator:

- Evaluate the effectiveness of advertising

Some events include additional performance indicators. These are:

EMDM   Explain the use of advertising agencies
Write content for use on the Internet

FMDM   Write direct-mail letters
Explain the use of advertising agencies

HMDM   Explain the use of advertising agencies

SMDM   Explain the use of advertising agencies
Write direct mail letters

TMDM   Explain the use of advertising agencies
Design a company's catalogs
Design a company's brochures

DECA PREP

Check your understanding of DECA performance indicators with the DECA activity in this chapter's review. For more information and DECA Prep practice, go to *marketingessentials* *.glencoe.com/20/DECA*

DECA events that require knowledge of print advertisements are described here. Discuss the performance indicators to make sure students understand how to demonstrate their understanding.

The events acronyms stand for:

AAAL: Apparel and Accessories Marketing Series, AL

AAML: Apparel and Accessories Marketing Series, ML

ADC: Advertising Campaign Event

BSM: Business Services Marketing Series

EMDM: E-Commerce Management Team Decision Making Event

FMAL: Food Marketing Series, AL

FMDM: Financial Analysis Management Team Decision Making Event

FFML: Food Marketing Series, ML

FSRM: Full Service Restaurant Management Series

HMDM: Hospitality Services Management Team Decision Making Event

MMS: Marketing Management Series

QSRM: Quick Serve Restaurant Management Series

RMAL: Retail Merchandising Series, AL

RMML: Retail Merchandising Series, ML

SMDM: Sports and Entertainment Marketing Management Team Decision Making Event

TMDM: Travel and Tourism Marketing Management Team Decision Making Event

TSE: Technical Sales Event

VPM: Vehicles and Petroleum Marketing Series

DECA PREP

Find timed DECA prep activities correlated to the Competitive Events Workbook for students and DECA tips for teachers at **marketingessentials.glencoe.com /20/DECA**

CHAPTER 20   Classroom Resources

For the Teacher

- TeacherWorks
- marketingessentials.glencoe.com
- Interactive Chalkboard
- **Exam***View*® Pro Test Generator
- Fast File Unit 6

For the Student

- *Marketing Essentials* Online Edition
- Student Activity Workbook
- Marketing Math Workbook
- Marketing Research Project Workbook
- School-to-Work Activity Workbook
- Competitive Events Workbook
- *BusinessWeek* Reader and Case Studies
- marketingessentials.glencoe.com

FOCUS

Introducing the Section

COLLABORATIVE ACTIVITY

Divide the class into groups of four or five. Have each group imagine that it manages a creative services department at an advertising agency. The department, which includes graphic designers and copywriters, is responsible for presenting ideas for an advertising campaign at a client meeting. Suggest that the client has created a new type of MP3 player geared toward the youth market. Have students suggest a name for the product and develop ideas for a photo or illustration, copy, and a catchy slogan.

Preteaching Key Terms

Write the terms for the parts of a print ad in one column of the board and the rest of the terms in another column. Display several print ads and ask students to identify the four parts of each ad and generate definitions for each term.

- advertising campaign
- advertising agencies
- headline
- copy
- illustration
- clip art
- signature
- slogan

Critical Thinking

Ask students: What is an example of a "global consumer brand" and why would it be important to tailor an advertising campaign to specific countries or ethnic groups?

422

OBJECTIVES

- Discuss how advertising campaigns are developed
- Explain the role of an advertising agency
- Identify the main components of print advertisements

KEY TERMS

- advertising campaign
- advertising agencies
- headline
- copy
- illustration
- clip art
- signature
- slogan

Essential Elements of Advertising

READ and STUDY

BEFORE YOU READ
Predict Think of print ads you have seen recently. What key elements do they have in common?

THE MAIN IDEA
Successful advertising campaigns help to sell products and services. Marketers must know what the essential elements are and how they are used to develop effective advertisements.

STUDY ORGANIZER
Use a chart like the one below to take notes about the components of a print ad.

The Advertising Campaign

To advertise a product or service, a company must plan an advertising campaign. An **advertising campaign** is a group of advertisements, commercials, and related promotional materials and activities that are designed as part of a coordinated advertising plan to meet the specific goals of a company. An integrated advertising campaign involves the creation and coordination of a series of advertisements around a particular theme.

WHILE YOU READ

Connect Think of a product you like. How would you advertise it?

READ and STUDY

BEFORE YOU READ
Have students describe print advertisements they remember, and encourage them to tell why they are so memorable.

THE MAIN IDEA
Ask students to identify what they think the essential elements of a successful print advertisement are.

STUDY ORGANIZER
Make your own study organizer, or download the one at **marketingessentials.glencoe.com**. As study continues, you and the class should work together to take notes.

WHILE YOU READ Model for the students a product you like and how you would advertise it.

Planning an integrated advertising campaign involves a series of steps:

1. **Identify the target audience** Advertisers must analyze the potential market and decide who should receive their messages.
2. **Determine objectives** They identify their goals, such as increasing brand awareness, or increasing knowledge about the product.
3. **Establish the budget** Advertisers decide what to spend over a specific period of time.
4. **Develop the message** They develop the theme and messages based on the product's features, benefits, and uses.
5. **Select the media** They choose which media, such as TV, radio, Internet, or print, will be most effective.
6. **Evaluate the campaign** Advertisers use market research to see if the campaign met its objectives.

Advertising Agencies

Advertising agencies are independent businesses that specialize in developing ad campaigns and crafting the ads for clients. Full-service agencies plan the entire advertising campaign by setting objectives, developing advertising messages and strategies, completing media plans, selecting media, and coordinating related activities, including sales promotion and public relations. Larger advertising agencies employ specialists, such as copywriters, graphic artists, media experts, marketing researchers, and legal advisers, to help with the development and execution of campaigns.

Limited-service agencies specialize in one aspect of the campaign, such as creative services, media planning, or media buying. Larger companies are increasingly selecting specialists, such as those who concentrate only on Internet advertising, to develop different aspects of the advertising campaign. Global consumer brands also make use of specialty agencies to develop or tailor campaigns to specific countries, ethnic groups, or other target markets.

Technology and e-commerce opportunities have led many businesses to employ in-house staff for some advertising functions, such as Web site development and maintenance. Some companies supplement in-house resources with the work of freelance professionals or limited-service agencies.

New Models for Advertising Agencies

New models for advertising agencies include business formats such as creative boutiques, project team agencies, and virtual agencies.

A creative boutique is a specialized service agency that helps businesses with creative production. In a creative boutique, the advertiser develops the message and copy but outsources the design and production of the advertisement to the boutique. This type of organization enables the advertiser to create ads much faster than a traditional agency could.

Agencies organized around a project team provide copywriting, creative execution, and media placement without the overhead of a larger agency. Teams can come together to do one project, then move on to the next when the ad campaign is complete.

In a virtual agency, one individual coordinates the work of a network of experienced freelancers. A freelancer is a self-employed person who sells work or services by the hour, day, or job, rather than working on a regular salary basis for one employer. One of the benefits of this type of agency is that it has lower overhead, which means lower costs for the client.

Developing Print Advertisements

Although they are only one part of an advertising campaign, print advertisements are very important to most campaigns. As Figure 20.1 shows, print advertisements have four key elements: headline, copy, illustrations, and signature. Some advertisements also include the company's slogan. Each of the four key elements enhances the overall theme. The four fundamental elements of a print advertisement are applicable for ads in other media, too. As you read this section,

TEACH

Discussion Starter

ADVERTISING AGENCIES

Ask students to break into small groups and discuss which department of an advertising agency they would prefer to work in and in what capacity. Ask each to consider if he or she would make the most valuable contribution in a creative, research, media, or client role. Based on their answers, encourage them to identify the skills they need to develop to excel in each type of work.

TEACHING POINTS

Clarify To clarify the idea of theme in an integrated advertising campaign, present students with a variety of recent consumer magazines. Have them search for different ads for the same product, service, or company and discuss how they relate to one another. Help them define the overall message that the advertiser is sending through the various ads.

Critical Thinking

Ask students: Why might it be important that an account executive be able to communicate effectively with copywriters and graphic designers as well as with clients?

Online Activity

Advertisements for Advertising Agencies

Have students study the Web sites of various advertising agencies, choose one, and write a paragraph or two describing the overall message the Web site sends to potential clients. Have them discuss how the copy and visuals used on the home page of the Web site support that message.

TEACH CONTINUED

Concept Development

HEADLINE

After students have read the section on headlines, ask volunteers to recall the characteristics of effective headlines as you list them on the chalkboard. Lists should include these characteristics:

- brief, fewer than seven words
- grab and hold the reader's attention
- contain the words *you, your, how,* and *new*
- appeal to an immediate need
- identify a benefit of the product or service
- evoke emotion
- use a familiar saying with a twist
- make use of opposites

Then have students suggest which characteristics are represented in the following slogans or phrases:

- **Plop, plop, fizz, fizz. Oh! What a relief it is!**
- **Things go better with Coke.**
- **Car Insurance at Low Cost—If You're A Careful Driver**
- **How I Improved My Memory in One Evening**
- **Play Guitar in 7 Days or Your Money Back**
- **What's Wrong With This Picture?**

TEACHING POINTS

Role Play Tell students they are members of an advertising agency team working on a campaign for a new client. Present a product or service with which students are familiar and lead a brainstorming session where students develop headlines and subheads for print advertisements for that product or service.

Figure 20.1 | **Parts of a Print Advertisement**

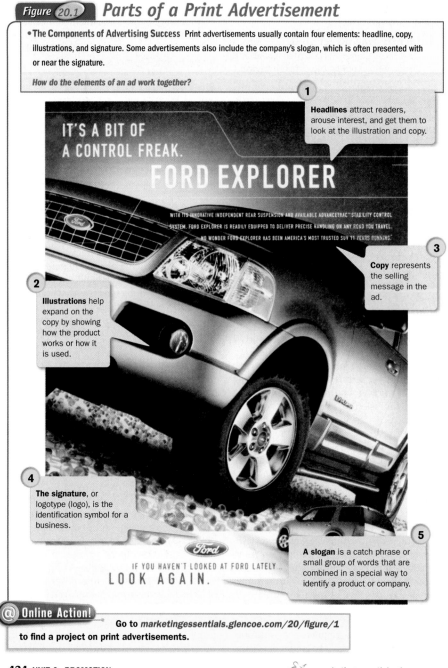

- **The Components of Advertising Success** Print advertisements usually contain four elements: headline, copy, illustrations, and signature. Some advertisements also include the company's slogan, which is often presented with or near the signature.

How do the elements of an ad work together?

1 Headlines attract readers, arouse interest, and get them to look at the illustration and copy.

2 Illustrations help expand on the copy by showing how the product works or how it is used.

3 Copy represents the selling message in the ad.

4 The signature, or logotype (logo), is the identification symbol for a business.

5 A slogan is a catch phrase or small group of words that are combined in a special way to identify a product or company.

@ **Online Action!** Go to *marketingessentials.glencoe.com/20/figure/1* to find a project on print advertisements.

marketingessentials.glencoe.com

Figure 20.1 | **Parts of a Print Advertisement**

Discussion Ask students to discuss each of the key elements presented and defined in the Ford Explorer ad. Which elements do they think are most effective? Are there any that could be improved? Focus attention on the headline, "It's a Bit of a Control Freak," and have volunteers tell what message they think the advertiser is trying to send.

Caption Answer Each of the four key elements enhances the overall theme of the ad.

@ **Online Action!** For instructions, ideas, and answer guide, go to the Teacher Center at marketingessentials.glencoe.com.

Follow Up As students what the slogan at the bottom of the ad might suggest.

think of ways these concepts would apply to preparing television and radio commercials, as well as online advertising.

Headline

The **headline** is the phrase or sentence that attracts the readers' attention to a particular product or service. Headlines must grab attention fast and hold it. They must convince the reader that it is in his or her best interest to read the ad. A headline should also lead readers into the ad's illustration and make them want to read the copy to learn more about the product's or service's benefits. Research shows that headlines that use words such as *you, your, how,* and *new* attract the most attention.

Writing Effective Headlines

Before writing a headline, a copywriter must know the needs of the target market. These needs might relate to price, delivery, performance, reliability, service, or quality. The headline must identify a benefit of the product or service, such as how it meets a consumer need. Effective headlines stress these benefits by making a promise, asking a question, posing a challenge, or using a testimonial.

Most headlines are brief. Research has shown people cannot process more than seven words at one time.

In a recent study, creative directors from major advertising agencies analyzed award-winning print ads to determine what their headlines had in common. They discovered that 32 percent of the headlines used familiar sayings with a twist. For example, "When it rains, it pours" (Morton Salt) or "I think, therefore IBM" (International Business Machines). About 23 percent of the headlines made use of opposites such as "up/down" and "lie/truth." For example, "Does she, or doesn't she?" (Clairol hair coloring) or "Hand-built by robots" (Fiat Strada).

Copy

The **copy** is the selling message of a written advertisement. It details how the product or service meets the customer needs identified in the headline. As with headlines, copy

should be developed only after the market is thoroughly researched. It should be based on the business objectives for the advertising campaign. For example, is your advertising designed to introduce a new product, build an image, attract new customers, answer inquiries, or generate sales to existing customers?

marketingessentials.glencoe.com

Chapter 20 - Print Advertisements 425

Enrichment

EFFECTIVE PAST HEADLINES

Challenge students to research the topic of effective ad headlines as a class. Have them interview older family members or acquaintances, asking them to recall memorable ad headlines or slogans from their youth. Suggest that the students group the responses according to the age of the respondents and compare the groups. Have them look for products and services and headline styles that characterize each generation or time period.

Concept Development

COPY AND ILLUSTRATION

After the students have read the information about copy and illustration in the text, call on volunteers to identify characteristics of effective copy and illustration in print advertisements. Keep track of their responses in list form on the chalkboard. Refer students back to the ads reprinted in the chapter, or to other ads you have displayed, and have the students describe how the characteristics they have listed are reflected in the ads. Ask students to pay special attention to how the headlines, copy, and illustrations work together in especially effective ads.

A MATTER OF ETHICS   Do You Want My Opinion?

Discussion Lead a discussion about who owns the media, pointing out that a few large organizations dominate. Ask students to tell why it might be difficult for a broad spectrum of ideas to be heard when the key media outlets are controlled by a few entities.

THINKING ETHICALLY   Answer: Those who feel that cross-media ownership is ethical might point out that the issue is not who owns the TV station or the newspaper, but whether they use their ownership position for the public good. Others will point out that if all important media outlets are owned by the same person or company, there will be less competition, and therefore less incentive to provide quality programming or content.

@ Online Action!   For instructions, ideas, and answer guide, go to the Teacher Center at
marketingessentials.glencoe.com

Extended Activity

Media News Comparison
Ask students to choose a recent news story and compare the coverage on TV and in the newspaper. Ask students to provide examples of the different viewpoints, as well as different tone and delivery.

Individualized Practice

COPYWRITING

L1 Have students rewrite the following sentences in the active voice:

1. SensorExcel™, the next revolution in shaving closeness, is brought to you by Gillette.

2. One Hundred Twenty images from Corel Professional Photos are profiled in *The World's Best Digital Photographs* (coffee-table book and companion CD-ROM).

3. A 3800 V6 engine, air conditioning, and many other luxury amenities are included as standard features of the Buick LeSabre.

L2 Ask students to combine the sentences to create one sentence that is written in the active voice:

Group 1:

1. The finest selection of quality internationally sourced leather sofas and sectionals are now offered by Jennifer Leather.

2. Jennifer Leather also offers internationally sourced loveseats, chairs, and ottomans.

Group 2:

1. Esquire is an extensive collection of handsome timepieces.

2. These timepieces have quality features and details.

3. The features and details of Esquire timepieces are rarely found in watches so affordable.

L3 Have students collect and critique a variety of print ads discussing the use of active and passive voices in a one-page analysis or a 10-minute oral presentation.

• **MOTIVATING a CUSTOMER** Every headline should have a single focus or main idea. Headlines should motivate the reader to try a product or service.

What is the main idea of this ad?

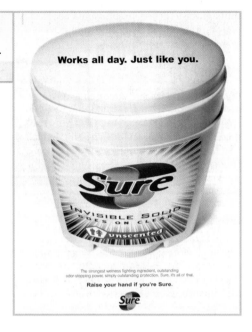

Here are some tips to create compelling, effective copy:

1. Your copy should be viewed as a conversation and written in a very personal, friendly manner.

2. Good copy, like a good headline, is simple and direct. Copy can vary from a few words to several paragraphs. Copy does not need to be extensive to get a message across. Copy can be viewed as an educational tool, a testimonial to the benefits of using the product, or a description of how an institution can help you.

3. Copy should appeal to the senses. Through the words, the customer should be able to see, hear, touch, taste, or even smell a product. This can be done through using descriptive adjectives and action words.

4. Your copy should tell the who, what, when, where, why, and how of your product. Remember that facts about your product are more powerful than claims.

Use case histories, statistics, performance figures, dates, and quotes from experts whenever possible.

5. Add desire and urgency to the copy. Use key words such as *new, improved, introducing, save,* and *easy* to establish immediate contact with the reader. They arouse interest, encourage awareness, and create desire and urgency.

6. Advertising copy should provide a personal call to action now or in the near future. It should always be in the second person and in the active rather than the passive voice. Including a phrase to encourage acting immediately, such as *last chance, limited supply, ends in two weeks,* or *special bonus offer,* helps create a sense of urgency and need for action.

Other techniques for keeping your copy personal include using contractions and short sentences. For example, "we are" would be written as "we're" and "you are" would be changed to "you're." Write in short sentences and avoid

426 UNIT 6 - PROMOTION

| AD GUIDE | MOTIVATING a CUSTOMER |

Discussion Lead students in a discussion of whether this ad is effective. Ask: what elements make it work or make it fail? Ask students to brainstorm other possible slogans for this ad.

Caption Answer The main idea is that the product is hardworking and lasts a long time.

Follow Up Ask students to list what they learn about the product from this ad.

the use of commas. Too many commas and long sentences will distract the reader.

Illustration

The **illustration** is the photograph, drawing, or other graphic elements used in an advertisement. Its primary functions are to attract and hold attention and to encourage action. It should also integrate the headline and copy. The illustration, together with the headline, should motivate the prospect to read at least the first sentence of the copy.

The illustration and graphic elements should transmit a message that would be hard to communicate with words alone. For example, illustrations can show the product, how the product works, and safety features. Illustrations should also project the desired image or benefit—for example, convenience, entertainment, leisure, or status.

Photographs should be used in advertisements when a sense of reality is necessary. Drawings are often used to show a part of a product that the reader would not normally see. Cut-away drawings and illustrations of constructed or manufactured products and equipment can help show important features not visible in a photograph. They can also help the reader understand how a product works.

Sources for Illustrations

Businesses often use clip art in their print advertisements. **Clip art** takes the form of images, stock drawings, and photographs. Suppliers, manufacturers, or trade associations often provide clip art for print advertisements. Clip art can also be found in published books, on CD-ROMs, and on the Web. Because clip art is ready for reproduction and printing, it is inexpensive, quick, and easy to use. When

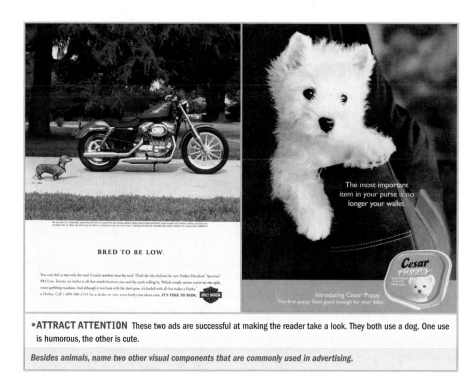

BRED TO BE LOW.

The most important item in your purse is no longer your wallet.

Cesar PUPPY

Introducing Cesar® Puppy. The first puppy food good enough for your baby.

• **ATTRACT ATTENTION** These two ads are successful at making the reader take a look. They both use a dog. One use is humorous, the other is cute.

Besides animals, name two other visual components that are commonly used in advertising.

ASSESS

Review Guide

CONCEPTS
Ask students to recall the parts of an effective print advertisement and the characteristics of each.

KEY TERMS
Have students review key terms, their spellings, and definitions in small groups.

ONLINE SELF-ASSESSMENT
Have students go to **marketingessentials.glencoe.com** for the Section 20.1 practice test.

Individualized Review

L1 Assign and review Chapter 20 activities in the Student Activity Workbook.

L2 Assign and review Chapter 20 activities in the Marketing Math Workbook.

L3 Assign and review Chapter 20 activities in the *BusinessWeek* Reader and Case Studies.

Marketing Practice

Have students choose an ad from a local or national magazine or newspaper and write a paragraph or two telling one reason why they think it is effective and one thing that might be done differently to make it more effective. Ask volunteers to present their ideas to the class.

AD GUIDE   ATTRACT ATTENTION

Discussion Lead students in a discussion of what is similar and different about these two ads. Ask students if they think the ads are targeted to a particular demographic, and if so, to describe it.

Caption Answer Answers may include certain colors, font styles, the inclusion of slogans, the use of children, or the use of cartoons.

Follow Up Ask students: What techniques or technology can buinesses use to track the effectiveness of print advertisements?

CLOSE

Ask students to recall and provide answers to the following questions.

- **What are the four essential elements of an effective print advertisement?**
  headline, illustration or photograph, copy, and signature. A slogan is sometimes a part of the signature.

- **What are some characteristics of an effective headline?**
  It is brief, grabs and holds the reader's attention, contains the words *you, your, how,* and *new,* appeals to an immediate need, identifies a benefit of the product or service, evokes emotion, uses a familiar saying with a twist, and makes use of opposites.

Online Activity

Fan Sites and Ad Dollars

These days, many personal or fan sites are funded through online sponsorship or ad placement. Ask students to explain why a business might advertise on a site that is not a commercial site.

---

stock artwork is not sufficient, professionals may be hired to photograph or illustrate situations or products.

Signature

The **signature**, or logotype (logo), is the distinctive identification symbol for a business. A well-designed signature gets instant recognition for a business. No advertisement is complete without it.

In national ads, the signature is the name of the firm. It may also include the corporate symbol and slogan. The signature in local advertisements usually includes the business's name, address, telephone number, business hours, or slogan. Many advertisers also include their Web site address in the signature.

Slogan

A **slogan** is a catchy phrase or words that identify a product or company. Each of these advertising slogans had the power to attract attention and arouse interest for the company or its product. To support a firm's signature, many businesses create and use slogans that help customers identify the firm and its image.

Here are techniques copywriters use when developing slogans for advertising campaigns:

- **Alliteration** uses repeating initial consonant sounds—"Welcome to the World Wide Wow" (AOL).
- **A paradox** is a seeming contradiction that could be true—"The taste you love to hate" (Listerine mouthwash).
- **Rhyme** uses rhyming words or phrases— "Give a hoot, don't pollute" (United States Forest Service).
- **A pun** is a humorous use of a word that suggests two or more of its meanings or the meaning of another word similar in sound—"Time to Re-Tire" (Fisk Tires).
- **A play on words** cleverly uses words to mean something else—"Let your fingers do the walking" (Yellow Pages).

 20.1 AFTER YOU READ

Reviewing Key Terms and Concepts

1. What steps should be followed when developing an advertising campaign?

2. Why are headlines so important in print advertisements?

3. What is the main purpose of advertising copy?

Integrating Academic Skills

Math

4. What is the cost per thousand (CPM) of a one-half-page display ad that costs $75 in a newspaper with a community circulation of 8,000?

Reading or Language Arts

5. Make up slogans for five products. Each slogan should use a different copywriting technique (alliteration, paradox, rhyme, pun, or play on words).

 Online Action! Check your answers at *marketingessentials.glencoe.com/20/read*

 AFTER YOU READ

Reviewing Key Terms and Concepts

1. Steps include: identify the target audience, determine objectives, develop the message, select the medium, and determine the results.

2. Headlines are so important in print advertisements because it is believed that 80 percent of the people who look at a print advertisement just read the headlines.

3. The advertising copy presents the selling message and stresses product features.

Integrating Academic Skills

4. $9.38; ($75 × 1,000) ÷ 8,000 = $9.38

5. Answers will vary. Responses should demonstrate an understanding of copywriting techniques.

Online Action! Answers at **marketingessentials.glencoe.com/20/read**

Advertising Layout

OBJECTIVES

- Explain the principles of preparing an ad layout
- List advantages and disadvantages of using color in advertising
- Describe how typefaces and sizes add variety and emphasis to print advertisements

KEY TERMS

- ad layout
- advertising proof

READ and STUDY

BEFORE YOU READ
Predict How do you think color affects the viewer's reaction to an ad?

MAIN IDEA
Advertisements have only a few seconds to attract a targeted audience. Advertisers need to understand effective design principles when developing ad layouts to attract the attention of the desired audience quickly.

STUDY ORGANIZER
Use a chart like the one below to take notes on the principles of ad design.

Tips for Developing Effective Ad Layouts

1. Leave white (unused) space. _____
2. _____
3. _____
4. _____

Developing Print Advertising Layouts

An **ad layout** is a sketch that shows the general arrangement and appearance of a finished ad. It clearly indicates the position of the headline, illustration, copy, and signature.

Components of Effective Ad Layouts

Ad layouts should be prepared in exactly the same size as the final advertisement. The illustrations should be large

WHILE YOU READ

Evaluation Think of a product you are interested in. How would you design an ad for it?

Chapter 20 - Print Advertisements **429**

FOCUS

Introducing the Section

COLLABORATIVE ACTIVITY
Organize students into small groups and challenge each to choose one of the following products and create a color palette for an ad for that product. The color palette should include two or three colors that work together to communicate a feeling or tone. Have them decide if they want the ad to be exciting, aggressive, and arresting, or if they think a soothing, softer approach would work better. Provide each group with old magazines and have them cut swatches from the printed pages that show the colors they have chosen. Have each group elect a spokesperson to explain to the class the product and the rationale for the colors they have chosen.

- sports car that goes from 0 mph to 60 mph in seconds
- boxed chocolate candy advertised as "fit for royalty"
- vacation resort located in the Caribbean
- new type of MP3 player

Preteaching Key Terms

Have students skim the chapter to find the key terms in context and read a few sentences around the term. Ask volunteers to suggest definitions for the terms based on the context in which they are used.

- ad layout
- advertising proof

READ and STUDY

BEFORE YOU READ
Point out that warm colors such as red, orange, and yellow make things appear to advance and cool colors such as blues and greens make things appear to recede.

THE MAIN IDEA
Ask volunteers to suggest principles of effective design.

STUDY ORGANIZER
Make your own study organizer, or download the one at marketingessentials.glencoe.com. As study continues, you and the class should work together to complete the organizer.

WHILE YOU READ Model for students how they can create a thumbnail sketch in pencil to indicate aspects of ad design, such as placement of the headline.

TEACH

Discussion Starter

USING COLOR IN PRINT ADVERTISEMENTS

Point out to students that color is not always required for an ad to be effective. Ask them to look in newspapers and magazines and find ads they think work effectively in black and white and share them in class; encourage students to support their opinions with specific examples. Suggest to students that they look for ads that have a strong call to action—ones that announce sales or provide a coupon for a substantial savings on a product with which most people are familiar.

Concept Development

SELECTING TYPEFACES AND TYPE SIZES FOR PRINT ADVERTISEMENTS

Ask students to look through textbooks or library books that are readily available and notice the characteristics of the typefaces used. Have them identify places in which serif faces are used most often and situations in which sans serif faces predominate.

TEACHING POINTS

Explain Point out that serif faces were invented to aid the reader. The serifs added to the letters are designed to help the word hold together so that it appears as a unit; this makes it easier for the brain to recognize and read. Tell students that serif faces are often used with running text such as the paragraphs in this textbook. Sans serif faces are often used in picture captions, callouts, and headlines.

MARKET TECH

In-Store Advertising Increases

In-store television advertising is gaining in popularity. Since more people are watching cable and satellite television channels, it has become difficult for national advertisers to reach a mass audience via regular network television. But a large and diverse number of people still shop on a regular basis at supermarket and discount chains. Tesco PLC, Britain's largest supermarket chain, is installing television sets in 300 of its stores. In between news clips, recipe tips, and beauty advice, the screens will show ads for products in the aisles. In the United States, Wal-Mart stores also have television sets that carry advertising messages.

How to Get Shoppers' Attention

To be effective, in-store ads must be very attention-getting, since customers are at the store to shop and not to watch television. In-store ads can be very creative and often use the actual store as a setting for the ad. For example, Unilever created an ad for its Axe deodorant that featured an attractive male using the product. The ad showed women in the store running after him because they were attracted to the scent.

THINK LIKE A MARKETER

What are some reasons why in-store TV advertising is becoming more popular with mass-market retailers?

@ Online Action!

Go to *marketingessentials.glencoe.com/20/tech* to find an activity on technology and advertising.

---

enough to show the product in use and grab attention through size, humor, or dramatic content. Ads that feature large visuals (60 to 70 percent of the total ad) are the best attention-getters. The image projected in the layout should be appropriate for the target audience.

The best ads contain a focal point and lines of force that guide the reader to the copy through photographs and illustrations. One technique is to create a Z layout. Place the most dominant item (typically the headline or illustration) on the top of the Z. Since a reader's eye will normally follow the path of the Z, place copy on the line going down and your signature and "call to action" at the bottom of the Z.

Using Color in Print Advertisements

A color ad is usually more realistic and visually appealing and commands the reader's attention more than a black-and-white advertisement does. In fact, research proves that color newspaper ads can increase the readership of ad copy by as much as 80 percent over black-and-white ads. Studies have also shown that full-color ads are usually more cost effective than two-color ads (usually black and another color) because of their increased response rates.

Adding another color can increase costs by as much as 35 percent. Therefore, when businesses use color in advertisements, the added cost must be continually measured against the desired results.

Select the appropriate colors for your product and target market. For example, red is used for passion, excitement, and power. It is often used in automobile and food advertising. Also, when developing ads for global markets or ethnic groups within the United States, an advertiser must be sensitive to the different meanings that color conveys to people of other cultures and countries.

 marketingessentials.glencoe.com

MARKET TECH

In-Store Advertising Increases

Discussion After students have read Market Tech, ask them to identify stores in the local area that might effectively use in-store advertising and suggest the types of products or services that might be advertised. Point out that this would be an appropriate way to advertise specials on merchandise that is not selling well, or, in grocery stores, perishable goods.

THINK LIKE A MARKETER Answer: Students might suggest that mass-market retailers have the most to gain from in-store advertising because shoppers usually spend more time in the stores, and the list of products that can be advertised is lengthy.

@ Online Action! For instructions, ideas, and answer guide, go to the Teacher Center at **marketingessentials.glencoe.com**

•**LETTERING** This ad is a good example of the use of fonts and type sizes to attract attention and impart information.

What is your reaction to the size of the words Break Out?

BREAK OUT

Go beyond black and white. Get stunning color that's surprisingly affordable with the Xerox Phaser 8200 printer. There's a new way to look at it.

XEROX.

Individualized Practice

EFFECTIVE AD LAYOUTS

L1 Ask students to list the components of an effective ad layout. Their lists should include attention-getting visuals that match the target audience, a focal point, type and type placement that aid the reader, and appropriate use of color.

L2 Ask students to list the components of an effective ad layout and show examples of each in actual ads they find in newspapers and magazines.

L3 Ask students to list the components of an effective ad layout and then critique several ads using the list as the criteria for effectiveness.

Online Activity

Web Fonts
Suggest to students that they research the number of fonts that are available on the Internet and have them bring in an example of a font they like to the class. Have them create the alphabet in that font and post the different fonts around the classroom.

Selecting Typefaces and Type Sizes for Print Advertisements

Many typefaces and type sizes are effective for use in print ads. Advertisers make sure to select styles and type sizes that are distinctive, yet appropriate for the business and target audience.

The look and appearance (design) of the type is called the typeface. A complete set of letters in a specific size and typeface is called a font. The appearance of the typeface affects the entire character of an advertisement.

Type size is measured in points. There are 12 points to one pica, and 6 picas to 1 inch. So a point is about $1/72$ of an inch. Your word processing program allows you to choose the size of type you want, usually within a range of 8 to 72 points.

One way to classify typefaces is to consider whether they are serif or sans serif. A serif typeface has short crosslines at the upper and lower ends of the letters. Times Roman and Palatino are two commonly used serif fonts. Here are examples of these fonts in 10-point and 24-point type. Can you see the crosslines at the top and bottom of the letters T and P?

Times Roman, 10-point
Times Roman, 24-point

Palatino, 10-point
Palatino, 24-point

A sans serif font is one that is *sans* (French for "without") any crosslines. These fonts are popular because their simple design makes them very easy to read. Some common sans serif fonts are Arial, Helvetica, and Futura. Here are some examples:

Chapter 20 - Print Advertisements 431

ASSESS

Review Guide

CONCEPTS

Ask students to recall the essential elements of an effective ad layout, including attention-getting visuals that match the target audience, a focal point, type and type placement that aid the reader, and appropriate use of color.

KEY TERMS

Have students review key terms, their spellings, and definitions in small groups

ONLINE SELF-ASSESSMENT

Have students go to marketingessentials.glencoe.com for the Section 20.2 practice test.

Individualized Review

L1 Assign and review Chapter 20 activities in the Student Activity Workbook.

L2 Assign and review Chapter 20 activities in the Marketing Math Workbook.

L3 Assign and review Chapter 20 activities in the *BusinessWeek* Reader and Case Studies.

Marketing Practice

For homework or as an in-class activity, give each student a copy from a print ad containing text that you have rewritten to include several errors. Give students 20 minutes to proofread the ad and create a sketch showing how they might produce a layout to show their client. Have them suggest the content and colors for an appropriate visual to be used within the ad.

Case Study

Advertising to Reach Young Males

Video games reach 18- to 34-year old males more effectively than perhaps any other medium. A recent Nielsen Media Research study found that young men were watching seven percent less prime-time television than a year earlier.

Activision, a Santa Monica, California, video game publisher, and Nielsen Entertainment are planning to help advertisers evaluate the effectiveness of video game ads. They are proposing an evaluation method that is similar to Nielsen Media Research's famous method of rating television shows.

Watching Gamers

The new system will track how many gamers see the ads in video game content, how often they see them, and how well they recall them. This system works with console-based games, by far the industry's largest sector, with real-time measurement data relayed through an Internet connection. It is estimated that video game product placement costs between $20,000 and $100,000, a fraction of the cost of a network TV ad. The new service, which is still in development, is likely to employ a small gadget to measure game-playing behavior, much as Nielsen's TV-rating service uses set-top devices to monitor TV-viewing habits. Gamers' ability to recall ads is likely to be measured using telephone surveys and other follow-up methods.

THINK STRATEGICALLY

What products would you advertise in video games?

@ Online Action! Go to *marketingessentials.glencoe.com/20/case* to find an activity on targeted advertising.

Arial, 10-point

Helvetica, 16-point

Futura, 24-point

The preferences and characteristics of the target market will dictate the choice of typeface. A study done by the Newspaper Advertising Bureau found that nearly one-third of readers over 65 were not reading ads because the type was too small. This means that a 14-point font would be a better choice than 10-point for ads designed to reach readers over 65. Type that is too small or difficult to read will lower the readership of an ad. Many companies use serif typefaces and 12-point font sizes in most ad copy.

 marketingessentials.glencoe.com

Case Study   Advertising to Reach Young Males

Discussion Have students read the Case Study and discuss the idea of including advertisements in video games. Have students who play video games describe how these ads differ from ads they see on television.

THINK STRATEGICALLY   **Answer:** Answers will vary; products might include global brands such as Nike and Pepsi, or products that align to particular game themes.

@ Online Action! For instructions, ideas, and answer guide, go to the Teacher Center at marketingessentials.glencoe.com

Large, bold type is usually chosen when the words contained in a headline are to be shouted. Smaller, lighter type is usually chosen when the words in a headline are to be whispered. In general, print advertisers should use one typeface for headlines and prices and another typeface for copy. You can add variety and emphasis by using different sizes of typefaces, italics, boldface, and combinations of capital and lowercase letters. The message may remain the same, however, capitalizing different words may change the effect.

Checking Advertising Proofs

When advertisements are first created, an **advertising proof** is developed. The advertising proof shows exactly how an ad will appear in print. Many proofs are now delivered in a digital format. This practice helps to cut production costs and speed up production.

The advertising proof is sent to the advertiser for review and approval. Before giving final approval of a written advertisement, the advertiser makes an evaluation based on the following criteria:

- The ad should be bold enough to stand out on a page, even if it is placed next to other ads.
- The overall layout should look clean and uncluttered and should guide the reader through the copy.
- The typefaces and type sizes should be easy to read and help to emphasize the message.
- The signature should be apparent and distinctive.
- The intended message and image projected must be appropriate for the target audience.

In addition, it is important to make sure that all prices are accurate and all brand names and company names are correctly spelled. Any errors found in the proof must be marked and returned for correction before the ad is published.

20.2 AFTER YOU READ

Reviewing Key Terms and Concepts
1. How can you create a focal point and eye movement in a print ad?
2. What size typeface would you use to attract attention in an ad? Why?
3. What is shown on an advertising proof?

Integrating Academic Skills
Math
4. If a Web banner ad has a click-through rate of one percent and was sent to 15,000 people, how many people visited the banner Web site?

Reading/Language Arts
5. Investigate the Better Business Bureau's (BBB) Code of Advertising. Select one of the BBB's basic advertising principles (comparative prices, claims of free, cents-off sales, etc.) to research and develop a short oral report on the standards for the specific advertising practice.

 Online Action!   Check your answers at *marketingessentials.glencoe.com/20/read*

marketingessentials.glencoe.com   **Chapter 20 - Print Advertisements 433**

Have students complete the following sentences:

- Graphic designers have several questions in mind when choosing an image for an ad, including _____ .
  Does it grab the viewer's attention; do the colors evoke appropriate feelings and emotions; is the image appropriate to the target audience; and is it the right size?

- Advertisers complete final evaluations of advertising proofs to ensure that _____ .
  The ad is bold enough to stand out on a page; the overall layout is clean and uncluttered and guides the reader through the copy; the typefaces and type sizes are easy to read and help to emphasize the company's message; the signature is apparent and distinctive; the intended message and image projected are appropriate for the target audience; and all information is accurate.

 Online Activity

Evocative Photos
Have students explore commercial and other photo sources online using a search engine to find images that could be used in certain ad situations to evoke emotions. Ask them to find images that could be used to convey comfort, and excitement.

AFTER YOU READ

Reviewing Key Terms and Concepts
1. Create a Z layout by placing the most dominant item (typically the headline or illustration) on the top of the Z. Then place copy on the line going down the Z and your signature and call to action at the bottom of the Z.

2. Answers will vary but should reflect a typeface that is distinctive, yet appropriate for the business and target audience.

3. The proof shows exactly how the ad will appear in print.

Integrating Academic Skills
4. 150 people (.01 click-through rate) $\times$ 15,000 people = 150

5. Answers will vary but should demonstrate research on advertising standards.

 Online Action!   Answers at **marketingessentials.glencoe.com/20/read**

BUILD SKILLS

18. Workplace Skills

The student should act professionally and try to meet the customer's needs in a non-confrontational manner, telling the customer that he or she will find the manager to help rectify the problem.

19. Technology Applications

Answers will vary, but each student should provide a rationale for why their ad layout addresses convenience, vanity, or health appeals.

20. Math Practice

$1,470; $42,000 × 3.5% = $1,470 advertising credit

DEVELOP CRITICAL THINKING

21. Investigating Advertising Agencies

Answers will vary; student summaries should include reasons for their decision.

22. Circulation and Ads

Space in newspapers and magazines for print ads are sold on the basis of how many impressions they can make—in other words, how many people will see them. Circulation figures for a publication are a way of gauging the number of people who will have an opportunity to view an ad. Publications that have a high circulation can charge more for ad space. The same concept works for other types of media as well.

BUILD SKILLS

18. Workplace Skills

Human Relations A customer wishes to purchase an item that was advertised improperly in a print advertisement. The item actually costs more than the advertised price. When told about the higher price, the customer is upset and angry, but she still wants the product. What procedures would you use to calm the customer and still complete the sale?

19. Technology Applications

Design an Ad Layout Using a desktop publishing program, select a product that you would advertise for a target audience of your choice. Develop an advertising proof and then write a paragraph describing why your layout would attract and appeal to your target audience.

20. Math Practice

Figure Out Advertising Credit Your hardware store has a cooperative arrangement with a manufacturer of garden tools. The store receives a 3.5 percent advertising credit on total yearly sales. What is your advertising credit on sales totaling $42,000?

DEVELOP CRITICAL THINKING

21. Investigating Advertising Agencies

Perform an Internet search for Advertiser and Agency Red Books. Select one of the top 25 advertising agencies by billings. Summarize the types of services it provides to clients. Would you select this company for your ad campaign? Why or why not?

22. Circulation and Ads

Why are media circulation numbers key to the business of print ads? What do they determine? To give examples that illustrate your answer, you should research advertising rates for one or two publications of your choice. As you work to find out this information, also note whether the publication you have selected is distributed nationwide or regionally. How does this type of information influence promotion decisions?

Formative Assessment

Formative assessment is an essential component of classroom work. This type of assessment provides information that is then used as feedback to modify teaching and meet student needs.

L1 Review key terms for this chapter. Ask students to write one sentence for each key term.

L2 Provide various examples of print advertisements. Have the students identify the essential elements of each and analyze the layout and design of the ads.

L3 Ask students to create a print ad for a product of their choice.

 Reteach **If results of this formative assessment seem low, consider the following activity:**

Have students work in pairs to analyze and explain the elements and layout principles used in one of the advertisements shown in the book.

APPLY CONCEPTS

23. Creating an Advertising Campaign

Design an advertising campaign of any length for a service, product, or company of your choice. Imagine that you will present the campaign to a prospective client. Research the appropriate budget and media.

Activity Prepare a summary of your campaign to present in class. Explain and justify your choices. Bring visuals such as a poster-sized sketch of your main ad or a graphic representation of all the campaign components and how they work together.

24. Creating an Advertising Layout

Select a product that interests you and develop an ad layout, including a sketch of the design, a headline, copy, illustration, and signature.

Activity Create an 8$^1/_2$" by 11" print advertising layout sketch. Prepare a summary explaining the parts of the ad and why you think they are effective.

NET SAVVY

25. Ad Research

Select a product or service that interests you and conduct an Internet search to find an ad for it. You might select either an ad, a banner, or a button. Analyze how this ad works and list three reasons you think it is effective.

CONNECTION

Role Play:
Ad Designer

Situation You are to assume the role of part-time employee of a locally owned jewelry store located in a small town. You are a high school student and a member of the school's field hockey team that has just won the state championship. The store's owner (judge) is thrilled and has decided to run an ad in the local newspaper to congratulate the team.

Activity The jewelry store owner (judge) has asked you to create a draft outline of the ad. The ad should contain the name of the store, the high school team name, and mention you as an employee. You are to present your draft of the ad to the jewelry store owner (judge).

Evaluation You will be evaluated on how well you meet the following performance indicators:

- Explain components of advertisements
- Analyze costs/benefits of company participation in community activities
- Explain the nature of positive customer/client relations
- Demonstrate appropriate creativity
- Prepare simple written reports

 Online Action!

For more information and DECA Prep practice, go to *marketingessentials.glencoe.com/20/*

CHAPTER 20 REVIEW

APPLY CONCEPTS

23. Creating an Advertising Campaign

Answer will vary; all the elements of an effective advertising campaign must be present.

24. Creating an Advertising Layout

Sketches will vary; student summaries should include an explanation of the parts of the ad and the reasons behind their effectiveness.

NET SAVVY

25. Ad Research

Answers will vary. Encourage students to research ads for several different products including appliances, clothing, business supplies, raw materials, commodities, etc. Similarly, encourage them to look for a variety of services individuals or businesses might seek, including repair and maintenance, legal, and risk management.

THE DECA CONNECTION

Students should be evaluated according to the performance standards noted in the role play. For another DECA role play, go to the Competitive Events Workbook or the Student Activity Workbook, or go to **marketingessentials.glencoe.com/20/DECA**

 Online Action! For instructions, ideas, and answer guide, go to the Teacher Center at **marketingessentials.glencoe.com**

DECA Advisors Corner

Reinforce student computer and advertising skills by getting involved in DECA's online advertising competitions. These competitions encourage DECA members to seek knowledge beyond traditional advertising media, and to develop a working appreciation of online advertising.

MINI-QUIZ

Read these sentences aloud to the students and have them supply the missing word or phrase.

1. The creation and coordination of a series of both broadcast and print advertisements around a theme is called _____ . (an advertising campaign)

2. The lettering, slogan, or saying that gets the reader's attention is called _____ . (a headline)

3. A rough draft that shows the general arrangement and appearance of a finished ad is called the _____ . (ad layout)

For an expanded chapter quiz, go to Chapter 20 in the TeacherWorks CD-ROM and to Chapter 20 in the **Exam View®** Pro Test Generator CD-ROM.

MARKETING INTERNSHIP

A SIMULATED **DECA** PRODUCT AND SERVICE MANAGEMENT EVENT

Pitch a New Client

 BASIC BACKGROUND

POGO is trying to get off the ground. The start-up air taxi service is looking for investors to put its business plan into action. It intends to offer short flights on six-seat mini-jets to and from small airports of the customer's choosing and on the customer's own schedule. Its plan calls for each of its mini-jets to fly 1,500 hours a year, or about 750 two-hour trips.

Expensive . . . and Economical Like a taxicab, the cost per mile is set, regardless of the number of passengers. It's pricey for someone flying alone, but if a company has four executives going to the same destination, POGO's price is pretty close to the cost of four first-class seats on a regular airline. The main selling point is convenience: There are no long waits at the airport and no fear of losing one's luggage. The target market is a mid-level executive who earns at least $150,000 a year and flies once every five or six weeks.

 YOUR OBJECTIVE

Your firm would like to sign POGO as a client. The plan is to sell the company on your firm's ability to promote the business to its target market. Your objective is to prepare an effective marketing proposal to present to POGO.

ASSIGNMENT AND STRATEGY

• **Get the background** To get started you will need to conduct the opportunities and threats portion of a SWOT analysis for POGO, and a competitive assessment. For example, look at the cost of first-class tickets on commercial airlines, as well as the cost to charter a small jet for routes that POGO might want to fly.

Research attitudes about air travel. Learn what annoys most airline travelers, especially business travelers, and how POGO's service could remove or reduce those annoyances.

Decide which media are best suited to reach POGO's target market.

• **Write the proposal** Begin your proposal by identifying POGO's main problem in one sentence. Then write a statement of purpose—what your firm intends to do to help POGO achieve its goals. Tell what you did to prepare for this

READ to WRITE

Race to the Stars

Have students research the race to launch a private spacecraft. Ask: What businesses are involved and what types of individuals are most likely to be the first customers? For example, in the summer of 2004, the first privately built craft flew into space. Ask students to research and discuss the interest in civilian spacecraft. Have them use the information they find to make a two-page brochure advertising the project to potential customers. Remind students to apply the concepts and guidelines for effective promotions provided in this unit. They should also keep their target market in mind when formulating their brochures.

presentation. Include a time line or work plan that outlines how to proceed.

Consider all the elements of a promotional mix: selling, advertising, sales promotion, and public relations. Provide rationale for your recommendations.

- **What your project should include** Be sure to tell how POGO will differentiate itself from its competitors. To make your project complete, create a sample of one or more of your promotional ideas.

 YOUR REPORT

Use a word processing program and presentation software to prepare a double-spaced report and an oral presentation for POGO. See a suggested outline and key evaluation points at *marketingessentials.glencoe .com/internship*

marketingessentials.glencoe.com

BUILD YOUR PORTFOLIO

Option 1 Internship Report
Once you have completed your Marketing Internship project and presentation, include your written report and a few printouts of key slides from your oral presentation in your Marketing Portfolio.

Option 2 Creating a Promotional Plan
A client (choose an existing company) wants a new, trendy promotional plan. Start with a SWOT analysis, a competitive assessment, and identify a target market. Then design a cutting-edge proposal that addresses your client's needs. Provide sample promotional materials. Prepare your written proposal using a word processing program and use presentation software for your oral presentation. See a suggested outline and key evaluation points at *marketingessentials.glencoe .com/portfolio*

@ Online Action!
Go to *marketingessentials.glencoe .com/Unit/6/DECA* to review promotion concepts that relate to DECA events.

UNIT 6

Unit Review

Now that students have completed the chapters in Unit 6, ask them to review their answers to the Analyze the Ad questions on page 359. Would they answer them differently? Why or why not?

Have students choose a job in the field of promotion that interests them and then research it online. If possible, have them job shadow a professional for part of the person's workday.

Ask students to write a two- to three-paragraph summary of their findings and discuss it with the class.

STEP AHEAD
Discuss with students the link between promotion and distribution. Effective promotion of a product or service should lead potential customers to the appropriate distribution channels. Have them think of examples of how one leads to the other.

Internship Wrap-Up

As a class, come up with ways to gain media coverage to promote POGO. Consider television, newspapers, magazines, and Web sites.

Options may include having journalists taking trips on the mini-jets or having celebrities endorsing POGO.

Then, have the class work in groups of four to five to outline one promotion strategy and present it to the class in a five-minute oral presentation.

BUILD YOUR PORTFOLIO

Explain to students that portfolios provide evidence of their knowledge and skills in working with data, people, and concepts. Developing a portfolio is a valuable career tool. Point out to students that they should tailor their portfolio to meet the needs and interests of certain employers. Encourage students to check the portfolio information available at **marketingessentials.glencoe.com/u6/internship.**

Peer Review
Fellow students who share common interests can serve as reviewers of the final portfolios. This review can be completed through the use of a checklist. Go to **marketingessentials.glencoe.com/u6/internship** to find a suggested checklist.

Unit Objectives

After completing this unit, students should be able to:

- Select the appropriate channels of distribution to effectively sell consumer and industrial products
- Explain the nature and scope of transportation systems and services
- Distinguish between purchasing agents and buyers
- Describe the buying process and the effect the Internet has had on the purchasing function
- Calculate the major entries in a merchandise plan
- Explain the stock-handling process
- Figure stock turnover rates
- Discuss the nature and the impact of technology on inventory management and inventory systems

Key to
Individualized
Activities

L1 Level 1 activities are basic activities and should fall within the range of all students.

L2 Level 2 activities are average activities and should be within the range of average and above average students.

L3 Level 3 activities are challenging activities designed for the ability range of above average students.

Enrichment Resources

PROFESSIONAL ORGANIZATIONS

Air Transport Association airlines.org

Council of Supply Chain Management Professionals csmp.org

MEDIA RESOURCES

Print or online editions of

American Shipper americanshipper.com

Industrial Distribution manufacturing.net/ind/

WRITING SUPPORT

Ask students to choose an item that can be found at a local retail store. Have them write a report that details the physical steps it might have taken from the manufacturer to the shelves, including transportation and warehouses. Ask them to keep and review this document as they study Unit 7.

UNIT 7 PLANNING GUIDE AND RESOURCES

CHAPTER	PRINT MATERIALS	TECHNOLOGY RESOURCES
Chapter 21 Section 21.1 Section 21.2	**From Unit 7 Fast File Booklet** Lesson Plans; Chapter Summaries; Reproducible Masters; Reproducible Tests **Print Ancillaries** Student Activity Workbook Marketing Math Workbook *BusinessWeek* Reader and Case Studies, Chapter 21 Competitive Events Workbook, Unit 7 Marketing Research Project Workbook School-to-Work Activity Workbook	Interactive Chalkboard classroom presentations marketingessentials.glencoe.com Online Student Edition, Chapter 21 TeacherWorks Exam*View*® Pro Test Generator, Chapter 21 Virtual Business
Chapter 22 Section 22.1 Section 22.2	**From Unit 7 Fast File Booklet** Lesson Plans; Chapter Summaries; Reproducible Masters; Reproducible Tests **Print Ancillaries** Student Activity Workbook Marketing Math Workbook *BusinessWeek* Reader and Case Studies, Chapter 22 Competitive Events Workbook, Unit 7 Marketing Research Project Workbook School-to-Work Activity Workbook	Interactive Chalkboard classroom presentations marketingessentials.glencoe.com Online Student Edition, Chapter 22 TeacherWorks Exam*View*® Pro Test Generator, Chapter 22 Virtual Business
Chapter 23 Section 23.1 Section 23.2	**From Unit 7 Fast File Booklet** Lesson Plans; Chapter Summaries; Reproducible Masters; Reproducible Tests **Print Ancillaries** Student Activity Workbook Marketing Math Workbook *BusinessWeek* Reader and Case Studies, Chapter 23 Competitive Events Workbook, Unit 7 Marketing Research Project Workbook School-to-Work Activity Workbook	Interactive Chalkboard classroom presentations marketingessentials.glencoe.com Online Student Edition, Chapter 23 TeacherWorks Exam*View*® Pro Test Generator, Chapter 23 Virtual Business
Chapter 24 Section 24.1 Section 24.2	**From Unit 7 Fast File Booklet** Lesson Plans; Chapter Summaries; Reproducible Masters; Reproducible Tests **Print Ancillaries** Student Activity Workbook Marketing Math Workbook *BusinessWeek* Reader and Case Studies, Chapter 24 Competitive Events Workbook, Unit 7 Marketing Research Project Workbook School-to-Work Activity Workbook	Interactive Chalkboard classroom presentations marketingessentials.glencoe.com Online Student Edition, Chapter 24 TeacherWorks Exam*View*® Pro Test Generator, Chapter 24 Virtual Business

National Marketing Education

CHAPTER	SECTION	PERFORMANCE INDICATOR
Chapter 21 **Channels of Distribution**	21.1	Explain the nature of channels of distribution (DIS)
		Explain the nature of channel members' relationships (DIS)
	21.2	Explain the nature and scope of distribution (DIS)
		Explain the nature of channel strategies (DIS)
		Select channels of distribution (DIS)
Chapter 22 **Physical Distribution**	22.1	Explain the nature and scope of distribution (DIS)
		Explain the shipping process (DIS)
	22.2	Explain storing considerations (DIS)
		Explain the nature of warehousing (DIS)
		Explain marketing and its importance in a global economy (BME)
Chapter 23 **Purchasing**	23.1	Explain the nature and scope of purchasing (BME)
		Plan purchases (BME)
	23.2	Explain the nature of the buying process (BME)
		Conduct a vendor search (BME)
Chapter 24 **Stock Handling and Inventory Control**	24.1	Explain the receiving process (DIS)
		Explain stock handling techniques used in receiving deliveries (DIS)
	24.2	Explain the nature of inventory control systems (DIS)
		Explain the types of inventory control systems (DIS)

BME Business, Management, Entrepreneurship   **DIS** Distribution

Standards Assessment Correlation

SECTION ASSESSMENT		CHAPTER ASSESSMENT						UNIT LAB
Reviewing Key Terms and Concepts	Integrating Academic Skills	Review Facts and Ideas	Build Skills	Develop Critical Thinking	Apply Concepts	Workplace Skills	Net Savvy	Marketing Internship
1, 2, 3	✓	17, 20, 22, 25	28	30	32			✓
1, 2	✓							
1, 2, 3		21, 22, 24–26	28	30	32		✓	✓
2, 3	✓	22, 23	27	30	32, 33	✓		✓
2			27	31	32, 33	✓	✓	✓
1, 2	✓	15, 16, 17, 20	21, 22	25	26, 27	✓	✓	✓
2, 3	✓		22	25	26, 27		✓	
1, 3	✓	18, 19	21			✓		
2, 3	✓	18, 19	21			✓		
		20		24				
1, 2, 3		6, 7, 8, 9	13	16	19	✓	✓	
	✓	7	13, 14	17	18	✓		
1, 2, 3	✓	6, 7, 8, 9	13	16	18, 19	✓	✓	
				16, 17	19			✓
1, 2, 3		21		30	32, 33		✓	
1, 2, 3	✓	21, 22, 25	27	30	32–34	✓	✓	
1, 2, 3	✓	21, 23–25	27	30, 31	33, 34	✓	✓	
1, 2, 3		23, 24		31	33, 34		✓	

@ Online Action! Check the latest updates for national standards and for your state's standards at **marketingessentials.glencoe.com**

UNIT 7

Unit Overview

Unit 7 presents the basics of buying and distribution.

Chapter 21 explores the place decision of the marketing mix—how products will be distributed and sold in domestic and foreign markets. Chapter 22 concentrates on the nature and scope of physical distribution such as transportation, systems, and storage. Chapter 23 considers the purchasing function in depth. Chapter 24 looks at the critical importance of stock handling, inventory control, and stock management.

MAKING IT RELEVANT

Inform students that distribution is what allows a product to reach the end user. Without a solid distribution plan, a business cannot satisfy its customers.

Unit Launch Activity

Have students share their first impressions of the ad this page. Ask students how the company visually conveys its freshness. They may note that the product and packaging are similar to those of other orange juices, but the text and visuals in the ad convey the freshness.

OUT OF TIME?
If class time is too short to cover all the chapters in this unit, go to Unit 7 in your Fast File Teacher Resources booklet and find the Chapter Summaries for Chapters 21, 22, 23, and 24.

440

UNIT 7 — Distribution

In this unit you will find

- **Chapter 21** Channels of Distribution

- **Chapter 22** Physical Distribution

- **Chapter 23** Purchasing

- **Chapter 24** Stock Handling and Inventory Control

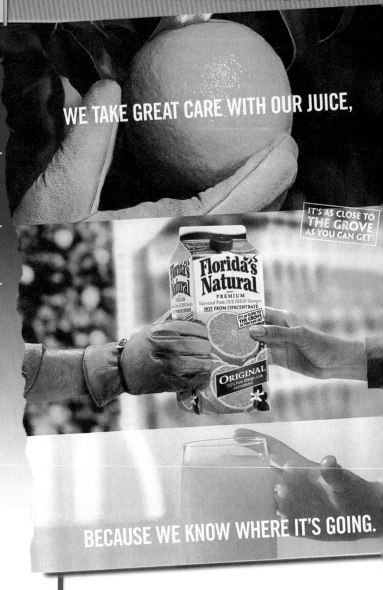

WE TAKE GREAT CARE WITH OUR JUICE,

IT'S AS CLOSE TO THE GROVE AS YOU CAN GET

Florida's Natural
PREMIUM
Squeezed From OUR FRESH Oranges
NOT FROM CONCENTRATE

ORIGINAL
100% Pure Orange Juice
PASTEURIZED

BECAUSE WE KNOW WHERE IT'S GOING.

440

 UNIT PROJECT

Researching Procedures for Routing Merchandise

Have chapter members investigate the policies, forms, and procedures used to receive, check, and route merchandise within a local business of their choice. Students should prepare a written report based on their research. They should evaluate the effectiveness of the policies, forms, and procedures used and then draw conclusions and make recommendations for improvement.

Assessment Guidelines Prepare a rubric for evaluation that includes number of topics, variety and coverage of topics, real-life examples, continuity, and quality of the written report. The presentation should cover the main points of the chapters in this unit.

Enrichment Assign and review Unit 7 activities in the Competitive Events Workbook.

Online Action! Go to *marketingessentials.glencoe.com/ u7/ad* for an extended activity.

Marketing Plan

ANALYSIS
SWOT
Economic
Socio-Cultural
Technological
Competitive
1

STRATEGY
Promotion
2 Place
Price
Product

IMPLEMENTATION
Organization
Management
Staffing
3

BUDGET
Cost of sales
Cost of Promotion
Incomes and Expenses
4

CONTROL
Evaluation
Performance Measures
Performance Analysis
5

In this unit

Foundations of Marketing
Business, Management, Entrepreneurship

Functions of Marketing
Distribution

Marketing Plan
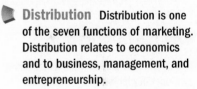

RELATE THE UNIT TO THE MARKETING PLAN

The four Ps of the marketing mix include product, place, pricing, and promotion. Unit 7 discusses distribution, a key factor in any company's place decision.

MARKETING PLAN OVERVIEW

Let students know that distribution is a key component of any product's marketing plan. Delivering a product quickly and for a fair price are crucial components in meeting the needs of customers.

Functions of Marketing

Point out to students that the Marketing Wheel shows the function of distribution and the foundation of business, management, and entrepreneurship.

▸ **Distribution** Distribution is one of the seven functions of marketing. Distribution relates to economics and to business, management, and entrepreneurship.

● **Business, Management, Entrepreneurship** Distributing the product so that it gets to the consumer intact and on time is one of the many responsibilities of business owners and managers. The channels of distribution should be well managed and maintained so that consumers receive their products in a reasonable amount of time, which helps to promote repeat business and customer referrals.

ANALYZE THE AD

Students' interpretations of the slogan will vary; most should note the direct connection from the earth (grove) to the consumer.

Market Talk Discuss with students the importance of distribution to Florida's Natural. The product—which does not have preservatives—must be transported quickly and cleanly.

Think and Write Answers will vary; some reasons to distribute nonfood items quickly may include conditions of the market that are likely to change quickly, such as with financial services regarding the stock market, or with fashion or entertainment items, which often have a brief shelf life. Other reasons may include merchandise that is marketable only around a season or holiday, or items must be quickly sold in order to free up inventory for a newer version of a product.

 Online Action! For instructions, ideas, and answer guide, go to the Teacher Center at **marketingessentials.glencoe.com**

Chapter Overview

This chapter presents fundamental information about channels of distribution. It also distinguishes the types of channels typical of the consumer and the industrial markets. Distribution planning involving e-commerce and foreign markets are also discussed in this chapter.

BUILD BACKGROUND

Bring a cotton T-shirt to class, and ask the students to brainstorm all the elements and steps involved in bringing it to market.

Raw cotton in the field, a farmer's harvest and labor, the collection and delivery of material to a manufacturer, the production line of the shirt, the warehousing of the shirt, the distribution, and the selling are all involved within the channels of distribution.

Why It's Important

The channel of distribution is an integral part in placing the product into the marketplace or the e-marketplace. Each vendor in the channel relies on timeliness, cost effectiveness, and reliability to make sure the process works.

Prepare to Read

Read aloud each of the vocabulary terms and ask students to write them on a sheet of paper. When they finish, write the terms on the board. Then have students guess at the meaning of each. Write their guesses next to each term. Leave this list on the board so students can see how close their guesses were to the actual definitions as they work through the chapter.

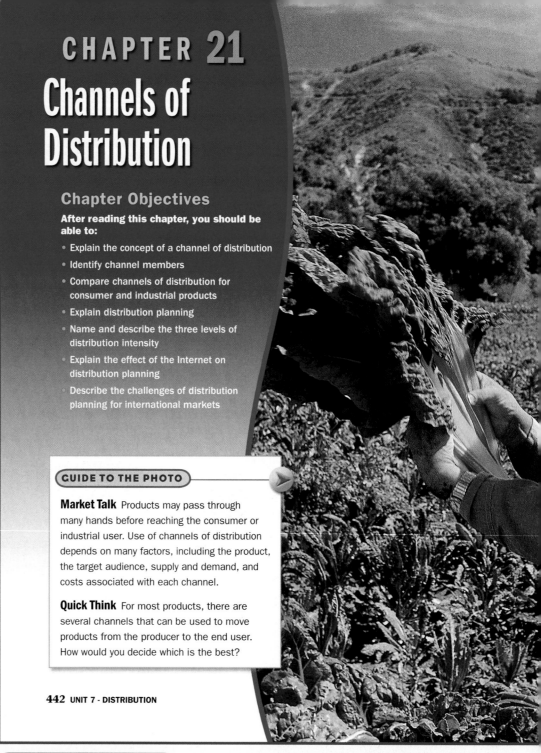

CHAPTER 21
Channels of Distribution

Chapter Objectives

After reading this chapter, you should be able to:

• Explain the concept of a channel of distribution
• Identify channel members
• Compare channels of distribution for consumer and industrial products
• Explain distribution planning
• Name and describe the three levels of distribution intensity
• Explain the effect of the Internet on distribution planning
• Describe the challenges of distribution planning for international markets

GUIDE TO THE PHOTO

Market Talk Products may pass through many hands before reaching the consumer or industrial user. Use of channels of distribution depends on many factors, including the product, the target audience, supply and demand, and costs associated with each channel.

Quick Think For most products, there are several channels that can be used to move products from the producer to the end user. How would you decide which is the best?

GUIDE TO THE PHOTO

Market Talk Point out the product visible in the photo; Swiss chard, a beet-like vegetable. Lead a discussion about the process it undergoes from conception to its delivery to the final user. Ask students to speculate about the various channels of distribution involved.

Quick Think Answers will vary; students may mention that the product itself often defines the type of distribution selected.

Follow Up Ask students to think of a product that is available at many different distribution outlets as well as another product that is available only at exclusive outlets. Have students share their responses in class.

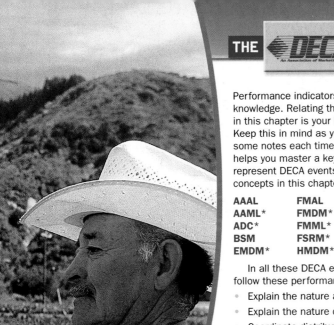

Performance indicators represent key skills and knowledge. Relating them to the concepts explained in this chapter is your key to success in DECA events. Keep this in mind as you read this chapter and write some notes each time you encounter material that helps you master a key concept. These acronyms represent DECA events that involve knowledge of concepts in this chapter.

AAAL	FMAL	MMS*	TMDM*
AAML*	FMDM*	QSRM*	TSE*
ADC*	FMML*	RMAL	VPM
BSM	FSRM*	RMML*	
EMDM*	HMDM*	SMDM*	

In all these DECA events you should be able to follow these performance indicators:

- Explain the nature and scope of distribution
- Explain the nature of channels of distribution
- Coordinate distribution with other marketing activities
- Explain the nature of channel-member relationships

All the events with an asterisk (*) also include these performance indicators:

- Explain the nature of channel strategies
- Select channels of distribution
- Evaluate channel members

Some events include additional performance indicators. These are:

BSM — Discuss the nature of service intermediaries

EMDM — Explain distribution issues and trends in e-commerce

DECA PREP

Check your understanding of DECA performance indicators with the DECA activity in this chapter's review. For more information and DECA Prep practice, go to *marketingessentials.glencoe.com/21/DECA*

DECA events that require knowledge of channels of distribution are described here. Discuss the performance indicators to make sure students understand how to demonstrate their understanding.

The events acronyms stand for:

AAAL: Apparel and Accessories Marketing Series, AL

AAML: Apparel and Accessories Marketing Series, ML

ADC: Advertising Campaign Event

BSM: Business Services Marketing Series

EMDM: E-Commerce Management Team Decision Making Event

FMAL: Food Marketing Series, AL

FMDM: Financial Analysis Management Team Decision Making Event

FMML: Food Marketing Series, ML

FSRM: Full Service Restaurant Management Series

HMDM: Hospitality Services Management Team Decision Making Event

MMS: Marketing Management Series

QSRM: Quick Serve Restaurant Management Series

RMAL: Retail Merchandising Series, AL

RMML: Retail Merchandising Series, ML

SMDM: Sports and Entertainment Marketing Management Team Decision Making Event

TMDM: Travel and Tourism Marketing Management Team Decision Making Event

TSE: Technical Sales Event

VPM: Vehicles and Petroleum Marketing Series

DECA PREP

Find timed DECA Prep activities correlated to the Competitive Events Workbook for students and DECA tips for teachers at **marketingessentials.glencoe.com/21/DECA**

CHAPTER 21 Classroom Resources

For the Teacher
- TeacherWorks
- marketingessentials.glencoe.com
- Interactive Chalkboard
- **Exam***View*® Pro Test Generator
- Fast File Unit 7

For the Student
- *Marketing Essentials* Online Edition
- Student Activity Workbook
- Marketing Math Workbook
- Marketing Research Project Workbook
- School-to-Work Activity Workbook
- Competitive Events Workbook
- *BusinessWeek* Reader and Case Studies
- marketingessentials.glencoe.com

FOCUS

Introducing the Section

COLLABORATIVE ACTIVITY

Ask students to name places where clothing, DVDs, gadgets, shoes, or other items can be bought. Remind students that in order to reach the public, manufacturers of those products have to consider those outlets in their decisions. Tell students that this chapter focuses on such decisions.

Preteaching Key Terms

Ask students to skim the section's key terms and then locate them as the boldface words in the running text. Have them read the sentence the boldface word appears in as well as those surrounding it to grasp the context of each word.

- channel of distribution
- intermediaries
- wholesalers
- rack jobbers
- drop shippers
- retailers
- brick-and-mortar retailers
- e-tailing
- agents
- direct distribution
- indirect distribution

Critical Thinking

Ask students: What do you think is the cause-and-effect relationship of a reliable channel of distribution and sales as opposed to an unreliable channel distribution and sales?

OBJECTIVES

- Explain the concept of a channel of distribution
- Identify channel members
- Compare channels of distribution for consumer and industrial products

KEY TERMS

- channel of distribution
- intermediaries
- wholesalers
- rack jobbers
- drop shippers
- retailers
- brick-and-mortar retailers
- e-tailing
- agents
- direct distribution
- indirect distribution

WHILE YOU READ

Compare List the different channels and how they are used to distribute products to consumers and to industrial users.

Distribution

READ and STUDY

BEFORE YOU READ

Predict What do you already know about distribution?

THE MAIN IDEA

As you know, the marketing mix includes decisions about product, place, price, and promotion. In this chapter, you will explore the place decision—where and how the product will be distributed and sold in the marketplace. Making the correct place decision has an impact on the entire operation of a business.

STUDY ORGANIZER

Draw the chart below. As you read this section, write in the routes taken to distribute products to consumers (A–E) and to industrial users (A–D).

Consumer Products	Industrial Products
A.	A.
B.	B.
C.	C.
D.	D.
E.	

Distribution: How It Works

How do you get somebody to buy your product? By marketing it! Now the question is how does that product get to your customers? This is the place decision, one of the four Ps of the marketing mix.

To make a place decision, marketers must decide on their channel of distribution. The **channel of distribution** is the path a product takes from its producer or manufacturer to the

READ and STUDY

BEFORE YOU READ

Remind students that this chapter focuses on the *place* of the promotional mix.

THE MAIN IDEA

Lead students in finding examples of good street vendor locations in their community.

STUDY ORGANIZER

Make a study organizer, or download the one at **marketingessentials.glencoe.com**. As study continues, you and the class should work together to complete the routes.

Encourage students to write the outline of the section on a piece of paper. As they read the chapter, have them write key words under each heading and discuss the types of distribution channels.

final user. When the product is purchased for use in a business, the final user is classified as an industrial user. When the product is purchased for personal use, the final user is classified as a consumer.

Using shampoo as an example, you can see how the same product may be classified as both a consumer and an industrial product. Manufacturers of shampoo sell their product to the customer through retail operations but

• **FASTER DELIVERY** Nissan, a Japanese auto manufacturer, has built a plant in Mississippi, so many Nissans sold in the U.S. are also built in the U.S.

What consequences do you think having a North American plant has in terms of distribution?

Chapter 21 - Channels of Distribution **445**

TEACH

Discussion Starter

IMPORTANCE OF DISTRIBUTION

Intermediaries are integral business entities that benefit the producer. The producer must trust that the intermediary has great expertise on the place at hand. Lead a discussion asking students to come up with ways in which a producer, intermediary, and user could build trust in their services.

Answers might include repeatability, reputation, track record, satisfaction, and overall excellence.

TEACHING POINTS

Explain In a world filled with competition to gain more market share, trust builds and solidifies relationships in business. If any one leg of the producer-intermediary-user tripod structure suffers, the end result for any one of them is less than successful.

Extended Activity

Exploring Distribution Options
Have students investigate distribution practices for perishable goods that are transported into and distributed in their city or state. Ask students to choose one perishable product and describe its distribution process in a two-paragraph summary.

AD GUIDE | **FASTER DELIVERY**

Discussion Ask students: Is purchasing a Nissan at a local dealer an example of direct distribution or indirect distribution? Have them explain their answer.

Caption Answer Answers will vary; possible answers include easier access to the destinations, more timely deliveries, alleviates import tariff and quotas on the vehicles, higher manufacturing standards, and so on.

Follow Up Ask students: In a global marketplace, how is outsourcing operations to other countries helping or hurting the U.S. economy? Have students research the issue and then discuss and debate their opinions in class.

TEACH CONTINUED

Concept Development

WHOLESALERS

Ask students if they believe that the Hershey Foods Corporation in Hershey, Pennsylvania, would be willing to distribute candy bars directly to their high school sporting and theater events. Why or why not? Have students give reasons for their responses. This activity will introduce the need for wholesalers and their role in the distribution process.

Most students will recognize that Hershey would not want to deal with such a small operation because the paperwork and shipping would be too costly and time consuming. Hershey Company might sell to the high school if it sold candy by the truckload, which is impractical.

TEACHING POINTS

Model To teach the concept of channels of distribution in the consumer market, put a diagram on the board (producer to consumer), and identify it as direct distribution. Then ask students to name products they have purchased directly from wholesalers, and have them describe the circumstances of the purchase.

Critical Thinking

Ask students to name reasons why small retailers tend to use the services of wholesalers. Answers may include that small retailers lack the storage space, capital, and customers to buy in large quantities.

NET MARKETING

How Will They Find You?

You have started an online auto parts business. You have great sources for parts, good relationships with your suppliers, and an attractive Web site. All you need is for customers to find your site among thousands of similar ones. Someone might search for "discount auto parts" on a search engine such as Google or Yahoo. What determines which merchants come up on top? Learning how search engines determine which sites are listed first is key to a successful Web business.

What Is a Good Web Page Design?

Your site's title should include words that will attract searchers—something like "Discount VW Vintage Auto Parts," where each word points to something a searcher might target. Each page of your site needs a different title. A meta-tag, a short but complete description of what is on the site, is also essential.

THINK LIKE A MARKETER

What can happen if you include words in your title that do not reflect the content of your Web page?

@ **Online Action!**

Go to *marketingessentials.glencoe.com/ 21/net* to find an activity on the Internet and distribution.

---

also may sell it to hair salons and hotel chains as an industrial product for use in a business.

Channel Members

Businesses involved in sales transactions that move products from the manufacturer to the final user are called **intermediaries** or middlemen. Intermediaries reduce the number of contacts required to reach the final user of the product. Suppose four customers wanted to buy a digital camera made by Nikon. If Nikon sells directly to consumers, it would have to make four separate sales transactions. By using an intermediary, such as CompUSA, the number of contacts Nikon must make is reduced to one.

Intermediaries are classified on the basis of whether they take ownership (title) of goods and services. Merchant intermediaries take title; agent intermediaries do not. Agent intermediaries, usually called agents, are paid a commission to help buyers and sellers get together. The two major types of merchant intermediaries are wholesalers and retailers.

Wholesalers

Businesses that buy large quantities of goods from manufacturers, store the goods, and then resell them to other businesses are called **wholesalers**. Their customers are retailers. Wholesalers may be called distributors when their customers are professional or commercial users, manufacturers, governments, institutions, or other wholesalers. In either case, they take title to the goods they buy for resale.

Two specialized wholesalers are rack jobbers and drop shippers. **Rack jobbers** are wholesalers that manage inventory and merchandising for retailers by counting stock, filling it in when needed, and maintaining store displays. As the name implies, they provide the racks for display of the product in a retail store. They bill the retailer only for the goods

marketingessentials.glencoe.com

NET MARKETING

How Will They Find You?

Discussion Lead a discussion about how people can use appropriate search words to find helpful Web pages among the huge number of pages on the Internet. Ask them how they select key words when browsing topics.

THINK LIKE A MARKETER Answer: Answers might include that if the title of the Web page does not accurately convey its precise message clearly and effectively, surfers will venture elsewhere. Intuitive design, smooth navigability, organized merchandise, and a secure Web site align with the trust issues between producer and (potential) customer.

@ **Online Action!** For instructions, ideas, and answer guide, go to the Teacher Center at marketingessentials.glencoe.com sold, not for all the items on display. Products that are handled by rack jobbers include CDs, hosiery, health products, and cosmetics.

Drop shippers own the goods they sell but do not physically handle the actual products. They deal in large quantities of items in bulk, such as coal, lumber, and chemicals that require special handling. Drop shippers sell the goods to other businesses and have the producer ship the merchandise directly to the buyers.

Retailers

Retailers sell goods to the final consumer for personal use. Traditional retailers, called **brick-and-mortar retailers**, sell goods to the customer from their own physical stores. These retail stores buy their products from manufacturers or wholesalers. They serve as the final link between the manufacturer and consumer. To build good customer relationships, they often have special services, such as offering credit or providing delivery.

A number of non-store retailing operations serve the customer. They include automatic retailing (vending machines), direct mail and catalog retailing, TV home shopping, and online retailing (or e-tailing).

Vending service companies buy manufacturers' products, such as drinks, snacks, and travelers items, and sell them through vending machines that dispense goods to consumers. These companies often place their vending machines in stores, office buildings, hospitals, airports, schools, and other institutions for free.

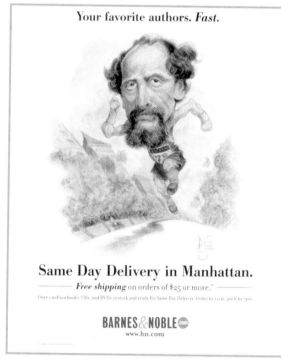

Your favorite authors. *Fast.*

Same Day Delivery in Manhattan.

Free shipping on orders of $25 or more.

Over 1 million books, CDs, and DVDs in stock and ready for Same Day Delivery. Order by 11am, get it by 7pm.

BARNES&NOBLE.com
www.bn.com

•**GETTING the GOODS to CUSTOMERS** Barnes & Noble stores in New York City provide an extra service to their customers: same-day delivery.

How does this illustrate the importance of thinking about distribution?

TEACH CONTINUED

Individualized Practice

RETAILERS

L1 Ask students if they think that electronic retail outlets will completely replace traditional brick-and-mortar stores. Have them support their opinions in a 150-word response.

L2 Ask students to imagine that intermediaries disappear overnight. Have them write a one-page essay on what would happen within a year to the variety of goods available to consumers and to production capabilities.
Answers will vary but might include that the former would be reduced and the latter limited, unless the Internet is able to generate enough business from manufacturers.

L3 Ask students to conduct a comparative shopping analysis of one book of their choice at the following locations: a local brick-and-mortar bookstore, an online store, a used local bookstore, and an online used bookstore. They should research a variety of measures, such as price (including taxes and shipping), time of delivery, condition of purchase (see the product's description on used sites), convenience factor, and so on. Ask students to record their data in a spreadsheet and indicate their proposed purchase plan in the end.

AD GUIDE   **GETTING the GOODS to CUSTOMERS**

Discussion Lead a discussion about consumers' desire for immediate gratification in an electronic marketplace. To spark this discussion, ask students how the Internet age has raised or lowered peoples' ability to wait for an online purchase.

Caption Answer Same-day delivery, particularly from a bookstore, entices customers to purchase even when they cannot be physically present at the brick-and-mortar store. Convenience and reliability are keys to sustaining business in the e-tailing environment.

Follow Up Ask students how they think businesses determine and locate their target audience for direct mail advertising.

TEACH CONTINUED

Concept Development

AGENTS

To teach the concept of agents, ask students to explain the job of a real estate agent.

Agents find buyers for sellers and sellers for buyers, tasks for which they receive a commission. A real estate agent deals with the buying and selling of property.

Then ask students if, in general, the real estate agents own the properties.

No, they are sales agents for the people who wish to sell their property.

Online Activity

Distribution Online

Have students find a retail store that offers product distribution via the Web as well as through brick-and-mortar stores. Have students list the advantages and disadvantages to the consumer of each type of distribution offered.

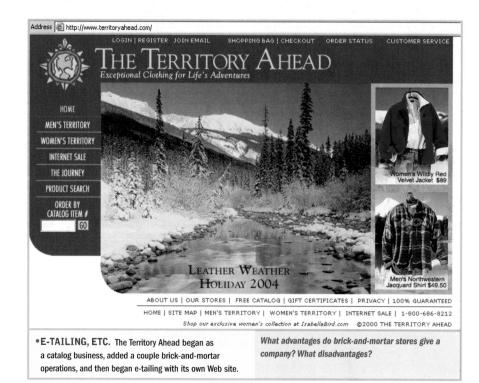

• E-TAILING, ETC. The Territory Ahead began as a catalog business, added a couple brick-and-mortar operations, and then began e-tailing with its own Web site.

What advantages do brick-and-mortar stores give a company? What disadvantages?

Direct mail and catalogs also reach the final consumer. Many large brick-and-mortar retailers produce their own catalogs to reach consumers who prefer shopping at home. There are also catalog houses that buy goods from different manufacturers and display them in a catalog for sale to the customer.

Television home shopping networks are TV stations that sell products to consumers. These companies buy the products in set quantities and sell them via television programs. Consumers phone in their orders while watching shows. One example of this is the Home Shopping Network (HSN).

Online retailing, or **e-tailing**, involves retailers selling products over the Internet to the customer. Some of the big e-tailing companies are found only on the Internet, such as amazon.com or overstock.com.

Not to be left out of the Internet revolution, many brick-and-mortar retailers, such as Target and Williams-Sonoma, have created Web sites. Some of the top e-tailing sectors are air travel, books, and hardware.

Agents

Unlike wholesalers and retailers, agents do not own the goods they sell. **Agents** act as intermediaries by bringing buyers and sellers together. There are two different types of agents: manufacturers' representatives and brokers.

Independent Manufacturers' Representatives

Independent manufacturers' representatives work with several related (but noncompeting) manufacturers in a specific industry. They are not on any manufacturer's payroll. Instead, they are paid commissions based on what they sell.

AD GUIDE — E-TAILING, ETC.

Discussion Ask students how they prefer to shop for clothes and shoes: catalog, brick-and-mortar store, or online? Have students explain their answers.

Caption Answer Answers will vary; possible answers may include that retailers may wish to fulfill the needs and preferences of different customers; customers who like tactile shopping prefer retail stores to other outlets, while other customers may prefer the convenience and speediness of Web transactions.

Follow Up Ask students to conduct research on Internet sales tax in their state. Have students share their findings in class.

An independent manufacturers' agent might carry a line of fishing rods from one manufacturer, lures from another, insulated clothing for hunters from a different manufacturer, and outdoor shirts from still another manufacturer.

Brokers

A broker's principal function is to bring buyers and sellers together in order for a sale to take place. Brokers usually do not have a continued relationship with either party. They negotiate the sale, are paid a commission, and then look for other customers. Food brokers, however, are an exception to this rule. Food brokers represent several manufacturers of products sold in supermarkets, convenience stores, and other specialty food stores.

Direct and Indirect Channels

Channels of distribution are classified as direct or indirect (see Figures 21.1 and 21.2). **Direct distribution** occurs when the producer sells goods or services directly

---

Case Study

Changing Channels

Gateway Computers was founded with a $10,000 loan by Theodore Waitt on his parents' Iowa farm in 1985. It grew to become a major computer producer, selling directly to consumers over the phone and on the Web. After acquiring eMachines, a low-end PC company, early in 2004, Gateway was the number three PC producer in the United States.

In 1996, Gateway became the first "bricks-and-clicks" computer seller (with both online sales and its own stores). There were over 300 Gateway stores where customers could order computers for delivery.

The Wrong Channel?

Company stores were never profitable, and in April 2004 Gateway closed all its stores, returning to phone and Web-based sales. eMachines had been available at other retail outlets, including Best Buy, and Gateway expanded into that channel for its own branded computers and consumer electronics.

Part of being a direct distributor is developing an especially close relationship with customers. Selling Gateway products in third party retail outlets will affect the control the company has over that relationship, but there is a trade-off in terms of a wider market for Gateway.

THINK STRATEGICALLY

What reasons can a direct distributor have to open brick-and-mortar or bricks-and-clicks operations?

 Online Action! Go to *marketingessentials.glencoe.com/21/case* to find an activity on channels of distribution.

TEACH CONTINUED

Individualized Practice

DIRECT AND INDIRECT CHANNELS

L1 Have students prepare a bulletin-board or multimedia display showing the channels of distribution used to get a product to final consumer. They can select something as simple as a pencil or as complex as a vehicle.

L2 Have students interview a local broker, wholesaler, or retailer. Have them develop questions that relate to current problems and/or challenges these businesspeople face today. Encourage students to summarize the results of their interview for the class.

L3 Have students research the new forms of interactive channels of distribution in the consumer and industrial markets. Specifically, tell them to see how e-commerce impacts the way business is being done. Have students create a two-page report on their findings on the trends and types of electronic equipment necessary for e-commerce to work.

Build Vocabulary

In this section, students learn that *agent* is synonymous with *broker*. Ask them to research and identify the various types of brokers and the purpose and function of each type.

Case Study   Changing Channels

Discussion Have students read the Case Study and discuss the differences between a brick-and-mortar company and a bricks-and-clicks company. Ask them to identify which type of company they might prefer to use for certain goods and why.

THINK STRATEGICALLY   **Answer:** The reasons vary, but might include development of a close relationship with customers, an opportunity to expand its market share, and another outlet to hike the profits of the company.

Online Action! For instructions, ideas, and answer guide, go to the Teacher Center at marketingessentials.glencoe.com

Concept Development

DISTRIBUTION CHANNELS FOR CONSUMER PRODUCTS AND SERVICES

Let students know that small retailers and independent business owners often cannot match the deep discounts and low prices that large retail operations or wholesalers offer due to their ability to buy directly from the manufacturer. Ask students to consider and list ways a smaller retailer could compete to keep or gain customers from wholesalers.

Answers might include offer a different selection, use a theme, and emphasize personal customer service.

Enrichment

UNDERSTANDING CHANNELS OF DISTRIBUTION

Divide the class into groups of three to five. Ask groups choose to one consumer product that interests them and research its path of distribution. Have students create a visual map of the distribution channels used to get the product to consumers. Encourage to use traditional art materials and/or graphic design software to complete this project. Have groups post their distribution maps in the classroom.

450

Figure 21.1 **Distribution Channels—Consumer Products**

• **Getting the Goods in Consumers' Hands** Products are distributed to consumers through five channels. Historically, most consumer goods were not distributed using direct distribution (channel A) because consumers became accustomed to shopping in retail stores. E-commerce is changing that for some products.

Which channel is used most often for items that go out of date quickly or need servicing?

CHANNEL A

Manufacturer/Producer Directly to Consumer

There are five ways in which direct distribution is used for consumer goods.
1. Selling products at the production site.
2. Having a sales force call on consumers.
3. Using catalogs or ads to generate sales.
4. Using telemarketing.
5. Using the Internet to make online sales.

CHANNEL B

Manufacturer/Producer to Retailer to Consumer

This is the most commonly used channel for merchandise that dates quickly or needs servicing.

CHANNEL C

Manufacturer/Producer to Wholesaler to Retailer to Consumer

This is the most common distribution method for staple goods, which are items that are always carried in stock and whose styles do not change frequently.

CHANNEL D

Manufacturer/Producer to Agents to Wholesaler to Retailer to Consumer

This is the channel for manufacturers who wish to concentrate on production and leave sales and distribution to others.

CHANNEL E

Manufacturer/Producer to Agents to Retailer to Consumer

This is the channel chosen by manufacturers who do not want to handle their own sales to retailers. The agent simply brings the buyer and seller together.

Manufacturers/Producers

Agents

Wholesalers

Retailers

Consumers

@ Online Action! Go to *marketingessentials.glencoe.com/21/figure/1* to find a project on distribution channels for consumer products.

marketingessentials.glencoe.com

Figure 21.1 **Distribution Channels—Consumer Products**

Discussion Of the indirect channels available, manufacturer/producer to retailer to consumer (channel B) is most commonly used in the consumer market. Ask students to read each channel on the figure, and discuss local businesses that fall within each category. Write their examples on the board.

Caption Answer Channel B is used most often for these items.

 Online Action! For instructions, ideas, and answer guide, go to the Teacher Center at **marketingessentials.glencoe.com**

Figure 21.2 · Distribution Channels—Industrial Products

•**Getting the Goods to Businesses** Industrial buyers have different needs than retail buyers, so they use different channels of distribution. The least common channel in the consumer market—direct distribution (channel A)—is the most common in the industrial market. Industrial products and services are distributed through four channels.

Which channel is most often used to distribute major equipment used in manufacturing?

CHANNEL A

Manufacturer/Producer Directly to Industrial Users

This is the most common method of distribution for major equipment used in manufacturing and other businesses. The manufacturer's sales force calls on the industrial user to sell goods or services. Note: All methods of direct distribution listed for the consumer market are used in the industrial market as well.

CHANNEL C

Manufacturer/Producer to Agents to Industrial Distributors to Industrial Users

Small manufacturers who do not have the time or money to invest in a direct sales force may prefer this channel. The agent sells the goods to the industrial wholesaler who stores, resells, and ships them to the industrial user.

CHANNEL B

Manufacturer/Producer to Industrial Distributors to Industrial Users

This channel is used most often for small standardized parts and operational supplies needed to run a business. Industrial wholesalers (distributors) take ownership of the products, stock them, and sell them as needed to industrial users.

CHANNEL D

Manufacturer/Producer to Agents to Industrial Users

This is another channel used when a manufacturer does not want to hire its own sales force. The agent represents the manufacturer for sale of the goods but does not take possession or title. The merchandise is shipped directly from the manufacturer to the industrial user.

 Online Action!
Go to *marketingessentials.glencoe.com/21/figure/2* to find a project on distribution channels for industrial products.

marketingessentials.glencoe.com

Figure 21.2 · Distribution Channels—Industrial Products

Discussion Manufacturers provide retailers with more than just goods. Because they are the best authorities on the use, quality, and content of their own products, they often supply retailers with other valuable offerings. Ask students to discuss what additional things the manufacturers offer retailers. This can be important to small retailers or those with limited budgets for advertising. Answers might include valuable product information, display materials, and advertising ideas.

Caption Answer Channel A is used most often.

Online Action! For instructions, ideas, and answer guide, go to the Teacher Center at **marketingessentials.glencoe.com**

TEACH CONTINUED

Individualized Math Skills

Have students use the following scenario to complete the leveled activity: A manufacturer sells an item priced at $75.59 to a discount chain store at 50 percent off the list (or suggested retail) price.

L1 Ask students to calculate the answer to the following question: If the item has a list price of $75.59, what does the discount chain store pay for it?
$75.59 \times 0.50 = \$37.80$

■ Tell students to assume that the same manufacturer that sells the item to the discount chain store at 50 percent off the list price gives a regular retailer only 40 percent off. Ask students to determine the dollar savings enjoyed by the chain store over a regular retailer.
Retailer cost: $75.59 \times 0.60 = \$45.35$;
Difference: $\$45.35 - \$37.80 = \$7.55$

L3 Tell students to assume that the manufacturer sells an item to two chain stores. The first chain store gets 50 percent off the list price. The second chain store does not get 50 percent off the list price, but rather the standard 40 percent off and an additional 10 percent for doing its own distribution. Ask students if the two discounts amount to the same dollar amount, and have them explain their answers.
No; the amounts differ because the discounts apply in sequence: $75.59 \times 0.60 = \$45.35$; $\$45.35 \times \$0.90 = \$40.82$

451

ASSESS

Review Guide

CONCEPTS

Ask students to create their own illustration of the consumer and industrial products and services for channels of distribution without refering to the textbook. Have them sketch what they can from memory, drawing and using text to recreate the concept. Once this is complete, allow them to go back and fill in their content holes with a different color pen or pencil.

KEY TERMS

Have students review key terms, their spellings, and definitions in small groups.

ONLINE SELF-ASSESSMENT

Have students go to marketingessentials.glencoe.com for the Section 21.1 practice test.

Individualized Review

L1 Assign and review Chapter 21 activities in the Student Activity Workbook.

L2 Assign and review Chapter 21 activities in the Marketing Math Workbook.

L3 Assign and review Chapter 21 activities in the *BusinessWeek* Reader and Case Studies.

Marketing Practice

Ask students to prepare and deliver a three-minute speech on a value created by intermediaries for producers in a specific channel of distribution.

---

to the customer, with no intermediaries. **Indirect distribution** involves one or more intermediaries. Both consumer markets and industrial markets use direct and indirect channels of distribution.

Examples of Channels of Distribution

Different channels of distribution are generally used to reach the customer in the consumer and industrial markets.

When selling to the industrial market, a manufacturer would sell paper napkins to industrial distributors who, in turn, would sell the napkins to restaurants.

When selling to the consumer market, the company would sell napkins to a wholesaler or use food brokers to sell to retailers such as grocery stores or party supply shops. Not every option works best for every kind of product or company.

Despite the potential for success that any product may seem to have, it can fail if the wrong channels of distribution are used.

Distribution Channels for Consumer Products and Services

Few consumer products are marketed using direct distribution (channel A) because consumers have become accustomed to shopping in retail stores. The most common indirect channel in the consumer market is Producer to Retailer to Consumer (channel B).

Manufacturer/Producer Directly to Consumer (Channel A)

Direct distribution can be used in five different ways to deliver products to consumers:

1. Selling products at the production site. Examples include factory outlets or farmers' roadside stands.
2. Having a sales force call on consumers at home. Examples include Avon and Tupperware.
3. Using catalogs or ads to generate sales.
4. Having sales representatives call consumers on the telephone (telemarketing). The

---

national do not call list has greatly limited this method.
5. Using the Internet to make online sales.

Manufacturer/Producer to Retailer to Consumer (Channel B)

This channel is used most often for products that become out of date quickly or need regular servicing. Clothing and automobiles are sold this way. Chain stores and online retailers use this channel.

Manufacturer/Producer to Wholesaler to Retailer to Consumer (Channel C)

This method of distribution is most often used for staple goods, which are items that are always carried in stock and whose styles do not change frequently. The manufacturer sells to the wholesaler, who then handles the sales, warehousing, and distribution of the goods to retailers. Consumer goods sold this way include supermarket items, flowers, candy, and stationery supplies.

Manufacturer/Producer to Agents to Wholesaler to Retailer to Consumer (Channel D)

Manufacturers who prefer to concentrate on production and leave sales and distribution to others use this channel. The agent sells to wholesalers who are involved in storage, sale, and transportation to retailers. The retailer then sells to consumers.

Manufacturer/Producer to Agents to Retailer to Consumer (Channel E)

Manufacturers who do not want to handle their own sales to retailers use this channel. The agent simply brings the buyer and seller together. Expensive cookware, meat, cosmetics, and many supermarket items are sold this way.

Distribution Channels for Industrial Products and Services

Industrial users shop differently and have different needs from consumers, so they use different channels of distribution. The least used channel in the consumer market—direct

---

Online Activity

E-Commerce as a Channel of Distribution

Ask students to conduct an online research project that answers the following questions: How has e-commerce changed the channels of distribution? Have students describe a business strategy used in this alternative form of distribution.

distribution (channel A)—is the most used channel in the industrial market.

Manufacturer/Producer Directly to Industrial Users (Channel A)

This method of distribution is most often used for major equipment used in manufacturing and other businesses. The manufacturer's sales force calls on the industrial user to sell goods or services. For example, a Xerox sales representative sells copiers directly to manufacturers and commercial businesses.

Manufacturer/Producer to Industrial Distributors to Industrial Users (Channel B)

This channel is used most often for small standardized parts and operational supplies needed to run a business. Industrial wholesalers (distributors) take ownership of the products, stock them, and sell them as needed to industrial users. For example, a restaurant supply wholesaler buys pots, pans, utensils, serving pieces, and paper products from various manufacturers to sell to restaurant owners.

Manufacturer/Producer to Agents to Industrial Distributors to Industrial Users (Channel C)

Small manufacturers who do not have time or money to invest in a direct sales force may prefer to use the services of an agent. The agent represents the manufacturer for sale of the goods but does not take possession or title. The agent sells the goods to the industrial wholesaler who stores, resells, and ships them to the industrial user.

Manufacturer/Producer to Agents to Industrial Users (Channel D)

This is another channel used when a manufacturer does not want to hire its own sales force. The merchandise is shipped directly from the manufacturer to the industrial user. Construction equipment, farm products, and dry goods are often marketed this way.

 21.1 AFTER YOU READ

Reviewing Key Terms and Concepts

1. What term describes the path a product takes from producer to final user?

2. What is the function of intermediaries?

3. Name the two main types of distribution channels.

Integrating Academic Skills

Math

4. Assume a manufacturer makes an item that costs $2.50 to produce. The markup when sold to the distributor is 35 percent. What is the cost to the distributor? When the distributor sells this item to the retailer, the markup is 40 percent. How much will the retailer pay for the item?

Language Arts

5. Using standard outline form, organize the following information into a Distribution Channel Members Outline: stores, wholesalers, retailers, merchant intermediaries, rack jobbers, agent intermediaries, drop shippers, intermediaries, direct mail operations, and independent manufacturers' representatives.

 Online Action!

Check your answers at *marketingessentials.glencoe.com/21/read*

marketingessentials.glencoe.com

Chapter 21 - Channels of Distribution **453**

SECTION 21.1

CLOSE

Ask students to provide answers to the following questions.

- Do you think e-tailing will eventually replace brick-and-mortar retailers? Explain.

  Answers will vary. Some students will say no because people want to see and touch the items they buy. Speed and convenience are also factors.

- Name the types of distribution channels that are used more frequently for consumer products and for industrial products.

  Indirect distribution channels are more frequently used for consumer products. Direct distribution channels are more frequently used for industrial products.

 Critical Thinking

Ask students: What are the short-term and long-term implications for finding the right channel of distribution for a product in the consumer market?

AFTER YOU READ

Reviewing Key Terms and Concepts

1. The term that describes the path a product takes from producer to final user is *Channel of distribution*.

2. Intermediaries link producers to the final users of a product.

3. The two main types of distribution channels are direct and indirect.

 Online Action! Answers at **marketingessentials.glencoe.com/21/read**

Integrating Academic Skills

4. The cost to the distributor is $3.375 per item. The retailer will pay $4.725 per item.

5. I. Intermediaries
  A. Agent Intermediaries
    1. Independent manufacturer's representative
  B. Merchant Intermediaries
    1. Wholesalers
      a. Rack jobbers
      b. Drop shippers
    2. Retailers
      a. Stores
      b. Direct mail operations

FOCUS

Introducing the Section

COLLABORATIVE ACTIVITY

Tell students that distributors in all industries tend to experience pressure from both customers and vendors. Ask students to speculate why distributors might feel pressure from both sides.

Preteaching Key Terms

Ask students to write the outline of this chapter in their journal. Include all the major headings as well as the boldface key terms under the appropriate heading.

- exclusive distribution
- integrated distribution
- selective distribution
- intensive distribution
- e-marketplace

 Critical Thinking

Tell students that the trend toward manufacturers opening their own stores is on the upswing (e.g., Apple Computer stores, NikeTown, and so on). Ask students to speculate how this kind of distribution might help independent retailers increase product awareness.

OBJECTIVES

- **Explain distribution planning**
- **Name and describe the three levels of distribution intensity**
- **Explain the effect of the Internet on distribution planning**
- **Describe the challenges of distribution planning for international markets**

KEY TERMS

- **exclusive distribution**
- **integrated distribution**
- **selective distribution**
- **intensive distribution**
- **e-marketplace**

Distribution Planning

READ and STUDY

BEFORE YOU READ

Predict What do you already know about distribution planning?

THE MAIN IDEA

Distribution decisions affect the entire company, so it is important for you to know how these decisions are made. It is also helpful to know how these decisions are carried out in different markets, including international markets and e-marketplaces.

STUDY ORGANIZER

In a chart like the one below, note the main components of distribution planning.

Multiple Channels

Distribution Planning

Control/Costs

WHILE YOU READ

Analyze Determine ways the Internet might facilitate the use of channels of distribution.

Understanding Distribution Planning

Distribution planning involves decisions about a product's physical movement and transfer of ownership from producer to consumer. In this chapter, we address only transfer of ownership concerns. Distribution decisions affect a firm's marketing program. Some of the major considerations are the use of multiple channels, control versus costs, intensity of distribution desired, and involvement in e-commerce.

READ and STUDY

BEFORE YOU READ

Review with students the channels of distribution outlined in Section 21.1. Re-create a flow chart of the distribution channels in consumer and industrial markets.

THE MAIN IDEA

Ask students to speculate how distribution decisions affect an entire company.

STUDY ORGANIZER

Make your own study organizer, or download the one at **marketingessentials.glencoe.com**. As study continues, you and the class should work together to complete the chart.

 Encourage students to create a story out of the information they acquire in this section to get the "big picture."

Multiple Channels

A producer uses multiple channels when its product fits the needs of both industrial and customer markets. J & J Snack Foods sells its pretzels, drinks, and cookies to supermarkets, movie theaters, stadiums, and other sports arenas. It also sells to schools, colleges, and hospitals. The producer must identify the best channel for each market.

Control Versus Costs

All manufacturers and producers must weigh the control they want to keep over the distribution of their products against costs and profitability.

Who Does the Selling?

A manufacturer must decide how much control it wants over its sales function. It can use its own sales force or hire agents to do the selling.

A direct sales force is costly. In-house sales representatives are on the company payroll, receive employee benefits, and are reimbursed for expenses. The manufacturer, though, has complete control over them. It can establish sales quotas and easily monitor each sales representative's performance.

With an agent, a manufacturer loses some of its control over how sales are made. This is because agents work independently, running their own businesses. However, the relative cost of using agents can be lower than hiring an in-house sales staff. No employee benefits or expenses must be paid because agents are independent businesspeople. Another benefit is that agents are paid a set percentage of sales, assuring that the cost of sales is always the same in relation to the sales generated.

Distribution Intensity

Distribution intensity has to do with how widely a product will be distributed. There are three levels of distribution intensity: exclusive, selective, and intensive.

Exclusive Distribution

Exclusive distribution involves protected territories for distribution of a product in a given geographic area. Dealers are assured that they are the only ones within a certain geographic radius that have the right to sell the manufacturer's or wholesaler's products. Prestige, image, channel control, and a high profit margin for both the manufacturer and intermediaries are characteristic of this distribution strategy. Franchised operations are examples of exclusive distribution planning.

Wholesalers may also sponsor voluntary groups in which a retailer agrees to buy and maintain a minimum inventory of the wholesaler's products. One example of a voluntary group sponsored by a wholesaler is the National Auto Parts Association (NAPA). Retailers affiliated with NAPA buy most of their stock from NAPA and participate in its promotions.

Some manufacturers own and run their own retail operations. This variation on exclusive distribution is **integrated distribution**. The manufacturer acts as wholesaler and retailer for its own products. The Gap sells its clothing in company-owned retail stores.

Selective Distribution

Selective distribution means that a limited number of outlets in a given geographic area are used to sell the product. The goal is to select channel members that can maintain the image of the product and are good credit risks, aggressive marketers, and good inventory planners.

Intermediaries are selected for their ability to cater to the final users that the manufacturer wants to attract. Dana Buchman sells its clothing only through top department stores that appeal to the affluent customers who buy its merchandise. It does not sell its goods in a chain megastore or a variety store with a very different target market.

Intensive Distribution

Intensive distribution involves the use of all suitable outlets to sell a product. The objective is complete market coverage, and the ultimate goal is to sell to as many customers as possible, wherever they choose to shop. Motor oil is marketed in quick-lube shops,

Chapter 21 - Channels of Distribution **455**

Online Activity

Agents Online

Ask students to go online to find real-world examples of companies that employ manufacturer's agents/representatives (those who work for several producers and carry noncompetitive, complementary merchandise) and selling agents (who represent a single producer). Have them create a table that indicates the company name, industry, and the job qualifications required.

Review Guide

CONCEPTS
Ask students to list the three levels of distribution intensity.
exclusive, selective, and intensive

KEY TERMS
Have students review key terms, their spellings, and definitions in small groups.

ONLINE SELF-ASSESSMENT
Have students go to **marketingessentials.glencoe.com** for the Section 21.2 practice test.

Individualized Review

L1 Assign and review Chapter 21 activities in the Student Activity Workbook.

L2 Assign and review Chapter 21 activities in the Marketing Math Workbook.

L3 Assign and review Chapter 21 activities in the *BusinessWeek* Reader and Case Studies.

Marketing Practice

Ask students to take an inventory of products in their home that are made in a foreign country. Direct them to create a table with the product in one column and the country in another. Then have them choose one product and think about its distribution process to the United States. Have them describe the process below their table.

farm stores, auto parts retailers, supermarkets, drugstores, hardware stores, warehouse clubs, and other mass merchandisers to reach the maximum number of customers.

E-Commerce

E-commerce is the means by which products are sold to customers and industrial buyers through the Internet. You already learned that e-tailing is retail selling over the Internet. This online shopping location is called the **e-marketplace**.

In 2004, Internet travel bookings were estimated at $54 billion, which was 23 percent of the travel industry's revenues. Consumers have also become accustomed to buying books, toys, and other goods online.

E-marketplaces for B2B operations provide one-stop shopping and substantial savings for industrial buyers. Online catalogs of products supplied by different companies make it easier for corporate buyers to compare prices and get the best deal. E-marketplaces provide smaller businesses with the exposure that they could not get elsewhere.

In each of the past five years, a greater proportion of B2B trade has taken place via the Internet. This trend is expected to continue for some time.

Legal and Ethical Considerations in Distribution

In most cases, businesses may use whatever channel arrangement they desire. Laws affecting channels generally prevent exclusionary tactics that might keep other companies from using a desired channel. The Clayton Antitrust Act of 1914 prevents exclusive arrangements that substantially lessen competition,

GLOBAL MARKET

Marketing Multiculturalism

Convention and visitors' bureaus in many American cities provide guides, maps, and other information about ethnic history and culture they hope will appeal to African Americans, Hispanics, or Asians. They act as marketing agents for their areas, indirectly bringing potential consumers to local businesses.

Destination Marketing Convention bureaus have always marketed their cities in different ways to different business or professional groups. Destination marketers recognize that focusing on ethnic history, food, and cultural events and activities can attract tourists and business travelers—and dollars—from different ethnic groups. In addition to convention bureaus, groups representing minority businesses, such as the African American Chamber of Commerce, publish brochures promoting black-owned businesses to African American visitors to their city. Such groups, along with many city governments, help support festivals and celebrations of ethnic holidays such as Chinese New Year, Cinco de Mayo, or Kwanzaa.

CRITICAL THINKING
How could businesses promote a city's Cinco de Mayo celebration to visitors?

@ Online Action!
Go to *marketingessentials.glencoe.com/21/ global* to find an activity on distribution and multicultural marketing.

GLOBAL MARKET

Marketing Multiculturalism

Discussion Ask students: How does multiculturalism influence mainstream interests, such as restaurants, fashion, books, music, and so on? Have students share their responses.

CRITICAL THINKING **Answer:** Answers will vary and may include a Web site, ads in newspapers and magazines with a heavy Latino readership, and ads on Spanish-language TV.

@ Online Action! For instructions, ideas, and answer guide, go to the Teacher Center at **marketingessentials.glencoe.com**

Follow Up Ask students to research the demographics of their town. Direct students to write a 100-word response on how they envision the changing face of their town over the next 25 years.

create a monopoly, or in which one party did not commit to the agreement voluntarily.

Some distribution practices meet legal requirements but may be ethically questionable. The American Marketing Association (AMA) Code of Ethics lists the following responsibilities in the area of distribution:

- Not manipulating the availability of a product for purpose of exploitation
- Not using coercion in the marketing channel
- Not exerting undue influence over the reseller's decision whether to handle the product.

Distribution Planning for Foreign Markets

Foreign market environments require that businesses adjust their distribution systems. They also give businesses a chance to experiment with different distribution strategies. For example, in the United States, General Motors distributes automobiles through franchised retail car dealerships. However, in Taiwan, GM owns its own retail dealerships and sells cars directly to consumers. In Taiwan, GM is free from franchise dealer constraints and has been able to test systems for selling cars to consumers directly over the Internet.

Cultural considerations should also be weighed when planning distribution in foreign markets. For example, when Reebok wanted to sell its athletic shoes in Europe, it studied European culture and found that Europeans visit sporting goods stores far less often than Americans. The company decided to distribute Reebok's shoes through hundreds of traditional retail shoe outlets. Within one year of adopting this distribution strategy, Reebok's sales in France doubled.

 21.2 AFTER YOU READ

Reviewing Key Terms and Concepts

1. Why might a company decide to use multiple distribution channels?
2. What are the factors a company must consider when choosing between a direct sales force and independent sales agents?
3. What are two advantages that e-commerce provides in B2B sales?

Integrating Academic Skills

Math

4. Assume manufacturer A had sales of $3,500,000 and sales expenses of 8 percent for outside sales agents. Manufacturer B, a rival company, had sales of $5,750,000 for the same period. Its sales expenses were $402,500. Which company had the lowest rate of sales expenses?

Language Arts

5. Look up the definitions for each of the following words in the American Marketing Association's Code of Ethics: *manipulate, availability, exploit, coercion, exert,* and *undue.* Then, rewrite each of the statements from the code in your own words.

 Online Action! Check your answers at *marketingessentials.glencoe.com/21/read*

marketingessentials.glencoe.com

Chapter 21 - Channels of Distribution **457**

Ask students to recall and provide answers to the following questions:

- Give two reasons for using a direct sales force instead of independent sales agents.

  A manufacturer may use a direct sales force when it wants complete control or when it only needs to service existing accounts.

- What problem might be created by a clothing manufacturer that establishes its own Web site to sell to the final consumer, while it also sells the same items to retailers for resale to consumers?

  Its supplier would become its competitor.

 Critical Thinking

Ask students to brainstorm some concepts being applied to the legal and ethical considerations in distribution.

AFTER YOU READ

Reviewing Key Terms and Concepts

1. A company may use multiple distribution channels when its product fits the need of both industrial and customer markets.

2. They must consider costs and control. A direct sales force is costlier to maintain but offers companies greater control over how its product is sold and allows for easier monitoring of sales agents; conversely, independent sales agents are cheaper to maintain but harder to monitor and control.

3. E-marketplaces for B2B operations provide one-stop shopping and the potential for substantial cost savings.

Integrating Academic Skills

4. Manufacturer A's sales expense = $280,000. Manufacturer B's rate = 7 percent. Manufacturer B's rate is lower.

5. Code of Ethics statements will vary; student rewrites should demonstrate an understanding of the terms.

 Online Action! Answers at **marketingessentials.glencoe.com/21/read**

CAREERS IN MARKETING

Lifelong Learning

CAREER INFORMATION

Have students go to marketingessentials.glencoe.com and find the Chapter 21 Careers page and click on the link for the American Marketing Association's Careers Strategies and Tips. Ask students to select one article, read it, and summarize it in three short paragraphs.

CHANNELS OF DISTRIBUTION

Knowing about distribution channels can make students better consumers and marketers. As technology makes home shopping easier, consumers need to evaluate products and their usefulness. Perceiving the pros and cons of each channel can help students determine the best one for each product.

Primary Source

Ask students to go to marketingessentials.glencoe.com to find Chapter 21 Resources. Ask them to click on the link for the American Marketing Association's marketing dictionary and read the definitions of terms relating to channels of distribution.

THINKING CRITICALLY

Good customer service aids in creating a loyal clientele and encourages the most effective marketing technique, word-of-mouth recommendations.

@ Online Action!

For instructions, ideas, and answer guide, go to the Teacher Center at marketingessentials.glencoe.com

---

JUSTIN STERLING MOODY
OWNER
FUSIONIST.COM

? What do you do at work?
I own and operate a network of online stores, focused on high-quality products from the hip-hop and underground youth cultures.
  We build everything, from the store section to the entire Web site. My resume includes bobmarley.com, fatburger.com, mearone.com, saberone.com, shopbelton.com, awolone.com and fusionist.com.
  I also manage the inventory and distribution of products sold through Fusionist, and I provide consultation concerning print media projects.

? What skills are most important to you?
My most important skill is customer service. Learning how to use a computer is absolutely essential, too. Although you don't need a degree to start your own business, everyone needs to experience college or some type of skill training school.

? What is your key to success?
My key to success is to never quit. If you try and try again, you are bound to get it right.

Aptitudes, Abilities, and Skills

Strong interpersonal skills, technical knowledge, and ability to maintain the IT back-end of a Web site

Education and Training

Many Web entrepreneurs are entirely self-taught, although courses do exist focusing on e-commerce and Web marketing.

Career Path

For many Web retailers, careers begin as a hobby, selling and shipping products that are of personal interest. Larger operations can often develop over time if demand is great enough, and if the logistics of the operation can keep up with this demand.

THINKING CRITICALLY

Why is customer service often considered the most valuable skill an entrepreneur can possess?

@ Online Action!

Go to *marketingessentials.glencoe.com/ 21/careers* to find a career-related activity.

Test-Taking Strategies

Ask students to take the headings from this chapter and turn them into questions. After they have completed their questions on a piece of paper, direct the students to exchange their questions. During the exchange, students will provide answers to each other's questions. Allow up to 10 minutes for students to fill in the answers or look them up in the text.

FOCUS on KEY POINTS

SECTION 21.1
- Manufacturers or producers may choose one or more paths (channels) to distribute products to the final user.

- The channels used to distribute consumer products usually differ from those used to distribute to the industrial market.

SECTION 21.2
- Manufacturers or producers may use multiple channels of distribution to reach different markets. Product distribution in foreign markets often requires special planning.

- Distribution intensity may be exclusive, selective, or intensive.

REVIEW VOCABULARY

Working in a group, choose a company and explain how it sells products to consumers and industrial buyers. Include the following terms:

1. channel of distribution (p. 444)
2. intermediaries (p. 446)
3. wholesalers (p. 446)
4. rack jobbers (p. 446)
5. drop shippers (p. 447)
6. retailers (p. 447)
7. brick-and-mortar retailers (p. 447)
8. e-tailing (p. 448)
9. agents (p. 448)
10. direct distribution (p. 449)
11. indirect distribution (p. 452)
12. exclusive distribution (p. 455)
13. selective distribution (p. 455)
14. intensive distribution (p. 455)
15. integrated distribution (p. 455)
16. e-marketplace (p. 456)

REVIEW FACTS and IDEAS

17. A marketer makes a place decision by selecting channels of distribution. What does this mean? (21.1)

18. What is another name for intermediaries? Name two types of intermediaries. (21.1)

19. Name five non-store retailing methods. (21.1)

20. What is the most common method of distribution for consumer products and services? For industrial products and services? (21.1)

21. What are the key questions a firm must consider in establishing a distribution plan? (21.2)

22. Explain why manufacturers sometimes use exclusive distribution. (21.2)

23. How do the costs of having a direct sales force differ from the costs of using independent sales agents? How do the controls differ? (21.2)

24. Name the three levels of distribution intensity and give one advantage of each. (21.2)

Chapter 21 - Channels of Distribution 459

REVIEW FACTS and IDEAS

17. This means that the marketer has decided what places the product will be distributed to reach potential buyers.

18. Another name for intermediaries is middlemen. Two types are merchant intermediaries and agent intermediaries.

19. Automatic retailers, direct mail retailers, catalog retailers, TV home shopping, and online retailing

20. Indirect channels; direct channels.

21. Key questions include the use of multiple channels, control of sales versus cost of sales, intensity of distribution desired, and use of e-commerce.

22. Manufacturers sometimes use exclusive distribution because their products are appropriate for both the industrial and the consumer markets.

23. A direct sales force is generally more expensive than sales agents. An in-house or direct sales force gives the producer more control over the product than they obtain with sales agents.

24. The three levels of distribution intensity are exclusive distribution, selective distribution, and intensive distribution. Exclusive distribution provides prestige, image control, and a high profit margin. Selective distribution maintains image, reduces credit risks, and insures more aggressive marketing. Intensive distribution provides maximum market coverage for the most sales possible.

FOCUS on KEY POINTS

Ask volunteers to read the summaries aloud in class and offer one real-life example of each concept.

REVIEW VOCABULARY

See glossary for definitions of **1–16.** Student explanations will vary but should include the terms listed and demonstrate an understanding of their definitions.

BUILD SKILLS

25. Workplace Skills
Memos will vary. Memos should use a professional, business like tone. The memo should clearly explain all appropriate channels of distribution with a rationale for each.

26. Technology Applications
Tables will vary; all tables should include quantities sold, per item cost, and shipping and handling charges.

27. Math Practice
You will save $1.56; $9.00 − [$6.20 + ($6.20 × 0.20)] = $1.56.

DEVELOP CRITICAL THINKING

28. Researching Key Concepts
Answers will vary. Suggest that students prepare for the interview with a list of questions about distribution channels.

29. Select a Level of Distribution
The exclusivity of the product often determines which type of distribution density is warranted.

BUILD SKILLS

25. Workplace Skills
Writing Your sporting goods manufacturing company wants to sell its exercise equipment products to fitness centers, schools, and individual consumers. As the assistant marketing manager, you have been asked to give your opinion on distribution channels. Write a memo (or an e-mail message) to your marketing manager identifying the channels that you think would best serve each market.

26. Technology Applications
Compare Shipping Costs Your company uses 24-inch mailing tubes to ship its products. Log onto the Internet and locate three distributors for this item. Using a word processing program, create a table comparing the information from each source such as quantities in which the tubes are sold and the stated per item cost. Also compare shipping and handling charges.

27. Math Practice
Calculate Savings The price of a best-selling paperback is $9.00 at a local bookstore. You can purchase the same book through an e-tailer for $6.20 plus 20 percent for shipping charges. How much will you save by purchasing the book through the e-tailer?

DEVELOP CRITICAL THINKING

28. Researching Key Concepts
Interview a marketing manager of a local manufacturer to learn what distribution channels the company uses to sell its products. Or, interview the buyer of a local retail business to learn which channels it uses to purchase its goods. Ask the person you are interviewing to explain how these decisions were made.

29. Select a Level of Distribution
Which level of distribution (intensive, selective, or exclusive) would you choose for the following products:
- Personal computers
- Cashmere sweaters
- A new brand of shampoo
- A new hybrid car

Formative Assessment

Formative assessment is an essential component of classroom work. This type of assessment provides information that is then used as feedback to modify teaching and meet student needs.

L1 Review key terms for this chapter. Ask students to write one sentence for each key term.

L2 Provide various examples of factors that affect distribution in story form. After each story, have the students identify which factors affect distribution.

L3 Ask students to create stories that illustrate effective channels of distribution.

 Reteach If results of this formative assessment seem low, consider the following activity:
Read the sections' objectives and subheads. Then, ask students to draw conclusions based on the concepts in this simple outline.

APPLY CONCEPTS

30. Determining Distribution Intensity

Design a product for a manufacturing company to produce. Define the market for your product. Then select the level of intensity that you think would be best for the distribution of your product.

Activity Use a word processing program to describe your product, your intended market, and your preferred distribution intensity. Provide your rationale for the level of intensity that you chose.

31. Compare E-Commerce to Brick-and-Mortar Shopping

Select a destination for a weekend trip. Log onto a travel site on the Internet. Using the Web site, determine what it will cost you to fly to your destination. Then investigate hotel expenses for a two-night stay. Record your information. Next, ask a local travel agent to help you plan the same trip.

Activity Write a brief report comparing the results of your two shopping experiences. Describe the pros and cons of each method.

NET SAVVY

32. Internet Searches and Marketing

Select a product you would like to purchase. Use a search engine to find e-tailers selling the product or log on to the Web sites of companies that you know would sell the product you wish to purchase.

 marketingessentials.glencoe.com

 THE ◀**DECA** CONNECTION

Role Play: Channels of Distribution

Situation You are to assume the role of assistant manager of a lighting and lamp store. Your store manager is considering adding a line of lamps from a new vendor. The vendor will ship lamps purchased from the line directly to the customer. The direct shipping means a delay of one day longer than your store delivery. This also means the store can sell the lamps at somewhat lower prices since the store does not have to store the lamps at the warehouse or deliver them to customers.

Activity You are to explain to a customer (judge) why waiting the extra day for delivery means lower prices for these lamps.

Evaluation You will be evaluated on how well you meet the following performance indicators:

- Explain the relationship between customer service and distribution
- Explain storing considerations
- Handle customer inquiries
- Explain channel-member relationships

 @ Online Action!

For more information and DECA Prep practice, go to *marketingessentials.glencoe .com/21/DECA*

Chapter 21 - Channels of Distribution **461**

APPLY CONCEPTS

30. Determining Distribution Intensity

Product reports will vary; students should provide a clear and convincing rationale.

31. Compare E-Commerce to Brick-and-Mortar Shopping

Comparisons will vary; students should describe both advantages and disadvantages of each method.

NET SAVVY

32. Internet Searches and Marketing

Purchasing decisions will vary. Accept all answers that show student understanding of e-tailing.

MINI-QUIZ

Administer the Mini-Quiz orally. Answers will be either true or false.

1. When one or more intermediaries are involved in a channel, the distribution is considered indirect. (true)

2. The path a product takes from producer or manufacturer is called its channel of distribution. (false, the process requires the inclusion of the final user as well)

3. All the businesses involved in sales transactions that move products from the manufacturer to the final user are called intermediaries or middlemen. (true)

For an expanded chapter quiz, go to Chapter 21 in the TeacherWorks CD-ROM and to Chapter 21 in the **ExamView®** Pro Test Generator CD-ROM.

 THE ◀**DECA** CONNECTION

Students should be evaluated according to the performance standards noted in the role play. For another DECA role play, go to the Competitive Events Workbook or the Student Activity Workbook, or go to **marketingessentials.glencoe.com/21/DECA**

 @ Online Action! For instructions, ideas, and answer guide, go to the Teacher Center at **marketingessentials.glencoe.com**

DECA Advisors Corner

Participating in an international marketing exchange program with an international partner school will teach your chapter members more about the global marketplace. Students can gain a wealth of knowledge through communicating with your international partners in person or via technology.

Chapter Overview

Chapter 22 examines physical distribution, which is the process of transporting, storing, order processing, stock handling, and inventory control of materials and products on the way from the manufacturer to the consumer.

BUILD BACKGROUND

Initiate a discussion about the various types of physical distribution available to businesses. Compile a list on the board as students reveal their answers. Then ask students to define product storage and list real-world examples of each type of distribution and storage.

Why It's Important

Businesses trust that their products are carried by a reliable and trustworthy distributor. Without this guarantee, businesses will select another carrier from the assortment of options.

Prepare to Read

Ask students to imagine that they are the authors of this chapter. Before writing it, they should create an outline to guide their writing. Make sure they do not look ahead in the chapter, but create an original outline on their own. This brief activity requires them to think critically about the topic of physical distribution. As they work their way through the chapter, they can compare and contrast their original outline with the chapter's structure.

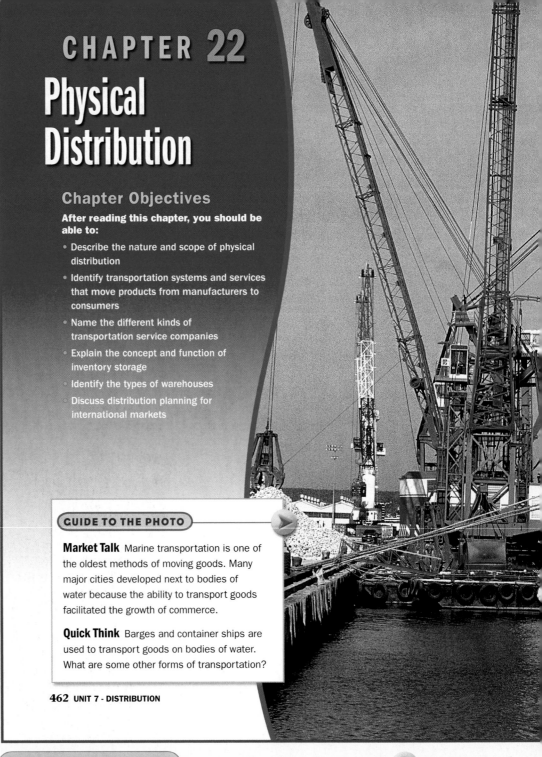

CHAPTER 22
Physical Distribution

Chapter Objectives

After reading this chapter, you should be able to:

- Describe the nature and scope of physical distribution
- Identify transportation systems and services that move products from manufacturers to consumers
- Name the different kinds of transportation service companies
- Explain the concept and function of inventory storage
- Identify the types of warehouses
- Discuss distribution planning for international markets

GUIDE TO THE PHOTO

Market Talk Marine transportation is one of the oldest methods of moving goods. Many major cities developed next to bodies of water because the ability to transport goods facilitated the growth of commerce.

Quick Think Barges and container ships are used to transport goods on bodies of water. What are some other forms of transportation?

462 UNIT 7 - DISTRIBUTION

GUIDE TO THE PHOTO

Market Talk Lead a discussion about the closest port to your community. This port may be in the same city or hundreds or thousands of miles away. Either way, allow the students to speculate where barges may arrive from based on the directional geography. Also, have students speculate about the types of goods available in those shipments based on the countries or places of origin.

Quick Think Student responses may include motor carriers, airplanes, pipelines, and railroads.

Follow Up Ask students to identify three major types of distribution that they have witnessed in their local area.

Performance indicators represent key skills and knowledge. Relating them to the concepts explained in this chapter is your key to success in DECA events. Keep this in mind as you read this chapter and take notes each time you encounter material that helps you master a key concept. These acronyms represent DECA events that involve knowledge of concepts in this chapter.

AAAL*	FMAL*	MMS	TMDM
AAML*	FMDM	QSRM	TSE
ADC	FMML*	RMAL*	VPM*
BSM	FSRM	RMML*	
EMDM*	HMDM	SMDM	

In all these DECA events you should be able to follow these performance indicators:

- Explain the nature and scope of distribution
- Explain the nature of warehousing
- Explain shipping processes
- Use an information system for order fulfillment

All the events with an asterisk (*) also include these performance indicators:

- Complete documents used in shipping goods
- Trace lost shipments
- Select best shipping method
- Analyze shipping needs

Some events include additional performance indicators. These are:

EMDM   Fulfill orders

Analyze capabilities of electronic business systems to facilitate order fulfillment

Assess order fulfillment processes

DECA PREP

Check your understanding of DECA performance indicators with the DECA activity in this chapter's review. For more information and DECA Prep practice, go to *marketingessentials .glencoe.com/22/DECA*

---

marketingessentials.glencoe.com

Chapter 22 - Physical Distribution **463**

THE **DECA** An Association of Marketing Students

CONNECTION

DECA events that require knowledge of physical distribution are described here. Discuss the performance indicators to make sure students understand how to demonstrate their understanding.

The events acronyms stand for:

AAAL: Apparel and Accessories Marketing Series, AL

AAML: Apparel and Accessories Marketing Series, ML

ADC: Advertising Campaign Event

BSM: Business Services Marketing Series

EMDM: E-Commerce Management Team Decision Making Event

FMAL: Food Marketing Series, AL

FMDM: Financial Analysis Management Team Decision Making Event

FMML: Food Marketing Series, ML

FSRM: Full Service Restaurant Management Series

HMDM: Hospitality Services Management Team Decision Making Event

MMS: Marketing Management Series

QSRM: Quick Serve Restaurant Management Series

RMAL: Retail Merchandising Series, AL

RMML: Retail Merchandising Series, ML

SMDM: Sports and Entertainment Marketing Management Team Decision Making Event

TMDM: Travel and Tourism Marketing Management Team Decision Making Event

TSE: Technical Sales Event

VPM: Vehicles and Petroleum Marketing Series

DECA PREP

Find timed DECA Prep activities correlated to the Competitive Events Workbook for students and DECA tips for teachers at **marketingessentials.glencoe.com /22/DECA**

CHAPTER 22   Classroom Resources

For the Teacher

- TeacherWorks
- marketingessentials.glencoe.com
- Interactive Chalkboard
- **Exam***View*® Pro Test Generator
- Fast File Unit 7

For the Student

- *Marketing Essentials* Online Edition
- Student Activity Workbook
- Marketing Math Workbook
- Marketing Research Project Workbook
- School-to-Work Activity Workbook
- Competitive Events Workbook
- *BusinessWeek* Reader and Case Studies
- marketingessentials.glencoe.com

SECTION 22.1

FOCUS

Introducing the Section

COLLABORATIVE ACTIVITY

Ask students to imagine a company's management team has asked them to evaluate its current transportation system. The company is deciding between a common carrier, its own private fleet, or a combination of both to transport its products. Ask the students to identify and share with the class the advantages and disadvantages of each transportation alternative.

Preteaching Key Terms

Ask students to read this section's key terms and create familiar words beside the unfamiliar ones found on that list.

- physical distribution
- transportation
- common carriers
- contract carriers
- private carriers
- exempt carriers
- ton-mile
- carload
- freight forwarders

Critical Thinking

Ask students to identify assumptions they can make about a distribution business that does not run smoothly. Answers may include dissatisfied customers and slow delivery.

OBJECTIVES

- Describe the nature and scope of physical distribution
- Identify transportation systems and services that move products from manufacturers to consumers
- Name the different kinds of transportation service companies

KEY TERMS

- physical distribution
- transportation
- common carriers
- contract carriers
- private carriers
- exempt carriers
- ton-mile
- carload
- freight forwarders

WHILE YOU READ

Read for Details
Keep a list of government agencies that regulate the physical distribution of goods.

464 UNIT 7 - DISTRIBUTION

Transportation Systems and Services

READ and STUDY

BEFORE YOU READ
Predict Why is distribution so important to the marketing concept of place?

THE MAIN IDEA
To succeed in today's business environment, a company must deliver its products to customers around the country and throughout the world in the most efficient and effective way.

STUDY ORGANIZER
Use a figure like the one below to list the advantages and disadvantages of each type of transportation system.

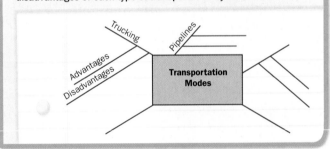

The Nature and Scope of Physical Distribution

After a company decides on its channels of distribution, it must plan for actually moving its products through those channels. Physical distribution is the key link between a business and its customers. **Physical distribution** comprises all the activities that help to ensure that the right amount

---

READ and STUDY

BEFORE YOU READ
Remind students that place utility involves having a product where customers can buy it.

THE MAIN IDEA
Ask students to list specific ideas about what makes a distributor efficient and how that benefits the user.

STUDY ORGANIZER
Model the study organizer for students by filling in an advantage. A full-size, downloadable study organizer can be found at marketingessentials.glencoe.com

  Ask students to visit the Web sites of these agencies and write down any questions they might have about the agencies' roles. Review the questions in discussion.

of product is delivered to the right place at the right time.

Physical distribution is also known as logistics. It involves order processing, transporting, storing, stock handling, and inventory control of materials and products. Figure 22.1 presents an overview of these functions. Physical distribution is the third-largest expense for most businesses. It is surpassed only by the costs of material and labor.

Businesses need to make the physical distribution system as efficient and cost effective as possible. At the same time, physical distribution needs to be coordinated with other business functions, such as purchasing, finance, production, packaging, and promotion. Suppose a business has planned to launch promotional ads for a new product available on a certain date. If the distribution system is unreliable, the product may not arrive at stores in time. This error will cost the business customers and cause the business to lose credibility.

Types of Transportation Systems

Transportation is the marketing function of moving a product from the place where it is made to the place where it is sold. Transportation costs are a significant part of each sale; therefore, manufacturers, wholesalers, and retailers look for the most cost-effective delivery methods.

There are five major transportation systems, or modes, which move products, including trucks, railroads, waterways, pipelines, and air carriers. Figure 22.2 shows the percentage of freight carried by each transportation mode.

Trucking

On certain U.S. highways, such as the Ohio Turnpike, about 30 percent of the miles driven are driven by commercial vehicles. Trucks, or motor carriers, are the most frequently used transportation mode. They carry higher-valued products that are expensive for a business to keep in inventory. They also carry products such as produce that have very limited shelf life. Lightweight shipments transported over moderate distances are generally handled by

trucks—nearly 80 percent of those shipments weigh less than 1,000 pounds each. Businesses use trucks for virtually all intracity (within a city) shipping and for 26 percent of the intercity (between cities) freight traffic in the United States.

State and federal transportation agencies regulate motor carriers used for interstate (between states) commerce. For example, they regulate the number of hours motor carrier operators can drive without stopping and the length of their rest periods. State transportation agencies regulate fuel taxes, safety issues, and rates charged for intrastate (within a state) trucking.

Types of Carriers

Businesses that use trucks to move their products have several different options. They can use for-hire carriers, private carriers, or a combination of both. For-hire carriers include common carriers and contract carriers.

Common carriers provide transportation services to any business in their operating area for a fee. Carriers can change their rates or geographical areas, as long as they do not charge rates that are different from their published rates. More than one-third of all motor freight is handled by common carriers. Less-than-truckload carriers provide shipments in which freight from multiple shippers are consolidated into a single truckload.

Contract carriers are for-hire carriers that provide equipment and drivers for specific routes, according to agreements between the carrier and the shipper. A contract carrier can provide services on a one-time basis or on a continuing basis.

Contract carriers usually transport goods for more than one business, and they can charge different rates to each business. However, they must file their contracts with the appropriate state or federal regulatory agency.

A major advantage of using for-hire carriers is that the business does not need to invest in transportation equipment. However, for-hire carriers offer less flexibility for special pick-ups or handling, rush deliveries, and direct shipments.

Chapter 22 - Physical Distribution **465**

TEACH

Discussion Starter

TYPES OF TRANSPORTATION SYSTEMS

Ask students to imagine they are in charge of the marketing campaign for Clean Air Week during May 24–30. Their campaign is to target transportation companies in the country. Have the students outline which distribution companies they will target—ones that might pollute the air the most. Then, they need to outline possible tangible solutions these companies can take for a week or longer to help clean up the environment. Ask students to prepare a 10-minute persuasive presentation on their campaign in front of the class.

TEACHING POINTS

Model Details and statistics are elements used in a persuasive campaign to bring home the realness of a topic. Bring these to class to illustrate the need for vigilant environmental awareness on the part of businesses as well as consumers.

Explain Give details on how Congress enacted the Clean Air Act Amendments. List how these have affected the transportation industry.

Critical Thinking

Companies are required to provide extensive lists of items in shipments now. Ask students how this affects the company. Answers might include expense and time to file and fill out the paperwork.

Extended Activity

Power Sources and Distribution

Ask students to speculate why public and private companies that provide distribution services might concern themselves with political and economic issues regarding energy sources, such as oil, gas, natural gas, hydroelectric power, and so on. Have students who are interested in this topic research distribution companies who are funding or using alternative energy sources and provide a brief summary of what they learned to the class.

Concept Development

PHYSICAL DISTRIBUTION

Ask students how federal agencies have placed heavy government regulations on the physical distribution system since the September 11, 2001, terrorist attack. Ask students if they think the regulations imposed will help or hamper the system of efficiency in the industry. Have students prepare a five-minute oral presentation on their findings.

Answers will vary; for example, the FDA receives 20,000 reports daily on food shipments in order to thwart any terrorist activity on the food supply.

TEACHING POINTS

Explain The Department of Transportation has increased regulations and background checks on passengers, crews, and cargo within the airline industry, which costs $100 million to implement; consumers defray the cost.

Demonstrate You may want to bring to class updated research on the Department of Transportation and the new policies and regulations it imposed on the industry. Use this information to discuss and contextualize the real-world distribution in today's world compared to 10 or 20 years ago.

Build Vocabulary

Ask students to differentiate *interstate* from *intrastate*. Then have them list interstate highway and intrastate roads in your region.

Interstate links two or more states; *intrastate* occur within a state.

Figure 22.1 *Physical Distribution*

• **Moving and Counting** Physical distribution involves the functions of order processing, transportation, storage, stock handling, and inventory control.

How does physical distribution work?

TRANSPORTATION

Transportation involves the actual physical movement of products. It is estimated that up to eight percent of a company's sales revenue is spent on the transportation function.

STOCK HANDLING

Receiving, checking, and marking items for sale are important steps in the physical distribution system.

ORDER PROCESSING

The purchase of a product initiates the movement of products through a physical distribution system.

STORAGE

The storage function facilitates the movement of products through the distribution channel as products are sold.

INVENTORY CONTROL

Proper inventory control ensures that products are kept in sufficient quantities and available when requested by customers.

@ Online Action! Go to *marketingessentials.glencoe.com/22/figure/1* to find a project on physical distribution.

 marketingessentials.glencoe.com

Figure 22.1 *Physical Distribution*

Discussion Ask students to indicate which type of physical distribution they would use to transport the following goods:

- coal
- fruit
- tulips from Holland to the U.S.
- exotic fish from Florida to California

- small overnight parcel
- coffee beans shipped from South America to the U.S.
- electronics equipment

Caption Answer Physical distribution begins when an order is processed. Handlers make sure the proper inventory is in stock in the storage facility before the product is transported to its final destination.

 @ Online Action! For instructions, ideas, and answer guide, go to the Teacher Center at **marketingessentials.glencoe.com**

Figure 22.2 Transportation Systems

• **The Importance of Single-Mode Transportation Systems** This pie chart shows the percentage of freight in ton-miles shipped by each mode of transportation.

Why do you think the percentage carried by trucks is so large?

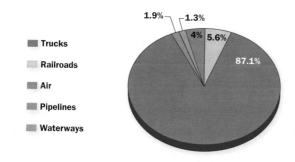

- ■ Trucks
- ■ Railroads
- ■ Air
- ■ Pipelines
- ■ Waterways

1.9% 1.3%
4% 5.6%
87.1%

Source: Bureau of Census, 1997

 Online Action!
Go to *marketingessentials.glencoe.com/22/figure/2* to find a project on modes of transportation.

Private Carriers

Private carriers transport goods for an individual business. The transportation equipment can be owned or leased to meet the specific transportation needs of the business. Significant capital investment is required, however, if a business decides to own and maintain its own private fleet.

Cost is a major factor in selecting transportation. Starting a private carrier operation requires a large investment in equipment and facilities. However, private carriers let a business maintain total control over equipment, maintenance, availability, routes, delivery times, and handling procedures. This also allows a business to rapidly change schedules, routes, and delivery times to meet customers' needs.

Many businesses use a combination of private and for-hire carriers. They may use their own trucks for local deliveries and common or contract carriers for shipments beyond their local service areas.

Exempt carriers are free from direct regulation of rates and operating procedures. In most cases, they carry agricultural products. Their rates are lower than those charged by common carriers because of their exempt status. Local transportation firms may also receive exempt status if they make short-distance deliveries within specified trading areas in cities.

Some disadvantages of trucks are that they cost more than rail and water carriers, and they are susceptible to delays due to traffic jams and road conditions. Trucks are also subject to size and weight restrictions, which can vary state-to-state.

Intermodal Transportation

Intermodal transportation combines two or more transportation modes to maximize the advantages of each. Piggyback service is carrying loaded truck trailers over land on railroad flatcars. Trucks will then take the trailers

marketingessentials.glencoe.com

Chapter 22 - Physical Distribution 467

TEACH CONTINUED

Individualized Practice

TYPES OF CARRIERS

L1 Ask students to create a table that lists various common carriers and defines the types of goods they transport in their local area.

L2 Ask students to imagine they have hired a residential moving common carrier to move household goods. They conducted their research online and found an inexpensive carrier but it required three-fourths payment upfront. Ask students to research any regulations governing residential moving carriers in a 150-word report. They should think about how regulations protect the consumer, particularly when it comes to transporting people's valuables?

L3 According to the Department of Homeland Security (DHS), within one year it tracked the following: 730 million travelers on commercial airlines, over 700 million pieces of baggage, 11.2 million trucks, and 2.2 million rail cars. Given these grand statistics, ask students to research and write a 500-word essay on the role and responsibility of the DHS. In their report, ask them to include how politics has influenced the formation of this department.

Critical Thinking

Ask students: Why might a business use more than one form of distribution?

Figure 22.2 Transportation Systems

Discussion Ask students to discuss why distribution centers can also be production centers. Have students suggest products that can be processed on their way to their final destination. Answers could include crude oil, which can be processed into gasoline, heating oil, and jet fuel; or cotton, which can be processed into thread and then textiles.

Caption Answer Answers might include that trucks are the most cost-effective method of transport and can easily cover both short and long distances to fulfill orders.

 Online Action! For instructions, ideas, and answer guide, go to the Teacher Center at **marketingessentials.glencoe.com**

Individualized Practice

RAILROADS

 L1 Ask students to create a list of regions and metropolitan areas in the United State that have a well-networked rail system for passenger travel.

L2 Ask students to imagine they are responsible for transporting dangerous goods by rail. They should research if there are any rules of compliance for carrying hazardous materials. Students should report their findings in a 100-word journal entry.

L3 Ask students to research the changes in the national security standards on the rail system over the past few years. They should prepare at least six minutes of material for a class presentation.

Critical Thinking

Ask the students how they think the natural world is impacted by infrastructure for transportation systems.

---

to their destinations. Fishyback service is shipping loaded truck trailers over water on ships and barges. Piggyback and fishyback services combine advantages of truck transportation with the lower costs of rail and marine transportation.

Railroads

Railroads are another major form of transportation in the United States. Trains transport nearly six percent of the total intercity ton-miles of freight. A **ton-mile** is the movement of one ton (2,000 lbs) of freight one mile.

Trains are important for moving heavy and bulky freight, such as coal, steel, lumber, chemicals, grain, farm equipment, and automobiles over long distances. Refrigerated cars keep perishable products such as milk or fresh vegetables from spoiling over long distances. Other specially designed freight cars haul combustible or hazardous materials, such as chemicals.

• **TWO IS BETTER THAN ONE** Often, intermodal transportation is used to get goods to the customer.

Why might a company use both rail and road shipping methods?

Pricing and Delivery Services

Shippers pay lower rail transportation rates if they fill an entire boxcar. A **carload** is the minimum number of pounds of freight needed to fill a boxcar. Carload weights are established for different classifications of goods. Once a shipment reaches the minimum weight, the shipper pays the lower rate, regardless of the physical size of the shipment. Rates charged for less-than-carload shipments are more expensive because partial carloads have to be unloaded at each destination.

Advantages and Disadvantages of Railroad Transportation

Railroads are one of lowest cost transportation modes because trains carry large quantities at relatively low per unit costs. Trains need 50 to 70 percent less energy than a motor carrier to transport freight, and they are seldom slowed or stopped by bad weather. This makes trains one of the safest modes of transportation.

The biggest disadvantage of rail transport is the lack of flexibility. Trains can pick up and deliver goods only at stations along designated rail lines.

Marine Shipping

Barges and container ships transport merchandise within the United States and around the world. Container ships carry their loads in either 20- or 40-foot-long standardized truck-size containers. The United States Maritime Commission regulates U.S. marine shipping.

Waterways

Inland shipping is shipping from one port to another on connecting rivers and lakes. The St. Lawrence Seaway, which is a combination of rivers, canals, and lakes, and the Mississippi and Ohio Rivers are all internal shipping routes that give ocean-going vessels access to the heartland of America.

Intracoastal shipping is the shipping of goods on inland and coastal waterways between ports along the same coast. For example, shipments can be sent from Virginia to North Carolina through the Great Dismal Swamp Canal.

PHOTO GUIDE — TWO IS BETTER THAN ONE

Discussion Ask students to discuss what kind of planning studies the state department of transportation might conduct. The students should also answer why the state spends money on such studies.

Caption Answer Possible answers include more efficiency, timeliness, and cost effectiveness (i.e., rail and water transportation cost less than truck transportation).

Follow Up Ask students to find the Bureau of Transportation Statistics online. They should browse the site and report to the class an interesting fact they learn.

International waterways are the oceans and rivers that connect continents and countries. Almost all overseas nonperishable freight is transported by container ships and barges because of the low cost. Products commonly shipped by international waterways include heavy equipment, steel, ore, forest products, grain, and petroleum.

Advantages and Disadvantages of Marine Shipping

The biggest advantage of marine transportation is the low cost: container ships and barges are the cheapest form of freight transportation. However, they are also the slowest form of transportation.

Marine shipping has other disadvantages. Buyers that are located far from the port city must have products off-loaded from container ships onto railroad cars or motor carriers to reach their destination. This added cost of distribution reduces some of the cost advantages of marine shipping.

Marine shipping is affected by bad weather and seasonal conditions. Great Lakes shipping, for example, is closed for two to three months in the winter.

Pipelines

Pipelines are usually owned by the company using them, and in these instances, they are considered private carriers. There are more than 200,000 miles of pipelines in the United States.

Pipelines are most frequently used to transport oil and natural gas. They move crude oil from oil fields to refineries, where it is processed. The refined products, such as gasoline, are then trucked to retail outlets such as your local gasoline station.

Advantages and Disadvantages of Pipelines

The construction of pipelines requires a high initial investment, but operational costs are relatively small. Pipeline transportation has the best safety record among all major transportation systems. Products carried through pipelines move slowly but continuously,

---

MARKET TECH

Scan and Bag as You Shop

National grocery chain, Albertsons, Inc., has introduced a Shop 'n' Scan system for shoppers who can scan and bag their groceries while they shop. Here are Albertsons' steps to using the system:

1. Take a Preferred Card to the Shop 'n' Scan display, scan the card, and wait for a handheld scanner to light up.
2. Use the scanner, store grocery bags, and a shopping cart while shopping.
3. Scan each item and place it in a bag.
4. If you return an item, scan it, and press the minus key.
5. If you can't remember whether you picked up something, scroll your list with the up and down keys.
6. Press the "i" key to see offers available only to Shop 'n' Scan customers.
7. At checkout, point the scanner at the "end of trip" bar code at the register and pull the trigger. That transfers your grocery list and prints a receipt. Pay as you would otherwise. There's no need to take your groceries out of the bags.
8. Place the scanner in a return rack.

THINK LIKE A MARKETER

What are some store and customer advantages and disadvantages for self-scanning devices?

@ Online Action!

Go to *marketingessentials.glencoe.com/22/tech* to find a project on scanning devices.

TEACH CONTINUED

Concept Development

PIPELINES

Inform students of the following facts: Pipelines carry about 24 percent of the ton-miles of freight transported in the United States. Air transportation is less than 1 percent of the ton-miles of freight shipped. Motor carriers ship 24 percent of the ton-miles of freight shipped; railroads ship one and one-half more.

Ask students to help create a pie chart titled Freight Shipment by Carrier that shows the percentage of ton-miles shipped by motor carrier, railroad, pipeline, air transportation, and waterways/others. They will have to determine the percentage of waterways/other, given the other statistics.

The graph should reflect the following percentages: motor carriers, 24 percent; railroads, 36 percent; pipelines, 24 percent; air transportation, 1 percent; waterways/other, 15 percent.

TEACHING POINTS

Demonstrate Use this as an example to help students find the percentage of ton-miles. Imagine motor carriers ship 24 percent of the ton-miles of freight in the United States. If railroads ship one and one-half times more freight than this, what percentage of the ton-miles ships by train?

36 percent; $1.5 \times 0.24 = 0.36$

 Critical Thinking

Ask students to identify how the protective packaging chosen by manufacturers is often determined by the type of transport.

MARKET TECH

Scan and Bag as You Shop

Discussion Ask students how technology and customer service interact within a retail environment. For example, students might relate an instance of how a store's technology has left them impressed or frustrated during a shopping experience.

THINK LIKE A MARKETER
Answer: Answers will vary; students may mention inventory issues, consumer control, efficiency, speed, convenience, timeliness, costs savings, customer service loss, and so on.

@ Online Action!
For instructions, ideas, and answer guide, go to the Teacher Center at **marketingessentials.glencoe.com**

ASSESS

Review Guide

CONCEPTS

Ask students to interview an adult about any online purchases they may have made. Ask them what swayed their decision to purchase a specific shipping method.

KEY TERMS

Have students review key terms, their spellings, and definitions in small groups.

ONLINE SELF-ASSESSMENT

Have students go to marketingessentials.glencoe.com for the Section 22.1 practice test.

Individualized Review

L1 Assign and review Chapter 22 activities in the Student Activity Workbook.

L2 Assign and review Chapter 22 activities in the Marketing Math Workbook.

L3 Assign and review Chapter 22 activities in the *BusinessWeek* Reader and Case Studies.

Marketing Practice

Convenience is worth the price in many instances when things are supposed to run smoothly. Ask students what products a store could sell with guaranteed timely delivery that would attract customers. Have students select a product and work in groups to create a 10-minute presentation on how that product will be delivered.

• **IT WILL BE THERE TOMORROW** Air transportation is a growing segment of the transportation industry.

What items are generally sent by air?

suffer minimal product damage or theft, and are not subject to delivery delays due to bad weather. The risk of a pipeline leak is low, but when a leak does occur, the damage to the environment can be extensive.

Air Cargo Services

Currently, air cargo services are less than one percent of the total ton-miles of freight shipped. High-value, low-weight, time-critical items such as overnight mail are often shipped by air. Certain high-value products, such as emergency parts, instruments, and medicines may also be shipped by air. Air cargo has space restraints, so products transported in smaller containers are well suited to this form of shipment.

The Federal Aviation Administration (FAA) regulates air transportation, but airlines and

air transport companies set their own rates. Air cargo service carriers offer such things as wide-bodied jets that can ship more goods and specialized packaging designed to help prevent damage.

Advantages and Disadvantages of Air Transportation

The greatest advantage for air transportation is its speed. This fast delivery time allows businesses to satisfy customers who need something quickly. It also reduces inventory expenses and storage costs.

The greatest disadvantage of air transportation is its cost. It is by far the most expensive form of distribution. Air cargo rates are at least twice as costly as truck rates. Other disadvantages of air cargo services include mechanical breakdowns and delays in delivery caused by bad weather.

Transportation Service Companies

Transportation service companies handle small- and medium-size packages. Some examples of these companies are the U.S. Postal Service, express delivery services, bus package carriers, and freight forwarders.

U.S. Postal Service

The U.S. Postal Service ships small packages by parcel post or first-class mail. For an extra fee, parcel post can be insured against loss or damage. Parcel post can also be express-mailed at higher rates to guarantee next-day delivery.

Express Delivery Services

Express delivery services specialize in delivering small, lightweight packages and high-priority mail usually weighing less than 150 pounds. Express delivery companies, such as Federal Express, DHL, and United Parcel Service, can deliver nationally or internationally by airplane, truck, bus, or train. Rates are based on speed of delivery, size and weight of package, distance to be sent, and type of service used. Regular service usually takes from two to three days; more expensive, next-day service is also available.

PHOTO GUIDE **IT WILL BE THERE TOMORROW**

Discussion Lead a discussion about the various overnight air cargo carriers students are most familiar with. Ask: What experiences do they have in sending and receiving high-priority packages?

Caption Answer High-value, low-weight, time-sensitive items; high-value products, such as emergency parts, instruments, and medicines, are often shipped by air.

Follow Up Ask students to compare prices among overnight air service providers for a work document that must leave their city and arrive in a destination of their choosing. The work papers fit inside a standard letter package. The providers' Web site allow users to select the size of package, priority status, and other options to offer a delivery cost. Ask: Which service would they select?

Over the last 35 years, express carriers have become a more important part of physical distribution. Federal Express, which began operations in 1971, transports an average of 3.1 million shipments daily. It has a worldwide fleet of 643 aircraft, 136,000 employees, and more than 1,000 service centers serving 215 countries.

DHL, a pioneering express delivery carrier, started shipping from San Francisco to Honolulu in 1969. It was the first carrier to introduce express international shipping via airplane to Eastern Europe in 1983 and to China in 1986. Today, DHL is the largest company that specializes in international express shipping. It can send packages to approximately 635,000 destinations in more than 233 countries and territories.

Bus Package Carriers

Bus package carriers provide transportation services for packages weighing less than 100 pounds. Bus package carriers, such as Greyhound, can provide same-day or next-day service to cities and towns along their scheduled routes. As with other forms of shipping, the cost of bus package transportation depends on the weight of the package and the distance it will travel.

Freight Forwarders

Freight forwarders are private companies that combine less-than-carload or less-than-truckload shipments from several different businesses and deliver them to their destinations. They gather small shipments into larger lots and then hire a carrier to move them, usually at reduced rates. By combining shipments, freight forwarders can often obtain truckload or carload rates and lower transportation costs for shippers. Freight forwarders also provide logistical services that help businesses select the best transportation methods and routes.

22.1 AFTER YOU READ

Reviewing Key Terms and Concepts
1. What is physical distribution?
2. Why is transportation important in marketing a product?
3. Which mode of transportation would you use to ship fresh flowers from Hawaii to New York? Why?

Integrating Academic Skills
Math
4. The *George A. Stinson* is the second largest freighter on the Great Lakes. Normally, it carries 57,000 tons of taconite ore each voyage between Superior, Wisconsin, and Detroit, Michigan. Now, due to lower lake levels, it can only carry 55,000 tons per trip. At an average cost of $5 per ton, how much revenue is lost per trip?

Civics and Government
5. The Transportation Security Administration (TSA) was established to protect the nation's transportation systems. Research and write a 200-word paper about security measures used to balance safety and security with ensuring freedom of movement for people and commerce.

 Online Action!

Check your answers at *marketingessentials.glencoe.com/22/read*

marketingessentials.glencoe.com

Chapter 22 - Physical Distribution 471

AFTER YOU READ

Reviewing Key Terms and Concepts
1. Physical distribution is all the activities (order processing, transportation, storage, stock handling, and inventory control) that get the right amount of product delivered to the right place at the right time.

2. Choosing the right mode of transportation can make a product more affordable to a customer or can make the product more desirable (for example, if it can arrive faster).

3. Students might cite air transportation, so that the flowers will still be fresh when they arrive in New York.

Integrating Academic Skills
4. 25,000; (57,000 tons × $6 = $285,000) − (52,000 tons × $6 = $260,000) = $285,000 − $260,000 = $25,000 in lost revenue

5. Answers will vary. However, students should investigate security challenges and related issues for highways, maritime, rail, and air transportation modes.

Online Action! Answers at *marketingessentials.glencoe.com/22/read*

Ask students to recall and provide answers to the following questions.

- **List four different examples of transportation service companies.**
  Express carriers, bus package carriers, freight forwarders, and the U.S. Postal Service.

- **Have students complete this statement: Physical distribution is the key link between _____ .**
  a business and its customers.

Extended Activity

Exploring Distribution Options
Have students research parcel post, one or more private parcel carriers, and one or more express carriers. They should obtain details about at least three services each provides, the time required to deliver, and the costs of the various services. Have students then use spreadsheet or graphic design software to construct a chart that compares the features and benefits of each service to use as a reference.

FOCUS

Introducing the Section

COLLABORATIVE ACTIVITY

Ask students to work in pairs to generate reasons why products need storage until they are sold. Take into consideration the needs of the producer, the manufacturer, the wholesaler, and the retailer. Have students brainstorm results and share them with the class.

Preteaching Key Terms

Ask students to take this section's key terms and write each in a sentence.

- storage
- private warehouse
- public warehouse
- distribution center
- bonded warehouse

Critical Thinking

Ask students if they think a business has the right to examine health records of employees who will operate heavy machinery in a warehouse.

OBJECTIVES

- Explain the concept and function of inventory storage
- Identify the types of warehouses
- Discuss distribution planning for international markets

KEY TERMS

- storage
- private warehouse
- public warehouse
- distribution center
- bonded warehouse

WHILE YOU READ

Analyze Think about products that need to be stored and others that do not. What are the differences between these types of goods?

Inventory Storage

READ and STUDY

BEFORE YOU READ
Predict How do you think inventory storage relates to a product's price?

MAIN IDEA
Inventory storage allows a business to keep its products for a certain period of time in a safe location until they are needed or ready to be sold.

STUDY ORGANIZER
In a chart like the one below, take notes about various types of warehouses.

Private Warehouse — Public Warehouse — Stores products until needed

The Storage of Goods

Some products, such as books, need to be manufactured in large quantities in order to be cost effective, and those products need to be kept safe and clean until they are sold. **Storage** is a marketing function and refers to the holding of goods until they are sold. The amount of goods stored is called an inventory. We will talk more about inventories in Chapter 24.

There are many reasons why storing goods is an essential activity for most businesses. First of all, products are stored until

READ and STUDY

BEFORE YOU READ
Some city zoning laws allow running a business from home, but not using the home for inventory storage. Ask: Where would small home business owners store their inventory? How would this affect their prices?

THE MAIN IDEA
Ask volunteers to name the various types of inventory shelving systems available.

STUDY ORGANIZER
Help students fill out their charts. A full-size, downloadable study organizer can be found at marketingessentials.glencoe.com

WHILE YOU READ Use student answers to lead to a discussion on the importance of the storage function.

orders are received from customers. Products might also need to be stored because production has exceeded consumption or demand decreases. Sometimes, agricultural commodities such as corn, wheat, and soybeans may only be available during certain seasons. Commodity storage makes these products available year-round and ensures that their price remains relatively stable. Some purchasers buy in quantity to get discounts on their purchases and then store the items until they are needed. Finally, products may be stored at convenient locations to provide faster delivery to customers.

The costs involved in storing products include space, equipment, and personnel. Storage also means spending money (or capital) on inventory rather than investing it in another activity that could provide a larger return.

Most products are stored in warehouses, or facilities in which goods are received, identified, sorted, stored, and dispatched for shipment.

Private Warehouses

A **private warehouse** is a facility designed to meet the specific needs of its owner. A private warehouse is valuable for companies that move a large volume of products. Specialized conditions, such as a temperature-controlled environment, may be built into the facility. Private warehouses often house other parts of the business operation, such as offices.

A disadvantage is that private warehouses are costly to build and maintain. In a recent survey, large retailers reported spending 51 percent of their total physical distribution costs on warehouse expenses; transportation costs accounted for the remaining 49 percent. Private warehouses should be considered only when a significant amount of merchandise needs to be stored, thus making the total operating costs lower than those of public warehouses.

Public Warehouses

A **public warehouse** offers storage and handling facilities to any individual or company that will pay for its use.

 marketingessentials.glencoe.com

Public warehouses not only rent space but also provide additional services to businesses. These services include shipment consolidation, receiving, unloading, inspecting, reshipping, order filling, and truck terminal operation services. Public warehouses are helpful to businesses that have low- to medium-volume storage needs or seasonal production.

Chapter 22 - Physical Distribution **473**

Discussion Starter

THE STORAGE OF GOODS

Businesses must continually assess the risk involved in the safety of its environment. Ask students to imagine they are risk appraisers for a company. Their mission is to assess the potential hazards in the inventory storage area. Have students create a list of possible violations.

TEACHING POINTS

Clarify Remind students that hazards may involve multiple factors, such as safety, health, environment, chemical substances, and hazardous substances.

Model On the board, create three categories: environmental, activity, and workplace. Within each category list one example of a possible hazard found within the inventory area.

Concept Development

PRIVATE WAREHOUSES

Ask students to identify when a private warehouse might be used and to give examples of the types of goods that might be stored in private warehouses.

A private warehouse is used to store a large amount of goods and are often proprietary to the company. These types of warehouses are often custom-built to fit the products which are being stored. An example of goods which might be stored in a private warehouse might be certain types of perishable goods, such as food items or flowers, which require a certain temperature to be maintained during storage and transport.

ASSESS

Review Guide

CONCEPTS

Write the following products on the board, then have the students tell you in which type of public warehouse each would likely be stored:

- broccoli cold storage
- cotton commodity
- chemicals bulk
- bicycle household goods
- apples cold storage
- washing machines general merchandise
- wheat commodity
- furniture household goods
- oil bulk
- toys general merchandise

KEY TERMS

Have students review key terms, their spellings, and definitions in small groups.

ONLINE SELF-ASSESSMENT

Have students go to **marketing.essentials.glencoe.com** for the Section 22.2 practice test.

Individualized Review

L1 Assign and review Chapter 22 activities in the Student Activity Workbook.

L2 Assign and review Chapter 22 activities in the Marketing Math Workbook.

L3 Assign and review Chapter 22 activities in the *BusinessWeek* Reader and Case Studies.

Marketing Practice

Ask students to brainstorm the various functions of a hypothetical software program used for distribution. They should offer their proposal of the software program to the class.

Case Study

Trucking and Wireless Technology

When Schneider National signed a deal in 1988 to equip its fleet with a satellite tracking and communication system from Qualcomm, the trucking giant was taking a big gamble on new and unproven technology.

The gamble paid off. The lines of drivers who once waited to use pay phones to call the home office, wasting precious on-duty hours, disappeared. Instead, drivers use text messaging to communicate with the home office via an in-cab or handheld wireless device.

Hot Spots and Wireless Modems

Instead of phone banks, truck stops are installing hot spots enabled with Wi-Fi technology. Drivers can log on to the Internet with laptops and PDAs equipped with wireless modems just by entering one of the hot spots and registering.

Schneider National now also writes its own software programs to integrate vehicle-location data and driver communications into its dispatch process and fleet management. In addition to new uses for existing data, Schneider National is also looking to add a tracking system that will locate trailers when doing intermodal transport.

THINK STRATEGICALLY

How do you think Schneider National's customers benefit from this technology?

@ Online Action! Go to *marketingessentials.glencoe.com/22/case* to find a research project on software and logistics.

Distribution Centers

A **distribution center** is a warehouse designed to speed delivery of goods and to minimize storage costs. The main focus in a distribution center is on sorting and moving products, not on storing them. Distribution centers are planned around markets rather than transportation requirements. They can cut costs by reducing the number of warehouses and eliminating excessive inventory.

Some businesses such as paint companies Sherwin-Williams and Benjamin Moore use their distribution centers to physically change the product for the final customer. Their distribution centers perform additional functions such as mixing ingredients, labeling, and repackaging for shipments to retailers.

Distribution centers also consolidate large orders from many sources and redistribute them as separate orders for individual

474 UNIT 7 - DISTRIBUTION

marketingessentials.glencoe.com

Case Study Trucking and Wireless Technology

Discussion Lead a class discussion on whether students foresee any privacy rights issues in relation to a company tracking an employee's exact location.

THINK STRATEGICALLY **Answer:** Using wireless technology improves customer service and gains a high payback in terms of return service. Schneider is able to track progress of shipments and let its customers know if a shipment will be late. Tracking allows Schneider's customers time to start planning contingencies such as using another shipping mode to honor service commitments.

@ Online Action! For instructions, ideas, and answer guide, go to the Teacher Center at **marketingessentials.glencoe.com**

accounts or stores within a chain. Merchandise normally stays only a very short time in a distribution center.

Bonded Warehouses

Bonded warehouses, either public or private, store products that require the payment of a federal tax. Imported or domestic products cannot be removed until the required tax is paid. Although they are charged storage fees, businesses can save on taxes by taking goods out of storage, and hence paying the tax, only when they are needed.

Distribution Planning for International Markets

Selling to customers in the international marketplace requires more planning than selling to domestic customers. Businesses that sell internationally must follow United States export laws as well as the import laws of the countries to which they are selling. Some countries also have legal restrictions about how products may be transported. Businesses frequently have to handle bureaucratic regulations, language barriers, and negotiations.

To deliver their goods successfully, businesses must understand other countries' physical transportation systems. In some less developed nations, the postal system may not be reliable enough to assure delivery of packages by mail. Other countries may not have well-developed roads and highway systems to support dependable truck deliveries. In China, for example, many goods are transported by bicycle or carts pushed by hand.

It is important to understand how retail institutions in other countries differ from American retail institutions. In some parts of the world, retailers have little or no capacity for refrigeration. American-style supermarkets are rare in developing countries due to the lack of refrigeration and storage facilities. In Japan, the term *supermarket* refers to a type of retail outfit that sells food as well as clothing, furniture, and appliances.

22.2 AFTER YOU READ

Reviewing Key Terms and Concepts

1. Give four reasons why merchandise is stored.
2. How does a distribution center differ from a warehouse?
3. What is a bonded warehouse?

Integrating Academic Skills

Math

4. One measure of warehouse productivity is the cost per order. Cost per Order = Total Warehouse Cost/Total Orders Shipped. What is the Cost per order for a company that has a total warehouse cost of $531,000 and shipped a total of 900 orders in a one-year period?

Language Arts

5. Use the Web sites for the American Trucking Association (ATA), the Association of American Railroads (AAR), the National Transportation Library, and other business news sources to research the latest issues impacting the transportation industry. Summarize these issues in a one-page report.

 Online Action!

Check your answers at *marketingessentials.glencoe.com/22/read*

marketingessentials.glencoe.com

Chapter 22 - Physical Distribution **475**

AFTER YOU READ

Reviewing Key Terms and Concepts

1. Reasons for storage: facilitate delivery to purchaser, production has outpaced demand, products require seasonal storage, to take advantage of quantity purchases, and to be located close to purchasers

2. Distribution centers focus on moving products rather than storing them.

3. A bonded warehouse can be either public or private and stores products that require the payment of a federal tax.

Integrating Academic Skills

4. The Cost per Order is $590; 531,000 ÷ 900 = $590

5. Answers will vary; issues might include a discussion of Internet services, Wi-Fi modems, PDAs, GPS locators, hand-held computers, local area networks for yard management Just-in-Time Pick up and delivery scanning equipment, RFID technology, Electronic Data Interchange and Voice Response, Quick Response Delivery, and integrated logistics planning and control.

 Online Action! Answers at **marketingessentials.glencoe.com/22/read**

CLOSE

Ask students to recall and to list answers to the following questions.

- **List at least three reasons why planning is important for distribution in international markets.**
  Language difficulties, bureaucratic regulations, and different legal customs

- **Given the evolution of technology what other products could evolve from physical to digital distribution?**
  Answers will vary but might include music videos, motions pictures, and games

Critical Thinking

Ask students how they think computer technology has affected inventory storage. Have students share their responses in class.

CAREERS IN MARKETING

Lifelong Learning

CAREER INFORMATION

Have students go to marketingessentials.glencoe.com and find the Chapter 22 Careers page and click on the link for the American Marketing Association's Careers Strategies and Tips. Ask students to select one article, read it, and summarize it in three short paragraphs.

PHYSICAL DISTRIBUTION

Students who are not planning careers in the physical distribution area of marketing might not be aware of innovations in methods of transportation or new regulations. However, these factors will impact students through prices they pay. Students can keep informed by reading business magazines, such as *BusinessWeek* and *The Wall Street Journal.*

Primary Source

Ask students to go to marketingessentials.glencoe.com find Chapter 22 Resources. Ask them to click on the link for the American Marketing Association's marketing dictionary and read the definitions of terms relating to physical distribution.

THINKING CRITICALLY

Loss prevention skills would be helpful because the physical distribution of products via an online store undergoes the same stresses and losses as those from a brick-and-mortar retail store.

@ Online Action!

For instructions, ideas, and answer guide, go to the Teacher Center at marketingessentials.glencoe.com

---

CAREERS IN MARKETING

STEVE ROBERTS
OWNER/OPERATOR
ZNRCDS.COM
MUSIC MAIL ORDER

? What do you do at work?
My duties include logistics, inventory management, and Web site inventory maintenance. Logistics includes everything from the physical tasks of pulling orders, stocking new product, and maintaining the warehouse, to making sure that the processes are in place and evaluated on a regular schedule for their effectiveness. Inventory management includes ordering product, re-ordering and re-stocking product as needed, and processing returns for defective or overstock products. Web site inventory maintenance means making sure that the site will allow the customer to order only those products currently in stock so as to minimize the occurrence of out-of-stock and back-ordered items.

? What skills are most important to you?
A background in inventory management and loss prevention is essential. Without these skills it would be impossible to manage a process during which you have no actual contact with the customer, such as an interactive e-commerce Web site. If the customer has no confidence that their order will be filled not only in a timely manner but also completely, they will likely find somewhere else to shop.

? What is your key to success?
First, put in place systems and processes that remove obstacles to customer service. Second, evaluate the effectiveness of the systems and processes on a regular schedule and make changes or adjustments as needed. Third, ask your customers what obstacles still exist, then, based on their input, revisit steps one and two.

Aptitudes, Abilities, and Skills

Inventory management, time management, strong computer skills, and organizational ability

Education and Training

High-level courses and degrees are offered in the areas of logistics and workflow, although many warehousing and inventory managers are entirely self-taught.

Career Path

Many on-the-floor warehouse jobs are entry level, while higher-level positions involve managing the overall process. Often, employees starting on the floor are promoted to managing positions as they stay with the company and develop new skills.

THINKING CRITICALLY

Why would skills in loss prevention, typically associated with running a retail store, be helpful to someone operating an e-commerce Web site?

Online Action!

Go to *marketingessentials.glencoe.com/ 22/careers* to Pnd a career-related activity.

marketingessentials.glencoe.com

Test-Taking Strategies

Tell the students to carefully and slowly read each test question before noting an answer. If they find any question to be confusing, they should go back and read it again, dissecting the parts they did not understand upon the first time they read the question.

FOCUS on KEY POINTS

SECTION 22.1

● Physical distribution links a business and its customers. Physical distribution comprises all the activities that help to ensure that the right amount of product is delivered to the right place at the right time. Physical distribution is also known as logistics. It involves transporting, storing, order processing, stock handling, and inventory control of materials and products. The different kinds of transportation include marine, air, pipeline, and land transportation, which includes both trucking and railroads.

SECTION 22.2

● Storage is the marketing function of holding goods until they are sold. Storing goods is an essential activity for most businesses. Products are stored in warehouses or distribution centers until orders are received from customers. Globalization is increasing the importance of international distribution.

REVIEW VOCABULARY

Define each of the below terms in a short sentence.

1. physical distribution (p. 464)
2. transportation (p. 465)
3. common carriers (p. 465)
4. contract carriers (p. 465)
5. private carriers (p. 467)
6. exempt carriers (p. 467)
7. ton-mile (p. 468)
8. carload (p. 468)
9. freight forwarders (p. 471)
10. storage (p. 472)
11. private warehouse (p. 473)
12. public warehouse (p. 473)
13. distribution center (p. 474)
14. bonded warehouses (p. 475)

REVIEW FACTS and IDEAS

15. Explain the components of physical distribution. (22.1)
16. Name transportation systems and services that are used to move goods from one place to another. (22.1)
17. What are the different kinds of transportation service companies? (22.1)
18. What is inventory storage? Explain how it is used. (22.2)
19. What are the different kinds of warehouses? (22.2)
20. Name at least three reasons why planning is important for distribution in international markets. (22.2)

Chapter 22 - Physical Distribution 477

FOCUS on KEY POINTS

Ask volunteers to read aloud the summaries and give one real-world example for each concept.

REVIEW VOCABULARY

See glossary for definitions of **1–14**.
A sample sentence might read:

1. *Physical distribution* is all the activities that help to ensure that the right amount of product is delivered to the right place at the right time.

REVIEW FACTS and IDEAS

15. Physical distribution involves order processing (initiates the movement of products through a physical distribution system), transportation (actual physical movement of products), storage (facilitates the movement of products through the distribution channel as products are sold), stock handling (receiving, checking, and marking items for sale), and inventory control (keeping product in sufficient quantities).

16. Major transportation systems include motor carriers, railroads, waterways, pipelines, and air carriers; service carriers include for-hire carriers, private carriers, or a combination of both.

17. The different kinds of transportation service companies are the U.S. Postal Service, express delivery services, bus package carriers, and freight forwarders.

18. Inventory storage refers to the holding of goods until they are sold. Storage of inventory is used while waiting for customers' orders and also when production has exceeded demand. Inventory storage is different than commodity storage which aims at making products available year-round and at keeping their prices consistent and stable.

19. The different kinds of warehouses include private warehouses, bonded warehouses, and public warehouses.

20. Reasons might include language difficulties, bureaucratic regulations, different countries or states have unique laws, and different storage and transportation systems.

BUILD SKILLS

21. Workplace Skills
Answers will vary; management would probably view this incident as possible grounds for dismissal, particularly if no attempts were made to properly record the damage.

22. Technology Applications
Presentations will vary; all presentations should demonstrate an understanding of the vocabulary term selected as well as facility with the presentation software.

23. Math Practice
$21,823.95; $75,255 × .29 = $21,823.95

DEVELOP CRITICAL THINKING

24. The Rise of International Distribution
Answers will vary; student lists should reflect an understanding of international physical distribution and how the Internet has affected it.

25. Shipping and Receiving
Memos will vary; all memos should include the pros and cons of each transportation alternative along with supporting details that explain the student's choice.

BUILD SKILLS

21. Workplace Skills
Human Relations You are a clerk in a warehouse. A carton of snack items has been damaged during a shipment. As you are filling out a report for the damaged merchandise, a coworker suggests you have some of the snacks because the warehouse will never miss them.

What would you say to your coworker? How do you believe management would view your coworker's suggestion?

22. Technology Applications
Prepare an Oral Presentation Select one of the vocabulary terms dealing with physical distribution. Use presentation software to develop a 10- to 15-minute presentation on different aspects associated with the term selected.

23. Math Practice
Calculate Price A large manufacturer can save 29 percent by using piggyback service. The cost of shipping the manufacturer's products without the piggyback service will total $75,255. How much money will the manufacturer save by using the service?

DEVELOP CRITICAL THINKING

24. The Rise of International Distribution
Why is knowledge of international physical distribution increasingly important? How has the Internet influenced the importance of international distribution? List three reasons why these developments are limited to free enterprise and the global economy.

25. Shipping and Receiving
Imagine you are a shipping and receiving supervisor for a large furniture manufacturer located in the midwestern part of the United States. Your distribution manager has asked you to evaluate the current distribution system used at your company. The company is deciding between a common carrier, its own private fleet, or a combination of both to transport its products.

Identify the pros and cons of each transportation alternative and write a memo to your manager detailing your analysis. Make sure to include supporting details.

Formative Assessment
Formative assessment is an essential component of classroom work. This type of assessment provides information that is then used as feedback to modify teaching and meet student needs.

L1 Review key terms for this chapter. Ask students to write one sentence for each key term.

L2 Provide various examples of factors that affect product distribution in story form. After each story, have the students identify which factors affect product distribution.

L3 Ask students to create stories that illustrate product distribution of a product of their choice.

Reteach **If results of this formative assessment seem low, consider the following activity:**
Have students read the section subheads, create an outline, and write one key idea underneath each subhead.

APPLY CONCEPTS

26. Investigating Intelligent Transportation Systems (ITS)

Perform an Internet search on the ITS program initiative of the U.S. Department of Transportation to add information technology to commercial vehicle operation.

Activity Write a one-page report detailing how technology is being used to improve safety, transportation time, and fuel costs.

27. Interviewing a Small-Business Owner

Interview a local businessperson about how product shipments are received within the business. Then select one specific transportation mode (such as trucking, air cargo carriers, etc.).

Activity Summarize in a one- to two-page report which products are received, how often, and what payment arrangements are involved.

NET SAVVY

28. Express Carriers

Using an Internet search engine, investigate a small-package express carrier (e.g. FedEx, DHL, UPS) or the U.S. Postal Service and prepare a report on its online services and technologies currently available to shippers. What are the goals of these online services? How can shippers use online technology and Web sites to market their own products and services?

THE CONNECTION

Role Play: Physical Distribution

Situation You are to assume the role of an experienced employee at the warehouse of a grocery supplier. You are familiar with the operation of the business and with filling orders from the individual grocery stores that your warehouse supplies. The warehouse manager has asked you to explain the warehouse operation to a new employee (judge).

Activity You are to explain to a new employee (judge) how the merchandise gets to your warehouse and how orders from the individual grocery stores you supply are filled and delivered.

Evaluation You will be evaluated on how well you meet the following performance indicators:

- Explain the nature of warehousing
- Explain the shipping process
- Explain storing considerations
- Explain the nature of channels of distribution
- Explain the nature of channel-member relationships

 Online Action!

For more information and DECA Prep practice, go to *marketingessentials.glencoe .com/22/DECA*

THE CONNECTION

Students should be evaluated according to the performance standards noted in the role play. For another DECA role play, go to the Competitive Events Workbook or the Student Activity Workbook, or go to **marketingessentials.glencoe.com/22/DECA**

 Online Action! For instructions, ideas, and answer guide, go to the Teacher Center at **marketingessentials.glencoe.com**

DECA Advisors Corner

In partnership with DECA, *USA Today*'s Student Business Program allows students first-hand knowledge of the marketing, distribution, sales, and advertising functions of the nation's newspapers. Additionally, your chapter can make money for each individual paper sold. This program is an excellent way to both reinforce marketing concepts and also raise funds.

APPLY CONCEPTS

26. Investigating Intelligent Transportation Systems (ITS)

Reports will vary; reported technologies could include those used for fleet administration, freight administration, electronic clearance, international border crossing clearance, weigh-in-motion (WIM), on-board safety monitoring, freight in-transit monitoring, or freight terminal management.

27. Interviewing a Small-Business Owner

Reports will vary depending on the business selected but should include an understanding of the transportation mode selected.

NET SAVVY

28. Express Carriers

Reports will vary; students may list a number of different available online services or technologies. Student reports should also demonstrate an understanding of the services and technologies.

MINI-QUIZ

Administer the Mini-Quiz orally. Students should select either true or false for their answer.

1. Physical distribution is also known as logistics. (true)

2. Contract carriers provide transportation services to any business in their operating area for a fee. (false)

3. A variation of the private and public warehouse is the distribution center. (true)

For an expanded chapter quiz, go to Chapter 22 in the TeacherWorks CD-ROM and to Chapter 22 in the **Exam*View*®** Pro Test Generator CD-ROM.

Chapter Overview

Chapter 23 examines the duties of organizational buyers, in both the industrial market and the reseller market. How buyers plan and calculate purchases is discussed, and students learn how to create a six-month merchandise plan. The three types of purchase situations—new-task, modified rebuy, and straight rebuy—are explored, and how the Internet is changing the purchasing function is discussed.

BUILD BACKGROUND

Have students generate a list of all the things they would need to purchase if they were to open a retail gift shop. Help students categorize the items into groups, such as items that will be used to operate the store (lighting and fixtures, for example) and gift items that will be made available for resale.

Why It's Important

The person who manages the purchasing function in any business is important because he or she has a direct impact on business expenses. The competence of the purchasing agent is crucial to the image, profitability, and success of the business.

Prepare to Read

List the section objectives and discuss them with the students. Have students skim the headings, subheadings, pictures and captions. Ask students which topics are covered in each section.

CHAPTER 23
Purchasing

Chapter Objectives

After reading this chapter, you should be able to:

- Define the terms used to describe organizational buyers
- Explain how planning purchases differs between an industrial market and a resellers' market
- Describe the six-month merchandise plan and explain its calculations
- Explain the concept of chain store buying
- List the three types of purchase situations
- Explain the criteria for selecting suppliers
- Name the factors involved in negotiating terms of a sale
- Describe the various Internet purchasing methods

GUIDE TO THE PHOTO

Market Talk Buyers in the apparel industry view designs before purchasing new collections. New designs are presented at private business meetings or at trade shows.

Quick Think What are some other sources of information about suppliers of products, materials, and services?

GUIDE TO THE PHOTO

Market Talk Explain that the people around the table in this photograph are making a purchasing decision at a trade show. Ask students if they or a family member has ever had to present a product or an idea to a potential buyer. Have students brainstorm different ways to convince a buyer to purchase a product for retail sale.

Quick Think Student responses may include trade journals, the Internet, and word-of-mouth.

Follow Up Ask students to select a store that interests them. Direct them to request an interview with the store's manager and ask questions about the purchasing process for that store.

Performance indicators represent key skills and knowledge. Relating them to the concepts explained in this chapter is your key to success in DECA events. These acronyms represent DECA events that involve knowledge of concepts in this chapter.

AAAL	FMAL	MMS*	TMDM*
AAML*	FMDM*	QSRM*	TSE*
ADC*	FMML*	RMAL	VPM
BSM*	FSRM*	RMML*	
EMDM*	HMDM*	SMDM*	

In all these DECA events you should be able to follow these performance indicators:

- Explain the nature and scope of purchasing
- Explain company buying/purchasing policies
- Explain the nature of the buying process
- Explain the nature of buyer reputation/vendor relationships
- Conduct vendor search

All the events with an asterisk (*) also include these performance indicators:

- Negotiate contracts with vendors
- Review performance of vendors

Some events include additional performance indicators. These are:

EMDM   Explain the impact of the Internet on purchasing

HMDM   Prepare food specifications (specs) for
FSRM   purchasing food items
QSRM   Plan quantities of food items to order

DECA PREP

Check your understanding of DECA performance indicators with the DECA activity in this chapter's review. For more information and DECA Prep practice, go to *marketingessentials* *.glencoe.com/23/DECA*

DECA events that require knowledge of purchasing are described here. Discuss the performance indicators to make sure students understand how to demonstrate their understanding.

The events acronyms stand for:

AAAL: Apparel and Accessories Marketing Series, AL

AAML: Apparel and Accessories Marketing Series, ML

ADC: Advertising Campaign Event

BSM: Business Services Marketing Series

EMDM: E-Commerce Management Team Decision Making Event

FMAL: Food Marketing Series, AL

FMDM: Financial Analysis Management Team Decision Making Event

FMML: Food Marketing Series, ML

FSRM: Full Service Restaurant Management Series

HMDM: Hospitality Services Management Team Decision Making Event

MMS: Marketing Management Series

QSRM: Quick Serve Restaurant Management Series

RMAL: Retail Merchandising Series, AL

RMML: Retail Merchandising Series, ML

SMDM: Sports and Entertainment Marketing Management Team Decision Making Event

TMDM: Travel and Tourism Marketing Management Team Decision Making Event

TSE: Technical Sales Event

VPM: Vehicles and Petroleum Marketing Series

DECA PREP

Find timed DECA Prep activities correlated to the Competitive Events Workbook for students and DECA tips for teachers at **marketingessentials.glencoe.com /23/DECA**

CHAPTER 23 Classroom Resources

For the Teacher

- TeacherWorks
- marketingessentials.glencoe.com
- Interactive Chalkboard
- **Exam*View*®** Pro Test Generator
- Fast File Unit 7

For the Student

- ***Marketing Essentials*** Online Edition
- Student Activity Workbook
- Marketing Math Workbook
- Marketing Research Project Workbook
- School-to-Work Activity Workbook
- Competitive Events Workbook
- ***BusinessWeek*** Reader and Case Studies
- marketingessentials.glencoe.com

FOCUS

Introducing the Section

COLLABORATIVE ACTIVITY

Organize the class into groups of five or six and tell them that they are part of a team responsible for opening a new restaurant. Their task is to purchase all of the goods required for table service in a 50-seat dining room. These goods include linens, flatware, dinnerware, and glassware. Suggest that they perform research to complete the activity. Have groups present a list of goods to purchase, a proposed budget, and list of vendors to contact.

Preteaching Key Terms

List the key terms on the board and have students skim the chapter looking for the terms in context. Have them propose definitions for the terms and write those meanings in their notebooks for use when studying.

- organizational buyers
- wholesale and retail buyers
- six-month merchandise plan
- open-to-buy (OTB)
- centralized buying
- decentralized buying

Build Vocabulary

Preview the following words by reading them in context. Ask students to explain what each word means.

- savvy
  know-how

- capacity
  the maximum amount that can be accommodated

OBJECTIVES

- Define the terms used to describe organizational buyers
- Explain how planning purchases differs between an industrial market and a resellers' market
- Describe the six-month merchandise plan and explain its calculations
- Explain the concept of chain store buying

KEY TERMS

- organizational buyers
- wholesale and retail buyers
- six-month merchandise plan
- open-to-buy (OTB)
- centralized buying
- decentralized buying

WHILE YOU READ

Compare List the similarities and differences of the four markets listed above.

The Role of the Buyer

READ and STUDY

BEFORE YOU READ

Predict What do you already know about the role of the buyer?

THE MAIN IDEA

The purchasing function in any business is important because the costs associated with running a business are often a direct result of the competence of the person responsible for buying the goods and services required to run the business.

STUDY ORGANIZER

Use a chart like the one below to write two or three sentences describing each of the following: industrial market, resellers market, government market, and institutional market.

Market	Notes
Industrial	
Resellers	
Government	
Institutional	

Planning Purchases

Organizational buyers purchase goods for business purposes, usually in much greater quantities than the average consumer. Much of what they buy requires technical knowledge and knowledge of the operations of the firm, especially in manufacturing and service operations. Having a handle on the business trends that affect their industry is also important, especially when buying for resale purposes.

READ and STUDY

BEFORE YOU READ

Ask students which is more important to buyers: price, quality, or quick availability?

THE MAIN IDEA

Suggest a common business, such as a retail clothes store, a sandwich shop, or a gas station, and have students list the types of goods that might need to be purchased in order for the business to operate.

STUDY ORGANIZER

Model the study organizer for students by filling in the first sentence. A full-size, downloadable study organizer can be found at marketingessentials.glencoe.com

WHILE YOU READ Model for students how they can list similarities and differences of the four markets as they read through the section.

Industrial Markets

In manufacturing and service businesses, the people responsible for purchasing may be called purchasing managers, industrial buyers, or procurement managers. Although the job titles may differ, the key function is to buy goods and services for use in the business.

In manufacturing businesses, planning purchases often requires industrial buyers to be directly involved with production planning. To get an idea of the responsibilities involved, consider the case of a purchasing manager for an outerwear apparel manufacturer.

The purchasing manager would review the company's master production schedule for details of production needed to meet sales requirements. Let's say that the marketing department predicts the company will sell 500 Style No. 1900 jackets in the coming season. The purchasing manager must know how much fabric, insulation, and thread and how many zippers it takes to produce one Style

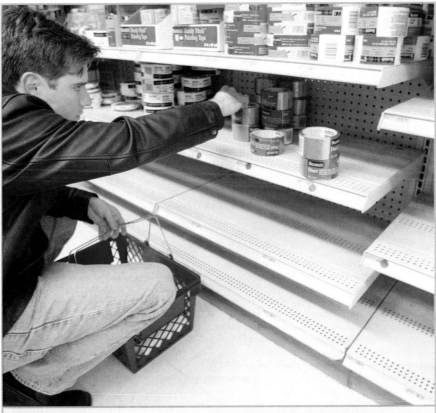

•**BUY to SELL** Purchasing and inventory control go hand in hand. Buyers need to know what sells and what does not. Companies need to figure out their projected sales to order the correct quantities of merchandise.

What can happen if a store's shelves run out of a popular item?

Chapter 23 - Purchasing **483**

TEACH

Discussion Starter

IMPORTANCE OF PLANNING PURCHASES

Ask students if they would enjoy shopping—with someone else's money. Then ask if any of them have ever considered becoming a buyer, either one who buys goods for a retail store or one who buys goods to operate a business. Point out that two types of buyers—industrial and resale buyers—will be discussed in this section. Ask them what they think each type of job entails, and to give their opinion as to whether the job would be fun, interesting, or challenging.

Build Vocabulary

Preview the following terms by reading them in context. Ask students to explain what each means and to name a synonym.

- **bill of materials**
  components

- **procurement**
  obtainment

- **Materials Requirement Planning (MRP)**
  a purchasing plan or analysis

PHOTO GUIDE   BUY to SELL

Discussion Lead a discussion about the implications of a poorly planned six-month merchandise plan. Point out that having too much or too little inventory can be a major problem for any business as it affects sales and profit.

Caption Answer If a store runs out of a popular item, demand will exceed supply; customers may be dissatisfied or upset.

Follow Up Ask students to find out what local stores do when they run out of an item that has been advertised as being on sale. For example, they could find out whether the store has a rain check policy.

Concept Development

INDUSTRIAL MARKETS AND RESELLERS

Ask students to think about resale and industrial buying situations. Ask: How are these two buying situations similar and different? What general kinds of tasks would be involved with both?

Both must plan purchases and evaluate vendors before making purchases. They differ in their purpose: Industrial buyers purchase materials used in making goods or providing services.

SIX-MONTH MERCHANDISE PLAN

To lead students through the six-month merchandise plan, provide different scenarios as you introduce each section of the plan.

- For planned sales, tell students that the economy appears to be in a period of recovery and continued growth is expected. Have them assume that unemployment figures have dropped from 6.9 percent to 4.5 percent, and inflation is low at 3 percent. Ask students how they would use this general economic information to project sales for the next six months.
  Students should recognize that there should be an increase in sales for the coming season.

- For BOM inventory, ask students how much inventory must be on hand to meet sales of $10,000 in a given month in a local retail store. Ask if $10,000 in inventory would be sufficient. Point out that you would have to have more than that on hand. Otherwise, the shelves would be bare.

- For retail reductions, ask students what they think would be included in this figure.
  employee discounts, markdowns, and shortages

No. 1900 jacket. This is called a bill of materials. The total of all the materials necessary to make one jacket can be multiplied by 500 to determine exactly what needs to be purchased to meet the sales goal.

To determine when to buy those items, the purchasing manager would be responsible for materials requirement planning (MRP). MRP includes an analysis of when to make the purchases so they are available when needed according to the production schedule. The purchasing manager must therefore know the capacity of the manufacturing facility. He or she must be sure the company has room for the supplies, raw materials, and inventory of finished goods.

Time lines and delivery of all supplies must be followed and checked on a regular basis to maintain the master production schedule. This ensures that everything is as it should be for manufacturing to progress at an appropriate rate.

Case Study

Maximizing Purchasing Power

Trader Joe's, a specialty grocer based in California, has 210 U.S. stores. It had estimated sales in 2003 of $2.5 billion, up 13 percent over 2002. The company operates differently from most grocers, selling only about 2,500 different items rather than the 40,000 a large chain supermarket carries. Buyers search for bargains around the world. When they find high-quality items at especially low prices, they buy large quantities, lowering the price further with volume discounts. Trader Joe's buys only from producers, not from wholesalers. Of its products, 20 percent to 25 percent are imported, and it has developed its own brands for about 80 percent of its products.

Guten Appetit!

Joe Coulombe began the business in 1958 as a chain of neighborhood convenience stores. He later expanded store space and began selling gourmet cheeses and wines at much lower prices than other food retailers. In 1979, the company was bought by Theo Albrecht, co-owner of the German Aldi food store chain, whose purchasing and marketing strategy is similar, focusing on a few items (700 in Aldi stores) and emphasizing store brands. Aldi sells to the low end of the market, focusing on budget items. Trader Joe's targets sophisticated buyers who still want to save money.

THINK STRATEGICALLY

From a purchasing standpoint, how can it benefit Trader Joe's to be owned by a German company? With a 13 percent increase in sales from 2002 to 2003, how much of an increase in purchases would you advise in a merchandise plan for Trader Joe's?

@ Online Action!

Go to *marketingessentials.glencoe.com/23/case* to find an activity about purchasing and the grocery business.

 marketingessentials.glencoe.com

Case Study — Maximizing Purchasing Power

Discussion Have students relate their experiences seeing ads for or shopping in low-price retail stores.

THINK STRATEGICALLY **Answer:** Answers will vary. Since Trader Joe's is a German company, its buyers may have easier access to goods from Eastern Europe, where prices are comparatively low. Increasing sales from 2002 to 2003 would be one factor in determining how much of an increase to advise for use in a merchandise plan. Other factors include whether more stores have opened or closed, whether there is more or less competition, the state of the economy, and whether prices from the producers have risen or fallen.

@ Online Action! For instructions, ideas, and answer guide, go to the Teacher Center at **marketingessentials.glencoe.com**

NET MARKETING

How to Choose a B2B?

Internet B2B suppliers have greatly increased in number as e-commerce has become mainstream. How can a purchaser wisely choose a vendor from the many thousands available? There are hundreds of directories listing B2Bs that simply provide links to their Web sites with no commentary. Services that provide directories, list the kinds of transactions vendors provide, and rate them on their performance are more helpful—and they do exist.

Online Information

Purchasinga2z is a Web site providing news reports about purchasing issues, research and ratings of B2B businesses and links to other sources of information. VerticalZOOM is another such service. It also features customer feedback on specific vendors, giving buyers an extra piece of the puzzle. The Internet may make purchasing easier, but it takes research to identify the right supplier when there are so many possibilities.

> ### THINK LIKE A MARKETER
>
> As the buyer for a new hip-hop fashion boutique, how will you find sources or know if a quoted price is reasonable?
>
> **@ Online Action!**
>
> Go to *marketingessentials.glencoe.com/23/net* to find activities about purchasing and the Internet.

Resellers' Markets

The resellers' market is found in wholesaling and retailing operations, where the person responsible for purchasing is simply called a buyer. **Wholesale and retail buyers** purchase goods for resale; they forecast customers' needs and buy the necessary products. Buyers must plan far in advance of the selling season to know how much of each item to purchase.

Six-Month Merchandise Plan

Buyers plan their purchases by preparing a **six-month merchandise plan**, the budget that estimates planned purchases for a six-month period.

The first figure calculated on a merchandise plan is the planned sales figure. In most cases, this is determined by using the previous year's monthly sales figures and adjusting them to reflect the firm's current-year sales goal.

Suppose sales for a particular month last year were $100,000, and this year's goal is to increase sales by 10 percent. This year's planned sales for the month would be calculated as follows:

Desired increase: $100,000 \times .10 = \$10,000$
Planned sales: $100,000 + \$10,000 = \$110,000$

You could also reach the same result in a single step:

$$\$100,000 \times 1.10 = \$110,000$$

The company goal for the current year is derived from a study of last year's sales, current market and economic conditions, and an analysis of the competition. Projection of accurate planned sales figures is important because all other figures on the merchandise plan are computed on the basis of this figure.

marketingessentials.glencoe.com

Chapter 23 - Purchasing **485**

TEACH CONTINUED

Individualized Math Practice

SIX-MONTH MERCHANDISE PLAN

Have students calculate the answers to the appropriate leveled activity:

L1 If the previous year's sales were $55,000, and planned sales for next year call for a 15 percent increase, what are planned sales for next year?
$55,000 \times 1.15 = \$63,250$

L2 BOM inventory for last July was $50,000, and the stock-to-sales ratio was 4:1. What were sales for last July?
$50,000 \div 4 = \$12,500$

L3 Last year's sales were $75,000, and planned retail reductions were 10 percent. Next year's planned sales assumes a 10 percent increase with planned retail reductions at 8 percent. What are planned retail reductions for next year?
$75,000 \times 1.10 = \$82,500$
$82,500 \times .08 = \$6,600$

TEACHING POINTS

Recall To help introduce the idea of planning sales for the future, ask students what socio-cultural, economic, and market factors should be considered when determining whether sales will increase or decrease from the previous year. Point out that population change, an increase or decrease in competition, changes in price, customer service, amount of advertising, and word-of-mouth from an established customer base are factors that affect future sales.

NET MARKETING

How to Choose a B2B?

Discussion Remind students that B2B stands for business-to-business. After students have read this feature, ask them to list and share the kinds of performance indicators they would look for on a Web site that rates various B2B vendors. Answers may include whether they offer competitive prices, the length of time they have been in business, the level of customer support they provide, how other customers rate them, etc.

THINK LIKE A MARKETER **Answer:** Fashion buyers learn about new designers and clothing manufacturers through various means, including trade shows, trade journals, and word-of-mouth. Prices can be compared to competitors' prices.

@ Online Action! For instructions, ideas, and answer guide, go to the Teacher Center at marketingessentials.glencoe.com

TEACH CONTINUED

RESEARCHING THE BOOKSTORE MARKET

Have students work in small groups to investigate buying trends in college bookstores and determine whether there is any application to high school bookstores. Ask them to look for new products that might be added to the existing line of goods carried in their own school store. Students should develop their suggestions by investigating the needs of their classmates and others in their school and by determining possible sources of supply for these goods. Have students present their findings and the rationale for their suggestions in a five-minute presentation or a two-page report.

Critical Thinking

Ask students to explain whose job is easier in terms of planning purchases—an industrial buyer's or a retail buyer's. Answers will vary. Each job has difficulties that depend on the scope of the job and its responsibilities.

Virtual Business

Introduce purchasing to students using Knowledge Matters' Virtual Business Retailing visual simulation, *Purchasing*. In this simulation, students explore the purchasing process of a retail store, how just-in-time inventory systems work, and why it is important to monitor sales and shrinkage.

Buyers must ensure that there is enough stock to accommodate the sales volume planned. This is also known as beginning-of-the-month (BOM) inventory. To project this figure, a buyer checks the previous year's records for how much stock was needed in relation to monthly sales. Sales were $40,000 in a given month and the BOM stock for that month was $120,000; therefore, the stock-to-sales ratio is 3 to 1. The buyer can apply that same ratio to the planned figure for another month if economic and market conditions are similar.

Here is how the BOM figure on the merchandise plan would be calculated. Suppose the stock-to-sales ratio is 2:1 (usually reported as 2). This means that to accommodate a given sales volume, it is necessary to keep twice that amount of stock on hand. BOM inventory should be twice the amount of anticipated sales; if sales are $5,000, then the BOM would be $10,000.

The end-of-the-month (EOM) stock figure is closely related to the BOM stock figure. The BOM stock figure for any given month is the EOM stock figure for the previous month.

Planned retail reductions take into account reductions in the selling price, shortages of merchandise caused by clerical mistakes, employee pilferage, and customer shoplifting. Such reductions in earnings and merchandise shortages ultimately affect the amount of money that must be planned for purchases.

Planned retail reductions can be calculated in two different ways. One is to calculate reductions as a percentage of planned sales. Suppose planned reductions have historically been 10 percent of planned sales. If planned sales for the month are $25,000, planned reductions for that month would be calculated as follows:

$$\$25,000 \times .10 = \$2,500$$

Some companies set goals of reducing planned reductions from the previous year. Assume that a firm's goal is to reduce this year's planned reductions by 5 percent from last year's figure. Last year's reductions were $700; therefore this year's planned reductions would be figured this way:

Desired decrease: $700 × .05 = $35
Planned reductions: $700 − $35 = $665

This result could also be reached
in a single step: $700 × .95 = $655

The planned purchase entry shows the retail-dollar purchase figures a firm needs to achieve its sales and inventory projections for

ATHLETA
Where women gear up.

We **love to shop** everything that's out there and **bring you the best** we can find, always with an eye for the **innovative, unique** and just **plain cool.**

While we were putting together our holiday collection we fell in love with the hip and curly **Poodle Hoodie** from **Mountain Hardwear.** Enough that we decided to see if we could get it in a bit early so we could share it with you now. Truly technical with a funky edge, this hoodie celebrates the bright colors of fall and will keep you warm all winter long.

SHOW ME THE HOODIE!

PURCHASING as a SALES TOOL Athleta, a catalog and e-tail business that targets women who play sports, sends advance notice of merchandise that has just been purchased.

How can the purchasing power and savvy of a company become a sales tool?

AD GUIDE   **PURCHASING as a SALES TOOL**

Discussion Lead a discussion about the importance of the role of the buyer for a company like Athleta. Point out that the buyer who founded the Poodle Hoodie, which is advertised here, created a marketing opportunity for the company it would not otherwise have had.

Caption Answer Purchasing power and marketing savvy can help a company create marketing opportunities faster and more often than the competition.

Follow Up Ask students to identify other gear that might be provided by this marketer of athletic clothing and equipment to women.

Figure 23.1 — Six-Month Merchandise Plan

- **Making Merchandise Plans** This nearly completed model merchandise plan is based on the following assumptions: sales are expected to increase by 10 percent over last year; last year's stock-to-sales ratios should be used to compute this year's BOM stock figures; this year's planned reductions should be 5 percent lower than last year's; and the planned BOM for August is $264,000.

What are the planned purchase figures for May through July?

Spring Season 20___ Department __Toys__ No. __6124__

		February	March	April	May	June	July	Total
Sales	Last year	82,000	96,000	90,000	100,000	94,000	80,000	
	Plan	90,200	105,600	99,000	110,000	103,400	88,000	
	Actual							
Retail Stock BOM	Last year	328,000	336,000	297,000	360,000	291,400	224,000	
	Plan	360,800	369,600	326,700	396,000	320,540	246,400	
	Actual							
Retail Reductions	Last year	12,300	14,400	13,500	15,000	14,100	12,000	
	Plan	11,685	13,680	12,825	14,250	13,395	11,400	
	Actual							
Purchases	Last year	N/A	N/A	N/A	N/A	N/A	N/A	
	Plan	110,685	76,380	181,125				
	Actual							

@ Online Action! Go to *marketingessentials.glencoe.com/23/figure/1* to find a project on merchandise plans.

each month. All the figures discussed previously—planned sales, BOM stock, and reductions—are needed to determine planned purchases (P). That includes planned sales (PS), planned EOM/BOM stock, and planned reductions (R). The formula for planned purchases is

$$(PS + EOM\ stock + R) - BOM\ stock = P$$

Assume that planned sales are $10,000, planned EOM stock is $25,000, planned reductions are $500, and BOM stock is $20,000.

Using the formula, planned purchases would be arrived at this way:

$$(\$10,000 + \$25,000 + \$500) - \$20,000 =$$
$$\$35,500 - \$20,000 = \$15,500$$

Figure 23.1 shows a nearly completed merchandise plan.

Open-to-Buy

During the buying season, a buyer may want to know the **open-to-buy (OTB)**. This is the amount of money left for buying goods

---

Enrichment

PURCHASING POWER

Point out to students that buyers in every type of wholesale and retail industry keep up with their field by reading trade journals. For example, *Progressive Grocer* and *Frozen Food Digest* are examples of trade journals read by buyers in the supermarket industry. Industrial buyers can keep abreast of their field by reading a journal called *Purchasing*. Have students choose a retail market and research trade journals that publish to that market. If possible, have students read one article that reports a trend what would be important to a buyer or purchasing agent. Ask them to prepare a two-minute oral presentation about the journals to explain their focus, editorial content, and advertising.

Individualized Math Practice

Have students complete the following leveled activities:

L1 B2B trade in the United States is estimated to be $6 trillion in 2005. Write the number six trillion in standard form.
6,000,000,000,000

L2 B2B trade in the United States is estimated to be $6 trillion in 2005. If organizational buyers account for 80 percent of all online transactions, what will be the value of organizational online buying in 2005?
$6 trillion $\times$ .80 = $4.8 trillion

L3 B2B trade in the United States is estimated to be $6 trillion in 2005. If this represents 42 percent of the total B2B U.S. nonservice market, what is the value of the U.S. nonservice market?
$6 trillion $\div$ .42 = $14.29 trillion

Figure 23.1 — Six-Month Merchandise Plan

Discussion After students have read **Figure 23.1**, point out that the plan has been designed to cover the spring season and includes the months February through July. Point out to students that some retail markets are very active only at certain times of the year. The market for candy, for example, centers around holidays such as Easter and Halloween. In such a case, it is important for a buyer to be able to project sales by month because the variation from month-to-month can be great.

Caption Answer The planned purchase figures are as follows: May—$48,790; June—$42,655; July—$117,000

@ Online Action! For instructions, ideas, and answer guide, go to the Teacher Center at marketingessentials.glencoe.com

ASSESS

Review Guide

CONCEPTS

Have students review the differences in the jobs of the industrial buyer and the reseller buyer.

The industrial buyer buys goods and services for use in the business. The wholesle or retail buyer must forecast customers' needs and buy products to meet those needs in a timely manner.

KEY TERMS

Have students review key terms, their spellings, and definitions in small groups.

ONLINE SELF-ASSESSMENT

Have students go to marketing.essentials.glencoe.com for the Section 23.1 practice test.

Individualized Review

L1 Assign and review Chapter 23 activities in the Student Activity Workbook.

L2 Assign and review Chapter 23 activities in the Marketing Math Workbook.

L3 Assign and review Chapter 23 activities in the *BusinessWeek* Reader and Case Studies.

Marketing Practice

Have students create a six-month merchandise plan for a line of power tools. They should base their plan on the following information: 1) For the six-month period last year, sales were about $20,000 each month. 2) Goal for the current year is a 12 percent increase. 3) The BOM figure at the beginning of this year's plan will be $50,000. 4) Retail reductions will be between 2 percent and 5 percent.

---

after all purchases received and on order have been considered. It is calculated this way:

P − (goods received + goods ordered) = OTB

Assume that merchandise received against the planned purchase figure computed above is $6,500 thus far and merchandise on order against it is $2,000. The present OTB would be as follows:

$$\$15,500 - (\$6,500 + \$2,000) = OTB$$
$$\$15,500 - \$8,500 = \$7,000$$

This $7,000 figure represents the retail value of the goods that the buyer may purchase at the time. However, the problem is not solved here.

There is a way to determine the actual money the buyer has to spend. You must calculate the markup percentage used by the buyer and deduct that figure from the retail value. Assume that the markup percentage is 45 percent based on the retail value of the merchandise. The formula for determining the OTB at cost is shown below:

$$100\% - \text{markup } \% =$$
$$\% \text{ attributed to cost of the item}$$
$$\% \text{ attributed to cost} \times \text{retail value} =$$
$$\text{OTB at cost}$$
$$100\% - 45\% \text{ markup} = 55\% \text{ (cost)}$$
$$55\% \text{ (cost)} \times \$7,000 \text{ (retail)} =$$
$$\$3,850 \text{ OTB at cost}$$

Therefore, in the end, the buyer has $3,850 to spend with all other costs considered. You can see how this extra step makes a big difference in the final amount.

Planning Purchases for a Chain Store Operation

Buying for all branches in a chain store operation is usually done in a central location (company headquarters) and is called **centralized buying**. Buyers involved in centralized buying generally buy all the items for a department or part of a department. There may be three buyers for women's shoes—one in charge of casual shoes, another of traditional shoes, and still another of better shoes.

To coordinate the efforts of those three buyers, there would be a merchandise or division manager. This person would oversee all shoe buyers, which may include those for men's, children's, and women's shoes.

Chain stores use centralized buying to create a unified image for the chain. Another benefit of centralized buying is the quantity discounts that stores can negotiate with vendors because of the large volume of goods that they purchase at one time.

Decentralized Buying

Sometimes, chain stores want to have special goods in their stores that are not available elsewhere in the chain. In these cases, local store managers or their designated buyers are authorized to make special purchases for their

---

PRACTICE

On a separate sheet of paper, practice the following calculations that are necessary for creating a six-month merchandise plan:

1. Last March a shop had sales of $7,300. The owner's goal is to increase sales by 8 percent for this year. What would be the planned sales for this March?
2. Last year's BOM for March was $10,950. Calculate the stock-to-sales ratio.
3. What should be the BOM stock figure for this March?
4. Planned reductions have historically been 10 percent of sales. Using this figure, what would be the planned reductions for this March? The owner would like to cut planned reductions by 5 percent this year. Last year's reductions for the month was $750, therefore what would be this year's target figure?
5. Using the figures given or calculated in numbers 1, 3, and 4, determine the planned purchases for the shop if the EOM stock figure for March is $12,000.
6. Assuming merchandise received and ordered amounted to $1,850, what would be the open-to-buy position at retail?
7. The customary markup for an item is 60 percent. What is OTB at cost?

Note: Answers to this practice set are available at *marketingessentials.glencoe.com*

 marketingessentials.glencoe.com

PRACTICE ANSWERS

1. $7,884
2. 1.5:1
3. $11,826
4. $788.40, $712.50
5. $8,770.50 [(PS + EOM + R) − BOM = P]
6. $6,920.50
7. $2,768.50

individual stores. This is **decentralized buying**. Decentralization is when authority for retail decisions is made at lower levels in the organization.

Retailers constantly make trade-offs between the efficiency gained through centralized buying and the greater sales potential obtained through decentralized buying decisions that tailor merchandise to local markets.

Government Markets

Just as there are special markets, such as industrial or resellers', there are also buyers for government markets. Government units are the federal, state, and local agencies responsible for purchasing goods and services for their specific markets. There are approximately 85,000 government units in the United States. These would include the Federal Aviation Administration (FAA), departments of sanitation, public libraries, and local school boards.

Government markets make up one of the largest single markets for retail goods and services in the world. In the United States, the federal government is a huge consumer of goods, ranging from food for school lunches to equipment for the military. A large portion of the federal government's buying is centralized. However, no one federal agency is responsible for all government buying.

Institutions

One final segment of the market cannot be overlooked when discussing buying power. This market includes institutions and non-profit organizations that do not compete in the business world in the same way retailers and wholesalers do. These institutions include hospitals, schools, colleges, churches, civic clubs, and foundations that do not work solely for profit. Institutions and nonprofit organizations may have unique buying requirements.

23.1 AFTER YOU READ

Reviewing Key Terms and Concepts

1. What are three job titles that can be used to describe people responsible for purchasing in manufacturing and service businesses?

2. How is a bill of materials used in planning purchases?

3. What are two benefits of centralized buying?

Integrating Academic Skills

Math

4. You are ordering tourist maps of your area for resale in your store. The cost of 500 maps is $625. The cost of 1,000 maps is $1,125. Calculate the per-item cost for each quantity of maps.

Geography

5. You want to become an industrial purchaser for the automobile manufacturing industry. Go to local car dealerships to research three different makes and models of cars. Obtain a brochure describing each model you research. Learn where each model is manufactured. Use your brochures to create a classroom map showing where each automobile is manufactured.

 Online Action!

Check your answers at *marketingessentials.glencoe.com/23/read*

marketingessentials.glencoe.com

Chapter 23 - Purchasing **489**

AFTER YOU READ

Reviewing Key Terms and Concepts

1. Three job titles that can be used to describe people responsible for purchasing in manufacturing and service businesses include: purchasing managers, industrial buyers, and procurement managers.

2. The bill of materials gives the total of all materials necessary to make one item. This can be multiplied by the total number of items to determine exactly how much must be purchased.

3. Centralized buying helps to create a unified image for the chain, merchandise can be transferred from one store to another where it is selling better, and quantity discounts can be negotiated due to large volume purchases.

Integrating Academic Skills

4. $1.25, $1.125

5. Brochures and sites will vary but should demonstrate a student understanding of industrial purchasing.

 Online Action! Answers at **marketingessentials.glencoe.com/23/read**

CLOSE

Ask students to recall and provide answers to the following questions.

- **What is the formula for calculating planned purchases?**
  (Planned sales + EOM stock + reductions) − BOM stock = Planned purchases, or (PS + EOM + R) − BOM = P

- **When is it appropriate for a chain store to use decentralized buying?**
  Decentralized buying allows individual stores to offer merchandise that is not available in other stores within the chain. This enables a store to meet a specific local demand for a product.

 Critical Thinking

Ask students: How does an organizational buyer for an industrial firm acquire the technical knowledge and knowledge about how the firm operates needed to do a good job? Answers might include that perhaps the buyer has worked at the firm, or another like it, in related jobs before becoming a buyer, or has acquired the technical knowledge in school.

FOCUS

Introducing the Section

COLLABORATIVE ACTIVITY

To prepare for reading this section, organize students in small groups and present them with this scenario: You are going off to college in a town that is 500 miles away. The others in your group are going to the same college, so you decide to pool your resources and purchase a house you can all share instead of living in a dorm. Tell students that their task is to create a list of steps the group will follow in order to make this buying decision together. Challenge them to think through how they will establish the needs they have, determine what real estate is available, and how the final decision will be made.

Preteaching Key Terms

Assign each term to a different group and have students skim the section to find the term in context. Call on volunteers to point out where the term occurs in the section, to read it in context, and to explain in their own words what it means.

- want slips
- consignment buying
- memorandum buying
- reverse auction

Critical Thinking

Ask students if they have ever purchased anything using the Internet and to cmpare that experience with shopping in a retail store.

OBJECTIVES

- List the three types of purchase situations
- Explain the criteria for selecting suppliers
- Name the factors involved in negotiating terms of a sale
- Describe the various Internet purchasing methods

KEY TERMS

- want slips
- consignment buying
- memorandum buying
- reverse auction

WHILE YOU READ

Compare List the differences among the types of purchase situation.

The Purchasing Function

READ and STUDY

BEFORE YOU READ
Predict What do you already know about the purchasing function?

THE MAIN IDEA
Knowing the details of the purchasing function will give you a better idea of what is involved in the overall job description. It is especially important to recognize the impact of the Internet on the purchasing function. You can expect changes in job descriptions for buyers in the near future due to the significant increase in online purchasing.

STUDY ORGANIZER
In a chart like the one below, write in three types of purchase situations and four criteria for selecting suppliers.

The Buying Process

There are many types of purchase situations. The ways suppliers are selected, how terms are negotiated, and how the Internet is used are changing the entire process.

Types of Purchase Situations

How difficult is the task of a purchasing manager or a buyer? The answer depends on which type of purchase situation is

READ and STUDY

BEFORE YOU READ
Lead students in a discussion about the tools buyers use to plan their purchases.

THE MAIN IDEA
After students have read the main idea, point out that in this section, they will learn more about techniques buyers use in making a purchase.

STUDY ORGANIZER
Model the study organizer for students by filling in the first purchase situation and criteria. A full-size, downloadable study organizer can be found at marketingessentials.glencoe.com

 WHILE YOU READ Model for students how to take notes about the different types of purchase situations and the characteristics of each.

considered. Let's review the three types of purchase situations: new task purchase, modified rebuy, and straight rebuy.

New-Task Purchase

In a new-task purchase situation, a purchase is made for the first time, possibly triggered by a formerly unrecognized need, a new manufacturing process, or organizational change. This can be the most complicated buying situation, because it involves a first-time purchase. In a retail or wholesale operation, salespeople prepare **want slips**. These are customer requests for items that are not carried in the store. The buyer evaluates want slips to determine if the requests warrant the purchase of new merchandise.

Modified Rebuy

In a modified-rebuy situation, the buyer has had experience buying the good or service, but some aspect of the purchase changes. Perhaps the buyer is purchasing from a new vendor because the previous vendor went out of business or increased prices significantly. Other reasons for investigating new vendors may come from an analysis of the competition (through comparison shopping) or from current trade information (found in trade journals or trade shows).

Finally, retail buyers may hire the services of a resident buying office. Resident buying offices are retailers' representatives in a geographic area where many suppliers of a given product are located. New York City's garment

GLOBAL MARKET

Stocking Challenge

Ikea is one of the largest privately held companies in the world, with over 200 furniture stores in 31 countries, employing over 75,000 people and generating over 12 billion in sales annually. It all started in 1956 in southern Sweden when a local entrepreneur figured out that he could transport furniture more easily by taking it apart and packing it flat. The customer would put it together and the furniture prices could be lowered. Several decades later, the concept still works.

Purchasing Stock for Stores Around the World Ikea owns and runs 14 major distribution centers, and purchases stock from 2,300 suppliers in more than 64 countries. In the past few years, Ikea acquired a number of its own factories, some of which function as training units and set standards for other suppliers for production economy, quality, and environmental awareness.

To secure supplies and help suppliers develop, Ikea is also partnering as joint owners or financiers in a number of countries including Poland, Slovakia, Russia, Romania, and Bulgaria.

CRITICAL THINKING

Why did Ikea decide to purchase its own factories?

@ Online Action!

Go to *marketingessentials.glencoe.com/23/global* to find an activity about purchasing and international business.

marketingessentials.glencoe.com

GLOBAL MARKET

Stocking Challenge

Discussion After students have read the information about working with international suppliers, have them create a list of all the questions they can think of needed to guide the selection of an international supplier.

CRITICAL THINKING **Answer:** Answers will vary but could include that Ikea wanted to have more control over its products and to reduce the cost of purchasing from suppliers.

@ Online Action! For instructions, ideas, and answer guide, go to the Teacher Center at **marketingessentials.glencoe.com**

TEACH

Discussion Starter

TYPES OF PURCHASE SITUATIONS

Have students discuss how they buy clothes to replace those that they have outgrown. Ask: Do you go back to the same source? Do you buy the same item as a replacement? What factors enter into your decision?

Write the students' answers on the board to help introduce the types of purchase situations: new-task, modified rebuy, and straight rebuy. Ask students to project how these three purchase situations affect the way resale buyers and purchasing agents purchase goods.

Answers will vary but should recognize the need for more research prior to purchase for a new-task and modified rebuy than with a straight rebuy.

TEACHING POINTS

Model Using an example from your own experience evaluating textbooks and other learning materials, model for students the modified rebuy purchasing situation involved in selecting and buying new materials. Point out that changes in curriculum, the need to present up-to-date material, and higher standards are factors that prompt the need to purchase new materials.

Critical Thinking

Ask students: What kinds of things are purchased by school officials that enable our school to run efficiently? Have students list individual items then group them into categories such as learning-related items; classroom equipment; and cafeteria.

TEACH CONTINUED

Concept Development

SELECTING SUPPLIERS

Ask students what criteria they would use for selecting a vendor. For example, tell them to imagine that they are in charge of buying T-shirts for a DECA fundraiser, and they have a choice of three local and three out-of-state firms. List student responses on the board. Have students categorize them under headings such as production capability, past experience with the vendor, range of product offerings, and buying arrangements.

Enrichment

SPECIAL SERVICES

Point out that some socially conscious companies and government units require vendors to supply proof that they employ or do business with minorities. For example, Ben & Jerry's Ice Cream company has such a requirement. Ask students if they believe that businesses have the right to impose ethical criteria on their suppliers.

TEACHING POINTS

Clarify Point out that such a requirement impacts an industrial buyer's ability to negotiate the best deal. The buyer may not be able to take advantage of the lowest price if the low-price vendor does not meet the requirement.

Extended Activity

Purchasing Perishables
Lead a discussion about how some of the food we buy in supermarkets is imported. Ask students to research how a certain perishable good is imported. Some issues to consider include currency exchange rates, guarantee of freshness, and transportation.

- **WHERE ARE CLOTHES MADE?** Clothes you buy in the U.S. are often manufactured abroad. Hong Kong is a central market for the garment industry.

Look at the tags on a few items of clothing (yours or at a store). List the countries where the clothes were made.

district, for example, is a central market for apparel. Resident buying offices send information to retail buyers on a regular basis. They inform buyers about new merchandise offerings, closeouts, or fashion trends.

Straight Rebuy

In a straight-rebuy situation, the buyer routinely orders the goods and services purchased from the same vendor(s) as in the past. Staple goods such as office supplies fall into the straight-rebuy category for wholesale and retail buyers. The purchase of certain manufacturing supplies may be considered a straight rebuy. (See Figure 23.2 for a recap of types of purchases.)

Selecting Suppliers

The criteria for selecting suppliers fall into a few key categories. They include production capabilities, past experience, product and special buying arrangements, and special services.

Production Capabilities

When dealing with a source for the first time, buyers may request specific information about the source's production capabilities. They may even visit a facility in person to see it in operation. Buyers may solicit business references to determine the source's reputation in the industry. These factors would be extremely important when selecting suppliers and transportation firms as partners in a just-in-time production arrangement.

Production capabilities for some companies go beyond the actual physical plant into ethical and social issues, such as a review of facilities to ensure that they are not sweatshops. Sweatshops are factories characterized by poor working conditions and negligent treatment of employees.

Past Experiences

Many buyers maintain resource files that document past experiences with vendors. All basic information, such as products carried,

---

PHOTO GUIDE   WHERE ARE CLOTHES MADE?

Discussion Ask students if they have heard of any bad publicity some clothing and toy manufacturers have had in the past regarding the mistreatment of manufacturing employees in foreign countries. Point out that, to combat this negative publicity, some companies have begun publicizing their efforts to work for improved labor standards in other countries.

Caption Answer Answers will vary but may include the United States as well as countries in Central America, South America, and Asia.

Follow Up Ask students to discuss why worker treatment and labor standards are ethical issues.

Figure 23.2 — Types of Purchases

•Stocking Up A purchasing manager may be faced with three buying situations: the new-task purchase, the modified rebuy, and the straight rebuy. The level of difficulty varies depending on the type of purchase.

What circumstances might lead to a modified rebuy type of purchase?

NEW-TASK PURCHASE

A new-task purchase is a first-time buy. This is the most complicated buying situation. It may be triggered by the identification of a previously unrecognized need or the decision to switch vendors. New-task purchases often involve input from a buying committee, as shown here.

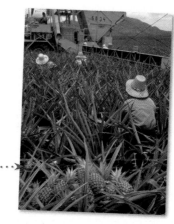

MODIFIED REBUY

In a modified rebuy, the buyer has had experience buying the item, but is changing something about the purchase: perhaps the product line, the vendor, or the grower.

STRAIGHT REBUY

With a straight rebuy, the buyer repeats a purchase that was made in the past. This buyer is reordering shoes he already carries in his store in order to replenish stock.

@ Online Action! Go to *marketingessentials.glencoe.com/23/figure/2* to find a project on types of purchases.

marketingessentials.glencoe.com

Concept Development

SPECIAL BUYING ARRANGEMENTS

Ask students to list the differences between consignment buying and memorandum buying. Then ask students to name who owns the inventory in consignment buying and why the distinction between consignment buying and memorandum buying is important.

In the case of consignment buying, the original supplier owns the inventory until it is sold. In the case of memorandum buying, the wholesaler or retailer owns the inventory, even though he or she may have certain return privileges. The distinction is important because of tax and insurance implications. In most situations, the entity that owns the inventory is responsible for taxes, and the entity that holds the goods is responsible for insuring them against loss.

TEACHING POINTS

Recall Remind students that ordinary dating terms are "2 percent within 10 days, net 30 days," or 2/10, net 30. This means that if the invoice is paid within 10 days the purchaser can deduct 2 percent as a discount. Otherwise, the invoice is due to be paid within 30 days of receipt.

Figure 23.2 — Types of Purchases

Discussion After students have read **Figure 23.2**, have them give examples of situations that would lead to each type of purchase.

Caption Answer Answers will vary and may include customer dissatisfaction, an error on the buyer or seller's part, or changing to a new vendor when the prior vendor is unable to fill the order.

@ Online Action! For instructions, ideas, and answer guide, go to the Teacher Center at **marketingessentials.glencoe.com**

Follow Up Ask students to tell which type of purchase would be prompted by these situations:

- a light bulb burns out (straight rebuy)
- family decides to get its first dog (new-task)
- your 20-year old washing machine breaks down and needs to be replaced (modified rebuy)

ASSESS

Review Guide

CONCEPTS
Have students list criteria for selecting suppliers.
production capabilities, range of product offerings, past experience with the vendor, and buying arrangements

Ask students to explain consignment buying, memorandum buying, dating terms, auctions, and reverse auctions.

KEY TERMS
Have students review key terms, their spellings, and definitions in small groups.

ONLINE SELF-ASSESSMENT
Have students go to marketingessentials.glencoe.com for the Section 23.2 practice test.

Individualized Review

L1 Assign and review Chapter 23 activities in the Student Activity Workbook.

L2 Assign and review Chapter 23 activities in the Marketing Math Workbook.

L3 Assign and review Chapter 23 activities in the *BusinessWeek* Reader and Case Studies.

Marketing Practice

To experience first hand what comparison shopping involves, have students identify competing stores in the area and specific items of merchandise to compare. Have students work in teams to compare those store items in terms of price, promotion, and merchandising/display. Have the teams report their findings to the class in a ten-minute presentation.

---

prices, delivery and dating terms, and the names of sales representatives, is recorded. Also noted are evaluations of products, delivery performance, and customer service. A major factor in selecting a supplier is the quality of goods it offers. Retail buyers keep accurate records of customer returns and the reasons for them. Returns relating to the quality of the goods may cause a vendor to be dropped as a supplier.

Special Buying Arrangements
Suppliers may have special policies regarding merchandise returns and sales arrangements. Two special types of sales and return policies are called consignment buying and memorandum buying.

In **consignment buying**, goods are paid for only after the final customer purchases them. The supplier owns the goods until the wholesaler or retailer sells them. Many suppliers offer consignment buying as an incentive when introducing a new line of goods. However, a problem arises with consignment buying when merchandise is stolen or damaged, raising the question of who is responsible and who must pay.

Memorandum buying occurs when the supplier agrees to take back any unsold goods by a certain pre-established date. The buyer pays for all the goods purchased but is later reimbursed for all the goods returned in accordance with the agreement. This buying arrangement allows for returns.

Special Services
Businesses today demand more services from their suppliers than just the basic return policy. Suppliers must keep up with these services to stay competitive.

One special service that many retailers are requesting or demanding is the placement by manufacturers of universal product codes (UPCs) on goods. Having the codes on all products saves the retailer time because individual items do not have to be marked with a price. It also helps retailers keep track of what they have in stock.

Negotiating Terms
Buyers must negotiate prices, dating terms, delivery arrangements, and discounts. You learned about dating terms and delivery arrangements in Chapter 16. Discounts are any reductions from the quoted price. Such reductions are generally granted for the buyer's performance of certain functions. These will be discussed in Chapter 26.

Dating terms include when a bill must be paid and the discount permitted for paying early. You learned about ordinary dating (2/10, net 30) in Chapter 16, but there are several variations for specific situations. A company may allow the dating terms to take effect later than the invoice date. This type of dating, which is known as advance dating, is sometimes offered to businesses as an incentive to buy before the buying season. An invoice may be dated January 15 and include the following advance dating terms: 2/10, net 30, as of March 1.

In other situations, additional days may be granted for the discount (called extra dating). This special dating may be used to encourage a buyer to purchase new merchandise. In still another situation, the terms begin when the buyer's firm receives the goods, which is called ROG dating (receipt of goods).

Internet Purchasing
Business-to-business (B2B) e-commerce has revolutionized the purchasing function for businesses in the industrial and reseller markets. Organizational buyers account for 80 percent of the total dollar value of all online transactions. Increased use of online buying is expected to continue. This is partly because organizational buyers have come to depend heavily on timely supplier information, and such information can be easily and quickly conveyed via the Internet. Another reason is that businesses have found that online purchasing dramatically reduces marketing costs for many types of products and services.

Most of the B2B e-commerce transactions are routine purchases of products such as

---

Extended Activity

Auctions
Help students experience the auction and reverse auction by dividing the class into two groups. Have one group decide on an item they want to buy and the other decide on an item they want to sell. Have each group conduct an auction. After the two auctions are completed, ask students to write a paragraph or two on each type of auction, describing their differences and similarities.

office supplies. The Internet makes the process more efficient.

Many companies have their own Web sites from which other companies may make purchases directly. Growing in popularity, however, are electronic exchanges where registered users can buy and sell their goods online. Most of these electronic exchanges are in specific industries, such as the NECX Global Electronics Exchange, an open market for electronic components, computer products, and networking equipment.

Another Internet purchasing trend involves online auction companies. An auction usually involves having a seller set an asking price and buyers try to outbid each other. In other cases, a reverse auction takes place. In a **reverse auction**, companies post what they want to buy and suppliers bid for the contract.

Purchasing online through third parties has both advantages and disadvantages.

The biggest advantage is lower prices. However, as with most businesses on the Internet, privacy is a problem. Some companies fear that competitors will know how much was paid for materials and supplies. To combat that problem, some big companies, like Intel and General Electric, have decided to run their own reverse auctions. GE spent just $15,000 to write its own reverse auction software. This has inspired other companies to follow.

GE's trading process network (TPN) enables GE buyers to post requests for quotes, negotiate, and place orders with global suppliers. The TPN has lowered GE's purchasing costs by over 20 percent.

Another problem with the online purchasing process, especially in a reverse auction, is that unknown companies could artificially deflate prices by bidding low prices. Such a practice would benefit buyers but cause bad relationships with suppliers.

23.2 AFTER YOU READ

Reviewing Key Terms and Concepts

1. What are three ways a buyer can acquire information that is helpful in a modified-rebuy situation.
2. How does the buyer's payment for goods differ between consignment and memorandum buying?
3. Name one advantage and one disadvantage of purchasing online.

Integrating Academic Skills

Math

4. Vendor A sells 144 (1 gross) coffee mugs at $496.50 with free shipping. Dating terms are 2/10, net 30. Vendor B's offer is $3.15 per mug for one gross, with shipping charges of $25, and payment is COD. Which vendor is offering the better deal?

Language Arts

5. You received a delivery that does not meet your specifications. Use a word processing program to write a letter to the supplier describing the problem and requesting the action you would like them to take.

 Online Action!

Check your answers at *marketingessentials.glencoe.com/23/read*

 marketingessentials.glencoe.com

Chapter 23 - Purchasing **495**

SECTION 23.2

CLOSE

Ask students to recall and provide answers to the following questions.

- **What are the three types of purchasing situations?**

  new-task, modified rebuy, and straight rebuy

- **What factors do buyers consider when evaluating a vendor?**

  production capabilities, past experience with the vendor, product offerings, and buying arrangements

- **What special buying arrangements might a buyer be looking for?**

  price, dating terms, shipping terms, return policy, and any special services available

Critical Thinking

Ask students to list advantages companies might have for having strict criteria for their suppliers.

AFTER YOU READ

Reviewing Key Terms and Concepts

1. A buyer should stay abreast of industry trends by reading general business publications, attending trade shows, and hiring resident buying services.

2. Consignment goods are paid for when they are purchased from the reseller. Memorandum goods are paid for when purchased from the supplier, but the price of unsold goods may be refunded to the reseller.

3. Answers will vary. Advantages include timely supplier information, reduction of costs, and ease. Disadvantages include potential privacy issues and unknown companies.

Integrating Academic Skills

4. Vendor A cost = $486.57. Vendor B cost = $478.60. Vendor B is a better deal.

5. Letters will vary; all letters should include the problem and the action requested.

Online Action! Answers at **marketingessentials.glencoe.com/23/read**

CAREERS IN MARKETING

Lifelong Learning

CAREER INFORMATION

Have students go to marketingessentials.glencoe.com and find the Chapter 23 Careers page and click on the link for the American Marketing Association's Careers Strategies and Tips. Ask students to select one article, read it, and summarize it in three short paragraphs.

THE PURCHASING FUNCTION

Ask students what qualities or skills they think are necessary to be a buyer. Tell students that to become a good buyer, they must stay abreast of trends in their industry and continue to comparison shop for the best possible suppliers and manufacturers. They should also keep in mind that technical skills are required to adequately create a reliable production plan.

Primary Source

Ask students to go to marketingessentials.glencoe.com and find Chapter 23 Resources. Ask them to click on the link for the American Marketing Association's marketing dictionary and read the definitions of the purchasing-related terms they find.

THINKING CRITICALLY

Answers might include the idea that love of one's work is an important ingredient for success in a career because it is a motivation to do one's best.

For instructions, ideas, and answer guide, go to the Teacher Center at marketingessentials.glencoe.com

JACOB SCHOENLY
OWNER
SYNTHETIC SPACE FURNITURE LIGHTING & ACCESSORIES

(?) What do you do at work?
The company is a small operation, and so I wear many hats. I maintain the Web site, select and purchase the vintage items that we resell, respond to customer inquiries, and process and ship orders.

(?) What skills are most important to you?
Perhaps the most important skill as a small business owner is the ability to multitask. Each day brings a variety of tasks that need to be fulfilled, and the person running a business has to ensure that everything is accomplished. This often means that if the owner wants something done, and done right, he has to do it himself. Beyond skills, there are important personality traits, such as honesty and reliability, that can help you make your business a success.

I am a strong believer in education. A solid liberal arts education is all that you need in order to begin a successful career. Such an education serves as a strong foundation for more specific on-the-job training that an employee might need. If someone is looking to start a business in a particular field, then prior work experience in that field can be helpful but is not an absolute requirement.

(?) What is your key to success?
Loving what I do. When you feel that way about your job, it no longer seems like work. I also strive to treat customers the same way that I would like to be treated, offering service that meets or exceeds their demands.

Aptitudes, Abilities, and Skills

Creativity, interpersonal skills and an outgoing personality, the ability to multitask and prioritize goals and demands

Education and Training

A liberal arts degree, coupled with real-world work experience in your chosen field, makes for a solid beginning.

Career Path

Retail store owners might begin their career working for someone else, or they might open up their own shop right away. Often, niche retailers are driven by the owner's personal interests and hobbies.

THINKING CRITICALLY

Why is a love for one's career so valuable?

 Online Action!

Go to *marketingessentials.glencoe.com/ 23/careers* to find a career-related activity.

Test-Taking Strategies

Suggest to students that they save time at the end of an exam to review the test questions and make sure they have not left out any answers or parts of answers. Students may find this difficult to do under the stress of an exam situation, but let them know that this kind of review can prevent inadvertent errors.

FOCUS on KEY POINTS

SECTION 23.1

● Organizational buyers in industrial and resellers' (wholesale and retail) markets purchase goods in much greater quantities than the average consumer.

● Buyers for government markets make purchases of goods and services for one of the largest single markets in the world.

SECTION 23.2

● The three types of purchase situations are new-task purchase, modified rebuy, and straight rebuy.

● The primary criteria for selecting suppliers are (1) production capabilities, (2) past experience, (3) special buying arrangements (such as consignment buying and memorandum buying), and (4) special services.

● The Internet has revolutionized purchasing in the industrial and resellers markets, and online buying is expected to grow in coming years.

REVIEW VOCABULARY

Write one sentence for each group of vocabulary terms, using each term in context.

1. organizational, wholesale, and retail buyers (pp. 482, 485)

2. six-month merchandise plan and open-to-buy (OTB) (pp. 485, 487)

3. centralized versus decentralized buying (pp. 488, 489)

4. want slips (p. 491)

5. consignment, memorandum buying, and reverse auction (pp. 494, 495)

REVIEW FACTS and IDEAS

6. List three titles for manufacturing or service business buyers. (23.1)

7. Identify the type of planning used to guide purchasing by organizational buyers and that used by buyers for the resale market. (23.1)

8. What is the six-month merchandise plan? What four figures must be calculated in order to complete a six-month merchandise plan? (23.1)

9. What method of buying is used by chain stores? Why? (23.1)

10. List three types of purchase situations that a buyer may encounter. (23.2)

11. What criteria do buyers use to evaluate suppliers? (23.2)

12. What factors are negotiable in determining the terms of a sale? (23.2)

REVIEW FACTS and IDEAS

6. Three titles are purchasing managers, industrial buyers, or procurement managers

7. Organizational buyers use production planning. Buyers for the resale market use six-month merchandise planning.

8. A six-month merchandise plan is a budget that estimates planned purchases for a six-month period. The four figures are planned sales, BOM/EOM, planned retail reductions, and planned purchases.

9. Centralized buying is used by chain stores to take advantage of the benefits of a unified image and the savings of quantity discounts.

10. Three types of purchase situations are new-task purchases, modified rebuy, and straight rebuy.

11. The criteria include production capabilities, past experiences, special buying arrangements, and special services.

12. Negotiable factors include prices, dating terms, delivery arrangements, and discounts.

FOCUS on KEY POINTS

Ask volunteers to read aloud the summaries to the class and give one real-world example for each concept.

REVIEW VOCABULARY

Sentences will vary and should include each of the key terms. See glossary for definitions of **1–5.** A sample answer might read:

1. *Organizational buyers* purchase goods for business purposes while *retail* and *wholesale* buyers purchase goods for resale.

BUILD SKILLS

13. Workplace Skills
Outlines and anticipated problems and solutions will vary but should include training for those who are not computer literate and a way for the buyers to maintain the good relationships they have built.

14. Technology Applications
Sample want slips and memos will vary but should include the correct elements.

15. Math Practice
$1,016.14 × 17 percent = $172.74
$1,016.14 − $172.74 = $843.40

DEVELOP CRITICAL THINKING

16. Analyzing Institutional Buying
Answers will vary depending on the interviewee and the business in which he or she works.

17. Internet Purchasing
Answers will vary but should include the idea that much industrial buying is concerned with purchasing commodities, such as raw materials, where there is very little or no difference in the products offered by the various vendors. Much of this type of purchasing is straight rebuy, which is well suited to the Internet.

BUILD SKILLS

13. Workplace Skills
Human Relations You are a division manager. Top-level management has instructed you to require your buyers to use online buying for the purchase of standardized products. Some of your longtime buyers are not computer literate and value the relationships they have established with their suppliers. Write an outline of the points you will present to your buyers. Make sure your outline includes:
- Problems you can anticipate
- How you would handle those problems

14. Technology Applications
Writing a Memo You work as a salesclerk in a men's clothing store. Several young customers have inquired about a popular line of clothing that you do not sell. You believe updating the young men's department would increase sales. Using a word processing program, create and complete a want slip for this line of clothing. Then write a memo to accompany your request, explaining to your buyer the merits of your proposal.

15. Math Practice
Discounts Suppose you own a craft supplies store, and you place an order with a fabric manufacturer for several bolts of printed cotton. The manufacturer offers you a 17 percent trade discount. The total list price is $1,016.14. How much do you have to pay?

DEVELOP CRITICAL THINKING

16. Analyzing Institutional Buying
Interview an institutional buyer in your community. Find out what kinds of products they buy and why, and what unique buying requirements they have. Report your findings to your class.

17. Internet Purchasing
Why is online buying popular in industrial markets? Explain your answer using two or three examples.

Formative Assessment
Formative assessment is an essential component of classroom work. This type of assessment provides information that is then used as feedback to modify teaching and meet student needs.

L1 Review key terms for this chapter. Ask students to write one sentence for each key term.

L2 Provide various examples of factors that affect purchasing in story form. After each story, have the students identify the factors that affected the purchasing situation.

L3 As students to create stories that illustrate the three types of purchasing situations: new-task, modified rebuy, and straight rebuy.

Reteach **If results of this formative assessment seem low, consider the following activity:**
Ask students to describe the following in their own words: 1) how purchases are planned for industrial and reseller markets; 2) types of purchasing situations.

APPLY CONCEPTS

18. Developing a Six-Month Plan Spreadsheet

Use a spreadsheet program to create a six-month merchandise plan using the data shown in Figure 23.1 of your text. Learn how to write formulas so that your worksheet will automatically calculate the figures for the current year's planned sales, BOM, planned reductions, and planned purchases.

Activity Note these formulas on the bottom of your worksheet. Change the expected sales increase to five percent and the planned reductions to 10 percent. Enter the data and complete the plan.

19. Selecting a Vendor

Do an Internet search on printer cartridge suppliers. Read the details from two of the top-rated suppliers. Using a word processing program, report on the services, prices, and product quality of each of these two suppliers.

Activity Report, as a buyer, which supplier you would use. Explain your rationale.

NET SAVVY

20. Chain Store Buyer

Conduct an Internet search using the phrase *popular chain stores.* Also search through a national online job board. Read through descriptions of store buyer positions and make a list of common qualifications for these positions.

THE DECA CONNECTION

Role Play: Fashion Buyer

Situation You are to assume the role of assistant buyer for the women's sportswear department of a large department store chain in the upper Midwest of the United States. Your department sells a large number of cotton turtleneck tops each year. The buyer (judge) has used one vendor for many seasons. The vendor can no longer supply seasonal fashion colors but is able to supply the basic colors. The buyer (judge) has asked you to help find a vendor to supply the fashion color turtlenecks in a comparable quality and price.

Activity You are to explain to the buyer (judge) how you will go about finding a new vendor for the turtlenecks.

Evaluation You will be evaluated on the following performance indicators:

- Conduct vendor search
- Explain the nature of buyer reputation/vendor relationship
- Explain company buying/purchasing policies
- Negotiate contracts with vendors
- Explain the nature of the buying process

 Online Action!

For more information and DECA Prep practice, go to *marketingessentials.glencoe .com/23/DECA*

APPLY CONCEPTS

14. Developing a Six-Month Plan Spreadsheet

Worksheets will vary; all worksheets should demonstrate understanding of merchandise plans and how to calculate formulas in the spreadsheet program.

15. Selecting a Vendor

Reports and rationales will vary; students should use criteria mentioned in the chapter.

NET SAVVY

16. Chain Store Buyer

Reports will vary; students should include a variety of job opportunities and descriptions.

THE DECA CONNECTION

Students should be evaluated according to the performance standards noted in the role play. For another DECA role play, go to the Competitive Events Workbook or the Student Activity Workbook, or go to **marketingessentials.glencoe.com/23/DECA**

 Online Action! For instructions, ideas, and answer guide, go to the Teacher Center at **marketingessentials.glencoe.com**

DECA Advisors Corner

Leadership skills, a portfolio, and a system of recognition reaching from the local to the national level—these are the rewards you can offer your chapter members through the DECA Leadership Education Action Program (LEAP). Students are encouraged to participate at their own pace.

MINI-QUIZ

Administer the Mini-Quiz either orally or on paper.

1. What are the people responsible for purchasing called in manufacturing and service businesses? (purchasing managers)

2. What is the formula for planned purchases?

$$[(PS + EOM + R - BOM) = P]$$

3. What is information about when a bill must be paid and the discount permitted for early payment called? (dating terms)

For an expanded chapter quiz, go to Chapter 23 in the TeacherWorks CD-ROM and to Chapter 23 in the **ExamView®** Pro Test Generator CD-ROM.

Chapter Overview

Chapter 24 discusses the key functions in the distribution system of stock handling and inventory control, including the steps in the receiving process for merchandise, the concept of inventory control, and the types of inventory systems. This chapter also exposes students to the concepts of unit and dollar control of inventory, stock turnover, and stock management. Finally, students will explore the impact of technology on inventory systems.

⊜ BUILD BACKGROUND ⊜

Have students think of some reasons why merchandise might arrive damaged at a storage facility or business.

Some possibilities include: poor packing of the product, either in its packing or in the carrier itself; mishandling merchandise before or after it is shipped; and bad weather conditions that made the physical transport of the merchandise unusually rough.

Why It's Important

To be successful and efficient, businesses must have stock handling and inventory systems in place. Together, they help control costs and ensure the operations can continue without interruption.

Prepare to Read

List the section objectives to discuss them with students. Have the students skim the chapter, looking at the pictures, reading the captions, and noting the heads. Ask questions to ensure students have a basic understanding of the chapter structure.

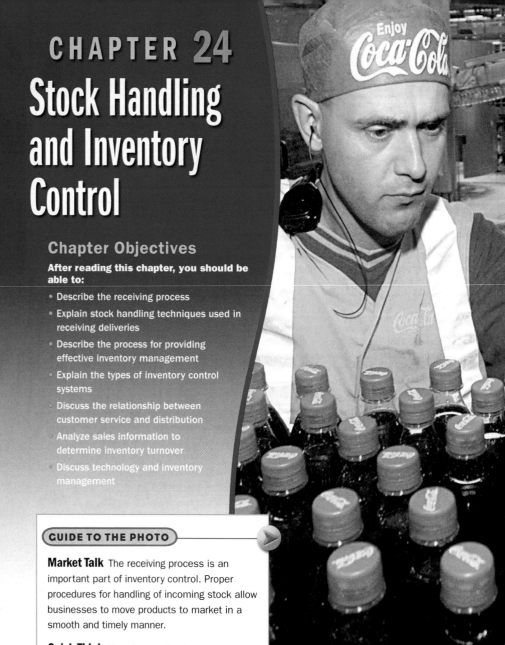

CHAPTER 24
Stock Handling and Inventory Control

Chapter Objectives

After reading this chapter, you should be able to:

- Describe the receiving process
- Explain stock handling techniques used in receiving deliveries
- Describe the process for providing effective inventory management
- Explain the types of inventory control systems
- Discuss the relationship between customer service and distribution
- Analyze sales information to determine inventory turnover
- Discuss technology and inventory management

⟩ GUIDE TO THE PHOTO

Market Talk The receiving process is an important part of inventory control. Proper procedures for handling of incoming stock allow businesses to move products to market in a smooth and timely manner.

Quick Think How does technology help control inventory?

500 UNIT 7 - DISTRIBUTION

GUIDE TO THE PHOTO

Market Talk Lead students in a discussion about possible problems that might arise in the inventory situation shown in the photograph. Ask students to identify factors that could lead to inefficiencies.

Quick Think Technology has simplified the way inventory is accounted for by making it easier to track items through the purchasing and distribution process.

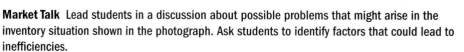 Follow Up Ask students if they have ever worked in an environment that had inventory management problems, such as lost or misplaced products. Have students discuss their experiences in class.

THE DECA CONNECTION

An Association of Marketing Students

Performance indicators represent key skills and knowledge. Relating them to the concepts explained in this chapter is your key to success in DECA events.

These acronyms represent DECA events that involve knowledge of concepts in this chapter.

AAAL*	FMAL*	MMS	TMDM*
AAML*	FMDM	QSRM*	TSE
ADC	FMML*	RMAL*	VPM
BSM	FSRM*	RMML*	
EMDM	HMDM*	SMDM	

In all these DECA events you should be able to follow these performance indicators:

- Explain the receiving process
- Describe the use of technology in the distribution process

Events with an asterisk (*) also include:

- Explain stock-handling techniques used in receiving deliveries
- Determine processing priorities
- Check incoming stock
- Reconcile shipping/receiving discrepancies
- File claims for lost/damaged goods
- Process returns to vendors
- Maintain inventory levels
- Complete inventory counts
- Explain the nature of inventory control systems
- Calculate inventory shrinkage

Some events include additional performance indicators. These are:

EMDM	Explain types of unit inventory control systems
AAAL/AAML	Transfer stock to/from branches
RMAL/RMML	Transfer stock to/from branches

DECA PREP

Check your understanding of DECA performance indicators with the DECA activity in this chapter's review. For more information and DECA Prep practice, go to *marketingessentials .glencoe.com/24/DECA*

Chapter 24 - Stock Handling and Inventory Control **501**

THE DECA CONNECTION

An Association of Marketing Students

DECA events that require knowledge of stock handling and inventory control are described here. Discuss the performance indicators to make sure students understand how to demonstrate their understanding.

The events acronyms stand for:

AAAL: Apparel and Accessories Marketing Series, AL

AAML: Apparel and Accessories Marketing Series, ML

ADC: Advertising Campaign Event

BSM: Business Services Marketing Series

EMDM: E-Commerce Management Team Decision Making Event

FMAL: Food Marketing Series, AL

FMDM: Financial Analysis Management Team Decision Making Event

FMML: Food Marketing Series, ML

FSRM: Full Service Restaurant Management Series

HMDM: Hospitality Services Management Team Decision Making Event

MMS: Marketing Management Series

QSRM: Quick Serve Restaurant Management Series

RMAL: Retail Merchandising Series, AL

RMML: Retail Merchandising Series, ML

VPM: Vehicles and Petroleum Marketing Series

TSE: Technical Sales Event

SMDM: Sports and Entertainment Marketing Management Team Decision Making Event

TMDM: Travel and Tourism Marketing Management Team Decision Making Event

DECA PREP

Find timed DECA Prep activities correlated to the Competitive Events Workbook for students and DECA tips for teachers at **marketingessentials.glencoe.com /24/DECA**

CHAPTER 24 Classroom Resources

For the Teacher

- TeacherWorks
- marketingessentials.glencoe.com
- Interactive Chalkboard
- **Exam*View*®** Pro Test Generator
- Fast File Unit 7

For the Student

- ***Marketing Essentials*** Online Edition
- Student Activity Workbook
- Marketing Math Workbook
- Marketing Research Project Workbook
- School-to-Work Activity Workbook
- Competitive Events Workbook
- ***BusinessWeek*** Reader and Case Studies
- marketingessentials.glencoe.com

FOCUS

Introducing the Section

COLLABORATIVE ACTIVITY

Ask students to help you brainstorm and write on the board topics that might be included in a fulfillment services policy for inventory handling and warehousing of incoming goods.

This policy might discuss the following topics: documentation, incoming shipments, storage/warehousing, security, and palletization.

Preteaching Key Terms

Ask students to view the section's key terms and predict information they expect to learn from these words. Have them write down these predictions in their journal. Next, ask them to recall related stories and experiences about those words. Lastly, allow the students to look up the meaning of the vocabulary words.

- receiving record
- blind check method
- direct check method
- spot check method
- quality check method
- source marking
- preretailing marking method

 Critical Thinking

Ask students to explain the importance and possible responsibilities of a receiving clerk at a manufacturing plant.

OBJECTIVES

- Describe the receiving process
- Explain stock handling techniques used in receiving deliveries

The Stock Handling Process

KEY TERMS

- **receiving record**
- **blind check method**
- **direct check method**
- **spot check method**
- **quality check method**
- **source marking**
- **preretailing marking method**

READ and STUDY

BEFORE YOU READ

Predict What are some ways to prepare merchandise to sell?

THE MAIN IDEA

All businesses must have a stock handling process in place to accept deliveries of materials or products. The receiving process must be done efficiently and correctly to insure that proper inventory levels are maintained at all times.

STUDY ORGANIZER

Copy the flow chart organizer below. Use the chart to identify key steps in the stock handling process.

Stock Handling Process

Receiving Merchandise

WHILE YOU READ

Question When an order for materials or products is received, what are some problems that might occur at delivery?

Stock Handling

Manufacturing companies depend on suppliers to deliver parts or raw materials used in making finished products accurately and on time. When these parts or materials are delivered to the warehouse, plant, or store, they must be received into stock and information about them must be recorded and tracked. For example, suppose a door handle manufacturer has a contract with an automobile assembly plant to supply door handles

502 UNIT 7 - DISTRIBUTION

READ and STUDY

BEFORE YOU READ
Ask students to list factors that make merchandise presentable and desirable for consumers.

THE MAIN IDEA
Ask volunteers to speculate about what happens when inventory levels are inaccurate.

STUDY ORGANIZER
Model the study organizer for students by filling in the second step in the flow chart. A full-size, downloadable study organizer can be found at **marketingessentials.glencoe.com**

 WHILE YOU READ Possible discrepancies might include: no purchase order on packing list, partial shipment, duplicate shipments, missing shipment, wrong item/model and/or color shipped, or damaged merchandise.

for pickup trucks. They deliver door handles almost every day to keep pace with production at the assembly plant.

Whether a business receives raw materials, parts, or merchandise for resale, it needs a process to handle the items. The steps in the stock handling process include receiving goods, checking them, marking the goods with information, if necessary, and delivering them to a place where they will be used, stored, or displayed for sale. The receiving clerk at the truck assembly plant who checks in the door handles must make sure that the correct part has been delivered, that the right number are there, and that they get to the assembly line in time to be installed on the pickup truck doors. The receiving clerk must also make sure that information about the parts is recorded in the system so that inventory levels are correct and the accounts payable department knows to pay the invoice from the door handle manufacturer.

Receiving Stock

Stock ordered by a business is received, checked, and, in retail settings, often marked with a selling price before it is transferred to the sales area.

Facilities

Where stock is placed when it is received depends on the type and size of the business. Smaller businesses may use a backroom or may even place items in store aisles when they are received. Many businesses, however, have enough space to devote an area of a loading dock, or first floor to receiving.

Large businesses and chain stores sometimes have separate warehouses or distribution centers where merchandise is received and stored before it is taken to the department or branch store that needs it. Facilities such as these have large bays with loading docks that open at the height of the bed of a truck for easy unloading.

Receiving Records

Every business records information about the goods it receives either manually or electronically in a **receiving record**. The items

on a receiving record depend on the needs of the business. They can include the following:

- A receiving number
- Person who received the shipment
- Shipper of the merchandise
- Place from which the goods were shipped
- Name of the carrier
- Number of the carrier
- Number of items delivered
- Weight of items delivered
- Condition of the goods received
- Shipping charges
- Department or store that ordered the merchandise
- Date the shipment was received

Each set of goods received is assigned a receiving number. Some businesses include this number on a record called an apron. An apron is a form that is attached to the invoice that accompanies the goods received before they move through checking and marking. The apron system helps prevent the payment of duplicate invoices because the invoice is only paid when the proper information is recorded on the apron.

The receiving number may be called an apron number for businesses using this system. In retail businesses, the apron is often prepared by a store's buyers. For example, Lydia buys accessories for a women's clothing shop. She prepares apron forms for a shipment of scarves she ordered when they arrive. These forms will travel through the system with the scarves as they are inspected, priced, prepared for display, and finally placed on the sales floor. The apron lists the steps the scarves take to reach the selling floor and includes the receiving number, the department number, the purchase order number, any terms on the purchase order and on the invoice, routing information, and the date the shipment was checked.

Checking Merchandise

Merchandise is checked to verify quantity and condition; cartons are checked for damage, and the goods are sorted and counted.

Chapter 24 - Stock Handling and Inventory Control **503**

Extended Activity

Inventory Criteria

Offer students the following scenario: They work for a manufacturer that ships products for domestic as well as international markets. Management has asked them to list the criteria to consider when selecting a freight carrier to move its products to market and help control the inventory. Ask students to identify what selection criteria they might need. Answers will vary; suggested criteria needed may include computerized inventory tracking systems and an electronic data interchange.

TEACH

IMPORTANCE OF STOCK HANDLING

Have students think about how they might receive inventory in the school store. Ask: How would they check it to verify quantity and condition? How would they mark it and move it to the sales area? If you do not have a school store, ask how students would verify quantity and condition.

TEACHING POINTS

Clarify Tell students that receiving, checking, and marking inventory are all considered part of the physical distribution process.

Concept Development

FACILITIES

Have students think of some ways that receiving, checking, marking, and transferring merchandise would be handled on these products: flowers and plants; produce; seafood and red meat; and animals received at a pet store.

All of these products would probably be more closely inspected than other products that are easier to check, such as packaged goods.

TEACHING POINTS

Clarify Remind students that those responsible for receiving and inspecting the products depend on the size of the company. Specially trained employees called receivers are responsible for checking merchandise in larger businesses, while smaller businesses may use sale associates, a manager, or even the owner to perform this activity.

Concept Development

METHODS OF CHECKING

At a business's year-end, a complete physical inventory for its annual audit is often required. For example, the U.S. government abides by this timeline: Inventory planning takes one to two months before inventory preparation, which takes one week; then there is the inventory day followed by post inventory completed within 30 days of the inventory. Ask students to list concerns that might appear under each section of the timeline.

TEACHING POINTS

Explain Tell the students that an annual audit is necessary for a variety of reasons, but most importantly, it discloses the accounting methods the company uses and determines the amount of money tied up in inventory.

Extend Tell students that damaged or obsolete goods are also part of the inventory audit. These types of goods are saleable at reduced prices. Ask students to consider why these items are considered part of inventory.

Answers may include that all items need to be accounted for.

Enrichment

INVENTORY COSTS

Ask students to create a bulleted list of five items that name costs a business incurs from carrying inventory.

Answers will vary; costs might include cost of moving inventory in warehouse and tracking receipts, overhead costs of warehouse where inventory is stored, insurance and taxes on inventory, physical inventory counting methods, shrinkage and obsolescence, and return on investment ratio from holding stock.

A MATTER OF ETHICS

Quality Control

Carlo had recently returned to work after raising a family. He got a job at a furniture manufacturer as a receiving clerk and was soon promoted to department manager. Upon receiving and inspecting a shipment of padding from a supplier, Carlo noticed that the quality of the padding was not according to the buyer's specifications that were listed on the purchase order.

Risk a Large Order or Not?

Carlo suspected that either a mistake had been made or the supplier had shipped the wrong merchandise. But when he reported his findings to the buyer, he was told to ignore the situation. The buyer said that the company needed the padding immediately to complete a large order. He said if the order was not completed by the end of the week, the company would lose the business altogether and that could jeopardize everyone's job.

THINKING ETHICALLY

Do you think that Carlo should report his findings or follow the buyer's request to ignore the situation? Explain.

@ Online Action!

Go to *marketingessentials.glencoe.com/ 24/ethics* to find a project on the use of inferior materials.

Some businesses use specially trained employees called receivers to inspect and record newly arrived merchandise.

In the past, checking merchandise was a time- and labor-intensive process. Today, however, electronic data interchange systems

---

minimize the time required for this process. For example, the door handle manufacturer's distribution center can notify the truck assembly plant in advance with information about which cartons of door handles to expect each day and the contents of each carton. Upon receipt at the assembly plant, coded shipping box labels are electronically scanned, the carton's contents are identified, and the information is automatically transferred to an inventory management computer system.

Methods of Checking

There are four methods that are frequently used to check merchandise: the blind check, the direct check, the spot check, and the quality check. Figure 24.1 illustrates the methods of checking merchandise.

The **blind check method** requires the receiver to write the description of the merchandise, count the quantities received, and list them on a blank form or dummy invoice. The list or dummy invoice is then compared to the actual invoice after the blind check is made. The blind check method is considered the most accurate checking method, but it can be time consuming. The blind check method is used when the merchandise needs to be moved quickly to the sales floor and the actual invoice has not yet been received from the seller. Invoices often follow the shipment of goods by two or more days.

With the **direct check method**, the merchandise is checked directly against the actual invoice or purchase order. This procedure is faster than the blind check method, but errors may not be found if the invoice itself is incorrect. Some receivers do not completely check the total number of items once they see the amount listed on the invoice: if the amount looks correct, they may not bother to take an actual count.

The **spot check method** is a random check of one carton in a shipment (such as one out of every twenty). The carton is checked for quantity, and then one product in the carton is inspected for quality. When the contents are as stated on the invoice, the remaining cartons

 marketingessentials.glencoe.com

A MATTER OF ETHICS — Quality Control

Discussion Lead a discussion about the possible emotional and professional issues Carlo may be facing with this dilemma.

THINKING ETHICALLY Answers will vary. This comes down to personal ethics whether or not someone reports this situation to the head of the department. It is always best to report the situation first to one's direct supervisor with documented evidence of such action.

@ Online Action! For instructions, ideas, and answer guide, go to the Teacher Center at marketingessentials.glencoe.com

Follow Up Ask for students to volunteer what they could do if they were in Carlo's situation. Have them explain their positions.

Figure 24.1 — Checking Merchandise

• Four Methods When a shipment is received, it must be checked to determine if the merchandise arrived in the right quantities and in good condition. Once a time- and labor-intensive process, it has been greatly simplified by electronic data interchange systems, which transfer information about the order to the receiver. The merchandise must still be checked manually for accuracy and quality assurance. Four methods of checking are commonly used.

What method would likely be used for new-task purchases?

BLIND CHECK

With this method, the receiver counts and records the quantities delivered on a dummy invoice. That information is then compared to the original invoice. This method is considered the most accurate but may be time consuming.

DIRECT CHECK

When using the direct check method, the receiver checks merchandise against the original invoice. This procedure is faster than the blind check. Errors may be introduced, however, if the receiver relies on the amount on the invoice rather than actually counting the merchandise delivered.

SPOT CHECK

A spot check is a random check of one carton in a shipment. The carton is checked for quantity and quality. If it passes inspection, the remaining cartons are assumed to be in the same condition. This method is often used for checking supermarket and drugstore deliveries.

QUALITY CHECK

A quality check is done whenever the workmanship and general characteristics of the merchandise received must be examined. This type of check is usually done for products such as furniture and products with artistic value, such as vases and paintings. Often this check is performed by the buyer, not a receiver.

@ Online Action! Go to *marketingessentials.glencoe.com/24/figure/1* to find a project on checking merchandise.

marketingessentials.glencoe.com Chapter 24 - Stock Handling and Inventory Control **505**

Figure 24.1 — Checking Merchandise

Discussion Tell students that U.S. consumers who buy items online or from catalogs often return merchandise through transportation service carriers, particularly around the holiday season in November and December. For example, the U.S. Postal Service allows small business owners to download and utilize a variety of its Web tool applications for return shipping labels, rate calculator, address information, shipping label information, and carrier pickup information. Ask students to brainstorm reasons why a company might generate customers' return shipping labels upon first sending the ordered item.

Caption Answer New-task purchases are best met with a quality check.

@ Online Action! For instructions, ideas, and answer guide, go to the Teacher Center at **marketingessentials.glencoe.com**

Individualized Practice

METHODS OF CHECKING MERCHANDISE

L1 Have students draw a concept map of the receiving-checking-marking transferring process. They may draw a receiving area and stick figures and use key terms to complete their maps.

L2 Have students visit a store in your community and choose three products they want to explore. For each product, they should report on the store's criteria and procedures for returning merchandise and getting credit or adjustments from the carrier or the seller. Have students write a 150-word report.

L3 Ask students to select a store with more than one location in your area to determine the store's transfer-of-stock policy. Then, have students present their findings to the class in an oral report.

Enrichment

HANDLING MERCHANDISE

If your school has a store, have students work together to receive, check, and mark merchandise for a defined period of time (perhaps two weeks to a month) in the store. After that time, they should assess how they could improve on the process of doing all three tasks and present a written report on how they would implement changes in the current receiving-checking-marking system.

ASSESS

Review Guide

CONCEPTS

Have students work in pairs to use their own words to explain the methods of receiving, checking, marking, and transferring merchandise. When students have finished, review these concepts with the class.

KEY TERMS

Have students review key terms, their spellings, and definitions in small groups.

ONLINE SELF-ASSESSMENT

Have students go to marketingessentials.glencoe.com for Section 24.1 practice test.

Individualized Review

L1 Assign and review Chapter 24 activities in the Student Activity Workbook.

L2 Assign and review Chapter 24 activities in the Marketing Math Workbook.

L3 Assign and Review Chapter 24 activities in the *BusinessWeek* Reader and Case Studies.

Marketing Practice

Ask students to create their own tag for an article of clothing. Have them create the clothing line name and its logo. Have students include all necessary information on the tag as if it were being sold in a store. Encourage students to use a word processing program or a graphics program for this assignment.

---

are assumed to be the same. Spot checking is often used for products such as canned goods, paper products, and pharmaceuticals.

The **quality check method** is done to inspect the workmanship and general characteristics of the received merchandise. Although a receiver can do a quality check, a buyer often performs this check. The merchandise is checked to determine whether the quality of the goods received matches the quality of the products, which were ordered. If the goods are damaged, a damage report is prepared. Damaged goods should not be discarded without the authorization of the supplier.

Returning Merchandise

Careful checking practices can save a business large amounts of money. All incorrect items, damaged merchandise, and items ordered but not received are identified and reported according to the policies of the business. When this is done, the business can get proper credit or adjustments from the carrier or the seller.

Upon return of the merchandise, the seller issues a credit memorandum. A credit memorandum is notification that the buyer's account has been credited for the value of the returned merchandise.

Marking Merchandise

After it has been received and checked, merchandise must be marked with the selling price and other information. Different methods may be used for various kinds of merchandise. The most common method of marking price is with a UPC, however a hand-operated pricing machine or pricing tickets can be used as well.

Universal Product Codes (UPCs) are widely used in business today for tracking merchandise (see Chapter 16). UPCs originate with the Uniform Code Council (UCC). A manufacturer pays an annual fee to the UCC for permission to use the UPC system. Many businesses receive goods that are preticketed with prices and UPCs.

UPCs are often used for **source marking**. With this method, the seller or manufacturer marks the price before delivering the merchandise to the retailer. Merchandise can be moved directly from the receiving area to the sales floor. The UPCs are scanned at the checkout area, and the price stored in the computer for that code is entered for the sale.

Some businesses use a **preretailing marking method** of marking merchandise. With the preretailing marking method, pricing information is marked in advance on the purchase order. This information is entered in the buyer's computer system, and prices are available for marking merchandise as soon as it is received. Preretailing marking is normally used for staple items that are unlikely to have price changes between the time of the order and receipt of the merchandise. It saves time because merchandise can be price marked immediately.

Finally, merchandise can be marked with the familiar price tickets. In large stores, price tickets are prepared by hand or by machine in a marking room or in a stock room. Gum labels are used on merchandise with a flat, hard surface such as books. Pin tickets are used on merchandise that will not be damaged by the pinholes, such as socks or scarves. String or plastic tags are used for larger articles, such as dresses, shirts, and suits. The pricing ticket also helps when a customer needs to return an item to a store as it is difficult to return an item that has no tags.

Price Ticket Information

The price ticket identifies the price of the merchandise. Other important information may also be included on the price ticket. Many businesses include information such as store numbers, model or style numbers, color, sizes, fabrics, manufacturer's number, and lot numbers. This information is useful for tracking merchandise. It helps a business determine which items, sizes, and colors are popular with customers.

 Extended Activity

Web Returns

Ask students to locate an online vendor and review its merchandise return policy. Have students use an instructional tone to write a set of instructions for a customer who wants to return merchandise to that vendor.

Transferring Merchandise

In a retail environment, once merchandise is received, checked, and marked, it is ready to be moved to the sales area. But if it remains on the shelf too long without being sold, it is often transferred to other departments or areas within the store. Older stock is generally transferred from a department or store to a warehouse at the beginning of each selling season. Old merchandise must be removed from the department sales areas to make room for new merchandise. The old merchandise is put on sale for a short time, and the merchandise that does not sell is transferred to a warehouse or distribution center.

Transferred merchandise is accompanied by a form describing the items, style numbers, colors, sizes, cost, and retail prices. Duplicate copies of the transfer forms are retained as a record of merchandise on hand.

Stock transfers between departments can occur when merchandise is carried by more than one department or when the demand for merchandise in one department creates a need for additional merchandise. Stock transfers can also occur when the merchandise is used for sales promotions, such as displays, advertising illustrations, or fashion shows or when the merchandise is used for installation or repairs in various departments.

Stock transfers between stores can occur to meet unexpected demand or to fill requests by customers. A customer may find the perfect pair of pants, but find that the branch of the store is sold out. Some stores will call another local store to have it send over the right size. Finally, stock transfers from store to distribution outlet can occur when off-season and nonsalable merchandise is moved to surplus or discount stores. A store may choose to transfer all of its winter clothing to an outlet store if the stock doesn't clear out during after-season sales.

 24.1 AFTER YOU READ

Reviewing Key Terms and Concepts
1. List the four main steps in the stock handling process.
2. What are the four methods used for checking merchandise?
3. How do UPC codes assist with the stock handling process?

Integrating Academic Skills
Math
4. A stationery store calculated the cost of price marking its merchandise to be $54,000 a year in employee time. The store estimates that it can save 33 percent of this cost by switching to source marking for most of its merchandise. What is the amount of the savings?

Social Studies
5. Research the history and development of the Universal Product Code (UPC). Use a word processing program to write a one-page paper on the beginning of UPC in the supermarket industry and its use on most manufactured products today.

 Online Action!

Check your answers at *marketingessentials.glencoe.com/24/read*

CLOSE

Ask students to recall and provide answers to the following questions.

- **What are some of the reasons for transferring merchandise between various store departments?**
Demand in one department exceeds the demand in another similar department; merchandise is used for sales promotions; or merchandise is used for installation or repairs.

- **Different methods are used for marketing merchandise depending on the product. Why are UPCs often used for source marking?**
With the UPC method, the price has already been placed on the product so that the product can be moved directly from the receiving area to the selling area.

 Critical Thinking

Ask students to brainstorm and list reasons why a retailer might attempt to sell damaged goods.

AFTER YOU READ

Reviewing Key Terms and Concepts

1. The four main steps in the stock handling process include receiving goods, checking them, marking the goods with information (if necessary), and delivering them to their selling or storing location.

2. The four methods used for checking merchandise are blind check, direct check, spot check, and quality check.

3. UPC bar codes allow the store to track sales and inventory levels.

Integrating Academic Skills

4. $17,820; $54,000 \times 0.33 = $17,820

5. Reports will vary. However, students should discover that Bernard Silver and Norman Woodland at Drexel Institute of Technology first invented bar codes in 1948. They were first used commercially in 1967. A consortium of supermarket retailers developed the present vertical bar system in 1973. About five billion barcodes are scanned worldwide each day.

Online Action!   Answers at **marketingessentials.glencoe.com/24/read**

FOCUS

Introducing the Section

COLLABORATIVE ACTIVITY

Ask students to define predict the meaning of the term *inventory management.* Then ask students to imagine they manage a store that offers different products (e.g., movie rental store, a sporting goods store, a restaurant). Have the class think of and list some reasons why inventory management would be challenging in this type of store.

Preteaching Key Terms

Let students know that sometimes unusual associations aid in remembering definitions of key words. Ask students to build mental imagery based on the connections they think of when hearing each key term.

- inventory
- inventory management
- just-in-time (JIT) inventory system
- perpetual inventory system
- physical inventory system
- cycle counts
- stockkeeping unit (SKU)
- dollar control
- unit control
- inventory turnover
- basic stock list
- model stock list
- never-out list
- real-time inventory systems

Critical Thinking

Ask students: Does inventory represent the entire assets of a business?

OBJECTIVES

- Describe the process for providing effective inventory management
- Explain the types of inventory control systems
- Discuss the relationship between customer service and distribution
- Analyze sales information to determine inventory turnover
- Discuss technology and inventory management

KEY TERMS

- inventory
- inventory management
- just-in-time (JIT) inventory system
- perpetual inventory system
- physical inventory system
- cycle counts
- stockkeeping unit (SKU)
- dollar control
- unit control
- inventory turnover
- basic stock list
- model stock list
- never-out list
- real-time inventory systems

WHILE YOU READ

Question How would shopping be different if there were no plan for inventory management?

Inventory Control

READ and STUDY

BEFORE YOU READ

Predict What would happen if stores and businesses did not maintain correct inventories?

MAIN IDEA

The inventory a business owns represents money tied up in products until the inventory is sold. A well-managed and controlled inventory increases the profits of a business.

STUDY ORGANIZER

Copy the concept map below. Use the map to record aspects of perpetual and physical inventory systems.

Inventory Management

Inventory refers to all the goods stored by a business before they are sold. Inventory includes raw materials, components purchased from suppliers, manufactured sub-assemblies, work in process, packaging materials, and finished goods. In a retail store, inventory includes all goods available for resale.

Inventory management is the process of buying and storing these materials and products while controlling costs for ordering, shipping, handling, and storage. This is usually the responsibility

---

READ and STUDY

BEFORE YOU READ

Ask students to brainstorm the effect low or high inventory might have on business success.

THE MAIN IDEA

Lead a discussion with the students about why inventory levels may change throughout the year.

STUDY ORGANIZER

Model the study organizer for students by filling in an aspect of inventory system. A full-size, downloadable study organizer can be found at **marketingessentials.glencoe.com**

 Answers will vary; students will probably indicate that there would be less store organization, more stock outages, and a less reliable way to purchase products. Encourage students to share answers in class.

•COUNTING the MERCHANDISE Inventory accuracy is important to any business.

What are three ways to monitor inventory?

of the supply chain manager whose job it is to maintain just the right level of inventory to meet the supply and demand needs of a business. Having the wrong merchandise in stock, holding too many slow-selling items, or storing too few fast-selling ones are problems the supply chain manager faces every day.

Unnecessarily high inventories can create many problems for a business. In addition to using up valuable storage space, they may increase personnel costs for security and warehouse staff, may cause higher inventory insurance premiums, and may lead to increased interest expenses for a business. Businesses lose money and reduce profits when they manage their inventories poorly.

Distribution, Inventory Management, and Customer Service

The most important goal of any department within a business is to meet the needs of its customers. Every department in today's business environment must be customer oriented if the overall business is to be successful.

Just-in-Time Inventory

A **just-in-time (JIT) inventory system** controls the flow of parts and material into assembly and manufacturing plants. A JIT inventory system coordinates demand and

supply such that suppliers deliver parts and raw materials just before they are needed for use. Plants keep only small stocks on hand to avoid tying up money and inventory space.

Computer link-ups tell suppliers and transportation companies which items are needed and when to deliver them to meet production needs. Parts are delivered on a schedule—just in time for use in the production process. A late shipment can bring an entire manufacturing operation to a standstill.

Inventory management is complex because a business has to correctly anticipate demand for its products while trying to keep overall inventory investment as low as possible. Retail businesses are expected to:

- Maintain the right quantities of merchandise without running out of stock
- Keep a wide product assortment (with low inventory investment) without compromising on customer needs and wants
- Purchase merchandise at large volumes to gain the lowest prices while not buying more than it will sell
- Keep a current inventory on hand

Good inventory management balances the costs of inventory with the benefits of maintaining a large inventory. The costs of

Chapter 24 - Stock Handling and Inventory Control **509**

TEACH

Discussion Starter

IMPORTANCE OF INVENTORY MANAGEMENT
Ask students to pick their favorite retail store and discuss its largest asset. Typically, inventory is the largest asset for a business.

TEACHING POINTS

Clarify Tell students about two types of inventory: those that require manufacturing and those in the service-related business. Goods for manufacturing often need assembly of some kind; the goods for a service business are for using on or for the customers.

Explain Tell students that most businesses pay for their inventory upon delivery or within 30 days of receipt.

Build Vocabulary

Ask students if they are familiar with the acronym *ASAP* (as soon as possible). Tell them that in the retail world, when someone wants something ASAP, it is often expected and delivered within that day. However, when a manufacturer is told it needs something ASAP, this means the good or service gets posted on the backlog.

PHOTO GUIDE   **COUNTING the MERCHANDISE**

Discussion Lead a discussion with students about the inventory management controls of paperless operations and timely and accurate inventory records.

Caption Answer Answers will vary; possible ways to monitor inventory include the use of UPC data, receiving records, sales checks, price tickets, cash register receipts, stock transfer records, etc.

Follow Up Ask students to discuss why bar codes are so important in today's business environment. Answers might include that bar codes simplify everything from grocery shopping to inventory of a large company. They also allow sales transaction data to be fed directly into a computer for efficient record-keeping and inventory control.

Concept Development

INVENTORY SYSTEMS

When students are acquainted with the concept of just-in-time buying and inventory control, ask them if they think it is a good idea for wholesale and retail buyers. Have them explain their opinions.

TEACHING POINTS

Clarify Tell students that at present there are many retail stores that use the JIT inventory system. As items are sold in the various retail stores, a computer transmits those records via satellite to a central location. Thus, all sales from every store are available to central buyers on a daily basis.

Explain Tell students that there are a variety of inventory control software companies that manufacturer and retail their programs.

Individualized Practice

PERPETUAL INVENTORY SYSTEMS

L1 Ask students to summarize the perpetual inventory systems in their journal. They can refer to their book, if needed. Have them write down the main points for each type of system.

L2 Have students explain what expectations are placed on a business that maintains a personal system inventory in a one-or-two paragraph response.

L3 Ask students to select a particular perpetual inventory system and investigate which company uses this type of system. Then have students complete a one-page report about how this system works well for the company.

---

inventory include not only the cost of the items in stock, but also storage, insurance, and taxes. Inventory ties up a business's working capital—money that could be used for other purposes. It is not effective for a company to maintain large inventory holdings if that money could be spent more effectively somewhere else or invested. Effective inventory management helps increase working capital and allows a business to use its savings to pay for other business expenses.

Inventory Systems

Two methods of tracking inventory are the perpetual inventory system and the physical inventory system.

Perpetual Inventory System

A **perpetual inventory system** tracks the number of items in inventory on a constant basis. The system tracks all new items purchased and returned, as well as sales of current stock. An up-to-date count of inventory is maintained for purchases and returns of merchandise, sales and sales returns, sales allowances, and transfers to other stores and departments. With a perpetual inventory system, a business keeps track of sales as they occur.

Manual Systems

In a manual system, employees gather paper records of sales and enter that information into the inventory system. These records can include receiving department records, sales checks, price tickets, cash register receipts, stock transfer requests, and other documents used for coding and tabulation.

Merchandise tags are used to record information about the vendor, date of receipt, department, product classification, color, size, and style. The merchandise tags from items sold are sent in batches to a company-owned tabulating facility or to an independent computer service organization where the coded information is analyzed through the use of computer software.

Computer-Based Systems

Computer-based systems to control inventory are increasingly popular, even among

smaller businesses. They are also faster and more accurate than manual systems. A point-of-sale terminal uses hand-held laser guns, stationary lasers, light pens, or slot scanners to feed sales transaction data directly from Universal Product Codes (UPCs), sales checks, or merchandise tags into a computer. Businesses then use computer-generated information printouts at different times for review and action.

Electronic Data Interchange (EDI) involves computer-to-computer information exchanges and relays of sales information directly to a supplier. The supplier then uses the sales transaction data to ship additional items automatically to the business.

Physical Inventory System

Under a **physical inventory system**, information about stock levels is not maintained on an ongoing basis. Rather, every so often, stock is visually inspected or actually counted to determine the quantity on hand. Inventory data can be captured in many ways, from high-tech methods to manual counts. Some of the most popular methods for larger retailers are scanned bar codes and keypad entry onto handheld devices.

Even if a perpetual inventory system is used, physical inventories are still conducted periodically or on a regular annual basis. A physical inventory allows a business to calculate its income tax, determine the correct value of its ending inventory, identify any stock shortages, and plan future purchases. There are several methods used for physical inventory control.

Inventory Counting Methods

To count inventory, businesses often use a combination of methods. Regular employees or outside inventory service companies can be used to count inventories. Larger national retailers tend to use outside companies such as Washington Inventory Services, RGIS, or smaller regional or local companies more than regular company employees. After the counting is finished, the total value of the inventory is determined. This value is reported on the business's financial statements.

Online Activity

Bricks-and-Clicks Industry Control

Ask students to research how a store that has both brick-and-mortar stores as well as online stores might handle their inventory. Have students create a multimedia presentation reporting what they learned.

Physical Inventory Method

The most popular method of inventory management is the physical inventory. Most businesses physically count inventory at least once a year, some conduct them on a semi-annual basis, and fewer on a quarterly or even more frequent basis. Inventory clerks usually work in pairs: one counts merchandise while the other records the count. Physical inventories are usually wall-to-wall store inventories which often require that the business close temporarily to conduct the inventory.

Cycle Count Method

Many businesses use **cycle counts** either in combination with an annual physical inventory or alone to track inventory. In this method, the entire inventory is never counted at one time. A small portion of the inventory is physically counted each day by stockkeeping units so that the entire inventory is accounted for on a regular basis. A **stockkeeping unit (SKU)** is a unit or a group of related items. Manufacturers' representatives do a variation of the cycle count method. The representative

Case Study

Bar Codes Meet New Standards

The Uniform Code Council, an industry group for retailers in the United States and Canada, is requiring that all bar code scanners read a new global Universal Product Code. Beginning in January of 2005 all point-of-sale scanners must be upgraded to read an extra number (up from 12 to 13 digits). Rather than the existing 12-digit bar code used in North America, the 13-digit bar code is widely used in Europe.

Global Codes

The new 13-digit code gives retailers information about the country of origin, the manufacturer, individual product information, and a single check digit to verify accuracy and to control inventory. The first two digits give country information. For example, numbers from 00–13 represent companies in the U.S. and Canada, while higher numbers represent other countries. The next five digits identify manufacturers from throughout the world who have registered their own unique code with regional authorities like the Uniform Code Council.

The next five numbers are assigned to individual products by each manufacturer. The previous 12 numbers are used mathematically to come up with a final number or check digit. The last number verifies that a product has been scanned correctly. Scanning and technical problems will occur for most retailers, because the software written for tracking sales, orders, and inventory control will need to be re-designed for the new bar code.

THINK STRATEGICALLY

While many consumer and retailers may experience initial technical difficulties with scanners and software, why are U.S. and Canadian retailers moving to the new 13-digit bar code standard?

 Online Action! Go to *marketingessentials.glencoe.com/24/case* to find a research project on UPCs and inventory.

marketingessentials.glencoe.com

Concept Development

INVENTORY COUNTING METHODS

Have students work in pairs to generate a list of types of goods that each of the following businesses would keep in its inventory: manufacturing, wholesaling, retailing, service, and extraction.

TEACHING POINTS

Summarize Physical inventory counting commences and ends at a specific time in a fiscal year. At this time, the inventory is counted and entered into the system. To sustain good inventory management controls, the inventory runs on 97 percent accuracy (i.e., a business only has a three percent margin of error—plus or minus—to keep the system valid).

Enrichment

CYCLE COUNT METHOD

To further explain the concept of cycle counting method for physical inventory, you might summarize the following recommendations from *Distribution Digest:*

- Set a level of acceptable accuracy for inventory reports.
- Determine how present inventory counting practices influence the accuracy of the records.
- Establish an initial inventory balance.
- During cycle counting, identify any patterns or issues.
- Complete inventory count before or after work.

Once you have read this bulleted list, ask the students to imagine setting these controls for a hypothetical retailer. Work as a class to discuss and set the needed controls.

Case Study Bar Codes Meet New Standards

Discussion Lead a discussion on whether students think the 13-digit codes will help a company's return on investment, considering the initial investment costs to update the systems and staff training.

THINK STRATEGICALLY **Answer:** Answers will vary; students might point out economic globalization as one reason. In addition, manufacturers will benefit by increased tracking, increased labor efficiency and more knowledge about out-of-stock items, inventory visibility, and items that can't be sold.

Online Action! For instructions, ideas, and answer guide, go to the Teacher Center at **marketingessentials.glencoe.com**

Follow Up Have students research how the 13-digit bar code is used in Europe.

Concept Development

STOCK CONTROL

On the board, draw a map that indicates where physical inventory resides as well as receiving and delivery areas for a warehouse. Have students draw routes that map the quickest and safest way from receiving an order to picking it up and dropping it off at the delivery area.

TEACHING POINTS

Explain Tell students that poor inventory control comes from not knowing where physical inventory is housed. Productivity on the warehouse floors decreases when retrieval becomes time-consuming.

Clarify Remind students that stock-outs for a product in demand (i.e., when there is no inventory of a product) hamper the success of the company by backlogging its orders (halting service).

Individualized Practice

INVENTORY CONTROL

L1 Ask students if goods for resale are accounted for on a financial accounting system.
Yes, and if goods are for resale, they are also nontaxable.

Also ask students to list the three ways in which inventory is typically classified.
Finished goods, work in progress, and raw materials.

L2 Ask students to research how inventory balances influence a balance sheet. Have them find a real-world spreadsheet and circle the inventory balances.

L3 If your school has a store, do the following: assign students in pairs to count the inventory, and have them develop written store inventory procedures.

---

visits a business on a regular basis, takes the stock count, and writes the order. Unwanted merchandise is removed from stock and returned to the manufacturer through a pre-determined, authorized procedure.

Visual Control Method

Visual control is sometimes used to monitor physical inventory levels. Smaller businesses often place stock cards on pegboards with stock numbers and descriptions for each item displayed. The stock cards specify the number of each item to be kept in stock. It can be somewhat inaccurate because it does not account for misplaced merchandise. The amount to reorder is the difference between the number on hand and the specified number to be stocked. The number to stock may be an estimate of sales for a typical period of time.

Trends in Inventory Methods

As business becomes increasingly more competitive, efficient and effective inventory management methods will be implemented. Some predicted future trends related to inventory methods will be the almost universal recording of inventories using SKU and/or UPC codes, greater use of technology in taking inventories, increased use and frequency of cycle counts by SKU, increased use of Internet technologies to link with vendors, and increased vendor participation.

Using Both Systems

A business does not have to choose between a physical inventory system and a perpetual inventory system. Most businesses find it most effective to use both systems. The perpetual system gives an up-to-date inventory record throughout the year. The physical system gives an accurate count that can be compared to the perpetual records to identify any errors or problems. The two systems actually complement each other.

The perpetual inventory records are used to help the business track sales and manage its merchandise. After a physical inventory is taken, the ending inventory amount becomes the beginning inventory for the year that follows. Purchases by the business during the

---

year are added to this amount, while sales are subtracted. Ending inventory is calculated in the example that follows.

Number of Items for 1/1/05 to 6/30/05		
Beginning inventory, 1/1/2005		1,000
Net purchases (purchases less purchases and allowances returned)	+ 300	
Merchandise available for sale		1,300
Less net sales (sales less returns and allowances)	− 1,050	
Ending inventory, 6/30/2005		250

Sometimes, the ending inventory shown in the perpetual inventory system does not match the physical count of inventory. When the physical count shows less merchandise than is supposed to be in inventory, a stock shortage or shrinkage has occurred. Employee and customer theft, receiving errors, incorrect counting, and selling errors can cause shortages for a business.

In the previous example, all records for purchases and sales are ongoing in a business; therefore the data represents a perpetual inventory system. The ending inventory figure of 250 items is the perpetual inventory. However, as you know, it is possible that this is not the most accurate count. If the physical inventory system showed ending inventory of 225, a stock shortage of 25 would have occurred $(250 - 225 = 25)$. It is not until the physical inventory is taken that the company really knows if its ending inventory records are correct. It is still helpful, however, to use the perpetual inventory as a good estimation.

Stock Control

Stock control involves monitoring stock levels and investments in stock so that a business is run efficiently. Planning those stock levels and monitoring them requires the use of several different systems. They include dollar versus unit control methods, inventory turnover calculations, and three stock lists (model, basic, and never-out).

Extended Activity

Online Inventory Systems

Have students read an article on inventory systems from an online article or from a periodical in the library. Ask students to write a 200-word summary on the article, being sure to include the title of the article, the source, and the date of publication.

Dollar Versus Unit Control

Inventory management involves both dollar control and unit control of merchandise held in inventory. **Dollar control** represents the planning and monitoring of the total inventory investment that a business makes during a stated period of time. A business's dollar control of inventory involves information about the amount of purchases, sales, dollar value of beginning and ending inventory, and stock shortages. This information helps a business determine the cost of goods sold and the amount of gross profit or loss during a given period of time. By subtracting operating expenses from the gross profit, the business can determine its net profit or loss.

Unit control refers to the quantities of merchandise that a business handles during a stated period of time. Unit control allows the business to keep inventory adjusted to sales and lets the business determine how to spend money available under a planned budget. In a unit control inventory system, merchandise is tracked by stockkeeping unit. Tracking the SKUs gives valuable sales information on those items that are successful and those that are not selling. A business can use this information to make better merchandising decisions. Sales promotions can be run to sell slow-moving items or to spotlight popular ones.

Unit control records also allow purchasing personnel to see what brands, sizes, colors, and price ranges are popular. By keeping track of this information, buyers can understand customer preferences and order accordingly. Finally, unit control records specify when items need to be ordered. When a minimum stock amount is reached, an order is placed for more stock. This system ensures that adequate assortments are available and helps avoid out-of-stock situations.

Inventory Turnover

The most effective way to measure how well inventory is being managed is to look at inventory turnover. **Inventory turnover** is the number of times the average inventory has been sold and replaced in a given period of time. The higher the inventory turnover rate, the more times the goods were sold and replaced. In retailing and wholesaling operations, the key is moving inventory so there is cash available to buy more fast-selling merchandise. High turnover rates mean that merchandise is selling quickly. That means higher profit for the business because its money is not tied up in inventory. Inventory turnover is also a good measure of success for businesses to use in evaluating vendors and products from year to year. Businesses use inventory turnover rates to compare a particular store's entire operation with the operations of similar stores.

Inventory turnover rates for selected retailers are available from trade associations and commercial publishers. One such publisher is Dun & Bradstreet, which publishes *Industry Norms and Key Business Ratios*. Inventory turnover rates can be calculated in dollars (retail or cost) or in units.

Stores that keep records of the retail value of stock compute their inventory turnover rates as follows:

$$\frac{\text{Net sales (in retail dollars)}}{\text{Average inventory on hand (in retail dollars)}}$$

When net sales during a period are $49,500 and average inventory is $8,250, the inventory turnover is 6:

$$\frac{\$49,500}{\$8,250} = 6$$

To determine the average inventory, use inventory amounts for each of the months included in the time period being considered. Total these, as shown in the second column below, and then calculate the average.

Month	Inventory	Net Sales
January	$ 50,000	$ 10,000
February	55,000	15,000
March	68,000	20,000
April	64,000	19,000
May	63,000	21,000
June	60,000	20,000
Totals	**$360,000**	**$105,000**

TEACH CONTINUED

Concept Development

INVENTORY TURNOVER
Ask students to discuss reasons why stock turnover rates often differ for similar businesses. Have them provide examples with their answers.

TEACHING POINTS
Demonstrate Take each inventory turnover formula and review the calculations. Plug in new figures to demonstrate how the formulas work.

Individualized Math Practice

L1 Have students complete the following problem: What is the inventory turnover when the net sales during a period are $23,500 and average inventory is $3,550?
6.6; 23,500 ÷ 3,550 = 6.6

L2 Ask students to write the correct answer to the following description: When a store wants to look at the number of items carried in relation to the number of items sold, it calculates its inventory turnover rates in units with this formula.
Number of units sold ÷ average inventory on hand in units

L3 Ask students to re-create their own inventory figures during a 12-month period and create a spreadsheet with vertically parallel columns that include: month, average inventory, and net sales. Once they have created this, have them find the inventory turnover rate for the 12-month period.

Online Activity

Turnover Rates
Ask students to conduct an online search to see if they can discover the inventory turnover rates for retailer. Encourage students to research online trade journals as well as business publications. Have students then write a 150-word paragraph about their findings.

Critical Thinking
Ask: In addition to letting buyers know when items need to be ordered, what are some other possible functions of unit control records?

513

Review Guide

CONCEPTS

Divide students into five groups. Assign to each group one of the concepts in this section—stock turnover, dollar control, unit control, perpetual inventory system, or physical inventory system. Have each group explain their concept to the class using an outline or symbolic drawing.

KEY TERMS

Have students review key terms, their spellings, and definitions in small groups.

ONLINE SELF-ASSESSMENT

Have students go to marketingessentials.glencoe.com for the Section 24.2 practice test.

Individualized Review

L1 Assign and review Chapter 24 activities in the Student Activity Workbook.

L2 Assign and review Chapter 24 activities in the Marketing Math Workbook.

L3 Assign and review Chapter 24 activities in the *BusinessWeek* Reader and Case Studies.

Marketing Practice

Inform students that one benefit of taking a marketing course is discovering that so many steps and people are involved in getting a product to market. Ask students to locate an article on stock handling and inventory management. Have students prepare an oral summary of the article and share it with the rest of the class.

514

MARKET TECH

Picking Up the Speed

Picking orders in distribution centers can represent 30 to 40 percent of the total labor cost. So, increasing the speed it takes for order picking and selection can save time and money. Radio frequency (RF) terminals can speed up order selection by showing a worker the best sequence to pick up requested orders. Speed is increased, because the order selector does not have to read the entire pick ticket to look for the items, arrange the pick sequence, and find the item location.

Initial Costs

However, warehouse management system (WMS) software must be purchased to use radio frequency picking. The computer program is needed to arrange the orders in the best possible picking sequence. The order selector, using a RF handheld terminal, sees only one item at a time shown on the terminal. Besides the software, handheld RF terminals costing about $4,000 each need to be purchased, and an RF network including installation, antennas, and access points needs to be erected. Extra RF terminals also need to be purchased for spares and for use by storage and distribution supervisors.

⬤ THINK LIKE A MARKETER

How would you justify to upper management a capital investment in distribution technology such as radio frequency terminals?

@ Online Action!

Go to *marketingessentials.glencoe.com/24/tech* to find a project on warehouse management software.

514 UNIT 7 - DISTRIBUTION

To get the average inventory for the six-month period, divide by the number of months.

$$\frac{\$360,000}{6} = \$60,000$$

Finally, to calculate inventory turnover, divide total net sales (see the third column above) by average inventory.

$$\frac{\$105,000}{\$60,000} = 1.75$$

This figure means that the average inventory was sold and replaced 1.75 times during the six-month period.

When only cost information about inventory is available, inventory turnover can be calculated with this formula:

$$\frac{\text{Cost of goods sold}}{\text{Average inventory on hand (at cost)}}$$

When a store wants to look at the number of items carried in relation to the number of items sold, it calculates its stock turnover rates in units with this formula:

$$\frac{\text{Number of SKUs sold}}{\text{Average SKUs on hand}}$$

Stock Lists

There are three plans used to monitor different types of goods—staple items, fashionable items, and very popular items. They are the basic stock list, model stock list, and never-out list.

A **basic stock list** is used for those staple items that should always be in stock. This list specifies products that a store should always carry based upon the type of business. A basic stock list in a men's clothing store would include items such as T-shirts, underwear, and dress socks. The basic stock list at a card store would include birthday cards, blank cards, thank you cards, and cards for special occasions, such as weddings and anniversaries.

Based on expected sales for a given period, a basic stock list specifies the minimum amount

 marketingessentials.glencoe.com

MARKET TECH

Picking Up the Speed

Discussion After students have read this feature, lead a discussion about the advantages and disadvantages of radio frequency terminals in distribution centers.

THINK LIKE A MARKETER **Answer:** Answers will vary. However, order picking is a very labor-intensive cost in distribution centers. Technologies used to reduce travel time can increase picking speed and improve accuracy. Time is money and locating items, verifying them and confirming the pick can increase delivery time of products for ultimate sale. The technology also saves on employee costs, since fewer order pickers might be required.

@ Online Action! For instructions, ideas, and answer guide, go to the Teacher Center at marketingessentials.glencoe.com

of merchandise that should be on hand for particular products. It shows the quantity of items that should be reordered, as well as the colors, styles, and sizes that should be carried. Retailers assign each product a code for ease in recording when the products are purchased and sold.

A **model stock list** is used for fashionable merchandise. Fashion items change relatively rapidly; therefore, these lists are less specific than basic stock lists. The information contained in model stock lists identifies goods by general classes (blouses, skirts, dresses, slacks) and style categories (short sleeve, long sleeve), sizes, materials, colors, and price lines. Style numbers are not included because each manufacturer's style numbers change each year. Although model stock lists identify how many of each type of item should be purchased, the buyer must actually select specific models at the market. A **never-out list** is used for best-selling products that make up a large percentage of sales volume. Items are added to or taken off the list as their popularity increases or declines.

The Future of Inventory Management

Because most customers who buy online expect their orders to be filled immediately, the ability to process and ship orders without delay has become essential to the success of e-businesses. This has brought about **real-time inventory systems**. Real-time inventory management is an Internet technology that connects applications, data, and users in real time. This technology lets a company constantly track every product it sells from when it is manufactured, or when it arrives in the warehouse, to when the customer orders it online, and to when it arrives at the buyer's door.

CLOSE

Ask students to recall and provide answers to the following questions:

- **Explain the concept of just-in-time inventory.**
  Suppliers deliver parts and raw materials just before they are needed in production.

- **Could the just-in-time inventory system be used in both retail and wholesale operations?**
  Yes, computers track daily inventory on goods in both kinds of businesses.

Extended Activity

Inventory Management
Ask students to locate a local business willing to discuss its inventory system. Students can then set up an appointment to see how the business's inventory management works, take organized notes, and share their findings.

24.2 AFTER YOU READ

Reviewing Key Terms and Concepts
1. Explain the difference between a perpetual and a physical inventory system.
2. Name the three different inventory counting methods.
3. What is the difference between dollar control and unit control as they relate to inventory management?

Integrating Academic Skills
Math
4. What is the inventory turnover rate (at cost) for a school store if the cost of goods sold equals $15,000 and the average inventory on hand (at cost) equals $3,000? What does your answer represent?

Science
5. Investigate smart cards or radio frequency identification (RFID) tags and develop a one-page report on the scientific principles involved with this technology.

 Online Action!
Check your answers at *marketingessentials.glencoe.com/24/read*

marketingessentials.glencoe.com

Chapter 24 - Stock Handling and Inventory Control 515

AFTER YOU READ

Reviewing Key Terms and Concepts
1. A perpetual inventory system tracks the number of items in inventory on a constant basis. Under a physical inventory system, stock is visually inspected or actually counted to determine the quantity on hand.

2. Three different methods include physical inventory, cycle counts, and visual control.

3. Dollar control: planning and monitoring total inventory investment. Unit control: merchandise quantities handled in a period of time.

Integrating Academic Skills
4. $15,000 ÷ $3,000 = 5. The answer (5) means that the average inventory was sold and replaced five times during the selected time period.

5. Answers will vary; reports should show an understanding of radio frequency identification (RFID) tags.

Online Action! Answers at **marketingessentials.glencoe.com/24/read**

CAREERS
IN MARKETING

Lifelong Learning

CAREER INFORMATION

Have students go to marketingessentials.glencoe.com and find the Chapter 24 Careers page and click on the link for the American Marketing Association's Careers Strategies and Tips. Ask students to select one article and summarize it in three short paragraphs.

STOCK HANDLING AND INVENTORY CONTROL

One benefit of taking a marketing course is discovering that so many steps and people are involved in the process of getting a product to consumers. Let students know that reading the business section of a daily newspaper or a trade magazine can help them be informed consumers about the products they use and buy.

Primary Source

Ask students to go to marketingessentials.glencoe.com and find Chapter 24 Resources. Ask them to click on the link for the American Marketing Association's marketing dictionary and read the definitions of the stock handling and inventory control-related terms they find there.

 THINKING CRITICALLY

Answers will vary; students might include that each industry has its own set of standards for technological use that can help businesses succeed.

@ Online Action!

For instructions, ideas, and answer guide, go to the Teacher Center at marketingessentials.glencoe.com

ANGIE VITTITOW
BUSINESS SYSTEMS ANALYST
UPS SUPPLY CHAIN SOLUTIONS

(?) What do you do at work?
I provide support for multiple clients in a third-party logistics environment. This includes supporting warehouse management order and inventory management systems. I train new employees, author documentation, and spec out modifications to improve the visibility of current inventory or to improve the quality of cycle counts and annual physical inventories. I work with the warehouse operations management to improve processes. I also work on new client implementations. Included in this are system design, warehouse layout, process design, and testing.

(?) What skills are most important to you?
Without a doubt, written and verbal communication skills are at the top of the list. I work with all levels of employees. I must be able to understand the operator's vision and translate that to specifications for software developers. When training, I must find a way to make sure the light bulb goes on for everyone, regardless of different learning styles. There is frequent interaction with our third-party clients. Presenting the company's best image to the client is very important.

(?) What is your key to success?
The ability to keep an open mind and good communication skills. Hard skills are important but soft skills will take you where you want to go.

Aptitudes, Abilities, and Skills

Excellent communication skills, organization, and time management

Education and Training

Technology-related degrees as well as degrees in general business are useful.

Career Path

Entry-level positions in logistics and operations can lead to a number of careers centered around the inner workings of a company.

 THINKING CRITICALLY

Why is keeping up with technology so crucial?

@ Online Action!

Go to *marketingessentials.glencoe.com/ 24/careers* to find a career-related activity.

Test-Taking Strategies

Remind students that the best way to overcome test anxiety is to walk into the testing session with confidence. This confidence comes with knowledge of the material, which itself comes from reviewing and studying over the course of several weeks.

FOCUS on KEY POINTS

SECTION 24.1

● Successful stock management procedures help control costs and ensure the continuation of business operations. The steps in the stock handling process include receiving goods, checking them, marking the goods with information, if necessary, and delivering them to their selling or storing location. Methods of checking merchandise include the blind check method, the direct check method, the spot check method, and the quality check method.

SECTION 24.2

● Inventory is one of the most costly parts of operations for many businesses. Inventory management is the process of buying and storing products for sale while controlling costs for ordering, shipping, handling, and storage. Inventory systems include perpetual inventory systems and physical inventory systems. Technology is changing the way inventory is controlled. Retail businesses have implemented standards such as UPCs, EDI, and SCM to take advantage of computerized systems. Real-time inventory systems let businesses track all stages of a product, from manufacture to delivery.

REVIEW VOCABULARY

Define each of the following key terms in a short sentence.

1. receiving record (p. 503)
2. blind check method (p. 504)
3. direct check method (p. 504)
4. spot check method (p. 504)
5. quality check method (p. 506)
6. source marking (p. 506)
7. inventory (p. 508)
8. inventory management (p. 508)
9. just-in-time (JIT) inventory system (p. 509)
10. perpetual inventory system (p. 510)
11. physical inventory system (p. 510)
12. cycle counts (p. 511)
13. stockkeeping unit (SKU) (p. 511)
14. dollar control (p. 513)
15. unit control (p. 513)
16. inventory turnover (p. 513)
17. basic stock list (p. 514)
18. model stock list (p. 515)
19. never-out list (p. 515)
20. real-time inventory system (p. 515)

REVIEW FACTS and IDEAS

21. Why is a receiving record important? (24.1)
22. What are stock handling techniques? (24.1)
23. What is the inventory management process? (24.2)
24. What are some methods used to monitor inventory under a physical inventory system? (24.2)
25. How do you calculate stock turnover rates? (24.2)
26. Give three examples of technological developments in the retail industry related to inventory management. (24.2)

Chapter 24 - Stock Handling and Inventory Control **517**

REVIEW FACTS and IDEAS

21. A receiving record is the document that describes the goods received by a business. It is important because it serves as a permanent record of delivery.

22. Stock handling techniques include receiving goods, checking them, marking the goods with information, and delivering them to their selling location

23. Inventory management is the process of buying and storing products for sale while controlling costs for ordering, shipping, handling, and storage.

24. Some methods include using scanned bar codes and keypad entry onto handheld devices.

25. Stock turnover can be calculated with this formula:

    cost of goods sold ÷ average inventory on hand (at cost)

    When a store wants to look at the number of items carried in relation to the number of items sold, it calculates its inventory turnover rates in units with this formula:

    number of units sold ÷ average inventory on hand in units

26. Examples of technological developments in the retail industry related to inventory management include the following: SCM, RFID, Warehouse Management Systems, UPC codes, Efficient Consumer Response (ECR), and Electronic Data Interchange (EDI).

FOCUS on KEY POINTS

Ask students to volunteer a few details they learned under each point in the sections. Students may want to work together and create a set of flashcards with the key points on one side and details on the other side. They can use these flashcards to quiz each other during class.

REVIEW VOCABULARY

See glossary for definitions of **1–20.**
A sample answer might read:

7. *Inventory* refers to all the goods stored by a business before they are sold.

CHAPTER 24 REVIEW

BUILD SKILLS

27. Workplace Skills

Answers will vary; students should demonstrate an understanding of the inventory turnover rate.

28. Technology Applications

Answers will vary; students should identify all relevant aspects of the article regarding privacy and radio frequency identification.

29. Math Practice

Average Inventory: $46,000,
$276,000 ÷ 6 = $46,000
Inventory Turnover rate: 3.5;
$161,000 ÷ $46,000 = 3.5

DEVELOP CRITICAL THINKING

30. Checking Merchandise

Merchandise must be checked after it is received to maintain and follow warehouse procedures in order to keep the inventory controllable. Merchandise that is not properly checked can result in incorrect inventory or price, poor quality, inefficiency, turnover cessation, and so on.

31. Real-Time Service

Real-time inventory service provides customers with the most recent product produced just for them; in this way, customers receive the appropriate product. A global business might be interested in real-time inventory systems because of the added time savings it might provide to different customers; other answers are possible.

BUILD SKILLS

27. Workplace Skills

Presenting Information Use the resources at a public library to research the inventory turnover rates of two competing companies.

28. Technology Applications

Presenting Information Find an article about potential privacy issues related to radio frequency identification at the library or on the Internet. Use a word processing program to prepare a summary focusing on the article's main points. Identify the name of the article, the author, source, and date of publication.

29. Math Practice

Calculating Inventory Turnover Calculate the inventory turnover rate (at retail) for the six-month period, given the following information.

Month	Average Inventory	Net Sales
July	$45,000	$15,000
August	$53,000	$20,000
September	$48,000	$21,000
October	$42,000	$32,000
November	$44,000	$35,000
December	$44,000	$38,000

DEVELOP CRITICAL THINKING

30. Checking Merchandise

Why must merchandise be checked after it has been received? Explain the consequences of not checking received merchandise properly.

31. Real-Time Service

Review the definition of real-time inventory system and research this inventory method on the Internet. After you read a few articles about it, answer the following questions: How can a real-time inventory system improve customer service? Why would a global business be particularly interested in real-time inventory systems?

Formative Assessment

Formative assessment is an essential component of classroom work. This type of assessment provides information that is then used as feedback to modify teaching and meet student needs.

L1 Review key terms for this chapter. Ask students to write one sentence for each key term.

L2 Provide various examples of factors that affect inventory control and stock handling. After each example, have students identify which factors affected each example.

L3 Ask students to create stories that illustrate effective ideas for management inventory issues.

Reteach If the results of this formative assessment seem low, consider the following activity: Ask students to read through the section objectives and have them try to answer the questions without referring to their book.

APPLY CONCEPTS

32. Researching Storage

Perform an Internet search on the potential hazards caused by the storage of goods and materials in warehouses, retail stores, or restaurants.

Activity Use a word processing program to compose a one-page report detailing some of the risks investigated and steps to minimize the risks. Organize your report by types of business.

33. Improving Inventory Management

Research business magazines to find an example of a company that has improved its inventory management system.

Activity Use presentation software to create an oral presentation describing the situation and how the solution increased profits.

34. Investigating Inventory Technologies

Use the Internet, your school media center, or local library to investigate how technologies such as RFID, Warehouse Management Systems, UPC codes, ECR computer systems, or Electronic Data Interchange are impacting inventory management.

Activity Use a word processing program to compose a one-page report with the source and date of your information cited.

NET SAVVY

35. Develop a Prospectus

Using an Internet search engine, identify a software company that specializes in inventory management systems. Use a word processing program to write a one-page prospectus on the company. Include its Web site address and some of the services the company offers.

marketingessentials.glencoe.com

THE **CONNECTION**

Role Play: Stock Handling and Inventory Control

Situation You are to assume the role of assistant grocery manager for a large grocery store. A customer has just returned a package of frozen broccoli that was purchased earlier today. The frozen broccoli is covered with ice crystals, appears to have freezer burn, and generally has an old appearance. The customer service clerk (judge) has refunded the customer's money and asks you how this situation could have occurred.

Activity You are to explain to the customer service clerk (judge) about stock handling and proper handling and rotation of frozen foods.

Evaluation You will be evaluated on how well you meet the following performance indicators:

- Explain storing considerations
- Store food products to prevent contamination and spoilage
- Explain stock-handling techniques used in receiving deliveries
- Process returned/ damaged products
- Inspect food deliveries

 Online Action!

For more information and DECA Prep practice, go to *marketingessentials.glencoe .com/24/DECA*

APPLY CONCEPTS

32. Researching Storage
Answers will vary depending on the type of business selected; reports should detail the risks and proper storage procedures.

33. Improving Inventory Management
Answers will vary; reports should demonstrate comprehension of the inventory management system used.

34. Investigating Inventory Technologies
Answers will vary; reports should demonstrate an awareness of how technology affects inventory management systems.

NET SAVVY

35. Develop a Prospectus
Answers will vary depending on the company selected. Students should demonstrate an understanding of a prospectus.

MINI-QUIZ

Administer the Mini-Quiz orally. Students should indicate if the following questions are true or false.

1. The *spot check method* involves a random check of a shipment in which the contents are assumed to be accurate for the entire shipment. (true)

2. A *perpetual inventory* system tracks the number of items in inventory on a random basis. (false; it tracks it on a constant basis)

3. In a *physical inventory system*, stock is visually inspected or counted to determine the quantity on hand. (true)

For an expanded chapter quiz, go to Chapter 24 in the TeacherWorks CD-ROM and to Chapter 24 in the **Exam***View*® Pro Test Generator CD-ROM.

THE **CONNECTION**

The students should be evaluated on the performance standards noted in the role play. For another DECA role play, go to the Competitive Events Workbook or the Student Activity Workbook, or go to **marketingessentials.glencoe.com/24/DECA**.

Online Action! For instructions, ideas, and answer guide, go to the Teacher Center at **marketingessentials.glencoe.com**

DECA Advisors Corner

Consider organizing a group of adults who might want to lend their expertise on an advisory committee. Choose four to five members with diverse marketing backgrounds. This group can provide guidance for the marketing program, assist with fundraising, help with media contacts, serve as classroom speakers, provide feedback and assistance on written projects, and more.

SET-UP

Discuss basic background to make sure students understand the simulation. Discuss with students how GPS systems might be used by museums and tourist attractions and contrast that with the original police, military, and aviation uses.

PROCEDURES

You may want to list procedures on the board and talk about any questions the students might have. Remind the students that a suggested outline for their project is available at **marketingessentials.glencoe.com/u7/ internship.**

TIME MANAGEMENT

Set goals, block schedules, and milestones. Assign interim deadlines for each step of the project.

ASSESSMENT

The rubrics for evaluation of the written, oral, and computer presentations are available at **marketingessentials.glencoe.com/u7/ internship.**

MARKETING INTERNSHIP

A SIMULATED **DECA** PRODUCT AND SERVICE MANAGEMENT EVENT

Sell GPS Technology to Consumers

➡ BASIC BACKGROUND

Your firm's newest client, Street-Smarts, specializes in Global Positioning System (GPS) products. GPS uses satellites to provide navigational information. The police, the military, and aviation used the technology for years before it became available on the consumer market. Other companies marketing GPS products include Timex, Garmin Inc., and Thales Navigation.

Pinpointing Locations

Some automobiles are equipped with GPS to help direct drivers to their destinations. Hand-held GPS devices are currently on the market for runners, hikers, cyclists, and outdoor sports enthusiasts. Geocaching and other games that make use of GPS are on the rise. Tourist attractions and museums are using the devices as tour guides.

Street-Smarts has asked for your firm's help in defining consumer markets, choosing products, and suggesting channels of distribution for its products.

➡ YOUR OBJECTIVE

Your objective is to suggest the products Street-Smart should market to consumers for personal use, who should be the target market(s), and the channel(s) of distribution that should be used to get the products into their hands.

➡ ASSIGNMENT AND STRATEGY

- **Conduct research** To get started, analyze Street-Smart's competitors and the market for GPS products. Learn about GPS technology, especially devices that are currently marketed to consumers for personal use. Research the emerging trends and markets for GPS. Examine the marketing of GPS products, including target markets, pricing, and distribution.

- **Develop the plan** Begin your proposal with an overview of the current consumer market for GPS technology, including emerging trends. Include a history of the growth of this market.

  Cover the four Ps of the marketing mix (product, place, price, and promotion). Then devise an effective distribution plan. Recommend products you think Street-Smarts should market, identify target markets, and suggest prices for the products.

READ to WRITE

Old Product, New Uses

Ask students if they can think of other items or services that were used by the police, military, or aviation industry before they were introduced to the general consumer market. Ask students to write a one-page report about products such as Hummer vehicles or the Internet and note how they were originally intended to be used and how they are now used on a commercial level. Ask students to consider how the previous use of the products by the police, military, or aviation industry might affect the marketing of the products for commercial use.

Discuss the distribution channels you would include, the costs involved, and the volume of products you suggest distributing. Provide reasons for your recommendations.

- **What your project should include** To make your project complete, suggest how Street-Smart should set up its sales and marketing departments for the consumer market. If you suggest working with resellers, include promotional materials that might be used to persuade resellers to carry this line of consumer GPS products. If you suggest a Web site, provide a sample site map and home page design.

YOUR REPORT

Use a word processing program and presentation software to prepare a double-spaced report and an oral presentation for Street-Smarts. See a suggested outline and key evaluation points at *marketingessentials .glencoe.com/internship*

BUILD YOUR PORTFOLIO

Option 1 Internship Report
Once you have completed your Marketing Internship project and presentation, include your written report and a few printouts of key slides from your oral presentation in your Marketing Portfolio.

Option 2 E-Commerce Plan
From books to groceries, electronics to entertainment, more and more e-commerce companies are succeeding. Create your own e-commerce business. Conduct a situation analysis to support the selection of the business. Develop ideas for purchasing, inventory control, warehousing, and shipping, as well as your Web site design. Prepare a written report and an oral presentation using word processing and presentation software. See a suggested outline and key evaluation points at *marketingessentials.glencoe .com/portfolio*

@ Online Action!

Go to *marketingessentials.glencoe .com/Unit/7/DECA* **to review distribution concepts that relate to DECA events.**

marketingessentials.glencoe.com

Marketing Internship **521**

Unit Review

Now that students have completed the chapters in Unit 7, ask them to review their answers to the Analyze the Ad activities on page 441. Would they answer them differently? Why or why not?

Have students select one product, such as apples, meat, or auto parts, and trace on a large posterboard its route from manufacturer to storage to distribution to final inventory before sale.

STEP AHEAD

Discuss with students how distribution affects pricing. Have them consider the cost of each step of distribution and how it must be factored into the final price.

Internship Wrap-Up

As a class, come up with events that could be used to promote GPS technology. Suggest urban treasure hunts, usage in reality TV shows, and demonstrations at locations such as ski slopes.

Divide the class into four roughly equal groups. Assign each group a promotion strategy and have them work together to create a distribution plan involving that strategy.

BUILD YOUR PORTFOLIO

Explain to students that portfolios provide evidence of their knowledge and skills in working with data, people, and concepts. Developing a portfolio can be a valuable career development and planning tool. Point out to students that group projects can be used as evidence of your teamwork and collaborative skills. Encourage students to check the portfolio information available at **marketingessentials.glencoe.com/u7/internship.**

Peer Review

Fellow students who share common interests can serve as reviewers of the final portfolios. This review can be completed through the use of a checklist. Go to **marketingessentials.glencoe.com/u7/internship** to find a suggested checklist.

- **Chapter 25**
  Price Planning

- **Chapter 26**
  Pricing Strategies

- **Chapter 27**
  Pricing Math

Unit Objectives

After completing this unit, students should be able to

- Explain the nature and scope of price planning
- Explain factors affecting price decisions
- Discuss the legal considerations of pricing
- Describe pricing concepts and policies for products in various stages of the life cycle
- Use pricing terminology and techniques correctly and effectively
- Use pricing math to calculate markups and markdowns
- Plan and implement a pricing strategy

Key to Individualized Activities

L1 Level 1 activities are basic activities and should fall within the range of all students.

L2 Level 2 activities are average activities and should be within the range of average and above average students.

L3 Level 3 activities are challenging activities designed for the ability range of above average students.

Enrichment Resources

PROFESSIONAL ORGANIZATIONS

Professional Pricing Society (PPR) pricingsociety.com

American Marketing Association (AMA) marketingpower.com

MEDIA RESOURCES

Print or online editions of

Discount Store News Retailing Today newspaper dsnretailingtoday.com

Wholesale Source magazine wsmag.com

WRITING SUPPORT

Ask students to list three products or services that interest them. Students should note the price of each item and write a paragraph each about why they think the price is justified or not. Ask students to keep and review this annotated list as they study Unit 8.

UNIT 8   PLANNING GUIDE AND RESOURCES

CHAPTER	PRINT MATERIALS	TECHNOLOGY RESOURCES
Chapter 25 Section 25.1 Section 25.2	**From Unit 8 Fast File Booklet:** Lesson Plans Chapter Summaries Reproducible Masters Reproducible Tests **Print Ancillaries** Student Activity Workbook, Chapter 25 Marketing Math Workbook, Chapter 25 *BusinessWeek* Reader and Case Studies, Chapter 25 Competitive Events Workbook, Unit 8 Marketing Research Activity Workbook School-to-Work Activity Workbook	Interactive Chalkboard classroom presentations, Chapter 25 Online Learning Center at **marketingessentials.glencoe.com** Online Student Edition, Chapter 25 TeacherWorks **Exam***View*® Pro Test Generator, Chapter 25 Virtual Business
Chapter 26 Section 26.1 Section 26.2	**From Unit 8 Fast File Booklet** Lesson Plans Chapter Summaries Reproducible Masters Reproducible Tests Print Ancillaries Student Activity Workbook, Chapter 26 Marketing Math Workbook, Chapter 26 *BusinessWeek* Reader and Case Studies, Chapter 26 Competitive Events Workbook, Unit 8 Marketing Research Project Workbook School-to-Work Activity Workbook	Interactive Chalkboard classroom presentations, Chapter 26 Online Learning Center at **marketingessentials.glencoe.com** Online Student Edition, Chapter 26 TeacherWorks, Chapter 26 **Exam***View*® Pro Test Generator, Chapter 26 Virtual Business
Chapter 27 Section 27.1 Section 27.2	**From Unit 8 Fast File Booklet** Lesson Plans Chapter Summaries Reproducible Masters Reproducible Tests Print Ancillaries Student Activity Workbook, Chapter 27 Marketing Math Workbook, Chapter 27 *BusinessWeek* Reader and Case Studies, Chapter 27 Competitive Events Workbook, Unit 8 Marketing Research Project Workbook School-to-Work Activity Workbook	Interactive Chalkboard classroom presentations, Chapter 27 Online Learning Center at **marketingessentials.glencoe.com** Online Student Edition, Chapter 27 TeacherWorks, Chapter 27 **Exam***View*® Pro Test Generator, Chapter 27 Virtual Business

National Marketing Education

CHAPTER	SECTION	PERFORMANCE INDICATOR
Chapter 25 **Price Planning**	25.1	Explain the nature and scope of the pricing function (PRI)
		Select approach for setting a base price (PRI)
		Determine cost of product (break-even, ROI, markup, price) (PRI)
	25.2	Explain factors affecting pricing decisions (PRI)
		Calculate break-even point (PRI)
		Explain legal considerations for pricing (PRI)
Chapter 26 **Pricing Strategies**	26.1	Explain the nature and scope of the pricing function (PRI)
		Explain the principles of supply and demand (ECO)
		Identify strategies for pricing new products (PRI)
	26.2	Determine cost of product (PRI)
		Explain factors affecting pricing decisions (PRI)
		Select approach for setting a base price (PRI)
		Set prices (PRI)
Chapter 27 **Pricing Math**	27.1	Explain the nature and scope of the pricing function (PRI)
		Describe the nature of profit-and-loss statements (BME)
		Set prices (PRI)
	27.2	Determine discounts and allowances that can be used to adjust base prices (PRI)

BME Business, Management, Entrepreneurship   **ECO** Economics   **PRI** Pricing

Standards Assessment Correlation

	SECTION ASSESSMENT		CHAPTER ASSESSMENT						UNIT LAB
	Reviewing Key Terms and Concepts	Integrating Academic Skills	Review Facts and Ideas	Build Skills	Develop Critical Thinking	Apply Concepts	Workplace Skills	Net Savvy	Marketing Internship
	1, 2, 3, 4	✓	1, 2, 3, 4	1, 2	1, 2	1, 2, 3	✓	✓	✓
	3	✓	4			1	✓		✓
	5		3	2	1	1	✓		✓
	1, 2, 3		5, 6, 7, 8			1, 3, 4	✓	✓	✓
	2	✓		1	1	1	✓		
	4		9, 10			2, 4		✓	
	1, 2, 3, 4	✓	1, 2, 3, 4	1, 2		2	✓	✓	✓
	2, 4	✓	2	2		1, 2			✓
	5		3	2					✓
	2, 4, 5	✓	6, 7, 8, 9	4	1, 2	1		✓	✓
	2, 3, 5		5, 6, 8, 9	2, 3, 4		1, 2	✓	✓	✓
	1, 2, 3, 4		8	3	1	1			✓
	5		7, 8		2	1, 2	✓		✓
	1, 2	✓	1, 2	1, 2		1, 2	✓	✓	✓
	1			1					
	2, 3	✓	1, 2, 3, 4,	2	1, 2, 3, 4,	1, 2	✓	✓	✓
	1, 2, 3	✓	7, 8, 9, 10	1, 2	2	1, 2	✓		

@ **Online Action!** Check the latest updates for national standards and for your state's standards at **marketingessentials.glencoe.com**

Unit Overview

Unit 8 examines pricing principles and practices.

Chapter 25 explores the importance of price and all the factors that affect the pricing decision. In Chapter 26, various pricing policies and strategies provide a wide range of ideas on how one goes about deciding on a price for products. Chapter 27 explains pricing computations, including how to calculate markups and markdowns, and discounts. Chapter 27 also ties the profit and loss statement to the concept of pricing.

MAKING IT RELEVANT

Ask students what would happen to a local business if it charged its customers the same amount it pays for the goods it sells.

The business would be losing money because there would be nothing left to pay operating expenses.

Unit Launch Activity

Have students create a list of their first impressions of the ad on this page. The lists should include comments on what the ad is about, what part of the ad they notice and why, and what the tone of the ad is.

OUT OF TIME?

If class time is too short to cover all the chapters in this unit, go to Unit 8 in your Fast File Teacher Resources booklet and find the Chapter Summaries for Chapters 25, 26, and 27.

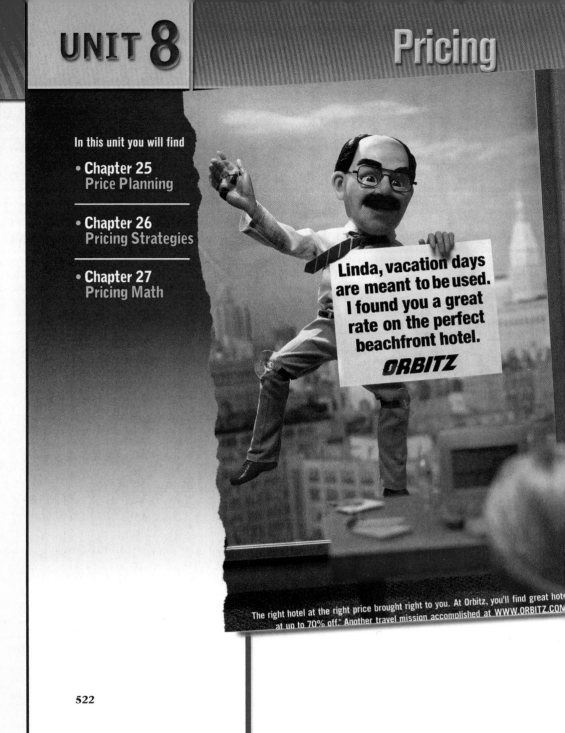

In this unit you will find

- **Chapter 25**
  Price Planning

- **Chapter 26**
  Pricing Strategies

- **Chapter 27**
  Pricing Math

Linda, vacation days are meant to be used. I found you a great rate on the perfect beachfront hotel. **ORBITZ**

The right hotel at the right price brought right to you. At Orbitz, you'll find great hotel at up to 70% off.* Another travel mission accomplished at WWW.ORBITZ.COM

522

DECA UNIT PROJECT

Pricing Principles and Practices

Have DECA chapter members use presentation technology to prepare a video or computer presentation about pricing principles and practices. Students can work in groups to decide what they should include in the presentation.

Assessment Guidelines Prepare a rubric for evaluation that includes time limits, number of topics, variety and coverage of topics, real-life examples, continuity, and quality of oral presentation. The presentations should be between five and ten minutes long, logically organized, and cover the key points of the unit.

Enrichment Assign and review Unit 8 activities in the Competitive Events Workbook.

Orbitz, an online company, provides travel services on its Web site. What does this ad say to you? How is Orbitz competing for Linda's business?

Market Talk Travel companies such as Expedia.com, Hotel.com, or Travelocity attract customers with competitive rates, powerful visuals, and fast, 24-hours-a-day service. Which of these three elements do you see in this Orbitz ad?

Think and Write Read the travel section of your local newspaper, browse the Internet to research competing travel Web sites. Make a list of companies in this market. Select two companies from your list and pick a travel destination. Find out about airfares, hotel and rental car rates from these two sites. Write a paragraph to explain which company you would select for your trip and why.

@ Online Action! Go to *marketingessentials.glencoe.com/u8/ad* for an extended activity.

Functions of Marketing

- Marketing-Information Management
- Financing
- Selling
- Professional Development
- Economics
- Business, Management, Entrepreneurship
- Communication, Interpersonal Skills
- Pricing
- Distribution
- Product/Service Management
- Promotion

Foundations — Concepts • Technology • Academic Concepts

Marketing Plan

1 ANALYSIS
SWOT
Economic
Socio-Cultural
Technological
Competitive

2 STRATEGY
Promotion
Place
Price
Product

3 IMPLEMENTATION
Organization
Management
Staffing

4 BUDGET
Cost of sales
Cost of Promotion
Incomes and Expenses

5 CONTROL
Evaluation
Performance Measures
Performance Analysis

In this unit

Foundations of Marketing
- Economics
- Business, Management, Entrepreneurship

Functions of Marketing
- Pricing

Ask students to share their opinions of the visual components of the Orbitz ad. Orbitz is competing for Linda's business by personalizing the approach.

Market Talk Discuss students' answers. Students may notice the humorous tone of the ad. They may also comment on the audience for this message: a person who works a lot and does not take time off. Make sure students notice the message about price at the bottom of the ad.

Think and Write To facilitate this assignment, you may want to bring a selection of travel-related documents to the classroom. For example, print the home page of competing travel Web sites, or bring in an online or print newspaper travel section. Discuss the variety of advertising formats with students.

@ Online Action! For instructions, ideas, and answer guide, go to the Teacher Center at **marketingessentials.glencoe.com**

Marketing Plan

RELATE THE UNIT TO THE MARKETING PLAN

The four Ps of the marketing mix are product, place, price, and promotion. Unit 8 addresses the price component of the marketing mix. Throughout this unit you will see how essential price is to a company's marketing plan and to its ultimate success or failure.

MARKETING PLAN OVERVIEW

Ask students if they can relate pricing to promotion, place, and product.
Students might mention that price is often something that is advertised. The type of product and the consumer's perception of that product influence the price. Place also plays a role in pricing: expensive products might be sold exclusively in high-end stores, for example.

Functions of Marketing

Point out to students that the Marketing Wheel shows the function of pricing and the foundations of economics and of business, management, and entrepreneurship.

- **Economics** Pricing determines revenue, profit, and return on investment (ROI) which are all key economic factors.

- **Business, Management, Entrepreneurship** Setting prices and pricing policy is one of the many responsibilities of business owners and managers. These decisions have a crucial impact on the health of a company. Pricing is often one of the most difficult decisions an entrepreneur has to make. Price should not turn consumers away, but it should cover all business expenses and provide the correct profit margin.

- **Pricing** is one the seven functions of marketing. Pricing relates to economics and to business, management, and entrepreneurship.

Chapter Overview

Chapter 25 introduces the goals and the different forms of price planning. Students will learn to differentiate market share from market position, and to define the four factors that affect price planning.

BUILD BACKGROUND

Initiate discussion about prices that students pay for items they need and want. Ask: Do students compare prices? Ask students to tell how they make their buying decisions. Tell them they are going to learn how businesses make their pricing decisions.

Why It's Important

Price (one of the four Ps of the marketing mix) is an essential element in marketing. The steps involved in determining price, together with company goals, the target market, and government regulations, are essential for business success.

Prepare to Read

Ask a volunteer to write all of the major headings on the board in outline format:

What Is Price?
Goals of Pricing
Market Factors Affecting Prices
Legal and Ethical Considerations for Pricing

Tell students to fill in the secondary (blue) headings as they preview or read the chapter. They will then have a thorough chapter outline to use as study notes.

CHAPTER 25
Price Planning

Chapter Objectives

After reading this chapter, you should be able to:

- Recognize the different forms of pricing
- Discuss the importance of pricing
- Explain the goals of pricing
- Differentiate between market share and market position
- List the four market factors that affect price planning
- Analyze demand elasticity and supply and demand theory
- Explain how government regulations affect price planning

GUIDE TO THE PHOTO

Market Talk Cell phone companies advertise in various ways to target very specific markets. Family plans that allow parents and children to stay connected during the day are very popular; so are plans geared toward college students.

Quick Think The first cell phone cost about $600. Now you can get a phone for free or for a modest sum when signing up for a plan. Think of three reasons why the price of cell phones has changed so much in recent years.

GUIDE TO THE PHOTO

Market Talk Lead a discussion about cell phone advertising that is aimed at young people or students. Which factors are likely to attract your students to a cellular plan? They may name minutes, rollover minutes, family and friends plans, phone-to-phone free calls, and more.

Quick Think Student responses may include: When cell phones were first introduced, the technology was new and expensive. As with many new technology products, mass production lowers manufacturing costs and brings savings to the customer.

Follow Up Ask students to name three items whose price has decreased over the years.

THE DECA CONNECTION

Performance indicators represent key skills and knowledge. Relating them to the concepts explained in this chapter is key to success in DECA events. These acronyms represent DECA events that involve knowledge of pricing concepts:

AAAL	FMAL	MMS	TMDM
AASL	FMDM	QSRM	TSE
ADC	FMSL	RMAL	VPM
BSM	FSRM	RMML	
EMDM	HMDM	SMDM	

In all these DECA events, you should be able to follow these performance indicators:

- Explain the nature and scope of the pricing function
- Describe the role of business ethics in pricing
- Explain the use of technology considerations for pricing

Some events include additional performance indicators. These are:

BSM	Explain the concept of price in services marketing
ADC	Explain the concept of price in the advertising industry
EMDM	Describe Internet pricing models
FMDM	Explain the concept of price in the financial services industry
HMDM	Explain the concept of price in the hospitality industry
SMDM	Explain the concept of price in sports and entertainment marketing
TMDM	Explain the concept of price in the travel and tourism industry

DECA PREP

Check your understanding of DECA performance indicators with the DECA activity in this chapter's review. For more information and DECA Prep practice, go to *marketingessentials .glencoe.com/25/DECA*

THE DECA CONNECTION

DECA events that require pricing knowledge and skills are described here. Discuss the performance indicators to make sure students understand how to demonstrate their understanding.

The events acronyms stand for:

AAAL:	Apparel and Accessories Marketing Series, AL
AAML:	Apparel and Accessories Marketing Series, ML
ADC:	Advertising Campaign Event
BSM:	Business Services Marketing Series
EMDM:	E-Commerce Management Team Decision Making Event
FMAL:	Food Marketing Series, AL
FMDM:	Financial Analysis Management Team Decision Making Event
FMML:	Food Marketing Series, ML
FSRM:	Full Service Restaurant Management Series
HMDM:	Hospitality Services Management Team Decision Making Event
MMS:	Marketing Management Series
QSRM:	Quick Serve Restaurant Management Series
RMAL:	Retail Merchandising Series, AL
RMML:	Retail Merchandising Series, ML
SMDM:	Sports and Entertainment Marketing Management Team Decision Making Event
TMDM:	Travel and Tourism Marketing Management Team Decision Making Event
TSE:	Technical Sales Event
VPM:	Vehicles and Petroleum Marketing Series

DECA PREP

Find timed DECA Prep activities correlated to the Competitive Events Workbook for students and DECA tips for teachers at **marketingessentials.glencoe.com /25/DECA**

CHAPTER 25 Classroom Resources

For the Teacher

- TeacherWorks
- marketingessentials.glencoe.com
- Interactive Chalkboard
- **ExamView** ® Pro Test Generator
- Fast File Unit 8

For the Student

- *Marketing Essentials* Online Edition
- Student Activity Workbook
- Marketing Math Workbook
- Marketing Research Project Workbook
- School-to-Work Activity Workbook
- Competitive Events Workbook
- *BusinessWeek* Reader and Case Studies
- marketingessentials.glencoe.com

SECTION 25.1

FOCUS

Introducing the Section

COLLABORATIVE ACTIVITY

Ask students what the sayings *put a price on something* or *name your price* mean to them. Have students consider the ways we use price when spending money or determining a product or service's value. Conclude by having students name all the forms price takes in situations other than purchasing goods.

Examples include: rent, tuition, dues, interest, wages, salaries, etc.

Preteaching Key Terms

Write the key terms and definitions on strips of paper. Place them in a container. Have volunteers each draw a strip of paper and read it out loud. Challenge students with the key terms to join the students with the correct definitions.

- price
- return on investment
- market share

Online Activity

Compare and Contrast

Not all products are the same price at different locations. Have students compare online prices to in-store prices at large retail stores such as Bloomingdale's or Wal-Mart.

OBJECTIVES

- Recognize the different forms of pricing
- Discuss the importance of pricing
- Explain the goals of pricing
- Differentiate between market share and market position

KEY TERMS

- price
- return on investment (ROI)
- market share

WHILE YOU READ

Analyze Find three main ideas in this section and jot them down on a piece of paper.

Price Planning Considerations

READ and STUDY

BEFORE YOU READ

Predict What do you already know about pricing?

THE MAIN IDEA

Price—one of the four Ps of the marketing mix—is an essential element in marketing a product to the correct target market. Price comes in a variety of forms. Pricing goals are directly related to a company's goals.

STUDY ORGANIZER

Use a chart like the one below to take notes about the scope and significance of pricing and the major goals of pricing.

Scope and Significance	Goals

What Is Price?

Price is the value in money (or its equivalent) placed on a good or service. It is usually expressed in monetary terms, such as $40 for a sweater. It may also be expressed in non-monetary terms, such as free goods or services in exchange for the purchase of a product. The oldest form of pricing is the barter system. Bartering involves the exchange of a product or service for another product or service, without the use of money. For example, a

---

READ and STUDY

BEFORE YOU READ

Ask students to identify how a product or service's price affects how they view it. For example, if a pair of shoes has a high price, does that prompt you to think they are of high quality? Why or why not? Answers might include: High prices are often given to luxury items, so this might affect how the customer views the shoes.

THE MAIN IDEA

Ask students to consider what the phrase *price planning* means, then state it in their own words.

STUDY ORGANIZER

Model the study organizer for students by filling in the first blank. A full-size, downloadable study organizer can be found at **marketingessentials.glencoe.com**

 WHILE YOU READ   Model for the students how they can use their own experience as consumers when learning about price.

business might exchange some of its products for advertising space in a magazine or newspaper. Some companies also will exchange advertising spots on their Web pages as a form of bartering, or an equal trade.

Relationship of Product Value

The value that a customer places on an item or service makes the difference in them spending $25,000 or $80,000 on a new auto or $20 or $150 on a concert ticket. Value is a matter of anticipated satisfaction—if consumers believe they will gain a great deal of satisfaction from a product, they will place a high value on it. They will also be willing to pay a high price.

A seller must be able to gauge where a product will rank in the customer's estimation—whether it will be valued much, valued little, or valued somewhere in between. This information can then be considered in the pricing decision. The seller's objective is to set a price high enough for the firm to make a profit and yet not so high that it exceeds the value potential customers place on the product.

Various Forms of Price

Price is involved in every marketing exchange. The fee you pay a dentist to clean your teeth, the amount you pay for a new pair of shoes, and minor charges such as bridge tolls and bus fares are all prices. Rent is the monthly price of an apartment. Interest is the price of a loan. Dues are the price of membership. Tuition is the price you pay for an education. Wages, salaries, commissions, and bonuses are the various prices that businesses pay workers for their labor. Price comes in many forms and goes by many names.

Importance of Price

Price is an important factor in the success or failure of a business. It helps establish and maintain a firm's image, competitive edge, and profits.

Many customers use price to make judgments about products and the companies that make them. A higher price means better quality from an upscale store or company to some customers; to other customers, a lower price means more for their money.

NET MARKETING

Let Your Fingers Do the Comparison Shopping

PriceGrabber.com is a fast, convenient way to locate and compare products, merchants, and prices online. Since 1999, PriceGrabber's innovative comparison shopping technology has made online shopping informative and effective. Savvy shoppers save time, money, and effort by using PriceGrabber to find the right product from the best merchant at the best price.

Ratings and Costs

Besides product pictures, descriptions, and specifications, PriceGrabber offers merchant and product ratings with narratives that give customers the lowdown on products and merchants.

A site feature called *BottomLinePrice* estimates total delivery costs, including applicable sales tax and shipping charges based on the delivery address.

● THINK LIKE A MARKETER

Could a comparison shop site be useful to a marketing manager working for an electronics company? Explain your answer.

@ Online Action!

Go to *marketingessentials.glencoe.com/ 25/net* to find a project on pricing sites.

marketingessentials.glencoe.com

NET MARKETING

Let Your Fingers Do the Comparison Shopping

Discussion After students have read Net Marketing, lead a discussion about the uses of pricing sites. Examples might be internet shopping or price comparison.

THINK LIKE A MARKETER Answer: Yes, a comparison shop site could be very useful to a marketing manager. Such sites are sources for research on competing products.

@ Online Action! For instructions, ideas, and answer guide, go to the Teacher Center at **marketingessentials.glencoe.com**

Follow Up Ask students to list three other products or services that have different prices at different locations.

TEACH

Discussion Starter

RELATIONSHIP OF PRODUCT VALUE

Begin the discussion by presenting the following example: When Apple came out with the iPod device, most computer industry observers felt that the product was overpriced. However, Apple has been overwhelmed by customer demand.

Ask students: Have you ever made a purchase based on a product's popularity? What was the product's price? Did it fit your expectations of the product's value? Answers will vary, but should highlight specific products, prices, and value judgments that were made.

TEACHING POINTS

Clarify Explain that *price* is one of the four Ps of the marketing mix. The other three are *product*, *place*, and *promotion*.

Build Vocabulary

Preview the following words by reading them in context with the section on product value. Ask students to explain what each word means. Then ask them to name a synonym.

- **avid** eager
- **objective** aim

Virtual Business

Introduce pricing to students using Knowledge Matters' Virtual Business Retailing visual simulation, *Pricing*. In this simulation, students explore the nature of pricing and discover its importance in the success of their virtual business.

Concept Development

VARIOUS FORMS OF PRICE

Have students think of the products and services they pay for on a weekly basis. As a class, develop a list of the many forms that price takes. Have students create a chart on the board with these headings: Price Name, Supplier, and Product or Service.

Answers will include a list products and services and their suppliers. For example, a bus fare would look like this on the chart:

Price Name: fare

Supplier: Metro

Product or Service: transportation

TEACHING POINTS

Demonstrate Bring in examples similar products and their prices sold in different retail stores, such as Macy's and Target. Demonstrate how company image can affect or drive the pricing of its products.

Clarify Remind students of the limitations of price-matching guarantees. Stores often expect customers to bring in a printed advertisement from a competitor's line before they will agree to match the price.

Critical Thinking

Ask students if an increase in price will always help to increase profits. Answers may include no, not if the costs and expenses increase more, or if sales volume goes down because of higher prices.

Advertising strategies are closely aligned to a firm's image. Wal-Mart's slogan, "Always Low Prices. Always." is a perfect example of how a company can use price as the main thrust of its advertising strategy. Some retailers stress that they offer the lowest prices in town or promise that they will beat any other store's prices. In such cases, price plays an important role in establishing the edge a firm enjoys over its competition.

Finally, price helps determine profits. Marketers know that sales revenue is equal to price times the quantity sold. In theory, sales revenue can be increased either by selling more items or by increasing the price per item. However, the number of items sold may not increase or even remain stable if prices are raised. Figure 25.1 shows what may happen.

It is also important to remember that an increase in price can increase profits only if costs and expenses can be maintained. You will explore this limitation later in the chapter.

Goals of Pricing

Marketers are concerned with earning a profit, or return on investment, as their primary goal of doing business. There are times, however, when two other pricing goals become important: gaining market share and meeting the competition.

Earning a Profit

Return on investment (ROI) is a calculation that is used to determine the relative profitability of a product. The formula for calculating rate of return on investment is as follows:

Rate of Return = Profit/Investment

Profit is another word for return, which explains the expression *return on investment*.

Assume your company sells watches to retailers for $9 each. Your cost to make and market the watches is $7.50 per unit. Remember that profit is money earned by a

Figure 25.1 *Projected Effects of Different Prices on Sales*

• **Increased Price or Increased Sales?** An increase in the price of an item may not produce an increase in sales revenue.

Explain why an increase in price does not always mean an increase in revenue.

Price per Item	× Quantity Sold	= Sales Revenue
$50	200	$10,000
$45	250	$11,250
$40	280	$11,200
$35	325	$11,375
$30	400	$12,000
$25	500	$12,500

@ Online Action!

Go to *marketingessentials.glencoe.com/25/figure/1* to find a project on pricing and sales.

Figure 25.1 *Projected Effects of Different Prices on Sales*

Discussion Lead students in a discussion about the relationship between pricing and quantity sold. Spark the discussion by mentioning that an increase in price might not produce an increase in sales revenue.

Caption Answer The number of people willing to buy at the higher price may decrease, and the quantity sold may decline.

@ Online Action! For instructions, ideas, and answer guide, go to the Teacher Center at marketingessentials.glencoe.com

Follow Up Have students recall the three goals of pricing.

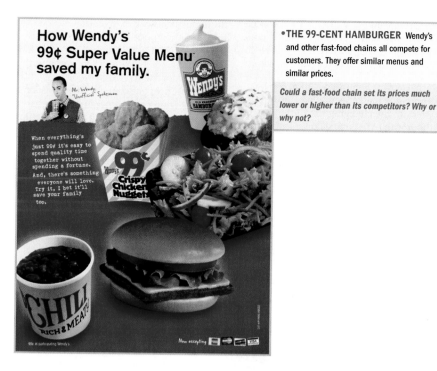

How Wendy's 99¢ Super Value Menu saved my family.

When everything's just 99¢ it's easy to spend quality time together without spending a fortune. And, there's something everyone will love. Try it, I bet it'll save your family too.

99¢ at participating Wendy's.

Now accepting

• **THE 99-CENT HAMBURGER** Wendy's and other fast-food chains all compete for customers. They offer similar menus and similar prices.

Could a fast-food chain set its prices much lower or higher than its competitors? Why or why not?

ASSESS

Review Guide

CONCEPTS

Have students review the different forms of pricing.

Have students then differentiate between market share and market position. Market share is a firm's percentage of the total sales volume generated by all competitors in a given market. Market position is the relative standing a business has in a given market in comparison to its competitors.

KEY TERMS

Have students review key terms, their spellings, and definitions in small groups.

ONLINE SELF-ASSESSMENT

Have students go to **marketingessentials.glencoe.com** for the Section 25.1 practice test.

Individualized Review

L1 Assign and review Chapter 25 activities in the Student Activity Workbook.

L2 Assign and review Chapter 25 activities in the Marketing Math Workbook.

L3 Assign and review Chapter 25 activities in the *BusinessWeek* Reader and Case Studies.

---

business minus costs and expenses, so that your profit on each watch is $1.50:

$$\$9 - \$7.50 = \$1.50$$

and your rate of return is 20 percent:

$$\$1.50/\$7.50 = .20$$

Your rate of return on investment is 20 percent.

A company may price its products to achieve a certain return on investment. Let's say that your watch company wants to achieve a return on investment of at least 25 percent on a new model. To determine the price at which the new watch would have to sell, you would work backward. Start with a target price, the price at which you want to sell the new watch. Then, determine how your company can get costs down so that price will generate your target return. When you take into consideration the suggested retail price you think consumers are willing to pay for the watch, target pricing takes on another

dimension. You will learn more about target pricing for the final consumer in Chapter 26.

Gaining Market Share

A business may forgo immediate profits for long-term gains in some other area. One goal, for example, might be to take business away from competitors. The business is trying to increase its market share in this case. For example, Nintendo's GameCube systems sold for $80 less than other similar systems, which helped to increase its market share from 19 percent to 37 percent in 2003. **Market share** is a firm's percentage of the total sales volume generated by all competitors in a given market. Businesses constantly study their market share to see how well they are doing with a given product in relation to their competitors.

Visualize the total market as a pie. Each slice of the pie represents each competitor's share of that market. The biggest slice of the pie represents the firm that has the largest percentage of

Chapter 25 - Price Planning 529

Marketing Practice

Ask students to select a product that was introduced to the market at one price, and then either the price dropped or the price increased. Have students determine what prompted this change in price and write a one-page report on their findings.

CLOSE

Have students complete the following statements:

- The key to pricing is understanding _____ . the value that buyers place on a product.

- Price helps establish and maintain a _____ . firm's image, competitive edge, and profits.

Critical Thinking

Ask students to discuss the advantages and disadvantages of an economy that uses bartering, which is the exchange of a product or service without the use of money.

---

the total sales volume. Marketers are also interested in their market position. Market position is the relative standing a competitor has in a given market in comparison to its competitors.

Improving Market Share and Market Position

To monitor market position, a firm must keep track of the changing size of the market and the growth of its competitors. Competitors are ranked according to their total sales volume. Thus, the company or brand with the highest sales volume would be ranked number 1.

Pricing is one means of improving market share and market position. Other means of accomplishing the same goals may involve increased advertising expenditures, changes in product design, and new distribution outlets.

Meeting the Competition

Some companies simply aim to meet the prices of their competition. They either follow

the industry leader or calculate the average price and then position their product close to that figure. Airline pricing appears to follow this pattern. Most airlines charge around the same price for the service provided.

How else does one compete when you don't want to rely on price alone? You compete on the basis of other factors in the marketing mix. These nonprice competing factors might include quality or uniqueness of product, convenience of business location or hours, and level of service. For example, Commerce Bank is open seven days a week and offers hours from 8:30 A.M. until 8:00 P.M. during weekdays. Automobile manufacturers are now competing with warranties and maintenance agreements, some offering coverage for five or ten years, or 50,000 or 100,000 miles, respectively. A computer store may offer free installation of software and training to teach you how to use your new software.

25.1 AFTER YOU READ

Reviewing Key Terms and Concepts

1. Provide an example of how pricing is related to a firm's image and promotion of that image.
2. What means, other than price, do marketers have to accomplish the goal of improving market share or market position?
3. Provide two examples of how businesses compete when they don't want to compete on price.

Integrating Academic Skills

Math

4. A cosmetic company has developed a new line of mascara. Each tube of mascara costs $6.50 to make and market and it is sold for $10. What is the rate of return on investment?

Geography

5. Why may the price of a concert ticket vary depending on where the concert is held within the United States? What if the concert is held in another country?

 Online Action!

Check your answers at *marketingessentials.glencoe.com/25/read*

marketingessentials.glencoe.com

AFTER YOU READ

Reviewing Key Terms and Concepts

1. Examples will vary. An example from this section is Wal-Mart's slogan "Always Low Prices. Always." This is a perfect example of how a company can use price as the main thrust of its promotion and image as a value-oriented retailer.

2. Increasing market share is done by increasing advertising expenditures, making

changes in product design, and creating new distribution outlets.

3. Examples may include: quality or uniqueness of product, convenience of business location or hours, and level of service.

Integrating Academic Skills

4. 53.8 percent rate of return on investment; $10 − 6.50 = $3.50; $3.50 ÷ $6.50 = .53846

Online Action! **Answers at** **marketingessentials.glencoe.com/25/read**

5. The cost of renting a venue may differ as well as the residents' standard of living, and demand for the various performers. Residents in different areas of the country and in different countries may place a different value on seeing a given concert. In other counties, you also must take the exchange rate into consideration and any special fees that performers may have to pay for the right to perform.

Factors Involved in Price Planning

OBJECTIVES

- List the four market factors that affect price planning
- Analyze demand elasticity and supply and demand theory
- Explain how government regulations affect price planning

KEY TERMS

- break-even point
- demand elasticity
- law of diminishing marginal utility
- price fixing
- price discrimination
- unit pricing
- loss leader

READ and STUDY

BEFORE YOU READ

Predict What are two factors that can influence prices?

THE MAIN IDEA

Pricing a product may seem like an easy task, until you take into consideration all the factors affecting that decision. Skipping even one aspect of this process could cost a business millions of dollars in lost sales or even in fines or lawsuits from not following the laws and ethics governing pricing decisions.

STUDY ORGANIZER

Draw the chart below. As you read this section, note each step of the pricing process and its consequence. Use these notes to review before a test.

Factors That Affect Price	Consequences
Costs and expenses	Determine a company's profits

Market Factors Affecting Prices

How do businesses make pricing decisions? The answer is not an easy one, as you have probably already realized. Constant changes in the marketplace force businesses to review their pricing decisions frequently. Four key market factors that must be considered when reviewing and establishing prices are: costs and expenses, supply and demand, consumer perceptions, and competition. Most price planning begins with an analysis of costs and expenses, many of which are related to current market conditions. The cost of raw materials may increase a manufacturer's costs to make an item.

WHILE YOU READ

Connect As you read this section think of what you have just learned about the goals of pricing.

Chapter 25 - Price Planning **531**

READ and STUDY

BEFORE YOU READ

Lead students in finding examples of factors. Have students work in small groups to list pricing factors. Answers might include competition's prices, manufacturing costs for the product, and discounts.

THE MAIN IDEA

Ask a volunteer to read the main idea aloud and ask another student to retell it in his or her own words.

STUDY ORGANIZER

Model the study organizer for students. A full-size, downloadable study organizer can be found at marketingessentials.glencoe.com

WHILE YOU READ Model for students how they can jot down notes on pricing as they read through the section.

FOCUS

Introducing the Section

COLLABORATIVE ACTIVITY

To prepare for reading this section, have students work as a group on a collaborative list of items whose prices they know. Examples might include CDs, DVDs, gasoline, fast meals, and clothing items. As they name items, write a price figure supplied by them. If students disagree or quote a wide range, write, for example, $12–$20 next to the item. Ask students how they think the pricing is determined for these items.

Preteaching Key Terms

Read the key terms aloud, or ask a volunteer to read them. Ask students to guess the meanings of these phrases:

- break-even point
- demand elasticity
- law of diminishing marginal utility
- price fixing
- price discrimination
- unit pricing
- loss leader

Tell students they can check their guesses as they read this section.

Build Vocabulary

Preview the following words by reading them in context. Ask students to explain what each word means. Ask them to name a synonym.

- gauge measure
- estimation valuation
- remedy solution

531

TEACH

Discussion Starter

IMPORTANCE OF PRICE

Ask the students to consider the following scenario: A family wins a raffle sponsored by a charitable organization. The prize is a sports car that the family doesn't want. For legal reasons, the charity cannot take it back. The family decides to sell the car. Ask students what the family should charge for the car. Have them consider the factors that would play a part in setting a price for the car.

TEACHING POINTS

Demonstrate Bring research material to class such as ads for cars (new and used); or the *Kelley Blue Book.* Help students figure out what would be a fair price by looking at these materials and add applicable taxes and fees.

Clarify The family will have to pay taxes on the car they won. They may also incur charges to register the vehicle.

Build Vocabulary

Preview the following words by reading them in context in the Case Study text:

- frugal
  economical
- net profit margins
  profit after costs and expenses

Discuss the meaning of these words with students.

Critical Thinking

Tell students to assume they can manufacture and distribute hair gel for $5 an ounce. Then ask: If you wish to sell this product in upscale department stores, is a suggested retail price of $10 appropriate? Why or why not?

532

Costs and Expenses

In today's competitive economic environment, businesses constantly monitor, analyze, and project prices and sales in the light of costs and expenses. They do this because sales, costs, and expenses together determine a firm's profit. Many factors have to be considered when raising or lowering prices even if the impulse to increase or decrease is a direct, seemingly logical reaction to events in the marketplace.

Responses to Increasing Costs and Expenses

When oil prices go up, you will often see an increase in rates charged by airlines, shipping companies, and gas stations. How else could businesses maintain their profit margins? Let's look at other options.

Some businesses have found that price is so important in the marketing strategy of a product that they hesitate to make any price changes. They will reduce the size of an item before they will change its price. A candy

---

Case Study

99¢ Only: Spending in Order to Earn

99¢ Only Stores' low-budget roots helped it increase sales to $863 million in 2003, up 21 percent over previous years. Their strategy? Cutting-edge warehouse and in-store stock-tracking and technology, and a frugal management culture that counts every penny.

Spend to Keep Prices Low

Expensive computer gear and cutting-edge automation are not exactly what you would expect to find behind the scenes at a retailer so price-conscious that it sells everything for $0.99 each. Net profit margins are 8.3 percent, which may not sound spectacular, but consider this: Kroger Co., the supermarket chain, has net margins of only 2.1 percent, while margins at the super-efficient Wal-Mart Stores Inc. come in at just 3.1 percent.

Yet, even with sales of $863 million, IT investments at 99¢ Only Stores are as spare as Robert Adams, Vice President of information services, can make them. 99¢ Only spends less than $5 million a year on IT, not a huge budget for a company this size.

Knowing Who Likes to Save

Where other dollar stores target low- to moderate-income neighborhoods, 99¢ Stores looks for areas with a high-income demographic. "Rich people like to save money too, and they do it in higher volumes," says founder David Gold. Case in point: The 18,000-square-foot 99¢ Only store adjacent to Beverly Hills rakes in the chain's highest annual gross sales, averaging $10 million.

THINK STRATEGICALLY
Why do you think 99¢ Only store management chose to invest in warehouse and in-store technology despite their reputation for containing costs?

Online Action!
Go to *marketingessentials.glencoe.com/25/case* to find a research project on discount stores.

532 UNIT 8 - PRICING

marketingessentials.glencoe.com

Case Study 99¢ Only: Spending in Order to Earn

Discussion Have students read the Case Study and discuss the pros (low prices, high net profit margins) and cons (low employee compensation, not enough budget for purchasing) of the 99¢ Only Stores' price planning strategy.

THINK STRATEGICALLY **Answer:** The key to success is low price and constant restocking. The more efficient the stocking operations are, the more profitable the business will be.

Online Action! For instructions, ideas, and answer guide, go to the Teacher Center at marketingessentials.glencoe.com

manufacturer might reduce a candy bar from 4 to 3.5 ounces rather than increase its price.

Manufacturers drop features their customers don't value. Some airlines have stopped serving meals and offer only beverages. Eliminating a small portion of its service helps the company to stay competitive.

Some manufacturers respond to higher costs and expenses by adding more features or upgrading the materials in order to justify a higher price. For example, the Ford Motor Company designed more comfortable supercabs on some of their trucks and charged more for those models.

Responses to Lower Cost/Expenses

Prices may occasionally drop because of decreased costs and expenses. Aggressive firms are constantly looking for ways to increase efficiency and decrease costs. Improved technology and less expensive materials may help create better-quality products at lower costs. Personal computers have fallen in price because of the improved technology.

Break-Even Point

Manufacturers are always concerned with making a profit. They are especially concerned, however, in two situations—when marketing a new product and when trying to establish a new price. In these circumstances, manufacturers carefully analyze their costs and expenses in relation to unit and dollar sales. To do this they calculate their break-even point.

The **break-even point** is the point at which sales revenue equals the costs and expenses of making and distributing a product. After this point is reached, businesses begin to make a profit on the product.

Suppose a toy manufacturer plans to make 100,000 dolls that will be sold at $6 each to retailers and wholesalers. The cost of making and marketing the dolls is $4.50 per unit, or $450,000 for the 100,000 dolls. How many dolls must the toy manufacturer sell to cover its costs and expenses? To calculate the break-even point, the manufacturer must divide the total amount of costs and expenses by the selling price:

$$450,000 \div \$6 = 75,000$$

To break even, the firm must sell 75,000 dolls. After 75,000 are sold, the firm will begin to make a profit.

Supply and Demand

In Chapter 3, you learned about supply and demand theory. You might recall that demand tends to go up when price goes down and down when price goes up. This statement is accurate as a general rule. However, demand for some products does not respond readily to changes in price. The degree to which demand for a product is affected by its price is called **demand elasticity**. Products are said to have either elastic demand or inelastic demand.

Elastic Demand

Elastic demand refers to situations in which a change in price creates a change in demand. Changes in the price of steak can serve as an example. If the price of steak were $8 per pound, few people would buy steak; if the price were to drop to $5, $3, and finally $2 per pound, however, demand would increase at each price level.

Law of Diminishing Marginal Utility

These increases would not continue indefinitely, however. At some point, they would be limited by another economic law—the **law of diminishing marginal utility**, which states that consumers will buy only so much of a given product, even though the price is low. Let's say that detergent went on sale, and you bought five bottles of it. Three weeks later a new sale is announced for the same detergent, but you already have enough to last for months; therefore, you don't take advantage of the new sale.

Inelastic Demand

Inelastic demand refers to situations in which a change in price has very little effect on demand for a product. If milk prices were to increase, parents with young children may still pay the higher price. During the holiday season, you may see parents willing to pay a

Online Activity

Costs and Expenses

Ask the students to select an online bookseller. Then ask them to browse and select a book they would like to order. Have the students list all the costs and expenses the company would incur to ship them the book.

TEACH CONTINUED

Concept Development

COSTS AND EXPENSES

After students have read the section on costs and expenses, ask them to imagine that they plan to manufacture a new brand of cologne. Ask students to list what they will need to buy in order to manufacture a bottle of cologne so it is ready to be sold.

Answers might include: a bottle, a label with a design, the cologne ingredients, packaging material, etc.

Individualized Math Skills

L1 Ask students to explain in their own words the formula for determining the break-even point.

Divide the total costs and expenses of making a product by the selling price. The result is the point at which the business begins to make a profit.

L2 The cost of making one backpack is $15 and All Outdoors, Inc. and the company expects to manufacture 60,000 backpacks. The selling price per backpack is $24. Have students calculate the number of backpacks All Outdoors, Inc. must sell to break even.

37,500 backpacks; ($15 × 60,000 = $900,000); $900,000 = 37,500 backpacks.

L3 Tell students that All Outdoors, Inc. has learned that its main competitor is charging only $20 for a backpack similar to its $24 model. Therefore, the company has decided to reduce the price of its backpack to $19.50. Have students calculate the new break-even point.

46,154 backpacks; ($15 × 60,000) ÷ $19.50 = 46,154 backpacks.

Concept Development

DEMAND ELASTICITY

To explain the concept of demand elasticity, ask students to suggest a product that is very popular with teenagers. Ask students how much they pay for the item. Increase the price until no student is willing to pay for the item. Then, tell students to assume that there is only one manufacturer of the item and one retailer selling it. Ask:

- Would you be willing to pay a higher price if the retailer did not expect a new shipment for two months?

- Would you buy it if a competitor were to produce a knockoff of the product at a lower price? Why or why not?

These questions will introduce the factors that affect demand elasticity: availability of substitutes, brand loyalty, price relative to income, luxury versus necessity, and immediacy of purchase.

TEACHING POINTS

Demonstrate Have students form groups. Have each group choose a price ranging between $5 and $50. Tell the students to write the price at the top of a page. Then, ask them to list or draw pictures of items at that price.

Extended Activity

Consumer Perceptions
Ask students to create a two-column chart. In one column, students should list goods or services that suggest status and luxury, In the other column, students should list goods or services that they think are more of a necessity. Ask students to choose one item on either list and write a two-paragraph explanation of why they categorized the item as either a luxury or a necessity.

---

higher price for a popular toy than they would normally pay. Since there is no substitute for that toy, it is an example of inelastic demand.

Factors Influencing Demand Elasticity

There are five factors that determine whether demand is elastic or inelastic. They are: brand loyalty, price relative to income, availability of substitutes, luxury versus necessity, and urgency of purchase. See Figure 25.2 for details.

Consumer Perceptions

Consumer perceptions about the relationship between price and quality or other values also play a role in price planning. Some consumers equate quality with price. They believe a high price reflects high quality. A high price may also suggest status, prestige, and exclusiveness.

Some businesses create the perception that a particular product is worth more than others by limiting the supply of the item in the market. They do this by coming out with a limited edition of a certain model and charging a higher price. Why? The reasoning is that the value of the item will increase as a result of its exclusiveness.

Service and Consumer Perceptions

Personalized service can add to a consumer's perceptions about price. Many consumers

---

Figure 25.2 Demand Elasticity

- **What Determines Demand Elasticity?** Demand elasticity varies with five factors. Most depend on the consumer's personal situation or attitudes about the purchase.

How does demand elasticity work?

1 Brand Loyalty
Some customers will not accept a substitute product, even though there are many competing brands. In such situations, demand becomes inelastic because customers are loyal to one brand.

2 Price Relative to Income
If the price increase is significant relative to one's income, demand is likely to be elastic.

3 Availability of Substitutes
When substitutes are readily available, demand becomes more elastic.

4 Luxury Versus Necessity
When a product is a necessity (such as medicine for a sick person), demand tends to be inelastic. When a product is a luxury, just the opposite is true.

5 Urgency of Purchase
If a purchase must be made immediately, demand tends to be inelastic.

@ Online Action!
Go to *marketingessentials.glencoe.com/25/figure/2* to find a research project on demand elasticity.

Figure 25.2 Demand Elasticity

Discussion Ask students to come up with an example of a product that illustrates each of the five factors. Ask them to explain why their example illustrates each factor that affect price elasticity. For example:

1. Brand loyalty: laundry detergent
2. Price relative to income: cosmetics
3. Availability of substitute: cars
4. Luxury vs. necessity: medicine (antibiotic) for a sick child
5. Urgency of purchase: gasoline

Caption Answer Demand elasticity refers to the degree to which demand for a product is affected by its' price. It involves brand loyalty, price relative to income, availability of substitutes, luxury versus necessity, and urgency of purchase.

 Online Action! For instructions, ideas, and answer guide, go to the Teacher Center at **marketingessentials.glencoe.com**

GLOBAL MARKET

GERMANY

Wal-Mart's Prices Too Low In Germany

In Germany, Wal-Mart was involved in a price war with its two major competitors, the Aldi and Lidl chains. Wal-Mart's response to its competitors' low prices for sugar was to lower its price for sugar to below cost. Wal-Mart also lowered its prices on margarine and milk, but not because of competition. When Wal-Mart experienced a sudden price increase by its suppliers of margarine, it decided not to risk losing market share by passing those increases on to its customers. Wal-Mart dropped milk prices to meet competitors' prices.

Supreme Court Ruling Germany's Superior Court ruled against Wal-Mart because its pricing practices were harmful for small- and medium-sized competitors. The basis of the Supreme Court's ruling questioned whether the pricing practices were "objectively justified" under the circumstances. The Supreme Court ruled that Wal-Mart did not violate the law with the price on margarine because it was only for a short period of time, as Wal-Mart looked for a new supplier. Wal-Mart's below-cost prices for milk were not justified because it was reacting to illegal pricing practices by its competitors, which hurt small businesses. The court maintained that Wal-Mart should have reported its competitors' pricing actions to the German Federal Cartel Office.

CRITICAL THINKING

Do you agree with the German court decision? Why or why not? How could have Wal-Mart avoided this legal tangle?

@ Online Action!

Go to *marketingessentials.glencoe.com/25/global* to find a research project about marketing and economic activity in Europe.

---

are willing to pay more for items purchased from certain businesses because of the service those businesses might offer.

Marketers can charge slightly higher prices because consumers are willing to pay for the added service. Five-star restaurants offer fancy place settings and an attentive wait staff to make your dining experience elegant.

Competition

Price must be evaluated in relation to the target market and is one of the four Ps of the marketing mix. A company can use a lower price when its target market is price conscious. When its target market is not price conscious, a company can resort to various forms of nonprice competition.

Nonprice competition minimizes price as a reason for purchase; instead, it creates a distinctive product through product availability and customer service. The more unusual a product is perceived to be by consumers, the greater the marketer's freedom to set prices above those of competitors.

Marketers change prices to reflect consumer demand, cost, or competition. When products are very similar, price often becomes the sole basis on which customers make their purchase decisions. Shoppers are more likely to buy the less expensive brand if they see no difference between products. Because of this, competitors must watch each other closely. When one company changes its prices, others usually react.

When competitors engage in a fierce battle to attract customers by lowering prices, a price war is the result. The problem with price wars is that firms reduce their profits while trying to undercut their competitors' prices and attract new customers. This may result in

marketingessentials.glencoe.com

GLOBAL MARKET

Wal-Mart's Prices Too Low in Germany

Discussion After students read Global Market, discuss how they would research pricing laws in a foreign country. Answers might include Web research or hiring consulting firms.

CRITICAL THINKING **Answer:** Answers will vary; students may agree and say that all companies doing business in Germany should be aware of its loss leader statute. Wal-Mart could have avoided this tangle by knowing German laws and reported illegal pricing practices to the Federal Cartel Office.

@ Online Action! For instructions, ideas, and answer guide, go to the Teacher Center at marketingessentials.glencoe.com

---

TEACH CONTINUED

Individualized Practice

COMPETITION

Tell students to imagine they work for a jeans manufacturer that wants to keep its prices low in order to remain competitive. The company has been losing money because its costs and expenses have been rising. If the company has another bad year, employees might be laid off, and the company may go bankrupt. The management team has asked employees for suggestions on how they can reduce the company's expenses.

Divide the students into groups. Ask each group to brainstorm ideas on how to reduce the company's costs and expenses.

L1 Tell students to select the three ideas they think are the most feasible.

L2 Tell students to select three feasible ideas. Ask them to identify the pros and cons of each idea and write a memo about it.

L3 Tell students to select three feasible ideas. Have one student from each group defend the group's ideas to the rest of the class. The class will represent the company's corporate board and question the group's ideas.

Build Vocabulary

Preview the following words by reading them in context in the Global Market feature. Ask the students to explain what they think those words mean.

- **loss leader**
  item that is sold below cost to draw customers into a store

- **market share**
  proportion of total sales held by each competitor

Review Guide

CONCEPTS

1. Ask students why marketers change prices.

Marketers change prices to reflect consumer demand, cost, or competition.

2. Ask students to list some legal and ethical considerations for pricing.

Answers will vary; legal and ethical considerations include price fixing, price discrimination, unit pricing, resale price maintenance, unfair trade practices, and price advertising.

KEY TERMS

Have student review key terms, their spellings, and definitions in small groups.

ONLINE SELF-ASSESSMENT

Have students go to marketingessentials.glencoe.com for the Section 25.2 practice test.

Individualized Review

L1 Assign and review Chapter 25 activities in the Student Activity Workbook.

L2 Assign and review Chapter 25 activities in the Marketing Math Workbook.

L3 Assign and Review Chapter 25 activities in the *BusinessWeek* Reader and Case Studies.

Marketing Practice

Have students select five products they have bought or observed for sale recently at a cheaper price than the going rate, or that they want to buy when the price goes down. Have students write a one-page report that describes the reasons for past and/or expected reductions.

---

excessive financial losses and, in some cases, actual business failure. According to *PC World*, it took two years for the home scanner market to stabilize after a two-year price war. The battle put many vendors out of business.

Legal and Ethical Considerations for Pricing

Federal and state governments have enacted laws controlling prices. Marketers must be aware of their rights and responsibilities regarding price fixing, price discrimination, resale price maintenance, minimum pricing, unit pricing, and price advertising. Some pricing practices, while legal, may not be ethical. Thus, ethical pricing considerations are also important.

Price Fixing

Price fixing occurs when competitors agree on certain price ranges within which they set their own prices. Price fixing can be proved only when there is evidence of collusion. This means that there was communication among the competing firms to establish a price range. Price fixing is illegal because it eliminates competition. The federal law against price fixing is the Sherman Antitrust Act of 1890, which outlawed monopolies.

Price Discrimination

Price discrimination occurs when a firm charges different prices to similar customers in similar situations. The Clayton Antitrust Act of 1914 defines price discrimination as creating unfair competition. The Robinson-Patman Act was passed in 1936 to strengthen the provisions of the Clayton Act. The Robinson-Patman Act prohibits sellers from offering one customer one price and another customer a different price if both customers are buying the same product in similar situations.

The Robinson-Patman Act was intended to help smaller retailers compete with the large chain stores.

Unit Pricing

A number of states have passed laws to make it easier for consumers to compare

---

similar goods that are packaged in different sizes or come in different forms (such as frozen and canned foods). **Unit pricing** allows consumers to compare prices in relation to a standard unit or measure, such as an ounce or a pound. Food stores have been most affected by these laws and have responded with shelf labels and computer records of unit prices.

Resale Price Maintenance

Manufacturers' resale price maintenance policies have come under scrutiny by legal authorities. Historically, manufacturers would set a retail price for an item and force retailers to sell it at that price. The manufacturer would punish retailers that sold the item for a lower price by withholding deliveries or refusing promised discounts or allowances. This practice of punishing retailers was outlawed in 1975 in the Consumer Goods Pricing Act.

A manufacturer may suggest resale prices in its advertising, price tags, and price lists. There can even be an agreement to fix the maximum retail price as long as the price agreement is not an "unreasonable restraint of trade" or considered "anti-competitive." A business cannot coerce current customers into adhering to such prices. It can tell customers in advance that they will not be permitted to sell its products if they break the established pricing policy. The difference between "coercing customers" and "telling them in advance" is the fine line manufacturers with such policies must walk.

Unfair Trade Practices Law

Unfair Trade Practices Law, also known as Minimum Price Law, prevents large companies with market power from selling products at very low prices to drive out their competition. In general the federal law prohibits pricing that has a predatory intent or that harms competition or consumers. Many states have enacted "sales below cost" or "unfair sales" statutes that may prohibit certain below-cost pricing, even though they would be permitted under federal law. The state laws were enacted to prevent retailers from selling goods below cost plus a percentage for expenses and profit. Some states

---

 Online Activity

Pricing Practices

Have students select three products that are advertised at very low cost online. Ask them to explore the situations: Are the prices listed real, or are they misrepresented? Are the products that are priced very low used as loss leaders? Is there any case of bait-and-switch? Ask students to keep organized notes and to be ready to present their findings in an oral report.

have passed such laws that cover all products, while others have included only specific products, such as gasoline, milk, or insurance.

In states where minimum price laws are not in effect, an item priced at or below cost to draw customers into a store is called a **loss leader**. This means the business takes a loss on the item to lead customers into the store. Retailers select highly popular, well-advertised products to use as loss leaders.

Price Advertising

The Federal Trade Commission (FTC) has developed guidelines for advertising prices. The FTC's price advertising guidelines forbid a company from advertising a price reduction unless the original price was offered to the public on a regular basis for a reasonable and recent period of time. Another rule says that a company may not say its prices are lower than its competitors' prices without proof based on a large number of items.

Also, a premarked or list price cannot be used as the reference point for a new sale price unless the item has actually been sold at that price.

Bait-and-switch advertising, in which a firm advertises a low price for an item it has no intention of selling, is illegal. For example, when a customer comes in and asks for the advertised item, salespeople switch the customer to a higher-priced item by saying that the advertised product is out of stock or of poor quality.

Pricing Ethics

Most ethical pricing considerations arise when interpreting pricing laws. Some businesses like computer chip makers and pharmaceutical companies spend a lot of money for research and development of new products. Once a product is created, its manufacturing cost may be small. When you compare its selling price to its manufacturing cost, the price may seem unusually high, but if you include the costs of development, the price may seem warranted. However, if you set a price higher than normal for a product in high demand, you are price gouging. Gouging is unethical and against the law in some states during national and state emergencies due to natural disasters or strikes.

25.2 AFTER YOU READ

Reviewing Key Terms and Concepts

1. In response to increased costs and expenses, what four pricing options might a business consider?

2. What five factors affect demand elasticity?

3. What U.S. government agency regulates price advertising?

Integrating Academic Skills

Math

4. Calculate the break-even point for a music CD that cost $12 to make and market and that will be sold for $15. The total quantity that will be sold at that price is 200,000.

Civics and Government

5. On the Internet or at your library, research the Robinson-Patman Act and list three forms of discrimination this legislation prevents.

 Online Action!

Check your answers at *marketingessentials.glencoe.com/25/read*

marketingessentials.glencoe.com

Chapter 25 - Price Planning 537

CLOSE

Ask students to recall and provide answers to the following questions:

- **What are factors that affect price planning?**

  Answers may include: costs and expenses, supply and demand, consumer perceptions, competition, and government regulations.

- **How does demand elasticity relate to supply and demand?**

  If a product is a necessity, demand is inelastic; if consumers demand a particular brand demand is also inelastic.

Extended Activity

Pricing Laws

Ask students to research the laws governing price discrimination and price fixing. Have students report on what they learned in a ten-minute oral presentation or a one-page summary. Laws chosen might include the Clayton Antitrust Act, which covers price discrimination; the Sherman Antitrust Act, which covers price fixing; the Robinson-Patman Act, which covers both.

AFTER YOU READ

Reviewing Key Terms and Concepts

1. Options might include: pass the costs to their customers; reduce the size of the item to keep the same price; drop some features their customers do not value; add more features or upgrade the materials to justify a higher price.

2. The five factors that affect demand elasticity are brand loyalty, price relative to income, availability or substitutes, luxury versus necessity, and urgency of purchase.

3. Federal Trade Commission (FTC)

Integrating Academic Skills

4. The break-even point is 160,000 CDs; 200,000 × $12 = $2,400,000 ÷ $15 = 160,000.

5. Three forms of discrimination the Robinson-Patman Act prevents are: price, discounts, and other preferential treatment if they lessen competition or hurt individual competitors.

Online Action! Answers at **marketingessentials.glencoe.com/25/read**

Lifelong Learning

CAREER INFORMATION

Have students go to marketingessentials.glencoe.com and find the Chapter 25 Careers page and click on the link for the American Marketing Association's Careers Strategies and Tips. Ask students to select one article, read it, and summarize it in three short paragraphs.

PRICE PLANNING

Newspapers and magazines may carry stories about companies that are under investigation for price fixing, price discrimination, or some other violation of pricing laws. These issues should remain of interest to students after they complete this course. As consumers and marketers, they will be affected by pricing legislation, court decisions, and investigations.

Primary Source

Ask students to go to marketingessentials.glencoe.com and find Chapter 25 Resources. Ask them to click on the link for the American Marketing Association's marketing dictionary and read the definitions of the price-related terms they find.

THINKING CRITICALLY

Companies often set prices without understanding the real economics behind their decisions. As a result, the easy-to-sell products are often underpriced.

 Online Action!

For instructions, ideas, and answer guide, go to the Teacher Center at marketingessentials.glencoe.com

---

CAREERS
IN MARKETING

John L Daly
Pricing Consultant
Executive Education, Inc.

(?) What do you do at work
I develop customized Microsoft Excel computer models for companies to price their products. My clients are usually manufacturing companies who are in highly competitive environments with thin profit margins. Most companies price their products using average accounting costs without an understanding of the real economics behind their pricing decisions. As a result, it is common for companies to overprice easy, high volume sales opportunities (what operating people would call gravy) and underprice difficult low-volume opportunities (what operations people would call dogs).

(?) What skills are most important to you?
In general, the discipline of marketing, which includes a knowledge of the customer and how much the customer is willing to pay, sets the upper limits of price. The lower limits must be set by a knowledge of the real economics of the selling situation. Pricing is a discipline that requires a strong knowledge of both marketing and cost accounting,

(?) What is your key to success?
I have a deep intuitive understanding of three disciplines: marketing, activity-based costing and information systems. Without any one of these three, I would not be able to do an effective job as a pricing professional. Pricing professionals should have an in-depth knowledge of the more quantitative aspects of marketing.

Aptitudes, Abilities, and Skills

Discipline and organizational skills, reading and research ability, strong mathematical and analytical skill

Education and Training

Advanced degrees in marketing, general business and accounting are very useful in this career.

Career Path

Careers in pricing may begin with entry-level research positions within established pricing firms.

THINKING CRITICALLY

Why is it common for companies to set prices incorrectly on products or services that are an easy sell?

@ Online Action!

Go to *marketingessentials.glencoe.com/ 25/careers* to find a research project on careers in marketing.

marketingessentials.glencoe.com

 ## Test-Taking Strategies

Give students the opportunity to ask for clarification of concepts and as needed. List concepts on the board, and ask student volunteers to define and discuss them in class. Work as a class to write a culminating statement on the board.

FOCUS on KEY POINTS

SECTION 25.1

● Price is the money value placed on a good or a service. There are many forms of price: fees, fares, tuition, rent, wages, commissions, etc.

● Pricing is a key factor in the success or failure of a product or service, and therefore of a business. It establishes an image, a competitive edge, and determines profits. Revenue = price × quantity sold.

● The goals of pricing are: earning a profit, gaining market share, and meeting the competition. Market share is a company's percentage of the total sales volume generated by all companies in a given market. Market position is the standing a company has in its market compared to its competitors.

SECTION 25.2

● Four factors affect pricing: costs and expenses, supply and demand, consumer perceptions, and competition.

● The law of supply and demand means that, in general, demand goes up when price goes down and demand goes down when price goes up. Demand elasticity is the degree to which demand affects price. If a change in price creates a change in demand, demand is said to be elastic. If change in price has little effect on demand, demand is inelastic.

● Legal and ethical issues play a key role in pricing. Government regulations control price fixing, price discrimination, resale price maintenance, minimum price, unit pricing, and price advertising.

REVIEW VOCABULARY

Define the key terms below.

1. price (p. 526)
2. return on investment (ROI) (p. 528)
3. market share (p. 529)
4. break-even point (p. 533)
5. demand elasticity (p. 533)

6. law of diminishing marginal utility (p. 533)
7. price fixing (p. 536)
8. price discrimination (p. 536)
9. unit pricing (p. 536)
10. loss leader (p. 537)

REVIEW FACTS and IDEAS

11. What are the different forms of pricing? (25.1)
12. Why is pricing important? (25.1)
13. What are the main goals of pricing? (25.1)
14. What is the difference between market share and market position? (25.1)

15. Name and explain the four market factors that affect price planning. (25.2)
16. What is demand elasticity and how does it alter supply and demand theory? (25.2)
17. What role do government regulations play in the pricing process? Give one example. (25.2)

Chapter 25 - Price Planning 539

REVIEW FACTS and IDEAS

11. The different forms of pricing are fees, tolls, fares, rent, interest, dues, tuition, wages, salaries, and commissions and bonuses.

12. Pricing is important in the success or failure of a business and for a firm's image, competitive edge, and profits.

13. The main goals of pricing are earning a profit, gaining market share, and meeting competition.

14. Market share is the percentage of the total sales volume generated by competitors, while market position is a firm's rank compared to that of competitors.

15. The four market factors that affect price planning are costs and expenses, demand elasticity, consumer perceptions, and competition.

16. Demand elasticity is the degree to which demand is affected by brand loyalty, price relative to income, availability of substitutes, and urgency of purchase.

17. Government regulations ensure legal and ethical pricing practices. One example is the Sherman Antitrust Act, which outlaws monopolies. Other examples are possible.

FOCUS on KEY POINTS

Ask volunteers to read the summaries aloud and give the classroom one real-life example for each concept.

REVIEW VOCABULARY

Sentences will vary. See glossary for definitions of **1–10.** A sample answer might read:

1. *Price* is the value of money placed on a good or service.

BUILD SKILLS

18. Workplace Skills

All memos should be addressed to the staff. The from should be the name of the student, the date the current date and the subject of the memo should be *Accurate Accounting*. The message should include how the consultants account for their time and the role they play in ethical pricing.

19. Technology Applications

Frozen Pizza Market

4%

- Salerno — 25%
- Ciccone — 20%
- Marie's — 15%
- Infantino — 14%
- Aurora's — 12%
- Angelo's — 10%
- Other — 4%

20. Math Practice

The return on investment for Ringo Wrango is 40 percent; $5.00 + $2.50 = $7.50; $10.50 − $7.50 = $3.00; $3.00 ÷ 7.50 = .4 = 40.0 percent.

The return on investment for Lingo Lango is 30.4 percent; $7.50 + $4.00 = $11.50; $15.00 − $11.50 = $3.50; $3.50 ÷ $11.50 = .304 = 30.4 percent.

Based on return on investment, Ringo Wrango is the more profitable toy for the company.

DEVELOP CRITICAL THINKING

21. Study the Competition

Student paragraphs will vary depending on the product they chose but should demonstrate an understanding of price and non-price competition.

22. Consumer Perceptions

Presentations will include aspects of the chosen products and analyze the pricing of competing products as it relates to the reputation of the product in the marketplace.

BUILD SKILLS

18. Workplace Skills

Interpersonal Communication Prepare a memo addressed to your staff of marketing consultants regarding the need for accurate accounting for the time they spend on their clients' projects. Explain the role they play in the ethical pricing practices of your firm. Include an explanation of the firm's rules regarding padding the bill and doing work for a client beyond the original contract.

19. Technology Applications

Spreadsheet Use a spreadsheet program to prepare a pie chart depicting market share enjoyed by competitors in a hypothetical $900 million market for specialty frozen pizza. Use these fictional figures to represent each brand's sales.

Brand	Sales (× 1,000)
Salerno	225,000
Ciccone	180,000
Marie's	135,000
Infantino	126,000
Aurora's	108,000
Angelo's	90,000
Other	36,000

20. Math Practice

Return on Investment Determine the return on investment for the following two toys:

	Ringo Wrango	Pingo Pango
Manufacturing costs	$ 5.00	$ 7.50
Marketing expenses	$ 2.50	$ 4.00
Selling price	$ 17.00	$ 14.75

Based on return on investment, which toy is more profitable for the company?

DEVELOP CRITICAL THINKING

21. Study the Competition

Select a product that interests you and note its price. Research other brands of that product and their prices. Which brands compete on price and which ones use nonprice competition to win customers? Summarize your findings in a 15-word paragraph.

22. Consumer Perceptions

Select a product and explain why and how consumer perceptions might have influenced its pricing. Write a short list of reasons and be prepared to discuss them in class.

 Formative Assessment

Formative assessment is an essential component of classroom work. This type of assessment provides information that is then used as feedback to modify teaching and meet student needs.

L1 Review key terms for this section. Ask students to write one sentence for each key term.

L2 Provide various examples of factors that affect price in story form. After each story, have the students identify which factor is affecting a price and explain how it does.

L3 Ask students to come up with stories that illustrate one or several factors that affect the price of an item of their choice.

Reteach If the results of this formative assessment seem low, consider the following activity:

Read the sections' subheads aloud and have students name two key facts or important details for each.

APPLY CONCEPTS

23. Identify Price

You must determine the price you will charge retailers for a box of disposable cleansing cloths, which is a new product. Competing brands retail for between $5.99 and $6.99. Assume your cost of manufacturing and marketing this new product is $2.75 per box. Remember to include a profit margin in the price you will charge retailers. To be competitive, you need to consider the suggested retail price that retailers will charge the final consumer. In this example, assume retailers will double the price they pay for the item when calculating the price they charge their customers. You expect to make 200,000 boxes of these disposable cloths at the price you will be charging retailers.

Activity What will be your break-even point? Use a word processing program to prepare a written report.

24. Research and Debate Price Gouging

Use the Internet to research the topic of price gouging from a legal and ethical standpoint. Find out if your state has a gouging law. Note specific instances and court decisions regarding price gouging. Include issues concerning prescription drugs in your research. Look at issues from a free market perspective and from a consumer's point of view.

Activity Use a word processing program to write a 200-word report of your findings and participate in a debate with classmates about price gouging.

NET SAVVY

25. A Fair Price?

Browse travel Web sites Travelocity, Orbitz, Expedia, and Priceline. Determine and list three differences in pricing factors between these dot-coms and brick-and-mortar travel agencies or major airlines.

 marketingessentials.glencoe.com

Role Play:
Management Trainee

Situation You are to assume the role of management trainee for a unisex clothing store that specializes in jeans and trendy clothing. The store's buyer (judge) wants your opinion about whether or not to carry a new brand of jeans that would sell for $10 more than your most expensive brand. Even at the $80 retail price, you think they will sell.

Activity In ten minutes, you will be meeting with the store buyer to share your thoughts and opinions. What will you say?

Evaluation You will be evaluated on how well you meet the following performance indicators:

- Explain the nature and scope of the pricing function
- Explain factors affecting pricing decisions
- Identify strategies for pricing new products
- Explain the nature of sales forecasts
- Persuade others

 Online Action!

For more information and DECA Prep practice, go to *marketingessentials.glencoe.com/25/DECA*

APPLY CONCEPTS

23. Identify Price

Students need to identify the gross margin percentage to be added to the cost to generate a profit for the manufacturer. Possible Answer: Suggested retail price: $5.99; 10%: Cost $2.75 × 1.10 = $3.025; $3.025 × 2 = $6.05, $6.05 adjusted to $5.99*

* *Adjustment made to match the actual price*

Break-even point: 181,818 boxes; $2.75 × 200,000 = $550,000; $550,000 ÷ $3.025 = 181,818.18 boxes, 181,818.18 boxes adjusted to 181,818*

* *Adjustment made to match the actual number of boxes*

24. Research and Debate Price Gouging

Research will vary by state. Both sides of the issue should be included in the report.

NET SAVVY

25. A Fair Price?

Answers might include costs and expenses (staff, office maintenance, advertising) as well as supply and demand.

MINI-QUIZ

Read these sentences to the students and have them volunteer the missing word(s).

1. The key to _____ is understanding value buyers place on a product. (pricing)

2. A firm's percentage of the total sales volume generated by all competitors in a given market is called its _____. (market share)

3. Most price planning starts with an analysis of _____. (costs and expenses)

For an expanded chapter quiz, go to Chapter 25 in the TeacherWorks CD-ROM and to Chapter 25 in the **Exam View®** Pro Test Generator CD-ROM.

THE DECA CONNECTION

The students should be evaluated on the performance indicators noted in the role play. For another DECA role play, go to the Competitive Events Workbook or the Student Activity Workbook, or go to **marketingessentials.glencoe.com/25/DECA**

Online Action! For instructions, ideas, and answer guide, go to the Teacher Center at **marketingessentials.glencoe.com**

DECA Advisors Corner

For mini-evaluations within the community, invite members of the business community into the classroom to role-play with each class member. Have advisors develop a case study to give to students a few days in advance. Students will then present their results to the visiting business-people in a role-play format. The business volunteers should then write a formal appraisal.

Chapter Overview

Chapter 26 explains a wide variety of pricing strategies: cost-oriented, demand-oriented, and competition-oriented strategies, product life cycle strategies, psychological strategies, and discount-based strategies.

BUILD BACKGROUND

Initiate a discussion about pricing strategies. Ask students: Do you think about how prices are set for certain items? Do you notice when prices go up or down? Do you think about why prices change? Tell students they are going to learn how prices are set and the strategies behind price setting.

Why It's Important

Pricing is a major factor in determining the profitability of any product. After deciding on pricing goals, marketers must establish pricing strategies that are compatible with the rest of the marketing mix. Understanding the various options helps businesses effectively execute the difficult task of pricing products.

Prepare to Read

Ask a volunteer to write all of the major headings on the board. Have students fill in the details under the headings as they preview or read the chapter. They will then have a thorough chapter outline to use as study notes.

CHAPTER 26
Pricing Strategies

Chapter Objectives

After reading this chapter, you should be able to:

- Name three pricing policies used to establish a base price
- Explain the two polar pricing policies for introducing a new product
- Explain the relationship between pricing and the product life cycle
- Describe pricing strategies that adjust the base price
- List the steps involved in determining a price
- Explain the use of technology in the pricing function

GUIDE TO THE PHOTO

Market Talk Product prices change all the time. Sometimes a new product or new technology becomes more common, so prices drop. At other times, retailers and service providers have sales and promotion events.

Quick Think Name a product you like whose price has changed in the past few years. Why did the price change?

GUIDE TO THE PHOTO

Market Talk Lead students in a discussion about pricing strategies. Have students suggest why prices change, especially when a new product or new technology becomes more common. Students might suggest these reasons for price variation: with increased product availability, the demand lessens and prices drop; if product availability decreases, the demand increases and prices rise.

Quick Think Answers will vary; students should try to identify the factors that caused the change in price.

 Follow Up Have students suggest three products that compete with the product they named in the Quick Think.

marketingessentials.glencoe.com

Performance indicators represent key skills and knowledge. Relating them to the concepts explained in this chapter is your key to success in DECA events. These acronyms represent DECA events that involve knowledge of concepts in this chapter.

AAAL	FMAL	MMS*	TMDM*
AAML*	FMDM*	QSRM*	TSE*
ADC*	FMML*	RMAL	VPM
BSM	FSRM*	RMML*	
EMDM*	HMDM*	SMDM*	

In all these DECA events you should be able to follow this performance indicator:

- Explain factors affecting pricing decisions

All the events with an asterisk (*) also include these performance indicators:

- Select approach for setting a base price
- Identify strategies for pricing new products
- Select product-mix pricing strategies
- Use psychological pricing to adjust base prices
- Select promotional pricing strategies used to adjust base prices
- Determine geographic pricing strategies to adjust base prices
- Identify segmented pricing strategies
- Set prices
- Adjust prices to maximize profitability

Some events include additional performance indicators. These are:

FMDM   Describe factors affecting the prices of financial services/products

ADC   Describe factors affecting the prices of advertising services

SMDM   Set event prices

TMDM   Set price of group tour

DECA PREP

Check your understanding of DECA performance indicators with the DECA activity in this chapter's review. For more information and DECA Prep practice, go to *marketingessentials .glencoe.com/26/DECA*

Chapter 26 - Pricing Strategies **543**

DECA events that require pricing strategy knowledge and skills are described here. Discuss the performance indicators to make sure students understand how to demonstrate their understanding.

The events acronyms stand for:

AAAL: Apparel and Accessories Marketing Series, AL

AAML: Apparel and Accessories Marketing Series, ML

ADC: Advertising Campaign Event

BSM: Business Services Marketing Series

EMDM: E-Commerce Management Team Decision Making Event

FMAL: Food Marketing Series, AL

FMDM: Financial Analysis Management Team Decision Making Event

FFML: Food Marketing Series, ML

FSRM: Full Service Restaurant Management Series

HMDM: Hospitality Services Management Team Decision Making Events

MMS: Marketing Management Series

QSRM: Quick Serve Restaurant Management Series

RMAL: Retail Merchandising Series, AL

RMML: Retail Merchandising Series, ML

SMDM: Sports and Entertainment Marketing Management Team Decision Making Event

TMDM: Travel and Tourism Marketing Management Team Decision Making Event

TSE: Technical Sales Event

VPM: Vehicles and Petroleum Marketing Series

DECA PREP

Find timed DECA Prep activities correlated to the Competitive Events Workbook for students and DECA tips for teachers at **marketingessentials.glencoe.com /26/DECA**

CHAPTER 26 Classroom Resources

For the Teacher

- TeacherWorks
- marketingessentials.glencoe.com
- Interactive Chalkboard
- **ExamView**® Pro Test Generator
- Fast File Unit 8

For the Student

- *Marketing Essentials* Online Edition
- Student Activity Workbook
- Marketing Math Workbook
- Marketing Research Project Workbook
- School-to-Work Activity Workbook
- Competitive Events Workbook
- *BusinessWeek* Reader and Case Studies
- marketingessentials.glencoe.com

FOCUS

Introducing the Section

COLLABORATIVE ACTIVITY

To prepare for reading this section, have students work as a group on a collaborative list of items whose prices they know have increased or decreased over time. Examples might be microwaves, DVD players, gasoline, and cars. As they name the items, write a plus or minus after the item to indicate whether the price has increased or decreased. Ask students why they think these prices have fluctuated.

Preteaching Key Terms

Read the key terms aloud, or ask a volunteer to read them. Ask students to predict the meanings of these phrases:

- markup pricing
- cost-plus pricing
- one-price policy
- flexible-price policy
- skimming pricing
- penetration pricing

Tell students they can check their predictions as they read this section.

 Critical Thinking

Ask students: Have you ever bought a product only to find it cheaper a few weeks or months later? What do you think caused the change in price? Have students share their answers with the class.

OBJECTIVES

- Name three pricing policies used to establish a base price
- Explain the two polar pricing policies for introducing a new product
- Explain the relationship between pricing and the product life cycle

KEY TERMS

- markup pricing
- cost-plus pricing
- one-price policy
- flexible-price policy
- skimming pricing
- penetration pricing

WHILE YOU READ

Analyze Identify policies and situations that marketers use to establish the base price for new and old products.

544 UNIT 8 - PRICING

Basic Pricing Policies

READ and STUDY

BEFORE YOU READ

Predict Name four reasons why prices vary.

THE MAIN IDEA

You already know the factors that influence pricing decisions. This will help you understand key pricing concepts. Establishing a base price from which price adjustments may be made is the focus of this section. This includes the various situations and company policies that can affect the pricing of a product.

STUDY ORGANIZER

Use a chart like the one below to take notes about the pricing policies that can affect the base price for a product.

Basic Pricing Concepts

A major factor in determining the profitability of any product is establishing a base price. Cost, demand, and competition influence pricing policies and are important in establishing a base price for a product. Each factor is the basis for a different method of setting the base price of any given product: cost-oriented pricing, demand-oriented pricing, and competition-oriented pricing.

READ and STUDY

BEFORE YOU READ

Have students work in small groups to list reasons. Answers might include: change in cost of materials needed to produce the product, or demand for the product or service.

THE MAIN IDEA

Ask a volunteer to read the main idea aloud and ask another student to retell it in his or her own words.

STUDY ORGANIZER

Model the study organizer for students by filling in notes for the first pricing policy. A full-size, downloadable study organizer can be found at marketingessentials.glencoe.com

 Model for students how they can identify policies and situations as they read through the section.

Cost-Oriented Pricing

In cost-oriented pricing, marketers first calculate the costs of acquiring or making a product and their expenses of doing business; then they add their projected profit margin to these figures to arrive at a price. Markup pricing and cost-plus pricing are two of the most common methods of cost-oriented pricing.

Markup Pricing

In **markup pricing**, resellers add a dollar amount (markup) to their cost to arrive at a price. For example, if an item cost $10 and the percentage of markup on cost is 40 percent, the retail price would be $14 ($10 × .40 = $4.00; $10 + $4 = $14). Thus, a markup, generally expressed as a percentage, is the difference between the price of an item and its cost. Markup pricing is used primarily by wholesalers and retailers, who are involved in acquiring goods for resale. The markup on products must be high enough to cover the expenses of running the business and must include the intended profit.

Cost-Plus Pricing

In **cost-plus pricing**, all costs and expenses are calculated, and then the desired profit is added to arrive at a price. Cost-plus pricing is used primarily by manufacturers and service companies. The method is more sophisticated than markup pricing because all fixed and variable expenses are calculated separately. Fixed expenses are those expenses that do not change based on production. Fixed expenses include things such as rent, interest on loans, executives' salaries, advertising, and insurance. Variable expenses are associated with the production of the good or service and include costs related to labor and supplies. When a manufacturer is running at full capacity, the percentage of fixed expenses allocated to each product becomes smaller. This permits the manufacturer to charge a lower unit price

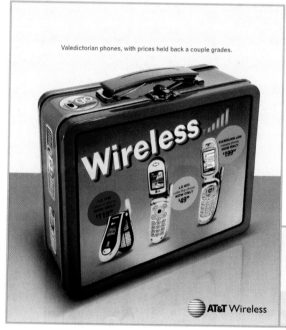

Valedictorian phones, with prices held back a couple grades.

AT&T Wireless

- **PRICING WIRELESS SERVICE** The demand for cell phone service has increased tremendously in the past years.

How has demand affected prices in this case?

Chapter 26 - Pricing Strategies **545**

Discussion Starter

COST-ORIENTED PRICING

Ask students to consider the following scenario: A charitable group that they belong to will be making and selling decorative T-shirts at an upcoming fundraiser. Have students list all the factors they must consider before they arrive at a price for the item they want to make.

TEACHING POINTS

Demonstrate Bring research material such as craft supply catalogs, to class, so that students can take into consideration how much it might cost them to produce the T-shirts.

Explain The amount of T-shirts they want to produce will affect the cost of the materials they need.

Concept Development

MARKUP PRICING

Ask students to respond to the following scenario: A wholesaler buys 100 wool suits at $30 apiece. How does the wholesaler determine the price at which he or she will resell the suits?

The wholesaler would investigate his or her competition to find out how much other companies are charging for the suits.

COST-PLUS PRICING

After students read the section on cost-plus pricing, ask them to imagine that they will be running a car wash. What types of expenses might they have to consider when determining a price to charge customers?

Answers might include: cost of water and soap, intended profit, cost of space rental, etc.

Concept Development

DEMAND-ORIENTED PRICING

After students have read the section on demand-oriented pricing, ask them to imagine that they will be making a hair grooming product to be sold exclusively at expensive salons. Ask: What types of things should they take into consideration when setting a price?

Customers at expensive salons expect to pay more for items than they would at discount or other stores.

Build Vocabulary

Preview the following words by reading them in context with the Competition-Oriented Pricing section.

- **elect**
  choose
- **going rate**
  standard; in line with the competition

Discuss the meaning of these words with students.

Critical Thinking

Ask students: Have you ever forgotten to pack an item, such as a toothbrush, for an airplane trip? Would you expect to pay more or less for the toothbrush at an airport than at a local drug store?

---

for goods. Figure 26.1 illustrates how cost-plus pricing can be used to calculate price for a manufacturer.

Demand-Oriented Pricing

Marketers who use demand-oriented pricing attempt to determine what consumers are willing to pay for given goods and services. The key to this method of pricing is the consumer's perceived value of the item. The price set must be in line with this perception or the item will be priced too high or too low for the target market. Inappropriate pricing could cause the product to fail.

Demand-oriented pricing relies on the basic premises of supply-and-demand theory and on demand elasticity factors. The higher the demand, the more a business can charge for a given good or service, even though the good or service and its cost do not change.

Competition-Oriented Pricing

Marketers may elect to take one of three actions after learning their competitors' prices: price above the competition, price below the competition, or price in line with the competition (going-rate pricing). There is no relationship between cost and price or between demand and price in this pricing method.

Competitive-bid pricing, one type of competition-oriented pricing strategy, determines the price for a product based on bids submitted by competitors to a company or government agency. In such cases, some companies will try to enter the lowest bid in order to obtain the contract.

Establishing the Base Price

To establish the base price or price range for a good or service, all three pricing approaches can be used.

Figure 26.1 **Cost-Plus Pricing for a Manufacturer**

- **Variable Costs** The example below is for a plain pair of pants.

  How would the addition of details, such as four pockets, affect the price to the business customer and ultimately to you, the final consumer?

PLENTY OF PANTS CLOTHING MANUFACTURER: UNIT PRICE FOR A PAIR OF PANTS

Materials (fabric, thread, zipper, buttons)	$7.50
Labor (piecework)	$1.50
Fixed expenses (overhead)	$.25
Intended profit	$2.25
Final price to business customer	$11.50

@ Online Action! Go to *marketingessentials.glencoe.com/26/figure/1* to find a project on cost-plus pricing for manufacturers.

Figure 26.1 **Cost-Plus Pricing for a Manufacturer**

Discussion Lead a discussion about how cost-plus pricing differs for service business and manufacturers.

Caption Answer The final price to the business customer and ultimately to the final consumer would go up because of the cost of purchasing the extra materials (for example, extra cloth and rivets), as well as the increased labor costs involved in applying those features to the garment.

 Online Action! For instructions, ideas, and answer guide, go to the Teacher Center at **marketingessentials.glencoe.com**

Case Study

Voice Over Internet Protocol

Once upon a time, there was only one telephone company in the United States. After the government broke up the monopoly in 1982, consumers had many more choices. The invention of mobile phones expanded the number of service providers, and the invention of telephoning through the Web (Voice over Internet Protocol) in the mid-1990s expanded that number again. With all those companies vying for customers, the competition is fierce.

Price Wars

Dozens of companies in the United States offer phone service through high-speed Internet connections. Some compete by adding features such as voice mail or call waiting, but most compete with price.

Verizon and AT&T charged $29.95 to $34.95 per month for unlimited calling in the U.S. in 2004. Some competitors charged $20 to $25 per month. Even cheaper plans limit the number of minutes. Skype uses a different business model, charging about 2.3 cents per minute for calls in the United States.

But some industry insiders warned there was no way to stay in business without charging $35 per month per customer, especially if the government decides VoIP providers need to collect the same taxes that traditional phone service providers collect.

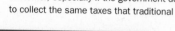 **THINK STRATEGICALLY**

What additional changes in this service do you predict for the future and how will those changes affect the pricing plans now offered by providers?

@ Online Action! Go to *marketingessentials.glencoe.com/26/case* to find an activity on new cost-saving technology.

Cost-oriented pricing helps marketers determine the price floor for a product, or the lowest price for which it can be offered and still make a profit. Demand-oriented pricing determines a price range for the product that is defined by the price floor and the ceiling price (the highest amount consumers would pay). Competition-oriented pricing may be used to ensure that the final price is in line with the company's pricing policies such as always offering prices lower than competitors. Combining pricing considerations offers a good

range within which a company can establish its base price. If a company decides to go with the competition-oriented pricing strategy, it still knows how much it can lower its prices if necessary, based on the cost-oriented pricing figures.

Reseller Considerations

Manufacturers may also consider the prices they will charge resellers (wholesalers and retailers) for their products in order to establish a base price. This can be done in one of

---

Individualized Practice

ESTABLISHING PRICES

L1 Tell students to imagine they run a snowplowing company. A local supermarket is accepting bids from companies to keep its parking lot clear of snow for the winter. As the manager of the company, you want the supermarket's business and plan to submit a bid. Ask students to brainstorm ideas on how to ensure that you will get the supermarket's business. Have students select three ideas they think are most feasible and orally present them to the class.

L2 Have students interview the owner or manager of an antique or consignment store regarding the pricing policy used by the store's sales staff. Do they use cost-oriented pricing, demand-oriented pricing, or competition-oriented pricing? Have students ask their interview subjects to explain why their chosen method is effective in their type of business. Have students report their findings in written form.

L3 Have students write a two-page report on the role of pricing for a particular product. In the report, students should compare and contrast the various pricing policies discussed in the text.

Concept Development

RESELLER CONSIDERATIONS

After students have read the section on reseller considerations, ask them to imagine they are resellers who must determine how much to charge a retailer for a shirt. Ask: which method would the students use and why?

Answers will vary; reasons may include: to make sure a profit is made, to keep the item in line with similar products, etc.

Case Study   Voice Over Internet Protocol

Discussion Have students read the Case Study and discuss how the improved technology has affected prices.

 THINK STRATEGICALLY   **Answer:** Answers will vary with regard to the future. Changes in service may include international calling and all the same services customers currently get with landline service once technology is improved.

@ Online Action! For instructions, ideas, and answer guide, go to the Teacher Center at **marketingessentials.glencoe.com**

Follow Up Let students know that if the government decides to increase its regulatory fee, prices charged to customers will have to reflect that increase.

TEACH CONTINUED

Individualized Practice

CALCULATING BASE PRICE

L1 Have students explain in their own words how to determine the retailer's base price to consumer using the pricing forward method.
The starting point is the manufacturer's cost. At each step, the reseller adds a markup to arrive at a new price. The reseller then charges its customers the new price. The final price is the price to the consumer.

L2 Have students calculate the answer to the following scenario: The manufacturer's cost for making a sweater is $10.00. The manufacturer's intended profit is 25% of the cost. The wholesaler's markup is 30% of its cost. The retailer's markup is 55.5% of its cost. What would the retailer's base price to consumers be?
$25.27; $10.00 + $2.50 + $3.75 + $9.02 = $25.27

L3 Have students calculate the answer to the following scenario: The manufacturer's cost for making a shirt is $5.00. The shirt sells at a 50% markup on cost to a retailer. If the manufacturer's cost increases by $1.00, from $5.00 to $6.00, by how many percentage points should he adjust his markup to keep the shirt at the same price to the retailer?
25%; $5.00 + (.5 × $5.00) = $5.00 + $2.50 = $7.50; $7.50 − $6.00 = $1.50; $1.50 ÷ $6.00 = 25%; 50% − 25% = 25%.

Figure 26.2 Pricing Backward From the Retail Price

- **Determining the wholesale price** One way for a manufacturer to arrive at a wholesale price is to subtract all the markups for channel members from the suggested retail price.

What problem would this manufacturer have if its costs and expenses totaled $37?

Manufacturer's suggested retail price (MSRP)	$75
Retailer's markup (40% of retail price)	−$30
Wholesaler's price to retailer (Subtract retailer's markup from MSRP)	$45
Wholesaler's markup (20% of wholesale price)	−$9
Manufacturer's price to wholesaler (Subtract wholesaler's markup from the price paid by wholesalers)	$36

- Remember this amount must cover costs, expenses, and profit for the manufacturer.

@ Online Action!
Go to
marketingessentials.glencoe.com/26/ figure/2 to find a project on pricing backward.

Figure 26.3 Pricing Forward From the Manufacturer's Cost

- **Marking up cost** In this pricing method, the starting point is the manufacturer's cost. At each step, a reseller adds a markup to arrive at a new price. The reseller then charges its customers the new price. The final price is the price to the consumer.

What do you see as the basic difference in markup percentage between calculating pricing forward and pricing backward?

Cost of producing the item	$30.00
Manufacturer's expenses and intended profit (20% of cost)	+6.00
Manufacturer's price to wholesaler (Cost plus expenses plus intended profit)	36.00
Wholesaler's markup (25% of price wholesaler paid for item)	+9.00
Wholesaler's price to retailer (Manufacturer's price to wholesaler + markup)	45.00
Retailer's markup (66.67% based on price paid to wholesaler)	+30.00
Retailer's base price to consumer	$75.00

@ Online Action!
Go to
marketingessentials.glencoe.com/26/ figure/3 to find a project on pricing forward.

---

two ways. You can work backward from the final retail price to find the price for the wholesalers. You can also do this in reverse, working forward from costs and expenses to the final retail price. Figures 26.2 and 26.3 illustrate these two methods.

In Figure 26.2, which describes the steps in working backward, the suggested retail price is set first, on the basis of consumer demand and competition. Next, the markups desired by the wholesalers and retailers are deducted sequentially from the suggested retail price. Finally, the base price that the manufacturer

548 UNIT 8 - PRICING

 marketingessentials.glencoe.com

Figure 26.2 Pricing Backward From the Retail Price

Discussion Point out that a manufacturer starts with the retail price and then subtracts all the markups. Lead a discussion as to why a retailer might employ pricing backward.

Caption Answer The manufacturer would have to find a way to reduce costs and expenses to maintain the $75 suggested retail price. Another option might be to raise the price to wholesalers and retailers, which would mean the suggested retail price would have to be higher than $75.

@ Online Action! For instructions, ideas, and answer guide, go to the Teacher Center at marketingessentials.glencoe.com

Follow Up Create a chart on the board to illustrate working backward from the final retail price and working forward from costs and expenses.

will charge the wholesaler is determined. Note that the price to the wholesaler must be high enough to cover the manufacturer's costs, any expenses, and the intended profit.

Figure 26.3 illustrates the steps for working forward from the manufacturer's cost. Expenses and intended profit must be considered, and then the wholesaler's and retailer's markups are added to the manufacturer's price to arrive at the base selling price. Competition and consumer demand may be left out of the pricing decision if the price is set at this point.

Pricing Policies and Product Life Cycle

A basic pricing decision every business must make is to choose between a one-price policy and a flexible-price policy. A business also needs to consider how a new product will be introduced into the marketplace. That choice will determine the pricing decisions that follow as the product moves through its life cycle.

One-Price Versus Flexible-Price Policy

A **one-price policy** is one in which all customers are charged the same prices. Prices are quoted to customers by means of signs and price tags, and no deviations are permitted. Most retail stores employ this policy. A one-price policy offers consistency and reliability. It also allows retailers to estimate sales and profit because they know the set price.

A **flexible-price policy** is one in which customers pay different prices for the same type or amount of merchandise. This kind of policy permits customers to bargain for merchandise. Most retail stores avoid using flexible pricing because it can cause legal problems and it may keep some customers away. A flexible-price strategy is common for goods such as used cars, artwork, antiques, furniture, and selected jewelry. One disadvantage of a flexible-price policy is that it does not offer consistent profits. It can be difficult to estimate sales revenue because of the fluctuations in price. However, with computer technology and huge databases, this may be changing.

Product Life Cycle

Products move through four stages: introduction, growth, maturity, and decline. Pricing plays an important role in this sequence of events.

New Product Introduction

A business may elect to price a new product above, in line with, or below its competitors depending on the philosophy of the business and market conditions. When a going-rate strategy is not used to introduce a new product, two methods may be used: skimming pricing or penetration pricing.

Method 1 Skimming pricing is a pricing policy that sets a very high price for a new

• **PRICING ELECTRONICS** Computers and other electronic appliances quickly go out of date as new technology emerges and becomes more common.

How does this fast product life cycle affect pricing?

Figure 26.3 — *Pricing Forward From the Manufacturer's Cost*

Discussion Point out that in pricing forward, a retailer uses the manufacturer's cost as a starting point. Lead a discussion as to why a retailer might employ pricing forward.

Caption Answer The basic difference between the markup percentages when calculating pricing forward and backward is that the markup percentage is greater when it is based on cost compared to retail. If market research indicated that consumers were willing to pay $80, the manufacturer could increase the price it charges wholesalers, which in turn provides a higher margin for the company and allows each channel member to make a little more on the item. The manufacturer could also elect to keep the same price and undercut the competition with the $75 price.

@ Online Action! For instructions, ideas, and answer guide, go to the Teacher Center at **marketingessentials.glencoe.com**

TEACH CONTINUED

Concept Development

ONE-PRICE VERSUS FLEXIBLE-PRICE POLICY

After students have read the section on pricing policies, ask them to identify a new product on the market. As a class, research the price of the new product, and find three similar products to see if the prices are higher, lower, or the same.

TEACHING POINTS

Clarify Remind students that businesses choose between two types of pricing policy: one-price or flexible-price policy.

Extend Present students with two buying opportunities: a leather-goods store at a mall and a leather-goods stall at a community market. Have students infer which pricing policy would be used at each location.

A one-price policy would be used at the mall, while a flexible-price policy would be used at a market.

AD GUIDE

PRICING ELECTRONICS

Discussion Lead a discussion about price changes by asking students what the ad tells them about the market for laptop computers. Have students explain their responses.

Caption Answer Newer products are likely to have higher prices than older products.

Follow Up Ask students to name two other products or services that were once very expensive, but are now available to the general public at more affordable prices.

ASSESS

Review Guide

CONCEPTS

Ask students to recall and to list the three basic pricing concepts.

There are three basic concepts for determining price: cost-oriented pricing, demand-oriented pricing, and competition-oriented pricing.

KEY TERMS

Have students review key terms, their spellings, and definitions in small groups.

ONLINE SELF-ASSESSMENT

Have students go to marketingessentials.glencoe.com for the Section 26.1 practice test.

Individualized Review

L1 Assign and review Chapter 26 activities in the Student Activity Workbook.

L2 Assign and review Chapter 26 activities in the Marketing Math Workbook.

L3 Assign and review Chapter 26 activities in the *BusinessWeek* Reader and Case Studies.

Marketing Practice

Have students select five products that they have bought in the past that are now selling for more or less than they paid. Tell students to research, outline, and write a two-page report that uncovers the reasons for the changes in price. Ask the students to relate these changes to the concepts presented in this chapter in their reports.

MARKET TECH

Pricing and Promotion Software

Chances are you have seen circulars in the mail or in the Sunday newspaper promoting special markdowns or "everyday low prices" at local stores. Stores used to rely on laborious calculations and even guesswork to set prices and decide what products to put on sale. Today, computer software can handle that job.

No More Guesswork

Retail chains including Radio Shack, Albertsons, and Longs Drugs use what is known as retail revenue management software or customer demand software to make pricing decisions.

The computer programs use information collected by point-of-sale terminals, such as sales volume and price. The software combines these data with other factors, including sales and volume goals, price sensitivity, and the prices that the chains pay for their goods.

After crunching the numbers, the software recommends prices and suggests products to put on sale or otherwise promote.

THINK LIKE A MARKETER

Why is the information collected at point-of-sale (POS) terminals not enough for this software to accomplish a complete price analysis?

@ Online Action!

Go to *marketingessentials.glencoe.com/26/tech* to find an activity on pricing and technology.

---

product. This kind of policy can be used any time demand is greater than supply. Such a policy is designed to capitalize on the high demand for a product during its introductory period.

Businesses that use this method recognize that the price will have to be lowered once the market for the product changes to more price-conscious customers. While the product is hot, the business will enjoy a high profit margin. Another advantage of skimming pricing is that the price may be lowered without insulting the target market.

One disadvantage of skimming pricing is that the high initial price generally attracts competition. In addition, if the initial price is far above what consumers are willing to pay, sales will be lost and profits diminished.

Method 2 Penetration pricing is the opposite of skimming pricing; the price for a new product is set very low. The purpose of penetration pricing is to encourage as many people as possible to buy the product and thus penetrate the market. This type of pricing is most effective in the sale of price-sensitive products (items with elastic demand). Sony used a penetration pricing strategy when it introduced its first PlayStation game console.

To penetrate the market quickly with penetration pricing, mass production, distribution, and promotion must be incorporated into the marketing strategy. The product should take hold in a short period of time. This allows the marketer to save on fixed expenses (through mass production) and to increase the profit margin (through volume sales).

The biggest advantage of penetration pricing is its ability to capture a large number of customers in a relatively short period of time. This blocks competition from other companies.

If the product is not in high demand, however, the lower price will cause the marketer to suffer a bigger loss than it would have if a higher initial price had been set.

 marketingessentials.glencoe.com

MARKET TECH

Pricing and Promotion Software

Discussion Ask students to give examples of other ways companies use technology.

THINK LIKE A MARKETER **Answer:** Sales and volume goals, price sensitivity, market share, as well as the prices that the chains pay for their goods, must be considered before a product can be promoted or put on sale.

@ Online Action! For instructions, ideas, and answer guide, go to the Teacher Center at marketingessentials.glencoe.com

Follow Up Divide students into two groups: one group that thinks pricing and promotion software is a good idea and one group that thinks the software is not a good idea. Have them debate the advantages and disadvantages.

Other Product Stages

Pricing during subsequent periods in a product's life cycle is determined by which pricing method was originally used, skimming or penetration. Sales increase rapidly during the penetration stage, and total costs per unit decrease because volume absorbs fixed costs. The main goal of marketers is to keep products in this stage as long as possible.

Sales of products introduced with skimming pricing should be monitored. Once sales begin to level off, the price should be lowered to appeal to the price-conscious target market.

Very little price change will be made in the growth stage for products introduced with penetration pricing. When demand decreases and sales begin to level off, competition is generally very keen. Marketers look for new market segments to hold the prices for their products. A baking soda marketer may stress noncooking uses for baking soda, such as deodorizing refrigerators.

The marketer's principal goal during the maturity stage is to stretch the life of a product. Some companies reduce their prices. Others choose to revitalize products in this stage by adding new features or improvements, or by looking for new target markets. Another option is to seek new markets in other nations in the global marketplace. Products that have been made obsolete in the United States by technological advances may be in the introductory or growth stage in other places. By using techniques like these, marketers can significantly extend a product's life cycle. When such efforts are not successful, however, a product moves into its decline.

Sales decrease and profit margins are reduced in the decline stage. Companies are forced to reduce the price to generate sales. To maintain profitability, marketers try to reduce manufacturing costs or cut back on advertising and other promotional activities. Once a product is no longer profitable, it is phased out.

CLOSE

Have students complete the following statement:

Going-rate pricing involves studying the competition's pricing to be sure that _____ .

the following one's own prices are in line with them.

Online Activity

Product Pricing on the Web

Ask interested students to choose an Internet product and research and report on what pricing strategies are used to market the product. Have students summarize their findings in a five- to ten-minute oral presentation.

26.1 AFTER YOU READ

Reviewing Key Terms and Concepts

1. Name and explain the two most common methods of cost-oriented pricing.
2. What is the key to demand-oriented pricing?
3. What three actions may marketers elect to follow in competition-oriented pricing?

Integrating Academic Skills

Math

4. Use the "pricing backward from retail price" approach to calculate the manufacturer's price to a wholesaler for a product that has a suggested retail price of $200. Assume that the retailer's markup on the retail price is 40 percent and the wholesaler's markup is 20 percent.

Civics and Government

5. What is competitive-bid pricing, and why must marketers understand this policy if they want to sell goods and service to the government?

@ Online Action!

Check your answers at *marketingessentials.glencoe.com/26/read*

marketingessentials.glencoe.com

Chapter 26 - Pricing Strategies **551**

AFTER YOU READ

Reviewing Key Terms and Concepts

1. The two most common methods of cost-oriented pricing are cost-plus pricing and markup pricing.

2. The key to demand-oriented pricing is the consumer's perceived value of the item.

3. Three actions marketers can take are: price above the competition, price below the competition, or price in line with the competition (going-rate pricing).

Integrating Academic Skills

4. $96; $200 × .40 = $80; $200 − $80 = $120; $120 × .20 = $24; $120 − $24 = $96

5. Competitive-bid pricing is a type of competition-oriented pricing that determines the price for a product based on bids submitted by competitors to a company or government agency. Laws require most government agencies to request bids based on certain specifications so they can select the company that offers the lowest prices.

@ Online Action! Answers at **marketingessentials.glencoe.com/26/read**

FOCUS

Introducing the Section

COLLABORATIVE ACTIVITY

To prepare students for reading this section, have students work in groups on a collaborative list of items they have bought at discounted or promotional prices. Examples might include cell phones, Internet service, and cars. As you write the items on the board, ask students why they think these items were offered at special prices.

Preteaching Key Terms

Read the key terms aloud, or ask a volunteer to read them. Ask students to predict the meanings of these phrases:

- product mix pricing strategies
- price lining
- bundle pricing
- geographical pricing
- segmented pricing strategy
- psychological pricing
- prestige pricing
- everyday low prices (EDLP)
- promotional pricing

Tell students they can check their predictions as they read this section.

Extended Activity

Energy Prices

Have students research local energy prices—for example, gasoline, natural gas, and electricity prices. Ask students to use spreadsheet software to create a table of the different types of energy sources, their cost, and their unit of measurement.

OBJECTIVES

- Describe pricing strategies that adjust the base price
- List the steps involved in determining a price
- Explain the use of technology in the pricing function

KEY TERMS

- product mix pricing strategies
- price lining
- bundle pricing
- geographical pricing
- segmented pricing strategy
- psychological pricing
- prestige pricing
- everyday low prices (EDLP)
- promotional pricing

WHILE YOU READ

Connect Note pricing strategy examples from your own experience.

Strategies in the Pricing Process

READ and STUDY

BEFORE YOU READ

Predict How and why do you think prices change?

THE MAIN IDEA

Now that you know how to establish a base price, you need to learn how and why price adjustments are made. Price adjustments are a marketer's way of being creative with pricing. These strategies help businesses stay competitive. Using the right pricing strategy can help increase sales and profitability for a company, as you will see in the examples provided.

STUDY ORGANIZER

Create an outline of this section to identify the strategies for adjusting prices and the steps in setting prices.

Price Adjustment Strategies
1. Product mix strategies
a. Price lining
b.
c.
d.
e.
2.

Adjusting the Base Price

Marketers can use specific pricing strategies to fit different economic and market conditions. To adjust base prices, marketers may employ any one or more of the following pricing strategies: product mix, geographical, international, segmented, psychological, and promotional pricing, as well as discounts and allowances. Using these strategies in the appropriate situations helps businesses remain competitive.

READ and STUDY

BEFORE YOU READ

Lead students in predicting how and why prices change by giving the example of seasonal produce and high availability leading to lower prices.

THE MAIN IDEA

Ask a volunteer to read the main idea aloud and other students to brainstorm reasons why price adjustments are made.

STUDY ORGANIZER

Model the study organizer for students by filling in the next letter in the outline. A full-size, downloadable study organizer can be found at **marketingessentials.glencoe.com**

WHILE YOU READ

Model a pricing strategy from your own experience for students.

Product Mix Strategies

Product mix pricing strategies involve adjusting prices to maximize the profitability for a group of products rather than on just one item. With this method, one product may have a small profit margin while another may be high to balance the effect of the lower priced one. They include price lining, optional product pricing, captive product pricing, by-product pricing, and bundle pricing.

Price Lining

Price lining is a special pricing technique that sets a limited number of prices for specific groups or lines of merchandise. A store might price all its blouses at $25, $35, and $50. When deciding on the price lines, marketers must be careful to make the price differences great enough to represent low, middle, and high quality items. Price lines of $25, $26, $27, and $28, for example, would confuse customers because they would have difficulty discerning their basis.

An advantage of price lining is that the target market is fully aware of the price range of products in a given store. In addition, price lining makes merchandising and selling easier for salespeople, who can readily draw comparisons between floor and ceiling prices.

Optional Product

Optional product pricing involves setting prices for accessories or options sold with the main product. One example is options for cars. All options need to be priced so that a final price for the main product can be established.

Captive Product

Captive product pricing sets the price for one product low but compensates for that low price by pricing the supplies needed to operate that product high. Ink-jet printers are low in price, but the ink cartridges required to operate the printers have high prices.

By-Product

By-product pricing helps business get rid of excess materials used in making a product by using low prices. Wood chips that are residual by-products from making furniture may be sold at a very low price to other manufacturing companies that use that material in making their products.

Bundle Pricing

With **bundle pricing**, a company offers several complementary products in a package that is sold at a single price. The one price for all the complementary products and the main item is lower than if a customer purchased each item separately. Computer companies use bundle pricing when they include software in the sale price of a computer. Bundling helps businesses sell items (parts of the package) that they may not have sold otherwise, which increases their sales and revenue.

Geographical Pricing

Geographical pricing refers to price adjustments required because of the location of the customer for delivery of products. The delivered price includes the cost of the item and delivery charges. In this pricing strategy, the manufacturer assumes responsibility for the cost and management of product delivery.

International Pricing

When doing business internationally, marketers need to set prices that take into consideration costs, consumers, economic conditions, and the monetary exchange rate. Costs may include shipping, tariffs, or other charges. Consumers' income levels and lifestyles will require adjustments to the price.

Segmented Pricing Strategies

A **segmented pricing strategy** uses two or more different prices for a product, even though there is no difference in the item's cost. Used correctly, this strategy helps businesses optimize profits and compete more effectively. Four factors can help marketers use segmented pricing strategies: buyer identification, product design, purchase location, and time of purchase.

Buyer Identification

Recognizing a buyer's sensitivity to price (demand elasticity) is one way to identify a

TEACH

Discussion Starter

PRODUCT MIX STRATEGIES

Ask students to imagine that they are planning a summer vacation for one week. Have them select a destination that would require airfare, hotel accommodations, and meals. First, have the students price the cost of each separately. Then have them find companies that offer the vacation as a package deal. Ask: Which option is more expensive? What are advantages and disadvantages of each? Answers will vary but students should be able to relate the advantages and disadvantages of each product mix.

TEACHING POINTS

Clarify Explain to students that some airlines offer special pricing at their Web sites to encourage traffic at their sites and buying directly from the airline.

Price Lining After students read the section on price lining, ask them to imagine they are selling a doll called the Merry Maddie Doll. The doll itself will be sold at $9.99 for a very low profit. Ask: How can you expect to make more on the doll using price-lining concepts? Answers will include: sell accessories for the doll, including clothes and toys for a higher profit, bundle it with other toys, etc.

Critical Thinking

Tell students that a small independent online record store has the latest Postal Service CD. The price is listed at $3 more than it is listed at a local large retail outlet. However, free shipping is included. Ask students to list reasons why a potential customer might prefer to order from the online site. Answers may include convenience or wanting to patronize the independent store rather than the large retailer.

Critical Thinking

Ask students if they have ever bought an item on sale only to spend more on accessories or options.

Concept Development

PSYCHOLOGICAL PRICING STRATEGIES

Ask students to name products that are usually sold using the odd-even pricing method. Ask: What products are sold at odd numbers, and what products are sold at even numbers?

Answers will vary. Odd-priced products might include cooking gadgets sold on television or sale items. Even-priced products might include food items.

TEACHING POINTS

Extend Ask students if they think there is a psychological difference between an item priced at $9.99 and one priced at $10. This type of question will help students understand the use of psychological pricing techniques.

Individualized Practice

PSYCHOLOGICAL PRICING

L1 Have students visit several different retail stores in their community to investigate psychological pricing strategies. Ask them to provide examples of products, their prices, and any psychological effects.

L2 Have students choose a specific method of psychological pricing, and then price and promote a product using this technique. Students should develop either store signs, TV or radio ads, or Internet ads for the promotion.

L3 Ask students to develop a system for having salespeople remind customers of a special. Have them prepare a memo explaining exactly what they want salespeople to do to encourage the sale of the specially priced merchandise.

customer segment. For example, to attract customers on fixed incomes, some businesses offer senior citizen and student discounts. Airlines offer different classes of travel—first class and coach. First-class travelers pay a significantly higher price to get to the same destination.

Product Design

Manufacturers may also create different prices for different product styles that do not reflect the cost of making the item but, rather, the demand for a given style.

Purchase Location

Purchase location involves pricing according to where a product is sold and/or the location of the good or service. Tickets for Broadway shows in New York City will be priced higher than those for the same show when it goes on the road.

Time of Purchase

Some types of businesses experience highs and lows in sales activity. During peak times, they are able to charge more because of increased demand. Telephone companies often charge more for long-distance calls made during business hours, a peak time.

Psychological Pricing Strategies

Psychological pricing strategies are pricing techniques that help create an illusion for customers. They are often based on a buyer's motivation for making a purchase and purchasing habits. Among common psychological pricing techniques are odd-even pricing, prestige pricing, multiple-unit pricing, and everyday low prices (EDLPs).

Odd-Even Pricing

A technique that involves setting prices that all end in either odd or even numbers is known as odd-even pricing. This strategy is based on the psychological principle that odd numbers ($.79, $9.95, $699) convey a bargain image. Even numbers ($10, $50, $100) convey a quality image. Whether or not this is true, you will find that many marketers follow the

odd-even technique in an effort to project a certain image.

Prestige Pricing

Prestige pricing sets higher-than-average prices to suggest status and high quality to the consumer. Many customers assume that higher prices mean better quality. Rolls-Royce automobiles, Waterford crystal, and Rolex watches are all prestige priced.

Multiple-Unit Pricing

Some businesses have found that pricing items in multiples, such as three for $1.00, is better than selling the same items at $.34 each. Multiple-unit pricing suggests a bargain and helps to increase sales volume.

Everyday Low Price

Everyday low prices (EDLP) are low prices set on a consistent basis with no intention of raising them or offering discounts in the future. Everyday low prices are not as deeply discounted as promotional prices might be, which creates sales stability. Other benefits include reduced promotional expenses and reduced losses due to discounting.

Promotional Pricing

Promotional pricing is generally used in conjunction with sales promotions where prices are reduced for a short period of time. Common types of promotional pricing are loss leader pricing (discussed in Chapter 25), special-event pricing, and rebates and coupons.

Loss Leader Pricing

Loss leader pricing is used to increase store traffic by offering very popular items of merchandise for sale at below-cost prices. The theory behind this practice is that customers will be attracted by the low price. Once in the store, they will buy regularly priced merchandise in addition to the loss leader item.

Special-Event

In special-event pricing, items are reduced in price for a short period of time, based on a specific happening, such as back-to-school,

Online Activity

Promotion Pricing on the Web

Have students research and identify the types of discounts or features offered by two or three companies when you purchase their products or services on their Web site rather than in-person or over the telephone. Have students share their research results with the class.

Presidents' Day, or anniversary sales. Manufacturers offer special promotions to wholesalers and retailers willing to advertise or promote a manufacturer's products.

Rebates and Coupons

Rebates are partial refunds provided by the manufacturer to consumers. To receive the rebate, a customer buys the product and then sends in a rebate form along with the product proof of purchase and a store receipt. Manufacturers offer rebates to wholesalers and retailers too, for purchasing certain quantities of goods prior to running promotions that will generate business for those resellers. Coupons allow customers to take reductions at the time of purchase. Coupons may be found in newspapers, advertisements, product packages, and even on sales receipts printed by retailers, such as supermarkets.

Discounts and Allowances

Discount pricing involves the seller offering reductions from the usual price. Such reductions are generally granted in exchange for the buyer's performance of certain functions. These include cash discounts, quantity discounts, trade discounts, seasonal discounts, and special allowances.

Cash Discounts

Cash discounts are offered to buyers to encourage them to pay their bills quickly. Terms are generally written on the invoice, for example, 2/10, net 30 means that a 2 percent discount is granted if the bill is paid in ten days.

Quantity Discounts

Quantity discounts are offered to buyers for placing large orders. Sellers benefit from large orders through the lower selling costs involved in one transaction as opposed to several small transactions. Quantity discounts also offer buyers an incentive to purchase more merchandise than they originally intended to purchase.

There are two types of quantity discounts: noncumulative and cumulative. Noncumulative quantity discounts are offered on one order, while cumulative quantity discounts are offered on all orders over a specified period of time. Cumulative discounts may be granted for purchases made over six months, for example, in which case all purchases for that period are used to determine the quantity discount offered. In other cases, buyers may be

marketingessentials.glencoe.com

Chapter 26 - Pricing Strategies **555**

A MATTER OF ETHICS

Reward or Punishment?

Some supermarkets offer special discounts on selected items to customers who have a frequent shopper card, but not to those without one. Consider two customers at the checkout counter, both purchasing the same loaf of bread. The customer with a card pays $2.00 for a loaf of bread, while the other without a card pays $2.99. Frequent shopper cards are available to all customers who request one.

Opting Out

Some customers simply do not want their purchases traced through participation in a frequent shopper program. They feel it is an invasion of their privacy. However, they also object to paying higher prices than other customers.

⬤ THINKING ETHICALLY

Are loyalty-card programs ethical?

@ Online Action!

Go to *marketingessentials.glencoe.com/26/ethics* to find an activity on ethics and pricing.

Concept Development

DISCOUNTS AND ALLOWANCES

Ask students if they have ever bought a product at a discount price. Was it a product they wanted and had been waiting for a special price, or was it something they had not thought of before but wanted once they saw the price? Have students share their responses. Then, ask students if they have ever considered buying a laptop. Have them consider the following offers:

- A local computer store is offering laptops at a low "Back to School" price of $499 as opposed to the regular price of $999. Ask students if they would take advantage of this offer.

- A local chain store is advertising a laptop at a special price of $599 with a free printer. Ask students how they might react to this offer.

TEACHING POINTS

Extend Ask students to imagine that they are responsible for grocery shopping. Coupons are everywhere—in the Sunday paper, in magazines, and even printed on your receipt. Ask: What are the advantages and disadvantages of using coupons? Advantages: You may save money on products you buy every week and some stores will double the amount of discount savings on the coupons. Disadvantages: You may buy a product you do not need just because you have a coupon, or the coupon may require you to buy more of the product than you need.

A MATTER OF ETHICS   Reward or Punishment?

Discussion Have students brainstorm how frequent shopping cards work.

THINKING ETHICALLY **Answer:** Students' opinions will vary. Most students will say the practice is ethical because all customers may get a loyalty card and benefit from its use. However, some students may point out that some customers do not use one because they feel that their privacy is being invaded when a business can track their purchases. Others are not inclined to take the time to complete the registration for a loyal program.

@ Online Action! For instructions, ideas, and answer guide, go to the Teacher Center at marketingessentials.glencoe.com

TEACH CONTINUED

Individualized Practice

DISCOUNTS AND CUSTOMER SERVICE

L1 Have students assume they work for a local retailer during a special end-of-season sale. All seasonal merchandise is reduced 25 percent to 50 percent off the original price. Unfortunately, some prices reflect markdowns that were taken prior to the sale. This confuses customers, because some expect the 25 percent or 50 percent discount to be taken off the ticketed price, instead of the original price. Ask students how they would explain the situation to the confused customers.

Students may explain that even though some merchandise was marked down previously, today's sale stipulates that the markdown is a percentage off the original price, not a prior sales price.

L2 Have students perform a role play between sales associates and customers in the following situation: have been leaving non-sale goods on the sale racks when they pick up sale items. A customer who selected a misplaced item has asked to receive a discount. Have students role-play this situation.

The students playing the customers may get very annoyed when told that they have selected an item that is not on sale, even though they found it on the sale rack. The students playing the sales associates should attempt to resolve the situation with tact.

L3 Tell students to assume that they are a store manager who has observed a sales associate giving a customer a discount on a non-sale item because the customer complained about the price. Have students brainstorm reasons why this discount, which is costing the store money in the short run, is an example of a promotional tactic.

Fulfilling the needs of customers and making them happy results in repeat business and increased sales.

556

required to sign a contract that guarantees a certain level of business. Advertisers who agree to use a specified number of column inches in their newspaper ads might be charged cheaper contract rates. Generally, the more you advertise, the less you pay per column inch.

Trade Discounts

Trade discounts are not really discounts at all but rather the way manufacturers quote prices to wholesalers and retailers. Many manufacturers establish suggested retail prices, or list prices, for their items. They grant discounts from the list price to members of the channel of distribution. A manufacturer might grant wholesalers a 40 percent discount from the list price and retailers a 30 percent discount.

The manufacturer might also quote the discounts in series, such as 25 percent and 10 percent for retailers and wholesalers, respectively. Series, or chain, discounts are calculated in sequence, with discounts taken on the declining balance as shown below. The example is based on a list price of $50.

Retailer's discount
$50 \times .25 = \$12.50$

Cost to retailer
$50 - \$12.50 = \$37.50$

Wholesaler's discount
$37.50 \times .10 = \$3.75$

Cost to wholesaler
$37.50 - \$3.75 = \$33.75$

In series discounts, note that the wholesaler's discount is based on the retailer's discount, not the original list price.

Seasonal Discounts

Seasonal discounts are offered to buyers willing to buy at a time outside the customary buying season. Manufacturers offer discounts to obtain orders for seasonal merchandise early so that production facilities and labor can be used throughout the year.

Other businesses use seasonal discounts to cut anticipated costs. Many retailers, for example, drastically reduce prices on swimsuits

after the summer season. Such retailers prefer to sell this merchandise at a lower markup than pay the costs of warehousing it until the following year. A variation on this device is used by vacation resorts. They offer vacationers lower rates to encourage use of resort facilities during the off-season.

Allowances

Trade-in allowances go directly to the buyer. Customers are offered a price reduction if they sell back an old model of the product they are purchasing. Consumers are generally offered trade-in allowances when purchasing new cars or major appliances. Companies are usually granted such allowances when purchasing machinery or equipment.

The Pricing Process and Related Technology

The pricing process is ongoing, as you will see in the steps of determining a price. As one of the four Ps of the marketing mix, pricing is the one of the most flexible because pricing strategies and prices can be changed quickly.

Steps in Determining Prices

There are six basic steps that are used to determine prices (see Figure 26.4):

Step 1: Establish pricing objectives
Step 2: Determine costs
Step 3: Estimate demand
Step 4: Study competition
Step 5: Decide on a pricing strategy
Step 6: Set prices

Step 1: Establish Pricing Objectives

The first step in the process of pricing a product is to determine the pricing objectives. Pricing objectives must conform to the company's overall goals: making profit, improving market share, and meeting the competition. To be effective, pricing objectives should be specific, time sensitive, realistic, and measurable. Increasing sales of a given product is not a good pricing objective. Increasing unit or dollar sales by 20 percent in one year compared

 Critical Thinking

Ask students to differentiate between promotional pricing and everyday low prices. A sample answer might be that promotional pricing is providing discount prices for a short period, while everyday low prices are set on a consistent basis and are not likely to be raised or lowered in the future.

Figure 26.4   Six Steps in Determining Price

• A Set Procedure Whether setting a price to launch a new product or adjusting the price of an existing product to increase sales, the process of determining price is the same.

What are some factors affecting this process?

STEP 1: ESTABLISH PRICING OBJECTIVES

The main goals of pricing are to make a profit, increase market share, and stay competitive. Remember that objectives should be time sensitive, realistic, and measurable. The objective for this product might be to increase market share by ten percent in the coming year.

STEP 2: DETERMINE COSTS

Costs are an important consideration in pricing. A company must price its product high enough above costs to make a profit. Costs for a soft drink manufacturer include raw materials, bottling, and labor.

STEP 3: ESTIMATE DEMAND

Through market research, a company must determine the size of the market and how much customers would be willing to pay for their product.

STEP 4: STUDY COMPETITION

Knowing what the competition charges for similar products is key to determining price. If a company prices its product too low, it misses out on potential profit, too high and it risks losing customers to the competition.

STEP 5: DECIDE ON A PRICING STRATEGY

The pricing strategy for a product depends on a variety of factors, including whether the product is being sold to segmented markets, whether there is a seasonal market, and where the product is sold. When a company sells soft drinks at a sporting event, purchase location is an important factor in determining price.

STEP 6: SET PRICES

Based on all the information gathered in the first five steps, a company sets a price for its product. Remember, though, that this price is subject to change.

@ Online Action!
Go to *marketingessentials.glencoe.com/26/figure/4* to find a project on pricing.

TEACH CONTINUED

Individualized Math Skills

L1 Ask students to determine the discount on a heating oil bill of $192 if a customer receives a 10 percent discount if the bill is paid within 10 days.
$19.20; $192 × .10 = $19.20

L2 Businesses that sign a contract guaranteeing three minutes of advertising over the course of a 24-hour period, receive a discount of 25 percent off the cost of a 30-second rate. The 30-second rate is $1,000, so three minutes would cost $6,000 at the regular rate. How much will a business save by buying three minutes all at once?
The company will save $1,500.

L3 A book has a list price of $29.95. The book distributor is offering a 25 percent discount to retailers and a 10 person discount to wholesalers. Have students calculate how much less the retailer is paying for the book than the wholesaler price. Have students round up to the nearest whole cent.
The retailer is paying $4.49 less than the wholesaler. $29.95 × .25 = $7.49; $29.95 − $7.49 = $22.46; $29.95 × .10 = $3.00; $29.95 − $3.00 = $26.95; $26.95 − $22.46 = $4.49

Figure 26.4   Six Steps in Determining Price

Discussion Lead a discussion about how businesses determine the price of their products. Ask students what they think the most important factors are when companies set prices.

Caption Answer Possible answers include: costs for materials and labor; the competition's prices; demand for the product; market; and purchase locations.

@ Online Action! For instructions, ideas, and answer guide, go to the Teacher Center at **marketingessentials.glencoe.com**

Review Guide

CONCEPTS

Ask students to recall various pricing strategies used to adjust the base price.

Answers will include product mix, geographical, international, segmented, psychological, and promotional.

KEY TERMS

Have students review key terms, their spellings, and definitions in small groups.

ONLINE SELF-ASSESSMENT

Have students go to marketingessentials.glencoe.com for the Section 26.2 practice test.

Individualized Review

L1 Assign and review Chapter 26 activities in the Student Activity Workbook.

L2 Assign and review Chapter 26 activities in the Marketing Math Workbook.

L3 Assign and review Chapter 26 activities in the *BusinessWeek* Reader and Case Studies.

Marketing Practice

Have students select an item or service they recently bought that they consider a bargain. Tell students to research, outline, and write a one- to two-page report that explains the concepts used to determine the price of the product. Ask students to relate these pieces to the concepts presented in this chapter.

---

with the previous year would be better. Why? Because the latter objective satisfies the requirements of being time-sensitive (one year) and it is specific and measurable (20 percent increase). At the end of one year, a company can evaluate the pricing objective to see if it was met. If not, the company can review the objective and the pricing strategies used to reach that objective.

Step 2: Determine Costs

For resellers (wholesalers and retailers), costs involved in the purchase of a product from their vendors and freight charges constitute the cost of the item. Businesses that provide services must take into account the cost of supplies used in conjunction with performing the service and the cost of labor help. A hair salon's shampoo, gels, hair spray, dyes, permanent wave solutions, and the like, as well as employee salaries, all need to be considered when determining the cost of providing those services. In manufacturing, the cost of materials and labor used in the manufacture of the product makes up the cost of an item. Costs can vary due to ever-changing economic conditions. A business needs to maintain accurate records and keep abreast of any change in its costs, which may affect its ultimate pricing decision.

Step 3: Estimate Demand

Marketers will study the size of the market to determine the total number of possible customers for a given product. For example, let's say the market is for a new soft drink. Sales of soft drinks for the past few years would be studied to see if sales were on the rise or the decline. Additional research might be conducted with consumers to see how they viewed soft drinks versus other beverages, such as water and juice alternatives. From their basic research, estimates would be made regarding the percentage of potential customers who might buy that new product. Much of this analysis is based on supply-and-demand theory and on the exceptions that occur because of demand elasticity.

Step 4: Study Competition

Studying your competitors is the next step in the process. You need to investigate what prices your competitors are charging for similar goods and services. Businesses subscribe to services that provide competitive information on a daily basis.

Step 5: Decide on a Pricing Strategy

Steps 2 through 4 help to establish a base price. In Step 5, you need to revisit the pricing objectives and decide on a pricing strategy or strategies that will help you accomplish your objectives. Everything you learned in Section 26.2 will help you in this endeavor. However, you must remember that as economic and market conditions change, strategies may require changes too.

Step 6: Set Prices

The final step is to set the price that will be quoted to customers, which is the published price that can be found on price tickets, company Web sites, and price sheets, as well as printed in catalogs and promotional materials. For that reason, it is important that all the above steps are carefully considered. Marketers must decide on how often they want to change their published prices. In addition to the cost of changing printed materials, customers' reactions to price changes must be considered.

Pricing Technology

Technology related to pricing can be seen in data that are now made available to marketers when making pricing decisions, as well as in the vehicles for providing price information to customers.

Smart Pricing

Smart pricing, as it is sometimes called, allows marketers to make intelligent pricing decisions based on an enormous amount of data that Web-based pricing technology crunches into timely, usable information. For example, Northern Group (a Canadian retailer) uses software that combines sales data with inventory data. The result is pricing

---

Critical Thinking

Ask: What would be the appropriate pricing strategy for a new product whose producer wanted to limit availability in the first year? Have students brainstorm specific pricing strategies and share their answers with the class.

recommendations that the pricing team can decide to accept or reject. Historical sales data are compared with current sales data from the store's point-of-sale system, as well as with its merchandising system, which includes the inventory levels for specific items. Combining all these data helps to suggest prices for new merchandise, as well as when to take markdowns, if any, on current merchandise in stock. This system gives this company the ability to adjust prices according to changing market conditions.

Communicating Prices to Customers

To compliment these advances in pricing decisions, electronic gadgets provide customers with real-time pricing information. Retailers that invest in electronic shelves and digital price labels can change prices quickly and easily. They also can send messages to shoppers while they are in the store alerting them to deals on goods of interest to the customer based on their buying habits.

We have already seen kiosks in retail stores where customers can scan a product to determine its price. In supermarket chains, we have seen self-check-out counters, where customers scan their own merchandise and pay for the products without the assistance of a clerk. With these new technological advances, price-marking techniques, such as printed price tags, are quickly becoming a thing of the past in certain industries.

Upcoming Technology: RFID

Upcoming technology that will revolutionize pricing and inventory control is called radio frequency identification, or RFID. RFID is wireless technology that involves tiny chips imbedded in products. A chip has an antenna, a battery, and a memory chip filled with a description of the item.

Have students complete the following sentence:

Loss leader pricing and special-event pricing are examples of _____ .
promotional pricing.

 Critical Thinking

Divide students into groups of three to five. Tell them to imagine that they are a sauce company, and they need to sell more jars of spaghetti sauce. Have students brainstorm ways they can use pricing strategies to increase sales.

 26.2 AFTER YOU READ

Reviewing Key Terms and Concepts

1. What is the key factor in deciding price lines?
2. Why does bundling discourage comparison shopping?
3. Name four factors that can help marketers use segmented pricing strategies.

Integrating Academic Skills

Math

4. Determine the price a wholesaler would pay for an item with a list price of $35 if the series trade discounts were 40 percent and 10 percent for retailers and wholesalers, respectively.

Geography

5. What factors would come into play when setting the price for a child's bicycle if you were selling it in Mexico or China?

 Online Action!
Check your answers at *marketingessentials.glencoe.com/26/read*

marketingessentials.glencoe.com

 AFTER YOU READ

Reviewing Key Terms and Concepts

1. The key factor in deciding price lines is to make the price differences great enough to represent low, middle, and high prices for the category of goods being offered.

2. Bundling discourages comparison shopping because it is often difficult to compare one package deal with another because each package deal contains different offerings.

3. Four factors that can help marketers utilize segmented pricing strategies are buyer identification, product design, purchase location, and time of purchase.

Integrating Academic Skills

4. For retailers $21, and for wholesalers $18.90; $35 × .40 = $14; $35 − $14 = $21; $21 × .10 = $2.10; $21.00 − $2.10 = $18.90

5. Answers will vary; factors that would come into play include: tariffs, quotas, monetary exchange rate, as well as economic and competitive situations in each country. You also would have to determine how much a customer in each of those countries would be willing to pay.

Online Action! **Answers at marketingessentials.glencoe.com/26/read**

Lifelong Learning

CAREER INFORMATION

Have students go to marketingessentials.glencoe.com and find the Chapter 26 Careers page and click on the link for the American Marketing Association's Careers Strategies and Tips. Ask students to select one article, read it, and summarize it in three short paragraphs.

PRICING STRATEGIES

Knowledge of how and why manufacturers and retailers set prices can help students as consumers to find the best products they can for the money. It can also convince them to stay informed about the more technical aspects of marketing. Combined with good consumer habits, this knowledge can save students both time and money.

Primary Source

Ask students to go to marketingessentials.glencoe.com and find Chapter 26 Resources. Ask them to click on the link for the American Marketing Association's marketing dictionary and read the definitions of the terms they find which are related to pricing strategies.

THINKING CRITICALLY

Answers will vary; possible answers include that businesses can monitor market information and compare its prices to those of competitors.

 Online Action!

For instructions, ideas, and answer guide, go to the Teacher Center at marketingessentials.glencoe.com

---

RYAN WILSON
CO-OWNER
VEGAN ESSENTIALS

❓ What do you do at work?
I run a new organic food store. With the hiring of additional employees, my position has become a bit more focused in the past year rather than running almost everything myself. Now, my primary focuses are setting a pricing policy, marketing, product research, customer service, and purchasing.

❓ What skills are most important to you?
General management skills from having to run so many aspects of a business. Internet marketing, customer and vendor relations, and product research are other much needed skills. Setting pricing, researching competition's prices and setting the right pricing policy for products that are not widely marketed is a challenge. In retrospect, the jobs I had to do working for others were far easier because my position was focused in one direction.

❓ What is your key to success?
Dedication. There have been countless 12–15 hour days, slow periods, vendor problems, and numerous other issues we've come across, and the only way to be successful has been to persevere through the rough times and keep looking forward. Never lose sight of what you want to accomplish with your business.

Aptitudes, Abilities, and Skills

Organizational skills, general business management, creativity, and flexibility

Education and Training

Many successful retailers have no higher education whatsoever, but general business, management, and accounting degrees can all be helpful.

Career Path

Retail careers often begin with entry-level positions in established stores. Niche retailers often spring from a personal hobby or interest (as in the case of this vegan-oriented store).

THINKING CRITICALLY

What can a business do to make sure its prices are competitive?

 Online Action!

Go to *marketingessentials.glencoe.com/26/careers* to find a career-related activity.

marketingessentials.glencoe.com

Test-Taking Strategies

List pricing strategies on the board, and ask student volunteers to define and discuss each strategy in class. Work as a class to create a culminating statement for each section on the board and have each student write the statement down in his or her own words.

CHAPTER 26 REVIEW

FOCUS on KEY POINTS

SECTION 26.1

● Establishing a base price for a product can be accomplished by combining cost-oriented, demand-oriented, and competition-oriented policies, as well as considering resellers' needs.

● Businesses must decide whether to use a one-price policy or a flexible pricing policy.

● The product life cycle needs to be considered in the pricing process. Two polar pricing strategies for the introduction of a product are skimming pricing and penetration pricing.

SECTION 26.2

● Once a base price is established, price adjustments are made with the use of specific pricing strategies. These strategies include product mix pricing, geographical pricing, international pricing, segmented pricing, psychological pricing, and promotional pricing, as well as discounts and allowances.

● There are six steps used to determine prices: establishing pricing objectives, determining costs, estimating demand, studying competition, deciding on a strategy, and setting the actual price.

● Pricing technology has revolutionized the way businesses make pricing decisions and adjustments to prices.

REVIEW VOCABULARY

Review each set of terms below. Note what they have in common.

1. markup pricing and cost-plus pricing (p. 545)

2. one-price policy and flexible-price policy (p. 549)

3. skimming pricing and penetration pricing (pp. 549, 550)

4. product mix pricing strategies, price lining, and bundle pricing (p. 553)

5. geographical pricing and segmented pricing strategy (p. 553)

6. psychological pricing, prestige pricing, everyday low prices (EDLP), and promotional pricing (p. 554)

REVIEW FACTS and IDEAS

7. List three pricing policies that can be used to establish a base price. (26.1)

8. What are two polar pricing methods that may be used when a new product is introduced into the market? (26.1)

9. Explain the relationship between pricing and the product life cycle. (26.1)

10. What are six types of pricing strategies that may be used to adjust the base price? (26.2)

11. List the six steps in the pricing process. (26.2)

12. Provide an example of how technology is used in pricing. (26.2)

Chapter 26 - Pricing Strategies 561

REVIEW FACTS and IDEAS

7. Three price policies that can be used to establish a baseprice are cost-oriented pricing, demand-oriented pricing, and competition-oriented pricing.

8. Two polar pricing methods used when a new product is introduced into the market are skimming pricing and penetration pricing.

9. Pricing in subsequent stages during a product's life cycle is dependent upon whether skimming or penetration pricing was used in the product's introduction. If a product is introduced with skimming pricing, prices can be lowered as more competitors enter the market. If the product was introduced with penetration pricing, the main goal is to keep products in this stage as long as possible.

10. Pricing strategies used to adjust the base price include: product mix, geographical, international, segmented, psychological, and promotional pricing, and discounts and allowances.

11. The six steps in the pricing process are: 1) Establish pricing objectives; 2) determine costs; 3) estimate demand; 4) study competition; 5) decide on a pricing strategy; 6) set prices.

12. Examples will vary; responses should show an understanding of how technology is used in pricing. One example might be kiosks which allow customers to scan items to determine price.

FOCUS on KEY POINTS

Ask volunteers to read the summaries aloud. Have the class brainstorm examples to reflect each bulleted summary.

REVIEW VOCABULARY

Student responses will vary. See glossary for definitions for **1-6.**

A sample answer might read:

1. *Markup pricing* and *cost-plus* pricing are both examples of cost-oriented pricing.

BUILD SKILLS

13. Workplace Skills

Answers will vary. Students may opt to refer to a store's policy regarding markdowns in each department being handled separately. For example, the employee may opt to refer the situation to the department manager who may or may not elect to give the customer the same discount that is printed on the price tag of the regularly-sized dress.

14. Technology Applications

Answers will vary depending on the pricing packages students use; spreadsheets should illustrate an understanding of pricing packages.

15. Math Practice

Snowboards: $4,802.50: 15 percent; CD players: $492.20; 8 percent

DEVELOP CRITICAL THINKING

16. Pick Your Discount

Cumulative discounts would be better because a small business would not have the space to store large orders.

17. Life Cycle

Answers will vary but should demonstrate an understanding of the product life cycle.

BUILD SKILLS

13. Workplace Skills

Human Relations You work for a department store in the women's dress department. A customer approaches you with two dresses that are identical, except that the one from the petite department is not marked down, while the other one is. None of the petite dresses have been marked down because the buyer for that department did not elect to do so.

How will you handle this customer who wants to buy that dress style in the petite size?

14. Technology Applications

Computer Skills Set up a spreadsheet to demonstrate bundle pricing of a computer and needed software. Show the savings to a customer when buying the advertised bundle price as compared with buying each item separately.

15. Math Practice

Incentives Promotional discounts are given to stores by manufacturers to place products in preferred locations or to pay for ads, displays, or in-store demonstrations. Calculate the store's net cost to stock the following items and the percentage of the discount given.

Item	Purchase Amount	Discount Amount	Net Cost to Store	Percent Discount
Snowboards	$5,650	$847.50	_____	_____
CD Players	$535	$42.80	_____	_____

DEVELOP CRITICAL THINKING

16. Pick Your Discount

If you were a small business with little storage space, which type of quantity discount would be better for you: cumulative or noncumulative? Why?

17. Life Cycle

Select a product that interests you and research its pricing history and its competition. You can complete these research steps on the Internet, through the company site and through competitors' sites; you can also research companies on their sites at your local library. Make a list of details such as how long a product has been on the market and any product improvements. In which product life cycle stage is it? Why?

Formative Assessment

Formative assessment is an essential component of classroom work. This type of assessment provides information that is used as feedback to modify teaching and meet student needs.

L1 Review key terms for this section. Ask students to write one sentence for each key term.

L2 Provide various example of pricing strategies in a story form. After each story, have students identify which pricing strategy or strategies are being used.

L3 Ask students to come up with stories that illustrate one or several pricing strategies that affect prices of items they want.

Reteach If the results of this formative assessment seem low, consider the following activity:

Read the section subheads aloud and have students name two key facts or important details for each.

APPLY CONCEPTS

18. Cost-Plus Pricing

Using cost-plus pricing, establish a price for a car wash fund-raiser. The local community center will allow you to use its parking lot and water supply for $10.00 per hour from 9:00 A.M. to 5:00 P.M. on a Saturday. To arrive at prices you can advertise, you must purchase all the cleaning supplies and determine how much you will use per auto. Since this is a learning experience, your labor costs will be $2 per hour per worker.

Activity Write a short report that outlines your pricing strategy and calculations and be ready to share it with your classmates.

19. Using the Six-Step Method for Determining Price

Use the six-step method for determining the price of a new hat fad. Competition for this hat will be with similar trucking hats. Your cost to make the hat is $15. Your company expects a gross profit from the sale of the hats to be at least 20 percent.

Activity Prepare a written report to depict the decisions you made in each step. Include all your research and calculations to justify the price you will charge retailers and the suggested retail price for this new hat.

NET SAVVY

20. Comparison Shopping

Browse computer companies' Web sites, such as Dell, IBM, HP, and Gateway, to see pricing strategies in action. Try to find the best price for a laptop computer for your firm. What pricing strategies made comparison shopping difficult?

marketingessentials.glencoe.com

THE DECA CONNECTION

Role Play: Assistant Buyer

Situation Assume the role of assistant buyer for a costume jewelry store. You are ordering a shipment of earrings in five styles from a supplier. The cost of the earrings is $1.50 per pair. You know that if you set too low a selling price the earrings will not sell well. The buyer (judge) has asked you to prepare a pricing strategy for the earrings. Among the decisions you must make is whether to price all the styles at one price point or to price the different styles at separate price points.

Activity Present your pricing strategy to your supervisor (judge).

Evaluation You will be evaluated on how well you meet the following performance indicators:

- Explain factors affecting pricing decisions
- Use psychological pricing to adjust base prices
- Select promotional pricing strategies used to adjust base prices
- Set prices
- Adjust prices to maximize profitability

@ Online Action!

For more information and DECA Prep practice, go to *marketingessentials.glencoe.com/26/DECA*

Chapter 26 - Pricing Strategies **563**

APPLY CONCEPTS

18. Cost-Plus Pricing
Reports will vary but should demonstrate an understanding of the selected pricing strategy. Encourage students to share their reports in class.

19. Using the Six-Step Method for Determining Price
All reports should include the following six steps:

Step 1: Establish Pricing Objectives

Step 2: Determine Costs

Step 3: Estimate Demand

Step 4: Study Competition

Step 5: Decide on a Pricing Strategy

Step 6: Set Prices

NET SAVVY

20. Comparison Shopping
Responses will vary; answers may include: bundling pricing, loss-leader pricing, everyday low pricing, rebates, and discounts.

MINI-QUIZ

Read these sentences to the students and have them volunteer the missing word(s).

1. In _____ resellers add a dollar amount to a product's cost to arrive at a price. (markup pricing)

2. Marketers who study their competitors to determine the prices of their products are using _____ pricing. (competition-oriented)

3. The purpose of _____ is to encourage as many people as possible to buy the product and thus penetrate the market. (penetration pricing)

For an expanded chapter quiz, go to Chapter 26 in the TeacherWorks CD-ROM and to Chapter 26 in the **Exam View®** Pro Test Generator CD-ROM.

THE DECA CONNECTION

Students should be evaluated according to the performance standards noted in the role play. For another DECA role-play, go to the Competitive Events Workbook or the Student Activity Workbook, or go to **marketingessentials.glencoe.com/26/DECA**

@ Online Action! For instructions, ideas, and answer guide, go to the Teacher Center at **marketingessentials.glencoe.com**

DECA Advisors Corner

Invite members of the business community into the classroom to help evaluate curriculum. These advisors should select a case study and give it to students a few days in advance. Students will then present their results to the visiting business people in a role play.

Chapter Overview

Chapter 27 presents the various mathematical formulas used by businesses to determine prices. It focuses on three principle areas: markup calculations, markdown calculations, and discount calculations.

�ö BUILD BACKGROUND ⌖

Have students recall situations in which they have purchased or seen ads for goods at a discount off the regular price. Ask students how they determined the price of the goods—guessing/estimating or calculating.

Why It's Important

Explain to students that understanding the principles of pricing and how to perform the related mathematical calculations are essential to understanding how a company maintains its profitability.

Prepare to Read

List the section objectives and discuss them with the students. Have students skim the headings, subheadings, pictures, and captions. Ask volunteers to tell the class what topics are covered in each section.

CHAPTER 27
Pricing Math

Chapter Objectives

After reading this chapter, you should be able to:

- Explain how a firm's profit is related to markup
- Use the basic formula for calculating a retail price
- Calculate dollar and percentage markup based on cost or retail
- Calculate markdown in dollars
- Calculate maintained markup in dollar and percent
- Utilize a general procedure for figuring discounts
- Calculate discounts in dollars and percentages
- Calculate net amounts

GUIDE TO THE PHOTO

Market Talk Many convenience stores are now offering coffee and other hot beverages, which offer high profit margins and bring in lots of repeat business.

According to *Supermarket News,* hot beverages delivered hefty gross margins in excess of 53 percent in 2002.

Quick Think Why do you think hot beverages bring in high profits?

GUIDE TO THE PHOTO

Market Talk Discuss with students the rise in popularity of coffee shops that serve light fare and feature a casual atmosphere for meeting with friends and associates. Ask students if these shops are good business ventures.

Quick Think In the case of hot beverages such as coffee, for example, the cost of goods includes the cost of the ingredients and the packaging needed to contain product for the customer, which is minimal, leaving a high gross profit margin.

 Follow Up You may want to remind students that factors that go into calculating gross margin are sales revenue and cost of goods sold and that revenue minus cost of goods equals gross profit.

marketingessentials.glencoe.com

THE DECA CONNECTION

Performance indicators represent key skills and knowledge. Relating them to the concepts explained in this chapter is your key to success in DECA events. These acronyms represent DECA events that involve knowledge of concepts in this chapter.

AAAL	FMAL	MMS*	TMDM*
AAML*	FMDM*	QSRM*	TSE*
ADC*	FMML*	RMAL	VPM
BSM	FSRM*	RMML*	
EMDM*	HMDM*	SMDM*	

In all these DECA events you should be able to follow this performance indicator:

- Explain factors affecting pricing decisions

All events with an asterisk (*) also include these performance indicators:

- Determine cost of product
- Determine discounts and allowances that can be used to adjust base prices
- Set prices
- Adjust prices to maximize profitability

Some events have additional performance indicators. These are:

ADC   Set price of advertising services

SMDM Set event prices

FMDM Describe factors affecting the price of financial services/products

        Set prices of financial services/products

EMDM Describe the impact of e-commerce on pricing decisions

DECA PREP

Check your understanding of DECA performance indicators with the DECA activity in this chapter's review. For more information and DECA Prep practice, go to *marketingessentials .glencoe.com/27/DECA*

Chapter 27 - Pricing Math **565**

THE DECA CONNECTION

DECA events that require knowledge of pricing math are described here. Discuss the performance indicators to make sure students understand how to demonstrate their understanding.

The events acronyms stand for:

AAAL: Apparel and Accessories Marketing Series, AL

AAML: Apparel and Accessories Marketing Series, ML

ADC: Advertising Campaign Event

BSM: Business Services Marketing Series

EMDM: E-Commerce Management Team Decision Making Event

FMAL: Food Marketing Series, AL

FMDM: Financial Analysis Management Team Decision Making Event

FMML: Food Marketing Series, ML

FSRM: Full Service Restaurant Management Series

HMDM: Hospitality Services Management Team Decision Making Event

MMS: Marketing Management Series

QSRM: Quick Serve Restaurant Management Series

RMAL: Retail Merchandising Series, AL

RMML: Retail Merchandising Series, ML

SMDM: Sports and Entertainment Marketing Management Team Decision Making Event

TMDM: Travel and Tourism Marketing Management Team Decision Making Event

TSE: Technical Sales Event

VPM: Vehicles and Petroleum Marketing Series

DECA PREP

Find timed DECA Prep activities correlated to the Competitive Events Workbook for students and DECA tips for teachers at **marketingessentials.glencoe.com /27/DECA**

FOCUS

Introducing the Section

COLLABORATIVE ACTIVITY

Organize the class into groups of five or six and tell them that they are responsible as a team for determining the costs of a week-long vacation for the group. They should consider air transportation, lodging, car rental, and meals. Have them figure out the costs for a trip they would all like to take. Then have them compute discounts at 15 percent off for off-season travel, and markups at 15 percent for high-season travel.

Preteaching Key Terms

List the key terms on the board and have the students skim the chapter looking for the terms in context. Suggest that they read the paragraph in which the term appears and, if necessary, the paragraph that comes before and after as well. Have them propose definitions for the terms and write those meanings in their notebooks for use when studying.

- gross profit
- maintained markup

Online Activity

Researching Markups

Ask interested students to find a consumer site or article online that talks about markup for a particular product. Have students summarize the article in a two- to three-paragraph written response.

OBJECTIVES

- Explain how a firm's profit is related to markup
- Use the basic formula for calculating a retail price
- Calculate dollar and percentage markup based on cost or retail
- Calculate markdown in dollars
- Calculate maintained markup in dollar and percent

KEY TERMS

- gross profit
- maintained markup

WHILE YOU READ

Connect How do you think profit relates to markup?

Calculating Prices

READ and STUDY

BEFORE YOU READ
Predict How do you think prices are calculated?

THE MAIN IDEA
Pricing and profit have a direct relationship to one another. Retailers use different formulas for calculating prices and related markups and markdowns.

STUDY ORGANIZER
Use a chart like the one below. Insert the basic formula for calculating a retail price in the middle circle. Use the other circles to record each formula you encounter in this chapter.

$$\frac{\text{Markup (MU)(\$)}}{\text{RP}} = \text{MU (\%)}$$

Basic Pricing Formula
Cost (C) + markup (MU) = retail price (RP)

Profit and Markup

A businessperson says, "We made a profit of $50—buying the radio for $100 and selling it for $150." The businessperson is only partially correct. The difference between the retail price of $150 (which is equal to 100 percent) and the $100 cost ($66\frac{2}{3}$ percent) is the markup, or margin, of $50 ($33\frac{1}{3}$ percent), not the profit. Profit is the amount left over from revenue after the costs of the merchandise and expenses have been paid. The

---

READ and STUDY

BEFORE YOU READ
Discuss the idea that the price of a product has to cover the original cost of the item, expenses related to the sale of the item, and profit.

THE MAIN IDEA
Ask a volunteer to read the main idea aloud and demonstrate how to change a percentage into a decimal.

STUDY ORGANIZER
Model the study organizer for students by filling in the first blank circle. A full-size, downloadable study organizer can be found at marketingessentials.glencoe.com

 WHILE YOU READ Have students propose their answers as they read and study the chapter. Ask volunteers to write answers on the board.

markup (margin) on an item, however, is the same as gross profit. **Gross profit** is the difference between sales revenue and the cost of goods sold. Expenses must still be deducted in order to get net (actual) profit. Therefore, a business must have a markup high enough to cover expenses and provide the profit needed to be successful.

Let's compare profit with retail markup by using the above figures and sales of 300 radios. Look at Figure 27.1 for this comparison. On an income statement, sales revenue would be $45,000 (100 percent), less cost of goods sold of $30,000 ($66\frac{2}{3}$ percent), which would equal gross profit of $15,000 ($33\frac{1}{3}$ percent). If expenses were $9,000 (20 percent), the gross profit ($33\frac{1}{3}$ percent) would be enough to cover expenses and earn a net profit of $6,000 or $13\frac{1}{3}$ percent ($6,000 divided by $45,000; or $33\frac{1}{3}$ percent − 20 percent).

Basic Markup Calculations

Retailers and wholesalers use the same formulas to calculate markup. We will use only retail prices here to make these formulas easier to understand. Note, however, that wholesale prices can be substituted in any of the formulas.

The most basic pricing formula is the one for calculating retail price. It states in mathematical terms a relationship that has been discussed in the last two chapters: retail price is a combination of cost and markup. Knowing these two figures will enable you to calculate retail price. Here's how.

Cost (C) + markup (MU) = retail price (RP)

For example,

$$\$14 + \$6 = \$20$$

Two other formulas can be derived from this basic formula—cost and markup.

Retail price (RP) − markup (MU) = cost (C)

$$\$20 - \$6 = \$14$$

Retail price (RP) − cost (C) = markup (MU)

$$\$20 - \$14 = \$6$$

 marketingessentials.glencoe.com

You will rely on these three formulas throughout this chapter. The formulas and their terms will be cited in abbreviated form (for example, as C + MU = RP).

PRACTICE 1

Use the retail price formula and its variations to do the following problems.

1. A calculator costs $3.50, and the markup is $1.49. What is its retail price?
2. A children's DVD retails for $29.99, and its markup is $10.04. What is its cost?

Note: Answers to all practice sets in this chapter at *marketingessentials.glencoe.com*

Percentage Markup

In the examples shown, markup was expressed as a dollar amount. In most business situations, however, the markup figure is generally expressed as a percentage. We will distinguish between these two forms of markup (dollar and percentage) throughout the rest of the chapter. In calculations, dollar markup will be represented with the abbreviation MU($) and percentage markup with the abbreviation MU(%).

Expressing markup in either dollar or percentage form is not the only choice that wholesalers and retailers have in making markup calculations. They may also elect to compute their markup on either cost or retail price if they choose to use the percentage form.

Most choose to base the markup on retail price for three reasons. First, the markup on the retail price sounds like a smaller amount. This sounds better to customers who know the markup percentage and can make the price seem reasonable.

Second, future markdowns and discounts are calculated on a retail basis. Third, profits are generally calculated on sales revenue. It makes sense to base markup on retail prices when comparing and analyzing data that play a role in a firm's profits.

Here are the steps that are used to calculate the percentage markup on retail. They will be

---

Discussion Starter

PROFIT AND MARKUP

Put an abbreviated profit and loss statement on the board. Next to it, put the parts of a retail price that correspond to items on the profit and loss statement. For example, next to *Sales Revenue*, put an arrow and note *Price;* and next to *Gross Profit*, note *Markup*. Ask students how markup is related to profit. Point out that the markup on an item must cover expenses related to selling the item in addition to profit.

TEACHING POINTS

Model Model how to convert percentages, decimals, and fractions by using a calculator. Have students convert the following percentages into decimals and fractions, the fractions into decimals and percentages, and the decimals into fractions and percentages:

$\frac{1}{3}$ 0.33, 33 percent
0.4 $\frac{2}{5}$, 40 percent
80 percent 0.8, $\frac{4}{5}$
0.667 $\frac{2}{3}$, $66\frac{2}{3}$ percent
$\frac{1}{12}$ 0.0833, $8\frac{1}{3}$

Concept Development

BASIC MARKUP CALCULATIONS

To introduce the basic markup calculations, draw a circle on the board, and label it *Retail Price*. Then, divide the circle into two parts, and label these parts *Costs* and *Markup*. Assign percentages or dollars to these parts. For example, make the markup 40 percent and the cost 60 percent for a total of 100 percent, or make the markup $2 and the cost $8 for a retail price of $10. Once students understand the basic formula, provide them with two of the three numbers and ask them to calculate the third.

Critical Thinking

Ask students why an oil painting might be marked up as much as 50 percent on a price basis while items such as sheets and towels, for example, would be marked up at a much lower percentage. Point out that the oil painting is a one-of-a-kind item, and the gallery only has one chance to sell it. A store selling towels and sheets, on the other hand, would have many units of the same item in stock and would sell them to many different customers.

PRACTICE 1 ANSWERS

1. $4.99
   ($3.50 + $1.49 = $4.99)
2. $19.95
   ($29.99 − $10.04 = $19.95)

TEACH CONTINUED

Enrichment

PROFIT AND LOSS STATEMENTS

Ask students why gross profit is an important number on a profit and loss statement. Point out that cost of goods is an unavoidable cost to the business. The business must buy or manufacture goods before they can be sold. Expenses, however, are more discretionary, even though they may be necessary. Therefore, if the manager of the business prepares a "pro forma" profit and loss statement when planning for sales and expenses, the gross profit number tells the manager how much he or she can spend on such things as marketing and still make a profit. Have students find an example of a pro forma profit and loss statement and point out the gross profit number.

Critical Thinking

Ask students: How is the market of a product related to the profit that a business expects to make? Answers may include that markup must be high enough to cover expenses and include profit if the company wishes to be financially successful.

Figure 27.1 — How Profit and Loss Relates to Markup

• **Calculating the Price** Before retailers or wholesalers set the price of an item, they must determine how much margin, or markup, they need on the item to sell it at a profit. That involves writing an income statement. Let's look at how these calculations work together to determine the markup.

How much markup is enough?

Sales revenue equals the price of an item times the quantity sold. This is the total amount of money generated by sales of a particular item. For example, if 300 radios are sold at $150/radio, sales revenue will be 300 × $15 = $45,000.

Cost of goods is the cost to purchase or make the items for sale. In the example of the radio, the cost to the retailer is $100/radio. For 300 radios, then, the cost is 300 × $100 = $30,000.

Gross profit is the difference between sales revenue and the cost of goods sold: $45,000 − $30,000 = $15,000.

Expenses are the costs of running the business that sells the item. In the case of the radio sales, these costs are $9,000.

Income Statement		
Sales revenue (300 items @ $150/item)	$45,000	100%
Cost of goods sold	$30,000	66 2/3%
Gross profit	$15,000	33 1/3%
Less expenses	$ 9,000	20%
Net profit	$ 6,000	13 1/3%

Net profit is the amount left over from revenue after the costs of the merchandise and expenses have been paid: $45,000 − $30,000 − $9,000 = $6,000. The owner of the electronics store decides that this is a sufficient profit and sets the retail price at $150.

The **retail price** is the price of the item to the customer, or the sticker price. The radio in our example will cost a customer $150.

The **unit cost** is the cost per item to the retailer or wholesaler. In our example, each radio costs the retailer $100.

Retail Pricing		
Retail price (unit price)	$150	100%
Unit cost	$100	66 2/3%
Markup (margin)	$ 50	33 1/3%

The **markup**, or **margin**, is the difference between the unit cost and the retail price, or the amount added to the unit cost to cover expenses and provide a profit. In our example, that is $150 − $100 = $50.

 Online Action! Go to *marketingessentials.glencoe.com/27/figure/1* to find a project on pricing.

Figure 27.1 — How Profit and Loss Relate to Markup

Discussion Lead a discussion about the profit and loss statement. Point out that if the markup on a product is not high enough, a loss will result. In such a case, net profit will be represented by a negative number.

Caption Answer The markup must be enough to cover business expenses and provide a profit. The amount is determined by the amount of these expenses and the desired profit.

Online Action! For instructions, ideas, and answer guide, go to the Teacher Center at marketingessentials.glencoe.com

Follow Up Ask students to tell what would happen to net profit in the example shown if the price were dropped by $10 to $140, but unit sales, cost of goods, and expenses stayed the same. (Net profit would be cut in half.)

easier to follow if we have an example to work with. Assume that you want to calculate the percentage markup on a pair of bookends that Wright's Department Store stocks for $49.50 (cost) and sells for $82.50 (retail price).

STEP 1 Determine the dollar markup.

RP − C = MU($)
$82.50 − $49.50 = $33.00

STEP 2 To change the dollar markup to the percentage markup, divide it by the retail price. The result will be a decimal.

MU($)/RP = MU(%) on retail
$33.00 divided by $82.50 = .4

STEP 3 Change the decimal to a percentage by shifting the decimal point two places to the right. This figure is the percentage markup on retail.

.40 = 40%

Retailers may find the percentage markup on cost to be helpful. The calculation is the same, except for Step 2. Using the same facts from above, you calculate the percentage markup on cost as follows:

STEP 1 Determine the dollar markup.

RP − C = MU($)
$82.50 − $49.50 = $33.00

STEP 2 To change the dollar markup to the percentage markup, divide by cost.

MU($)/C = MU(%) on cost
$33.00 divided by $49.50 = .6667

STEP 3 Change the decimal to a percentage. This figure is the percentage markup on cost.

.6667 = 66.67%

PRACTICE 2

Calculate the percentage markup in each of these situations.

1. The retail price of a music CD is $11.99 and the cost is $7.80. (A) What is the percentage markup based on cost price? (B) Based on retail price? Round your markup percentages to the tenths place.
2. A gas grill costs $220, and its markup is $179.99. (A) Find its percentage markup on cost price. (B) Calculate the retail price, and then (C) calculate its percentage markup on retail price. Round percentages to the tenths place.
3. A gallery sells a framed print for $100, and its markup is $50. (A) What is its percentage markup on cost price? (B) On retail price?

Markup Equivalents Table

You would notice a correlation between the two figures if you calculated enough problems using the formulas for computing percentage markup based on cost and retail. This correlation led marketers to develop a calculation aid called a Markup Equivalents Table, a portion of which is shown in Figure 27.2. The table lists markup percentages based on retail and the equivalent percentages based on cost. To use the table, you locate the percentage markup on retail and read its cost equivalent in the adjacent column or vice versa.

PRACTICE 3

Use the markup equivalents table in Figure 27.2 to answer the following questions:

1. When the markup on retail is 31 percent, what is its equivalent markup on cost?
2. The markup on cost is 22 percent; what is its equivalent markup on retail?

Cost Method of Pricing

Sometimes marketers know only the cost of an item and its markup on cost. In such a situation, they use the cost method of pricing.

Chapter 27 - Pricing Math 569

Concept Development

PERCENTAGE MARKUP

Explain to students that there are two approaches to percentage markup. One is based on the cost of the item and the other is based on the retail price of the item. To illustrate the difference, present this example:

A set of matching napkins and tablecloth costs a retailer $69.74. The store's markup is $23.25. What is the percentage markup based on cost?
33 percent; $23.25 ÷ $69.74 = 0.333 = 33 percent

What is the percentage markup based on retail price?
25 percent; $69.74 + $23.25 = $92.99; $23.25 ÷ $92.99 = 0.250 = 25 percent

TEACHING POINTS

Clarify Point out to students that, in this case, the markup of $23.25 is 33 percent (or ⅓) of the cost, and 25 percent (or ¼) of the retail price.

PRACTICE 2 ANSWERS

1. (A) 53.7 percent on cost ($11.99 − 7.80 = $4.19; $4.19 ÷ 7.80 = .5371); (B) 34.9 percent on retail price ($11.99 − 7.80 = $4.19; $4.19 ÷ $11.99 = .3494).
2. (A) 81.8 percent on cost ($179.99 ÷ $220 = .8181); (B) retail price $399.99 ($179.99 + 220 = $399.99); (C) 45 percent on retail ($179.99 ÷ $399.99 = .4499).
3. (A) 100 percent on cost ($50 ÷ 50 = 1); (B) 50 percent on retail price ($50 ÷ $100 = .5)

PRACTICE 3 ANSWERS

1. 45 percent
2. 18 percent

TEACH CONTINUED

Individualized Math Skills

MARKUP AND PERCENTAGES

L1 Have students determine the retail price of a product that has a cost of $75.49 and a markup of $38.41.
$114; $75.49 + $38.51 = $114

L2 Have students determine the markup percentage of a product that has a cost of $75.49 and a markup of $38.41.
$38.51 ÷ $114 = 0.3378 = 33.78%

L3 Tell students that a product originally cost $75.49 and had a markup of $38.41 But the cost of purchasing a product has gone up 10%, and the selling price must be increased accordingly. Have students determine the new selling price and markup using the original markup percentage.
The new cost is $83.04: $75 × 1.10 = $83.04; the markup percentage on cost is 66.22%: $75.49 + $114 = 0.6622 = 66.22%; the new selling price, P, is $125.40: P = $83.04 + 0.6622 = $125.40; The markup is $42.36: $125.40 − $83.04 = $42.36.

Online Activity

Online Auctions
Ask students to select a specific category of goods or services and research various auction shopping sites to find the site that offers the widest array of offerings in that category. Have students write three or four paragraphs evaluating the various sites they researched.

Consider a board game that a toy store buys for $8.50 and sells for cost plus a 40 percent markup on cost. To arrive at the retail price, follow these steps:

STEP 1 Determine the dollar markup on cost. Multiply the cost by the percentage markup on cost in decimal form.

C × MU(%) = MU($)
$8.50 × .40 = $3.40

STEP 2 Add the dollar markup to the cost to get the retail price.

C + MU($) = RP
$8.50 + $3.40 = $11.90

Often, the situation is not that simple. Suppose you have the cost, but the only markup figure you know is the markup on retail. What will you do? You cannot use the markup percentage on retail to calculate the markup in dollars unless you know the retail price. This is the perfect time to use the Markup Equivalents Table (see Figure 27.2). You can convert the markup on retail to the markup on cost and apply it to the cost of the item to arrive at the markup in dollars.

Here is an example: A marketer knows that the customary markup for a particular cosmetics firm is 33.3 percent based on retail and that the cost of its most popular lipstick is $8.00. To project the lipstick's retail price, follow these steps:

STEP 1 Use the markup equivalents table to get all the information in the same form (cost). Find the cost equivalent of a 33.3 percent markup on retail.

Markup Percent on Retail	Markup Percent on Cost
32.0	47.1
33.3	50.0
34.0	51.5

STEP 2 Apply the cost method to determine the retail price. First calculate the dollar markup on cost.

C × MU(%) = MU($)
$8.00 × .50 = $4.00

NET MARKETING

Shopping Auctions

Internet shopping auctions provide a means for buyers and sellers to get the merchandise they want through a bidding system. The seller establishes a price where bidding starts. Buyers respond by placing bids for the goods they want to purchase. One of the largest Internet shopping auctions is eBay. However there are others. Some of them are even specialized, like ones for sports memorabilia.

Setting a Price
Some items are in great supply or there is not a lot of demand for them. Usually the prices on those items are relatively low, such as a cookbook for $3 or a chair for $6. For other items that are more rare, prices can soar; for example, a 1961 Mickey Mantle baseball card for $102.

● THINK LIKE A MARKETER

Identify an item you own that you might want to auction off on the Internet. At what price would you start the bidding?

@ Online Action!

Go to *marketingessentials.glencoe.com/ 27/net* to find an activity on online pricing.

NET MARKETING

Shopping Auctions

Discussion Lead a discussion about the growing popularity of shopping auctions. Ask students to relate any experiences they or someone they know may have had purchasing items through such auctions.

THINK LIKE A MARKETER **Answer:** Answers will vary. Students might conduct research on prices for the item or to see if it is in demand, valuable, or worth selling before they determine the price.

@ Online Action! For instructions, ideas, and answer guide, go to the Teacher Center at marketingessentials.glencoe.com

Figure 27.2 — Markup Equivalents

• **Markup Equivalents Table** This sample markup equivalents table allows users to convert markups on retail to markups on cost and vice versa.

A 23.1 percent markup based on retail is equal to what markup percent based on cost?

Markup on Retail	Markup on Cost	Markup on Retail	Markup on Cost
4.8%	5.0%	25.0%	33.3%
5.0	5.3	26.0	35.0
6.0	6.4	27.0	37.0
7.0	7.5	27.3	37.5
8.0	8.7	28.0	39.0
9.0	10.0	28.5	40.0
10.0	11.1	29.0	40.9
10.7	12.0	30.0	42.9
11.0	12.4	31.0	45.0
11.1	12.5	32.0	47.1
12.0	13.6	33.3	50.0
12.5	14.3	34.0	51.5
13.0	15.0	35.0	53.9
14.0	16.3	35.5	55.0
15.0	17.7	36.0	56.3
16.0	19.1	37.0	58.8
16.7	20.0	37.5	60.0
17.0	20.5	38.0	61.3
17.5	21.2	39.0	64.0
18.0	22.0	39.5	65.5
18.5	22.7	40.0	66.7
19.0	23.5	41.0	70.0
20.0	25.0	42.0	72.4
21.0	26.6	42.8	75.0
22.0	28.2	44.4	80.0
22.5	29.0	46.1	85.0
23.0	29.9	47.5	90.0
23.1	30.0	48.7	95.0
24.0	31.6	50.0	100.0

@ Online Action! Go to *marketingessentials.glencoe.com/27/figure/2* to find a project on markups.

Concept Development

MARKUP EQUIVALENTS

To prove the reliability of the Markup Equivalents table, have students calculate the markup percentage on retail and the markup percentage on cost for three different situations:

- **RP = $100 and C = $80**
  MU = $20 or 20 percent on retail and 25 percent on cost

- **RP = $85 and C = $68**
  MU = $17 or 20 percent on retail and 25 percent on cost

- **RP = $95 and C = $76**
  MU = $19 or 20 percent on retail and 25 percent on cost

Enrichment

COST AND RETAIL PRICE

Remind students that they learned about cost and retail price in Chapter 23. To be sure they understand the significance of the distinction, help them cite some analogies. Note that the percentage markup based on retail price should be used with other price-based figures. Similarly, the percentage markup based on cost should be used only with other cost-based figures. Ask students to suggest some other math situations in which the same general rule applies.

Answers will vary; for example, if you were figuring the area of a rectangle, you would have to convert all of the dimensions to the same unit of measure; if you were adding fractions, you would have to convert all of the addends so that they have a common denominator.

Figure 27.2 — Markup Equivalents

Discussion Lead a discussion on how the table works. Model how to use the table by naming a percentage from one of the columns and asking the students to find its equivalent.

Caption Answer A 23.1 percent markup on retail is equivalent to a 30.0 percent markup on cost.

@ Online Action! For instructions, ideas, and answer guide, go to the Teacher Center at **marketingessentials.glencoe.com**

Follow Up Ask students to estimate the markup on cost of a 38.5 percent markup on retail (approximately 62.7 percent).

TEACH CONTINUED

Individualized Math Skills

MARKUPS

L1 Ask students to solve the following word problem:

A restaurant has determined that each item on the menu must have a markup of at least 40 percent over cost. The ingredients for a sub sandwich cost a restaurant $2.50. What is the lowest price the restaurant could sell the sub sandwich for?

$2.50 × 140 percent = $3.50. The restaurant has to charge at least $3.50.

L2 Ask students to solve the following word problem:

For all items at an office supply store, the standard dollar markup on cost is 50 percent. If a ream of paper costs the store $1.72, can they sell it for $2.49 and meet their standard?

$1.72 × 150 percent = $2.58. No, $2.49 does not meet the standard.

L3 Ask students to solve the following word problem:

A grocer buys eggs from a farmer at $0.60 per dozen. If the grocer marks up the eggs 80 percent on cost, how many dozen does he have to sell in order to make a gross profit of $100?

$0.60 × 80 percent = $0.48
$100 ÷ $0.48 = 208.33
The grocer must sell 209 dozen to make a gross profit of $100.

Critical Thinking

Ask students: why might a retail business make its markup percentages proprietary information?

STEP 3 Then calculate the retail price.

$$C + MU(\$) = RP$$
$$\$8.00 + \$4.00 = \$12.00$$

Retail Method of Pricing

Another way to compute the retail price when all you know are cost and the markup on retail is to use the retail method. This method is based on changing the information that you already have into retail figures.

Let's consider an example: The owner of a sporting goods store wants to know what the markup and retail price should be for a sun visor that costs $6.75. His customary markup based on the retail price is 40 percent. The steps that he follows in his calculation are as follows:

Case Study

The Vuitton Money Machine

Luxury Priced Right

Louis Vuitton handbags and rivals Gucci, Prada, Coach, and Hermes price their handbags very high to attract the luxury market. The Vuitton machine is running mighty smoothly right now. With $3.8 billion in annual sales, it is about twice the size of runners-up Prada and Gucci. Vuitton maintained double-digit sales growth and the industry's fattest operating margins as rivals staggered through a global downturn that started early in 2001. That power was underscored in March 2003, when Vuitton reported a record-high 45 percent operating margin. Some Vuitton bags retail for $1,000 or more. And no Vuitton bag is ever marked down.

Manufacturing Differences

According to Andrew Gowen, an analyst who visited the factories of Vuitton and competitor Hermes, they are "worlds apart. Vuitton's factory is still labor-intensive, but there is a balance between mechanization and handmade. At Hermes, it looks like you stepped into the 14th century, just rows and rows of people stitching." Hermes bags cost more, but the company's operating margins are only about 25 percent, which is the industry's average margin.

THINK STRATEGICALLY

What word could you use instead of "margin" if you were speaking about the pricing function? Why do you think Louis Vuitton's margins are so high in comparison to its competitors and the industry in general?

@ Online Action!

Go to *marketingessentials.glencoe.com/27/case* to find an activity on luxury pricing.

Case Study — The Vuitton Money Machine

Discussion Lead a discussion about marketing techniques for luxury products. Point out to students that Vuitton never discounts its products as a marketing feature to attract the wealthy, luxury-minded customer.

THINK STRATEGICALLY **Answer:** In terms of pricing, the word *margin* is a synonym for *markup*. Vuitton achieves higher margins because some of the processes used in making its handbags are automated and do not rely on expensive labor.

@ Online Action! For instructions, ideas, and answer guide, go to the Teacher Center at marketingessentials.glencoe.com

Follow Up Ask students to find ads for Vuitton, Hermès, Gucci, and Prada in fashion magazines and compare the messages that each ad sends.

GLOBAL MARKET

CHINA

China's Auto Industry and the WTO

When China joined the World Trade Organization (WTO) in 2001, it lowered tariffs and raised quotas on automobiles. Tariffs on imported cars dropped from a range of 70 percent to 80 percent of the list price to 50 percent to 60 percent. By 2006, duties should have sunk to 25 percent, which is still high by world standards but low enough to put autos within the reach of China's growing upper middle class.

New Designs What is good for buyers is bad news for China's automakers, which will experience intense competition from imported autos. As the state phased out rules dictating which models each manufacturer can assemble, manufacturers were free to design new cars aimed at quality- and cost-conscious buyers. Eventually, lower prices and wider choices should create a thriving auto industry.

By 2004, China's auto production ranked fourth in the world, according to peoplesdaily.com. However, an increase in import quotas and further tariff cuts put pressure on domestic manufacturers' margins according to John Bailey, a director at Standard & Poor's Corporate Ratings and Infrastructure Ratings in Hong Kong.

CRITICAL THINKING

How do changing tariffs and quotas on imported autos sold in China affect Chinese automakers' margins?

@ Online Action!

Go to *marketingessentials.glencoe.com/27/ global* to find an activity on price and international marketing.

STEP 1 Determine what percentage of the retail price is equal to cost. This is a matter of subtracting the known retail markup percent from 100 percent, which represents the retail price.

RP(%) − MU(%) = C(%)
100% − 40% = 60%

STEP 2 To determine the retail price, divide the cost by the decimal equivalent of the percentage calculated in Step 1.
$6.75 divided by .60 = $11.25

STEP 3 Calculate the dollar markup.

RP − C = MU($)
$11.25 − $6.75 = $4.50

STEP 4 Check your work by multiplying the retail price you calculated in Step 2 by the percentage markup on retail given originally. The answer will match the dollar markup you calculated in Step 3, if your retail price is correct.

RP × MU(%) = MU($)
$11.25 × .40 = $4.50

You can use a visual device called the retail box (see Figure 27.3) to help you remember this sequence of calculations. This retail box organizes your information and makes it simple to check your work.

marketingessentials.glencoe.com

Chapter 27 - Pricing Math 573

TEACH CONTINUED

Concept Development

COST AND RETAIL METHODS OF PRICING

To help students think about the relationship between the cost and retail methods of pricing, ask them to tell how they would figure the markup in dollars and the retail price of an item if they only knew its cost and the markup percentage on retail. Point out that they could use the markup equivalents table or the retail method of pricing.

TEACHING POINTS

Practice Use flash cards to teach the basic math formulas for the cost method of pricing and the retail method of pricing. Show students a formula and have them identify what the formula is for. Then provide the student with a problem related to the formula they have just identified.

Online Activity

Car Price Markups
Have students go online to research *Consumer Reports, Kelley Blue Book,* or other similar sources to determine the cost to a dealer for a particular car. Have students research the sticker price for the car (the retail price) at a particular dealer and calculate the dealer's dollar and percentage markup.

GLOBAL MARKET

China's Auto Industry and the WTO

Discussion Ask students to recall the purpose of the WTO. If necessary, remind them that the WTO is an international body dealing with the rules of trade between nations.

CRITICAL THINKING **Answer:** Tariffs increase the cost of an item and quotas limit the number of items that can be imported into a country. When tariffs are lowered and quotas are raised, retail prices can be lowered on imported autos and more autos can be imported into China. These two actions impact Chinese automakers adversely because to be competitive with imported autos, they must lower their prices. Lowering their prices reduces their margins.

@ Online Action! For instructions, ideas, and answer guide, go to the Teacher Center at marketingessentials.glencoe.com

Discussion Starter

CALCULATIONS FOR LOWERING PRICES

Discuss with students how to calculate markdowns. To launch the discussion, have them draw on their personal experience in buying things on sale. Ask them how they calculate a price when they select something from a rack posted "20 percent off ticketed prices." Show them that their methods are similar to, if not exactly the same as, the methods described in the text for calculating markdowns.

PRACTICE 4 ANSWERS

1. (A) $1.89 (100% − 4% = 96%; $1.81 ÷ .96 = $1.89); (B) $.08 ($1.89 − $1.81 = $.08). (C) Double-check: $1.89 × .04 = .0756 or $.08 markup.
2. (A) $50 (100% − 60% = 40%; $20 divided by .40 = $50); (B) $30 ($50 − $20 = $30). (C) Double-check: $50 × .60 = $30 markup.

PRACTICE 4

Calculate retail price and markup in these two problems by using the retail method. Then double-check your answer to see if your retail price is correct.

1. (A) Find the retail price and (B) dollar markup for a bag of chips that costs $1.81 and has a 4 percent markup on retail. (C) Double-check your answer.
2. A lamp costs the retailer $20 and has a 60 percent markup on retail. Calculate this lamp's (A) retail price and (B) dollar markup. (C) Double-check your answer.

Calculations for Lowering Prices

When a business lowers its prices, a new sale price must be calculated, as well as a new markup. Let's look at the steps used in calculating markdowns (lowered prices), maintained markups, and the actual sale prices derived from these calculations.

Markdowns

To reduce the quantity of goods in stock, a business will sometimes mark down merchandise by a certain percentage (MD[%]).

This reduction is based on the retail price. Consider as an example a record store that wants to mark down by 25 percent CDs that originally sold for $16. The steps for calculating the sale price (SP) are as follows:

STEP 1 Determine the dollar markdown. Multiply the retail price by the percentage markdown.

$$RP \times MD(\%) = MD(\$)$$
$$\$16 \times .25 = \$4$$

STEP 2 To determine the sale price, subtract the markdown from the retail price.

$$RP - MD(\$) = SP$$
$$\$16 - \$4 = \$12$$

Another way to arrive at the same answer is to consider what percentage of the original price will equal the sale price. The procedure is still two steps long, but the percentage calculation is so easy that you can probably do it in your head and save some time. Here are the steps involved.

STEP 1 Determine what percentage of the original price will equal the sale price. This is simply a matter

---

Figure 27.3 *Retail Box*

	$	%		$	%
Retail Price	M 11.25	J 100	Retail Price	M	J 100
Markup	N 4.50	K 40	Markup	N	K
Cost	O 6.75	L 60	Cost	O	L

Computation:
L = J − K   L = 100 − 40 = 60%
M = O ÷ L   M = $6.75 ÷ .60 = $11.25
N = M − O   N = $11.25 − $6.75 = $4.50

Check: M × K = N   11.25 × .40 = $4.50

- **The Retail Method** To compute the retail price using the retail method, fill in the boxes following the letter sequence (J-O). Note that the box labeled "J" (RP%) is always 100 percent. The amounts that go in the boxes labeled K (MU%) and O (C$) are usually known.

Why is this retail box an example of the retail method for calculating markup?

@ Online Action! Go to *marketingessentials.glencoe.com/27/figure/3* to find a project on retail pricing.

Figure 27.3 *Retail Box*

Discussion Lead a discussion of how the table works and why it is an example of the retail method for calculating markup.

Caption Answer The retail box is considered a retail method because all figures are converted to retail figures for computation purposes.

@ Online Action! For instructions, ideas, and answer guide, go to the Teacher Center at marketingessentials.glencoe.com

Follow Up Ask students to use spreadsheet software to create a retail box.

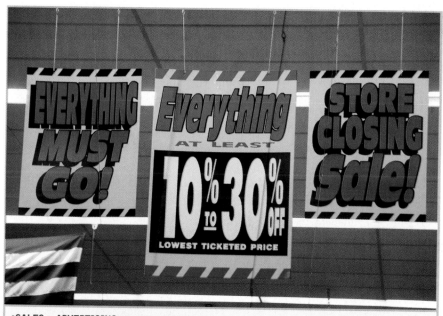

•SALES as ADVERTISING Many stores widely publicize their sales as a way of attracting shoppers.

Why would a store that is closing put its merchandise on sale?

of subtracting the markdown percentage from 100 percent.

RP(%) − MD(%) = SP(%)
100% − 25% = 75%

STEP 2 To find the sale price, multiply the retail price by the decimal equivalent of the percentage calculated in Step 1.

RP × SP(%) = SP
$16 × .75 = $12

PRACTICE 5

Calculate the sale price.

1. A suit that sells for $350 is to be marked down by 40 percent. What is its new price?

Maintained Markup

When a marketer marks down goods, the markup and markup percentage change. The difference between an item's final sale price and its cost is called the **maintained markup**.

Maintained Markups and Pricing Strategies

Businesses must plan for markdowns; doing so is part of being profitable and competitive in the marketplace. Reductions in the original retail price include employee discounts, damaged goods allowances, and special sales events. For businesses to enjoy the profit margin they need to be successful, they must take these factors into account.

The concept of maintained markup becomes extremely important in planning the original price of the item and all future markdowns.

Chapter 27 - Pricing Math 575

SECTION 27.1

CLOSE

Ask students to complete the following statements:

- Gross profit is the difference between sales revenue and _____.
  cost of goods sold

- Markups and markdowns can be expressed as a dollar amount or as a _____.
  percentage

- Retail price equals cost plus _____.
  markup

- A markdown is a reduction based on the item's _____.
  retail price

PRACTICE 6 ANSWER

1. (A) $239.99 sale price
($299.99 × .80 = 239.992);
(B) $113.99 MM$ ($239.99 −$126 = $113.99);
(C) 47.5 percent ($113.99 ÷ $239.99 = .475)

Let's consider an example. Assume that a video game that cost Zap Electronics $25 to manufacture and originally sold for $50 is marked down 20 percent. The maintained markup (expressed in both dollars and as a percentage) is calculated as follows:

STEP 1 Calculate the new sale price.

100% − 20% = 80%
$50 × .80 = $40

STEP 2 To determine the maintained markup in dollars (MM$), subtract the cost from the sale price.

SP − C = MM($)
$40 − $25 = $15

STEP 3 To determine the maintained markup percentage, divide the

maintained markup in dollars by the sale price. Note: Round percents to the tenths place.

MM($) ÷ SP = MM(%)
$15 ÷ $40 = .3750
.375 = 37.5%

PRACTICE 6

Now try the same type of computation on your own.

1. A digital audio player that costs the retailer $126 to stock sells for $299.99 (retail price). The retailer wants to mark down the player 20 percent. (A) Determine the sale price and (B) maintained markup in dollars, and then (C) calculate the maintained markup percentage. Round the markup percentage to the tenths place.

 27.1 AFTER YOU READ

Reviewing Key Terms and Concepts

1. What income statement term is the same as markup?
2. What steps are used to calculate prices according to the cost method?
3. When is the initial markup the same as the maintained markup? Explain.

Integrating Academic Skills

Math

4. Determine the retail price of an item that cost the business $89 and has a markup of $50.

Writing

5. Write a two-page paper on research comparing prescription drug prices in Canada with prices for the same drugs sold in the United States.

@ Online Action! Check your answers at *marketingessentials.glencoe.com/27/read*

marketingessentials.glencoe.com

 AFTER YOU READ

Reviewing Key Terms and Concepts

1. Margin is the same as markup.

2. Cost Method: Step 1) Determine the dollar markup on cost by multiplying the cost by the percentage markup on cost in decimal form. Step 2) Add the dollar markup to the cost to get the retail price.

3. When no markdowns are taken the initial markup and maintained markup are the same.

Integrating Academic Skills

4. $139; $89 + $50 = $139

5. Reports will vary. The conclusion may be that prescription drugs are less expensive in Canada than they are in the United States. Students may include the fact that many U.S. citizens are purchasing their prescription drugs from Canada because of the lower prices and that the U.S. government is checking into that practice.

 @ Online Action! Answers at *marketingessentials.glencoe.com/27/read*

Calculating Discounts

OBJECTIVES

- Utilize a general procedure for figuring discounts
- Calculate discounts in dollars and percentages
- Calculate net amounts

KEY TERMS

- employee discounts

READ and STUDY

BEFORE YOU READ

Connect When did you last purchase a discounted item?

THE MAIN IDEA

Discounts affect the final price a customer will pay. Therefore, it is essential that you learn how to calculate discounts and the net price payable.

STUDY ORGANIZER

In the center of the diagram below record the procedures for calculating discounts and the net amount payable. In the other circles, note examples of discounts.

Discounts — Employee discounts

Discount Formulas

$P \times D (\%) = D(\$)$
$P - D (S) = NP$

Discounts

Discounts

Discounts and allowances are price adjustments often taken by employees for purchases and offered by vendors to their customers. Knowing how to calculate discounts and the resulting net amounts is important because they affect the prices customers ultimately pay for the products you are selling or buying.

Recall that a discount is a reduction in the price of goods and services sold to customers. Retailers may offer discounts to their employees as a job benefit or to encourage their employees to

WHILE YOU READ

Predict Compare the two methods of calculating discounts and net amounts to decide when each method should be used.

FOCUS

Introducing the Section

COLLABORATIVE ACTIVITY

Have students work in groups to develop their own quantity discount plan for the school store. Tell them that the markets they will be targeting are school sports teams and the parents' sports association.

Have students begin their plan with specialized T-shirts designed for each targeted group. Explain that the cost per T-shirt to the school store will be $10. Suggest that they first determine the retail price for one T-shirt and then work out the details for the quantity discounts.

Groups should summarize their discount pricing plans in chart form. They should prepare a written report as well, spelling out the rationale for the plan.

Preteaching Key Terms

List the key term on the board and have students skim the chapter looking for the term in context. Suggest that they read the paragraph in which the term appears and, if necessary, the paragraph that comes before and after as well.

- employee discounts

Extended Activity

Exploring Discounts

Have students look at discounts offered at one retail store. Students may choose a brick-and-motor store or an online store. Ask students to find at least three examples of discounts. If the discount is a percentage, have students calculate the actual cost of the item compared to the original price. If the discount is a flat fee, have students calculate the cost of the item compared to the original price and also calculate the discount percentage.

READ and STUDY

BEFORE YOU READ

Lead students in discussing how discounts are calculated. Have students offer examples of discounts they have received and show how the discounted price was determined.

THE MAIN IDEA

Calculating discounts is an important skill that is used in figuring discounts offered by manufacturers to retailers, employers to employees, and retailers to customers.

STUDY ORGANIZER

Model the study organizer for students by filling in the first circle. A full-size, downloadable study organizer can be found at **marketingessentials.glencoe.com**

WHILE YOU READ Model for students how they can take notes as they read the section.

TEACH

Discussion Starter

DISCOUNTS

Ask students if any of them work for a business that offers employee discounts, or if they know someone who does. Ask what conditions or stipulations are attached to using the discount privilege. List students' answers on the board for their reference as they read and study the chapter.

Common conditions or stipulations might be that discounts can only be applied to the employee and sometimes his or her immediate family. Frequently, a manager must authorize or initial the purchase sales check.

TEACHING POINTS

Practice After students have read about the various types of discounts, give them a clue, such as those below, associated with each type of discount and have them tell you which type of discount the clue illustrates:

- 1–12 items at 8 cents each, 13–20 items at 6 cents each
  quantity discount

- 15 percent off if you buy your back-to-school stock in May
  seasonal discount

- 30 percent off anything you can wear on the job
  employee discount

- $4300 off your total purchase if you feature the item in a newspaper ad
  promotional discount

---

purchase their goods. Vendors offer discounts to their customers to encourage prompt payment and stimulate business. There are two different ways you can go about calculating discounts and net amounts.

The first way is to calculate the discount and then subtract the discount from the original price. You would use this method if you wanted to know the dollar amount of the discount and the net amount. Here is an example of this two-step method.

STEP 1 Multiply the price (P) by the discount percentage [D(%)] to get the dollar amount of the discount [D($)].

$$P \times D(\%) = D(\$)$$

STEP 2 Subtract the discount from the price to get the net price (NP), or the amount that the customer will actually pay.

$$P - D(\$) = NP$$

Here is an example. A business is offering a 35 percent discount on an item that sells for $150.

$$\$150 \times .35 = \$52.50$$
$$\$150 - 52.50 = \$97.50$$

When you simply want to know the net amount due, you can also follow a two-step process. Using the above example, those calculations would be as follows:

STEP 1 Subtract the discount percent from 100 percent. This figure represents the net price's percentage equivalent (NPPE).

$$100\% - D(\%) = NPPE$$
$$100\% - 35\% = 65\%$$

STEP 2 Then multiply the original price by that net price's equivalent percentage to get the net price.

$$P \times NPPE = NP$$
$$\$150 \times .65 = \$97.50$$

Employee Discounts

Discounts offered by employers to their workers are **employee discounts**. Employee discounts encourage employees to buy and use their company's products. In so doing, businesses hope employees will project confidence in and enthusiasm for those products. This is especially important for the sales staff and customer service representatives, so they can speak about the products from firsthand experience. Employee discounts can range from 10 percent to 30 percent for entry-level employees and as high as 50 percent or more for top-level executives.

Discounts from Vendors

Some common types of discounts offered by manufacturers and distributors are cash, trade, quantity, seasonal, and promotional, all of which were already explained in Chapter 26. The following section explains how each of these types of discounts is calculated.

Cash Discounts

Recall from Chapter 26 that a cash discount is a discount offered to buyers to encourage them to pay their bills quickly. Consider the invoice terms 3/15, net 60.

Recall that the first number (3) represents the percentage of the discount applicable to the invoice total. When that total is $1,000 and the customer takes advantage of the discount, the calculations are as follows:

STEP 1 Determine the dollar discount.

$$P \times D(\%) = D(\$)$$
$$\$1,000 \times .03 = \$30$$

STEP 2 Determine the net price.

$$P - D(\$) = NP$$
$$\$1,000 - \$30 = \$970$$

Cash discounts can also be calculated on a unit basis. The net unit price listed on the invoice for 100 items at $10 each is determined as follows:

Extended Activity

Calculate Trade Discounts

Have students calculate the following: If a manufacturer offers a trade discount of 50 percent plus terms of 2/10 net 30, what is the total discount percentage the retailer can take if it pays the invoice the day it is received? (52 percent)

STEP 1 Determine the dollar discount.

$$P \times D(\%) = D(\$)$$
$$\$10.00 \times .03 = \$.30$$

STEP 2 Determine the net price.

$$P - D(\$) = NP$$
$$\$10.00 - \$.30 = \$9.70$$

The net amount payable by the customer would still be the same, of course—$970 ($9.70 × 100).

If you wanted to determine the net price simply, you could subtract 3 percent from 100 percent and take 97% of $10 ($10 × .97 = $9.70).

Trade Discounts

Trade discounts are based on manufacturers' list prices. They are not really discounts but are the way manufacturers quote prices to wholesalers and retailers. They are called trade discounts because different prices are offered to different lines of trade (for example, wholesalers versus retailers), in a series, such as 40 percent and 20 percent. The 40 percent discount is offered to the retailer and the series of discounts 40 percent and 20 percent is offered to the wholesaler. To figure 40 percent and 20 percent trade discounts for a wholesaler's invoice totaling $8,450, you would do the following:

STEP 1 Determine the first dollar discount.

$$P \times D(\%) = D(\$)$$
$$\$8,450 \times .40 = \$3,380$$

STEP 2 Determine the declining balance.

$$P - D(\$) = DB$$
$$\$8,450 - \$3,380 = \$5,070$$

STEP 3 Take the second discount off the declining balance in Step 2

$$DB \times D(\%) = D(\$)$$
$$\$5,070 \times .20 = \$1,014$$

STEP 4 Determine the net price

$$DB - D(\$) = NP(\$)$$
$$\$5,070 - \$1,014 = \$4,056$$

Sometimes, retailers or wholesalers want to calculate the net unit price of individual items listed on an invoice. In those cases, using the result of subtracting the discounts from 100 percent would be faster. Assuming one of the items on that above invoice was $84.50, you would multiply $84.50 × .60 = $50.70; then you would multiply $50.70 × .80 = $40.56 (net unit price).

PRACTICE 7

Determine the amounts payable by the following customers.

1. Alliance Trucking receives an invoice in the amount of $325,000 showing the terms 2/10, net 30. The invoice lists five trucks at $65,000 each. (A) If Alliance takes advantage of the discount, what will be the net amount due on the invoice? (B) The net price per truck?

2. A manufacturer gives retailers a 55 percent trade discount. The invoice received by Oliver's Department Store totals $2,907.40. (A) What is the dollar amount of the store's discount? (B) What is the amount payable to the manufacturer?

3. A manufacturer gives wholesalers discounts of 40 percent and 10 percent. The invoice received by Industrial Wholesaler totals $193,300. What is the net amount payable to the manufacturer?

Quantity Discounts

Quantity discounts are offered to buyers for placing large orders. Sellers benefit from large orders because the selling costs for one transaction are lower than for several small transactions. Quantity discounts are meant to encourage buyers to buy in bulk and purchase more merchandise than they originally intended to purchase. These discounts may be quoted either as a percentage of price or as part of a quantity price list like this:

No. of items	1–24	25–48	49–72
Unit price	$.95	$.90	$.85

Using the above table, if you purchased 50 items, you would pay $.85 each. Your total bill would be $42.50 ($.85 × 50).

Chapter 27 - Pricing Math **579**

Critical Thinking

Have students describe a situation in which receiving an employee discount would be an incentive to working for a company. What other kinds of incentives would encourage them to seek employment? Answers will vary according to the tastes and goals of the students, but may include working for a clothing store that offers a discount. Other incentives include tuition reimbursement.

TEACH CONTINUED

Concept Development

DISCOUNTS FROM VENDORS

To introduce discounts from vendors, such as manufacturers and distributors, ask students to recall what they learned about them in Chapter 26. Have students identify the principal types of discounts (cash, quantity, trade, promotional, and seasonal) and write the terms on the board. Then have students explain how each type of discount is used.

TEACHING POINTS

Model Walk students through calculating the price of a $40 sweater marked 20 percent off.
$32; $40 × 0.20 = $8;
$40 − $8 = $32

Expand Tell students that retailers such as Costco and Best Buy are able to mark up goods only around 10 percent, while other, full-service retailers must mark up their products 25 percent to be profitable. Explain that the bare-bones warehouses, small sales staffs, tight control on inventory, and other factors keep costs low so markup does not have to be as high to ensure profitability.

PRACTICE 7 ANSWERS

1. (A) Net amount on invoice $318,500 ($325,000 × .98)
   (B) Net amount per truck $63,700 ($65,000 × .98)
2. (A) $1599.07 discount ($2907.40 × .55);
   (B) $1308.33 amount payable ($2907.40 − 1599.07).
3. $104,382 (100% − 40% = 60%; $193,300 × .60 = $115,980; 100% − 10% = 90%; $115,980 × .90 = $104,382)

ASSESS

Review Guide

CONCEPTS
Have students review the key formulas presented in this chapter for the various types of discounts.

KEY TERMS
Have students review key terms, their spellings, and definitions in small groups.

ONLINE SELF-ASSESSMENT
Have students go to marketingessentials.glencoe.com for the Section 27.2 practice test.

Individualized Review

L1 Assign and review Chapter 27 activities in the Student Activity Workbook.

L2 Assign and review Chapter 27 activities in the Marketing Math Workbook.

L3 Assign and review Chapter 27 activities in the *BusinessWeek* Reader and Case Studies.

Marketing Practice

Have students sign up to interview the managers or personnel directors of selected retail stores in the community to learn about their employee discount policies. Areas of inquiry should include the discount percentage for entry-level employees, conditions of the discount, and what the store gains by offering discounts. Have students present their findings in a one- to three-page written report or an oral presentation of no more than 10 minutes.

•**SCHOOL SUPPLIES DISCOUNTS** The price of school supplies varies depending on the time of year.

When are school supplies likely to be discounted and why?

Sometimes, businesses offer cumulative quantity discounts, whereby a certain minimum purchase must be made during a specified period of time for the discount to be activated. A firm may offer a 2 percent cumulative quantity discount to any company that purchases $3,000 worth of products in a six-month period. If a firm's purchases total $2,500 during that period, no discount is given; if they total $4,000, however, the discount is allowed.

For example, let's say a manufacturer offers a 5 percent cumulative quantity discount for purchases that total at least $5,000 in a three-month period. Suppose Kathy's Flowers placed the following orders:

January 15: $1,000; February 28: $2,000; March 10: $3,000. The total purchases of $6,000 would meet the dollar requirement within the three-month period. Thus, Kathy's net amount payable would be $5,700 ($1,000 + $2,000 + $3,000 = $6,000 × .95 = $5,700). If Kathy's Flowers had not placed the March 10 order, the total for the three-month period would be only $3,000, so no discounts would be permitted.

Promotional Discounts

Promotional discounts are given to businesses that agree to advertise or in some other way promote a manufacturer's products. When the promotional discount is quoted as a percentage, it is calculated in the same way as a cumulative discount.

Sometimes, marketers are granted a dollar amount as a promotional discount. In such cases, they may want to determine the net purchase price or the percentage of the promotional discount for themselves. Consider an example. The Cycle Shop buys Speedy bicycles for $10,000 and is granted a $250 promotional discount for displaying the bikes in its store window during the month of March. To determine the percentage discount, follow these steps:

STEP 1 Divide the dollar discount by the original price. The answer will be a decimal.

D($) divided by P = D(%)
$250 ÷ $10,000 = .025

STEP 2 Change the decimal to a percentage by shifting the decimal point two places to the right. This figure is the percentage discount. When necessary, round the percentage to the tenths place.

.025 = 2.5%

PHOTO GUIDE **SCHOOL SUPPLIES DISCOUNTS**

Discussion Lead a discussion on how seasonal items are priced. Ask students why they think retailers price items in such a way and how those prices affect their bottom line.

Caption Answer School supplies are likely to be discounted in the winter, as that is when the school session is already in full swing. Retailers earn greater profits from school supplies in the fall, right before school begins, and are less likely to offer discounts then.

Follow Up Ask students to think of three other items that are priced seasonally.

Seasonal Discounts

Sellers offer seasonal discounts to encourage buyers to purchase goods long before the actual consumer buying season. Purchasing beach towels before January 27 or ski apparel before May 1 might qualify retailers for seasonal discounts.

Seasonal discounts are calculated in the same way as other discounts. PNC, Inc. offers an 8 percent seasonal discount to all buyers who purchase winter coats before August 1. An order placed on July 20 for $1,500 worth of decorations would qualify for the discount. However, if that order was placed on August 1, PNC, Inc. would not grant the 8 percent discount.

PRACTICE 8

Now try these problems involving quantity, promotional, and seasonal discounts.

1. Suppose a firm is required to buy $10,000 worth of goods by September 15 in order to qualify for a 10 percent cumulative quantity discount. (A) Would a firm that purchased $8,000 worth of goods on September 1 get the discount? (B) What about one that purchased $11,500 worth on September 20?

2. A manufacturer offers a retailer $3,775 as a promotional discount for advertising a certain product. What is the percentage discount if the total invoice was $75,500? Round percentage discount to the tenths place.

3. Regal Shoe Company offers retailers a 6 percent discount for placing orders by May 1. A retailer takes advantage of the offer and purchases $117,344 worth of shoes by the cutoff date. What is the net amount payable on the invoice?

27.2 AFTER YOU READ

Reviewing Key Terms and Concepts

1. The dating terms on a $7,000 invoice are 3/10, net 30. If the buyer takes advantage of the cash discount, what will be the net amount due?
2. If a promotional discount involved receiving a free case of items you purchased, how can you calculate the percent of the discount offered?
3. Why do sellers offer seasonal discounts to customers?

Integrating Academic Skills

Math

4. How much would you charge a customer who purchased 80 items, based on the following quantity price list?

Number of items	0–12	13–36	37–49	50–74
Unit price	$4.50	$4.25	$4.00	$3.75

Art

5. Prices for artwork vary immensely. Use the Internet to locate artwork that appeals to you. Price the artwork and write a short report on the variations you found in prices and any discounts offered.

 Online Action!

Check your answers at *marketingessentials.glencoe.com/27/read*

CLOSE

1. **Have students name as many of the discounts associated with pricing as they can.**

   employee, cash, trade, quantity, seasonal, and promotional

2. **Ask students to identify the kind of discounts represented by each of the following situations:**

   - **1–2 items at 8 cents each and 13–20 items at 20 cents each**
     quantity discount

   - **15 percent off if you buy your winter clothing in summer**
     seasonal discount

   - **30 percent off any company product**
     employee discount

PRACTICE 8 ANSWERS

1. (A) No, because the minimum quantity is $10,000. (B) No, because the deadline date was September 15.
2. 5 percent ($3,775 ÷ $75,500 = .05)
3. $110,303.36 (100% − 6% = 94%; $117,344 × 0.94 = $110,303.36)

AFTER YOU READ

Reviewing Key Terms and Concepts

1. $6,790; $7,000 × .03 = $210; $7,000 − $210 = $6,790
2. The price for those free goods would be given a dollar value based on the price noted on the invoice for one case of the items purchased. The value of the free goods would be divided by the invoice's total to arrive at the promotional discount percent.
3. Seasonal discounts are offered to encourage buyers to order long before the actual consumer buying season.

Integrating Academic Skills

4. $300; 80 × $3.75 = $300
5. Answers will vary depending on the artwork selected but should include all relevant information on the pricing of the paintings.

 Online Action! Answers at **marketingessentials.glencoe.com/27/read**

CAREERS IN MARKETING

Lifelong Learning

CAREER INFORMATION

Have students go to marketingessentials.glencoe.com and find Chapter 27 Careers page and click on the link for the American Marketing Association's Careers Strategies and Tips. Ask students to select one article, read it, and summarize it in three short paragraphs.

PRICING MATH

Understanding and performing basic pricing calculations enhances students' confidence as future employees and consumers. Encourage students to use these equations at school or work. Repetition and practical application of math concepts will increase familiarity, speed, and accuracy. Checking math at home and at work also provides good practice.

Primary Source

Ask students to go to marketingessentials.glencoe.com and find Chapter 27 Resources. Ask them to click on the link for the American Marketing Association's marketing dictionary and read the definitions of the terms related to pricing math that they find.

THINKING CRITICALLY

Answer will vary; students might should include the idea that economics involves the study of supply and demand. Pricing is related to those factors.

@ Online Action!

For instructions, ideas, and answer guide, go to the Teacher Center at marketingessentials.glencoe.com

---

BILL BUCKALEW
PRICING CONSULTANT
DEMAND CURVE, INC.

Aptitudes, Abilities, and Skills

Analytical skills, strong computer and technical ability, and mathematical aptitude are all critical.

(?) What do you do at work?
My job is to help companies achieve financial goals through better pricing. A good strategy puts the company in a position to be successful, while a bad strategy assures that the company will fail. As a pricing consultant, it is important to know which pricing strategy will increase the company's chances for success.

Education and Training

Degrees in economics are essential in this career; other math-intensive courses are also helpful to the pricing analyst.

(?) What skills are most important to you?
Price analysis requires the ability to access and manipulate large data sets. It is important for a good consultant to be able to pull data from many diverse data sources and transform that data into information that people can use to make decisions. Skills that are important, then, are data query, statistical analysis, and reporting. Some tools that can be used to assist this process are SQL, MS-Access, MS-Excel, and report-generators like Crystal Reports or Business Objects.

Career Path

Entry-level positions can begin in the accounting department of any major company; many price analysts also work in a freelance capacity.

(?) What is your key to success?
To consistently increase the value of the products or services the company is supplying. Increasing the value of the product or service forces upward price pressure in the marketplace. When customers realize the benefits of the company's offering they are willing to pay more to purchase... and the pricing consultant gets paid!

THINKING CRITICALLY

Why is a thorough understanding of basic principles of economics so important for this career?

@ Online Action!

Go to *marketingessentials.glencoe.com/ 27/careers* to find a career-related activity.

 marketingessentials.glencoe.com

Test-Taking Strategies

Inform students of the following test-taking strategies:

1. As you study the material in your textbook or notes, turn the main points of each topic or heading into questions. Check to see if the answers come to you quickly and correctly. Write your questions and answers down and review them before the test.

2. Encourage students to create flash cards to practice the basic pricing math formulas. Students can write the formula on one side of the card, and what the formula is used for on the other side of the card. They can also put a problem related to the formula they have identified.

FOCUS on KEY POINTS

SECTION 27.1

● Gross profit on an income statement is the same as gross margin or markup in pricing. The basic formula for markup is Cost + Markup = Retail Price. Markups may be computed on cost or retail prices and in dollars or percentages.

● To calculate a markdown, multiply the markdown percent by the retail price. To arrive at the sale price, subtract the dollar markdown from the original retail price.

● Maintained markup is the difference between sale price and cost.

SECTION 27.2

● The procedure for calculating discounts is to multiply the price by the discount percentage and then to subtract that amount from the original price to arrive at the net price. Another method for calculating the net price is to subtract the discount percent from 100 percent. Multiply the resulting percentage by the original price to arrive at the net price.

● Cash discounts are offered to customers with dating terms such as 2/10, net 30. The "2" represents the discount percentage. Trade discounts are often quoted in series, such as 40 percent and 20 percent. To calculate the net price with a series of discounts, multiply each sequential discount by the declining balance.

● Quantity discounts may be quoted on a quantity price list that provides unit prices for specific quantities purchased. Promotional discounts are often granted in dollar amounts. To determine the percentage of discount offered in a promotion, divide the promotional discount by the original price paid for the merchandise in an order. Seasonal discounts have qualifying purchase date requirements.

REVIEW VOCABULARY

Explain the meanings of the following terms by giving an example of each.

I. gross profit (p. 567)

2. maintained markup (p. 575)

3. employee discounts (p. 578)

REVIEW FACTS and IDEAS

4. Explain how a firm's profit is related to markup. (27.1)

5. What is the most basic formula you need in order to calculate retail price? (27.1)

6. How are the dollar and percentage markups calculated, based on cost and based on retail? (27.1)

7. What is the two-step procedure for calculating a discount and net amount? What is the two-step procedure for calculating just the net price? (27.2)

8. A company is granted a $250 promotional discount for including a product in its flyer. What percentage is this discount of the $5,000 invoice? (27.2)

Chapter 27 - Pricing Math 583

REVIEW FACTS and IDEAS

4. Markup is similar to gross profit. Gross profit is the difference between sales revenue and the cost of goods sold.

5. Cost plus markup equals retail price (C + MU = RP).

6. First calculate the dollar markup ($19.99 − $13.99 = $6.00). To calculate the markup percentage on cost, you divide the dollar markup by cost ($6.00 ÷ $13.99 = .4288). Then you change the decimal answer to a percent by moving the decimal place two places to the left and adding a percent sign (42.88%). You may also want to round the percent to the tenth place (42.9%). To determine the markup percentage based on retail you divide the dollar markup by the retail price: $6.00 MU ÷ $19.99 RP = .30001 or 30 percent (MU%).

7. The two-step procedure for calculating a discount and net amount: Step 1) multiply the discount by the price to get the dollar discount; Step 2) Subtract the dollar discount from the price to get the net amount. The two-step procedure for just calculating the net price: Step 1) subtract the discount from 100 percent. Step 2) Multiply the price by the percent calculated in Step 1.

8. 5 percent; $250 ÷ $5,000 = .05

FOCUS on KEY POINTS

Ask volunteers to read the summaries out loud and give one real-world example for each concept.

REVIEW VOCABULARY

See glossary for definitions of **I–3.** Dollar amounts will vary in the example. A sample answer might read:

I. *Gross profit* the difference between sales revenue and cost of goods sold. Example: Sales revenue $10,000 − cost of goods sold $6,500 = $3,500 gross profit.

BUILD SKILLS

9. Workplace Skills
Answers will vary. However, most students should realize that it is not only unethical to give discounts that don't apply to merchandise, but is also stealing from the company.

10. Technology Applications
Spreadsheets will vary. Accept all that demonstrate understanding of how retail prices are calculated using the retail method.

11. Math Practice
(A) 81.6 percent on cost ($4.49 MU ÷ $5.50 C = .8163) (B) 44.9 percent on retail ($5.50 C + $4.49 MU = $9.99 RP; $4.49 C ÷ $9.99 RP = .4494)

DEVELOP CRITICAL THINKING

12. What Is the Retail Price?
One way is to use the equivalents table to determine the equivalent markup on cost in order to use the cost method. The other is the retail box method, where the markup on cost is subtracted from 100 percent and then divided into the cost to determine the retail price. Cost method: 20 percent markup on retail is equivalent to 25 percent on cost, so $300 × .25 = $75 markup; $300 + $75 = $375 retail price. With the retail box method, the calculations would be: 100 percent − 20 percent = 80 percent; $300 ÷ .80 = $375 retail price.

13. Company Discounts
$11,280; $8,000 + $4,000 = $12,000; 100 percent − 6 percent = 94 percent; $12,000 × .94 = $11,280

BUILD SKILLS

9. Workplace Skills
Business Ethics The store where you are working as a cashier is having a huge sale with selected items marked down 30 to 50 percent. The discounts are taken at the register. Your friend asks you to take a 50 percent markdown on an item that is not on sale. What would you do?

10. Technology Applications
Computing Prices Prepare a spreadsheet that shows how retail prices are calculated using the retail method. Use a 40 percent markup on retail and the following items and their costs:

Item	Retailers Cost
Model #314	$20
Model #315	$35
Model #316	$42

Record the formulas you used in your spreadsheet calculations.

11. Math
Calculate: Percentage Markup A card store buys boxes of candy for $5.50 and puts a $4.49 markup on each box. (A) What is the percentage markup on cost? (B) The percentage markup on retail?

DEVELOP CRITICAL THINKING

12. What Is the Retail Price?
Suppose a buyer wanted to buy goods that cost $300 and the customary markup on retail was 20 percent.

Demonstrate two methods that could be used to calculate the retail price. Identify each method when showing your calculations. Finally, explain why you chose the two calculation methods.

13. Company Discounts
A vendor offers Company XYZ a cumulative discount of six percent on orders of at least $10,000 placed within a six-month period. Company XYZ purchases $8,000 within three months and $4,000 a month later.

What is the amount payable by Company XYZ? Make sure you show all the steps in your calculations.

Formative Assessment

Formative assessment is an essential component of classroom work. This type of assessment provides information that is then used as feedback to modify teaching and meet student needs.

L1 Review key terms for this chapter. Ask students to write one sentence for each key term.

L2 Provide various examples of factors that affect pricing math in story form. After each story, have the students identify the factors that affected the pricing situation.

L3 As students to create stories that illustrate cost method and retail method of pricing.

Reteach If the results of this formative assessment seem low, consider the following activity: Ask students to skim the chapter and be able to describe the following in their own words: 1.) the relationship of profit and loss and markup; 2.) how to calculate markdowns and markups; 3.) planning for maintained markup

APPLY CONCEPTS

14. Trade Discounts and Maintained Markup

Local schools and businesses have inquired about receiving a discount if they purchase bagels for resale. Prepare a discounted price list that shows at least five different price options for different quantities purchased. Assume your cost to make and market one bagel is $.35. At present, you sell one bagel in your retail store for $.60. Be sure your trade discounts still generate gross margins of no less than 27 percent, which is essential to remain profitable.

Activity What trade discounts would you offer these resellers?

15. Understanding Markup and Gross Profit

Trade organizations often publish average markup (margins) for a given product category. Research the retail prices of two competing products from each of the three categories noted below.

Product Category	Average Retail Markup Percent
Small Appliances	30%
Videos	25%
Clothing	50%

Activity Use a spreadsheet to calculate the cost of those items. Analyze the costs and markup in dollars you calculated, as well as the sales volume required to generate $100,000 in gross profit for each of the products you researched.

NET SAVVY

16. Free Goods and Coupons

Find a Web site that offers free goods and coupons. Do manufacturers' coupons affect the retailer's markup percentages?

Role Play: Pricing Math

Situation Assume the role of manager of the children's department of a department store. The buyer (judge) has asked you to select three slow selling merchandise styles for markdowns. The styles you have selected are 10 infant sleepers that currently are selling for $20 each; 6 girls cotton crewneck sweaters selling for $25 each; and 11 boys wool sweaters selling for $30 each. The buyer has asked you to take a 30 percent markdown on each item.

Activity Determine the new selling price for each of the styles receiving a markdown, and send a buyer a report of those new prices.

Evaluation You will be evaluated on how well you meet the following performance indicators:

● Determine discounts and allowances that can be used to adjust base prices

● Explain the nature and scope of the pricing function

● Explain factors affecting pricing decisions

● Demonstrate orderly and systematic behavior

 Online Action!

For more information and DECA Prep practice, go to *marketingessentials.glencoe.com/27/DECA*

APPLY CONCEPTS

14. Trade Discounts and Maintained Markup

Answers will vary. However, the lowest possible discount is 20 percent; more than that would exceed the goal of a 27 percent maintained markup (100% − 20% = 80%; $.60 × .80 = $.48 unit price; $.48 − .35 = $.13 MU; $.13 divided by $.48 = .271 = 27.1%.

15. Understanding Markup and Gross Profit

Answers will vary based on products selected. A sample spreadsheet is provided below:

Item	Dirt Devil	Video	Jeans
Retail Price	$79.99	$19.99	$49.99
Retail Markup %	30%	25%	50%
Markup in $ (RP × MU%)	$24.00	$5.00	$25.00
# of Units needed for gross profit of $100,000 ÷ MU	4,167 (4166.66)	20,000	4,000

NET SAVVY

16. Free Goods and Coupons

No. Even though the retailer provides customers with the discounts at the register, retailers are reimbursed by the manufacturers for coupons that they redeem.

 MINI-QUIZ

Read these sentences to the students and have them volunteer the missing words.

1. The difference between the retail price and the cost of an item is the _____. (markup)

2. The difference between an item's final sale price and its cost is called the _____. (maintained markup)

For an expanded chapter quiz, go to Chapter 27 in the TeacherWorks CD-ROM and to Chapter 27 in the **ExamView®** Pro Test Generator CD-ROM.

THE **CONNECTION**

The students should be evaluated on the performance indicators noted in the role play. For another DECA role play, go to the Competitive Events Workbook or the Student Activity Workbook, or go to **marketingessentials.glencoe.com/27/DECA**

Online Action! For instructions, ideas, and answer guide, go to the Teacher Center at **marketingessentials.glencoe.com**

DECA Advisors Corner

Use the guidelines for DECA's Learn and Earn Event to plan the following activity: Select a worthy charity to benefit from a fundraising activity students will design. Students will use their math skills in projecting how much the project will gross.

SET-UP

Discuss basic background to make sure students understand the simulation. You may want to bring in a few ads for toys and point out the key messages in the ads and on the packaging. Introduce the students to the Consumer Product Safety Commission (CPSC) Web site, particularly the section of the site that deals with labeling information.

PROCEDURES

You may want to list procedures on the board and talk about any questions the students might have. Remind the students that a suggested outline for their project is available at **marketingessentials.glencoe.com/u8/ internship.**

TIME MANAGEMENT

Set goals, block schedules, and milestones. Assign interim deadlines for each step of the project.

ASSESSMENT

The rubrics for evaluation of the written, oral, and computer presentations are available at **marketingessentials.glencoe.com/u8/ internship.**

MARKETING INTERNSHIP

A SIMULATED DECA PRODUCT AND SERVICE MANAGEMENT EVENT

Pricing Toys

BASIC BACKGROUND

Tri-Star Toys is introducing two new products influenced by Japanese pop culture. One is a trading card game called Laszot. The other is a line of 12-inch stuffed animals called Mie Dolls. Each doll is supposed to have a unique trait, such as being friendly or mischievous.

Setting a Price Tri-Star Toys wants your firm's help deciding how to price these two new products. The biggest cost factor with the trading card games is creating the stories and characters. Assume a cost of $.25 per card for the initial production. For the dolls, assume an initial cost of $4.50. Marketing expenses are $0.05 per trading card and $1.00 per doll. Demand for both items depends on conditions in the marketplace, which you will need to determine.

YOUR OBJECTIVE

 Your objective is to prepare an effective pricing and retail strategy for Tri-Star's two new products. The company wants to make a 15 percent profit off the products in the first year. You will need to identify a price for sale to wholesalers, retailers, and e-commerce sites, as well as a suggested retail price for those businesses to charge their customers. Base your conclusions on research and analysis of current market conditions.

ASSIGNMENT AND STRATEGY

- **Get the background** To get started you will need to conduct a situation analysis and competitive assessment for these two new products made by the Tri-Star Toy Company. Learn all you can about the markets for trading card games and dolls, some of which may be collectibles.

    You may want to look at the introductions of other trading card games, including Pokemon and Yu-Gi-Oh, and other dolls, such as Ugly Dolls and Beanie Babies.

- **Write the pricing proposal** Begin your proposal by reviewing the reason the client hired your firm.

    Then, provide background information you learned from your situation analysis and competitive assessment.

    Use your research to justify your assumptions as you go through the six steps of pricing a product.

READ to WRITE

New Product Development

Have students research and read about an existing product and find a new use for it, or report on how this product has found a new use in the marketplace. Suggest using the Internet and searching with key words such as "products with multiple uses" or "new product applications." You may want to share this example: The strong breathable fabric trademarked as Gortex® was introduced in the 1980s as the component of artificial ligaments grafted during knee surgery. Gortex is now used in boots, gloves, and jackets as an insulating yet breathable fabric. Ask students to prepare a short written report about their findings.

The six steps are: (1) establish pricing objectives; (2) determine costs; (3) estimate demand; (4) study competition; (5) decide on a pricing strategy; and (6) set prices.

- **What your project should include** Show the math you used to arrive at suggested prices for wholesalers, retailers, and e-commerce sites, as well as the suggested prices for retail customers. Also create a table that depicts your competitive price analysis. Create other tables and figures as needed to show relationships among data.

YOUR REPORT

Use a word processing program and presentation software to prepare a double-spaced report and an oral presentation for Tri-Star Toys. See a suggested outline and key evaluation points at *marketingessentials.glencoe.com/internship*

marketingessentials.glencoe.com

BUILD YOUR PORTFOLIO

Option 1 Internship Report
Once you have completed your Marketing Internship project and presentation, include your written report and a few printouts of key slides from your oral presentation in your Marketing Portfolio.

Option 2 Multi-tiered Pricing Strategies
A designer of high-priced apparel is thinking of also designing moderate-priced fashions. After doing some research, including a situation analysis, create a pricing plan for this designer. It should include a suggested target market and customer profile, distribution, and pricing strategies. Prepare a written report and an oral presentation using word processing and presentation software. See a suggested outline and key evaluation points at *marketingessentials.glencoe.com/portfolio*

@ Online Action!

Go to *marketingessentials.glencoe.com/Unit/8/DECA* to review pricing concepts that relate to DECA events.

Marketing Internship **587**

Unit Review

Now that students have completed the chapters in Unit 8, ask them to review their answers to the Analyze the Ad questions on page 523. Would they answer differently? Why or why not?

Then ask students if they think supply and demand affect prices on discount travel sites.

Prices are affected when the demand of tickets for one destination is so high that the discounter runs out of deeply discounted tickets. For example, if a student tries to book a flight to Hawaii two days before spring break, there will be very few, if any, discounted tickets available. The discounter's price is then likely to be the same as the airlines'.

Have students write a three-paragraph summary of what they learned about price planning strategies and pricing.

STEP AHEAD
Students have explored the relationship between pricing, branding, and promotion. Ask them to consider other phases of the marketing plan (analysis, objective, budget, evaluation) and make a list of possible ways pricing relates to these key steps.

Internship Wrap-Up

Ask students which main steps of product development are demonstrated in the process of creating a new toy. Have students prepare a one-page outline detailing one step of product development for a toy product of their choice.

Steps may include generating ideas, screening ideas, developing the business proposal, developing the product, market testing, and commercialization.

BUILD YOUR PORTFOLIO

Explain to students that portfolios provide evidence of their knowledge and skills in working with data, people, and concepts. Developing a portfolio can be a valuable career development and planning tool. Point out that portfolios should also include personal documents such as a résumé. Encourage students to check the portfolio information available at **marketingessentials.glencoe.com/u8/internship.**

Peer Review
Fellow students who share common interests can serve as reviewers of the final portfolios. This review can be completed through the use of a checklist. Go to **marketingessentials.glencoe.com/u8/internship** to find a suggested checklist.

- **Chapter 28**
  Marketing Research

- **Chapter 29**
  Conducting Marketing Research

Unit Objectives

After completing this unit, students should be able to:

- Discuss the nature, importance, and usage of marketing research in planning and implementing marketing strategies
- Explain the function of marketing information systems
- Describe four important types of marketing research
- Describe the steps used in conducting marketing research
- Construct effective marketing research questionnaires

■ Key to
■ Individualized
■ Activities

L1 Level 1 activities are basic activities and should fall within the range of all students.

L2 Level 2 activities are average activities and should be within the range of average and above average students.

L3 Level 3 activities are challenging activities designed for the ability range of above average students.

Enrichment Resources

PROFESSIONAL ORGANIZATIONS

Advertising Research Foundation (ARF) arfsite.org

Council of American Survey Research Organizations casro.org

ESOMAR (World Association of Opinion and Marketing Research Professionals) esomar.org

MEDIA RESOURCES

Print or online editions of

Advertising Age adage.com

Journal of Marketing Research marketingpower.com/content504.php

WRITING SUPPORT

Ask students to think of an item that they would like to sell. Have them write an essay about the research they would conduct to make sure that the item sells and ensure they can make a profit from it. Ask students to keep and review this document as they study Unit 9.

Management

CHAPTER	PRINT MATERIALS	TECHNOLOGY RESOURCES
Chapter 28 Section 28.1 Section 28.2	**From Unit 9 Fast File Booklet** Lesson Plans Chapter Summaries Reproducible Masters Reproducible Tests **Print Ancillaries** Student Activity Workbook, Chapter 28 Marketing Math Workbook, Chapter 28 *BusinessWeek* Reader and Case Studies, Chapter 28 Competitive Events Workbook, Unit 9 Marketing Research Project Workbook School-to-Work Activity Workbook	Interactive Chalkboard classroom presentations, Chapter 28 Online Learning Center at marketingessentials.glencoe.com Online Student Edition, Chapter 28 TeacherWorks **Exam***View*® Pro Test Generator, Chapter 28 Virtual Business
Chapter 29 Section 29.1 Section 29.2	**From Unit 9 Fast File Booklet** Lesson Plans Chapter Summaries Reproducible Masters Reproducible Tests **Print Ancillaries** Student Activity Workbook, Chapter 29 Marketing Math Workbook, Chapter 29 *BusinessWeek* Reader and Case Studies, Chapter 29 Competitive Events Workbook, Unit 9 Marketing Research Project Workbook School-to-Work Activity Workbook	Interactive Chalkboard classroom presentations, Chapter 29 Online Learning Center at marketingessentials.glencoe.com Online Student Edition, Chapter 29 TeacherWorks **Exam***View*® Pro Test Generator, Chapter 29 Virtual Business

CHAPTER	SECTION	PERFORMANCE INDICATOR
Chapter 28 **Marketing Research**	28.1	Describe the need for marketing information (MIM)
		Explain the nature of marketing research in a marketing-information function (MIM)
	28.2	Explain the nature and scope of the marketing-information management function (MIM)
		Identify information monitored for marketing decision making (MIM)
		Identify the nature of sales forecasts (MIM)
Chapter 29 **Conducting Marketing Research**	29.1	Explain the nature and scope of the marketing-information management function (MIM)
		Describe sources of secondary data (MIM)
		Use data for information analysis (MIM)
	29.2	Collect marketing information from others (MIM)
		Describe the use of technology in the marketing-information management function (MIM)

MIM Marketing-Information Management

Standards Assessment Correlation

	SECTION ASSESSMENT		CHAPTER ASSESSMENT						UNIT LAB
	Reviewing Key Terms and Concepts	Integrating Academic Skills	Review Facts and Ideas	Build Skills	Develop Critical Thinking	Apply Concepts	Workplace Skills	Net Savvy	Marketing Internship
	1	✓	17	20	24	26	✓		✓
	2, 3	✓	13–15	20, 21	23	26	✓	✓	✓
	2, 3	✓	11, 12, 14, 15	20, 21	23, 24	26	✓	✓	✓
	1, 2, 3	✓	13, 14		24	26		✓	✓
	1, 2, 3	✓				25			✓
	1, 2, 3	✓	14, 16, 18, 19, 20	23	26, 27	28	✓	✓	✓
	1, 2, 3	✓	15	23	27		✓		✓
	1, 2, 3	✓		23	26, 27	29	✓		✓
	1, 2, 3	✓	14, 16, 17,	23	27	29	✓		✓
				24				✓	✓

@ Online Action! Check the latest updates for national standards and for your state's standards at marketingessentials.glencoe.com

Unit Overview

Unit 9 explores marketing information management—its importance, the major areas of marketing research, and the steps performed in the marketing research process. Chapter 28 introduces the process of getting the marketing information needed to make sound business decisions through systematic gathering, recording, and analyzing of data. Chapter 29 defines the five steps of the marketing research process—problem definition, obtaining data, data analysis, recommending solutions to the problem, and implementing the findings.

MAKING IT RELEVANT
Ask students why marketing information is essential to business success.

Marketing information systems can help businesses predict and solve the problems they face.

Unit Launch Activity

Have students share their first impressions of the ad on this page. Ask students how a business such as Coca-Cola might have decided to target the market shown in the ad and what strategies they may have used to research that market.

Answers will vary; students may suggest demographic research or personal surveys.

In this unit you will find

- **Chapter 28**
  Marketing
  Research

- **Chapter 29**
  Conducting
  Marketing
  Research

588

 UNIT PROJECT

Perform a Research Study
If your program has a school store, have chapter members develop a research study to determine the market potential for products to be offered in the store. Students should develop the survey, conduct the research, analyze the data, and write a report on the findings to give to the school administration.

Assessment Guidelines Prepare a rubric for evaluation that includes completeness of the survey used, thoroughness of the research conducted, a sound analysis of the data, and clearly written and thought out reporting of the students' findings.

Enrichment Assign and review Unit 9 activities in the Competitive Events Workbook.

OUT OF TIME?
If class time is too short to cover all the chapters in this unit, go to Unit 9 in your Fast File Teacher Resources booklet and find the Chapter Summaries for Chapters 28 and 29.

Marketing Plan

Coca-Cola decided to target one demographic group and promote just one of its many beverages in this ad. Does the ad appeal to other demographic groups, as well?

Market Talk Marketing research can analyze results by demographic factors, including income, age, and ethnicity. Companies often make marketing decisions based on the results of their research.

Think and Write Imagine you visit friends in a neighboring state and find out everybody at your friends' high school wears a different brand of jeans than people at your high school wear. List four questions you would ask your friends to discover why a different brand of jeans is popular in their state.

@ Online Action! Go to *marketingessentials.glencoe.com/ u9/ad* for an extended activity.

Functions of Marketing

- Marketing-Information Management
- Financing
- Selling
- Pricing
- Distribution
- Product/Service Management
- Promotion

Foundations
- Professional Development
- Economics
- Business, Management, Entrepreneurship
- Communication, Interpersonal Skills

Concepts • Technology • Academic Concepts • Technology • Academic Concepts • Technology • Academic Concepts

Marketing Plan

1 ANALYSIS
SWOT
Economic
Socio-Cultural
Technological
Competitive

2 STRATEGY
Promotion
Place
Price
Product

3 IMPLEMENTATION
Organization
Management
Staffing

4 BUDGET
Cost of sales
Cost of Promotion
Incomes and Expenses

5 CONTROL
Evaluation
Performance Measures
Performance Analysis

In this unit

Foundations of Marketing
- Business, Management, Entrepreneurship

Functions of Marketing
- Marketing Information Management

 marketingessentials.glencoe.com

589

Marketing Plan

RELATE THE UNIT TO THE MARKETING PLAN

The four Ps of the marketing mix include product, place, pricing, and promotion. An effective marketing plan cannot be made without conducting marketing research, which is explained in Unit 9.

MARKETING PLAN OVERVIEW

Let students know that conducting effective marketing research and analysis will help increase a business's chances to succeed and profit in the face of fierce competition and the changing marketplace.

Functions of Marketing

Point out to students that Chapters 28 and 29 will deal with the marketing function of marketing information management and the marketing foundation of business, management, and entrepreneurship.

- **Marketing Information Management** For businesses to be successful, they must continually gather marketing information and know how to analyze and manage it for maximum benefit to the business.

- **Business, Management, Entrepreneurship** Business managers and entrepreneurs have to be careful about the marketing research they conduct, tailoring it specifically to answer the questions they have about the market. They must then correctly analyze the data collected before implementing changes based on those data. The changes should be geared toward improving a business's functionality and performance.

Answers will vary; characteristics might include 1) young, 2) college student, and 3) traveling frequently back home. Other types of customers might include business travelers or families taking a summer vacation.

Market Talk Ask students to brainstorm other possible demographic factors.

Think and Write Questions will vary; questions may deal with aspects such as environment, brand loyalty and availability, types of and amount of advertising, or color preference.

@ Online Action! For instructions, ideas, and answer guide, go to the Teacher Center at **marketingessentials.glencoe.com**

Chapter Overview

Chapter 28 explains the purpose of marketing research and identifies ways of gathering information and methods of conducting research. Students will also read about trends and limitations in marketing research.

BUILD BACKGROUND

Initiate a discussion of what factors influence students' purchasing decisions. How would the companies that make the products they buy benefit from understanding the reasons behind purchase decisions? Ask students what factors are important for companies to know. Tell students they will learn how companies compile and use such information in marketing their products and services.

Why It's Important

A great deal of time and money are spent on marketing research before a new product or service is launched, but marketing research continues throughout the life of a product or service. It is essential for businesses to understand factors which affect the purchasing of their product or service. Marketing research is necessary to compile, analyze, and implement that information.

Prepare to Read

Ask a volunteer to write all of the major headings on the board in outline format. Tell students to fill in the secondary headings as they preview or read the chapter. They will then have a thorough chapter outline to use as study notes.

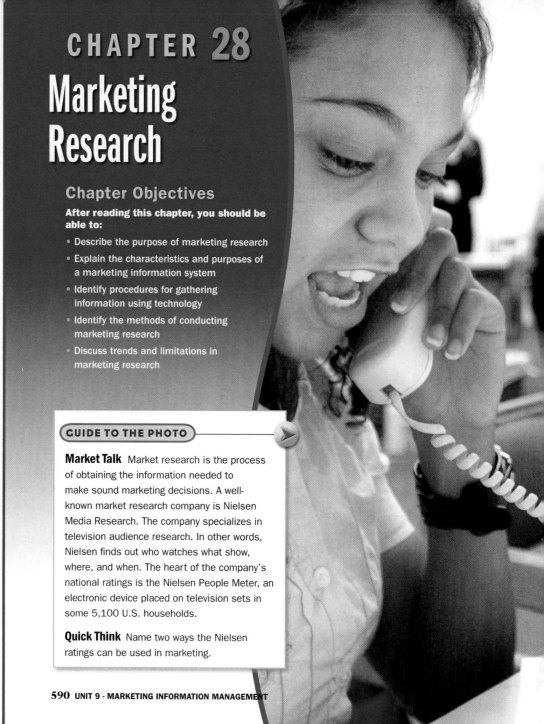

CHAPTER 28
Marketing Research

Chapter Objectives

After reading this chapter, you should be able to:

- Describe the purpose of marketing research
- Explain the characteristics and purposes of a marketing information system
- Identify procedures for gathering information using technology
- Identify the methods of conducting marketing research
- Discuss trends and limitations in marketing research

GUIDE TO THE PHOTO

Market Talk Market research is the process of obtaining the information needed to make sound marketing decisions. A well-known market research company is Nielsen Media Research. The company specializes in television audience research. In other words, Nielsen finds out who watches what show, where, and when. The heart of the company's national ratings is the Nielsen People Meter, an electronic device placed on television sets in some 5,100 U.S. households.

Quick Think Name two ways the Nielsen ratings can be used in marketing.

590 UNIT 9 - MARKETING INFORMATION MANAGEMENT

GUIDE TO THE PHOTO

Market Talk Lead a discussion about Nielsen Media Research and the type of information they collect about television audiences. Ask: What type of programs do your students watch, if any? At what time and on what stations? Why is this information valuable to TV networks? How is it valuable to advertisers?

Quick Think Student responses may include: Networks can use ratings to persuade advertisers of the value of advertising on a certain program. Advertisers can use ratings to match their product with the appropriate audience demographic. Advertisers can use ratings to choose when to run their commercial for the most exposure.

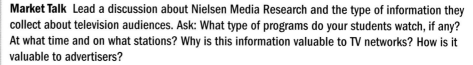 **Follow Up** Ask students to name another company similar to Nielsen Media Research which collects research information for an industry other than television.

THE DECA CONNECTION

Performance indicators represent key skills and knowledge. Relating them to the concepts explained in this chapter is your key to success in DECA events.

These acronyms represent DECA events that involve knowledge of concepts in this chapter.

AAAL	FMAL	MMS	TMDM*
AAML*	FMDM	QSRM*	TSE
ADC	FMML*	RMAL	VPM
BSM	FSRM*	RMML*	
EMDM	HMDM*	SMDM	

In all these DECA events you should be able to follow these performance indicators:

- Describe the need for marketing information
- Explain the nature and scope of the marketing-information management function
- Explain the role of ethics in marketing-information management
- Explain the nature of marketing research in a marketing-information management system
- Explain the use of databases in organizing marketing data
- Design a database for information analysis
- Use a database for information analysis

All the events with an asterisk (*) also include this performance indicator:

- Describe information helpful to retailers in planning

Some events include additional performance indicators. These are:

BSM/SMDM	Identify research methods used to evaluate service quality
EMDM	Explain privacy issues in e-commerce
	Explain the nature of data mining

DECA PREP

Check your understanding of DECA performance indicators with the DECA activity in this chapter's review. For more information and DECA Prep practice, go to *marketingessentials .glencoe.com/28/DECA*

marketingessentials.glencoe.com

Chapter 28 - Marketing Research 591

THE DECA CONNECTION

DECA events that require marketing research knowledge and skills are described here. Discuss the performance indicators to make sure students understand how to demonstrate their understanding.

The events acronyms stand for:

AAAL: Apparel and Accessories Marketing Series, AL

AAML: Apparel and Accessories Marketing Series, ML

ADC: Advertising Campaign Event

BSM: Business Services Marketing Series

EMDM: E-Commerce Management Team Decision Making Event

FMAL: Food Marketing Series, AL

FMDM: Financial Analysis Management Team Decision Making Event

FMML: Food Marketing Series, ML

FSRM: Full Serve Restaurant Management Series

HMDM: Hospitality Services Management Team Decision Making Event

MMS: Marketing Management Series

QSRM: Quick Service Restaurant Management Series

RMAL: Retail Merchandising Series, AL

RMML: Retail Merchandising Series, ML

SMDM: Sports and Entertainment Marketing Management Team Decision Making Event

TMDM: Travel and Tourism Marketing Management Team Decision Making Event

TSE: Technical Sales Event

VPM: Vehicles and Petroleum Marketing Series

DECA PREP

Find timed DECA Prep activities correlated to the Competitive Events Workbook for students and DECA tips for teachers at **marketingessentials.glencoe.com /28/DECA**

CHAPTER 28 Classroom Resources

For the Teacher

- TeacherWorks
- marketingessentials.glencoe.com
- Interactive Chalkboard
- **Exam**View® Pro Test Generator
- Fast File Unit 9

For the Student

- *Marketing Essentials* Online Edition
- Student Activity Workbook
- Marketing Math Workbook
- Marketing Research Project Workbook
- School-to-Work Activity Workbook
- Competitive Events Workbook
- *BusinessWeek* Reader and Case Studies
- marketingessentials.glencoe.com

SECTION 28.1

FOCUS

Introducing the Section

COLLABORATIVE ACTIVITY

To prepare for reading this section, have students split into groups and choose two products, one that is successful and one that failed in the marketplace. Have students brainstorm how marketing research may have contributed to the success and failure of each product. Ask students to consider how consumers' attitudes and preferences might have been taken into better consideration to make the failed product more successful. Have groups share their ideas in class.

Preteaching Key Terms

Read definitions of each key term aloud one at a time. Have students write down on a piece of paper which key term they think matches each definition. Tell students they can see if they guessed correctly as they read the chapter.

- marketing research
- marketing information system
- database marketing
- database

 Critical Thinking

Ask students if they have ever tried a new product and disliked it. Ask them to come up with reasons that the company thought their product would be successful.

OBJECTIVES

- Describe the purpose of marketing research
- Explain the characteristics and purposes of a marketing information system
- Identify procedures for gathering information using technology

KEY TERMS

- marketing research
- marketing information system
- database marketing
- database

WHILE YOU READ

Analysis Compare and contrast the terms *market* and *marketing research*.

Marketing Information Systems

READ and STUDY

BEFORE YOU READ

Predict List some reasons why you think that some new businesses have almost immediate success while others fail miserably.

THE MAIN IDEA

Successful companies must be able to understand the needs and wants of customers. Marketing research provides information to help a business plan, solve problems, and make decisions regarding its products and services.

STUDY ORGANIZER

Use a chart like the one below to take notes about the main concepts in this section.

Defining Marketing Research

One of the largest American sports shoe manufacturers wants to introduce its new, best-selling shoe in overseas markets. A famous basketball player in the United States wears the shoe and the ad shows him shooting hoops in locations around the world. The commercial is aired in three European countries, translated into each country's official language. However, the sales are disappointingly low. What went wrong?

 READ and STUDY

BEFORE YOU READ

Write "Succeed" on one side of the board and "Fail" on the other side. Lead students in brainstorming reasons why new businesses succeed or fail. Write the reasons on the board under the appropriate heading.

THE MAIN IDEA

Ask students to give examples of how understanding customer needs and wants can help a business plan.

STUDY ORGANIZER

Make your own study organizer, or download one at **marketingessentials.glencoe.com**. As study continues, the class should work together to take notes.

WHILE YOU READ Model for students how they can make a simple, two-column graphic organizer. Name one column *marketing* and the other *marketing research*.

Even though the ad has a global focus, it does not have global appeal, at least not in Europe. Careful marketing research would have shown that basketball is not as popular in Europe as it is in the United States. Few people purchased the shoe because there were few people who could relate to the sport associated with product.

According to the Marketing Research Association, **marketing research** involves the process and methods used to gather information, analyze it, and report findings related to marketing goods and services. Information obtained through marketing research is used to identify marketing opportunities, solve marketing problems, implement marketing plans, and monitor marketing performance.

Marketing research is most often used by companies to:

- Determine consumers' attitudes and preferences
- Test product features
- Determine market size and growth potential
- Learn about competitive products
- Determine buying cycles
- Understand how the company is perceived by the public

Before developing a product, marketers can conduct research to determine the type of product customers want. The research can minimize potential losses when introducing the new product. Consumers accept only one out of every ten new products introduced into the marketplace; therefore, gaining information about consumer likes and dislikes is important.

Why Is Marketing Research Important?

Businesses that do not pay attention to what consumers are buying and why are likely to make costly marketing mistakes.

The information obtained from research helps businesses increase sales and profits.

Research answers questions about what products to produce, at what price to sell the products, who will buy the products, and how the products will be promoted.

Research also helps businesses solve marketing problems and gauge the potential of new ideas. For example, Stouffer's spent almost 13 years doing marketing research and development before starting its Lean Cuisine product line. Stouffer's studied consumers' interest in health and dieting. They conducted consumer panels to find out what dieters liked and disliked about diet meals. Using the information, the company developed its product, tested its package design, and held pilot sales of the product in several large cities before national distribution. The product was a tremendous success, with over $125 million in sales after the first year of national distribution.

Research also helps a company keep track of what is happening with its current markets. Through research, a company can determine its major competitors, what its competitors are offering, which products consumers prefer, and how satisfied customers are with its product.

Who Uses Marketing Research?

Small businesses usually do not have separate research specialists or departments. There, marketing research is done informally by the owners, managers, or employees, or they hire outside service providers who specialize in market research. Larger companies often have in-house research departments and marketing personnel to plan and conduct marketing research. But even larger companies sometimes contract with outside research companies because of their specialized expertise. It is estimated that $6.2 billion was spent in 2001 on marketing research conducted in the United States by the largest 180 marketing research firms and in-house groups.

Trade associations representing various manufacturers, wholesalers, and retailers conduct marketing research. Industry trade associations, such as the National Retail Federation, collect

---

 Extended Activity

Database Marketing—Rewards Cards

Lead a discussion of supermarket reward cards as an example of database marketing. Ask students what type of information may be collected from such cards. (Answers may include household demographics, lifestyle, and purchase behavior.) Ask how many students use such cards or know people who do. Possible questions may include:

- Did you know the supermarket was collecting this information when you signed up for the card?

- Does knowing your purchases are being tracked make you more or less likely to use the card?

Ask students to list other possible ways in which businesses collect information that consumers might not be aware of.

TEACH

Discussion Starter

DEFINING MARKETING RESEARCH

Ask students to imagine that they must come up with a new product idea. They have one year before the launch of their new product. Which factors must they research before they begin product development? What information must they collect from consumers? In class, have students brainstorm questions to ask consumers and then rank responses in order of importance regarding the success of their product.

TEACHING POINTS

Demonstrate Bring in examples of consumer surveys conducted by companies performing marketing research for new products. Help students identify common types of questions asked on such surveys.

Concept Development

WHO USES MARKETING RESEARCH?

After students read the section on who uses marketing research, brainstorm types of organizations other than individual businesses that use marketing research. Ask students to focus on marketing research for their own school. On the board, list groups that their school could collect information from.

Answers may include students, family members, local residents, teachers, etc.

Divide students into groups and have each group create a short survey aimed at one of the target groups. Have groups share their surveys and lead discussion about how each group's opinions could help the school function better and which group's opinions should be most important.

ASSESS

Review Guide

CONCEPTS

Ask students to recall the purpose of marketing research.

To identify marketing opportunities, solve marketing problems, implement marketing plans, and monitor marketing performances.

KEY TERMS

Have students review key terms, their spellings, and definitions in small groups.

ONLINE SELF-ASSESSMENT

Have students go to marketingessentials.glencoe.com for the Section 28.1 practice test.

Individualized Review

L1 Assign and review Chapter 28 activities in the Student Activity Workbook.

L2 Assign and review Chapter 28 activities in the Marketing Math Workbook.

L3 Assign and review Chapter 28 activities in the *BusinessWeek* Reader and Case Studies.

Marketing Practice

Have students select a product currently on the market that they view as having room for improvement. Tell students to research the product and write a two-page report outlining a marketing research plan to improve the product's sales.

A MATTER OF ETHICS

Conducting Research

Fun Foods has hired Manuel's marketing firm to learn what 20- to 30-year-old women want in a nutrition bar. Manuel's bosses have written a 20-minute marketing survey and sent him and his colleague, Jason, to the mall to interview young women. But when Manuel tells shoppers how long the survey will take, they don't want to participate.

Misleading Respondents

Jason has had no trouble finding women to interview. When they take their lunch break, Manuel asks Jason the secret of his success. Jason says, "I say the survey will take only five minutes. When they realize more than ten minutes have gone by and they look uneasy, I tell them we're almost done."

THINKING ETHICALLY

Is Jason's behavior ethical? If Manuel decides to keep telling the truth, what should he do when he and Jason submit their results to their bosses?

@ Online Action!

Go to *marketingessentials.glencoe.com/ 28/ethics* to find an activity about ethics and marketing research.

---

industry data to help their members understand the markets for their products.

Nonprofit organizations, such as hospitals, conduct patient satisfaction surveys to improve on programs and services.

Marketing Information Systems

The data collected in marketing research must be sorted and stored so that the results can be put to good use. Many businesses have sophisticated marketing information systems to organize, collect, and store marketing research data for future decisions. A **marketing information system** is a set of procedures and methods that regularly generates, stores, analyzes, and distributes information for use in making marketing and other business decisions. Most marketing information systems rely heavily on data about current customers, overall product sales reports, and inventory levels. Marketers use marketing information systems in many ways, including designing advertising campaigns, developing promotional plans, and selling directly to customers. Data that should be part of a marketing information system include:

- Customer profile data, such as the results of previous marketing studies regarding buying behavior, shopping patterns, customer demographics, and lifestyles research
- Company records, such as sales results, expenses, supplier data, and production schedules
- Competitors' records, such as their prices, products, and market share
- Government data, such as price trends, new regulations and laws, and future projections for the economy
- Marketing research reports that are produced and sold by research firms

Database Marketing

Information technologies have made the collection and analysis of data for decision making much easier. **Database marketing**, or customer relationship management (CRM), is a process of designing, creating, and managing customer lists. These customer lists contain information about individuals' characteristics and transactions with a business. Customer lists are developed from customer touch points such as face-to-face sales, direct-mail responses, telephone or e-mail purchases, service requests, or Web site visits. Marketing lists can also be obtained through third-party companies that specialize in selling databases of names and addresses to specific markets.

A MATTER OF ETHICS — Conducting Research

Discussion Lead a discussion on the ethics of marketing research by asking what, if any, kinds of behavior might be unethical in market research.

THINKING ETHICALLY **Answer:** Answers will vary; most students should understand that intentionally misleading people is unethical. Students might have a hard time deciding if Manuel should tell his bosses that Jason misled people. They might recommend that Manuel wait for his bosses to ask why Jason did so much better than he did.

@ Online Action! For instruction, ideas, and answer guide, go to the Teacher Center at marketingessentials.glencoe.com

Follow Up Ask students to brainstorm ways that Jason and Manuel could achieve their research goal without falsifying information or misleading interviewees.

Once a customer list is developed, it can be used for locating, selecting, and targeting customers with special programs and services.

Ways To Collect Data

Many businesses create special programs to assist in data collection by furnishing "valued customer cards," which add the customer's identity to the purchase. Customers complete an application, which entitles them to special rewards. Over time, the store collects data on customer purchases and analyzes it to better understand household demographics, lifestyles, and purchase behavior.

Consumer Databases

Information about consumers and their buying habits are stored in computer databases. A **database** is a collection of related information about a specific topic. For example, REI, an outdoor recreational products retailer, has a database of people to whom it sends its catalogs. American Express maintains a database of its card members and their

addresses, plus what they buy, where they buy it, where they eat out, and how much money they spend. The company uses the information to send their card members special offers on products, hotels, restaurants, and travel.

Many companies that collect information about their customers often sell that information to others. Banks that provide mortgage loans often share the names and addresses of the borrowers with insurance companies that then send information about mortgage insurance to the borrower. This exchange of information among businesses has led to complaints of invasion of privacy.

Consumer Privacy

The government has created regulations regarding protecting the privacy of consumers. Banks now offer detailed privacy statements that ensure the protection of clients' personal information. Other businesses offer their clients the option of being added to mailing lists, instead of automatically making their contact information available.

SECTION 28.1

CLOSE

Ask students to recall and provide answers to the following questions:

- **Who uses marketing research?**
  Small businesses, large companies, trade associations, government departments, nonprofit organizations

- **What are the difficulties of marketing information systems?**
  They require a significant investment of time and money, and they need trained personnel to maintain and analyze the data.

Critical Thinking

Ask students: Have you ever taken a survey or participated in a focus group for marketing research purposes? What kind of questions were you asked? Have students share their responses in class.

28.1 AFTER YOU READ

Reviewing Key Terms and Concepts

1. Why is marketing research important?

2. Besides individual businesses, who else conducts marketing research?

3. What is a marketing information system?

Integrating Academic Skills

Math

4. According to the European Society for Opinion and Marketing Research, $16 billion was spent on marketing research in 2003. The world's top 25 marketing research companies had total revenues of $10.5 billion. What percentage of the overall research dollars does this represent?

Communication

5. Use the Internet, school media center, or local library to investigate the concept of customer relationship management (CRM). Write a one-page paper on the benefits of business-to-consumer relationships and the specific strategies that can be used to establish them.

 Online Action!
Check your answers at *marketingessentials.glencoe.com/28/read*

marketingessentials.glencoe.com **Chapter 28 - Marketing Research 595**

 (duplicate marker)

AFTER YOU READ

Reviewing Key Terms and Concepts

1. Marketing research is important because it lets producers know what products to produce, it identifies consumer wants, needs, and preferences, it helps solve marketing problems, and it enables businesses to keep track of competition. Marketing research is also necessary to evaluate the effectiveness of marketing plans.

2. Besides individual businesses, various manufacturers, wholesalers, retailers, departments within local, state, and federal governments, and nonprofit organizations conduct marketing research.

3. A marketing information system is a set of procedures and methods that regularly generates, stores, analyzes, and distributes information for use in making marketing decisions.

Integrating Academic Skills

4. $10.5 billion ÷ $16 billion = 0.656, or about 66 percent

5. Papers will vary; all papers and demonstrate an understanding of customer relationship management.

Online Action! Answers at **marketingessentials.glencoe.com/28/read**

FOCUS

Introducing the Section

COLLABORATIVE ACTIVITY

To prepare for reading this section, divide students into groups and have each group flip through a magazine and choose a product advertisement. Have students brainstorm types of marketing research they could conduct to help market this product. Then have each group choose the method that would work best for their particular product and present it to the class. Lead a discussion about why different types of marketing research may work better for different products.

Preteaching Key Terms

Divide students into groups, and have them guess the meanings of the key terms and write them down. Write the key terms across the top of the board and have groups write the meaning under each term. As students read the chapter, they can see which groups guessed correctly.

- quantitative research
- qualitative research
- attitude research
- market intelligence
- media research
- product research

Critical Thinking

Ask students: In what ways can using more than one type of marketing research help a business better identify its target market?

OBJECTIVES

- Identify the methods of conducting marketing research
- Discuss trends and limitations in marketing research

KEY TERMS

- quantitative research
- qualitative research
- attitude research
- market intelligence
- media research
- product research

Types, Trends, and Limitations of Marketing Research

READ and STUDY

BEFORE YOU READ

Predict Many new products are introduced to the marketplace every year. What do you think would happen if marketing research were not used in product development?

THE MAIN IDEA

Using more than one type of research often improves a business's ability to solve problems and successfully market a product.

STUDY ORGANIZER

Use a chart like the one below to note the differences between quantitative and qualitative research.

Types of Marketing Research

Quantitative Research
1.
2.

Quantitative and Qualitative Research

Qualitative Research
1. Attitude Research
2.

WHILE YOU READ

Predict What kinds of marketing research do successful businesses conduct?

Types of Marketing Research

The type of research businesses conduct depends on the problem that they are trying to solve. **Quantitative research** answers questions that start with "how many" or "how much." This type of research usually gathers information from large numbers of people. Quantitative research relies heavily on surveys or questionnaires to obtain information.

596 UNIT 9 - MARKETING INFORMATION MANAGEMENT

READ and STUDY

BEFORE YOU READ

Have students list new products that have come out in the last year. Write these on the board and discuss which products have failed and if students think marketing research was used in their development.

THE MAIN IDEA

Ask students how using different types of research helps a product succeed.

STUDY ORGANIZER

Make your own chart, or download the one at **marketingessentials.glencoe.com**. As study continues, you and the class should work together to complete the chart.

WHILE YOU READ

Model for students how to keep a running list of kinds of marketing research as they read through the section.

Qualitative research focuses on smaller numbers of people (usually fewer than 100) and tries to answer questions about "why" or "how." This type of research relies heavily on in-depth interviews, rather than surveys that have been constructed ahead of time. Most marketing research efforts combine both quantitative and qualitative methods. (See Figure 28.1 for a breakdown of money typically spent on market research in the United States.)

Research is not limited to products; it is also conducted to answer questions about attitudes and behaviors, market segments, advertising media, brands, prices, employees, and every other aspect of marketing. (See Figure 28.2.)

Attitude Research

Attitude research, also known as opinion research, is designed to obtain information on how people feel about certain products, services, companies, or ideas. Satisfaction studies conducted by mail surveys or telephone interviews are the most common ways to get at individuals' opinions. Customers are usually asked to rate "how satisfied" they are with a product or service they purchased or used.

Opinion polls are another example of attitude research. The Gallup Organization conducts opinion polls on politics, elections, business and the economy, social issues, and public policy. Based on random samples of the population, opinion poll results can be generalized to the entire population. A business considering a major expansion might be interested in the attitude of the general population toward the economy.

Consumer panels, also called focus groups, are groups of people who are questioned to provide information on research issues.

Market Intelligence

Market intelligence is concerned with the size and location of a market, the competition, and the segmentation within the market for a particular product or service. Existing market data and new research are used to assemble a profile of present and potential customers, competitors, and the overall industry. Market intelligence helps define potential

---

Figure 28.1 — U.S. Market Research Spending by Category

• **How Marketing Research Dollars Are Spent** In 2001, syndicated spending represented the largest segment of U.S. marketing research expenditures.

What type of research is represented by the survey segment in this figure?

Segment	Annual Spending ($ million)	Percent of Total	Percent Increase Over Previous Year
Qualitative	1,120	18.2	+5.2
Syndicated	2,573	41.8	+9.2
Survey	2,466	40.0	−1.4

Source: *Marketing News Supplement,* June 11, 2002

 Online Action!
Go to *marketingessentials.glencoe.com/28/figure/1* to find a project on marketing research spending.

 marketingessentials.glencoe.com

Chapter 28 - Marketing Research 597

Figure 28.1 — U.S. Market Research Spending by Category

Discussion Ask students to name types of research they think would fall under each category in **Figure 28.1**. Lead a discussion about why companies would spend more money on syndicated and survey research methods than on qualitative research. Answer: Qualitative research usually focuses on small numbers of people and thus costs less than other methods administered to large numbers of people.

Caption Answer Quantitative research is represented by the survey segment.

Online Action! For instructions, ideas, and answer guide, go to the Teacher Center at **marketingessentials.glencoe.com**

TEACH

Discussion Starter

TYPES OF MARKETING RESEARCH
Have students imagine they own a small electronics store. Sales have been down for the last year. They want to conduct marketing research to find out what customers are looking for. Should they conduct quantitative or qualitative research? *Students should answer quantitative.*

Have students brainstorm appropriate survey questions. Ask students what kind of research they do after changes are implemented. *Students should answer qualitative.*

TEACHING POINTS

Demonstrate You may want to bring in examples of quantitative surveys. Ask students to think of similar surveys they have filled out in the past.

Clarify Remind students that marketing research is not restricted to products. Ask students to list questions pertaining to other areas, such as attitude, behavior, market segments, advertising media, brands, etc.

Extend Have students go to a local business and interview the owner or manager, asking if they survey their customers and how they pick their survey questions.

Concept Development

ATTITUDE RESEARCH
Divide students into small groups and have each group create a satisfaction survey about food in the school cafeteria. Have each student in the group write out a copy of the survey; then have groups exchange and fill out each other's surveys. Ask volunteers to discuss how the survey they created was different than the one they filled out. Lead a discussion about the various types of questions that can be on such surveys.

597

TEACH CONTINUED

Concept Development

MARKET INTELLIGENCE

Make photocopies of a market research report covering a specific industry, such as consumer electronics, cosmetics, carbonated beverages, etc. Have students read over the report and jot down notes on the type of information included, such as sales data, sales forecasts, customer demographics, and competitor profiles. Lead a discussion about the information in the report and write an outline on the board as students list the sections.

TEACHING POINTS

Explain Explain to students that many companies pay large amounts of money to purchase market information. Ask students why they think companies find market information so valuable.

Extend Have students keep the market research report and work in class to create a brief summary of the key points of the report.

Extended Activity

Types of Marketing Research
Have students choose one type of marketing research and write a one-page report describing a scenario that uses that type of marketing research.

Figure 28.2 *Types of Marketing Research*

• **What Do Marketers Need to Know?** Marketing research covers all the activities used to gather, analyze, and report information related to marketing. This broad field can be broken down by types of research and defined by the purpose of the research.

How do you find out the kind of marketing information you need to know?

ATTITUDE AND OPINION RESEARCH

Marketers conduct this type of research to discover how people feel about their products, services, or ideas. Satisfaction surveys, such as those sent after a visit to the hospital, and opinion polls, such as those used by political campaigns, are examples of this type of research.

MARKET INTELLIGENCE

Research is used to gather information about an existing or potential market for market intelligence. It defines the size, location, and makeup of the market. This type of research is often done before a new product launch. It is used to guide the marketing efforts for the new product.

MEDIA RESEARCH

This type of research is used to determine the effectiveness of the various media to advertise a good or service. It can be conducted before or after a media campaign.

PRODUCT RESEARCH

This type of research is used to gather information about a product's design, packaging, and usage. It is used to discover how customers react to a new product design or packaging. It can also be used to gather information about how a competing product is designed and packaged.

@ Online Action!
Go to *marketingessentials.glencoe.com/28/figure/2* to find a project on types of marketing research.

Figure 28.2 *Types of Marketing Research*

Discussion On slips of paper write various types of information companies might want to research, such as opinion on customer service, the size of the market for big-screen TVs, response to a commercial, or preference for toothpaste packaging. After students read **Figure 28.2**, have them pull slips of paper from a bowl, read aloud, and identify which type of research would be appropriate. Ask other students whether they agree or disagree with each choice and lead discussion about matching research with purpose.

Caption Answer The type of problem to be solved determines the type of marketing research that is conducted and tells you what you need to know.

@ Online Action! For instructions, ideas, and answer guide, go to the Teacher Center at **marketingessentials.glencoe.com**

target markets for a particular product or service and how to reach potential customers.

A company's existing and projected sales data are part of market intelligence. Sales data help businesses project the potential sales for a product and anticipate problems related to future sales. Sales trends for various products may also be compared to determine whether a product's sales are increasing or declining.

Sales Forecasting

Sales forecasting is an attempt to estimate the future sales of an existing product. A total estimate of a market is calculated, company and competitor sales are analyzed, and then an individual share is estimated for a business.

The share that is assigned to a business is called its market share or sales penetration of

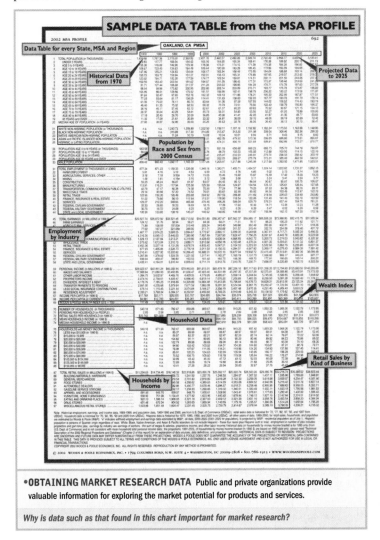

SAMPLE DATA TABLE from the MSA PROFILE

•OBTAINING MARKET RESEARCH DATA Public and private organizations provide valuable information for exploring the market potential for products and services.

Why is data such as that found in this chart important for market research?

TEACH CONTINUED

Individualized Math Skills

L1 Ask students to research and explain how to calculate the market share of a company.
Divide the company's total sales by the total market sales. The result is the company's market share.

L2 Ask students to solve the following problem: A candy company's yearly sales are $250 million. The total candy market for the year is $5 billion. What is the candy company's market share?
$250 million ÷ $5 billion equals 0.05, or 5 percent. The company's market share is 5 percent.

L3 Give students copies of a chart showing two years of sales data (such as 2002 and 2003 data) for various markets. For each market, have students calculate the percentage increase from the previous year and then forecast sales for 2004.

Extended Activity

Sales Forecasting Careers
Ask students to research two to three careers that involve sales forecasting and to list the skill sthat might be necessary in those careers in a brief, one-page summary.

PHOTO GUIDE **OBTAINING MARKET RESEARCH DATA**

Discussion Lead a discussion on some possible uses for this information. Ask students how they think this kind of information was obtained.

Caption Answer The data in this chart provide demographic information that helps define a market (in this case, Oakland, California).

Follow Up Have students select a particular type of information from this profile that could be used to market a certain product, for example, a new type of environmentally friendly automobile.

TEACH CONTINUED

Concept Development

MEDIA RESEARCH

Make transparencies of ten advertisements from a print magazine or newspaper. Allow students to view each ad for about five to ten seconds before switching to the next one. After students have viewed all the ads, have them write down the subject of as many as they can remember. Then ask them to try to remember key details, such as illustrations, colors, slogans, etc. Lead a discussion about which ads stuck most in students' minds and why. Also discuss if students were more likely to remember the type of product or the brand name.

TEACHING POINTS

Extend Have students pretend they are an advertiser. Have students design an effective ad for a product, using construction paper, magazine clippings, markers, etc.

Build Vocabulary

Preview the following words by reading them in context under the heading Media Advertising Measures. Discuss the meaning of these words with the students.

- **audience**
  homes/people exposed to ad

- **frequency**
  times viewer sees/hears ad

- **reach**
  percentage that will see/hear ad

- **ratings**
  total impressions delivered

the market. Based on its research findings, the business can then try to increase its market share through changes in the product, pricing, promotion, or distribution strategies.

Market share estimation and market segmentation research studies are used for new products and services in both consumer and industrial markets. The goal of market share and segmentation studies is to investigate the potential markets for new products and to define characteristics of the target market.

Specialized software programs can assist with forecasting. These computer programs analyze current market data and use this information to predict future sales.

Economic Forecasting

Economic forecasting is an attempt to predict the future economic conditions of a city, a region, a country, or other part of the world. This research requires extensive knowledge of economic statistics and trend indicators.

Case Study

Ad Agency Launches a Video Game Unit

Young & Rubicam, a large, full-service advertising agency, teamed up with Bounce, an event marketing group, in 2004 to start a video game promotional unit called Bounce Interactive Gaming (BIG).

Ad agencies became more interested in video games in 2003, when Nielsen data showed that that men aged 18 to 34—an appealing demographic group for advertisers—were watching less prime-time TV. And Jupiter Research expects that, by 2009, 63 million people in the U.S. will spend at least five hours a week playing video games.

Target Audience

BIG markets products to fans of video games. The company signs deals with video game makers to embed products in the games in the form of a brand of beverage or car, for example. It also hosts video game events sponsored by its products. These events include tournaments for top players or live-satellite feeds to watch tournaments in action.

Captive Audience

Advertising through video games has advantages over advertising on TV. Gamers stay in the room during the course of the game, unlike TV watchers, who sometimes leave the room during commercial breaks. Gamers keep their attention focused on the screen, while TV watchers can lose their concentration. A gamer might also like a product just because it is used by the gamer's onscreen character.

THINK STRATEGICALLY

What are some strategic reasons for a large full-service advertising agency to establish a video game promotional unit?

 Online Action! Go to *marketingessentials.glencoe.com/28/case* to find an activity about advertising and market research.

Case Study   Ad Agency Launches a Video Game Unit

Discussion Have students discuss the advantages and disadvantages of video game advertising versus television advertising. Ask: How are the target audiences different?

THINK STRATEGICALLY **Answer:** It is a new way to reach the gaming audience. A video game promotional unit capitalizes on the increasing popularity of video games and could be more effective than promotion through TV. It is also an opportunity to get into the business before competitors do.

 Online Action! For instructions, ideas, and answer guide, go to the Teacher Center at **marketingessentials.glencoe.com**

Several federal agencies collect information on key economic indicators, such as new building construction, inflation rates, money supply, and consumer and producer price indexes. Most businesses rely on government data to predict economic conditions, and then they adjust their business activities accordingly.

Businesses use research on general economic conditions to help plan for long-range expansion. This research helps to determine whether to cut costs when unfavorable economic conditions, such as higher interest rates or raw materials costs, are predicted.

Media Research

Media research, also known as advertising research, focuses on issues of media effectiveness, selection, frequency, and ratings. Businesses often conduct research to determine which media are most effective for getting an advertising message to a particular market.

Media research studies brand awareness, advertising recall, brand image, effectiveness of advertising copy, and audience size for a particular type of advertising.

Media Advertising Measures

Important statistics for media measurement include audience, frequency reach, and ratings. Audience is the number of homes or people exposed to a particular advertising medium. Frequency is the number of times a viewer in the audience sees or hears an ad. Reach is the percentage of the target audience that will see or hear an ad at least once, while ratings are the total number of audience impressions delivered over a set period of time.

To obtain these important media advertising measures, businesses often request information from the print, broadcast, and electronic media of interest to them. In most cases, the information received would include a rate card listing the advertising costs, its circulation or viewership figures, deadline dates, and other requirements for submission of an advertisement. Other information might

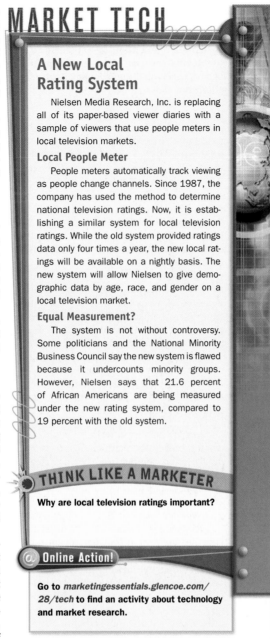

MARKET TECH

A New Local Rating System

Nielsen Media Research, Inc. is replacing all of its paper-based viewer diaries with a sample of viewers that use people meters in local television markets.

Local People Meter

People meters automatically track viewing as people change channels. Since 1987, the company has used the method to determine national television ratings. Now, it is establishing a similar system for local television ratings. While the old system provided ratings data only four times a year, the new local ratings will be available on a nightly basis. The new system will allow Nielsen to give demographic data by age, race, and gender on a local television market.

Equal Measurement?

The system is not without controversy. Some politicians and the National Minority Business Council say the new system is flawed because it undercounts minority groups. However, Nielsen says that 21.6 percent of African Americans are being measured under the new rating system, compared to 19 percent with the old system.

THINK LIKE A MARKETER

Why are local television ratings important?

Online Action!

Go to *marketingessentials.glencoe.com/28/tech* to find an activity about technology and market research.

TEACH CONTINUED

Enrichment

NEW PRODUCT DEVELOPMENT

Have students talk to the manager of a local supermarket to discuss which products have been test marketed in the store within the last few years. How was their store chosen to participate in the test? How did the manufacturer promote the products? Are the products now sold regularly in the store? How was customer feedback solicited on these products? Were changes made to the product as a result of customer feedback? Have students summarize their findings in a two- to three-page report.

Extended Activity

Consumer Privacy

Have students search newspapers, magazines, and online media for stories concerning consumer privacy issues. Article topics may include litigation over privacy issues, new technology that affects consumer privacy, or new laws concerning privacy.

MARKET TECH

A New Local Rating System

Discussion Lead a discussion about the advantages and disadvantages of switching from paper-based viewer diaries to people meters. Ask students why they think the results are different for popular minority shows under the new system.

THINK LIKE A MARKETER | **Answer:** Local television ratings are important because they enable marketers to determine which ads to run on which channels in order to reach their target market. TV ratings are an important measure of TV audience, reach, and frequency. Ads on higher-rated TV shows generate more money for the TV station.

Online Action! For instructions, ideas, and answer guide, go to the Teacher Center at marketingessentials.glencoe.com

SECTION 28.2

ASSESS

Review Guide

CONCEPTS

Ask students to recall the four types of marketing research and give examples of each type.

Attitude and opinion research, market research, media research, and product research. Examples may include: political surveys (attitude/opinion); economic forecasting (market); Nielsen ratings or Internet tracking (media); new product test marketing or product usage surveys (product).

KEY TERMS

Have students review key terms, their spellings, and definitions in small groups.

ONLINE SELF-ASSESSMENT

Have students go to the Section 28.2 practice test at
marketingessentials.glencoe.com

Individualized Review

L1 Assign and review Chapter 28 activities in the Student Activity Workbook.

L2 Assign and review Chapter 28 activities in the Marketing Math Workbook.

L3 Assign and review Chapter 28 activities in the *BusinessWeek* Reader and Case Studies.

Marketing Practice

Have students work in groups of three to four to create a new product they would like to put on the market. Have students research the market their product will be entering and devise a plan to conduct new product development, research competitive products, and conduct product usage research once their product is launched. Have students write a three- to five-page report explaining their plan.

concern the age, income, interests, hobbies, occupations, and attitudes of readers, subscribers, or viewers. Another way to measure advertising research on the various media is to subscribe to *Standard Rate and Data Service* (SRDS), which publishes rates and data for the advertising industry.

Researching Print Advertisements

Marketing researchers can use different techniques to get people's reactions to an advertisement. To determine the ad's effectiveness, readers are asked about the extent to which they noticed the ad, remembered it, and associated it with the advertised brand. The ad is also measured on its ability to change the consumer's beliefs, attitudes, or intended behavior. Using consumer panels is another technique for measuring print advertising effectiveness.

Readership in print media is measured by surveys or estimated by circulation. The Audit Bureau of Circulations provides circulation data on more than 1,500 daily and weekly newspapers and 1,000 periodicals. Mediamark Research and Simmons Market Research Bureau provide audience data. They conduct recent reading studies to see if participants can recall a magazine logotype, have read the magazine, and can remember where they read it during in the past month.

Researching Broadcast Media

Most broadcast ad testing research is done on television commercials. Testing research can use quantitative or qualitative research techniques, such as personal interviews, theater tests, in-home testing, or focus groups, to get reaction to planned TV advertisements.

Nielsen Media Research, Inc. provides audience measurement information for the television industry. Nielsen estimates the audience by measuring the viewing habits of 13,000 people in 5,000 homes. Nielsen's measurement information is recorded by "people meters" on TV sets, VCRs, cable boxes, and satellite dishes that automatically monitor program viewing. Nielsen counts the number of viewers in meter-equipped households to get the number of households using TV, the share of the audience that is tuned to a particular station, and the rating, or percentage of viewers, for a particular television program at a particular time. Broadcast and cable network providers, program developers, distributors, and advertisers use this information to decide on which television programs to advertise.

The Arbitron Ratings Company assembles important data on radio advertising. Arbitron produces radio audience measurements and sells software that analyzes advertising expenditure data. Continuous audience measurement in 267 local markets serving 2,300 radio stations makes it the largest radio audience service in the world. Arbitron contacts more than two million consumers a year and collects more than one million diaries to compile its radio station rating reports. Diaries are records on which people report such viewer data as who is watching or listening to a station and what programs are tuned in.

Using the Internet

The effectiveness of Internet advertising is often measured with tracking studies. Tracking studies can be either Web-centric or user-centric. The Web-centric method logs the total number of people who have visited a Web site and stores the results on the Internet provider's network. The user-centric method involves metering software in a sample household or business that tracks computer usage and Web sites that are visited. The information gained from user-centric tracking can be compiled and analyzed to get an audience profile for a certain Web site.

Product Research

Product research centers on evaluating product design, package design, product usage, and consumer acceptance of new and existing products. Many new products and their packages are designed, tested, changed, and introduced each year. Product research is also conducted to collect information about competitive products. Concept testing is often used in the early stages of product

602 UNIT 9 - MARKETING INFORMATION MANAGEMENT

Online Activity

Online Surveys

Ask students to find an online survey site and take one or more surveys on that site. Have students note if they had to register and what kind of information they had to submit. Ask students how they think the survey company will use their information. Have students share their findings in a one-page analysis.

development (see Chapter 30). Concept testing, product positioning, and pricing studies are frequently done with focus groups or in-depth interviews to get initial consumer reaction to a product or service idea.

Trends in Marketing Research

The nature and scope of marketing research is rapidly changing to keep pace with a changing marketplace. The trend toward a global marketplace means increased international competition for U.S. companies, which must improve or change products frequently to hold on to their customers. In this environment, product quality and customer satisfaction are the keys to business success. Research that measures these qualities has become the fastest growing form of marketing research.

Another important trend is the use of both internal and external information in managing a business. Total quality management (TQM) programs place a premium on gathering and using database research in improving business operations.

Limitations of Marketing Research

The amount of information that can be gathered is limited by the amount of money and time a company can afford to spend on the equipment and by the number of personnel needed to conduct the research.

Marketing research information also has its limitations. Customers in a test market situation may say they want a particular product, but there is no guarantee they will actually buy the product when it is sold.

CLOSE

- Divide students into groups of three or four and have each group choose a topic pertaining to their school about which they will conduct an opinion poll (such as extracurricular activities, academics, school lunches, parking, housing, etc.). Have students make up poll questions that ask about opinions. Each group will then poll a random sample of students and combine their answers. Have groups present their results to the class and discuss how their results can be generalized to the entire student population.

- Lead a discussion comparing and contrasting Web-centric and user-centric tracking. Divide students into small groups of two or three and have them write down examples of when each type of study would be appropriate.

  Examples may include: comparing hits on a company's Web site versus hits on their competitors' sites (Web-centric); studying which Web sites are popular among a demographic (user-centric).

Critical Thinking

Ask students what makes them want to try a new product. Does receiving a free sample or a coupon influence their decision to try a new product? Have students share their responses in class.

28.2 AFTER YOU READ

Reviewing Key Terms and Concepts

1. What are the two types of marketing research?

2. What are the four major areas within marketing research?

3. List at least two trends facing marketing researchers today.

Integrating Academic Skills

Math

4. Assume that you are planning to purchase an exercise and fitness center targeted to women aged 21 to 49 in your city. By doing market research using results from the Consumer Expenditure Surveys and the U.S. Census Bureau, you learn that 1,550 households in your target market spend $475 a year on fitness and recreation. There is one other fitness center that serves 25 percent of your target market. What would be your annual sales forecast for the center?

Geography

5. Investigate a country of your choice and develop a two-page paper on its location, population demographics, and its culture. As part of your report, indicate recommendations for conducting marketing research in the country.

 Online Action!

Check your answers at *marketingessentials.glencoe.com/28/read*

marketingessentials.glencoe.com

AFTER YOU READ

Reviewing Key Terms and Concepts

1. Quantitative and qualitative research.

2. Four major areas of marketing research are attitude research, market research, media research, and product research.

3. Any two of the following: increased emphasis on customer satisfaction; emphasis on total quality management; more integration

of marketing research data with other source; total quality management (TQM) programs. Global trends, technological advances, and concern for privacy are additional answers.

Integrating Academic Skills

4. Sales forecast = $552,187.50
Step 1: 100% − 25% = 75%
Step 2: 1,550 × .75 = 1,162.5 households
Step 3: 1,162.5 × $475 = $552,187.50

5. Reports will vary. Accept all reports that include required elements and demonstrate an understanding of marketing research.

Online Action! Answers at **marketingessentials.glencoe.com/28/read**

CAREERS IN MARKETING

Lifelong Learning

CAREER INFORMATION

Have students go to marketingessentials.glencoe.com and find Chapter 28 Careers page and click on the link for the American Marketing Association's Careers Strategies and Tips. Ask students to select one article, read it, and summarize it in three short paragraphs.

MARKETING RESEARCH

There are many ways to study marketing research. Most community colleges or extension programs will offer classes and seminars on marketing research topics, including questionnaire design, focus group techniques, statistics courses, and methods of analysis for survey information. These courses are often taught by professional market researchers from local businesses.

Primary Source

Ask students to go to marketingessentials.glencoe.com and find Chapter 28 Resources. Ask them to click on the link for the American Marketing Association's marketing dictionary and read the definitions of any terms related to marketing research they find.

THINKING CRITICALLY

The consumer information provided by market surveys lets businesses know what current customers and potential customers want and need.

@ Online Action!

For instructions, ideas, and answer guide, go to the Teacher Center at marketingessentials.glencoe.com

MICHELLE DAY
SENIOR RESEARCH ANALYST
THE STEVENSON COMPANY

? What do you do at work?
Clients and I work together to develop a survey tool to question current or potential customers. We implement this survey and analyze the results to gain a better understanding of customers' opinions of the question at hand. This information is compiled into a format that is presented to clients, who are then able to meet the needs of their customers and make better business decisions based on the results.

? What skills are most important to you?
Computer skills and communication skills are critical to this job. Other important skills are analyzing, organizing, and time management. Communication is also very important, both effective oral communication with the client to understand their questions and objectives, and written communication to draft the surveys and present the results to the client in a clear and logical format.

? What is your key to success?
Both continuing to learn and receiving constructive criticism have helped me succeed in my job. I have continued to learn by completing an MBA, attending applicable training seminars, and asking questions of those who are more experienced than I am. I welcome constructive criticism from these more experienced professionals, who can help me improve upon the skills I have.

Aptitudes, Abilities, and Skills

Computer skills, communication skills, time management, an analytical mind

Education and Training

Degrees in marketing, communication, or general business are helpful.

Career Path

A successful career path can begin with an assistant position in a marketing department, and continue with responsibilities as market research data analyst.

THINKING CRITICALLY

How are market surveys useful to a business?

@ Online Action!

Go to *marketingessentials.glencoe.com/28/careers* for a career-related activity.

Test-Taking Strategies

Have students create a visual study aid by dividing a piece of paper into four sections and writing one of four types of market research in each section (attitude research, market research, media research, and product research). In each section, have students write key terms and/or draw pictures that relate to each type of research.

FOCUS on KEY POINTS

SECTION 28.1

● Marketing research involves the marketing function that links the consumer, customer, and public to the marketer through information. Marketing information is used to identify marketing opportunities, solve marketing problems, implement marketing plans, and monitor marketing performance. A marketing information system is a set of procedures and methods that regularly generates, stores, analyzes, and distributes marketing information for use in making marketing decisions.

SECTION 28.2

● Marketing research is usually divided into two broad types of research: quantitative and qualitative. Marketing research involves the process and methods used to gather information, analyze it, and report findings related to marketing goods and services. The nature and scope of marketing research are rapidly changing to keep pace with a changing marketplace. Marketing research information provides much information but does have limitations.

REVIEW VOCABULARY

Write each of the following vocabulary terms on the front of a 5" × 8" index card with the correct definition on the reverse. Review the terms and definitions by quizzing another marketing student.

1. marketing research (p. 593)
2. marketing information system (p. 594)
3. database marketing (p. 594)
4. database (p. 595)
5. quantitative research (p. 596)

6. qualitative research (p. 597)
7. attitude research (p. 597)
8. market intelligence (p. 597)
9. media research (p. 601)
10. product research (p. 602)

REVIEW FACTS and IDEAS

11. What is marketing research? (28.1)
12. What is the primary function of a marketing information system? (28.1)
13. What is a marketing database? (28.1)
14. How does quantitative research differ from qualitative research? (28.2)
15. What is attitude research? (28.2)
16. What is market intelligence? (28.2)

17. Why do businesses conduct media research? (28.2)
18. Give an example of one research technique used for new product development and one for product usage research. (28.2)
19. Name one trend and one limitation of marketing research. (28.2)

Chapter 28 - Marketing Research 605

FOCUS on KEY POINTS

Ask volunteers to read the summaries aloud and give the classroom one real-life example for each concept.

REVIEW VOCABULARY

See glossary for definitions of **1–10.**
A sample answer might read:

1. *Marketing research* involves the process and methods used to gather information, analyze it, and report findings related to marketing goods and services.

REVIEW FACTS and IDEAS

11. Marketing research involves the process and methods used to gather information, analyze it, and report findings related to marketing goods and services.

12. To generate, store, analyze, and distribute marketing information.

13. A marketing database is a collection of information on a specific topic, for example, information about the preferences, opinions, habits, trends, and plans of potential customers.

14. Quantitative research deals with evaluations, opinions, attitudes, and behaviors about current and potential customers. Qualitative research focuses on smaller numbers of people (usually less than 100) and tries to discover the basic reasons behind their buying decisions or actions.

15. Attitude research, also known as opinion research, is designed to obtain information on how people feel about certain products, services, companies, or ideas.

16. Market intelligence is concerned with the size and location of a market, the competition, and the segmentation within the market for a particular product or service.

17. Media research is used to determine the effectiveness of the various media to advertise a good or service.

18. New product development: concept testing, pricing studies, brand research, choice study or blind test, test marketing. Product usage: industrial, customer, or employee satisfaction studies.

19. Answers will vary; marketing research trends include the global marketplace, the use of internal and external information in managing a business, and total quality management (TQM). Marketing research limitations include money, time, and the number of personnel needed to conduct the research.

BUILD SKILLS

20. Workplace Skills

Responses will vary; student answers should demonstrate an understanding of ethical business practices. Making changes to incomplete or missing responses will affect the validity of the survey.

21. Technology Applications

Reports will vary; students may choose to focus on one or more companies in the pharmaceuticals market.

22. Math Practice

Total cost: $16,140; 1500 names $\times$ $.30 = $450 (mailing list); 1500 $\times$ $.10 = $150 (printing); 1500 $\times$ $.36 = $540 (mailing costs); $450 + $150 + $540 + $15,000 (writing and analysis) = $16,140

DEVELOP CRITICAL THINKING

23. Press Review

Answers will vary; reports should demonstrate an understanding of a research activity.

24. Marketing Across the Planet

Answers will vary; student explanations and examples should include reference to the difficulties of conducting marketing research across different cultures, such as taking cultural differences into account.

BUILD SKILLS

20. Workplace Skills

Human Relations You have a part-time job in the marketing research department of a large corporation. You and three coworkers are gathering information through mailed surveys. Your supervisor wants each of you to complete at least 30 surveys a day, which can be difficult. One coworker makes changes to incomplete or missing responses on some surveys that have been returned. What should you do?

21. Technology Applications

Analyzing International Trends Use presentation software to present an oral report on the international trends affecting marketing research efforts in the pharmaceuticals market.

22. Math Practice

The Cost of Direct Mail Research Assume that your company plans to send a marketing questionnaire to 30 percent of the names on a mailing list of 5,000 people. The mailing list was purchased from another company for $0.30 per name. Each questionnaire costs $0.10 to print; mailing costs are $0.36 (including the envelope and return envelope) each; and the cost of writing the questionnaire, analyzing the information, and preparing the report is $15,000. What is the total cost?

DEVELOP CRITICAL THINKING

23. Press Review

Review current business publications such as the *Wall Street Journal, Business Week, Forbes, Money, Advertising Age, Brandweek,* and *Sales & Marketing Management.* Find one current research activity and write a one-page report on the nature and scope of the research activity.

24. Marketing Across the Planet

Select a country and an industry or product that interests you. Research this industry or this product in the country of your choice and in the United States, consider how it is marketed, who the target market is, whether there is any import or export exchange. Take notes as you conduct research on the Internet and at the library. Be ready to explain your answer and provide examples. How has the global economy affected marketing research?

 ## Formative Assessment

Formative assessment is an essential component of classroom work. This type of assessment provides information that is then used as feedback to modify teaching and meet student needs.

L1 Have students write a one-page summary of the chapter using all key terms.

L2 Provide scenarios in which each of the four types of marketing research is used. Have students identify they type of marketing research in each scenario.

L3 Have students create flashcards with a marketing research technique on one side and an example of that technique on the other. Flashcards should include the four types of marketing research and the various techniques associated with each type.

 Reteach   **If the results of the formative assessment seem low, consider the following activity:**

Read section subheads aloud and have volunteers give a summary of the section.

APPLY CONCEPTS

25. Identifying Market Factors

Use the Internet to find the U.S. Census Bureau Web site and research your city or state's population, income, education, trading area, and purchasing power. Consult city or state offices for additional market information. For example, you may contact your area's chamber of commerce.

Activity Using presentation software, create an oral report highlighting these marketing factors.

26. Evaluating Research Agencies

Use the Internet to investigate companies that provide customer research, online database searches, and information-brokering services.

Activity Identify four questions that you would ask of a large research agency before you would use its services for media research.

NET SAVVY

27. Researching Market Researchers

Visit the Web site for the American Marketing Association to find Marketing Research Services. Investigate one of the listed companies.

Develop a company profile in 100 to 150 words, describing the company's history, number of employees, and the marketing research that it conducts.

THE **DECA** **CONNECTION**

Role Play: Marketing Research

Situation You are to assume the role of assistant manager of a small hardware store. The store's sales have been steady, but not growing at the rate they should. The store's owner (judge) is concerned about the lack of sales growth and has asked you for some ideas about how to remedy this situation.

Activity You are to suggest some ways to determine the solution to the lack of sales growth and make your suggestions to the hardware store's owner (judge).

Evaluation You will be evaluated on how well you meet the following performance indicators:

- Describe the need for marketing information
- Assess marketing-information needs
- Identify information monitored for marketing decision making
- Demonstrate interest and enthusiasm
- Address people properly

@ Online Action!

For more information and DECA Prep practice, go to *marketingessentials.glencoe.com/28/DECA*

Chapter 28 - Marketing Research **607**

CHAPTER **28** REVIEW

APPLY CONCEPTS

25. Identifying Market Factors
Reports will vary depending on student's selected city and state. Accept all reports containing required elements.

26. Evaluating Research Agencies
Students might ask about the company's data sources, computer technology and related software capabilities, research services offered, professional references, and previous work/contracts.

NET SAVVY

27. Researching Market Researchers
Profiles will vary depending on company chosen. Accept all reports containing required elements: company history, number of employees, and the marketing research it conducts.

THE **CONNECTION**

The students should be evaluated on the performance indicators noted in the role play. For another DECA role play, go to the Competitive Events Workbook or the Student Activity Workbook, or go to **marketingessentials.glencoe.com/28/DECA**

 Online Action! For instructions, ideas, and answer guide, go to the Teacher Center at **marketingessentials.glencoe.com**

DECA Advisors Corner

Acquaint your chapter members with National DECA. Pair up members of your chapter and give them a list of questions that can be answered by viewing DECA's Web site (**www.deca.org**). Have students describe DECA's home page, for instance, identify the national officers.

MINI-QUIZ

Read these sentences to the students and have them volunteer the missing word(s).

1. _____ is the marketing function that links the consumer, customer, and public to the marketer through information. (Marketing research)

2. A set of procedures and methods that regularly generates, stores, analyzes, and distributes marketing information is called a(n) _____. (marketing information system)

3. A collection (or file) of related information on a specific topic is known as a(n) _____. (database)

For an expanded chapter quiz, go to Chapter 28 in the TeacherWorks CD-ROM and to Chapter 28 in the **ExamView®** Pro Test Generator CD-ROM.

CHAPTER 29

Chapter Overview

Chapter 29 introduces the methods used to collect data for marketing research. Students will learn how to differentiate primary data from secondary data and how to design and conduct surveys.

BUILD BACKGROUND

Initiate discussion about how businesses decide to introduce new products and eliminate old ones. For example, what factors might prompt restaurants to add low-fat meals to its menu? How can the restaurant determine if its customers are pleased with this addition? Tell students they are going to learn how businesses conduct marketing research.

Why It's Important

Businesses that want to increase their customer base must have information about the attitudes and behaviors of current and prospective customers. Marketing research provides data for the development of strategies that will increase sales and profits.

Prepare to Read

Ask a volunteer to write all of the major headings on the board in outline format:

The Marketing Research Process Constructing the Questionnaire

Tell students to fill in the secondary headings as they preview or read the chapter. They will then have a thorough chapter outline to use as study notes.

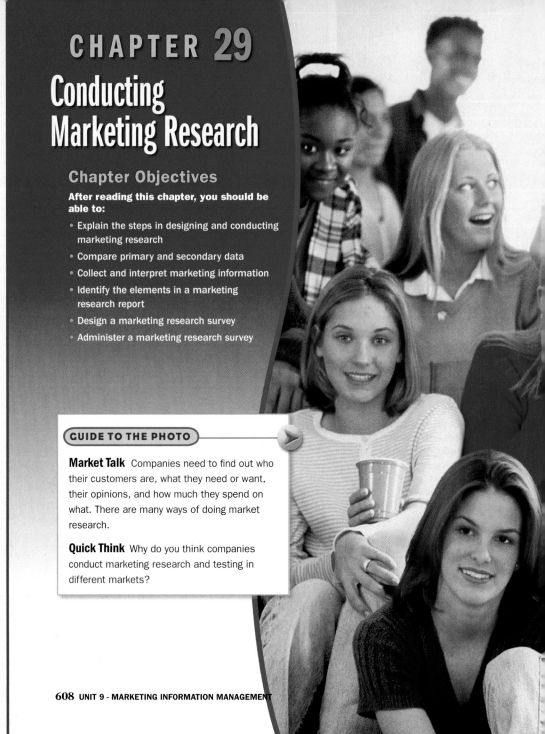

CHAPTER 29
Conducting Marketing Research

Chapter Objectives

After reading this chapter, you should be able to:

- Explain the steps in designing and conducting marketing research
- Compare primary and secondary data
- Collect and interpret marketing information
- Identify the elements in a marketing research report
- Design a marketing research survey
- Administer a marketing research survey

GUIDE TO THE PHOTO

Market Talk Companies need to find out who their customers are, what they need or want, their opinions, and how much they spend on what. There are many ways of doing market research.

Quick Think Why do you think companies conduct marketing research and testing in different markets?

GUIDE TO THE PHOTO

Market Talk Lead a discussion about marketing research surveys. Ask students if they have ever participated in a survey. Ask: What was the format of the survey? What kinds of questions did they answer? They may name questions about age, gender, income, products purchased, satisfaction with these products, and more.

Quick Think Student responses may include: Customers in different markets may have different needs and preferences. Companies must determine how to adapt their products or services to each market.

 Follow Up Ask students to name three factors that may differentiate one market from another.

THE DECA CONNECTION

An Association of Marketing Students

Performance indicators represent key skills and knowledge. Relating them to the concepts explained in this chapter is your key to success in DECA events. These acronyms represent DECA events that involve knowledge of concepts in this chapter.

AAAL	FMAL	MMS	TMDM*
AAML	FMDM	QSRM	TSE
ADC	FMML	RMAL	VPM
BSM	FSRM	RMML	
EMDM	HMDM*	SMDM	

In all these DECA events you should be able to follow these performance indicators:

- Identify information monitored for marketing decision making
- Describe sources of secondary data
- Search the Internet for marketing information
- Monitor internal records for marketing information
- Collect marketing information from others
- Conduct an environmental scan to obtain marketing information
- Describe the use of technology in the marketing-information management function
- Describe techniques for processing marketing information
- Interpret descriptive statistics for marketing decision making
- Write marketing reports
- Present report findings and recommendations

Events with an asterisk (*) include this performance indicator: Complete a property analysis. **HMDM** and **FMDM** also include additional performance indicators: Explain the concept of product in the hospitality industry and in the financial services industry respectively.

DECA PREP

Check your understanding of DECA performance indicators with the DECA activity in this chapter's review. For more information and DECA Prep practice, go to *marketingessentials .glencoe.com/29/DECA*

Chapter 29 - Conducting Marketing Research **609**

THE DECA CONNECTION

An Association of Marketing Students

DECA events that require knowledge of how to conduct marketing research are described here. Discuss the performance indicators to make sure students understand how to demonstrate their understanding.

The events acronyms stand for:

AAAL:	**Apparel and Accessories Marketing Series, AL**
AAML:	**Apparel and Accessories Marketing Series, ML**
ADC:	**Advertising Campaign Event**
BSM:	**Business Services Marketing Series**
EMDM:	**E-Commerce Management Team Decision Making Event**
FMAL:	**Food Marketing Series, AL**
FMDM:	**Financial Analysis Management Team Decision Making Event**
FMML:	**Food Marketing Series, ML**
FSRM:	**Full Service Restaurant Management Series**
HMDM:	**Hospitality Services Management Team Decision Making Event**
MMS:	**Marketing Management Series**
QSRM:	**Quick Serve Restaurant Management Series**
RMAL:	**Retail Merchandising Series, AL**
RMML:	**Retail Merchandising Series, ML**
SMDM:	**Sports and Entertainment Marketing Management Team Decision Making Event**
TMDM:	**Travel and Tourism Marketing Management Team Decision Making Event**
TSE:	**Technical Sales Event**
VPM:	**Vehicles and Petroleum Marketing Series**

DECA PREP

Find timed DECA Prep activities correlated to the Competitive Events Workbook for students and DECA tips for teachers at **marketingessentials.glencoe.com /29/DECA**

CHAPTER 29 Classroom Resources

For the Teacher

- TeacherWorks
- marketingessentials.glencoe.com
- Interactive Chalkboard
- **Exam***View*® Pro Test Generator
- Fast File Unit 9

For the Student

- *Marketing Essentials* Online Edition
- Student Activity Workbook
- Marketing Math Workbook
- Marketing Research Project Workbook
- School-to-Work Activity Workbook
- Competitive Events Workbook
- *BusinessWeek* Reader and Case Studies
- marketingessentials.glencoe.com

FOCUS

Introducing the Section

COLLABORATIVE ACTIVITY

To prepare for reading this section, have students work in groups to discuss the following situation: A bakery specializing in cakes for special occasions serves customers who are mostly middle-class, two-income families with children. The owner would like to expand her business by adding a breakfast/lunch restaurant. How would she decide whether or not her target market would support this addition? On the board, list students' suggestions under the appropriate step in marketing research.

Preteaching Key Terms

Write the key terms on the board. Then read aloud the definitions, but not in order. Ask students to match the key terms with their definitions.

- problem definition
- primary data
- secondary data
- survey method
- sample
- observation method
- point-of-sale research
- experimental method
- data analysis

Tell students to write down the key terms and their definitions as they read this section.

Critical Thinking

Ask students: When conducting marketing research, why must a company define the problem before attempting to collect data?

OBJECTIVES

- Explain the steps in designing and conducting marketing research
- Compare primary and secondary data
- Collect and interpret marketing information
- Identify the elements in a marketing research report

KEY TERMS

- problem definition
- primary data
- secondary data
- survey method
- sample
- observation method
- point-of-sale research
- experimental method
- data analysis

WHILE YOU READ

Predict Consider the sequence of steps in marketing research. What would happen if one of the steps were omitted?

The Marketing Research Process

READ and STUDY

BEFORE YOU READ
Predict Why do you think that an organized process is necessary to conduct marketing research?

THE MAIN IDEA
Businesses that want to increase their customer base must have information about the attitudes and behaviors of current and prospective customers. Marketing research can provide insight for strategies that will increase sales and profits.

STUDY ORGANIZER
Construct a flow chart like the one below to record the steps in conducting marketing research.

The Marketing Research Process

Step 1: Define the Problem

The Marketing Research Process

The five steps that a business follows when conducting marketing research are defining the problem, obtaining data, analyzing the data, recommending solutions, and applying the results. Each step is performed sequentially to arrive at solutions to a problem or research issue. Figure 29.1 provides more details about each step in the research process.

610 UNIT 9 - MARKETING INFORMATION MANAGEMENT

READ and STUDY

BEFORE YOU READ
Lead students in identifying consequences of conducting marketing research without an organized process.

THE MAIN IDEA
Ask a volunteer to read the main idea aloud. Then ask students to suggest specific ways a business might gather information about the attitudes and behaviors of customers.

STUDY ORGANIZER
Model the study organizer for students by filling in the second step in the chart. A full-size, downloadable study organizer can be found at marketingessentials.glencoe.com

WHILE YOU READ Students might indicate that all steps need to be followed to make the marketing research process effective.

Figure 29.1 · The Marketing Research Process

• **Five Steps** Marketing research helps businesses find solutions to problems. There are five steps in the marketing research process, beginning with defining the problem or research issue and ending with applying the results of the research. Following the steps in sequence is important, since each step depends on the steps that preceded it.

What can researchers do after the data are analyzed?

1 DEFINING THE PROBLEM

The problem or research issue is identified and goals are set to solve the problem.

2 OBTAINING DATA

Researchers obtain data from primary and secondary sources.

3 ANALYZING DATA

Researchers compile, analyze, and interpret the data.

4 RECOMMENDING SOLUTIONS

Researchers come up with potential solutions to the problem and present them in a report.

5 APPLYING THE RESULTS

The research results are put into action.

 Online Action! Go to *marketingessentials.glencoe.com/29/figure/1* to find a project on the marketing research process.

marketingessentials.glencoe.com   Chapter 29 - Conducting Marketing Research **611**

TEACH

Discussion Starter

STEP 1: DEFINING THE PROBLEM

Have students brainstorm five or six issues that need to be addressed in your school. By group consensus, choose the four most pressing problems. Then divide students into four groups and assign one problem to each group. Have each group set goals to solve the problem and present their solutions to the class.

TEACHING POINTS

Model Organize a mock school board meeting where each group presents an argument for why and how the assigned problem needs to be addressed. If the administration can only address one problem at the moment, which would it choose, based on the groups' arguments? Have students vote for the most convincing presentation.

Extend Encourage the groups to find alternative, creative solutions that involve less time, money, or resources than their selected plan.

Build Vocabulary

Preview the following words by reading them in context. Ask students to explain what each word means. Then ask them to name a synonym.

• **sequentially** in order
• **facilities** services
• **pose** present or ask

Figure 29.1 · The Marketing Research Process

Discussion After students read **Figure 29.1**, discuss the five steps in the marketing research process. Ask students to identify a problem a company might face, and then discuss how to solve this problem using the steps.

Caption Answer The researchers come up with potential solutions and present them. Then, the research results can be put into action.

Online Action! For instructions, ideas, and answer guide, go to the Teacher Center at **marketingessentials.glencoe.com**

Follow Up Divide the students into small groups. Have each group brainstorm three possible solutions that the company might apply.

Concept Development

STEP 2: OBTAINING DATA

Ask students to determine if the following data are primary or secondary.

- a personal interview response to a new cereal packaging design (primary)

- a U.S. government demographic report (secondary)

- statistics from the SBA on the number of small business start-ups (secondary)

- IBM's five-year sales figures (secondary)

- marketing research conducted by Procter & Gamble for a new dishwashing liquid (primary)

- a jewelry store's customer buying records (secondary)

- census data from the State of Ohio (secondary)

- an opinion research poll conducted by IBM for a new computer it plans to introduce in a year (primary)

- a survey conducted in a supermarket by a representative of a new ice cream manufacturer (primary)

- statistics from a magazine on population in the South (secondary)

Step 1: Defining the Problem

The most difficult step in the marketing research process is defining the problem. **Problem definition** occurs when a business clearly identifies a problem and what is needed to solve it. That is, the business identifies a research question and the information that is necessary to answer it.

Take, for example, a convention and resort center that wants to know if its staff, services, and facilities are meeting the needs of its guests. The business needs this information so that it can continually improve its services as a resort and convention destination.

With the problem defined, the researcher can create objectives for the study that will help answer the research problem. Objectives might include: determine how satisfied different categories of guests are with reservation procedures, accommodations, guest services, and meeting and recreational facilities.

Objectives are used to develop the actual questions that will be included in the research instrument. You will learn more about writing questions later in this chapter. For now you simply need to know that objectives and questions must correlate with one another. Here are two examples:

- **Objective:** Determine guest satisfaction with facilities.
  Question: On a scale of 1 to 5, with 1 being poor and 5 being excellent, how would you rate the following resort facilities? (list of facilities)
- **Objective:** Determine if vacationers and convention-goers differ in levels of satisfaction with the resort and convention center.
  Question: What was the primary purpose of your visit?

This question is necessary so that ratings by guest type can be analyzed separately. If this question was not included in the research instrument, the above objective could not be accomplished.

Because money and time are limited, each business has to determine which problems and issues are the most important to address at a given time.

Step 2: Obtaining Data

The second step in the marketing research process is obtaining data. During this second step, data are collected and examined in terms of the problem or problems being studied.

The word *data* means facts. There are two types of data used in marketing research: primary and secondary. **Primary data** are data obtained for the first time and used specifically for the particular problem or issue under study. **Secondary data** have already been collected for some purpose other than the current study. Secondary data are less expensive to collect than primary data. Therefore, it is most cost effective for a company to decide what secondary data it can use before collecting any primary data.

How Secondary Data Are Obtained

Secondary data are obtained from both internal sources (sources within the company) and external sources (sources outside the company). An excellent source of internal secondary data is the marketing information system of a business. As explained in Chapter 28, a marketing information system is an internal method of getting data used to measure monthly sales, determine the geographic distribution of customers, track customer buying patterns, and identify popular items on the market. Secondary data are most often collected in the following ways:

Internet Sources

The Internet has increased the availability of secondary data from a variety of sources. Since most companies have a Web address, some secondary information is available for free through a company's home page. A company's description of its products, services offered, locations, sales revenue, number of employees, product specifications, and pricing is often available. But since Web site information is used primarily for promotional

Online Activity

Data Finder

Ask students to use FedWorld or the Federal Web Locator to locate government Web sites which contain demographic data. Have students use this data to create a one-page profile for a particular part of the country. Have students share their profiles in class.

Extended Activity

Types of Data

After students have read the section on obtaining data, ask them to imagine that a television service company wants to expand its premium package to include five more channels. The company needs to know which additional channels would most please their current and prospective customers. Have students brainstorm types of primary and secondary data that could provide this information.

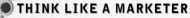

NET MARKETING

Paying Your Bills Online

One in four American households now pays bills online each month. Online bill pay makes paying bills quick and convenient. Some services even allow users to establish their own payment schedule.

There are two approaches to Internet bill payment. Each month a person may go to a specific company's Web site and pay a particular bill, such as the water bill. This usually means making stops at the Web sites of several companies.

One-Stop Bill Pay

The other method uses consolidation. Banks, credit card companies, and portals such as Yahoo, MSN, and Quicken let consumers pay multiple bills in one place. Most portals charge a monthly fee. AOL Bill Pay is an exception: America Online subscribers can make Internet bill payments for free.

AOL does not act as a payment intermediary, but it provides links to the Web sites of each company, where transactions take place directly between the consumer and merchant. AOL says its research shows that most people prefer to make payments at a merchant's Web site, because they get faster credit for last-minute payments. Payments handled by an intermediary can take five days or longer to clear.

> ### ● THINK LIKE A MARKETER
> Why is AOL offering a free online bill paying service, rather than charging for the service?
>
> **@ Online Action!**
>
> Go to *marketingessentials.glencoe.com/ 29/net* to find an activity about the Internet and marketing research.

---

purposes, all information should be verified through other, more objective sources.

Digital dossiers, which provide company profiles on public corporations, income statements, and balance sheets, are also available online. These reports and databases can be purchased for a fee from business clearinghouses, such as Hoover's Online, Factiva, Standard and Poor's NetAdvantage, LexisNexis, and Mergent Online.

U.S. and State Government Sources

State departments of commerce and small business development centers assist with business and economic development activities and can also provide useful information.

Data collected by U.S. government agencies regarding population demographics, specific markets, industries, products, economic news, export information, and legislative trends

can be accessed on the Internet for free or for a nominal cost. FedWorld and the Federal Web Locator are two Web directories with links to most government Web sites that provide such data. The Small Business Administration, U.S. Department of Commerce, U.S. Census Bureau, U.S. Securities and Exchange Commission, and the Bureau of Labor Statistics can also be excellent sources for secondary data.

Publications such as the *Census of the Population* and the *Statistical Abstract of the United States* contain hundreds of tables, graphs, and charts that can be useful when analyzing information, such as income, age, and family size, in areas as small in size as zip codes.

Specialized Research Companies

An active and growing number of specialized research companies, or syndicated services, also offer secondary data for business needs.

 marketingessentials.glencoe.com

Chapter 29 - Conducting Marketing Research 613

NET MARKETING

Paying Your Bills Online

Individualized Practice

HOW SECONDARY DATA ARE OBTAINED

L1 Have students make a list of objective sources they could use to verify data collected from a company's Web site.

L2 Ask students to suggest secondary sources where they might obtain information for the following three scenarios:

- A company wants to know if consumers will continue to purchase 35mm cameras five years from now.
- A company wants to determine whether there is a demand for household cleaners in the international market.
- A clothing company wants to know its chief competitor's current prices for long-sleeved T-shirts.

L3 Have students select a company with a Web site. Tell them to imagine they are working for a competing company. Ask students to write a thorough report about the other company, using data obtained from that company's Web site. Make sure they include suggestions for their own company's improvement based on the information obtained.

Discussion After students have read Net Marketing, lead a discussion about the advantages and disadvantages of paying bills online.

● THINK LIKE A MARKETER **Answer:** AOL is hoping free bill payments will help stop people from leaving its dial-up Internet access for high-speed services. AOL hopes that by offering free online bill payments, customers who take the trouble to set up the accounts will remain more loyal than those who do not.

@ Online Action! For instructions, ideas, and answer guide, go to the Teacher Center at **marketingessentials.glencoe.com**

TEACH CONTINUED

Concept Development

ADVANTAGES AND DISADVANTAGES OF SECONDARY DATA

Ask students to identify the specific advantages and disadvantages of secondary data in the following scenario: An athletics company wants to introduce an innovative running sandal to its existing line of footwear. The company must collect data to determine if enough customers would purchase the new sandal to outweigh the production costs.

Answers might include the following: advantages—the company will save money and time; disadvantages—there is no existing data for running sandals, meaning the company does not have a price to match and no way of knowing customer demand for this product.

To follow up, ask students to suggest a situation in which a company might rely solely on secondary data.

Individualized Practice

HOW PRIMARY DATA ARE OBTAINED

L1 Have students list three examples of data that could only be attained through primary research.

L2 Divide students into small groups. Ask each group to devise a situation in which a small company might benefit from hiring a research organization to collect primary data.

L3 Ask students to select a national research organization. Ask them to research the organization and write a review of the organization's services, fees, and special interests.

Specialized companies sell demographic data, five-year forecasts, consumer purchase information, business data, census information, and consumer classification reports to businesses. Syndicated services make this data available in print and electronic formats.

An example is Mediamark Research, Inc. (MRI), which provides comprehensive demographic, lifestyle, product usage, and exposure data to all forms of advertising media. MRI is the nation's leading producer of multimedia audience research for advertisers, agencies, and magazines. The company also provides research in consumer marketing, brand loyalty, promotional opportunities, and trade marketing services, as well as many other types of market research services.

Business Publications and Trade Organizations

Secondary data can also be obtained in business publications such as *Forbes, BusinessWeek,* the *Wall Street Journal,* and *Sales & Marketing Management.* National and statewide trade associations often publish secondary data in articles, reports, and books.

Examples of trade associations for marketing research include the Advertising Research Foundation, American Association for Public Opinion Research, American Marketing Association, Council of American Survey Research Organizations, and the Marketing Research Association. Check the *Small Business Sourcebook* or the *Encyclopedia of Business Information Sources* to identify major books, trade journals, and organizations for specific business categories.

Advantages of Secondary Data

The greatest advantage of secondary data is that they can be obtained easily, because the data are on the Internet; in corporate, public, and college libraries; or available for purchase from syndicated services. The U.S. Census Bureau can provide nationwide data that would cost any firm a great deal of time and money to research on its own.

Disadvantages of Secondary Data

There are two major disadvantages associated with secondary data. First, the existing

---

data may not be suitable for the problem under study.

The other disadvantage is that secondary data may sometimes be inaccurate. Federal census data are collected every ten years. As a result, projections based on the most recent census may not be correct for the current year.

How Primary Data Are Obtained

Primary research data can be obtained through company research projects or specialized research organizations. Large companies frequently have their own marketing research staff to conduct primary research for the company. However, both large and small companies make use of research organizations. National research organizations often contract with businesses and organizations to provide attitude and opinion, market, media, and product research services. AC Nielsen, Arbitron, Synovate, IMS Health, and Westat are some of the leading research organizations in the United States. Primary data may be collected using three methods: the survey method, the observation method, and the experimental method.

The Survey Method

The **survey method** is a research technique in which information is gathered from people through the use of surveys or questionnaires. It is the most frequently used method of collecting primary data.

When designing a survey, marketers must determine the number of people to include in their survey. Researchers can survey the entire target population if it is small. This is called a census. Usually, though, researchers cannot survey the entire target population, because the population is too large, and time and money are limited. Instead, researchers use a sample of the entire target population to get survey results. A **sample** is a part of the target population that represents it accurately. The size of the sample depends on the amount of money the company has to spend and the degree of accuracy that is needed. Generally speaking, the larger the sample, the more accurate the results.

Extended Activity

Focus Group Interviews

Ask students: What procedures might companies use to select participants for a focus group interview? Have interested students find online or other focus groups and give a brief, five-minute oral summary of what they found in class.

After determining the size of the population to survey, a marketer must decide what type of survey to conduct. Surveys can be conducted in person, by phone (using personal calls and prerecorded messages), by mail (regular and e-mail), or by using the Internet. When the marketer has decided exactly how to conduct the survey, he or she then writes the questions according to the specific needs of that survey type.

Technological Methods

Survey research can now be conducted through online surveys and focus group chat sessions on the Internet. Fax broadcasting allows businesses to send questionnaires to a select group of fax numbers. Automated dialers increase the number of telephone survey responses by placing multiple calls and automatically rejecting those with busy signals and answering machines. Digital surveys allow a prerecorded voice to qualify a respondent and then ask a series of survey questions. Interactive voice response is similar to voicemail as callers are greeted by a recorded voice that leads them through a series of questions. Responses can be given using the telephone keypad.

Interviews

The personal interview involves questioning people face-to-face. Since door-to-door interviews are expensive, researchers often conduct interviews in central locations. Because this type of interview began in shopping malls, it is called a mall intercept interview.

A form of personal interview is the focus group interview. A focus group interview involves eight to twelve people who are brought together to evaluate advertising, a particular product, package design, or a specific marketing strategy under the direction of a skilled moderator.

The moderator must direct the discussion to accomplish the objectives of the study. Focus group facilities usually include conference rooms, observation rooms, and audiotape and videotape equipment.

•**MARKET RESEARCH** Conversations with consumers are essential to market researchers who need accurate market intelligence on which to base their strategies.

How would research about an existing product differ from research about a brand new one?

A major advantage of personal interviews is that it is often easier to get people to respond to personal interviews than to mail, phone, or Internet surveys. A disadvantage, however, is the cost associated with personal interviews. Personal surveys are easy to administer, but it takes time to get survey responses tabulated for data analysis.

The telephone interview is quick, efficient, and relatively inexpensive. However, this method is now limited by the new do-not-call-list rules.

A mail survey is a relatively inexpensive way to reach a potentially large audience. With a direct-mail survey, a business can use visual presentation techniques. Respondents are generally honest in their responses, and they find mail surveys to be less intrusive.

Unfortunately, even a successful response rate for mail surveys is only ten percent. Average response rates can be improved for questionnaires by offering some type of incentive to complete them.

Internet-based surveys are quick and eliminate data entry, since the responses are automatically tabulated when the survey is completed.

Internet-based research allows for real-time data collection, multiple-choice questions, and

Chapter 29 - Conducting Marketing Research **615**

Individualized Practice

INTERVIEWS

L1 Tell students to imagine they work for an ice cream business that would like to conduct mall intercept interviews. Have students identify at least three central locations that might be ideal for gathering customer feedback.

L2 Ask students to brainstorm additional incentives that companies might offer for people willing to complete and return their mail questionnaires. Ask: What factors determine the incentives a company could realistically offer?

L3 Ask students to write a five-paragraph essay explaining how to improve the participation rate of the telephone interview.

Enrichment

ATTITUDE AND OPINION RESEARCH

Have students investigate how three different companies conduct attitude and opinion research. Make sure students include at least one local business in their exploration, such as a grocery store, post office, or restaurant. In these cases, students may visit the business and interview a manager. For other companies, have students look online for examples of attitude and opinion surveys. Do all three companies conduct research in the same way? How do their approaches differ? Ask students to prepare a brief, one- to two-page report on their findings.

PHOTO GUIDE   MARKET RESEARCH

Discussion Lead a discussion about consumer market research by asking students if they have ever been interviewed for or participated in market research.

Caption Answer Market research about a new product requires finding out if there is a need for a new product. Researching an existing product involves asking for consumers' reviews and opinions, competition analysis, and finding information about the usage of the product.

Follow Up If students have not participated in market research, ask them to imagine their reaction to being approached for a mall intercept or telephone interview.

ASSESS

Review Guide

CONCEPTS

Ask students to explain the process of data analysis.

Answer suggestion: The process involves compiling, analyzing, and interpreting the results of primary and secondary data collection. Then this data may be organized in a chart or other visual aid to clearly present the results.

KEY TERMS

Have students review key terms, their spellings, and definitions in small groups.

ONLINE SELF-ASSESSMENT

Have students go to **marketing.essentials.glencoe.com** for the Section 29.1 practice test.

Individualized Review

L1 Assign and review Chapter 29 activities in the Student Activity Workbook.

L2 Assign and review Chapter 29 activities in the Marketing Math Workbook.

L3 Assign and review Chapter 29 activities in the *BusinessWeek* Reader and Case Studies.

Marketing Practice

Divide the class into groups of four or five students. Have each group develop a list of 15 questions for a survey on the impact of window displays. Appoint a presenter from each group to share the questions they would ask shoppers. As a class, select the best questions and compile a survey. Have the students administer the survey and write a one-page report explaining the results.

---

open-ended, text-based answers. A drawback is that Internet surveys are limited to individuals who have access to the Web. Also, many people dislike receiving uninvited e-mail surveys.

The Observation Method

The **observation method** is a research technique in which the actions of people are watched and recorded either by cameras or by observers. Properly performed and recorded observations supply better results than those obtained with survey techniques.

Another use of observation called mystery shopping is used to view the interaction between customers and employees. A mystery shopper is a researcher who poses as a customer and goes into a business to observe employees and operations.

One disadvantage of the observation method is that it cannot measure attitudes or motivation. Observation provides information on what the person does, but not why the person does it.

Observation research is faster than personal interviews, and people are unaware that they are being observed, so they are acting as they normally would. This type of research is also cost effective.

Point-of-sale research is a powerful form of research that combines natural observation with personal interviews to get people to explain buying behavior. Point-of-sale researchers observe shoppers to decide which ones to choose as research subjects. After observation, researchers approach the selected shoppers and ask them questions. They can easily remember the reason why they purchased a product because customers have just made the decision to buy.

The Experimental Method

The **experimental method** is a research technique in which a researcher observes the results of changing one or more marketing variables while keeping other variables constant under controlled conditions. The experimental approach is often used to test new package designs, media usage, and new promotions.

The experimental method is infrequently used for marketing research because of the cost of setting up the research situation and the inaccuracy of the responses.

Step 3: Analyzing the Data

The third step in the marketing research process is data analysis. **Data analysis** is the process of compiling, analyzing, and interpreting the results of primary and secondary data collection.

A-P Super Service, Inc., surveyed customers about the quality of the auto mechanics' repair service. The number of customers who returned the survey was 120. Answers to questions were organized so that the percentage of men and women responding to each question could be shown clearly. Data were cross-tabulated to determine such things as how men and women differ in their perceptions of the service. The answers to a question about the quality of service might be presented as shown below. The number of respondents is given in parentheses after the question.

Question: How would you rate the quality of service provided by A-P Super Service, Inc? (N = 120)

Rating	Men	Women
Excellent	30%	60%
Good	15%	10%
Average	20%	20%
Fair	20%	5%
Poor	15%	5%

As you can see, female customers of A-P Super Service, Inc., have a more favorable impression of the quality of service than the male customers do. This information shows the owner that the shop's image among its male customers needs to be improved.

Data Mining

Data mining is a computer process that uses statistical methods to extract new information from large amounts of data. A database may contain subtle relationships or patterns that only a mathematical search process can identify.

Extended Activity

The Observation Method

After students have read the section on the observation method, ask them to imagine that they work for the research department of a cookie company. The company wants to know more about its current and potential consumers so it can update its marketing approach. Ask students to devise a research plan based on the observation method. Ask: What factors must they take into consideration? Have students share their responses in class.

Step 4: Recommending Solutions to the Problem

The conclusions drawn from the research are usually presented in an organized and well-written report. Recommendations must be clear and well supported by the research data. A typical research report includes the following:

- Title page
- Acknowledgments of people who assisted in the research effort
- Table of contents
- List of tables, figures, charts, and graphs
- Introduction (includes the problem under study, its importance, definitions, limitations of the study, and basic assumptions)
- Review of the research information (including the results of any secondary data reviewed for the research effort)
- Procedures used (research technique or techniques used to obtain primary data)
- Findings
- Recommendations
- Summary and conclusions
- Appendixes
- Bibliography

Step 5: Applying the Results

In evaluating the research, managers may find that the research was inconclusive, additional research is needed, or the research suggests specific courses of action. After the research has been completed and changes made, a business should carefully monitor the results. A business needs to know whether the specific actions taken are successful. The research effort has been a success if decisions made as a result lead to increased profits through better sales, increased efficiency, or reduced expenses.

29.1 AFTER YOU READ

Reviewing Key Terms and Concepts

1. Name four sources of information to use in collecting secondary data.
2. What are two advantages and two disadvantages of using secondary data?
3. How does survey research differ from observation research?

Integrating Academic Skills

Math

4. Research indicates that 80 percent of a flower shop's customers live within one mile of the store, another 15 percent live within two miles of the store, and the remaining 5 percent live within five miles of the store. Compute the number of customers who live within the various trading areas if the population of the entire area is 14,240.

Reading and Language Arts

5. Research a company in your community to find out how it collects demographic information about its customers. Write a 250-word report on how customer information (name, address, phone, occupation, age, spending patterns, etc.) is collected and used.

 Online Action!

Check your answers at *marketingessentials.glencoe.com/29/read*

marketingessentials.glencoe.com **Chapter 29 · Conducting Marketing Research** 617

SECTION 29.1

CLOSE

Ask students to recall and provide answers to the following questions:

- **How does data mining aid in data analysis?**
  As a computer process, it helps analyze data by extracting new information that only a mathematical search can identify.

- **After completing all five steps of the marketing research process, how will a company know if its research effort was a success?**
  The company should monitor the decisions made as a result of the research; if the decisions lead to increased profits through better sales, increased efficiency, or reduced expenses, then the research was a success.

Critical Thinking

Ask students: How can the results of a mystery shopping experience improve customer service?

AFTER YOU READ

Reviewing Key Terms and Concepts

1. Answers include any four of the following: a business's marketing information system, Internet sources, government sources, specialized research companies, business publications, and trade organizations.

2. Answers will vary; two advantages might include that secondary data can be obtained easily and inexpensively. Two disadvantages might include that secondary data might not be suitable for the problem under study and can be out of date or otherwise inaccurate.

3. The survey method gathers information through surveys or questionnaires. The observation method collects data by observing people.

Integrating Academic Skills

4. Within one mile: 11,392; 14,240 × .80 = 11,392. Between one and two miles: 2,136; 14,240 × .15 = 2,136. Between two and five miles: 712; 14,240 × .05 = 712

5. Answers will vary; all reports must include the name of the company and an explanation of how customer information is collected and used.

 Online Action! Answers at *marketingessentials.glencoe.com/29/read*

SECTION 29.2

FOCUS

Introducing the Section

COLLABORATIVE ACTIVITY

Have students brainstorm a list of three problems for which a business might use marketing research. Write each problem as a column heading on the board. Have each student choose one of the three problems and write three questions that could be asked about it on a research questionnaire. Write students' questions under the appropriate column. Then, ask students to identify the questions as open-ended or force-choice.

Preteaching Key Terms

Read the key terms aloud, or ask a volunteer to read them. Ask students to guess the meanings of the terms by using each one in a sentence.

- validity
- reliability
- open-ended questions
- forced-choice questions

Critical Thinking

Ask students: What are the advantages and disadvantages of using open-ended questions and forced-choice questions on surveys?

OBJECTIVES

- Design a marketing research survey
- Administer a marketing research survey

KEY TERMS

- validity
- reliability
- open-ended questions
- forced-choice questions

The Marketing Survey

READ and STUDY

BEFORE YOU READ

Predict Why is the survey method an important tool for obtaining information?

THE MAIN IDEA

Businesses need valid and reliable data to make good decisions. Marketing researchers need to know how to construct survey instruments that provide the necessary information to assist in the decision-making process.

STUDY ORGANIZER

Complete an outline of Section 29.2 by listing headings, subheadings, and key concepts.

WHILE YOU READ

Compare and Contrast How do written survey instruments and scripted interviews differ?

Constructing the Questionnaire

As a major form of quantitative research, questionnaires should provide data that have validity. A questionnaire has **validity** when the questions asked measure what was intended to be measured. A researcher designs a questionnaire to measure a retail store's customer service. Questionnaires that are poorly written or that do not address customer service will not have validity.

READ and STUDY

BEFORE YOU READ

Lead students in suggesting reasons why the survey is an important tool for obtaining information. Answers might include: surveys collect customer feedback in an organized way.

THE MAIN IDEA

Ask a volunteer to read the main idea aloud and ask another student to retell it in his or her own words.

STUDY ORGANIZER

Model the study organizer for students by filling in the first numbered blank. A full-size, downloadable study organizer can be found at marketingessentials.glencoe.com

 WHILE YOU READ Let students know that both methods usually survey a sample of the target population and may include an incentive for people to participate.

Research questionnaires should also have reliability. **Reliability** exists when a research technique produces nearly identical results in repeated trials. Reliability requires that the questions ask for the same type of information from all the respondents. Questions should be clear and easily understood so that all participants understand the question in the same way. Asking a respondent in a restaurant survey, "Was your food hot?" would not yield a reliable answer. "Hot" could be interpreted as either the level of spiciness or the temperature of the food.

To be valid and reliable, a questionnaire must be properly written, formatted, and administered.

Writing Questions

Survey questions can be either open-ended or forced-choice. **Open-ended questions** ask respondents to construct their own response to a question. "What changes or additions to this coat would you recommend?" is an example of an open-ended question. Some surveys have a space for general comments or suggestions on the survey instrument. This is also a type of open-ended question. Open-ended questions generate a wide variety of responses that are sometimes difficult to categorize and tabulate. As a result, most researchers prefer forced-choice questions.

Forced-choice questions ask respondents to choose answers from possibilities given on a questionnaire. Forced-choice questions are the simplest questions to write and the easiest to tabulate. They can be two-choice questions, multiple-choice questions, rating or ranking scales, and level of agreement scales.

Yes/No Questions

Two-choice questions give the respondent only two options, usually yes or no. Yes/no questions should be used only when asking for a response on one issue. You could use a yes/no question to ask "Was our facility clean?" or "Was our facility well maintained?", but not to ask "Was our facility clean and well

maintained?" The customer may have different answers for the two issues that the question addresses. Having a question that asks about more than one issue decreases validity and reliability.

Yes/no questions are most often used as filter questions. Filter questions help to guide respondents to answer only those questions that apply.

In cases where there is a range of choices and yes/no questions are not appropriate, you would use multiple-choice questions, rating scale questions, or level of agreement questions.

Multiple-Choice Questions

Multiple-choice questions give the respondent several choices. When constructing multiple-choice questions, it is important to make the options mutually exclusive and comprehensive enough to include every possible response. In order to be sure that all options are covered, many surveys have a space for the option "other." A rental company might ask its customers the following question:

When you have a choice of all the car rental companies listed below, which do you prefer? (check only one)

☐ Alamo   ☐ Hertz
☐ Avis   ☐ National
☐ Budget   ☐ Thrifty
☐ Dollar   ☐ Other _____
☐ Enterprise

Offering the choice of "other" increases reliability. If "other" was not an option, respondents who use an unlisted car rental service might not answer at all or might pick an inaccurate answer from the list just to give an answer. This action would cause misleading results.

Rating Scale Questions

Other forced-choice questions may ask respondents to rate a product or service based upon a scale. A variety of scales may be used, such as a rating scale from very satisfied to very dissatisfied, or from excellent to poor.

Chapter 29 - Conducting Marketing Research **619**

Extended Activity

Multiple-Choice Questions

Bring in examples of multiple-choice surveys from the Internet. Have students guess what kind of company distributed each survey. Then ask students to guess the problem the survey was designed to address. Next, ask students to select a topic that interests them. Have them create a survey about this topic to distribute to their classmates. The survey should be comprised of 10–20 good multiple-choice questions. Have students complete the surveys and compile the results.

TEACH

Discussion Starter

WRITING QUESTIONS

Ask students to consider the following: A small health and fitness club has been losing customers since the opening of a larger facility. Some customers have mentioned that the new facility has a swimming pool and a cafeteria—amenities that the small club lacks. The owners are willing to expand their facility, but need to know what customers want. Ask students what questions the owners should ask if they distribute a survey to their current customers.

Concept Development

YES/NO QUESTIONS

To explain the concept of Yes/No questions, give students the following example questions and ask them to explain why they are poorly constructed. Then, ask students to improve the questions:

- **Was your hotel experience enjoyable and problem-free?**
  the respondent may have different answers to "enjoyable" and "problem-free": Was your hotel experience enjoyable? Was your hotel experience problem-free?

- **Do you support the mayor's view on education?**
  the question assumes the respondent already has this knowledge: The mayor's official view on education is_____. Do you support her view on education?

- **Will you ever return to San Francisco?**
  the respondent may not know his or her future plans: Do you plan to return to San Francisco within the next year?

Explain to students that sometimes a question cannot be asked in forced-answer format; the question may need to be completely rewritten.

TEACH CONTINUED

Concept Development

BASIC GUIDELINES FOR WRITING QUESTIONS

Explain to students that a prescreening is helpful before distributing a survey. If a question is biased, the research results could be unreliable. Have students work in small groups to create three survey questions. Ask each group to write one intentionally biased question. Collect and redistribute the surveys among the groups. Ask the groups to identify the biased question. Have the groups rewrite the question so it is no longer biased.

Online Activity

Internet Surveys

Ask students to search the Internet for a survey designed especially for teens. Ask students to complete the survey online. Have them print a copy of the survey questions and bring it to class. Be sure to have students check the Web site to see the survey results.

Virtual Business

Introduce marketing research to students using Knowledge Matters' Virtual Business Retailing visual simulation, *Market Research*. In this simulation, students learn how to collect market information using surveys and how to use the information to make their businesses more successful.

GLOBAL MARKET

Test Marketing for the Hispanic Market

There are many all-purpose household cleaning products available in the United States, but not many of them have been targeted specifically at Hispanic consumers.

Colgate-Palmolive began marketing its Mexican brand, Fabuloso, in the United States in 1997. Since then, its market share has been growing. It rolled out a fabric softener called Suavitel at the same time. Suavitel's share of the Hispanic market in the United States has already topped 10 percent.

Challengers Procter & Gamble added to the competition by introducing Gain fabric softener, in addition to its Gain and Ariel detergents that were already targeted at Hispanic consumers.

SC Johnson challenged Fabuloso all-purpose cleaner by introducing Glade Cleaner-Limpiador. "Limpiador" means "cleaner" in Spanish. The company test-marketed the product in upstate New York in 2004. Glade Cleaner-Limpiador was priced at $2.35 for 30.4 ounces at one store in Rochester, New York. It comes in red and purple bottles that look similar to Fabuloso's packaging. Companies that are introducing new products for the Hispanic market often use stronger scents than in their other products. Glade considered scents including country meadow and lavender for its all-purpose cleaner.

CRITICAL THINKING

Which type of primary research data and methods might these manufacturers have used?

@ Online Action!

Go to *marketingessentials.glencoe.com/29/global* to find an activity about international marketing research.

The following is an example of a rating question that might be used to rate the front desk staff of a resort.

How would you rate your reception by the front desk staff?

Helpfulness
Excellent   Good   Fair   Below Average
Check-In Speed
Excellent   Good   Fair   Below Average
Offering Info About Resort
Excellent   Good   Fair   Below Average
Use of Your Name
Excellent   Good   Fair   Below Average

Level of Agreement Questions

When assessing attitudes or opinions, it is often a good idea to write statements that describe those attitudes or opinions. Then you can ask respondents for their level of agreement with the statements. Commonly used options include *strongly agree* (SA), *agree* (A), *neutral* (N), *disagree* (D), and *strongly disagree* (SD). The following are examples of statements that might be used in a health-related questionnaire.

Indicate your level of agreement with the following statements based on your personal preference:

"I am extremely health conscious."
   SA   A   N   D   SD
"I do not like vegetables."
   SA   A   N   D   SD
"Eating low-cholesterol foods is important to me."
   SA   A   N   D   SD
"The cafeteria should serve heart-healthy foods."
   SA   A   N   D   SD

620 UNIT 9 - MARKETING INFORMATION MANAGEMENT

 marketingessentials.glencoe.com

GLOBAL MARKET

Test Marketing for the Hispanic Market

Discussion After students read Global Market, discuss what factors would be important to consider when constructing a survey primarily for Hispanic customers. Answers might include making the survey available in Spanish.

CRITICAL THINKING **Answer:** Primary research data might include sales records for the test market. Methods could include observation and point-of-sale research.

@ Online Action! For instructions, ideas, and answer guide, go to the Teacher Center at marketingessentials.glencoe.com

As you can see, if someone had to answer yes or no to these questions, the researcher might not get an accurate picture. That is why it is often easier to use descriptive statements for research on attitudes and opinions.

Basic Guidelines for Writing Questions

Each question should be written clearly and as briefly as possible. Use the same ranking or rating scales for all similar questions. It is important not to ask leading questions, which suggest a correct answer. An example of a leading question is: "Do you prefer X or the more reasonably priced Z?" The phrase "more reasonably priced" could cause respondents to answer Z.

You should avoid any bias, which is a systematic error introduced by encouraging one outcome or answer over the others. It is also important to avoid questions that might cause a respondent to guess at the meaning of your question. The following is an example of a question that might cause a respondent to guess:

Case Study

Re-Inventing the Potato

The United States Potato Board wanted to find out why potato sales revenue had not kept up with population growth or the consumer price index.

The Board contracted with the Perishables Group, a specialized research group for growers, shippers, suppliers, commodity boards, and retailers to do the research.

Digging In

The Perishables Group used secondary data: consumer research related to meal trends, food consumption diaries, focus groups, consumer intercepts, lifestyle issues, and census data. To obtain primary data, they interviewed grocery store executives. Category concept testing was done on packaging, cross-merchandising, and secondary locations.

A New Recipe

Research by the Potato Board and the Perishables Group led to the following recommendations: Minor packaging changes were needed, sales could be increased by displaying potatoes in or near meat departments, and better merchandising of bag and bulk varieties was needed. The partners also developed a Retail Marketing Toolkit that provided consumer, trade, and new merchandising concept research, as well as recommendations for assortment, pricing, promotion, and a menu of merchandising options to increase potato sales.

Welcome to the United States Potato Board online information resource for the U.S. Potato industry.

Click on a button below or select a category to continue.

Growers / Industry
Consumer Information
International Buyer
Healthy Potato Resource Center
Media Information

- [International Buyer] - [Consumer Information] - [Media Inform

THINK STRATEGICALLY

Why did the United States Potato Board contract with a research group to study sales of potatoes?

 Online Action!   Go to *marketingessentials.glencoe.com/ase* to find an activity about marketing research.

TEACH CONTINUED

Individualized Practice

FORMATTING

L1 Have students list five ways to strengthen the visual appearance of a questionnaire.

L2 Ask students to find or create an example of a well formatted and a poorly formatted survey. Have them explain why each element is effective or ineffective using one or two sentences.

L3 Have students imagine that their coworker has designed a survey. Both the appearance and content are too casual, using language that would only be acceptable among friends. Ask students to write a memo to the coworker, tactfully explaining how the survey could be revised.

Enrichment

DEVELOPING A SURVEY

Identify one marketing research problem in your community, or have students identify a research problem for a local business. Have students create a ten-question survey for this problem. The survey should contain both open-ended and forced-choice questions.

Critical Thinking

Ask students: Why might a survey be pretested by someone unaffiliated with the company conducting the research?

Case Study   **Re-Inventing the Potato**

Discussion Have students read the Case Study and discuss why a survey alone would not have been an effective method for determining customer satisfaction with potatoes.

THINK STRATEGICALLY   **Answer:** The United States Potato Board needed specialized research assistance to re-invent the potato category and improve the business climate for retailers, shippers and growers. The challenge was to respond to consumer trends and provide retailers with critical information in order to make informed decisions concerning potato category management and development.

Online Action!   For instructions, ideas, and answer guide, go to the Teacher Center at **marketingessentials.glencoe.com**

ASSESS

Review Guide

CONCEPTS

Ask students to describe four kinds of forced-choice questions.

Answers should include basic definitions for yes/no, multiple-choice, rating scale, and levelof agreement questions.

KEY TERMS

Have students review key terms, their spelling, and definition in small groups.

ONLINE SELF-ASSESSMENT

Have students go to marketing.essentials.glencoe.com for the Section 29.2 practice test.

Individualized Review

L1 Assign and review Chapter 29 activities in the Student Activity Workbook.

L2 Assign and review Chapter 29 activities in the Marketing Math Workbook.

L3 Assign and review Chapter 29 activities in the *BusinessWeek* Reader and Case Studies.

Marketing Practice

RESEARCH RESULTS

Have students find a newspaper or magazine article that presents the results of a research survey. Ask: What kinds of questions were included in the survey? In addition to the survey results, what other information did the article provide about the company and the survey? How will the company apply the results? Make sure students look for evidence showing that the survey is valid and reliable. Have students present their findings in a five-minute oral report.

How many students in your high school drink coffee on a daily basis?

☐ Less than 10
☐ 10–49
☐ 50–99
☐ 100–149
☐ 150–199
☐ over 200

Without asking every student, the respondent cannot answer the question without guessing.

When a survey questionnaire is finished, it is a good idea to pretest the wording of the questions. This pretest allows for correction of any misleading questions, directions, or problems on the questionnaire.

Formatting

Questionnaires must have excellent visual appearance and design to appeal to respondents. You should use dark ink, preferably black, on light paper and type that is easy to read. The questionnaire should be short enough to be answered quickly. Section headings or numbers should be placed on all individual survey sections. Numbers should be placed on all individual questions. If your questionnaire requires more than one page, place a note at the bottom of each page to continue to the next page.

Content Formatting

Directions for completing the questionnaire must be clear for each section or group of questions.

General demographic questions about gender, age, ethnic background, and education are typically grouped together at the end of

• **RATING SCALES** Some forced-choice questions ask respondents to reply based on a rating scale.

Why do businesses often use rating scales to measure customer satisfaction?

PHOTO GUIDE   RATING SCALES

Discussion Lead a discussion about rating scale questions by asking why they are helpful in determining customer satisfaction.

Caption Answer Answers may vary; students may suggest that rating scales employ forced-choice questions, which are easy to write, and the results of which are easy to tabulate.

Follow Up Ask students to explain why the Yes/no question, "Were you satisfied?" might not necessarily be a reliable way to determine what services might need improvement.

a questionnaire. This is because respondents are more likely to answer personal questions after completing the other questions. The only time such information is placed at the beginning of a questionnaire is to qualify a respondent. For example, if an interviewer wanted to study the views of people in their twenties, he or she might ask, "Are you between the ages of 20 and 30?" If the person answers yes, the interviewer would administer the survey. If the answer is no, then the person would not be included in the study.

Administering the Questionnaire

All surveys should have deadlines for completion. A mailed questionnaire should be sent first-class with a hand-signed cover letter, and it should be personalized if the potential respondent is known. The cover letter should explain the purpose of the survey and the deadline for returning the questionnaire. A postage-paid return envelope should be included with the questionnaire for the respondent's convenience.

In-Person Surveys

Questionnaires that are not mailed should have a brief explanation of the survey's purpose placed on the questionnaire itself. A plan should be established for selecting participants in an unbiased way. In a personal interview, reactions to visual materials such as ads or actual product samples can be collected.

Incentives

Many questionnaires offer incentives to encourage people to participate. For example, a company may enter each respondent's name into a drawing for a cash prize. Or, each participant may receive a coupon for the company's product.

29.2 AFTER YOU READ

Reviewing Key Terms and Concepts

1. When is a survey valid?
2. What guidelines should be followed to ensure that a questionnaire is effective?
3. Name three techniques to make the format of a questionnaire appealing.

Integrating Academic Skills

Math

4. A retailer conducts a traffic study to estimate yearly sales. Use the following data to estimate yearly sales for the retailer: 1,500 people pass the store each day, seven percent enter the store and spend an average of $14, and the store is open 360 days during the year.

Civics and Government

5. Find a newspaper article dealing with an opinion poll on a local, state, or national issue. Write a 100-word summary of when and how the poll was conducted, and what the results indicated.

 Online Action!
Check your answers at *marketingessentials.glencoe.com/read*

CLOSE

Ask students to recall and provide answers to the following questions:

- **What are the two qualities that a research questionnaire should have?**
  validity and reliability

- **What are four ways to administer a questionnaire?**
  by mail, through the Internet, by telephone, and in person

- **What are some factors to consider when administering a survey in-person?**
  Answers may include dress in a businesslike manner, carry a clipboard to hold your questionnaires, be polite, establish a plan for selecting participants in an unbiased way.

 Online Activity

Research Organizations
Assign each student a research firm from American Marketing Research's list of the top 50 U.S. research organizations, which is available online. Ask students to research the firm's research specialty, some of its major clients, and the cost of its services. Have students prepare a one- to two-page report detailing their findings.

AFTER YOU READ

Reviewing Key Terms and Concepts

1. A survey is valid when the questions measure what was intended to be measured.

2. Surveys must be properly written, formatted, and administered.

3. Any of the following techniques are acceptable: excellent appearance and design; section headings or numbers; clear directions; demographic questions grouped together; a variety of question types.

Integrating Academic Skills

4. $529,200; 1,500 × .07 = 105 people; 105 × $14/person = $1,470 a day; $1,470 × 360 days = $529,200

5. Students should identify the issue, the type of campaign (local, state, or national), how the opinion poll was conducted, and the results.

Online Action! Answers at **marketingessentials.glencoe.com/29/read**

CAREERS IN MARKETING

Lifelong Learning

CAREER INFORMATION

Have students go to marketingessentials.glencoe.com, find the Chapter 29 Careers page, and click on the link for the American Marketing Association's Careers Strategies and Tips. Ask students to select one article, read it, and summarize it in three short paragraphs.

MARKETING RESEARCH

Conducting marketing research requires a particular skill set. It may be an attractive career to detail-oriented individuals who thrive on the challenging of predicting customer responses and who enjoy using their analytical skills and technology skills in their work. Defining the problem and selecting the necessary data to solve the problem are skills that will benefit students now and in the future.

Primary Source

Ask students to go to marketingessentials.glencoe.com and find Chapter 29 Resources. Ask them to click on the link for the American Marketing Association's marketing directory and read the definition of any marketing research-related terms they find.

✺ THINKING CRITICALLY

Public speaking is a valuable skill because being able to communicate well with others is essential in school, in one's personal life, and in many professions.

@ Online Action!

For instructions, ideas, and answer guide, go to the Teacher Center marketingessentials.glencoe.com

---

CAREERS IN MARKETING

D. CLAY KELLY
DIRECTOR OF MARKETING
STRAND ASSOCIATES, INC.

❓ What do you do at work?
My primary job is to support the efforts of our staff as we seek new work opportunities. Our "product" is professional services, namely engineering design. I make visits to city and county leaders as well as state and federal officials whose jobs are related to construction and capital improvements projects that require engineering services. My goal is to develop a relationship between the decision makers and our firm so that we are completely in tune with the needs of the client.

❓ What skills are most important to you?
People skills are the most important. I fully believe that everyone is a salesperson or a marketer, regardless of their position or chosen career. This applies to almost anyone, whether you're a farmer selling cattle, a businessperson trying to increase market share, or a religious leader creating interest in a specific belief.

❓ What is your key to success?
You have to believe in what you're marketing. In my case, I'm marketing the professional capabilities of my fellow engineers. I am convinced they are among the best in our business and they are dedicated to helping our clients succeed. A reputation is built over a lifetime, but can be destroyed in a moment. Protect your integrity as you would your life and success will be yours in the richest sense of the word.

Aptitudes, Abilities, and Skills

Verbal, written, and interpersonal skills are crucial; public speaking is equally essential.

Education and Training

General business degrees are helpful, along with degrees in marketing and economics, and industry-specific courses.

Career Path

Marketing careers arise within virtually all medium to large companies, often through entry level jobs, marketing or otherwise.

✺ THINKING CRITICALLY

Why is public speaking such a valuable skill?

@ Online Action!

Go to *marketingessentials.glencoe.com/careers* to find a career-related activity.

◨ Test-Taking Strategies

Use a piece of notebook paper to model for students how to write down key terms and names of concepts in one column and their definitions and explanations in another column. Show that by folding the paper in half, they have a study guide.

FOCUS on KEY POINTS

SECTION 29.1

● The five steps that a business follows when conducting marketing research are defining the problem, obtaining data, analyzing the data, recommending solutions, and applying the results. The steps are performed sequentially to arrive at solutions to a problem or research an issue.

SECTION 29.2

● Questionnaires should provide data that are valid and reliable. Marketing surveys may include open-ended and forced-choice questions. Forced-choice questions include yes/no, multiple-choice, rating scale, and level of agreement questions.

● To obtain unbiased data and increase response rates, market researchers must follow guidelines when constructing, formatting, and administering surveys.

REVIEW VOCABULARY

Write one correct sentence on conducting marketing research for each of the following terms.

1. problem definition (p. 612)
2. primary data (p. 612)
3. secondary data (p. 612)
4. survey method (p. 614)
5. sample (p. 614)
6. observation method (p. 616)
7. point-of-sale research (p. 616)
8. experimental method (p. 616)
9. data analysis (p. 616)
10. validity (p. 618)
11. reliability (p. 619)
12. open-ended questions (p. 619)
13. forced-choice questions (p. 619)

REVIEW FACTS and IDEAS

14. Identify in correct order the five steps used in designing and conducting a research study. (29.1)

15. What is the difference between primary and secondary data? Why should researchers consider one type first? (29.1)

16. Identify the three methods used to collect primary data. (29.1)

17. What is the survey method of research? Describe four ways to conduct surveys. (29.1)

18. Identify the elements in a final marketing research report. (29.1)

19. When constructing the options for multiple-choice questions, what is important to remember? (29.2)

20. When do you use level of agreement questions on a questionnaire? (29.2)

21. Name two examples of how bias can be introduced into a questionnaire. (29.2)

22. What can be done when administering a question to encourage people to participate? (29.2)

Chapter 29 - Conducting Marketing Research **625**

FOCUS on KEY POINTS

Ask a volunteer to read the summaries aloud. Then ask another student to explain the key points in his or her own words.

REVIEW VOCABULARY

See glossary for definitions of **1-13.**
A sample sentence might read:

10. A marketing research questionnaire has *validity* when the results measure what was intended to be measured.

REVIEW FACTS and IDEAS

14. The five steps are: 1.) defining the problem; 2.) obtaining data; 3.) analyzing data; 4.) recommending solutions; and 5.) applying the results.

15. Primary data are obtained specifically to address the problem under consideration. Secondary data were collected for some other purpose. Secondary data are also readily available at little or no cost and should be used before gathering primary data. Therefore, researchers should consider secondary data first, because it is less expensive to obtain.

16. The three methods of collecting primary data are the survey method, the observation method, and the experimental method.

17. Survey method: A research technique of which information is gathered from people directly through the use of questionnaires. Surveys can be conducted by mail, telephone, Internet, or by personal interview.

18. Title page: acknowledgments; table of contents; lists of illustrations; introduction; review of the literature; procedures used to obtain primary data; findings; recommendations; summary and conclusions; appendices; and bibliography.

19. It is important to remember to make the options mutually exclusive and comprehensive enough to include every possible response.

20. You use these questions on a questionnaire when accessing attitudes or opinions.

21. Answers will vary but should demonstrate an understanding of the concept of bias; bias could be introduced by asking leading questions or asking questions that require respondents to guess the answer because they do not have the knowledge to answer them.

22. Incentives can be offered to encourage participation.

BUILD SKILLS

23. Workplace Skills

Answers will vary; students may suggest letting a supervisor or manager handle the situation.

24. Technology Applications

Data will vary by county. Graphic representations can include sketches, bar graphs, pictures, and other visual aids.

25. Math Practice

Phone = $5.50/survey ($250 + $1250 + $1250 = $2750) ÷ 500 = $5.50

Mail = $5.00/survey ($500 + $2,000 = $2,500) ÷ 500 = $5.00

Internet = $.51/survey = ($250 + $5.00 = $255) ÷ 500 = $.51

DEVELOP CRITICAL THINKING

26. Language Arts

Student should state that despite the best marketing research and planning, businesses cannot escape risk in the marketplace.

27. Conducting a Focus Group

Student responses should demonstrate that they understand the purpose of a focus group. Alternatives include: 1) Conduct a focus group with customers in the shop (learn what existing customers think). 2) Ask attendees at a cosmetics convention to participate in an informal focus group (learn what professionals think). 3) Conduct a focus group at the local mall (find out what non-customers think).

BUILD SKILLS

23. Workplace Skills

Human Relations You are employed in a shopping mall where a natural observation study is occurring. Your coworker thinks that this research technique is an invasion of privacy and is threatening to tell customers that they are being observed. How should you handle this situation?

24. Technology Applications

Using Secondary Data Sources Locate the U.S. Census Bureau's Web site and the County Business Patterns Economic Profile for your county. Use this profile to identify the number of employees in your county and the annual payroll for your county. Find the total estimated employment by size of business and locate the industry area in your county that employs the most people. Make a graphic representation of the data that you found.

25. Math Practice

Research Costs What would be the per person costs to complete a phone, mail, or Internet survey for 500 people given the following costs:
Phone: $250 for phone; $1250 for interviewers; $1250 for data entry
Mail: $500 for printing/postage; $2,000 to open envelopes and enter data
Internet: $250 create/deliver; $5 to convert data.

DEVELOP CRITICAL THINKING

26. Language Arts

Write a one- to two-page paper addressing the question, "Can business risks be eliminated by conducting marketing research?" Provide a supporting rationale for your answer. Explain what types of risk can be eliminated and why. Try to give specific company examples each time.

27. Conducting a Focus Group

The owner of a cosmetics boutique wants to conduct a focus group to determine whether carrying some organic beauty products would be a good business move. However, this owner does not have a marketing budget and is unwilling to pay several thousand dollars to an outside market research company.

What could the owner do to still have a focus group while keeping costs down?

List at least three ideas and explain why each idea would bring in valuable market research data.

Formative Assessment

Formative assessment is an essential component of classroom work. This type of assessment provides information that is then used as feedback to modify teaching and meet student needs.

L1 Have students identify and define key terms.

L2 Provide various examples of a company gathering data in story form. After each story, have the students identify the data as primary or secondary.

L3 Ask students to create stories that illustrate how a company might gather data.

 Reteach If the results of this formative assessment seem low, consider the following activity:

Ask students to create a chapter quiz for each subhead. Then redistribute the quizzes throughout the class and have them answer the questions.

APPLY CONCEPTS

28. Finding a Marketing Research Firm

Locate the Web page of *Quirk's Marketing Research Review*. Search for a firm in your state or city that performs marketing research.

Activity Develop a one-page profile that includes the company name, a company description, research services it provides, and the industries, markets, or audiences served.

29. Constructing a Questionnaire

Construct a 15-item written survey instrument that would assess student satisfaction with a current policy affecting your school community, such as student parking. Use a combination of yes/no, multiple-choice, rating scale, and level of agreement questions.

Activity Share your final document in class. Brainstorm on possible improvements. Form groups of two or three and administer the questionnaire to students on campus during lunch and recess breaks. Share the results and the experience in class.

NET SAVVY

30. Market Research Online

Perform an Internet search for the WorldOpinion Web site. Select "Periodicals" then click on "The Frame." Look in the archives for an article about a recent trend or issue within the field of marketing research. Identify the title of the article, date, and author, and complete a 50-word summary of the trend or issue.

marketingessentials.glencoe.com

CONNECTION

Role Play: Marketing Research

Situation You are to assume the role of researcher at a marketing research company. You have recently been assigned a high school student as a summer intern (judge). The duties are that the intern (judge) assist you with your tasks and in turn, you are to provide the intern (judge) training in the marketing research your company conducts. Today you are going to explain the sources of marketing data, particularly secondary data.

Activity You are to explain to the intern (judge) the importance of secondary data and sources of that data.

Evaluation You will be evaluated on how well you meet the following performance indicators:

- Identify information monitored for marketing decision making
- Describe sources of secondary data
- Search the Internet for marketing information
- Monitor internal records for marketing information
- Collect marketing information from others (e.g., customers, staff, vendors)

 Online Action!

For more information and DECA Prep practice, go to *marketingessentials.glencoe .com/29/DECA*

Chapter 29 - Conducting Marketing Research **627**

APPLY CONCEPTS

28. Finding a Marketing Research Firm

Answers will vary based upon the city or state where the students are located.

29. Constructing a Questionnaire

Students responses should demonstrate they understand how to use the different kinds of questions and how to create questions that can provide useful data.

NET SAVVY

30. Market Research Online

Student summaries will vary; all summaries should demonstrate an understanding of the marketing research trend and identify the source of the article.

MINI-QUIZ

Read these sentences to the students and have them volunteer the missing word(s).

1. The most difficult step in the marketing research process is _____. (problem definition)

2. Specialized research companies that provide secondary data for businesses are known as _____. (syndicated services)

3. The most popular method of collecting primary data is the _____ method. (survey)

For an expanded chapter quiz, go to Chapter 29 in the TeacherWorks CD-ROM and to Chapter 29 in the **Exam***View*® Pro Test Generator CD-ROM.

THE DECA CONNECTION

The students should be evaluated according to the performance standards noted in the role play. For another DECA role play, go to the Competitive Events Workbook or the Student Activity Workbook, or go to **marketingessentials.glencoe.com/29/DECA**

 Online Action! For instructions, ideas, and answer guide, go to the Teacher Center at **marketingessentials.glencoe.com**

DECA Advisors Corner

Encourage members to participate in either individual or chapter written events. Form a support network/advisory panel for students to utilize during the research and writing process. Appropriate business professionals and teachers make excellent members of advisory panels. It is also helpful for students to read previous winning entries.

MARKETING INTERNSHIP

A SIMULATED ◀DECA PRODUCT AND SERVICE MANAGEMENT EVENT

Research Male Grooming Products

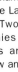

BASIC BACKGROUND

The male grooming industry is big—with estimates between $5 billion and $8 billion in annual sales, and it's still growing. Some large companies already active in this market include Unilever, Procter & Gamble, Estee Lauder, and Nivea. Two smaller companies enjoying success are American Crew and Sharps. Sharps' brands include products such as Kid Glove Shave Gel and Guck-in-a-Puck for hair styling.

Branching Out Your firm's client, G&G Cosmetics, is looking to take advantage of the trend of sales growth in male grooming by starting a new line of products for the "modern-day guy." Currently G&G makes cosmetics and personal grooming products for young women of different ethnic backgrounds. Its competitively priced products are sold in department stores. To grow its business, however, it now must expand into other markets.

YOUR OBJECTIVE

Your objective is to conduct a marketing research study of the target market. You need to provide G&G Cosmetics with a customer analysis and recommendations on how to create and market products for this new target market.

ASSIGNMENT AND STRATEGY

- **Get the background** To get started you need to conduct secondary research on the personal grooming industry for men. Find out sales figures, profitability, pricing strategies, and the most popular products. Then, identify questions to ask in a marketing research study.

  You will need to learn what grooming products are used by the target market, what their motivations are, what needs and wants are not being met, where they shop, and what media are part of their daily or weekly routine.

- **Conduct the research and write the report** State G&G Cosmetics' main problem and the objectives of the study.

- **Choose a format** Decide on the marketing research format(s) that will work best to achieve the objectives. Identify the target population and how participants will be selected.

READ to WRITE

Men's Grooming Around the World
Ask the class to research the men's cosmetics market in Europe and Asia. Have students find out how the market has been developing in those regions and apply their findings to the American market. Students should then write a one-page essay detailing the information they found about foreign markets, and have them create guidelines for a domestic version of the market. Encourage students to be specific about their product(s) and their target market(s).

Design the instrument you will use (written questionnaire, focus group questions, etc.).

Conduct the study and take note of any incidents that may create bias or limit your study's conclusions. Highlight the most important findings and include tables and charts to make it easy to see the details of your findings.

Use your data to provide recommendations and a plan to implement those recommendations for the client. Include a section on the limitations of your study.

- **What your project should include** Include samples of all materials used in your marketing research study and examples of any marketing ideas in your recommendations.

 ### YOUR REPORT

Use a word processing program and presentation software to prepare a double-spaced report and an oral presentation for G&G Cosmetics. Use Glencoe's *Marketing Research Project Workbook* as a resource. See a suggested outline and key evaluation points at *marketingessentials.glencoe.com/internship*

marketingessentials.glencoe.com

BUILD YOUR PORTFOLIO

Option 1 Internship Report
Once you have completed your Marketing Internship project and presentation, include your written report and a few printouts of key slides from your oral presentation in your Marketing Portfolio.

Option 2 Conducting a Customer Satisfaction Study Design a customer satisfaction survey for a company of your choice. After conducting the study, explain the methodology, conclusions from your findings, limitations, and recommendations. Prepare your written report using a word processing program and use presentation software for your oral presentation. See a suggested outline and key evaluation points at *marketingessentials.glencoe.com/portfolio* and use Glencoe's *Marketing Research Project Workbook* as an additional resource.

@ Online Action!
Go to *marketingessentials.glencoe.com/Unit/9/DECA* to review information management concepts that relate to DECA events.

Marketing Internship **629**

Unit Review

Make sure students understand the importance of marketing research for making sound business decisions, and that marketing research involves a process in which the steps must be followed sequentially to obtain the best results. Have students create a visual representation of the marketing research process and the various types of marketing research. Display their work on the bulletin board.

STEP AHEAD
Discuss with students how marketing research can be used to plan the creation of new products. Ask them to describe the pitfalls of offering new products without conducting marketing research.

Internship Wrap-Up

Explain to students that many men are not comfortable with men's skin care or anything that can be considered somehow not masculine. Ask students how they would market a concept that may seem socially radical to some.

Answers may include focusing on very precise markets, such as those who wear couture fashions, or presenting it as scientifically based—and not aesthetic—grooming.

BUILD YOUR PORTFOLIO

Explain to students that portfolios provide evidence of their knowledge and skills in working with data, people, and concepts. Developing a portfolio can be a valuable career development and planning tool. Point out to students that they should include a variety of work to show their versatility. Encourage students to check the portfolio information available at **marketingessentials.glencoe.com/u9/internship**.

Peer Review
Fellow students who share common interests can serve as reviewers of the final portfolios. This review can be completed through the use of a checklist. Go to **marketingessentials.glencoe.com/u9/internship** to find a suggested checklist.

UNIT 10 | Product and Service

Chapter 30
Product Planning

Chapter 31
Branding, Packaging, and Labeling

Chapter 32
Extended Product Features

Unit Objectives

After completing this unit, students should be able to:

- Explain how businesses plan what products to produce and sell and how they position and manage these products
- Explain the nature and scope of product planning, product mix, and product development
- Explain the concept of a product life cycle
- Identify strategies to position products in various life cycles
- Explain the nature and scope of branding, packaging, and labeling in product planning
- Identify the importance of branding, branding elements, and branding strategies to product/service management
- Explain the importance of warranties and credit to product planning
- Discuss the importance of warranties as extended product features

■ Key to
■ Individualized
■ Activities

L1 Level 1 activities are basic activities and should fall within the range of all students.

L2 Level 2 activities are average activities and should be within the range of average and above average students.

L3 Level 3 activities are challenging activities designed for the ability range of above average students.

Enrichment Resources

PROFESSIONAL ORGANIZATIONS

Consumer Federation of America consumerfed.org

Institute of Packaging Professionals iopp.org

MEDIA RESOURCES

Print or online editions of

Manufacturing Talk manufacturingtalk.com

Packaging Digest packagingdigest.com

📖 WRITING SUPPORT

Ask students to think of a manufacturer they prefer, such as a clothing company, music label, or auto manufacturer. Have them write an essay describing at least three reasons why they are loyal to it. Ask students to keep and review this document as they study Unit 10.

Management

UNIT 10 PLANNING GUIDE AND RESOURCES

CHAPTER	PRINT MATERIALS	TECHNOLOGY RESOURCES
Chapter 30 Section 30.1 Section 30.2	**From Unit 10 Fast File Booklet** Lesson Plans Chapter Summaries Reproducible Masters Reproducible Tests **Print Ancillaries** Student Activity Workbook, Chapter 30 Marketing Math Workbook, Chapter 30 *BusinessWeek* Reader and Case Studies, Chapter 30 Competitive Events Workbook, Unit 10 Marketing Research Project Workbook School-to-Work Activity Workbook	Interactive Chalkboard classroom presentations, Chapter 30 Online Learning Center at marketingessentials.glencoe.com Online Student Edition, Chapter 30 TeacherWorks **Exam**View® Pro Test Generator, Chapter 30 Virtual Business
Chapter 31 Section 31.1 Section 31.2	**From Unit 10 Fast File Booklet** Lesson Plans Chapter Summaries Reproducible Masters Reproducible Tests **Print Ancillaries** Student Activity Workbook, Chapter 31 Marketing Math Workbook, Chapter 31 *BusinessWeek* Reader and Case Studies, Chapter 31 Competitive Events Workbook, Unit 10 Marketing Research Project Workbook School-to-Work Activity Workbook	Interactive Chalkboard classroom presentations, Chapter 31 Online Learning Center at marketingessentials.glencoe.com Online Student Edition, Chapter 31 TeacherWorks **Exam**View® Pro Test Generator, Chapter 31 Virtual Business
Chapter 32 Section 32.1 Section 32.2	**From Unit 10 Fast File Booklet** Lesson Plans Chapter Summaries Reproducible Masters Reproducible Tests **Print Ancillaries** Student Activity Workbook, Chapter 32 Marketing Math Workbook, Chapter 32 *BusinessWeek* Reader and Case Studies, Chapter 32 Competitive Events Workbook, Unit 10 Marketing Research Project Workbook School-to-Work Activity Workbook	Interactive Chalkboard classroom presentations, Chapter 32 Online Learning Center at marketingessentials.glencoe.com Online Student Edition, Chapter 32 TeacherWorks **Exam**View® Pro Test Generator, Chapter 32 Virtual Business

National Marketing Education

CHAPTER	SECTION	PERFORMANCE INDICATOR
Chapter 30 **Product Planning**	30.1	Explain the nature and scope of the product/service management function (PSM)
		Explain the concept of product mix (PSM)
		Plan product mix (PSM)
	30.2	Identify the impact of product life cycles on marketing decisions (PSM)
		Describe factors used by marketers to position products/businesses (PSM)
Chapter 31 **Branding, Packaging, and Labeling**	31.1	Explain the nature of branding (PSM)
		Explain branding strategies (PSM)
	31.2	Explain the functions of packaging (PSM)
		Explain labeling laws (PSM)
Chapter 32 **Extended Product Features**	32.1	Explain warranties and guarantees (PSM)
		Indentify consumer protection provisions of appropriate agencies (PSM)
	32.2	Explain the purposes and importance of credit (FIN)
		Explain the purposes and importance of obtaining credit (business) (FIN)
		Describe legal issues affecting business (BME)

BME Business, Management, Entrepreneurship   **FIN** Financing   **PSM** Product/Service Management

Standards Assessment Correlation

	SECTION ASSESSMENT		CHAPTER ASSESSMENT						UNIT LAB
	Reviewing Key Terms and Concepts	Integrating Academic Skills	Review Facts and Ideas	Build Skills	Develop Critical Thinking	Apply Concepts	Workplace Skills	Net Savvy	Marketing Internship
	1	✓	8, 9	15	18	20, 21	✓		✓
	2, 3		6, 7, 10		18	20, 21			✓
	2, 3		8						✓
	3	✓	10, 11, 12, 13	16	18				✓
	1, 2		8, 9, 14	15		20, 21	✓		✓
	1, 2, 3	✓	24, 25	28	32	34	✓	✓	✓
	3	✓	24, 26, 27	28, 30	31, 32	33, 34	✓	✓	✓
	1, 2			29	31, 32	34			✓
	3	✓				34			✓
	1, 2	✓	14–18	25	27				
	3	✓			27	29			✓
	1, 2, 3		19	24, 26	28	30	✓	✓	
			22			30		✓	
		✓	23	26	27, 28	29			

@ Online Action! Check the latest updates for national standards and for your state's standards at **marketingessentials.glencoe.com**

UNIT 10

Product and

Unit Overview

Unit 10 discusses the decisions a business makes in the production and sale of its products. Chapter 30 shows how businesses plan what products to produce and sell. Chapter 31 introduces the nature and scope of branding in product planning. Lastly, Chapter 32 discusses the various types of warranties and credit offerings provided by businesses to support products.

MAKING IT RELEVANT

Ask students to brainstorm why businesses need to know how to introduce new products while keeping other products successful in the marketplace.

Unit Launch Activity

Have students share their first impressions of the ad on this page. Ask them to discuss what kind of product information is given in this ad and to describe how the information is conveyed (for example, through visual elements). Then ask students to decide which components of the ad are most effective at conveying product features and quality.

In this unit you will find

- **Chapter 30**
  Product Planning

- **Chapter 31**
  Branding, Packaging, and Labeling

- **Chapter 32**
  Extended Product Features

More, please

More choice. All the nutrition. Great taste. Friskies® gives your cat the most out of every meal. And more out of life. 49 wet foods, 5 dry and 7 treats.

Friskies for More™

OUT OF TIME?

If class time is too short to cover all the chapters in this unit, go to Unit 10 in your Fast File Teacher Resources booklet and find the Chapter Summaries for Chapters 30, 31, and 32.

 UNIT PROJECT

Presenting Products
Have chapter members complete a 15-minute sales presentation for an item to be sold to a company for resale. Students should stress the product features, brands, warranties, packaging, labeling, and related extended product features. Refer to your guidelines or the guidelines developed by the National DECA Delta Epsilon Chi division for the Sales Representation Event.

Assessment Guidelines Prepare a rubric for evaluation that includes the guidelines developed by National DECA for the Sales Representation Event, or prepare your own guidelines that include the effectiveness and thoroughness of the presentation.

Enrichment Assign and review Unit 10 activities in the Competitive Events Workbook.

Service Management

ANALYZE THE AD

Friskies is a leading cat food brand sold in the United States and in several foreign countries. How does this ad try to appeal to cat owners?

Market Talk Many cat food brands, including Friskies, 9Lives, and Whiskas, feature pictures of cats on their packaging. Iams and Hill's Science Diet are exceptions. Why would they choose not to feature pictures of cats?

Think and Write Look through a grocery store and find five items with appealing packaging that makes you more inclined to buy the product. For each product, note what makes the packaging effective. Does effective packaging have any similarities, even for different kinds of products? Does it make you willing to pay more for the product?

 Online Action! Go to *marketingessentials.glencoe.com/ u10/ad* for an extended activity.

Functions of Marketing

- Marketing-Information Management
- Financing
- Selling
- Pricing
- Distribution
- Product/Service Management
- Promotion

Foundations — Professional Development, Economics, Business, Management, Entrepreneurship, Communication, Interpersonal Skills

In this unit

Foundations of Marketing
- Business, Management, Entrepreneurship

Functions of Marketing
- Product/Service Management

marketingessentials.glencoe.com

631

Marketing Plan

1. **ANALYSIS**
   - SWOT
   - Economic
   - Socio-Cultural
   - Technological
   - Competitive

2. **STRATEGY**
   - Promotion
   - Place
   - Price
   - **Product**

3. **IMPLEMENTATION**
   - Organization
   - Management
   - Staffing

4. **BUDGET**
   - Cost of sales
   - Cost of Promotion
   - Incomes and Expenses

5. **CONTROL**
   - Evaluation
   - Performance Measures
   - Performance Analysis

Marketing Plan

RELATE THE UNIT TO THE MARKETING PLAN

The four Ps of the marketing mix include product, place, pricing, and promotion. Unit 10 focuses on the product aspect.

MARKETING PLAN OVERVIEW

Let students know that all of the decisions a business makes in the production and sale of its products involve aspects of product and service management.

Functions of Marketing

Point out to students that Chapters 30, 31, and 32 will deal with the marketing function of product and service management and the marketing foundation of business, management, and entrepreneurship.

- **Product/Service Management** Branding is an important component to product/service management, as customer perception of a company is a crucial element in determining a business's success.

- **Business, Management, Entrepreneurship** Managers and entrepreneur must juggle many tasks in order to keep a business going. They must know how to introduce new products while keeping old products successful and how to build on their business's success.

ANALYZE THE AD

Answers will vary; students may say that this ad appeals to cat owners by featuring an image of a cat and anthropomorphizing it (making it "speak").

Market Talk These ads may wish to stress the brand itself or the scientific or health benefits of their product, or even to distinguish their brand from all other products that use similar images.

Think and Write Comparisons of packaging will vary; all responses should compare and contrast the appeal of the packaging being presented and offer sound reasoning.

 Online Action! For instructions, ideas, and answer guide, go to the Teacher Center at
marketingessentials.glencoe.com

Chapter
Overview

This chapter introduces students to the nature and scope of product planning. It discusses the concept of product mix and the importance of product mix strategies and their impact on product planning. The strategies used in each stage of the product cycle are described, along with a discussion of product positioning and category management.

BUILD BACKGROUND

Ask students to name a brand of clothes they like. Then ask them to describe what characterizes that brand, including style, colors, where sold, and the more subtle characteristics such as the messages the clothes symbolize. Tell students they are going to learn how brands are developed and positioned in the marketplace.

Why It's Important

Product planning is crucial to the launch and success of most products. A product not launched and positioned correctly in the market could fail, even though if marketed differently, it might be successful. The steps in product planning help ensure the successful launch of a product and the successful movement of a product through its life cycle.

Prepare to Read

Ask a volunteer to write all of the major headings on the board in outline format. Tell students to fill in the secondary headings as they preview or read the chapter. They will then have a thorough chapter outline for use as study notes.

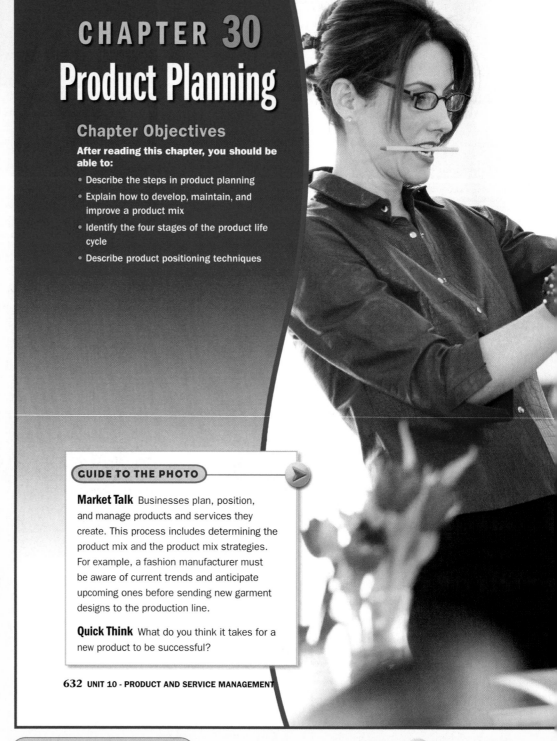

CHAPTER 30
Product Planning

Chapter Objectives

After reading this chapter, you should be able to:

- Describe the steps in product planning
- Explain how to develop, maintain, and improve a product mix
- Identify the four stages of the product life cycle
- Describe product positioning techniques

GUIDE TO THE PHOTO

Market Talk Businesses plan, position, and manage products and services they create. This process includes determining the product mix and the product mix strategies. For example, a fashion manufacturer must be aware of current trends and anticipate upcoming ones before sending new garment designs to the production line.

Quick Think What do you think it takes for a new product to be successful?

GUIDE TO THE PHOTO

Market Talk Lead a discussion about the positioning of clothes in the marketplace. Ask: What values do students look for in clothes? For example, do they want to look casual, stylish, cool, or sporty? How are these values represented in the clothes they buy? How has the manufacturer positioned the clothes they like in the marketplace with physical characteristics, advertising, and distribution channels?

Quick Think Answers will vary; student responses may include good design and good marketing.

Follow Up Ask students to create three innovations in sportswear that might be introduced into the market as a part of the product mix for running shoes.

marketingessentials.glencoe.com

Performance indicators represent key skills and knowledge. Relating them to the concepts explained in this chapter is your key to success in DECA events. These acronyms represent DECA events that involve knowledge of concepts in this chapter.

AAAL	FMAL	MMS*	TMDM*
AAML*	FMDM*	QSRM*	TSE*
ADC*	FMML*	RMAL	VPM
BSM	FSRM*	RMML*	
EMDM*	HMDM*	SMDM*	

In all these DECA events you should be able to follow these performance indicators:

- Explain the nature and scope of the product/service management function
- Identify the impact of product life cycles on marketing decisions
- Describe the use of technology in the product/service management function
- Explain business ethics in product/service management
- Explain the concept of product mix
- Describe factors used by marketers to position products/businesses

The events with an asterisk (*) include these indicators:

- Plan product mix
- Determine services to provide customers
- Explain the role of customer service in positioning/image
- Develop strategies to position product/business

HMDM and **FMDM** include additional performance indicators: Explain the concept of product in the hospitality industry and in the financial services industry respectively.

DECA PREP

Check your understanding of DECA performance indicators with the DECA activity in this chapter's review. For more information and DECA Prep practice, go to *marketingessentials .glencoe.com/30/DECA*

Chapter 30 - Product Planning **633**

DECA events that require knowledge of product planning are described here. Discuss the performance indicators to make sure students understand how to demonstrate their understanding.

The events acronyms stand for:

AAAL: Apparel and Accessories Marketing Series, AL

AAML: Apparel and Accessories Marketing Series, ML

ADC: Advertising Campaign Event

BSM: Business Services Marketing Series

EMDM: E-Commerce Management Team Decision Making Event

FMAL: Food Marketing Series, AL

FMDM: Financial Analysis Management Team Decision Making Event

FFML: Food Marketing Series, ML

FSRM: Full Service Restaurant Management Series

HMDM: Hospitality Services Management Team Decision Making Event

MMS: Marketing Management Series

QSRM: Quick Serve Restaurant Management Series

RMAL: Retail Merchandising Series, AL

RMML: Retail Merchandising Series, ML

SMDM: Sports and Entertainment Marketing Management Team Decision Making Event

TMDM: Travel and Tourism Marketing Management Team Decision Making Event

TSE: Technical Sales Event

VPM: Vehicles and Petroleum Marketing Series

DECA PREP

Find timed DECA Prep activities correlated to the Competitive Events Workbook for students and DECA tips for teachers at **marketingessentials.glencoe.com /30/DECA.**

CHAPTER 30 Classroom Resources

For the Teacher
- TeacherWorks
- marketingessentials.glencoe.com
- Interactive Chalkboard
- **ExamView**® Pro Test Generator
- Fast File Unit 10

For the Student
- *Marketing Essentials* Online Edition
- Student Activity Workbook
- Marketing Math Workbook
- Marketing Research Project Workbook
- School-to-Work Activity Workbook
- Competitive Events Workbook
- *BusinessWeek* Reader and Case Studies
- marketingessentials.glencoe.com

FOCUS

Introducing the Section

COLLABORATIVE ACTIVITY

To prepare for reading this section, have students imagine they are going to open a retail business and they must determine the types and number of products to be carried. Have them write the following on a separate sheet of paper:

1. Type of retail business they would like to open (for example, a beauty supply store).

2. Four general categories of merchandise they would like to carry (for example, shampoo, hair coloring, nail polish and cosmetic brushes).

3. Factors that would determine the type and number of products they will carry.

Preteaching Key Terms

Read the key terms aloud or ask a volunteer to read them. Ask students to predict the meaning of these phrases and write the phrases and their meaning on a separate sheet of paper.

- product planning
- product mix
- product line
- product item
- product width
- product depth
- product modification

As students read through the chapter, they can check their predictions against the information contained in the chapter and refine their definitions.

OBJECTIVES

- Describe the steps in product planning
- Explain how to develop, maintain, and improve a product mix

KEY TERMS

- product planning
- product mix
- product line
- product item
- product width
- product depth
- product modification

Product Planning, Mix, and Development

READ and STUDY

BEFORE YOU READ

Connect Recall a recent shopping trip. Can you name a new consumer product you discovered?

THE MAIN IDEA

Product planning allows a business to design marketing programs that increase sales by making products that customers want.

STUDY ORGANIZER

With a flow chart like the one below, represent the seven key steps in product development.

New Product Development

Step 1 Generate Ideas → ☐ → ☐ → ☐

☐ → ☐ → ☐

WHILE YOU READ

Analysis What marketing activities must occur prior to launching a new product?

Product Planning

A product is anything a person receives in an exchange. A product can be a tangible item (a notebook PC), a service (auto repair), an idea (a plan for a marketing campaign), some other abstract good (an education), or a combination of all of these concepts. A product, therefore, includes its physical features, the seller's reputation, the seller's services, and the way the product is viewed by people. **Product planning** involves making

634 UNIT 10 - PRODUCT AND SERVICE MANAGEMENT

READ and STUDY

BEFORE YOU READ

Answers will vary; many students will find it very hard to identify one new consumer product even though advertisers spend large amounts of money to introduce new products every year.

THE MAIN IDEA

Ask a volunteer to read the main idea aloud and ask another student to retell it in his or her own words.

STUDY ORGANIZER

Model the flow chart for students. A full-size, downloadable study organizer can be found at **marketingessentials.glencoe.com**

 WHILE YOU READ Encourage students to identify generating ideas, screening ideas, developing proposals/plans, product development, and testing.

decisions about what features should be used in selling a business's products, services, or ideas. These decisions relate to product features, such as packaging, labeling, and branding, as well as to services, such as product warranties, that are necessary to support the product. Product planning allows a business to coordinate existing products and features offered to customers, add new products, and delete products that no longer appeal to customers. Product planning requires creativity as well as the ability to interpret current customer needs and forecast new trends.

Product Mix

Product mix includes all the different products that a company makes or sells. A large manufacturer may have a variety of products in different categories. For example, Kraft Foods, the second-largest food and beverage manufacturer in the world, has hundreds of products in five areas: snacks, beverages, cheese, groceries, and convenience meals. Kraft's key brands include Kraft, Kool-Aid, Maxwell House, Nabisco, Oscar Mayer, and Post products.

A retailer's product mix is made up of all of the different products the store sells. Retail stores must plan their product mix carefully because they cannot offer all the products that customers may want.

Variations in Product Mixes

Have you ever heard of *El Caserio* or *Trakinas?* Both are brands that Kraft sells outside the United States. El Caserio is a popular cheese in Spain. Trakinas is a cookie sold in Brazil, Thailand, and China. Kraft has a diverse international market and therefore carries different product mixes for different customer needs across the world.

The type and number of products to be carried must be based on the objectives of the business, the image the business wants to project, and the market it is trying to reach. This makes product mixes unique to each business. Even similar types of businesses can offer different product mixes.

Product Items and Lines

A **product line** is a group of closely related products manufactured or sold by a business. Examples include all the car models produced by the Pontiac division of General Motors or all the cereals produced by Kellogg's. Retailers frequently sell more than one product line.

A **product item** is a specific model, brand, or size of a product within a product line. Typically, retailers carry several product items for each product line they sell. A Harley-Davidson motorcycle dealer might carry several Softail models, such as the Night Train, Deuce, or Heritage Softail Classic.

Product Width and Product Depth

The width and depth of its product offerings define a product mix. **Product width** refers to the number of different product lines a business manufactures or sells. **Product depth** refers to the number of items offered within each product line.

A retailer that sells three brands of jeans—Levi's, Lee, and Guess—has a product width of three. The product depth is the number of sizes, price ranges, colors, fabric type, and styles for each brand.

Product mix strategies vary with the type of business. Red Lobster restaurants, which specialize in seafood dinners, have considerable product depth within a narrow product line (seafood entrées). Other restaurants may offer broader menus that include steak, chicken, pork, and pasta dinners as well as seafood. Their product mix may have greater width but less depth than Red Lobster's.

Both manufacturers and retailers must decide on the width and depth of their product mix. To determine its product mix, a business needs to identify its target market, its competitors, and the image it wants to project. After a target market and an image are identified, a business must determine which product lines and items to manufacture or sell. Businesses must also periodically review whether its existing product lines need to be expanded, modified, decreased, or eliminated.

Chapter 30 - Product Planning 635

TEACH

Discussion Starter

PRODUCT WIDTH AND PRODUCT DEPTH

Ask the students to consider the following scenario: You decide to start a pet store. What types of things do you need to consider in determining the width and depth of product offerings? For example, are there other places where people can buy pet food in the neighborhood? Where do they buy pets? What brands of pet food should you carry?

TEACHING POINTS

Demonstrate Talk about the Iams pet foods to illustrate how one business established a unique line of products. Iams is sold in pet stores.

Extended Activity

Product Positioning

Have students research the types of pet foods that exist today and how they differentiate themselves from one another. Then, have students perform the same research for another product.

Online Activity

Developing Hybrid Cars

Have students research hybrid cars for an existing product line using the library, the Internet, and other sources as needed. Ask students why they believe the hybrid car was introduced and to account for the length of time it took for the car to be produced. Have students summarize their findings in a one-page report.

Discussion Starter

PRODUCT MIX STRATEGIES

Ask students to imagine that they have decided to go forward with their pet store. Discuss the factors students need to consider to determine the mix of products they will offer, such as how practical it is to stock different food and pet toys, cages, etc.; how long it will take to stock certain products; how much space they will have; and other factors that will help them to determine their product mix.

Concept Development

PRODUCT MIX STRATEGIES

After students have read the section on product mix strategies, ask them to list possible product mixes for the following:

- teas
  fruit teas, decaffeinated teas, blends of teas, English teas, Chinese teas
- grooming supplies
  brushes, shampoos, make up, shaving implements
- cars
  convertibles, coupes, SUVs

TEACHING POINTS

Clarify Tell students that introducing a new product into a product mix is a decision not made lightly. It involves several different departments or business units, such as marketing, research and development, manufacturing, and finance. All parties have to try to understand not only whether the product will be successful but whether it will complement the other products in the mix. They must answer the questions: Will this product confuse consumers, will it weaken brand loyalty to the other products in the line, will it take market share away from the other products in the line?

- **TARGETING CAT PEOPLE and DOG PEOPLE** Iams offers pet food for both cats and dogs.

Why does Iams make both varieties of pet food?

Product Mix Strategies

A product mix strategy is a plan for determining which products a business will make or stock. Businesses can use different product mix strategies depending on their resources and objectives. Some businesses develop completely new products to add to their existing product lines. Others expand or modify their current product lines. Sometimes businesses drop existing products to allow for new product offerings.

To make these decisions, a business must take an objective look at sales as well as other factors such as current trends. A product that has experienced success in the past may not continue to thrive if it fails to respond to changing consumer wants and needs.

Developing New Products

Successful new products can add substantially to a company's overall sales and boost its market share. Often a slight variation of the original or existing product can lead to increased sales.

Procter & Gamble (P&G), the number-one U.S. maker of household products, devotes roughly 15 percent of its research and development budget to developing new products. Innovative P&G products that have created new consumer-goods categories include Febreze odor removers, the Swiffer dry-mop system, and the Dryel home dry-cleaning kit.

According to one study, new products (those less than five years old) account for about 35 percent of total sales for major consumer and industrial goods companies. New products also can help a company's image by building a reputation among customers as an innovator and leader. In addition, a new product may increase markups and profits to sellers because its price tends to be 10 to 15

AD GUIDE

TARGETING CAT PEOPLE and DOG PEOPLE

Discussion Lead a discussion with students on this issue: How can a company extend its product mix in the future? Ask: What are the possibilities for introducing new products later on? For developing their brand more distinctly? Have students share their responses and provide examples.

Caption Answer Cat and dog food are made of similar ingredients but target different markets: owners of cats and owners of dogs.

Follow Up Ask students what other products Iams might include in its product mix.

percent higher than that of older, comparable products.

New product development generally involves seven key steps (see Figure 30.1):

1. Generating ideas
2. Screening ideas
3. Developing a business proposal
4. Developing the product
5. Testing the product with consumers
6. Introducing the product (commercialization)
7. Evaluating customer acceptance

Generating Ideas

New product ideas come from a variety of sources, including customers, competitors, channel members, and company employees. Current and existing customers are frequently involved in focus groups or idea sessions designed to generate new product concepts in as many categories as possible. Creativity is essential for new product development.

Many companies that manufacture consumer packaged goods use a task force approach to new product development. With this approach, employees from different departments, such as marketing, sales, manufacturing, finance, and research and development, take a new concept from the idea stage through the steps of product development. Companies that manufacture and sell industrial products often establish venture teams that are independent of any particular department. Venture teams normally develop new products that are not part of the existing business.

Screening Ideas

During the screening process, ideas for products are evaluated. They are matched against the company's overall strategy, which defines customers, target markets, competitors, and existing competitive strengths.

During the screening process, new ideas are evaluated for potential conflicts with existing products.

A screening might involve concept testing with consumers. Consumers would be asked to identify attributes they liked and disliked about the new concept and to indicate how willing they would be to buy such a product. The purpose of the screening stage is to find the products that deserve further study. A large number of products are rejected in the screening stage, making it an important preliminary step.

Developing a Business Proposal

A product idea that makes it through the screening process is evaluated in terms of its profit potential. A business proposal is developed to evaluate the new product in terms of the size of the market, potential sales, costs, profit potential, technological trends, overall competitive environment, and level of risk. During this stage, production requirements must be considered. How long will it take to create and introduce the new product? Can it be produced efficiently and at a competitive price? The business plans a program to study the feasibility of making and marketing the new product.

Developing the Product

During product development, the new product idea takes on a physical shape, and marketers develop a marketing strategy. The company makes plans relating to production, packaging, labeling, branding, promotion, and distribution.

During this phase of product development, technical evaluations are made to see whether the company can produce the new product and whether it is practical to do so. The Ben & Jerry's ice cream company had difficulties when it first developed Cherry Garcia ice cream. The original idea was to add whole chocolate-coated cherries to the ice cream. But the whole cherries were too large to go through the production machinery, which caused the chocolate to break off the cherries. After numerous tests, the company finally added the cherries and the chocolate separately.

In addition to detecting difficulties with product production, tests are conducted on products to see how they will hold up

Chapter 30 - Product Planning 637

Critical Thinking

Ask students: How do you think manufacturers can position their products in the marketplace using different distribution channels? Encourage students to provide concrete examples and to share their responses in class.

TEACH CONTINUED

Individualized Math Skills

DEVELOPING NEW PRODUCTS

Provide students with the following scenario to use for the levelled activities: You have decided to open a pet store. Your monthly expenses, including rent for the store space, utilities, and advertising, will be $1,300.

L1 You need to pay yourself a salary of $2,000 a month. How much should you budget for these expenses in the first year?
Expenses, including your salary, will be $39,600.

L2 The landlord has decided to raise the rent on the space you occupy for your pet store by 15% a year. Your utilities and advertising also have gone up 15%. You were paying $1,300 a month for these expenses. How much more will you have to pay.
You will now have to pay $1,495 a month, and additional $195.

L3 In your first year of operating a pet store, you made a gross profit of $12,500 on sales of pet food. If the markup on pet food is 40%, what is total sales of pet food for the year?
$12,500 ÷ 40% = $31,250

TEACHING POINTS

Demonstrate Have a local pet store owner come in and talk about how he or she determines the store's product mix and makes enough money to keep the store going.

Online Activity

Product Testing
Have students research product testing online. Have students write a one-page report summarizing their findings.

TEACH CONTINUED

Individualized Practice

PRODUCT LINES

L1 Think of a food product you or someone you know consumes often. List what might be some other products in this product line.

Example: if an individual consumes ice cream, other products might include frozen yogurts, ice cream bars, frozen fruit bars.

L2 List three different ways a company might categorize its products into different product lines.

By type of product, by geographical area in which it is sold, by its distribution channel.

L3 Develop a one-page written proposal for a new product line of cat foods. Include the products in the line, the rationale for the line, how the different products will enhance the other products in the line, how the products will be marketed.

Critical Thinking

Ask students: What are the factors that influence a company's product mix? Students may mention consumer preferences, the cost of launching and promoting a new product, the existing product mix, and how the new product fits in with the existing product mix.

Figure 30.1 ## The Steps in New Product Development

• **Getting an Idea Into a Consumer's Hands** Developing new products involves several key steps.

How does an idea lead to a product?

Steps 1 and 2
GENERATING AND SCREENING IDEAS

Generating involves tracking cultural trends and observing customer behaviors to generate ideas. Screening ideas for new products includes eliminating possibilities until one or two ideas are selected for development and a business proposal is written.

Steps 3, 4, and 5
WRITING A BUSINESS PROPOSAL/ DEVELOPING THE PRODUCT/ TESTING THE PRODUCT

A business proposal evaluates the proposed product in terms of size of market, potential sales, costs, profit potential, technology, the competition, and the level of risk involved. During the development stage, a prototype is made for testing.

Step 6
INTRODUCING THE PRODUCT

If customer response is favorable, the product is introduced into the marketplace.

Step 7
EVALUATING CUSTOMER ACCEPTANCE

After the product has been introduced, marketers track customer acceptance.

 Online Action!
Go to *marketingessentials.glencoe.com/30/figure/1* to find a project on the process of new product development.

Figure 30.1 ## The Steps in New Product Development

Discussion Review the product development steps with students and ask them to give an example of each for one product in a line of cars. Have students give reasons for their responses and share them with the class.

Caption Answer The idea is the critical first step in new product development. It is a creative process that perceives a need and a way to fill it. If the idea passes the screening process, a product is developed, tested, and introduced to the market.

 Online Action! For instructions, ideas, and answer guide, go to the Teacher Center at **marketingessentials.glencoe.com**

during normal and not-so-normal use by the consumer. A new product may be tested for durability in the lab by machines that will reproduce the actions or motions that the product will undergo during use. Technical problems should be detected at this stage so that they can be corrected before full-scale production begins.

The government requires extensive testing in various stages for some products, such as prescription drugs and genetically engineered food products. These tests end with testing on human beings to determine side effects and problems with the product's safety. Getting final approval from the government for use by the general public can take years.

Testing the Product with Consumers

New products frequently are test-marketed in certain geographic areas to see whether consumers will accept them. Larger companies establish research and development departments that work with marketing staff, marketing research staff, and outside research companies to develop and test new products.

Not every new product needs to be test-marketed. A focus group evaluation during development can provide additional input into final product design, uncovering potential problems before production.

In some cases, the costs of test marketing, focus group evaluations, or direct marketing tests to sample households may be too high. Marketers may forgo testing of other products because they do not yet have a product to be evaluated. Sometimes a company delays test marketing because it does not want to give competitors information that might help them get a competing product on the market.

Introducing the Product

This stage is also called commercialization. Introducing a new product can be expensive. For example, to convince adults to use Crest Whitening Expressions toothpaste in cinnamon, citrus, and herbal mint flavors, Procter & Gamble spent $80 million dollars on a marketing campaign.

marketingessentials.glencoe.com

A MATTER OF ETHICS

Hold the Sugar

Suppose you are developing a new low-sugar doughnut. The new doughnut is designed to attract dieters and diabetics. A regular, glazed doughnut has 10 grams of sugar and 200 calories. More than half of the calories come from 12 of grams fat.

Fast-food makers are introducing lower-calorie products because of changing diet trends. In addition, consumers have filed lawsuits in which they claim that their health has been adversely affected by foods that are high in fat and sugar.

Lawmakers Weigh In

In 2004, the U.S. House of Representatives passed legislation that would ban lawsuits seeking damages because fast food caused weight gain or health problems resulting from obesity. Proponents of the so-called cheeseburger bill argue that such lawsuits are frivolous and ignore personal responsibility for healthy eating. Opponents of the bill argue that the fast-food industry should not be given federal protection from such lawsuits.

THINKING ETHICALLY

Do you think that companies should be immune from lawsuits over their food content?

@ Online Action!

Go to *marketingessentials.glencoe.com/30/ethics* to find an activity about ethics and product development.

New products must be advertised to introduce their benefits to consumers. A new or revised distribution network may be needed. The company may need to develop training programs for its sales force. To pay these costs,

A MATTER OF ETHICS   Hold the Sugar

Discussion Tell students that fast food restaurants have tried to change their product mix to make themselves less vulnerable to lawsuits by introducing more healthy meals. See if students can name some of these changes.

THINKING ETHICALLY
Answer: Answers will vary. Some students may say that it is an individual's responsibility to watch what one eats, while others may say that a corporation should be responsible for providing accurate nutritional information and/or informing the consumer about potentially dangerous or healthy ingredients in their products.

@ Online Action!
For instructions, ideas, and answer guide, go to the Teacher Center at **marketingessentials.glencoe.com**

Follow Up
Ask students to look for advertisements for healthy fast-food.

TEACH CONTINUED

Concept Development

INTRODUCING THE PRODUCT

Tell students that 70 percent of new product introductions fail at the retail level. Ask students to discuss some of the reasons for failure of new products.

Answers may include Consumer preferences, not a compelling need, not marketed to the right audience, not promoted adequately.

TEACHING POINTS

Demonstrate Show students a documentary on how a certain product was invented, developed, and marketed.

Individualized Practice

DEVELOPING PRODUCTS

L1 Have students generate three ideas for pet food products.

Answers might include food for young cats, food for advanced age cats, food for cats with kidney problems—all in dry and wet, and food for nursing cats

L2 Have students generate three ideas for pet food products and develop a focus group of several fellow students to see how they would react to these products. Have students summarize their results in a one-page report.

L3 Have students generate three ideas for pet food products and list the factors in scientific, medicine and food research that might make them change your pet product mix within the next few years.

For example, new medical techniques might make it possible to diagnose cat diseases more easily; advanced medical techniques might make it possible to give cats the right nutrition to make them live longer.

ASSESS

Review Guide

CONCEPTS

Ask students to list the steps for new product development.

Generating ideas, screening ideas, developing a business proposal, developing the product, testing the product, introducing the product (commercialization), and evaluating customer acceptance.

KEY TERMS

Have students review key terms, their spellings, and definitions in small groups.

ONLINE SELF-ASSESSMENT

Have students go to marketingessentials.glencoe.com for the Section 30.1 practice test.

Individualized Review

L1 Assign and review Chapter 30 activities in the Student Activity Workbook.

L2 Assign and review Chapter 30 activities in the Marketing Math Workbook.

L3 Assign and review Chapter 30 activities in the *BusinessWeek* Reader and Case Studies.

Marketing Practice

Divide the class into four groups. Have groups select one existing product line and list a number of products in that line. Then ask them to develop one new product to fit into the existing line.

---

the company must get its new products into the market as quickly as possible.

Evaluating Customer Acceptance

The purpose of this step is to evaluate customer acceptance of the product and the marketing strategies used to introduce the product.

One way to obtain customer responses is to study sales information. Scanning equipment and computer systems can be used to compile large amounts of sales and market data on existing and new products. From this information, customized reports can be prepared. These reports help answer key questions such as:

- How often do customers buy the new product?
- When did customers last buy the new product?
- Where are the best customers for our new product?
- What new products are customers buying?

Developing Existing Products

Companies constantly review their product mix to see if they can further expand their product lines or modify existing products. They do this in order to build on an already established image, to appeal to new markets, and to increase sales and profits. Companies that have successful product lines often add products to those lines in order to take advantage of customers' positive attitudes toward the brand name.

One disadvantage of adding new products to a company's product mix is the cost factor. Adding products or product lines increases inventory, promotion, storage, and distribution costs. New products also may take sales away from existing products and may require additional training for sales representatives who sell the products. Finally, when a brand or corporate name is placed on a new product and the product proves to be unpopular, poorly made, or harmful, all products with the corporate name suffer.

Two ways of developing existing products are line extensions and product modifications.

Line Extensions

Companies can expand product offerings by adding new product lines, items, or services, which may or may not be related to current products. To illustrate this strategy, think of all the varieties of Tylenol, such as Tylenol Flu, Tylenol Cold, and Tylenol Allergy Sinus. These products also come in a variety of forms, such as tablets, caplets, and gel caps. Each of these products is a line extension of the original Tylenol product.

A line extension is intended to be a different product that appeals to somewhat different needs of consumers. In essence, the company wants to provide a wider range of choices to increase product depth within a line. Line extensions are easy to market because customers are already familiar with the original product on which the extension is based.

Product Modifications

A **product modification** is an alteration in a company's existing product. Modified products may be offered in new and different varieties, formulations, colors, styles, features, or sizes. Product modifications are a relatively quick and easy way to add new products to a company's product line.

When modifying a product, the old product often is phased out. Packaging may be modified to appeal to consumers and attract them to the new product.

Deleting a Product or Product Line

Sometimes companies decide that they will no longer produce or sell a particular product or, even a whole product line. There can be many reasons for this move.

Obsolescence

Changes in customer interests and technology have caused many products to be dropped. For example, older models of desktop computers have been dropped because

---

 Extended Activity

Product Modifications

Tell students that companies are always thinking of ways to improve their existing products. This is often how new products and product lines are born. Read the story of Classic Coke in the text. Ask students to think of another product that was modified in a similar way, or to think of how a current product might be modified and then marketed in the same way. For example, the Volkswagen Bug was redesigned to be bigger and more comfortable.

newer models are faster and less expensive to produce.

Loss of Appeal

As consumer tastes change, companies drop products that no longer appeal to the old tastes. These products may have some lasting loyalties that generate revenue, but the manufacturers must decide whether these benefits are really worth the expense of keeping the item in their product mixes.

Changes in Company Objectives

Sometimes a product does not match a company's current objectives. In 1993, Sears sold one of its subsidiaries, Coldwell Banker real estate company, for this reason. For several years, Sears had lost market share to other retailers. The company sold some unrelated businesses to focus on its retail objectives.

Replacement with New Products

To encourage retailers to cover costs of putting a new product onto limited shelf space, manufacturers pay slotting fees. Slotting fees for cereal and paper goods often reach $50,000 or more. According to a Federal Trade Commission study in 2003, a nationwide product launch might cost $2 million in slotting fees alone. Slotting fees help the retailer balance the costs associated with accepting a new product. A retailer must mark down eliminated products and pay for software, labor, and materials to change price labels and enter a new product into the inventory.

Lack of Profit

Product developers may drop products when sales reach such a low level that the return on sales does not meet company objectives.

Conflict With Other Products in the Line

Sometimes products take business away from other products in the same product line. Increased sales of one product can cause decreased sales of another product.

 30.1 AFTER YOU READ

Reviewing Key Terms and Concepts

1. Why is product planning important to a business?

2. What is the difference between product planning and product mix?

3. What are the three major strategies for developing an effective product mix?

Integrating Academic Skills

Math

4. According to Productscan Online, a new product database, there were 33,677 new product introductions in 2003, compared to 21,986 in 1993. By what percentage did new product introductions increase during that decade?

Reading/Language Arts

5. Perform an Internet search or visit your school or local library to obtain information about slotting fees. Write a one- to two-page paper on the advantages and disadvantages of slotting fees from a manufacturer's and retailer's perspective.

@ Online Action!

Check your answers at *marketingessentials.glencoe.com/30/read*

marketingessentials.glencoe.com   Chapter 30 - Product Planning **641**

CLOSE

Ask students to recall and provide answers to the following questions:

- **What is product modification and why is it used?**
  A product modification is an alteration in a company's existing product. It is a relatively quick and easy way to add new products to a company's product line.

- **What are the factors that might make a company discontinue a product?**
  Changes in customer interests and technology, products no longer appeal, doesn't match the company's current objectives, doesn't make enough profit, conflicts with other products in the line.

- **What is a line extension of a product line? Give an example.**
  A different product that appeals to somewhat different needs of consumers. An example is Tylenol caplets and gel caps, which extend the original Tylenol product.

Critical Thinking

Tell students that the United States is becoming a service economy. New services are just as important as new products. Ask students to brainstorm what types of services could extend a cell phone product line. Examples might include text messaging.

 AFTER YOU READ

Reviewing Key Terms and Concepts

1. It allows a business to coordinate existing products and features offered to customers, add new products, and delete products.

2. Product planning involves making decisions about those features needed to sell a business's products, services, or ideas. Product mix includes all the products that a company makes or sells.

3. Three major strategies include: developing new products, developing existing products, or deleting a product or product line.

Integrating Academic Skills

4. 53% increase; 33,677 − 21,986 = 11,691; 11,691 ÷ 21,986 = 53%

5. Answers may include: Manufacturer Advantage: shelf space availability, access to consumers. Disadvantage: high costs;

Retailer Advantage: pays for costs to add product to inventory. Disadvantage: must take markdowns on discontinued items.

@ Online Action! Answers at **marketingessentials.glencoe.com/30/read**

FOCUS

Introducing the Section

COLLABORATIVE ACTIVITY

To prepare for reading this section, have students think of one product that has been around most of their lives—for example, Coke. Then ask students to see if they can define the different ways in which the product was marketed at different times. Explain that products go through the life cycle stages of introduction, growth, maturity and decline, and require different marketing strategies in each cycle. Product positioning is a way to position the product differently for the different phases of its life cycle.

Preteaching Key Terms

Read the key terms aloud or ask a volunteer to read them. Ask students to predict meaning of these phrases and write the phrases and their meaning on a separate sheet of paper.

- product life cycle
- product positioning
- category management
- planograms

As students read through the section, they can check their predictions against the information contained in the chapter and refine their definitions.

Online Activity

Assistive Technology

Have students research voice command software or other assistive technology and give a short presentation on how companies are currently marketing it or how it could be marketed in the future.

OBJECTIVES

- Identify the four stages of the product life cycle
- Describe product positioning techniques

KEY TERMS

- product life cycle
- product positioning
- category management
- planograms

Connect Think of why you purchase certain products or services.

Sustaining Product Sales

READ and STUDY

BEFORE YOU READ

Contrast How do you think marketing strategies differ for a new product and for an established one?

THE MAIN IDEA

After products are introduced in the marketplace, they go through different stages of growth and decline. It is important to understand the different marketing strategies used to sustain product sales over time.

STUDY ORGANIZER

Create a chart like the one below to record each stage in the product life cycle. List each stage's sales characteristics and marketing strategies.

Stages in the Product Life Cycle

Stages	Sales Characteristics	Marketing Strategies
Introduction		

The Product Life Cycle

A **product life cycle** represents the stages that a product goes through during its life. There are four stages of the life cycle: introduction, growth, maturity, and decline (see Figure 30.2). As each stage in the product life cycle is reached, marketers must adjust their product mix and their marketing strategies to ensure continued sales.

READ and STUDY

BEFORE YOU READ

Answers will vary; students should be able to explain that marketing strategies used for products have to change as products move through a life cycle.

THE MAIN IDEA

Ask a volunteer to read the main idea aloud and ask another student to retell it in his or her own words.

STUDY ORGANIZER

Model the study organizer for the students. A full-size, downloadable study organizer can be found at **marketingessentials.glencoe.com**

WHILE YOU READ Answers will vary; students may indicate product features, packaging, color, labeling, and promotional efforts.

Managing During the Introduction Stage

When the product is introduced to the market, the company focuses its efforts on promotion and production. The major goal is to draw the customer's attention to the new product. The company works to build its sales by increasing product awareness. Special promotions may get the customer to try the new product. The costs of introducing a product are high. Therefore, this is usually the least profitable stage of the life cycle.

Managing During the Growth Stage

During the growth phase of the product life cycle, the product is enjoying success as shown by increasing sales and profits. Much of the target market knows about and buys the product. Advertising may now focus on consumer satisfaction, rather than on the benefits of new products. By this time, the competition is aware of the success of the product and is likely to offer new products in order to compete. To keep its product sales growing, the company may have to introduce new models or modify the existing product to offer more than the competition.

Managing During the Maturity Stage

A product reaches the maturity stage when its sales level off or slow down. The product may have more competition now, or most of the target market may already own the product.

Figure 30.2 The Product Life Cycle

- **Understanding the Product Life Cycle** The life cycle of a product can be divided into four stages: introduction, growth, maturity, and decline.

Why are sales relatively flat during the maturity stage?

@ Online Action!
Go to *marketingessentials.glencoe.com/30/figure/2* to find a project on the product life cycle.

 marketingessentials.glencoe.com

Figure 30.2 The Product Life Cycle

Discussion **Figure 30.2** shows the relationship between the time a product has been in the market and the amount of profit it earns. Have students think of familiar products that have been in the market a long time. What stage of the life cycle do students think these products are in? Have any of them been reinvented for a new target audience?

Caption Answer Sales are relatively flat during the maturity stage because many people in the target market may own the product or there may be more competition for the product.

@ Online Action! For instructions, ideas, and answer guide, go to the Teacher Center at **marketingessentials.glencoe.com**

Follow Up Ask students to think about the stages of product life cycle the next time they go to the store. Ask: What products have been reinvented to give them a longer life?

TEACH

Discussion Starter

THE PRODUCT LIFE CYCLE

Ask the students to consider the following scenario: You have invented a new type of computer that allows the user to issue voice commands. There is no keyboard. Discuss how you would spend your marketing dollars during the four phases of the product life cycle. List student responses on the board.

Concept Development

MANAGING DURING THE MATURITY STAGE

After students have read the section of managing during the various stages of a product's life, ask them to discuss how Coke, which is in its mature stage, is managed. They should address these questions:

- What competitive products must Coke manage against?
  Pepsi, other colas, other soft drinks
- What advertising campaigns has Coke put into place to manage against competition?
  The Real Thing campaign, for one
- What distribution strategies help Coke manage against the competition?
  served exclusively in some restaurants
- What other strategies has Coke employed?
  introduction of Classic Coke

Have students share their responses in class.

TEACHING POINTS

Demonstrate Discuss other soft drink management strategies, such as contests in which you win a prize according to what appears on a bottle cap and tie-ins with fast food chains.

643

Individualized Practice

PRODUCT STAGES

Give students the following leveled activities:

L1 Think of one product that is in its mature stage. List how you think the company is managing the product, in terms of advertising, promotions, distribution channels, and changes to the product.

L2 Assume you have a line of pet foods and they have now reached the mature stage. There is new competition in the form of healthy pet food on the market. What strategies would you adopt to cope with the competition?
reinvent the foods for a healthier emphasis, sell them at a discount

L3 Pick one product currently being sold in the market. Write a one-page essay or give a five-minute oral presentation on how you would reinvent the product for greater sales.
Possible answer: Purina Cat Chow—add cat foods for young kittens, older cats, cats with kidney problems.

Enrichment

PRODUCT POSITIONING

Using the example of the personal care-line OT found in the text, ask students to invent some names for these imaginary products in the line:
• bar soap
• bubble bath
• shower gel
• deodorant

TEACHING POINTS

Demonstrate Bring in an ad for a grooming or personal care product that shows product positioning. Use the example of to talk about how the product is positioned by the ad.

Case Study

Snowboarding Without Snow

Winter snowboarding has grown in popularity. From 1997 to 2002, the number of snowboarders doubled to 5.6 million, according to the National Sporting Goods Association. A new product now allows snowboarders to do urban snowboarding after the snow melts. No bindings, boots, or warm clothing is required.

The new boards have a long, hourglass shape, center wheels, and wide-set wheels to simulate a snowboarding ride. The boards are designed to allow riders to slalom down steep streets better than they can with skateboards.

A New Product for an Existing Market

In 1996, Steen Strand designed a prototype of the new board as a project for his master's degree in design at Stanford University. Strand's Freebord X-80 gives the sensation of snowboarding because it has the ability to rotate 360 degrees while on descent. The Freebord X-80 offers two swiveling wheels that sit near the nose and tail of the board. Weight is displaced from the center of the board to the wheels, which spins the board in circles as well as turns it sharply uphill to control speed.

Sales of the Freebord X-80 are expected to double this year. Freebords are so hot in Asia that a Taiwanese company has already developed its own version of the board.

THINK STRATEGICALLY

Compare Freebords X-80s to skateboards in the product life cycle. What marketing strategies would you use for the Freebord X-80?

@ Online Action! Go to *marketingessentials.glencoe.com/30/case* to find an activity about product development.

During this stage, a company spends more of its marketing dollars fighting off the competition. As advertising expenses climb, the company may have to decide whether it can continue to improve the product to gain additional sales.

Managing During the Decline Stage

During the decline stage, sales fall. Profits may reach the point where they are smaller than the costs. Management will need to decide how long it will continue to support the product. Besides dropping the product, the company can use other product mix strategies to try to gain further sales from a declining or failing product. These strategies include selling or licensing the product, recommitting to the product line, discounting the product, regionalizing the product, and modernizing or altering the product.

Sell or License the Product

Many companies sell or license their poorly performing products to risk-taking companies. Risk-taking companies try to rejuvenate

 marketingessentials.glencoe.com

Case Study — Snowboarding Without Snow

Discussion The Freeboard is an example of taking an idea that has proved popular and extending it to create new product. Ask students to think of other examples of this.

THINK STRATEGICALLY **Answer:** Freeboard X-80s are in the introduction stage, while skateboards are in the maturity stage. The focus of the marketing efforts should be on promotion and production. The major goal is to draw the customer's attention to the new product. The company should build its sales by increasing product awareness. Special promotions may get the customer to try the new product.

@ Online Action! For instructions, ideas, and answer guide, go to the Teacher Center at
marketingessentials.glencoe.com

the product by changing the product's image or introducing it to a new market.

Recommit to the Product Line

Some companies decide that a declining product has other possible uses that can help improve sales.

Even with recommitment and advertising of new product uses, there is no guarantee that a product will continue to have enough sales. Eventually, it may need to be discontinued.

Discount the Product

Many declining product lines can be saved from deletion by discounting them to compete with cheaper store or private brands.

Regionalize the Product

Sometimes companies decide to sell declining products only in the geographical areas where there is strong customer loyalty. The Nabisco Food Group markets its My-T-Fine desserts only in northeastern states where it still has a significant customer base. By marketing its product only in that area, the company avoids the cost of national advertising and distribution.

Modernize or Alter the Product Offering

Some products can be altered or modernized to avoid deletion. Products can be completely redesigned, packaged differently, or reformulated. Tide laundry detergent—available in powder form in a box—was redesigned as New Tide. The product was also introduced in liquid form and repackaged in a plastic bottle.

Companies spend large amounts of money to develop and promote consumer and industrial products. As a result, they are reluctant to delete products without trying one of the above strategies. When products must be dropped, a company needs to plan the move carefully to avoid disappointing customers and damaging the company's overall image.

Product Positioning

The focus of **product positioning** is the image that a product projects. The goal of product positioning is to set the product apart from the competition. Product positioning refers to the efforts a business makes to identify, place, and sell its products in the marketplace. To position their products, businesses identify customer needs and determine how their products compare to the competition. A number of strategies are used to position products in the marketplace.

Positioning by Price and Quality

Companies frequently position their products in a product line on the basis of price and quality. A company may offer an economy line, a mid-priced line, and a luxury line. Positioning by price and quality stresses high price as a symbol of quality or low price as an indication of value.

The Ford Motor Company deliberately positions its Focus as an economical compact car while still emphasizing quality. It positions its Mustang as a high-performance car. Promotional efforts are aimed at creating price and quality images for these products. This strategy enables Ford to give each of its products a unique position in the marketplace.

Positioning by Features and Benefits

Products are often associated with a feature, attribute, or customer benefit. OT, a line of personal care products for boys ages 9 to 16, was introduced in 2004. Research had indicated that preteen and teenage boys were dissatisfied with choices available in personal care products. The product line includes shampoo, deodorant, body wash, hair gel, and pomade with rugged names such as Pit Defense and Body Slam. Procter & Gamble, under a licensing agreement with OT Overtime LLC, is promoting the products with bold product names, formulas, and colors to match the intensity of overtime play in sports.

Positioning in Relation to the Competition

Some businesses position their products to compete directly with the products of other companies. Positioning in relation to

Critical Thinking

Discuss how the camera phone may have evolved and whether ethical concerns were thought through by phone producers initially. It is possible this phone will be banned in certain situations because of privacy concerns. Ask students to consider how ethical concerns or legal applications can affect the life of a product and to discuss their responses in class.

TEACH CONTINUED

Individualized Practice

MARKETING THROUGH THE PRODUCT LIFE CYCLE

L1 Ask students to list the strategies used to manage a product during the declining stage of its life cycle.

L2 Ask students to list the strategies used to position a product in the marketplace and to give an example of each.

L3 Give students the following scenario: Assume you are the product manager for a new product in cellular telephones— a cell phone/TV. List the strategies you might use to position the product in the marketplace.

Answers might include emphasize the price of the TV feature, the convenience of having a small television you can carry with you, how having a television and cell phone beats all other cell phone products, etc.

Concept Development

CATEGORY MANAGEMENT

Ask students to define the concept and aim of category management.

Category management is a process that involves managing product categories as individual business units. The aim of the process is to put manufacturers in closer touch with customer needs.

TEACHING POINTS

Extend Ask students: Why is placement on shelf space so important in many retail stores?

Products placed near one another can complement or compete. Some placements will appeal to target audiences, such as children's cereals or toys down low on the shelf where they will be more visible.

ASSESS

Review Guide

CONCEPTS

Ask students to recall the steps for new product development.
1) Generate ideas, 2) screen ideas, 3) develop a business proposal, 4) develop the product, 5) test the product, 6) introduce the product, and 7) evaluate customer acceptance.

KEY TERMS

Have students review key terms, their spellings, and definitions in small groups.

ONLINE SELF-ASSESSMENT

Have students go to marketingessentials.glencoe.com for the Section 30.2 practice test.

Individualized Review

L1 Assign and review Chapter 30 activities in the Student Activity Workbook.

L2 Assign and review Chapter 30 activities in the Marketing Math Workbook.

L3 Assign and review Chapter 30 activities in the *BusinessWeek* Reader and Case Studies.

Marketing Practice

Have students research online or go to the grocery store to find a product that is targeted to their regional market. (For example, Campbell's Soup offers specialized products to their Mexican and Canadian markets.) Ask students to adapt the product to a different regional market. Have them write a one-page report summarizing what about the product would change and use art materials or graphic design software to create a label for the product.

MARKET TECH

DVR Benefits at a Low Cost

A digital video recorder, or DVR, is a neat way to watch TV. With a DVR system, you can pause or rewind live TV and can record any program for viewing later without complicated programming and the need to keep blank tapes handy.

But buying a DVR can be costly. What if your budget is limited?

A Cheaper Alternative

If you have a plain old Windows PC, you can turn it into a DVR by using a product from SnapStream Media, a small company from Houston. SnapStream's Beyond TV 3 includes DVR software for Windows and the necessary hardware—an external TV tuner from Hauppauge Computer Works that plugs into the computer with a simple USB cable. This package is sold on the SnapStream.com Web site. No service fee is charged.

Because this bundled product is really two products that are only loosely integrated, there are multiple installation processes—one for the Hauppauge tuner, one for the most recent tuner hardware updates, and a third installation of the Beyond TV 3 software itself.

THINK LIKE A MARKETER

What potential problems can you foresee with bundled products that try to replicate more expensive products at a lower cost? Do you think that this product will be successful?

@ **Online Action!**

Go to *marketingessentials.glencoe.com/ 30/tech* to find an activity about technology and product development.

---

the competition is a common strategy when a firm is trying to solidify an advantage over another firm.

It is not always a good idea to compete head-to-head with the industry leader. It might be better to compete by showing that you are the underdog. Southwest Airlines does a good job of that by telling potential customers that they are the low-fare alternative to full-service airlines.

Positioning in Relation to Other Products in a Line

Individual products may be positioned in relation to other products in the same line. Starting with the original Palm Pilot fit-in-your-pocket organizer, the company has introduced other handheld products that not only organize information but have added features. For example, the Zire handheld will play MP3s, show photos, and play video clips. The Tungsten handheld allows the user to use e-mail and surf the Web, and the Treo line has all these features plus a phone.

Category Management

Many manufacturers and retailers are adopting a process for marketing and selling their products known as category management. **Category management** is a process that involves managing product categories as individual business units. A category may include a group of product lines with the same target market and distribution channels. The process is designed to put manufacturers and retailers in closer touch with customer needs.

The category manager is responsible for all the brands for one generic product category, such as foods, beverages, or health and beauty products. The category manager is responsible for the profits or losses of the product mix and product lines in the category. The position evolved out of the position of product manager. The difference between the two job titles is that a category manager is responsible for a generic category and has more

marketingessentials.glencoe.com

MARKET TECH

DVR Benefits at a Low Cost

Discussion Ask students to discuss the advantages and disadvantages of bundling technology for the consumer, the producer, and the retailer.

THINK LIKE A MARKETER **Answer:** Answers will vary. However, most students should recognize that bundled products require special technical expertise to properly install the software and equipment. For most customers, the three step process would be confusing, and since the software is available only online, technical assistance is limited. Unless the product installation process can be simplified, most people probably will prefer to save their money for one of the more expensive DVR units.

 Online Action! For instructions, ideas, and answer guide, go to the Teacher Center at marketingessentials.glencoe.com

interaction with other managers from finance, production, and research and development. A product manager handles a particular product and has more direct interaction with the company's sales force.

The manufacturer can customize a product mix within a category according to customer preference on a store-by-store basis. Using scanned data on product sales and other market data, manufacturers assist retailers with their product mix. In examining product mix, a manufacturer determines which of its products a particular retailer does not carry. It also identifies products that would have strong sales potential for both the retailer and the manufacturer. This analysis helps the manufacturer to recommend an optimum product mix by projecting sales volume and profits for a retailer. The manufacturer then suggests

adding or deleting certain items to its product mix. If the category manager feels that one product is decreasing sales of other products in the same category, this product may be discontinued.

Another way manufacturers can help retailers is through **planograms**. A planogram is a computer-developed diagram that shows retailers how and where products within a category should be displayed on a shelf at individual stores. This maximizes a product's potential. Placement can also be used to highlight other products that can be used in conjunction with a product. Manufacturers can even customize planograms for specific types of stores. Each store can then stock more of the products that appeal to people in its trading area and fewer products that have limited appeal to its customers.

 30.2 AFTER YOU READ

Reviewing Key Terms and Concepts
1. What is the focus and goal of product positioning?
2. List four strategies used to position products in the marketplace.
3. What is category management?

Integrating Academic Skills
Math
4. The Dryers Company has two declining products and is considering deleting one of them from its product line. Product A costs $65 per unit to produce and sells for $110. The storage, distribution, and promotion costs average $4.30 per unit. Last year, 19,500 units were sold. Product B costs $38 to produce and sells for $72. Its storage, distribution, and promotion costs average $7.50 per unit. Last year, 56,000 units were sold. Of the two products, which is the less profitable and should be deleted?

History
5. Perform an Internet search or visit a school or local library to investigate the history of a popular consumer product. Write a one-page report on when and where it was introduced, how it is used, and who manufactures it today.

 @ Online Action!
Check your answers at *marketingessentials.glencoe.com/30/read*

marketingessentials.glencoe.com   **Chapter 30 - Product Planning 647**

AFTER YOU READ

Reviewing Key Terms and Concepts
1. The focus is the image a product projects. The goal is to set the product apart from the competition.

2. Stress price and quality, stress product features and benefits, stress unique characteristics, compare the product to the competition, show a relationship to other products in the line.

3. Category management is a process that involves managing product categories as individual business units.

Integrating Academic Skills
4. Product A is less profitable. Product A: $110 (RP) × 19,500 units = $2,145,000; ($65 + $4.30) × 19,500 units = $1,351,350 costs; $2,145,000 − $1,351,350 = $793,650 net profit.

Product B: $72 (RP) × 56,000 units = $4,032,000; ($38 + $7.50) × 56,000 units = $2,548,000 costs; $4,032,000 − $2,548,000 = $1,484,000 net profit.

5. Reports will vary; all reports should demonstrate an understanding of the product's life cycle.

@ Online Action!   Answers at **marketingessentials.glencoe.com/30/read**

SECTION 30.2

CLOSE

Ask students to recall and provide answers to the following questions:

- **What is the product life cycle? Name the four stages.**

  The product life cycle is the stages a product goes through during its life span. There are four stages: introduction, growth, maturity, and decline.

- **How can a manufacturer's planogram assist retailers?**

  A planogram is a computer-developed diagram that shows retailers how and where products within a category should be displayed on a shelf at individual stores. This helps to maximize a product's potential. Placement can also be used to highlight other products that can be used in conjunction with the product.

Virtual Business

Introduce merchandising to students using Knowledge Matters' Virtual Business Retailing visual simulation, *Merchandising*. In this simulation, students learn how product placement within a store can affect sales.

CAREERS IN MARKETING

Lifelong Learning

CAREER INFORMATION

Have students go to marketingessentials.glencoe.com and find Chapter 30 Careers page and click on the American Marketing Association's Careers Strategies and Tips. Ask students to select one article, read it, and summarize it in three short paragraphs.

PRODUCT PLANNING

For students who do not wish to pursue a career in product development, the most relevant information in this chapter may be understanding the product life cycle in terms of a planned purchase. The best time to buy a product may not be at the moment it is introduced. Tell students that by keeping informed of new products in development or changes to already existing products, they can learn to be educated consumers.

Primary Source

Ask students to go to marketingessentials.glencoe.com and find Chapter 30 Resources. Ask them to click on the link for the American Marketing Association's marketing dictionary and read the definitions of the terms they find that are related to product planning.

● THINKING CRITICALLY

Continuing education is crucial in most careers because workers must adapt to changes in technology and the marketplace.

@ Online Action!

For instructions, ideas, and answer guide, go to the Teacher Center at marketingessentials.glencoe.com

CAREERS IN MARKETING

MACK HANAN
PRINCIPAL
GREENSTREEM.COM LLC

(?) What do you do at work?
I specialize in the creation and take-to-market implementation of fast-growth business models, both for mature businesses of Fortune 500 corporations, and for start-up and early stage companies. I specialize in companies that deal with high-tech or cutting-edge technologies in one way or another.

(?) What skills are most important to you?
It is important to have a strong market sense, as well as an up-to-date understanding of technology. I also have to stay informed on the interplay between social trends and government policy compliance. Strategic creativity is important, as are the ability to lead the adoption of change and people skills as a team leader.

(?) What is your key to success?
I am a zealous advocate of creative strategies, and I work hard to ensure their effective application. It is important to always remain dedicated to my client's objectives. Also, I understand that my compensation is based solely on the performance of my work. In other words, the old adage that the customer is king is still true. So is the rule that good, expert work will be rewarded.

Aptitudes, Abilities, and Skills

Strong understanding of technology as it applies to your chosen industry

Education and Training

High-level business degrees are helpful, with an emphasis on studies in your chosen field of specialty.

Career Path

High-level consultants might begin their careers as employees of a firm, helping apply technology to business and marketing needs. The path of such a career is largely determined by interests, passion, and aptitude.

● THINKING CRITICALLY

Why is continuing education crucial in most careers?

@ Online Action!

Go to *marketingessentials.glencoe.com/ 30/careers* to find a career-related activity.

 marketingessentials.glencoe.com

Test-Taking Strategies

Suggest that if students do not know the answer to a test question, they can skip the question and come back to it as time allows. Inform students that sometimes they will find they know the answer when they return to the question a second or third time.

FOCUS on KEY POINTS

SECTION 30.1

● Product planning involves deciding what features are needed to sell a business's products, services, or ideas. A product mix strategy is the plan for how the business determines which products it will make or stock. Businesses can use different product mix strategies depending on their resources and their objectives.

SECTION 30.2

● A product life cycle represents the stages that a product goes through during its life (introduction, growth, maturity, and decline). The goal of product positioning is to set the product apart from the competition. Category management is a process that involves managing product categories as individual business units.

REVIEW VOCABULARY

Contrast the following groups of vocabulary terms.

1. product planning (p. 634)/product mix (p. 635)

2. product line (p. 635)/product item (p. 635)

3. product width (p. 635)/product depth (p. 635)

4. product modification (p. 640)/product life cycle (p. 642)

5. product positioning (p. 645)/category management (p. 646)/planograms (p. 647)

REVIEW FACTS and IDEAS

6. What is the difference between a product item and a product line? (30.1)

7. Compare and contrast product depth and product width. (30.1)

8. What types of criteria are used to screen new product ideas? (30.1)

9. Explain how marketers evaluate customer acceptance of a new product. (30.1)

10. What are four reasons for expanding a product line? (30.1)

11. What strategies might a business use during a product's growth stage? (30.2)

12. What strategies might a business use during a product's maturity stage? (30.2)

13. List the strategies that a company can use during a product's decline stage. (30.2)

14. Explain the concept of product positioning. (30.2)

REVIEW FACTS and IDEAS

6. A product item is a specific model, brand, or size of product within a product line. A product line is a group of closely related products that are manufactured and/or sold by a business.

7. Product width is the number of different product lines a business carries. Product depth is the number of product items offered within each product line.

8. The types of criteria are general product, marketing, and production characteristics.

9. Marketers use marketing research techniques during product development and continued monitoring of product performance after introduction to evaluate customer acceptance.

10. To build on an already established image, to increase sales and profits, to offer customers complementary products, and to appeal to new markets.

11. Strategies might include heavy advertising and other means of promotion, such as in-store displays, to draw customers' attention.

12. Strategies might include advertising to compete with similar products and improving the product.

13. Sell or license, recommit, discount, regionalize, modernize, or alter the product.

14. Product positioning refers to the efforts of a business to identify, place, and sell its products in the marketplace.

FOCUS on KEY POINTS

Ask volunteers to read the summaries aloud and give the classroom one real-life example for each concept.

REVIEW VOCABULARY

Anwers will vary. See glossary for definitions of **1–5.** A sample answer might read:

2. A *product item* is a specific model, brand, or size of product within a *product line*.

649

CHAPTER 30 REVIEW

BUILD SKILLS

15. Workplace Skills

Answers will vary; students should be tactful in their responses to the customer.

16. Technology Applications

Reports will vary, but should describe the effects of one technological achievement in today's cars.

17. Math Practice

At most, 12 stores (2 mass market stores and 10 small retail chain stores); $90,000 - (2 \times \$20,000) = \$50,000$; $\$50,000 \div \$5,000 = 10$

DEVELOP CRITICAL THINKING

18. Investigating New Product Development

Student reports will vary; all reports should identify the product, its intended users, and their rationale for believing that the product will or will not be successful.

19. Green Products for Green Marketing

Answers will differ depending on the products chosen; students should demonstrate an understanding of the concepts of product modification, ecologically sound product, and green market.

BUILD SKILLS

15. Workplace Skills

Human Relations You are the manager of a large grocery store that has recently remodeled. An exasperated customer confronts you because he cannot find a product. He complains that the new organization of products makes no sense. What might you do to pacify the customer and encourage him to continue shopping at the store?

16. Technology Applications

Technology and Car Features Investigate how technological improvements have impacted cars in the past five years. Using a word processing program, prepare a written report of 150 to 200 words about one technological development and its effect on the kinds of features offered in today's cars.

17. Math Practice

Slotting Fees Retailers sometimes charge manufacturers slotting fees for helping to introduce merchandise. Assume that a small retail chain charges $5,000 per store for a new brand of hot dogs, while a mass market merchandiser charges $20,000 per store for the same product. To how many stores could you sell your brand of hot dogs if your company has a slotting allowance budget of $90,000 and must include at least two mass market stores?

DEVELOP CRITICAL THINKING

18. Investigating New Product Development

Perform an Internet search for a sports-related product that is being introduced. Write a one-page report on the product, its intended users, and your rationale for believing that the product will or will not be successful.

19. Green Products for Green Marketing

In response to the development of a market for ecologically sound products, manufacturers are designing products that are safe for the environment, or they are adapting current products to fit the green market.

Choose a company that interests you, describe their current product line, and suggest ways one or several products could be modified to be environmentally friendly. Finally, explain how the product modifications you are suggesting would affect the company's marketing strategies.

 Formative Assessment

Formative assessment is an essential component of classroom work. This type of assessment provides information that is used as feedback to modify teaching and meet student needs.

L1 Review key terms for this section. Ask students to write one sentence for each key term.

L2 Provide examples of factors that affect product positioning in story form. After each, have the students identify which factor is affecting product positioning and explain how it does so.

L3 Ask students to come up with stories that illustrate one or several factors that affect how a product is positioned.

 Reteach If the results of this formative assessment seem low, consider the following activity:

Read the sections' subheads aloud and have students name two key facts or important details for each.

APPLY CONCEPTS

20. Identifying Product Mix

Explore a Web site for a car manufacturer, such as Ford, General Motors, DaimlerChrysler, Honda, Toyota, or another one of your choice. Identify the product mix offered by the car manufacturer.

Activity Write an outline detailing one product line and the primary market for each product in that product line.

21. Presenting Width and Depth of a Product Line

Investigate a consumer product, such as digital cameras, cellular phones, handheld gaming devices, cosmetics, or sporting equipment, by a specific manufacturer. Identify the width and depth of the selected product line.

Activity Prepare a chart presenting your findings. List each product line as a separate column heading. Then list particular product names in the columns under the appropriate product line. See Figure 30.1 for an example.

NET SAVVY

22. Product Line Extensions

Find a food product manufacturer's Web site (Campbell's Soup, J. M. Smucker, Dean Foods, Kellogg's, Hershey Foods, General Mills, H. J. Heinz, Kraft, Del Monte) to obtain five examples of product line extensions. Use presentation software to give an oral report on the name of the original product and the line extensions for the product.

CONNECTION

Role Play: Product Planning

Situation You are to assume the role of sales associate for a store that sells decorative pillows for the home. The store's owner (judge) has decided to introduce a new line of tapestry pillows imported from England. The store's owner (judge) has asked you for ideas and suggestions to help introduce this new line. The new pillow line will have a retail selling price of $70 to $80 each. This is 10 percent higher than current selling prices.

Activity You are to present your ideas and suggestions for introducing the new pillow line to the store's owner (judge).

Evaluation You will be evaluated on how well you meet the following performance indicators:

● Explain the concept of product mix

● Plan product mix

● Describe factors used by marketers to position products/businesses

● Develop strategies to position products/ businesses

● Explain the nature and scope of product/ service management function

 Online Action!

For more information and DECA Prep practice, go to *marketingessentials.glencoe.com/30/DECA*

APPLY CONCEPTS

20. Identifying Product Mix
Answers will vary with product line selected. Each outline must detail each product item (car brand) in the product line and identify a primary target market for the product.

21. Presenting Width and Depth of a Product Line
Graphic representations will vary; all representations should show student understanding of the information contained in the graph.

NET SAVVY

22. Product Line Extensions
Some examples might include Frito-Lays potato chips, Frito-Lays barbecue, sour cream and onion, etc.; Miracle Whip mayonnaise, Miracle Whip low-calorie mayonnaise; Häagen-Dazs ice cream; Häagen-Dazs sorbet.

MINI-QUIZ

Read these sentences to the students and have them volunteer the missing word(s).

1. The category manager is responsible for all the _____ for one generic product category such as foods, beverages, or health and beauty products. (brands)

2. The manufacturer can customize a product mix within a category according to _____ preference on a store-by-store basis. (customer)

For an expanded chapter quiz, go to Chapter 30 in the TeacherWorks CD-ROM and to Chapter 30 in the **Exam***View*® Pro Test Generator CD-ROM.

CONNECTION

Students should be evaluated according to the performance standards noted in the role play. For another DECA role play, go to the Competitive Events Workbook or the Student Activity Workbook, or go to **marketingessentials.glencoe.com/30/DECA**

Online Action! For instructions, ideas, and answer guide, go to the Teacher Center at **marketingessentials.glencoe.com**

DECA Advisors Corner

If you have a DECA operated, school-based enterprise, have students analyze how your products are selling to determine if products need to be added or deleted from your selection. Have chapter members conduct research among your school's population to determine their interests.

651

Chapter Overview

Chapter 31 explains the role of branding in product planning, including the various branding elements and types of brands. Students will learn the principal functions of product packaging and labels.

BUILD BACKGROUND

Initiate conversation about branding. Ask students to name as many brands as they can. Ask students what they think makes up a brand: how do brands affect their purchasing choices? Ask students how packaging and labeling are related to branding: how do packaging and labeling affect their purchasing choices?

Why It's Important

Branding, packaging, and labeling are all integral components of product planning. Brands identify products and connote benefits, features, and qualities, so it is important that a brand appropriately projects the company's image and culture. Similarly, packaging and labeling must be carefully planned to create a good impression and sell the product.

Prepare to Read

Ask a volunteer to write the chapter's three topics on the board:

- branding
- packaging
- labeling

Tell students to fill in the section headings as they preview or read the chapter. They will then have a thorough chapter outline to use as a study guide.

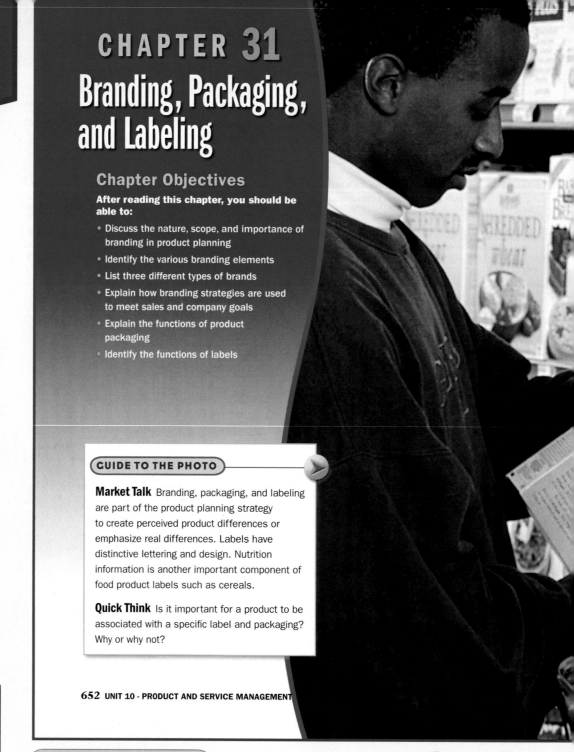

CHAPTER 31
Branding, Packaging, and Labeling

Chapter Objectives

After reading this chapter, you should be able to:

- Discuss the nature, scope, and importance of branding in product planning
- Identify the various branding elements
- List three different types of brands
- Explain how branding strategies are used to meet sales and company goals
- Explain the functions of product packaging
- Identify the functions of labels

GUIDE TO THE PHOTO

Market Talk Branding, packaging, and labeling are part of the product planning strategy to create perceived product differences or emphasize real differences. Labels have distinctive lettering and design. Nutrition information is another important component of food product labels such as cereals.

Quick Think Is it important for a product to be associated with a specific label and packaging? Why or why not?

GUIDE TO THE PHOTO

Market Talk Lead a discussion about how labeling on a product has influenced students' decisions or actions as consumers. Allow them to provide specific examples of times packaging has "sold" them on an item.

Quick Think Answers will vary. Packaging is used to create an image for a product. Labels help consumers identify a product that they may like or be comfortable with. For this reason, companies rarely abandon a label design once a product establishes itself in the marketplace.

Follow Up Ask students to discuss shopping experiences when they thought they bought one product but ended up with something else. Have students explain how the label led them to make a mistaken purchase.

Performance indicators represent key skills and knowledge. Relating them to the concepts explained in this chapter is your key to success in DECA events. These acronyms represent DECA events that involve knowledge of concepts in this chapter.

AAAL*	FMAL*	MMS	TMDM
AAML*	FMDM	QSRM	TSE
ADC	FMML*	RMAL*	VPM*
BSM	FSRM	RMML*	
EMDM*	HMDM	SMDM	

In all these DECA events you should be able to follow these performance indicators:

- Explain the nature of branding
- Describe the uses of grades and standards in marketing

All the events with an asterisk (*) also include this performance indicator:

- Explain the use of brand names in selling

Some events include additional performance indicators. These are:

EMDM	Use the Internet to build brand equity
	Optimize a business's Web site placement with major search engines and directories
HMDM	Explain the nature of product extensions in the hospitality industry
TMDM	Explain the nature of product extensions in the travel and tourism industry
SMDM	Explain the use of branding in sports and entertainment marketing, Explain logo rights
AAML	Explain fashion-brand images
AAAL	Explain fashion-brand images
FMML	Identify major product categories and classifications of food products in grocery stores

DECA PREP

Check your understanding of DECA performance indicators with the DECA activity in this chapter's review. For more information and DECA Prep practice, go to *marketingessentials .glencoe.com/31/DECA*

Chapter 31 - Branding, Packaging, and Labeling 653

CHAPTER 31 Classroom Resources

For the Teacher
- TeacherWorks
- marketingessentials.glencoe.com
- Interactive Chalkboard
- **Exam*View*®** Pro Test Generator
- Fast File Unit 10

For the Student
- *Marketing Essentials* Online Edition
- Student Activity Workbook
- Marketing Math Workbook
- Marketing Research Project Workbook
- School-to-Work Activity Workbook
- Competitive Events Workbook
- *BusinessWeek* Reader and Case Studies
- marketingessentials.glencoe.com

DECA events that require knowledge of branding, packaging, and labeling are described here. Discuss the performance indicators to make sure students understand how to demonstrate their understanding.

The events acronyms stand for:

AAAL:	Apparel and Accessories Marketing Series, AL
AAML:	Apparel and Accessories Marketing Series, ML
ADC:	Advertising Campaign Event
BSM:	Business Services Marketing Series
EMDM:	E-Commerce Management Team Decision Making Event
FMAL:	Food Marketing Series, AL
FMDM:	Financial Analysis Management Team Decision Making Event
FMML:	Food Marketing Series, ML
FSRM:	Full Service Restaurant Management Series
HMDM:	Hospitality Services Management Team Decision Making Event
MMS:	Marketing Management Series
QSRM:	Quick Serve Restaurant Management Series
RMAL:	Retail Merchandising Series, AL
RMML:	Retail Merchandising Series, ML
SMDM:	Sports and Entertainment Marketing Management Team Decision Making Event
TMDM:	Travel and Tourism Marketing Management Team Decision Making Event
TSE:	Technical Sales Event
VPM:	Vehicles and Petroleum Marketing Series

DECA PREP

Find timed DECA Prep activities correlated to the Competitive Events Workbook for students and DECA tips for teachers at **marketingessentials.glencoe.com /31/DECA.**

FOCUS

Introducing the Section

COLLABORATIVE ACTIVITY

Divide students into groups of two or three and have each group choose a brand with which they are all familiar. Have each group answer the following questions about their brand:

- Is it selling a product, service, or idea?

- Is it a name, term, symbol, or combination of these elements?

- Does it identify one product, a family of related products, or all products of a company?

- What benefits, features, or qualities does the brand connote?

Preteaching Key Terms

List the vocabulary terms on the board. Have students discuss each term and reach a consensus on each term's meaning. Write class definitions on the board so students can check their definitions as they read the section.

- brand
- brand name
- trade name
- brand mark
- trade character
- trademark
- national brands
- private distributor brands
- generic brands
- brand extension
- brand licensing
- mixed brand
- co-branding

OBJECTIVES

- Discuss the nature, scope, and importance of branding in product planning
- Identify the various branding elements
- List three different types of brands
- Explain how branding strategies are used to meet sales and company goals

KEY TERMS

- brand
- brand name
- trade name
- brand mark
- trade character
- trademark
- national brands
- private distributor brands
- generic brands
- brand extension
- brand licensing
- mixed brand
- co-branding

Branding Elements and Strategies

READ and STUDY

BEFORE YOU READ

Connect Have you or a member of your family recently shopped for or purchased an automobile? How did you know about the benefits and characteristics of the vehicle before you saw it in person?

THE MAIN IDEA

The name of a company and the names of its products or services need to project a positive image. Selecting, promoting, and protecting that image, or brand, is an integral part of the marketing function.

STUDY ORGANIZER

In a chart like the one below, take notes on the branding process.

WHILE YOU READ

Analyze Why are brands so important to the success of a business?

Branding

Branding is an important component of the product planning process. A **brand** is a name, term, design, symbol, or combination of these elements that identifies a product or service and distinguishes it from its competitors. A brand can be used to identify one product, a family of related products, or all products of a company. Brands connote any number of benefits,

READ and STUDY

BEFORE YOU READ

Lead students in listing benefits and characteristics about a car before they see it.

THE MAIN IDEA

Ask students to give an example of a product or service that projects a company in positive light.

STUDY ORGANIZER

Draw the organizer on the board. A full-size downloadable study organizer can be found at marketingessentials.glencoe.com. As study continues, work together to complete the organizer.

WHILE YOU READ

Model for students how they can list the important aspects of branding as they read the section.

features, or qualities. For example, a company may want to cultivate a brand that connotes quality and reliability. Another company may want to cultivate a brand that connotes fun and excitement. Brands are one of a company's most important assets and are powerful tools in the marketing and selling process.

Elements of Branding

Brands are developed to target customers' needs and preferences and include elements such as brand names, trade names, brand marks, trade characters, and trademarks. These elements are often combined to form a firm's corporate symbol or name.

Effective brands have tremendous value and frequently become global brands. Global brands appeal to consumers beyond cultural or political boundaries. For example, McDonald's is an effective global brand. The company's brand seeks to project an image of consistent quality in food and service, but it adapts its

menu to meet the needs of consumers in individual countries.

Brand Name

A **brand name**, also called a product brand, is a word, group of words, letters, or numbers that represent a product or service. An effective brand name should be easy pronounced, distinctive, and recognizable. Examples include PT Cruiser, Pepsi, Barbie, Pop-Tarts, and Big Mac.

Trade Name

A **trade name**, or corporate brand, identifies and promotes a company or a division of a particular corporation. The trade name is the legal name that a company uses when it does business and is used to promote a positive image of the organization such as quality, value, and reliability. Procter & Gamble, Dell, Disney, Kellogg's, Nike, and Yahoo are all examples of trade names. The trade name

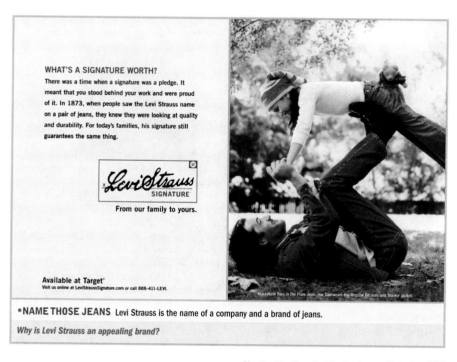

WHAT'S A SIGNATURE WORTH?
There was a time when a signature was a pledge. It meant that you stood behind your work and were proud of it. In 1873, when people saw the Levi Strauss name on a pair of jeans, they knew they were looking at quality and durability. For today's families, his signature still guarantees the same thing.

Levi Strauss
SIGNATURE

From our family to yours.

Available at Target®
Visit us online at LeviStraussSignature.com or call 888-411-LEVI.

Mackenzie flies in the Flare Jean. Her Dad wears the Regular Fit Jean and Trucker Jacket.

• **NAME THOSE JEANS** Levi Strauss is the name of a company and a brand of jeans.

Why is Levi Strauss an appealing brand?

Chapter 31 - Branding, Packaging, and Labeling **655**

Concept Development

BRAND MARK AND TRADE CHARACTER

Write a brand name on the board that does not have a brand mark or trade character. Have students give suggestions for brand marks or trade characters and write suggestions on the board. Be sure to tell students that brand marks and trade characters should not be too complicated, as simple marks and characters are often more visually appealing and easily recognizable.

Individualized Practice

GENERATING BRAND NAMES

L1 Ask students to list ten branded products that they know of and to then list another brand of that product if possible.

L2 Ask students to make three columns on a sheet of paper. In the first column, have students list products for which they will only buy one brand. In the second, have students list products for which they will buy any brand. In the third, have students list products for which they will buy a store brand or generic product.

L3 Ask students to choose a brand that they view as outdated. Have students write up a plan to reposition the brand, including changes to brand name, image, brand mark or trade character, advertising, etc.

TEACHING POINTS

Demonstrate You may want to bring in examples of brand name products, store brand products, and generic products. You may also want to bring in an example of a repositioned brand, showing the product before and after the change.

---

supports the product brands offered by the company.

Brand Mark and Trade Character

Many brands incorporate a unique symbol, coloring, lettering, or other design elements known as a **brand mark**. A brand mark is recognizable visually and does not need to be pronounced. Some examples of brand marks are the U.S. Postal Service's eagle or Apple Computer's apple. On the other hand, a **trade character** is a specific type of brand mark, one with human form or characteristics. Some examples of trade characters include Green Giant's Jolly Green Giant, the Pillsbury Doughboy, and the Keebler Elves.

Trademark

A **trademark** is a word, name, symbol, device, or a combination of these elements that is given legal protection by the federal government. Trademarks are used to prevent other companies from using a similar element that might be confused with the trademarked one. For example, the image of the golden arches is a trademark of McDonald's. The colorful peacock is a trademark for NBC. No other company can use these symbols. The U.S. Patent and Trademark Office grants trademark rights. Disputes regarding trademarks are settled in federal courts.

Sometimes companies try to extend trademark branding of products and services to include additional elements of sound, color, and smell. Boston Duck Tours, a sightseeing tour company, received a sound trademark for the sound of a human voice making ducklike quacking noises.

Trademarks are followed by a registered trademark symbol (®). When brand names, brand marks, trade characters, and other elements of branding are registered as trademarks, they cannot be used or misused by other companies.

Importance of Brands in Product Planning

Branding establishes an image for a product or company and projects that image to

---

its customers and the marketplace. The use of brands is important in product planning for several reasons.

- **To build product recognition and customer loyalty** It is important that satisfied customers be able to easily recognize a company's branded products when they return to make repeat purchases.

- **To ensure quality and consistency** Through branding, companies communicate to customers that they can expect consistent quality and performance, purchase after purchase. Branding connotes consistency. For example, nine out of ten people will pay 25 percent more to buy GE Soft White light bulbs rather than select another brand. The GE Soft White brand is perceived by customers to be of higher quality and a better value than lower-priced competitors.

- **To capitalize on brand exposure** Branding helps companies extend their products or services into new target markets. It also helps introduce new product lines or categories. Customers and prospects are more willing to try new products that carry a familiar brand name.

With careful planning, companies can also adjust or reposition a brand to capitalize on changes in the market.

Generating Brand Names

It is estimated that 75 percent of all companies introduce a new product name every year. The U.S. Patent and Trademark Office registered over 79,000 trademarks in 1999, for example. It is understandable, therefore, why some companies find it increasingly difficult to secure desirable corporate or product names—so many names are already taken!

How does a company create a brand name? Some companies turn to computer software programs that specialize in generating brand names. These programs will check to see if a name is already owned and trademarked by another company. Other companies hire branding agencies, naming consultants, or

---

Extended Activity

Trademark

Lead a discussion about well-known trademarks. You may want to bring in examples of well-known trademarks, such as a logo, as well as more unusual trademarks such as color. Then, ask students to think of companies that have successfully trademarked sounds, colors, or smells. Ask: What makes these elements distinct enough to trademark? Divide students into small groups of two or three and have them list elements that should be able to be trademarked, and elements that should not be able to be trademarked. Have each group present their lists and then lead class discussion about where the line should be drawn.

public relations firms to generate and check the availability of brand names.

Branding is so important to product planning that over 60 percent of all companies conduct market research to test new brand names before they are released. After a name has been generated and researched, companies will then conduct brand-loyalty research to gauge the brand's effectiveness.

Once established, brand names are carefully protected and rarely changed.

Types of Brands

Wholesalers and retailers also brand their products. As a result, there are three classifications of brands, one for each type of company that brands its products: national brands (manufacturers), private distributor brands (wholesalers and retailers), and generic brands.

National Brands

National brands, also called producer brands, are owned and initiated by national manufacturers or by companies that provide services. Examples of national brands for consumer goods include Hershey Foods, Colgate-Palmolive, Whirlpool, Sunoco, and

Ford. Examples of service companies that generate national brands are Northwest Airlines, Hilton, Avis, Bank One, and AFLAC.

The Importance of National Brands

National brands generate the majority of sales for most consumer product categories. Approximately 70 percent of all food products, 65 percent of all appliances, 80 percent of all gasoline, and 100 percent of all automobiles are sold under national brands.

Electronic commerce has created a new category of national brand: the Internet brand. There are Internet brands for both consumer products and services. Examples of Internet consumer product brands include Amazon.com and eBay, while examples of service brands include Monster, Google, and Yahoo.

Private Distributor Brands

Private distributor brands, also called private brands, store brands, dealer brands, or private labels, are developed and owned by wholesalers and retailers. The manufacturer's name does not appear on the product. Some examples of private distributor brands are Radio Shack, Kohl's Villager, and Wal-Mart's George.

NET MARKETING

Free Entertainment

Video games can be expensive, but there is a way to play games for free. Advergames let Web site visitors play free of charge, as long as the gamers are willing to see advertising while they are playing. Several of Kraft's best known brands have games. At Nabiscoworld.com, visitors can play *Ritz Bits Sumo Wrestling*. Players control either the Creamy Marshmallow or the Chocolatey Fudge cracker. After quite a bit of belly smacking, the result is the S'more-flavored cracker.

Advergames Come Under Criticism

Some critics worry that advergames can be too influential and that children may not realize they are seeing advertising.

THINK LIKE A MARKETER

Why are many consumer products manufacturers using advergaming?

@ Online Action!

Go to *marketingessentials.glencoe.com/31/net* to find a project on advertising in games.

marketingessentials.glencoe.com

Chapter 31 - Branding, Packaging, and Labeling **657**

NET MARKETING

Free Entertainment

Discussion Ask students who have played advergames to share their experiences with the class. Lead the discussion by asking the following question: Is playing the game for free a fair tradeoff for seeing the advertising and brand messages?

THINK LIKE A MARKETER **Answer:** Advergaming is an effective way to expose both youth and adults to a company's products. According to online usage data from Nielsen Net Ratings, advergaming is becoming increasingly popular. The typical player spends a half-hour on a game site, often replaying a single game 15 times or more.

@ Online Action! For instructions, ideas, and answer guide, go to the Teacher Center at marketingessentials.glencoe.com

Concept Development

GENERATING BRAND NAMES

Have students list new products that have come out in the last year, then ask them the following questions: Are these products extensions of existing products or new products? Is the brand name based on an existing product or entirely new? Have students explain their responses.

TEACHING POINTS

Extend Write four or five new product names on the board and lead discussion about why the companies might have chosen the brand names. Then, divide students into small groups of two or three and give each group a foreign language dictionary. Ask students to choose one of the brand names on the board and come up with a brand name to use for the product in the other language. Remind students to take into account what their brand name might sound like or mean in the other language.

Concept Development

NATIONAL BRANDS

Ask a volunteer to write four headings on the board: food, appliances, gasoline, and automobiles. Ask students to list brand names for each category, both national and private distributor brands. Note the number of national versus private distributor brands in each category and lead a discussion about how their list compares to the percentages listed in the text (70 percent of food products, 65 percent of appliances, 80 percent of gasoline, and 100 percent of automobiles are national brands). Ask students why they think lower percentages of food products and appliances are national brands, compared to the higher percentage of gasoline and the 100 percent share of automobiles.

ASSESS

Review Guide

CONCEPTS

1. Ask students to list the various branding elements and give examples of each element.
brand name, trade name, brand mark and trade character, trademark

2. Ask students to list the three types of brands.
national, private distributor, and generic

KEY TERMS

Have students review key terms, their spellings, and definitions in small groups.

ONLINE SELF-ASSESSMENT

Have students go to marketingessentials.glencoe.com for the Section 31.1 practice test.

Individualized Review

L1 Assign and review Chapter 31 activities in the Student Activity Workbook.

L2 Assign and review Chapter 31 activities in the Marketing Math Workbook.

L3 Assign and review Chapter 31 activities in the *BusinessWeek* Reader and Case Studies.

Marketing Practice

Have students choose a national brand product they recently bought. Have students research the product's branding strategy, as well as the competitors' branding strategies. Have students outline and write a two- to three-page report which relates their findings to the concepts found in Section 31.1.

Private distributor brands appeal to customers who desire the quality and performance of national brands at a lower price. Many large supermarket and retail chains have private distributor brands. For example, in the supermarket industry, private brands represent 45 percent of the market in Switzerland, 37 percent in England, 22 percent in Canada, and 12 percent in the United States. At some major department stores, such as J.C. Penney, private labels make up 40 percent of total sales; at Target, they account for 80 percent of apparel sales.

The Increasing Popularity of Private Brands

Private distributor brands are increasing their market share in most product categories worldwide. In 2003 in the United States, approximately 800 categories of private label goods existed in clothing, paper products, medications, vitamins, and pet foods.

Private brands are popular with retailers because they usually carry higher gross margins and thus are more profitable for the seller than manufacturer brands. Also, because private brands cannot be sold at competitors' stores, they help cultivate customer loyalty.

Generic Brands

Generic brands are products that do not carry a company identity. The packaging for generic products usually features a description of the product, such as "pancake mix" or "paper towels." Generic brands are generally sold in supermarkets and discount stores. These unbranded products are often priced 30 to 50 percent lower than manufacturer brands and 10 to 15 percent lower than private distributor brands. Companies that manufacture and sell generic brands do not heavily advertise or promote these products and, therefore, can pass on savings to customers.

The Jewel supermarket chain in Chicago was the first to introduce generic products in the 1970s. Generic products have expanded to include more than 300 product categories, including vitamins, auto parts, food staples, and pharmaceuticals. Generic products are now offered in more than 250 retail chains

---

throughout the United States, and more than 75 percent of all U.S. supermarkets carry generic items.

Branding Strategies

Companies develop and rely on a variety of branding strategies to meet sales and company objectives. Some of these strategies include brand extensions, brand licensing, mixed branding, and co-branding. Effective use of different brand strategies can increase sales of branded products and maximize company profits.

Brand Extension

Brand extension is a branding strategy that uses an existing brand name to promote a new or improved product in a company's product line. For example, Ocean Spray extended its cranberry juice drink product line by adding flavors, including Cran®Apple, Cran®Cherry, and Cran®Grape fruit blends. Launching new products is costly, and the failure rate for new products is high. Sometimes companies can reduce this risk by using an already established brand name.

One risk that companies face when they employ a brand extension strategy is overextending a product line and diluting the brand. When does brand dilution occur? If a brand includes too many products, the original brand and other selections in the product line may lose recognition and appeal with customers.

Brand Licensing

Some companies allow other organizations to use their brand, brand mark, or trade character through **brand licensing**. This authorization is a legal licensing agreement for which the licensing company receives a fee, such as a royalty, in return for the authorization. The agreement delineates all the terms and conditions under which the brand may be used.

Companies license their brands to increase revenue sources, enhance company image, and sell more of their core products. For example, the National Football League (NFL) has

---

 Critical Thinking

Ask students if they are more likely to purchase national, private distributor, or generic brands. Does the product category make a difference in their decision, such as if they are buying food rather than clothing? Have students share their responses in class.

---

licensing arrangements with Pepsi and Visa. Pepsi and Visa use the NFL name and logo in their promotions to try to attract customers loyal to the NFL.

Mixed Brands

Some manufacturers and retailers use a **mixed-brand** strategy to sell products. They offer a combination of manufacturer, private distributor, and generic brands. A manufacturer of a national brand will agree to make a product for sale under another company's brand. For example, Michelin manufactures its own brand of tires as well as tires for sale at Sears under the Sears brand name. A mixed-brand strategy enables a business to maintain brand loyalty through its national brand and reach several different target markets through private brands, thus increasing its overall product mix. It can maximize its profits by selling a private brand product without damaging the reputation and the sales of its national brand product.

Co-Branding

Have you noticed that Kellogg's Pop-Tarts are made with Smucker's fruit filling? This is an example of a **co-branding** strategy. A co-branding strategy combines one or more brands in the manufacture of a product or in the delivery of a service. This strategy enables companies to capitalize on the popularity of other companies' products and services to reach new customers and, ideally, increase sales for both companies' brands. Co-branding can work with one or many partners.

Co-branding can also work when two or more retailers share the same location. Starbucks Coffee Co. has an agreement with Barnes & Noble to open coffee shops inside their bookstores.

CLOSE

Provide newspapers, magazines, or online advertisements to the class. Have students choose an ad and point out the following: brand name, trade name, brand mark or trade character, or trademark. Then, have them decide whether it is a national brand or private distributor brand. Repeat with another ad.

Extended Activity

Brand Loyalty

Ask students to interview a friend, family member, or other person about a brand that they have remained loyal to over the years. They might ask, "What about the brand has made them stay loyal? How has the brand changed over the years?" Have students summarize their interviews in a one-page report.

31.1 AFTER YOU READ

Reviewing Key Terms and Concepts

1. What is the difference between a brand name and a trade name?
2. List the three types of brands.
3. What are the different types of branding strategies?

Integrating Academic Skills

Math

4. According to a *Forbes* magazine study in 2004, General Electric had a trade name or corporate brand value of $54.2 billion, compared to Nike's brand value of $19.7 billion. How many times larger was the brand value of GE than Nike?

Language Arts

5. Kellogg's sells a cereal called Frosted Flakes in the United States, but it is called Frosties in most European countries and *Zucaritas* in Italy. Write a 150-word paper explaining why consumer product companies, such as Kellogg's, use different names for the same product in various countries.

 Online Action!

Check your answers at *marketingessentials.glencoe.com/31/read*

marketingessentials.glencoe.com

Chapter 31 - Branding, Packaging, and Labeling **659**

 AFTER YOU READ

Reviewing Key Terms and Concepts

1. A brand name or product brand is the word, group of words, letters, or numbers representing a brand that can be spoken. A trade name or corporate brand identifies the company or company division.

2. Three types of brands: national (consumer product, service, and Internet), private distributor, and generic.

3. Four types of branding strategies include brand extension, brand licensing, mixed brands, and co-branding.

Integrating Academic Skills

4. 2.751 times as large; $54.2 ÷ $19.7 = 2.751

5. Answers will vary; students should be able to state that large companies have traditionally attempted to build brand equity in different countries by addressing advertising and promotions based upon the unique culture of the country. However, with the rise of a global economy, many companies see the advantage of having a single brand.

Online Action! Answers at *marketingessentials.glencoe.com/31/read*

FOCUS

Introducing the Section

COLLABORATIVE ACTIVITY

To prepare for reading this section, bring several types of products to class in the amounts in which they are usually packaged (such as 12 pencils, 2 cookies, 4 rolls of tape, 50 paper clips or rubber bands, etc.). Also bring in the packaging but keep it out of sight. Ask students how each product is normally packaged for retail sale, and then place the package with the product. Divide students into small groups of two or three and give each group one of the products. Ask groups to brainstorm other types of packaging that could be used for their product.

Preteaching Key Terms

Bring in an example of a package or label fitting each of the key terms (some might fit more than one term). Ask students to guess which package or label goes with each term. As students read chapter, they can see if they guessed correctly.

- package
- mixed bundling
- price bundling
- blisterpacks
- aseptic packaging
- cause packaging
- label
- brand label
- descriptive label
- grade label

 Critical Thinking

Ask students what would happen if all products were packaged in the same way. What would happen to competition if all labels looked alike?

OBJECTIVES

- Explain the functions of product packaging
- Identify the functions of labels

KEY TERMS

- **package**
- **mixed bundling**
- **price bundling**
- **blisterpacks**
- **aseptic packaging**
- **cause packaging**
- **label**
- **brand label**
- **descriptive label**
- **grade label**

Packaging and Labeling

READ and STUDY

BEFORE YOU READ

Predict Most consumer products are packaged and labeled. Why do you think companies go to the expense of packaging and labeling consumer products?

THE MAIN IDEA

While branding gives a specific company or product brand personality, packaging and labels put a "face" on a product. Effective packaging and labels create a good impression, help sell the product, and communicate benefits to customers.

STUDY ORGANIZER

In a chart like the one below, take notes about the functions of packaging.

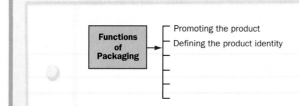

WHILE YOU READ

Connect Consider how packaging and labeling help you as a consumer.

Packaging

A **package** is the physical container or wrapping for a product. Developing a product's package is an integral part of product planning and promotion. It is estimated that ten percent of a product's retail price is spent on developing, designing, and producing just the package.

READ and STUDY

BEFORE YOU READ

Lead students in brainstorming reasons why companies package and label their products.

THE MAIN IDEA

Read the main idea aloud and ask volunteers to give specific examples of packaging and labeling that create a good impression, help sell the product, and communicate benefits.

STUDY ORGANIZER

Model the study organizer for students by filling in the next blank. A full-size, downloadable study organizer can be found at **marketingessentials.glencoe.com**

 WHILE YOU READ Model for students how to create a two-column, two-row chart to keep track of benefits of packaging and labeling.

Functions of Packaging

A package does much more than hold a product; it is also a selling tool. Companies take great care when designing or redesigning their products' packages.

Packaging fulfills several functions, including promoting and selling the product, defining product identity, providing information, expressing benefits and features, ensuring safe use, and protecting the product, among others (see Figure 31.1).

Promoting and Selling the Product

Customer reaction to a product's package and its brand name is an important factor in its success or failure in the marketplace. Attractive, colorful, and visually appealing packages have promotional value and can carry important messages about the product's performance, features, and benefits. As more and more stores become self-service, a product's package serves an increasingly important marketing function.

Sometimes marketers package or bundle two or more complementary products or services together in one package. The practice of packaging different products and services together is known as **mixed bundling**. Usually the mixed bundled price is cheaper than purchasing all the products separately. **Price bundling** occurs when two or more similar products are placed on sale for one package price.

A container's design can minimize sales lost to competitors' products. It can even create new sales opportunities. Pump soap containers were designed to be neater, cleaner, and easier to use than bar soaps. These new containers have not replaced bar soaps; instead, they provide a choice for customers. Pump-type dispensers created new sales and started an entire new line of soap products.

Defining Product Identity

Packages are often used to promote an image such as prestige, convenience, or status.

Providing Information

A package provides information for the customer. Many packages give directions for using the product and information about its contents, product guarantees, nutritional value, or potential hazards.

Expressing Customer Needs

Product packages often come in various sizes to meet the needs of different market segments. Family packs are designed to meet the needs of larger families, while smaller packages are made for individuals. Specific examples include multipacks of beverages such as soda and juice, bulk sizes of paper packages, single-serving cans of soup, and family meals at fast-food outlets.

Both products and package designs must also keep up with changing lifestyles. Lunch kits with sliced meats and snack kits with cookies did not exist 25 years ago. Now, this product category is estimated to be a $1 billion business.

Ensuring Safe Use

A package can also improve product safety for the customer. For example, many products formerly packaged in glass now come in plastic containers. To avoid misuse or product tampering, many nonprescription drugs, cosmetics, and food items are now sold in tamper-resistant packages such as blisterpacks and jars and plastic containers with sealed lids. **Blisterpacks** are packages with preformed plastic molds surrounding individual items arranged on a backing.

Countless other products are packaged in childproof containers. These types of containers feature lids that are more difficult to open, thereby reducing the chances of accidental spills and poisonings.

Protecting the Product

In addition to helping sell the product, a package must also protect a product during shipping, storage, and display. The package design should also prevent or discourage tampering, prevent shoplifting, and protect against breakage and spoilage.

Airtight containers are especially important with perishable food products such as cheese or lunch meat.

Chapter 31 - Branding, Packaging, and Labeling **661**

 Online Activity

Online Product Information

Some companies, such as fast food restaurants, provide product information on their company Web site rather than on their product packaging. Have students choose a restaurant, visit their company Web site, and list the information they provide on their Web site that is not printed on their packaging. Have students share their findings with the class. Then, spark a discussion by asking students why companies might prefer not to have some information on their packaging.

TEACH

Discussion Starter

FUNCTIONS OF PACKAGING

Ask students to consider the following scenario: A company wants to increase sales of its peanut butter. All of its competitors sell peanut butter in jars, and it wants to take a new bold packaging stand. Ask: What other packaging should the company consider? As students brainstorm packaging ideas, have a volunteer write ideas on the board. Lead a discussion about the advantages and disadvantages of using each type of packaging for peanut butter.

Concept Development

PROVIDING INFORMATION

Bring in examples of product packaging that provides a lot of information, such as food packaging or medicine packaging. Divide students into small groups of two or three and give each group a product package. Ask: What information is required by law? How do companies indicate which information is most important? Have groups list all the information they can find on the package and present their findings to the class.

TEACHING POINTS

Model You may want to look at one product package as a class and model for students how to identify the various types of product information on the package.

Individualized Math Skills

PROMOTING AND SELLING THE PRODUCT

L1 Ask students to explain how consumers save money through mixed bundling or price bundling.
Consumers buy two or more complementary products or two or more similar products in a package for less than the price of buying the individual products separately.

L2 The price of one bottle of shampoo is $2.49. The price of two bottles of shampoo price-bundled is $3.99. How much is the consumer saving by purchasing the price-bundled shampoo instead of buying two separate bottles?
The consumer saves $.99; $2.49 × 2 = $4.98; $4.98 − $3.99 = $.99

L3 Provide students with a list of various personal care products such as soap, shampoo, conditioner, body wash, etc. and their individual prices. Products should all be from the same brand. Have students choose products that complement each other and come up with various mixed bundling ideas. Have students price each mixed bundle and calculate the consumer savings over buying the products individually.

Enrichment

PROTECTING THE PRODUCT

Have students choose partners and tell them that they will be designing a new form of packaging for eggs. They should consider product safety during shipping, storage, and display, as well as preventing tampering and shoplifting and protecting against breakage and spoilage. Have each pair draw and label plans for their new packaging.

Figure 31.1 *The Functions of Packaging*

• **Buy Me!** Packaging serves many purposes, from product protection to attracting customers' attention. It is a selling tool that promotes and sells the product, defines the product's identity, provides information, ensures safe use, and protects the product.

How can nutritional information on packaging help promote a product, as well?

PROMOTING AND SELLING THE PRODUCT

A well-designed package is a powerful point-of-purchase selling device because it can make a product stand out from its competition.

DEFINING PRODUCT IDENTITY

Packaging can be a crucial part of an overall marketing strategy for a product—particularly its advertising component.

PROVIDING INFORMATION

Packaging gives customers useful information through labels: directions for use, nutritional information, and instructions for care.

MEETING CUSTOMERS' NEEDS

When designing packages, product planners analyze customer lifestyles and create packaging that meets customers' needs for size and convenience.

ENSURING SAFE USE

Proper packaging, such as childproof caps, helps to eliminate potential injuries or misuse of a product.

PROTECTING THE PRODUCT

Packaging can protect a product from damage or spoilage.

@ Online Action!
Go to *marketingessentials.glencoe.com/31/figure/1* to find a project on packaging

---

Figure 31.1 *The Functions of Packaging*

Discussion Ask students to explain how they think each product featured in **Figure 31.1** serves the corresponding function of packaging. For each packaging function (promoting and selling the product, defining product identity, providing information, ensuring safe use, and protecting the product), have students brainstorm examples of other products whose packaging serves that same function.

Caption Answer Nutritional information on a label will help sell a product to someone who is health-conscious, on a specialized diet, or has food allergies.

@ Online Action! For instructions, ideas, and answer guide, go to the Teacher Center at **marketingessentials.glencoe.com**

If product planners do not consider these factors when designing packaging, companies run the risk of losing business as well as eroding their brand images.

Contemporary Packaging Issues

Product packaging offers companies unique opportunities to incorporate the latest technologies and address lifestyle changes as well as environmental, social, and political concerns.

Aseptic Packaging

Aseptic packaging incorporates a technology that keeps foods fresh without refrigeration for extended periods. The process involves separately sterilizing the package and the food product, and filling and sealing the package in a sterile environment. Canning and bottling are aseptic methods of food storage.

Environmental Packaging

Companies are trying to develop packages that respond to consumer demand for environmentally sensitive designs. Recent public opinion surveys show that most Americans support less wasteful packaging. They are even willing to pay more for products that reduce waste. In response to consumer concern, companies are making more packages that are reusable, recyclable, and safer for the environment.

Many companies that manufacture spray products such as hair products, air freshener, and paint have switched from using aerosol cans to pump dispensers, which do not release ozone-destroying chlorofluorocarbons, or CFCs, into the atmosphere.

Cause Packaging

Some companies are also using their packages to promote social and political causes.

GLOBAL MARKET

They Got Sole

High fashion can have very humble beginnings. Dr. Martens boots, known as Doc Martens, are the invention of a British orthopedic physician who wanted to create work shoes for people with foot problems. They were an immediate hit among fashion trendsetters, became a British cultural symbol, and are now popular on many continents.

Their popularity is in part due to their broad appeal. In the United States, musicians and rockers of the grunge, alternative, garage band, and ska scenes wore them in the late 1980s and 1990s. But they were also part of the mainstream marketplace.

Regional Differences But not everyone likes the same Docs. Europeans wear Doc Martens in bright colors, such as reds, greens, and blues. In Japan, younger women and some men like classic mid-calf-high boots in colors. Americans prefer black, brown, and tan. Americans are more likely to buy hiking boot styles because of a more casual lifestyle.

Aside from the color differences, all Doc Martens have certain design elements in common. According to the company's marketing director, all Docs have a thick, deeply treaded sole that extends beyond the upper and heavy stitching, often in white, along its seams.

CRITICAL THINKING

How can marketers develop a global brand but still address local needs?

@ Online Action!

Go to *marketingessentials.glencoe.com/31/ global* to find a project on global marketing of brands.

marketingessentials.glencoe.com

Chapter 31 - Branding, Packaging, and Labeling **663**

GLOBAL MARKET

They Got Sole

Discussion Lead a discussion about why different cultures prefer different styles. Ask students if they agree with the statement that Americans prefer the hiking boot style in black, brown, and tan.

CRITICAL THINKING **Answer:** Maintaining a global brand involves keeping an eye on what is popular in each local market and adjusting to different customer preferences. If the basic product is appealing, it has a good chance of being adopted with modifications appropriate to that culture.

@ Online Action! For instructions, ideas, and answer guide, go to the Teacher Center
marketingessentials.glencoe.com

TEACH CONTINUED

Concept Development

ENVIRONMENTAL PACKAGING

Ask students to list the typical foods they eat during a day and describe the packaging used for each food: Do they recycle the packaging or throw it away? Of the packaging they throw away, could any of it be recycled? On a two-column chart, have students list in one column foods they eat whose packaging can be recycled, and in the other column list foods whose packaging cannot be recycled. On the board, create a class chart of recyclable and non-recyclable food packaging. Lead a discussion about which column is longer and whether students feel it is important to be able to recycle food packaging.

TEACHING POINTS

Explain Explain to students what types of materials are recyclable. You may want to have a city representative come in to class and explain the city's recycling program, or pass out materials explaining the different types of recyclable materials.

Extend Ask students to choose a product from their list of non-recyclable products. Have students brainstorm how to change that product's packaging to be recyclable.

Critical Thinking

Ask students if they have ever bought a product only to find it was broken. Ask: Was this a result of poor packaging? How did their experience affect their view of the brand? Have students explain their answers.

Concept Development

CAUSE PACKAGING

Give students a worksheet with a list of brands or products on one side and the causes they promote on the other side. Have students match which brands/products they think go with each cause. Give students the correct answers and discuss if each brand/product is related to the cause on its packaging. Ask students if they feel companies should use their product packaging to promote social or political causes. Ask students to make a list of causes they think would be acceptable to the general public, and a list of causes they think are too controversial to be used on packaging.

TEACHING POINTS

Demonstrate Bring in examples of cause packaging and lead discussion about the different ways companies use packaging to promote a cause.

Follow Up Have students select a cause and a brand or product they think would be a good match with that cause. Have students write a letter to the president of the company persuading them to promote their cause through cause packaging.

Enrichment

LABELING LAWS

Make a list of various federal, state, and local labeling laws. Assign a law to each student and have students research the law, including the requirements of the law, when it was established, why it was established, products affected by the law, and any court cases regarding the law. Have students present their findings in an oral report and supply a visual aid showing the part of the product label to which their law pertains.

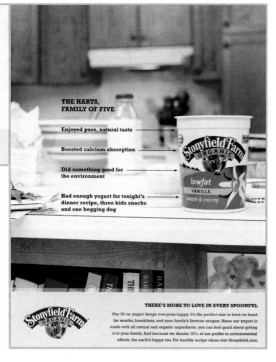

• **YOGURT on a MISSION** The Stonyfield Farm yogurt company prints messages on the lids of its containers. For example, in October 2004, they advertised a sweepstakes for schools in selected states to win the use of a refrigerated vending machine free of charge for one year. Stonyfield Farm donates ten percent of its profits each year to efforts that help protect or restore the Earth.

What message is the labeling of this product sending?

THE HARTS, FAMILY OF FIVE

Enjoyed pure, natural taste

Boosted calcium absorption

Did something good for the environment

Had enough yogurt for tonight's dinner recipe, three kids snacks and one begging dog

THERE'S MORE TO LOVE IN EVERY SPOONFUL

This practice is known as **cause packaging**. The issues on the packages may be totally unrelated to the products inside. Ben & Jerry's ice cream cartons promote saving the rain forests and express opposition to the use of bovine growth hormone to stimulate milk production in cows.

Printing messages on packages encourages consumers to participate in or think about issues. In many ways, cause packaging is also a company's attempt to differentiate its products from those of its competitors.

Labeling

A **label** is an information tag, wrapper, seal, or imprinted message that is attached to a product or its package. The main function of a label is to inform customers about a product's contents and give directions for use. Labels also protect businesses from legal liability if a consumer is injured during the use of its product. Fear of litigation, consumer pressure, government regulation, and concern for consumer safety are all factors that have compelled manufacturers to place more detailed information on labels.

There are three kinds of labels: brand, descriptive, and grade.

The **brand label** gives the brand name, trademark, or logo. For example, some bananas are stamped with the Chiquita brand label. Although this is an acceptable form of labeling, it does not supply sufficient product information.

A **descriptive label** gives information about the product's use, construction, care, performance, and other features. For example, food labels include product illustrations, weight statements, dating and storage information, ingredients, product guarantees,

---

AD GUIDE — YOGURT on a MISSION

Discussion Point out that this ad appeals to consumers' concern for the environment. Ask students if they would be more likely to buy a product that addresses environmental concerns and have them give reasons for their decision.

Caption Answer Answers may include: The word *organic* suggests that the yogurt is good for your body, and that the product is environmentally friendly. *Lowfat* would appeal to calorie-conscious shoppers.

Follow Up Organic products often project an image of being environmentally friendly. Have students research organic brands, choose one, and write a one-page report detailing in what way a particular organic brands helps support a sustainable environment.

and the manufacturer's name and address. Product illustrations must represent what is in the package. Weight statements give the net weight of the entire product minus the package or liquid in which it is packed.

Date and storage information is necessary for food items. Date information includes the "packed on" date (date food was packed), the "sell by" date (last date product should be sold), the "best if used by" date (last date for use for top quality), and the expiration date (date after which the product should not be used). Storage information tells how the product should be stored to have the least waste and best quality. Descriptive labels do not necessarily always contain all the information that consumers need when making a buying decision.

Nonfood labels usually provide consumers with instructions for the proper use and

Case Study

Looking for the Cool Factor

The Wrigley company has not spent a lot of time remaking its products over the years. It has been making its Juicy Fruit and Spearmint flavors for more than 100 years, and its Doublemint brand for more than 90 years. But recently the company wanted to expand its sales and extend its brand. So the company turned to Skippies for advice.

Ask the Teens

Skippies, short for School Kids with Income and Purchasing Power, are a target market segment that is getting more attention from market researchers. Teenagers spent $170 billion on products for themselves or their family households in 2003, up from $155 billion in 2000 according to a survey conducted by Teenage Research Unlimited.

Once Wrigley consulted with the Skippies, it introduced a new kind of Juicy Fruit in Strappleberry and Grapermelon flavors. Instead of having the normal long, flat shape with shiny foil around each stick, the new gum is candy-coated individual pieces packaged in blisterpacks. The gum package is flatter and wider than the traditional gum package and it has an inner case that slides out. The company also launched a tongue-twister contest on its Web site, offering free gum to winners. The traditional Juicy Fruit sticks are still on the market.

> **THINK STRATEGICALLY**
> Why are companies attempting to make connections with the youth market? Are there any problems with remixing a traditional brand?

@ Online Action! Go to *marketingessentials.glencoe.com/31/case* to find a project on marketing to teens.

 marketingessentials.glencoe.com

Chapter 31 - Branding, Packaging, and Labeling **665**

Case Study — Looking for the Cool Factor

Discussion After students read the Case Study, ask volunteers to give their opinion on the new Juicy Fruit gum. Ask: Have students tried the new gum or seen the advertisements? Does the fact that the new gum is a brand extension of the original Juicy Fruit positively or negatively impact their opinion?

> **THINK STRATEGICALLY** **Answer:** Marketers view this market as huge and want to capitalize on it. The packaging, name changes, and games are attempts to appeal to young people. The danger is that the company will dilute its original market and alienate long-time customers.

@ Online Action! For instructions, ideas, and answer guide, go to the Teacher Center at **marketingessentials.glencoe.com**

TEACH CONTINUED

Individualized Practice

LABELING

L1 Ask students to list the three types of labels and give an example of each.
Examples will vary; sample answers follow: brand label—Chiquita brand label on bananas; descriptive label—food labels with dating and storage information or nonfood labels with care instructions; grade label—eggs labeled with a quality grade.

L2 Ask students to create a visual aid showing the three types of labels. Have students write the three types of labels on a poster board and have students list characteristics of each label type and draw pictures of examples.
Types of labels include: brand, descriptive, and grade; pictures will vary.

L3 Give students examples of products that would be labeled with each of three types of labels (such as the labels on an apple, a box of cookies, and a carton of eggs). On three sheets of paper, have students draw a mock label for each product, including all the elements that would be on each label. On the descriptive label, have students identify all the parts of the label.
Product illustrations, weight statements, dating and storage information, universal product code, product guarantees, and the manufacturer's name and address.

TEACHING POINTS

Demonstrate You may want to bring in products that have examples of each type of label.

Model On the board, draw a large square and fill in all the parts of a descriptive label, including product illustrations, weight statements, dating and storage information, universal product code, product guarantees, and the manufacturer's name and address.

ASSESS

Review Guide

CONCEPTS

1. Ask students to list the functions of product packaging.
Promoting and selling the product, defining product identity, providing information, expressing benefits and features, ensuring safe use, and protecting the product.

2. Ask students to recall the three types of labels.
Brand, descriptive, and grade.

KEY TERMS

Have students review key terms, their spellings, and definitions in small groups.

ONLINE SELF-ASSESSMENT

Have students go to marketing.essentials.glencoe.com for the Section 31.2 practice test.

Individualized Review

L1 Assign and review Chapter 31 activities in the Student Activity Workbook.

L2 Assign and review Chapter 31 activities in the Marketing Math Workbook.

L3 Assign and review Chapter 31 activities in the *BusinessWeek* Reader and Case Studies.

Marketing Practice

Have students select a branded product, such as a food product. Have students redesign the product packaging and labeling for that product. Their descriptive label must include all required elements. Have students write a two- to three-page report explaining their redesign and the reasons for their choices. Reports may include diagrams or examples of the new designs.

care of products. They also give manufacturers a convenient place to communicate warranty information and product use warnings. Notices of electrical hazard, flammability, and poisonous ingredients are required on the labels of certain categories of products. Due to increased international business, labels might contain symbols in addition to words. These symbols give graphic instructions on how to wash, cook, or care for the product.

The manufacturer's name and address is provided so consumers can write for more information or to register a complaint. Many packages include the company's Web address, encouraging consumers to visit for more information. Some labels include a customer service phone number that consumers can contact for questions or problems.

A **grade label** states the quality of the product. For example, eggs are grade-labeled AA, A, and B; corn and wheat are grade-labeled 1 and 2; and canned fruit is often grade-labeled A, B, or C.

Labeling Laws

In the past, the public has criticized companies for failing to offer complete and truthful information on product labels. Consumers also complained about the lack of uniformity in labeling. As a result of these complaints and concerns, labeling laws were established. Many package labels must now meet local, state, and federal standards. Federal mandates require that the name and address of the manufacturer, packer, or distributor and the quantity of contents appear on labels. These standards prevent manufacturers from misleading consumers with deceptive or incomplete packaging labels.

The Fair Packaging and Labeling Act (FPLA) of 1966 established mandatory labeling requirements and authorized the U.S. Food and Drug Administration (FDA) and the Federal Trade Commission (FTC) to establish packaging regulations. A 1992 amendment to the FPLA called for packages of selected products to include metric measurements. The amendment, which went into effect in 1994,

mandates that product weight be listed in American and metric weights and measures.

In today's global marketplace, companies must also consider the labeling laws of other countries. Some countries require bilingual labels. Others require that every ingredient in a product be listed on the label.

The Federal Food and Drug Administration

The federal Nutrition Labeling and Education Act passed in 1990 and enacted in 1994 protects consumers from deceptive labeling. This act, which is administered by the FDA, requires that labels give nutritional information on how a food fits into an overall daily diet. Labels must clearly state the amount of calories, fat, carbohydrates, sodium, cholesterol, and protein in each serving, as well as the percentage of a daily intake of 2,000 calories. The act also regulates health claims and defines descriptive terms to make them consistent on all products. These terms and phrases include *light* and *lite, free* (as in *fat free, salt free, cholesterol free*), *low, reduced,* and *good source of.*

The FDA also requires that manufacturers of certain products place health warnings on their packages. Beginning in 1989, all alcoholic beverage labels had to carry the following statement: "According to the Surgeon General, women should not drink alcoholic beverages during pregnancy because of the risk of birth defects. Consumption of alcoholic beverages impairs the ability to drive a car or operate machinery and may cause health problems." Similar warnings of health risks are required on cigarette package labels.

The FDA also has proposed new regulations on genetically modified foods. The FDA is developing guidelines for voluntary labeling as to whether food products contain genetically modified organisms.

The Federal Trade Commission

Another federal agency involved with product labeling is the Federal Trade Commission (FTC). The FTC is also responsible for monitoring advertising that is false or misleading.

666 UNIT 10 - PRODUCT AND SERVICE MANAGEMENT

 Extended Activity

Labeling Laws

Have students go to the FDA Web site and read the Federal Nutrition Labeling and Education Act. Have students research the act and write a one-page report summarizing the major points of the act that affect labeling, or have interested students give an oral presentation. Encourage students to create and use visual aids in their presentations.

The Care Labeling Rule, first introduced in 1972, requires that care labels be placed in textile clothing. The care labeling rules ensure that specific information about the care of garments be detailed on labels, including information related to washing, drying, and ironing.

The FTC released guidelines in 1992 for companies to follow when making environmental claims on product labels. Previously, many environmental terms had definitions that were not clear. When using the term *recycled* to describe the content of its products, a company must now show proof that it has retrieved or recovered a designated amount of scraps or materials from the waste stream. The term *recyclable* can be used only if the product or package can be re-used as raw material for a new product or package. The terms *ozone safe* and *ozone friendly* can be used only if the products do not contain any ozone-depleting chemicals. The terms *degradable, biodegradable,* and *photodegradable* can be used only if the product will decompose into elements found in nature within a reasonably short period of time after disposal.

U.S. Department of Agriculture

The rise of specialty markets for organic foods, which totaled $11 billion in sales in 2002, has compelled the U.S. Department of Agriculture (USDA) to issue legal standards and certification requirements for organic labels. The National Organic Rule dictates that companies must reserve the words *100 percent organic* and *organic* for use with foods that are produced without hormones, antibiotics, herbicides, insecticides, chemicals, genetic modification, or germ-killing radiation. The certified organic label requires both products and producers to be certified.

The Country of Origin Labeling (COOL) Act signed in 2002 will take effect in September of 2006. This new law is also administered by the USDA and will require that a country-of-origin label be placed on all fruits, vegetables, peanuts, meats, and fish in the future.

31.2 AFTER YOU READ

Reviewing Key Terms and Concepts

1. Why is a package important to product planning?

2. What are the main functions of product packaging?

3. What three federal agencies regulate labeling laws?

Integrating Academic Skills

Math

4. Robinson & Provost, Inc., a name branding agency, was paid $15,000 by Happy Wanderers Travel Agency for the research and development of the agency's corporate trade name and trademark. Robinson & Provost's graphic designer was paid $6,475 for her creative work on this project. Her salary was what percentage of the entire amount?

Civics and Government

5. Use the Internet or library resources to study one of the federal labeling laws explained in this chapter. Write a one- to two-page report on how the government enforces the law that you investigated.

 Online Action!

Check your answers at *marketingessentials.glencoe.com/31/read*

marketingessentials.glencoe.com   Chapter 31 - Branding, Packaging, and Labeling **667**

AFTER YOU READ

Reviewing Key Terms and Concepts

1. A package represents the size, shape, and final appearance of a product at the time of sale and helps to sell the product, which makes it important to product planning.

2. Functions of packaging include promoting and selling the product, defining product identity, providing information, expressing benefits and features, ensuring safe use, and protecting the product.

3. The agencies are the Federal Food and Drug Administration, Federal Trade Commission, and the U.S. Department of Agriculture.

Integrating Academic Skills

4. 43.1 percent; $6,475 ÷ $15,000 = 43.1 percent

5. Answers will vary; students should identify the name and purpose of the law, the agency that administers it, and how the law affects product labeling.

Online Action! Answers at **marketingessentials.glencoe.com/31/read**

CLOSE

Have students complete the following statements:

- **The purposes of packaging are** _____.

  to hold the product, to promote it, to help define its identity, to provide product information, to meet customer needs with various sizes available, to ensure safe use, and to protect the product

- **The main functions of labels are** _____.

  to give product content and directions for use, and to protect businesses from legal liability for mishaps involving their products

 Critical Thinking

Ask students what would happen if product labels were not regulated by law. What problems might occur? Have students discuss their answers in class.

CAREERS IN MARKETING

CAREERS IN MARKETING

Lifelong Learning

CAREER INFORMATION

Have students go to marketingessentials.glencoe.com, find Chapter 31 Careers page, and click on the link for the American Marketing Association's Careers Strategies and Tips. Ask students to select one article, read it, and summarize it in three short paragraphs.

BRANDING

Newspapers and magazines often cover consumer and industry branding news, including stories on national and private label brands and the future of branding. Branding news should remain of interest to students throughout their careers, whether as consumers purchasing brands or marketers selling brands.

Primary Source

Ask students to go to marketingessentials.glencoe.com and find Chapter 31 Resources. Ask them to click on the link for the American Marketing Association's marketing dictionary and read the definitions of any terms related to branding, packaging, and labeling they find.

THINKING CRITICALLY

A marketing degree will help an entrepreneur understand the process of identifying, advertising, and selling to a target market.

@ Online Action!

For instructions, ideas, and answer guide, go to the Teacher Center at marketingessentials.glencoe.com

---

TRACEY MCFALL
OWNER
**KINDHEARTED WOMEN,
BABY CARE PRODUCTS**

(?) What do you do at work?
I develop and create formulas and recipes for cosmetic and body care products such as lotions, body butters, hair conditioners, baby care products, and the like. I test, package, label, and advertise my products myself. I have a partner who makes baby diapers and diapering supplies. Development of effective formulas requires not only knowledge of raw materials and how they do what they do, but some knowledge of basic chemistry as well.

(?) What skills are most important to you?
The ability to listen to customer feedback. Sometimes I may love a product, but it is not selling. I need to do a little troubleshooting and find out why. Adjustment may be needed in ingredients, marketing, and/or pricing. Sometimes the problem is as simple as a label design flaw or an unappealing bottle or jar—I guess another important skill is the ability to be a bit of a detective.

(?) What is your key to success?
Secure financial backing; research and know your market. Set aside a fair amount for advertising and track what works and what doesn't, be diverse while remembering you can't do it all—you still need a niche. Never sacrifice product quality or your moral values for sales. Most of all, be patient, and remember that most small businesses fail within the first year.

Aptitudes, Abilities, and Skills

Creativity, research skills, product knowledge, customer service and communication skills

Education and Training

Degrees in marketing, communication, and general business are useful.

Career Path

This is an entrepreneurial career, which means it can start anywhere. Product development positions at large corporations are high-level positions, though, and require substantial marketing and product design experience.

THINKING CRITICALLY

How might someone in this entrepreneurial career benefit from a marketing degree?

@ Online Action!

Go to *marketingessentials.glencoe.com/ 31/careers* to find a career-related activity.

Test-Taking Strategies

Read aloud all chapter heads and subheads, pausing after each to give students time to write down main ideas from each section. Review any concepts students are unsure of or confused aboutand instruct students to spend extra time studying these concepts.

FOCUS on KEY POINTS

SECTION 31.1

● A brand is a name, term, design, or symbol (or combination of these elements) that identifies a product or service. Brands can include a number of elements, such as a trade name, brand name, brand mark, trade character, and trademark. Branding strategies include brand extensions, brand licensing, mixed branding, and co-branding. Effective use of different brand strategies can increase sales of branded products and maximize company revenues.

SECTION 31.2

● The functions of packaging include promoting and selling the product, defining product identity, providing information, expressing benefits and features to customers, ensuring safe use, and protecting the product. The main function of a label is to inform customers about a product's contents and give directions for use. Labels also protect businesses from legal liability that may occur if a consumer misuses the product.

REVIEW VOCABULARY

Define each of the key terms below.

1. brand (p. 654)
2. brand name (p. 655)
3. trade name (p. 655)
4. brand mark (p. 656)
5. trade character (p. 656)
6. trademark (p. 656)
7. national brands (p. 657)
8. private distributor brands (p. 657)
9. generic brands (p. 658)
10. brand extension (p. 658)
11. brand licensing (p. 658)
12. mixed brand (p. 659)
13. co-branding (p. 659)
14. package (p. 660)
15. mixed bundling (p. 661)
16. price bundling (p. 661)
17. blisterpack (p. 661)
18. aseptic packaging (p. 663)
19. cause packaging (p. 664)
20. label (p. 664)
21. brand label (p. 664)
22. descriptive label (p. 664)
23. grade label (p. 666)

REVIEW FACTS and IDEAS

24. What is the difference between brand extension and brand licensing? (31.1)
25. Why is a mixed-brand strategy used in product planning? (31.1)
26. What is a grade label? (31.2)
27. Name three types of packaging and explain their uses. (31.2)

Chapter 31 - Branding, Packaging, and Labeling 669

REVIEW FACTS and IDEAS

24. Brand extension extends a familiar or original brand name for other items in the product line. Brand licensing is the legal authorization by a brand owner to allow another company to use the brand, logo, or trademark for a fee.

25. In a mixed-brand strategy, a national brand product is sold under another company's brand. This enables the manufacturer to maximize profits by reaching new markets through the use of private brands while maintaining customer loyalty to its national brand.

26. A grade label states the quality, or grade, of a product.

27. Answers should include three types of packaging and their uses. Examples include: mixed bundling, used to sell different products together; price bundling, used to sell similar products in one package; and blisterpacks, used to prevent tampering.

FOCUS on KEY POINTS

Ask volunteers to read the summaries aloud and give the classroom one real-life example for each concept.

REVIEW VOCABULARY

See glossary for definitions of **1–23.**
A sample answer might read:

1. A *brand* is a name, term, design, symbol, or combination of these elements that identifies a product or service and distinguishes it from its competitors.

CHAPTER 31 REVIEW

BUILD SKILLS

28. Workplace Skills

Research reports will vary; reports should demonstrate an understanding of the concepts product line and brand. Students should explain the differences and similarities among the products in the product line chosen.

29. Technology Applications

Charts will vary; students should record and describe the specific process used for recycling an identified item.

30. Math Practice

Reports will vary; all reports should indicate an understanding of the mathematical method used to calculate brand valuation.

DEVELOP CRITICAL THINKING

31. For Kids Only

Answers may include: This segment of the market is as large as the baby boom generation. Companies want to capitalize on this portion of the marketplace and create products that target children in order for them to influence families' purchasing choices.

32. Global Brands

Answers will vary; companies may study cultural etiquette, rhetorical connotations, customs, and so on before finalizing the name and packaging of a product in different countries. They may also consider competing products.

BUILD SKILLS

28. Workplace Skills

Research Skills Select one line of products that is of interest to you. Identify the various brands sold in that product line. Use the Internet and corporate Web sites to find out specific product information. List the similarities and differences among the products.

29. Technology Applications

The Recycling Process Research the process used to recycle paper, cardboard, glass, plastic, wood, or other packaging materials. Create a chart that illustrates and describes the type of recycling process for the material selected.

30. Math Practice

Brand Valuation Perform an Internet search on the mathematical method used by Interbrand to determine brand valuation. Summarize the procedure in a written one-page report.

DEVELOP CRITICAL THINKING

31. For Kids Only

A few brands of yogurt now package their product in soft plastic tubes that can be squeezed. The concept is that it is yogurt on the go. This idea might have targeted a broad market segment, but instead, those companies have single-mindedly chosen to target primary and middle-school-aged children and their families.

Why do you think manufacturers chose this market segmentation? How does the packaging relate to the target market?

32. Global Brands

Large multinational companies often sell their products all around the globe. For example, Unilever sells a deodorant soap called Rexona in Africa, Australia, and the Middle East, and in most of Europe. In Great-Britain, the same soap is called Sure while in the United States it is called Degree.

What factors do you think companies such as Unilever consider before introducing a product with a specific label and packaging to a specific market?

 Formative Assessment

Formative assessment is an essential component of classroom work. This type of assessment provides information that is then used as feedback to modify teaching and meet student needs.

L1 Have students explain how each key term relates to branding, packaging, and labeling.

L2 Give students examples of well-known brands and have students write a paragraph about each brand, using the key terms and concepts from the chapter.

L3 Have students write an essay relating the concepts of branding, packaging, and labeling.

Reteach If the results of this formative assessment seem low, consider the following activity:
Read each of the major section heads aloud and have students fill in the subheads for each section.

APPLY CONCEPTS

33. Investigating Brand Licensing

Investigate an existing brand licensing arrangement. Use business publications or online sources such as *Brandweek, Adweek, BusinessWeek, Fortune, Forbes, Marketing News,* or Creative Magazine.com to find applicable information.

Activity In a one-page paper, summarize the companies involved and how the licensing arrangement was established.

34. Understanding Product Packaging

Locate the Web site of a food products manufacturer of your choice, such as Hormel, Hershey's, General Mills, Kellogg's, H.J. Heinz, Del Monte, or Campbell's. Review the site and the company's product lines. Select one product line and identify how the package for the product fulfills one or more of the functions of packaging identified in this chapter.

Activity Use presentation software to create a report based on your research.

NET SAVVY

35. Advergames

Locate an advergame Web site. Some possible choices include the sites of Procter & Gamble, Wrigley, Kellogg's, Kraft, Pepsi, McDonald's, General Mills, or Hershey's. Play one of the sponsored games. Prepare an oral presentation with an accompanying electronic presentation describing the game, how it is played, and what you liked and disliked about the game.

marketingessentials.glencoe.com

Role Play: Branding, Packaging, and Labeling

Situation You are to assume the role of assistant manager of a discount store. Your store carries merchandise with well-known manufacturer brands, merchandise with the store's brand, and some merchandise with generic branding. Many new employees find the different types of brands difficult to understand and explain to customers.

Activity You are to explain the three types of brands to the store's sales staff (judge) during an upcoming staff meeting. Be sure to include examples of each type of brand in your presentation.

Evaluation You will be evaluated on how well you meet the following performance indicators:

- Explain the nature of branding
- Describe factors used by marketers to position products/businesses
- Develop strategies to position products/businesses
- Explain the concept of product mix
- Conduct staff meetings

 Online Action!

For more information and DECA Prep practice, go to *marketingessentials.glencoe.com/31/DECA*

Chapter 31 - Branding, Packaging, and Labeling **671**

APPLY CONCEPTS

33. Investigating Brand Licensing

Reports will vary. Accept all reports which demonstrate an understanding of the brand licensing arrangement.

34. Understanding Product Packaging

Reports will vary; students should demonstrate an understanding of packaging and use presentation software to create a report.

NET SAVVY

35. Advergames

Presentations will vary depending on advergame chosen and should show a student understanding of both the game and the advertising component.

The students should be evaluated on the performance indicators noted in the role play. For another DECA role play, go to the Competitive Events Workbook or the Student Activity Workbook, or go to **marketingessentials.glencoe.com/31/DECA**

 Online Action! For instructions, ideas, and answer guide, go to the Teacher Center at **marketingessentials.glencoe.com**

DECA Advisors Corner

Invite a state officer or former DECA members to your school and/or chapter meeting to make presentations to your marketing classes. They can speak to other classes, to your co-op sponsors, or to fellow educators. This is a first-hand method of demonstrating the vast role that DECA plays in developing leadership, marketing, and managements skills in America's youth.

Chapter Overview

Chapter 32 introduces the concept of extended product features used in product planning. It emphasizes the use of warranties and credit to sell products and services. The chapter also explains the laws and agencies involved with product safety and the use of credit.

☞ BUILD BACKGROUND ☜

Have students imagine that they work in the service department of an electronics store. Their store offers warranties with plasma televisions and computers. To assess their knowledge of product and service planning, their supervisor has asked them to explain the importance of warranties in product planning. Ask the students what sources they will use to research and verify the report on service warranties.

Why It's Important

Depending on how warranties are used and the quality of the product or service, they can either boost sales or become a major problem for a business. Extending credit to customers or accepting credit cards for purchases is an important part of product planning. The wise use of credit can be as a great benefit to a business and its customers.

Prepare to Read

Ask the students to familiarize themselves with the entire chapter by reading the section introductions, headers, and questions. This strategy allows the students to understand the breadth of issues covered.

CHAPTER 32
Extended Product Features

Chapter Objectives

After reading this chapter, you should be able to:

- Identify different types of warranties
- Explore the importance of warranties in product planning
- Identify the major provisions of product safety legislation
- Explain consumer responsibilities and rights related to product performance
- Describe the importance of credit
- Explain various sources of consumer credit
- Identify the types of credit accounts extended to consumers
- Discuss how businesses use trade credit

GUIDE TO THE PHOTO

Market Talk Extended product features such as warranties and the use of credit affect product planning and relate to consumer rights and responsibilities. If a consumer buys a pair of shoes and the soles fall apart on the first day the customer wears the shoes, the product might be defective and might be covered by a manufacturer's warranty.

Quick Think Would a warranty cover the same shoes if they fall apart after a month of wear? Explain your opinion.

GUIDE TO THE PHOTO

Market Talk Lead a discussion with students about the importance of product testing. Ask them how companies can save money in the long run by conducting trial runs and preliminary field tests before a product hits the market.

Quick Think Answers will vary, but typically the manufacturer should cover its product under normal wear and tear. If the retail store does not replace the shoe at no cost, the customer can contact the manufacturer directly for a replacement pair.

 Follow Up Ask students whether, when they are purchasing an item from a retailer, they might inquire about the product's warranty. Have them discuss why or why not.

THE DECA CONNECTION

Performance indicators represent key skills and knowledge. Relating them to the concepts explained in this chapter is your key to success in DECA events. These acronyms represent DECA events that involve knowledge of concepts in this chapter.

AAAL	FMAL	MMS*	TMDM
AAML	FMDM*	QSRM	TSE
ADC	FMML	RMAL	VPM
BSM	FSRM	RMML	
EMDM*	HMDM	SMDM	

In all these DECA events you should be able to follow these performance indicators:

- Explain warranties and guarantees
- Identify consumer protection provisions of appropriate agencies
- Explain business ethics in product/service management
- Describe legal issues affecting businesses
- Explain the purpose and importance of credit

The events with an asterisk (*) also include:

- Make critical decisions regarding acceptance of credit cards

Some events include additional indicators:

VPM	Describe the role of warranties and guarantees used in vehicle and petroleum marketing
AAML/MML	Explain factors affecting extension of credit. Determine credit worthiness of customers. Close credit accounts. Establish collection procedures.
FMDM	Determine credit worthiness. Place a hold on customer accounts. Analyze credit rating system. Collect receivables.

DECA PREP

Check your understanding of DECA performance indicators with the DECA activity in this chapter's review. For more information and DECA Prep practice, go to *marketingessentials .glencoe.com/32/DECA*

THE DECA CONNECTION

DECA events that require knowledge of extended product features are described here. Discuss the performance indicators to make sure students understand how to demonstrate their understanding.

The events acronyms stand for:

AAAL:	**Apparel and Accessories Marketing Series, AL**
AAML:	**Apparel and Accessories Marketing Series, ML**
ADC:	**Advertising Campaign Event**
BSM:	**Business Services Marketing Series**
EMDM:	**E-Commerce Management Team Decision Making Event**
FMAL:	**Food Marketing Series, AL**
FMDM:	**Financial Analysis Management Team Decision Making Event**
FMML:	**Food Marketing Series, ML**
FSRM:	**Full Service Restaurant Management Series**
HMDM:	**Hospitality Services Management Team Decision Making Event**
MMS:	**Marketing Management Series**
QSRM:	**Quick Serve Restaurant Management Series**
RMAL:	**Retail Merchandising Series, AL**
RMML:	**Retail Merchandising Series, ML**
SMDM:	**Sports and Entertainment Marketing Management Team Decision Making Event**
TMDM:	**Travel and Tourism Marketing Management Team Decision Making Event**
TSE:	**Technical Sales Event**
VPM:	**Vehicles and Petroleum Marketing Series**

DECA PREP

Find timed DECA Prep activities correlated to the Competitive Events Workbook for students and DECA tips for teachers at marketingessentials.glencoe.com /32/DECA

CHAPTER 32 Classroom Resources

For the Teacher

- TeacherWorks
- marketingessentials.glencoe.com
- Interactive Chalkboard
- **Exam***View*® Pro Test Generator
- Fast File Unit 10

For the Student

- ***Marketing Essentials*** Online Edition
- Student Activity Workbook
- Marketing Math Workbook
- Marketing Research Project Workbook
- School-to-Work Activity Workbook
- Competitive Events Workbook
- ***BusinessWeek*** Reader and Case Studies
- marketingessentials.glencoe.com

FOCUS

Introducing the Section

COLLABORATIVE ACTIVITY

Ask students to recall the definition of the term *product feature*; write it and its meaning on the board. Then, have students define the term *extended product feature*. Have them brainstorm ways a product's features could be extended.

Preteaching Key Terms

Have students predict definitions for the key terms in class. Then have volunteers check those definitions against the ones found in the text.

- warranty
- express warranty
- full warranty
- limited warranty
- implied warranty
- warranty of merchantability
- warranty of fitness for a particular purpose
- disclaimer

Online Activity

Consumer Protection Laws

Have students research and report on any local, state, or federal consumer protection or product safety laws that are available for viewing or download over the Internet. Tell students that this information is often available through the Web sites of local, state, or federal agencies. Ask students to present a brief summary of the law they chose in a five-minute oral report. Encourage students to use presentation software in their reports.

OBJECTIVES

- Identify different types of warranties
- Explore the importance of warranties in product planning
- Identify the major provisions of product safety legislation
- Explain consumer responsibilities and rights related to product performance

KEY TERMS

- warranty
- express warranty
- full warranty
- limited warranty
- implied warranty
- warranty of merchantability
- warranty of fitness for a particular purpose
- disclaimer

Warranties

READ and STUDY

BEFORE YOU READ

Predict Why do you think warranties are a good marketing tactic?

THE MAIN IDEA

Sellers use warranties to encourage customers—wholesalers, retailers, or consumers—to purchase a product or service. Warranties can boost sales, but they can also pose product and customer service problems.

STUDY ORGANIZER

In a chart like the one below, take notes about extended features and warranties.

WHILE YOU READ

Analysis Why are warranties and guarantees both essential components of product planning?

Warranties

Extended product features offered after the sale, such as warranties, often determine the likelihood of repeat sales. A **warranty** is a promise or guarantee given to a customer that a product will meet certain standards. Typically, these standards apply to materials, workmanship, and performance.

Guarantee is another term for warranty. The major difference between a guarantee and a warranty is the promotional value

---

READ and STUDY

BEFORE YOU READ

Have students suggest ways warranties might help to market a product. Answers may include that they suggest that the product meets certain standards.

THE MAIN IDEA

Lead a discussion with students about whether they think warranties are useful sales tools.

STUDY ORGANIZER

Model the study organizer for students by filling in the first blank. A full-size, downloadable study organizer can be found at marketingessentials.glencoe.com

 Answers will vary. Warranties and guarantees are important elements of product planning because they help to increase sales and profits.

of the promise. The term guarantee (or guaranteed) is usually used in conjunction with promotional phrases such as money-back guarantee, results guaranteed, guaranteed for 1,000 hours of use, or satisfaction guaranteed.

A warranty, on the other hand, is usually framed as a series of specific promises. An example is, "Norm's Body Shop will repair any defects in workmanship billed on the repair invoice unless caused by or damaged from unreasonable use, maintenance, or care of the vehicle, excluding paint work if the vehicle's original finish is defective."

Typical warranties set time or use limits for coverage and restrict the seller's liability. The most familiar language is usually found in auto warranties: "Warranty ends at 36 months or 36,000 miles, whichever occurs first."

Role of Warranties in Product Planning

Warranties are an important element of product planning because they help increase sales and profits (see Figure 32.1). Customers often make purchasing decisions based on warranties.

Businesses are not required by law to issue warranties, although most do to assure their customers that their products and services meet quality standards. For some companies, notably automobile manufacturers, warranties play a prominent role in product advertising. Warranties are also significant to businesses because:

- They direct a company to focus on customer satisfaction.
- They require a company to adhere to performance standards.
- They generate customer feedback.
- They encourage quality in product development.
- They boost promotional efforts.

Warranties come in two different forms, express and implied. These forms, in turn, can be divided into specific types.

Express Warranties

An **express warranty** is one that is explicitly stated, in writing or verbally, to encourage a customer to make a purchase. A written warranty can appear in a number of places: on the product packaging, in the product literature, in an advertisement, or as part of a point-of-purchase display. The location of the warranty should be accessible to customers before purchase. The warranty must always be clearly worded so that customers can easily understand its terms. Spoken warranties, however, even if clearly worded, may not be enforceable unless they are also in writing.

Here is an example of how an express warranty works. A broadcast advertisement shows that a portable MP3 player will operate while the user jogs. You purchase the player and discover almost immediately that it shorts out when you jog. You are entitled to whatever relief the warranty specifies. Now imagine that the MP3 product package features a runner using the product in the rain. You find that the product shorts out in the rain. Once again, you are entitled to warranty relief because the illustration constitutes a promise of performance, even though the promise is not a written one. There are two types of written warranties: a full warranty and a limited warranty.

Full Warranty

A **full warranty** guarantees that if a product is found to be defective within the warranty period, it will be repaired or replaced at no cost to the purchaser. A manufacturer who offers a full warranty agrees to repair a defective product "within a reasonable time and without charge."

Limited Warranty

A **limited warranty** may exclude certain parts of the product from coverage or require the customer to bear some of the expense for repairs resulting from defects. It is not uncommon, for example, for a limited warranty to specify that the manufacturer will pay

 Extended Activity

Extended Auto Warranties

Ask students to research an extended auto warranty. Ask students to then use word processing software to write a 200-word compare and contrast paper on the value of purchasing an extended warranty for an auto of their choice. In the papers conclusion, students should outline their personal stance on such a warranty, its value, and whether they would purchase it. The students should cite their sources either in the report or in a bibliography.

TEACH

Discussion Starter

WARRANTIES

Many students may be familiar with the concept of product warranties. Read to the students the sample warranty below. While reading it, ask the students to keep the following items in mind: 1) promises to repair defects in material, 2) under certain conditions, and 3) within a certain period of time. Then have the class brainstorm limited warranty language for a mobile phone.

Sample limited one-year warranty is as follows: This product is warranted to be free from manufacturing defects for a period of one year from the date of purchase, subject to the following: that it is not misused and/or taken apart and that it has not been used for commercial purposes. This warranty does not cover failure caused by build-up of food matter or water deposits. If this appliance becomes defective under the terms of this one-year warranty, we will repair it free of charge, including both materials and labor, provided it is returned to our nearest Authorized Service Center.

Concept Development

EXPRESS WARRANTIES

Lead the students in a discussion about a company's concern for warranty cost management. Ask students to identify some challenges a company might have to consider when manufacturing a product and putting it into the marketplace.

Answers might include that the company must consider ways to reduce warranty costs, to reduce the risk of a product's failure, to reduce the risk of product recall, and so on.

675

TEACH CONTINUED

Individualized Practice

UNDERSTANDING WARRANTIES

L1 Ask the students to choose a product and to brainstorm and list at least four extended product features (in addition to a warranty) for this product.

L2 Ask students to imagine this scenario: The business college they attend requires each student to purchase a laptop computer and a DVD that includes their textbook and course packets needed for the years to come until graduation. The upfront cost is between $3,000 and $6,000. Ask students to write a 300-word paper discussing the advantages and disadvantages of such an agreement versus the traditional method of buying textbooks and borrowing a school computer.

L3 Ask students why they think a state's Department of Education requires teachers to be certified. Ask students to investigate what the word certified means. Does this process guarantee a good teacher? Students should defend their answer in a one-page essay. Answers will vary, but requiring teacher certification is the state's attempt to ensure that teachers are technically competent in the subject area and have mastered entry-level teaching skills.

 Critical Thinking

Ask students what kinds of internal activities a company might impose on a product to ensure total quality in a product before it hits the market. Answers will vary, but might include design reviews, field trials, quality audits, analysis of engineering, and so on.

676

Figure 32.1 **Warranties and Product Planning**

• **Appealing to the Customer** Following are some of the ways warranties affect product planning.

Why do companies issue warranties?

FOCUS ON CUSTOMER NEEDS

Warranties help to guide expectations for product performance.

SET CLEAR STANDARDS OF PERFORMANCE

Warranties and company policies that set specific standards tell the customer how the product is manufactured or how it will perform.

GENERATE CUSTOMER FEEDBACK

Product or warranty registrations help provide customer feedback about the product.

ENCOURAGE QUALITY CONTROL

Quality manufacturing is necessary, since products that are defective or cannot be repaired must be replaced under a warranty program.

BOOST PROMOTIONAL EFFORTS

Long-term warranties speak for the reputation of the company and the confidence it has in its products.

@ Online Action!

Go to *marketingessentials.glencoe.com/32/figure/1* to find a project on the role of warranties.

676 UNIT 10 - PRODUCT AND SERVICE MANAGEMENT

marketingessentials.glencoe.com

Figure 32.1 *Warranties and Product Planning*

Discussion Lead a discussion about why product warranties would encourage quality control. Answers might include that it is less expensive for a company to produce a quality product than to replace a defective one.

Caption Answer Warranties help companies focus on customer needs, deliver products that meet specific standards (and build the company's image), generate customer feedback (through warranty registrations), control quality, and promote their products.

@ Online Action! For instructions, ideas, and answer guide, go to the Teacher Center at **marketingessentials.glencoe.com**

Follow Up Ask students to share their experiences of having to return a purchase.

for replacement parts but charge the customer for labor or shipping.

Implied Warranties

Most major consumer purchases are covered by written warranties provided by manufacturers. When there are no written warranties, implied warranty laws apply. An **implied warranty** is one that takes effect automatically by state law whenever a purchase is made. There are two types of implied warranties: a warranty of merchantability and a warranty of fitness for a particular purpose.

Warranty of Merchantability

A **warranty of merchantability** is the seller's promise that the product sold is fit for its intended purpose. Some examples are a gasoline-powered lawnmower that will cut the grass or an electric power saw that will cut wood.

Warranty of Fitness

A **warranty of fitness for a particular purpose** is used when the seller advises a customer that a product is suitable for a particular use, and the customer acts on that advice. A customer, for example, might buy a small truck based on a salesperson's recommendation that it will pull a trailer of a certain weight. The dealership must take back the truck and refund the buyer's money if it turns out that the truck cannot tow the anticipated load.

Warranty Disclaimers

Warranties often have disclaimers to protect the businesses issuing them. A **disclaimer** is a statement that contains exceptions to and exclusions from a warranty. Disclaimers are used to limit damages that can be recovered by a customer. A common form of disclaimer limits recovery to a refund of the purchase

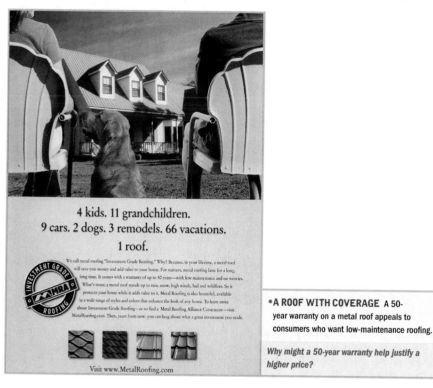

4 kids. 11 grandchildren.
9 cars. 2 dogs. 3 remodels. 66 vacations.
1 roof.

We call metal roofing "Investment Grade Roofing." Why? Because, in your lifetime, a metal roof will save you money and add value to your home. For starters, metal roofing lasts for a long, long time. It comes with a warranty of up to 50 years—with low maintenance and no worries. What's more, a metal roof stands up to rain, snow, high winds, hail and wildfires. So it protects your house while it adds value to it. Metal Roofing is also beautiful, available in a wide range of styles and colors that enhance the look of any home. To learn more about Investment Grade Roofing—or to find a Metal Roofing Alliance Contractor—visit MetalRoofing.com. Then, years from now, you can brag about what a great investment you made.

Visit www.MetalRoofing.com

• **A ROOF WITH COVERAGE** A 50-year warranty on a metal roof appeals to consumers who want low-maintenance roofing.

Why might a 50-year warranty help justify a higher price?

Chapter 32 - Extended Product Features **677**

TEACH CONTINUED

Concept Development

ROLE OF EXTENDED WARRANTIES

Ask students to name products that are usually covered under service contracts. The students should speculate on the amount of revenue that service contracts bring into a retailer.

TEACHING POINTS

Clarify Tell students that companies often offer extended service contracts not only as good customer service but also as major sources of revenue. The warranties generate more sales revenue (and more profits if the product performs as expected) on the original sale of the product.

Enrichment

CONSUMER LAWS AND AGENCIES

The Federal Trade Commission (FTC) states that education is the key to avoiding consumer injury. It offers various tips and reminders to prevent becoming a victim of fraud. Ask students to brainstorm some tips they and other smart consumers can follow when shopping online.

TEACHING POINTS

Summarize Remind students that they should never be deprived of knowing and acting on their consumer rights. For example, you might mention that before a purchase is complete, the consumer should read the fine print, check the refund or return policy, check the delivery dates, and assess the warranty.

Clarify Remind students that to ensure safe and secure online shopping not only during the holidays but anytime, the consumer should have updated anti-virus software installed, they should not enclose their financial information in an e-mail, and they should be wary opening any e-mail attachment.

678

A MATTER OF ETHICS

Using Credit Wisely

Credit card issuers make money on credit card interest rates and special fees. Late payment fees can run from $15 on small balances to up to $39 dollars on larger balances. Late payment fees or additional fees are charged to customers who exceed their authorized credit limits, do not pay their minimum charges within the payment grace period, take cash advances, or transfer balances from one card to another. For example, to get a cash advance, a credit card user has to pay a minimum fee of two to three percent of the advanced amount plus a minimum charge of $2 to $10. Late payment and cash advance fees increased at the same time many credit card issuers have introduced introductory rates of zero to three percent to attract new customers. The average U.S. household's credit card debt is nearly $9,000.

THINKING ETHICALLY

Do you think that late payment fees are fair to customers? Why or why not?

@ Online Action!

Go to *marketingessentials.glencoe.com/ 32/ethics* to find an activity about ethics and credit.

---

price. It can specifically exclude any other costs that may have been incurred by the owner as a result of product failure. Another common disclaimer waives customers' rights under implied-warranty laws.

Role of Extended Warranties

Extended warranties or service contracts provide repairs or preventive maintenance for a specified length of time beyond a product's normal warranty period. Customers pay extra for such a contract at the time of purchase or shortly afterward. Costs range from a few dollars on a low-cost item to hundreds or even thousands of dollars on a higher-priced item, such as a car. There is often a deductible amount, which the customer pays before work is performed.

Extended warranties are beneficial to both businesses and customers. Businesses benefit by receiving additional money (and more profit, if the product performs as expected) on the original sale of a product. Customers benefit from the assurance of long-term satisfaction with their purchase.

There are also disadvantages to service contracts. *Consumer Reports* magazine estimates that only 12 to 20 percent of people who buy extra repair or service protection ever use it.

Other Extended Product Features

In addition to warranties, product planners create additional extended product features to boost customer satisfaction. These features include delivery, installation, billing, service after the sale, directions for use, technical assistance, and training.

Businesses gain feedback by conducting customer service and satisfaction surveys. After an initial purchase, customers are frequently asked to submit product registration cards to gain customer data and ideas for product and service improvements.

Consumer Laws and Agencies

Business people need a working knowledge of relevant federal, state, and local laws. Manufacturers must be sure that their products meet all legal requirements. They must be safe, adequately labeled, and properly advertised; if they are not, the manufacturer could face fines or product recalls.

Larger companies often employ consumer affairs or legislative specialists to advise management about legal requirements. Smaller companies often join trade associations to stay informed about existing and pending laws that affect their products.

A MATTER OF ETHICS   Using Credit Wisely

Discussion Lead a discussion with students about the various costs associated with credit card use: charges for interest, late payments, exceeding credit limits, etc.

THINKING ETHICALLY Answer: Answers will vary. Some students may say that, because credit card companies are lending consumers money, they can charge whatever fees they want for late payments. If users want to avoid such fees, they should pay their bills on time. Others will suggest that such fees take advantage of consumers, who have come to depend on the cards for doing business.

@ Online Action! For instructions, ideas, and answer guide, go to the Teacher Center at marketingessentials.glencoe.com

Follow Up Ask students to research statistics on personal bankruptcy.

Federal Statutes

Making sure products meet all federal product safety standards is an important function of product planning. Cars and trucks, for example, have their emission standards set by the Environmental Protection Agency (EPA), their price stickers regulated by the Federal Trade Commission, and any potentially dangerous design flaws investigated by the National Highway Traffic Safety Administration.

Magnuson-Moss Consumer Product Warranty Act

Many of the warranty features have their origins in a federal statute called the Magnuson-Moss Consumer Product Warranty Act of 1975. This statute governs written warranties for all consumer products costing $15 or more. It sets minimum standards for such warranties, rules for making them available before a product is sold, and provisions for lawsuits against manufacturers if a warranty is not fulfilled. The Federal Trade Commission enforces this act.

Consumer Product Safety Act

Other federal statutes protect consumers by forcing companies to manufacture and sell safe products. The Consumer Product Safety Act of 1972, for example, established the Consumer Product Safety Commission (CPSC). This agency monitors the safety of more than 15,000 nonfood items, such as toys; household, outdoor, sports, recreation, and specialty products; and appliances. The agency issues standards for the construction, testing, packaging, and performance of these products to protect the public from unreasonable risks of serious injuries or deaths. When the CPSC finds any product defective or dangerous, it can do any of the following:

- Issue a product safety alert.
- Require that warning labels be attached to the product.
- Recall the product and order repairs.
- Withdraw the product or prohibit its sale.

Since its inception, the CPSC has recalled more than 4,000 products. In June of 2004, Payless ShoeSource, Inc., voluntarily recalled 441,000 Smart Fit and Teeny Toes athletic shoes because the eyelet lace holder can detach, posing a choking hazard for children.

To ensure consumer awareness of product recalls, notices for unsafe children's products, appliances, toys, and other items are placed in all U.S. Postal Service offices.

Food, Drug, and Cosmetic Act

The Food, Drug, and Cosmetic Act of 1938 is another federal statute designed to ensure that products will be safe. Safe in this case means pure, wholesome, and effective. It covers features such as informative labels and truthful advertising. The Food and Drug Administration is responsible for the safety of drugs, medical devices, foods, and some food supplements; it also enforces the act. The agency also regulates the advertising and sale of imported and exported foods, drugs, cosmetics, medical devices, animal drugs, animal feed, and products that emit radiation.

State Statutes

Many states have passed their own consumer protection laws. Most are aimed at preventing poorly made or poorly serviced products.

The most common form of state regulation affects service businesses. Most states require certain individuals such as auto mechanics, realtors, and police and fire safety officers to meet training requirements. It is necessary to hold a license or state certification before legally practicing in those professions. The process frequently involves testing and the payment of a substantial fee.

Lemon Laws

Nearly all states have lemon laws to protect customers. Lemon laws are statutes designed to protect consumers from poorly built cars. Under most lemon laws, a car is a lemon if it is out of service at least 30 days during the first year of ownership or if four attempts have been made to fix the same problem. Lemon owners are entitled to a refund or a comparable replacement car.

 Extended Activity

Comparing Warranties

Asks students to conduct a price comparison for a warranty on two different brands of the same type of appliance (for example, a washer or a dishwasher). Have students create a spreadsheet including the service contracts, quote price, and details of the warranty for both products. They can then summarize the information in a brief oral or written statement.

TEACH CONTINUED

Enrichment

FEDERAL STATUTES

Lead students in a discussion of whether and in what way corporations should comply with federal statues which protect consumers, the environment, and businesses. However, some corporations choose to pay the fines for violating the statues rather than complying with them. Ask students whether they feel that this is ethical behavior. Then ask students how environmental policies have influenced businesses' ethics and their social responsibilities.

Individualized Math Skills

L1 Have students complete these basic mathematical problems. Explain that these kinds of functions are required to calculate finance charges on credit cards.

1. $(12 \times 400) + (19 \times 300) =$

_____

2. 320×1.75 percent =_____
$10,500; $5.60

L2 A business has to pay a credit card company an additional 4 percent for each purchase charged. If the items of a purchase total $78, how much does the business pay the company?
$3.12; $78 \times 0.04 = $3.12

L3 Give students the following problem to solve: Their zero-percent interest charge account statement arrives in the mail for the billing period of 4/13 through 5/12. It shows a previous balance of $160. The statement lists new purchases of $30 on 4/16. It also states that their payment of $100 was posted on 4/20. The credit card company uses new purchases to figure the average daily balance. Calculate the average daily balance.
$111.03; [($160 \times 3 days) + ($190 \times 4 days) 1 ($90 \times 22 days)] \div 29 days = $111.03

ASSESS

CONCEPTS

Have the students study product packaging at home or in a local store for product warnings. Have students give reasons that warnings for seemingly obvious hazards are often included in product packaging. If the warnings are not included, a customer can always say he or she did not know about the potential hazards of using the product and can sue the manufacturer if injured while using the product. Product warnings are included with food products for this reason.

KEY TERMS

In small groups, have students review key terms, spellings, and definitions.

ONLINE SELF-ASSESSMENT

Have students go to marketingessentials.glencoe.com for the Section 32.1 practice test.

Individualized Review

L1 Assign and review Chapter 32 activities in the Student Activity Workbook.

L2 Assign and review Chapter 32 activities in the Marketing Math Workbook.

L3 Assign and review Chapter 32 activities in the *BusinessWeek* Reader and Case Studies.

Marketing Practice

Ask students to write a warning to accompany a product of their own choosing. Also ask them to indicate where the warning is placed—on the item, on the packaging, in both places, and so on. Once students complete this assignment, ask them to prepare a five-minute presentation for the class.

•**CHECKING SAFETY** Underwriters Laboratories (UL) is a multinational corporation that tests products for safety. Products that pass the tests can bear a UL mark.

Why might a consumer prefer to buy a product with a UL mark?

Many states have incorporated arbitration programs into their lemon laws. In arbitration, an impartial third party, such as a representative of the Better Business Bureau, decides the crucial issues—for example, whether a vehicle is a lemon and how much the refund should be. In most cases, the arbitrator's ruling is not binding on the parties. The owner can sue the carmaker in a court of law if he or she is not satisfied with the outcome. The principal benefit of arbitration is that it saves all parties the long delays and excessive costs often associated with a lawsuit.

Consumer Rights and Responsibilities

Consumers have a right to expect quality products at fair prices. What happens when the extended features fail? Consumers can take several steps when they have not been adequately protected by a warranty.

- The consumer should contact the business that sold the product or provided the service via phone, letter, or the Internet.
- If the problem is still unresolved, the consumer should contact the local, state, or federal offices that can assist with consumer complaints. Contact information can be found on the World Wide Web or in a telephone directory.
- Finally, if the problem is still not resolved, consumers can take legal action.

Consumers can sue manufacturers or retailers on at least three grounds: breach of federal law (written warranty), breach of state law (implied warranty), and negligence. Negligence means failure to take proper or reasonable care.

When a company does not fulfill its warranty or when it shows carelessness, con-

680 UNIT 10 - PRODUCT AND SERVICE MANAGEMENT

AD GUIDE   CHECKING SAFETY

Discussion Ask students what they can surmise from this ad. Have them tell you what the company does, a little about its history, and so on. Ask the students if they think this is an effective ad.

Caption Answer The mark of an independent testing service may give the consumer added assurance. Where safety is a concern, as with electronic products, the products are tested; the results of the test passed on to the consumer.

Follow Up Ask students why such an independent, not-for-profit product-safety testing center is needed in the business world. Have them explain why companies cannot guarantee their own quality assurance and control units.

sumers have the right to take a case to court. Courts have held manufacturers and retailers liable for defects in products or when injury is caused by use of the product. Individuals can also bring food suppliers to court if unhealthy practices or bad food cause sickness.

Consumers, cities, and states can file class action suits against manufacturers who make unsafe products. Class action suits are lawsuits filed by more than one party. It is estimated that Bridgestone/Firestone has spent over $1.5 billion in product recalls and legal fees since 2000 on cases related to some of its tires being involved in SUV rollover accidents.

Businesses can take steps to minimize liability suits during product planning. Manufacturers should examine product design and consider what might go wrong. Products should be tested thoroughly. Besides federally mandated tests, there are extensive use tests that manufacturers can do to make suggestions for recommended product use.

Manufacturers should give special attention to package design and provide warnings on the package and labels about any potential hazards involved in using the product. When a manufacturer suspects a problem with a product, it is often more cost effective to recall that product than to risk liability and a damaged reputation.

Private distributors can limit their liability by questioning manufacturers before accepting a product for sale. They should obtain the manufacturer's test data and determine the company's ability to stand behind the product before it is put on store shelves.

As a final line of defense against product liability, businesses should encourage their customers to be responsible consumers. They should take every opportunity to remind customers of their duty to be informed. Customers are responsible for reading and following the safety directions provided with products. This is especially important with items for children, such as car seats, cribs, and even toys.

 32.1 AFTER YOU READ

Reviewing Key Terms and Concepts
1. List the different types of warranties.
2. What is the role of warranties in product planning?
3. What are the basic provisions of federal product safety laws?

Integrating Academic Skills
Math
4. In 2004, the state of Michigan gave $47.8 million of the $1 billion it received from the 1998 national tobacco award settlement to biomedical research and new business development. What percentage of Michigan's settlement award does this amount represent?

Communication
5. Warranties are written in legal terms and many consumers find them hard to understand. Using a warranty from a household appliance, electronic equipment, or other consumer product you or your family recently purchased, rewrite the warranty in language that is clear and easy to understand.

 Online Action!
Check your answers at *marketingessentials.glencoe.com/32/read*

marketingessentials.glencoe.com

Chapter 32 - Extended Product Features **681**

 SECTION 32.1

CLOSE

Ask students to recall and provide answers go the following questions:

• **Many unsafe and potentially dangerous toys enter the country from other countries. What should the federal government do to prevent this from happening?**
It can involve the U.S. Customs Service and Consumer Product Safety Commission to prevent dangerous toys from entering the country.

• **What can consumers do when they feel that a product's warranty has not adequately protected them?**
Consumers can sue the company, possibly return it, or throw it away.

Critical Thinking
Ask students why reading or watching the news can help make them better consumers.

AFTER YOU READ

Reviewing Key Terms and Concepts
1. Types of warranties include: 1) express warranties (including full warranties and limited warranties); 2) implied warranties (including warranties of merchantability and warranties of fitness); and 3) extended warranties.

2. Warranties are important because they focus on customer needs, set clear standards of performance, generate customers, encourage quality control, and boost promotional efforts.

3. Products must be safe, adequately labeled, and advertised in an honest manner.

Integrating Academic Skills
4. 4.78 percent; $47,800,000 ÷ $1,000,000,000 = 4.78 percent
5. Answers will vary, but each student should rewrite the warranties using terms that are easily understood.

Online Action! Answers at **marketingessentials.glencoe.com/32/read**

681

FOCUS

Introducing the Section

COLLABORATIVE ACTIVITY

First ask students to define the term *credit*. Ask them to brainstorm two lists: (1) things that people normally buy on credit and (2) things that businesses buy on credit. They may have a more difficult time with the latter, since they may not have considered the fact that businesses buy things on credit.

Preteaching Key Terms

Ask the students to skim the section, paying attention to headers and key terms. This technique allows students to grasp the context of the text ahead.

- credit
- 30-day accounts
- installment accounts
- revolving accounts
- budget accounts

Extended Activity

Credit Reports

Ask students to research agencies which publish credit reports. Have students choose at least one credit reporting agency and summarize the content of what is found on a personal credit report from that agency. Have students report on their findings in class, and lead a discussion on the uses of consumer credit reports.

OBJECTIVES

- Describe the importance of credit
- Explain various sources of consumer credit
- Identify the types of credit accounts extended to consumers
- Discuss how businesses use trade credit

KEY TERMS

- credit
- 30-day accounts
- installment accounts
- revolving accounts
- budget accounts

WHILE YOU READ

Connect Based on your prior knowledge about credit, what are the advantages and disadvantages of using credit for purchases?

Credit

READ and STUDY

BEFORE YOU READ

Predict Over 185 million U.S. consumers have at least one credit card. Why do you think credit cards are so popular?

THE MAIN IDEA

Extending credit to customers or accepting credit cards for purchases is an important part of product planning. The wise use of credit can be a great benefit to a business and its customers.

STUDY ORGANIZER

In a chart like the one below jot notes about credit's features.

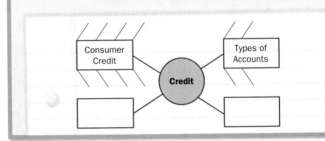

Credit and Its Importance

Credit enables businesses or individuals to obtain products or money in exchange for a promise to pay later. Credit allows most consumers to make major purchases such as homes, autos, appliances, furniture, and recreational vehicles. Consumers also use credit to make less costly purchases, such as meals, clothing, groceries, and movies.

READ and STUDY

BEFORE YOU READ

Lead students in a discussion about why credit cards appeal to consumers. Answers may include convenience or the ability to buy high-cost items and receive them at once.

THE MAIN IDEA

Ask students to discuss why a business might extend credit to its customers.

STUDY ORGANIZER

Model the study organizer for students by filling in a feature of consumer credit. A full-size, downloadable study organizer can be found at **marketingessentials.glencoe.com**

 Students may indicate that one advantage is the ability to purchase items that would not be available for cash. A disadvantage is the high interest.

The use of credit is essential to the U.S. and global economies. According to CardWeb, in 2004 there were over 185 million credit cardholders.

Role of Credit

Businesses and consumers alike use credit to purchase goods and services. Credit is also used between manufacturers, wholesalers, and retailers to buy materials, equipment, supplies, and services for use either within their businesses or to sell to other businesses.

Millions of people and thousands of businesses would not be able to buy necessary goods and services without credit. By extending credit to its customers, a business provides a purchasing incentive and enhances its sales and profits.

Consumer Credit

Companies that offer credit, such as banks, department stores, and oil companies, typically issue credit cards. Customers fill out credit applications to provide information about their sources of income and credit history. If they meet the company's lending criteria, they are issued a credit card and agree to a credit contract that establishes the rules governing the use of the card.

Credit cards are issued with credit limits based on customers' ability to pay and their payment histories. A credit limit is a preapproved dollar amount. Customers can accumulate balances up to that amount. Credit limits can range from as little as $500 for first-time cardholders to tens of thousands of dollars.

Purchases made by credit cards go through a computerized preapproval process prior to the purchase. This assures the company that a customer has not exceeded his or her credit limit.

Bank Credit Cards

Banks or their subsidiaries issue bank credit cards. Visa and MasterCard sponsor bank credit cards, but these companies do not issue them directly. Banks such as BankOne and Citibank that issue credit cards set their own fees and interest rates.

An annual fee is a flat yearly charge similar to a membership fee. Interest rates are tied to other lending rates such as the prime rate or the Treasury bill rate. These are called variable-rate plans. Others are not explicitly tied to changes in other rates and are called fixed-rate plans.

Retailers who belong to a bank credit card system either electronically process credit card sales or mail the credit card forms to the bank for payment. First, the bank deducts a service fee from the sale amount. Then, it remits the balance to the retailer.

Store and Gasoline Cards

Some businesses are large enough to offer their own credit cards, known as proprietary or house cards. Examples of stores and gasoline companies that issue credit cards are Home Depot, Target, and Shell. Usually, proprietary cards do not have an annual fee, but they do have high interest rates. A business also prefers when customers use proprietary cards because it receives income from finance charges. Finance charges on unpaid credit card balances are very expensive. Interest rates of 18 percent or even 21.6 percent are high, but not uncommon.

Travel and Entertainment Cards

Some travel and entertainment companies such as American Express, Diners Club, and Discover issue charge cards with annual fees and service charges; they require that transaction balances be paid in full each month. These types of cards are often accepted for nontravel and entertainment-related goods and services. Travel and entertainment charge card companies also charge retailers higher service fees than credit card companies do for processing the payment. Some businesses are unwilling to pay these fees, so these cards are not universally accepted.

Rebate Cards

Rebate cards offer some type of reward or incentive to consumers who use them. These cards are frequently co-branded and offer rewards in cash, airline miles,

Chapter 32 - Extended Product Features 683

Online Activity

Credit Card Options

Ask students to go to the American Express Web site to research the various credit card options that it offers. They should input the information into a spreadsheet to create a comparative chart. Then have them compare the American Express offerings to another credit card company of their choosing. They should include this other credit card company in another column on the comparison sheet.

TEACH

Discussion Starter

ROLE OF CREDIT

Discuss with students that credit card companies have promoted their cards as status symbol items. For example, American Express offers tiers of membership: the green card, the gold card, the platinum card, the blue card, and the black card (also known as the Centurion™ Card). Each tier has certain benefits and credit lines.

TEACHING POINTS

Recall Remind students credit card companies are a billion-dollar industry—the most successful sector of the U.S. banking system—because of the need or desire for people to borrow money.

Concept Development

CONSUMER CREDIT

On the fifth business day of each month the Federal Reserve issues an up-to-date report on consumer credit. Over a six-year span ending in 2004, outstanding consumer credit has increased $523.1 billion. Lead students in a discussion about why people might have been spending more and saving less during that time period.

TEACHING POINTS

Explain Tell students as a responsible credit card holder, he or she can pay the statement's minimum balance, a sustainable amount of the balance, or the balance in full.

Individualized Practice

CONSUMER CREDIT

L1 Ask students to write down the general types of information a credit card application requests from its potential customers. Have students summarize this information in written form.

L2 Ask students to write a 50-word response stating whether they agree or agree with the following statement and why: "Both consumer credit and business credit are essential to the U.S. economy. Without it, many people and businesses would not be able to buy products when they need them. Ultimately, extending credit to consumers can give them an incentive to buy and thus increase a business's profits."

L3 Ask students to interview a credit manager from a local bank, who can talk to them about the types of credit that banks commonly offer. They should take detailed notes during the interview as well as request take-home brochures or pamphlets regarding the bank's credit services. Then, ask students to prepare a 10-minute presentation that summarizes their findings as well as items they learned while reading the credit application.

Build Vocabulary

Small business owners and entrepreneurs often resort to financial institutions for *working capital*. Ask students to find out what working capital is and how it helps these types of businesspeople.

Case Study

Rewards Cards

Rewards cards pay a consumer one point per dollar charged. Since many card issuers no longer charge annual fees to have a card, consumers who pay off their balances each month actually earn money by using rewards cards.

Citibank recently introduced a diamond rewards card that enables cardholders to buy CDs and videos for 1,700 to 2,150 points. Gift certificates are awarded after 500 points are earned. Buy-to-save rewards programs have been launched in the last few years. Upromise is a college savings plan and Nestegg puts a portion of cardholders' spending into retirement accounts.

A Good Deal?

Consumers who do not pay their balance off every month find that the interest charges cost many times more than the free merchandise. For example, if you charge $5,000 to a rewards card, you would receive credits worth about $50. But every month that the balance goes unpaid costs the consumer $41.25 (based on a 9.9 percent annual interest rate).

Only about a quarter of cardholders pay off their balances every month! Rewards programs are targeted to the cardholders who maintain revolving balances. Experts estimate that about 20 to 40 percent of Americans have rewards cards today.

THINK STRATEGICALLY

Why are credit card companies issuing rewards cards?

@ Online Action! Go to *marketingessentials.glencoe.com*Base to find an activity about rewards cards.

---

telecommunication service, or special merchandise offers. Individuals who plan to carry balances on a rebate credit card should search for a card with the lowest interest rate. Those who use a credit card for convenience, however, and pay the balance every month may find that rebate cards offer the best deal. Rebate cards have higher interest rates because they are subsidizing membership costs by offering special incentives on future purchases. The Chase PerfectCard Visa, for example, enables you to earn three percent back on your credit

purchases for gasoline and one percent on all other purchases. However, the card carries a high annual rate.

Affinity Cards

Affinity cards are credit cards issued by banks to demonstrate a consumer's loyalty to a team, university, charity, business, or other organization. The organization solicits its members or customers to offer them an affinity card to help with brand promotion. The card issuer returns a small percentage

 marketingessentials.glencoe.com

Case Study Rewards Cards

Discussion Ask students how proprietary cards benefit the store that issues them.

THINK STRATEGICALLY **Answer:** To compete with competitors who offer low introductory rates for balance transfers, credit card companies have started loyalty programs that make rewards commonplace, immediate, and obtainable in the short run.

@ Online Action! For instructions, ideas, and answer guide, go to the Teacher Center at **marketingessentials.glencoe.com**

Follow Up Have students research one credit card rate and calculate how much interest they would pay for six months on an unpaid store credit card balance.

(usually less than one percent) of the interest to the organization and reward points or miles to the customer.

Debit Cards

A variation of the credit card is the debit card. When consumers pay for purchases with a debit card, they are authorizing the seller to withdraw funds directly from their bank account at the time of sale to pay for the purchase.

Special Customer Cards

These cards enable customers to receive reduced prices or reward certificates for cash discounts on future purchases. For the business, they provide marketing research information about customers' purchase patterns. Examples include grocery store club cards.

Secured and Unsecured Loans

Loans are also a form of credit. Consumers and businesses can obtain secured loans and unsecured loans for the purchase of goods and services. In secured loans, something of value, such as property, motor vehicles, machinery, or merchandise is pledged as collateral (security). The collateral helps to ensure that a loan will be repaid; if the loan is not repaid, the lender keeps the secured items to cover the debt.

Consumers and businesses can also obtain unsecured loans, which represent a written promise to repay a loan. Unsecured loans do not require collateral but rely on the excellent credit reputation of the borrower who pledges to repay the loan.

In either case, a credit contract is signed to detail payment terms and penalties for not meeting those terms.

Types of Accounts

Four major consumer credit plans are in use today: regular or 30-day accounts, installment accounts, revolving accounts, and budget accounts. The dollar amount a customer pays to use credit is called the finance charge. A finance charge may include interest costs and other charges associated with transactions.

Regular

Regular charge accounts, or **30-day accounts**, enable customers to charge purchases during a month and pay the balance in full within 30 days after they are billed. There is no finance charge for this type of credit plan as long as the bill is paid on time.

Installment Accounts

Installment accounts, or time payment plans, allow for payment over a period of time. Installment accounts are normally used for large purchases, such as a college education, travel, automobiles, appliances, and furniture. Installment accounts offer a certain interest rate over a set period of time. Installment accounts sometimes require a down payment and a separate contract for each purchase.

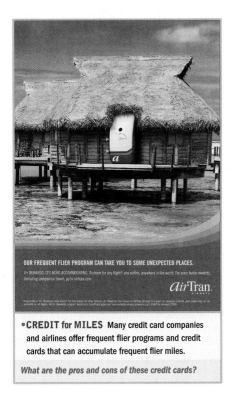

OUR FREQUENT FLIER PROGRAM CAN TAKE YOU TO SOME UNEXPECTED PLACES.

*air*Tran.

•**CREDIT for MILES** Many credit card companies and airlines offer frequent flier programs and credit cards that can accumulate frequent flier miles.

What are the pros and cons of these credit cards?

Chapter 32 - Extended Product Features **685**

ASSESS

Review Guide

CONCEPTS
Ask students to explain how credit works. Credit allows consumers and businesses to buy goods and services when they are needed in exchange for a promise to pay later.

KEY TERMS
In small groups, have students review key terms, their spellings, and definitions.

ONLINE SELF-ASSESSMENT
Have students go to marketingessentials.glencoe.com for the Section 32.2 practice test.

Individualized Review

L1 Assign and review Chapter 32 activities in the Student Activity Workbook.

L2 Assign and review Chapter 32 activities in the Marketing Math Workbook.

L3 Assign and review Chapter 32 activities in the *BusinessWeek* Reader and Case Studies.

Marketing Practice

Ask students to call a credit representative at three local business establishments (i.e., retail stores, gas stations, department stores, etc.). Have students should determine what types of credit accounts they offer. Have students report their findings to the class in a five-minute oral report.

MARKET TECH

Cash or Charge?

McDonald's customers are now able to pay for their burgers and fries in about 6,000 of the restaurants using credit and debit cards. The world's largest restaurant chain, with 31,000 restaurants in 199 countries, McDonald's has signed agreements with Visa, MasterCard, American Express, and Discover. As of 2004, McDonald's did not plan to launch credit or debit cards with its own logo.

A Happy Meal for Credit Cards

In the past, if McDonald's franchises (80 percent of its restaurants are franchises) wanted to accept credit or debit cards, they had to negotiate individual agreements with credit card companies and banks. The company's agreement with major credit card brands, however, saves its franchises the trouble of negotiating individual agreements. Prior to 2004, only 3,000 McDonald's restaurants accepted cashless payments.

Credit cards, which were once used mostly for big-ticket items, are now being used for the everyday transactions such as paying tolls, buying gasoline and groceries, or reserving movie tickets to build up frequent-flier miles or promotional bonus points.

THINK LIKE A MARKETER

Why have fast-food restaurants like McDonald's been slow to accept payment by credit card?

@ Online Action!

Go to *marketingessentials.glencoe.com/ tech* to find an activity about technology and product features.

 marketingessentials.glencoe.com

Revolving Accounts

With **revolving accounts**, the retailer determines the credit limit and payment terms. The minimum payment is usually a certain percentage on the balance owed or a minimum dollar amount, such as $15. The customer can choose to pay more than the minimum payment to reduce the balance owed. An interest charge is added to the unpaid balance for the billing period.

Customers can make purchases up to the credit limit when using a revolving account. Under most credit card arrangements, regular accounts become revolving accounts if the full amount is not paid for the billing period. Most billing cycles are 25-day periods.

Budget Accounts

Budget accounts allow for the payment of a purchased item over a certain time period without a finance charge. The most typical interest-free time period is 90 days, but some businesses have extended the time period to as much as one year. Some retailers who handle expensive products, such as furniture and appliances, offer budget accounts. Budget accounts do not require the customer to pay any interest charges if the amount owed is paid within the interest-free time period. Finance charges are applied if the amount is not paid within the specified time period. Offering budget accounts is one way that a company can stay competitive.

Business Credit

Business credit, or trade credit, is similar to consumer credit in that money is lent for goods and services. Suppliers sell raw materials, equipment, and inventory to businesses that agree to pay for these items with credit. Businesses often use credit for the same reasons that individual consumers do.

Unlike consumer credit, trade credit does not involve the use of a card. Credit memorandums, letters of credit, and credit drafts are used in trade credit arrangements. Money is lent and the parties involved in the transaction agree to payment terms.

MARKET TECH

Cash or Charge?

Discussion Lead students in a discussion how credit card processing might influence a business's efficiency and quality control.

THINK LIKE A MARKETER **Answer:** Answers may vary. Fast-food restaurants may have traditionally relied upon cash because they were concerned credit card transactions would slow down the payment process. New technologies, however, have made it possible to process credit card payments faster than cash, and this, in turn, has opened up a new profit stream for the fast-food restaurant industry—customers who prefer using credit cards.

@ Online Action! For instructions, ideas, and answer guide, go to the Teacher Center at marketingessentials.glencoe.com

Legislation Affecting Credit

Many government regulations protect consumers and their credit standing along with providing information on the proper use of credit.

The Truth in Lending Act of 1968 requires that lenders disclose information about annual percentage rates, the name of the company extending credit, and the amount financed. It also requires lenders to provide the total purchase price minus any down payments and taxes, the actual finance charge in dollars, a payment schedule, and late payment penalties.

The Fair Credit Reporting Act of 1971 requires that a lender report the name and address of the credit bureau that was used when a consumer is denied credit. The act gives consumers the opportunity to check their credit histories for errors that prevent them from obtaining credit.

The Equal Credit Opportunity Acts of 1975 and 1976 set guidelines for the review of applications for credit. These acts also prohibit discrimination based on age, gender, race, religion, or marital status.

The Fair Debt Collection Act of 1980 prevents businesses from harassing or abusing customers to collect debts.

The Fair Credit and Charge Card Disclosure Act of 1988 helps consumers by requiring credit card issuers to provide information about card costs to open credit and charge accounts.

The Fair and Accurate Credit Transactions Act of 2003 requires businesses to verify identities and addresses before opening accounts to fight identity theft. Consumers will also be able to receive free credit reports each year, correct errors more easily in their credit files, and opt out of sharing their information for marketing purposes.

CLOSE

Ask students to recall and provide answers to the following questions:

- **Why do some businesses issue proprietary or house credit cards?**
  These cards have high interest rates. Businesses also prefer for customers to use these cards because the business receives income from finance charges.

- **Why might some businesses set a minimum total dollar amount before they allow the user to charge a purchase to a bank credit card?**
  Banks charge the business a service fee for processing each card purchase. By setting a dollar minimum on these card purchases, businesses are hoping to reduce their service fee costs.

- **Why do federal and state governments pass legislation regulating credit?**
  It is necessary due to the tremendous impact credit has on the economy and its individuals.

Critical Thinking

Ask students if they think credit cards encourage people to live beyond their means. Have students share their responses in a class discussion.

32.2 AFTER YOU READ

Reviewing Key Terms and Concepts

1. Why is credit important as an extended product feature?

2. What are five sources of consumer credit?

3. List the four major consumer credit plans.

Integrating Academic Skills

Math

4. The average American charges $3,000 per year on a credit card. How many years would it take to earn 25,000 miles for a free airline trip, if the rebate was two miles earned per $1 spent with an airline affinity card?

Civics and Government

5. Perform Internet or library research on one of the federal laws regarding consumer credit. Prepare a 150-word paper on the purpose and provisions of the selected legislation.

 Online Action! Check your answers at *marketingessentials.glencoe.com/read*

marketingessentials.glencoe.com

AFTER YOU READ

Reviewing Key Terms and Concepts

1. Credit enables consumers and businesses to buy goods and services when needed in exchange for a promise to pay later.

2. Answers may include: bank credit cards, store and gasoline credit cards, travel and entertainment cards, secured and unsecured loans.

3. Regular or 30-day accounts, installment accounts, revolving accounts, and budget accounts.

Integrating Academic Skills

4. 4.16 years: Step 1: $3,000 total purchases × (2 ÷ $1/purchases) = $6,000; Step 2: 25,000 miles ÷ 6,000 = 4.16 years

5. Answers will vary; student reports should give an example of consumer credit laws.

Online Action! Answers at **marketingessentials.glencoe.com/32/read**

CAREERS IN MARKETING

Lifelong Learning

CAREER INFORMATION

Have students go to **marketingessentials.glencoe.com**, find Chapter 32 Careers page, and click on the link for the American Marketing Association's Careers Strategies and Tips. Ask students to select one article, read it, and summarize it.

PRODUCT DEVELOPMENT

Consumers can research products that had problems because they were rushed to market, had manufacturing issues, were found to be hazardous, or where the business employed poor or unethical testing. Knowledge of past issues can inform consumers to make educated purchasing decisions and can help businesses decide what issues to look for when developing similar products.

Primary Source

Ask students to go to **marketingessentials.glencoe.com** and find Chapter 32 Resources. Ask them to click on the link for the American Marketing Association's marketing dictionary and read the definitions of the terms related to extended product features.

THINKING CRITICALLY

Answers will vary. Students may state that being able to imagine and visualize in 3D is important for the product planning stage because complete visualization helps creators analyze potential problems and issues.

@ Online Action!

For instructions, ideas, and answer guide, go to the Teacher Center at **marketingessentials.glencoe.com**

JEFF KRAUSE
PRODUCT DEVELOPMENT CONSULTANT

? **What do you do at work?**
Industrial design encompasses nearly every discipline needed to take any product from a mere idea to a more or less completely functional physical reality. I create sketches, hand renderings or computer-generated renderings, non-functional or functional physical examples of the concept, as well as 3D computer-generated models of the design. If an industrial designer is properly experienced, he or she can also supply most of the specifications needed for the product to be "tooled" and actually manufactured.

? **What skills are most important to you?**
A modern industrial designer uses a blend of aesthetic skills, mechanical design, and a knowledge of numerous manufacturing processes. This includes the ability to mentally visualize shapes and mechanisms in 3D, and create mock-ups, appearance prototypes, and even working prototypes. Advanced skills include Computer-Aided Design (CAD).

? **What is your key to success?**
Success as an industrial designer means being good at interpreting the concepts of others and maintaining their intent throughout. But they do need to make the originator's vision their own, and along the way they evolve that vision into a product that can be manufactured inexpensively in the real world.

Aptitudes, Abilities, and Skills

An artistic eye, strong computer skills, and a real-world understanding of what products work

Education and Training

Helpful courses include graphic design, arts, mechanical design, and CAD.

Career Path

Most industrial designers begin work within an established firm, but the market is ripe for freelancers with experience under their belt and a portfolio of their work.

THINKING CRITICALLY

Why is it important for an industrial designer to be able to imagine and visualize in 3D?

@ Online Action!

Go to *marketingessentials.glencoe.com/ 32/careers* to find a career-related activity.

Test-Taking Strategies

As students study for section, chapter, or unit tests, tell them to review the chapter objectives. They should write them down on a piece of paper and then write everything they remember about the content from that particular objective. Once their memory list is finished, they can go back to the textbook and fill in the gaps in their notes.

FOCUS on KEY POINTS

SECTION 32.1

● Warranties are an important element of product planning because they help to increase sales and profits. Customers often base their purchasing decisions on the availability of warranties. A working knowledge of relevant federal, state, and local laws regarding warranties is essential for businesspeople.

SECTION 32.2

● Credit enables businesses or individuals to obtain products or money in exchange for a promise to pay later. The use of credit is essential to our economy. Many government regulations protect consumers and their credit standing along with providing information on the proper use of credit.

REVIEW VOCABULARY

Construct a crossword puzzle using the following vocabulary terms. Below the puzzle, include appropriate clues for the down and across spaces.

1. warranty (p. 674)
2. express warranty (p. 675)
3. full warranty (p. 675)
4. limited warranty (p. 675)
5. implied warranty (p. 677)
6. warranty of merchantability (p. 677)
7. warranty of fitness for a particular purpose (p. 677)
8. disclaimer (p. 677)
9. credit (p. 682)
10. 30-day accounts (p. 685)
11. installment accounts (p. 685)
12. revolving accounts (p. 686)
13. budget accounts (p. 686)

REVIEW FACTS and IDEAS

14. What is a warranty? (32.1)
15. What is the difference between an express warranty and an implied warranty? (32.1)
16. How does a full warranty differ from a limited warranty? (32.1)
17. What is a warranty disclaimer? (32.1)
18. Explain the advantages and disadvantages for extended warranties or service contracts. (32.1)
19. Compare and contrast credit and credit limits. (32.2)
20. What is the difference between a credit card and a debit card? (32.2)
21. How do travel and entertainment charge cards differ from bank, store, and gasoline credit cards? (32.2)
22. What is the difference between consumer and business credit? (32.2)
23. How does the Fair and Accurate Credit Transactions Act of 2003 assist consumers? (32.2)

Chapter 32 - Extended Product Features 689

FOCUS on KEY POINTS

Ask students to volunteer a few details they learned under each section's bulleted point.

REVIEW VOCABULARY

Students should consult the glossary for definitions for **1–13,** which they can paraphrase when using them as clues in the crossword puzzle. You might suggest that students browse the Internet for free puzzle-making downloadable software to create their crossword puzzle.

REVIEW FACTS and IDEAS

14. A warranty is a promise, or guarantee, given to a customer that a product will meet certain standards.
15. An express warranty is explicitly stated in writing or verbally. An implied warranty is one that exists automatically by state law whenever a purchase takes place.
16. Under a full warranty, a product found to be defective within the warranty period will be repaired or replaced at no cost to the purchaser. A limited warranty offers less coverage.
17. A disclaimer is a statement that contains exceptions to and exclusions from a warranty.
18. Advantages: 1) customers benefit from continued satisfactory product performance; and 2) peace of mind that comes with a preventative maintenance program. Disadvantages: 1) some contracts overlap existing coverage while the manufacturer's warranty is in effect, and 2) most people never need them.
19. Credit is a promise to pay later. A credit limit is a preapproved dollar amount that can be spent to purchase items on credit.
20. Credit cards are issued with a credit limit based upon customers' ability to pay and their payment history. Debit cards allow funds to be withdrawn directly from a checking account and transferred to the place of purchase.
21. Travel and entertainment cards require the payment in full for charges incurred each month. Bank, store, and gasoline cards do not.
22. Business or trade credit is similar to consumer credit in that money is loaned for goods and services. Unlike consumer credit, trade credit does not involve the use of credit cards.
23. Consumers receive free credit reports each year, correct errors more easily in credit files, and can opt out of sharing their information for marketing purposes.

BUILD SKILLS

24. Workplace Skills

Answers will vary but students should identify the name of the card, features, current interest rate, and grace period for payment.

25. Technology Applications

Answers will vary, but students should attempt to gather this information without directly contacting the business. Students should be able to find this information by searching online and checking Web sites.

26. Math Practice

The customer will spend less money for the year with the existing situation.

Existing Situation
$9,000 × 0.03 = $270 per month
$270 × 12 = $3,240/year

Different Situation
$9,000 × 0 percent = $0 for 3 months
$9,000 × 0.05 = $450
$450 × 9 = $4,050/year

Based upon minimum payments only, the customer should not switch. However, the customer needs to compare the interest rates charged for the new and existing cards. If the interest rate was lower on the new card and the customer continued to pay the minimum payment, it would be beneficial to change.

DEVELOP CRITICAL THINKING

27. Defective Warranty

Answers might include return the product, contact the retailer or manufacturer regarding an extended warranty feature, contact the appropriate government office, and so on.

28. Consumer Credit Regulations

It is necessary due to the tremendous impact credit has on the economy and individuals. These laws regulate companies issuing cards to consumers and protect consumers' credit standing.

BUILD SKILLS

24. Workplace Skills

Communication Perform an Internet search on available credit cards from a selected bank, store, gasoline, or travel and entertainment credit card company. Write a one- to two-paragraph description of the card, features, current interest rate, and grace period for payment.

25. Technology Applications

Obtaining a Warranty Quote Use the Internet to find a direct marketer of extended warranties. Obtain a quote for the following items:

- A car
- A recreational vehicle
- A motorcycle
- A boat

26. Math Practice

Consolidating Debt A household has $9,000 in credit card debt and pays three percent per month interest on all credit card payments. The family gets an offer for a new card. It promises no minimum payment for three months on all balance transfers and then a five percent interest rate thereafter.

Assuming that the household pays only the interest each month on a $9,000 balance, under which scenario will the customer spend less money over the course of a year? What other information would you need to know to advise the customer about consolidating credit cards?

DEVELOP CRITICAL THINKING

27. Defective Warranty

What steps should consumers follow if they believe a product's warranty has not adequately protected them?

28. Consumer Credit Regulations

List three reasons why it is necessary to have federal and state legislation regulating consumer credit.

Formative Assessment

Formative assessment is an essential component of classroom work. This type of assessment provides information that is then used as feedback to modify teaching and meet student needs.

L1 Review key terms for this chapter. Ask students to write one sentence for each key term.

L2 Provide various examples of factors that affect extended product features or credit. Have the students identify which factors affect each one.

L3 Ask students to create stories that illustrate ideas for successfully utilizing consumer or commercial credit.

 Reteach If the results of the formative assessment seem low, consider the following activity:

Assign and review the answers to section assessments in class.

APPLY CONCEPTS

29. Finding the Better Business Bureau

Research a Better Business Bureau located in your state.

Activity Use presentation software to create an oral report that summarizes the various services it provides and where it is located.

30. Comparing Credit Cards

Locate the Web site for the Board of Governors of the Federal Reserve System and find information about comparison shopping for bank credit cards. The board's site provides information on interest rates, grace periods, annual fees, and telephone numbers for the 150 largest banking institutions offering credit cards.

Activity Prepare a spreadsheet using computer software that compares the advantages and disadvantages of three credit cards. Compare annual fees, annual percentage rates, and other pertinent information.

NET SAVVY

31. Learn How to Use Credit

Use the library or the Internet to investigate how to use credit wisely. Research by reading advice in personal finance columns in newspapers and on Web sites. Prepare a one-page report on tips for using credit wisely.

marketingessentials.glencoe.com

Role Play: Extended Product Features

Situation You are to assume the role of sales associate for a costume jewelry store. The store carries earrings, necklaces, bracelets, and watches that are appealing to younger customers. The merchandise price points are at the high end of the range for costume jewelry. All the merchandise carries a lifetime guarantee. If a watch needs to be repaired or items need stones replaced, the item must be sent to the customer service center, not returned to the store.

Activity You are to explain the store's lifetime guarantee to a customer (judge) who is purchasing a watch for $175.

Evaluation You will be evaluated on how well you meet the following performance indicators:

● Explain warranties and guarantees

● Interpret business policies to customers/clients

● Explain the nature of positive customer/client relations

● Handle customer inquiries

● Address people properly

 Online Action!

For more information and DECA Prep practice, go to *marketingessentials.glencoe.com*

Chapter 32 - Extended Product Features **691**

APPLY CONCEPTS

29. Finding the Better Business Bureau
Presentations should express an understanding of the services provided by the Better Business Bureau.

30. Comparing Credit Cards
Spreadsheets should contain pertinent information related to credit cards.

NET SAVVY

31. Learn How to Use Credit
Students might look for articles about people who used credit wisely as well as those who did not. Suggest that they offer a realistic portrait of the advantages and disadvantages to using credit.

MINI-QUIZ

Administer the Mini-Quiz orally. Students should answer these questions as either true or false.

1. An arrangement whereby businesses or individuals can obtain products or money exchanged for a promise to pay later is called a warranty.
(false, it is called credit.)

2. A promise to a customer that a product will meet certain standards is called credit.
(false, it is called a warranty.)

3. A service contract that provides service or preventative maintenance for a specified period beyond a product's normal warranty period is called an extended warranty.
(true)

For an expanded chapter quiz, go to Chapter 32 in the TeacherWorks CD-ROM and to Chapter 32 in the **Exam View**® Pro Test Generator CD-ROM.

The students should be evaluated on the performance indicators noted in the role play. For another DECA role play, go to the Competitive Events Workbook or the Student Activity Workbook, or go to marketingessentials.glencoe.com/32/DECA

 Online Action! For instructions, ideas, and answer guide, go to the Teacher Center at marketingessentials.glencoe.com

DECA Advisors Corner

To build leadership skills, break students into small groups and ask them to discuss the following questions: 1) What are the most important skills for tomorrow's leaders?; 2) How has technology changed leadership?; 3) How can high school students develop their own leadership skills?

MARKETING INTERNSHIP

A SIMULATED **DECA** PRODUCT AND SERVICE MANAGEMENT EVENT

SET-UP

Discuss basic background to make sure students understand the simulation. Ask students to discuss what they know about low-carb diets. Are they healthy, and do they work? Have students debate whether it is preferable for a food company to feed customers what they want or market a less popular but healthier diet.

PROCEDURES

You may want to list procedures on the board and talk about any questions the students might have. Remind the students that a suggested outline for their project is available at marketingessentials.glencoe.com/u10/internship.

TIME MANAGEMENT

Set goals, block schedules, and milestones. Assign interim deadlines for each step of the project.

ASSESSMENT

The rubrics for evaluation of the written, oral, and computer presentations are available at marketingessentials.glencoe.com/u10/internship.

Create a New Exciting Food Product

BASIC BACKGROUND

Mainstream Foods wants to create healthy food for people on the go. Its competitors have already flooded the market with meal replacement products and low-carbohydrate alternatives to their existing foods.

Who Is Doing What? Unilever has a low-carb product line called Carb Options®, which includes salad dressings, peanut butter, iced tea, steak sauce, and a chocolate chip brownie bar. Keto carries an even broader line of low-carb foods, including spaghetti, elbow macaroni, pizza dough, macaroni and cheese, tortilla chips, cereal, ice cream, and ketchup. Russell Stover has low-carb candies and DeBoles offers low-carb spaghetti. Manufacturers have developed meal replacement bars such as Balance®, Atkins®, and Zone® bars, which target adults, and milk and cereal bars which target children.

YOUR OBJECTIVE

You are on the team of research and development (R&D) scientists and marketing staff members. The team's role is to develop a new line of low-carb foods or meal replacement products. The clock is ticking: Mainstream Foods wants the new products introduced in six months because it wants to capitalize on the active-lifestyle and low-carbohydrate crazes and popular diets such as Atkins, South Beach, Zone, and 40-30-30.

ASSIGNMENT AND STRATEGY

- **Get the background** You will have to conduct an environmental scan to identify threats and opportunities for Mainstream Foods. Include the popular diets and products noted above and any food labeling laws or other relevant government regulations.

  Research what competitors have already done to capitalize on these trends. Do your research at a library or on the Internet, as well as in food stores and supermarkets. Trade publications that may be helpful include *Brandweek, Advertising Age,* and *Supermarket News.*

- **Develop the product concept** Use the steps for new product planning to design one or more products or product lines for Mainstream Foods.

READ to WRITE

History of Diet Foods

Ask the class to research the history of diet foods. Ask them to detail the turning points (such as the introduction of artificial sweeteners such as saccharin or aspartame) and trends (like the creation of low-carb drinks) and summarize the developments in a two-page essay. Encourage students to focus on a single company, a single product, or an industry-wide trend. Students should include information on the types of information about diets and nutrition available to the public, the sources of that information, and whether and how businesses adapted food products in response to that information. Have students discuss the current and future markets for diet foods.

Once your team has developed a new product or product line, conduct marketing research with the intended target market(s) to see if any changes should be made. Include the product concept, its packaging, and the other marketing mix strategies in your market research study.

- **What your project should include** Your ideas for your product and/or product line should include its name, packaging, labeling, warranty or guarantee, and other marketing mix strategies (place, price, promotion). Be sure to conclude with a strong argument as to why this new product or product line will be successful.

 YOUR REPORT

Use a word processing program and presentation software to prepare a double-spaced report and an oral presentation for Mainstream Foods. See a suggested outline and key evaluation points at *marketingessentials.glencoe.com/internship*

BUILD YOUR PORTFOLIO

Option 1 Internship Report
Once you have completed your Marketing Internship project and presentation, include your written report and a few printouts of key slides from your oral presentation in your Marketing Portfolio.

Option 2 Designing a New Product Develop a new product or service of your choice. Use the steps in product development to decide on a new product. Analyze current market and PEST (political, economic, socio-cultural, and technological) conditions. Prepare a comprehensive written report and an oral presentation noting the target market, product name, packaging, labeling, price, place, and promotion. See a suggested outline and key evaluation points at *marketingessentials.glencoe.com/portfolio*

@ **Online Action!**

Go to *marketingessentials.glencoe.com/Unit/10/DECA* to review product and service management concepts that relate to DECA events.

marketingessentials.glencoe.com

Marketing Internship **693**

Unit Review

Now that students have completed the chapters in Unit 10, ask them to review their answers to the Think and Write activity on page 631. Would they answer it differently? Why or why not?

Conclude this unit with a general review of all elements of product planning, including new product development, product mix, branding, packaging, labeling, warranties, and credit. Have products such as Liquid Paper, Post-Its, or other handy products available to use as specific examples.

Ask students to visit the supermarket and find a product that is labeled as new or improved. Have them simulate the product's planning, conveying the process as a series of steps.

STEP AHEAD
Have the students suppose they have invented a new product and are about to create a business to produce and sell it. Ask them what steps might be taken to prepare for entrepreneurship.

Internship Wrap-Up

Have students research the government regulations on manufacturing and selling food products of their choice. Direct them to the Food and Drug Administration to find out what is required in terms of the food product preparation and packaging.

BUILD YOUR PORTFOLIO

Explain to students that portfolios provide evidence of their knowledge and skills in working with data, people, and concepts. Developing a portfolio can be a valuable career development and planning tool. Point out to students that quality is more important than the quantity of entries. Encourage students to check the portfolio information available at marketingessentials.glencoe.com/u10/internship.

Peer Review
Fellow students who share common interests can serve as reviewers of the final portfolios. This review can be completed through the use of a checklist. Go to marketingessentials.glencoe.com/u10/internship to find a suggested checklist.

Unit Objectives

After completing this unit, students should be able to:

- Identify the risks, rewards, advantages, and disadvantages of entrepreneurship
- Identify the different forms of business ownership
- Explain the types of business risks and different methods used to handle them
- Identify the three major sections of a business plan
- Develop a business plan with appropriate documentation
- Prepare financial statements used by entrepreneurs to report income and analyze a business's financial status

■ Key to
■ Individualized
■ Activities

L1 Level 1 activities are basic activities and should fall within the range of all students.

L2 Level 2 activities are average activities and should be within the range of average and above average students.

L3 Level 3 activities are challenging activities designed for the ability range of above average students.

Enrichment Resources

PROFESSIONAL ORGANIZATIONS

The American Small Business Association asbaonline.org

Small Business Administration sba.gov

Young Entrepreneurs' Organization yeo.com

MEDIA RESOURCES

Print or online editions of

Entrepreneur Magazine entrepreneur.com

Inc. inc.com

WRITING SUPPORT

Ask students to list at least three qualities that are needed by an entrepreneur. In a two-page essay, have students explain these qualities and suggest ways to cultivate these qualities. Ask students to keep and review this document as they study Unit 11.

Finance

UNIT 11 PLANNING GUIDE AND RESOURCES

CHAPTER	PRINT MATERIALS	TECHNOLOGY RESOURCES
Chapter 33 Section 33.1 Section 33.2	**From Unit 11 Fast File Booklet** Lesson Plans; Chapter Summaries; Reproducible Masters; Reproducible Tests **Print Ancillaries** Student Activity Workbook Marketing Math Workbook *BusinessWeek* Reader and Case Studies, Chapter 33 Competitive Events Workbook, Unit 11 Marketing Research Project Workbook School-to-Work Activity Workbook	Interactive Chalkboard classroom presentations marketingessentials.glencoe.com Online Student Edition, Chapter 33 TeacherWorks Exam*View*® Pro Test Generator, Chapter 33 Virtual Business
Chapter 34 Section 34.1 Section 34.2	**From Unit 11 Fast File Booklet** Lesson Plans; Chapter Summaries; Reproducible Masters; Reproducible Tests **Print Ancillaries** Student Activity Workbook Marketing Math Workbook *BusinessWeek* Reader and Case Studies, Chapter 34 Competitive Events Workbook, Unit 11 Marketing Research Project Workbook School-to-Work Activity Workbook	Interactive Chalkboard classroom presentations marketingessentials.glencoe.com Online Student Edition, Chapter 34 TeacherWorks Exam*View*® Pro Test Generator, Chapter 34 Virtual Business
Chapter 35 Section 35.1 Section 35.2	**From Unit 11 Fast File Booklet** Lesson Plans; Chapter Summaries; Reproducible Masters; Reproducible Tests **Print Ancillaries** Student Activity Workbook Marketing Math Workbook *BusinessWeek* Reader and Case Studies, Chapter 35 Competitive Events Workbook, Unit 11 Marketing Research Project Workbook School-to-Work Activity Workbook	Interactive Chalkboard classroom presentations marketingessentials.glencoe.com Online Student Edition, Chapter 35 TeacherWorks Exam*View*® Pro Test Generator, Chapter 35 Virtual Business

National Marketing Education

CHAPTER	SECTION	PERFORMANCE INDICATOR
Chapter 33 **Entrepreneurial Concepts**	33.1	Explain the concept of private enterprise (ECO)
		Identify speculative business risks (BME)
		Explain the types of business risk (BME)
		Identify desirable personality traits important to business (PD)
	33.2	Explain employment opportunities in business (PD)
		Explain the types of business ownership (BME)
		Explain legal issues affecting business (BME)
Chapter 34 **Risk Management**	34.1	Explain the nature of risk management (BME)
		Explain types of business risk (BME)
	34.2	Explain routine security precautions (BME)
		Develop business plan (BME)
Chapter 35 **Developing a Business Plan**	35.1	Plan and organize the work efforts of others (BME)
		Explain the nature of marketing plans (BME)
	35.2	Explain the nature and scope of financing (FIN)
		Determine financing needed to start a business (FIN)
		Explain the nature of marketing plans (BME)
		Explain the nature and scope of financing (FIN)
		Determine financing needed to start a business (FIN)
		Describe sources of financing for businesses (FIN)
Chapter 36 **Risk Management**	36.1	Explain the nature and scope of financing (FIN)
		Explain the nature of business plans (BME)
		Interpret financial statements (BME)
	36.2	Explain the concept of accounting (BME)
		Explain the nature of balance sheets (BME)
		Describe the nature of cash-flow statements (BME)

BME Business, Management, Entrepreneurship   **ECO** Economics   **FIN** Financing   **PD** Professional Development

Standards Assessment Correlation

	SECTION ASSESSMENT		CHAPTER ASSESSMENT						UNIT LAB
	Reviewing Key Terms and Concepts	Integrating Academic Skills	Review Facts and Ideas	Build Skills	Develop Critical Thinking	Apply Concepts	Workplace Skills	Net Savvy	Marketing Internship
	1, 2	✓	15	21	24	26	✓	✓	✓
			16, 17	21		27	✓		✓
			16, 17	22	24				✓
		✓	18	21		26	✓	✓	
	1		16–20	21		26, 27	✓	✓	
				21		26, 27	✓		✓
	2, 3	✓		22					✓
		✓	10, 13, 14	16	19, 20	21, 22	✓		✓
	1, 2, 3	✓	11	16, 17	20	21	✓		✓
	1, 2, 3	✓	12, 14	16	19, 20	21	✓	✓	✓
	2		13	16		22	✓		✓
			14	18		23, 24	✓	✓	✓
	1, 2	✓	11, 13, 15	19	21	23, 24		✓	✓
	3		13, 17	19	21, 22	23, 24		✓	✓
	3		12, 17	19	21, 22	23, 24		✓	✓
	1, 2, 3		11, 13, 15	18, 19	21	23, 24	✓	✓	✓
	2, 3	✓	13, 17	19	22	23, 24		✓	✓
	1	✓	12, 17	19	21, 22	23, 24		✓	✓
	1, 3	✓	12, 17	19	21, 22	28	✓		✓
	1, 2, 3	✓	15, 16, 20	23, 24	26, 27	28	✓		✓
	3	✓	14–16	24	27	28		✓	✓
	1, 2		17, 20–22	23, 25	26, 27	28, 29	✓		✓
	1, 2, 3	✓	18–20, 22	23	26, 27	28	✓		✓
	3	✓	18, 19, 22	23		29	✓		✓
			18, 22	23		29	✓		✓

@ Online Action! Check the latest updates for national standards and for your state's standards at marketingessentials.glencoe.com

Unit Overview

Unit 11 describes entrepreneurship and the financial planning required in entrepreneurship. Chapter 33 introduces students to the process of starting and managing a business. Chapter 34 then discusses the economic, natural, and human risks inherent in business ownership. Chapter 35 discusses how potential business owners create a business plan to give an overall picture of a proposed business to potential investors and lenders. Lastly, Chapter 36 shows students how to identify capital needs for a business and develop a financial plan that will meet those needs.

MAKING IT RELEVANT

Ask students why entrepreneurship is an important part of the U.S. economy. Entrepreneurship is important to the U.S. economy because it affects change in the marketplace and provides jobs for about 55 percent of the labor force.

Unit Launch Activity

Have students share their first impressions of the ad on this page. Inform students that the children of entrepreneurs are likely to become entrepreneurs themselves. Ask students to create a list of reasons this is the case. Have the class compare and combine their lists. Save and revisit the combined list at the end of the unit.

OUT OF TIME?

If class time is too short to cover all the chapters in this unit, go to Unit 11 in your Fast File Teacher Resources booklet and find the Chapter Summaries for Chapters 33, 34, 35, and 36.

694

In this unit you will find

- **Chapter 33**
  Entrepreneurial Concepts

- **Chapter 34**
  Risk Management

- **Chapter 35**
  Developing a Business Plan

- **Chapter 36**
  Financing the Business

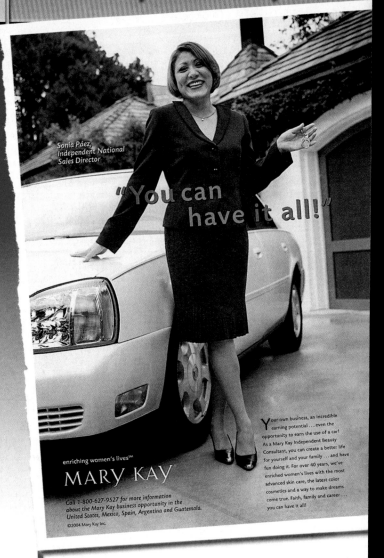

Sonia Páez, Independent National Sales Director

"You can have it all!"

enriching women's lives℠
MARY KAY

Your own business, an incredible earning potential . . . even the opportunity to earn the use of a car! As a Mary Kay Independent Beauty Consultant, you can create a better life for yourself and your family . . . and have fun doing it. For over 40 years, we've enriched women's lives with the most advanced skin care, the latest color cosmetics and a way to make dreams come true. Faith, family and career . . . you can have it all!

Call 1-800-627-9527 for more information about the Mary Kay business opportunity in the United States, Mexico, Spain, Argentina and Guatemala.
©2004 Mary Kay Inc.

694

DECA UNIT PROJECT

Small Business Ownership in America

Have students research the role of small business ownership in American society since the 1700s. What role did small business play in the society of the late 1990s? What role will it probably play in the 21st century? How is small business ownership reflective of current economic and sociological trends in our society? Have students write their findings in a one-page report.

Assessment Guidelines Prepare a rubric for evaluation that includes thoroughness of the reports presented by students. Students should consider the differences between small businesses of today and those of the 1700s, and how their economic and sociological impact has changed as society has evolved.

Enrichment Assign and review Unit 11 activities in the Competitive Events Workbook.

and Finance

ANALYZE THE AD

Mary Kay sells its cosmetics through more than 1.3 million independent representatives who earn commissions. What is this ad selling?

Market Talk Most cosmetics companies sell through department stores or drugstores. Mary Kay and the much larger Avon both depend on independent representatives. The direct sales method lets representatives grow their businesses as much as they want. This flexibility appeals to entrepreneurs.

Think and Write An entrepreneur can start a business, be an independent salesperson for a company, or open a franchise. Choose the most appealing scenario and list three reasons for your preference.

 Online Action! Go to *marketingessentials.glencoe.com/u11/ad* for an extended activity.

Functions of Marketing

Marketing Plan

1 ANALYSIS
SWOT
Economic
Socio-Cultural
Technological
Competitive

2 STRATEGY
Promotion
Place
Price
Product

3 IMPLEMENTATION
Organization
Management
Staffing

4 BUDGET
Cost of sales
Cost of Promotion
Incomes and Expenses

5 CONTROL
Evaluation
Performance Measures
Performance Analysis

In this unit

Foundations of Marketing
- Business, Management, Entrepreneurship
- Economics

Functions of Marketing
- Financing

ANALYZE THE AD

The ad is selling the idea of the advantages of being an independent Mary Kay consultant.

Market Talk Ask students to brainstorm possible advantages and disadvantages of the career advertised in this ad.

Think and Write Answers will vary; encourage students to share their preference and the reasons behind their choice in small groups.

 Online Action! For instructions, ideas, and answer guide, go to the Teacher Center at **marketingessentials.glencoe.com**

Marketing Plan

RELATE THE UNIT TO THE MARKETING PLAN
The four Ps of the marketing mix include product, place, pricing, and promotion. Unit 11 focuses on small business and touches on its use of the marketing mix.

MARKETING PLAN OVERVIEW
Let students know that an effective marketing plan will help increase an entrepreneur's odds of succeeding in the marketplace.

Functions of Marketing
Point out to students that Chapters 33, 34, 35, and 36 will deal with the marketing function of financing and the marketing foundations of economics and of business, management, and entrepreneurship.

▶ **Financing** Understanding the basic principles of financing is essential for starting and growing a business. Without a thorough consideration of the marketplace and how it will impact lenders and investors, a new business could have trouble staying solvent.

● **Business, Management, Entrepreneurship** Business managers and entrepreneurs must have a good grasp of economics and financing if they want to be successful businesspeople, and they must know how each part relates to the others.

● **Economics** A business can be supported only by a marketplace that welcomes its products. Understanding the economics of the global marketplace or even a local town in which a small business is based helps a business-person determine whether the financial climate will support the business.

Chapter Overview

This chapter introduces entrepreneurship and its advantages and disadvantages. The chapter also lists the personal characteristics needed to become a successful entrepreneur. The legal steps taken in establishing a business are also explored in Chapter 33.

BUILD BACKGROUND

Ask students if they or someone they know has any experience being self-employed. Give some examples, such as providing childcare, developing Web sites, mowing lawns, or cleaning pools. Ask them what the rewards and drawbacks of working for themselves were. Tell students that by working for themselves, they were acting in an entrepreneurial manner.

Why It's Important

A large sector of the American economy is based on entrepreneurs, many of whom operate small businesses. Small businesses are currently showing strong growth, and many future jobs are predicted to come from this sector.

Prepare to Read

Discuss the section objectives with students. Have students skim the chapter, looking at pictures, reading captions, and noting the headings. Ask questions to ensure that students have an understanding of the chapter structure.

Entrepreneurial Concepts

Chapter Objectives

After reading this chapter, you should be able to:

- Define entrepreneurship
- Detail the advantages of entrepreneurship
- Explain the risks and disadvantages of entrepreneurship
- List the characteristics and skills of entrepreneurs
- Understand the importance of small business in the U.S. and global economies
- Identify the forms of business ownership
- Name the legal steps to take in establishing a business

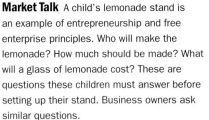

GUIDE TO THE PHOTO

Market Talk A child's lemonade stand is an example of entrepreneurship and free enterprise principles. Who will make the lemonade? How much should be made? What will a glass of lemonade cost? These are questions these children must answer before setting up their stand. Business owners ask similar questions.

Quick Think Name at least two other questions entrepreneurs (or lemonade-stand owners) must answer before starting a new business.

GUIDE TO THE PHOTO

Market Talk Lead a discussion about the type of small business featured in this photograph. Then have students discuss high-profile entrepreneurs that started out tackling small-scale business ventures.

Quick Think Answers will vary. Students should recognize how need in the marketplace can define the types of entrepreneurships developed.

 Ask students to name two businesses that are entrepreneurships. Then ask students to discuss whether they would be interested in running such a business, and why.

marketingessentials.glencoe.com

Performance indicators represent key skills and knowledge. Relating them to the concepts explained in this chapter is your key to success in DECA events. These acronyms represent DECA events that involve knowledge of concepts in this chapter.

AAAL	FMAL	MMS*	TMDM*
AAML*	FMDM*	QSRM*	TSE*
ADC*	FMML*	RMAL	VPM
BSM	FSRM*	RMML*	
EMDM*	HMDM*	SMDM*	

In all these DECA events you should be able to follow these performance indicators:

- Determine the relationship between government and business
- Explain the concept of private enterprise
- Determine factors affecting business risk
- Explain the role of business in society
- Explain types of business ownership
- Describe current business trends
- Describe legal issues affecting business
- Explain the nature of legally binding contracts

All the events with an asterisk (*) also include these performance indicators:

- Explain the nature of tax regulations on business

Some events include additional performance indicators. These are:

FMDM Explain the nature of regulations affecting the financial services industry

TMDM Explain the nature of regulations affecting the travel and tourism industry

HMDM Explain the nature of regulations affecting the hospitality industry

EMDM Describe legal considerations in e-commerce

DECA PREP

Check your understanding of DECA performance indicators with the DECA activity in this chapter's review. For more information and DECA Prep practice, go to *marketingessentials.glencoe.com/33/DECA*

DECA events that require knowledge of entrepreneurial concepts are described here. Discuss the performance indicators to make sure students understand how to demonstrate their understanding.

The event acronyms stand for:

AAAL: Apparel and Accessories Marketing Series, AL

AAML: Apparel and Accessories Marketing Series, ML

ADC: Advertising Campaign Event

BSM: Business Services Marketing Series

EMDM: E-Commerce Management Team Decision Making Event

FMAL: Food Marketing Series, AL

FMDM: Financial Analysis Management Team Decision Making Event

FMML: Food Marketing Series, ML

FSRM: Full Service Restaurant Management Series

HMDM: Hospitality Services Management Team Decision Making Event

MMS: Marketing Management Series

QSRM: Quick Serve Restaurant Management Series

RMAL: Retail Merchandising Series, AL

RMML: Retail Merchandising Series, ML

SMDM: Sports and Entertainment Marketing Management Team Decision Making Event

TMDM: Travel and Tourism Marketing Management Team Decision Making Event

TSE: Technical Sales Event

VPM: Vehicles and Petroleum Marketing Series

DECA PREP

Find timed DECA Prep activities correlated to the Competitive Events Workbook for students and DECA tips for teachers at marketingessentials.glencoe.com/33/DECA

CHAPTER 33 Classroom Resources

For the Teacher

- TeacherWorks
- marketingessentials.glencoe.com
- Interactive Chalkboard
- **Exam***View*® Pro Test Generator
- Fast File Unit 11

For the Student

- ***Marketing Essentials*** Online Edition
- Student Activity Workbook
- Marketing Math Workbook
- Marketing Research Project Workbook
- School-to-Work Activity Workbook
- Competitive Events Workbook
- ***BusinessWeek*** Reader and Case Studies
- marketingessentials.glencoe.com

FOCUS

Introducing the Section

COLLABORATIVE ACTIVITY

Give students five minutes to write a list of what they would consider to be the advantages and the disadvantages of entrepreneurship.

Examples might include: advantages—personal freedom, increased income, personal satisfaction, own work schedule; disadvantages—high stress, potential loss of income, high risk.

Preteaching Key Terms

Read the key terms aloud, or ask a volunteer to read them. Ask students to predict the meanings of these words:

- entrepreneurship
- entrepreneurs

Tell students they can check their predictions as they read this section.

Build Vocabulary

Define the term *altruism* (unselfish regard for the welfare of others). A good understanding of this term will help focus the discussion. Ask each student to each think of an example of altruism that relates to entrepreneurs. Write the examples on the board.

Answers might include: Bill and Melinda Gates Foundation—brings innovations in health and learning to the global community.

OBJECTIVES

- **Define entrepreneurship**
- **Detail the advantages of entrepreneurship**
- **Explain the risks and disadvantages of entrepreneurship**
- **List the characteristics and skills of entrepreneurs**
- **Understand the importance of small business in the U.S. and global economies**

KEY TERMS

- **entrepreneurship**
- **entrepreneurs**

WHILE YOU READ

Connect Compare the characteristics of an entrepreneur to your own personality. Would you make a good entrepreneur?

Entrepreneurship

READ and STUDY

BEFORE YOU READ

Predict Do you know any successful entrepreneurs? Make a list of reasons for their success.

THE MAIN IDEA

Entrepreneurship has advantages and disadvantages. Although it involves accepting risks, it can lead to personal freedom and financial reward.

STUDY ORGANIZER

Draw a diagram like the one below and list the characteristics of entrepreneurship as you read this section.

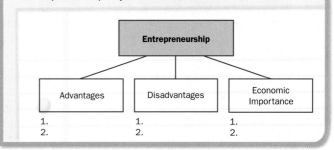

Advantages	Disadvantages	Economic Importance
1.	1.	1.
2.	2.	2.

What Is Entrepreneurship?

Entrepreneurship is the process of starting and operating your own business. **Entrepreneurs** are people who create, launch, organize, and manage a new business and take the risk of business ownership. You are an entrepreneur already if you have provided babysitting services or cut someone's lawn for pay.

Entrepreneurs make major contributions to our economy. Entrepreneurs often have an idea, or business concept, that

698 UNIT 11 - ENTREPRENEURSHIP AND FINANCE

READ and STUDY

BEFORE YOU READ

Ask students to identify the personal attributes needed for a successful entrepreneur. Answers might include: they are self motivated, creative, and work hard; they have good social skills, etc.

THE MAIN IDEA

Ask students to define risks and personal freedoms. Discuss their definitions.

STUDY ORGANIZER

Model the study organizer for students by filling in the first numbered blank. A full-size, downloadable study organizer can be found at marketingessentials.glencoe.com

 WHILE YOU READ Model for students how they can compare their own personal attributes to those of a successful entrepreneur.

drives their business. When an entrepreneur combines this vision with the means to manufacture the product (or provide the service) and market it, the contributions to the economy both within and outside the United States can be remarkable. The results of entrepreneurship can change our lives in other ways, too. Consider the following examples:

- Henry Ford introduced the mass production of automobiles, making them affordable to the average person. His entrepreneurship revolutionized transportation and transformed lifestyles.
- William Hewlett and David Packard started a small business in Packard's garage near Stanford University in California. They invented the three-and-a-half-inch floppy disk and the first pocket calculator. Their business grew into the giant Hewlett-Packard Corporation, which produces a vast array of computer products, including

laser printers. These products changed the speed with which people process information.

These entrepreneurs became famous and wealthy as a result of starting their own businesses, but not all entrepreneurs achieve such success. Some start companies simply because they want to be their own bosses and make their own business decisions.

Advantages of Entrepreneurship

The advantages of entrepreneurship can include personal freedom, personal satisfaction, increased self-esteem, and increased income. Entrepreneurs set their own work schedules and make their own decisions. They are able to try out their own new ideas and direct their energies into business activities, take control of their businesses and their work settings.

Many business owners are willing to put in the extra effort to make their businesses succeed because of financial rewards. With

NET MARKETING

E-Training Anyone?

What do you need to do to earn second place on the *Fortune* Small Business 100 list? You need to be very good at providing technology-based products and services to pharmaceutical, bio-technological, medical device, and contract resource companies. eResearch Technology, Inc., sells centralized electrocardiographic (diagnostic) services as well as technology and services to streamline the clinical trial process.

Online Training for Customers

The company's Web site takes full advantage of the power of the Internet and Web marketing. One of its key e-commerce features is Web-based training through its eResearch Community's eHealth Education. This service lets customers access a series of sophisticated, interactive, Web-based training programs to learn clinical research processes and procedures.

THINK LIKE A MARKETER

If eResearch Technology, Inc., sells products and services, why does it bother with online training?

@ **Online Action!**

Go to *marketingessentials.glencoe.com/33/net* to find an activity about the Internet and entrepreneurship.

NET MARKETING

E-Training Anyone?

Discussion After students have read Net Marketing, lead a discussion about the uses of e-training. Examples might include: for full-time employees who want to study outside normal business hours, for long-distance learning, etc.

THINK LIKE A MARKETER **Answer:** By offering online training, eResearch Technology, Inc., creates another reason for consumers to use and purchase their products.

@ **Online Action!** For instructions, ideas, and answer guide, go to the Teacher Center at marketingessentials.glencoe.com

Follow Up Ask students to find the eResearch Technology Web site and note what else is offered on the site. Have them report their findings to the class.

TEACH

Discussion Starter

WHAT IS ENTREPRENEURSHIP?

Many people have strong altruistic motives for becoming entrepreneurs. Have students discuss why altruism plays a part in some people's desire to become entrepreneurs.

Some people feel they are investing in the local community by contributing to the local labor force.

TEACHING POINTS

Make Comparisons Begin discussion about the entrepreneurs featured on the page. Ask: In what ways are they alike?

Answers may include they stared their own business out of original ideas.

Concept Development

ADVANTAGES OF ENTREPRENEURSHIP

As a class, discuss the advantages to entrepreneurship. Have students develop a list of advantages and write them on the board.

Answers will include: personal freedom, personal satisfaction, increased self-esteem and income, etc.

To expand the discussion, as a class, link the personal attributes discussed in the Before You Read section with the advantages listed.

TEACHING POINTS

Explain Bring examples of national and international entrepreneurs to class. Explain the advantages and personal attributes that contributed to each entrepreneur.

Clarify Remind students of the limitations of entrepreneurship. Without financial backing, small businesses can suffer from cash flow restrictions.

Individualized Practice

ENTREPRENEURSHIP AS A CAREER CHOICE

L1 Have students choose a specific type of entrepreneurship, such as opening a Web design company. Tell them to list both the specific skills and general attributes needed to succeed in this business.

L2 On a three-column chart, have students compare three entrepreneurs using these categories: specific skills, general attributes, and challenges conquered.

L3 Ask students to research a famous entrepreneur. In a two-page expository essay, have them explain the steps their entrepreneur took to build his or her business, the entrepreneur's personal attributes, and their specific skills.

Build Vocabulary

Preview the following words by reading them in context in the Case Study:

- **prestigious** celebrated
- **lavish** extravagant
- **loyalty** faithfulness

Discuss the meanings of these words with students.

Online Activity

Online Entrepreneurship
Ask the students to use the Internet to research an online entrepreneurship. Ask them to bring their findings to class to illustrate the wide range of online businesses.

Case Study

Entrepreneur in the Kitchen

Housewife Estee Lauder began her cosmetics business in the 1930s, mixing up face creams in her New York kitchen and going into beauty salons to offer free demonstrations to women sitting under hair dryers. Her creams were high quality, and people who tried them usually bought them.

In 1948, Lauder persuaded a buyer at the prestigious retailer Saks Fifth Avenue to order her product. That first order sold out in two days.

Product Line Diversification

Over the years, Lauder developed a full line of cosmetics under her own name and sold it selectively through high-end department stores around the world. Her company also developed the Clinique, Aramis, Prescriptives, and Origins lines—each targeted to a slightly different market.

A Marketing Genius

Estee Lauder originated the "gift with purchase" concept, which has become very important in cosmetics sales. If a customer purchases one item, he or she receives a gift package containing many other items worth more than the amount spent. It is a creative way of developing customer loyalty. Lauder was the only woman in *Time* magazine's listing of the 20 most influential business geniuses of the twentieth century.

THINK STRATEGICALLY

How could it make sense to give away products worth more money than the item purchased? What qualities of an entrepreneur does that idea display?

@ Online Action! Go to *marketingessentials.glencoe.com/33/case* to find an activity about entrepreneurship.

---

success often comes money, and this potential motivates many entrepreneurs.

Disadvantages of Entrepreneurship

Being an entrepreneur has disadvantages, too. These include a high level of stress, possible setbacks, the risk of failure, potential loss of income, long and irregular hours, the need to handle multiple tasks, and the required strong self-discipline.

Most new businesses have a restricted cash flow because of start-up costs. As a result, an entrepreneur may not meet his or her personal financial needs during the first year of operation, or even longer. Increased income comes only when the business succeeds.

Entrepreneurs are not 40-hours-per-week people. To succeed, they must meet the needs of the marketplace, which often means long and irregular hours.

marketingessentials.glencoe.com

Case Study — Entrepreneur in the Kitchen

Discussion Have students read the Case Study and discuss the pros (such as possibility of success, chance to develop her own product and try her own ideas) and cons (long hours, unknown business identity, risk) Estee Lauder faced when beginning her entrepreneurship.

THINK STRATEGICALLY
Answer: By giving away sample products as gifts, Lauder builds great customer loyalty. Answers might include: creativity, daring, good social skills.

@ Online Action! For instructions, ideas, and answer guide, go to the Teacher Center at **marketingessentials.glencoe.com**

Follow Up Ask students to think of two other scenarios in which a company might give away samples as gifts with a purchase.

Running a business requires doing many tedious, time-consuming tasks. To save money, new business owners may do many of these jobs themselves. Among the tasks they may perform are time-consuming paperwork, such as accounts payable, accounts receivable, payroll, and government forms.

The Risks of Entrepreneurship

Starting a new business requires a major commitment of time, money, and effort. A new business owner must be a risk taker. It is often necessary to quit a job, work long hours, invest savings, and borrow money—all with no guarantee that the new business will succeed. Seven out of ten small-business owners started their businesses with less than $20,000, according to the 1998 report *The Wells Fargo/National Federation of Independent Business Series on Business Starts and Stops.* In fact, in 2002, 14 percent of *Inc.* magazine's 500 fast-growing companies started with less than $1,000.

The risk of failure with a new business is very real. Only two-thirds of new businesses survive at least two years, and about half survive at least four years. When a company fails, often much of the money invested in it is lost. Failure also means loss of employment.

Entrepreneurship as a Career Choice

Being an entrepreneur can be exciting and greatly rewarding, but it is not for everyone. Those who succeed have certain skills and personal characteristics that enable them to meet the challenges of business ownership.

First, entrepreneurs must have the skills necessary to run their business. Someone starting an online magazine should know how to write and have a good grasp of Internet technology. Beyond specific skills, most successful entrepreneurs share a number of characteristics.

Characteristics of Successful Entrepreneurs
- Determination
- Self-motivation
- Self-confidence
- Strong organizational skills
- Leadership ability
- Self-discipline
- Creativity
- Willingness to work hard
- Spirit of adventure
- Good social skills

Do You Have What It Takes?

You can answer this question by doing a self-evaluation—an assessment of your personal qualities, abilities, interests, and skills. The self-evaluation in Figure 33.1 on page 702 was developed by the Small Business Administration (SBA). Take a few minutes to answer each question and write your answers on a piece of paper. Think before you answer and be honest. Answering "yes" to most or all of these questions suggests that you may have the right characteristics for success.

Before you start a business, ask family members, friends, and other businesspeople who are in the same or a similar business about their experiences. Do research on the type of business you want to start. All this information should give you a good indication of whether you are ready to join the millions of small-business owners in the United States.

Marketing and Entrepreneurship

Although entrepreneurs may have the business and technical skills they need to produce and provide a quality product or service, they may overlook the importance of marketing. Entrepreneurs who possess a good understanding of marketing have an advantage over those who do not.

Many resources exist for entrepreneurs who need help with marketing. For example, The American Marketing Association has a special interest group devoted to helping entrepreneurs develop marketing skills, the Marketing & Entrepreneur Special Interest Group. The National Federation of Independent Businesses has an award-winning online library of business management information called the *Business Toolkit.*

Concept Development

MARKETING AND ENTREPRENEURSHIP

Advertising in print media plays a key role in marketing. To illustrate the effect of printing schedules on advertising, collect three magazines based on the same topic, such as gardening. The magazines should be published at different intervals, such as monthly, quarterly, and yearly. Ask students to identify the format, content, and number of ads contained in each magazine. Have students discuss how a magazine's printing schedule might affect the types or numbers of advertisements that are placed in the magazine.

Enrichment

IDENTIFY THE TARGET MARKET

Collect two kitchen appliance advertisements from magazines. Ask students to identify the target market for each ad, based on its content, format, and size. Remind students that magazines are often printed a month or two in advance, which can affect which advertisements are used. Have students keep detailed notes of their evaluations and present their findings in an oral report.

Extended Activity

Business Growth

Have students consider why small businesses can often generate growth at such a fast rate. Then ask students to research such a business and describe that business in a two-paragraph summary. Have students then give reasons that business was able to generate such growth in a one-paragraph response.

Review Guide

CONCEPTS

Have students list the advantages and disadvantages of entrepreneurship. Advantages: personal freedom and satisfaction, increased self-esteem and income; disadvantages: high stress, risk of failure, setbacks, loss of income

KEY TERMS

Have students work in small groups to review key terms, their spellings and definitions.

ONLINE SELF-ASSESSMENT

Have students go to marketingessentials.glencoe.com for the Section 33.1 practice test.

Individualized Review

L1 Assign and review Chapter 33 activities in the Student Activity Workbook.

L2 Assign and review Chapter 33 activities in the Marketing Math Workbook.

L3 Assign and Review Chapter 33 activities in the *BusinessWeek* Reader and Case Studies.

Marketing Practice

Ask students to select a product or service they would like to build a business around. Have them create a three-paragraph paper to persuade potential investors to fund the business venture. Students should identify the target market, the competition, and explain how their business approach is unique.

Figure 33.1 *Self-Evaluation*

• **Know Yourself** Be honest as you answer each of these self-evaluation questions. Having a clear understanding of your personal strengths and skills will help you decide whether or not to become an entrepreneur.

What do your answers say about you?

The first seven questions relate to your personality characteristics.	YES	NO
1. Do you like to make your own decisions?	——	——
2. Do you enjoy competition?	——	——
3. Do you have willpower and self-determination?	——	——
4. Do you plan ahead?	——	——
5. Do you like to get things done on time?	——	——
6. Can you take advice from others?	——	——
7. Can you adapt to changing conditions?	——	——

The next series of questions relates to your physical, emotional, and financial well-being.

8. Do you understand that owning your own business may entail working 12 to 16 hours a day, probably six days a week and maybe on holidays?	——	——
9. Do you have the physical stamina to handle a business?	——	——
10. Do you have the emotional strength to withstand the strain?	——	——
11. Are you prepared to lower your living standard for several months or years?	——	——
12. Are you prepared to lose your savings?	——	——
13. Do you know which skills and areas of expertise are critical to the success of your business?	——	——
14. Do you have these skills?	——	——
15. Does your idea for a business use these skills?	——	——
16. Can you find the people who have the expertise you lack?	——	——
17. Do you know why you are considering this business?	——	——
18. Will your business meet your career aspirations?	——	——

@ Online Action!

Go to *marketingessentials.glencoe.com/33/figure/1* to find a project on self-evaluation.

The Role of Entrepreneurship in the Domestic and Global Economy

Entrepreneurs and small to medium businesses play a key role in the domestic and the global economy: They generate growth at a rate that is much faster than other larger and more established businesses. Eighty percent of the new jobs created annually come from businesses that are less than five years old.

The National Federation of Independent Businesses reported in its 2000 *Small Business Policy Guide* that more than 60 percent of all businesses in the United States employ four or fewer people. The Global Entrepreneurship Monitor (GEM) reports a strong correlation between national economic growth and the level of national entrepreneurial activity. Firms with fewer than 500 employees were responsible for 50 percent of the gross domestic product (GDP)—the measure of the

702 UNIT 11 - ENTREPRENEURSHIP AND FINANCE

 marketingessentials.glencoe.com

Figure 33.1 *Self-Evaluation*

Discussion Discuss the personality characteristics and physical, emotional, and financial factors to take into account before beginning a small business. Ask students: Do any surprise you? Which seem most important? Discuss their answers.

Caption Answer Answers will vary, but students should identify any strengths or weaknesses that might affect their decision to run a small business.

@ Online Action! For instructions, ideas, and answer guide, go to the Teacher Center at marketingessentials.glencoe.com

Follow Up Have students choose the question that most interests them and discuss their responses in class.

goods and services produced using labor and property in the United States.

Small businesses benefit the economy and society in other ways, too. They offer consumers more choices of goods and services, and they help improve products and processes.

Entrepreneurship and the Global Economy

New businesses are a sign of an economy's vitality and readiness to find or invent new opportunities in a world market that has become more and more challenging.

The U.S. Small Business Administration (SBA) is finding new ways to help small businesses in the very competitive global economy. In 2004, SBA loaned more than $17 billion and trained two million small-business owners. A new SBA Web site provides business owners with helpful information. This includes access to government services, help with regulations, and applications for help, money, and training. The SBA is also providing more opportunities to work with government buyers and ways to compete in international markets.

Trends in Entrepreneurship

Entrepreneurship is on the rise. According to the SBA, the number of incorporated self-employed persons was 5.2 million in March 2004, up from an average of 4.4 million for the years 1999, 2000, and 2001. Several recent trends in the marketplace have fostered this growth:

- The availability of technology
- Increased global communication
- The rise of the Internet and e-commerce
- A society and a market that are more and more diversified

Smart entrepreneurs are always looking for business opportunities and trends that affect their business. They watch socio-economic and political trends such as dual-income families, changes in eating habits, and national and international security issues to get ideas.

CLOSE

Have students complete the following statements:

- **Smart entrepreneurs are always looking for _____ .**
  business opportunities and trends that affect their business.

- **Entrepreneurs are people who _____ .**
  create, launch, organize, and manage a new business and take the risk of business ownership.

 Critical Thinking

Ask students to name recent trends in entrepreneurship and to brainstorm reasons for these recent trends. Have students share their responses in class.

 33.1 AFTER YOU READ

Reviewing Key Terms and Concepts

1. How is being an entrepreneur different from being an employee?

2. Study the personal characteristics required of an entrepreneur and list the ones that describe you.

3. How do small businesses contribute to the U.S. economy?

Integrating Academic Skills

Math

4. There are 3,000 new business start-ups per year. How many business start-ups is this per week? Statistically, how many of these businesses will remain open at the end of four years?

Language

5. Etymology is the study of the origin and history of words. Use a dictionary to discover the etymology of the word *entrepreneur*. Look up the meaning of the prefix *en*. How are the words *entrepreneur* and *enterprise* related? Write a brief report on the history and meaning of the word *entrepreneur*.

 Online Action!
Check your answers at *marketingessentials.glencoe.com/33/read*

marketingessentials.glencoe.com   **Chapter 33 - Entrepreneurial Concepts 703**

 AFTER YOU READ

Reviewing Key Terms and Concepts

1. Entrepreneurs organize, manage, and assume the risk of owning and operating a business. Employees work for owners.

2. Lists will vary but may include: determined, self-motivated, self-confident, organized, having leadership ability, self-disciplined, creative, willing to work hard, willing to take risks, and having good social skills.

3. Answers may include: they employ 60 percent of the labor force and produce 50 percent of the GDP.

Integrating Academic Skills

4. There will be 57 start-ups per week. Half of those, or 1,500, will be open after four years.

5. The prefix *en* means to cause, from the Old French *entreprendre*, meaning to undertake. Enterprise is an undertaking. Student reports will differ but should draw connections between the history and meanings of the words *entrepreneur* and *enterprise*.

Online Action! Answers at **marketingessentials.glencoe.com/33/read**

FOCUS

Introducing the Section

COLLABORATIVE ACTIVITY

Clip several "business for sale" ads for franchises from a local or national newspaper. Read the ads to students. Ask them to generate a board list of the things they would consider before buying each business.

Preteaching Key Terms

Divide the key terms into two roughly equal groups. Divide the class in half and give each half of the terms. Have each group research the definitions of their key terms and report the definitions back to the class.

- franchise
- sole proprietorship
- unlimited liability
- partnership
- general partnership
- limited partnership
- corporation
- stockholders
- limited liability
- foreign corporation
- limited liability company (LLC)
- Doing Business As (DBA)
- Articles of Incorporation

Critical Thinking

Have students discuss why small business ownership has become important to the U.S. society and economy.

704

OBJECTIVES

- Identify the forms of business ownership
- Name the legal steps to take in establishing a business

KEY TERMS

- franchise
- sole proprietorship
- unlimited liability
- partnership
- general partnership
- limited partnership
- corporation
- stockholders
- limited liability
- foreign corporation
- limited liability company (LLC)
- Doing Business As (DBA)
- Articles of Incorporation

Analyze Compare the advantages and disadvantages of the four forms of business organization.

Logistics of Business Ownership

READ and STUDY

BEFORE YOU READ

Predict If you were to start a business, what would it be? What steps do you think you would have to take before opening the business?

THE MAIN IDEA

Going into business involves deciding how to enter business, determining the organizational form the business will take, and following the steps necessary to establish the business legally.

STUDY ORGANIZER

Think of yourself as an entrepreneur and write down the steps you need to take to establish your new business in a chart like the one below.

Purchase an Existing Nonfranchise Business — Ways to Own a Business

Business Ownership Opportunities

There are four ways to enter business: (1) purchase an existing nonfranchise business, (2) take over the family business, (3) start a new business, or (4) purchase a franchise business.

Purchase an Existing Nonfranchise Business

When an entrepreneur buys an existing nonfranchise business, there is usually little or no help from the previous owner. The prospective buyer must investigate the reasons for the

---

READ and STUDY

BEFORE YOU READ

Ask students to predict the legal steps they would need to take before opening a new business.

THE MAIN IDEA

Ask a volunteer to read the main idea aloud and ask another student to retell it in his or her own words.

STUDY ORGANIZER

Model the study organizer for students by filling in the first oval. A full-size, downloadable study organizer can be found at **marketingessentials.glencoe.com**

 Guide students to use their own experiences as organized learners when analyzing the four forms of business organization.

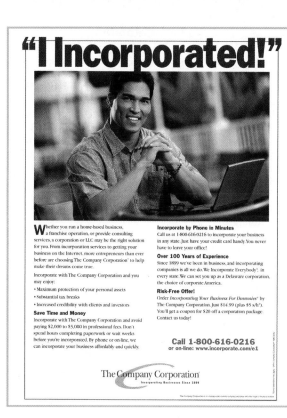

"I Incorporated!"

•STARTING YOUR OWN BUSINESS There are many different forms of business and various ways of organizing a company. This ad promotes a company that helps new owners through the incorporation process.

Why would an entrepreneur need assistance with setting up a business?

---

sale of the business. Likewise, business records, the condition of the property, and inventory must be carefully examined. The reputation of the business in the community must be considered as well. In some cases, the new owner may contract the services of the previous owner to assist with management during a transition period.

Take Over the Family Business

Many of the same considerations for purchasing an existing business apply to taking over a family business. The difference, in this case, is that the previous owner is a family member. Will this help or hinder the new owner in taking control? The new owner must explore potential conflicts and concerns with family members. Succession planning (transition to the next generation), managing growth, and family relations are some of the challenges of taking over and running a family business.

Start a New Business

Starting a new business gives an entrepreneur great freedom of choice. The new business owner can start the business of her choice and plan it from the ground up. She can decide where it is located, what it sells, and how it is organized. There are no old debts to settle and no bad reputation to overcome. On the other hand, it is up to the new owner to establish the business's reputation and build a customer base.

Chapter 33 - Entrepreneurial Concepts 705

TEACH

Discussion Starter

FORMS OF BUSINESS OWNERSHIP

Discuss with students the value of networking to help launch a new business. Remind students that entrepreneurs network constantly to keep up on innovations in their field, to build their list of resources and contacts, and to keep themselves visible in the community.

TEACHING POINTS

Make Connections Have students discuss the ways they network now. Encourage examples of how they may have contacted acquaintances for help in finding a job.

Extend Each year, *Entrepreneur's Franchise 500* publishes a list of top ten franchises. Have students research to find out the top ten for this year. Tell students to bring the list to class and discuss them, especially if there are any unfamiliar businesses.

 Online Activity

Terms of a Franchise
Have students research the franchise terms for two or more parent companies, such as Subway or Burger King. Ask students to research and identify which parent company offers the entrepreneur more personal freedom.

AD GUIDE   **STARTING YOUR OWN BUSINESS**

Discussion Lead a discussion about the entrepreneurial opportunities and services outlined in this ad.

Caption Answer Answers will vary; students might conclude that there are many tasks involved in setting up a business and outsourcing or delegating those tasks may reduce the amount of time or ease the workload of the entrepreneur.

Follow Up Have students investigate the Web site listed in this ad and report one characteristic or service they discovered to the class.

TEACH CONTINUED

Individualized Practice

PURCHASE A FRANCHISE BUSINESS

L1 Have students conduct research to find the 16 career clusters of the States' Career Cluster Initiative. Then have them choose one that interests them. Tell them to find and research three franchise companies within their chosen career cluster. Have students report the results of their research in a one-page response.

L2 Have each student contact a company that offers franchises and write a 250-word report that summarizes:

1. The amount of money it takes to buy the franchise.

2. The training provided by the franchiser.

3. The restrictions on the types of products one can sell in the franchise outlet.

4. Other relevant information one would need to know about buying a franchise from this company.

L3 Using the self-evaluation survey in **Figure 33.1** on page 702, have students identify a particular set of skills in which they are strong. Then have students find a franchise company that would best suit those skills. In a short essay, have students explain why their personal attributes would allow them to succeed in that particular type of business.

Purchase a Franchise Business

A **franchise** is a legal agreement to sell a parent company's product or services in a designated geographic area. McDonald's Corporation and Taco Bell are examples of companies that sell franchises. They are franchisors. The franchisee (the person buying the business) has to invest money to buy the franchise and also pays an annual fee and a share of the profits. In exchange, the franchisor provides a well-known name, a business plan, advertising, and the proven methods and products of the parent company.

In franchise businesses, new business owners have a lot of help. All the business planning is done by the franchisor. Planning generally includes management training, merchandising, and day-to-day operations.

One disadvantage of franchising is the initial cost. A significant amount of capital is needed to purchase most franchises. The franchisee must also pay high initial fees to begin operations. In addition, the franchisor is often very strict about how the business is run.

Forms of Business Organization

The choice of legal organization or structure a new business should have is a critical decision. It may make the difference between success and failure. It determines how fast business decisions are implemented and how well the business competes in the marketplace. There are four possible forms of business organization (see Figure 33.2):

- sole proprietorship
- partnership
- corporation
- limited liability company (LLC)

The choice depends on the financial and tax situation of the owner, the type of business, the number of employees who will be hired, and the level of risk involved in the new business. As a business grows, these factors may change and may require reorganization. A business could start out as a sole proprietorship, grow into a partnership, and ultimately wind up as a corporation.

Sole Proprietorship

A **sole proprietorship** is a business owned and operated by one person. This is the most common form of business ownership. Approximately 70 percent of all U.S. businesses are sole proprietorships. Sole proprietors usually have a special skill by which they can earn a living; for example, plumbers, contractors, and many entrepreneurs who start Web site businesses are often sole proprietors. The sole proprietor must provide the money and management skill to run the business. In return for all this responsibility, the sole proprietor is entitled to all the profits.

Advantages and Disadvantages of Sole Proprietorship

A sole proprietorship is easy to start. The sole proprietor provides the money to start the business. For instance, a plumber will spend money on tools, a truck, office space and supplies, and possibly advertising. The sole proprietorship is generally taxed less than other forms of business, and there is more freedom from government regulation. Because the owner is usually the only investor in the business, that person is entitled to all the profits. A sole proprietorship also gives a business owner great control over the business.

However, this also means that the owner is responsible for all business debts and legal judgments against the company. If the debts of a business exceed its assets, creditors can claim the owner's personal assets, such as a home, cars, and savings. This is called **unlimited liability**, which means that a business owner's financial liability is not limited to investments in the business, but extends to his or her total ability to make payments.

The Partnership

A **partnership** is a legal agreement between two or more people to be jointly responsible for the success or failure of a business. Partnerships represent about 10 percent of U.S. businesses. Common partnerships in your community may include real estate agencies, law offices, and medical offices.

Critical Thinking

Ask the students to recall the self-evaluation survey they completed in **Figure 33.1** on page 702. Ask: Which of the four forms of business organization would best suit your personality? Have students explain their answers in class. Answers will vary; students should identify specific personality traits and the form of business organization that best suits those personality traits.

Figure 33.2 *Business Organization*

• **The Four Forms of Business Ownership** The legal organization of a business is a key decision for an entrepreneur. It determines how fast business decisions can be made, how well the business will compete in the marketplace, and how quickly it can raise money.

Which form of business ownership is easiest to establish?

SOLE PROPRIETORSHIP

A sole proprietorship gives an entrepreneur the greatest control over business decisions and all the profits. It also exposes the owner to greater risks.

PARTNERSHIP

Partners share decision-making responsibility as well as the business's profits and losses. In a limited partnership, a limited partner is responsible for losses only to the level of his or her investment in the business. The general partner is fully responsible for losses.

LIMITED LIABILITY COMPANY

The limited liability company (LLC) is a cross between a partnership and a corporation. Its owners (called members) have only limited liability, and it has tax benefits over a corporation.

CORPORATION

Corporations are owned by stockholders, who may range in number from one to millions. Each stockholder owns a portion of the business and is responsible for losses only to the level of his or her investment. In a corporation, the owners may not be involved in the day-to-day decision making for the business. With this type of organization, the benefits and risks are shared among the stockholders. Corporations can raise money relatively easily, but the decision-making process can be slow.

 Online Action!

Go to *marketingessentials.glencoe.com/33/figure/2* **to find a project on entrepreneurship.**

marketingessentials.glencoe.com

Chapter 33 - Entrepreneurial Concepts **707**

Figure 33.2 *Business Organization*

Discussion After students have read **Figure 33.2**, discuss the different ways to enter business. Ask students to define each method in their own words.

Caption Answer A sole proprietorship is the easiest to establish because it involves just one person and no legal agreement.

 Online Action! For instructions, ideas, and answer guide, go to the Teacher Center at **marketingessentials.glencoe.com**

Follow Up Ask students: How does a limited liability company differ from a corporation?

TEACH CONTINUED

Concept Development

SOLE PROPRIETORSHIP
Clip several "business for sale" ads for sole proprietors from a local or national newspaper. Read the ads to students. Ask them to generate a list of the things they would consider before buying each business using these headings: Money Needed to Invest, Products Sold, Legal Requirements for Start-Up, and Location.

TEACHING POINTS
Model Invite a sole proprietor to the class to talk about his or her experience in launching an entrepreneurship.

Clarify Explain to students that partnerships can take two forms: general and limited. Discuss the advantages and disadvantages of both.

Extended Activity

Calculating Franchise Costs
Give students the following scenario: It costs $75,000 to obtain a franchise for a Sport Store sporting goods store. Have students calculate the percentages for each of the following items:
a) Franchise fee: $13,500
b) Inventory: $35,000
c) Fixtures and Equipment: $6,500
d) Leasehold Improvements: $15,000
e) Working Capital: $5,000

Answers should read:
a) 18%; $13,500 ÷ $75,000 = .18;
b) 47%; $35,000 ÷ $75,000 = .47;
c) 9%; $6,500 ÷ $75,000 = .09;
d) 20%; $15,000 ÷ $75,000 = .2;
e) 7%; $5,000 ÷ $75,000 = .07

TEACH CONTINUED

Concept Development

THE CORPORATION

Have students create a chart that compares each type of business ownership using these headings: Initial Investment, Level of Risk, Taxes, Ease/Difficulty of Starting a Business.

TEACHING POINTS

Model Bring in examples of private and public corporation materials. These materials should detail each company's business units, board of directors, contact information, etc. Discuss the structure of each company with students.

Clarify Explain to students that the phrase *foreign corporation* often means a company that does business in another state, not another country.

Extended Activity

Stock Exchanges and Public Companies

Have students define IPO, or initial public offering. Ask students to research a past or recent IPO that took place on a major exchange, such as NYSE, AMEX, or NASDAQ, and to share the results of their research with the class.

A partnership is formed by a partnership agreement, usually prepared by an attorney, which specifies the responsibilities of each partner. Partners share the profits if the business is a success and the losses if it fails. Profits are usually divided according to the amount of time and money each partner invested. There are two kinds of partnerships: general and limited.

General Partnership

In a **general partnership**, each partner shares in the profits and losses. As in the sole proprietorship, each partner has unlimited liability for the company's debts. Also, each partner's share of the profits is taxed as personal income.

Limited Partnership

In a **limited partnership**, each limited partner is liable for any debts only up to the amount of his or her investment in the company. Every limited partnership, however, must have at least one general partner who has unlimited liability. In exchange for their limited liability, limited partners have no voice in the management of the partnership. The withdrawal of a limited partner does not dissolve the partnership.

Advantages and Disadvantages of Partnerships

There are several advantages to a partnership. It combines the skills of the owners. A partnership may make more capital (money)

GLOBAL MARKET

GERMANY

Promotion and Soccer

German electronics and engineering company Siemens is known in the United States for domestic appliances. However, its major businesses worldwide are transportation and communication systems and large power turbines.

Siemens deals mostly with governments and large corporations, not consumers. The company is huge, with almost $90 billion in sales in 190 countries.

Global Promotion Siemens is also a cell phone manufacturer in Europe. To compete with big names Nokia and Motorola, it needs to get the company name in the public eye.

The strategy Siemens has chosen is corporate sponsorship of sports, choosing teams that are extremely popular in its target markets of Europe, Latin America, and Asia. Siemens is the major sponsor of the Real Madrid Spanish soccer team. Soon after the Siemens deal, Real signed two soccer superstars, Brazilian Ronaldo and Englishman Beckham. Once the Siemens logo was on the jerseys of the team, Siemens's share of the cell phone market tripled in Latin America. The effect was strongest in Brazil.

CRITICAL THINKING

What effects on its major engineering business could come from Siemens being more visible in consumer markets?

@ Online Action!

Go to *marketingessentials.glencoe.com/33/global* to find an activity about international entrepreneurship.

GLOBAL MARKET

Promotion and Soccer

Discussion After students read Global Market, discuss how Siemens used its corporate sponsorship of soccer to promote its name and products in a new market.

CRITICAL THINKING **Answer:** Siemens might shift more development of its engineering business toward consumer products, such as cell phones, when it becomes more visible in consumer markets.

@ Online Action! For instructions, ideas, and answer guide, go to the Teacher Center at **marketingessentials.glencoe.com**

Follow Up Have students suggest three companies that are direct competitors of Siemens.

available, allowing easier operation and expansion. It gives each partner a voice in the management of the business. A partnership is taxed solely on the profits of the business and regulated less heavily than a corporation.

What are some of the disadvantages of partnerships? The owners may not always agree on business decisions, yet the actions of one partner are legally binding on the other partners. This means that all partners must assume their share of the business debt. They must also be responsible for the shares of any partners who cannot pay. Finally, the business is dissolved if one partner dies. It can be reorganized as a new partnership, but the process is time consuming and costly.

The Corporation

A **corporation** is a legal entity created by either a state or a federal statute authorizing individuals to operate an enterprise. In other words, a corporation is a business that is owned by several people but is considered to be just one person or entity under the law. A corporation has several unique features:

- **Legal permission to operate** To operate a business as a corporation, the owners must file an application with state officials for permission. Once the application is approved, this document becomes the corporation's charter.
- **Separate legal entity** A corporation is a separate legal entity that is created by law. A corporation can borrow money, sign contracts, buy or sell property, and sue and be sued in court.
- **Stockholders** The ownership of a corporation is divided into shares of stock. If the corporation sells stocks, it is one way to raise money. The owners of a corporation are the stockholders.
- **Board of directors** Stockholders own the corporation, but often they do not manage it. Instead, the stockholders elect a board of directors that is responsible for major decisions that affect the company.

Corporations offer owners limited liability. **Limited liability** means that the personal assets of the owners cannot be taken if the company does not meet its financial obligations or if it gets into legal trouble. Unlike a partnership, a corporation is not affected by the death, incapacity, or bankruptcy of an officer or a shareholder.

Types of Corporations

There are many types of corporations, but the two main categories are private and public corporations. A public corporation is a business entity created by the federal, state, or local government. This group can include incorporated cities as well as school, transit, and sanitation districts.

A private corporation is formed by private persons. This category is very broad and includes closely held corporations (or "close corporations") and publicly held corporations (sometimes these are called public corporations even though they are subject to different rules than the public corporations described above).

A closely held corporation is owned by a few persons or a family. Shares or stocks of a closely held corporation are not sold to the public. On the other hand, a publicly held corporation is one whose stock (shares) is owned by a large group of people. Selling stock helps a corporation raise capital. In the United States, stocks or shares of a publicly held corporation are usually sold on the New York Stock Exchange (NYSE), the American Stock Exchange (AMEX), or the National Association of Securities Dealers Automated Quotations (NASDAQ) system. Microsoft is an example of a publicly held corporation whose stock is traded on NASDAQ.

If a corporation succeeds, the value of the stock rises and stockholders benefit. Stockholders own their shares with limited liability. For example, if a stockholder purchased $1,000 worth of Dell Computers stock and the company failed, the investor would lose the investment amount but would not be responsible for the company's debt.

TEACH CONTINUED

Enrichment

ORGANIZATIONS FOR ENTREPRENEURS

Have students find the Web site or written materials about one of the following national organizations and write a 250-word report on the benefits of membership in each organization:

- **National Small Business Association**
- **Small Business Service Bureau**
- **National Association for the Self-Employed**
- **Small Business Benefit Association**

Build Vocabulary

Preview the following words by reading them in context. Discuss the words' meanings with students.

- **liability** vulnerability
- **incorporate** organize together

Critical Thinking

Ask students: Why might certain groups of professionals, such as doctors, attorneys, accountants, and other professionals, form corporations? Answers will vary but could include the following: to limit liability, share costs of doing business, share work responsibilities, etc.

Online Activity

Online Store

Have students choose and analyze an online store. The store can sell products, services, or a combination of both products and services. Ask students decide what an entrepreneur who wishes to have an online store must take into account and report their conclusions in a one-page response.

ASSESS

Review Guide

CONCEPTS

1. Have students review and list the four forms of business ownership.
These include: sole proprietorship, partnership, corporation, and limited liability company.

2. Ask students to list the legal steps involved in setting up a company:
Legal steps include: find help, register the business, and obtain licenses.

KEY TERMS

In small groups, have students review key terms, their spellings, and definitions.

ONLINE SELF-ASSESSMENT

Have students go to
marketingessentials.glencoe.com
for the Section 33.2 practice test.

Individualized Review

L1 Assign and review Chapter 33 activities in the Student Activity Workbook.

L2 Assign and review Chapter 33 activities in the Marketing Math Workbook.

L3 Assign and Review Chapter 33 activities in the *BusinessWeek* Reader and Case Studies.

Marketing Practice

Have students select a form of business ownership. Then have them choose a product or service the company would offer to customers. Ask students to write a short advertisement that would encourage potential investors to invest in the new company. Students might focus on a product or service niche, or an improvement on an existing product or service. Have students share their advertisements in class.

710

Forming a Corporation

Forming a corporation is a complicated process. An entrepreneur must determine the company's internal corporate structure, which is defined by its bylaws, and the processes for selecting a board of directors and electing officers (those who handle the day-to-day operations). In small corporations, members of the board of directors are frequently elected as the officers of the corporation.

An entrepreneur must also choose the state in which to incorporate (establish) the company. For small companies, it is generally best to do this in the state where the company will do business.

A **foreign corporation** is one that is incorporated under the laws of a state that differs from the one in which it does business. (*Foreign* here means another state, not another country.) Foreign corporations must register with each state in which they intend to do business.

Advantages and Disadvantages of Corporations

Why would an entrepreneur decide to incorporate his or her business? There are four main advantages of incorporation:

1. Each owner has limited liability.
2. It is easier to raise capital (money) with corporations than with other forms of business. Capital is often needed for expansion.
3. Owners can easily enter or exit the business simply by buying or selling stock.
4. Management is shared—each area of the business is handled by someone with expertise in that area.

Disadvantages include the following:

1. Complexity of formation
2. Increased government regulation
3. Corporate profits are taxed. Shareholders are taxed on dividends they earn as well as on profits made from the sale of a stock.
4. Intricate accounting and record keeping

The Limited Liability Company

The **limited liability company (LLC)** is a relatively new form of business organization. This business structure is a hybrid of a partnership and a corporation. Its owners (called members) are shielded from personal liability, and all profits and losses pass directly to the owners without taxation of the entity itself.

Legal Steps to Establishing a Business

Before an entrepreneur can officially open the doors of a new business, he or she must take specific steps to legally establish and protect the business. These steps vary depending on whether the business will be a sole proprietorship, partnership, corporation, or limited liability company.

Step 1: Find Help

New business owners may wish to consult an accountant, attorney, or other business advisor to determine the best organization for their new businesses. When a corporation is formed, the laws of many states require that an attorney be hired to guide the entrepreneur through the complicated process of incorporation. The entrepreneur must check the laws of the state in which she or he is incorporating.

Step 2: Register the Business

To form a sole proprietorship or partnership, a business owner must file for a DBA at the local county clerk's office. A **DBA (Doing Business As)** is the registration by which the county government officially recognizes that a new proprietorship or partnership exists.

A DBA also protects the name of the business for a certain number of years. This name protection applies only to the county where the business is registered. There is usually a filing fee for registration.

To form a corporation, an entrepreneur must file Articles of Incorporation with the corporation and securities bureau in the state department of commerce.

Articles of Incorporation identify the name and address of a new corporation, its purpose, the names of the initial directors,

Online Activity

Legal Steps and Online Businesses

Ask students to research any regulations required for registering businesses that conduct operations over the Internet. Encourage students to choose one company or organization which conducts its business over the Internet and describe at least two characteristics of that business which relate to the Internet. Have students summarize their findings in a one-page report.

and the amount of stock that will be issued to each director.

There is a filing fee, but the business becomes protected and no other business may register under that business's name. The necessary forms, applications, and information on filing fees can be obtained from the state department of commerce.

An LLC is established by filing Articles of Organization with the state. This document describes the LLC and lists the names of its members and initial managers. Many states also require LLCs to have an operating agreement. For the company to have the tax advantage of an LLC, this document must show that the company is distinct from a corporation.

Step 3: Obtain Licenses

Depending on the type of business and where it is located, a new owner may have to obtain one or more licenses. Licenses estab-lish minimum standards of education and training for people who practice in a particular profession. They also regulate where businesses can locate, and they protect neighborhoods and the environment.

Individual states license many businesses and occupations, such as doctors, accountants, cosmetologists, barbers, marriage counselors, and pharmacists.

Licensing is done to protect the public from unqualified people practicing in a business and to maintain the health and welfare of the citizens.

In addition to state licenses, the community may require special local licenses or permits to comply with zoning ordinances, building codes, and safety standards.

Local governments use licensing as a way to regulate people who plan to enter certain types of businesses. Most communities require a business owner to obtain a license before opening a hotel, restaurant, or movie theater.

33.2 AFTER YOU READ

Reviewing Key Terms and Concepts
1. List the four ways to become a business owner.
2. What are the four legal forms of business organization and which is the most common?
3. What is one advantage of a limited liability company?

Integrating Academic Skills
Mathematics
4. An entrepreneur works 11 hours a day, five days a week, 51 weeks a year. How many hours does this person work annually? To how many 40-hour workweeks is this equivalent?

Government
5. The U.S. government protects entrepreneurs by issuing trademarks, copyrights, and patents. Research each of these terms and write a description of the type of protection provided by each.

 Online Action!

Check your answers at *marketingessentials.glencoe.com/33/read*

marketingessentials.glencoe.com

Chapter 33 - Entrepreneurial Concepts **711**

SECTION 33.2

CLOSE

Have students complete the following statements:

- **Entrepreneurs must have the skills necessary _____.**
  to run the business.

- **To form a sole proprietorship or partnership, _____.**
  a business owner must file for a DBA.

 Extended Activity

The History of the Corporation
Encourage students to research the history of corporations in the United States. Ask students to provide the legal definition of a corporation and to describe how this definition affords corporations certain types of advantages that previously were held only by individuals. Then have students list the potential advantages and disadvantages of corporations when it comes to holding a business liable (legally responsible) for physical, emotional, or environmental damages from products, industrial processes, and ethical and legal standard violations.

AFTER YOU READ

Reviewing Key Terms and Concepts
1. four ways to become a business owner include start a new business, purchase a franchise, purchase an existing business, and take over a family business.
2. Four legal forms of business organization are sole proprietorship, partnership, corporation, and limited liability company. Sole proprietorship is the most common.

3. Advantages of a limited liability company include: it has tax benefits and its owners are shielded from personal liability.

Integrating Academic Skills
4. This person works 2,805 hours; $11 \times 5 \times 51 = 2,805$. This is equivalent to 70.125 40-hour work weeks; $2,805 \div 40 = 70.125$.

5. A trademark is a symbol, word, phrase, or design that identifies the source of goods; it can be used legally only by the owner of the trademark. A copyright protects an original artistic or literary work. A patent protects an invention.

Online Action! Answers at *marketingessentials.glencoe.com/33/read*

CAREERS
IN MARKETING

Lifelong Learning

CAREER INFORMATION

Have students go to marketingessentials.glencoe.com to find the Chapter 33 Careers page and click on the link for the American Marketing Association's Careers Strategies and Tips. Ask students to select one article, read it, and summarize it in three short paragraphs.

MANAGEMENT SKILLS

Creativity, knowledge of online consumers' behavior, and dynamic decision-making skills contribute to Jermaine Griggs' success at the online company. Being aware of the internal and external drives of consumers, coworkers, competitors, and other decision-makers allows marketers and managers to remain competitive in the marketplace.

Primary Source

Ask students to go to marketingessentials.glencoe.com and find Chapter 33 Resources. Ask them to click on the link for the American Marketing Association's marketing dictionary and read the definitions of the terms related to entrepreneurial concepts.

💥 THINKING CRITICALLY

Answers will vary. Students should demonstrate an understanding that during start-up, many companies have few employees; it is common for entrepreneurs to perform tasks at all levels.

@ Online Action!

For instructions, ideas, and answer guide, go to the Teacher Center at marketingessentials.glencoe.com

JERMAINE GRIGGS
CEO AND FOUNDER,
HEARANDPLAY.COM

❓ What do you do at work?
In the beginning, I was head customer service representative, phone operator, fulfillment manager, and Web designer. As the business grew, the day-to-day operations began to be automated, allowing me to focus more on building and growing the business. I now focus on attracting joint-venture partners, building and cultivating relationships with affiliates, product development, and implementation of new strategies. Lastly, because of the power of the Internet to split-test different versions of a Web site, I am regularly testing and changing sales copy, advertisements, order form layouts, and other sections of our Web site to better improve conversion rates, visitor values, and overall sales.

❓ What skills are most important to you?
A manager who has had wide success in the offline world is not necessarily guaranteed success on the Internet. If I had to rely totally on employees for Web design, e-mail marketing, search engine optimization, and other functions, I would truly be lost! To know at least the minimum rules of the game is essential. The ability to be aware of trends, consumer behaviors online, and audience interaction, and to be able to respond and alter strategic plans accordingly is vital. Also, patience and the ability to watch extraordinarily good days pass as well as all-time low days are definitely attributes of a net entrepreneur.

❓ What is your key to success?
My eagerness to learn. I never stop learning.

Aptitudes, Abilities, and Skills

Creativity, knowledge of the Internet and the product/service being offered

Education and Training

Many net entrepreneurs have no degrees at all, although business degrees can definitely be useful and provide valuable skills.

Career Path

Web entrepreneurs come from all walks of life—this has historically been a field in which people can succeed, if they have the right idea and the willingness to follow through.

💥 THINKING CRITICALLY

Why is it a good idea for net entrepreneurs to perform many of the tasks that might ordinarily fall to employees?

@ Online Action!

Go to *marketingessentials.glencoe.com/33/careers* to find a career-related activity.

Test-Taking Strategies

Show students how they can create a chapter outline by recording the different levels of headings as they read. They can then record their notes on the outline and use the outline to review chapter concepts.

FOCUS on KEY POINTS

SECTION 33.1

● Being an entrepreneur involves risk taking, but it can bring both personal and financial rewards.

● Advantages of entrepreneurship include being your own boss and earning a high income if the business succeeds. Entrepreneurs can try out their own ideas, set their own work schedules, and make their own business decisions. Disadvantages of entrepreneurship include the risk of failure, long working hours, and the potential loss of income.

● Entrepreneurship is important to our economy. It creates jobs, which provide income to individuals and communities.

SECTION 33.2

● The four ways to become a business owner are (1) purchase an existing business, (2) take over the family business, (3) start a new business, and (4) purchase a franchise business.

● The four forms of business organization are (1) sole proprietorship, (2) partnership, (3) corporation, and (4) limited liability company.

REVIEW VOCABULARY

Work with your classmates as part of a team. Your teacher will call out the terms below. The team that correctly defines the term first gets a point. The team with the most points wins.

1. entrepreneurship (p. 698)
2. entrepreneur (p. 698)
3. franchise (p. 706)
4. sole proprietorship (p. 706)
5. unlimited liability (p. 706)
6. partnership (p. 706)
7. general partnership (p. 708)
8. limited partnership (p. 708)
9. corporation (p. 709)
10. stockholders (p. 709)
11. limited liability (p. 709)
12. foreign corporation (p. 710)
13. limited liability company (LLC) (p. 710)
14. Doing Business As (DBA) (p. 710)
15. Articles of Incorporation (p. 710)

REVIEW FACTS and IDEAS

16. Define entrepreneurship. (33.1)
17. What risks are involved in being an entrepreneur? (33.1)
18. What are the advantages of being an entrepreneur? (33.1)
19. List the personal characteristics and skills needed to be a successful business owner. (33.2)
20. Why are small businesses important to the U.S. economy? (33.2)
21. List four opportunities for becoming a business owner. (33.2)

Chapter 33 - Entrepreneurial Concepts 713

REVIEW FACTS and IDEAS

16. Entrepreneurship is starting and managing your own business.

17. Potential failure, loss of income, and poor health.

18. Advantages include personal freedom, satisfaction, increased income, and increased self-esteem.

19. Characteristics include: like making decisions, enjoy competition, have will power and self-determination, plan ahead, get things done on time, take advice from others, and adapt to changing conditions.

20. Small businesses employ 55 percent of the labor force and produce 50 percent of GDP.

21. Opportunities include starting a new business, purchasing a franchise, purchasing an existing business, and taking over a family business.

FOCUS on KEY POINTS

Ask volunteers to read the summaries aloud and give one real-life example for each concept.

REVIEW VOCABULARY

See glossary for definitions of **1–15.** The team with the most points wins the Marketing Quiz Bowl. A sample answer might read:

1. *Entrepreneurship* is the process of starting and operating your own business.

BUILD SKILLS

22. Workplace Skills
Responses will vary and might include: a sound business structure, contract, the ability to work together, and finances are factors to consider.

23. Technology Applications
Student reports will vary depending on the type of business; all reports should include: the name of the business and the procedures for filing for a DBA locally.

24. Math Practice
$76,500 is left after buying equipment; $90,000 − ($900,000 × 0.15) = $76,500.

DEVELOP CRITICAL THINKING

25. Innovation and Entrepreneurship
Answers will vary but may include: Entrepreneurs often have an idea, or business concept, that drives their business. It may be a perceived need in the marketplace, a new product, or a variation of an existing product. These new ideas are innovations. Examples will vary.

26. Opening Your Own Restaurant
Student answers will differ. They might research the market, the competition, a location, financing available, and the potential of the business to generate income. Students may consider the following factors when choosing a type of organization: number of people involved, source of financing, willingness to take risk. Their research steps and reasons will vary.

BUILD SKILLS

22. Workplace Skills
Human Relations A very good friend of yours wants to start a bicycle rental shop. Both of you are bicycle enthusiasts, and you decide to explore this possibility together. What important factors should you consider so that becoming business partners does not destroy your friendship?

23. Technology Applications
Filing a DBA Continue to explore the business opportunity described in the previous exercise. Create a name for your new business. Using the Internet, research the procedures and fees for filing for a DBA at your county clerk's office. Also determine whether another business is using this business name. Use a word processing program to write a report of your findings.

24. Math Practice
Business Numbers Your company had sales revenue of $2,000,000 last year. Profit was $90,000. Of that you decide to allocate 15 percent of that profit to new equipment. How much is left after you have bought the equipment you need?

DEVELOP CRITICAL THINKING

25. Innovation and Entrepreneurship
Why is entrepreneurship associated with innovation? List three reasons and three examples of companies that have been innovators. Explain briefly why each company you have selected is an example of innovation.

26. Opening Your Own Restaurant
Imagine that you have a talent for cooking Italian food and that you would like to open an Italian restaurant in your neighborhood. Consider the following questions:

- What kind of research would you do to finalize your decision?
- How would you go about choosing which type of organization your business would be?

List the research steps you would take to answer each question and the reasons for your final decision.

 Formative Assessment

Formative assessment is an essential component of classroom work. This type of assessment provides information that is then used as feedback to modify teaching and meet student needs.

L1 Have students identify the four forms of business organization.

L2 Have students write an evaluation of the effectiveness of small business.

L3 Have students create a corporation promoting a product or service of their choice. Have students outline the structure of their company and discuss the legal steps they need to take to set up the company.

 Reteach   If the results of this formative assessment seem low, consider the following activity:

Read each of the key terms aloud. Have students define the key terms and use them in a sentence. Address any questions that students may have.

APPLY CONCEPTS

27. Investigating Small Business

Use the Internet or the periodicals section of your library to find an article about the rising number of women entrepreneurs.

Activity Summarize the article and print your summary to share with your classmates.

28. Buying a Franchise

Interview the owner of a local franchise. Learn how he or she decided to purchase this particular franchise, what kind of support he receives from the company, what his job is like, and advice he would give to someone considering purchasing a franchise.

Activity Use presentation software to create a report of what you learned.

NET SAVVY

29. Spotting Hot New Market Trends

Entrepreneurs often look into the future to find new market possibilities. Using the publication *The Futurist,* research a new market trend in your field of interest (go to *www.marketingessentials.glencoe.com/33/resources* and look for a link to the World Future Society Web site or find the publication in your library). Write an essay about what you find and describe how your skills would help you to enter this field.

THE ◆DECA◆ CONNECTION

Role Play: Entrepreneurial Concepts

Situation You are to assume the role of experienced employee of a local nursery and garden center. You have focused your studies in that direction and worked at the nursery to gain experience. You want to own a nursery and feel the time is right to do so. The owner of the nursery you work at is retiring and plans to sell the business. You have several options. You could purchase the nursery you work at, you could start a new nursery business, or you could purchase a franchise nursery business.

Activity You are to explain each of the options to your banker (judge) who will be offering you advice about your decision.

Evaluation You will be evaluated on how well you meet the following performance indicators:

● Explain the types of business ownership

● Explain the concept of private enterprise

● Describe legal issues affecting businesses

● Explain the types of business risk

● Address people properly

 Online Action!

For more information and DECA Prep practice, go to *marketingessentials.glencoe.com/33/DECA*

APPLY CONCEPTS

27. Investigating Small Business

Accept written summaries that demonstrate student has done the research.

28. Buying a Franchise

Research and interviews will vary. Accept responses that show student has done the work and understands the concept.

NET SAVVY

29. Spotting Hot New Market Trends

Encourage students to read their essays aloud to the rest of the class and use their essays to motivate discussion.

MINI-QUIZ

Read these sentences to the students and have them volunteer the missing words:

1. _____ attempt to earn money and make profits by taking the risk of owning and operating a business. (Entrepreneurs)

2. A legal agreement between two or more people to be jointly responsible for the success of a business is called a _____. (sole proprietorship)

3. The people who actually own a corporation are known as its _____. (stockholders)

For an expanded chapter quiz, go to Chapter 33 in the TeacherWorks CD-ROM and to Chapter 33 in the **ExamView®** Pro Test Generator CD-ROM.

THE ◆DECA◆ CONNECTION

The students should be evaluated on the performance indicators noted in the role play. For another DECA role play, go to the Competitive Events Workbook or the Student Activity Workbook, or go to marketingessentials.glencoe.com/33/DECA

 Online Action! For instructions, ideas, and answer guide, go to the Teacher Center at marketingessentials.glencoe.com

DECA Advisors Corner

One approach to DECA Week is to highlight a different aspect of DECA each day during that week. Brainstorm with chapter members to plan specific activities for each day during the national DECA Week and use the conceptual foundation of the organization, the DECA diamond.

Chapter Overview

Chapter 34 introduces students to the concept of business risk and risk management; it also identifies the different economic, natural, and human risks faced by businesses. The chapter also explains how businesses limit risk.

⌁ BUILD BACKGROUND ⌁

Ask students to consider the risks they take in their own lives. Point out that most human activity carries with it some element of risk. Have students discuss the ways they minimize the risk of potential problems. They may, for example, mention that they try to eat right in order to stay healthy and study hard to maintain good grades.

Why It's Important

Businesses must manage risks in ways that accommodate public interest, human safety, environmental concerns, and state and federal laws. Risk management is necessary for effective financial, marketing, production, and human resource management decisions. Risk management reduces the adverse effects of risk on business resources, cash flow, and profits.

Prepare to Read

Ask a volunteer to write all of the major headings on the board in outline format. Tell students to fill in secondary headings as they preview or read the chapter. They will then have a thorough chapter outline to use as a study guide.

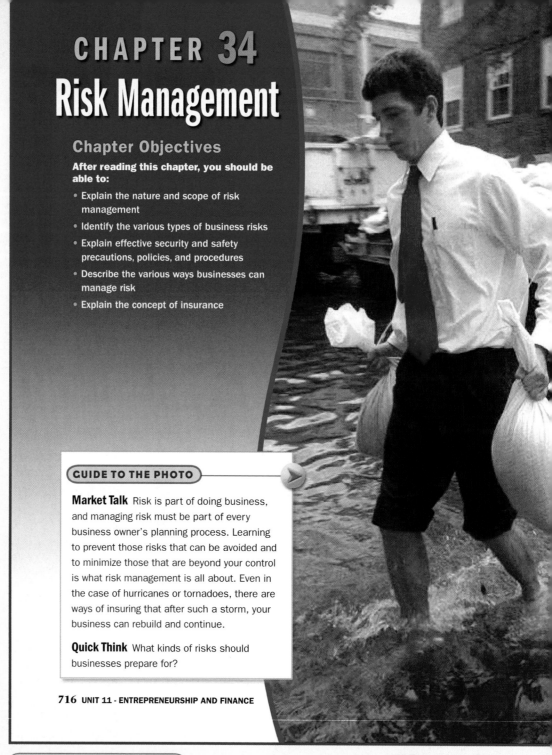

CHAPTER **34**
Risk Management

Chapter Objectives

After reading this chapter, you should be able to:

- Explain the nature and scope of risk management
- Identify the various types of business risks
- Explain effective security and safety precautions, policies, and procedures
- Describe the various ways businesses can manage risk
- Explain the concept of insurance

▶ GUIDE TO THE PHOTO

Market Talk Risk is part of doing business, and managing risk must be part of every business owner's planning process. Learning to prevent those risks that can be avoided and to minimize those that are beyond your control is what risk management is all about. Even in the case of hurricanes or tornadoes, there are ways of insuring that after such a storm, your business can rebuild and continue.

Quick Think What kinds of risks should businesses prepare for?

GUIDE TO THE PHOTO

Market Talk Lead a discussion about how natural disasters can cause a business to lose revenue. Point out that such risks are often weather related and differ by region. Also point out that certain kinds of businesses are vulnerable to certain natural disasters. For example, an agricultural business might be severely hurt by a prolonged drought, but a manufacturing business in the same area may not be affected.

Quick Think Student responses will vary but may include weather, natural disasters or disasters caused by humans, as well as financial and business risks.

 Follow Up Ask students to name the weather-related and other natural disasters that may affect businesses in the local area.

Performance indicators represent key skills and knowledge. Relating them to the concepts explained in this chapter is your key to success in DECA events. These acronyms represent DECA events that involve knowledge of concepts in this chapter.

AAAL	FMAL	MMS*	TMDM*
AAML*	FMDM*	QSRM*	TSE*
ADC*	FMML*	RMAL	VPM
BSM	FSRM*	RMML*	
EMDM*	HMDM*	SMDM*	

In all these DECA events you should be able to follow these performance indicators:

- Determine factors affecting business risk
- Explain types of business risk
- Describe the concept of insurance
- Explain routine security precautions
- Follow safety precautions
- Explain procedures for handling accidents
- Explain procedures for dealing with workplace threats

Events with an asterisk (*) include these indicators:

- Correct hazardous conditions
- Establish a fire-prevention program
- Establish safety policies and procedures
- Establish policies/procedures for preventing internal theft
- Develop policies and procedures for preventing vendor theft

SMDM Describe risk management for event planning

EMDM Identify strategies for Web site and customer transaction protection

---

DECA PREP

Check your understanding of DECA performance indicators with the DECA activity in this chapter's review. For more information and DECA Prep practice, go to *marketingessentials .glencoe.com/34/DECA*

DECA events that require knowledge of risk management are described here. Discuss performance indicators to make sure students understand how to demonstrate their understanding.

The event acronyms stand for:

AAAL: Apparel and Accessories Marketing Series, AL

AAML: Apparel and Accessories Marketing Series, ML

ADC: Advertising Campaign Event

BSM: Business Services Marketing Series

EMDM: E-Commerce Management Team Decision Making Event

FMAL: Food Marketing Series, AL

FMDM: Financial Analysis Management Team Decision Making Event

FMML: Food Marketing Series, ML

FSRM: Full Service Restaurant Management Series

HMDM: Hospitality Services Management Team Decision Making Event

MMS: Marketing Management Series

QSRM: Quick Serve Restaurant Management Series

RMAL: Retail Merchandising Series, AL

RMML: Retail Merchandising Series, ML

SMDM: Sports and Entertainment Marketing Management Team Decision Making Event

TMDM: Travel and Tourism Marketing Management Team Decision Making Event

TSE: Technical Sales Event

VPM: Vehicles and Petroleum Marketing Series

DECA PREP

Find timed DECA Prep activities correlated to the Competitive Events Workbook for students and DECA tips for teachers at **marketingessentials.glencoe.com /34/DECA.**

CHAPTER 34 **Classroom Resources**

For the Teacher

- TeacherWorks
- marketingessentials.glencoe.com
- Interactive Chalkboard
- **Exam***View*® Pro Test Generator
- Fast File Unit 11

For the Student

- *Marketing Essentials* Online Edition
- Student Activity Workbook
- Marketing Math Workbook
- Marketing Research Project Workbook
- School-to-Work Activity Workbook
- Competitive Events Workbook
- *BusinessWeek* Reader and Case Studies
- marketingessentials.glencoe.com

SECTION 34.1

FOCUS

Introducing the Section

COLLABORATIVE ACTIVITY

To prepare for reading this section, have students work in groups of five or six to compose their own tales about Sad Sam's Service Station, a place where everything seems to go wrong. Encourage students to incorporate a wide variety of disasters involving employees, customers, the weather, etc. Have each group share its story and categorize the risks described on the board under the headings such as *economic, natural,* and *human.*

Preteaching Key Terms

List the key terms on the board and ask the students which one could be a category name that describes three of the other terms.

- business risk
- risk management
- economic risks
- natural risks
- human risks

Business risks include economic, human, and natural risks.

Build Vocabulary

Preview the following words and phrases by reading them in context. Ask students to explain their meaning.

- guarantee
  assurance of quality or length of use

- obsolescence disuse

 Critical Thinking

Bring in items such as cassette tapes as examples of product obsolescence. Ask students how product obsolescence is an economic risk.

OBJECTIVES

- Explain the nature and scope of risk management
- Identify the various types of business risks

KEY TERMS

- business risk
- risk management
- economic risks
- natural risks
- human risks

Risk Management for Business

READ and STUDY

BEFORE YOU READ
Predict What are some kinds of business risks?

THE MAIN IDEA
Risk is part of doing business. Businesses must manage risks in ways that accommodate public interest, human safety, the environment, and state and federal laws.

STUDY ORGANIZER
In a chart like the one below, note the main kinds of risks and some examples of each kind of risk.

What Is Risk Management?

To achieve our goals, all of us make decisions each day that involve taking risks. The possibility of financial loss is what is known as **business risk**. Business risks are situations that can lead to financial gain, loss, or failure.

A business cannot eliminate all risk, but marketers can reduce and manage their risks. According to the American Risk and Insurance Association, **risk management** is the systematic

WHILE YOU READ

Question Is it possible for a business to eliminate risks completely ?

READ and STUDY

BEFORE YOU READ
Have students brainstorm different business risks and classify them as *economic, natural,* or *human.*

THE MAIN IDEA
Have a volunteer give an example of a business managing risk.

STUDY ORGANIZER
Model the study organizer for students by filling in the first blank. A full-size, downloadable study organizer can be found at marketingessentials.glencoe.com.

WHILE YOU READ   Answers will vary. A business cannot eliminate all risk, but marketers can reduce and manage potential risks.

process of managing an organization's risks to achieve objectives in a manner consistent with public interest, human safety, environmental needs, and the law. Risks are managed by using the best available marketing information, analyzing opportunities, and making wise decisions.

Types of Business Risks

Economic, natural, and human risks are among the types of risks that a business may experience. (See figure 34.1)

Economic Risks

Economic risks are risks that result from changes in overall business conditions. These changes can include the level or type of competition, changing consumer lifestyles, population changes, limited usefulness or style of some products, product obsolescence, government regulation, inflation, or recession.

Businesses that fail to change their products when competitors offer more features and benefits lose sales and experience economic risk. Foreign competition is also an economic risk for many U.S. companies, because foreign products can often be produced and sold for less than similar domestic products.

Consumer lifestyles and population changes are other economic risks facing modern businesses if they fail to adapt products or services to meet customers' changing interests and needs.

The limited usefulness or style of some products is another potential economic risk. Prices are frequently reduced on products to sell them at the end of the season. Every price reduction reduces both revenue and profits.

Some products inevitably become obsolete or outdated. Known as product obsolescence, this type of economic risk frequently impacts businesses that depend on the latest trends to market goods and services. Obsolescence occurs because new products are constantly being developed.

Changes in the general business environment caused by inflation or recession can present economic risks. For example, businesses in an area experiencing high unemployment will suffer through reduced product sales.

Government Regulations

Government laws and regulations can also result in economic risks. Laws that require businesses to pay for such things as special licenses or permits, street and sewer improvements, environmental clean-ups, parking, and general upkeep will reduce profits.

Product recalls, or even the threat of recalls, by government agencies can affect sales and profits. Companies that have to recall products often face high legal costs in addition to expensive repairs and replacements. In 2003, a Texas court ordered the tire company Bridgestone/Firestone to pay $70 million to replace tires, $41 million to manufacture new tires, $15.5 million on a consumer education campaign, and $19 million in legal fees for 14.4 million tires recalled in 2000. The company incurred costly expenditures because it had to notify all owners by mail, provide free replacements, and then pay the legal settlement costs.

Natural Risks

Natural risks are risks that are caused by natural occurrences. They can result in loss or damage of property and may cause a business to be shut down for any length of time. Common natural risks can include catastrophes such as floods, tornadoes, hurricanes, fires, lightning, droughts, and earthquakes. Some risks that are caused by people are also called natural risks: power outages, civil unrest, oil spills, arson, terrorism, and even war are classified as natural risks. Businesses can insure against unexpected losses from some natural risks, but not all. For example, a typical business insurance policy may not cover damage caused by acts of war or riots; special insurance may be required to cover regional threats such as earthquakes or floods.

Weather is an example of a natural risk. Some businesses and products depend on predictable weather conditions for success.

Chapter 34 - Risk Management 719

 Extended Activity

Business Conditions

Display headlines and articles from local print or online newspapers discussing current business conditions. Lead a discussion about the general business environment in your area. Ask students if business is going through an inflationary or a recessionary period and to describe some of the risks associated with these factors. Point out that recessions often lead to higher unemployment, which leads to lower revenues for local businesses, which in turn feeds higher unemployment as businesses cut costs and lay off workers.

TEACH

Discussion Starter

TYPES OF BUSINESS RISKS
Ask students to tell what kinds of risks they face in everyday life and how those risks are managed. Encourage them to discuss how insurance helps with the management of risks such as illness, vehicle accidents, and loss of life.

Concept Development

ECONOMIC RISKS
Ask students: Why is competition good for consumers and for general business conditions?
Competition keeps the price of products low and quality high. It promotes innovation and investment in new ideas and keeps upward pressure on the standard of living.

Discussion Starter

NATURAL RISKS
Point out to students that the text states that natural events, such as floods, tornadoes, hurricanes, fires, earthquakes, and unexpected changes in weather conditions can create risks. Have students brainstorm examples of how natural occurences can financially damage a business.

Guide students to understand that such disasters can physically damage property, including the place of business, or destroy off-site equipment such as delivery trucks and service lines or cables. Weather-related events can also lead to injuries to customers or employees for which the business may be liable. Hurricanes can destroy neighborhoods and reduce economic activity in an entire region.

Individualized Practice

HUMAN RISKS

L1 Ask students to identify and list human risks that a retail grocery store or supermarket faces.

L2 Ask students to identify and write a one-page report on a common workplace hazard.

L3 Have students research and report on the Sarbanes-Oxley Act of 2002, which established a set of rigorous accounting standards for public companies in the wake of the Enron scandal. Have students explain how Sarbanes-Oxley will help public companies better manage business risk.

Enrichment

RISK MANAGEMENT

Using the Internet, the *Reader's Guide to Periodical Literature,* or the newspaper/magazine database in your media center or library, have students research and obtain a copy of an article on risk management. Have students write a 50- to 100-word abstract of the article and develop an outline of it. Ask students to prepare a five-minute oral presentation on the contents of the article. Students can report on such topics as how businesses respond to a natural disaster and steps businesses can take to prevent shoplifting.

TEACHING POINTS

Review Write the terms *economic risk, natural risk,* and *human risk* on the board. Have each student give one example of each.

Figure 34.1 — Types of Business Risk

• **Preparing and Coping** There are three main categories of business risk.

How do businesses manage risks?

ECONOMIC RISKS

These include overestimating demand for merchandise. This store bought more summer styles than its customers wanted and now has to sell them at prices near cost to make room for the fall lines. Better planning could help manage this risk.

NATURAL RISKS

These include unexpected weather conditions as well as catastrophes, such as hurricanes. Earthquakes and fires are other natural risks to businesses. Both prevention and risk transfer are important in managing this kind of risk.

HUMAN RISKS

These include risks related to on-the-job safety as well as employee dishonesty and error. Training in the use of potentially dangerous machinery is an important part of managing safety risks.

@ Online Action! Go to *marketingessentials.glencoe.com/34/figure/1* to find a project on handling business risks.

Figure 34.1 — Types of Business Risk

Discussion After students read **Figure 34.1**, ask them to identify additional business risks that could be included under each category. For example, underestimating demand for a product and buying too few items might be considered an economic risk because it might lead to the loss of good customers to other stores. Market research and better planning could help manage this risk. Have students share and give reasons for their responses.

Caption Answer Answers may include: take preventive measures to avoid risks, transfer risks (for instance, by buying insurance), assume responsibility for the risks, and avoid risks.

@ Online Action! For instructions, ideas, and answer guide, go to the Teacher Center at **marketingessentials.glencoe.com**

Follow Up Ask students to name types of risks that can be anticipated.

A mild winter season or below-normal snow-fall represents lost revenues and a natural risk for ski resorts.

Protecting your business property against the risk of loss by fire is a direct way to manage risk. Installing smoke detectors, portable fire extinguishers, and automatic sprinklers, for example, will help to protect your staff, property, and revenue.

Human Risks

Human risks are risks caused by human mistakes or dishonesty, or other risks that can be controlled by humans. They range from the financial impact of robbery or embezzlement to job-related injury or illness.

Customer Dishonesty

Loss caused by customer theft, fraudulent payment, or nonpayment is a human risk. In 2001, the National Retail Federation determined that shoplifting cost retailers $10.2 billion that year. This loss is passed on to all of us in the form of higher prices for every product to cover inventory shortages, pay for security personnel, and install theft prevention systems. Additional examples of customer dishonesty include the nonpayment of accounts or paying for goods and services with fraudulent checks or credit cards.

Employee Risks

Employees represent another human risk for business. For example, members of management at the energy trading giant Enron Corporation and its accounting firm, Arthur Andersen LLP, used questionable accounting techniques that inflated profits and hid losses. These fraudulent practices resulted in the company declaring bankruptcy in 2001—which was, at that time, the largest bankruptcy in U.S. history. Thousands of Enron employees lost their jobs, and many people lost savings they had invested in Enron stock. In addition, Arthur Andersen LLP, previously one of the top five accounting firms in the United States, lost its auditing license and sold its assets to competitors.

marketingessentials.glencoe.com

A MATTER OF ETHICS

A Difficult Choice

Herring's Auto Supply has been in business for twenty years, but a new discount store opened nearby six months ago, and sales have been off ever since. Herring's has had four low sales months in a row. Bills from vendors are piling up, and Mr. Herring is concerned that if he pays all the bills, there will not be enough cash on hand to pay all his employees when payday comes around at the end of next week. This situation has never happened in all his years of business.

Mr. Herring asks the store's manager what she thinks they should do. The manager thinks it is more important to pay the employees than to pay the vendors. After all, they work for Mr. Herring. Mr. Herring points out that the vendors have employees they need to pay, too.

THINKING ETHICALLY

What is the ethical thing for Mr. Herring to do in this situation? Explain your reasoning.

@ Online Action!

Go to *marketingessentials.glencoe.com/ 34/ethics* to find a project on ethics and risk management.

Skills and Working Environment

In a restaurant, failing to properly cook or handle food can lead to customers becoming ill or hospitalized. To reduce risks of this type, many companies have instituted safety programs that stress the importance of proper food handling.

Chapter 34 - Risk Management **721**

ASSESS

Review Guide

CONCEPTS·

Ask students to list the three types of risk businesses face and to provide an example of each.
Economic risks include changes in taste and style, product obsolescence, and technology advancement; natural risks include storms, earthquakes, or even war; human risks include employee error or negligence and customer dishonesty.

KEY TERMS

Have students review key terms, their spellings, and definitions in small groups.

ONLINE SELF-ASSESSMENT

Have students go to **marketingessentials.glencoe.com** for the Section 34.1 practice test.

Individualized Review

L1 Assign and review Chapter 34 activities in the Student Activity Workbook.

L2 Assign and review Chapter 34 activities in the Marketing Math Workbook.

L3 Assign and review Chapter 34 activities in the *BusinessWeek* Reader and Case Studies.

Marketing Practice

Ask students to undertake a comprehensive risk assessment of their school store or a local business. Have students cover the major functions of a business, including administration, production, and marketing. Have them find solutions to the most common business risks for that business. Encourage them to use visual aids in a ten-minute oral presentation of their risk assessment.

A MATTER OF ETHICS A Difficult Choice

Discussion Lead a discussion about the moral dilemma faced by Herring's Auto Supply. Encourage students to think of themselves as the store's manager who must advise the owner on which course of action to take. Point out that the store manager is also an employee of Herring's and will be personally affected by this decision.

THINKING ETHICALLY **Answer:** Answers will vary. However, students may say that the business has a legal and moral obligation to pay both vendors and employees. A business that cannot meet its obligations must file for bankruptcy or go out of business.

@ Online Action! For instructions, ideas, and answer guide, go to the Teacher Center at **marketingessentials.glencoe.com**

Follow Up Have students investigate recent changes in bankruptcy laws.

721

CLOSE

Ask students to answer the following questions:

- **What is business risk?**
  The possibility of business loss or failure.

- **What is risk management?**
  The systematic process of managing an organization's risk exposure to achieve objectives consistent with public interest, human safety, environmental factors, and law.

Extended Activity

Product Risks

Have students list some products that are no longer on the market because they are obsolete and have been replaced by newer, better versions. Then, have students research product recalls and report to the class how these recalls came about and how they affected the businesses concerned. Encourage students to find examples that relate to computer technology, which changes very quickly.

The business environment or work setting itself often becomes a risk. Customer or employee accidents are potential human risks. Commercial airlines, for example, prepare crews for emergencies not only caused by mechanical problems but also by human factors. A passenger might fall in a crowded aisle, break an arm, and sue the airline. Employees could also be overcome by toxic fumes or sickened by other environmental hazards. Another type of risk sometimes faced by employers is the threat of sexual harassment or physical violence in the workplace.

Computer-Related Crime

Over the past decade, computer-related crime has emerged as a significant new human risk for businesses. Malicious programs called computer worms or viruses can be downloaded inadvertently by employees and can wreak havoc on internal computer networks and communications systems.

Individuals may also penetrate the security of computer systems to gain access or information for mischievous or criminal purposes, including industrial espionage such as stealing proprietary company information or client lists.

Computer crime is committed by many different kinds of people, from current or past employees to professional cyberthieves. Protecting a business from computer crime requires securing the computer network using passwords, encoded firewall programs, and virus detectors. It also requires being vigilant about scanning for operational or human security risks that affect technology and keeping up to date on security alerts released by soft-ware producers. Training employees on privacy policies and the proper handling of confidential information related to voice mail, e-mail and Internet use is necessary to minimize risk of computer intrusion or information theft.

34.1 AFTER YOU READ

Reviewing Key Terms and Concepts

1. Why does product obsolescence pose an economic risk?
2. What are three examples of natural risks?
3. What causes human risks for businesses?

Integrating Academic Skills

Math

4. It is estimated that three to four percent is added to the price of a product to cover shoplifting losses. Calculate the price of a $29.99 skateboard without the four percent "hidden tax" due to shoplifting losses.

Social Studies/Language Arts

5. Perform an Internet search or library research on recent bankruptcies. Choose one company and write a short paper on the causes and effects of that company's bankruptcy.

 Online Action!

Check your answers at *marketingessentials.glencoe.com/34/read*

AFTER YOU READ

Reviewing Key Terms and Concepts

1. Product obsolescence poses an economic risk because new products are being developed, and many businesses depend on marketing the latest trend. If the products are not sold before they become obsolete, prices have to be reduced.

2. Answers will vary, possible answers include floods, tornadoes, hurricanes, fires, lightning, droughts, earthquakes, terrorism, power outages, arson, war, and unexpected changes in normal weather conditions.

3. Human risks are caused by human mistakes, dishonesty as well as the unpredictability of customers, employees, or a failure to maintain a safe work environment.

Integrating Academic Skills

4. Price without shoplifting: $28.79; $29.99 × .04 = $1.20; $29.99 − $1.20 = $28.79

5. Answers will vary, students should be able to identify the cause and effect of a company's bankruptcy.

Online Action! Answers at **marketingessentials.glencoe.com/34/read**

SECTION 34.2

Handling Business Risks

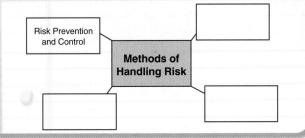

FOCUS

OBJECTIVES

- Explain effective security and safety precautions, policies, and procedures
- Describe the various ways businesses can manage risk
- Explain the concept of insurance

KEY TERMS

- insurance policy
- extended coverage
- fidelity bonds
- performance bonds

READ and STUDY

BEFORE YOU READ

Predict A business faces many risks to earn a profit. What methods do you think a business might use to handle its risks?

THE MAIN IDEA

Businesses use certain strategies to help prevent, avoid, and protect against accidents, injuries, fires, thefts, defective products, and environmental and other disasters.

STUDY ORGANIZER

Copy the chart below. As you read, fill in the boxes with the different methods of handling risk.

Risk Prevention and Control → Methods of Handling Risk

Introducing the Section

COLLABORATIVE ACTIVITY

To prepare for reading this section, have students work in small groups of five or six to identify how their school administration protects the school against natural and human risks. Have them list safety-related rules and regulations they follow in the school environment and describe ways these rules are communicated. For example, they might identify such ways as signs in hallways, student orientation sessions and handbooks, assembly programs, fire drills, or safety rules related to participation in sports. Conduct a class discussion about the findings with representatives from each group serving on a discussion panel.

Preteaching Key Terms

Read the key terms aloud and ask students to predict their meanings:

- insurance policy
- extended coverage
- fidelity bonds
- performance bonds

Have students take notes on the meaning of each term as they read the section.

Ways of Handling Business Risks

There are four basic ways that businesses can handle risks: risk prevention and control, risk transfer, risk retention, and risk avoidance. An effective risk prevention program for a business should use a combination of all these methods.

WHILE YOU READ

Question Which method of handling risks do you think is most important for a business?

Chapter 34 - Risk Management **723**

Critical Thinking

Ask students to brainstorm some of the risks a company might face by marketing its products globally. For example, obtaining payment from customers located in certain countries might be difficult for certain companies.

READ and STUDY

BEFORE YOU READ

Lead students in finding examples of ways businesses can lessen the risks they face.

THE MAIN IDEA

Ask students to read the main idea and then discuss how they can protect against similar risks in the home. Have them brainstorm what precautions they take to lessen the chance of injury or loss.

STUDY ORGANIZER

Model the study organizer for students by filling in the first box. A full-size, downloadable study organizer can be found at **marketingessentials.glencoe.com**

WHILE YOU READ Suggest to students that they come back to this question after reading the section and see if they answer it differently.

Discussion Starter

RISK PREVENTION AND CONTROL

Ask the class to brainstorm techniques that they are familiar with that employers use to screen future employees. Have students volunteer their experiences applying for jobs or volunteer your own experience. Have them relate what kinds of questions they were asked on application forms and in interviews. Ask: Were they asked to provide documents such as a driver's license? What might a prospective employer learn about someone from his or her driver's license? Ask students if they have ever had to provide references when applying for a job and to explain why they think an employer would contact a reference before deciding to hire someone.

Build Vocabulary

Preview the following phrases by reading them aloud. Discuss the basic meaning of each, then ask students to do research to find out more about them.

- **drug testing**
  testing for illegal substance use

- **injuries due to improper lifting**
  a workplace injury

Extended Activity

Have students, research information about and/or visit the Web site of OSHA, the U.S. Department of Labor Occupational Safety & Health Administration. Ask students to choose one section of the site and summarize its contents in a five-minute oral presentation.

• **DETERRING THEFT** Closed-circuit television systems can help to deter both employee and customer theft.

What other systems do retailers use to help prevent theft?

Risk Prevention and Control

Business risks can be handled through prevention and control. Many common types of risks can be controlled and minimized by screening and training employees, providing safe working conditions and sufficient safety instruction, preventing external theft, and deterring employee theft.

Screening and Training Employees

The best way to prevent the human risk of employee carelessness and incompetence is through effective employee screening, orientation, and training. Background screening on all job applications, checking references, and requiring driver licenses are often used to assist in new employee selection. Many employers also use pre-employment tests for basic and technical skills to find the right people. Larger companies and some smaller ones now require prospective employees to undergo testing for illegal drugs before being hired. Drug abuse can lead to increased human risk by making employees careless and more likely to ignore or forget safety rules.

When employees begin a new job, some form of orientation, training, and instruction is normally provided. The training may be brief verbal instruction or extensive training that lasts several weeks or months. Workers should be trained in rules and regulations relating to safety.

Providing Safe Conditions and Safety Instruction

According to the National Safety Council, in 2002 there were 4,900 workplace deaths in the United States due to unintentional injuries. Another 3.7 million workers suffered disabling injuries. The financial impact of workplace accidents leading to wage loss, medical expense, and workers' compensation disability payments is staggering.

Based on these numbers alone, safety and health information must be provided to all employees. When employees receive safety instruction and have safe working conditions, the potential for on-the-job accidents is greatly reduced.

To manage such risks, businesses can design all employee work zones and customer selling areas for efficient foot traffic and storage. They can also provide training on proper ways to safely lift and store merchandise.

Many companies address workplace safety by developing accident management programs, which include:

PHOTO GUIDE — DETERRING THEFT

Discussion Discuss with students the problem of theft in a retail environment. Point out that both employee and customer theft present a risk to the business owner.

Caption Answer Answers will vary; clothing retailers often use tagging systems or security guards to deter shoplifting. Business watch programs, similar to neighborhood watch programs, are used to discourage burglary.

Follow Up Invite a store manager to talk to the class about how his or her business deters employee theft and shoplifting.

- Creating a health and safety committee to check for hazards
- Correcting hazards before accidents occur
- Complying with all state and federal health and safety regulations
- Investigating and recording all workplace incidents and accidents
- Providing employees with protective clothing and equipment
- Placing first aid kits near workstations

- Posting the address and phone number of nearby healthcare facilities
- Offering employee classes in first aid and CPR
- Tracking how many workdays were missed due to accidents or injuries
- Scheduling regular safety meetings and training
- Preparing and distributing written safety and health plans

Case Study

Some Risks Pay Off

Cirque du Soleil is not your average circus. You will not see lion tamers, but you will see world-class acrobats and dancers performing amazing feats combined with fantastic sets, lighting, and music. Each Cirque show has a theme, and the company introduces one new show each year, after three years of development.

The company was started in 1984 by 23-year-old fire eaters Guy Laliberté and Daniel Gauthier. They persuaded the Quebec government to fund a show by street performers in a Montreal festival. Success led to well-received shows across Canada.

Taking a Gamble

Production companies offered to take Cirque on the road with traveling companies. Despite the temptation of having the shows in different locations with different casts to bring in more revenue faster, Cirque's managers decided that each show should only have one cast to maintain the highest level of performance. This allowed Cirque to raise ticket prices significantly. Forgoing immediate profits was a risk that paid off.

 THINK STRATEGICALLY
What kinds of business risks do you see associated with Cirque du Soleil's business, including transporting people and sets around the world? How would you manage such risks?

@ Online Action! Go to *marketingessentials.glencoe.com/34/case* to find an activity on business risks.

marketingessentials.glencoe.com

Individualized Practice

PROVIDING SAFE CONDITIONS AND SAFETY INSTRUCTION

L1 Tell students to imagine that they have been hired for the summer to work on the janitorial and grounds crew at school. Ask them to identify what safety training and equipment they would expect to receive at their orientation session.

L2 Ask students to write a one-page memo detailing an effective workplace safety training program for a computer-oriented business.

L3 Ask students to research why some states have banned lie detectors for job screening. Have them document their findings in a one-page report.
Possible reasons include unreliability of equipment, misinterpretation of test results, invasion of privacy, and constitutional limits on self-incrimination.

Critical Thinking

Ask students why they think many businesses are required to post written health and safety regulations.

Case Study Some Risks Pay Off

Discussion Have students discuss the risks that were facing the founders of the company when they started out. Ask how those risks differ from the ones they face today.

THINK STRATEGICALLY **Answer:** The circus has human and economic risks. Human risks involve the selection of trained performers who can be entertaining and work without injury. Transportation of props and people represents an economic risk. Skillful screening of performers is necessary to assess their required technical skills; the purchase of insurance is necessary to minimize economic risk associated with this type of entertainment.

@ Online Action! For instructions, ideas, and answer guide, go to the Teacher Center at **marketingessentials.glencoe.com**

725

Concept Development

PREVENTING THEFT

After students have read the material about preventing external theft, lead a discussion about shoplifting, burglary, robbery, and the difference among them. Make sure students understand the difference between a misdemeanor and a felony. A misdemeanor is a less serious crime, such as shoplifting. A felony is a more serious crime, such as auto theft or bank robbery. Point out that state laws differ in their definitions of what constitutes a felony.

TEACHING POINTS

Extend Have students brainstorm ways employees can steal from employers. You might suggest that taking office supplies for use at home, use of the telephone for personal calls and long distance, personal use of photocopiers and fax machines, and inappropriate use of office postage and mail services are considered by many employers to be theft.

 Critical Thinking

Ask students why sexual or racial harrassment can be considered a workplace risk.

- Offering incentives such as prizes or bonuses for improved safety records
- Addressing workplace threats such as sexual harassment or violence

Preventing Theft

One of the largest and most costly forms of human risk is theft by employees and customers. Internal theft by employees and external theft by customers in retail stores is high. The 2004 National Retail Security Survey estimated that inventory theft from retail stores costs the American public over $33 billion every year.

Shoplifting is external theft that involves stealing merchandise from a business. Shoplifting is one of the fastest-growing crimes against property in the country. While shoplifting losses vary by store type, it is estimated that one-third of lost inventory is caused by shoplifting.

There are many ways to deter shoplifting. Businesses can educate store employees about shoplifting prevention guidelines. Adequately lighting store layouts, storing expensive items in locked display cases, or tagging products with electronic anti-theft devices can cut down on shoplifting. Many stores use security personnel and security devices such as high-zoom digital recorders, electronic gates, closed-circuit television, and wall or ceiling mirrors to cut down on the risk of theft.

Apprehending shoplifters is a significant risk. Merchants can be sued for allegations of false arrest, false imprisonment, malicious prosecution, excessive use of force, or physical assault. To limit their liability, retailers must know acceptable shoplifter detention policies and be sure that employees are trained in these practices.

Robbery is stealing of money or merchandise by violence or threat. Many local police departments provide instruction on how to prevent and handle robberies. Businesses can lower their risk from robberies by:

- Limiting the amount of money that is kept on hand

- Handling bank deposits discreetly
- Installing video cameras to help identify robbers
- Hiring extra employees to assure double coverage
- Hiring security guards
- Installing bulletproof glass in cashier cubicles
- Opening back doors only for freight or trash
- Installing switches that allow employees to lock outside doors
- Increasing lighting inside and outside of the establishment
- Making sure doors are locked and alarms are set at night

Controlling Employee Theft

Employee theft represents 48 percent (compared to shoplifting's 31 percent) of all business losses due to theft. Most employee theft occurs at the point-of-sale (POS) terminal, or cash register. To protect against employee theft, many businesses have installed closed-circuit television systems and POS terminals that generate computerized reports.

POS computerized reports monitor void transfers, cash discrepancies, sales reports, refunds by employees, employees' discounts, and cash register transactions. By carefully analyzing these data, businesses improve the chances of apprehending dishonest employees.

Closed-circuit television systems used in conjunction with POS terminals also lower the risk of employee theft. Closed-circuit systems include cameras concealed in mannequins, ceilings, or walls. Usually operated by security personnel in a control room, they are backed up with a video recorder.

Internal business standards regarding policies to prosecute dishonest employees must be established. Open discussion about employee honesty and company policies keep all employees aware of expectations. Another prevention technique is pre-employment psychological testing to detect attitudes about honesty.

 Online Activity

Stopping Shoplifting

Divide the class into three- to five-member teams to work on an anti-shoplifting campaign for your community and school. Suggest that they start by searching the Internet using such terms as *anti-theft, anti-shoplifting* and *loss prevention.* Have each team develop ideas and an action plan for the campaign. Suggest that they include an educational component to focus on the cost of shoplifting to all consumers, and the legal penalties associated with this crime. You might have students document the entire effort by following the guidelines of the Civic Consciousness Project provided by DECA.

•**TRANSFERRING
RISK** Insurance policies are a way of transferring risk from the business owner to an insurance company. How much you pay for such insurance depends on how high the risk of loss appears to the insurer.

How can an insurer help a business determine its insurance needs?

TEACH CONTINUED

Concept Development

RISK TRANSFER

Ask students to discuss the business purpose of insurance. Point out that businesses often purchase insurance to transfer some of the risks of doing business. An insurance policy represents a contract between the business and the insurance company to cover certain business risks in the event of a loss. Explain that insurance companies not only sell insurance, but they also educate their clients about ways to reduce risk. They typically assist business owners in identifying potential risks by conducting a walk-through and recommending changes that can be made to warn customers and employees of potential hazards.

Extended Activity

Are There Uninsurable Risks?
Have students investigate why insurance companies might not cover a particular kind of risk. For example, some property policies may not protect against floods or earthquakes. Have students share their findings in a class discussion.

Risk Transfer

Some business risks can be handled by transferring the risk of loss to another business or to another party. Risk transfer methods include purchasing insurance, establishing product and service warranty periods, and contractual risk transfer.

Purchasing Insurance

A business can insure property and people against potential loss by purchasing insurance policies. An **insurance policy** is a contract between a business and an insurance company to cover a specific business risk. A business can buy an insurance package that combines two or more types of insurable risks of loss.

Insurance companies estimate the probability of loss due to natural risks such as fire, lightning, and wind damage, and human risks such as theft and vandalism. The insurance company then looks at the business's location, past experience, limits, and type of business to determine an insurance rate.

One of the most common forms of business insurance is property insurance. Property insurance covers the loss of or damage to buildings, equipment, machinery, merchandise, furniture, and fixtures. Coverage can be

Chapter 34 - Risk Management 727

Concept Development

PURCHASING INSURANCE

After students have read the material about transferring risk, divide the class into four groups and assign each group one or two types of insurance: (1) property insurance, (2) personal liability and product liability insurance, (3) life insurance and credit insurance, and (4) workers' compensation insurance. Give each group several magazines, a large sheet of poster board, several large sheets of paper, colored markers, and tape. Have each group use its materials to create a poster on the types of insurance assigned to them. If students cannot find appropriate pictures in magazines, they may draw them. Have each group write a definition for each type of insurance on the poster board, tape the relevant pictures on the board, and write words or phrases that illustrate the types of insurance. Ask each group to share their posters in class.

Extended Activity

Small Business Crime Prevention

The Small Business Association offers numerous publications on crime prevention in small business. Have each student acquire one of these publications or have several copies of each publication available. Ask students to read and summarize information and present a brief oral report to the class.

• **MANAGING RISKS** There are different kinds of insurance for different kinds of risks.

Why might a business have different providers for property insurance and life insurance?

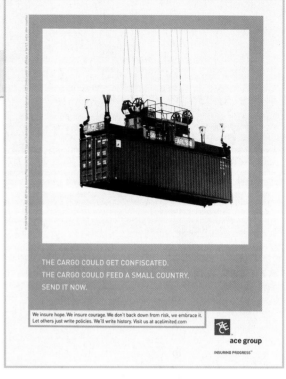

THE CARGO COULD GET CONFISCATED.
THE CARGO COULD FEED A SMALL COUNTRY.
SEND IT NOW.

We insure hope. We insure courage. We don't back down from risk, we embrace it. Let others just write policies. We'll write history. Visit us at acelimited.com

ace group
INSURING PROGRESS

---

purchased for up to the full replacement value of the building, inventory, or other values.

In addition, property insurance may be extended to cover off-premise property, valuable papers and records, fire department service charges, and personal property of others, including theft. Property insurance typically includes the following features:

- **Replacement Cost Coverage** This will reimburse the business owner for the replacement cost of buildings and other personal property. A co-insurance penalty may apply if the insured business purchases less than the reconstruction value of property. This means, for example, that the insurance company

might pay 80 percent of the covered items and the insured pays the balance.

- **Automatic Increase Protection** This policy feature automatically adjusts the coverage to compensate for inflation on both the building and contents.
- **Business Interruption** This feature compensates a business for loss of income during the time that repairs are being made to a building after a natural disaster. This coverage will also reimburse other expenses that continue during the repair period, such as interest on loans, taxes, rent, advertising, and salaries.

Property insurance policies can be purchased with an extended coverage endorsement. An

---

AD GUIDE   MANAGING RISKS

Discussion Lead a discussion about the different types of insurance companies. Explain that insurance companies specialize in managing risk in different areas.

Caption Answer Answers will vary; students should understand that companies can specialize in insuring for different types of risk. For example, certain companies specialize in health insurance, others in life insurance. In addition, specific industries may be targeted by a particular insurance company.

Follow Up Ask interested students to research different insurance companies, such as the Ace Group, Blue Cross, and Metropolitan Life, to determine the types of insurance they offer. Have students share their findings with the class.

extended coverage endorsement provides protection against types of loss that may not be covered under a basic property insurance policy. Water leakage or sewer back-up are typical examples.

Liability Insurance

Business liability insurance protects a business against damages for which it may be held legally liable, such as an injury to a customer or damage to property of others. Primary business liability insurance is usually provided for claims up to $1 million. This type of insurance may be extended to cover business premises, company operations, customer medical expenses, and product and advertising liability claims.

Product liability insurance protects against business losses resulting from personal injury or property damage caused by products manufactured or sold by a business. Many businesses purchase product liability insurance to protect against potential customer claims even though private laboratories and government agencies may have tested the products extensively.

Fidelity bonds protect a business from employee dishonesty. Businesses usually require employees who handle money, such as bank tellers and cashiers, to be bonded. If a bonded employee steals money or merchandise, the bonding company pays the loss. Individuals who are to be bonded are subject to background checks before a bond is issued.

Performance bonds, also called surety bonds, provide financial protection for losses that might occur when a construction project is not finished due to the contractor's impaired financial condition.

Life insurance is often purchased to protect the owners or managers of a business. A sole proprietor (individual business owner) is usually required to have life insurance in order to borrow money. The policy will guarantee that there will be money to pay off the sole proprietor's debts and obligations if he or she dies.

MARKET TECH

Power Paper

Have you ever opened up a greeting card and heard it play *Happy Birthday to You*? Ultra-thin silicon technology makes the generation of music possible, but where does it get its power? Power Paper is an Israeli company that makes batteries as thin as a piece of paper to power such cards, among hundreds of other uses.

Work and Play

One powerful application of Power Paper technology is PowerID, which integrates radio frequency identification (RFID) with the company's power source. Merchandise tagged with PowerID can be tracked from manufacturer to retailer, even if stored in boxes or around materials that interfere with radio transmission. The labels can be read from as far as 40 feet away. This helps all members of a supply chain manage the risks of theft and other losses, as well as keep better track of the level of inventory on hand.

For the retail market, Power Paper has created products that incorporate printed clocks, simple games, or calculators into the covers of notebooks. Hasbro, the toy company, has incorporated Power Paper batteries into products such as thin LCD watches and touch-activated musical-instrument-shaped stickers that play tunes.

THINK LIKE A MARKETER

What other products can you think of that could be improved with batteries as thin as a piece of paper?

@ Online Action!

Go to *marketingessentials.glencoe.com/34/tech* to find an activity on technology and risk management.

Enrichment

BECOMING BONDED

Some students may one day have to be bonded. Have students research this process. Ask: What happens when you become bonded? How does the bonding company determine how much money will be reimbursed to a person who makes a claim against a bonded employee? Who is not eligible to become bonded? Under what circumstances is bonding revoked? Have students present their findings in a 250-word report.

Extended Activity

Orientation and Risk

Have students who are or have been employed and have gone through an orientation program write a 100- to 250-word report on the orientation program used at their place of employment. Tell them to discuss the strengths and weaknesses of the program, what types of risks it explained, and how the program could be improved. Have students express what they learned from the program and what they would like to know or find out more about.

MARKET TECH

Power Paper

Discussion Ask students if they have ever purchased or received a singing greeting card. Have students share their responses to the technology.

THINK LIKE A MARKETER **Answer:** Answers will vary; this activity may generate discussion about how certain consumer products can be improved using technology. Encourage students to think creatively.

@ Online Action! For instructions, ideas, and answer guide, go to the Teacher Center at marketingessentials.glencoe.com

ASSESS

Review Guide

CONCEPTS

- Ask students to list the various types of business risks.
  economic, natural, and human

- Have students explain the concept of insurance.
  Answer suggestion: an insurance policy is a contract between a business and an insurance company to cover a specific business risk.

KEY TERMS

In small groups, have students review key terms, spellings, and definitions.

ONLINE SELF-ASSESSMENT

Have students go to **marketingessentials.glencoe.com** for the Section 34.2 practice test.

Individualized Review

L1 Assign and review Chapter 34 activities in the Student Activity Workbook.

L2 Assign and review Chapter 34 activities in the Marketing Math Workbook.

L3 Assign and review Chapter 34 activities in the *BusinessWeek* Reader and Case Studies.

Marketing Practice

Have students select a business risk such as theft and develop a prevention program aimed at reducing this business risk for a particular company or industry. Have students research, outline, and write the steps they would take to reduce this business risk in a two-page document.

Purchasing life insurance on a partner can provide the money needed for other partners to continue the business when the partners are named as beneficiaries and receive the money from the policy.

Credit insurance protects a business from losses on credit extended to customers. Credit life insurance pays off the balance due for loans granted by banks, credit unions, and other financial institutions in the event the borrower dies.

Workers' compensation insurance covers employees who suffer job-related injuries and illness and protects employers from lawsuits filed by an employee injured on the job. All states require employers that regularly employ a predetermined minimum number of employees for prescribed time periods to purchase workers' compensation insurance coverage.

Product and Service Warranties

Warranties are promises made by the manufacturer or distributor with respect to the performance and quality of a product.

Transferring Risks Through Business Ownership

In a sole proprietorship, the individual owner assumes all risks. Partnerships enable the partners to share in the business risks.

- **AVOIDING RISK** Many companies that provide businesses with insurance are also involved in helping them create effective risk management plans.

Why might an insurance company want its clients to minimize risks?

AD GUIDE — AVOIDING RISK

Discussion Lead a discussion about what risk management companies do and how they work. Point out to students that they help companies evaluate the risks associated with doing business and help them find ways to transfer, avoid, or retain risk.

Caption Answer Answers will vary; students may offer that minimized client risk means that insurance companies can keep their costs down and offer their services at lower cost to the client.

Follow Up Have interested students talk with people in the insurance field to find out how they minimize and manage their own risk.

Corporations allow the stockholders, as owners, to share the business risks. The corporate form of ownership offers the most protection from losses.

Risk Retention

In some cases, it is impossible for businesses to prevent or transfer certain types of risks, so they retain or assume financial responsibility for the consequences of loss. This process is called risk retention. A business has to assume the loss—or retain the risk—if customer trends change and merchandise remains unsold. Most retail shops assume the loss of a certain percentage of goods due to damage or theft.

It is possible to underestimate the risk, such as when merchandise is purchased in anticipation of high demand but weather, fashion trends, or customers' purchasing habits change. A business may attempt to generate a profit by taking a risk, such as purchasing land for future development or sale through subdivision.

Risk Avoidance

Certain risks may be anticipated in advance. Risk avoidance means that a business refuses to engage in a particularly hazardous activity. Market research can lead businesses to conclude that investment in a product or service is not worth the risk. All business decisions should be made with the consideration of both potential benefits and potential risks. Avoiding unacceptable business risks should be a key consideration in any marketing decision.

CLOSE

Have students answer the following questions.

- **What is risk retention?**
  Risk retention means that a business elects to retain or assume responsibility for some business risks.

- **What is risk avoidance?**
  Risk avoidance means that a business refuses to engage in a particular activity. Each method is similar, since both are ways of handling risk.

Critical Thinking

Ask students how a SWOT analysis or a PEST scan can help a company assess its risks.

34.2 AFTER YOU READ

Reviewing Key Terms and Concepts

1. What are the four basic ways to handle business risks?

2. What strategies can be used by businesses for risk prevention and control?

3. Identify three different ways that a business can transfer risks.

Integrating Academic Skills

Math

4. The total cost of theft from retail stores in 2004 was estimated at $33 billion. Calculate the individual costs of internal and external theft if internal theft represented 48 percent and shoplifting represented 31 percent.

Language Arts

5. Perform library research on the topic of shoplifting. Write a 100-word article abstract on the topic of shoplifting. In your article abstract identify the name of the article, its publication date and name of publication, and summarize the article.

 Online Action!

Check your answers at *marketingessentials.glencoe.com/34/read*

marketingessentials.glencoe.com

Chapter 34 - Risk Management 731

AFTER YOU READ

Reviewing Key Terms and Concepts

1. Four basic ways to handle business risks are risk prevention and control, risk transfer, risk retention, and risk avoidance.

2. Providing safe working conditions and safety instruction, screening and training of employees, preventing external theft, and controlling employee theft.

3. Three ways to transfer risk include purchasing insurance, providing product and service warranties, and transferring risks through business ownership.

Integrating Academic Skills

4. Internal theft = $15,840,000,000; external theft = $10,230,000,000.

5. Answers will vary; student articles should demonstrate an understanding of shoplifting as well as identify the source of the article.

 Online Action! **Answers at marketingessentials.glencoe.com/34/read**

Lifelong Learning

CAREER INFORMATION

Have students go to marketingessentials.glencoe.com, find the Chapter 34 Careers page, and click on the link for the American Marketing Association's Careers Strategies and Tips. Ask students to select one article and summarize it.

RISK MANAGEMENT

Risk management is a profession that can be applied to a variety of departments within business operations. For example, workplace safety can be managed by many different departments. Students interested in the field of risk management may benefit from taking courses in human resources, labor relations, and industrial or technological risk management specific to their industry of choice.

Primary Source

Ask students go to marketingessentials.glencoe.com and find Chapter 34 Resources. Ask them to click on the link for the American Marketing Association's marketing dictionary and read the definitions of the terms that are related to risk management and assessment.

THINKING CRITICALLY

Answers will vary; students may mention human risks as well as financial risks.

@ Online Action!

For instructions, ideas, and answer guide, go the Teacher Center at marketingessentials.glencoe.com

732

CAREERS IN MARKETING

Billy Hardison
Independent Talent Buyer and Concert Promoter

(?) What do you do at work?
As an independent talent buyer in a secondary market, marketing is just one of the necessary skills for survival. At the micro level every concert promoter negotiates as fiscally responsible a deal as possible with every artist on a case-by-case basis. Advertising the upcoming event is an obvious next step. Marketing, however, exists at the macro level. Marketing not only influences advertising decisions, it also effects the buying of the talent itself. Branding must be consistent. Shows that are bought, choice of sponsors (if any), use of mass media and to what degree, visibility to the common public, ideology, religion and eating habits are all factors that must be addressed when defining the brand.

(?) What skills are most important to you?
The intangibles are the ability to communicate to the audience, even if it is not your audience, humility, diplomacy, foresight, street smarts, blue-collar skills and work ethic. The tangibles are the ability to communicate through all mediums, computer skills, an appreciation of the arts, a college degree.

(?) What is your key to success?
This is a hard nut to crack. Drive is the most important quality, regardless of the formal training. We have a saying in the "biz": "This is the hardest business to get into and the hardest business to get out of."

Aptitudes, Abilities, and Skills

Strong interpersonal and people skills, versatility, sales aptitude, ability to manage several projects

Education and Training

A bachelor's degree can be helpful, although the exact nature of the degree is often not important.

Career Path

Many concert promoters start small, organizing local shows with friends; opportunities also exist within larger entertainment firms.

THINKING CRITICALLY

What type of business risks do you think this type of work include?

@ Online Action!

Go to marketingessentials.glencoe.com/34/careers to find a career-related activity.

Test-Taking Strategies

Have students choose one or two concepts in the chapter for which they need clarification, and write a 50-word summary of each concept in their own words. The summarizing practice will help reinforce key chapter ideas and concepts.

FOCUS on KEY POINTS

SECTION 34.1

● Business risks are situations that can lead to financial gain, loss, or failure. Risk management is the process of managing risk in an ethical way.

● Business risks fall into three categories: economic, natural, and human. Economic risks such as recession or population changes result from changes in overall business conditions. Natural risks such as floods or arson result from natural or sometimes human occurrences. Human risks are caused by human mistakes or things that can be controlled by humans, such as the working environment.

SECTION 34.2

● There are various ways that businesses can manage risks of financial loss, including loss prevention, control, transfer, retention, and avoidance. Establishing and maintaining safe conditions and controlling external and internal theft can reduce financial loss.

● Insurance is a common way to transfer risks. You can also transfer risk through warranties or business ownership changes.

REVIEW VOCABULARY

Define each of the following terms in a short sentence.

1. business risk (p. 718)
2. risk management (p. 718)
3. economic risks (p. 719)
4. natural risks (p. 719)
5. human risks (p. 721)
6. insurance policy (p. 727)
7. extended coverage (p. 729)
8. fidelity bonds (p. 729)
9. performance bonds (p. 729)

REVIEW FACTS and IDEAS

10. What is risk management, and why is it an important marketing function? (34.1)
11. What are the different types of business risk? Give an example of each type. (34.1)
12. How do safety and security policies reduce risks for businesses? (34.2)
13. Describe at least two ways businesses can manage risks. (34.2)
14. What is the purpose of an insurance policy? (34.2)
15. Name two types of bonds and the purpose of each. (34.2)

Chapter 34 - Risk Management **733**

REVIEW FACTS and IDEAS

10. Risk management is the systematic process of managing an organization's risks to achieve objectives in a manner consistent with public interest, human safety, environmental needs, and the law. Risk management is an important marketing function because it is necessary for effective financial, marketing, production, and human resource management decisions. Risk management also reduces the adverse effects of risk on business resources, cash flow, and profits.

11. Economic, natural, and human risks are among the types of risks that a business may experience. Examples will vary.

12. Safety and security policies reduce risk because they help communicate to all employees specific ways to minimize risk in these areas.

13. Answers may include: Insurance is a common way to manage risks. You can also transfer risk through warranties or business ownership.

14. The main purpose of an insurance policy is to transfer risk from one company or party to another.

15. Fidelity bonds protect a business from employee dishonesty. Performance bonds provide financial protection for losses that might occur when a construction project is not finished due to a contractor's impaired financial condition.

FOCUS on KEY POINTS

Ask volunteers to read the summaries aloud and give the class one real-life example for each concept.

REVIEW VOCABULARY

See glossary for definitions of 1–9.
A sample sentence might read:

1. A *business risk* is a possibility of financial loss.

733

BUILD SKILLS

16. Workplace Skills
Answers will vary but should outline the importance of hygiene and other good practices in the workplace and mention the risks that could result from failing to follow appropriate cleanliness guidelines.

17. Technology Applications
Answers will vary but should list the top five most costly natural disasters in your state.

18. Math Practice
$29,616; $1,234,000 × .024 = $29,616

DEVELOP CRITICAL THINKING

19. Selecting Insurance
Answers will vary; explanations should reflect that a business should match its needs to the types of insurance it purchases and the types of insurance companies it deals with. It is possible to spend too much money on insurance relative to the risk a business faces.

20. Extended Warranties
Answers will vary; responses may include that companies offer extended product warranties as a means to increase their profitability. The warranty is supposed to make the consumer feel that he or she has an extra layer of protection should the product malfunction.

BUILD SKILLS

16. Workplace Skills
Interpersonal Communication Suppose you are the manager of a sandwich shop. Prepare a memo to your staff of food workers on the importance of hygiene and other good practices in the workplace. Explain the kinds of risks that both employees and others may face.

17. Technology Applications
Creating Charts Using the Internet or other resources, research the top five most costly natural disasters in your state's history. Use a spreadsheet or graphic design program to create a chart listing the five disasters and their costs.

18. Math Practice
Counting the Losses Calculate the amount of net sales lost to an apparel specialty store with annual sales of $1,234,000 and a shoplifting rate of 2.4 percent.

DEVELOP CRITICAL THINKING

19. Selecting Insurance
Different companies have different needs. Choose a company or a type of business that interests you. Research the type of risks your chosen business typically encounters.

As you research and find out facts about the business type you selected, try to answer the following questions:

- Are there any risk factors that the company you selected should not have to consider?
- What factors should this business consider when selecting an insurance company?

Explain your answers.

20. Extended Warranties
Why does a company sell extended warranties to its customers if its advertising stresses the product's quality and durability? Does this imply that the company's products are likely to malfunction? Explain your answers and give two product examples.

Formative Assessment

Formative assessment is an essential component of classroom work. This type of assessment provides information that is then used as feedback to modify teaching and meet student needs.

L1 Review key terms for this chapter. Ask students to write one sentence for each key term.

L2 Provide examples of risks that affect different types of businesses. After each story, have students connect the risks with the businesses.

L3 Have students develop scenarios that illustrate a specific type of risk.

 Reteach   If the results of this formative assessment seem low, consider the following activity:
Read each of the key terms aloud. Have students define the key terms and use them in a sentence. Clarify any issues students may have.

APPLY CONCEPTS

21. Improving Workplace Safety

Perform Internet or library research about workplace safety laws or regulations. Select a particular aspect of employment laws affecting workplace safety. Take notes about the law, including its name, date it went into effect, and protections found in the law.

Activity Review the information and use presentation software to prepare an oral report on one aspect of workplace safety.

22. Understand Insurance

Locate an insurance provider using the Internet or other sources. Select a provider that lists details such as type and length of coverage.

Activity Using presentation software, describe the nature and scope of the insurance company from the materials reviewed.

NET SAVVY

23. Business and the Environment

Find the Web site for the U.S. Environmental Protection Agency (EPA). The EPA plays a significant role in preventing, correcting, and eliminating potential environmental problems. Write a one-page summary about a recent situation involving a business and what actions were taken by the EPA to protect the public interest.

marketingessentials.glencoe.com

CONNECTION

Role Play:
Assistant Manager

Situation You are to assume the role of an assistant manager for a 24-hour self-service gas station and convenience store. Your store has been experiencing an increasing number of drive-offs. Drive-offs happen when individuals leave the station without paying. Your store manager has asked you to design a procedure for handling external theft (shoplifting). Your procedure must avoid annoying regular customers.

Activity You are to prepare an oral presentation explaining your plan for reducing external theft without jeopardizing customer goodwill and employee safety.

Evaluation You will be evaluated on how well you meet the following performance indicators:

● Explain routine security precautions

● Explain procedures for handling shoplifting

● Follow safety precautions

● Demonstrate problem-solving skills

● Demonstrate effective oral presentation skills

 Online Action!

For more information and DECA Prep practice, go to *marketingessentials.glencoe.com/34/DECA*

APPLY CONCEPTS

21. Improving Workplace Safety

Presentations will vary and should reflect an understanding of the workplace safety.

22. Understand Insurance

Presentations will vary; each presentation should include general information about the company and the nature and scope of its insurance operations.

NET SAVVY

23. Business and the Environment

Summaries will vary; students should identify a case involving a business, the actions taken by the EPA to penalize or correct the problem, and how the EPA's actions affected the public interest.

THE DECA CONNECTION

The students should be evaluated on the performance indicators noted in the role play. For another DECA role play, go to the Competitive Events Workbook or the Student Activity Workbook, or go to **marketingessentials.glencoe.com/34/DECA**

 Online Action! For instructions, ideas, and answer guide, go to the Teacher Center at **marketingessentials.glencoe.com**

DECA Advisors Corner

Hold an employer appreciation breakfast. Invite your business supporters, key teachers, school administrators, etc. A student presentation about DECA should be the main component of the agenda. Many advisors utilize this time to recognize those who helped make the DECA year a success.

MINI-QUIZ

Read these sentences to the students and have them volunteer the missing word(s):

1. The possibility of financial loss is called _____. (business risk)

2. The systematic process of managing an organization's risk exposure is known as _____. (risk management)

3. A strategy used when it is impossible for a business to prevent or transfer risks is known as _____. (risk retention)

For an expanded chapter quiz, go to Chapter 34 in the TeacherWorks CD-ROM and to Chapter 34 in the **ExamView®** Pro Test Generator CD-ROM.

Chapter Overview

This chapter introduces students to the business plan. It stresses the importance of business planning in developing a business idea and in evaluating results. The chapter details how to conduct a self-analysis and a marketing analysis for a new business and ways to obtain capital to start a business.

BUILD BACKGROUND

Ask students to consider which method would be the best way to reach a destination: 1) using a road map, or 2) relying on your intuition. Write "business plan" and "road map" on the board. Tell students that a business plan is a road map that helps people choose the best route and mark progress. Tell them that the business plan also helps determine if a business idea will work.

Why It's Important

Business planning is important for three reasons: 1) It helps to obtain financing. Most potential lenders and investors will want to see a detailed business plan before lending or investing money. 2) It serves as a guide in opening a business. New business owners need a guide during business start-up to identify the legal procedures. 3) It helps in business management because it lays out the steps you must take to ensure profitable operation.

Prepare to Read

List the section objectives on the board. Have students skim the chapter, looking at the pictures, reading the captions, and noting the heads. Ask questions to ensure that the students have a basic understanding of the chapter structure.

CHAPTER 35
Developing a Business Plan

Chapter Objectives

After reading this chapter, you should be able to:

- Explain the purpose and importance of a business plan
- Identify external planning considerations
- Develop a business's organization plan
- Construct a marketing plan
- Identify the financial elements of a business plan
- Describe financing sources for businesses

GUIDE TO THE PHOTO

Market Talk By the time a business opens its doors, it should have a business plan and a marketing plan in place. While the marketing plan outlines market analysis and marketing strategies, the business plan defines the larger picture and includes a mission statement and a detailed financial plan for all functions of the business. Entrepreneurs must look at all available sources of funding and opportunities to raise capital.

Quick Think Why must a small business entrepreneur make creative funding decisions when planning a new business or expanding an existing one?

GUIDE TO THE PHOTO

Market Talk Have students discuss what some of the difficulties of opening a new business might be. Discussion will vary, but topics might include: having enough capital to get started, knowing what customers want, knowing where to get the best supplies, hiring good employees.

Quick Think Answers will vary. Many entrepreneurs will encounter financial needs when planning a new business or expanding a business so it is important to explore all possible sources of capital.

 Follow Up — Ask students to think of three businesses they would like to start someday. As students share their ideas, list the types of businesses on the board.

Performance indicators represent key skills and knowledge. Relating them to the concepts explained in this chapter is your key to success in DECA events.

These acronyms represent DECA events that involve knowledge of concepts in this chapter.

AAAL	FSRM*	TSE*	FMAL
FMML*	VPM	TMDM*	RMAL
RMML*	SMDM*	BSM	FMDM*
HMDM*	ADC*	QSRM*	
AAML*	MMS*	EMDM*	

In all these DECA events you should be able to follow these performance indicators:

- Conduct an environmental scan to obtain marketing information
- Explain the nature and scope of financing
- Assess personal interests and skills needed for success in business

Events with an asterisk (*) also include:

- Explain the nature of business plans
- Develop company objectives (for a strategic business unit)
- Develop strategies to achieve company goals/objectives
- Explain external planning considerations
- Develop business plan

Some events include one additional indicator: Conduct location feasibility study. These events are:

AAML	FMDM
FMML	HMDM
QSRM	SMDM
RMML	TMDM

DECA PREP

Check your understanding of DECA performance indicators with the DECA activity in this chapter's review. For more information and DECA Prep practice, go to *marketingessentials .glencoe.com/35/DECA*

marketingessentials.glencoe.com

DECA events that require knowledge of developing a business plan are described here. Discuss the performance indicators to make sure students understand how to demonstrate their understanding.

The event acronyms stand for:

AAAL: Apparel and Accessories Marketing Series, AL

AAML: Apparel and Accessories Marketing Series, ML

ADC: Advertising Campaign Event

BSM: Business Services Marketing Series

EMDM: E-Commerce Management Team Decision Making Event

FMAL: Food Marketing Series, AL

FMDM: Financial Analysis Management Team Decision Making Event

FMML: Food Marketing Series, ML

FSRM: Full Service Restaurant Management Series

HMDM: Hospitality Services Management Team Decision Making Event

MMS: Marketing Management Series

QSRM: Quick Serve Restaurant Management Series

RMAL: Retail Merchandising Series, AL

RMML: Retail Merchandising Series, ML

SMDM: Sports and Entertainment Marketing Management Team Decision Making Event

TMDM: Travel and Tourism Marketing Management Team Decision Making Event

TSE: Technical Sales Event

VPM: Vehicles and Petroleum Marketing Series

DECA PREP

Find timed DECA Prep activities correlated to the Competitive Events Workbook for students and DECA tips for teachers at **marketingessentials.glencoe.com /35/DECA**

CHAPTER 35 Classroom Resources

For the Teacher

- TeacherWorks
- marketingessentials.glencoe.com
- Interactive Chalkboard
- **Exam*View*®** Pro Test Generator
- Fast File Unit 11

For the Student

- ***Marketing Essentials*** Online Edition
- Student Activity Workbook
- Marketing Math Workbook
- Marketing Research Project Workbook
- School-to-Work Activity Workbook
- Competitive Events Workbook
- ***BusinessWeek*** Reader and Case Studies
- marketingessentials.glencoe.com

FOCUS

Introducing the Section

COLLABORATIVE ACTIVITY

Have several copies of fairly detailed business plans available. Have students work in groups of three or four. Ask them to skim each section of the business plan and write down why each section is useful, e.g., the competition analysis tells how needed the new business is. Ask them also to evaluate whether they as investors would invest in this new business and why. After students are finished have each group share their responses with the whole group.

Preteaching Key Terms

Give students 10 minutes to look through the chapter, write down each key term, and attempt to define the term. When students are finished, check their understanding of each term.

- business plan
- business philosophy
- trading area
- buying behavior

 Critical Thinking

Ask students to think about what lenders and investors gain from providing start-up funds to new businesses. Answers will vary but should include the fact that investors will get a share of the profits of the new business if it is profitable, and lenders will get interest on their loans.

OBJECTIVES

- Explain the purpose and importance of a business plan
- Identify external planning considerations

The Business Plan

KEY TERMS

- business plan
- business philosophy
- trading area
- buying behavior

READ and STUDY

BEFORE YOU READ
Predict What do you think would happen if you started a business without planning first?

THE MAIN IDEA
A business plan helps an entrepreneur develop business goals, determine necessary resources, and identify how the new business will operate. This plan also helps potential lenders or investors assess if the business is a good financial risk.

STUDY ORGANIZER
In a chart like the one below, identify the elements in the first component of a business plan.

Description and Analysis	

WHILE YOU READ

Connect Suppose you want to launch a business. List three questions a lender would ask you before loaning you funds.

Developing the Business Plan

If you want to establish your own business, you will probably need financial assistance. A business plan will help you secure that assistance. A **business plan** is a proposal that outlines a strategy to turn a business idea into a reality. It describes a business opportunity, such as a new business or plans to expand an existing one, to potential investors and lenders. They will review the business plan before granting you credit or start-up capital.

738 UNIT 11 - ENTREPRENEURSHIP AND FINANCE

READ and STUDY

BEFORE YOU READ
Tell students that, to convince a lender to offer financial backing, you must develop a business plan that describes the proposed business; and details the organization, marketing, and financial plan for the business.

THE MAIN IDEA
Ask students to briefly state the reasons new businesses need a business plan.

STUDY ORGANIZER
Model the study organizer for students by filling in the first blank. A full-size, downloadable study organizer can be found at marketingessentials.glencoe.com

 Ask students to jot down notes as they read indicating questions a lender might ask.

In addition to helping you obtain financing, a business plan will guide you as you open the business and plan for its management.

Your business plan should convince investors and lenders that your business idea is profitable, identify procedures necessary to legally establish the business, and work as a management tool to identify the month-to-month steps necessary to operate a profitable business. A business plan must be well organized and easy to read. It should contain three main components:

- Description and analysis of the proposed business
- Organizational and marketing plan
- Financial plan

Although the formats of business plans vary, the outline in Figure 35.1 on page 740 is an excellent model.

Description and Analysis of the Proposed Business

The description and analysis section introduces the proposed business concept. This section should clearly identify the products and services the business will sell. It includes your personal business philosophy, as well as a self-analysis that describes your business experience, education, and training. This section of your business plan also includes a trading area analysis, a market segment analysis, and an analysis of potential locations.

When preparing your plan, be as factual as possible. Where can you get up-to-date information online and off? For regional and national business information, consult recent issues of *BusinessWeek, Entrepreneur, Fortune, Money,* the *Wall Street Journal,* and other business publications. Trade and professional associations as well as industry groups can also be a source of data. Tap into research conducted by local and state economic advisory boards, councils, and government agencies. The U.S. Small Business Administration and the Senior Core of Retired Executives (SCORE) can also refer you to potential sources of information and classes for aspiring entrepreneurs.

Business Philosophy and Products

Begin your plan with a description of the type of business you want to open. In this section, you will present marketing research data and review significant trends that will influence the success of your business. Explain how a current or changing situation has created an opportunity for the business to fulfill consumer demand.

Business Philosophy

Next, state your **business philosophy**, which explores how you think the business should be run and demonstrates your understanding of your business's role in the marketplace. It reveals your attitude toward your customers, employees, and competitors. Your business philosophy will help you attract new customers and maintain existing customers once you start a business.

Wal-Mart's business philosophy is that it will not be undersold, and the return policy is that customers can always return merchandise if they are dissatisfied with it.

Type of Product or Service

After identifying your business philosophy, describe the product or service you will offer. Explain the potential consumer benefits and why your product or service will be successful. Include as many facts, trends, and statistics as you can, and be thorough in your research and documentation. Speculation and statements of belief do not convince investors and lenders to lend you money.

Self-Analysis

The next part of your business plan includes a self-analysis, a description of your personal education, training, strengths, and weaknesses, and a plan for personal development.

Experiences, Skills, and Plans

In this part of the business plan, you need to highlight your strengths and skills in your chosen area. You should also describe how you will acquire the skills you lack through additional training or by hiring other professionals.

Chapter 35 - Developing a Business Plan 739

TEACH

Discussion Starter

BUSINESS PHILOSOPHY AND PRODUCTS

Ask students to consider the following business philosophies and discuss what kind of business each philosophy would be appropriate for:

1. We get it there on time.
2. We provide the highest-quality product.
3. We pamper the customer.

This exercise will allow students to see the variety of philosophies possible. Discussion will vary, but the first philosophy might be good for a restaurant delivery service or a mailing service. The second might be good for a furniture maker or other crafts person. The third might be good for a spa, gym, or luxury hotel.

TEACHING POINTS

Demonstrate Bring in a variety of ads that show a business philosophy. Have students browse through the ads and determine the business philosophy expressed in the ad.

Clarify Explain to students how a business philosophy guides business decisions. A hotel focusing on pampering the customer might buy the thickest beach towels even though the towels are expensive, while a hotel focusing on attracting business travelers might buy less expensive towels but provide free Internet access.

Concept Development

OUTLINE FOR A BUSINESS PLAN

To help students understand the outline, have them imagine what would happen if a business did not have one or two of the elements of the business plan. For example, ask students what would happen if a business did not have a management team plan or an organizational plan.

Answers will vary; the lack of a management team plan might result in confusion about who is in charge of what.

TEACHING POINTS

Explain Make sure students understand that an executive summary summarizes the business plan. It lets readers quickly indentify the main points of the plan.

Role Play Role play an entrepreneur pitching a new business to a lender or investor, then ask students to perform similar role plays. The entrepreneur should give the business a name, explain to the lender or investor the information that will be included in the business plan, and tell the lender or investor why it is important that he or she read the business plan.

Critical Thinking

Have students debate which part of the business plan is most important. Help students understand that ultimately, each part is equally important.

Figure 35.1 **Outline for a Business Plan**

• **Business Plan Outline** Developing a business plan is like outlining a strategy for turning your business idea into a reality.

Why should a business plan be a continuing work-in-progress?

BUSINESS PLAN OUTLINE

1

Section 1 describes the general concept of the proposed business, outlines the entrepreneur's special skills, and analyzes the potential market.

I. Description and analysis of the proposed business situation
   A. Type of business
   B. Business philosophy
   C. Description of good or service
   D. Self-analysis
      1. Education and training
      2. Strengths and weaknesses
      3. Plan for personal development
   E. Trading area analysis
      1. Geographic, demographic, and economic data
      2. Competition
   F. Market segment analysis
      1. Target market
      2. Customer buying behavior
   G. Analysis of potential location

II. Organization and marketing plan
   A. Proposed organization
      1. Type of ownership
      2. Steps in establishing business
      3. Personnel needs
   B. Proposed good/service
      1. Manufacturing plans and inventory policies
      2. Suppliers
   C. Proposed marketing plan
      1. Pricing policies
      2. Promotional activities

2

Section 2 discusses how the business will be organized, describes the product or service to be offered, and details the marketing plan.

III. Financial plan
   A. Sources of capital
      1. Personal sources
      2. External sources
   B. Projected income and expenses
      1. Personal financial statement
      2. Projected start-up costs
      3. Projected personal needs
      4. Projected business income
      5. Projected business expenses
      6. Projected income statement(s)
      7. Projected balance sheet
      8. Projected cash flow

3

Section 3 identifies the sources of capital and projects income and expenses.

 Online Action! Go to *marketingessentials.glencoe.com/35/figure/1* to find a project on business plans.

Figure 35.1 **Outline for a Business Plan**

Discussion Have students think of a business they have worked for or another local business. Ask them to speculate on what might be contained in each part of the business plan for this business. Relating the business plan outline to a business students know will help them understand the parts of the business plan.

Caption Answer As time passes, the market, the business, and the competition will all change. The business plan will need to be revised to account for these changes.

 Online Action! For instructions, ideas, and answer guide, go to the Teacher Center at **marketingessentials.glencoe.com**

 Follow Up Ask students to think of a type of business they would like to start. Ask each student to complete one section of the business plan with this new business in mind.

Indicate the education and training you have had so far to prepare you for operating your new business. Your educational and work experience shows potential lenders that you can understand the industry and have the required skills for running a successful business.

Licenses

Some businesses require applying for a special license. In this section, you should explain if you already have this license or are in the application process.

Personal Traits

Finally, include the special personal traits and work habits you possess that will help you to operate the proposed business. Examples of past leadership activities, personal initiatives, and willingness to work hard all add strength to your business plan.

Trading Area Analysis

Following an explanation of your personal strengths and skills, define your trading area. A **trading area** is the geographical area from which a business draws its customers. Before going into business, you must analyze the trading area to become familiar with geographic, demographic, and economic data, as well as with the competition.

Information about the population in your trading area is available from your local chamber of commerce or state department of commerce. You can also consult the most recent local U.S. census data in your library or on the Internet.

Geographic, Demographic, and Economic Data

Geographic data include population distribution figures: how many people live in a certain area. Demographics are identifiable and measurable population statistics such as age, gender, marital status, and race/ethnicity. Knowing the demographics of your trading area will help you identify market trends that may have a direct impact on your business.

Prevailing economic conditions are among the major factors affecting a business. Economic factors include economic growth projections, trends in employment, interest rates, business mergers, and governmental regulations. Tax increases or decreases levied by the local, state, and federal governments will affect consumer buying power.

NET MARKETING

Using the Web Wisely

Even if your dream business is a conventional one, use of the Internet can still be part of your business plan. Donna Boone, a swim school instructor, profited from an electronic alternative to word-of-mouth marketing in building a customer base for her swim school in suburban Washington, D.C. Providing excellent personal service to small classes of students, she counted on parents to sing her praises through community online newsletters and Web logs, or blogs. One former student's online letter of praise resulted in 36 new pupils.

Expansion Plans

Boone's marketing plan was successful. She is now the owner of a profitable school, and she has plans to open four more in the next five years. Though her business is land- or water-based, her marketing plan made good use of the virtual universe.

THINK LIKE A MARKETER

What other aspects of a business plan could the Internet help you to address?

@ Online Action!

Go to *marketingessentials.glencoe.com/35/net* to find an activity about the Internet and business plans.

marketingessentials.glencoe.com

Chapter 35 - Developing a Business Plan **741**

NET MARKETING

Using the Web Wisely

Discussion Have students think of the last time they visited an online business. Ask what attracted them to the site, what they found helpful, and what they found unhelpful.

THINK LIKE A MARKETER Answer: Answers will vary. Through the Internet an entrepreneur can obtain geographic, demographic, and economic data, information about steps to be taken to establish a business, pricing and promotional policies used by competitors, location of competitors, templates for financial statements, and sources of capital to assist with the development of a business plan.

@ Online Action!
For instructions, ideas, and answer guide, go to the Teacher Center at **marketingessentials.glencoe.com**

TEACH CONTINUED

Individualized Practice

SELF-ANALYSIS

L1 Have students write a four-paragraph self-analysis. The first paragraph should include their education and training. The second should explore their strengths. The third should describe their weaknesses. The fourth should contain their plan for personal development.

L2 Have students choose a type of business they would like to operate. Then, have them research the training and education needed to be successful in that field. Ask each student to give a five-minute oral report on their findings.

L3 Ask students to work in pairs to interview one another about their self-analysis. Each should take turns asking each other to describe education and training, strengths, weaknesses, and plans for personal development. Then, each student should introduce his or her partner to the class by describing their partner's self-analysis.

TEACHING POINTS

Model Write your own self-analysis and share it with the class.

Demonstrate Invite a lender or investor to visit the class. Have the lender talk about what he or she expects for a business plan, especially the self-analysis section.

Build Vocabulary

Preview the following words by reading them in context:

- trends directions
- potential lenders financial backers
- licenses per units

Discuss the meaning of these words with the students. Encourage students to name synonyms.

Concept Development

TRADING AREA AND COMPETITION

Have students select two small businesses in your community that are in direct competition (for example, two dry cleaners). Have students determine: 1) what each business does to differentiate itself from the competition, 2) how each business keeps abreast of the competition, and 3) what indirect competition each business faces. Ask students to define *indirect competition.*

Indirect competition is created by products that are the same as yours but offered through a different outlet or through a newly applied technology.

TEACHING POINTS

Clarify Ask students to generate a list of popular local businesses. Then, ask students to work in groups of three or four to group the businesses according to their trading areas. For example, stores selling popular music might all have the same trading area, whereas stores selling groceries would have a different trading area. Ask each group to write a few sentences explaining each trading area. Emphasize that there are no right answers.

Enrichment

LOCATION ANALYSIS

Have students list five different types of successful businesses in your community and analyze why each is located where it is. They should consider such things as accessibility to the public, to suppliers, and to transit routes. (For example, manufacturers and wholesalers value low space costs and good access to transit routes over accessibility by the public.) Encourage students to share their findings in class.

It is important to include how much disposable income the potential consumers in your trading area have. This is the personal income remaining from wages after all taxes are taken out. Disposable income is also referred to as buying income.

A special measurement called a buying power index (BPI) has been developed to help new business owners determine the buying power for a given target market. The BPI index factors total population, total income, and total retail sales figures to determine an overall indicator of an area's sales potential. A market can be a state, region, county, or metropolitan statistical area (MSA). These factors are then expressed as a percentage of total potential U.S. sales. You can find more information on buying power indexes in *Demographics USA* (formerly known as the *Survey of Buying Power Index*), which is published annually by Trade Dimensions International.

A good source of information on local economic conditions is your local bank. Bank officials often have business projections for major geographical areas and for most types of businesses located in their immediate area. In addition, the Small Business Administration (SBA) has funded over 1,100 small business development centers (SBDCs) to provide counseling, training, and technical assistance to small businesses and new entrepreneurs. Since 1980, over nine million rural and urban entrepreneurs have received services from SBDCs. Other good sources of information are related business publications available at schools, public libraries, colleges, and universities, or on the Internet.

Competition

As a new business owner, you must analyze your competition. List all the competitors in your trading area: products, prices, locations, general quality of products, and strengths and weaknesses. Try to estimate your competitors' sales volume and identify how they promote and sell their products. You should be able to use these factors to demonstrate how your business will be superior to the competition.

• A BIG EXCEPTION Usually, businesses do not locate right next to competitors, but auto dealerships are an exception. An "auto row" with multiple dealerships lets customers see all of their options.

What kind of location do auto dealerships prefer?

PHOTO GUIDE   A BIG EXCEPTION

Discussion Discuss with students why auto dealers are an exception to the rule of not locating a business near competitors. Answers might include: Each dealer sells a different brand of auto, and customers may shop with their minds set on a particular brand. Locating near other auto dealers offers convenience to shoppers and provides visibility.

Caption Answer Most dealerships prefer to be near competitors. They are often near freeways or on major streets where people can see them easily.

Follow Up Ask students what types of shops offer goods or services that are complementary to auto dealers. Where are they located?

Some good sources of information about your competitors can be found through annual reports, the local chamber of commerce, trade associations, the Yellow Pages, the Internet, business publications, and reports such as those published by Dun & Bradstreet.

Market Segment Analysis

The next part of your business plan should contain a market segment analysis, a description of your target market, and the buying behavior of your potential customers.

Target Market

As you know, your target market is the specific group of people you want to reach. You can identify your target market by common geographic characteristics such as region, county size, size of city, density of population, and climate of the area. You can also categorize it by demographic characteristics such as age, gender, marital status, family size, income, occupation, education, religion, culture, or ethnic background.

You must carefully identify your target market so that you will know the needs and wants of different markets for your goods and services. Your task as an entrepreneur is to decide which market to target and how to do it.

Customer Buying Behavior

After you have identified your target market, you will need to explain how the market's buying behavior will be good for your business. **Buying behavior** is the process individuals use to decide what they will buy, where they will buy it, and from whom they will buy it.

Analysis of Potential Locations

The decision where to locate your store is vital to your success. You can select your location after you have analyzed your trading area and your market segment, including your target market and your competition. You need to consider several additional factors.

Buy, Lease, or Build?

Should you buy, lease, or build your facility? The advantages of leasing outweigh the other options for most new businesses. With leasing,

you avoid a large initial outlay of cash, your risk is reduced by the shorter commitment, and your lease expenses are tax deductible. The process of buying or building is more complex and almost always requires major financing.

Regardless of whether you buy, lease, or build, you need to compare certain terms of each potential method of financing your property. Those terms include monthly rent or payments and the length of commitment. You will also need to find out who is responsible for insurance.

You should have an attorney review any lease or contract before you sign it. He or she will help you fully understand your obligations and negotiate the best possible terms before completing the deal.

Competing and Complementary Businesses

Before you decide, consider the number and size of potential competitors in the area. If your business is similar in size and merchandise to its competitors, you may want to locate near them. This can encourage comparison shopping. On the other hand, a larger business that offers more variety than the competition should be able to generate its own customers and therefore can be situated away from the competition.

A complementary business is one that would help generate store traffic. A shoe or accessories store located next to a clothing store is one example of a complementary business.

Hours of Operation

The nature of your business will dictate if you locate your business in a mall, neighborhood shopping center, freestanding location, or online. That location, in turn, will determine your hours of operation and the number of customers who will see and patronize your business.

Visibility

Restaurants and other businesses that rely on high visibility or prime locations may spend the extra money to locate in a high-traffic location. Such a site may not be a priority or profitable for all businesses.

Extended Activity

Marketing to Differences

Tell students that, even though a professional 40-year-old man with children and a single 20-year-old man with no children might both buy computers, businesses would market computers differently to the two people. Have students discuss the potential differences in marketing to these two people. For example, the 20-year-old man might be sold on real-time e-mail access to friends, while the 40-year-old man might be more interested in online shopping to save time.

ASSESS

Review Guide

CONCEPTS

Ask students to recall the purpose of a business plan.

Answers should include that a business plan is a proposal that outlines a strategy to turn business ideas into a reality. It describes a business opportunity, such as a new business or plans to expand an existing one, to potential investors and lenders.

KEY TERMS

Have students review key terms, their spellings, and definitions in small groups. Students might work in pairs to quiz one another on the key term definitions.

ONLINE SELF-ASSESSMENT

Have students go to marketingessentials.glencoe.com for the Section 35.1 practice test.

Individualized Review

L1 Assign and review Chapter 35 activities in the Student Activity Workbook.

L2 Assign and review Chapter 35 activities in the Marketing Math Workbook.

L3 Assign and review Chapter 35 activities in the *BusinessWeek* Reader and Case Studies.

Marketing Practice

Have students work in pairs to interview a successful business owner about his or her business plan. Students should work together to come up with three to five questions to ask the business owner. Then one should ask the questions while the other records the business owner's answers. Together, the students should take turns writing paragraphs that summarize the business owner's answers.

CLOSE

Ask students to complete the following statement:

The three key functions of a business plan are _____.

obtain financing, guide opening business, and manage the business successfully.

Critical Thinking

Ask students how the geography of a country might affect what is sold there. For example, if you have a store in a warm part of the country like Florida, does that mean you can never sell seasonal winter gear?

Safety

Customer safety should be a consideration when choosing a business location. Research the community's crime rate. You do not want to open your operation in an area where customers feel uncomfortable or are reluctant to visit. Find out whether the fire department is a volunteer or municipal one; contact them to inquire about safety codes, if any, that apply to your business.

Customer Accessibility

Make sure your customers can get to your location easily. Identify the highways, streets, and public transportation options that they would have to use in getting to your site. Will traffic be an obstacle? Will they find sufficient parking easily and for a reasonable charge? Are the location, route, and parking wheelchair accessible?

Zoning and Other Regulations

Now, you are ready to find a specific site. Your first step should be to learn about any local ordinances or laws that may affect your business. Research any restrictions that might prevent you from locating in a particular area. Plans to build or renovate will require the necessary building permits. Operating a regulated business, such as a service station, will call for the necessary local zoning approvals and state licenses.

35.1 AFTER YOU READ

Reviewing Key Terms and Concepts

1. Why is it important to develop a business plan?

2. Identify the three major parts of a business plan.

3. What is a trading area?

Integrating Academic Skills

Math

4. Compute the buying power index for city A, given the following formula and information

Buying Power Index =
.5 × Area's Percentage for U.S. Effective Buying Power
+ .3 × Area's Percentage of U.S. Retail Sales
+ .2 × Area's Percentage of U.S. Population
City A Percentage of U.S. Effective Buying Power = .0103
City A Percentage of U.S. Retail Sales = .0099
City A Percentage of U.S. Population = .008

Economics

5. Investigate what economic and demographic data are available for your community by consulting with your local chamber of commerce, the city government, the U.S. Census Bureau, or the Internet. Include such factors as employment levels, major industries, income, education, etc. Summarize your findings in a one-page written report.

 Online Action!

Check your answers at *marketingessentials.glencoe.com/35/read*

AFTER YOU READ

Reviewing Key Terms and Concepts

1. A business plan is important because 1) it describes the proposed business to potential investors or lenders, 2) it guides you as you open the business, and 3) it helps you to manage the business profitably.

2. Description and analysis of the business situation, organization and marketing plan, and financial plan for the proposed business.

3. A trading area is the geographical area from which a business draws its customers. Before going into business, you must analyze the trading area with respect to geographic, demographic, and economic data, as well as competition.

Integrating Academic Skills

4. Buying Power Index = .00972; (.5 × .0103) + (.3 × .0099) + (.2 × .008) = .00515 + .00297 + .0016 = .00972

5. Answers will vary; students should include such factors as employment levels, major industries, income, education, cultural/ethnic characteristics, etc., in their reports.

Online Action! Answers at **marketingessentials.glencoe.com/35/read**

The Marketing and Financial Plans

OBJECTIVES

- Develop a business's organization plan
- Construct a marketing plan
- Identify the financial elements of a business plan
- Describe financing sources for businesses

READ and STUDY

BEFORE YOU READ

Predict What do you think a lender would be looking for in the marketing plan section of a business plan?

THE MAIN IDEA

The marketing plan section of the business plan outlines how you intend to organize the business. It also explains how you will use advertising and promotional activities to help your business grow and prosper in the competitive marketplace.

STUDY ORGANIZER

Complete a chart like the one below and identify the components of a marketing plan.

KEY TERMS

- job descriptions
- organization chart
- equity capital
- debt capital
- collateral
- credit union

Organizing the Plan

The second section of the business plan explains how you will organize the new business. It describes your current and anticipated staffing needs. It also reviews how you plan to sell your product and how you intend to reach and satisfy customers. The details of your proposed product are explained along with your potential suppliers, manufacturing or selling

WHILE YOU READ

Connect Think of a business you know or have heard about and list facts it might use in its marketing plan.

Chapter 35 - Developing a Business Plan **745**

FOCUS

Introducing the Section

COLLABORATIVE ACTIVITY

Have each student pick a partner in the class. Each pair should brainstorm a list of the things that might be included in (1) the organization plan and (2) the marketing plan. Review students, answers, creating a board list of their answers under column headings marked *organization plan* and *marketing plan.*

Preteaching Key Terms

Have one student dictate the key terms, while another writes them on the board. Ask students to guess the meanings of the words and then check the meanings in the text.

- job descriptions
- organization chart
- equity capital
- debt capital
- collateral
- credit union

Critical Thinking

Ask students: Why is it important to anticipate staffing? Answers may include the fact that it sometimes takes a while to advertise new jobs, interview candidates, and make hires. Therefore, it is good to know in advance what staffing needs will be.

READ and STUDY

BEFORE YOU READ

Tell students that a lender will be looking at your plans for operation including your proposed organization, including type of ownership; personnel needs; and proposed products or services. Under your marketing plan the lender will be looking for your pricing and promotional plans for the business.

THE MAIN IDEA

Have students list possible components of the marketing and financial sections of the business plan.

STUDY ORGANIZER

Model the study organizer for students by filling in the first blank. A full-size, downloadable study organizer can be found at **marketingessentials.glencoe.com**

WHILE YOU READ Answers might include ideas related to pricing and promotional activities.

TEACH

Discussion Starter

PROPOSED ORGANIZATION AND JOB DESCRIPTIONS

Have students think of a job description they have read. Provide examples from want ads if your students are unfamiliar with job descriptions. Ask students to list and describe the common elements of job descriptions.

Answers should include the purpose and/or title of the job, the qualifications and/or skills needed, the duties of the job, and often the equipment to be used.

TEACHING POINTS

Clarify Ask students to discuss what might be on a job description for a teacher or principal at your school. Then, show students the actual job descriptions so that they can check their understanding of job descriptions.

Expand Have students think of a job they have had or would like to have. Then, have them write a one-page job description for that job. Be sure they include the purpose of the job, the qualifications and skills needed, the duties to be performed, and the equipment to be used.

Critical Thinking

Ask students to write a two- to three-paragraph essay on why it is important that job descriptions be rewritten when a job itself changes.

Case Study

Design Is About More Than Looks!

The designers of Apple's first computer mouse and the first laptop computer formed IDEO in 1991. Throughout the 1990s, the company was a design leader in the tech field, focusing on making products user-friendly. Adding capabilities in psychology and architecture, it has become well-known for designing environments and processes, in addition to products and services. IDEO's innovative approach to design and solving problems has resulted in rave reviews from its clients, who range from Amtrak to clothing designer Prada.

The New Office

The popular comic strip Dilbert focuses on the challenges of working in a typical office cubicle. Scott Adams, Dilbert's creator, worked with IDEO to create a cubicle that would answer people's complaints about lack of privacy, space, tools, and control of the cubicle environment.

The walls of Dilbert's Ultimate Cubicle are snap-in modular blocks, some hollow for storage. Workers can choose from a catalog of different floor and wall modules and furnishings, including a hammock that snaps out of sight, an aquarium, or a hamster wheel. Floor modules flip over to reveal different textures and colors. Extra storage is found in hollow floor blocks, and seating folds down from the cubicle wall.

The cubicle is playful, but also efficient and comfortable. Rather than building expensive new space, IDEO redesigns spaces to be more pleasant, often saving companies money while enhancing the working environment for everyone.

THINK STRATEGICALLY
How would a design consulting firm like IDEO fit into a business plan for a neighborhood coffee shop?

@ Online Action! Go to *marketingessentials.glencoe.com/35/case* to find an activity about business plans.

---

methods, and inventory policies. Finally, it includes your marketing plan. Your marketing plan details your pricing strategies and promotional plans.

Proposed Organization

The organizational section of your business plan is a blueprint or a foundation for the structure of your proposed business. You must construct a clear, solid foundation around which to build the rest of your business.

Types of Ownership

There are three main types of business ownership structures: sole proprietorships, partnerships, and corporations. In this part of the business plan, you will identify which structure you have chosen and why. The structure you choose for your business will impact the remainder of the plan.

Steps in Establishing Your Business

Next, you will outline the steps you plan to take to establish your business. The specific

marketingessentials.glencoe.com

Case Study Design Is About More Than Looks!

Discussion Ask students to think about and describe places where they have worked or have seen others working. Was the space efficient or inefficient? Comfortable or uncomfortable? Have students explain their responses.

THINK STRATEGICALLY **Answer:** Answers will vary. IDEO might design comfortable tables and chairs, an area for games, a section for reading and storing magazines, a way of providing Internet access, or even a more efficient area for making coffee.

@ Online Action! For instructions, ideas, and answer guide, go to the Teacher Center at **marketingessentials.glencoe.com**

Follow Up Ask students to use graph paper or computer software to design an office cubicle. Make sure they include room for a chair, computer, and telephone.

steps you will take depend on how you organize your business.

Staffing

You need to demonstrate to potential investors and lenders that you know how to staff the business so that it operates efficiently and successfully. List your personnel needs in your business plan and identify the people who will perform those jobs. For example, if you are opening a small coffee shop, what staffing needs will you have?

Many new businesses begin as one-person operations. It is not unusual for an entrepreneur to handle everything from management to financial oversight to advertising and promotion.

Job Descriptions

Prepare job descriptions for your partners, employees, and yourself. **Job descriptions** are written statements listing the requirements of a particular job and the skills needed to fulfill those requirements. Each job description includes the purpose of the job, qualifications and skills needed, duties to be performed, equipment to be used, and expected working conditions. Detailed job descriptions help employees know exactly what is expected of them and help you measure their performance against those expectations.

Organization Chart

Once you have completed the job descriptions, develop an organization chart to establish the chain of command within your business. An **organization chart** is a diagram of the company's departments and jobs with lines of authority clearly shown. Your organization chart tells employees to whom they report and to whom they can turn with problems or questions. It also establishes department responsibilities.

Outside Experts

Trained professionals will help you avoid mistakes that could damage your prospects for success. If you decide to use outside professionals, identify them and their responsibilities on your organization chart. Professionals who can help include accountants, attorneys, bankers, and insurance agents.

You can also use technical assistance to identify employment practices in your state or locality. State agencies such as state departments of civil rights, commerce, labor, licensing, and regulation publish many inexpensive or free publications and offer technical assistance to help new entrepreneurs understand various employment laws, rules, and regulations.

Proposed Product or Service

One part of your business plan should include information on the types of products and services you will offer, as well as your potential suppliers, manufacturing plans, and inventory policies. Your investors or lenders will also want to know what the associated costs will be.

If you are selling a product, you will need to develop a plan that details all of the purchasing or manufacturing requirements as well as your inventory policy and the anticipated costs. You need to show how you will manage the products you purchase or manufacture. How much, for example, will you keep on hand? How will you keep track of what to order and what has been sold? Where will you store the products that you have in stock?

Your inventory system depends on the size and scope of your proposed business. Trade associations and many suppliers can give you suggestions for the best inventory control system for your business.

For a service business, you need to develop a plan that addresses who will provide the service to your customers and how and when that will happen. In your plan, state the services provided by your competitors. Then describe the additional or distinct services you will provide and estimate their costs. Point out your edge over the competition.

Proposed Marketing Plan

You are now ready to develop your marketing policies, that is, the way you will price and promote your product. Both promotion of

TEACH CONTINUED

Concept Development

PROPOSED PRODUCT OR SERVICE

Ask students to provide an example of a business they might like to start, such as a café or a video store. Then, have the class list all the information they would need to gather on this product or service. Lists will vary. Make sure students note information on inventory needed, methods of storing and tracking the inventory, services provided, and methods of providing these services.

TEACHING POINTS

Model Invite a local businessperson to class to talk about inventory storage and tracking at his or her business or visit a local business to see inventory storage and tracking firsthand.

Clarify Explain to students that storing inventory can be expensive. Introduce the concept of "just in time" delivery. This method of delivering products only as they are needed cuts down on storage costs.

 Critical Thinking

Ask students: Why might lenders and investors read the financial section of a business plan more closely than other parts of the plan? A sample answer might be that they want to make sure the business is profitable so that they do not lose money.

 Extended Activity

A Business Plan

Use the Internet to obtain SBA copies of the **Business Plan for Retailers,** the **Business Plan for Small Manufacturers,** and the **Business Plan for Home-Based Businesses.** Give each student a copy of each business plan. Have each student compare and contrast these plans, and write a maximum three-page report on the information.

Discussion Starter

SOURCES OF CAPITAL

Read the introductory paragraph to this section aloud. Then ask students to respond to the following question: If you were an investor who was asked to put money into a business that had no business plan, what factors would determine whether or not you would do it?

Possible responses include: whether the potential owner is starting a brand new business or buying an existing business; if the latter, whether or not the existing business is successful; the potential owner's experience with the type of business; and local market needs for the business.

TEACHING POINTS

Demonstrate Have a loan officer from a local lending institution speak about obtaining financing for business start-up. Ask this person to bring to class copies of loan applications so students can become familiar with the terminology and documentation needed to begin the loan application process.

---

product and wise pricing policies are vital to the success of your business (see Figure 35.2).

Pricing Policies

Your business plan must outline your pricing policies. As you learned in Unit 8, you must be able to set a price high enough to cover your costs and make a profit, but competitive enough to attract customers.

Reread Chapters 25, 26, and 27 to review the important factors in pricing.

Promotional Activities

Once pricing policies have been established, you need to describe your promotional activities. Identify how to reach the greatest number of potential customers in your target market in the most efficient and effective way.

You will need visibility, too. That comes from the promotional mix. A firm's promotional mix encompasses advertising, public relations, promotions, and personal selling. Your business plan will outline the mix that will be most effective in persuading prospects (wholesalers, retailers, and consumers) to do business with you. The plan will explain why you have selected this mix and what costs you anticipate. Specify an annual budget for each activity.

Financial Section of the Business Plan

In the financial section of a business plan, lenders and investors can see what monies are needed to start and operate the business. They will also review the entrepreneur's statements of personal and external sources of capital. In addition, the financial section contains statements of projected income and expenses for at least the first year of operation.

Sources of Capital

Capital is the funding needed to finance the operation of a business. It includes all goods used to produce other goods. In business, capital may include owned property and cash resources. In this chapter, the term *capital* refers to anything that can be converted into money.

Equity Capital

Raising money from within your company or by selling part of the interest in the business is called using **equity capital**. The advantage of using equity capital is that you do not need to repay the money or pay interest. However, the investor becomes a co-owner in your business. The larger the share of your business that you sell, the more control you relinquish to your investors. Equity capital sources include personal savings, partners, and shareholders.

Personal Savings

The most common method of financing a business is using personal savings. Although you may not prefer this option, you probably cannot avoid investing part of your savings. As you know, starting any new business involves risk. Your prospective investors and lenders will expect you to share in that risk.

Partners

Having partners is another way to raise capital for your business. Partners may bring in their own money and have access to other sources. As with equity investors, you may have to share control of the business when you bring in a partner.

Shareholders

You may sell stock to shareholders as a way of raising capital. You will need to form a corporation first (see Chapter 33). Shareholders have some influence over general corporate policy decisions, but as long as you hold a majority of the shares, you control the corporation's daily activities.

Debt Capital

Debt capital is a term used to describe borrowed funds that must be repaid. Some debt capital sources are banks, credit unions, the Small Business Administration, friends, relatives, suppliers, and previous business owners.

Debt capital can work to your advantage when you finance a new business because borrowing money and repaying it on a timely basis builds a good credit standing. In turn, a

---

 Extended Activity

Business Financing

Tell students that in a 1999 Levi Institute Survey of Small Businesses, 20 percent of the small companies surveyed relied on a variety of non-bank forms of financing. Ask students if they think state economic development agencies should use public dollars to create economic development loans for small businesses. Ask students to list advantages and disadvantages of such an arrangement. A sample advantage might be that new business expansions create jobs and help the economy. A sample disadvantage might be that the government would be using public tax dollars and public employees to aid private businesses.

Figure 35.2 Organization and Marketing

• **How It Will Work** The second part of a business plan describes the organization of the company and outlines the marketing efforts that will be used to promote the company's products and services. Below are the three aspects of a business summarized in this part.

What factors affect a company's organization?

ORGANIZATION

These three entrepreneurs have decided to become partners in an Internet café, and are signing partnership agreements that set out their responsibilities. They have already identified the perfect location and are negotiating a lease. Their business plan calls for the three partners to be the sole employees until the business becomes profitable, and they are willing to work 70–80 hours a week to make the café a success.

PRODUCTS AND SERVICES

This partner is arranging for Internet service. In the meantime, another is negotiating with coffee wholesalers and equipment suppliers, while the third is working with designers to choose furnishings and fixtures.

MARKETING

The partners' business plan calls for low pricing early on to build a customer base. The owners have confidence that the great pastries and coffee drinks will keep people coming in after the price for online service is increased. Another planned marketing move is putting a sandwich board ad in front of the café.

Online Action!
Go to *marketingessentials.glencoe.com/35/figure/2*
to find a project on planning a business's organization and marketing.

marketingessentials.glencoe.com

Chapter 35 - Developing a Business Plan **749**

Concept Development

EQUITY CAPITAL

Ask students to list some advantages and disadvantages of using equity capital to finance a business.

Advantages might include that the business owner does not have to pay back or pay interest on the equity capital. Disadvantages might be that the owner might lose his or her personal savings, and that taking on partners or shareholders may decrease the amount of control the business owner has of the business.

TEACHING POINTS

Demonstrate Invite a business owner to come to class and talk about how the owner financed his or her business.

Critical Thinking

Ask students: Before taking on a financial partner, what might the business owner want to know about the person? Answers will vary but might include knowing the person's background, education, work experience, business philosophy, and financial situation.

Figure 35.2 Organization and Marketing

Discussion Have students discuss what a potential lender might look for in the three aspects of business outlined in this section. Answers might include: A lender would look at 1) organization to be sure a startup includes employees adequate to the job; 2) products and services, to determine the cost and market potential of products; and 3) marketing, to be sure the products will be aggressively marketed.

Caption Answer Answers may include that organization may be affected by the investment of money, availability of time, and expertise and experience of those involved.

Online Action! For instructions, ideas, and answer guide, go to the Teacher Center at **marketingessentials.glencoe.com**

ASSESS

Review Guide

CONCEPTS

Ask students to recall the purpose of the marketing section of the business plan. The marketing section outlines how you intend to organize the business and explains how you will use advertising and promotional activities to help your business grow and prosper.

KEY TERMS

Have students review key terms in small groups. For example, students can each take turns using one of the key terms in an original sentence.

ONLINE SELF-ASSESSMENT

Have students go to marketingessentials.glencoe.com for the Section 35.2 practice test.

Individualized Review

L1 Assign and review Chapter 35 activities in the Student Activity Workbook.

L2 Assign and review Chapter 35 activities in the Marketing Math Workbook.

L3 Assign and review Chapter 35 activities in the *BusinessWeek* Reader and Case Studies.

Marketing Practice

Have students consider a business they would like to start. Then have them list five ideas for promoting their business such as providing high-quality products or services, having excellent customer service, offering special deals, or providing quick service. Ask students to choose one of these promotional ideas and develop a one-page written plan for its implementation. Then ask students to list and describe at least one strategy for financing their plan.

750

---

good credit standing makes it easier for you to borrow additional money. Although interest must be paid with the loan, that interest becomes a tax-deductible business expense. In addition, by financing with debt capital, you do not share control of the business with lenders.

There is a major disadvantage to debt capital, however. If you cannot pay back your debt, you could be forced into bankruptcy. That does not always mean the business must close, but creditors might take control of the company away from the owner.

Banks

Commercial banks are one of the most common sources of business financing. They know their local areas and economies well and offer a number of different loans and services on competitive and government-regulated terms.

To evaluate a business owner's credit-worthiness, banks rely on the following criteria, called the six Cs of credit: capital, collateral, capability, character, coverage, and circumstances.

- How much of your own money, or capital, is to be invested in your new business? Banks, like other potential investors, will want to know how much capital you are willing to invest into your new venture.
- What assets (anything of value that you own) can be used as collateral for a loan? **Collateral** is something of value that you pledge as payment for a loan in case of default. Lenders will usually require that the value of the collateral be greater than the amount of the loan. Some businesses may use accounts receivable, which is the sum of money owed to a

GLOBAL MARKET

LATIN AMERICA

Targeting the Market

Cellular and long-distance phone companies know that marketing to the Hispanic population is good business. Hispanic Americans use cell phones 10 percent more than the national average.

Immigrants from Mexico and Central and South America tend to call their families back home more than other Americans call these areas. Plans that offer inexpensive rates for calls to countries in Latin America compete for the Hispanic phone dollar. Plans that allow unlimited calling between family members in the States are also more popular with Hispanic customers. And the lack of computers and scarcity of e-mail in many Central American countries means that the phone gets more use by people doing business with vendors in those countries.

Phone companies have learned it is important to distinguish between different segments of the Hispanic market. People whose first language is English have different phone needs than those whose first language is Spanish. It is important for phone companies to target their marketing campaigns to the right customer base, or they will be unsuccessful.

CRITICAL THINKING

In creating a marketing campaign targeted to an ethnic group, what factors would you want to know about the group?

@ Online Action!

Go to *marketingessentials.glencoe.com/35/ global* to find an activity about business plans and international business.

GLOBAL MARKET

Targeting the Market

Discussion Tell students that high school students are also a group that phone companies might market to. Ask students to share what they might want in a phone service.

CRITICAL THINKING **Answer:** When marketing to specialized markets such as an ethnic group, it is important to know about the particular culture, social habits, and lifestyles of that group.

@ Online Action! For instructions, ideas, and answer guide, go to the Teacher Center at marketingessentials.glencoe.com

Follow Up Have students imagine that they are marketing a phone service to immigrants who want to make frequent international calls to friends and family. Ask students to select their market and create appropriate ads.

business by its customers, as collateral. Banks want to know that your loan will be repaid, even if your business fails.

- A résumé of your previous training and related work experience, including professional and personal references, will answer questions about your capability and character. Your personal credit history will also be reviewed to see if you regularly pay your bills on time.
- Banks will want to know the amount of insurance coverage that you carry and the general circumstances of your business. This is outlined in the description and analysis section of your business plan.

Credit Unions

A **credit union** is a cooperative association formed by labor unions or groups of employees for the benefit of its members. Credit unions often charge lower interest rates on loans than banks do. To borrow money from a credit union, however, you must be a member. Check with your parents, guardians, and relatives to determine your eligibility, since credit unions often accept memberships for relatives. Credit unions also use the six Cs of credit to decide whether they will accept your loan application.

Financial Statements

After you have identified your source or sources of capital, the last part of your business plan is to develop your financial statements. Your financial statements display your business's projected income and expenses and help persuade investors to lend you money. (See Chapter 36.)

35.2 AFTER YOU READ

Reviewing Key Terms and Concepts
1. What are the three major parts in the organization and marketing section of the business plan?
2. How is an organization chart used in a business?
3. What are the six Cs of credit?

Integrating Academic Skills

Math
4. A relative decides to lend you $12,500 at a simple 4.5 percent interest rate, payable one year after the start of your new business. How much will you owe at the end of the year?

Economics
5. Investigate a five-year balloon loan from a local lending institution in your community. Find out the rate of interest on a five-year balloon loan of $25,000. Identify the lending source, your monthly loan payment, and the total amount of interest that you would be charged over the five-year period.

 Online Action!

Check your answers at *marketingessentials.glencoe.com/35/read*

marketingessentials.glencoe.com

Chapter 35 - Developing a Business Plan **751**

AFTER YOU READ

Reviewing Key Terms and Concepts
1. Proposed organization (including types of ownership, steps in organizing the business, personnel needs) proposed good or service, and proposed marketing plan.
2. An organization chart is a diagram of the various jobs and functions that are found in a company. It establishes clear lines of authority and official reporting responsibilities for organizations.
3. The six Cs of credit include capital, collateral, capability, character, coverage, and circumstances.

Integrating Academic Skills
4. $13,062.50; Original loan $12,500 + Interest $562.50 (12,500 × .045) = $13,062.50
5. Answers will vary but each student should identify the lending source, the monthly loan payment, and the total amount of interest charged over the five-year period.

 Online Action! Answers at *marketingessentials.glencoe.com/35/read*

CLOSE

- Have students write a 50- to 100-word summary that describes the contents of the organization and marketing section of a business plan.
- Ask students to recall the purpose of the financial section of the business plan.
  The purpose is to estimate the money needed to state and operate the business and to ensure the business will be profitable.

Extended Activity

A Small Business Plan
Have students contact a small business owner and review his or her business plan. Have students report on: difficulties creating the plan; how the difficulties were overcome; and how the plan helps find investors. Ask students to summarize their findings in a 10-minute oral presentation.

Lifelong Learning

CAREER INFORMATION

Have students go to marketingessentials.glencoe.com and find Chapter 35 Careers page and click on the link for the American Marketing Association's Careers Strategies and Tips. Ask students to select one article, read it, and summarize it in three short paragraphs.

BUSINESS AND MARKETING PLANS

Due to the importance of the business plan, encourage students to further research this area of marketing and business. Business magazines and books devoted to the subject include *Inc.* magazine's *How to Write a Successful Business Plan*. Taking courses on writing a business plan would also be valuable.

Primary Source

Ask students to go to marketingessentials.glencoe.com and find Chapter 35 Resources. Ask them to click on the link for American Marketing Association's marketing dictionary and read the definitions of any terms related to developing a business that plan they find.

● THINKING CRITICALLY

Benefits include making all the decisions, keeping all the profits, and variety in what you do. Downsides include having to do all the work and assuming all the risks.

@ Online Action!

For instructions, ideas, and answer guide, go to the Teacher Center at marketingessentials.glencoe.com

---

BARBARA DAY, M.S., R.D., C.N.
PUBLISHER
KENTUCKIANA HEALTH FITNESS MAGAZINE

Aptitudes, Abilities, and Skills

Organization, strong communication skills, sales ability, and an outgoing personality

? What do you do at work?
As a publisher, assignments editor, marketing specialist, writer, operations manager, proofreader, radio talk show host, and television guest, my normal working day is very diverse. I juggle many tasks during the course of my workday and I really thrive in that type of environment. My workday starts at 6:00 A.M. answering e-mails and writing columns. Working seven days a week is not unusual.

Education and Training

General business degrees are helpful with running the behind-the-scenes aspects of the business, although many niche publishers are entirely self-taught.

? What skills are most important to you?
Flexibility, organization, and good communication skills are essential as an entrepreneurial business person. To be a publisher, I have had to learn as I go. I am the only full-time person in my organization, so if a job needs to be done, I generally have to do it myself or contract the work out. Having a business background is essential for balancing the budget. I have an undergraduate degree in dietetics and institution administration and a master's degree in community nutrition with an emphasis on exercise science. Every type of job I have had since I graduated from college has been laced with program development—I have developed quite the entrepreneurial spirit—from self-publishing books to starting health promotion programs for the Department of Defense to local programs.

Career Path

Niche publications can be started by anyone, at any time—but to ensure success, study both the topic and the marketplace to see if they are a good fit. Larger alternative weeklies make good training grounds for this career.

? What is your key to success?
Believing in your product and yourself. When I hit an obstacle or roadblock, instead of accepting the situation, I regroup and go in another direction.

● THINKING CRITICALLY

What are some of the benefits of running a one-person company? What might be some of the down-sides?

Online Action!

Go to *marketingessentials.glencoe.com/ 35/careers* to find a career-related activity.

Test-Taking Strategies

Give students the opportunity to review their notes or ask questions before giving in-class assignments. For example, you might list the parts of a business plan on the board, and then ask students to explain why each part is important.

CHAPTER **35** REVIEW

FOCUS on KEY POINTS

SECTION 35.1

● The three components of a business plan are description and analysis of the proposed business; organizational and marketing plan; and financial plan.

● The description and analysis should include: type of business; business philosophy; product or service; self-analysis; trading area analysis; market segment analysis; and location analysis.

SECTION 35.2

● The organization and marketing plan outlines how the business will be organized and how it will be promoted.

● Most entrepreneurs need to borrow money to start a business. Investors and lenders want to see financial information about a business before they commit to making an investment.

● The financial plan should include sources of capital for the business and its projected income and expenses.

REVIEW VOCABULARY

Review the definitions for the following vocabulary terms with a classmate.

1. business plan (p. 738)

2. business philosophy (p. 739)

3. trading area (p. 741)

4. buying behavior (p. 743)

5. job descriptions (p. 747)

6. organization chart (p. 747)

7. equity capital (p. 748)

8. debt capital (p. 748)

9. collateral (p. 750)

10. credit union (p. 751)

REVIEW FACTS and IDEAS

11. Why should aspiring entrepreneurs conduct a self-analysis as part of a business plan? (35.1)

12. Why is it important to know the disposable income of potential customers? (35.1)

13. What sources can an entrepreneur access to research the competition for a proposed product or service? (35.1)

14. Why should personnel needs be identified in a business plan? (35.2)

15. What is the best way to promote a new business? (35.2)

16. What are debt capital and equity capital? (35.2)

17. What is the most common method of financing a business? (35.2)

Chapter 35 - Developing a Business Plan 753

REVIEW FACTS and IDEAS

11. Self-analysis identifies your personal education, strengths, weaknesses, and a plan for personal development. It is important because it shows potential lenders that you can understand the industry and have the required skills for running a successful business.

12. Disposable income is personal income minus taxes. You need to know if the potential market has enough customers with enough buying income to support a proposed business.

13. The Internet, *Yellow Pages*, annual reports, trade associations, the local Chamber of Commerce, Small Business Development Centers, and business publications.

14. Potential investors need to know that you can identify the essential jobs your business will need to run properly.

15. Promotion plans will differ depending on the product. You must identify your target market and determine the promotional mix that will best reach that market.

16. Debt capital is money that is raised from lenders. Equity capital is money that raised by selling part of the business.

17. The most common method of financing a business is personal savings.

FOCUS on KEY POINTS

Ask volunteers to read each summary aloud. After each one, give students a few minutes to ask questions for clarification.

REVIEW VOCABULARY

See glossary for definitions of **1–10.** A sample definition might read:

1. A *business plan* is a proposal that outlines a strategy for turning a business idea into a reality.

BUILD SKILLS

18. Workplace Skills
Papers will vary; students should display an understanding of the concept of government involvement via licensing.

19. Technology Applications
Lists will vary and should display an understanding of the resources needed by an entrepreneur.

20. Math Practice
Jonesville has the larger BPI and is a more favorable location.

Jonesville Buying Power Index = .02277; (.5 × .0271) + (.3 × .0194) + (.2 × .017) = .02277

Leadville = .01431; (.5 × .0151) + (.3 × .013) + (.2 × .0143) = .01431

DEVELOP CRITICAL THINKING

21. Researching Small Business Services
Answers will vary; reports should show an understanding of why the selected resources can help a business develop a business plan.

22. Decide for Yourself
Student answers will differ but should demonstrate an understanding of the consequences of failing to repay debt discussed in the chapter. While some investors or co-owners may not force bankruptcy, they may insist on telling the owner how to run the business.

BUILD SKILLS

18. Workplace Skills
Legal Some businesses and their employees must be licensed before they can open or perform their duties. Prepare a 250-word paper on the reasons that government agencies often require a license for certain business owners and their employees.

19. Technology Applications
Finding Resources Research on the Internet all the sources of business information that may be useful to an entrepreneur. List your findings and organize the information and URLs into broad categories such as government resources, trade organizations, and so on.

20. Math Practice
Number Crunching Given the facts below, determine the buying power indexes for the cities of Jonesville and Leadville. Which city would be a more favorable location for a new business?

Buying Power Index = .5 × Area's Percentage for U.S. Effective Buying Power + .3 × Area's Percentage of U.S. Retail Sales + .2 × Area's Percentage of U.S. Population

Jonesville Percentage of U.S. Effective Buying Power = .0271
Jonesville Percentage of U.S. Retail Sales = .0194
Jonesville Percentage of U.S. Population = .017

Leadville Percentage of U.S. Effective Buying Power = .0151
Leadville Percentage of U.S. Retail Sales = .013
Leadville Percentage of U.S. Population = .0143

DEVELOP CRITICAL THINKING

21. Researching Small Business Services
The Senior Corps of Retired Executives (SCORE) is a voluntary group of counselors who help America's small businesses. SCORE provides many resources to help individuals write business plans. Locate the SCORE Web site and find the address of the SCORE office nearest to your school. List at least three resources available from SCORE to help you develop a comprehensive business plan. Explain why and how these resources will help.

22. Decide for Yourself
"While debt capital can work to your advantage when establishing a business, there are many disadvantages if you cannot pay back your debt. Bankruptcy is one of these disadvantages, however it may not be the worst one." Explain what this statement means and decide whether you agree or disagree.

 ## Formative Assessment

Formative assessment is an essential component of classroom work. This type of assessment provides information that is then used as feedback to modify teaching and meet student needs.

L1 Read definitions of the key terms and have students name the corresponding term.

L2 List all the parts of the business plan on the board. Ask students to provide examples of what might go in each part.

L3 Ask students to create an outline for a business plan for a business thy would like to start.

 Reteach **If the results of this formative assessment seem low, consider the following activity:**

Write the elements of a business plan on the board in a random order. Have students rewrite them in correct order and describe the purpose of each.

APPLY CONCEPTS

23. Describing and Analyzing a Business Situation

Begin developing a business plan using information in this chapter, from your instructor, or from DECA Entrepreneurship Event guidelines. Describe the type of business, the product/service involved, factors that make the business appealing, and the factors you think will make it successful. Describe your aspirations and career objectives, education, and related work experiences. Finally, make a chart of your potential advantages over your competitor(s).

Activity Use a word processing program to prepare your project. Be ready to present it to your class.

24. Developing an Organization and Marketing Plan

Continue the business plan that you created in the previous activity. Create an organization chart for your proposed business. The plan should contain a budget, pricing policies, and a method to evaluate its effectiveness. List special promotional events for each month of the year for your business.

Activity Using a word processing program and a spreadsheet program, organize a presentation for your classmates as if they were potential lenders.

NET SAVVY

25. Finding Small Business Resources

Find the U.S. Small Business Administration (SBA) Web site. Summarize at least five resources that are available through the SBA for new business start-ups in a one- to two-page written report.

marketingessentials.glencoe.com

Role Play: Developing a Business Plan

Situation You are to assume the role of loan officer for a community bank. You are having a chat with a friend (judge) you have known for several years who has been working as assistant manager of a local restaurant for the past three years. Your friend (judge) has decided to purchase and operate a coffee shop and is informally discussing the possibility of applying for a loan from your bank. Your friend (judge) has several questions about completing a business plan.

Activity You are to explain to your friend (judge) the importance of each of the three sections of a good business plan.

Evaluation You will be evaluated on how well you meet the following performance indicators:

- Explain the nature of business plans
- Develop company objectives
- Explain the nature and scope of financing
- Develop a business plan
- Explain loan evaluation criteria used by lending institutions

 Online Action!

For more information and DECA Prep practice, go to *marketingessentials.glencoe.com/35/DECA*

The students should be evaluated on the performance indicators noted in the role play. For another DECA role play, go to the Competitive Events Workbook or the Student Activity Workbook, or go to **marketingessentials.glencoe.com/35/DECA**

Online Action! For instructions, ideas, and answer guide, go to the Teacher Center at **marketingessentials.glencoe.com**

DECA Advisors Corner

Using the guidelines for the Entrepreneurship Participating Event from the DECA Guide, have each student develop a business prospectus for starting his or her own business. The advisor can put together judges and have a competition to decide which plans will be entered in state competition.

APPLY CONCEPTS

23. Describing and Analyzing a Business Situation

Projects should describe the type of business, the product/service involved, factors that make the business appealing, the factors that the student thinks will make it successful, and a chart which compares and contrasts the competition. Career and work objectives and experiences should also be relayed.

24. Developing an Organization and Marketing Plan

Presentations should contain a budget, selection of media, promotional events, and a plan to evaluate effectiveness.

NET SAVVY

25. Finding Small Business Resources

Reports will vary; students should demonstrate an understanding of the resources available on the SBA Web site.

MINI-QUIZ

Administer the Mini-Quiz orally. Have students fill in the blanks.

1. A proposal that describes every part of a new business to an investor is called a(n) _____. (business plan)

2. A business _____ tells how an individual thinks a business should run and demonstrates an understanding of its role in the marketplace. (philosophy)

3. Written statements about the requirements of a particular job are known as _____. (job descriptions)

For an expanded chapter quiz, go to Chapter 35 in the TeacherWorks CD-ROM and to Chapter 35 in the **ExamView®** Pro Test Generator CD-ROM.

Chapter Overview

This chapter tells how to identify and plan for the capital needs of a proposed business by developing the financial section of a business plan. It discusses estimating start-up costs and personal financial statement. It explains the need for and preparation of an income statement, balance sheet, and cash flow statement.

⊘ BUILD BACKGROUND ⊜

Work with the class to develop a sample personal budget for a college student for one month, listing their assets and their liabilities, or debts. Encourage students should make rough estimates of the costs of tuition, rent, food, and bills, as well as per month income and the value of assets such as a car. Tell students that this information can be used to prepare a personal financial statement.

Why It's Important

No company can run without capital. The most common reason for writing a business plan is to outline the finances needed to start and continue a business. Investors and lenders want to know why their money is needed, how the money is used, and how the money is paid back. The financial section of the business plan provides this information.

Prepare to Read

Before the students read the text, ask them to read all the figures and their accompanying captions. Have them study the various financial statements, worksheets, financing sources, expenses, income statement, and so on. This allows the students to get a jumpstart on comprehension by visually digesting complex business jargon.

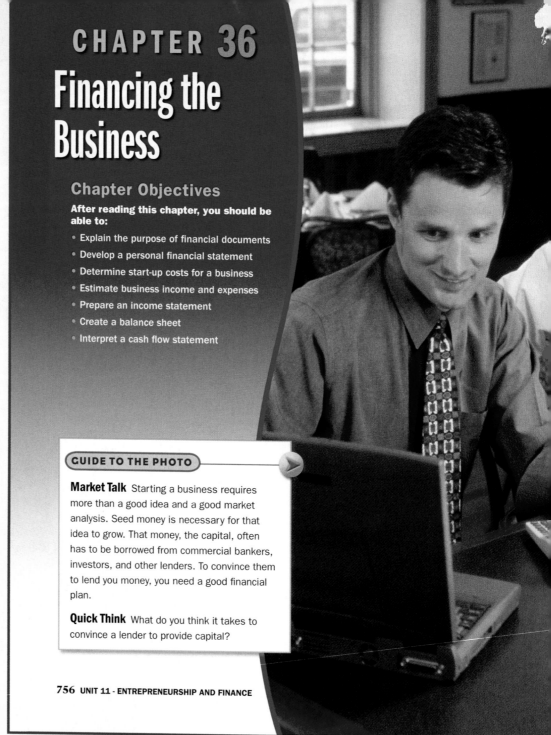

CHAPTER 36
Financing the Business

Chapter Objectives

After reading this chapter, you should be able to:

- Explain the purpose of financial documents
- Develop a personal financial statement
- Determine start-up costs for a business
- Estimate business income and expenses
- Prepare an income statement
- Create a balance sheet
- Interpret a cash flow statement

> **GUIDE TO THE PHOTO**
>
> **Market Talk** Starting a business requires more than a good idea and a good market analysis. Seed money is necessary for that idea to grow. That money, the capital, often has to be borrowed from commercial bankers, investors, and other lenders. To convince them to lend you money, you need a good financial plan.
>
> **Quick Think** What do you think it takes to convince a lender to provide capital?

GUIDE TO THE PHOTO

Market Talk Ask students if they think it is better to overestimate or underestimate expenses in the financial plan section of a business plan. Have them defend their reasoning.

Quick Think Answers might include accurate numbers, a repayment plan, a profitable margin, and a convincing marketing plan.

Follow Up Ask students on whom they would rely to assist them in the preparation of the financial section of a business plan.

marketingessentials.glencoe.com

THE DECA CONNECTION

Performance indicators represent key skills and knowledge. Relating them to the concepts explained in this chapter is your key to success in DECA events. These acronyms represent DECA events that involve knowledge of concepts in this chapter.

AAAL	FMAL	MMS*	TMDM*
AAML*	FMDM*	QSRM*	TSE*
ADC*	FMML*	RMAL	VPM
BSM	FSRM*	RMML*	
EMDM*	HMDM*	SMDM*	

In all these DECA events you should be able to follow these performance indicators:

- Explain the nature of overhead/operating costs
- Explain an employee's role in expense control
- Explain the concept of accounting
- Calculate net sales
- Describe the nature of cash flow statements
- Explain the nature of balance sheets
- Describe the nature of profit and loss statements
- Describe the nature of business records
- Describe the nature of budgets

All the events with an asterisk (*) also include these performance indicators:

- Analyze cash flow patterns
- Calculate financial ratios
- Interpret financial statements
- Analyze operating results in relation to budget/industry
- Prepare financial statements for audit
- Develop expense-control plans
- Develop a company's budget

DECA PREP

Check your understanding of DECA performance indicators with the DECA activity in this chapter's review. For more information and DECA Prep practice, go to *marketingessentials.glencoe.com/36/DECA*

Chapter 36 - Financing the Business 757

THE DECA CONNECTION

DECA events that require knowledge of financing the business are described here. Discuss the performance indicators to make sure students understand how to demonstrate their understanding.

The events acronyms stand for:

AAAL:	Apparel and Accessories Marketing Series, AL
AAML:	Apparel and Accessories Marketing Series, ML
ADC:	Advertising Campaign Event
BSM:	Business Services Marketing Series
EMDM:	E-Commerce Management Team Decision Making Event
FMAL:	Food Marketing Series, AL
FMDM:	Financial Analysis Management Team Decision Making Event
FMML:	Food Marketing Series, ML
FSRM:	Full Service Restaurant Management Series
HMDM:	Hospitality Services Management Team Decision Making Event
MMS:	Marketing Management Series
QSRM:	Quick Serve Restaurant Management Series
RMAL:	Retail Merchandising Series, AL
RMML:	Retail Merchandising Series, ML
SMDM:	Sports and Entertainment Marketing Management Team Decision Making Event
TMDM:	Travel and Tourism Marketing Management Team Decision Making Event
TSE:	Technical Sales Event
VPM:	Vehicles and Petroleum Marketing Series

DECA PREP

Find timed DECA Prep activities correlated to the Competitive Events Workbook for students and DECA tips for teachers at **marketingessentials.glencoe.com/36/DECA**

CHAPTER 36 Classroom Resources

For the Teacher

- TeacherWorks
- marketingessentials.glencoe.com
- Interactive Chalkboard
- **ExamView®** Pro Test Generator
- Fast File Unit 11

For the Student

- *Marketing Essentials* Online Edition
- Student Activity Workbook
- Marketing Math Workbook
- Marketing Research Project Workbook
- School-to-Work Activity Workbook
- Competitive Events Workbook
- *BusinessWeek* Reader and Case Studies
- marketingessentials.glencoe.com

FOCUS

Introducing the Section

COLLABORATIVE ACTIVITY

Divide students into four groups, each one representing a type of business: manufacturing, wholesale, retail, or service. Give each group five to 10 minutes to brainstorm a list of capital requirements for its start-up business.

Preteaching Key Terms

Ask students to write the key terms in their journal. Under each word, leave a few blank lines. They should write *definition* and *example* directly below the key term. On the definition line, ask students to write a phrase or two for the meaning of the word; on the *example* line, ask students to write a sentence using the word. When they come across the key word in the text, they can check their notes and rewrite their definitions or examples as necessary.

- personal financial statement
- asset
- liability
- net worth
- start-up costs

Online Activity

E-Dictionary

Tell students that in order to demystify business jargon, it is important to rely on a business and finance dictionary. Ask students to find a reputable and free online business dictionary they can consult throughout this chapter. If they come across a term or concept for which they want greater clarification, they can write it down in their journal and consult the e-dictionary.

OBJECTIVES

- Explain the purpose of financial documents
- Develop a personal financial statement
- Determine start-up costs for a business

KEY TERMS

- personal financial statement
- asset
- liability
- net worth
- start-up costs

Preparing Financial Documents

READ and STUDY

BEFORE YOU READ
Predict Why would you need to include financial documents in a new business plan?

THE MAIN IDEA
The most common reason for writing a business plan is to obtain financing for a business. To get the money you need to start your business, you will need to prepare many financial statements.

STUDY ORGANIZER
In a chart like the one below, outline the steps in the preparation of a financial statement.

Organized Financing

1. Prepare financial documents.
2. _____
3. _____

WHILE YOU READ
Connect Why do you think it is necessary to develop personal and start-up financial statements?

The Financial Part of a Business Plan

Financial information is a major component of a business plan. In your business plan, you will include financial documents that describe your personal finances as well as the financial needs of your business. By preparing financial statements, you will be able to determine the amount of money needed to operate the business as well as the amount that must be borrowed, if any.

READ and STUDY

BEFORE YOU READ
Financial documents help to determine how much money can be made by the business.

THE MAIN IDEA
Ask students to think about all the possible categories they might expect to see on financial spreadsheets.

STUDY ORGANIZER
Model the study organizer for students by filling in the first blank. A full-size, downloadable study organizer can be found at **marketingessentials.glencoe.com**

WHILE YOU READ
Explain that a personal financial statement shows your net worth and how you manage money; start-up costs show what it will cost to start the business.

When you borrow money, the lender will want to see proof that you are able to repay a loan. The lender will examine your credit history, collateral (items you own that can be sold to pay off the loan), and prospects for business success. The financial documents you include in your business plan will help show that you will be able to pay off your loan.

The five important financial documents in a business plan are the personal financial statement, the start-up cost estimate, the income statement, the balance sheet, and the cash flow statement. In this section, you will learn about the first two.

The Personal Financial Statement

The **personal financial statement** is a summary of your current personal financial condition—a snapshot of your finances. It is an important part of any loan application for a new business. It measures your financial progress to date and shows how well you have met your personal financial obligations in the past. It compares your assets and liabilities at a particular point in time. An **asset** is anything of monetary value that you own, such as cash, checking and savings accounts, real estate, or stocks. A **liability** is a debt that you owe to others, such as credit card debt, school loans, car payments, or taxes.

Assets

To develop a personal financial statement, you first list your assets. Be realistic about the current value of your assets. For example, if you have a car worth $11,700, do not round it up to $12,000. Be sure to list all your cash assets (checking and savings accounts), any investments (stocks, bonds, mutual funds, and retirement funds), and personal assets (furniture, cars, clothes, and home). You will need to estimate the present value of each item. A lender will look for assets that you can sell to

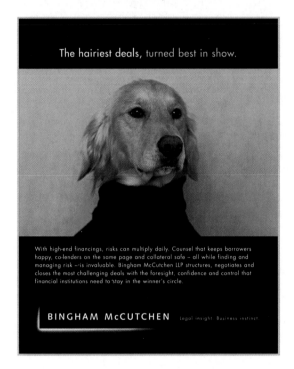

The hairiest deals, turned best in show.

With high-end financings, risks can multiply daily. Counsel that keeps borrowers happy, co-lenders on the same page and collateral safe – all while finding and managing risk – is invaluable. Bingham McCutchen LLP structures, negotiates and closes the most challenging deals with the foresight, confidence and control that financial institutions need to stay in the winner's circle.

BINGHAM McCUTCHEN   *Legal insight. Business instinct.*

THE LENDER'S POINT of VIEW This ad is for a national legal firm that handles high-level financial transactions. It facilitates deals and advises lenders and borrowers.

Why would an entrepreneur need such financial and legal guidance?

Chapter 36 - Financing the Business **759**

TEACH

Discussion Starter

THE PERSONAL FINANCIAL STATEMENT

Ask students to identify for themselves which of the following categories best describes their personal cash flow situation: *spend every penny they earn, spend today and accumulate debt,* or *assets are greater than the spending.* Ask them to reflect on their own personal financial situation including their own spending and savings habits.

TEACHING POINTS

Clarify Remind students that, for many people, more than one of these categories may apply.

Model Bring into class the personal financial statement form found on the Small Business Administration Web site. Fill in a hypothetical person's financial information. Discuss this person's cash flow versus spending habits.

Online Activity

Check Your Credit

Invite students to research how they can checking their credit report for free at one of several online credit reporting sites. Individuals are allowed to check their credit reports for free through such services once a year. Remind students that checking your credit report is a good deterrent against identity theft.

Virtual Business

Introduce financing to students using Knowledge Matters' Virtual Business Retailing visual simulation, *Financing.* In this simulation, students evaluate different financing methods to finance their start-up businesses.

TEACH CONTINUED

Concept Development

ASSETS AND DEBTS

Ask students to generate a list of assets and debts people who want to start a business might typically have.

TEACHING POINTS

Explain Tell students that financial health is as responsible and important as a person's health. Knowing your financial situation allows you to set financial goals, which might include starting a business, owning a car or house, attending college, saving for retirement, and so on.

Summarize Expand the discussion of assets and liabilities (debts). Give students examples of liquid assets and various liabilities (debts). Explain that these are specific types of assets and liabilities (debts).

Enrichment

ESTIMATING START-UP COSTS

Tell students that they are business consultants and entrepreneurs come to them with questions regarding starting a business. Ask them to generate a list of questions new business owners might bring to their attention.

PRACTICE 1 ANSWERS

1. Total assets are $25,200
   ($15,000 + $5,000 + $1,000 + $1,700 + $2,500 = $25,200)
2. Total Liabilities are $16,500
   ($10,000 + $5,000 + $1,500 = $16,500)
3. Net worth is $8,700 ($25,200 − $16,500 = $8,700)

A MATTER OF ETHICS

Borrowing From Parents

Serena, Frank, and Dominick are three friends who are going into business together. They plan to open a small sunglasses shop in a large mall. They have a clear business plan and are certain the shop will be a success if they can get the financing they need. In preparation for meeting with a bank loan officer, each of them has prepared a personal financial statement. Being young, they do not have a lot of assets, and they are concerned the bank will not consider them good risks for a loan.

Inflating Assets

Dominick asked his parents if they would add his name to the title of their house, just until the start-up financing comes in. They agreed, so Dominick has listed the family home as an asset. That has increased his net worth by $200,000. He feels the bank will look more favorably on the loan application as a result.

THINKING ETHICALLY

If you were one of his partners, what would you say to Dominick about this arrangement?

@ Online Action!

Go to *marketingessentials.glencoe.com/36/ethics* to find an activity on ethics and capital loans.

---

pay off the business loan if your business does not do as well as expected. Provide a total value for each asset and a grand total for all assets.

Debts

Next, list your debts, including your charge accounts, mortgage balance, and school

---

and automobile loans. Calculate a total for each type of debt and a grand total for all debts.

Net Worth

Next, calculate your personal net worth. Your **net worth** is the difference between your assets and your liabilities. To find a business's net worth, subtract its debts from its assets. For corporations, net worth is called stockholders' equity; for partnerships and sole proprietorships, it is called owner's equity.

Your personal financial statement is one way to determine whether you and your business are good credit risks. A lender will require a copy of your personal tax returns to see how you have earned money in the past. A lender will also request a credit report to determine how well you have paid past debts. If you plan to continue working at another job, the lender will be interested in whether that income can cover your personal expenses until your new business becomes profitable.

PRACTICE 1

1. You have assets of $15,000 (car), $5,000 (savings), $1,000 (cash value of life insurance), $1,700 (cash), and personal property worth $2,500. What are your total assets?
2. You have liabilities of $10,000 (car loan), $5,000 (student loan), and $1,500 (credit card balances). What are your total liabilities?
3. What is your net worth?

Note: Answers to all practice sets at *marketingessentials.glencoe.com*

Estimating Start-Up Costs

Before starting your business, you need to know how much it will cost. **Start-up costs** are projections of how much money you will need for your first year of operation (see Figure 36.1). You also need an estimate of the long-term operating costs that you anticipate after the first year.

By assessing these start-up costs prior to getting involved in a project, you are protecting

 marketingessentials.glencoe.com

A MATTER OF ETHICS   Borrowing From Parents

Discussion Ask students to discuss the advantages and disadvantages of starting a business with several friends.

THINKING ETHICALLY **Answer:** Answers will vary. Dominick's parents have pledged their home as collateral for the new business. If the business fails, his parents' home equity may be at risk for any unpaid bills. While his partners may like the opportunity to increase their personal asset statement, they and Dominick's parents are taking a huge risk.

@ Online Action! For instruction, ideas, and answer guide, go to the Teacher Center at **marketingessentials.glencoe.com**

Follow Up Ask students how interest might interfere with paying back the loan to the lender when the store's sales are barely breaking even.

Figure 36.1 — Start-Up Cost Worksheet

• **Estimating Costs** The SBA provides many forms and worksheets to help new business owners project monthly expenses.

Why is a start-up worksheet helpful to a new entrepreneur?

ESTIMATED MONTHLY EXPENSES

Item	Your estimate of monthly expenses based on sales of $_____ per year Column 1	Your estimate of how much cash you need to start your business (See column 3) Column 2	What to put in column 2. (These figures are typical for one kind of business. You will have to decide how many months to allow for your business.) Column 3
Salary of owner	$	$	2 times column 1
All other salaries and wages			3 times column 1
Rent			3 times column 1
Advertising			3 times column 1
Delivery expenses			3 times column 1
Supplies			3 times column 1
Telephone and Internet			3 times column 1
Other utilities			3 times column 1
Insurance			Payment required by insurance company
Taxes, including Social Security			4 times column 1
Interest			3 times column 1
Maintenance			3 times column 1
Legal and other professional fees			3 times column 1
Miscellaneous			3 times column 1
STARTING COSTS YOU ONLY HAVE TO PAY ONCE			Leave column 2 blank
Fixtures and equipment			See separate worksheet
Decorating and remodeling			Talk it over with a contractor
Installation of fixtures and equipment			Talk to suppliers from whom you buy these
Starting inventory			Supplies will probably help you estimate this
Deposits with public utilities			Find out from utility companies
Legal and other professional fees			Lawyer, accountant, and so on
Licenses and permits			Find out from city offices what you need
Advertising and promotion			Estimate what you'll use for opening
Accounts receivable			What you need to buy more stock until credit customers pay
Cash			For unexpected expenses or losses, special purchases, etc.
Other			Make a separate list and enter total
TOTAL ESTIMATED CASH YOU NEED TO START	$	$	Add up all the numbers in column 2

 Online Action!

Go to *marketingessentials.glencoe.com/36/figure/1* to find a project on start-up costs.

marketingessentials.glencoe.com

Chapter 36 - Financing the Business **761**

Figure 36.1 — Start-Up Cost Worksheet

Discussion After students have reviewed **Figure 36.1**, discuss how students would find the various figures needed to complete the worksheet. Ask them to give specific examples for particular items.

Caption Answer This worksheet will help an entrepreneur predict the one-time start-up costs as well as the ongoing costs of a new business.

 Online Action! For instructions, ideas, and answer guide, go to the Teacher Center at **marketingessentials.glencoe.com**

 Follow Up Have students research, using one of the resources given in the text, to determine the start-up costs for a selected business. Then have them use those numbers to create this worksheet.

TEACH CONTINUED

Individualized Math Skills

L1 Give students the following scenario: You estimate that your business start-up costs will be $10,200. You have $8,400.

a. What percentage of the total amount do you have?
   82%; $8,400 ÷ $10,200 = 0.82 = 82%

b. What percentage of the total amount do you need?
   18%; $10,200 − $8,400 = $1,800; $1,800 ÷ $10,800 = 0.1766 or 0.18. Or 1.00 − 0.82 = 0.18 = 18%

L2 Give students the following scenario: You estimate that your business start-up costs will be $10,200. You have $8,400.

a. What percentage of the total amount do you have?
   $8,400 ÷ $10,200 = 0.82 = 82%

b. What percentage of the total amount do you need?
   $10,200 − $8,400 = $1,800; $1,800 ÷ $10,800 = 0.1766 or 0.18; 0.18 = 18%

c. Subtract the decimal numbers you calculated for a and b. What is your answer?
   0.82 − 0.18 = 0.64

d. Multiply the decimal numbers you calculated for a and b. What is your answer?
   0.82 × 0.18 = 0.1476

e. Divide your answer for a by your answer for b. Round your answer to the hundredth.
   4.56; 0.82 ÷ 0.18 = 4.55555 or 4.56

L3 Give students the following scenario: You refigured your business start-up costs and determined that you will need about 15 percent more than the amount you originally anticipated, which was $10,200. How much money will you need altogether to start your business?
   $11,730; or $10,200 × 0.15 = $1,530; $10,200 ÷ $1,530 = $11,730

761

Review Guide

CONCEPTS

Ask students to list the start-up costs for a new business.

Answers may include the nature of the proposed business, the size of the business, the amount of inventory needed, the timing of cash revenues and expenses, and the time between using start-up funds from personal assets or potential lenders and the first sales of the business.

KEY TERMS

Have students review key terms, their spellings, and definitions in small groups.

ONLINE SELF-ASSESSMENT

Have students go to marketingessentials.glencoe.com for the Section 36.1 practice test.

Individualized Review

L1 Assign and review Chapter 36 activities in the Student Activity Workbook.

L2 Assign and review Chapter 36 activities in the Marketing Math Workbook.

L3 Assign and review Chapter 36 activities in the *BusinessWeek* Reader and Case Studies.

Marketing Practice

Ask students to use a word processing program to create a letter to the state department of commerce requesting general information about the steps involved with starting a business in your state.

Figure 36.2 **Financing Sources**

• **Finding Funding** There are several funding sources for new businesses.

What is the difference between a primary and a secondary source of financing?

Primary Sources		Secondary Sources	
Long-term financing	*Short-term financing*	*Long-term financing*	*Short-term financing*
• Personal financing	• Personal financing	• Business alliances	• SBA CAPLines
• Family and friends	• Family and friends	• SBA regular 7(a) program	• Consumer finance companies
• Private investors	• Credit cards	• Venture capital	• Commercial finance companies
• Equity financing	• Credit unions	• SBICs	• State and local public financing
• Leasing	• Trade credit	• State and local public financing	
• Credit unions	• Banks	• Franchising	
• SBA LowDoc	• SBA Microloans	• Asset-based financing	
	• SBA LowDoc		

@ Online Action! Go to *marketingessentials.glencoe.com/36/figure/2* to find a project on financing a business.

yourself and helping to ensure the viability of the business. You will need to spend money on goods and services ranging from furniture to advertising. The costs vary depending on the type of business.

Although start-up costs vary, they are based on factors such as:

- **The nature of your proposed business** Manufacturing, wholesale, and retail businesses all have different needs and requirements.
- **The size of your business** Small businesses usually do not require as much money to start as big ones.
- **The amount and kind of inventory needed** For example, it is much more costly to purchase inventory for a large supermarket than for a neighborhood convenience store.
- **The estimated time between starting the business and earning income from the first sales.**
- **The operating expenses** Expenses must be paid before cash is received from sales.

Business start-up costs may be one-time costs or continuing costs.

- **One-time costs** are expenses that will not be repeated after you begin the business. Examples of one-time costs are licenses

and permits; deposits for telephone installation; and charges for installation of equipment, fixtures, and machinery.
- **Continuing costs** are operating expenses you will pay throughout the life of the business. Examples of continuing costs are payroll, monthly rent, advertising, supplies, insurance, repairs, maintenance, and taxes. Most businesses are not profitable immediately, so include at least three months of continuing costs when estimating the amount of cash you will need to get started.

You can get information from several sources to help you plan your financial needs. The Small Business Administration (SBA) provides information to people who want to start a new business. The SBA offers a wide variety of loan programs. These programs help small businesses borrow money at reasonable interest rates from traditional lenders. The SBA has developed a worksheet for estimating start-up costs and operating expenses for new businesses.

You can also get estimates of start-up costs from people who are already in a similar business or from a trade association. State and local government agencies, such as your state

 marketingessentials.glencoe.com

Figure 36.2 **Financing Sources**

Discussion After students have reviewed **Figure 36.2**, ask them to brainstorm and discuss some basic differences between primary and secondary sources.

Caption Answer A primary source of financing has the borrower using personal means to acquire funding, whereas a secondary source of financing relies on outside lenders to provide the funds for a new business.

@ Online Action! For instructions, ideas, and answer guide, go to the Teacher Center at marketingessentials.glencoe.com

Follow Up Ask students whether they would prefer to use primary or secondary sources of financing to start a new business. Have them explain their answers to the class.

department of commerce and local chamber of commerce, are valuable sources of cost information (see Figure 36.2).

PRACTICE 2

1. Your business has one-time costs of $25,000 and average monthly costs of $3,600. What are your total costs for the first quarter of operation? Using the same average monthly costs, what are your total costs for the year?

Personal Costs

Unless you are starting your new business while still working at another job, you will need money to live on during the start-up phase. Your personal costs are those expenses that are necessary for you to live. You will need to project your monthly living expenses and household cash needs for at least the first

year of business. When starting a new business, you may be able to meet your personal expenses by working at another job or by relying on income from your parents or a spouse.

You may choose not to work outside your business or seek any other source of income, but you must plan to have enough cash on hand to pay your personal expenses. Some experts suggest you have enough start-up capital to pay for up to six months of living expenses.

Set aside the money for living expenses in a savings account or another account from which you can withdraw money without penalty. Do not use the money for any other purpose. This fund will help you get through the start-up period. The amount should cover living expenses such as regular monthly payments, household operating expenses, food expenses, personal expenses, and tax expenses.

CLOSE

Ask students to recall and provide answers to the following questions:

- **Why is financial information included as part of a business plan?**
  It helps determine how the business will operate financially. Lenders want to see financial documents you need for a loan.

- **Why would a bank would require a borrower to insure property that the bank would hold as collateral?**
  In case of the property's damage or loss, the insurance company will repay the lender.

- **Have students generate a list of one-time start-up costs and the continuing costs for running a school store.**
  Answers will vary. Possible one-time costs include renovation of existing space in the school. Continuing costs include ongoing purchase of inventory and fixtures, purchase of supplies, repairs, and so on.

36.1 AFTER YOU READ

Reviewing Key Terms and Concepts
1. What is a personal financial statement?
2. Define asset, liability, and net worth.
3. How are one-time costs different from continuing costs?

Integrating Academic Skills
Math

4. Calculate the total start-up costs for an online business by using the Starting Cost Calculator on the U.S. Small Business Administration Web site and the following data:
   - Initial expenses: legal: $500; office supplies: $300; office equipment: $1,500; design: $150; brochures: $150; Web site: $500; other: $700.
   - Money needed for reserve for a total of six months: monthly payroll: $2,500; monthly rent: $750; and monthly expenses: $550.
   - Start-up inventory: $2,000.

   What are the total start-up costs for a six-month period?

Economics

5. Perform an Internet or library search on the factors that are considered by new business start-ups when locating in a particular state. Summarize the results of your research in a one-page paper.

 Online Action!
Check your answers at *marketingessentials.glencoe.com/36/read*

marketingessentials.glencoe.com   **Chapter 36 - Financing the Business 763**

PRACTICE 2 ANSWER

1. Total costs for the first quarter are $35,800 [$25,000 + ($3,600 × 3) = $35,800]. Total costs for the year are $68,200 [$25,000 + ($3,600 × 12) = $68,200].

AFTER YOU READ

Reviewing Key Terms and Concepts

1. The personal financial statement is a summary of your current personal financial condition.

2. An asset is anything of monetary value that you own. A liability is a debt that you owe. Net worth is the difference between assets and liabilities.

3. One-time costs are expenses that will not be repeated after you begin operating the business. Continuing costs are operating expenses you will pay throughout the life of the business.

Integrating Academic Skills

4. Start-up costs = $28,600; $3,800 + $22,800 + $2,000 = $28,600
   Step #1: Initial expenses = $3,800

Step #2: Money for reserve = $22,800 or ($2,500 + $750 + $550 = $3,800) × 6 months = $22,800
Step #3: Start-up Inventory = $2,000

5. Answers will vary; each student should identify economic factors, including prevailing wage rates, availability of trained personnel, cost of doing business, such as business taxes, workers' compensation rates, and cost of property.

 Online Action!   Answers at **marketingessentials.glencoe.com/36/read**

FOCUS

Introducing the Section

COLLABORATIVE ACTIVITY

Tell students that estimating is one of the crucial skills required for forecasting on the financial section of the business plan. Ask students to briefly write some of the ways that they would estimate income and expenses for an existing business as well as for a start-up. Then ask students what factors would help them estimate revenue for a new business.

Preteaching Key Terms

Ask students to test themselves at regular intervals with this section's key terms. This will help them learn the vocabulary words more completely. Also, encourage them to practice using the vocabulary terms in class as much as possible.

- income statement
- gross sales
- net sales
- net income
- interest
- principal
- balance sheet
- cash flow statement

Build Vocabulary

Remind students of the term *gross income*. This is a term they will come across quite frequently on financial forms and statements.

Financial Aspect of a Business Plan

OBJECTIVES

- Estimate business income and expenses
- Prepare an income statement
- Create a balance sheet
- Interpret a cash flow statement

KEY TERMS

- income statement
- gross sales
- net sales
- net income
- interest
- principal
- balance sheet
- cash flow statement

READ and STUDY

BEFORE YOU READ
Predict Why do you think so many new businesses fail?

THE MAIN IDEA
Financial institutions and investors will want to know why you need their money, how you are going to use it, and how you plan to repay them. The financial section of a business plan provides this information to prospective lenders.

STUDY ORGANIZER
In a chart like the one below, create an outline that lists key information about financial documents.

Organized Financing *(continued)*

1. Prepare an income statement.
2. _____
3. _____

WHILE YOU READ

Connect Suppose you want to start your own company. List the specific financial needs you would have as you read this section.

Estimating Business Income and Expenses

After you estimate your start-up costs and personal living expenses, the next step is to estimate the money you expect to earn and to spend while operating your business. Many small businesses fail because they do not bring in enough revenue to pay their costs and expenses. Estimating your business income and expenses is a key part of your business plan. Lenders will want to see your estimates to help them decide whether to lend you money.

764 UNIT 11 - ENTREPRENEURSHIP AND FINANCE

READ and STUDY

BEFORE YOU READ
Lead students to understand that new businesses fail because the timing or amounts of revenues and expenditures are different from those planned.

THE MAIN IDEA
Discuss with students the skills entrepreneurs need to convince financial institutions to lend them money.

STUDY ORGANIZER
Model the study organizer for students by filling in the first blank. A full-size, downloadable study organizer can be found at marketingessentials.glencoe.com

WHILE YOU READ Have students take notes on the different items needed for a new business that would require financing.

If you are buying an existing business, you will have previous operating results to use as a guide. If you are starting a new business, you will need to estimate your potential revenue and the costs and expenses of operating the business.

The Income Statement

The financial document used to calculate revenue, costs, and expenses is the income statement. The **income statement** is a summary of income and expenses during a specific period such as a month, a quarter, or a year. This statement is often called a profit and loss statement.

The income statement for an existing business shows the previous year's income, costs, and expenses. The income statement for a new or planned business estimates earnings and expenses for the first few months (or the first year) of operation. Figure 36.3 shows a sample projected quarterly income statement. Refer to this figure as you read about the different parts of the income statement.

Income statements have several major parts: total and net sales, cost of goods sold, gross profit, expenses of operating the business, net income from operations, other income or expenses, net profit before income taxes, and net profit after income taxes. Each item on the income statement is added to or subtracted from total sales to find the amount of net profit or loss.

       Total Sales
− Returns and Allowances
= Net Sales
− Cost of Goods Sold
= Gross Profit
− Operating Expenses
= Net Income from Operations
− Other Expenses (Interest)
= Net Profit (Loss) Before Taxes
− Taxes
= Net Profit (Loss) After Taxes

Now we will see how to calculate the amounts for each part of the income statement.

Estimating Total Sales

The income generated by a business depends on the yearly volume of sales. Most new businesses grow slowly in the beginning, so you should be conservative in estimating your first-year sales.

Most people who start a new business have some idea about where they will sell their products. You may already have discussed your new product with potential buyers. You may even have a contract to produce a certain number of items. Suppose you are starting a new T-shirt printing business. You have a contract for 2,000 shirts, which you will sell at $8 each wholesale. Your estimated total sales will be $16,000. You would estimate your total sales at $160,000 if you think you can produce and sell ten times that amount during your first year.

It is important to calculate a reasonable estimated sales volume. You must verify your estimated sales volume by comparing it with projected industry figures for your size of business and location. Trade associations, bankers, and industry publications can help you make sales and income estimates.

The accuracy of your sales estimates will also depend on the quality of your market analysis. Losses rather than profits are common during the first year of business. In your business plan, you will need to show how you will cover any losses by investing more capital or reducing your operating expenses.

Calculating Net Sales

The total of all sales for any period of time is called **gross sales**. Your gross sales will simply be the total of all cash sales if your company sells only on a cash basis. When your company accepts credit and charge cards, sells gift certificates, or offers merchandise on account, then all of these different types of sales transactions must be totaled to arrive at gross sales.

Most businesses have some customer returns and allowances (credit granted to customers for damaged or defective goods kept by the customer); therefore, the gross sales figure does not reflect the actual income from sales.

TEACH

Discussion Starter

ESTIMATING BUSINESS INCOME AND EXPENSES

Ask the class to select an existing or new manufacturing, retail, or service business in your community. Have students discuss what factors the owners of each business had to consider when estimating earnings and expenses.

TEACHING POINTS

Expand Remind students that calculating sales volume for a service business involves establishing an hourly rate and multiplying that by the number of hours worked annually, and then dividing the result by 12 for a monthly income figure. Keep in mind industry averages and market trends. A service business cannot start out charging more than the industry average unless it offers something extra.

Clarify Remind students that estimating business expenses is like estimating personal living expenses. Entrepreneurs should estimate and calculate all pre-opening expenses as well as those for the first 90 days of business.

Critical Thinking

Ask students to think about why the University of Pennsylvania has a research center dedicated to risk management and the decision-making process. Have them investigate and discuss how such research might influence government and business policies.

Extended Activity

Estimating Income and Expenses

Have students practice estimating income and expenses by choosing a product they buy frequently, such as a CD, and assume a royalty of 10% and a manufacturing cost of $1.80 per product, including packaging. Ask students to estimate income based on the price students typically pay, considering that the wholesale price will be less. Remind students that not all products will sell well.

TEACH CONTINUED

Concept Development

PROJECTING BUSINESS EXPENSES

Ask students the following: If you were a banker or investor reviewing a business plan in anticipation of lending or investing money for a business start-up, what questions would you ask the potential business owner regarding how he or she will use your money?

Answers might include the following: How will the money make the business profitable? How will the business repay the money? Who will be making decisions regarding the use of the money? How qualified is this person to run a business? How knowledgeable about this particular business is this person? What experience does this person have in this area of business? How do the projections compare to the actual numbers of similar businesses?

TEACHING POINTS

Explain Remind students that some businesses are riskier than others, and lenders will take this fact into consideration before granting a loan. Among the businesses with the highest failure rates are those providing recreation services and oil and gas extraction. Health services and private education services have one of the lowest failure rates.

Clarify Remind students of the difference between gross sales and net sales. Net sales is gross sales less returns and allowances.

Figure 36.3   *Projected Quarterly Income Statement*

• **Financial Statement** An income statement summarizes a business's income and expenses for a specific period of time. It gives a snapshot of the business's health, showing profits or losses. This is often used to attract investors or to show lenders. Because a new business doesn't have a business history, it develops a projected income statement that estimates expected income and expenses for a period of time.

How might a new business gather the information needed to project income and expenses?

	Month 1	Month 2	Month 3	TOTAL
Sales	30,900	34,000	36,400	101,300
Less Returns & Allowances	900	1,000	1,400	3,300
NET SALES	30,000	33,000	35,000	98,000
Cost of Goods Sold	19,500	21,000	22,750	63,250
GROSS PROFIT	10,500	12,000	12,250	34,750
Operating Expenses				
Variable Expenses				
Advertising	300	350	350	1,000
Automobile	450	400	525	1,375
Dues and Subscriptions	15	20	18	53
Legal and Accounting	300	400	350	1,050
Miscellaneous Expenses	360	480	420	1,260
Office Supplies	120	160	140	420
Security	300	400	350	1,050
Telephone	90	120	105	315
Utilities	90	120	105	315
Total Variable Expenses	2,025	2,450	2,363	6,838
Fixed Expenses				
Depreciation	180	180	180	540
Insurance	300	300	300	900
Rent	800	800	800	2,400
Salaries and Payroll Taxes	5,600	5,600	5,600	16,800
Total Fixed Expenses	6,880	6,880	6,880	20,640
TOTAL EXPENSES	8,905	9,330	9,243	27,478
NET INCOME FROM OPERATIONS	1,595	2,670	3,007	7,272
Other Income	0	0	0	0
Other Expenses (Interest)	300	300	300	900
NET PROFIT (LOSS) BEFORE TAXES	1,295	2,370	2,707	6,372
Taxes	325	590	680	1,595
NET PROFIT (LOSS) AFTER TAXES	970	1,780	2,027	4,777

Net Sales is determined by subtracting returns and allowances from total sales.

Gross Profit is the difference between net sales and the cost of goods sold.

Operating Expenses are the costs of operating a business. They are divided into variable and fixed expenses.

Total Expenses is determined by adding the total variable expenses to the total fixed expenses.

Net Income From Operations is found by subtracting total expenses from gross profit.

Net Profit Before Taxes is calculated by adding other income to net income from operations, then subtracting interest expense.

Net Profit After Taxes is found by subtracting taxes from net profit before taxes. This amount represents the actual profit after income taxes are paid from operating the business for a certain period of time.

 Online Action!

Go to *marketingessentials.glencoe.com/36/figure/3* to find a project on personal finance.

Figure 36.3   *Projected Quarterly Income Statement*

Discussion Ask students to discuss if they have ever watched or read a business broadcast or article about a public company's projected quarterly income. Have them discuss the purpose of making this kind of information available to the public.

Caption Answer New business owners can get this information from the Small Business Administration, the local chamber of commerce, similar businesses, or trade associations.

Online Action! For instructions, ideas, and answer guide, go to the Teacher Center at marketingessentials.glencoe.com

Follow Up Have students perform research, using the sources listed above, to find the projected quarterly expenses for a business of their choice.

The total of all sales returns, discounts, and allowances is subtracted from gross sales to get **net sales**. The net sales figure is the amount left after gross sales have been adjusted for returns and allowances. Look at Figure 36.2 to find the net sales for each month.

Cost of Goods Sold

The total amount spent to produce or to purchase the goods that are sold is called the cost of goods sold. To calculate cost of goods sold, add goods purchased during the period to the beginning inventory value. Then subtract the amount of the ending inventory.

Beginning Inventory
+ Net Purchases, or Production Costs
− Ending Inventory
= Cost of Goods Sold

As you learned in Chapter 24, you count the stock on hand and calculate its value to determine beginning and ending inventory amounts.

Most service businesses do not provide goods to their customers. Therefore, they do not have to determine the cost of goods sold. Their gross profit is the same as net sales. Other businesses that produce or purchase products to sell must calculate the cost of goods sold.

Determining Gross Profit

Gross profit or gross margin on sales is the difference between the net sales and the cost of goods sold.

The formula for calculating gross profit is:

Net Sales
− Cost of Goods Sold
= Gross Profit

Once you know the cost of goods sold, you can calculate your gross profit by subtracting the cost of goods sold from net sales.

Suppose you are employed by Downhill Racers, a company that sold $115,765 worth of mountain bikes last year. The company books show a total of $3,220 in sales returns and allowances. When you subtract the sales

returns and allowances from total (gross) sales, you get net sales of $112,545. The cost of goods sold for last year totals $69,459; therefore, your gross profit is: $112,545 − $69,459 = $43,086.

Projecting Business Expenses

The next major part of the income statement is the operating expenses—the costs of operating the business, including variable and fixed expenses.

Calculating Variable Expenses

Variable expenses change from one month to the next. Variable costs can fluctuate depending upon the sales volume of the business. Variable expenses include items such as advertising, office supplies, telephone bills, and utilities.

Variable expenses are often calculated as a percentage of some baseline amount. Advertising expenses, for example, may average 5 percent of total sales.

Calculating Fixed Expenses

Fixed expenses are costs that remain the same for a period of time. These types of expenses stay fixed for months regardless of sales volume. Depreciation, insurance, rent, salaries, and payroll taxes are examples of fixed expenses.

Depreciation is a complicated fixed expense. Depreciation represents the amount by which an asset's value has fallen because of age, wear, or deterioration in a given period of time. IRS laws and rules govern the time period over which you can depreciate assets. An accountant can help you determine the asset depreciation schedule and amounts to use in listing assets on your income tax return.

Projecting other fixed expenses usually is easier because you simply add all your fixed costs, such as rent or insurance. Employee wages may be a significant part of your business expenses. Let's look at how to calculate payroll costs.

Calculating Payroll Expenses

To calculate payroll expenses, you must first estimate the number of employees you

TEACH CONTINUED

Individualized Practice

BUSINESS EXPENSES

L1 Ask students to memorize the formulas for the cost of goods sold, gross profit, and net pay. They can write the formulas on flash cards and work with a partner to quiz each other.

L2 Ask students to create a spreadsheet with an income statement for a hypothetical business. They should review the differences between variable expenses and fixed expenses before starting.

L3 Ask students to locate specific IRS laws or rules regarding the time period over which someone can depreciate assets. Ask students to write a few paragraphs on why this is such a complicated issue under fixed expenses.

Critical Thinking

Ask students what strategies they might use to budget based on variable income.

Virtual Business

Introduce financial statements to students using Knowledge Matters' Virtual Business Retailing visual simulation, *Financial Statements*. In this simulation, students learn to read and interpret financial statement information to understand the health of a business.

Critical Thinking

Explain to students that discretionary income is what is left after the fixed monthly expenses are paid. Have students discuss how a person or a business might use this discretionary income differently. Encourage students to give concrete examples.

TEACH CONTINUED

Concept Development

CALCULATING VARIABLE EXPENSES

Ask students to propose budgeting advice for someone who went from a steady paycheck to a variable one. Have students review the meaning of variable expenses and fixed expenses.

TEACHING POINTS

Explain Remind students that moving from a steady paycheck to a variable one requires financial discipline when it comes to saving. It's best to have nine months of income saved in case of unemployment or minimal work cycles.

Summarize Remind students of the importance of keeping track of expenses, personally or professionally. Various software programs, such as Quicken, Microsoft Money, and Excel are built for creating and tracking budget plans, payments, and forecasts.

Exenteded Activity

Presenting Financials

Ask students to select one company that they want to learn more about and research it using online resources, newspapers, and possibly broadcasts. Their objective is to understand the company's financial situation and hypothesize where the company is going. Ask students to create a presentation as if they are going to speak to the company's board of directors. Have them outline the company's future goals, market its current situation, and defend the findings. Students should prepare a 10-minute presentation. Encourage other students to ask the presenters questions after the presentation ends.

need to operate your business. Then, research typical salaries in your area for the work the employees will perform. You can get help on salary information by consulting your state employment security agency (SESA) office and by reviewing the help-wanted ads in the newspaper for similar jobs. You can also use the minimum wage as a starting point and decide how much more to pay for more skilled workers, recognizing that a skilled worker should have a higher salary than an unskilled one.

When setting up your business, you need to give careful attention to your payroll records. Payroll records are important to your employees and to your company. They are also used to prepare income tax returns, so the federal and state governments are also concerned with their accuracy.

Your bank, your accountant, a bookkeeping service, or a computer software program can help you set up a system to calculate and record payroll and cut checks.

Case Study

Two Men and a Truck

The sons of Mary Ellen Sheets started a local moving service when they were in high school. They used an old pickup to transport people's belongings around Lansing, Michigan, after school. In 1985, the boys' mother bought the company's first truck to keep the business going while the boys were away in college. In 1988, Two Men and a Truck became the first local moving company in the United States to offer franchises. By 2003, there were 125 local franchises in 25 states with revenues of $122 million. Sheets's sons, Brig and Jon Sorber, are still part of management.

Advice on Starting a Business

Sheets has advice for people starting a new business: Get your finances in order and keep accurate accounts. For years, she kept company receipts in a shoebox under her desk. As the company grew and annual audits were required, auditors would groan as they searched through boxes of paper receipts.

What stopped Sheets from getting accounting help was her idea that it was too expensive. When she finally hired an accountant, however, the errors he found in his first month on the job saved the company enough money to pay his first year's salary. Her advice to new businesses is: Either learn about finance or hire financial professionals.

TWO MEN AND A TRUCK®
"Movers Who Care®"

| Why Us | Moving | Packing | Boxes | Hiring a Mover

THINK STRATEGICALLY

Why is it necessary for a business to keep good financial records?

 Online Action! Go to *marketingessentials.glencoe.com/36/case* to find an activity on financials and starting a business.

Case Study   Two Men and a Truck

Discussion Ask students to discuss what kind of trouble a business can get into if it fails to keep accurate records (either knowingly or unknowingly).

THINK STRATEGICALLY **Answer:** Good financial record-keeping is a must for any business. Accurate records allow a business to meet all credit obligations and provide precise cash flow information for business operations as well as investors, leaders, and auditors.

Online Action! For instructions, ideas, and answer guide, go to the Teacher Center at **marketingessentials.glencoe.com**

Follow Up Have students brainstorm other employee positions that might "pay for themselves" through money generated or saved.

Your payroll records may be part of the cash disbursements journal where you keep records of all cash payments. You may prefer to keep your payroll records in a separate payroll journal. When using a separate journal for payroll records, use a separate record for each employee. Each record will show one employee's pay period, hours worked, earnings, deductions, and net pay.

The amount earned by an employee is that person's gross pay. Net pay is what the employee receives after deductions for taxes and insurance, and voluntary deductions. Nancy Baker earns $11 an hour and worked 40 hours during the week; therefore, her gross pay is $440 ($11 × 40 hours).

Nancy's deductions total $125.66, so you would calculate her net pay by subtracting the deductions from her gross pay:

$440 − $125.66 = $314.34 (net pay)

Tax tables are available for calculating the amount to be deducted from each employee's pay for local, state, and federal income tax. The percentage of gross pay to be deducted for FICA (Social Security and Medicare taxes) changes frequently. Get the latest information from your local Social Security office.

Example: Find the net pay for Rosarita Romerez, who worked a total of 44 hours during a week at $13 per hour. She is paid time-and-a-half for overtime (hours worked beyond 40 hours in a week). Her deductions totaled $105.25 for the week.

STEP 1 **Calculate the gross pay.**

$520.00 ($13 × 40 hours)
+ 78.00 ($13 × 4 hours × 1.5)
$598.00 (gross pay)

STEP 2 **Subtract deductions.**

$598.00 (gross pay)
− 105.25 (total deductions)
$492.75

In estimating your total payroll expenses, you will need to use current tax rates for local, state, and federal income taxes. Remember that as the employer, you will also pay FICA and unemployment payroll taxes on your employees' earnings. You will need to include those amounts in your total payroll expense estimate.

Calculating Total Expenses

Once you have calculated all your operating (variable and fixed) expenses, you are ready to total your expenses. To calculate total expenses, add the variable expenses to the fixed expenses.

Total Variable Expenses
+ Total Fixed Expenses
= Total Expenses

Net Income From Operations

After calculating your total expenses, the next step is to calculate net income from operations. **Net income** is the amount left after the total expenses are subtracted from gross profit.

The formula for calculating net income from operations is:

Gross Profit on Sales
− Total Expenses
= Net Income From Operations

Suppose you own the "I Can Do That" Home Remodeling Company, which had gross profit on sales of $153,156 during the year. Your total operating expenses for the year were $88,991, so your net income from operations was:

$153,156 − $88,991 = $64,165

During the first years of operation, a business may have a net loss from operations. A net loss results when total expenses are larger than the gross profit on sales. The financial plan should address how the business intends to pay its debts in the short term, especially if a loss is probable during the first months of operation.

Online Activity

E-Customer Loyalty

Ask students to use the Internet to research an e-business or other company where customer loyalty has enabled a business to become a successful brand. Have students summarize their findings in a one-page response.

Individualized Math Skills

L1 Ask students to find federal tax tables (both single persons and married persons weekly payroll) either online or in an annual tax booklet. Ask them to use the appropriate table to find the following FIT amount withheld from the paychecks: a single person earning over $350 a week and claiming one allowance; a married person earning over $370 a week and claiming two allowances.

Answers will vary; check current tax tables to determine correct answers.

L2 Tell students that they calculate taxable wages by subtracting personal exemptions from annual gross pay. Use this formula to solve the problem: Rosa Lopez's gross pay is $72,000 a year. The state income tax rate is 4 percent of taxable wages. Lopez takes a married exemption for her and her husband. How much is withheld from her gross earnings for state income tax within one year? Note: For this problem, students need to know that a married person's personal exemption is $3,000.

$2,760; ($72,000 − $3,000) − ($69,000 × 0.04) = $2,760

L3 Ask students to calculate the following problem: Eric Wong is single and earns an annual salary of $25,000. The personal exemption in his state is $1,500. The state tax rate is 2.5 percent of his taxable wages. What are his taxable wages? What is the annual tax withheld from his salary for state income tax?

Eric's taxable wages are $23,500; annual tax withheld is $587.50.

TEACH CONTINUED

Concept Development

CALCULATING INCOME AND EXPENSES

Divide students into four groups, each representing a type of business—manufacturing, wholesale, retail, or service. Help each group make an appointment with the owner and/or general manager of each type of business assigned. Each group should interview this person regarding how income and expenses were initially projected, and how that compares with ongoing projections. Students should write a report of their findings and present it to the class.

TEACHING POINTS

Clarify Remind students that in the business world, they might hear the acronyms, *NOI* (net operating income), *NOPAT* (net operating profit after taxes), or *NOPLAT* (net operating profit less adjusted taxes).

Extend Students may have heard "creative accounting" in the media on occasion. Company executives have been prosecuted for wiping expenses off the income statement as well as incorrectly classifying expenses as reoccurring or one-time.

Build Vocabulary

Introduce students to the accounting term, *GAAP (generally accepted accounting principles)*. In the U.S., these rules are set by the Financial Accounting Standards Board (FASB).

Critical Thinking

Ask students if they think a Web domain can be considered a long-term asset or a long-term liability.

Calculating Other Income

In the Net Income From Operations section of the income statement, list money earned from sources other than sales. You may earn dividends on stocks or interest on your savings or checking accounts. **Interest** is the money paid for the use of money borrowed or invested.

To estimate your interest earnings, check with local banks and find the current interest rate paid on similar accounts. It is likely that you will use some of this money during the year, so you will need to calculate interest only on the amount actually on deposit. Unless the interest income you expect to earn is significant, you may want to list this amount as zero in your business plan.

Calculating Other Expenses

You will pay interest on any money that you borrow to start your business. The amount you borrowed is called the **principal**. Interest is expressed as a percentage of the principal and is called the rate of interest.

For example, if you borrow $100 at 6 percent, the principal is $100 and the rate of interest is 6 percent. To find the amount of interest for one year, multiply the principal (p) times the rate of interest (r) times the length of time (t). This formula is stated as:

$$i = prt$$
$$(\$100 \times .06 \times 1 = \$6).$$

You would pay $6 in interest for the example above.

The units in the rate of interest and time must agree. That is, if the rate of interest is expressed in years, then the time must be expressed in years as well. Both may be expressed in months. Check this before you do your math so that your answers will be correct. If the rate is given without reference to a time period, you can assume that it is for one year.

Suppose you are quoted a yearly rate and need to convert it to a monthly rate. There are 12 months in a year, so you would divide the yearly rate by 12 to get the monthly rate.

When you are quoted a monthly rate and want to convert it to a yearly rate, multiply the monthly rate by 12.

Once you decide how much money you will need to borrow and how long it will take you to repay the loan, you can calculate your total annual (or monthly) interest. This amount is listed on the financial statement as Other Expenses (Interest).

Net Profit or Loss Before Taxes

Net profit or net loss before taxes is calculated by adding other income to net income from operations and then subtracting other expenses from the total.

> Net Income From Operations
> + Other Income
> − Other Expenses
> ─────────────────
> = Net Profit (or Loss) Before Taxes

Net Profit or Loss After Taxes

Net profit (or loss) after taxes is the amount of money left over after federal, state, and local taxes are subtracted. This amount represents the actual profit from operating the business for a certain period of time.

The projected income statement should be done on a monthly basis for new businesses. After the first year, projected income statements can be prepared on a quarterly basis.

The steps that follow are a summary of how to prepare a monthly projected income statement.

STEP 1 Estimate total sales.

STEP 2 Subtract sales discounts, returns, and allowances from total sales to calculate net sales.

STEP 3 List the estimated cost of goods sold.

STEP 4 Subtract the cost of goods sold from net sales to find gross profit on sales.

STEP 5 List each monthly operating expense, categorizing each as a variable or fixed expense.

Online Activity

Projecting Business Expenses

To improve their understanding of projecting business expenses, have students analyze several examples of income statements and balance sheets from existing businesses to determine the current and fixed assets and the current and long-liabilities. Students should be able to find current income statements on financial or company Web sites.

STEP 6 Total the monthly operating expenses.

STEP 7 Subtract total operating expenses from gross profit on sales to find net income from operations. Put parentheses around any projected losses; for example, a projected loss of $1,000 would be identified as ($1,000).

STEP 8 Add other income such as interest on bank deposits and subtract other expenses, such as interest expense, from net income from operations. The result is net profit (or loss) before income taxes.

STEP 9 Estimate total taxes on the net income and subtract that amount from net profit. The result is net profit (or loss) after taxes.

PRACTICE 3

Using the income statement shown below, answer the following questions:

1. How much did Mountain Air pay for the bikes it sold?
2. How much was the gross profit for the year?
3. How much were total operating expenses?
4. Which operating expense was the most costly?
5. How much net income was earned during the year?

Mountain Air Bikes
Income Statement for the Year Ended December 31, 20--

Net Sales	$202,736
Cost of Goods Sold	$124,375
Gross Profit	$?
Operating Expenses	
Salaries	$ 28,022
Rent	$ 14,211
Utilities	$ 5,214
Advertising	$ 3,422
Total Operating Expenses	$?
Net Income From Operations	$?

MARKET TECH

Creating Loyalty

Encouraging customer loyalty has always been a goal of marketers. Marketing technology has pioneered many ways of getting customers to come back again and again. "New marketing" targets individuals rather than groups, because the software behind it collects specific information about each person.

Targeted Rewards

Harrah's, an entertainment, resort, and casino company, asks each customer to sign up for its Total Rewards loyalty program. Customers use their rewards cards whenever they make a purchase at the resort.

Harrah's tracks the results and offers special deals and privileges to consumers who return often even if they do not spend a lot of money on their visits.

The rewards offered are related to what the consumer has purchased in the past—free concert tickets to music lovers, for example.

The company tracked an increase of 20 percent in customer loyalty after the program's first year.

THINK LIKE A MARKETER

Where would you list on an income statement the expenses for the software necessary to track customer purchasing?

@ Online Action!

Go to *marketingessentials.glencoe.com/ 36/tech* to find an activity on technology and starting a business.

TEACH CONTINUED

Individualized Practice

STARTING A NEW BUSINESS

L1 Have students use an Internet search engine to research the U.S. Small Business Administration's guidelines about starting a new business specifically targeted to women and minority business owners.

L2 Ask students to create a chart. Have them identify and label separate columns for the financial documents discussed in this chapter. Under each column, have them identify the reasons for including a document as part of the financial section of a business plan.

L3 Have students obtain a copy of a recent annual report. The students should develop a two-page paper summarizing the letter to the stockholders, identifying any goods and services planned for the future, the company's total sales, the operating income and expenses, new income, and cash flow.

PRACTICE 3 ANSWERS

Mountain Air Bikes
Income Statement for the Year Ended December 31, 20--

Net Sales	$202,736
Cost of Goods Sold	$124,375
Gross Profit	$ 78,361
Operating Expenses:	
Salaries	$ 28,022
Rent	$ 14,211
Utilities	$ 5,214
Advertising	$ 3,422
Total Operating Expenses	$ 50,869
Net Income from Operations	$ 27,492

1. $124,375
2. $78,361
3. $50,869
4. Salaries
5. $27,492

MARKET TECH

Creating Loyalty

Discussion Ask students to discuss what customer loyalty does for a business.

THINK LIKE A MARKETER Software necessary to track customer purchasing would be listed as an operating expense on an income statement.

@ Online Action! For instructions, ideas, and answer guide, go to the Teacher Center at **marketingessentials.glencoe.com**

Follow Up Ask students: What other business expenses might be incurred while building customer loyalty? Answers might include: expenses for marketing efforts to reach repeat customers and build a rewards program.

TEACH CONTINUED

Concept Development

THE BALANCE SHEET

Give each student a copy of a complete balance sheet that contains all of the elements in the balance featured in this text. As a class, write a letter to a friend, describing the formula for how each of the following were achieved: assets, liabilities, and equity.

TEACHING POINTS

Clarify Tell students that some companies have found that sharing financial statements with employees can be a significant tool for motivating employee performance. To help employees who lack a financial background, the financial statement is annotated to explain the meaning of each line in the statement.

Extend Introduce students to the importance of the Sarbanes-Oxley Act of 2002, also known as "SarBox." This Act was approved by Congress in response to many of the questionable ethical activities surrounding modern corporate culture. Sarbox requires companies to establish and strictly abide by their own formal documentation of internal controls. It is intended to improve corporate and individual responsibility.

Build Vocabulary

Introduce students to the concept of terminal value. Stockholders are aware of a company's *terminal value*, meaning that one day the company will close, liquidate everything, and divide it among shareholders.

The Balance Sheet

A **balance sheet** is a summary of a business's assets, liabilities, and owner's equity.

Assets

Assets are anything of monetary value that you own. They are classified as either current or fixed.

- Current assets are cash and anything of value that can be converted into cash in a year. Examples of current assets are cash in the bank, accounts receivable (money owed to you by your customers), and inventory.
- Fixed assets are used over a period of years to operate your business. Fixed assets cannot be changed into cash within a year. Examples of fixed assets include land, buildings, equipment, furniture, and fixtures. The assets of the business are important because they are needed to operate the business. When borrowing money to start a business, assets are also often used as collateral for the loan.

Liabilities

Liabilities are listed in another section of the balance sheet. Liabilities are the amounts that the business owes—for example, money owed for merchandise purchased. Liabilities are classified as either current or long-term.

- Current liabilities are the debts the business must pay during the upcoming business year. Examples of current liabilities are accounts payable (money owed to suppliers), notes payable (money owed to a bank), taxes payable, and money owed to employees for salaries.
- Long-term liabilities are debts that are due after 12 months. Some examples are mortgages and long-term loans.

Equity

Equity, or net worth, is the third section of the balance sheet. When you start a new business, you will most likely invest some savings in the business. The amount of the savings is your equity, or ownership interest, in the business. The money invested will be used to buy assets and to operate the business. The assets owned by the business and the debts the business owes impact your equity. Remember, net worth is the difference between the assets of a business and its liabilities: Assets − Liabilities = Net Worth (Equity).

Analysis of Financial Statements

Lenders use ratio analysis to determine how a business is performing as compared to other businesses in the industry. Ratios indicate whether a business has too much debt, is carrying too much inventory, or is not making enough gross profit. Information on the balance sheet and the income statement may be used to calculate these ratios. Lenders use ratio analysis to determine whether your business would be a good investment risk and whether it could repay a loan.

Figures on the balance sheet will show you the amount of your ownership interest (owner's or stockholders' equity) and the financial strength of a business on a given date. The data on the income statement can give you an idea of how well the business is operating over a period of time. Sometimes you will need information from both statements to calculate the ratios.

The following are some of the most basic operating ratios and how they may be used to analyze or interpret financial statements. A number of sources and directories exist to help you determine the common business ratios for your type of business. These include *Financial Studies of Small Business* published by the Financial Research Associates, *Industry Norms and Key Business Ratios* by Dun & Bradstreet, and *Almanac of Business and Industrial Financial Ratios* by Leo Troy.

Liquidity Ratios

Liquidity ratios are used to analyze the ability of a firm to meet its current debts. One liquidity ratio is current ratio. Its formula is current assets divided by current liabilities. In this case, it is better to have a high ratio.

Critical Thinking

Ask students if they think a company's stockholders are interested in the company's liquid assets—those that are easily converted to cash. Have them explain their answers in class. Remind students that the cash flow statement shows how a company's cash and its equivalents enter and exit its establishment. This is to help the investors see how the money is spent and how the company is running.

The acid test, or quick ratio, is used to see if the company can meet its short-term cash needs. Its formula is cash plus marketable securities plus accounts receivables divided by current liabilities.

Activity Ratios

Activity ratios are used to determine how quickly assets can be turned into cash. One such ratio is called accounts receivable turnover, which indicates the number of days it takes to collect the money owed by customers. To calculate this ratio, divide net sales by average trade receivables. In this case, it is better to have a lower ratio.

The stock turnover ratio measures how many days it takes to turn over, or sell, the inventory. Excessive inventory ties up cash that a company can use to grow its business. The basic formula for this ratio is cost of goods sold divided by average inventory.

Profitability Ratios

Profitability ratios measure how well the company has operated during the past year. One ratio is profit margin on sales, which shows the rate of profit in percentages. This information is found on the income statement. Its formula is net income divided by net sales. Another profitability ratio is the rate of return on assets, which shows how well you are doing when compared to other companies. The formula for this ratio is net income divided by average total assets.

Cash Flow Statement

A **cash flow statement** is a monthly plan that tracks when you anticipate that cash will come into the business and when you expect to pay out cash. A cash flow statement helps you determine whether you will have enough money to pay your bills on time.

Businesses need cash to pay bills and their employees, and to use for unexpected expenses. The cash flow statement itemizes how much cash you started with, what your projected cash expenditures are, and how and when you plan to receive cash. It also shows when you will need to find additional funds and when you will have cash remaining. Most lenders will require you to estimate cash flow for the first year of operation.

Cash Payments

When operating a business, one of your largest payments of cash will be for your merchandise. You will most likely have to pay for part of the merchandise in cash and part on credit.

When estimating sales for the income statement, you include both cash and credit sales. In contrast, the cash flow statement shows only the amount you expect to receive in cash (for cash sales and payments for credit sales) during the month.

Chapter 36 - Financing the Business 773

Online Activity

IRS Services

Ask students to visit the Web site for the Internal Revenue Service. Have students visit an area of the site that is designated for businesses and write a one-page summary of one or more of the services offered.

Concept Development

CASH FLOW STATEMENT

Have students review the sales from the school store during the last year. Then have students project the income and expenses for the store for the next year.

TEACHING POINTS

Summarize Remind students that one of the most common reasons for business failure is inadequate cash flow. Being successful means not only selling the product, but also collecting the money for it within a reasonable time.

ASSESS

Review Guide

CONCEPTS

Create index cards with the chapter's key terms and concepts written on them. Divide the students into two groups. Allow the first team to choose one index card from the stack. (Do not allow the students to see the cards they choose.) Allow the first team 30 seconds to give a definition to the term on the card. If no team member can give a correct definition, allow the other team to try. Reward the winning team. Review the terms for which neither team could give a correct answer.

KEY TERMS

Have students review key terms, their spellings, and definitions in small groups.

ONLINE SELF-ASSESSMENT

Have students go to **marketingessentials.glencoe.com** for the Section 36.2 practice test.

Individualized Review

L1 Assign and review Chapter 36 activities in the Student Activity Workbook.

L2 Assign and review Chapter 36 activities in the Marketing Math Workbook.

L3 Assign and review Chapter 36 activities in the *BusinessWeek* Reader and Case Studies.

Marketing Practice

Ask students to research a business that used a creative advertising campaign to strengthen sales that had fallen flat. Students will have to review the campaign and its relation to the company's financial statement. Ask students work in pairs and give a brief presentation to the class with their findings.

You may receive payment for most of your credit sales 30 days after the sales. You will also need to calculate your monthly costs for operating the business.

How to Prepare a Cash Flow Statement

Use the following steps to prepare a cash flow statement.

STEP 1 Add the total cash on hand (in bank accounts) and money received from any loans to find your total start-up money.

STEP 2 Subtract the start-up costs to determine the amount of cash left for operation.

STEP 3 Enter the estimated cash you expect to receive from cash sales and credit sales for each month during the first year. Enter the amount of any income from business investments or additional loans.

STEP 4 Add all sources of cash receipts to find the total cash income for the month.

STEP 5 List the cost of goods that you will buy for your inventory. This cost should be separated into purchases for which you will pay cash and purchases on credit, which you will pay for the next month.

For example, the cash flow statement shows goods bought on credit in Month 1.

This is a payment for items bought on credit prior to the opening of the business. Add the cash and credit purchases to find the total cost of inventory purchases.

STEP 6 List the expenses you expect to pay during the month. These amounts are the same as those listed on the income statement, except for the depreciation expense.

Depreciation is a means of spreading the cost of an asset over a period of years. The amount of depreciation is not an actual payment made by the business, so it is not listed on the cash flow statement.

STEP 7 Total all expenses for the month.

STEP 8 List amounts that will be paid out for capital expenditures. A capital expenditure is money paid for an asset used to operate the business. The purchase of a delivery truck would be a capital expenditure.

STEP 9 List any other payments that will be made, such as repayment of the principal and interest for the loan.

STEP 10 Add all the cash expenditures (cost of inventory purchased, expenses, capital expenditures, and other payments).

Subtract the total cash payments from the total cash received during the month to determine net cash flow.

The amount of any cash payments that are higher than cash receipts should be placed in parentheses to show a loss.

STEP 11 Add the beginning cash balance from the start-up column to the net cash flow for the month.

The result is the cash surplus for the month. When the costs of operating the business are higher than income added to the beginning of the cash balance, the business will have a deficit rather than a surplus.

In that case, the business will need additional cash for its operations. The amount is listed on the Cash Needs line.

The income statement does not take into account how long it may take a business to collect the cash from sales made on credit.

 marketingessentials.glencoe.com

 Online Activity

Dividends

Ask students why they think stable companies offer dividends to their shareholders. Have students research and find dividend statements online and share them with the class. Dividend statements can usually be found on public company Web sites or financial services Web sites.

Loans

What can you do if your cash flow statement indicates you will need additional money during the year? You should be able to borrow money if your business has potential and your balance sheet shows enough assets to serve as collateral.

A loan can help you keep the business going during the start-up period and during slow sales months. When your cash flow projections indicate that you need to borrow money to meet monthly expenses, you will want to include monthly payments on the loan as a part of your cash needs for the rest of the year.

> **PRACTICE 5**
>
> 1. You have total cash of $23,000 to start your business and start-up costs of $12,000.
> What amount of cash is available for operating the business?
>
> 2. Suppose cash income for the first three months is $100, $750, and $980. Total expenses for these same months are $4,800, $3,400, and $2,700.
> What is the cash flow for each month?
>
> 3. What is the cumulative amount of cash available at the end of each month?

CLOSE

Ask students to recall and provide answers to the following questions.

- **What steps can a company take to improve its cash flow?**

  Answers include: Invoice promptly to customers with good credit; manage payables by making timely, accurate payments, and correct overbilling; and control overhead costs.

36.2 AFTER YOU READ

Reviewing Key Terms and Concepts

1. How is gross profit calculated on an income statement?
2. What is the difference between variable and fixed expenses on an income statement?
3. What is a balance sheet?

Integrating Academic Skills

Math

4. Total first-quarter sales for the Bad Frog Beverage Company were $315,000. Goods returned by customers amounted to $6,100. The cost of goods sold to customers was $212,000. The company's total fixed and variable expenses were $94,500. Calculate the following amounts: net sales, gross profit, net income from operations.

Reading and Language Arts

5. Investigate the concept and purpose of cash flow statements. Write a one-page paper on how a business owner could improve cash flow.

 Online Action!

Check your answers at *marketingessentials.glencoe.com/36/read*

> **PRACTICE 5 ANSWERS**
>
> 1. The amount of cash available for business operations is $11,000 ($23,000 − $12,000 = $11,000).
> 2. The cash flow is as follows: month 1: −$4,700 ($100 − $4,800 = −$4,700); month 2: −$2,650 ($750 − $3,400 = −$2,650); month 3: −$1,720 ($980 − $2,700 = −$1,720).
> 3. The cumulative cash available at the end of each month is as follows: month 1: −$6,300 ($11,000 − $4,700 = $6,300); month 2: $3,650 ($6,300 − $2,650 = $3,650); month 3: $1,930 ($3,650 − $1,720 = $1,930).

AFTER YOU READ

Reviewing Key Terms and Concepts

1. Gross profit or gross margin on sales is the difference between the net sales and the cost of goods sold. The formula for calculating gross profit is: Net Sales − Cost of Goods Sold = Gross Profit

2. Variable expenses change from one month to the next. Variable costs can fluctuate up or down depending upon the sales volume of the business. Fixed expenses are costs that remain the same for a period of time regardless of sales volume.

3. A balance sheet is a summary of a business' assets, liabilities, and owner's equity.

Integrating Academic Skills

4. Net sales = $308,900 ($315,000 − $6,100); Gross profit = $96,900 ($308,900 − $212,000); Net income from operations = $2,400 ($96,900 − $94,500)

5. Answers may include prompt invoicing to customers with good credit; managing payables by making timely, accurate payments, correcting overbilling, and controlling overhead costs.

Online Action! Answers at **marketingessentials.glencoe.com/36/read**

CAREERS
IN MARKETING

Lifelong Learning

CAREER INFORMATION

Have students go to marketingessentials.glencoe.com and find Chapter 36 Careers page and click on the link for the American Marketing Association's Careers Strategies and Tips. Ask students to select one article read it, and summarize it.

FINANCING BUSINESS

To enhance their knowledge of financial information related to business, students may take business classes, including accounting, small business management, entrepreneurship, and computer classes to use financial and spreadsheet software. Such classes are offered at most community colleges, by the Small Business Administration, and as regular college courses. Many companies will pay for continuing education.

Primary Source

Ask students to go to marketingessentials.glencoe.com and find Chapter 36 Resources. Ask them to click on the link for the American Marketing Association's marketing dictionary and read the definitions of the finance-related terms they find.

THINKING CRITICALLY

This knowledge is crucial. Anyone in finance or accounting needs to have a thorough understanding of the principles involved in generating numbers that show a business's financial profile.

@ Online Action!

For instructions, ideas, and answer guide, go to the Teacher Center at marketingessentials.glencoe.com

---

CAREERS IN MARKETING

JAMES KAISER
FINANCIAL MANAGER
AMERICAN GREETINGS CORP.

(?) What do you do at work?
Gathering specific financial information related to an investment (expected investment versus expected return) and developing financial performance goals, then structuring the terms of the relationship in a manner that is most beneficial to American Greetings, while coaching the executive management team in developing customer-oriented strategies.

(?) What skills are most important to you?
The most valuable technical skill important to success is in-depth knowledge and understanding of corporate finance, including profitability analysis (discounted cash flows, internal rate of return, net present value, return on net capital employed). The most valuable soft skill important to success is a broad knowledge of marketing, including product position/differentiation and product life cycle (what competitive advantages the product offers over competition, where the product is in its life cycle, and how these attributes affect product profitability).

(?) What is your key to success?
There are two keys to be successful as a financial manager that recommends corporate profitability strategies to executive management teams. The first is financial knowledge, the ability to correctly and accurately analyze financial information. The second is presentation, the ability to market and defend your finding/results to a broad audience in a manner that achieves your objectives.

Aptitudes, Abilities, and Skills

Knowledge of finance and marketing, attention to detail, and presentation and communication skills

Education and Training

Degrees in marketing and general business; advanced degrees in finance and business administration are especially important.

Career Path

Finance careers often begin with entry-level positions in accounting, bookkeeping or similar departments.

THINKING CRITICALLY

How important is a thorough understanding of the workings of corporate finance in this career?

@ Online Action!

Go to *marketingessentials.glencoe.com/36/careers* to find a career-related activity.

Test-Taking Strategies

Ask students to rewrite or highlight their notes using different color ink pens a week before the test. Certain colors represent levels of knowledge—high, medium, and low. When it comes time to study, students can focus on the colors that represent their areas which need the most study.

FOCUS on KEY POINTS

SECTION 36.1

● Five important financial documents are the personal financial statement, the start-up cost estimate, the income statement, the balance sheet, and the cash flow statement. The personal financial statement is a summary of your current personal financial condition. Start-up costs are a projection of how much initial money you will need for your first and continuing years of operation. You also need an estimate of your personal living expenses.

SECTION 36.2

● The next step is to estimate the money you expect to earn and to spend operating your business. The financial document that is used to calculate a business's revenue, costs, and expenses is the income statement. A balance sheet is a summary of a business's assets, liabilities, and owner's equity. A cash flow statement is a monthly plan that indicates when you anticipate cash coming into the business and when you expect to pay out cash. A cash flow statement shows whether you will have enough money to pay your bills.

REVIEW VOCABULARY

Use each of the following terms in a sentence.

1. personal financial statement (p. 759)
2. asset (p. 759)
3. liability (p. 759)
4. net worth (p. 760)
5. start-up costs (p. 760)
6. income statement (p. 765)
7. gross sales (p. 765)
8. net sales (p. 767)
9. net income (p. 769)
10. interest (p. 770)
11. principal (p. 770)
12. balance sheet (p. 772)
13. cash flow statement (p. 773)

REVIEW FACTS and IDEAS

14. What financial information should be included as part of a business plan? (36.1)
15. What factors determine start-up costs for a new business? (36.1)
16. How do start-up costs differ from personal costs? (36.1)
17. What are the major categories that are calculated on the income statement? (36.2)
18. How is a cash flow statement used? (36.2)
19. What is the purpose of a balance sheet? (36.2)
20. What is an asset? (36.2)
21. What does net worth tell a business owner? (36.2)
22. What kinds of financial information are presented on an income statement, a balance sheet, and a cash flow statement? (36.2)

REVIEW FACTS and IDEAS

14. Business plans should include a financial statement, personal living expenses, start-up costs, income statement, balance sheet, and cash flow statement.

15. Factors include the nature of proposed business, the size of business, the amount of inventory needed, the time between using start-up funds from personal assets or from potential lenders and first sales, and the timing of cash revenues and your expenses.

16. Start-up costs are a projection of how much initial money you will need for your first year of operation. Personal costs are your required living expenses.

17. The major categories that are calculated on an income statement include net sales, cost of goods sold, gross profit, operating expenses, net income from operations, and net income before and after taxes.

18. A cash flow statement is used to determine whether you will have enough money to pay your bills on time.

19. The purpose of a balance sheet is to show the amount of ownership interest and the financial strength of a business on a given date.

20. An asset is anything of value owned by a business. Current assets can be converted into cash in the upcoming year. Fixed assets are used over a period of years to operate a business.

21. Net worth is the difference between the assets of a business and its liabilities.

22. The income statement projects revenue and expenses. The balance sheet presents the assets and liabilities of the business. The cash flow statement shows how cash will flow into and out of the business.

FOCUS on KEY POINTS

Ask students to volunteer a few details they also learned and remembered under each point in the sections.

REVIEW VOCABULARY

Student sentences will vary. See glossary for definitions of 1–13. Make sure the students demonstrate understanding of the word in its context. Encourage students to combine numerous words in one sentence to demonstrate higher-level writing skills.

BUILD SKILLS

23. Workplace Skills

Answers will vary. Students should encourage the friend not to ignore personal living expenses, but to complete the financial forms mentioned in the chapter to ensure adequate capitalization to be completely successful in his new enterprise.

24. Technology Applications

Answers will vary, depending on the choice of business and the template found. Students should complete a form requiring the same basic information found in the Start-Up Cost Worksheet shown in **Figure 36.1** on page 761.

25. Math Practice

Answers will vary. Student budgets should include the personal expense items discussed in the chapter. Living expenses could be reduced by sharing the apartment, food, and some of the regularly occurring expenses such as phone, Internet, and utilities with roommates.

DEVELOP CRITICAL THINKING

26. Business Ratios

Answers will vary; students should be able to identify and explain business ratios and their importance to the particular business.

27. Economic Development Loans

Answers will vary; a suggested answer is that local banks have an interest in community development. Also, there are more banks than federal or state agencies.

BUILD SKILLS

23. Workplace Skills

Human Relations After high school, a friend has decided to open a landscaping business for cottage owners who live around a small inland lake. He believes that he will not need extra capital for personal living costs because the business will generate enough revenue to cover this. Should your friend be concerned about his personal living costs? If so, discuss the reasons why your friend should be concerned.

24. Technology Applications

Cash Requirement Worksheets Perform an Internet search for initial cash requirements worksheets. Use one of these templates to estimate expenses and calculate the total amount of cash needed to start a new business.

25. Math Practice

Develop a Budget Suppose that you are renting an apartment and earn a yearly salary of $24,000. Develop a cost-of-living budget. Be sure to include all regular monthly payments, household operating costs, food, and personal expenses. How might you help pay for your expenses?

DEVELOP CRITICAL THINKING

26. Business Ratios

Select an industry that interests you. Research several companies and contact the person in charge of finances at one or two companies. Interview each person to find out about three business ratios that have proven helpful to him or her in running the business.

Identify each ratio and write a one-paragraph summary on why each ratio was important.

27. Economic Development Loans

Many states and the federal government have economic development programs devoted to the needs of small businesses. Research such programs available in your state. Also look into business loans available from local and national banks. Why do a majority of economic development loans originate from banks rather than from the state or federal agencies?

 ### Formative Assessment

Formative assessment is an essential component of classroom work. This type of assessment provides information that is then used as feedback to modify teaching and meet student needs.

L1 Review key terms for this chapter. Ask students to write one sentence for each key term.

L2 Provide various examples of factors regarding financing a business. After each example, have the students identify the factors contained in each one.

L3 Ask students to create stories that illustrate effective ideas for business financing.

 Reteach If the results of this formative assessment seem low, consider the following activity: Ask students to create a balance sheet from scratch based on their hypothetical numbers for a business of interest.

APPLY CONCEPTS

28. Investigating Start-Up Costs

Select a business and investigate its start-up costs for the financial section of a business plan. Use the following resources to find the information: people in the business, suppliers, trade associations, Service Corps of Retired Executives (SCORE), Small Business Administration, local chambers of commerce, and business start-up guides and magazines.

Activity Develop a start-up worksheet for the business and be ready to present your project in class.

29. Cash Flow Statement and Income Statement

Locate the Microsoft Office Downloads Online Web site. Under "Templates," find the link for preparing a cash flow statement. Then, find the link for preparing an income statement.

Activity Develop a 12-month cash flow statement for the business that you selected for the financial section of the business plan. Develop a 12-month profit and loss projection based on the business that you selected for the financial section of the business plan.

NET SAVVY

30. Research Franchise Opportunities

Locate the International Franchise Association Web site on the Internet. Find an existing franchise opportunity to investigate. Use a word processing program to write a report describing the franchise opportunity, including the type of franchise, primary product or service, potential for growth, and other pertinent facts about it.

marketingessentials.glencoe.com

THE DECA CONNECTION

Role Play: Financing the Business

Situation You are to assume the role of branch manager for a large regional bank. You have a great deal of experience with business loan applications. You have been asked to make a presentation to a group of students (judge) enrolled in an entrepreneurship class. Your presentation is to focus on the financial part of a business plan. You are to prepare an outline of the information you plan to present.

Activity You are to make your presentation to the entrepreneurship students (judge).

Evaluation You will be evaluated on how well you meet the following performance indicators:

● Determine financing needed to start a business
● Determine financing needed for business operations
● Describe the nature of cash-flow statements
● Describe sources of financing for businesses
● Make oral presentations

 Online Action!

For more information and DECA Prep practice, go to *marketingessentials.glencoe.com/36/DECA*

APPLY CONCEPTS

28. Investigating Start-Up Costs

Answers will vary by type of industry; financial requirements should be identified and worksheets should demonstrate an understanding of start-up costs.

29. Cash Flow Statement and Income Statement

Answers will vary by type of business; each student should be able to download the cash flow statement, worksheets and income, and complete the templates.

NET SAVVY

30. Research Franchise Opportunities

Answers will vary depending on the franchise chosen. Student reports should demonstrate an ability to conduct an Internet search and prepare a report using a word processing program, and should include the information requested.

THE DECA CONNECTION

The students should be evaluated on the performance indicators noted in the role play. For another DECA role play, go to the Competitive Events Workbook or the Student Activity Workbook, or go to marketingessentials.glencoe.com/36/DECA

 Online Action! For instructions, ideas, and answer guide, go to the Teacher Guide at marketingessentials.glencoe.com

DECA Advisors Corner

Team up with a local charity and conduct a local fundraising event. Bring in businesspeople from your DECA Advisory Committee. Students can form committees and work with the businesspeople to provide all the public relations functions for the event.

MINI-QUIZ

Administer the Mini-Quiz orally. Answers are either true or false.

1. Something of monetary value that you own is called an asset. (true)

2. A debt that you owe is called a liability. (true)

3. A summary of a business's assets, liabilities, and owner's equity is called the balance sheet. (true)

For an expanded chapter quiz, go to Chapter 36 in the TeacherWorks CD-ROM and to Chapter 36 in the **Exam***View*® Pro Test Generator CD-ROM.

779

MARKETING INTERNSHIP

A SIMULATED ◆DECA **PRODUCT AND SERVICE MANAGEMENT EVENT**

SET-UP

Discuss basic background to make sure students understand the simulation. Ask students what a bicycle store might do to draw baby boomers who do not already have an interest in cycling. Ideas may include attending health fairs, promoting the health benefits, and stocking bicycles that fit the needs of middle-aged riders.

PROCEDURES

You may want to list procedures on the board and talk about any questions the students might have. Remind the students that a suggested outline for their project is available at **marketingessentials.glencoe.com/u11/ internship.**

TIME MANAGEMENT

Set goals, block schedules, and milestones. Assign interim deadlines for each step of the project.

ASSESSMENT

The rubrics for evaluation of the written, oral, and computer presentations are available at **marketingessentials.glencoe.com/u11/ internship.**

Start a Bicycle Business

 BASIC BACKGROUND

Your firm has a new client, a cycling enthusiast, who wants to open a bicycle shop. As former vice president of marketing for a small manufacturer, she took early retirement with a $200,000 severance package, which she is willing to invest in this new venture.

Picking Up Speed

Your client believes there's a growing interest in cycling because of Lance Armstrong's influence, and she says baby boomers are looking for exercise that is easier on the joints than running. That, combined with the client's passion for the sport of cycling, her business experience, and her capital resources, can mean potential success for your firm. Now all she needs is a good business plan to obtain the financing to begin her second career as a bicycle shop owner.

 YOUR OBJECTIVE

Your objective is to prepare a complete business plan for a new cycling shop for our client. A detailed financial section is important because this plan will be used to secure a loan and/or to interest investors in this new business venture.

 ASSIGNMENT AND STRATEGY

- **Get the background** Conduct research on the sport of cycling, as well as on different types of bicycles and accessories. Research suppliers of these items.

  Conduct a SWOT analysis and an assessment of the competition in your area. Study the geographic, demographic, and economic factors that could influence where the store is located. Consider what economic, socio-cultural, and technological factors might affect this business. Look for ways your client can differentiate her business from her competitors.

- **Figure out startup costs** Research the costs of opening the store, such as renovation of a local retail space that is available for lease or purchase, buying the initial inventory, and promotions, as well as fixed expenses to operate the business for the first year.

  Investigate ways of obtaining needed financial resources.

READ to WRITE

Variety in Bicycling

Ask the class to research at least two varieties of bicycles and their markets in a local, domestic, or international context. Examples may include BMX bicycles, mountain bikes, tandem bikes, and beach cruisers. Have students describe the different types of cycles, to whom they generally appeal, and how they are marketed. Then have students summarize the descriptions of the bicycles and their markets in a two-page report. Encourage students to add examples of advertisements or other marketing material and submit them with their reports.

- **Develop the business plan** Prepare a business plan that includes an introduction, an analysis of the business situation, proposed organization (such as the type of ownership and needed staffing), proposed marketing mix decisions, and a complete financial analysis and plan.

- **What your project should include** To make your project complete, include a suggested store layout, sample promotional materials, and detailed projected financial statements, such as a projected income statement, cash flow statement, and balance sheet.

YOUR REPORT

Use a word processing program and presentation software to prepare a double-spaced report and an oral presentation for your client. See a suggested outline and key evaluation points at *marketingessentials .glencoe.com/internship*

BUILD YOUR PORTFOLIO

Option 1 Internship Report
Once you have completed your Marketing Internship project and presentation, include your written report and a few printouts of key slides from your oral presentation in your Marketing Portfolio.

Option 2 Start Your Own Independent or Franchised Business
Assuming you had $100,000 to start a new business, what type of business would you open? Select a business (independent or franchise) you would like to open some day and write a complete business plan for it. Assume this plan will be used to obtain additional financing. Prepare your written report using a word processing program and use presentation software for your oral presentation. See a suggested outline and key evaluation points at *marketingessentials.glencoe .com/portfolio*

@ Online Action!

Go to *marketingessentials.glencoe .com/Unit/11/DECA* to review entrepreneurship concepts that relate to DECA events.

marketingessentials.glencoe.com

Marketing Internship **781**

Unit Review

Now that students have completed the chapters in Unit 11, ask them to review their answers to the Analyze the Ad question on page 695. Would they answer them differently? Why or why not?

Next, ask students if they were inspired by studying this unit to pursue an entrepreneurial endeavor. Were they influenced to consider entrepreneurship as a career? What conclusions can they draw about entrepreneurship from their study of this unit? Have students organize their thoughts about entrepreneurship in a brief essay. Call on volunteers to share their writing with the class.

STEP AHEAD
Ask students: How do entrepreneurs improve their abilities and develop their skills?

Internship Wrap-Up

Inform students that baby boomers who take up cycling will also need information about safety gear and rules for the road. Have the class design a course that could be offered by the business, outlining its benefits, how it would be run, and a fair price to charge.

BUILD YOUR PORTFOLIO

Explain to students that portfolios provide evidence of their knowledge and skills in working with data, people, and concepts. Developing a portfolio can be a valuable career development and planning tool. Point out to students that verbiage should be active, brief, and grammatically correct. Encourage students to check the portfolio information available at **marketingessentials.glencoe.com/u11/internship.**

Peer Review
Fellow students who share common interests can serve as reviewers of the final portfolios. This review can be completed through the use of a checklist. Go to **marketingessentials.glencoe.com/u11/internship** to find a suggested checklist.

Unit Objectives

After completing this unit, students should be able to:

- Assess personal values, goals, interests, and abilities for career decision making
- Participate in career planning activities using various sources of career information
- Develop a career plan based on career assessment and planning activities
- Identify job search strategies
- Write a letter of application, a résumé, and cover letter, and complete an application form
- Prepare for and conduct themselves properly during a job interview
- Follow up a job interview

■ Key to
■ Individualized
■ Activities

L1 Level 1 activities are basic activities and should fall within the range of all students.

L2 Level 2 activities are average activities and should be within the range of average and above average students.

L3 Level 3 activities are challenging activities designed for the ability range of above average students.

Enrichment Resources

PROFESSIONAL ORGANIZATIONS

American Marketing Association marketingpower.com

DECA deca.org

MEDIA RESOURCES

Print or online editions of

Fast Company Fastcompany.com

WRITING SUPPORT

Ask students to list three careers they are interested in pursuing. For each career, have them write a paragraph listing steps they can take in preparation. Ask students to keep and review this document as they study Unit 12.

Career Development

CHAPTER	PRINT MATERIALS	TECHNOLOGY RESOURCES
Chapter 37 Section 37.1 Section 37.2	**From Unit 12 Fast File Booklet** Lesson Plans Chapter Summaries Reproducible Masters Reproducible Tests **Print Ancillaries** Student Activity Workbook Marketing Math Workbook *BusinessWeek* Reader and Case Studies, Chapter 37 Competitive Events Workbook, Unit 12 Marketing Research Project Workbook School-to-Work Activity Workbook	Interactive Chalkboard classroom presentations, Chapter 37 Online Learning Center at **marketingessentials.glencoe.com** Online Student Edition, Chapter 37 TeacherWorks **Exam***View*® Pro Test Generator, Chapter 37 Virtual Business
Chapter 38 Section 38.1 Section 38.2	**From Unit 12 Fast File Booklet** Lesson Plans Chapter Summaries Reproducible Masters Reproducible Tests **Print Ancillaries** Student Activity Workbook Marketing Math Workbook *BusinessWeek* Reader and Case Studies, Chapter 38 Competitive Events Workbook, Unit 12 Marketing Research Project Workbook School-to-Work Activity Workbook	Interactive Chalkboard classroom presentations, Chapter 38 Online Learning Center at **marketingessentials.glencoe.com** Online Student Edition, Chapter 38 TeacherWorks **Exam***View*® Pro Test Generator, Chapter 38 Virtual Business

National Marketing Education

CHAPTER	SECTION	PERFORMANCE INDICATOR
Chapter 37 **Identifying Career Opportunities**	**37.1**	Identify tentative occupational interest (PD)
		Assess personal interests and skills needed for success in business (PD)
	37.2	Analyze employer expectations in the business environment (PD)
		Identify desirable personality traits important to business (PD)
		Identify sources of career information (PD)
		Explain employment opportunities in business (PD)
		Identify skills needed to enhance career progression (PD)
Chapter 38 **Finding and Applying for a Job**	**38.1**	Utilize job-search strategies (PD)
		Identify sources of career information (PD)
	38.2	Complete a job application (PD)
		Write a letter of application (PD)
		Prepare a résumé (PD)
		Interview for a job (PD)
		Write a follow-up letter after job interviews (PD)

PD Professional Development

Standards Assessment Correlation

	SECTION ASSESSMENT		CHAPTER ASSESSMENT					UNIT LAB
Reviewing Key Terms and Concepts	Integrating Academic Skills	Review Facts and Ideas	Build Skills	Develop Critical Thinking	Apply Concepts	Workplace Skills	Net Savvy	Marketing Internship
1, 2, 3	✓		21, 22	24, 25	26, 27	✓	✓	✓
1, 2, 3	✓	14, 15	21, 22	24, 25	26, 27	✓	✓	✓
		16	21, 22	25	27	✓		✓
1	✓		21, 22	24, 25	27	✓	✓	✓
		18	22	24	26		✓	✓
1, 2		20	22	24	26, 27		✓	✓
		20	21, 22	24	26, 27	✓	✓	✓
1, 2, 3	✓	10, 11, 12		22	23, 24		✓	
3	✓	10		22	23, 24		✓	
1				22	23			
3				22	23			
2, 3		14		22				
1, 2, 3		15, 16	18, 19	21		✓		
		17						

@ Online Action! Check the latest updates for national standards and for your state's standards at marketingessentials.glencoe.com

Unit Overview

Unit 12 describes the practical aspects of planning a career. Chapter 37 introduces the means for identifying and researching career possibilities and suggests that a student prepare a plan of action when a career choice has been made. Chapter 38 includes proven methods for conducting a job search.

MAKING IT RELEVANT

Ask students to brainstorm three to four possible marketing careers and to describe the types of skills, training, and education they think are needed to succeed in those careers. This unit will help students find and get a job that is satisfying and rewarding.

Unit Launch Activity

Have students share their first impressions of the ad on this page. Ask them who it appeals to and what its goal is. They may suggest that the main target market of the ad may be those who may have distorted views of American Indians. The ad is meant to enlighten readers and stir support for a cause. Other students may suggest that the ad is designed to inform American Indians about the career planning resources and career opportunities available to them.

In this unit you will find

- **Chapter 37**
  Identifying Career Opportunities

- **Chapter 38**
  Finding and Applying for a Job

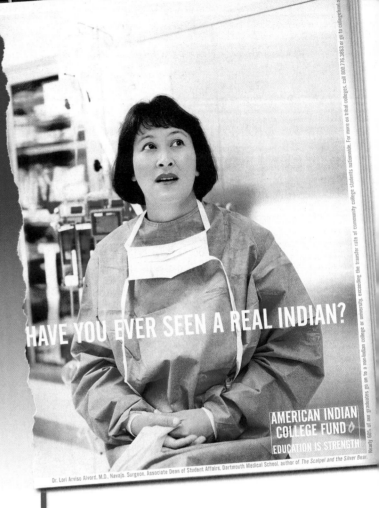

HAVE YOU EVER SEEN A REAL INDIAN?

AMERICAN INDIAN COLLEGE FUND ◊
EDUCATION IS STRENGTH

Dr. Lori Arviso Alvord, M.D., Navajo. Surgeon. Associate Dean of Student Affairs, Dartmouth Medical School, author of *The Scalpel and the Silver Bear.*

Nearly 60% of our graduates go on to a non-Indian college or university, exceeding the transfer rate of community college students nationwide. For more on tribal colleges, call 800.776.3863 or go to collegefund.org.

782

OUT OF TIME?

If class time is too short to cover all the chapters in this unit, go to Unit 12 in your Fast File Teacher Resources booklet and find the Chapter Summaries for Chapters 37 and 38.

DECA
An Association of Marketing Students

UNIT PROJECT

Preparing for the Interview

Have students prepare a file that includes their career profile, plan of action, sample job application, résumé, cover letter, references, and answers to common interview questions. Have them go through a simulated job interview with an adult, such as a faculty member, who will act as the interviewer. Ask the interviewers to provide feedback on an evaluation sheet.

Assessment Guidelines Prepare a rubric for evaluation that includes an honest and thorough assessment of the student's performance in the simulated interview. The interviewer should judge the students on such qualities as attitude, posture, thoughtfulness of responses, presentation of résumé, eye contact, and questions for the interviewer.

Enrichment Assign and review Unit 12 activities in the Competitive Events Workbook.

Career Development

ANALYZE THE AD

This ad promotes a nonprofit organization that supports education for American Indian youth. How does this ad relate to finding and pursuing a career path?

Market Talk Nonprofit and community-action organizations can use the power of marketing to help their causes. The nonprofit American Indian College Fund supports 34 tribal colleges and grants scholarships. What is the most powerful component of this ad?

Think and Write Many organizations help students with their educational and career goals. Look through Web sites and magazine and newspaper articles on education to find sources of support that could help you. Choose the most suitable or most promising options for you. Write out step-by-step plans for contacting the top three organizations on your list.

@ Online Action! Go to *marketingessentials.glencoe.com/u12/ad* for an extended activity.

Functions of Marketing

marketingessentials.glencoe.com

Marketing Plan

1. **ANALYSIS**
   SWOT
   Economic
   Socio-Cultural
   Technological
   Competitive

2. **STRATEGY**
   Promotion
   Place
   Price
   Product

3. **IMPLEMENTATION**
   Organization
   Management
   Staffing

4. **BUDGET**
   Cost of sales
   Cost of Promotion
   Incomes and Expenses

5. **CONTROL**
   Evaluation
   Performance Measures
   Performance Analysis

In this unit

Foundations of Marketing
- Communication, Interpersonal Skills
- Professional Development

783

Marketing Plan

RELATE THE UNIT TO THE MARKETING PLAN

Unit 12 will help students choose the career that is right for them. Most careers will involve marketing and the four Ps of the marketing mix: product, place, pricing, and promotion.

MARKETING PLAN OVERVIEW

Inform students that knowing how to create an effective marketing plan will benefit them in any career they choose.

Functions of Marketing

Point out to students that Chapters 37 and 38 will deal with the marketing foundations of professional development; and communications and interpersonal skills.

○ **Professional Development** Professional development is a natural part of any career trajectory. Students will learn this as they begin to think of where they see themselves professionally in a year's time, five years' time, and in 10 years.

○ **Communications, Interpersonal Skills** Composing a résumé and cover letter, handling an interview and its follow-up, and inquiring about jobs all require students to utilize their communications and interpersonal skills. Once they get the job, they will need these skills even more.

ANALYZE THE AD

The ad links access to an education to success in a career. The American Indian College Fund assists Native Americans in gaining an education and becoming skilled professionals.

Market Talk Answers will vary; many students may say that the most powerful component of the ad is the sentence, "Have you ever seen a real Indian?" It dismantles the stereotypes of Native Americans shown in Western movies or other media and, instead, shows a successful professional.

Think and Write Plans for contacting organizations that help students with their education and career goals will vary, but may include phone calls, e-mails, or visits.

@ Online Action! For instructions, ideas, and answer guide, go to the Teacher Center at *marketingessentials.glencoe.com*

Chapter Overview

In this chapter, students will look at the factors that will affect and influence their career decisions and plans. They will also read about the different career opportunities available in the field of marketing. they will also read about the different career opportunities available in the field of marketing.

Initiate a discussion about jobs students have had. What factors in a job make it satisfying? What kind of skills or preparation did they need to do the job? Did they need to know basic math operations? Ask students to discuss the different facets of and training for past jobs. Tell them they are going to learn how to choose and prepare for the careers best suited to them.

Why It's Important

Working in a field that best suits a person's lifestyle and interests makes for a more satisfying career. Being properly prepared to work in a chosen field helps ensure more success for any worker.

Prepare to Read

Ask a volunteer to write all of the major headings on the board in outline format:

Choosing a Career
Develop an Action Plan and Reach Your Goal
Is Marketing a Career for You?
Marketing Occupational Areas
Job Levels in Marketing

Tell students to fill in the secondary (blue) headings as they preview or read the chapter. They will then have a thorough chapter outline to use as study notes.

CHAPTER **37**
Identifying Career Opportunities

Chapter Objectives

After reading this chapter, you should be able to:

- Assess your goals, values, interests, skills, and aptitudes
- Appraise your personality
- Complete a career assessment
- Locate career research resources
- Develop a plan to reach your career goals
- Explain the importance of marketing careers to the U.S. economy

GUIDE TO THE PHOTO ▶

Market Talk According to the American Marketing Association, there are over 750,000 marketing professionals working in the United States and Canada. A vast array of opportunities awaits you. You may want to work with the public, spend your days in a quiet office with a computer, or be outdoors coordinating a promotional event for a customer. Jobs in marketing are found in varied environments throughout the United States and around the world.

Quick Think Now is the time to start narrowing your choices down to find the career that will satisfy you the most. How will you begin?

GUIDE TO THE PHOTO

Market Talk Lead a discussion about different fields and jobs that involve marketing. Ask students to brainstorm what kinds of jobs are involved in marketing. Students may name sales representatives, ad campaign managers, telemarketers, and more.

Quick Think Student responses may include weighing interests and abilities when choosing a career. Other things to consider may involve overall lifestyle goals.

Follow Up Ask students to describe several jobs they would not want and why those would not be good career choices for them.

Performance indicators represent key skills and knowledge. Relating them to the concepts explained in this chapter is your key to success in DECA events.

These acronyms represent DECA events that involve knowledge of concepts in this chapter.

AAAL*	FMAL*	MMS	TMDM*
AAML*	FMDM*	QSRM*	TSE*
ADC*	FMML*	RMAL*	VPM*
BSM	FSRM*	RMML*	
EMDM*	HMDM*	SMDM*	

In all these DECA events you should be able to follow these performance indicators:

- Assess personal interests and skills needed for success in business
- Use feedback for personal growth
- Make decisions
- Set personal goals
- Analyze employer expectations in the business environment
- Identify sources of career information
- Identify tentative occupational interest
- Explain employment opportunities in marketing
- Explain employment opportunities in business
- Describe techniques for obtaining work experience
- Explain the need for ongoing education as a worker
- Explain possible advancement patterns for job
- Identify skills needed to enhance career progression

All the events with an asterisk (*) also include this performance indicator:

- Describe/Explain career/employment opportunities in (that respective industry)

DECA PREP

Check your understanding of DECA performance indicators with the DECA activity in this chapter's review. For more information and DECA Prep practice, go to *marketingessentials .glencoe.com/37/DECA*

marketingessentials.glencoe.com

Chapter 37 - Identifying Career Opportunities **785**

DECA events that require knowledge of identifying career opportunities are described here. Discuss the performance indicators to make sure students understand how to demonstrate their understanding.

The event acronyms stand for:

AAAL: Apparel and Accessories Marketing Series, AL

AAML: Apparel and Accessories Marketing Series, ML

ADC: Advertising Campaign Event

BSM: Business Services Marketing Series

EMDM: E-Commerce Management Team Decision Making Event

FMAL: Food Marketing Series, AL

FMDM: Financial Analysis Management Team Decision Making Event

FMML: Food Marketing Series, ML

FSRM: Full Service Restaurant Management Series

HMDM: Hospitality Services Management Team Decision Making Event

MMS: Marketing Management Series

QSRM: Quick Serve Restaurant Management Series

RMAL: Retail Merchandising Series, AL

RMML: Retail Merchandising Series, ML

SMDM: Sports and Entertainment Marketing Management Team Decision Making Event

TMDM: Travel and Tourism Marketing Management Team DecisionMaking Event

TSE: Technical Sales Event

VPM: Vehicles and Petroleum Marketing Series

DECA PREP

Find timed DECA Prep activities correlated to the Competitive Events Workbook for students and DECA tips for teachers at **marketingessentials.glencoe.com /37/DECA**

CHAPTER 37 Classroom Resources

For the Teacher

- TeacherWorks
- marketingessentials.glencoe.com
- Interactive Chalkboard
- **ExamView®** Pro Test Generator
- Fast File Unit 12

For the Student

- *Marketing Essentials* Online Edition
- Student Activity Workbook
- Marketing Math Workbook
- Marketing Research Project Workbook
- School-to-Work Activity Workbook
- Competitive Events Workbook
- *BusinessWeek* Reader and Case Studies
- marketingessentials.glencoe.com

SECTION 37.1

FOCUS

Introducing the Section

COLLABORATIVE ACTIVITY

Divide students into groups of four to five. Have students create a collaborative list of facets of jobs. Examples may include work hours, level of training, travel, variety in daily tasks, level of independence, environmental factors, and amount of responsibility. Ask students to think about the work environment they would prefer.

Preteaching Key Terms

Read the key terms aloud, or ask a volunteer to read them. Ask students to look up each word in a dictionary:

- lifestyle
- values
- aptitude
- *Occupational Outlook Handbook (OOH)*
- career outlook
- O*NET
- internship
- planning goals
- specific goal
- realistic goal

Tell students to compare the dictionary definitions with the definitions from this section.

Extended Activity

Job Description

Name a specific job in the field of marketing, such as Director of Public Relations for a local sports team. Ask students to describe a good director of public relations, including that person's skills, preferences, and lifestyle. Descriptions may include an outgoing person who loves sports, doesn't mind working evenings and weekends, and manages others well.

OBJECTIVES

- Assess your goals, values, interests, skills, and aptitudes
- Appraise your personality
- Complete a career assessment
- Locate career research resources
- Develop a plan to reach your career goals

KEY TERMS

- lifestyle
- values
- aptitude
- *Occupational Outlook Handbook (OOH)*
- career outlook
- O*NET
- internship
- planning goals
- specific goal
- realistic goal

Define Goals

READ and STUDY

BEFORE YOU READ
Predict Are you interested in the careers of any of your family members or neighbors? Why or why not?

THE MAIN IDEA
Understanding yourself is the first step in finding a career you will enjoy. You need to know yourself well in order to select the most satisfying career. This section will help you begin to assess your attributes so you can match them to the right career for you. Then you will compare your needs to the opportunities for careers you have identified and researched.

STUDY ORGANIZER
Use a chart like the one below to note key aspects of the six steps in the self-assessment process.

The Self-Assessment Process	
What do I do well?	

WHILE YOU READ

Compare Which of the six self-assessment areas will have the greatest effect on your career choice?

Choosing a Career

Your career is the work you will do to earn a living over a period of years, perhaps a lifetime. A career often includes a series of progressively more responsible jobs in one field or in related fields. Choosing a career requires careful thought and preparation. This six-step process for decision making can help guide you in making important career choices:

786 UNIT 12 - EMPLOYABILITY AND CAREER DEVELOPMENT

READ and STUDY

BEFORE YOU READ
Answers will differ. Lead students to understand that people with similar interests, abilities, and values are likely to have common career goals.

THE MAIN IDEA
Have students predict the steps to defining their goals after reading the key terms and section headings.

STUDY ORGANIZER
Model the study organizer for students by filling in the second blank. A full-size, downloadable study organizer can be found at **marketingessentials.glencoe.com**

 WHILE YOU READ Remind students to think about the goals, skills, and interests that are most important to them. Tell them that each person's will be different.

1. Define your lifestyle goals.
2. Conduct a self-assessment.
3. Identify possible career choices and gather information on each.
4. Evaluate your choices.
5. Make your decision.
6. Plan how you will reach your goal.

In this section, we will explore how to define lifestyle goals, conduct a self-assessment, and identify possible career choices by gathering information.

Define Your Lifestyle Goals

The first step in choosing a career requires that you do a bit of reflecting. You need to think about what kind of life you would like to live—your **lifestyle**. What type of lifestyle do you want? How do you want to spend your time, energy, and money? The answers to these questions will help you set lifestyle goals to make possible the life you want to have in the future.

Your career has a great effect on lifestyle. Some careers will fit your lifestyle goals better than others. If spending time with your family is important to you, then you probably will not want a career that requires a lot of travel. Similarly, if you cherish weekends for religious or leisure activities, you probably will not look for a job that requires working weekends. Knowing your lifestyle goals will help you find a career that enhances your lifestyle.

As a student, your life revolves around school, friends, and family. As an adult, your lifestyle will be influenced by:

- where you live (city, suburbs, or rural area)
- the type of housing in which you live
- the cultural environment in which you live, including the kinds of shopping and leisure activities you enjoy
- your mode of transportation
- your relationships with your family and friends
- the work you do to earn a living

Your career is the key to your lifestyle because it will provide the earnings needed to support your lifestyle. Before you can determine how compatible a career will be with lifestyle goals, you need to assess what your goals are.

Conduct a Self-Assessment

Be prepared to record your findings in a notebook. Label the notebook *Self-Assessment File*. Summarize your various assessments in paragraph form or, where appropriate, by using a rating scale.

Your Values

Values are beliefs that guide the way we live. Just as people have different abilities and personalities, they also have different values. Defining your system of values is essential in choosing a career.

•**CITY or COUNTRY?** Living in the city can be exciting yet demanding. A rural setting offers a quieter, more relaxed lifestyle.

In which setting would you feel most comfortable, urban or rural?

TEACH

Discussion Starter

CHOOSING A CAREER

Ask students to consider the following scenario: All her life Selena's family encouraged her to become a teacher. Many family members worked in education and enjoyed their careers. Selena became an elementary-school teacher, but is frustrated by her students' dependence on her, as well as the long hours of preparation needed. She wants to start over in another field, but she is not sure what she wants to do. Ask students where Selena should start. Have them brainstorm a list of questions they could ask her to get her thinking about a new career.

TEACHING POINTS

Model Have a student help you act out an interview between Selena and a career counselor (with you as counselor). Select your questions from a career inventory or from a personality index.

Explain Tell students that choosing a career more suited to her interests and lifestyle will help Selena lead a happier life. This may be the first time in her life that Selena really thought about her own goals and values regarding her career. Students may be in a similar situation.

 Online Activity

Self-Assessment

Have students find different Web sites with free personality and career assessments. Each student should complete at least one assessment.

Lead a discussion about the results. Did their findings surprise students or did they confirm what the students already knew about themselves?

PHOTO GUIDE — CITY or COUNTRY?

Discussion Lead a discussion about the lifestyle of the person in the picture. Ask students: How do you think the lifestyle this person has chosen affects her choice of career?

Caption Answer Student answers will differ but should tell them something about their desired lifestyle.

Follow Up Ask students to name three marketing careers they think would fit this persons's supposed lifestyle goals and three that would not.

TEACH CONTINUED

Concept Development

YOUR INTERESTS

After students have read the section on interests, ask them to imagine doing their favorite hobby for a living. Ask students to explain in a one-paragraph response how they could use their hobby in a career.

Sample answer: someone who enjoys playing computer games could study programming and become a game creator or tester

Discussion Starter

IDENTIFY POSSIBLE CAREER CHOICES AND GATHER INFORMATION

Ask students to brainstorm reasons that it is important to research a career outlook for more than one career.

Answers may include that it is easier to get a job in a growing field. If a career outlook is decreasing, so will the number of job opportunities in that field. It would be better to train in a career that is growing.

Identify your values by focusing on the beliefs and actions that are important to you. If you are willing to work very hard to succeed, you value achievement. Another possible value is the opportunity to express yourself.

Your Interests

Most people spend between 30 and 40 years working, so it makes sense to choose work that interests you. When you can clearly define your interests, you can gain a clearer picture of a career that will be fulfilling to you.

To evaluate your interests, write down the things you like to do. Include leisure activities, school activities, favorite classes, sports, and social activities.

Another way to find out about your interests is to take a career interest survey. Such surveys are similar to tests, but there are no right or wrong answers. You are given a long list of activities, and you decide how much you would like doing each of them. Then you score the survey yourself to learn which careers best match your interests. Your school counselor or marketing teacher can probably arrange for you to take one of these surveys.

Your Skills and Aptitudes

To be successful in any career, you will need specific skills and aptitudes.

An **aptitude** may be an ability or natural talent, or it may be the potential to learn a certain skill. Pursuing a career without having an aptitude for the required skills may be a struggle instead of a pleasure, and real success will be hard to achieve. Once you know what skills are required to perform a job, you can determine if you have the aptitude to acquire those skills.

You may have already developed skills that will be useful in a career that interests you. Do you find it easy to sell cookies, candy bars, or other items to raise funds for your DECA chapter? Are you good at organizing committees and getting others to do their jobs? Is math easy for you? Have you won any prizes for your creative efforts? List your skills and aptitudes on a separate sheet of paper in your self-assessment file, and update your list as you develop new skills.

Your Personality

Your personality is the combination of all of the unique qualities that make you who you are. Understanding your personality characteristics will help you to determine what types of work situations will best suit you. Personality tests, available through your guidance counselor, can help you identify your personality type. Think about how you respond to stress. Do you find it an enjoyable challenge, or do you avoid it? As you perform this exercise, remember that there is no right or wrong kind of personality. There are only different kinds of people.

Your Work Environment Preferences

Your work environment refers to where you work—the place and its working conditions. Working conditions include sights, sounds, and smells.

You do not have to know all your preferences about working conditions now, but you should start thinking about them. For example, do you prefer to work indoors or outdoors? Sitting down or standing up?

Your Relationship Preferences

All jobs require working with information and ideas, people, or objects—alone or in some combination. These categories can form the basis for describing different kinds of careers. Since any career you choose will likely involve an overlap of these categories, think about which interests you most. Do you like working with others, or do you prefer to work alone? Are you comfortable handling interpersonal conflicts at work? The answers to these questions, too, can help you understand your relationship preferences.

Identify Possible Career Choices and Gather Information

To research careers, you will need to gather information from a variety of sources. You will find current information at libraries or on the Internet. You can also learn a great deal through informational interviews, professional and trade organizations, and actual work experience.

Online Activity

Searching the *OOH*

Have students visit the Web site of the *Occupational Outlook Handbook.* Point out the different ways to conduct a search on the Web site; for instance, students could search by occupational clusters such as sales. Have students use the Web site to find the projected outlook for marketing careers in the next 10 years.

Case Study

The Career of Stan Ovshinsky

One secret to a successful career is being open to change and willing to explore new possibilities. Stanley Ovshinsky has done just that. Born over 80 years ago, he has made discoveries and inventions in the world of physics and chemistry since 1960 that have had commercial uses in everything from cell phones to space stations.

Hero of the Planet

Time magazine named Ovshinsky a Hero of the Planet in 1999 for his development of small-scale solar electric systems that allow even remote villages to have electricity.

Ovshinsky's physics discoveries led to the development of the rechargeable, "green," NiMH battery. This technology powers not only millions of cell phones, digital cameras, and other small electronic devices but also the first consumer electric vehicle, the EV-1. His work on phase-change optical memory has been applied in rewritable DVD and CD products.

In recent years, Ovshinsky, together with Toyota, has built a prototype hydrogen hybrid car that produces no exhaust emissions and goes from 0 to 74 mph in 6 seconds. His goal is to have a commercially viable solid hydrogen system ready to fuel a zero-emission vehicle for the automotive industry by 2010. As he moves towards his 90th birthday, Ovshinsky shows no signs of resting on his laurels.

THINK STRATEGICALLY

Ovshinsky started out running a machine shop, and he was always interested in metals and their properties. What interests do you have that could lead to a successful career?

 Online Action! Go to *marketingessentials.glencoe.com/37/case* to find an activity on career development.

Libraries

A publication you will find in the library is the ***Occupational Outlook Handbook (OOH)***. The U.S. Department of Labor publishes a revised edition of the *OOH* every two years and the *OOH Quarterly* four times each year. The *OOH* describes what workers do on the job, working conditions, the training and education needed, earnings, and expected job prospects in a wide range of occupations. These publications will give you valuable information on the number and types of jobs available in any field, known as the **career outlook**.

Professional and Trade Associations

Professional and trade associations serve individuals and businesses with common interests. These are excellent sources for current information about careers in many professions.

Members are usually people working in or associated with the same industry. Some associations serve individuals in particular careers,

---

Case Study — The Career of Stan Ovshinsky

Discussion Have students read the Case Study and discuss how running a metal shop could have led to Ovshinsky's other achievements.

THINK STRATEGICALLY **Answer:** Answers will vary. One interest can often lead to the development of another. For example, Ovshinsky saw a need in his machine shop for more efficient energy. This probably led to him thinking about and then developing, his own inventions. These inventions took him out of the machine shop and into an inventor's lab.

Online Action! For instructions, ideas, and answer guide, go to the Teacher Center at marketingessentials.glencoe.com

Follow Up Have students do an online search to learn more about Stan Ovshinsky. It may surprise students to know that Ovshinsky never went to college.

Individualized Practice

DEFINE SKILLS AND APTITUDES

L1 Have students put a checkmark beside the skills on their lists that they are using in their current job. (Remind students that being a full-time student can be considered a job.) Next, have students put a star beside the skills that they would like to use in a career. Have them brainstorm ways they can use or develop these skills.

L2 Read the following biography to the students as an example of a biography of a particular worker: "I like telling people where to go. I enjoy researching about different places and will even visit to do a thorough job. I am outgoing, so I work well with people. I am good at discovering the type of vacation others most prefer. This may include types of transportation, activities, as well as temporary housing." Ask students to name a career area that this biography might represent.
Possible career areas include travel, tourism/hospitality, and marketing.

L3 Ask students to create a one-page biography based on the life of someone in a particular career. The description should only include the skills, goals, and personality of the worker without stating the job.

Build Vocabulary

Preview the following words by reading them in context in the Case Study text:

- **prototype** example or standard
- **laurels** honors, accolades

Have students propose definitions. Then, discuss the meaning of these words with students.

TEACH CONTINUED

Individualized Practice

SELF-EVALUATION

L1 Ask students the following questions about their relationship preferences: Do you feel that you do your best brainstorming in a group? Or do you feel more inspired when working alone? Do you want lots of feedback about your performance? Or do you feel that supervision takes up time better used elsewhere? Ask students to respond to these questions in writing.

L2 Have students write a two-page biographical essay about their self-assessments. It should include the topics discussed in this section: values, interests, skills, aptitudes, personality, work environment preferences, and relationship preferences.

L3 Have students pair up and act out giving each other career counseling. Ask them to take turns asking each other assessment questions. At the end of each turn, have the "counselor" give the other as many career options as possible that the other should consider.

Critical Thinking

Have students explain why a more reserved person who prefers working alone might not be the best person to be a travel agent.

790

---

such as the American Marketing Association or the Direct Marketing Association.

These associations promote pooling of resources, technology cooperation, common standards, and marketing strategies. Information is disseminated in newsletters, journals, and reports.

The Internet

Much of the information previously available in print at libraries is now available online. **O*NET**, the Occupational Information Network, has replaced the *Dictionary of Occupational Titles,* which was the primary source of occupational information for fifty years. The O*NET database includes information on skills, abilities, knowledge, work activities, and interests associated with occupations. The O*NET site provides information on how to use the O*NET database. The *Occupational Outlook Handbook (OOH),* described previously in the section on libraries, is also available online. Directions for locating career information are given on the *OOH* site.

You can also find a wealth of resources for research from America's Career InfoNet Web site. The College Board has a section on its Web site devoted to helping you research careers.

Informational Interviews

You may want to set up an informational interview with a professional who works in a career that interests you. You can learn about the demands and opportunities of a career by talking with someone who has experience. You also get the opportunity to learn about the day-to-day realities of a job. Those who have met the challenges of a career are usually happy to talk about it.

Ask both your teacher and your counselor for suggestions about whom you should interview. They may have lists of people in the community who enjoy talking with young people about their work. Family members and friends of the family can also sometimes give you leads.

If you do not get some good suggestions from these sources, contact the public affairs

NET MARKETING

College While You Work

If your career goal is a high-level job in any area of marketing, you will want to continue your education past high school into college, and probably beyond a bachelor's degree to an MBA or other graduate degree. What if you have already begun your career path, and do not feel able to take time off for college or an advanced study? An online degree program could be the solution.

There are many fully accredited universities offering degrees in a variety of business areas to students who want to do some or most of their degree work in an online environment. Many online students are already working in fields related to their studies. Bachelor's, master's, and doctoral programs are all available online. Studying online means that students download lectures at their own pace and on their own schedules. Students receive and submit assignments and get instructor feedback by e-mail. They have access to online research libraries as well as to other students with whom they can discuss course content. The market for these services might include you.

 THINK LIKE A MARKETER

List three pros and three cons of an online degree program.

@ Online Action!

Go to *marketingessentials.glencoe.com/ 37/net* to find an activity about online degrees.

NET MARKETING

College While You Work

Discussion Have students discuss the advantages and disadvantages of online degree programs. You may want to preprint information from an online education Web site about their program to spark discussion.

THINK LIKE A MARKETER **Answer:** Pros may include: working at one's own pace, working at unscheduled hours, not having to commute or pay for parking, etc. Cons may include: not being able to meet other students, not getting immediate feedback from the instructor, having to be self-disciplined, etc.

@ Online Action! For instructions, ideas, and answer guide, go to the Teacher Center at **marketingessentials.glencoe.com**

• **INTERVIEW for SUCCESS** An interview with a prospective employer offers you an opportunity to collect information about a job or career.

What other opportunities does the interview offer the interviewer and the interviewee? Do you think an interview is a good resource in gathering information about a career of interest to you? Why or why not?

or public relations officer at a professional association. Ask if the organization sponsors career nights or other opportunities where you can speak with people who are currently working in the field.

Before any interview, prepare a list of questions that you want to ask. Here are some suggestions:

- How do you spend most of your time on the job?
- Which work activities do you like most?
- What skills will I need to do this type of work?
- What skills will I need to advance?
- What education and training will I need?
- Can I complete some of the training after I begin working?
- How much time do you spend working with ideas and information? With people? With objects?
- Will there be an increase in job opportunities in this field over the next several years? What impact will automation and new technology have on job opportunities in the next few years?

On-the-Job Experience

Many students work part-time after school, on weekends, or during the summer months. If you have an idea of a career you might be interested in pursuing, an entry-level position in that field will offer you great experience.

On-the-job experience offers you many benefits. You can:

- try out some of the work activities in your career field and decide how much you like doing them;
- experience the work environment associated with that career;
- develop work habits that will help you succeed in your career;
- broaden your understanding of the world of work and smooth the transition from school to work;
- make career contacts who can serve as mentors or assist you when you are searching for a job later; and
- build up your résumé, which will grow as you gain more working experience.

You may also look into an internship program at a company or organization that interests you. An **internship** offers students direct work experience and exposure to various aspects of a career, either with or without pay.

The value of an internship is in the experience and the contacts that you make. Employers seriously consider internship experience when reviewing candidates for new positions.

Chapter 37 - Identifying Career Opportunities 791

TEACH CONTINUED

Individualized Practice

CHOOSING A CAREER

L1 Ask students to research one marketing job that interests them. Based on their research, have them write a 100-word job description for the career choice. The description should include such things as job duties, salary range, work environment, education requirements, and pathway for advancement.

L2 Have students write a one-page self-assessment that states reasons they would do well at a chosen job. Students should list all their resources and attach any ads used as source material. Encourage students to review their source material and resources in class.

L3 Have each student role-play an internship interview with another student, asking such questions as "What skills do you already have that will help you do this job?" and "What kind of training have you had that has prepared you for this position?"

TEACHING POINTS

Clarify Point out that students' self-assessments would help prepare them for a job interview for that particular career.

Figure 37.1 **Personal Career Profile**

• **Is It a Match?** A personal career profile helps you compare your self-assessment with a particular career assessment.

Based on this career profile, how does Joan Smith's personal information match the information about a teaching career? Rank each category from 1 to 5, with 5 being the best match.

Name Joan Smith   Date September 4, 20--

Personal Information	Career Information	Match (1–5, with 5 being the best match)
Your Values: The value scales I took showed that I like to help other people (humanitarianism). I like to be a leader. Doing creative things is fun, too.	**Values:** As a teacher I would have a chance to help others—that's what it's all about. Teachers certainly have plenty of opportunities to be leaders, too. Teachers also need to be creative!	
Your Interests: My hobby interests have always been photography, reading, and theater. My career interest survey showed that I might like a career in leading/influencing, selling, the arts, or maybe a humanitarian career.	**Career Duties and Responsibilities:** As a teacher, I would present information, and direct student discussions and activities in class. I would help each student individually, too. (Maybe I could teach marketing or general business.) A teacher's working conditions would be good in most schools. (Summers off!)	
Your Personality: I like people, and I have a good attitude toward learning. I have an open mind. I'm enthusiastic, too. However, I don't have the energy and drive that some people have. I don't know if I could work night after night.	**Type of Personality Needed:** A teacher must like kids, even when they aren't very likeable. I would have to prepare my lessons every day—couldn't just forget about them. Teachers need to be organized, too.	
Data-People-Things Preferences: I think I like working with people most of all. I wouldn't want to be stuck in an office all day with only "data" to talk to. I also wouldn't like working only with things. Some data would be all right, though.	**Data-People-Things Relationships:** Teachers work mostly with people—their students, the principal, parents. They work with data (information), too, though. I don't think they work much with things.	
Skills and Aptitudes: I may have some natural teaching skills—the kids at the YMCA always come to me for help. I helped several kids in Miss Moore's class. Business classes are easy for me.	**Skills and Aptitudes Needed:** Being able to present information so students can understand it is a very important skill. Of course, you must know your subject. An appetite for learning new approaches to teaching is important, too.	
Education/Training Acceptable: I sure never thought I would go to college—I never even liked doing the homework in high school. However, here I am a senior with no real prospects of a good job. Maybe college is the answer.	**Education/Training Required:** Four years of college (it sounds like forever, but I guess it does go fast) are required before you can begin teaching in most states. Some states require course work beyond that.	

 Online Action! Go to *marketingessentials.glencoe.com/37/figure/1* to find a project on career assessment.

Figure 37.1 **Personal Career Profile**

Discussion Ask students to discuss how Joan assessed herself. For example, did Joan make honest assessments? Ask students to brainstorm where this self-assessment might lead her.

Caption Answer Rankings will vary. Most students, however, will agree that Joan's strongest career matches are the Values, Interests, and Skills and Aptitudes sections. Her weakest match is Education/Training Acceptable.

 Online Action! For instructions, ideas, and answer guide, go to the Teacher Center at marketingessentials.glencoe.com

Follow Up Have students create their own Personal Career File. Ask them to have someone who knows them well rank each category for them. Have them compare this profile with their own ranking of themselves.

GLOBAL MARKET

Marketing Yourself Globally

Have you ever thought about living in another country? Imagine you spot the information below on a Web site dedicated to working abroad.

- The New Zealand government will grant up to 500 young citizens of the United States of America (USA) work visas for a working holiday annually.
- Visas allow a working holiday of 12 months.

To be eligible you must:

- be a citizen or resident of the USA
- prove that your main reason for coming to New Zealand is to visit
- have a valid American passport
- hold a return ticket or sufficient funds to purchase such a ticket
- have a minimum of NZ$4,200 in available funds to meet your living costs while in New Zealand
- hold medical and comprehensive hospitalization insurance for the length of your stay

CRITICAL THINKING

How would working in a foreign country help your long-term career plan?

@ Online Action!

Go to *marketingessentials.glencoe.com/37/global* to find an activity on technology and career planning.

It demonstrates high interest and a willingness to put in time to gain valuable experience.

Evaluate Your Choices

Once you identify one or even several interesting careers, it is time to compare and contrast that potential career with your self-assessment. In this way, you can determine if a career that seems of interest is really a good match for you.

Organize your task before you begin for better efficiency. Gather all of your self-assessment notes and research on different careers. It is helpful to begin this matching process on paper. Create a personal career profile, using an evaluation format that allows you to compare your self-assessment side-by-side with a particular career assessment (see Figure 37.1).

On the left side of the profile, write down the information about yourself. Then make several photocopies of this form—one for each career that you researched and that interests you. Using these copies, fill in the career information on the right by referring to your notes. After you complete each profile, reread all the information carefully. The following questions will guide you as you evaluate your choices.

- Do the work values in this field match my values?
- Will this career support my lifestyle goals?

marketingessentials.glencoe.com

Chapter 37 - Identifying Career Opportunities **793**

GLOBAL MARKET

Marketing Yourself Globally

Discussion Ask students how global work experience might make them more desirable to stateside companies.

CRITICAL THINKING **Answer:** Answers will vary; answers may include that working abroad shows commitment to an occupation, curiosity about the world, tenacity, and global thinking capabilities; useful qualities in any career.

@ Online Action! For instructions, ideas, and answer guide, go to the Teacher Center at **marketingessentials.glencoe.com**

Concept Development

EVALUATE YOUR CHOICES

After evaluating their potential careers, many students may decide that the career would not be a good match for them after all. Remind students that changing career choices is not wrong, but will be good for them in the long run. Direct them back to the beginning of the section to choose a new career path. Ask students the following questions:

- What have you learned about yourself after walking down a path and finding that it wasn't the best route to take?
- What skills and abilities did you learn that you were able to apply to something you did enjoy?

 Extended Activity

Your Own Pros and Cons List
Ask students to list factors they would have to consider about their own lives if they are offered an internship. Have volunteers share their individual decisions about taking an internship. Have them list the three biggest factors in their decisions.

Critical Thinking

Ask students to brainstorm ways how knowing about marketing could be useful in other fields or aspects of life. For example, marketing might be useful when developing a new product or medicine, or it could help a volunteer organization solicit donations.

TEACH CONTINUED

Concept Development

DEVELOPING A CAREER PLAN

After students have read **Figure 37.2**, ask them to explain that setting career goals can be like a roadmap. Ask students to brainstorm what the landmarks in a career plan might be.

Answers may include: A roadmap helps you reach a destination, a goal. Sometimes there is more than one way to reach the destination. Usually when you get directions to a place, there are landmarks along the way that help you know you are going in the right direction. Landmarks in a career plan are short- and medium-term goals that help you reach your long-term goal (the final destination).

TEACHING POINTS

Compare Explain to students that people often use a roadmaps even though they have written directions as well. In the same way, visualizing the distance between your goals on your career plan can help you decide which path to take to reach your goal.

Extended Activity

Making Career Decisions

Tell students that many of them may not feel ready to make a decision about what career to pursue. Tell students that one way to help determine career is to determine what kind of lifestyle you want. Also tell students that they should write those lifestyle or career goals down. They can then go back and read these goals when they are faced with a decision that affects their future. Have students write down at least two examples of career goals. An example might include "Become a buyer for a department store within 5 years of graduation from high school."

- Do the responsibilities match my skills and aptitudes?
- How suited is the job to my personality?
- Does the work environment match my needs?
- Does the career offer the work relationships I am seeking?

Develop an Action Plan and Reach Your Goal

A plan does not guarantee success, but outlining the steps that you need to follow to reach your ultimate goal will provide a path.

Formulate Planning Goals

The small steps you take to get from where you are now to where you want to be are **planning goals**. They give your life a sense of direction and move you steadily toward your ultimate career goal. Every time you reach a goal, you gain confidence to move on to the next one (see Figure 37.2).

Be Specific

The best way to make progress toward your ultimate goal is to make your planning goals specific. A **specific goal** is stated in exact terms and includes some details. The goal statement "I want to become a success" is not specific. "I want to complete my class in marketing this semester and earn at least a B" is specific. It is the type of planning goal that moves you forward. The more specific you are about your career goals, the more likely you are to formulate a plan to reach those goals.

Be Realistic

Planning goals must also be realistic. A **realistic goal** is one that you have a reasonable chance of achieving. Think about all of the different skills and aptitudes that you possess. They will guide you in identifying both your ultimate career goal and your planning goals.

Work Backward

When you set your planning goals, begin with your ultimate career goal. Then decide what objectives you must reach along the way

---

to achieve your ultimate goal. Work backward, starting with your most distant, long-term goal, and move toward the present to determine the necessary medium- and short-term goals.

For example, suppose your ultimate career goal is to become a chef. A long-term goal may be to study with a world-class chef. To earn the credentials you need to get such an opportunity, you may set a medium-term goal of earning a degree from a culinary institute. Another medium-term goal may be to get a job at a well-respected restaurant in your town or city. To prepare for that opportunity, you may set a short-term goal to work in a local kitchen to gain practical experience. Another short-term goal may be to investigate what type of training you will need. So, you may subscribe to a cooking magazine or keep up-to-date with new cookbooks.

Having a progressive series of goals allows you to test your ultimate career goal and make corrections along the way. While progressing toward your career goal, your experiences may reinforce your career decision or lead to your changing your career goal. You may discover another career that you find more interesting. On the basis of work experience in a kitchen, you may discover that you would rather own a restaurant than be a chef. At any point along the way, you can adjust your path and your ultimate goal.

Professional Development

Whatever your career choice, you will need a plan of action to reach your goal. Your plan must include the concepts and strategies needed for personal and professional growth.

Choosing education is much like choosing a career. Follow the complete decision-making process to select the best program and the best school for you. Your school counselor is a good place to start. Your school and public libraries are likely to have useful information. You can also search the Internet and visit the Web sites of those schools that interest you.

Due to the continuing changes brought about by technology and the competition of a global economy, all professionals must

---

Online Activity

Education Options

Ask students to find at least five Web sites for places to pursue further education or training in marketing. Have students include at least one school offering online classes. Encourage students to explore the site, perhaps by using the site map. Have the students document important information such as information about the program, cost, etc. Students could present information by printing up a page from each site, by using a spreadsheet program, or by creating a graph to compare schools.

Figure 37.2 Developing a Career Plan

• **Steps to Take** After you have completed a self-evaluation to determine your personal strengths and weaknesses and researched possible career paths, you should be ready to write a career plan and begin to act on it.

What is your plan?

STEP 1: SET CAREER GOALS

You need a road map to get from where you are to your final destination. The specific, realistic, short- and medium-term goals you set are the mile markers on your map. Achieving each one takes you that much closer to your final career goal.

STEP 2: DEVELOP AN EDUCATION/ PROFESSIONAL DEVELOPMENT PLAN

Choosing how much and what kind of education or training you need for your career is one of the most important decisions you will make. Develop short- and long-term education and training goals, including internships with employers in the fields that attract you.

STEP 3: DRAW UP A PLAN OF ACTION

Create your plan, including both the work experience goals and the educational goals you will need to reach your ultimate career. Be realistic about the timing of each step of your plan. Know that you will likely revise it as time goes on and circumstances change.

@ **Online Action!** Go to *marketingessentials.glencoe.com/37/figure/2* to find a project on career planning.

marketingessentials.glencoe.com **Chapter 37 - Identifying Career Opportunities** 795

Figure 37.2 Developing a Career Plan

Discussion Based on the information shown in the pictures, have students guess what the student's long-term career goal might be (e.g., scientist, magazine publisher). Ask: How might these short- and medium-term goals differ for different careers?

Caption Answer Plans will vary; all plans should follow the three steps: setting career goals, developing an education plan, and having a plan of action.

Follow Up Have students use their career plans to create one of the following options:

• A fictional story with the writer as the main character, who uses the plan of action to reach the career goal as the plot in the story.

• A roadmap including short-, medium-, and long-term goals.

• A flow chart or sequence diagram with arrows leading to the next goals.

Review Guide

CONCEPTS

1. Ask students to recall the categories of self-assessments needed when choosing a career.
lifestyle, values, interests, skills, aptitudes, personality, work environment, and relationship preferences

2. Have students list different sources where they can find career information.
libraries, the Internet, informational interviews, on-the-job experience, and professional and trade associations

KEY TERMS

Have students review key terms, their spellings, and definitions in small groups.

ONLINE SELF-ASSESSMENT

Have students go to **marketingessentials.glencoe.com** for the Section 37.1 practice test.

Individualized Review

L1 Assign and review Chapter 37 activities in the Student Activity Workbook.

L2 Assign and review Chapter 37 activities in the Marketing Math Workbook.

L3 Assign and review Chapter 37 activities in the *BusinessWeek* Reader and Case Studies.

Marketing Practice

Divide students into small groups. Find several copies of the *Occupational Outlook Handbook (OOH)* and give each group an OOH, or direct the students to the OOH Web site. Give each group a slip of paper with an occupation on it. Have groups find the career and create a 10-minute presentation about that career for the class.

CLOSE

1. Have students complete this statement: The most valuable thing I learned in this lesson regarding career planning was _____.
Answers will vary. Students may mention setting goals, researching careers, or performing self-assessments.

2. Have students choose a career and perform a self-assessment where they match up their skills and abilities to that career. Have students then create a plan for developing the necessary skills for that career. Have students document their results in a two-page report.

Extended Activity

Entry-Level Positions

Ask students to write a one-page essay on how starting any career at an entry-level position can prepare them for a higher skill level position. Student essays might mention that, in order to be successful at a highly skilled level, you should understand the jobs at lower levels or, while you are at an entry-level position, you can observe those over you and then choose one as a role model for your future position.

---

upgrade their existing skills and acquire new ones. It is no surprise, then, that lifelong learning is key to any successful career.

If you are planning for education and training beyond high school, consider the following questions:

- What is my ultimate career goal?
- What course can I take now that will help me to reach that career goal?
- What education and training beyond high school is required to reach my career goal?
- How much of this education and training must I complete before I enter this career?
- Where can I get this education and training?
- How much will this education and training cost, and how will I get the money?
- How much education and training can I get on the job?

Outlining Your Plan

After you have answered these questions, begin writing your personal plan of action. Write down all of your goals, the date that you plan to begin working toward each one, and the date you expect to reach each goal. Identify the skills you will need to enhance progression in your career. This will help keep you on track toward your ultimate career goal—the one that turns your dream lifestyle into reality.

 37.1 AFTER YOU READ

Reviewing Key Terms and Concepts

1. What are the first two basic steps in choosing a career?
2. List three considerations that will help you formulate planning goals.
3. List six areas to explore when conducting a self-assessment.

Integrating Academic Skills

Math

4. Assume that you will work for 40 years before you retire. You invest $5,000 in a retirement fund at the end of your first year. It compounds at a 7 percent annual rate of return for the next 39 years. How much will be in the account when you retire? Use the following equation to find the amount that will be in the account: Amount = $5000 \times (1.07)^{39}$ where $(1.07)^{39}$ is 13.9948204.

Language Arts

5. Use your library, school career center, local bookstore, or online bookstore to obtain two books on choosing a career. Browse through each book and read the chapters devoted to self-assessment. Then, make a chart comparing the information both books give about the steps to self-assessment.

 Online Action! Check your answers at *marketingessentials.glencoe.com/37/read*

 AFTER YOU READ

Reviewing Key Terms and Concepts

1. Conduct a self-assessment and choose a career that is right for you.

2. Planning considerations include specific, realistic goals; training and education; costs; time frames; and short-, medium-, and long-term goals.

3. Self-assessment includes values, interests, skills, aptitudes, personality, and work environment and relationship preferences.

Integrating Academic Skills

4. The account will amount to $69,974.10 by the time you retire.

5. Charts will vary; all charts should demonstrate an understanding of self-assessment and how to conduct a self-assessment.

Online Action! Answers at **marketingessentials.glencoe.com/37/read**

Careers in Marketing

OBJECTIVES

- Explain the importance of marketing careers to the U.S. economy

KEY TERMS

- occupational area

READ and STUDY

BEFORE YOU READ
Predict What do you already know about careers in marketing?

THE MAIN IDEA
If you are considering a career in marketing, you will need to learn about the requirements, opportunities, rewards, and trends in this exciting field. The more career information you have, the easier it will be to reach a career decision.

STUDY ORGANIZER
In a chart such as the one below write in the benefits, trends, and job levels of marketing careers.

Questions About a Marketing Career

1. _____
2. Are there many jobs available? _____
3. _____

Is Marketing a Career for You?

As you study marketing, you have the opportunity to evaluate marketing as a potential career. Even if you decide that marketing is not for you, the skills and knowledge you gain from your study will help you in school and on the job. These skills include writing, researching, communication, and analytical skills, among others.

Analyze List three pros and three cons of a career in marketing.

Chapter 37 - Identifying Career Opportunities **797**

READ and STUDY

BEFORE YOU READ
Have students name all the marketing careers they can. List them on the board, then discuss what students know about each one.

THE MAIN IDEA
Ask a volunteer to retell the main idea in his or her own words.

STUDY ORGANIZER
Model the study organizer for students by filling in the first blank. A full-size, downloadable study organizer can be found at **marketingessentials.glencoe.com**

WHILE YOU READ Point out that what some people would consider pros, others may consider cons.

FOCUS

Introducing the Section

COLLABORATIVE ACTIVITY
Have students brainstorm list of marketing jobs they know. Examples might include advertising executive, entrepreneur, and sales clerk. As students name jobs, have them also give a salary range. Ask students how they think salary is determined for these jobs.
Answers may include level of education or training, level of responsibility, or commissions.

Preteaching Key Terms

Read the key term aloud. Ask students to give examples of the key term.

- occupational area
Answers will vary; students may mention well-known occupational areas such as health care, entertainment, or sales.

TEACH

Discussion Starter

IS MARKETING A CAREER FOR YOU?
Ask the students to consider the following scenario: Kelis is a display specialist for a large downtown store. She loves her job, but hopes to someday be store manager. She has been offered a promotion to the position of buyer. Although she knows that this would get her one step closer to her goal of store manager, she does not think she would like the job. She would especially miss being off the sales floor and away from customers and sales-clerks. Ask students to list pros and cons for Kelis in her decision.

Review Guide

CONCEPTS

Remind students that a marketing career can lead to a good income and interesting work. Have them list the five job levels of a marketing career.

entry-level, career-sustaining, specialists, supervisors, and managers and CEOs/owners

ONLINE SELF-ASSESSMENT

Have students go to marketing.essentials.glencoe.com for the Section 37.2 practice test.

Individualized Review

L1 Assign and review Chapter 37 activities in the Student Activity Workbook.

L2 Assign and review Chapter 37 activities in the Marketing Math Workbook.

L3 Assign and review Chapter 37 activities in the *BusinessWeek* Reader and Case Studies.

Marketing Practice

Have students pick a career of their choice. Students should research the projected outlook for the job and write a two-page description of the outlook, including job responsibilities, salary range, training needed, and advancement opportunities.

Critical Thinking

Ask students to brainstorm the qualities needed by a good CEO. Answers may include such traits as self-motivated, patient, diplomatic, knowledgeable about all jobs in the company, aggressive, goal-oriented, and ethical.

An Overview of Marketing Careers

Marketing provides perhaps the greatest diversity of opportunities of any career field—from purchasing merchandise, to selling, to designing ads, to steering the company as president. About 33 million Americans earn a living in marketing. Careers in marketing span an array of activities required to develop, promote, and distribute goods and services to consumers. When considered in this broad sense, marketing activities account for about one in every three American jobs.

Benefits of a Marketing Career

The most obvious benefit of a career in marketing is the opportunity to make an above-average income. Even in an entry-level job, it is nice to know that potential earnings in marketing are excellent.

There are usually more opportunities to advance in a marketing career than in almost any other area of business. This is because of the high visibility that many marketing positions have.

People who work in marketing frequently present and shape their ideas in meetings with company managers and executives. People who work in sales get constant feedback on their efforts in the form of sales figures that are regularly reviewed by upper-level management. People who work in advertising may develop ad campaigns that win critical acclaim from professional associations. In terms of a job, this means winning promotions faster in marketing than in many other careers.

A career in marketing can be stressful, however, because there are pressures to succeed, and results of one's efforts are highly visible.

Employment Trends in Marketing

The Bureau of Labor Statistics (BLS) projects that employment in marketing and sales will continue at a high level through 2012. The rapid growth of e-commerce provides many opportunities.

Department of Labor projections indicate that managerial jobs in marketing-related fields will continue to be plentiful, regardless of the industry.

Changes in the marketplace have created the need for more rather than fewer marketing professionals. The rise in the number of single-person households, changing preferences in recreational activities, and the increase in foreign competition must all be monitored through market research and marketing information systems. To track these and other quickly developing trends, companies are expanding their marketing programs and staffs.

Marketing Occupational Areas

An **occupational area** is a category of jobs that involves similar interests and skills. Focusing on one or two areas makes it much easier to find information about the career area that most interests you. Listed below are the 21 generally accepted areas or career applications within the field of marketing.

- Advertising
- Customer Service
- E-Commerce
- Entrepreneur
- Fashion Merchandising
- Financial Services
- Food Marketing
- Hospitality Marketing
- Importing/Exporting
- International Marketing
- Marketing Research
- Pharmaceutical/Medical Marketing
- Product Management
- Professional Sales
- Public Relations
- Real Estate
- Restaurant Management
- Retail Management
- Sales Management
- Service Marketing
- Sports Marketing
- Travel/Tourism/Hospitality Marketing

Extended Activity

Employment Trends in Marketing

Have students choose one of the 21 career applications. Have them find projections for the specific area and even for specific jobs in the field for the next 5, 10, and 20 years. Remind students of places to find the information, such as the Department of Labor Web site. You could also invite a marketing professional to come to class and talk about how they began their career.

Job Levels in Marketing

Many jobs exist within each of the occupational areas, or career applications, of marketing. Jobs in each marketing area can be categorized according to five skill levels.

- **Entry-level jobs** usually require no prior experience and involve limited decision-making skills.
- **Career-sustaining jobs** require a higher level of skill and more decision making than entry-level jobs.
- **Marketing specialist employees** must show leadership ability and make many decisions on a daily basis. Being a marketing specialist is a long-term career goal for many in marketing.

- **Marketing supervisors** must have good management skills, the ability to make many decisions on a daily basis, and excellent marketing skills. This is the highest career level to which many people aspire. The prestige and income are generally quite high, and there is less risk involved than at the top management level.
- **Managers and CEOs/owners** are at the top level. People at this level are capable of running an entire company or a significant part of it. They must be highly skilled in a number of areas. They are responsible for the final success of the enterprise.

 37.2 AFTER YOU READ

Reviewing Key Terms and Concepts

1. What are three benefits of a career in marketing?
2. There are ten major areas you should consider when investigating careers. Rank them by importance level, with number 1 being your highest priority and number 10 being your lowest.
3. Name five resources for researching careers.

Integrating Academic Skills

Math

4. Use the *Occupational Outlook Handbook* in the library or online to find the current annual salaries for two marketing jobs of interest to you. What is the difference between these two salaries? Assume that in two years, the salary for each job increases by 12 percent. What will be the new salary for each job?

Government and Economics

5. Government agencies and the policies they implement have a strong effect on our market economy. Select one of the following agencies to research: Federal Communications Commission, Federal Reserve Board, Federal Trade Commission, Food and Drug Administration, or Internal Revenue Service. Write a one-page report on the agency and what it does. Explain how the agency impacts the economy.

 Online Action!

Check your answers at *marketingessentials.glencoe.com/37/read*

CLOSE

Ask students to recall and provide answers to the following questions:

- What are some benefits of a marketing career?
  varied and interesting work, good salary, room for advancement, and perks
- What are projected employment opportunities in marketing?
  The need for marketing specialists is projected to increase steadily.
- What are the five job levels in marketing?
  entry-level, career-sustaining, specialists, supervisors, and managers and CEOs/owners

 Online Activity

Researching Careers Online

Have students select one of the 21 areas from the list to conduct an online search. Model typing in an online search engine, putting quotation marks around titles with more than one word. Have students write a paragraph about the particular field based on the information they found. Be sure they list the pages they used.

AFTER YOU READ

Reviewing Key Terms and Concepts

1. Benefits include varied and interesting work, good salary, room for advancement, and perks.
2. Rankings will vary but should include: lifestyle goals, values, interests, skills, aptitudes, personality, environment preferences, relationship preferences, career goals, and employment trends.

3. Resources may include: someone in the field, the *OOH,* Department of Labor brochures, training courses and seminars, internships, and trade associations and Web sites.

Integrating Academic Skills

4. Answers will vary according to which two careers are chosen. Ask students to use a calculator to check their answers for the increased salaries.
5. Reports will vary; encourage students to research these federal agencies at the government Web site for each one.

Online Action! Answers at **marketingessentials.glencoe.com/37/read**

Lifelong Learning

CAREER INFORMATION

Have students go to marketingessentials.glencoe.com and find Chapter 37 Careers page and click on the link for the American Marketing Association Career Center. Ask students to select one article, read it, and summarize it in three short paragraphs.

MARKETING CAREER OPPORTUNITIES

Any financial magazine, such as *Forbes,* often features marketing specialists. Students should also know about even more specific trade magazines, such as *Sales & Marketing Management* or *Target Marketing.* They should read these magazines to stay abreast of trends in the marketing industry, as this knowledge will help them advance in their careers.

Primary Source

Ask students go to marketingessentials.glencoe.com and find Chapter 37 Resources. Ask them to click on the link for the American Marketing Association's marketing dictionary at the bottom of the page. Have students read the definitions of the marketing career-related terms they find.

THINKING CRITICALLY

Working at no charge can build skills and generate contacts for both networking and future work opportunities. Instances will vary.

@ Online Action!

For instructions, ideas, and answer guide, go to the Teacher Center at marketingessentials.glencoe.com

NICK CORCODILOS
PRESIDENT, NORTH BRIDGE GROUP, INC.
ASKTHEHEADHUNTER .COM

? What do you do at work?
Companies turn to me to find great talent to do jobs that impact the bottom line positively. Finding great people does not involve running ads or searching for résumés on online job boards. A good headhunter serves as a hub of insider information in the industry he or she services. In other words, my job is to know the best people in the field I service, and to help those people meet one another and stay in touch. In essence, a good headhunter helps useful but sensitive information flow among the people who make an industry click.

? What skills are most important to you?
Street smarts (the most useful form of intelligence), self-motivation, persistence, and enthusiasm are the keys to success as a headhunter. My most important skill is the ability to see connections where others do not. You cannot learn the business from a book, a course, or a workshop. You must work closely with a good headhunter who can teach you the business, and who you can observe closely at work. I think it is imperative to have a college degree.

? What is your key to success?
Doing nice things for others for free. For every placement I make to earn a fee, I probably wind up helping 30 people make connections that somehow pay off for them. I have a lot of friends as a result.

Aptitudes, Abilities, and Skills

Outgoing personality, strong social and interpersonal skills, ability to make connections and think creatively

Education and Training

General business and marketing degrees are common; degrees in psychology can also be useful. Apprenticeships and internships are crucial.

Career Path

Industry contacts are crucial, so aspiring headhunters often begin their careers at established agencies.

● THINKING CRITICALLY

Why is it sometimes beneficial to do work at no charge? What are some instances you can think of in which this might be valuable?

@ Online Action!

Go to *marketingessentials.glencoe.com/ 37/careers* to find a career-related activity.

Test-Taking Strategies

List key chapter concepts on the board, and ask student volunteers to define and discuss them in class. Work as a class to write a culminating statement about the concept on the board. Answer any questions students might have.

FOCUS on KEY POINTS

SECTION 37.1

- Good career choices are based on a comprehensive self-assessment of values, interests, skills, aptitudes, personality, and lifestyle preferences.
- Career planning includes looking at work values, lifestyle fit, and the education and training required. It also includes learning about the duties and skills required, and at helpful personality traits, work environment, and work relationships.
- Your plan of action to reach your career goal requires setting specific and realistic short- and medium-range planning goals.

SECTION 37.2

- Consider the benefits, employment trends, occupational areas, and job levels in marketing.

REVIEW VOCABULARY

Use these vocabulary terms in a paragraph on career research.

1. lifestyle (p. 787)
2. values (p. 787)
3. aptitude (p. 788)
4. *Occupational Outlook Handbook (OOH)* (p. 789)
5. career outlook (p. 789)
6. O*NET (p. 790)
7. internship (p. 791)
8. planning goals (p. 795)
9. specific goal (p. 795)
10. realistic goal (p. 795)
11. occupational area (p. 798)

REVIEW FACTS and IDEAS

12. Define values, lifestyle goals, interests, and aptitudes. Why is it important to assess these when choosing a career? (37.1)

13. What are two methods for appraising your personality? (37.1)

14. What is a work environment? What three categories are involved in relationship preferences? (37.1)

15. What areas should be investigated when completing a career assessment? (37.1)

16. Name two online career research resources. What resources are available at libraries? Name three other possible resources. (37.2)

17. What purpose does a personal career profile serve? (37.2)

18. What are three occupational areas in marketing? (37.2)

Chapter 37 - Identifying Career Opportunities **801**

REVIEW FACTS and IDEAS

12. Values are beliefs that guide how a person lives. Lifestyle goals include where people choose to live, how they relate to others, and how they earn a living. Interests are things that a person enjoys doing in his or her leisure time. Aptitudes are a person's natural abilities. These factors should be taken into account to better choose a satisfying career.

13. You can appraise your personality by taking a personality test or by listing your own personality traits.

14. Work environment is the place and conditions where a person works. Relationship preferences involve working with others, working alone, and handling interpersonal conflicts.

15. All the following areas should be researched for a career assessment: lifestyle goals, values, interests, skills, aptitudes, personality, environment preferences, relationship preferences, career goals, and employment trends.

16. Online career resources may include the *OOH* online and O*NET. Besides free access to the Internet, libraries also have books, trade magazines, pamphlets, films, videos, and special references with information about careers. Other resources are professional associations, informational interviews, and on-the-job experience, including internships.

17. A personal career profile can help a person easily see if his or her own interests match those of a successful worker in that field.

18. Student answers may include any three of the 21 areas listed on page 798 of Section 37.2 under the heading Marketing Occupational Areas.

FOCUS on KEY POINTS

Ask volunteers to read the summaries for the two sections aloud. Have students provide real-life examples that relate to the concepts discussed in each section.

REVIEW VOCABULARY

See glossary for definitions of **1–11.** Paragraphs will vary; all paragraphs should mention that each term is an essential part in choosing a career to research.

BUILD SKILLS

19. Workplace Skills

Paragraphs will vary; the Web site address for the personality test should be included in the paragraph.

20. Technology Applications

Student research will vary; the results of the research should demonstrate that the student has an understanding of how to use online resources to find career information.

21. Math Practice

The college graduate earns $14,000, or 53.8 percent, more than the high school graduate; $40,000 − $26,000 = $14,000; $14,000 ÷ $26,000 = 53.8 percent

DEVELOP CRITICAL THINKING

22. Preview Careers

Answers will vary; students' lists should show evidence that the student has an understanding of how to use the O*NET Web site.

23. Assess Your Values

Answers will vary but may include one's upbringing and one's personal beliefs. Personal values often have a profound effect on a person's career choice and career goals.

BUILD SKILLS

19. Workplace Skills

Human Relations Use a search engine on the Internet to do a search on personality tests. Find a site that will let you take a personality test for free. Print out the result of your test. Then write a brief paragraph explaining how this information might help you relate to others.

20. Technology Applications

Research Salary Ranges A possible career choice might be some type of research in marketing. You have considered your lifestyle goal and know that you want to have a comfortable lifestyle. Use the Internet to find the salary ranges of some specific jobs in marketing research. Name one or more specific jobs that meet your criteria. Then consider job opportunities in four marketing-related careers: computer technology, finance, business management, and economics. Go to the O*NET site to explore the outlook for job opportunities in these careers.

21. Math Practice

Calculating a Wage If the average national wage for an employee with a high school diploma is $26,000 while the average wage for an employee with a four-year degree is $40,000, how much more does the second employee earn? (Provide your answer in dollars and in percentage.)

DEVELOP CRITICAL THINKING

22. Preview Careers

Log on to the O*NET site (use a search engine to find the URL) and use the following steps:
- Click on the Skills Search and follow the directions.
- Once you have selected the skills you have or skills you wish to obtain, click on GO. (This search will identify occupations that use the skills you chose.)
- Prepare a list of the skills you selected and the occupations that were identified.

23. Assess Your Values

How do you think your values were formed? What effects do you think your personal values will have on the career you choose?

Formative Assessment

Formative assessment is an essential component of classroom work. This type of assessment provides information that is used as feedback to modify teaching and meet student needs.

L1 Review key terms for this chapter. Ask students to write one sentence for each key term.

L2 Provide various examples of avenues leading to separate career choices in story form. After each story, have the students identify another way (if any) to reach the same career goal.

L3 Ask students to create their own personality profiles for a worker in a particular career in marketing.

 Reteach   If the results of this formative assessment seem low, consider the following activity:

Have students quiz each other using key terms and section reviews.

APPLY CONCEPTS

24. Long-Range Goals

One of your strong interests is plants and flowers. You have decided that your long-range career goal is to own a retail garden shop. You have an opportunity to work in a local garden shop as soon as you graduate, get on-the-job training, work your way up, and eventually buy into the business. Your parents want you to go to college first. Do some research into horticultural (gardening) programs offered at two- or four-year colleges. Use this information to formulate your decision.

Activity Write a brief plan of action for achieving your career goal. Present this plan to your parents.

25. Prepare for an Interview

Select a career that interests you. Prepare a list of six or more questions that you would like to ask someone who works in that field. Locate and arrange to interview such a person.

Activity Use a word processing program to write up your questions and the answers that you received. Share this information with your classmates.

NET SAVVY

26. Job Search

Access a job listing site on the Web and key in a search for the job of your dreams. Analyze the results of your search and develop a plan of action to obtain your favorite job on the list.

marketingessentials.glencoe.com

THE **DECA** CONNECTION

Role Play: Career Opportunities

Situation You are to assume the role of high school junior. You plan to attend college upon graduation. You feel that you should explore some career areas that interest you. You know that you are interested in business and want to explore career opportunities in that field. You have decided to begin your career exploration at the library and on the Internet.

Activity You are to prepare an outline of your career exploration findings. You will discuss your findings with your parents (judge).

Evaluation You will be evaluated on how well you meet the following performance indicators:

- Assess personal interests and skills needed for success in business
- Analyze employer expectations
- Identify sources of career information
- Identify tentative occupational interest
- Explain employment opportunities in business

 Online Action!

For more information and DECA Prep practice, go to *marketingessentials.glencoe .com/37/DECA*

APPLY CONCEPTS

24. Long-Range Goals

Plans of action will vary, but may include business courses, botany courses, or working part-time at the garden shop.

25. Prepare for an Interview

Summaries of interviews will vary, but should include information such as name of the interviewee, position, and job responsibilities.

NET SAVVY

26. Job Search

Plans of action will differ depending on the results of the students' searches and the jobs chosen. Student plans should outline specific steps to be taken to reach a goal; steps should be specific and realistic.

MINI-QUIZ

Administer the Mini-Quiz orally. Have the students fill in the blank with the correct vocabulary word.

1. _____ is the first step in a career search. (Self-assessment)

2. A(n) _____ is an ability or a potential for learning a certain skill. (aptitude)

3. A(n) _____ offers students direct work experience and exposure to various aspects of a career, either with or without pay. (internship)

For an expanded chapter quiz, go to Chapter 37 in the TeacherWorks CD-ROM and to Chapter 37 in the **Exam***View*® Pro Test Generator CD-ROM.

THE **DECA** CONNECTION

The students should be evaluated on the performance indicators noted in the role play. For another DECA role play, go to the Competitive Events Workbook or the Student Activity Workbook, or go to **marketingessentials.glencoe.com/37/DECA**

 Online Action! For instructions, ideas, and answer guide, go to the Teacher Center at **marketingessentials.glencoe.com**

DECA Advisors Corner

Coordinate a Career Day with a local business community group. Ask the business volunteers to draw up a short list of jobs within their industry and provide job descriptions. Students will develop their résumés and research a job and a company. One class day can be spent role-playing interviews. On DECA Career Day, business volunteers can give valuable feedback to students.

CHAPTER 38

Chapter Overview

In this chapter, students explore the process of finding and applying for a job. Such factors include creating a résumé, filling out an application, and interviewing for a job.

BUILD BACKGROUND

Everyone has a better chance at success with the proper planning. While this is true in business, it is also true of people marketing themselves to find the right job. Ask students to think about the entry-level position for their chosen career—the career that will occupy their adult life. Have them take some time to reflect on what they have learned in this course, and then have them consider how they plan to market themselves to a potential employer. The students should organize an individualized job-finding program.

Why It's Important

By utilizing the best resources and sources to locate job leads, students will start on their chosen career path. Each step along the way on a career involves small but crucial increments. Filling out an application and preparing a résumé are two tasks every applicant must successfully complete in order to gain a first interview.

Prepare to Read

Have the students familiarize themselves with all of the vocabulary terms in this chapter. Review terms out loud with the class. Write the unfamiliar terms on the board for the students. Continue to reference them throughout the chapter.

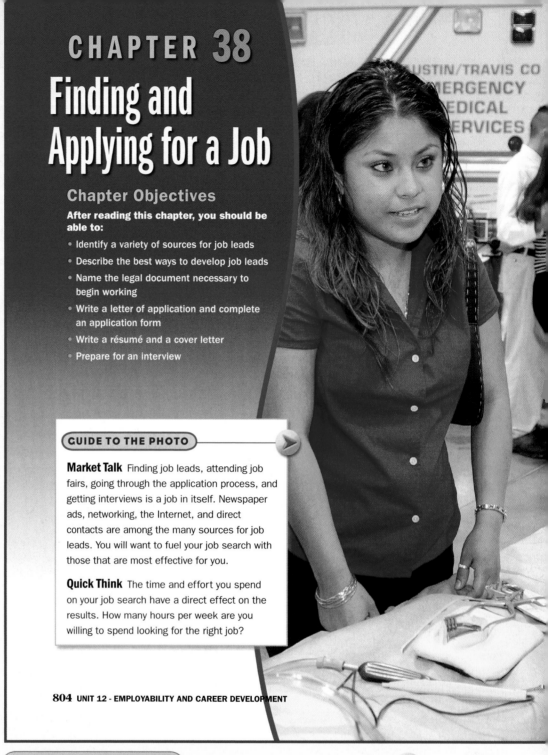

CHAPTER 38
Finding and Applying for a Job

Chapter Objectives

After reading this chapter, you should be able to:

- Identify a variety of sources for job leads
- Describe the best ways to develop job leads
- Name the legal document necessary to begin working
- Write a letter of application and complete an application form
- Write a résumé and a cover letter
- Prepare for an interview

GUIDE TO THE PHOTO

Market Talk Finding job leads, attending job fairs, going through the application process, and getting interviews is a job in itself. Newspaper ads, networking, the Internet, and direct contacts are among the many sources for job leads. You will want to fuel your job search with those that are most effective for you.

Quick Think The time and effort you spend on your job search have a direct effect on the results. How many hours per week are you willing to spend looking for the right job?

GUIDE TO THE PHOTO

Market Talk Lead the students in a discussion about the importance of art of small talk when getting to know a potential future employer.

Quick Think Answers will vary, but remind students they will need to commit to finding a job as if it were their job. It takes diligence, follow-through, and persistence to land the job of their dreams.

 Follow Up Ask students to name one of their dream jobs. Then, discuss a potential plan for working toward that career path.

Performance indicators represent key skills and knowledge. Relating them to the concepts explained in this chapter is your key to success in DECA events. These acronyms represent DECA events that involve knowledge of concepts in this chapter.

AAAL	FMAL	MMS	TMDM*
AAML	FMDM	QSRM	TSE*
ADC*	FMML	RMAL	VPM
BSM*	FSRM	RMML	
EMDM	HMDM*	SMDM*	

In all these DECA events you should be able to follow these performance indicators:

- Assess personal interests and skills needed for success in business
- Analyze employer expectations in the business environment
- Utilize job-search strategies
- Complete a job application
- Interview for a job
- Write a follow-up letter after job interview
- Write a letter of application
- Prepare a résumé
- Utilize resources that can contribute to professional development
- Use networking techniques for professional growth
- Identify skills needed to enhance career progression

All the events with an asterisk (*) also include this performance indicator:

- Assess the services provided by professional organizations in (that industry)

DECA PREP

Check your understanding of DECA performance indicators with the DECA activity in this chapter's review. For more information and DECA Prep practice, go to *marketingessentials .glencoe.com/38/DECA*

DECA events that require knowledge of finding and applying for a job are described here. Discuss the performance indicators to make sure students understand how to demonstrate their understanding.

The events acronyms stand for:

AAAL: Apparel and Accessories Marketing Series, AL

AAML: Apparel and Accessories Marketing Series, ML

ADC: Advertising Campaign Event

BSM: Business Services Marketing Series

EMDM: E-Commerce Management Team Decision Making Event

FMAL: Food Marketing Series, AL

FMDM: Financial Analysis Management Team Decision Making Event

FMML: Food Marketing Series, ML

FSRM: Full Service Restaurant Management Series

HMDM: Hospitality Services Management Team Decision Making Event

MMS: Marketing Management Series

QSRM: Quick Serve Restaurant Management Series

RMAL: Retail Merchandising Series, AL

RMML: Retail Merchandising Series, ML

SMDM: Sports and Entertainment Marketing Management Team Decision Making Event

TMDM: Travel and Tourism Marketing Management Team Decision Making Event

TSE: Technical Sales Event

VPM: Vehicles and Petroleum Marketing Series

DECA PREP

Find timed DECA Prep activities correlated to the Competitive Events Workbook for students and DECA tips for teachers at **marketingessentials.glencoe.com /38/DECA.**

CHAPTER 38 Classroom Resources

For the Teacher

- TeacherWorks
- marketingessentials.glencoe.com
- Interactive Chalkboard
- **Exam**View® Pro Test Generator
- Fast File Unit 12

For the Student

- **Marketing Essentials** Online Edition
- Student Activity Workbook
- Marketing Math Workbook
- Marketing Research Project Workbook
- School-to-Work Activity Workbook
- Competitive Events Workbook
- **BusinessWeek** Reader and Case Studies
- marketingessentials.glencoe.com

FOCUS

Introducing the Section

COLLABORATIVE ACTIVITY

Applying for a job is a process that begins with the job search and ends with the post-interview follow up. Have students generate a list of things one must do to obtain and follow up a job interview. Answers may include: get a work permit; search for job openings and leads; apply for a job with cover letters, résumés, and application forms; prepare for the interview; interview; and follow up with a phone call or personalized note.

Preteaching Key Terms

Read the key terms aloud, or ask one of the students to read them:

- job lead
- networking
- public employment agencies
- private employment agencies
- staffing/temporary agencies

Have students predict their meanings. Tell students they can check their predictions as they read the section.

Build Vocabulary

Introduce students to the word *nepotism*. Ask students to define the word. Outline the pros and cons associated with nepotism in the workplace, particularly when it comes to landing a job.

 Critical Thinking

Ask students to think of reasons job candidates might not be offered an employment opportunity. Have them write down their reasons and share them with the class.

OBJECTIVES

- Identify a variety of sources for job leads
- Describe the best ways to develop job leads

KEY TERMS

- job lead
- networking
- public employment agencies
- private employment agencies
- staffing/temporary agencies

Finding a Job

READ and STUDY

BEFORE YOU READ

Predict How did your family members and friends find their jobs? What job-hunting techniques can you learn from them?

THE MAIN IDEA

This section will help you learn how to locate job leads to find the job that will start you on your way to success in your chosen career.

STUDY ORGANIZER

In a chart like the one below, write in seven types of sources of job leads.

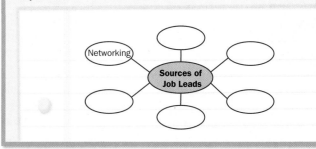

WHILE YOU READ

Compare Think about which sources for job leads would be most productive for you.

Finding Job Openings

Developing effective job search and interview skills will help you make the most of your time and effort when looking for a job. How do you uncover job opportunities?

The best way to start is by contacting all of the sources available to you that might produce a job lead. A **job lead** is information about a job opening. Sometimes you may have to act like a detective, following up skimpy leads and researching

READ and STUDY

BEFORE YOU READ

Ask students to recall job-hunting experiences they have had or witnessed.

THE MAIN IDEA

Ask a volunteer to discuss how he or she would find a desirable job opportunity.

STUDY ORGANIZER

Model the study organizer for students by filling in the first oval. A full-size, downloadable study organizer can be found at marketingessentials.glencoe.com

 Remind students as they read to think of how the information can assist them market themselves to potential employers.

information about a company to plan the best approach. Finding the right job requires getting as many leads as possible and following up on them.

Networking

Often, the best source for job leads will be people you know—family, friends, schoolmates and their families, former employers, professionals, teachers or professors, local business owners, coaches, members of a religious or community group to which you belong, and even acquaintances. These people form your network.

Networking is the art of building alliances. Finding contacts among those in your network is, without a doubt, the most effective way to find a job. Most businesses welcome applications from friends of employees because they trust their employees' opinions. Make a list of all your contacts, including addresses, phone numbers, and e-mail addresses. Keep this list current and add to it as your career and education progress.

Let your contacts know you are seeking employment, the type of work you are suited for, what you have to offer, and the types of companies or careers that interest you.

Politely ask them if they would be comfortable letting you know if they hear of any openings that might suit you or meet your requirements. They may not immediately know of the perfect job for you, but they can keep you in mind and even ask their friends and coworkers about openings.

Networking is a mutual exchange, so be prepared to help them when they ask or when the need is apparent. Always let them know when you have responded to one of their leads and thank them for helping you.

School Counselor

When you are building your network, remember to include your school guidance counselor. Local retail stores and other businesses frequently call school counselors for names of qualified students for part-time or temporary jobs.

Professional People In Your Personal Life

You probably have occasional contact with professional people in your personal life—doctors, businesspeople, dentists, or lawyers. If you have established a good relationship with these people, they will probably be happy to help you in your job search. Since they are part of your network, you can ask them for names of people to contact or for advice about job prospects or the career you are pursuing.

Former Employers

Even if they were temporary or part-time jobs, your former employers may be good sources of job leads. It is likely that they will want to help you find a job if they were pleased with your work.

Cooperative Education and Work Experience Programs

Cooperative education teachers have contacts in the business community because they place and supervise students in part-time jobs. Students enrolled in cooperative work experience programs receive course credit and are sometimes paid, as well.

Newspaper and Magazine Ads

For many years, the Help Wanted section of the local newspaper, especially the Sunday edition, was perhaps the best place to find job openings. However, do not overlook your daily local newspaper. Look in the employment sections every day. Most papers organize listings of job openings by type.

These Help Wanted sections also teach you about the local job market. You will learn the qualifications required for different types of jobs. You may find information about salaries and benefits as well.

Follow up immediately on every ad that might lead to the job you want. Be aware, however, if an ad requires you to pay money or enroll in a course, it may be a disguised attempt to sell something rather than a genuine job offer.

In business newspapers and magazines, you can look for information about local and regional companies that are expanding, opening

---

Online Activity

Visit a Job Search Site

Ask students to visit the Monster.com (or other career search) Web site and select a feature article about résumés, networking featured employer, or career advice. Once they have read the article, ask them to summarize the article, relate it to the text of this section, and share their findings with the class.

TEACH

Discussion Starter

NETWORKING

Ask students, "Who is currently working?" Then ask, "How did you obtain your job?" If no one in the class is working, ask them where they could begin in order to find a job. Their answers will help you introduce the concept of networking, as well as the other means of developing job leads, such as newspaper ads, online job postings, signs in store windows, and so on.

TEACHING POINTS

Demonstrate Once the students have a substantial list of ways to get a job, ask them what skills they think are needed to get the job interview.

Concept Development

NEWSPAPER AND MAGAZINE ADS

Collect a week's worth of local newspapers and pass out the classified sections to the students. Ask them to read over the ads and draw conclusions about the local job market.

TEACHING POINTS

Explain Remind students that although companies may not have a current opening, they keep applications and résumés on file in the event a job opens. A human resources representative skims the file first when thinking about filling a new or existing position.

Summarize Remind students that employers have a limited space in ads to write their information regarding a job. If a job sounds interesting and a candidate is somewhat qualified, encourage that candidate to apply anyway.

Individualized Practice

COOPERATIVE EDUCATION AND WORK EXPERIENCE PROGRAMS

L1 Ask students to create a list of the types of individuals they would seek for career advice. Have them explain what characteristics these people possess that make them successful.

L2 Ask students to investigate any school cooperative education and work experience programs. They could meet with the groups to learn the benefits and opportunities available from such programs. Have students write a one-page reflective response in their journal about this experience.

L3 Ask students to conduct a role play in front of the class, where one student is the school counselor and the other is a student who needs a career plan. The student playing a school counselor may want to search the Internet for career questions or a career survey.

Build Vocabulary

1. Introduce students to the term *cold call.* A cold call is a telephone call made directly to a potential workplace or customer without prior contact. Explain what this is, what types of jobs often require it, and how to become effective at it.

2. Introduce the students to the term *headhunter.* A headhunter is a recruiter, especially for corporate and high-level positions. Explain to them the meaning of this term, who uses this type of career placement, and what industries most often use a headhunter.

---

a new office, entering a new market, winning a bid for new business, or introducing a new product. These are the types of companies who are hiring.

Many professionals depend on their association's magazine to alert them to job openings. Some may be available in your library or a local college library. If not, you may be able to access them online.

Employment Agencies

Employment and temporary staffing agencies match workers with jobs. Most cities have several types of employment agencies—public, private, and staffing/temporary agencies. **Public employment agencies** are supported by state or federal taxes and offer free services to both job applicants and employers. **Private employment agencies** and **staffing/temporary agencies**, which are not supported by taxes, must earn a profit to stay in business. They charge a fee for their services, which is paid by either the job applicant or the employer.

Public employment agencies are identified by the names of the states in which they are located. The Texas Employment Commission and the California Employment Development Department are examples. In some cities, the state employment service is the only one available. When you fill out an application form at the public employment agency near you, you will be interviewed to determine your qualifications and interests. The agency will call you if they find a job that is a good match. You will be told about the company and the duties of the job, then referred for an interview if you are interested.

Many times, private employment agencies have job leads that are not listed with public agencies. Remember, however, that private agencies charge a fee if they place you on a job. Make sure you know who is expected to pay the fee—it might be you. This will be stated in a contract you will be asked to sign. The employer often pays the fee for matching workers with higher-level jobs. The employee usually pays the placement fee for an entry-level job. The fee is usually a

percentage of salary for the first several months or even the first full year of employment.

Staffing services or temporary help agencies will test you, interview you, and match you with jobs that last from one day to several months. You will be assigned to a company, but the staffing service is your employer. Do your best work, because temporary assignments can lead to permanent positions for the right candidate.

Company Personnel Offices

In large companies, the personnel office (often known as Human Resources, or HR) handles employment matters, including the hiring of new workers. If you have a networking contact within a large company whom you can ask about job openings, that is great. If not, visit the organization's Web site and click on the "Jobs," "Careers," or "Join Us" links to see what positions are available. While you are visiting the company's Web site, try to find the name of the head of the department in which you are interested in working. Many sites include the names of key employees and their contact information. Although some companies welcome phone inquiries about job openings, most do not. Be sure to ask a contact if a phone call or drop-in visit to inquire about openings is acceptable. A few large companies and most government agencies such as the United States Postal Service may post job openings on public bulletin boards.

Searching the Internet

Employers are using the Internet extensively, and millions of jobs are posted at any given time. In addition to searching company Web sites for openings, search for opportunities at employment portals such as Hotjobs.com, Monster.com, or America's Job Bank. For jobs in marketing, also check MarketingJobs.com and many of the professional associations that serve the field, such as the American Marketing Association, the Direct Marketing Association, the Public Relations Society of America, and the International Association of Business Communicators. Check the listings on their local chapter sites, too.

Extended Activity

The Electronic Job Search

Ask students to think about how electronic résumés and online job searching have influenced the landscape of hiring and job placement. Have students write a one-page response on the advantages and disadvantages of using the Internet to help them search for job leads and procure employment.

Case Study

It's a Monster!

Monster.com is the world's largest job search firm. The company's roots go back more than 30 years. It began as a Yellow Pages advertising sales company. The now familiar online Monster was created in 1994, and in 2003, it had 24 million résumés posted online, more than Yahoo's HotJobs and CareerBuilder.com combined. In 2004, a subscriber could search more than 800,000 available jobs. The company has sites in 20 different languages to serve job seekers and employers worldwide.

An estimated 80 percent of human resources managers now look for potential employees by searching online résumés, and an estimated 96 percent of those seeking jobs post their résumés online. For a fee, potential employers can post jobs, search Monster's résumé bank, or screen and track job candidates. More than 30 percent of Monster's 2003 revenue came from its résumé service alone. Job seekers pay to subscribe, search through postings, and apply for jobs online using the site. They can also get career advice and information about everything from résumés to typical salaries to relocation.

In 2000, Monster started Monstermoving.com, a companion site offering its own services related to relocating, as well as a portal to such businesses as real estate and moving companies around the country.

THINK STRATEGICALLY
Why would job seekers pay for Monster's service?

@ Online Action!
Go to *marketingessentials.glencoe.com/Base* to find an activity on job searches.

On employment portals, search for up-to-date listings—nothing more than a month old. Many job search engines and portals enable you to search by location, job type, industry, date of posting, and even salary. Some enable you to subscribe to an e-mail alert to notify you when positions are posted. Check to see if there is a charge for this service. It is a great way to learn about opportunities as soon as they become available.

marketingessentials.glencoe.com

Contacting Your Job Leads

A letter of inquiry and a polished résumé will help you contact the company by regular mail or via e-mail.

If you call for an appointment, it is usually best not to discuss the job on the telephone. You will probably get more consideration by inquiring about the job after you arrive in person. If you are not sure about the best contact strategy, place a quick

Chapter 38 - Finding and Applying for a Job 809

Case Study It's a Monster!

Discussion Have students read the Case Study and discuss the job market from a global perspective. Ask them how services such as Monster are making the world of work smaller.

THINK STRATEGICALLY **Answer:** Monster provides job seekers with a service (finding employment opportunities for them). Most job seekers are willing to pay for this service.

@ Online Action! For instructions, ideas, and answer guide, go to the Teacher Center at **marketingessentials.glencoe.com**

Follow Up Have students research online employment services and compare the fees they charge both employers and job-seekers for various services. Ask them to share their findings with the class.

ASSESS

Review Guide

CONCEPTS
Have students generate at least three job leads from various sources. They should write the leads on a sheet of paper and tell how they found them.

KEY TERMS
Have students review key terms, their spellings, and definitions in small groups.

ONLINE SELF-ASSESSMENT
Have students go to **marketingessentials.glencoe.com** for the Section 38.1 practice test.

Individualized Review

L1 Assign and review Chapter 38 activities in the Student Activity Workbook.

L2 Assign and review Chapter 38 activities in the Marketing Math Workbook.

L3 Assign and review Chapter 38 activities in the *BusinessWeek* Reader and Case Studies.

Marketing Practice

Ask students to use Internet search engines to locate online sites where job openings are posted. They should compile a list of jobs they are interested in. Next to each opportunity, have them explain in a short paragraph why they find that particular job interesting.

 Critical Thinking

Ask students to define the types of skills and traits a future employer looks for in a candidate.

CLOSE

Have students complete the following statements:

- **A résumé is** _____ .
  a brief summary of personal information, education, skills, work experience, activities, and interests

- **Examples of online employment portals include** _____ .
  Monster.com, America's Job Bank, MarketingJobs.com, CareerBuilder.com, and so on

Online Activity

Government Job Sites

Ask students to research local, state, and federal job search sites. Have students choose two sites and summarize the contents and characteristics of both in a bulleted list or one-page report.

---

call to the personnel or human resources department to inquire what the company prefers. You will be better prepared if you have conducted your research about the organization. If the company sells consumer products, you should familiarize yourself with its products by studying the products and those of its competitors in stores.

As you research the company, make a note of key words used in the ad. You will learn below how these can be helpful in preparing your job application.

The goal is to be fully prepared—as if you are going to an actual interview—whenever you contact a company in any manner. Bring your résumé even if you expect just to fill out an application.

Letters of Inquiry

As you are learning, the Internet is a valuable research tool for any job search. In most situations, you can learn about openings on a company's Web site, through networking contacts, and via direct contact. If these activities do not yield the information you need about potential openings, you can write a letter of inquiry.

Before writing a letter of inquiry, you should have conducted your research about the company and found the name and contact details of the person to whom you should address your correspondence. Now you are ready to write a letter of inquiry. See Chapter 8 to review the elements of a business letter. Include your résumé with your letter of inquiry. That is being proactive.

38.1 AFTER YOU READ

Reviewing Key Terms and Concepts

1. What is a job lead?
2. What is the most effective way to find a job?
3. List nine possible sources of job leads.

Integrating Academic Skills

Math

4. Your employer is encouraging workers to ride the bus to work by providing bus passes at the reduced rate of $8.00 per week. If you drive to work, your travel costs per week include $7.25 for gas, $12 for parking, and $10.00 for toll fares. Assuming you work 48 weeks per year, how much will you save if you ride the bus?

Government

5. Employers often state in their employment ads that they are equal opportunity employers. Research the various equal opportunity federal employment laws. Write a brief summary of the kinds of discrimination that are prohibited by these laws.

 Online Action!

Check your answers at *marketingessentials.glencoe.com/read*

Reviewing Key Terms and Concepts

1. A job lead is information about a job opening.
2. The most effective way to find a job is through contacts among the members of your network.
3. Possible answers for sources of job leads include family and friends, school counselor, professionals, former employers, cooperative education and work experience programs, newspaper ads, employment agencies, company personnel offices, and the Internet.

Integrating Academic Skills

4. You will save $1,020 by riding the bus; [($7.25 + $12 + $10) × 48] − ($8.00 × 48) = $1,020.

5. Summaries will vary but should include race, color, religion, gender, national origin, age, and disabilities.

Online Action! Answers at *marketingessentials.glencoe.com/38/read*

Applying for a Job

OBJECTIVES

- Name the legal document necessary to begin working
- Write a letter of application and complete an application form
- Write a résumé and a cover letter
- Prepare for an interview

KEY TERMS

- standard English
- references
- cover letter
- résumé

READ and STUDY

BEFORE YOU READ
Predict Ask several of your networking contacts how they have applied for jobs. What experiences do they have in common?

THE MAIN IDEA
You have assembled some job leads and found a few jobs that interest you; your next step is to apply for them. This is done by completing application forms, writing letters of application, and preparing your own résumé.

STUDY ORGANIZER
In a chart like the one below, list ideas about how you would go about applying for a job.

Applying for a Job

1. Get a work permit.
2. _____
3. _____
4. _____

Getting a Work Permit

A work permit establishes that it is legal for a young worker to do the type of work offered. In some states, work permits must specify the exact duties and hours of work. In these cases, both the employer and the worker fill out sections of an application for the permit. The employer, worker, and the worker's

WHILE YOU READ

Analyze Study both the application form and résumé in this text, so that you will be familiar with their form and content.

Chapter 38 - Finding and Applying for a Job **811**

FOCUS

Introducing the Section

COLLABORATIVE ACTIVITY
Give each student a copy of a generic application form or an application form from a familiar local business. Have students fill out the application for a specific job (for example, a retail sales associate or coffee barista). Allow them to use any resources they may have with them (such as an address book). Allow 10 to 15 minutes for this activity.

Preteaching Key Terms

Write the key terms on the board and ask students to predict their meanings:

- standard English
- references
- cover letter
- résumé

Ask students to think of and write in their journal specific examples relevant to standard English.

Standard English examples: not *there's* but *there is*; do not use contractions when writing a formal letter.

 Critical Thinking

Ask students to consider why employers find bilingual applicants desirable. Have students write a one- to two-paragraph response explaining why the ability to speak multiple languages is considered a highly marketable skill.

READ and STUDY

BEFORE YOU READ
Ask students to share this information with the class and discuss what they can learn from their contacts' experiences.

THE MAIN IDEA
Ask students what kind of information is needed to complete applications, résumés, and cover letters.

STUDY ORGANIZER
Model the study organizer for students by completing the second blank. A full-size, downloadable study organizer can be found at **marketingessentials.glencoe.com**

 WHILE YOU READ Provide the class with examples of both good and bad résumés.

811

APPLYING FOR A JOB

Ask students to discuss some common ways of submitting job application forms and résumés. Have them to speculate on the reasons companies increasingly use high-tech recruitment and screening measures.

Résumés can be submitted through mail, fax machines, Web sites, e-mail, or in person. Web-based recruitment has become a popular strategy for companies looking to gain a competitive advantage over their competitors.

FILLING OUT APPLICATION FORMS

Ask students to list some concerns employers have about candidates filling out their job applications. Write the list on the board.

Remind the students that honesty, legibility, and information are often ranked as the top three concerns.

TEACHING POINTS

Summarize In an employer's mind, filling out an employment application is not necessarily the same thing as applying for a job. Many employers use the application as a screening tool for potential interviewees. Therefore, it is essential to make a good impression with a neat, complete application.

Clarify Remind students that they should fill out a written application in blue or black ink, never in pencil or colorful ink.

 Critical Thinking

Ask students why employers might conduct a background checks.

---

parent or guardian must sign the application before a work permit is issued.

Ask your marketing teacher or counselor whether you will need a work permit and, if so, where you can get one. A designated school official usually issues work permits. Check on this now so you can avoid possible delays when you are ready to go to work.

Applying for a Job

Companies are looking for the most qualified people to fill their jobs. The decision to hire is based on three criteria:

1. How well can you do the job?
2. How willing are you to do the job?
3. How well will you fit in?

The decision about whether to hire you will depend on information you provide in your résumé or application form and during the interview. The way you present the information and yourself are also very important.

Many employers ask job applicants to fill out an application form. Some request additional documents, such as a separate letter of application or a résumé. Throughout this course, you have been building your employment portfolio including examples of some of your best marketing-related efforts. You will want to add a copy of your résumé to your portfolio. Many employers administer one or more employment tests to applicants. Most companies today do background checks for any criminal activity and also do some type of drug testing.

Using Standard English

Everything you write and say to a prospective employer should be in standard English. **Standard English** is the formal style of writing and speaking that you have learned in school. It is standard because it means the same thing to everyone.

Standard English employs correct grammar, spelling, pronunciation, and usage. The repeated use in conversation of the interjections *you know* or *like* is also not advisable.

Nonstandard pronunciations are another common lapse. An accent, however, either regional or foreign, is considered acceptable.

Employers will have several opportunities to evaluate your communication skills. Your letter of application or résumé will indicate your writing skills. Finally, when you are interviewed, the employer will evaluate your verbal communication skills and your ability to listen and interact in a businesslike manner.

Filling Out Application Forms

Most application forms are short (from one to four pages) and ask similar questions. More and more companies are asking applicants to complete online forms. Companies usually design their own application forms, so you may find differences among various applications.

The application form provides information about your qualifications so company personnel can decide whether to interview you. The first rule of filling out an application form is to complete the form neatly. Spell all words correctly. Complete the form at the place of employment, use a pen with blue or black ink. Do not use colored inks.

Answer every question that applies to you. Write "NA" for those questions that are not applicable. This shows that you did not overlook the item.

Use your full name, not a nickname, on the form. On most applications, your first name, middle initial, and last name are requested. Provide your complete address, including your zip code.

List a specific job title if asked about your job preference; do not write "anything" as an answer. Employers expect you to know what type of work you can and want to do.

Most application forms include a section on education. Write the names of all the schools you have attended and the dates of attendance. There will also be a section on previous work experience. You may not have had much work experience, but you can include short-term or unpaid jobs. Fill out this section in reverse chronological order—begin with

---

 Critical Thinking

Companies often juggle the dual recruitment metric: efficiency versus effectiveness. A company wants to find the right candidate, but it has to contemplate how long it is willing to wait for the "perfect" person to fit the job. Ask students to consider the following statement: Hiring the right person is better than hiring someone right away. Have students brainstorm and discuss the advantages and disadvantages of having this job recruitment philosophy.

your current or most recent job and end with your first job.

Be prepared to list several references. **References** are people who know your work habits and personal traits well and will recommend you for the job. Make sure you ask permission of your references before listing them on an application form. Try to use professional references, such as your teachers, friends established in business, or former employers. Do not list classmates, relatives, or personal friends. Sign your name using your first name, middle initial, and last name. Your signature should be written, never typed or printed.

Writing Cover Letters

Writing a **cover letter** is like writing a sales pitch about yourself. You must convince an employer that you are the best person to fill a specific job opening. Your cover letter should reflect your understanding of the company and how you may be able to meet its needs. Cover letters can be submitted via mail, e-mail, or fax. They usually accompany a résumé. A cover letter should be personalized for each position and addressed to an individual.

Tell why you are interested in the position and describe your special qualifications for it.

Write a first draft to get down most of the main points. Next, revise your letter until you are pleased with the end result. Ask a teacher, parent or guardian, or friend in business to read and critique your letter. Then put the final touches on it and print out a copy.

Describe how you learned about the job opening in the first sentence.

The second paragraph should contain a description of how your education and experience qualify you for the job. Emphasize facts that make you especially well qualified for the job. Do not repeat the information in the résumé; instead, demonstrate how that experience or education qualifies you for this position. If you have a lot to say about both your education and job experience, use a separate

paragraph for each. Mention classes you have taken that are related to the job.

Finally, in your last paragraph, ask for an interview at the employer's convenience. State when you will be available, and provide your telephone number and e-mail address.

Many companies receive dozens of cover letters with résumés every week. Businesses that advertise jobs in the newspaper may receive hundreds of letters. Businesses interview only a small portion of those who write—those who qualify for the position and make an effective written presentation. Your cover letter can give you a big advantage over other applicants. Take the time to develop an effective letter of which you are really proud. Once you write a letter, you can adapt it for other jobs, personalizing the details to each position.

As with any sales pitch, a good first impression counts. Use the spell-check function of your word processing program to eliminate any spelling errors. Before you send your letter, make sure you have read it over for accuracy.

Your letter must not only be neat and clear but also follow the rules outlined in this section. Be sure to include all the elements of a business letter. In particular, use the salutation and a formal closing, as shown.

Print your cover letter with black ink on white or off-white paper; use paper that matches the kind you use for your résumé. Keep in mind that colored paper does not fax well. For electronic submission, be sure to apply the formatting suggestions that are discussed in the next section to your electronic cover letter.

Preparing Résumés

A cover letter and a résumé convey your qualifications in writing and sell your abilities. You can see an example of a traditional printed résumé in Figure 38.1. A **résumé** is a summary of personal information, education, skills, work experience, and activities. A résumé organizes the facts about you that are

TEACH CONTINUED

Concept Development

WRITING COVER LETTERS

Have students imagine that they are a human resources manager and receive a poorly written cover letter from a prospective candidate. For example, the letter might not specify the position the person wants, the letter is written in slang, or it does not offer any details on education or work history. Ask the students to write a professional letter in response to this candidate's cover letter.

TEACHING POINTS

Clarify Remind students that a company will toss a candidate's application and supporting documents aside if the person's cover letter and résumé are filled with grammatical mistakes. Tell students that it is important not only to carefully read the letter crafted, but also to have two other people read it before sending it.

Model Bring into class a collection of cover letters. Explain the positive and negative points about each so students can understand how their letters should read in the future.

Extended Activity

Analyze Cover Letters

Ask students to search the Internet or the library for cover letters they could utilize when they job hunt. Ask them to take the letters' language into consideration as they write their own letter for a real position or a hypothetical one. Remind them to keep the letter to three paragraphs and never have it run longer than a page.

Extended Activity

Ethical Considerations

Ask students to contemplate this scenario: They are a human resources manager and receive a student's résumé with blatantly false information. (For example, the position asks for a high-school diploma and the candidate has not graduated from high school.) Ask students what impression an employer might receive from such an applicant. Have students share their responses in class.

TEACH CONTINUED

Individualized Practice

WRITING A RÉSUMÉ

L1 Ask students to use the Internet to research the various résumé databases available. For example, have them analyze how one job site differs from another. Have students create a table with the pros and cons of each Web site's function for building and posting an online résumé.

L2 Ask students to write a one-page paper on tips for résumé writing. They should write these tips to a general audience. Have them describe and give examples of the importance of action verbs, scannable résumé formats, the role of keywords, and so on.

L3 Ask students to research sample résumé forms using the Internet or the library. The students should select one they like the best. Have them recreate their own résumé using the desired format located.

Enrichment

ELECTRONIC RÉSUMÉS

Ask students to research tips for creating an e-résumé. They should learn basic formatting issues desired when submitting an e-résumé. Then, have students create their own résumé or create one for a hypothetical person looking for an entry-level position at a local retailer.

 Critical Thinking

Ask students to identify various ways they can become competitive in today's job market. Have students write down their responses and keep them for future use.

MARKET TECH

Tomorrow's Office

Innovations in office technology have been coming at lightning speed since the middle of the 1980s. The office of tomorrow is likely to be as unrecognizable to us as today's office full of computers and fax machines would be to your grandparents.

Technology on the Go

The next wave of new office technologies will simplify complex tasks, interact with their users, and allow people to take their work with them wherever they go. The driving force is increasing productivity.

Wireless Connections

Wireless connections make it possible to set up an electronic office anywhere wireless networks are available.

Turning tabletops into plasma computer screens makes it possible for everyone at a meeting to see a presentation on the table in front of him or her, or for people at a restaurant to order from electronic menus. Microsoft is developing software that allows e-mail or voice messages to arrive at the nearest computer.

THINK LIKE A MARKETER

As a potential employee in a marketing-related business, how could keeping informed about new technologies help you get a job?

@ **Online Action!**

Go to *marketingessentials.glencoe.com/38/tech* to find an activity on job searches and office technology.

related to the job, which saves the employer time before and during an interview.

Your résumé outlines your qualifications for a particular job. When you send an employer a résumé, include a cover letter. The résumé makes filling out job applications a simpler process because you have already organized all the information. Many people prepare a résumé as the first step in the job application process. Even if you are not hired, many employers will keep your résumé on file for a certain period of time. If they have an opening for which you qualify in the future, they may call you.

Electronic Résumés

If you are applying for a position online, you may be required to submit an electronic résumé. First, compose your electronic résumé using a word processing program.

Electronic Formatting Issues

The format of your electronic résumé should be text only. Save your résumé as a text file; this is the easiest way to transmit and read electronic files. Avoid bold type, italics, and underlining, which do not transmit well and make your résumé difficult to read. Stick to a commonly used traditional font, such as Times New Roman, and keep the font size between 12 and 14 points. Do not use tabs; use the space bar instead.

Using Key Words

Companies that accept résumés electronically will usually search for job qualifications by looking for key words. It is very likely that a computer program, not a person, will first scan your résumé. In the scanning process, the computer searches for key words and phrases, and the résumé is summarized and ranked among other qualified candidates.

Because of this, it is important to use key words to describe what you can do. What are key words? Key words consist primarily of nouns and are usually divided into three categories: job title, industry, and personal traits. If you have done your preliminary research about the company, industry, and job—using methods such as the Internet, publications, or

MARKET TECH

Tomorrow's Office

Discussion Lead students in a discussion about how technology has influenced various occupations and career pathways.

THINK LIKE A MARKETER **Answer:** Answers will vary and might include that it helps candidates remain competitive in an aggressive marketplace, it assists in implementing new technologies in a stagnant workplace, and so on.

@ **Online Action!** For instructions, ideas, and answer guide, go to the Teacher Center at marketingessentials.glencoe.com

Figure 38.1 Résumé

What Information Should You Include? Your résumé should show off your education, skills, and experience in the best way possible—and do it in one page.

What are some tips for writing a résumé?

① Objective Your objective statement should indicate the type of job you want. Change this item if you use the same résumé to apply for a different job.

② Identification Include your name, address, telephone number, and e-mail address.

Frank Johnson
1235 East Tenth Avenue
Ventura, CA 93003
(805) 555-6264
frankjohnson@yourname.com

Objective:
A marketing analyst position that would complement my academic and work experience.

③ Experience List experience related to the specific job for which you are applying, including volunteer work.

Experience:
9/04-present Assistant Marketing Analyst
Ventura Volvo
6580 Leland Street
Ventura, CA 93003

Used computer to estimate sales by model and make recommendations for inventory. Accessed databases using computer terminal to study inventory in relation to buying estimates. Studied historical applications, including media ads, price and color changes, and impact of season.

9/03-9/04 Marketing Assistant
KVEN Radio
Ventura, CA 93003

Assisted Communications Manager in publishing articles and ads, sales presentations, vendor contracts, and trade shows. Contacted vendors for advertising needs (charts, overheads, banners).

④ Education List schools attended from high school on, the dates of attendance, and diplomas or degrees earned. It is fine to emphasize the courses that are related to the job you are applying for.

Education:
2002-2004 Ventura College. AA in Marketing. Dean's Honor Roll two semesters.
Courses included:
Marketing I and II
Marketing Information Systems
Advertising
Economics I and II
Computer Science
1999-2002 Ventura High School, Graduated in upper 10 percent of class. Served as Vice President of DECA two years.

⑤ Activities and Awards List school clubs or sports awards, and any recognition you received at work, school, or extracurricular settings.

Personal:
Hobbies include writing computer programs, tennis, and photography.

⑥ References Include up to three references on a short résumé. Or, indicate that they are available. Always ask people ahead of time if they are willing to be listed as references for you.

References:
Available upon request.

 Online Action!

Go to *marketingessentials.glencoe.com/38/figure/1* to find a project on résumés.

Figure 38.1 Résumé

Discussion Ask students to discuss how they should write a résumé if they have never had a job before. Answer may include: Provide information about experiences and awards related to school, community involvement, and extracurricular activities.

Caption Answer Answers might include highlight accomplishments and extracurricular, volunteer, and leadership experiences; describe duties; and limit the information to one page.

 Online Action! For instructions, ideas, and answer guide, go to the Teacher Center at **marketingessentials.glencoe.com**

Follow Up Have each student write a résumé and bring it to class. Ask students to exchange their résumés with a partner. Students should critique their partners' résumés, judging how well they followed the guidelines for résumé writing.

TEACH CONTINUED

Concept Development

PREPARING RÉSUMÉS

Ask students to write a hypothetical career timeline from now until retirement. They should include about education, possible opportunities, and location moves that might benefit their career. When the timelines are complete, ask students to share them in class.

TEACHING POINTS

Clarify Remind students to drop the "I" in their résumé. This takes the narrator out and instead focuses on the action.

Summarize Remind students when writing a résumé to demonstrate how their strengths and experiences can benefit a future employer.

Build Vocabulary

Introduce students to the career counseling strategy of *assessment testing*. Explain to them that unlike a school test that tests one's knowledge of a subject, this assessment is designed to aid the applicant in finding his or her career. Encourage students to find a career assessment test online that they can take for free.

Extended Activity

Job-Specific Tests
Tell students that some companies require job applicants to write an essay or take a test (for example, personality tests, job expertise tests, and so on). Ask students to imagine they are applying for a sales position at a local store. Have students write a 100-word response on why a store would make them craft an essay as part of the application process.

Enrichment

REVIEWING RÉSUMÉS

Have students review each other's résumés to provide constructive criticism. Allow all students the opportunity to revise the first draft of their résumé in order to improve it. Also, have students adjust their own résumé to match one of the cover letters they prepared earlier. Tell them to save both of these documents in their notebooks for future use.

Discussion Starter

PREPARING FOR AN INTERVIEW

Ask students why they think an interview is so important in the hiring process. Have students share their responses in class and give reasons for their conclusions.

TEACHING POINTS

Model Bring into class a variety of interview strategy guides or books. Share with the class various points that relate to the content discussed in this textbook.

Critical Thinking

Ask students to respond to whether they agree with the following statement and why: "If you believe in yourself, so will others." Have students share their responses in class.

---

networking—you will have developed a list of key words or phrases that are mentioned.

It is important to include industry-specific jargon, as many employers will search by industry language. Be sure to spell out all acronyms—mention your membership in the Distributive Education Clubs of America (DECA), not just DECA. You may not be considered for a job for which you are qualified if key words do not appear on your résumé.

Confidentiality is an issue when you post your résumé on the Internet. Remember that once posted on a career Web site, your résumé is a public document that is out of your control. When you give information so that a potential employer can contact you, you have the option of limiting your personal information by including only an e-mail address or post office box. Since most employers prefer to contact applicants by telephone or e-mail, make sure your answering machine message is professional, and check your messages and e-mails daily so you can respond promptly.

Before e-mailing your résumé to employers, e-mail a copy to yourself so that you can review the message.

How to Submit Your Résumé

When you have completed your cover letter and résumé, you can submit them as part of an e-mail. It is best to "cut and paste" the résumé into the body of an e-mail message rather than including it as an attached file. Attached files can be difficult to read if the file is created in a word processing program different from the one used by the employer. Also, some employers may be hesitant to open file attachments because of the risk of computer viruses. Some companies will specify what type of electronic form they prefer; read online submission directions carefully to avoid having your résumé rejected.

Traditional/Print Résumés

In addition to your electronic résumé, prepare a print résumé for positions that require a cover letter and résumé to be mailed or faxed. If you print your own résumé, use black ink on white or off-white paper; ideally, the paper

should match the kind you use for your cover letter. Some applicants use local printing companies to print their résumés. If you have your résumé printed in this manner, inquire about prices and ask to look at samples of actual résumés. Shop around—some printing companies offer package deals that include matching paper for your cover letters, as well as envelopes.

Print Formatting Issues

As you can see in Figure 38.1, your printed résumé has formatting that helps organize the material and enables the reader to find the information easily. To review additional styles and formatting options for printed résumés, look at the many résumé sample books that can be found in your library or bookstore. Many online job search sites also feature samples and free advice about preparing résumés and covers. Enter "resume samples" on your favorite search engine to be directed to many sites where you can view résumés. Many sites are free, but some do charge.

Some students hire writers to help them develop their résumés. You can find these experts in your local Yellow Pages. Online résumé writing services can also be a resource. Prices, quality, and turnaround time vary; again, shop around.

What happens during an interview is usually what determines an employer's choice of one applicant over another. It is critical to prepare yourself carefully. Your plan should include three steps: preparing for the interview, conducting yourself properly during the interview, and following up the interview.

Preparing for an Interview

The employer's first impression of you will impact his or her hiring decision. Appropriate grooming and dress, body language that shows confidence, and use of standard English all combine to make a good first impression.

Dress and Grooming

Recently, employees in many stores and offices have adopted a dress code known as

816 UNIT 12 - EMPLOYABILITY AND CAREER DEVELOPMENT

Extended Activity

Make a Career Plan

Ask students to create a self-survey of personal interests regarding their hobbies, academic interests, overall disposition, social skills, and motivating factors. This can help them pinpoint employment areas or career paths that might interest them. Then ask students to contemplate a career that interests them. They can research the experience and education needed for this career using the *Occupational Outlook Handbook* and other resources. Have students create a one-page document in essay, timeline, or bulleted list that documents steps to take to achieve that career.

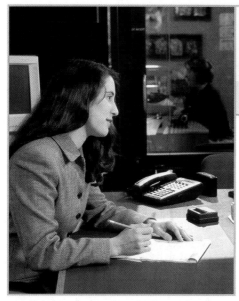

• THE INTERVIEW There are a few common sense basics to remember when interviewing for a job: Look at the interviewer, pay attention, do not hesitate to ask questions, and answer questions as precisely as you can.

Why is it a good idea to prepare a few questions before the interview?

corporate casual. This does not mean, however, that you should dress casually for an interview. It is better to make the extra effort to make a good impression by dressing in a more formal way.

Your clothes should be neat, clean, and wrinkle-free for every interview. In some cases, appropriate interview dress depends on the job. In sales, for example, people dress formally and conservatively to make a good impression on customers.

Regardless of its style, your hair should be clean and neat. Remember, the interviewer will be looking to see how well you will fit in, so a conservative hairstyle is usually most appropriate.

Employers will notice whether your hands are clean and your nails are neatly trimmed. Wearing a great deal of jewelry, for both men and women, can be distracting in an interview. Too much makeup on women can also distract the interviewer. Also, it is a good idea not to wear any perfume or cologne to an interview. Strong scents can be overwhelming and distracting, and some people are allergic to them.

Things to Know

Once you call for an interview appointment, write down the date and time and ask for the interviewer's name. Check the spelling and make sure you can pronounce it correctly. Ask the receptionist how to pronounce the name if it is unfamiliar to you.

Before your interview, carefully review your résumé. Be ready to answer any questions about your education, work experience, or other qualifications.

The research you have conducted about a company will once again come in handy in an interview situation. Your knowledge will help you make a better impression because you will be able to talk intelligently about the company's products and operations. It will show that you are interested in the firm.

Chapter 38 - Finding and Applying for a Job 817

TEACH CONTINUED

Individualized Practice

INTERVIEWING

L1 Ask students to write the answers to the questions under the header Things to Know (on page 818) in their journal.

L2 Ask students to use the Internet and research various things candidates should not say in an interview. Have students make a list and share it with the class.

L3 Ask students to create a role play in which one person interviews another. This mock interview can last five to 10 minutes. Make sure the interviewer comes with a prepared list of questions.

Enrichment

DRESS AND GROOMING

Ask students to list tips men and women can follow when dressing and grooming for an interview. Encourage students to use visual aids or presentation software to show appropriate and inappropriate examples.

Build Vocabulary

Introduce students to the phrase "dress for success." Explain why dress might sway a hiring manager's decision between two equally talented candidates.

PHOTO GUIDE THE INTERVIEW

Discussion Ask students: Why do you think this job candidate has a pencil and paper? Discuss their answers.

Caption Answer You will seem more informed and interested in the job and the employer. It can also help you answer important questions about whether you want to work for this employer.

Follow Up Have students ask one adult they know what helped and hurt them in a job interview. Ask them to share their stories with the class.

 Critical Thinking

Ask students if they think it is right for a potential hiring manager to judge a candidate based on his or her attire and appearance. Ask: Do they consider this a form of discrimination? Have students discuss their responses.

Concept Development

THINGS TO KNOW

Tell students that research indicates that within the first five minutes of an interview, the interviewer has made up his or her mind about whether or not to hire the candidate. Ask students what they might do to make a great first impression.

TEACHING POINTS

Clarify Remind students that if they carry a cell phone or any other technological devices, they should turn them off before entering an interview.

Summarize Remind students that it is best to arrive 10 to 15 minutes ahead of time at the interview in order to check themselves over in the restroom mirror, get a drink of water, and sit comfortably in the waiting room. Remind them not to fidget while waiting or while in the interview. They should instead offer each individual they meet a handshake, smile, and sincere eye contact.

Extended Activity

Interview Questions

Ask students to research and find a list of questions commonly used during an interview. Once they have located these questions, ask them to take some time to create complete answers as though they were in an actual interview.

The following questions are often asked of job applicants during interviews. Write the answers to these questions, then practice answering them. Ask a family member, teacher, or friend to help you by asking the questions and giving you feedback on your reply.

- Why do you want to work for this company?
- Do you want permanent or temporary work?
- Why do you think you can do this job?
- What jobs have you had? Why did you leave?
- What classes do you like best in school?
- In what school activities have you participated?
- What do you want to be doing five years from now?
- Do you prefer working alone or with others?
- What is your main strength?
- What salary do you expect?

- What grades have you received in school?
- How do you feel about working overtime?
- How many days were you absent from school last year?
- Why should I hire you?
- When can you begin work?

Under federal law, employers cannot make employment decisions on the basis of race or ethnicity, gender, religion, marital status, age, country of origin, sexual preference, and physical and/or mental status. Questions should address only the factors that bear on the ability of a job applicant to carry the work required. Therefore, questions about these topics should not be asked. If asked such a question, you have three choices (The latter is usually the best way to handle such questions.):

1. You can answer truthfully if you feel your answer will not harm you.
2. You can mention to the interviewer that the question is inappropriate because

•ABILITY Federal law makes it illegal to discriminate in hiring decisions based on disabilities, unless it would cause the employer significant hardship.

According to this ad, what qualities do many disabled people have that would make them good employees?

AD GUIDE ABILITY

Discussion Ask students: Why do you think the federal government enacted laws to protect those with disabilities from discrimination in hiring? Discuss student responses.

Caption Answer Many disabled people overcome challenges every day, and they have a strong desire to succeed.

Follow Up Ask students to research and report back to the class on job assisting services for people with disabilities.

of laws against discrimination in hiring—but this will likely end any chance of getting the job.

3. You can sidestep the question and base your answer on the requirements of the job and your ability to perform it.

Conducting Yourself Properly During an Interview

Always go alone for a job interview. If someone must accompany you on the day of the interview, ask that person to wait for you outside in a public location. Plan to arrive for your interview five to ten minutes early. Always allow some extra time in case you run into delays. Do not be too early, though. Waiting outside the interviewer's door for half an hour is not comfortable for you or the employer.

Before you meet the interviewer, you may meet a receptionist, administrative assistant, or other employee. Be courteous and polite to anyone you meet; these people might be your future coworkers.

If you have not already completed an application form, you may be asked to do so before or after the interview. Be prepared by bringing a good pen or two with black or blue ink. You may also need to supply your social security number and your references. Bring along two copies of your résumé to the interview, one to leave with your interviewer if he or she wants it and one to help you fill out an application form.

Remain standing until you are asked to sit down. When you do sit down, lean forward slightly toward the interviewer to show your interest. Relax and focus on your purpose: to make the best possible impression.

Place your purse or briefcase on the floor by your chair. Never put anything on the interviewer's desk, even if there is room. This may appear disrespectful or too casual.

It is normal to feel a little nervous at the beginning of an interview. You will relax as the interview progresses. Keep your hands in your lap, and try to keep them still. Never place your hands on the interviewer's desk. Look the interviewer in the eye most of the time and listen to him or her carefully. Be confident and be yourself. The employer has taken the time to interview you because he or she has confidence that you are a qualified candidate.

What to Say in an Interview

Most interviewers begin by asking specific questions. Answer each question honestly. If you do not know the answer to a particular question, say so. The interviewer will probably realize it if you try to fake an answer. Keep your answers short and to the point.

Two particular questions often cause problems for young job applicants. These questions are, "What type of work would you like to do?" and "What wage (or salary) do you expect?" You can answer the first question by giving the name of the specific job you want. The question about expected wage or salary is a little more difficult if you do not have a specific wage or salary in mind or if you are unsure of what the typical pay bracket is for the job. The best answer is something like, "What do you usually pay for this type of work?" Try to turn the question back to the interviewer. If you must answer, offer a pay range.

Wages and benefits are usually discussed toward the end of an interview. If your interviewer does not mention pay, wait until the interview is almost over; then ask how much the job pays. If you know that there will be a second interview before the job is offered, you may wait until then to ask about salary. You also may want to ask about benefits if you are applying for a full-time, permanent job. Benefits may include a paid vacation and insurance coverage.

The interviewer will expect you to ask some questions. Specific questions show the interviewer that you have done your research and are interested in learning more. Job applicants often ask questions like those listed below:

- Why is the position vacant?
- What are the typical responsibilities for this position?
- Would I work individually or with a team?
- With what other areas of the company would I interact on a regular basis?
- What type of training or orientation would I receive?

TEACH CONTINUED

Concept Development

WHAT TO SAY IN AN INTERVIEW

Ask students to prepare a five-minute sales pitch as if they were marketing themselves to a potential employer during an interview. Their pitch should exhibit their personality and work style.

TEACHING POINTS

Clarify Remind students that in an interview, it is not the time to rely on modesty. With only a few minutes to promote themselves, it is important to discuss their strengths and accomplishments as they relate to the possible position at hand. They should focus on the talents an employer will find beneficial to it.

Extend Remind students not to label their successes as a matter of luck. They should avoid using such disclaimers as "I was lucky enough..." or "I don't mean to brag, but...." Explain that these statements can be interpreted as a sign of insecurity on the candidate's part.

Extended Activity

Following Up After an Interview
Ask students to write a thank-you note to a hiring manager for a position they really want to obtain for the summer. Make sure the note follows basic business structure. When the notes are complete, share some of the more successful ones with the class.

Extended Activity

Interview Behavior
Ask students to research and write a list of good and bad interview behaviors. Students should place a check mark next to any of the behaviors they might have exhibited before. Ask them to pay attention to how their actions are perceived by others.

ASSESS

Review Guide

CONCEPTS

1. Ask students to review the basic functions of the cover letter and résumé.

2. Review with students the highlights of good interview techniques. Also, ask students to answer some of the most commonly asked interview questions. Have students connect those questions with specific jobs.

KEY TERMS

Have students review key terms, their spellings, and definitions in small groups.

ONLINE SELF-ASSESSMENT

Have students go to **marketingessentials.glencoe.com** for the Section 38.2 practice test.

Individualized Review

L1 Assign and review Chapter 38 activities in the Student Activity Workbook.

L2 Assign and review Chapter 38 activities in the Marketing Math Workbook.

L3 Assign and review Chapter 38 activities in the *BusinessWeek* Reader and Case Studies.

Marketing Practice

Ask students to create a career resource file. The purpose of the career resource file is for students to begin a lifelong process of self-analysis and career assessment. Have students write a self-assessment, including information about their interests, aptitudes, and personal traits. Students should include career research and career preparation information in the file as well. Ask students to write a reflective paragraph on the ever-changing nature of careers and the need for continual self-improvement.

820

A MATTER OF ETHICS

Keeping One's Word?

Kendall worked for five years at Genaro's Music, a store selling recorded music and some DVDs. He learned a great deal from Genaro, his boss, and over the years did everything from stocking shelves to keeping track of sales. In exchange for teaching Kendall the business, Genaro asked Kendall to agree that, if he went into business himself, he would not compete directly with Genaro's.

Kendall feels ready to start his own business. He is thinking of focusing on world music, selling CDs and tapes, DVDs of concerts, and also unusual musical instruments from around the world. Genaro's does not have a big world music section, so Kendall does not feel he is competing directly with Genaro. When he tells Genaro about his plans, his boss disagrees and says that starting the business would violate the agreement not to compete.

THINKING ETHICALLY

Is it ethical for Kendall to start the new store? If the store turns out to take business away from Genaro's, what should Kendall do? Explain the reasons for your answers.

@ Online Action!

Go to *marketingessentials.glencoe.com/38/ethics* to find an activity on ethical conduct in the workplace.

- What are some of the issues the person hired will need to address immediately?
- Please tell me about the department in which I would work.
- What is the typical career path for someone starting in this position? What are the opportunities for advancement?

- Will I have regular evaluations or reviews?
- How are the company and the department structured?
- To whom would I report?
- Will I need to take any tests as part of the interview process?
- What is the dress code?
- What are the hours of work?
- Would I be expected to work on the weekend?
- Does the position require any travel?
- Is overtime common on this job?
- What benefits do you offer?
- When do you expect to be making your hiring decision?

Closing the Interview

At the close of the interview, one of several things can happen. You may be offered the job, or you may be told that you will not be hired. More likely, however, you will be told that a decision will be made later. You may be asked to a second interview with someone else in the company, such as a department head. This usually means you have made a good impression in your first interview, and your chances of being offered the job are good.

If you are interested in the position, let the interviewer know. You can ask for the job or ask for the next interview if another interview is required. Be a good salesperson and say something like, "I am very impressed with what I've seen and heard here today, and I am confident that I could do an excellent job in the position you've described to me. When might you be in a position to make an offer?"

If an offer is extended, accept it only if you are ready. If you are sure that you want it, accept it on the spot. If you want some time to think it over, be courteous and tactful in asking for that time. It is not unreasonable to want to think about this decision before making a commitment. Set a definite date when you can provide an answer (usually no more than 24 to 48 hours).

You will be able to sense when the interview is almost over. Then you should stand, smile, and thank your interviewer for his or

---

A MATTER OF ETHICS   Keeping One's Word?

Discussion Ask students to discuss the binding of a verbal agreement versus the binding of a written agreement.

THINKING ETHICALLY   **Answer:** Answers will vary. The decision may come down to whether Kendall signed a noncompete clause while working for Genaro's Music. If he did not, then Genaro simply asked Kendall out of respect for the business not to enter the market with a competing store.

@ Online Action!   For instructions, ideas, and answer guide, go to the Teacher Center at marketingessentials.glencoe.com

Follow Up   Ask students how a person's words and actions create a certain kind of persona.

her time and consideration. Shake hands and go. Be sure to thank the receptionist or administrative assistant on your way out.

Following Up After an Interview

A thank-you letter is an appropriate way to follow up most interviews. Simply thank the employer for the time given you and reaffirm your interest in the job.

Include any information that you may have forgotten to mention during the interview that will help qualify you for the position. Your letter may be either handwritten or typed, but it must be neat.

Many employers check references and call your school for a recommendation. This may take several days. Unless you were told not to call, it is all right to telephone the employer five or six days after the interview. Ask to speak with the person who interviewed you. Then give your name and ask if he or she has made a decision on the job. This will let the employer know that you are still interested.

After You Are Hired

After you begin a new job, there are several steps you can take to enhance your career growth and future job searches:

- Thank all those who interviewed you.
- Make a list of your accomplishments and awards you may have received individually or as part of a team or department.
- Keep samples of your work, unless the material is confidential.
- Save copies of reviews and evaluations.
- Take advantage of any opportunity to learn new skills or receive training.
- Continue to build your networking contacts.
- Volunteer for committee responsibilities that are outside the scope of your job. These opportunities help you stand out in the company and may uncover the next step in your career path.
- Be a team player and work to the best of your ability.

CLOSE

Ask students to recall and provide answers to the following questions:

- **Name the four different ways employers can get information from a job applicant.**
  Application form, résumé, cover letter, and employment tests.

- **What elements should a cover letter include?**
  How one learned about the job, a description of qualifications, a list of references, and a request for an interview. A cover letter introduces someone and states how he or she can do a good job for a company.

- **How would you follow up a job interview?**
  Send a short thank-you note and place a telephone call a few days later.

- **What can an interviewer tell about a candidate's body language during an interview?**
  Comfort level, maturity, self-confidence level, social mores, etc.

38.2 AFTER YOU READ

Reviewing Key Terms and Concepts

1. List the basic information categories you would list in a résumé.
2. What three steps can you take to help you achieve a successful interview?
3. Describe how you can learn about a company in order to prepare for an interview.

Integrating Academic Skills

Math

4. You have been offered a job at $12.00 per hour for 40 hours plus an additional 5 hours per week at time-and-a-half. You will work 50 weeks per year. If the combined withholding of taxes on your pay is 22 percent, what will your total annual net pay?

History

5. Research gender pay equity issues in the United States. Write a one-page report on the history of this issue and on current developments in this area.

 Online Action!

Check your answers at *marketingessentials.glencoe.com/38/read*

 Online Activity

Interviewing

Have students search the Web for sites that give advice or offer techniques to master the interview process. Have students take notes on a technique that interests them. Ask volunteers to walk the class through one technique.

AFTER YOU READ

Reviewing Key Terms and Concepts

1. Basic information categories include personal identification, objective, experience, education, activities and awards, and list of references.

2. Three steps you can take to help you achieve a successful interview are to prepare for the interview, conduct yourself properly during the interview, and to follow up the interview.

3. Different ways to learn about a company include read company brochures or catalogs, visit the company's Web site, look for print or online articles, and ask members of your network.

Integrating Academic Skills

4. Your total annual net pay is $25,080; $480 + 90 (overtime) = $570 per week; $570 × 50 weeks = $28,500 per year; $28,500 × .88 = $25,980.

5. Reports will vary; student findings should reflect an understanding of gender pay equity in the United States.

Online Action! Answers at **marketingessentials.glencoe.com/38/read**

CAREERS
IN MARKETING

Lifelong Learning

CAREER INFORMATION

Have students go to marketingessentials.glencoe.com and find the Chapter 38 Careers page. Click on the link for the American Marketing Association's Careers Strategies and Tips. Ask students to select one article, read it, and summarize it in three short paragraphs.

THE CAREER SEARCH PROCESS

Career coaches often conduct public seminars and workshops on career search, interview, and résumé and cover letters or offer their career counseling services privately for a fee. Students can use the Internet and print advertisements to see what kinds of topics are included in such a seminar.

Primary Source

Ask students go to marketingessentials.glencoe.com and find the Chapter 38 Resources. Ask them to click on the link for the American Marketing Association's marketing dictionary at the bottom of the page. Have students read the definitions of any career or job-search related terms they find.

● THINKING CRITICALLY

Answers might include that such a career requires looking at an individual's work experience, and personality and suggesting new, creative ways to succeed.

@ Online Action!

For instructions, ideas, and answer guide, go to the Teacher Center at marketingessentials.glencoe.com

CAREERS
IN MARKETING

KAREN BATTOE
PRESIDENT AND FOUNDER
PERSONAL SUCCESS
SYSTEMS, INC.

(?) What do you do at work?
I am a certified professional coach and president and founder of Personal Success Systems, Inc., a corporate and individual coaching and consulting firm in Orlando, Florida. I work with managers and executives who are stuck, and want to learn a more creative approach to being successful in the job market. I coach clients through the exploration and self-discovery process, partner with them on all aspects of the job search, and continue to coach them through their first 60 days on the job.

(?) What skills are most important to you?
Listening, observation, objectivity, the ability to ask thought-provoking questions, the ability to think outside of the box, creativity, and innovation. I recommend that anyone who wants to be a coach should experience working with a coach. Enroll in one of the coaching schools. Get your certifications. Once you learn the coaching process, then you can choose your specialty. If you want to specialize in career management, make sure you choose a coach who specializes in that area.

(?) What is your key to success?
Over 20 years in the employment field. Before founding Personal Success Systems, Inc., I was an executive for several multinational corporations. I also am very intuitive when it comes to people, and have spent years building my credibility.

Aptitudes, Abilities, and Skills

Outgoing personality, ability to think creatively and ask unusual questions, strong interpersonal skills

Education and Training

Degrees in psychology, business, marketing, or management are useful.

Career Path

Coaching schools provide access to certifications necessary for this career; once certified, students can find entry-level work within the human resources department at large corporations, or can attempt to freelance.

● THINKING CRITICALLY

Why is creativity so important in this career?

@ Online Action!

Go to *marketingessentials.glencoe.com/ 38/careers* to find a career-related activity.

 ## Test-Taking Strategies

Ask students to pair up with a partner to quiz each other on the definitions of the key terms and the section reviews. Encourage students to create a dialogue when discussing the chapter to make the content more user-friendly rather than strictly sticking to the textbook verbiage.

FOCUS on KEY POINTS

SECTION 38.1
● You can find job leads through many sources, and you should make use of most of them. Among the best are networking contacts, newspaper and magazine ads, employment and temporary staffing agencies, and the Internet.

SECTION 38.2
● You may apply for a job by filling out an application form or by submitting a résumé with a cover letter.

● The decision to hire is almost always made during or following the interview. Therefore, it is very important to be well prepared.

● For each job interview, conduct yourself properly during the interview, and follow up after each interview.

REVIEW VOCABULARY

Use the following vocabulary terms in a paragraph describing an effective job search.

1. job lead (p. 806)
2. networking (p. 807)
3. public employment agencies (p. 808)
4. private employment agencies (p. 808)
5. staffing/temporary agencies (p. 808)
6. standard English (p. 812)
7. references (p. 813)
8. cover letter (p. 813)
9. résumé (p. 813)

REVIEW FACTS and IDEAS

10. What will most likely be your best source of job leads? (38.1)
11. Name two methods of contacting job leads and describe one advantage of each method. (38.1)
12. What is one technique of expanding your list of job leads? (38.1)
13. What is a work permit, and what purpose does it serve? (38.2)
14. What information does a résumé contain? (38.2)
15. What should you do to make a good first impression at a job interview? (38.2)
16. What are some rules of conduct to follow during the interview? (38.2)
17. What are appropriate ways to follow up after an interview? (38.2)

Chapter 38 - Finding and Applying for a Job 823

REVIEW FACTS and IDEAS

10. Your best source of job leads is often your friends and family. Other sources may include school counselor, professionals, former employers, cooperative education and work experience programs, newspaper ads, employment agencies, company personnel offices, and the Internet.

11. Student answers may include by phone, e-mail, and regular mail. Advantages will vary and may include timeliness.

12. One technique of expanding your list of job leads is to ask each contact for another lead.

13. A work permit is a legal document that is often required for a worker under the age of 18. It establishes that it is legal for a young worker to do the type of work offered.

14. A résumé should contain your personal identification, objective, experience, education, activities and awards, and your references.

15. Answers may include: dress appropriately, use body language that shows confidence, and use standard English.

16. Answers may include: go to the interview alone, arrive a few minutes early, be courteous, bring copies of your résumé, remain standing until you are asked to sit, respect the interviewer's personal space.

17. Appropriate ways to follow up after an interview include call, write a thank-you letter, and visit.

FOCUS on KEY POINTS

Ask students to volunteer a few details they also learned under each point in the sections.

REVIEW VOCABULARY

See glossary for definitions of 1–9. Student responses will vary. Judge the completeness of the paragraph not only on their utilizing the key terms, but also on their using them in the correct context. They should support the key terms with content they learned in this chapter and the overall course. A sample sentence might read:

An effective job search often starts with *networking:* contacting friends and acquaintances to get *job leads.*

BUILD SKILLS

18. Workplace Skills
Responses will vary. You might suggest that a hiring manager or whoever booked the interview verify the date and time. Advise the student not to leave the company until the date and time have been double-checked with a supervisor.

19. Technology Applications
Questions and answers will vary. Advise students to research the array of questions, including behavioral-style questions that are popular in interview situations. Encourage the students to write full answers, with general comments and specifics about their experiences.

20. Math Practice
Your average rate of pay is $14.67 per hour: $[(\$14 \times 3) + (\$15.68 \times 2)] \div 5 = \$14.67$.

DEVELOP CRITICAL THINKING

21. Interview Question
Answers will vary due to the multitude of tough interview questions available. Interviewees often have a hard time listing their weaknesses while still casting themselves in a positive light.

22. To Call or Not to Call?
Often hiring managers write the "do not call" request on the ad due to the high volume of applications they receive. Phone calls might be considered a burden to the company insider. Sending a follow-up e-mail is often more acceptable today. Applicants can call, knowing that the company insider may not appreciate it. Be mindful that if the company is interested in the candidate, it will contact him or her for an interview.

BUILD SKILLS

18. Workplace Skills
Human Relations You are scheduled for a job interview. You arrive at the receptionist's desk about ten minutes before the interview. The receptionist checks her schedule and says she does not have your name on her list for today. A further check shows that she has you scheduled for tomorrow at the same time. You are certain that you wrote the appointment correctly on your calendar. What should you say?

19. Technology Applications
Preparing for an Interview Conduct a search on the Internet to learn more about job interviewing. Look for examples of tough questions that an interviewer might ask. Using a word processing program, list three of these questions. Write the answer you would give for each one if you were asked such a question during an interview.

20. Math Practice
Calculate a Pay Rate You work full time for a local retailer as a floor manager. For three days a week, you work a standard nine-to-five shift. For two days a week, you work a split shift. Your pay is $14.00 per hour. However, on the two days you work a split shift, you receive a 12 percent pay differential, which makes your pay $15.68 per hour for those two 8-hour days. What is your average rate of pay for the 40-hour week?

DEVELOP CRITICAL THINKING

21. Interview Question
Give an example of an interview question that might be difficult to answer, and explain how it could be handled.

22. To Call or Not to Call?
Suppose you spot an ad in an online listing. You think this is the perfect job for you, so you e-mail your résumé and cover letter. The ad warns, "no phone calls, please." However, you have researched the company thoroughly and you are convinced you match the job description. Should you call the company's Human Resources department? Why or why not? What else could you do to stand out among the applicants?

Formative Assessment

Formative assessment is an essential component of classroom work. This type of assessment provides information that is then used as feedback to modify teaching and meet student needs.

L1 Review key terms for this chapter. Ask students to write one sentence for each key term.

L2 Ask students to create stories that illustrate effective ideas for self-promotion during the interview process.

L3 Ask students to create a 10-minute presentation that models the steps for locating and securing employment. Encourage students to use multimedia in their presentations.

 Reteach If the results of this formative assessment seem low, consider the following activity:

Have students identify characteristics of effective cover letters, résumés, and interview strategies.

APPLY CONCEPTS

23. Finding Jobs in Marketing

Locate an ad for a marketing job that interests you in the employment section of a newspaper. Make a copy of this ad. Then do some research in your library or on the Internet to learn more about cover letters. Read several examples of cover letters. Also, research the company that placed the ad and the type of position that is advertised. Use this information to target your writing.

Activity Using a word processing program, write your own cover letter in response to the newspaper ad you selected. Display your ad and letter in your classroom.

24. Creating a Networking System

Use a database or spread sheet program to create a file listing all the friends, family members, professionals, and former employers who might be able to help you find work. Your networking file should contain the following categories: names and titles, company associations, addresses, phone numbers, fax numbers, and e-mail addresses. You should also include a category for noting dates of contact and brief summaries of what was discussed.

Activity Use the information you have gathered to list the types of jobs for which you could apply and the areas of industry that are covered by your networking contacts.

NET SAVVY

25. Internet Job Search

Find job search Web sites and narrow your search to focus on advertising. Select several areas in the United States and review the jobs that are offered. Compare and contrast the job offerings.

marketingessentials.glencoe.com

CONNECTION

Role Play: Finding a Job

Situation You are to assume the role of high school junior. You are enrolled in a marketing class and want to find a part-time job that will enhance your experience in your marketing class. Part of your class work is an assignment to prepare an outline of the process for finding and then applying for a job that you will find interesting and do a good job for your employer.

Activity You are to prepare your job-seeking assignment and present it to your marketing teacher (judge).

Evaluation You will be evaluated on how well you meet the following performance indicators:

● Utilize job-search strategies
● Prepare a résumé
● Complete a job application
● Interview for a job
● Write a follow-up letter after job interviews

@ Online Action!

For more information and DECA Prep practice, go to *marketingessentials.glencoe.com/38/DECA*

Chapter 38 - Finding and Applying for a Job **825**

CHAPTER **38** REVIEW

APPLY CONCEPTS

23. Finding Jobs in Marketing
Letters and ads will vary; letters should demonstrate comprehension of the job listed.

24. Creating a Networking System
Student files should demonstrate an understanding of networking.

NET SAVVY

25. Internet Job Search
Job ads will vary depending on position and location. Typically, the position titles are relatively boilerplate, which generalize duties for the most part. Usually in smaller companies, job titles are often inflated more than the same title at larger companies.

MINI-QUIZ

Administer the Mini-Quiz orally. Students should respond as either true or false.

1. Many electronic résumés are not initially read by a person, but are scanned by a computer program, which looks for key words and phrases. (true)

2. When applying for a job, it is a good idea to prepare a cover letter and résumé, which outline your qualifications for a particular job. (true)

3. A thank-you note is an appropriate way to follow up an interview. (true)

For an expanded chapter quiz, go to Chapter 38 in the TeacherWorks CD-ROM and to Chapter 38 in the **Exam**View® Pro Test Generator CD-ROM.

  CONNECTION

The students should be evaluated on the performance indicators noted in the role play. For another DECA role play, go to the Competitive Events Workbook, or the Student Activity Workbook, or go to **marketingessentials.glencoe.com/38/DECA**

@ Online Action! For instructions, ideas, and answer guide, go to the Teacher Center at **marketingessentials.glencoe.com**

DECA Advisors Corner

This project will serve the needs of all students seeking employment. Put together a job-seeking skills packet by copying appropriate materials from your teaching resources. Compose a cover letter to all students in the DECA chapter and include a copy of the packet.

MARKETING INTERNSHIP

A SIMULATED ⬥DECA PRODUCT AND SERVICE MANAGEMENT EVENT

SET-UP

Discuss basic background to make sure students understand the simulation. Ask students to describe training programs or employment tests they might have taken. Have them explain whether if the programs were effective and what they learned from them.

PROCEDURES

You may want to list procedures on the board and talk about any questions the students might have. Remind the students that a suggested outline for their project is available at marketingessentials.glencoe.com/u12/ internship.

TIME MANAGEMENT

Set goals, block schedules, and milestones. Assign interim deadlines for each step of the project.

ASSESSMENT

The rubrics for evaluation of the written, oral, and computer presentations are available at marketingessentials.glencoe.com/u12/ internship.

Design an Employment Test

⟩ BASIC BACKGROUND

On the hit reality show *The Apprentice,* contestants competed for a six-figure salary in a job with Donald Trump's organization. They were divided into teams and given tasks to perform to prove their skills. Some of the tasks included

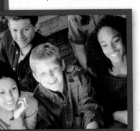

selling lemonade in New York City, designing an ad campaign for a jet rental company, buying and selling items from a flea market, and managing a restaurant.

From Reality Show to Real Life This show gave your firm the idea to give its clients training programs or interview tools that use real-life situations.

⟩ YOUR OBJECTIVE

Your objective is to develop a real-life training program or a real-life employment test for a specific position within a company. The company you select may be a manufacturer or retailer of apparel, food, toys, sports equipment, a fast-food or full-service restaurant chain, a bank, a hotel chain, an e-commerce company, a professional sports team, an amusement park, or any of the clients identified in Units 1–11. Your training program or employment test must be realistic, evaluate the skills required for that position, and be highly customized for that specific client.

⟩ ASSIGNMENT AND STRATEGY

- **Get the background** Research the job position for which you will develop the training program or employment test. What education, experience, skills, and aptitudes are required for this position?

  Learn as much as you can about the position's specific tasks, as well as the interpersonal and communication skills that are useful in the position. To get the inside scoop, you might interview someone or spend a few hours shadowing a person who holds that position.

- **Design the program** Prepare the actual scenario(s) that will be part of the training program or employment testing. Explain where each scenario will take place, what the task is, and how the trainee or applicant will be evaluated. If the program is for job training, provide follow-up activities to help new hires learn how to improve their skills.

- **What your project should include** In addition to writing the proposal to pitch the client, refer to Unit 5 to review how to make an

READ to WRITE

Broad-Based Appeal of Training Programs

Have students research training or extended learning programs that are marketed to professionals and corporate clients. What are some popular topics? Is it possible for such classes to appeal to people who work in different fields or industries? Have students describe their findings and explain their answers in a one-page essay.

Encourage students to explore at least two different types of training programs (such as technology skills-building programs and workplace cultural sensitivity programs) while conducting their research.

effective sales presentation. Such preparation steps might include an analysis of competing companies that offer similar services. You should also consider preparing a feature-benefit chart. Think about what your potential customers' objectives and motives might be and what type of decision-making process they are likely to follow. Prepare sample materials for training or testing, and use presentation software for your oral presentation. Add any additional materials you will need to reach your goal, which is selling your proposal to the client.

➤ YOUR REPORT

Use a word processing program and presentation software to prepare a double-spaced report and an oral presentation for the client. See a suggested outline and key evaluation points at *marketingessentials .glencoe.com/internship*

marketingessentials.glencoe.com

BUILD YOUR PORTFOLIO

Option 1 Internship Report
Once you have completed your Marketing Internship project and presentation, include your written report and a few printouts of key slides from your oral presentation in your Marketing Portfolio.

Option 2 Preparing for a Job Interview
Select and research a job for which to apply. Prepare a cover letter, résumé, references, portfolio of your work, and a sample thank-you note you would send to the person who interviewed you. Prepare responses to ten common interview questions. Find another person to pretend to interview you for the job and videotape the session. Use the videotape to evaluate your performance. See a suggested outline and key evaluation points at *marketingessentials.glencoe .com/portfolio*

@ Online Action!

Go to *marketingessentials.glencoe .com/Unit/12/DECA* to review employment concepts that relate to DECA events.

Marketing Internship **827**

Unit Review

Now that students have completed the chapters in Unit 12, ask them to review their answers to the Think and Write activity on page 783. Would they answer it differently? Why or why not?

Next, have students meet in small groups to discuss their career directions and how to use career research resources.

Finally, ask each student who participated in a job interview experience to evaluate his or her job interview simulation experience. Have students write their strengths and weaknesses and what they can do to improve their performance.

STEP AHEAD
Ask students if they feel ready to enter the job market. Lead a class discussion on what they can do to further prepare themselves.

Internship Wrap-Up

Let students know that some businesses often take employees on retreats to build teamwork and leadership skills. Ask students to research such activities and explain how they benefit the workplace and the workers and to share their findings in class in a brief, informal oral report.

BUILD YOUR PORTFOLIO

Explain to students that portfolios provide evidence of their knowledge and skills in working with data, people, and concepts. Developing a portfolio can be a valuable career development and planning tool. Point out to students that it should be as professional looking as possible. Encourage students to check the portfolio information available at **marketingessentials.glencoe.com/u12/internship.**

Peer Review
Fellow students who share common interests can serve as reviewers of the final portfolios. This review can be completed through the use of a checklist. Go to **marketingessentials.glencoe.com/u12/internship** to find a suggested checklist.

GLOSSARY

A

accounting The discipline that keeps track of a company's financial situation.

Ad Council A nonprofit organization that helps produce public service advertising campaigns for government agencies and other qualified sponsors.

ad layout A sketch that shows the general arrangement and appearance of a finished ad.

adaptation Changing an existing product and/or promotion to better suit the characteristics of a targeted country or region.

adjacent colors Colors that are located next to each other on the color wheel and share the same undertones; also known as analogous colors.

advertising A form of nonpersonal promotion in which companies pay to promote ideas, goods, or services in a variety of media outlets.

advertising agencies Independent businesses that specialize in developing ad campaigns and crafting the ads for clients.

advertising campaign A group of advertisements, commercials, and related promotional materials and activities that are designed as a part of a coordinated advertising plan to meet the specific goals of a company.

advertising proof A representation of an ad that shows exactly how it will appear in print.

agents Intermediaries who bring buyers and sellers together and do not own the goods they sell.

agreement A specific commitment that each member makes to the group.

allowance A partial return of the sale price for merchandise that the customer has kept.

aptitude An ability or natural talent; the potential to learn a certain skill.

Articles of Incorporation A document filed with a state department of commerce that identifies the name and address of a new corporation, its purpose, the names of the initial directors, and the amount of stock that will be issued to each director.

aseptic packaging A food storage process that keeps foods fresh without refrigeration for up to six months.

assertiveness Standing up for what you believe.

asset Anything of monetary value that a person owns, such as cash, checking and savings accounts, real estate, or stocks.

attitude research A type of research designed to obtain information on how people feel about certain products, services, companies, or ideas; also known as opinion research.

B

balance of trade The difference in value between a nation's exports and its imports.

balance sheet A summary of a business's assets, liabilities, and owner's equity.

bar graph A drawing made up of parallel bars whose lengths are proportional to the qualities being measured.

barriers Obstacles that interfere with the understanding of a message.

basic stock list A list used for those staple items that should always be in stock.

Better Business Bureau (BBB) One of the oldest nonprofit organizations that establishes self-regulation among businesses.

blind check method The receiver of a delivery writes the description of the merchandise, counts the quantities received, and lists them on a blank form or dummy invoice.

blisterpack Packaging with preformed plastic molds surrounding individual items arranged on a cardboard backing.

bonded warehouses Public or private warehouses that store products requiring the payment of a federal tax.

boomerang method A selling method that converts a customer's objection into a selling point.

brand A name, term, design, symbol, or combination of these elements that identifies a business, product, or service and distinguishes it from its competitors.

brand extension A branding strategy that uses an existing brand name to promote a new or improved product in a company's product line.

brand label Label giving the brand name, trademark, or logo.

brand licensing A legal authorization by a trademarked brand owner to allow another company (the licensee) to use its brand, brand mark, or trade character for a fee.

brand mark A unique symbol, coloring, lettering, or other design elements.

brand name A word, group of words, letters, or numbers that represent a product or service; also known as a product brand.

break-even point The point at which sales revenue equals the costs and expenses of making and distributing a product.

brick-and-mortar retailers Traditional retailers that sell goods to customers from physical stores, rather than over the Internet.

broadcast media Radio and television.

budget accounts Accounts that allow the payment of a purchased item over a certain time period without a finance charge.

bundle pricing A pricing technique in which a company offers several complementary products in a package that is sold at a single price.

business cycle Recurring changes in economic activity, such as the expansion and contraction of an economy.

business philosophy Beliefs about how a business should be run that demonstrate an understanding of the business's role in the marketplace.

business plan A proposal that outlines a strategy to turn a business idea into a reality.

business risk The possibility of financial loss.

business-to-business selling Sales that take place in a manufacturer's or wholesaler's show room (inside sales) or in a customer's place of business (outside sales).

buying behavior The process individuals use to decide what they will buy, where they will buy it, and from whom they will buy it.

buying signals The things customers do or say to indicate a readiness to buy.

C

career outlook Valuable information on the number and types of jobs available in any field.

carload The minimum number of pounds of freight needed to fill a boxcar.

cash flow statement A monthly plan that tracks when a person anticipates that cash will come into their business and when they expect to pay out cash.

cash on delivery (COD) sale A transaction that occurs when a customer pays for merchandise at the time of delivery.

category management A process that involves managing product categories as individual business units.

cause packaging Packaging that is used by companies to promote social and political causes.

centralized buying Buying process for all branches in a chain store operation, usually done in a central location, such as company headquarters.

channel of distribution The path a product takes from its producer or manufacturer to the final user.

channels The avenues through which messages are delivered.

circle graph A pie-shaped geometric representation of the relative sizes of the parts of a whole; also called a pie chart.

clip art Images, stock drawings, and photographs used in print advertisements.

closing the sale The process of obtaining a positive agreement from the customer to buy.

co-branding A combination of one or more brands in the manufacture of a product or in the delivery of a service.

cold canvassing The process of locating as many potential customers as possible without checking out leads beforehand.

collateral Something of value that a person pledges as payment for a loan in case of default.

color wheel A circular illustration of the relationships between colors.

command economy An economic system in which the government decides what, when, and how much will be produced and distributed.

common carriers Trucking companies that provide transportation services to any business in their operating area for a fee.

communication The process of exchanging messages between a sender and a receiver.

communications programs Software applications that enable users to electronically communicate through computers with people around the world.

competition The struggle between companies to attract new customers, keep existing ones, and take away customers from other companies.

complementary colors Colors that are opposites on the color wheel and are used to create high contrast.

consensus A decision on which all members of a team agree.

consignment buying Paying for goods only after the final customer purchases them.

consultative selling Sales that provide solutions to customers' problems by finding products that meet their needs.

consumer market Consumers who purchase goods and services for personal use.

consumer price index (CPI) Measurement of the change in price over a period of time of approximately 400 retail goods and services used by the average urban household.

Consumer Product Safety Commission (CPSC) Federal agency responsible for overseeing the safety of all products except food, drugs, cosmetics, medical devices, tobacco products, firearms and ammunition, motor vehicles, pesticides, aircraft, boats, and fixed site amusement rides.

consumer promotions Sales strategies that encourage customers and prospects to buy a product or service.

contract carriers For-hire trucking companies that provide equipment and drivers for specific routes.

GLOSSARY

contract manufacturing The process of hiring a foreign manufacturer to make products according to certain specifications.

controlling The process of setting standards and evaluating performance.

cooperative advertising A cost-sharing arrangement whereby both a supplier and a local advertiser pay for advertising.

copy The selling message of a written advertisement.

copyright The exclusive right to reproduce or sell a work authored by an individual, such as writings, music, and artwork.

corporation A legal entity created by either a state or a federal statute authorizing individuals to operate an enterprise.

cost-plus pricing All costs and expenses are calculated, and then the desired profit is added to arrive at a price.

coupons Certificates that entitle customers to discounts on goods and services.

cover letter A letter written by an applicant to an employer describing why that applicant is the best person to fill a specific job opening.

credit The opportunity for businesses or individuals to obtain products or money in exchange for a promise to pay later.

credit union A cooperative association formed by labor unions or groups of employees for the benefit of its members.

cross-training A process that prepares a team member to do many different activities.

customer benefits The advantages or personal satisfaction a customer will get from a good or service.

customer profile A list of information about a target market, such as age, income level, ethnicity, occupation, attitudes, lifestyle, and geographic residence.

customer relationship management (CRM) Identifying and understanding customers to form a strong, long-lasting relationship.

customization The process of creating products or promotions for certain countries or regions.

cycle counts A small portion of the inventory is physically counted each day by stockkeeping units so that the entire inventory is accounted for on a regular basis.

D

data analysis The process of compiling, analyzing, and interpreting the results of primary and secondary data collection.

database A collection of related information about a specific topic.

database marketing A process of designing, creating, and managing customer lists that contain information about an individual's characteristics and transactions with a business; also known as customer relationship management (CRM).

database programs Software applications that store and organize information.

debt capital Borrowed funds that must be repaid.

decentralized buying Local chain store managers or their designated buyers who are authorized to make special purchases for their individual stores.

decimal number A fraction or mixed number whose denominator is a multiple of 10.

demand Consumer willingness and ability to buy products.

demand elasticity The degree to which demand for a product is affected by its price.

demographics Statistics that describe a population in terms of personal characteristics such as age, gender, income, marital status, ethnicity, education, and occupation.

denominator The bottom number in a fraction; it represents how many parts make up a whole.

depression A period of prolonged recession.

derived demand The demand for industrial goods based on the demand for consumer goods and services.

descriptive label A label that gives information about the product's use, construction, care, performance, and other features.

desktop publishing programs A software application that is part word processor and part graphics application, and enables users to edit and manipulate both text and graphics in one document.

digit The ten basic symbols that compose the numbering system: 0, 1, 2, 3, 4, 5, 6, 7, 8, and 9.

direct check method The merchandise is checked directly against the actual invoice or purchase order.

direct close A closing method in which a salesperson asks for the sale.

direct distribution Sales of goods or services directly to the customer, with no intermediaries.

direct marketing A type of advertising directed to a targeted group of prospects and customers rather than to a mass audience.

disclaimer A statement that contains exceptions to and exclusions from a warranty.

discretionary income The money left over from a consumer's income after paying for basic living necessities such as food, shelter, and clothing.

display The visual and artistic aspects of presenting a product to a target group of customers.

disposable income The money left over after taxes are taken out of a consumer's income.

distractions Things that compete with the message for the listener's attention.

distribution center A warehouse designed to speed delivery of goods and to minimize storage costs.

Doing Business As (DBA) registration The registration by which a county government officially recognizes that a new proprietorship or partnership exists.

dollar control The planning and monitoring of the total inventory investment that a business makes during a stated period of time.

domestic business A business that sells its products only in its own country.

drop shippers Businesses that own the goods they sell but do not physically handle the products.

E

economic risks Risks that result from changes in overall business conditions.

economy The organized way a nation provides for the needs and wants of its people.

e-marketplace The online shopping location where products are sold to customers and industrial buyers through the use of the Internet.

embargo A total ban on specific goods coming into and leaving a country.

emotional barriers Biases against the sender's opinions that prevent a listener from understanding.

emotional motive A feeling experienced by a customer through association with a product.

empathy An understanding of a person's situation or frame of mind.

employee discounts Discounts offered by employers to their workers.

empowerment Encouragement of team members to contribute and take responsibility for the management process.

endless chain method The process of asking previous customers for names of potential customers.

enterprise resource planning (ERP) Sophisticated software that integrates all parts of a company's business management.

entrepreneurs People who create, launch, organize, and manage a new business and take the risk of business ownership.

entrepreneurship The process of starting and operating your own business.

enumeration Listing items in order.

Environmental Protection Agency (EPA) Federal agency that protects human health and our environment.

environmental scan An analysis of outside influences that may have an impact on an organization.

Equal Employment Opportunity Commission (EEOC) Federal agency responsible for the fair and equitable treatment of employees with regard to hiring, firing, and promotions.

equity The concept of equal rights and opportunities for everyone.

equity capital The process of raising money from within your company or by selling part of the interest in the business.

e-tailing Retailers selling products over the Internet to the customer; also known as online retailing.

ethics Basic values and moral principles that guide the behavior of individuals and groups.

European Union (EU) European trading bloc.

everyday low prices (EDLP) Consistently low prices with no intention of raising them or offering discounts in the future.

exclusive distribution Sales involving protected territories for distribution of a product in a given geographic area.

excuses Reasons for not buying or not seeing the salesperson.

executive summary A brief overview of an entire marketing plan.

exempt carriers Trucking companies that are free from direct regulation of rates and operating procedures.

exit interview An interview arranged by the human resources department when an employee leaves a company.

expansion A time when the economy is flourishing; also called prosperity.

experimental method A research technique in which a researcher observes the results of changing one or more marketing variables while keeping certain other variables constant under controlled conditions.

exports Goods and services sold to other countries.

express warranty A warranty that is explicitly stated, in writing or verbally, to encourage a customer to make a purchase.

extended coverage An endorsement that provides protection against types of loss that may not be covered under a basic property insurance policy.

extensive decision making The process used when there has been little or no previous experience with an item.

F

factors of production Economic term for the four categories of resources: land, labor, capital, and entrepreneurship.

feature-benefit selling Sales that match the characteristics of a product to a customer's needs and wants.

GLOSSARY

Federal Trade Commission (FTC) Federal agency responsible for enforcing the principles of a free enterprise system and protecting consumers from unfair or deceptive business practices.

feedback A receiver's response to a message.

fidelity bonds A type of insurance that protects a business from employee dishonesty.

finance A business function that involves money management.

firewall Hardware or software that protects a computer from attacks by hackers.

fixtures The principal installations in a store; permanent or movable store furnishings that hold and display merchandise.

flexibility Behavior that allows you to adapt to changing circumstances.

flexible-price policy A price policy that lets customers bargain for merchandise.

flextime A program that allows workers to choose their work hours.

focal point An area in a display that attracts attention first, above all else.

Food and Drug Administration (FDA) Federal agency that regulates labeling and safety of food, drugs, and cosmetics sold in the United States.

forced-choice questions Questions that ask respondents to choose answers from possibilities given on a questionnaire.

foreign corporation A company that is incorporated under the laws of a state that differs from the one in which it does business.

foreign direct investment (FDI) Investments in factories, offices, and other facilities in another country that are used for a business's operations.

formal balance When a large item is placed on one side of a display,

a similarly large item should be placed on the other side.

for-profit business A business that seeks to make a profit from its operations.

fractions Numbers used to describe or compare parts of a whole.

franchise A legal agreement to sell a parent company's product or services in a designated geographic area.

free enterprise system A system that encourages individuals to start and operate their own businesses in a competitive market, without government involvement.

free trade Commercial exchange between nations that is conducted on free market principles, without tariffs, import quotas, or other restrictive regulations.

free-on-board (FOB) The price for goods includes delivery at the seller's expense to a specified point and no further.

freight forwarders Private companies that combine less than carload or truckload shipments from several businesses and deliver them to their destinations.

full warranty A warranty that guarantees that if a product is found to be defective within the warranty period, it will be repaired or replaced at no cost to the purchaser.

G

general partnership A way to organize a business in which each partner shares in the profits and losses.

generalization A statement that is accepted as true by most people.

generic brands Products that do not carry a company identity.

geographical pricing A pricing technique that makes price adjustments because of the location of the customer for delivery of products.

geographics Segmentation of the market based on where people live.

global business A business that sells its products to more than one country.

globalization The process of selling the same product and using the same promotion methods in all countries.

goods Tangible items of monetary value that satisfy needs and wants.

grade label A label that states the quality of the product.

graphics and design programs Software applications for creating and modifying images.

green marketing Producing and promoting environmentally safe products.

greeting approach A way to approach a customer that focuses on welcoming the customer to the store.

gross domestic product (GDP) The output of goods and services produced by labor and property located within a nation.

gross national product (GNP) The total dollar value of goods and services produced by a nation.

gross profit The difference between sales revenue and the cost of goods sold.

gross sales The total of all sales for a given period of time.

H

headline The phrase or sentence that captures the readers' attention, arouses their interest, and entices them to read the rest of the ad.

home page The main page of a Web site that clearly and quickly lets people know what site they are visiting.

horizontal organization A structure where top management shares decision making with self-managing teams of workers who set their own goals and make their own decisions.

human risks Risks that are triggered by errors or omissions as well as the unpredictability of customers or of working environments.

hypertext markup language (HTML) A detailed code used to write Web pages.

hypertext transfer protocol (HTTP) The global computer protocol used to identify and locate Web pages on the Internet.

I

illustration The photograph, drawing, or other graphic elements used in an advertisement.

implied warranty A warranty that takes effect automatically by state law whenever a purchase is made.

imports Goods and services purchased from other countries.

incentives Products earned or given away through contests, sweepstakes, and rebates.

income statement A summary of income and expenses during a specific period of time; also known as profit and loss statement.

indirect distribution Sales of goods or services to the customer through one or more intermediaries.

Industrial market Businesses that buy products to use in their operations; also called the business-to-business market (this can be abbreviated as B-to-B or B2B).

industry A group of establishments primarily engaged in producing or handling the same product or group of products or in rendering the same services.

inflation A period of rising prices.

informal balance The placement of several small items with one large item within a display.

infrastructure The physical development of a country,

including its roads, ports, sanitation facilities, and utilities.

initiative The process of taking action and doing what needs to be done without being asked.

installment accounts Accounts that allow for payment over a period of time; also known as time payment accounts.

institutional advertising The process used to try to create a favorable image for a company and foster goodwill in the marketplace.

institutional promotion A promotion method used to create a favorable image for a business, help it advocate for change, or take a stand on trade or community issues.

insurance policy A contract between a business and an insurance company to cover a specific business risk.

integrated distribution A distribution system in which manufacturers act as wholesaler and retailer for their own products.

intensive distribution Sales involving the use of all suitable outlets to sell a product.

interest The money paid for the use of money borrowed or invested.

intermediaries Businesses involved in sales transactions that move products from the manufacturer to the final user; also known as middlemen.

Internet A worldwide network of computer networks, allowing a free flow of information.

Internet service providers (ISPs) Companies that provide Internet access for businesses, organizations, and individuals.

internship An opportunity that offers students direct work experience and exposure to various aspects of a career, either with or without pay.

inventory All the goods stored by a business before they are sold.

inventory management The process of buying and storing

materials and products while controlling costs for ordering, shipping, handling, and storage.

inventory turnover The number of times the average inventory has been sold and replaced in a given period of time.

invoice An itemized list of goods that includes prices, terms of sales, total, taxes and fees, and amount due.

J

jargon Specialized vocabulary used by members of a particular group.

job descriptions Written statements listing the requirements of a particular job and the skills needed to fulfill those requirements.

job lead Information about a job opening.

joint venture A business enterprise that different companies set up together; often, the venture involves a domestic company and a foreign company.

just-in-time (JIT) inventory system An inventory system that controls the flow of parts and material into assembly and manufacturing plants.

K

kiosks Interactive point-of-purchase displays that are typically four feet high, have pedestal-mounted high-tech screens, and take up only a few square feet of floor space.

L

label An information tag, wrapper, seal, or imprinted message that is attached to a product or its package.

GLOSSARY

law of diminishing marginal utility An economic law stating that consumers will buy only so much of a given product, even though the price is low.

layaway A sales method that keeps merchandise in storage until the customer finishes paying for it.

layman's terms Words the average customer can understand.

liability A debt that a person owes to others, such as credit card debt, school loans, car payments, or taxes.

licensing The process of letting another company (licensee) use a trademark, patent, special formula, company name, or some other intellectual property for a fee or royalty.

lifestyle The kind of life a person lives.

limited decision making The process used when a person buys goods and services that he or she has purchased before but not regularly.

limited liability The personal assets of the owners cannot be taken if the company does not meet its financial obligations.

limited liability company (LLC) A relatively new form of business organization that is a hybrid of a partnership and corporation.

limited partnership A form of business organization in which each limited partner is liable for any debts only up to the amount of his or her investment in the company. The business's general partner is liable for all debts.

limited warranty A warranty that excludes certain parts of the product from coverage or requires the customer to bear some of the expense for repairs resulting from defects.

line graph A line that joins points representing changes in a variable quantity, usually over a period of time.

loss leader An item priced at or below cost to draw customers into a store.

M

maintained markup The difference between an item's final sale price and its cost.

management The business function of planning, organizing, and controlling all available resources to achieve company goals.

market People who share similar needs and wants and are capable of buying products.

market economy An economic system in which individuals and companies decide what will be produced, when, and how it will be distributed.

market intelligence Information about the size and location of a market, the competition, and the segmentation within the market for a particular product or service.

market segmentation The process of analyzing and classifying customers in a given market to create smaller, more precise target markets.

market share A company's percentage of total sales volume generated by all competition in a given market.

marketing The process of planning, pricing, promoting, selling, and distributing products to satisfy customers' needs and wants.

marketing concept Businesses should satisfy customers' needs and wants while making a profit.

marketing information system A set of procedures and methods that regularly generates, stores, analyzes, and distributes information for use in making marketing and other business decisions.

marketing mix The four basic marketing strategies, called the four Ps: product, place, price, and promotion.

marketing plan A formal written document communicating the goals, objectives, and strategies of a company.

marketing research The process and methods used to gather information, analyze it, and report findings related to marketing goods and services.

marketing strategy Identification of target markets and determination of marketing mix choices that focus on those markets.

markup pricing The process where resellers add a dollar amount (markup) to its cost to arrive at a price.

marquee An architectural canopy that extends over a store's entrance.

mass marketing Use of a single marketing plan to reach all customers.

media The avenues through which messages are delivered; also known as channels.

media planning The process of selecting the advertising media and deciding the time or space in which the ads should appear to accomplish a marketing objective.

media research A type of research focusing on the issues of media effectiveness, selection, frequency, and ratings; also known as advertising research.

memorandum buying A buying process in which the supplier agrees to take back any unsold goods by a certain pre-established date.

merchandise approach A way to approach a customer that focuses on making a comment or asking questions about a product in which the customer shows interest.

middle management Managers who implement the decisions of top management.

mini-nationals Midsize or smaller companies that have operations in multiple countries.

mission statement A brief paragraph or two that describes the ultimate goals of a company.

mixed brand A combination of manufacturer, private distributor, and generic brands as a strategy to sell products.

mixed bundling The practice of packaging different products and services together.

mixed number A whole number and a fraction written together.

model stock list An inventory monitoring plan used for merchandise that quickly goes out of fashion.

monopoly Exclusive control over a product or the means of producing it.

multinationals Large corporations that have operations in multiple countries.

N

national brands Brands that are owned and initiated by national manufacturers or service companies; also known as producer brands.

natural risks Risks that result from natural occurrences, such as an earthquake or bad weather.

negotiation The process of working with different parties to find a resolution to their conflict.

net income The amount left after the total expenses are subtracted from gross profit.

net sales The amount left after gross sales have been adjusted for returns and allowances.

net worth The difference between the assets of a business and its liabilities.

networking The art of building business contacts and alliances.

never-out list An inventory monitoring plan used for best-selling products that make up a large percentage of sales volume.

news release An announcement that is sent by a business or organization to media outlets.

nonprice competition Competition based on factors that are not related to price, such as product quality, service and financing, business location, and reputation.

nonprofit organization An organization that can function like a business but uses the money it makes to fund the cause identified in its charter.

nonverbal communication Expressing oneself without the use of words.

North American Free Trade Agreement (NAFTA) An international trade agreement among the United States, Canada, and Mexico.

numerator The top number in a fraction; it represents the number of parts being considered.

O

objection analysis sheet A document that lists common objections and possible responses to them.

objections Concerns, hesitations, doubts, or other honest reasons a customer has for not making a purchase.

observation method A research technique in which the actions of people are watched and recorded either by cameras or by observers.

occupational area A category of jobs that involve similar interests and skills.

Occupational Information Network (O*NET) An online database that includes information on skills, abilities, knowledge, work activities, and interests associated with occupations.

Occupational Outlook Handbook (OOH) A publication that describes what workers do on the job, working conditions, the training and education needed, earnings, and expected job prospects in a wide range of occupations.

Occupational Safety and Health Administration (OSHA) Federal agency that provides guidelines for workplace safety and enforces those regulations.

on-approval sale An agreement permitting a customer to take merchandise (usually clothing) home for further consideration.

one-price policy All customers are charged the same price for the goods and services offered for sale.

online advertising A form of advertising that uses either e-mail or the World Wide Web.

open-ended questions Questions that require respondents to construct their own answers.

opening cash fund A limited amount of money for the cash register provided by a manager or other designated person at the beginning of each business day.

open-to-buy (OTB) The amount of money left for buying goods after all purchases received and on order have been considered.

organization chart A diagram of a company's departments and jobs with lines of authority clearly shown.

organizational buyers Buyers who purchase goods for business purposes, usually in much greater quantities than the average consumer buys.

organizing Establishment of a time frame in which to achieve a goal, assigning employees to the project, and determining a method for approaching the work.

GLOSSARY

P

package The physical container or wrapping for a product.

paraphrase To restate something in a different way.

partnership A legal agreement between two or more people to be jointly responsible for the success or failure of a business.

patent A government-issued exclusive right to make, use, or sell an invention for up to 20 years.

penetration pricing A pricing policy that sets the initial price for a new product very low.

percentage A number expressed in parts per 100.

performance bonds A type of insurance that provides financial protection for losses that might occur when a construction project is not finished due to the contractor's impaired financial condition; also known as surety bonds.

performance standard An expectation of performance that reflects a company's goals and marketing plan objectives.

perpetual inventory system An inventory system that tracks the number of items in inventory on a constant basis.

personal financial statement A summary of a person's current personal financial condition.

personal selling Any form of direct contact between a salesperson and a customer.

persuade The process used to convince someone to change a perception in order to get them to do what you want.

physical distribution Activities to deliver the right amount of product to the right place at the right time.

physical inventory system An inventory system where every so often, stock is visually inspected or actually counted to determine the quantity on hand.

pie chart A pie-shaped geometric representation of the relative sizes of the parts of a whole; also called a circle graph.

planning The process of setting goals and determining how to reach them.

planning goal The small steps you take to get from where you are now to where you want to be.

planogram A computer-developed diagram that shows retailers how and where products within a category should be displayed on a shelf at individual stores.

point-of-purchase displays (POPs) A sales promotion device; manufactured units with bold graphics and signage that hold, display, or dispense products.

point-of-sale research A form of research that combines natural observation with personal interviews to get people to explain buying behavior.

point-of-sale system The process of combining a cash register with a computer, making it possible to capture information about the transaction at the time of sale, then applying it to different functions.

pre-approach The preparation for the face-to-face encounter with potential customers.

premiums Low-cost items given to consumers at a discount or for free.

presentation software Software application that produces slide shows or multimedia presentations.

prestige pricing A pricing technique that sets higher-than-average prices to suggest status and high quality to the consumer.

price The value (in money or its equivalent) placed on a product.

price bundling Two or more similar products are placed on sale for one package price.

price competition The sale price of a product; the assumption is that consumers will buy the product with the lowest price.

price discrimination Charging different prices to similar customers in similar situations.

price fixing When competitors agree on certain price ranges within which they can set their own prices.

price gouging Pricing products unreasonably high when there is a high demand resulting from a monopoly or a natural disaster.

price lining A special pricing technique that sets a limited number of prices for specific groups or lines of merchandise.

primary data Data obtained for the first time and used specifically for the particular problem or issue under study.

principal Money that is borrowed, sometimes to start a business.

print media Newspapers, magazines, direct mail, signs, and billboards used in advertising.

private carriers Trucking companies that transport goods for an individual business.

private distributor brands Brands that are developed and owned by wholesalers and retailers; also known as private brands, store brands, dealer brands, or private labels.

private employment agencies Employment agencies that are not supported by taxes and must earn a profit to stay in business.

private sector Businesses not associated with government agencies.

private warehouse A facility designed to meet the specific needs of its owner.

problem definition The process by which a business clearly identifies a problem and what is needed to solve it.

producer price index (PPI) Measurement of wholesale price levels in the economy.

product depth The number of items offered within each product line.

product features Basic, physical, or extended attributes of a product or purchase.

product item A specific model, brand, or size of a product within a product line.

product life cycle The stages that a product goes through during its life.

product line A group of closely related products manufactured or sold by a business.

product mix All the different products that a company makes or sells.

product mix pricing strategies Adjusting prices to maximize the profitability for a group of products rather than just one item.

product modification An alteration in a company's existing product.

product planning Making decisions about the features and services of a product or idea that will help sell that product.

product positioning The image a product projects that sets it apart from the competition.

product promotion A promotion method businesses use to convince consumers to select its products or services.

product research The evaluation of product design, package design, product usage, and consumer acceptance of new and existing products.

product width The number of different product lines a business manufactures or sells.

production The process of creating, expanding, manufacturing, or improving on goods and services.

productivity The output per worker hour that is measured over a defined period of time, such as a week, month, or year.

profit The money earned from conducting business after all costs and expenses have been paid.

promotion Decisions about advertising, personal selling, sales promotion, and publicity used to attract potential customers.

promotional advertising Advertising designed to increase sales.

promotional mix A combination of strategies and a cost effective allocation of resources.

promotional pricing A pricing technique in which prices are reduced for a short period of time, generally used in conjunction with sales promotions.

promotional tie-ins Sales promotional arrangements between one or more retailers or manufacturers; also known as cross-promotion and cross-selling campaigns.

proportion The relationship between and among objects in a display.

prospect A potential customer; also known as a lead.

protectionism A government's establishment of economic policies that restrict imports to protect domestic industries.

psychographics Studies of consumers based on social and psychological characteristics.

public employment agencies Employment agencies that are supported by state or federal taxes and offer free services to both job applicants and employers.

public relations (PR) Activities that help an organization influence a target audience

public sector Local, state, and federal government agencies and services, such as public libraries and state universities.

public warehouse Storage and handling facilities offered to any individual or company that will pay for its use.

publicity A tactic that public relations professionals use to bring information about an organization to the public's attention.

pull policy A process that directs promotion towards consumers.

purchase order (PO) A legal contract between a buyer and a supplier to purchase a specified number of products at a specified price.

push policy A manufacturer uses a mix of personal selling, advertising, and buying discounts to promote a product to large retailers that sell its products.

Q

qualitative research A type of research that focuses on smaller numbers of people (usually fewer than 100) and tries to answer why or how questions.

quality check method The merchandise is checked to determine whether the quality of goods received matches the quality of the products, which were ordered

quantitative research A type of research that answers questions that start with how many or how much.

quota A limit on either the quantity or monetary value of a product that may be imported.

R

rack jobbers Wholesalers that manage inventory and merchandising for retailers by counting stock, filling it in when needed, and maintaining store displays.

rational motive A conscious, logical reason for a purchase.

real-time inventory system An Internet technology that connects applications, data, and users in real time.

GLOSSARY

realistic goal A goal that a person has a reasonable chance of achieving.

receiving record Information recorded by businesses about the goods they receive.

recession A period of economic slowdown that lasts for two quarters, or six months.

recovery A period of renewed economic growth followed by a recession or depression.

references People who know a job applicant's work habits and personal traits well and will recommend that person for the job.

referrals The names of other people who might buy a product, given to salespeople by satisfied customers.

reliability When a research technique produces nearly identical results in repeated trials.

remedial action Using preventive discipline or corrective discipline to encourage appropriate workplace behavior.

resources All the things used in producing goods and services.

résumé A brief summary of personal information, education, skills, work experience, activities, and interests.

retailers Channel of distribution that buys goods from wholesalers or directly from manufacturers and resells them to the consumer.

return on investment (ROI) A calculation that is used to determine the relative profitability of a product.

revolving accounts Charge accounts where the retailer determines the credit limit and payment terms.

risk management The systematic process of managing an organization's risks to achieve objectives in a manner consistent with public interest, human safety, environmental needs, and the law.

routine decision making The process used when a person needs little information about a product to make a decision because he or she buys it regularly.

S

sales check A written record of a sales transaction that includes such information as the date of the transaction, items purchased, purchase prices, sales tax, and the total amount due.

sales forecasts The projection of probable future sales in units or dollars.

sales promotion All marketing activities--other than personal selling, advertising, and public relations--that are used to stimulate purchasing and sales.

sales quotas Dollar or unit sales goals set for the sales staff to achieve in a specified period of time.

sales tax A percentage fee placed by the government on the sale of goods and services.

sample A part of the target population that is assumed to represent the entire population.

scarcity The difference between what consumers want and need and what the available resources are.

secondary data Data that has already been collected for some purpose other than the current study.

Securities and Exchange Commission (SEC) Federal agency that regulates the sale of securities (stocks and bonds), licenses brokerage firms and financial advisers, and investigates dealings among corporations.

segmented pricing strategy A pricing strategy that uses two or more different prices for a product, even though there is no difference in the item's cost.

selective distribution A limited number of outlets in a given geographic area are used to sell the product.

service approach A way to approach a customer that focuses on asking the customer if he or she needs assistance.

service close A way to close a sale in which a salesperson explains services that overcome obstacles or problems.

services Intangible items of monetary value that satisfy needs and wants.

setting The circumstances under which communication takes place.

signature The distinctive identification for a business; also known as logotype or logo.

situation analysis The study of the internal and external factors that affect marketing strategies.

site map An outline of what can be found on each page within the Web site.

six-month merchandise plan The budget that estimates planned purchases for a six-month period.

skimming pricing A pricing policy that sets a very high price for a new product.

slogan A catchy phrase or words that identify a product or company.

sole proprietorship A business owned and operated by one person.

source marking The seller or manufacturer marks the price before delivering the merchandise to the retailer; the marking often uses a universal product code (UPC).

specialty media Relatively inexpensive, useful items featuring an advertiser's name or logo that are given away; also known as giveaways or advertising specialties.

spot check method The receiver of a delivery conducts a check of one carton in a shipment to see if the right kind and quantity of goods were delivered.

spreadsheet programs Software applications used to organize, calculate, and analyze numerical data.

staffing/temporary agencies Employment agencies that are not supported by taxes and must earn a profit to stay in business.

standard English The formal style of writing and speaking that is taught in school.

standing-room-only close A method of closing a sale that is used when a product is in short supply or when the price will be going up in the near future.

start-up costs Projections of how much money a new business owner will need for the business's first year in operation.

stockholders The owners of a corporation with limited liability.

stockkeeping unit (SKU) A unit or a group of related items in a unit control inventory system; the smallest unit used in inventory control.

storage A marketing function that refers to the holding of goods until they are sold.

store layout The ways that stores use floor space to facilitate and promote sales and serve customers.

storefront The exterior of a business that includes a store's sign or logo, marquee, outdoor lighting, banners, planters, awnings, windows, the exterior design, ambiance, landscaping, and lighting of the building.

substitution method A selling method that involves recommending a different product that would still satisfy the customer's needs.

suggestion selling A method of selling in which the salesperson recommends additional goods or services to the customer.

superior-point method A selling technique that permits the salesperson to acknowledge objections as valid yet still offset them with other features and benefits.

supervisory-level management Managers who supervise the activities of employees who carry out the tasks determined by middle and top management.

supply The amount of goods producers are willing to make and sell.

survey method A research technique in which information is gathered from people through the use of surveys or questionnaires.

SWOT analysis An assessment of a company's strengths and weaknesses and the opportunities and threats that surround it; SWOT: strengths, weaknesses, opportunities, threats.

T

target market A group of people identified as those most likely to become customers.

tariff A tax on imports; also known as a duty.

teamwork Work done by a group of people to achieve a common goal.

telecommuting A program that involves working at home, usually on a computer, with completed jobs transmitted by e-mail or mail-in disk.

telemarketing The process of selling over the phone.

terms for delivery The final delivery arrangement between the buyer and seller.

third-party method A selling method that involves using a previous customer or other neutral person who can give a testimonial about the product.

30-day accounts Accounts that enable customers to charge purchases during a month and pay the balance in full within 30 days after they are billed.

till The cash drawer of a cash register.

time management The process of budgeting time to accomplish tasks on a certain schedule.

ton-mile The movement of one ton (2,000 lbs) of freight one mile.

top management Managers who make decisions that affect the whole company.

trade character A specific type of brand mark, one with human form or characteristics.

trade name A phrase or symbol that identifies and promotes a company or a division of a particular corporation; also known as a corporate brand.

trade promotions Sales promotion activities designed to get support for a product from manufacturers, wholesalers, and retailers.

trademark A brand name, brand mark, trade name, trade character, or a combination of these elements that is given legal protection by the federal government.

trading area The geographical area from which a business draws its customers.

traditional economy Traditions and rituals that answer basic questions of what, how, and for whom.

transit advertising Advertising found on public transportation.

transportation The marketing function of moving a product from the place where it is made to the place where it is sold.

triadic colors Three colors that are equally spaced on the color wheel.

trial close An initial effort to close a sale.

GLOSSARY

U

uniform resource locator (URL) The address of a file that is available on the Internet, usually on the World Wide Web.

unit control A method of stock control that measures the quantities of merchandise that a business handles during a period of time.

unit pricing Including price information for a standard unit or measure so that consumers can compare prices more easily.

universal product code (UPC) A combination bar code and number used to identify a product and manufacturer.

unlimited liability A business owner's financial liability is not limited to investments in the business, but extends to his or her total ability to make payments.

utility An attribute of a product or service that makes it capable of satisfying consumers' wants and needs.

V

validity When questions asked on a questionnaire measure what was intended to be measured.

values Beliefs that guide the way people live.

vertical organization A hierarchical, up-and-down organizational structure in which the tasks and responsibilities of each level are clearly defined.

visual merchandising Coordinating the physical elements in a place of business to project the right image to customers.

W

want slips Customer requests for items that are not carried in the store.

warranty A promise or guarantee given to a customer that a product will meet certain standards.

warranty of fitness for a particular purpose A warranty used when the seller advises a customer that a product is suitable for a particular use, and the customer acts on that advice.

warranty of merchantability The seller's promise that the product sold is fit for its intended purpose.

which close A method of closing a sale that encourages a customer to make a decision between two items.

whistle-blowing Reporting an illegal action by one's employer.

wholesale and retail buyers Buyers who purchase goods for resale.

wholesalers Channel of distribution that obtains goods from manufacturers and resells them to industrial users, other wholesalers, and retailers.

Wi-Fi Technology that establishes a wireless fidelity Internet connection using radio frequencies.

word processing programs Software applications designed to create documents that are primarily text but may contain a few graphics.

World Trade Organization (WTO) A global coalition of more than 140 governments that makes rules governing international trade.

World Wide Web (www) A subset of the Internet that is a collection of interlinked electronic documents.

INDEX

INDEX

INDEX

INDEX

INDEX

INDEX

Photo Credits

INTRODUCTION

Overview

Current educational theory stresses that students with all types of special needs learn and perform better when they are part of a mixed group rather than assigned with others having similar needs to contained "special education" classrooms. As a result, you may use *Marketing Essentials* with a very wide range of learners. The purpose of this guide is to aid you in helping all the students in your class get the most from this course by defining special needs and offering teaching strategies to help you integrate special needs students into the classroom.

ENGLISH LANGUAGE LEARNERS

Overview

Students learning English as a second language will come to your classroom with varying degrees of skill in English. In addition, social and cultural differences may affect their comfort and academic performance. With *Marketing Essentials*, you have a unique opportunity to help these students assimilate the ways of their new home while allowing them to share likenesses and differences between this culture and the one of their birth.

General Strategies

- Remember that students' ability to speak English does not reflect their academic ability.

- Don't fall into the habit of speaking in an extra-loud voice to students still acquiring English proficiency.

- Bilingual aides can be very helpful, especially in cases where all English language learners in the class speak the same first language. However, if a number of different languages (and dialects) are represented in your classroom, an aid speaking one of these will be of limited value. Try to develop connections within the community to help with homework assignments as well as translations of letters to parents and other home/school communications.

- Provide outlines of planned class content to English language learners in advance so that they can look up new vocabulary and preview material at their own pace.

- Allow "thinking time" between any question or comment you make and student response. Don't let class discussion fall into the format of a game show, where only a few who are good at quickly shouting out a response can be "winners." All students benefit from being given time to process information before answering, and this is especially true of the English language learner.

- Pair native English speakers and second-language learners as appropriate for class activities.

- Write numerals on the board as you say them. Use pantomime and visuals whenever possible to illustrate both concrete terms and ideas.

STUDENTS WITH VISION IMPAIRMENTS

Overview

The term *vision impairment* refers to those learners whose sight is impaired to varying degrees as well as those who are blind. Abilities of students with vision impairments cover a range as wide as that among their sighted peers. However, vision impairment may affect cognitive, motor, and social development. The suggestions that follow are designed to help you successfully include students with vision impairments in your class as well as offer them the individual guidance necessary for effective teaching and learning.

General Strategies

- Speak clearly; but unless a student with a vision impairment also has hearing loss, do not shout or speak in an unnaturally loud voice.

- Be specific in your instructions and references. Describe what you are doing as you do it. Use specific references such as "on the table near the door" or "in the bookcase in the back of the room" as opposed to "up here" or "over there."

- Make it a matter of course to have sighted students work with students with vision impairments, giving oral descriptions of illustrations and other visuals in the text or classroom.

- Seat students with vision impairments or who are blind near the front of the classroom. In the case of those who are partially sighted, avoided standing between them and light sources such as windows. Ask the individuals what seating works best for them.

- Build a classroom library of audiotaped readings. You and selected students might record chapters from the textbook until the entire book is available on audiotape. (These tapes will also prove helpful for English language learners and those honing reading skills.)

- Locate pre-recorded audiotapes of books and other print materials that might expand and enrich course content.

- Determine whether your students with vision impairments use Braille; if so, locate sources for materials in Braille and secure any materials related to the class.

- Look for community resources such as schools, charitable organizations, and special education departments at local colleges devoted to working with the blind and partially sighted. Help students and their families connect with any suitable services, and check out any help these sources might offer you as an educator.

- Use the Internet to continue your own professional development. Check for guidance offered online by colleges, government agencies, and other organizations devoted to the education of persons with visual impairments. A search using the keywords *teaching the visually impaired* will result in a large and ever-changing listing of Web sites on this topic.

STUDENTS WITH HEARING IMPAIRMENTS

Overview
Students with hearing impairments range from those with partial to total loss of hearing. These students may communicate using sign language or by speaking. They may read lips, use a hearing aid or a cochlear implant (a device surgically implanted and operated through a box that can be worn around the waist), come to class with an interpreter, or make use of a combination of these. Ability range is similar to that of hearing students; but, as is the case with other special needs, the hearing loss may affect cognitive, motor, social, and speech development.

General Strategies

- Determine the means individual students use to communicate and then talk to them individually about how you can create a classroom that aids rather than detracts from their efforts. For example, you might determine the best seating arrangements, minimize background noise, and make sure you and other students face students with hearing impairments when you are speaking.

- Watch for misconceptions. One teacher was put off by what he read as the enraged expression on the face of a deaf student in his class. When he talked about this with her interpreter, he commented that he found her obvious anger almost frightening. The interpreter explained that the look was not one of rage but of fierce concentration as the girl struggled in the early stages of learning to read lips.

- Write out instructions on paper or on the board. Consider using an overhead projector, which allows you to maintain eye contact as you write.

- Unfamiliar words can be difficult to lip-read or sign without prior exposure. If materials for a lesson involve technical terminology or new vocabulary, supply word lists in advance to students and their interpreters.

- Pair students with hearing impairments with hearing partners. This benefits both students in that hearing students will gain knowledge about how students with hearing impairments meet this challenge. They can also help the partner with a hearing impairment by: repeating the words of others spoken with their backs turned to the student with a hearing impairment; monitoring the level of environmental noise in the classroom; and, repeating public address and other such announcements.

- Make a class project of learning sign language. Have students obtain a copy of the alphabet for American Sign Language and practice using this means of communication. They might then work in groups to translate and present a favorite poem or song in this medium.

- Have a student explain what Cloze Captioning is and how it works.

- Check Internet resources. Colleges, organizations for the persons with hearing impairments, and family/school support groups are all well established and offer myriad services.

STUDENTS WITH BEHAVIOR DISORDERS

Overview
Students with behavior disorders deviate, usually to a marked degree, from expectations of acceptable classroom behavior. Such students impair not only their own functioning but that of classmates as well. Abilities of those students with behavior disorders range from gifted through learning disabled.

General Strategies

- Be prepared, but don't prejudge. Students with behavior disorders are probably made known to you before class begins. You may have met with counselors, deans, school psychologists and other personnel; and you probably have heard informal comments by former teachers. However, approaching the class with the expectation that everybody in it will live up to behavioral norms can be the first step in breaking individual behavior patterns.

- Determine the student's interests and learning modalities, and make use of this information when forming collaborative groups and making assignments.

- Make sure that rules for behavior are clearly defined. When deviations from these rules occur, intervene at once, modeling more appropriate forms of behavior.

- Make sure goals and expectations for the course are clearly defined at the beginning, and refer to these often throughout the course.

- Don't be discouraged if you do not have immediate success; work toward long-term improvement.

- Check Internet resources. A search using the keywords *teaching students with behavior disorders* will yield a significant number of sources ranging from guidelines issued by boards of education in various states through sites designed to be visited by students with such problems who are then offered tips for building self-esteem and coping skills. It is worth noting that many of these sites tend to lump all special needs, from physical impairments to behavior disorders, together. It's strongly urged that you preview any sites before suggesting students visit them.

STUDENTS WITH LEARNING DISABILITIES

Overview
Students with learning disabilities have problems in one or more areas, including academics, language development, perception, social/emotional adjustment, memory, or ability to pay attention. As a rule, they require more support and structure in the classroom setting. However, like their peers who do not come to class with these problems, most students with learning disabilities will benefit from instruction that incorporates a wide variety of learning modalities, including visual, kinesthetic, auditory, and so forth.

General Strategies
- Make sure that guidelines for classroom behavior, preparation of assignments, and other duties and responsibilities for the class are clearly defined at the beginning of the school year. Take care to stress these as often as necessary with students with learning disabilities.

- Make clear the understanding that students with learning disabilities are expected to adhere to the same standards as all the other students in the class. This can be done as necessary in your individual conferences to discuss the progress of students with learning disabilities

- Break the more complex tasks into steps, and make periodic informal checks to see that students understand the purpose of the work and are not falling behind.

- Distributing outlines of material to be presented in class can help the student with learning disabilities both preview and review content as necessary.

- When possible, have the student with learning disabilities work with a partner who is not learning disabled. Encourage the sharing and comparing of notes taken during class, homework assignments, and preparations for class projects.

- Create a library of audiotaped readings of the chapters in the text and of any other related print materials. (See also the section on English language learners.) Encourage students with learning disabilities to use these to stay current with course content and to improve reading comprehension skills.

STUDENTS WITH PHYSICAL IMPAIRMENTS

Overview
Students with physical impairments might be very broadly classified into two groups, those for whom the use of one or more limbs is severely restricted and those with other health impairments such as inability to breathe without assistance from a respirator or other such device, uncontrollable body movements, and so forth. Some students must rely on wheelchairs while others make use of crutches, leg braces, and other such aids. Students in wheelchairs may or may not have use of their arms.

General Strategies
- Before classes begin, determine the needs of students with physical impairments and make sure the basic layout of your classroom allows them the necessary access.

- Although recent events and national concerns have heightened awareness about the need for solid preplanning of evacuation of the classroom and school building, make doubly sure that such plans are in place, and go over these with the entire class until everybody is familiar with them.

- Teachers of students with physical impairments are almost unanimous in their championing of a teaching approach that includes integration into the curriculum of the visual arts, music, and where suitable kinesthetic and tactile activities. In short, what is proving to work well for the student who is not physically impaired also is the most effective approach for those who are.

- As the course progresses and all students become more comfortable speaking their minds to you, individually talk with students with physical impairments about what they perceive to be the strong and weaker points of the classroom setting and instructional approach, given their particular physical impairment. Decide together how these issues might be addressed.

- Check resources in your community. Look for organizations that offer services to those with physical impairments. If there is a need, work to connect the families of students with physical impairments with these organizations and the services they offer.

STUDENTS WITH SPEECH IMPAIRMENTS

Overview

Students with speech impairments may have impediments ranging from problems with articulation or voice strength to inability to speak at all. Such impairments can also include stuttering, chronic hoarseness, and difficulty in expressing an appropriate word or phrase. In many cases, these students attempt to refrain from any class participation.

General Strategies

- Students with speech impairments cover as wide a range of aptitudes and abilities as do students without such problems.
- Use normal communication patterns, in particular, refrain from completing statements or thoughts for the student.
- Talk with any specialists and counselors who see learners with speech impairments outside of your classroom in "pull-out" programs, one-to-one instruction, or individual or group therapy. These professionals may be able to provide guidelines for your work in the classroom, such as when to encourage or require that a particular student with a speech impairment enter group discussion and when not, how to alter or defuse situations that seem to aggravate the speech problem, and so forth.
- Once you and individual students with speech impairments have begun to get to know and be comfortable with each other, talk with them one-on-one about what classroom approaches do and do not work for them. Are there ways to make the class more effective and comfortable?
- Those students who rely on electronic speaking devices or use body language to communicate should be encouraged in these efforts.
- Allow students who have questions about a particular lesson to submit these in writing. Set aside time to go over the questions with the student.

GIFTED STUDENTS

Overview

Although no formal definition exists, gifted students can be described as having above average ability, task commitment, and creativity. When working to their full potential, they rank in the top 5 percent of their classes. However, not all gifted students perform equally well in all areas; a student showing signs of being extremely gifted in some subjects may not, for a variety of reasons, achieve to that degree in others. Further, some successful teaching practitioners argue that every student has the potential to be gifted in some areas, and that many are indeed gifted in ways not covered by the definition, including their mastery of basic coping and survival skills. The suggestions that follow are designed to help you creatively extend class content for students who fit the general definition, but they also offer ways to provide creative extensions to all students in your class.

General Strategies

- In teaching gifted students, educators are encouraged to provide instruction that involves a number of different modalities, is built around project-based learning, features collaborative learning, and offers enrichment of all types.
- But it is also repeatedly and successfully argued that these approaches are ones that work best for all students, whether they have special needs or not. In fact, few things can be more discouraging for the student with other special needs or the student considered closer to average than to be relegated to rote learning while those considered to be the "smart kids" get to do projects involving arts integration and all the other "fun stuff." These suggestions provide some ways to encourage the gifted within the atmosphere of a classroom where everybody has the opportunity to take part in the best the curriculum has to offer.
- When it is necessary to provide additional work for gifted students, make assignments that tie into instruction but take that instruction further by widening or deepening the experience.
- Build your classroom into a community of learners. Stress the collaborative nature of all projects, pointing out ways in which all students can both help and learn from other students.